THE ROUGH GUIDE TO

Malaysia
Singapore & Brunei

There are more than one hundred and fifty Rough Guide titles
covering destinations from Amsterdam to Zimbabwe

Forthcoming titles include

Alaska • Copenhagen • Ibiza & Formentera • Iceland

Rough Guide Reference Series

Classical Music • Country Music • Drum 'n' Bass • English Football
European Football • House • The Internet • Jazz • Music USA • Opera
Reggae • Rock Music • Techno • Unexplained Phenomena • World Music

Rough Guide Phrasebooks

Czech • Dutch • Egyptian Arabic • European Languages • French • German
Greek • Hindi & Urdu • Hungarian • Indonesian • Italian • Japanese
Mandarin Chinese • Mexican Spanish • Polish • Portuguese • Russian
Spanish • Swahili • Thai • Turkish • Vietnamese

Rough Guides on the Internet

www.roughguides.com

ROUGH GUIDE CREDITS

Text editor: Richard Lim
Series editor: Mark Ellingham
Editorial: Martin Dunford, Jonathan Buckley, Jo Mead, Kate Berens, Amanda Tomlin, Ann-Marie Shaw, Paul Gray, Helena Smith, Judith Bamber, Orla Duane, Olivia Eccleshall, Ruth Blackmore, Geoff Howard, Claire Saunders, Gavin Thomas, Alexander Mark Rogers, Polly Thomas, Joe Staines, Lisa Nellis, Andrew Tomičić, Duncan Clark, Peter Buckley, Sam Thorne, Lucy Ratcliffe (UK); Andrew Rosenberg, Mary Beth Maioli, Don Bapst, Stephen Timblin (US)
Production: Susanne Hillen, Andy Hilliard, Link Hall, Helen Ostick, Julia Bovis, Michelle Draycott, Katie

Pringle, Robert Evers, Mike Hancock, Robert McKinlay, Zoë Nobes
Cartography: Melissa Baker, Maxine Repath, Ed Wright
Picture research: Louise Boulton, Sharon Martins
Online: Kelly Cross, Anja Mutić-Blessing, Jennifer Gold (US)
Finance: John Fisher, Gary Singh, Edward Downey, Mark Hall, Tim Bill
Marketing & Publicity: Richard Trillo, Niki Smith, David Wearn, Jemima Broadbridge, Chloë Roberts, Birgit Hartmann (UK); Simon Carloss, David Wechsler (US)
Administration: Tania Hummel, Demelza Dallow, Julie Sanderson

ACKNOWLEDGEMENTS

The authors would like to thank the following people:

Charles: No trip to KL would be the same without help from Stevie, the wonder host from the *Backpackers Travellers Inn* and *Lodge*. Thanks also to David Nathan, *Liquid*'s Marketing Manager, and to Indy Manicka and team at the *Travellers Station* for eager email correspondence. I am also indebted to Professor Khoo Kay Kim, now in Singapore, for his many insights into the rich history of the region. Across the South China Sea in Kuching, Wayne Tarman and Mike Reed of Travelcom Asia are the most excellent drinking partners for any thirsty traveller, and thanks also to Audrey Wan Ullock at the *Telang Usan Hotel*. Up the Rajang it was a relief to meet the wonderfully enthusiastic Nyaring Bandar from the *Pelagus Rapids Resort*, and in Miri, many thanks to Gracie Geikie and team at Seridan Mulu Tours and to Lemi Imau at the *Rihga Royal*. At Long San, I am grateful to Anthony Lawai for being such a true gentleman. In Brunei, Leslie Chiang and Anthony Chieng at Sunshine Borneo Tours opened up the country for me and showed me the way to *Voctech*, Tim Ringrose, at Borneo Outdoors, helped broaden my knowledge of the Sultan's domain too. In

Kota Kinabalu, masterful photographer Albert Teo shared his passion for Sabah; round the tip in Sandakan, Chris Perez got me out to his jungle camp and Peter in Semporna kindly filled in some important details. Also thanks to Peter and Sabina Davison for top-quality socializing; and, as always, the deepest thanks to my brother David and sister-in-law Fiona. Last but not least, thanks to editor Richard, and to Karen for her support and love.

Mark: Thanks to my wife, Susie, and my family for their love and support.

Arnold: Ms Khoo Sien Wah at the tourist info centre in the KOMTAR building in Georgetown, and all the staff at the tourist office in Melaka.

Pauline: Anuar and Badriah; Jack and Fatimah; Helena on Sibu; Simon from HTD; Pim and Liz; Nana; and Ross.

The editor thanks Narrell Leffman and Gerrard Kennedy for additional Basics research; Mike Hancock for typesetting; The Map Studio, Romsey, Hants and Maxine Repath for the maps; and Russell Walton for vigilant proofreading. Thanks also to John Gee for accurate tips as always, Kemal for Bahasa pointers and Arnold for the Persian gossip.

PUBLISHING INFORMATION

This third edition published November 2000 by
  Rough Guides Ltd, 62–70 Shorts Gardens,
  London WC2H 9AH.
Distributed by the Penguin Group:
Penguin Books Ltd, 27 Wrights Lane, London W8 5TZ
Penguin Putnam, Inc., 375 Hudson Street, NY 10014, USA
Penguin Books Australia Ltd, 487 Maroondah Highway,
  PO Box 257, Ringwood, Victoria 3134, Australia
Penguin Books Canada Ltd, 10 Alcorn Avenue, Toronto,
  Ontario, Canada M4V 1E4
Penguin Books (NZ) Ltd, 182–190 Wairau Road,
  Auckland 10, New Zealand
Typeset in Linotron Univers and Century Old Style to an
  original design by Andrew Oliver.
Printed in the UK by Clays Ltd, St Ives PLC
Illustrations in Part One and Part Three by Edward Briant.

Illustrations on p.1 & p.615 by Henry Iles
© Charles de Ledesma, Mark Lewis and Pauline Savage
  2000
No part of this book may be reproduced in any form without permission from the publisher except for the quotation of brief passages in reviews.
688pp – Includes index
A catalogue record for this book is available from the British Library
ISBN 1-85828-565-8

THE ROUGH GUIDE TO

Malaysia
Singapore & Brunei

written and researched by

Charles de Ledesma, Mark Lewis
and Pauline Savage

with additional accounts by

Arnold Barkhordarian

**ROUGH
GUIDES**

THE ROUGH GUIDES

TRAVEL GUIDES • PHRASEBOOKS • MUSIC AND REFERENCE GUIDES

 We set out to do something different when the first Rough Guide was published in 1982. Mark Ellingham, just out of university, was travelling in Greece. He brought along the popular guides of the day, but found they were all lacking in some way. They were either strong on ruins and museums but went on for pages without mentioning a beach or taverna. Or they were so conscious of the need to save money that they lost sight of Greece's cultural and historical significance. Also, none of the books told him anything about Greece's contemporary life – its politics, its culture, its people, and how they lived.

So with no job in prospect, Mark decided to write his own guidebook, one which aimed to provide practical information that was second to none, detailing the best beaches and the hottest clubs and restaurants, while also giving hard-hitting accounts of every sight, both famous and obscure, and providing up-to-the-minute information on contemporary culture. It was a guide that encouraged independent travellers to find the best of Greece, and was a great success, getting shortlisted for the Thomas Cook travel guide award,

and encouraging Mark, along with three friends, to expand the series.

The Rough Guide list grew rapidly and the letters flooded in, indicating a much broader readership than had been anticipated, but one which uniformly appreciated the Rough Guide mix of practical detail and humour, irreverence and enthusiasm. Things haven't changed. The same four friends who began the series are still the caretakers of the Rough Guide mission today: to provide the most reliable, up-to-date and entertaining information to independent-minded travellers of all ages, on all budgets.

We now publish more than 150 titles and have offices in London and New York. The travel guides are written and researched by a dedicated team of more than 100 authors, based in Britain, Europe, the USA and Australia. We have also created a unique series of phrasebooks to accompany the travel series, along with an acclaimed series of music guides, and a best-selling pocket guide to the Internet and World Wide Web. We also publish comprehensive travel information on our Web site:

www.roughguides.com

HELP US UPDATE

We've gone to a lot of effort to ensure that the third edition of *The Rough Guide to Malaysia, Singapore & Brunei* is accurate and up-to-date. However, things change – places get "discovered", opening hours are notoriously fickle, restaurants and rooms raise prices or lower standards. If you feel we've got it wrong or left something out, we'd like to know, and if you can remember the address, the price, the time, the phone number, so much the better.

We'll credit all contributions, and send a copy of the next edition (or any other *Rough Guide* if you prefer) for the best letters. Please mark letters: "Rough Guide Malaysia, Singapore & Brunei Update" and send to:
Rough Guides, 62–70 Shorts Gardens, London WC2H 9AH, or Rough Guides, 4th Floor, 345 Hudson St, New York, NY 10014.
Or send email to: mail@roughguides.co.uk
Online updates about this book can be found on Rough Guides' Web site at **www.roughguides.com**

THE AUTHORS

Freelance journalist **Charles de Ledesma** was born in Miri, Sarawak. An inveterate music traveller, Charles loves nothing better than attending festivals in the back of beyond. He's contributed to the *Rough Guide to World Music* and can frequently be heard on the USA's National Public Radio covering the latest – as well as retro – music trends, and on BBC London Live's Robert Elms Show. Additionally, Charles writes occasionally for the travel pages of the *Independent*.

After graduating from the University of Bristol, **Mark Lewis** spent a year teaching English in Singapore, during which time he regularly contributed book reviews to the *Singapore Straits Times*. Author of *The Rough Guide to Singapore* and co-author of *The Rough Guide to Vietnam*, Mark is now Features Editor of *Computer Weekly* magazine.

After leaving university, **Pauline Savage** travelled extensively throughout Asia. Although she now works as a desk-bound editor in London, she maintains a keen interest in the area and returns whenever she has the opportunity.

READERS' LETTERS

Thanks to all the people who wrote in with comments on the previous edition of the guide and suggestions for this edition, in no particular order:

Jeanette Thornhill, Simon Loft, Joyce Reed, Jo Yuen, Steve and Jane Winn, Oliver Brooks, David Truman, Neil Kingham, Louise Melville, Kestrel Gerrard, Keith Davies, Laurent d'Guyot, Lisa Burrows, Chris and Leesa, Andrew and Jo Preshaus, Bernard Horrocks and Glenn Sontag, Charlotte and Crispin Worthington, Peter Ray, Peter Cunningham, Dave Brighouse and Melanie Boyce, Craig Powers, Roy Koerner, Suzanne Kay, Annalisa Henderson, Jan Uhde, Stephen Aguilar, Mike Ashton, Margit Waas, Heather Abbott, Phoebe McLeod, Rachel Yarrow, Anne Briggs, Mike Sykes, Wendy Fox, Stephen Carter, Alex Henry, Daniel Milson, Emma Stagg, Vicky Johnstone, G. Duckworth, Jenny Cook, Peter Jenkins, Jane Floweth, Philip Reeves, Paul Lawlor, Allan Spence, John Gee, Maureen O'Keeffe, Mark and Vanessa Scott, Neil Rae, Karen Mann and Kevin Marren, Kate Cole, M.H. Sharpe, H.H. Saffery, Ben Mandelson, I.R. Nelson, Monica Mackaness and John Garratt, Eckehard, Barry Barnes, Rob and Liz Noble, Deborah Hegarty, Fredrik Ygge, Paul and Lesley Glendenning, Justin Wastnage, Ben Davies and Stuart Clarke.

CONTENTS

PART THREE CONTEXTS 615

LIST OF MAPS

MAP SYMBOLS

———	Railway	♛	Castle	@	Cybercafé
═══	Highway	⚇	Public Gardens	Ⓗ	Hospital
═══	Road	⌒	Cave	ⓘ	Tourist office
-----	Path	▲	Peak	⊠	Post office
– – –	Ferry route	⥁	Viewpoint	ⓒ	Telephone
~~	Waterway	☥	Lighthouse	⚷	Golf Course
– – –	Chapter division boundary	⚑	Waterfall	■	Building
▪–▪–▪	International borders	⚘	Marshland	➕	Church
–– ··	Malaysian state boundary	★	Bus Stop	⁺⁺⁺	Christian Cemetery
☦	Church (regional maps)	✕	Airport	⌖	Muslim Cemetery
☪	Mosque	Ⓟ	Parking	▨	Park
✿	Buddhist Temple	⚠	Campsite	▨	National Park
♣	Hindu Temple	⬠	Refuge	▨	Pedestrianized area
✡	Synagogue	◉	Accommodation	⸬	Area market
∴	Ruins	■	Restaurant/café		

INTRODUCTION

At first glance there seems little to link **Malaysia**, **Singapore** and **Brunei**, not even geographical proximity. Six hundred kilometres of the South China Sea separates Peninsular Malaysia (also called West Malaysia or the Malay Peninsula) from the Malaysian states of Sarawak and Sabah (also called East Malaysia) in the north of Borneo. And Bangkok is as close to Kuala Lumpur and Singapore as is the Bruneian capital Bandar Seri Begawan. But all three countries are born of a common history and ethnic composition that links the entire Malay archipelago, from Indonesia to the Philippines. Each became an important port of call on the trade route between India and China, the two great markets of the early world, and later formed the colonial linchpins of the Portuguese, Dutch and British empires. However, Malaysia has only existed in its present form since 1963, when the federation of the eleven Peninsular states, along with Singapore and the two Bornean territories of Sarawak and Sabah, became known as Malaysia. Singapore left the union in 1965, gaining independence in its own right; Brunei, always content to maintain its own enclave in Borneo (it decided not to join the Federation of Malaysia in 1963), only lost its British colonial status in 1984.

Since then, Malaysia, Singapore and Brunei have been united in their **economic dominance** of Southeast Asia. While the tiny Sultanate of Brunei is locked into a paternalistic regime, using its considerable oil wealth to guarantee its citizens an enviable standard of living, the city-state of Singapore has long been a model of free-market profiteering, transformed from a tiny port with no natural resources into one of the world's capitalist giants. Malaysia is the relative newcomer to the scene, though it has an ambitious manifesto by which it aims to achieve First World status by 2020. This will involve doubling the size of the economy and increasing personal income fourfold by that time, with tourism massively expanding in the process. The most ambitious part of this project is the building of the Multimedia Super Corridor, a belt of hi tech development stretching 50km south from the capital Kuala Lumpur, and including a new, purportedly paperless, administrative city, Putrajaya.

Though Malaysia, Singapore and Brunei don't have the grand ancient ruins of neighbouring Thailand, their rich **cultural heritage** is apparent, with traditional architecture and crafts thriving in the rural kampung (village) areas, and on display in cultural centres and at exhibitions throughout the modern cities. The dominant cultural force in the region has undoubtedly been the Malay adoption of **Islam** in the fourteenth century, while in Singapore, **Buddhism** and **Taoism** together hold sway among half the population. But it's the commitment to religious plurality – there are sizeable Christian and Hindu minorities – that is so attractive, often providing startling juxtapositions of mosques, temples and churches. What's more, the region's diverse **population**, a blend of indigenous Malays, Chinese and Indians, has spawned a huge variety of annual **festivals** as well as a wonderful mixture of **cuisines**.

As well as a rich cultural life, the region has astonishing **natural beauty**. With parts of Thailand starting to suffer from overexposure to tourism, it comes as a welcome surprise to discover Peninsular Malaysia's unspoiled east-coast **beaches**, while both the Peninsula and the Bornean states have some of the world's oldest tropical **rainforest**. The national parks are superb for cave exploration, river-

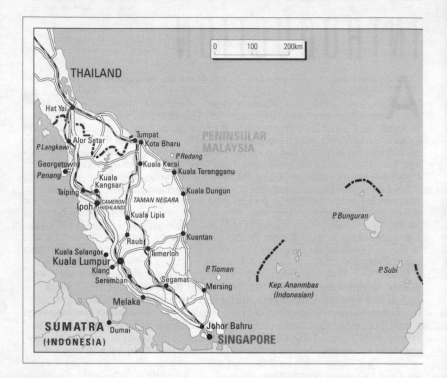

rafting and wildlife-watching, and provide challenging **treks**, including that to the peak of one of Southeast Asia's highest mountains, Mount Kinabalu in Sabah.

Malaysia

Malaysia's fast-growing capital, **Kuala Lumpur** (often simply referred to as KL) makes much the same initial impression as does the city-state of Singapore, with high-rise hotels and air-conditioned shopping malls, and characterful areas like Chinatown and Little India. KL is also the social and economic driving force of a nation eager to better itself, a fact reflected in the growing number of designer bars and restaurants in the city, and in the booming manufacturing industries surrounding it. But this is a city firmly rooted in tradition, where the same Malay executives who wear suits to work dress in traditional clothes at festival times. And although the city is changing quickly, life on the busy streets still has a spontaneous feel, with markets and food stalls crowded in amongst new banks and businesses.

Less than three hours' drive south of the capital lies the birthplace of Malay civilization, **Melaka**, a must on anybody's itinerary. Much further up the **west coast** is the first British settlement, the island of **Penang**, with old colonial buildings and a vibrant Chinatown district adorning its capital, **Georgetown**. In between KL and Georgetown is a string of old tin-mining towns, such as **Ipoh** and **Taiping**, which provided the engine of economic change in the nineteenth century. For a

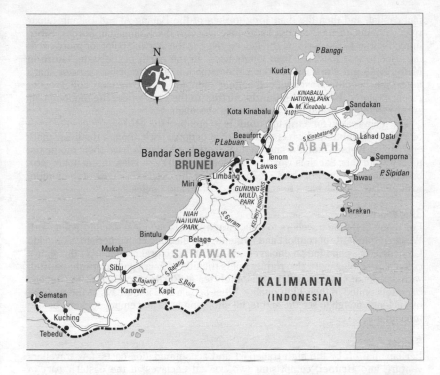

taste of Old England, head for the hill stations of **Fraser's Hill** and **Cameron Highlands**, where cooler temperatures and lush countryside provide ample opportunities for walks, rounds of golf and cream teas. North of Penang, there's a more Malay feel to the country, with **Alor Setar** the last major town before the Thai border. This far north, the premier tourist destination is **Pulau Langkawi**, a popular duty-free island.

Routes down the Peninsula's **east coast** are more relaxing, running past the sleepy kampungs of the mainland – **Merang**, **Cherating** and **Marang** – and the stunning islands of **Pulau Perhentian** and **Pulau Tioman**. The state capitals of **Kota Bharu**, near the northeastern Thai border, and **Kuala Terengganu**, further south, are showcases for the best of Malay traditions, craft production and performing arts.

Crossing the Peninsula's mountainous interior by road or rail allows you to venture into the unsullied tropical rainforests of **Taman Negara**. The park's four thousand square kilometres has enough to keep you occupied for weeks: trails, salt-lick hides for animal-watching, an aerial forest-canopy walkway, limestone caves and waterfalls. Other interior routes can take in a ride on the **jungle railway**, which links east and west coasts, and visits to the southern **lakes**, which retain communities of indigenous peoples, the Orang Asli.

Across the sea from the Peninsula are the East Malaysian states of Sarawak and Sabah. For most travellers, their first taste of **Sarawak** is **Kuching**, the old colonial capital, and then the Iban **longhouses** of the Batang Ai and Batang Lupar river systems, or the Bidayuh longhouse close to the Kalimantan border. **Sibu**, much further to the north on the Rajang river, is the starting point for more exciting trips to less touristed Iban longhouses. In the north of the state, **Gunung Mulu National Park** is the principal destination, its extraordinary razor-sharp limestone needles providing demanding climbing. More remote still are the rarely explored **Kelabit Highlands**, further to the east, where the mountain air is refreshingly cool and flora and fauna is abundant.

The main reason for a trip to **Sabah** is to conquer the 4101-metre granite peak of **Mount Kinabalu**, which is set in its own national park, though the lively modern capital **Kota Kinabalu** and its idyllic offshore islands have their moments, too. Beyond this, Sabah is worth a visit for its **wildlife**: turtles, orang-utans, proboscis monkeys and hornbills are just a few of the exotic residents of the jungle, while Pulau Sipadan has a host of sharks, fishes and turtles.

Singapore

For many first-time travellers to Asia, **Singapore** is the ideal starting point, with Western standards of comfort and hygiene, and dazzling consumerism, alongside Chinese, Malay and Indian enclaves and the architectural remnants of the state's colonial past. Singapore also rightly holds the title of Asia's **gastronomic capital**, with snacks at simple hawker stalls, high tea at **Raffles**, and exquisite Chinese banquets united in their high quality. Most people find a few days in the metropolis is long enough to see the sights, fill shopping bags and empty pockets, before moving on.

Brunei

Perhaps put off by the high transport and accommodation costs, few travellers venture into **Brunei**, comprising two coastal enclaves in the eastern part of Sarawak, near the border with Sabah. For those who do pass through, however, there are few more stirring sights than the spectacle of the main mosque in the capital **Bandar Seri Begawan**, towering over the water village below. The sparsely populated Temburong district now offers the chance to visit unspoilt rainforest at the **Ulu Temburong National Park**. A million miles away from all of these, culturally speaking, is the state's Disneyland-style **Jerudong Playground**.

When to go

Temperatures vary little in Malaysia, Singapore and Brunei, constantly hovering around 30°C (22°C in highland areas), while humidity is high all year round. The major distinction in the seasons is marked by the arrival of the **monsoon** (also called "the rainy season" locally), which particularly affects the east coast of Peninsular Malaysia, the northeastern part of Sabah, Brunei and the western end of Sarawak from November to February. Monsoon brings heavy and prolonged downpours, sometimes lasting two or three hours and prohibiting more or less all activity for the duration; boats to most of the islands in affected areas will not attempt the sea swell during the height of the rainy season. It's worth noting, too, that tropical climates are prone to showers all year round, often in the mid-afternoon, though these short, sheeting downpours clear up as quickly as they arrive. In mountainous areas like the Cameron Highlands, the Kelabit Highlands and any of the hill stations, you may experience more frequent rain as the high peaks gather clouds more or less permanently. See the climate chart below for more precise information about temperature and rainfall.

The **ideal time** to visit is during the first half of the year, between March and July, thereby avoiding the worst of the rains. Arriving just after the monsoon – say, in early March – affords the best of all worlds: an abundant water supply, verdant countryside and bountiful waterfalls. If you brave the heavy showers, the months

CLIMATE CHART											

Average daily temperatures (°C, max and min) and monthly rainfall (mm)

	Jan	Feb	March	April	May	June	July	Aug	Sept	Oct	Nov	Dec
Bandar Seri Begawan												
max °C	30	30	31	32	32.5	32	31.5	32	31.5	31.5	31	31
min °C	23	23	23	23.5	23.5	23.5	23.5	23.5	23	23	23	23
rainfall mm	133	63	71	124	218	311	277	256	314	334	296	241
Cameron Highlands												
max °C	21	22	23	23	23	23	22	22	22	22	22	21
min °C	14	14	14	15	15	15	14	15	15	15	15	15
rainfall mm	120	111	198	277	273	137	165	172	241	334	305	202
Kota Bharu												
max °C	29	30	31	32	33	32	32	32	32	31	29	29
min °C	22	23	23	24	24	24	23	23	23	23	23	23
rainfall mm	163	60	99	81	114	132	157	168	195	286	651	603
Kota Kinabalu												
max °C	30	30	31	32	32	31	31	31	31	31	31	31
min °C	23	23	23	24	24	24	24	24	23	23	23	23
rainfall mm	133	63	71	124	218	311	277	256	314	334	296	241
Kuala Lumpur												
max °C	33	33	33	33	33	32	32	32	32	32	31	31
min °C	22	22	23	23	23	23	23	23	23	23	23	23
rainfall mm	159	154	223	276	182	119	120	133	173	258	263	223
Kuching												
max °C	30	30	31	32	33	33	32	33	32	32	31	31
min °C	23	23	23	23	23	23	23	23	23	23	23	23
rainfall mm	683	522	339	286	253	199	199	211	271	326	343	465
Mersing												
max °C	28	29	30	31	32	31	31	31	31	31	29	28
min °C	23	23	23	23	23	23	22	22	22	23	23	23
rainfall mm	319	153	141	120	149	145	170	173	177	207	359	635
Penang												
max °C	32	32	32	32	31	31	31	31	31	31	31	31
min °C	23	23	24	24	24	24	23	23	23	23	23	23
rainfall mm	70	93	141	214	240	170	208	235	341	380	246	107
Singapore												
max °C	31	32	32	32	32	32	31	31	31	31	31	30
min °C	21	22	23	23	23	23	22	22	22	22	22	22
rainfall mm	146	155	182	223	228	151	170	163	200	199	255	258

of January and February are particularly rewarding for **festivals**, especially Chinese New Year and the Hindu celebration of Thaipusam. By sticking to Singapore and the west coast of the Peninsula, you not only miss the most severe rains but, coincidentally, find yourself in the most important areas for Chinese and Hindu culture. Arrive in Sabah a little later, in May, and you'll be able to take in the Sabah Fest, a week-long celebration of Sabahan culture. In Sarawak, June's *gawai* festival is well worth attending, when longhouse doors are flung open for two days of rice-harvest merry-making, with dancing, eating, drinking and music. Similarly, the pre-monsoon month of September, just around harvest time, is a fruitful time for the Malaysian east coast in terms of cultural activity.

PART ONE

THE
BASICS

GETTING THERE FROM BRITAIN

There are frequent flights to Kuala Lumpur (KL) and Singapore from London Heathrow and from Manchester. Flights to Bandar Seri Begawan, though not quite as frequent, have the advantage of giving access not only to Brunei but also to East Malaysia (there are no direct flights from Britain to Sabah and Sarawak). On these routes, Malaysia Airlines (MAS), Singapore Airlines, Royal Brunei Airlines, BA and Qantas are the main operators, with return fares typically going for around £500 return, though prices rise by about £100 during high season (July, Aug & Dec). Flying from a regional city adds £50–60 to the cost; the airline you're flying to KL with can usually arrange your connecting flight to Heathrow or Manchester. Alternatively, consider an indirect flight with KLM via Amsterdam, where you pick up their flight to KL or Singapore; their fares from over a dozen regional airports, including Teeside, Aberdeen and Cardiff, cost the same as flying from London.

Airlines occasionally advertise competitive promotional fares in the media – it's not a bad policy to check with them first to see what they've got to offer. However, you're usually better off booking your flight through an established **discount agent**, as this is generally significantly cheaper than buying directly from the airline. There's a list of reliable discount agents on p.5; others can be found by consulting the advertisements in the weekend national papers, especially the *Times* on Saturdays and the *Observer* and *Sunday Times*.

London's *Evening Standard* newspaper and *Time Out* magazine, and major regional newspapers and listings magazines, like the Manchester-based *City Life*, are also useful. Likewise the Internet is increasingly a sensible place to make a start – check out *www.cheapflights.co.uk* and *www.ebookers.com*, among others.

If you're a full-time **student** or **under 26**, you may be eligible for additional discounts on flights, or be able to obtain flexible tickets (incurring minimal or no charges should you change your travel plans) without paying a premium fare. It's worth consulting a student and youth travel specialist, such as usit CAMPUS or STA (see p.5), as to what's on offer.

Those visiting Malaysia or Singapore as part of a longer Southeast Asian tour may want to consider getting discounted flights to **Bangkok** in Thailand. Though this route is little cheaper than flying directly to KL or Singapore, it offers the opportunity to travel overland by train or bus into Peninsular Malaysia – see "Getting there from Southeast Asia", p.17, for details. You can also get to the region with a **Round-the-World** flight or an **open-jaw** ticket, the latter letting you fly out to one city and back home from another. For details of both types of tickets, see p.5.

There's an increasing number of **package holidays** and **adventure tours** available, too, ranging from fly-drive holidays to Malaysia and specialist trekking trips in Sarawak to Singapore city breaks. Although usually not the cheapest way of travelling, these deals can be worthwhile if you have a specific interest or are on a tight itinerary (see p.6).

MALAYSIA FLIGHTS AND FARES

The quickest way to get to **West Malaysia** is on a **nonstop** flight to **Kuala Lumpur** from **London Heathrow** or **Manchester**, which takes around thirteen hours. From Heathrow, you can fly with either Malaysia Airlines (MAS) or BA; only MAS does nonstop flights from Manchester. On these flights, APEX tickets – valid for one month and requiring booking and payment at least seven days in advance – cost around £500 in low season; however, note that you can't get a full refund on your booking if you're unable to travel – the cancellation fee is around £100. More flexible

PEX or SUPERPEX tickets (minimum stay seven days, maximum three months; refundable apart from a £50 cancellation fee) come at greatly increased cost, around £900 return in low season. Both airlines have occasional seat **sales**, however, where you can pick up a return flight for as little as £420, though you're still liable for a £100 cancellation fee should you cancel your trip. Discount agents can sometimes sell you a flight on either airline for about £100 less than the APEX fare.

Flying with any other airline to KL involves at least one stop en route. Such flights sometimes work out considerably cheaper than flying nonstop, but take up to eight hours longer; on the other hand, they offer the chance of a **stopover** in another country. Options include Air India (via Bombay), KLM (via Amsterdam), Air Lanka (via Colombo), Thai (via Bangkok), Turkish Airlines (via Istanbul or Dubai) and Gulf Air (via Abu Dhabi). In terms of price, there's little to choose between these airlines; any reliable specialist agent can sell you a ticket on one of these routes, usually for between £400 and £500 in low season,

though you might find prices slightly higher at other times.

SABAH AND SARAWAK

If you're headed for **East Malaysia**, you have two choices of route, neither particularly direct. The first is to fly direct to **Brunei** (see opposite) and travel into **Sabah** or **Sarawak** by bus, car or boat, or on another flight; the combined cost of your flight to Brunei and onward travel is around £550 in low season. The second option is to fly to **KL** or **Singapore** and connect with an MAS internal flight to **Kuching** or **Kota Kinabalu**. The total flight time can vary enormously, depending on what day (and what time of day) you fly. There are around ten daily flights leaving KL for Kuching, and a similar number for Kota Kinabalu; the best connection adds around two hours to your journey, though on an indirect flight (many stop off at Johor Bahru), you could be looking at more like four hours on top of the journey time from London.

MAS' low-season return fares from London or Manchester to Kuching and Kota Kinabalu are

---

AIRLINES

Air India ☎020/8560 9996, *www.airindia.com* Three flights a week to KL and six weekly flights to Singapore (with a stop in Delhi or Bombay, usually lasting several hours).

Air Lanka ☎020/7930 4688, *www.airlanka.com* Five flights weekly to Singapore and three a week to KL, all with stopovers in Colombo.

British Airways ☎0845/7222111, *www.british-airways.com* Four daily nonstop Singapore flights, plus one daily flight to KL, from Heathrow.

Finnair ☎020/7408 1222, *www.finnair.com* Four flights a week from London to Singapore, via Helsinki.

Gulf Air ☎020/7408 1717, *www.gulfairco.com* One daily flight to Singapore via Bahrain, and three to KL via Abu Dhabi.

KLM ☎0870/5074074, *www.klm.com* Flies daily via Amsterdam to both KL and Singapore.

Kuwait Airways ☎020/7412 0007. Flies twice a week from Heathrow to Singapore, via Kuwait.

Malaysia Airlines (MAS) ☎0870/607 9090, *www.mas.com.my* The efficient Malaysian national airline flies nonstop to KL twice daily from Heathrow and three times a week from Manchester. There are regular connections on to

Kuching, Kota Kinabulu and Penang, and less frequent flights to Brunei.

Pakistan International Airways ☎020/7499 5500. Three flights a week from Heathrow to Singapore via Karachi.

Qantas ☎0845/7747 767, *www.qantas.com.au* Flies from Heathrow to Singapore nonstop twice daily, and three times a week to KL.

Royal Brunei Airlines ☎020/7584 6660, *www.bruneiair.com* Flies from London Heathrow to Brunei daily, with stops in Dubai and Singapore.

Singapore Airlines (SIA) ☎020/8747 0007, *www.singaporeair.com* Singapore's national carrier does three daily flights to Singapore from Heathrow, with one flight a day from Manchester. From Singapore, they offer some conveniently timed connections to KL, Penang, Kota Kinabalu, Kuching and Brunei.

Thai International ☎020/7499 9113, *www.thaiair.com* Daily flights to Bangkok from where you can travel overland to KL and Singapore.

Turkish Airlines ☎020/7766 9300, *www.turkishairlines.com* Flies from Heathrow to Singapore via Istanbul four times a week, and four times a week to KL, via Istanbul and Dubai.

simply the price of the KL leg plus the regular fare from KL to each city – around £75 for Kuching, and £120 for Kota Kinabalu. If you intend to make additional internal flights in Malaysia, consider buying an MAS **Discover Malaysia Pass**, only available in conjunction with an MAS ticket into or out of Malaysia; see p.40 for details.

SINGAPORE AND BRUNEI FLIGHTS AND FARES

Singapore Airlines has daily **nonstop** scheduled flights from **London Heathrow** and from **Manchester** to **Singapore**; the flight takes around thirteen hours. From Heathrow, British Airways, Royal Brunei and Qantas also fly direct to Singapore. A low-season return ticket on SIA, valid for three months, costs around £520 from London or Manchester. Flying on BA, Qantas or Royal Brunei costs the same or very slightly more than flying on SIA, though on Qantas and Royal Brunei, these prices may be available only through discount agents.

On other airlines, a scheduled flight to Singapore involves at least one stop en route, typically at the airline's hub city. It generally

takes around seventeen hours in total to reach Singapore this way, though the journey can last as long as 22 hours. Fares from London airports start from around £400 in low season (with slightly cheaper fares sometimes available, particularly from January to March), Pakistan Airways and Finnair are usually about the cheapest.

BRUNEI

The only airline that flies directly to Brunei is their national carrier, Royal Brunei Airlines, which flies daily from **London Heathrow** to **Bandar Seri Begawan**, a sixteen-hour journey with brief stops in Dubai and Singapore. A specialist discount agent is your best bet for this flight (their prices start at £400 return in low season, rising to £550 in high season). It's worth noting that flights in July and December are regularly busy.

RTW AND OPEN-JAW TICKETS

There are a bewildering number of **Round-the-World** (RTW) tickets on offer. One example is the World Discover ticket, sold by BA and Qantas for

SPECIALIST TOUR OPERATORS

Asia World Travel, third floor, Waterloo House, 11–17 Chertsey Rd, Woking, Surrey GU21 5AB (☎01483/730808). Fly-drive holidays, city breaks in Singapore, trips to Sarawak and Mount Kinabalu in Sabah, and tours of both west and east coast Peninsular Malaysia. Recommended, but not budget-priced.

Bales Tours, Bales House, Junction Rd, Dorking, Surrey RH4 3HB (☎01306/885991). Especially recommended for guided tours in Sarawak and Sabah, as well as tailor-made trips incorporating the Eastern & Oriental trip from Singapore to Bangkok.

British Airways Holidays, Astral Towers, Betts Way, London Rd, Crawley, West Sussex RH10 (worldwide ☎0800/242 4243). Five-night city breaks in Singapore, KL or Penang starting at £565.

Exodus Expeditions, 9 Weir Rd, London SW12 0LT (☎020/8675 5550). Their six-week Southeast Asia tour from Hong Kong to Singapore (£1200 excluding flights) incorporates three weeks in Peninsular Malaysia. They also do a fifteen-day "Borneo Explorer" trip which includes visits to Gunung Mulu in Sarawak, and Mount Kinabalu and Sungei Kinabatangan in Sabah (£1300–1600, including flights).

Explore Worldwide, 1 Frederick St, Aldershot, Hants, GU11 1LQ (☎01252/760000, *www.explore .co.uk*). Among other trips to Malaysia, they offer a twelve-day tour of Sarawak, including nights in longhouses near Kuching; this costs around £750, including flights and twin-sharing accommodation.

Kuoni Worldwide, Kuoni House, Dorking, Surrey RH5 4AZ (☎01306/740500). Peninsular and East Malaysia tours and city breaks, including a twelve-night "Malaysia Discovery" tour, visiting Singapore, Penang, Melaka, Cameron Highlands and Kota Bharu, costing £1000 for two people in twin-sharing accommodation (flights extra).

Magic Of The Orient, 2 Kingsland Court, Three Bridges Rd, Crawley, West Sussex RH10 1HL (☎01293/537700). Varied adventure tours in East Malaysia to suit most budgets; their six-day "Wildlife of Sabah" tour, taking in the eastern islands and Sungei Kinabatangan, costs £425 excluding flights to the region. Also specializes in fly-drive packages on the Peninsula.

MAS, 61 Piccadilly, London W1V 9HL (☎020/7341 2020). Their Road to Freedom scheme involves booking hotels and car hire ahead: prices run from £350 per person, based on two people travelling together, including car and hotels (flights extra). They can also arrange river-rafting trips starting at around £400 per person for six nights (not including airfare).

Reliance Holidays Asia, 12 Little Newport St, London WC2 (☎020/7437 0503). Does numerous tours to Malaysia; their "Borneo Connection" trip covers Sarawak and Sabah (8 days £700; 10 days £1200; price covers twin-share accommodation and flights). Also does coach tours around the Peninsula.

Thomas Cook, 45 Berkeley St, London W1X 5AE and High Streets across London and the UK (☎0990/666522, *www.tch.thomascook.com*). Varied escorted and independent tours to all points in the region – fly-drives, city breaks and beach holidays.

---

around £850; it allows you to make six stopovers en route from London to Australia. Usefully for a wider trip through the Far East, all these stops can be in Southeast Asia should you wish – you could visit Bangkok, KL, Singapore and Jakarta along the way, for example.

Open-jaw tickets have the convenience of allowing you to fly back from a different airport to your initial destination, which often means you can avoid backtracking to catch your flight home; low-season fares for a ticket out to Bangkok and back from Singapore start at around £450.

ORGANIZED TOURS AND PACKAGE HOLIDAYS

There are an increasing number of organized **tours** and **package holidays** available to both Singapore and Malaysia (see box, above, for a list of tour operators). For city breaks, five nights in Singapore, including flights and accommodation in a three-star hotel, go for around £600 (£800 in high season), a figure which rises to £800–1000 for two weeks. Standard two-week packages to Malaysia usually include nights in KL, Cameron Highlands, Melaka, Penang and beach destinations like Kota Bharu, or island locations like Tioman, Langkawi or the Perhentians, ending up (or starting) in Singapore; these cost just over £1000 in high season, perhaps £150–200 less in low season.

Specialist operators can also arrange itineraries which include **trekking** through the rainforest, guided **adventure tours** in the national parks, and even a ride on the extremely swish

Eastern & Oriental Express train which plies between Singapore and Bangkok (see p.38). These tours tend to be expensive, but sometimes include activities that would be very difficult or impossible to arrange for yourself. Operators like Explore Worldwide and Exodus usually offer competitive prices; for example, the former's "Borneo Adventure", a 21-day trip to Sarawak and Sabah, including visits to a longhouse and various national parks, costs £1000 including flights. The box opposite contains a list of companies operating specialist tours and details of what they offer. You can usually arrange less expensive tours once you're already travelling – details of local tour operators and prices are given where appropriate in the *Guide*.

Several companies – including MAS – offer **fly-drive** packages to Malaysia and Singapore, which include a return flight, the use of a small car and prebooked accommodation in three-star hotels; the standard fourteen-day route starting in Singapore and visiting Melaka, Kuala Lumpur, the Cameron Highlands, Penang, Kota Bharu and Kuantan costs £1000–1400. If you book under MAS' Road to Freedom programme (see box, opposite), you get to choose what grade of hotel you stay in, and which type of car you hire. Some companies – like Magic of the Orient and Asia World – organize a tailor-made fly-drive tour, which gives you the chance to get a little off the beaten track and visit the interior and Taman Negara National Park. A two-week tour, inclusive of flights, accommodation and car, starts at around £1000 per person.

GETTING THERE FROM IRELAND

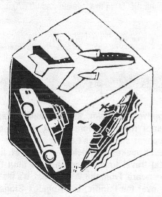

There are two indirect options to get to **Malaysia and Singapore from Ireland: you can either get a flight to London or** **Manchester, where you pick up nonstop flights to Kuala Lumpur and Singapore or get a flight to KL or Singapore via the hub city of an airline based outside Britain, such as Air France or Lufthansa. If you are flying from Northern Ireland, your best bet is generally flying via London or Manchester. The most straightforward way to reach Brunei from any part of Ireland is also to get a flight to London, where you pick up Royal Brunei's direct flight to Bandar Seri Begawan. For details of flights to KL, Singapore and Bandar Seri Begawan from Britain, see p.3.**

If you are flying with Malaysian Airlines (MAS) from Heathrow, they arrange your flight to London with British Midland, which adds around IR£70 on top of their cost of the onward flight. It's a little cheaper to bypass Britain; Lufthansa's Dublin–KL fare via Frankfurt is around IR£420 in low season,

---

DISCOUNT AGENTS AND TOUR OPERATORS

Joe Walsh Tours, 34 Grafton St, Dublin 2 (☎01/671 8751); 69 Upper O'Connell St , Dublin 2 (☎01/872 2555); 8–11 Baggot St, Dublin 2 (☎01/676 6091); 117 St Patrick St, Cork (☎021/277959). Knowledgeable discounted-flight agent with city tours in Kuala Lumpur and Penang from £829, including flights.

usit NOW, Fountain Centre, College St, Belfast BT1 6ET (☎028/9032 4073); Aston Quay, Dublin 2 (☎01/602 1600), and branches elsewhere in the Republic; *www.usitnow.ie* Ireland's main outlet for youth and student fares.

AIRLINES

Aer Lingus In the Republic ☎01/886 8888; in Northern Ireland ☎0645/737747; *www.aerlingus.ie*

Air France In the Republic ☎01/844 5633; in Northern Ireland ☎0845/084 5111; *www.airfrance.fr* One daily flight from Dublin to Singapore via Paris; the onward leg from Paris is nonstop.

British Airways In the Republic ☎1800/626747; in Northern Ireland ☎0845/722 2111; *www.british-airways.com* Offers connecting services from Northern Ireland to London, where you pick up their flight to KL or Singapore.

British Midland In the Republic ☎01/283 8833; in Northern Ireland ☎0870/607 0555; *www.britishmidland.co.uk* Flies from the Republic and Northern Ireland to London or Manchester, where you can pick up onward flights to Singapore, KL and Bandar Seri Begawan.

Lufthansa In the Republic ☎01/844 5544; in Northern Ireland ☎0845/773 7747; *www.lufthansa.co.uk* Flies from Dublin to KL, with a two-hour stop in Frankfurt.

Royal Jordanian ☎061/360800, *www.rja.com.jo* Flies from Shannon to Amman on Sunday, connecting with their nonstop flight to KL.

Malaysia Airlines In the Republic ☎01/676 1561; in Northern Ireland ☎0870/607 9090; *www.mas.com.my* Flies to KL from London and Manchester; they arrange connecting flights with British Midland to either airport from the Republic and Northern Ireland.

Singapore Airlines In the Republic ☎01/671 0722; in Northern Ireland ☎020/8747 0007, *www.singaporeair.com* Fly from Manchester and London Heathrow to Singapore; can arrange connections with Aer Lingus or British Midland from Dublin.

---

rising to IR£500 in high season; Royal Jordanian fly from Shannon, via Amman, to Kuala Lumpur for around IR£500 in low season and IR£600 in high. You can also get to Singapore for a little less this way; Air France fly from Dublin via Paris for around IR£550 in low season and IR£670 in high.

GETTING THERE FROM THE US AND CANADA

Malaysia, Singapore and Brunei are roughly halfway around the world from the East Coast of North America, and so whether you plan on flying eastward or westward, you're going to have a long flight with at least one stopover. However, the eastbound (transatlantic) route is more direct as the usual stopover cities aren't as far out of the way, which makes it quicker – about 21 hours' total travel time – and cheaper than flying westward. From the West Coast, it's faster to fly over the Pacific; Los Angeles–Singapore can be done in as little as nineteen hours, for example. That said, flying via Europe – which may suit your itinerary better – doesn't cost that much more.

The greatest choice of flights are to **Singapore** and **Kuala Lumpur** (KL), from where there are onward connections to Penang (on the Malaysian west coast), Kuching (in Sarawak), Kota Kinabalu (in Sabah) and Bandar Seri Begawan (in Brunei). Malaysia Airlines (MAS) is the only airline operating direct flights to KL from North America, while Singapore Airlines does direct flights to Singapore; there are no nonstop flights to Brunei, however.

AIRLINES IN NORTH AMERICA

Air Canada ☎1-888/247-2262, *www.aircanda.ca* Nonstop daily flights to Hong Kong or Seoul from Vancouver, Montréal and Toronto; they have onward arrangements with other carriers flying to Singapore, KL, Penang, Kuching, Kota Kinabulu, and Bandar Seri Begawan.

Air France In US ☎1-800/237-2747, Canada ☎1-800/667-2747; *www.airfrance.fr* Daily nonstop flights to Paris from major North American and Canadian cities, with onward connections to Singapore and arrangements with other carriers for connections to KL, Penang, Kuching, Kota Kinabalu and Bandar Seri Begawan.

Asiana Airlines ☎1-800/227-4262, *www.flyasiana.com* Daily flights to Singapore via Seoul from Los Angeles, San Francisco, Washington DC and New York.

British Airways ☎1-800/247-9297, *www.british-airways.com* Daily nonstop service from twenty-one US gateway cities, and from Montréal, Toronto and Vancouver, to London, with connections to Singapore and KL.

Canadian Airlines ☎1-800/426-7000, *www.cdnair.ca* Daily flights from Montréal/Toronto and Vancouver to Hong Kong, Tokyo, Osaka and Taipei, with connections on other carriers to Singapore and KL.

Cathay Pacific In US ☎1-800/233-2742, Canada ☎1-800/555-1212; *www.cathay-usa.com* Daily flights to Hong Kong from Vancouver, Toronto, Los Angeles, New York and San Francisco, with connections to KL and Singapore.

China Air Lines ☎1-800/227-5118, *www.china-airlines.com* Daily flights to Taipei from New York, Los Angeles, San Francisco, Honolulu and Anchorage, with onward connections to KL and Singapore.

EVA Airlines ☎1-800/695-1188, *www.evaair.com* This Taiwanese carrier has daily flights to Singapore, KL and Penang, via Taipei, from New York, Seattle, San Francisco and Los Angeles.

Japan Airlines ☎1-800/525-3663, *www.japanair.com* Daily flights to KL and Singapore, via Tokyo, from New York, Chicago, Dallas, San Francisco, Los Angeles and Vancouver.

Korean Airlines ☎1-800/438-5000, *www.koreanair.com* Flying via Seoul, it has daily flights to Singapore and three flights a week to KL, Penang, Kuching and Kota Kinabalu from all major US cities, as well as from Vancouver and Toronto. A Seoul stopover costs around US$50/CDN$75.

Malaysia Airlines (MAS) ☎1-800/552-9264, *www.malaysiaair.com* Three flights a week from New York and four flights a week from Los Angeles to KL, with connections to Singapore, Penang, Kuching, Kota Kinabalu and Bandar Seri Begawan. Also does two flights a week to KL from Vancouver, via Taipei. MAS can arrange connecting flights from US and Canadian cities to Los Angeles and New York, using other carriers.

Northwest/KLM In US ☎1-800/374-7747, Canada ☎1-800/361-5073, *www.klm.com* Serving all major US and Canadian cities, they offer daily flights to KL and Singapore from the East Coast via Amsterdam, and from the West Coast via Osaka or Tokyo.

Pakistan International Airlines (PIA) ☎1-800/221-2552. Five flights a week from New York to Karachi, with connections to Singapore and KL.

Philippine Airlines ☎1-800/435-9725, *www.philippineair.com* Flies three or four times a week from Los Angeles, Honolulu and San Francisco to Manila, with connections to KL, Singapore, Kuching and Kota Kinabalu.

Singapore Airlines ☎1-800/742-3333; *www.singaporeair.com* Flies to Singapore twice daily from Los Angeles and San Francisco, once daily from New York and three times a week from Vancouver, with connections to KL, Penang, Kuching, Kota Kinabalu and Bandar Seri Begawan. Stopovers in Hong Kong or Tokyo en route to Singapore cost US$100/CDN$150 extra.

Thai International In US ☎1-800/426-5204, Canada ☎1-800/668-8103, *www.thaiair.com* Flies from Los Angeles, New York, Washington DC, San Francisco, Dallas and Miami to Bangkok, with connecting flights to KL, Penang, Singapore and Bandar Seri Begawan.

United Airlines ☎1-800/538-2929, *www.ual.com* Daily flights from all major US and Canadian cities to Hong Kong and Tokyo, with connections on to Singapore.

Airfares from North America to Southeast Asia are highest from around early June to late August, and again from early December to early January. All other times are considered low season. The price difference between the two seasons is only about US$200–300/CDN$200–300 on a typical round-trip fare, but bear in mind that to travel during high season, it's best to book as far in advance as possible to get the best deal on tickets. Note that flying at weekends ordinarily adds about

DISCOUNT AGENTS, CONSOLIDATORS AND TRAVEL CLUBS IN NORTH AMERICA

Air Brokers International, 150 Post St, Suite 620, San Francisco, CA 94108 (☎1-800/883-3273 or 415/397-1383; www.airbrokers.com). Consolidator and specialist in RTW and Circle-Pacific tickets.

Air Courier Association, 15000 W Sixth Ave, Suite 203, Golden, CO 80401 (☎1-800/282-1202 or 303/215-9000; www.aircourier.org). Courier-flight broker.

Council Travel, Head Office, 205 E 42nd St, New York, NY 10017 (☎1-800/226-8624, 1-888/COUNCIL or 212/822-2700, www.counciltravel.com) and branches in many other US cities. Student travel organization.

Educational Travel Center, 438 N Frances St, Madison, WI 53703 (☎1-800/747-5551 or 608/256-5551, www.edtrav.com). Student/youth discount agent.

Flight Centre, South Granville St, Vancouver, BC (☎1-877/321-4255, www.flightcentre.com), and branches all over British Columbia and Ontario. Discount airfares from Canada.

Gateway Express, 7760 France Ave S, Edina, MN 55435 (☎612/831-3525, www.gatewayexpress.com). Discounts on flights to Asia.

High Adventure Travel Inc., 442 Post St, Suite 400, San Francisco, CA 94102 (☎1-800/350-0637 or 415/912-5600, www.airtreks.com). RTW and Circle-Pacific tickets. Their Web site features an interactive database that lets you build and price your own RTW itinerary.

Last-Minute Travel Club, 100 Sylvan Rd, Suite 600, Woburn, MA 01801 (☎1-800/LAST-MIN, www.lastminutetravel.com). Travel club specializing in stand-by deals.

Moment's Notice, 7301 New Utrecht Ave, Brooklyn, NY 11204 (☎212/486-0500). Discount-travel club.

Now Voyager, 74 Varick St, Suite 307, New York, NY 10013 (☎212/431-1616, fax 334-5243). Courier-flight broker.

Overseas Tours, 199 California Drive, Millbrae, CA 94030 (☎1-800/323-8777). Discount tickets and tours.

Pan Express Travel, 6 Wellesley St E, Suite 303, M41-186, Toronto, ON (☎416/964-6888). Discount airfares.

STA Travel, 10 Downing St, New York, NY 10014 (☎1-800/777-0112), and branches in other major cities; www.sta.com. Worldwide specialist in independent and student travel.

Travel Avenue, 10 S Riverside Plaza, Suite 1404, Chicago, IL 60606 (☎1-800/333-3335 or 312/876-6866, www.travelavenue.com). Travel agent that offers discounts in the form of rebates after you've bought your ticket with them.

Travel CUTS, 187 College St, Toronto, ON M5T 1P7 (☎1-800/667-2887 or 416/979-2406), and other branches across Canada (mostly on, or near, university campuses); www.travelcuts.com Student-travel specialists, with discounted fares for non-students too.

Worldtek Travel, 111 Water St, New Haven, CT 06511 (☎1-800/243-1723, www.worldtek.com). Discount travel agency.

US$100/CDN$100 to the round-trip fare; price ranges quoted in the sections below assume mid-week travel. If you are flying indirectly via an Asian city, you may want to take advantage of a **stopover** there; many airlines will allow you to do this for US$50–100 extra on top of the round-trip fare.

If you're flying with MAS to KL, it doesn't cost any extra to get a connecting flight from KL to Penang or Kuching; however, connections to Kota Kinabalu cost around US$100/CDN$150. Those who want to use internal flights to get around Malaysia may find it worthwhile getting a **Discover Malaysia air pass**, costing US$100/CDN$150 or US$200/CDN$300 depend-

ing on the type of pass; it's available from MAS in conjunction with round-trip tickets only (see p.40). **Round-the-World** tickets (see p.12) are worth considering if you want to see Malaysia, Singapore and Brunei as part of a much wider-ranging trip.

Though your travel agent should have details of airlines' up-to-the-minute fares, occasionally you'll turn up better deals by calling the airlines directly (be sure to ask about seasonal promotions). Whatever the airlines have on offer, however, there are any number of specialist travel agents trying to offer a better deal, details of which can be found in their advertisements in the Sunday newspaper travel sections. Some of these agents are **consolidators**, who buy up large blocks of tickets to sell on at a discount. Note that airlines generally won't alter tickets sold through a consolidator, so you can only make changes through the consolidator, and will often have to pay a very steep fee to change the dates of your flights. Like consolidators, **discount agents** deal in blocks of tickets off-loaded by the airlines, and typically offer a range of other travel-related services as well, such as insurance, youth and student ID cards, car rentals and tours. **Discount travel clubs** are worth considering if you travel a lot; most charge an annual membership fee, in return for which you get discounts on air tickets, car rental and the like. The **Internet** is also a useful resource; try *www.cheaptickets.com* and *www.lastminute.com* to compare prices, book flights and find last-minute deals. Be aware that there are a certain number of sharks among the travel companies – *never* deal with a company that demands cash up front or refuses to accept payment by credit card.

FLIGHTS TO MALAYSIA

From the US, Malaysia Airlines (MAS) operates **direct flights** to Kuala Lumpur from Los Angeles (via Taipei or Tokyo) and from New York (via Dubai), and also offer connections to other cities in Malaysia. Many other airlines can get you to Malaysia, though you need to change planes in their hub cities; Korean Airlines' flights from major US cities to KL, via Seoul, are among the cheapest, especially if tickets are bought through a discount travel agent.

The cheapest **fares** from the East Coast to KL run from about US$850 in the low season to US$1100 in the high season; from the West Coast the corresponding fares are US$800 and US$1000.

FROM CANADA

Canadian Airlines has daily flights from Montréal, Toronto and Vancouver to Hong Kong, Seoul, Tokyo, Osaka and Taipei. Their onward connections to KL are generally arranged with other carriers, although from Vancouver, Canadian has two weekly direct flights to KL via Taipei – as does Malaysia Airlines. Korean Air also operates flights out of Vancouver and Toronto to Seoul and onto Singapore and KL. Fares from Vancouver range from CDN$2200 in low season to

CDN$2400 in high season; the corresponding fares from Toronto and Montréal are CDN$2300 and CDN$2600.

FLIGHTS TO SINGAPORE

From the US, Singapore Airlines offers the most frequent departures to Singapore, with direct flights from New York (via Frankfurt) and Los Angeles and San Francisco (via Tokyo, Seoul, Taipei or Hong Kong). Taking an indirect flight with another airline or using a combination of airlines won't necessarily increase your journey time, and can often be a cheaper option. The cheapest flights are on Asiana Airlines, which make connections via Seoul, and on Korean Airlines, which flies from all major US cities to Singapore via Seoul.

From the East Coast, the cheapest fares range from US$900 in the low season to US$1100 in the high season; fares start at US$800 from the West Coast in low season, rising to US$1000 in high.

FROM CANADA

Canadian Airlines have daily flights from Montréal, Toronto and Vancouver to several Asian cities, with connecting flights on other carriers to Singapore. Both Singapore Airlines and Korean Airlines fly to Singapore via Seoul, with Singapore Airlines flying from Vancouver and Korean Airlines flying from Vancouver and Toronto. Other airlines, such as EVA and Northwest, have connections via Taiwan and Japan respectively. Fares from Vancouver range from CDN$2000 in low season to CDN$2300 in high; from Toronto and Montréal CDN$2200 to CDN$2400.

FLIGHTS TO BRUNEI

In recent times **Brunei** has become a lot cheaper to fly to, but it is still pretty much off the beaten track – only MAS and Singapore Airlines fly there directly from North America.

Besides using these airlines, you could pick up a cheap ticket to London, Singapore or KL, and fly on from any of these cities with Royal Brunei Airlines, MAS or Singapore Airlines (see "Getting There from Britain", p.3), though discount agents in North America are unlikely to be able to sell you a ticket for the final leg. APEX fares with MAS or Singapore from New York are around US$850 in low season, rising to US$1100 in high; from Los Angeles,

US$900/US$1100; and from Vancouver, CDN$2050/CDN$2300.

RTW AND COURIER FLIGHTS

Round-the-World (RTW) and **Circle-Pacific** tickets usually allow you to touch down in about half a dozen cities, and so can be very good value if you're planning a trip involving several stops. A lot of travel agents offer "off the shelf" RTW/Circle-Pacific tickets which include a myriad of ready-built itineraries; it's also possible to create a customized itinerary, but a ticket for this is more expensive. Fares with Singapore and Malaysia stopovers start at around US$1200 (around CDN$2100 for Canadian departures). As an example, a RTW ticket for the New York–Hong Kong–Penang–Kuala Lumpur–London–New York route costs around US$1300. It's worth checking out flight-agent Web sites, as some have lists of itineraries and sample fares.

NORTH AMERICAN TOUR OPERATORS

Abercrombie & Kent, 1520 Kensington Rd, Oak Brook, IL 60521 (☎1-800/323-7308, *www.ambercrombiekent.com*). Deluxe tours built around the Eastern & Oriental Express.

Adventure Center, 1311 63rd St, Suite 200, Emeryville, CA 94608 (☎1-800/227-8747, *www.adventurecenter.com*). Adventure tours and hikes combining Singapore, Malaysia and Thailand. A ten-day nature-watching trip in East Malaysia, including some mountain climbing, starts at around US$650, excluding flights.

Adventures Abroad, Suite 2148-20800 Westminster Hwy, Richmond, BC V6V 2W3 (☎1-800/665-3998, *www.adventures-abroad.com*). Small-group (maximum 21 participants) adventure tours to Malaysia. Their eight-day jungle trip costs CDN$3000, including the flight from the West Coast of Canada.

Asian Affair Holidays, Singapore Airlines (☎1-800/742-3133, *www2.singaporeair.com/americas/aah.htm*). Packages including airfare from the US, hotels and sightseeing. A three-day Singapore or KL package costs from US$1400.

Asian Pacific Holidays, 90101 Reseda Blvd, Suite 227, North Ridge, CA 91324 (☎1-800/825-1680, *www.asianpacificadventures.com*). Specializes in off-the-beaten-track tours offering in-depth cultural explorations throughout Malaysia and Southeast Asia. For example, their "Headhunters, hornbills, and orangutans" tour of East Malaysia, lasting fourteen days, costs US$1750 plus airfare.

Cathay Pacific Holidays (☎1-800/762-8181, *www.cathay-usa.com*). City-break packages and discounts on hotels. Their four-day Singapore package costs US$300 including accommodation, though not flights.

Earthwatch, 680 Mt Auburn St, Watertown, MA 02272-9104 (☎1-800/776-0188, *www.earthwatch.org*). Runs eco-oriented conservation programmes involving volunteer participation.

The fourteen-day "Green turtles of Malaysia" tour starts at US$1700 excluding airfare.

Japan & Orient Tours, 4025 Camino del Rio South, Suite 200, San Diego, CA 92108 (☎1-800/377-1080, *www.jot.com*). Regional tours, city breaks to KL, Penang and Singapore, cruises, fly-drives, E&O Express. Their four-night package to Singapore starts at US$800, including flights and accommodation.

Journeyworld International, 551 Fifth Ave, Suite 1923, New York, NY 10176 (☎1-800/635-3900). Offers general Malaysian vacations, city breaks and E&O Express packages.

Pacific Bestour, 228 River Vale Rd, River Vale, NJ 07675 (☎1-800/688-3288, *www.bestour.com*). Organizes regional tours, Singapore city breaks, and packages on the E&O Express.

Pacific Holidays, 2 W 45th St, Suite 1102, New York, NY 10036-4212 (☎1-800/355-8025, *www.pacificholidaysinc.com*). Offers inexpensive group tours: their fifteen-day tour through Peninsular Malaysia, flying into KL and out of Singapore, starts at around US$1900 including airfare.

Saga Holidays, 222 Berkeley St, Boston, MA 02116 (☎1-800/234-8220, *www.sagaholidays.com*). Inexpensive coach tours. Their thirteen-night "Borneo: the Mystical Wilderness" tour to East Malaysia starts at US$1600, with departures from Los Angeles or New York.

TBI Tours, 53 Summer St, Keene, NH 03431 (☎1-800/221-2216, *www.generaltours.com*). Offers a variety of packages in Singapore and Malaysia.

Vacationland, 150 Post St, Suite 680, San Francisco, CA 94108 (☎1-800/245-0050, *www.vacation-land.com*). Malaysia Airlines' tour arm, they offer an extensive range of city breaks, fly-drive packages, regional tours and the like. Tours of Singapore start at around US$1000 for seven days, departing from the West Coast (US$200 more from New York City).

Round-trip **courier flights** to Singapore and Kuala Lumpur cost around US$300/CDN$450, with last-minute specials booked within three days of departure as low as US$100/CDN$150.

PACKAGES AND ORGANIZED TOURS

Tours in Malaysia and Singapore range from sweaty jungle treks to five-star city breaks and sightseeing excursions. Inevitably, these packaged journeys are more expensive than they would be if done independently, but can be worth it for a hassle-free experience, particularly if you only have a limited amount of time for your journey.

North American operators don't really offer budget tours – a two-week adventure vacation taking in Sabah and Sarawak costs around US$2500/CDN$3700, including airfare, for example. **Fly-drive** packages, starting at around US$1800/CDN$2700, at least allow you to keep costs down by giving you more independence; for even greater flexibility, you can buy a package covering accommodation, airport transfers, some meals and sightseeing, though not flights; these start at around US$250/CDN$370 for three days.

For a taste of opulent splendour, consider a package trip on board the Eastern & Oriental (E&O) Express train (see p.38); packages, starting at US$1200/CDN$1800, invariably include several days' worth of luxurious side trips, along with the two-night train journey from Singapore to Bangkok prices.

Note that your local travel agent should be able to book any tour for you at the same price as buying directly from the tour operator. For a list of North American tour companies, see box opposite.

GETTING THERE FROM AUSTRALIA AND NEW ZEALAND

There's a good choice of flights to Malaysia, Singapore and Brunei, with each country regularly served by its own national airline – Malaysian Airlines (MAS), Singapore Airlines or Royal Brunei respectively – as well as by other carriers. Singapore is generally the most frequently used gateway to the region.

The market for flights to Southeast Asian destinations is very competitive, so it's best to shop around, though note that tickets purchased direct from the airlines are usually expensive (it's more than likely you'll be quoted the undiscounted rate). The travel agents listed in the box overleaf can fill you in on all the latest deals and any special offers. If you're a **student** or under 26, you may be able to obtain a further reduction of ten or twenty percent off the normal discounted fare; a student travel specialist, like STA, is a good place to start.

It's well worth taking advantage of a **stopover** en route – Asian airlines fly via their home base giving you a perfect opportunity to explore a bit more of the area – or an **open-jaw** ticket that allows you to fly into one city and out of another, and travel overland in between. For those visiting the region as part of a wider trip, there are several good-value options worth considering, such as multistop **Circle Asia** fares and **Round-the-World** (RTW) tickets; see "Getting There from Southeast Asia", p.17, for details of routes into Malaysia, Singapore and Brunei from Thailand and Indonesia. If you intend to use internal flights within Malaysia, it's worth getting MAS' **Discover Malaysia Pass**, available only to those travelling to Malaysia itself with MAS (see p.40 for details).

AIRLINES

Air New Zealand In Australia ☎13 2476, in New Zealand ☎0800/737 000 or 09/357 3000. Flies daily from Auckland to Singapore, in combination with Singapore Airlines.

Ansett In Australia ☎13 1414 or 02/9352 6444, in New Zealand ☎09/379 6409; *www.ansett.com.au* Three flights a week from Sydney to Singapore and Kuala Lumpur: code-shares with Singapore Airlines to provide daily services.

British Airways In Australia ☎02/8904 8800, in New Zealand ☎09/356 8690. Operates daily flights a week from Sydney to Singapore.

Egypt Air, Australia ☎02/9232 6677, no NZ office. Flies twice a week from Sydney to Singapore.

Garuda In Australia ☎1300/365 330, 09/366 1855 or 1800/128 510. Flies daily from Sydney, Melbourne and Perth, three times weekly from Brisbane and Auckland and twice weekly from Cairns, Adelaide and Darwin to Singapore and separately to Kuala Lumpur, via Denpasar. Has connections to Bandar Seri Begawan and major Malaysian cities.

Malaysia Airlines In Australia ☎13 2627, in New Zealand ☎09/373 2741 or 0800/657 472, *www.mas.com.my* Daily to Kuala Lumpur from Brisbane, Sydney, Melbourne and Perth; and twice a week from Darwin, Cairns and Adelaide; with connections to Singapore, Bandar Seri Begawan, Kota Kinabalu, Kuching, Penang and other major Malaysian cities.

Qantas In Australia ☎13 1313, in New Zealand ☎0800/808 767, *www.qantas.com.au* Daily from Australian gateway cities to Singapore.

Royal Brunei Airlines In Australia ☎07/3221 7757, no NZ office; *www.bruneiair.com* Three flights a week from Brisbane and two from Darwin and Perth to Singapore, Kuala Lumpur, Kuching and Kota Kinabalu, via Bandar Seri Begawan.

Singapore Airlines In Australia ☎13 1011, in New Zealand ☎09/303 2129 and ☎0800/808 909. Daily flights to Singapore from Sydney, Melbourne, Brisbane, Perth and Auckland, and several flights a week from Cairns and Adelaide, with connections to Bandar Seri Begawan, Kuala Lumpur, Penang, Kota Kinabalu and Kuching.

Thai Airways In Australia ☎1300/651 960, in New Zealand ☎09/377 3886. Daily from Sydney and Melbourne, and several times a week from Brisbane, Perth, Cairns and Auckland to Singapore, Bandar Seri Begawan, Kuala Lumpur and Penang, via Bangkok.

Virgin Atlantic Airways In Australia ☎07/3407 7188, in New Zealand ☎09/308 3377. Flies from Brisbane and Sydney to Kuala Lumpur, in collaboration with MAS and Ansett.

TRAVEL AGENTS

Anywhere Travel 345 Anzac Parade, Kingsford, Sydney (☎02/9663 0411 and 018/401 014, *anywhere@ozemail.com.au*)

Budget Travel 16 Fort St, Auckland, plus branches around the city (☎09/366 0061 or 0800/808 040).

Destinations Unlimited 87 Albert St, Auckland (☎09/373 4033).

Flight Centres Australia 82 Elizabeth St, Sydney, plus branches nationwide (☎02/9235 3522, nearest branch ☎13 1600). New Zealand: 350 Queen St, Auckland (☎09/358 4310), plus branches nationwide; *www.flightcentre.com.au*

Northern Gateway 22 Cavenagh St, Darwin (☎08/8941 1394, *oztravel@norgate.com.au*).

STA Travel 855 George St, Sydney; 256 Flinders St, Melbourne; other offices in state capitals and major universities (nearest branch ☎13 1776, telesales ☎1300/360 960); 10 High St, Auckland (☎09/309 0458, telesales ☎09/366 6673), plus branches in Wellington, Christchurch, Dunedin, Palmerston North, Hamilton and at major universities; *www.statravel.com.au*

Student Uni Travel, 92 Pitt St, Sydney (☎02/9232 8444) plus branches in Brisbane, Cairns, Darwin, Melbourne and Perth.

Thomas Cook, 175 Pitt St, Sydney (☎02/9231 2877) plus branches in Melbourne and state capitals (local branch ☎13 1771, telesales ☎1800/801 002); 191 Queen St, Auckland (☎09/379 3920); *www.thomascook.com.au*

Trailfinders, 8 Spring St, Sydney (☎02/9247 7666) and 91 Elizabeth St, Brisbane (☎07/3229 0887).

Travel.com.au 76–80 Clarence St, Sydney (☎02/9262 3555, *www.travel.com.au*)

usit BEYOND, cnr Shortland St and Jean Batten Place, Auckland (☎09/379 4224 or 0800/788 336) plus branches in Christchurch, Dunedin, Palmerston North, Hamilton and Wellington; *www.usitbeyond.co.nz*

FLIGHTS AND FARES

Fares vary according to **season**. High season is from mid-May to August and Dec to mid-January, shoulder from March to mid-May and September to mid-October, and low the rest of the year; return fares climb by A$200/NZ$200 from low to shoulder season and again from shoulder to high season. On any one airline, airfares from the main Australian east-coast cities are priced pretty much the same (though they vary from one airline to another), with Ansett and Qantas providing a shuttle service from other cities and towns to the point of departure; flights from Perth and Darwin are around A$100–200 cheaper. From New Zealand, you can expect to pay about NZ$150–300 more from Christchurch or Wellington than from Auckland. All the sample fares we give below are low-season prices.

Malaysia Airlines, Singapore Airlines, Royal Brunei, Garuda, Qantas and Ansett all have regular services **from Australia** to Malaysia and Singapore; all these airlines, except Qantas and Ansett, also fly to Brunei. On the whole, return fares to Kuala Lumpur, Singapore and Bandar Seri Begawan from Brisbane, Sydney or Melbourne and Cairns are roughly A$900 in low season for a return; one-way fares are about A$300–400 less. Flying into Singapore, from where you can easily get a train into Malaysia (see p.35 for details), is sometimes a little cheaper than into Kuala Lumpur. The real bargains are often with Middle Eastern airlines keen to fill flights for the leg to Singapore before they head for home; Egypt Air, for example, flies twice a week from Sydney for about A$600 return. Royal Brunei offer some excellent deals to Singapore, Kuala Lumpur, Kuching or Kota Kinabalu via Brunei from Brisbane and Cairns (return fares start at A$850), Perth and Darwin (A$750–800).

From New Zealand, Air New Zealand, British Airways, Garuda, Qantas, Singapore Airlines and Malaysia Airlines, among others, fly from Auckland to Singapore and Kuala Lumpur, with return fares starting at NZ$1300 in low season (one-way fares are around NZ$400–500 cheaper). A connecting flight to Brunei (there are no direct flights from New Zealand at time of writing) adds around NZ$550 to the total cost.

OPEN-JAW AND RTW TICKETS

An **open-jaw ticket** doesn't add hugely to the cost and saves on backtracking, as it allows you to fly in to one city and out of another. If you intend to visit the region as part of a wider trip, then it's worth considering **Round-the-World** (RTW) and **Circle Asia** tickets. Put together by an alliance of airlines, these allow you to travel via two or more Asian cities en route, and offer greater flexibility than a simple return flight. For example, prices for a RTW ticket from Sydney to Singapore, Bangkok, London, New York, Los Angeles, Auckland and back to Sydney start at around A$2400/NZ$3000; and a round trip to Brunei from Singapore or Kuala Lumpur will add an extra A$450/NZ$550 to the basic price. Ultimately your choice will depend on where you want to travel before or after Malaysia and Singapore.

PACKAGES, CITY BREAKS AND SPECIALIST TOURS

Package holidays can be an economical and hassle-free way of sampling the delights of Malaysia, Singapore or Brunei, especially if you can only manage a short visit and are happy to base yourself in one city or resort. Inexpensive five-night packages in Penang, for example, start at around A$1000/NZ$1250, including return airfare from eastern Australia, transfers, twin-share accommodation and breakfast. Though there are fewer package holidays departing from Perth or Darwin, those that are available generally cost about A$200 less per person.

City breaks, fly-drive options and **coach tours** run by a host of operators, including Ansett Australia Holidays, Creative Tours, Asian Explorer Holidays, Qantas Holidays, Singapore Asian Affair Holidays and Venture Holidays, can be bought through your travel agent; most can also arrange add-on trips to resort islands, Sabah and Sarawak, cruises from Singapore, air passes, rail travel and can book accommodation in regional Malaysia. Sample city-break prices are four nights in Singapore from A$1000/NZ$1150, or five nights in Kuala Lumpur (A$1150/NZ$1200), with the exact price depending on the type of accommodation chosen. Two-night extensions to Langkawi or Tioman cost from A$250/NZ$300; to Sarawak, approximately A$400/NZ$450; and to Sabah, A$650/NZ$800 (all including air transfers from KL).

Extended journeys through the region cater to all tastes – from those in search of thrills and adventure to those who simply prefer to tour in a group. Operators such as Peregrine, Explore

SPECIALIST TOUR OPERATORS

Abercrombie & Kent, 90 Bridport St, Albert Park, Melbourne (☎03/9699 9766 or 1800/331 429), plus branches in Brisbane and Sydney; 1/88 Rockfield Rd, Penrose, Auckland (☎09/579 3369); *www.abercrombiekent.com* Upmarket tours of Southeast Asia, including travel on the Eastern & Oriental Express.

Adventure Specialists, 1/69 Liverpool St, Sydney (☎02/9261 2927). Overland and adventure tour agent for a load of companies including Peregrine and Intrepid.

The Adventure Travel Company, 164 Parnell Rd, Parnell, Auckland (☎09/379 9755). Agents for Intrepid, Peregrine, Guerba Expeditions, Encounter Overland and a host of other adventure-travel tour operators.

Adventure World, 73 Walker St, North Sydney (☎02/9956 7766 or 1800/221 931), plus branches in Adelaide, Brisbane, Melbourne and Perth; 101 Great South Rd, Remuera, Auckland (☎09/524 5118, *www.adventureworld.com.au*). Agents for a vast array of international adventure-travel companies including Explore Worldwide. For example, they take bookings for Explore's thirteen-day "Malay Peninsula" trip, taking in the islands of Penang and Pangkor, the Cameron Highlands, Melaka and Singapore (around A$1300/NZ$1600 excluding airfare).

Always Padi Travel, 4/372 Eastern Valley Way, Chatswood, Sydney (☎1800/259 297, *www.padi.com*). All-inclusive dive-package holidays to prime dive sites in Malaysia.

Intrepid Adventure Travel, 12 Spring St, Fitzroy, Melbourne (☎1300/360 667, *info @intrepidtravel.com.au*). Small-group tours to Southeast Asia with the emphasis on cross-cultural contact. Apart from all-inclusive tours, they organize packages that exclude flights (for example, a three-day "Cameron Highlands Escapade" from A$200/NZ$300), and homestays with Malaysian families (from A$150/NZ$200 for two days)

Peregrine Adventures, 258 Lonsdale St, Melbourne (☎03/9662 2700) plus offices in Brisbane, Sydney, Adelaide and Perth; *www.peregrine.net.au* Organizes adventure travel for small groups, with a range of graded trips. Their nine-day "Sabah Adventure" costs around A$1100/NZ$1400.

San Michele Travel, 81 York St, Sydney (☎02/9299 1111 or 1800/222 244), plus branches in Melbourne and Perth. Offers customized rail tours throughout Southeast Asia; a favourite is their thirteen-day Singapore–Bangkok journey (A$1600/NZ$2100 including accommodation). They also do city breaks, sightseeing trips and cruises out of Singapore, and extended overland tours of Northern Borneo, including Brunei.

Silke's Travel, 263 Oxford St, Darlinghurst, Sydney (☎1800/807 303, 807 860, 02/9380 5835 or 9380 6244, *www.silkes.com.au*). Specially tailored packages for gay and lesbian travellers.

Worldwide and Intrepid have a range of itineraries covering Malaysia and Singapore; among Peregrine's and Intrepid's tours are some more challenging jaunts, such as Intrepid's thirteen-day "Sabah" tour (from A$1200/NZ$1550 excluding airfare) which, in addition to taking in the rainforests and wildlife of the region, includes a strenuous two-day ascent of Mt Kinabalu.

GETTING THERE FROM SOUTHEAST ASIA

Vietnam (whose national airlines created this scheme), it allows you to fly among the participating states, beginning and ending in the country where you bought the pass; you're allowed to stay for a minimum of three nights and a maximum of three months in each one. The price of the pass depends on which of these countries you start from and the number of stopovers you want to make. A Circle ASEAN pass beginning and ending in Malaysia or Brunei costs around £300/US$500 with two stopovers, £350/US$550 with three stopovers and £425/US$650 with four, five or six stopovers.

The train is the most attractive overland route to Peninsular Malaysia; from Bangkok, it's only a sixteen-hour trip to the Malaysian border, from where you can continue down the main Malaysian line (which runs down the west coast of the Peninsula, to Penang and KL, and ends in Singapore). There are, of course, other possible routes into either Malaysia or Singapore from Southeast Asia: by ferry, bus or taxi from various southern Thai towns, by sea from points in the Philippines and Sumatra and North Kalimantan in Indonesia, or by road from West Kalimantan to Sarawak. There's a round-up below of the most popular border crossings, and details of the routes are included in the text throughout.

Getting a long-haul flight into a Southeast Asian hub city outside Malaysia, Singapore and Brunei used to be cheaper than flying straight into KL or Singapore, even though you had to continue your journey on a local flight from, say, Bangkok, Jakarta or Hong Kong. However, increased competition on long-haul routes into KL and Singapore now means that any saving to be made by flying via another Southeast Asian country is most likely during high season (June–Aug) only.

A good-value option if you're on a wider tour of Southeast Asia is a **Circle ASEAN Pass**. Only available in Brunei, Indonesia, Malaysia, the Philippines, Singapore, Thailand and

FROM THAILAND

The most popular way of getting to Malaysia from Thailand is to catch the **train from Bangkok**. Trains leave Bangkok's Hualamphong station (book at least a day in advance at the station ticket office) four times a day for Hat Yai, where the line divides. One daily train goes south via the Malaysian border town of Padang Besar and on to Butterworth (see p.37) for the Malaysian west-coast route, which continues on to KL (journey from Bangkok takes 24hr; around £50/US$75 one-way) and Singapore (30hr; £60/US$90 one-way). Two daily trains from Hat Yai follow an easterly route to the Thai border town of Sungei Golok, a short walk from the Malaysian border crossing at Rantau Panjang (see p.37); once there, you can catch a local bus or taxi for the thirty-kilometre-journey to Kota Bharu. In all, the journey from Bangkok to Kota Bharu takes around twenty hours and costing £45/US$70.

There are also frequent **flights** from Bangkok on Thai Airways International to KL (2 weekly; one-way £140/US$225) and Singapore (4 weekly; £250/US$400); but no direct flights to Sarawak or Sabah. From Hat Yai, there are services to KL (7 weekly; £66/US$105) and Singapore (1 daily; £150/US$250). MAS does flights from Bangkok to Kuala Lumpur (5 daily; one-way £150/US$250) and Penang (4 daily; £100/US$150). Flights can be booked from travel agents in Bangkok; students and under-26s can probably undercut these prices by booking through STA, 14th Floor, Room 1406 Wall Street Tower, 33 Suriwong Rd (☎02/236 0262, *www.statravel.co.th*); NS Tours, c/o *Vieng Thai Hotel*, Ram Bhuttri Rd, Banglamphu (☎02/629 0509); or Pacto PC & C, Room 100 in the Hualamphong station concourse (☎02/226 5711).

Scheduled **ferry** services sail from the most southwesterly Thai town of **Satun** to the Malaysian west-coast town of Kuala Perlis (3 daily; 30min) and to Pulau Langkawi (3 daily; 1hr 30min). Boats leave when full from Thammalang pier, 10km south of Satun. Departing Thailand by sea for Malaysia, you should get your passport stamped at the immigration office at the pier to avoid problems with the Malaysian immigration officials when you arrive. Another option is the ferry from the southern Thai town of Ban Taba to the Malaysian town of Pengkalan Kubor, where you get frequent taxis and buses to Kota Bharu, 20km away. There are buses to Ban Taba from the provincial capital, Narathiwat (90min).

The easiest **road** access from Thailand is via the rail junction town of Hat Yai, from where buses and shared taxis run regularly to Butterworth and Georgetown, around a six-hour trip. From the interior Thai town of Betong on Route 410, there's a road across the border to the Malaysian town of Keroh, from where Route 67

SOUTHEAST ASIA

leads west to meet Route 1 at Sungei Petani; shared taxis run along the route. You can also get a taxi from Ban Taba the few kilometres south to Kota Bharu.

FROM INDONESIA

There are a variety of ways to reach **West Malaysia** and **Singapore** from Indonesia, with frequent **flights** from Jakarta to Singapore (2hr) and KL (3hr), and from Medan in Sumatra to Penang (20min) and Singapore (40min).

A **ferry** service operates twice daily from Medan in northern Sumatra to Penang (4hr) and, from Dumai further south, there's a daily service to Melaka (2hr). There are also services from Pulau Batam in the Riau archipelago (accessible by plane or boat from Sumatra or Jakarta) to Johor Bahru (2 daily; 30min) or Singapore (2 daily; 30min); and a minor ferry crossing from Tanjung Balai (2 daily; 45min) to Kukup (see p.325), just to the southwest of Johor Bahru.

EAST MALAYSIA

From Pontianak in Kalimantan, Garuda does a **flight** to Kuching in **Sarawak** (3 weekly; 1hr). It's possible to reach Sarawak from Indonesian Kalimantan on just one **road** route, through the border town of Entikong and onwards to Kuching in the southwest of the state. The bus trip from the western city of Pontianak to Entikong takes seven hours, crossing to the Sarawak border town

of Tebedu (see p.386); you can stay on the same bus for another three hours to reach the Sarawak capital, Kuching. There are five or six buses a day plying the route, the earliest one, the Super Executive, run by the SJS bus company. It departs from Pontianak at 6am, arriving at the border at around 1pm and Kuching around 4pm. Other buses running through the rest of the day are less plush and correspondingly less expensive.

There are daily **ferries** to Tawau (see p.498) in **Sabah** from Nunakan (1hr) and Tarakan (3hr) in Eastern Kalimantan. There are also **flights** from Tarakan to Tawau, departing twice a week.

FROM HONG KONG

Both Cathay Pacific and MAS operate two daily nonstop flights from Hong Kong to KL. There are five daily flights to Singapore with Cathay Pacific and two more on Singapore Airlines. New regulations in Hong Kong make it impossible for most travellers who aren't residents of Hong Kong to enter without a return ticket. But if you are using Hong Kong as a base and wanting to travel onwards from there, only to later return, then remember that fares bought there aren't particularly good value. For the better deals, visit one of the following travel agents in Hong Kong: Shoestring Travel, Flat A, Fourth Floor, Alpha House, 27–33 Nathan Rd (☎2723 2306, fax 2721 2085); or Hong Kong Student Travel, Hang Lung Centre, Yee Wo St, Causeway Bay (☎2833 9909).

VISAS AND RED TAPE

Nationals of the UK, Ireland, the US, Canada, Australia and New Zealand don't need visas to stay in Malaysia, Singapore or Brunei for up to fourteen days, longer in some cases. In practice though, it's not necessary to apply for a visa in advance, as you're given permission to enter the country when you arrive, and it's straightforward to extend your permission to stay. That said, it's always a good idea to check with the embassy or consulate of the country you're visiting (see the boxes below and opposite for addresses), as the rules on visas are complex and subject to change. Ensure that your passport is valid for at least six months from the date of your trip, and has several blank pages for entry stamps.

MALAYSIA

When **British, Irish**, **US**, **Canadian, Australian** and **New Zealand** nationals enter Malaysia, a stamp is put in their passport entitling them to a **two-month stay** (visitors who enter via Sarawak receive a one-month stamp; see below). It's a straightforward matter to **extend** this permit to stay by applying at the Immigration Department, who have offices (listed in the *Guide*) in Kuala Lumpur and major towns. If you're in the south of the Peninsula, though, it's simpler just to cross into Singapore and back, whereupon you'll be granted a fresh Malaysia entry stamp. In theory, visitors can extend their stay for up to six months, although this is subject to the discretion of the official you encounter. In practice, there's rarely a problem with extending your stay to three months.

Tourists travelling from the Peninsula to **East Malaysia** (Sarawak and Sabah) must carry a valid passport and be cleared again by immigration; visitors to Sabah can remain as long as their original entry stamp is valid.

SARAWAK

Sarawak has its own rules when it comes to visiting. When you **arrive** in Sarawak, you receive an entry stamp permitting you to stay for **one month**, easily extendable for an additional month at the immigration offices in Kuching, Bintulu or Miri. If Sarawak is also the place where you

MALAYSIAN EMBASSIES AND CONSULATES ABROAD

Australia 7 Perth Ave, Yarralumla, Canberra, ACT 2600 (☎06/273 1543).

Brunei 437 Kg Pelambayan, Jalan Kota Batu, PO Box 2826, Bandar Seri Begawan (☎02/228410).

Canada 60 Boteler St, Ottawa, ON K1N 8Y7 (☎613/237-5182).

Indonesia 17 Jalan Imam Bonjol, 10310 Jakarta Pusat (☎021/336438).

Ireland No office; contact their UK representation.

Netherlands Runtenburweg 2, 2517 KE, The Hague (☎070/350 6506).

New Zealand 10 Washington Ave, Brooklyn, Wellington (☎04/852 439).

Singapore 301 Jervois Rd, Singapore 1024 (☎2350111).

Thailand 35 South Sathorn Rd, Bangkok 10120 (☎02/286 1390).

UK 45 Belgrave Square, London SW1X 8QT (☎020/7235 8033).

USA 2401 Massachusetts Ave NW, Washington, DC 20008 (☎202/328-2700); Two Grand Central Tower, 140 45th St, 43rd Floor, New York, NY 10017 (☎212/490-2722); 350 Figueroa St, Suite 400, World Trade Centre, Los Angeles, CA 90071 (☎213/621-2991).

SINGAPOREAN EMBASSIES AND CONSULATES ABROAD

Australia 17 Forster Crescent, Yarralumla, Canberra, ACT 2600 (☎06/273 3944).

Brunei PO Box 2159, Bandar Seri Begawan 1921, Negara Brunei Darussalam (☎02/262741).

Canada Suite 1305, 999 Hastings St, Vancouver, BC V6C 2W2 (☎604/669 5115).

Indonesia Block X/4 Kav No. 2, Jalan H.R. Rasuna Said, Kuningan, Jakarta (☎021/520 1489).

Ireland No office; contact their UK representation.

Malaysia 209 Jalan Tun Razak, Kuala Lumpur 50400 (☎03/2161 6404).

Netherlands Rotterdam Plaza, Weena 670 3012 CN Rotterdam (☎020/404 2111).

New Zealand Johnsonville PO Box 13-140, Wellington (☎04/479 2076).

Thailand 129 South Sathorn Rd, Bangkok (☎02/286 2111).

UK 9 Wilton Crescent, Belgravia, London SW1X 8SP (☎020/7235 8315).

USA 3501 International Place NW, Washington, DC 20008 (☎202/537-3100); 2424 SE Bristol, Suite 320, Santa Ana Heights, CA 92707 (☎714/476-2330).

BRUNEIAN EMBASSIES AND CONSULATES ABROAD

Australia 16 Bulwarra Close, O'Mally, Canberra, ACT 2606 (☎06/290 1801).

Canada 395 Laurier Ave, Ottawa, ON, KIN 6R4 (☎613/234-5656)

Indonesia Wisma Bank Central Asia Building, Eighth Floor, Jalan Jendral Sudirman, KAV 22-23, Jakarta (☎021/5/1 2124).

Ireland No office; contact their Australia representation.

Malaysia Eighth Floor, Wisma Sin Heap Lee, Jalan Tun Razak, Kuala Lumpur (☎03/2161 2800).

New Zealand No office; contact their Australia representation.

The Philippines, Eleventh Floor, BPI Building, Ayala Ave, Paseo De Roxas, Makati City, Metro, Manila (☎81/62836).

Singapore 325 Tanglin Rd (☎7339055).

Thailand 154, Soi E Kamai 14, Su Khumvit 63, Bangkok (☎02/515766).

UK 19/20 Belgrave Square, London SW1X 8PG (☎020/7581 0521).

USA Watergate, Suite 300, 2600 Virginia Ave, NW, Washington, DC 20037 (☎202/342-0159).

entered the country, and you want to head to the Peninsula or Sabah subsequently, you need to go to the immigration office in Kuching (see p.375) and have your passport stamped with the usual two-month pass granted to travellers arriving in Malaysia via the Peninsula or Sabah. However, if you arrived in Sarawak after entering Malaysia through the Peninsula or Sabah, note that your original entry stamp must be valid in order for you to return to either. It's straightforward to have the stamp renewed at the immigration office in Kuching; note also that it doesn't matter if the stamp lapses while you're in Sarawak, as long as your presence is covered by a valid Sarawak entry stamp. Certain trips within Sarawak also require special **travel permits**; details are given in the text.

SINGAPORE

Upon arrival in Singapore, citizens of the UK, Ireland, the US, Canada, Australia and New Zealand are normally stamped in for fourteen days, though they are given a month's stay if they request this. **Extending** your stay for up to three months is possible, at the discretion of the Immigration Department (see p.612); extensions beyond three months are not unknown, but less common. If you have any problems extending your stay, there's always the option of taking a bus up to Johor Baru just inside Malaysia, then returning to Singapore, whereupon you're given a new entry stamp.

BRUNEI

US nationals don't need visas to visit Brunei for up to ninety days, while British nationals don't need a visa to visit Brunei for up to thirty days. Canadian, Australian and New Zealand passport holders don't need visas for up to fourteen days in Brunei. Once you're in Brunei, extending your permission to stay is usually a formality; apply at the Immigration Department in Bandar Seri Begawan.

DRUGS: A WARNING

In Malaysia, Singapore and Brunei, the **possession of illegal drugs** – hard or soft – carries a hefty prison sentence. If you are caught smuggling drugs into or out of the country, at best you face a long stretch in a foreign prison; at worst, you could be hanged. This is no idle threat, as the authorities have, in the recent past, shown themselves to be prepared to pass the death sentence on Western travellers. The simple advice, therefore, is not to have anything to do with drugs in any of these countries, and never agree to carry anything through customs for a third party.

CUSTOMS ALLOWANCES

Malaysia's duty-free **allowances** let you bring in 200 cigarettes, 50 cigars or 250g of tobacco, and wine, spirits or liquor not exceeding 75cl. In addition, no duty is paid on electrical goods, cameras, watches, cosmetics and perfumes. There's no customs clearance for passengers travelling from Singapore or Peninsular Malaysia to East Malaysia, nor for people passing between Sabah and Sarawak.

Entering **Singapore** from anywhere other than Malaysia (with which there are no duty-free restrictions), you can bring in 1 litre each of spirits, wine and beer duty-free; duty is payable on all tobacco. Other duty-free goods in Singapore include electronic and electrical items, cosmetics, cameras, clocks, watches, jewellery, and precious stones and metals.

Visitors to **Brunei** may bring in 200 cigarettes, 50 cigars or 250 grams of tobacco, and 60ml of perfume; non-Muslims over 17 can also import two quarts of liquor and twelve cans of beer for personal consumption (any alcohol brought into the country must be declared upon arrival).

INSURANCE

A typical travel insurance policy usually provides cover for the loss of baggage, tickets and – up to a certain limit – cash or cheques, as well as cancellation or curtailment of your journey. Most of them exclude so-called dangerous sports unless an extra premium is paid: in Malaysia, this can mean scuba-diving, trekking or climbing Mount Kinabalu. Read the small print and benefits tables of prospective policies carefully; coverage can vary wildly for roughly similar premiums. Many policies can be chopped and changed to exclude coverage you don't need – for example, sickness and accident benefits can often be excluded or included at will.

If you do take **medical** coverage, ascertain whether benefits will be paid as treatment proceeds or only after return home, and whether there is a 24-hour medical emergency number. When securing **baggage** cover, make sure that the per-article limit will cover your most valuable possession. If you need to make a **claim**, you should keep receipts for medicines and medical treatment, and in the event you have anything stolen, you must obtain an official statement from the police.

Bank and credit cards often have certain levels of medical or other insurance included, and you may automatically get travel insurance if you use a major credit card to pay for your trip.

ROUGH GUIDES TRAVEL INSURANCE

Rough Guides now offer their own travel insurance, customized for our readers by a leading UK broker and backed by a Lloyds underwriter. It's available for anyone, of any nationality, travelling anywhere in the world, and we are convinced that this is the best-value scheme you'll find.

There are two main Rough Guide insurance plans: Essential, for effective, no-frills cover, starting at £23.03 for two weeks in Asia; and Premier – more expensive but with more generous and extensive benefits. Each offer European or Worldwide cover, and can be supplemented with a "Hazardous Activities Premium" if you plan to indulge in sports considered dangerous,

such as skiing, scuba-diving or trekking. Unlike many policies, the Rough Guides schemes are calculated by the day, so if you're travelling for 27 days rather than a month, that's all you pay for. Alternatively, you can take out annual multi-trip insurance, which covers you for all your travel throughout the year (with a maximum of 60 days for any one trip).

For a policy quote, call the Rough Guides Insurance Line on UK freephone ☎0800/015 0906, or, if you're calling from outside Britain, on ☎(+44) 1243/621046. Alternatively, you can get a quote and buy your insurance online at *www.roughguides.com/insurance*

Americans and **Canadians** should also check that they're not already covered. Canadian provincial health plans usually provide partial cover for medical mishaps overseas. Holders of official student/teacher/youth cards are entitled to meagre accident coverage and hospital in-patient benefits. Students will often find that their student health coverage extends during the vacations and for one term beyond the date of last enrolment. Homeowners' or renters' insurance often covers theft or loss of documents, money and valuables while overseas, though conditions and maximum amounts vary from company to company.

HEALTH

No inoculations are required for visiting Malaysia, Singapore or Brunei, although the immigration authorities may require proof of a yellow-fever vaccination (administered within the last ten years) if you're arriving from a country that has a long history of this disease.

However, it's a wise precaution to visit your doctor no less than two months before you leave to check that you are up to date with your **polio**, **typhoid**, **tetanus** and **hepatitis A** inoculations, and to check the malarial status of the areas you are visiting. If you intend to travel for an extended period, or in rural areas, your doctor may also recommend protection against **Japanese B encephalitis, hepatitis B, tuberculosis** and **rabies. North Americans** will have to pay for these inoculations, available at an **immunization centre** – there's one in every city of any size – or most local clinics. Most general practitioners in the **UK** have a travel surgery from which you can obtain advice and certain vaccines on prescription, though they may not administer some of the less common immunizations.

For up-to-the-minute information, make an appointment at a specialized **travel clinic**. All these clinics sell travel-associated **accessories**, including mosquito nets and first-aid kits.

MEDICAL RESOURCES FOR TRAVELLERS

UK AND IRELAND

British Airways Travel Clinic, 156 Regent St, London W1 7RA (no appointment necessary; Mon–Fri 9.30am–5.15pm, Sat 10am–4pm; ☎020/7439 9584). There are also appointment-only branches at 101 Cheapside, London EC2 (Mon–Fri 9–11.45am & 12.15–4.45pm; ☎020/7606 2977) and at the BA terminal in London's Victoria Station (Mon–Fri 8.15–11.30am & 12.30–3.40pm; ☎020/7233 6661). BA also operate around thirty regional clinics throughout the country (call ☎01276/685040 for the one nearest to you, or check *www.british-airways.com*).

Hospital for Tropical Diseases, St Pancras Hospital, 4 St Pancras Way, London NW1 0PE (☎020/7388 9600). Travel clinic and recorded-message service (☎0839/337733; 49p per minute) which gives hints on hygiene and illness prevention as well as listing appropriate immunizations.

MASTA (Medical Advisory Service for Travellers Abroad), London School of Hygiene and Tropical Medicine. Operates a Travellers' Health Line (☎0906/822 4100; 60p per minute; 24hr), giving written information tailored to your journey by return of post.

Travel Medicine Services, PO Box 254, 16 College St, Belfast 1 (☎028/9031 5220). Medical advice for travellers heading abroad.

Tropical Medical Bureau, Grafton St Medical Centre, 34 Grafton St, Dublin 2 (☎01/671 9200); Dun Laoghaire Medical Centre, 5 Northumberland Ave, Dun Laoghaire, Co. Dublin (☎01/280 4996). Offers medical advice before a trip and medical care afterwards.

US AND CANADA

Canadian Society for International Health, 170 Laurier Ave W, Suite 902, Ottawa, ON K1P 5V5 (☎613/230-2654). Distributes a free pamphlet, *Health Information for Canadian Travellers*, containing an extensive list of travel-health centres in Canada.

Center for Disease Control, 1600 Clifton Rd NE, Atlanta, GA 30333 (☎404/639-3311, *www.cdc.gov/travel*). Information on outbreaks of disease and suggested inoculations; their Web site is very useful.

International Association for Medical Assistance to Travellers (IAMAT), 417 Center St, Lewiston, NY 14092 (☎716/754-4883, *www.sentex.net/iamat*) and 40 Regal Rd, Guelph, ON

N1K 1B5 (☎519/836-0102). A non-profit organization supported by donations, it can provide a list of English-speaking doctors, climate charts and leaflets on various diseases and inoculations.

Travel Medicine, 351 Pleasant St, Suite 312, Northampton, MA 01060 (☎1-800/872-8633, *www.travmed.com*). Sells first-aid kits, mosquito netting, water filters and other health-related travel products.

Travelers Medical Center, 31 Washington Square, New York, NY 10011 (☎212/982-1600). Consultation service on immunizations and treatment of diseases for people travelling to developing countries.

AUSTRALIA AND NEW ZEALAND

Travellers' Immunization Service, 303 Pacific Hwy, Sydney (☎02/9416 1348).

Travellers' Medical and Vaccination Centre 7/428 George St, Sydney (☎02/9221 7133); 1/170 Queen St, Auckland, (☎09/373 3531); plus

branches in other major Australian cities; *www.tmvc.com.au* This travel-health specialist operates a chain of clinics, stocks first-aid kits and provides general information on keeping healthy while travelling.

MEDICAL PROBLEMS

The levels of hygiene and medical care in Malaysia, Singapore and Brunei are higher than in much of the rest of Southeast Asia; with any luck, the most serious thing you'll go down with is a cold or an upset stomach.

It's wise, though, to take a few precautions and be aware of health risks beforehand. In a tropical

climate it's especially important to be vigilant about **personal hygiene**. Wash your hands often, especially before eating; keep all cuts clean, treating them with iodine or antiseptic, and covering them to prevent infection. Be fussier about sharing things like drinks and cigarettes than you might be at home; never share a razor or toothbrush. It is also inadvisable to go around barefoot – and best to wear flip-flop sandals even in the shower. In addition, make sure you maintain a sufficient calorie intake (an unfamiliar diet may reduce the amount you eat) and **get enough sleep** and rest (it's easy to get run-down if you're on the move a lot, especially in a hot climate).

HEAT PROBLEMS

Travellers unused to tropical climates periodically suffer from **sunburn** and **dehydration**. The easiest way to avoid this is to restrict your exposure to the midday sun, use high-factor sun screens, wear sunglasses and a hat. You should also drink plenty of water and, if you do become dehydrated, keep up a regular intake of fluids. Weak black tea and clear soups are useful for mineral salts, and a rehydration preparation such as Dioralyte also does the trick (the DIY version is a handful of sugar with a good pinch of salt added to a litre of water, which creates roughly the right mineral balance). **Heat stroke** is more serious and can require hospitalization: its onset is indicated by a high body temperature, dry red skin and a fast pulse. To prevent **heat rashes**, **prickly heat** and **fungal infections**, use a mild antiseptic soap and dust yourself with prickly-heat talcum powder, which you can buy all over Malaysia and Singapore.

STOMACH PROBLEMS: FOOD AND WATER

The most common complaint is a **stomach problem**, which can range from a mild dose of diarrhoea to full-blown dysentery. Ninety-five percent of stomach bugs are unpleasant, but basically unthreatening; however, if you notice blood or mucus in your stools, then you may have amoebic or bacillary **dysentery**, in which case you should seek medical help immediately.

Since stomach bugs are usually transmitted by **contaminated** food and water, steer clear of raw vegetables and shellfish, always wash unpeeled fruit, and stick to freshly cooked foods, avoiding anything reheated. But however careful you are, food that's spicy or just different can sometimes upset your system, in which case, try to stick to relatively bland dishes and avoid fried food.

Tap water is drinkable throughout Malaysia, Singapore and Brunei (and in major towns in Sarawak and Sabah), but in rural areas you should buy bottled water, which is widely available. If you're going trekking in the national parks, or travelling upriver in Sarawak, you might want to invest in a **water purifier** (see box below). In addition, drinking excessive amounts of alcohol is a common cause of diarrhoea, and in a tropical environment you may encounter bugs unfamiliar at home, to which you have less resistance.

MALARIA AND OTHER DISEASES

It's highly unlikely that you'll catch anything very serious while in Malaysia, Singapore or Brunei, though long-term travellers may have brought something with them from elsewhere, so it's

---

WATER PURIFICATION

Contaminated water is a major cause of diseases such as diarrhoea and gastroenteritis, typhoid, cholera, dysentery, poliomyelitis, hepatitis A, giardiasis and bilharziasis. The microorganisms which cause these can be present even when water looks clean and safe to drink. If you're trekking in the back of beyond, or travelling upriver in deepest Sarawak, all drinking water should be regarded with caution.

Apart from drinking **bottled water**, there are various ways to avoid disease by treating your water source, whether it be a tap, a river or stream. **Boiling,** the time-honoured method, is effective in sterilizing water, although it will not remove unpleasant tastes. A minimum boiling time of ten minutes (longer at higher altitudes) is sufficient to kill microorganisms.

Chemical sterilization can be carried out using either chlorine or iodine tablets (it's essen-

tial to follow the manufacturer's dosage), or a tincture of iodine liquid – add a couple of drops to one litre of water and leave to stand for twenty minutes. Iodine tablets are preferable to chlorine as the latter leaves an unpleasant taste in the water and isn't effective in preventing such diseases as amoebic dysentery and giardiasis. A water **filter** is also useful, not least to improve the taste. However, note that a water filter alone will not remove viruses which, due to their microscopic size, will pass through into the filtered water.

Purification, a two-stage process involving both filtration and sterilization, gives the most complete treatment. Portable water purifiers range in size, weighing from as little as 60 grams (these units can be slipped into a pocket) up to 800 grams (a backpack is one way to carry these around).

important to recognize the early stages of some possible diseases. Although the risk of catching **malaria** is pretty low, if you're planning to travel for a long time or think you might be staying in remote areas, then you should consider protection against it. The illness, which cannot be passed directly from one person to another, begins with flu-like symptoms, with a fluctuating high fever. The prevention of mosquito bites is the most reliable way to avoid the disease: apply **insect repellent** at regular intervals and sleep with a mosquito net where possible – some places provide these but it is safer to take your own. Mosquito coils, which you light to release smoke that deters the insects, are very cheap and widely available in shops throughout Malaysia and Singapore.

Most doctors will advise the additional use of **malaria tablets**. Although these aren't completely effective in protecting against malaria, they do at least help reduce the symptoms should you develop the disease. You have to start taking the tablets one week before you arrive in a malaria zone, and continue taking them throughout your trip as well as for four weeks after you return; if you don't complete the course, you won't be protected. Your GP will be able to advise you as to which course of tablets is most effective for the region you intend to visit.

Dengue fever is caused by a family of viruses which are transmitted by the mosquito bite in a similar way to malaria, and tends to occur seasonally and in epidemics. While it is a very common cause of fever and non-specific flu-like symptoms in Southeast Asia, generally speaking the disease is not serious – deaths in adults are very rare. However, the symptoms – severe headache, pain in the bones (especially of the back), fever and often a fine, red rash over the body – can be serious enough to keep you in bed for a few days. There's no specific treatment, just plenty of rest, an adequate fluid intake and painkillers when required.

Typhoid is a lethal disease that is spread by contact with infected water or food. It begins with a headache and a consistently high fever, followed by red spots on the chest and back, dehydration and occasional diarrhoea. If you think you have these symptoms you should seek immediate medical treatment.

Hepatitis is an inflammation of the liver, which may manifest itself as jaundice – a yellow discolouration of the skin and eyes – though extreme tiredness is a common characteristic. Viral hepatitis is most commonly hepatitis A or B. **Hepatitis A** is one of the most likely infections encountered in Asia, and is spread via contaminated food and water. Rest, lots of fluids and a total abstinence from alcohol are the major elements in the cure, as well as a simple, bland diet. A new and rather expensive vaccine, Havrix, provides immunity against hepatitis A for up to ten years; one jab is required. The rarer **Hepatitis B** is transmitted through infected blood and blood products, so intravenous drug-users, together with those who have had unprotected sex, are most at risk. The Hepatitis B vaccine (three jabs over six months, plus a booster after five years) is recommended to anyone falling into one of these high-risk categories, and to those travelling in rural areas with access to only basic medical care.

Cholera, outbreaks of which are reported in Malaysia from time to time, is caught by contact with infected water and food. The disease begins with fever, severe vomiting and diarrhoea, followed by weakness and muscle cramps – seek medical help immediately and watch out for dehydration. There is a vaccine, though it's considered so ineffectual nowadays that there's little point in having it.

Rabies is spread by the bite or even the lick of an infected animal – most commonly a dog or cat. If you suspect that you have been bitten by a rabid animal, wash the wound immediately and thoroughly with antiseptic and seek medical help. Even if you have been inoculated, you'll require further injections.

CUTS, BITES AND STINGS

Wearing protective clothing when swimming, snorkelling or diving can help avoid sunburn and protect against any sea stings. **Sea lice**, minute creatures which cause painful though harmless bites are the most common hazard; more dangerous are **jellyfish**, whose stings must be doused with vinegar to deactivate the poison before you seek medical help. **Coral** can also cause nasty cuts and grazes. Any wounds should be cleaned vigorously, since retained coral particles are a common cause of prolonged deep infection. After cleaning, make sure you keep the wound as dry as possible until it's properly healed. The only way to avoid well-camouflaged **sea urchins** and **stone fish** is by not stepping on the seabed: even thick-soled shoes don't provide total protection against their long, sharp spines, which can be removed by softening the skin by holding it over a steaming pan of water.

Jungle **trekking** presents a few potential health problems, too. Poisonous **snakes** are rare, but if you are bitten you must remain absolutely still and calm until help arrives. Meanwhile, get someone to clean and disinfect the wound thoroughly (alcohol will do if nothing else can be found), and apply a bandage with gentle pressure to the affected area. It helps if you can kill the snake and take it to be identified. Poisonous **spiders** are relatively rare; as with snake bites, keep calm and seek medical help as soon as possible. **Leeches** are a far more common bother and, though harmless, cause an unpleasant sensation. Long trousers and socks help deter them, but once on your skin, they can be hard to remove. If flicking or pulling them off doesn't work, burning leeches off with a lighter or cigarette is effective, as is rubbing them with alcohol or tobacco juice. See "Outdoor pursuits", p.75, for more.

TREATMENT: PHARMACIES, DOCTORS AND HOSPITALS

Medical services in Malaysia, Singapore and Brunei are excellent, with staff almost every-where speaking good English and using up-to-date treatments. In the *Guide*, we've included details of local pharmacists and hospitals in the "Listings" sections for cities and major towns.

The main towns in Malaysia always have a **pharmacy**, well stocked with familiar brand-name drugs; opening hours are usually Monday to Saturday 9am–6pm (except in Kelantan, Terengganu, Kedah and Perlis states, where Friday and not Sunday is the day of closing). Pharmacists can recommend products for skin complaints or simple stomach problems, though it always pays to get a proper diagnosis. Private **clinics** are found even in the smallest towns – your hotel or the local tourist office will be able to recommend a good English-speaking doctor. A visit costs around RM30, not including the cost of any prescribed medication. Don't forget to keep the receipts for insurance-claim purposes. Finally, the emergency department of each town's **General Hospital** will see foreigners (usually allowing you to jump the queue) for the token fee of RM1, though obviously costs rise rapidly if continued treatment or overnight stays are necessary.

Services in **Singapore** are broadly similar to those in Malaysia; for the location of Singapore pharmacies and hospitals, turn to p.611. Brunei actually offers free medical treatment; see p.517.

INFORMATION AND MAPS

You can get plenty of information before you leave by calling or writing to the relevant national tourist organizations, which have offices in most foreign countries. Much of the information put out on Malaysia is fairly general, though you should be able to get hold of good maps and lots of glossy brochures. For Singapore, it's easier to get hold of information in advance of your trip, right down to bus timetables and museum opening hours. For hard information on Brunei and on the more remote areas, especially Sarawak and Sabah, you'll often have to wait until you get there; even when you do, information is often frustratingly hard to come by. The Visitors' Centre in KL (p.86) is a good first stop for material on East Malaysia.

There are many Web sites about each country (see box, overleaf), the region having taken to the **Internet** in a big way; even in small towns, getting online at Internet cafés and computer stores isn't a problem.

MALAYSIA WEB SITES

www.asiahype.com Excellent site on KL's eating, nightlife and entertainment scenes.

www.newmalaysia.com A Malaysian search engine with plentiful information and links on Malaysian news, music, travel and more.

www.sarawak.com.my/travel_features/ Excellent site stuffed full of articles on Sarawakian culture.

www.malaysiakini.com One of a number of sites offering political coverage and views from outside the mainstream.

www.mns.org.my The Malaysian Nature Society's site has useful material on the national parks, including trails and ecological information, and details of other nature sites throughout the country.

www.tourism.gov.my Comprehensive, up-to-date site put together by Tourism Malaysia in KL.

www.sarawaktourism.com The Web site of the Sarawak Tourism Board.

SINGAPORE WEB SITES

www.newasia-singapore.com The Singapore Tourism Board's official site, featuring a tour planner, attractions, current events, a virtual "tour" of the island and an accommodation search by price range.

www.makansutra.com Quirky Web site maintained by the foodies who annually publish the *Makansutra* food guide to Singapore. Carries fascinating essays about the cultural and culinary facets of eating out in Singapore.

www.straitstimes.com.sg The online version of the *Singapore Straits Times*.

BRUNEI WEB SITES

www.sunshineborneo.com This travel-agent-run site contains lots of useful information on the oil-rich state, plus great pictures.

www.bruneiair.com The Web site of Brunei's national air carrier includes a section on visiting Brunei.

www.brunet.bn/news/bb/ The online version of the independent Brunei English-language paper, the *Borneo Bulletin*. Brunei news tends to be limited to stories like the results of local tug-of-war competitions, but the paper is worth a read for their occasionally interesting coverage of neigbouring Sarawak and Sabah.

TOURIST OFFICES AND INFORMATION

The **Malaysian Tourism Promotion Board** (MTPB; *www.tourism.gov.my*) is the government tourist organization, often referred to as Tourism Malaysia. It operates tourist offices, variously called Visitors' Centres or Tourist Information, in most major towns, which are generally open Monday to Friday 8am–12.45pm and 2–4.15pm, Saturday 8am–12.45pm; though in Kelantan and Terengganu, offices close on Friday and open Sunday instead. As a rule, the offices are more than happy to furnish you with glossy brochures and leaflets, organized on a state-by-state basis, but are less helpful for hard information about areas off the beaten track. The best publication is the *Malaysia Travel Planner*, available from Tourism Malaysia offices abroad, which rounds up all thirteen states' attractions as well as listing practical information (like train timetables). In most cases, the offices maintain local accommodation lists, though this doesn't necessarily guarantee any particular standard. There'll always be someone on hand who can speak at least some English. All of Malaysia's national parks also have information offices (Taman Negara even has a small library) stocked with maps and leaflets, and staffed by English speakers. Most, however, won't be able to give you much in-depth information, the exceptions being at Sarawak's Bako National Park, where photocopied scientific reports are available, and some of the parks in Sabah, especially Mount Kinabalu, for which extensive fold-out brochures are published by the Sabah Parks office (see p.448).

In Singapore, tourist information is put out by the **Singapore Tourist Board** (STB; *www.newasia-singapore.com*), which has three downtown branches with English-speaking staff and toll-free information lines (see p.536 for details). Each branch has a huge range of handouts, the

TOURISM MALAYSIA OFFICES ABROAD

Australia 56 William St, Perth (☎09/481 0400, fax 321 1421, *tourmal@omen.com.au*); 65 York St, Sydney (☎02/299 4441, fax 262 2026, *amir@iaccess.com.au*).

Canada 830 Burrard St, Vancouver, BC V6Z 2K4 (☎604/689-8899, fax 689-8804, *mtpb-yvr@msn .com*).

Ireland No office.

New Zealand No office.

UK 57 Trafalgar Square, London WC2N 5DU (☎020/7930 7932, fax 7930 9015, *info@malaysia org uk*)

US 595 Madison Ave, Suite 1800, New York, NY 10022 (☎212/754-1113, fax 754-1116, *mtpb@aol .com*).

SINGAPORE TOURIST BOARD OFFICES ABROAD

Australia 2/226 James St, Perth (☎08/9228 8166); Level 11, AWA Building, 47 York St, Sydney (☎02/9290 2888).

Canada Standard Life Centre, 121 King St W, Suite 1000, Toronto, ON M5H 3T9 (☎416/363-8898).

Ireland No office.

New Zealand 3rd floor, 43 High St, Auckland (☎09/358 1191).

UK 1st floor, Carrington House, 126–130 Regent St, London W1R 5FE (☎020/7437 0033).

US 12th floor, 590 Fifth Ave, New York, NY 10036 (☎212/302-4061); Prudential Plaza, 180 N Stetson Ave, Suite 1450, Chicago, IL 60601 (☎312/938-1888); 8484 Wiltshire Blvd, Suite 510, Beverly Hills, CA 90211 (☎213/852-1901, *www.singapore-usa.com*

biggest and best of which is the "Singapore Official Guide", featuring good maps, including the free (and very useful) *Map of Singapore*.

Brunei has a fledgling tourist industry, and the only offering from the Economic Development Board, which handles tourism and maintains a booth at the airport (see p.500), is the *Explore Brunei* booklet, which has some useful information but few hard facts. You won't fare much better even if you contact your local Bruneian embassy or consulate prior to departure.

MAPS

Maps of Malaysia are widely available abroad, the best general maps being either the detailed Nelles 1:650,000 *West Malaysia* (not including Sabah and Sarawak) and Berndtson and Berndtson's *Malaysia*; both include plans of major Malaysian towns. The 1:2,000,000 Bartholomew *Singapore & Malaysia World Travel Map* shows the entire region and the *Globetrotter Travel Map* of the Peninsula has around a dozen extra area plans, including Tioman and Penang. Road maps available in Malaysia are better than the ones abroad; if driving, you'll want to arm yourself with the free 1:1,000,000 *Road Map of Malaysia*, available for RM10 from any tourist office. The excellent

Petronas Heritage *Mapbook of Peninsular Malaysia* has 43 double-page spreads showing the Malaysian road system from town to town, with descriptions of all points of interest on each route. In theory, it's available for RM15 from the larger Petronas service stations, though, in practice, it can be quite hard to come by.

The range of maps of **Sarawak** and **Sabah** are more limited; very few show the extensive river systems of the interior of the two states adequately. The Land and Survey Department's 1:500,000 relief map of Sarawak is the most available, and can be obtained from the bookshop at the Kuching *Holiday Inn* (see p.363), but the recently updated *Periplus Sarawak* map (1:1,000,000) is quite OK for most purposes. The best coverage of Sabah is provided by the Nelles *East Malaysia* map, and there's a new Periplus one to choose from as well.

The **hiking maps** provided by information offices in places like Cameron Highlands and Taman Negara are barely adequate, but they are the best you'll find. If you're following hiking routes marked on sketch maps (including those in this book), it's always wise to ask local advice before setting off.

The best available maps of **Singapore** are the 1:22,500 *Nelles Singapore* and the *Cartographia*

MAP OUTLETS IN THE UK

CAMBRIDGE
Heffers Map and Travel, 3rd Floor, in Heffers Stationery Department, 19 Sidney St, Cambridge CB2 3HL (☎01223/568467, *www.heffers.co.uk*).

GLASGOW
John Smith and Sons, 57–61 St Vincent St, Glasgow G2 5TB (☎0141/221 7472, fax 248 4412, *www.johnsmith.co.uk*).

LONDON
National Map Centre, 22–24 Caxton St, SW1 (☎020/7222 4945, *www.mapsworld.com*).
Stanfords, 12–14 Long Acre, WC2 (☎020/7836 1321, *sales@stanfords.co.uk*).
The Travel Bookshop, 13–15 Blenheim Crescent, W11 2EE (☎020/7229 5260, *www .thetravelbookshop.co.uk*).

MAP OUTLETS IN NORTH AMERICA

CHICAGO
Rand McNally, 444 N Michigan Ave, IL 60611 (☎312/321-1751, *www.randmcnally.com*).

MONTRÉAL
Ulysses Travel Bookshop, 4176 St-Denis, PQ H2W 2M5 (☎514/843-9447, *www.ulyssesguides .com*).

NEW YORK
The Complete Traveler Bookstore, 199 Madison Ave, NY 10016 (☎212/685-9007).
Rand McNally, 150 52nd St, NY 10022 (☎212/758-7488, *www.randmcnally.com*).

SAN FRANCISCO
The Complete Traveler Bookstore, 3207 Fillmore St, CA 92123 (☎415/923-1511).
Rand McNally, 595 Market St, CA 94105 (☎415/777-3131, *www.randmcnally.com*).

SEATTLE
Elliot Bay Book Company, 101 S Main St, WA 98104 (☎206/624-6600, *www.elliottbaybooks .com*).
Wide World Books and Maps, 4411 Wallingfor Ave N, Seattle, WA 98103 (☎206/634-3453, *www .travelbooksandmaps.com*).

TORONTO
Open Air Books and Maps, 25 Toronto St, ON M5R 2C1 (☎416/363-0719).

VANCOUVER
International Travel Maps′and Books, 552 Seymour St, BC V6B 3J5 (☎604/687-3320, *www.itbm.com*).

WASHINGTON DC
Rand McNally, 1201 Connecticut Ave NW,

MAP OUTLETS IN AUSTRALIA AND NEW ZEALAND

Washington, DC 20036 (☎202/223-6751, *www .randmcnally.com*).
ADELAIDE
The Map Shop, 16a Peel St (☎08/8231 2033).

AUCKLAND
Specialty Maps, 58 Albert St (☎09/307 2217).

BRISBANE
Worldwide Maps and Guides, 187 George St

(☎07/3221 4330).

CHRISTCHURCH
Mapworld, 173 Gloucester St, Christchurch (☎03/374 5399, fax 374 5633, *maps@mapworld .co.nz, www.mapworld.co.nz*)

MELBOURNE
Mapland, 372 Little Bourke St, (☎03/9670 4383)

West Malaysia, the latter containing a good map of the island. The *Singapore Street Directory*, from all bookshops, is a must if you're renting a car.

There are few specific maps of **Brunei** available, though *Nelles East Malaysia* includes an adequate Brunei map; coverage of the state on other general maps of East Malaysia/Borneo tends to be rather scant. The Bruneian government produce a map of Bandar Seri Begawan and its environs, which is available in the capital's bookshops and stationers.

TRAVELLERS WITH DISABILITIES

Of the three countries, Singapore is the most accessible to travellers with disabilities; hefty tax incentives are provided for developers who include access features for the disabled in new buildings. In contrast, Malaysia makes few provisions for its own disabled citizens, a state of affairs that clearly affects the tourist with disabilities.

In both countries, life is made a lot easier if you can afford the more upmarket hotels (which usu-ally have specially adapted elevators) and to shell out for taxis and the odd domestic flight. Similarly, the more expensive international **airlines** tend to be better equipped to get you there in the first place: MAS, British Airways, KLM and Qantas all carry aisle wheelchairs and have at least one toilet adapted for disabled passengers. However, few, if any, tour operators offering holidays in the region accommodate the needs of those with disabilities.

CONTACTS FOR TRAVELLERS WITH DISABILITIES

UK

Holiday Care Service, second floor, Imperial Building, Victoria Rd, Horley, Surrey RH6 7PZ (☎01293/774535). Provides free lists of accessible accommodation abroad – European, American and long-haul destinations – plus a list of accessible attractions in the UK. Information on financial help for holidays available.

RADAR (Royal Association for Disability and Rehabilitation), 12 City Forum, 250 City Rd, London EC1V 8AF (☎020/7250 3222; Minicom ☎020/7250 4119). Produces an annual holiday guide for the UK (£7, includes p&p) and separate guides for long-haul and for Europe (both £5 inc. p&p) alternate years.

Tripscope, Brentford Community Resource Centre, Alexandra House, Brentford High Street, Brentford, Middlesex TW8 0NE (☎0845/758 5641). This registered charity provides a national telephone-information service offering free advice on international transport and travel for those with a mobility problem.

NORTH AMERICA

Directions Unlimited, 123 Green Lane, Bedford Hills, NY 10507 (☎914/241-1700). Travel agency specializing in custom tours for people with disabilities.

Information Center for People with Disabilities, Fort Point Place, 27–43 Wormwood St, Boston, MA 02210 (☎617/727-5540). Clearing house for information, including travel.

Mobility International USA, PO Box 10767, Eugene, OR 97440 (Voice and TDD ☎541/343-1284, *www.miusa.org*). Information and referral services, access guides, tours and exchange programmes. Annual membership $35 (includes quarterly newsletter).

Society for the Advancement of Travel for the Handicapped (SATH), 347 Fifth Ave, Suite 610, New York, NY 10016 (☎212/447-7284, *sathtravel@aol.com*). Non-profit travel-industry referral service that passes queries on to its members as appropriate; allow plenty of time for a response.

Travel Information Service, Moss Rehabilitation Hospital, 1200 Tabor Rd, Philadelphia, PA 19141 (☎215/456-9600). Telephone-information service and referral.

Twin Peaks Press, Box 129, Vancouver, WA 98666 (☎360/694-2462 or 1-800/637-2256). Publisher of the *Directory of Travel Agencies for the Disabled*, listing more than 370 agencies worldwide; *Travel for the Disabled*; the *Directory of Accessible Van Rentals*; and *Wheelchair Vagabond*, loaded with personal tips.

AUSTRALIA AND NEW ZEALAND

ACROD (Australian Council for Rehabilitation of the Disabled), PO Box 60, Curtin, ACT 2605 (☎02/6282 4333). Provides lists of travel agencies and tour operators for people with disabilities.

Barrier Free Travel, 36 Wheatley St, North Bellingen, NSW 2454 (☎02/6655 1733). Independent consultant which draws up individual itineraries for people with disabilities.

Disabled Persons Assembly, PO Box 10, 138 The Terrace, Wellington (☎04/472 2626). Provides lists of travel agencies and tour operators for people with disabilities.

Singapore's **National Council of Social Service**, at 11 Penang Lane (☎3361544), can provide you with a free copy of *Access Singapore*, a thorough and informative brochure detailing amenities for the disabled in Singapore's hotels, hospitals, shopping centres, cinemas and banks. Access is improving, slowly, and most hotels now make some provision for disabled guests, though often there will only be one specially designed bedroom in an establishment – always call first for information, and book in plenty of time. Getting around the city is less straightforward: buses are not accessible to wheelchairs and there

are no elevators in the MRT system. However, one taxi company, TIBS (see p.540 for details), has several cabs big enough to take a wheelchair, and there are acoustic signals at street crossings.

In Malaysia, wheelchair users will have a hard time negotiating the uneven pavements in most towns and cities, and will find it difficult to board buses, trains, ferries and the LRT metro system in Kuala Lumpur, none of which has been adapted for wheelchairs. Although most modern hotels in KL and Georgetown have good access, much budget accommodation is located up narrow stairways and presents difficulties for the disabled.

COSTS, MONEY AND BANKS

cial deals on tickets that help keep costs down (see "Getting Around" for more).

Bargaining is *de rigueur* throughout Malaysia and Singapore, especially when shopping or renting a room for the night, though note that you don't haggle for meals.

TAKING MONEY ABROAD

The safest and most convenient method of carrying your money is as **traveller's cheques** – either sterling or US dollar cheques are acceptable. Available at a small commission from most banks, and from branches of American Express and Thomas Cook, traveller's cheques can be cashed at Malaysian, Singaporean and Bruneian banks, licensed moneychangers and some hotels, upon presentation of a passport. Some shops will even accept traveller's cheques as cash.

Major **credit cards** are widely accepted in the more upmarket hotels, shops and restaurants throughout the region, though beware of the illegal surcharges levied by some establishments – check before you pay that there's no surcharge; if there is, contact your card company and tell them about it. Banks will often **advance cash** against major credit cards; moreover, with American Express, Visa and MasterCard, it's possible to withdraw money from **automatic teller machines** (ATMs) in Singapore and all Malaysian cities and towns. To make sure your card will work in the regions you intend to travel, contact your card company before you leave home. To report lost or stolen traveller's cheques

Those entering Malaysia from Thailand will find their daily budget remains pretty much unchanged; approaching from Indonesia, on the other hand, costs will take a step up. Once in the region, daily necessities like food, drink and travel are marginally more expensive in Singapore than in Malaysia; over in East Malaysia, room rates tend to be a little higher than on the Peninsula, and you'll also find yourself forking out for river trips and nature tours.

Travelling in a group helps keep accommodation and eating costs down. The region affords no savings for senior citizens, though an **ISIC student card** might occasionally pay dividends. Most tourist attractions offer discounted entrance fees for **children**, while Malaysia's **public transport** network has a variety of spe-

or credit cards, call: **Visa** in Malaysia (☎1-800/801066), in Singapore (☎1-800/3451345); **MasterCard** in Malaysia (☎1-800/964767), in Singapore (☎1-800/3451345); **American Express** in Malaysia (☎0044 1273 696933 or 526122), in Singapore (☎2998133).

If your funds run out, you can arrange for cash to be transferred from home. **Wiring money** – which can take anything from two to seven working days – incurs a small fee in Southeast Asia and a larger one back home. You'll need, first, to supply your home bank with details of the local branch to which the money should be sent, after which it'll be issued to you upon presentation of some form of ID.

MALAYSIA

Basic food, accommodation and public transport costs in **Peninsular Malaysia** are extremely reasonable. If you're prepared to live frugally – staying in the most spartan lodging houses, roughing it on local transport, and eating and drinking at roadside stalls – it's quite feasible to manage on £10/US$15 a day. You'll not want to live like this for too long, though, and once you start to treat yourself to a few luxuries, the figures soon add up: an air-conditioned room, a meal at a decent restaurant, and a beer to round off the day could easily bump your **daily budget** up to a more realistic £20/US$32 a day. From there, the sky's the limit, with Malaysia's plush hotels, swanky restaurants and exclusive nightclubs well capable of emptying even the fullest wallet. You'll find living costs roughly similar in **East Malaysia**, though you can expect room rates to be up to fifty percent more expensive than on the mainland. Moreover, just getting around in Sarawak and Sabah can be fairly expensive, since you'll often have to organize your own transport; there are more details at the beginning of the relevant chapters.

Malaysia's unit of **currency** is the Malaysian **ringgit** (denoted "RM" before the price, and often informally called a "dollar"), divided into 100 sen. **Notes** come in RM1, RM5, RM10, RM20, RM50 and RM100 denominations; **coins** are minted in 1 sen, 5 sen, 10 sen, 20 sen, 50 sen and RM1 denominations.

At the time of writing, the **exchange rate** was around RM5.5 to £1, RM3.50 to US$1. Up-to-the-minute rates are posted daily in banks and exchange kiosks, and published in the *New Straits Times*. There is no currency black market in Malaysia, and no limit on the amount of foreign currency you can carry in or out of the country, although it must be declared at customs. There is however a limit of RM1000 on the amount of ringgit allowed into or out of Malaysia.

Major banks represented in Malaysia include the United Malayan Banking Corporation, Maybank, Bank Bumiputra, Oriental Bank, Hong Kong Bank and Standard Chartered; Ban Hin Lee Bank (BHL), a bank found only in major cities, doesn't charge any commission for changing American Express traveller's cheques. **Banking hours** are generally Monday to Friday 10am–3pm and Saturday 9.30–11.30am, though in the largely Muslim states of Kedah, Perlis, Kelantan and Terengganu, Friday is a holiday and Sunday a working day. Licensed **moneychangers**' kiosks, found in bigger towns all over the country, tend to open later, until around 6pm, with some opening at weekends and until 9pm, too; some hotels will exchange money at all hours. Exchange rates tend to be more generous at banks, but as you might be charged a higher commission fee, using a moneychanger can sometimes work out cheaper. It's not generally difficult to change money in Sabah or Sarawak, though if you are travelling along a river in the interior for any length of time, it's a wise idea to carry a fair amount of cash, in smallish denominations.

SINGAPORE

In Singapore, as in neighbouring Malaysia, if money is no object, you'll be able to take advantage of hotels, restaurants and shops as sumptuous as any in the world. But equally, with budget dormitory accommodation in plentiful supply, and both food and internal travel cheap in the extreme, you'll find it possible to live on a **budget** of less than £10/US$16 a day. Upgrading your lodgings to a private room in a guesthouse, eating in a restaurant and having a beer or two requires £20/US$32 a day. Once you are housed, fed and watered, Singapore has much of interest that costs hardly anything at all.

The currency is the **Singapore dollar**, written simply as $ (or – occasionally in this book – S$ to distinguish it from other dollars) and divided into 100 cents. **Notes** are issued in denominations of $1, $2, $5, $10, $20, $50, $100, $500, $1000 and $10,000; **coins** come in denominations of 1, 5, 10, 20 and 50 cents, and $1. The current **exchange rate** is around $2.60 to £1, $1.70 to US$1.

Singaporean dollars are not accepted in Malaysia, but are legal tender in Brunei (see below).

Singapore **banking hours** are generally Monday to Friday 10am–3pm and Saturday 9.30am–11.30am, outside of which you'll have to go to a moneychanger in a shopping centre (see p.611 for locations), or to a hotel. **Major banks** represented include the Overseas Union Bank, the United Overseas Bank, the OCBC, the Development Bank of Singapore, Standard Chartered Bank, Hong Kong and Shanghai Bank and Citibank. Rates at moneychangers are as good as you'll find in the banks. No currency black market operates in Singapore, nor are there any restrictions on carrying currency into or out of the state.

BRUNEI

Costs for everything except accommodation in Brunei are roughly the same as in Singapore. However, there's only one budget place to stay in the capital and if you can't get in there, you're looking at around £30/US\$45 minimum per night in a hotel, which means an average **daily budget** in Brunei is likely to start at around £40–50/US\$60–75. In addition, if you want to see anything of the surrounding countryside, you are largely dependent on expensive taxis since the public transport network, though slowly being developed, is still minimal.

Brunei's currency is the **Brunei dollar**, which is divided into 100 cents; you'll see it written as B\$, or simply as \$. The Bruneian dollar has parity with the Singapore dollar and both are legal tender in either country. Notes come in \$1, \$5, \$10, \$50, \$100, \$500, \$1000 and \$10,000 denominations; coins come in denominations of 1, 5, 10, 20 and 50 cents.

Brunei **banking hours** are Monday to Friday 9am–3pm and Saturday 9–11am, with **banks** represented in Bandar including the International Bank of Brunei, Citibank, Standard Chartered Bank and the Overseas Union Bank – all of which charge a transaction fee of a few dollars for cashing traveller's cheques.

GETTING AROUND

Public transport in Malaysia, Singapore and Brunei is reasonably reliable, though not as cheap as in other Southeast Asian countries. Apart from in Singapore, where there's a comprehensive island-wide public transport system (see p.537 for the details), most of your travelling, particularly in Peninsular Malaysia, will be by bus, minivan or, less often, long-distance taxi. That said, the Malaysian train system has its uses, especially on the long haul up the west coast from Singapore and into Thailand. By and large, the roads in Peninsular Malaysia are reasonable and recent road construction has speeded up journey times: the North–South Highway runs the length of the west coast from Johor Bahru to Bukit Kayu Hitam, while the East–West Highway connects Kota Bahru with Penang.

Sabah and **Sarawak** have their own travel peculiarities – in Sarawak, for instance, you're reliant on boats, and occasionally planes, for most long-distance travel although the bus service from Kuching in the south to Kuala Baram in the north has improved immensely in recent years. Brunei's bus service, covering routes through the main towns, is supplemented by boats in remote areas such as the Temburong district. The chapters on Sarawak, Sabah and Brunei contain detailed travel information for each area. The main thing to note is that there is no boat service linking Peninsular Malaysia or Singapore with East Malaysia or Brunei; consequently, flights are the only way to get between the two regions.

BUSES

The national bus network is generally the easiest and quickest way of getting around Malaysia, with regular services between all major towns. In addition to the government-run Transnational bus company (☎03/201 1430) and individual state bus operators, a large number of private companies operate services along specific routes (one of the largest is Plusliner; ☎03/232 0763 or 230 4180, *parkmayberhad@hotmail.com*). Each town bus station usually contains one or more bus company offices, where you buy your ticket; since prices are fairly similar on each route, it matters little which company you choose.

Buses for long-distance routes (those over 3hr) typically leave in clusters in the early morning and late evening, while shorter or more popular routes are served regularly throughout the day. In most cases you can just turn up immediately prior to departure, though on some of the more popular routes – Kuala Lumpur to Penang, or Kuantan to Singapore – it's advisable to reserve a ticket at least a day in advance at the relevant ticket office (particularly during the major holiday periods of Christmas, Easter and Hari Raya). The departure time of the company's next bus is usually displayed. Fares are eminently reasonable: the seven-hour run from KL to Georgetown, for exam-

ple, costs around RM19; for other fares, see the box below. Many towns and cities have more than one bus station, serving different regions or companies; the text and maps detail where you should go to catch your bus. The long-distance station is often located on the edge of town, needing a local bus or taxi ride to reach. Local buses usually, though not always, operate from a separate, more central station. They serve routes within the state and are consequently cheaper, but also slower, less comfortable and without air-conditioning. It's not possible to book a seat – buy your ticket on the bus.

Various buses ply the long-distance routes across **Sabah**, but they are heavily outnumbered by the **minibuses** that buzz around the state, which generally leave from the same terminals. Faster and slightly more expensive than the scheduled bus services, minibuses only leave when jam-packed and are often very uncomfortable as a result; the journey from Kota Kinabalu to Kudat or Sandakan costs RM15 or RM20 respectively. Also prevalent in Sabah are **Land Cruisers**, outsized jeeps which take only eight passengers, and whose fares are at least twenty percent higher than going by minibus.

In Sarawak, modern air-con buses ply the trans-state coastal road between Kuching and the Brunei border, serving Sibu, Bintulu and Miri en route. The trip from Kuching to Miri costs RM70 and takes 15 hours; Kuching to Sibu costs around RM30. In addition, local buses serve the satellite towns and villages around the state's main settlements. These buses are particularly useful when exploring southwestern Sarawak and for the cross-border trip to Pontianak in Indonesian Kalimantan. Land Cruisers are increasingly coming into use for navigating the logging tracks which have opened up remote inland areas; details of routes are given in the *Guide*.

TRAINS

The Peninsula's **train** service, operated by Keretapi Tanah Melayu Berhad (KTMB; *www.ktmb.com.my*), is limited in scope, relatively expensive and extremely slow, making it for the most part an unappealing alternative to the bus except for travel along the west-coast main line. However, it is virtually the only way to reach some of the more interesting places in the interior and there's still a certain thrill in arriving at some of the splendidly solid colonial stations, built when the train was the prime means of transport.

SAMPLE EXPRESS BUS ROUTES AND FARES

Kuala Lumpur to:

Alor Setar	5hr	RM21.20
Padang Besar	7hr	RM24.00
Butterworth	4hr	RM17.10
Cameron Hglds	5hr	RM12.10
Ipoh	4hr	RM9.40
Johor Bahru	5hr	RM16.50
Kota Bharu	9hr	RM25.00
Kuala Lipis	4hr	RM7.90
Kuala Terengganu	8hr	RM21.60
Kuantan	4hr	RM12.10
Lumut	4hr	RM12.20
Melaka	2hr 30min	RM6.80
Penang	4hr 30min	RM18.00
Singapore	5hr	RM21.30
KL–Melaka Express	2hr 30min	RM6.80

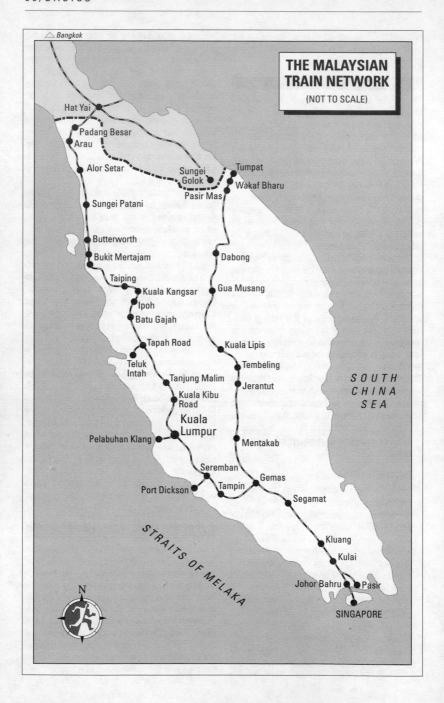

THE MALAYSIAN
TRAIN NETWORK
(NOT TO SCALE)

SAMPLE TRAIN ROUTES AND FARES						
All fares are given in ringgit.	EXPRESS			ORDINARY		
	1st	2nd	3rd	1st	2nd	3rd
Kuala Lumpur to:						
Alor Setar	79.00	37.00	23.00	70.50	30.60	17.40
Butterworth	67.00	34.00	19.00	58.50	25.40	14.40
Gemas	35.00	20.00	11.00	27.00	11.70	6.70
Ipoh	40.00	22.00	12.00	31.50	13.70	7.80
Kuala Lipis	–	–	–	56.00	36.50	18.00
Padang Besar	92.50	45.50	25.30	81.00	35.10	20.00
Taiping	53.00	28.00	16.00	45.00	19.50	11.10
Tapah Road	32.00	19.00	10.00	23.30	10.10	5.80
Tumpat	–	–	106.50	46.50	29.00	–
Singapore	68.00	34.00	19.00	60.00	26.00	14.80
Singapore to:						
Alor Setar	142.30	66.70	37.80	133.30	58.10	33.70
Butterworth	127.00	60.00	34.00	118.50	51.40	29.90
Gemas	43.00	23.00	13.00	34.50	15.00	8.50
Kuala Lipis	–	–	–	67.50	29.30	16.70
Kuala Lumpur	68.00	34.00	19.00	60.00	26.00	14.80
Padang Besar	152.50	71.10	40.30	134.00	62.50	35.50
Tumpat	–	–	–	112.50	48.80	27.70

A free **timetable** for the whole country is available from the train station in Kuala Lumpur and other major towns; it details all the services on the various routes except for some additional local services on the jungle railway (see p.230). All stations have departure and arrival times posted near the platform.

ROUTES AND SERVICES

From the southern Thai town of Hat Yai, the main **west-coast line** runs via Padang Besar on the Malaysian border south through Butterworth (for Penang), Ipoh, Tapah Road (for the Cameron Highlands) and KL, where you usually have to change trains before continuing on to Singapore. Between KL and Singapore the train route splits at Gemas, 58km northeast of Melaka, from where a second line runs north through the mountainous interior – a section known as the **jungle railway** – via Kuala Lipis, skirting Kota Bharu (nearest station is at Wakaf Bharu) on its way to the northeastern border town of Tumpat. It's possible to get to Thailand on this line by leaving the train at Pasir Mas and catch a bus or taxi to the border crossing at Rantau Panjang; once across the border, at Sungei Golok, you can catch a train northwest to Hat Yai (see p.253 for details).

East Malaysia's only rail line is in **Sabah**, where there's a 55-kilometre narrow-gauge link between **Tanjung Aru**, 5km south of Kota Kinabalu, and **Tenom**. The service is slow and jarring, and only really worth following between Beaufort and Tenom, when it traces a dramatic path along Sungei Padas; for the details, see p.467.

There are two main types of trains in the Peninsula. **Express trains**, which stop only at principal stations, run on the west-coast line only; **local trains** (labelled "M" on timetables), run on both lines and stop at virtually every station. Both types of train are divided into three classes, with the option of air-con; the advantage of choosing an express train on a west-coast route is that it can knock anything up to three hours off your journey time. You don't need to book in advance for local trains, but you may want to **reserve** a day or two in advance (which incurs a small charge and must be done at the station) for express trains, particularly if you require an overnight berth.

On the west coast, there are three trains a day between Singapore and KL, and four between KL and Padang Besar; of these, only one is a local train. In addition, there is a once-daily Kedah Line service, which runs along the west-coast line between Butterworth and Arau only, and one **international express** a day between Butterworth and **Bangkok**, for which additional charges apply (see below). Thus travelling from Singapore to Bangkok involves changing at both KL and Butterworth, unless you catch the once-daily Ekspres Raykat train ("ER" on the timetable) from Singapore, which stops briefly at KL before continuing on to Butterworth (where you'll have to wait until the next day to pick up the Bangkok connection). Two daily services between Kluang and Singapore, and one daily between Gemas and Singapore, augment the west-coast schedule. All the trains on the interior route are local trains, with the exception of the Tumpat Express, which runs three times weekly between Singapore and Tumpat. There's also a once-daily train from Gemas to Tumpat.

TICKETS AND PASSES

Fares vary according to class of travel and type of train; for main routes and prices see the box overleaf. Second-class is usually roomy and comfortable enough for most journeys; the only real advantage of first-class travel, which is nearly twice as expensive as second class, is the air-conditioning. Third-class, although only around half as much as second, is inevitably more crowded, with fewer comforts. On overnight sleepers, only first- and second-class berths are available, though second class offers air-con as an option.

A berth on the international express between Butterworth and Bangkok costs around RM29 first-class, from RM23 in second-class air-con and from around RM8 in non-air-con, depending on whether you want an upper or lower berth. Charges for berths on all other overnight trains are marginally higher.

The **Malaysia and Singapore Rail Pass** is available to anyone who is under 26 or a holder of ISIC (International Student Identity Card) or full-time students of any age. Allowing unlimited second-class train travel on KTM in Peninsular Malaysia and Singapore, the pass is valid for 7 (£24/US$39), 14 (£33/US$52) or 21 (£39/US$63) days, though to get your money's worth, you have to be prepared to travel almost exclusively by train. The pass also covers the cost of seat reser-

vations, but not the use of sleeper berths. It's available from specialist rail agents, such as usit CAMPUS in London (see p.5), or from student-oriented travel agents in Kuala Lumpur and Singapore, where it costs roughly the same in the local currencies.

TRANS-MALAYSIAN ROUTES

Other than the Malaysian journeys, one long-distance route you might consider is the train ride from Singapore to Bangkok, which takes nearly thirty hours. While all trains bar one necessitate changing in KL (the exception being the Ekspres Raykat, which runs from Singapore through to Butterworth; see above), you never usually have to wait longer than an hour in KL to catch an onward service to Butterworth. Unfortunately there are no convenient connections from Butterworth with the international express to Bangkok; you either need to make an overnight stop in Butterworth or, at best, endure a six-and-a-half-hour wait. It's a tiring journey done in one go, particularly if you don't book a berth on the overnight leg between Butterworth and Bangkok (see above for charges). One-way tickets for the entire Singapore–Bangkok route cost around S$100 first-class and S$45 second-class; a Malaysia and Singapore Rail Pass (see above) is valid up until the Thai border.

Following the same route in considerably more luxury, the **Eastern & Oriental Express** departs on certain Sundays from Singapore to Bangkok (returning on Thursdays), stopping briefly at Kuala Lumpur and longer at Butterworth (where there's time for a three-hour tour of Penang island, which you can book as part of your ticket); there's also a longer stop at Kanchanaburi, south of Bangkok. Taking altogether three days and two nights, the trip costs £850/US$1400 per person. Bookings can be made at Eastern & Oriental Express, Sea Containers House, 20 Upper Ground, London SE1 (☎020/7805 5060, *www.orient-express.com*); through some of the tour operators listed on p.12 and p.16; in Singapore at E&O Services, #32-01/03 Shaw Towers, 100 Beach Rd (☎3923500); or in Bangkok, E&O Services, c/o *Tong Poon Hotel*, 130 Rong Muang soi, Rama V1 Rd (☎02/216 8661).

LONG-DISTANCE TAXIS

Most towns in Malaysia have a **long-distance taxi rank** (usually right next to the express bus station). The taxis charge fixed-price, per-person fares on long-distance routes throughout the country; you can usually reckon on paying between 100 and 200 percent more than the regular bus fare. You have to wait until the car has its full complement of four passengers before departure, but in most major towns the wait should never take more than thirty minutes.

Prices are chalked up on a board in the station, so there's no danger of being ripped off – in fact, taxis are generally very reliable and a lot quicker than the buses. From Kuala Lumpur, you're looking at fares of around RM33–40 to Butterworth, RM20–25 to Ipoh and RM45–50 to Kota Bharu. As a foreigner you may be pressured to charter the whole car (at four times the one-person fare), which makes it expensive unless you're in a group. For long-distance journeys, it's best to arrive at the taxi rank early in the morning (7–8am) as there are more departures then.

FERRIES AND BOATS

Ferries sail to all the major islands off Malaysia's east and west coasts. The traditional **bumboats** – originally used for fishing – are rapidly being replaced by faster, sleeker express models; if you want to experience an old-style bumboat ride, you can still do so in Singapore (see p.541). On most ferries, you buy your ticket in advance from booths at the jetty (on some you can pay on the boat as well); all the relevant details are given in the text. Barring rainy-season storms, there are daily services from the mainland to Tioman and the Perhentian islands, and a regular catamaran service from Singapore to Tioman. Kapas and Redang are almost wholly off-limits during the rainy season though; you'll have trouble chartering a boat there even if your wallet stretches that far. The only regular service between two Malaysian offshore islands is the daily boat between Penang and Langkawi (see p.171).

Within **Sarawak**, the most common form of public transport, buses aside, are the long and narrow express boats which ply the state's river systems. A lifeline for the inhabitants of the interior, these low-lying craft run to a regular timetable; buy your ticket on board. On the smaller tributaries, travel is by longboat, which can turn out to be more expensive if you have to charter the whole vessel, although you rarely need to do so. For more details on getting around Sarawak by boat, see p.356.

Sabah has no express-boat river services, though regular ferries connect Pulau Labuan with Kota Kinabalu, Sipitang and Menumbok, all on the west coast; details are given in the text. In **Brunei**, there are some useful boat services, including the speedboat service from the capital, Bandar Seri Begawan, to Bangar for Temburong Park, and the regular boats from Bandar to Lawas or Limbang in Sarawak and Pulau Labuan in Sabah; see p.510 for details.

PLANES

The Malaysian national airline, MAS, operates a comprehensive range of **domestic flights**, though services between major towns on the Peninsula are often routed via Kuala Lumpur, making them long-winded and uneconomical. But some routes are definitely worth considering: although expensive, the flight from KL to Langkawi (RM135 one way) takes just 55 minutes, as compared to the lengthy eleven-hour bus journey followed by an hour's ferry ride. MAS has **booking offices** in every major town and city on the Peninsula, as well as in Sarawak, Sabah and Singapore; addresses and phone numbers are given throughout the text.

SPECIAL FARES

Though there are no student discounts for anyone studying outside Malaysia, a range of **special fares** offer considerable discounts to tourists, families, those travelling in groups, and disabled travellers. Designated **night tourist flights** can halve the price of a one-way flight between KL and Alor Setar (normally around RM120); similar reductions are available between KL and Kota Bharu, Kota Kinabalu, Kuching, Penang and Johor Bahru. In addition, one-way and return **excursion fares** apply between Johor Bahru and Kota Kinabalu, Kuching and Penang, and between KL and Kota Kinabalu, Kuching, Labuan and Miri, representing savings of ten to fifteen percent over regular MAS fares. Within Malaysia, it's also possible to obtain **family fares**: if one family member pays the full fare, the accompanying spouse and/or children get a 25 percent discount, though the return trip must be made within thirty days of the outward journey.

Two types of **group fare** exist: between Peninsular Malaysia and East Malaysia and between Sabah and Sarawak, three or more passengers travelling together receive a fifty- percent discount; for other routes in Malaysia, a 25-percent discount applies. To qualify, the return journey must be made between four and thirty days after the outward journey, and full payment must be made at least seven days prior to departure. **Blind** or **disabled** passengers are entitled to a fifty-percent discount on these routes, with a 25 percent reduction for a companion.

AIR PASSES

To keep internal flight costs down, it's worth buying a **Discover Malaysia Pass**, only available in conjunction with an MAS flight into Malaysia from abroad. The pass costs approximately £60/US$100 for a maximum of five flights within one of Malaysia's three air-travel sectors (Sarawak, Sabah and the Peninsula) and £125/US$200 for any five internal flights. Passes are valid on a specific pre-booked itinerary within a 28-day period, although, after the first flight, dates of subsequent flights can be changed for free and the route can be altered for a fee of around £16/US$25 per change. The flights are completely of your choosing – for example from KL to all Peninsular destinations count as one sector – but the same sector cannot be used more than once except for the purpose of making an immediate flight connection. See the "Getting There" sections on pp.1–16 for details of MAS tickets and offices in your own country.

MAIN ROUTES

The most frequent service within the Peninsula is the shuttle between KL and Singapore, on either MAS or Singapore Airlines, with departures every half-hour at peak times for a standard one-way fare of RM170/S$150; the journey takes 55 minutes. For Penang, there's also an hourly MAS service from KL (45min; RM100 one way) and a Singapore Airlines service from Singapore (3 daily; S$175 one way). The Singapore Airlines subsidiary, SilkAir, connects Singapore with Tioman, Langkawi and Kuantan.

Flights to East Malaysia operate mainly out of Kuala Lumpur, with Johor Bahru providing additional services to Kuching and Kota Kinabalu. Although direct services from KL take roughly 1 hour 40 minutes to Kuching, and 2 hours 30 minutes to Kota Kinabalu, many flights are routed via Johor Bahru, with some Sabah-bound flights then making several more stops in Sarawak on the way.

Within Sarawak and Sabah, numerous nineteen-seater Twin Otter and thirty-eight seater Fokker flights help maintain communications with the remote provinces. There are regular rural air services from Miri to many quite isolated destinations, such as Lawas, Limbang, Ba Kelalan, Marudi, Gunung Mulu and Bario; from Kota Kinabalu to Kudat, Lawas, Limbang and Sandakan; and from Lawas to Ba Kelalan and Limbang. Flights to the more remote of these areas are susceptible to delays and cancellations due to weather conditions; it's as well to note that some routes – like Miri–Mulu and Miri–Bario – are very popular indeed and require booking weeks in advance, ideally.

DRIVING AND VEHICLE RENTAL

The condition of the **roads** in Peninsular Malaysia is generally excellent, making driving there a viable prospect for tourists. It's mostly the same story in Sarawak and Brunei, though Sabah is the odd one out; around a quarter of roads there are rough, unpaved and highly susceptible to flash flooding.

On the Peninsula, the pristine **North–South Highway** (reckon on paying approximately RM1 toll for every 7km travelled) runs nearly 900km up the west coast from Johor Bahru to the border with Thailand, with Route 1, its predecessor, shadowing it virtually all the way. At Kuala Lumpur, Route 2, a notorious accident blackspot, cuts through the central region to connect the capital with the east-coast town of Kuantan, while much further to the north, the East–West Highway (Route 4) traces the Thai border to link Butterworth with Kota Bharu. The mountainous interior is sliced in two by the narrow and winding Route 8, which leaves Route 2 roughly 50km from Kuala Lumpur, passing through Kuala Lipis and Kuala Kerai before reaching Kota Bharu. The east coast is served by Route 3, a relatively traffic-free road that begins in Kota Bharu and terminates in Johor Bahru, 700km to the south. Typical journey times are two and a half hours from Kuala Lumpur to Melaka, seven hours for KL to Penang, and four hours for KL to Singapore.

Note that the streets of major cities like Kuala Lumpur, Kuantan and Georgetown are particularly traffic-snarled, with confusing one-way systems to boot, not ideal for the disoriented driver. That said, the main highways are hassle-free, making fly-drive holidays on the Malaysian

CAR RENTAL AGENCIES

UK
Avis ☎0990/900500
Budget ☎0800/181181
Hertz ☎0990/996699

Ireland
Avis ☎01/874 5844
Budget ☎0800/973159
Hertz ☎01/676 7476

North America
Avis ☎1-800/331-1084
Budget ☎1-800/527-0700
Hertz ☎1-800/654-3001

Australia
Avis ☎1800/225 533
Budget ☎1300/362 848
Hertz ☎1800/550 067

New Zealand
Avis ☎09/526 2800
Budget ☎0000/652 227
Hertz ☎0800/655 955

Peninsula a popular option. Several travel agencies (see "Getting There" sections on pp.3–16) offer pre-booked routes, or you can choose your own route, booking accommodation in hotels as you go.

CAR AND BIKE RENTAL

To **rent a vehicle** in Malaysia, Singapore and Brunei, you must be 23 or over and have held a clean driving licence for at least a year; a national driving licence, particularly if written in English, is sufficient, though there's no harm in acquiring an International Driving Licence.

The major international car-rental **agencies** represented in Malaysia and Singapore are Avis, Budget, Hertz and National; you'll find at least one of their offices in each major town and at the airports. There are also a handful of local companies, including Mayflower and Thrifty, which charge about the same; we've given addresses and phone numbers for rental companies in the accounts of cities and major towns. Note that the international rental agencies need between three and seven days' notice for a prepaid booking before you leave your home country (see box,

above, for their contact details) or at least two days' notice if you're booking and paying locally, though you may be fortunate enough to turn up and rent a car on the spot.

In Malaysia, rates begin at around RM150 (£28/US$45) per day for a basic Proton Saga, including unlimited mileage and personal insurance. A collision damage waiver of up to RM2000 is usually included also, otherwise an additional charge of around RM15 per day is levied. Rates for periods longer than three days are better value: a week's rental costs around RM800–900 (£150–175/US$220–270). If you want to take the car into Singapore, a surcharge of RM$80 a day applies.

In Singapore, rental deals vary according to whether the three-percent tax and collision damage waiver is included, but the rate, again for a Proton Saga, averages around S$170 (£60/US$90) a day and around S$1000 (£400/US$600) a week. Taking the car into Malaysia incurs a surcharge of S$25 per day. Rental offices usually require two days' notice and a deposit of around S$100; this can be avoided by prebooking abroad. Car rental in **Brunei** is relatively cheap, with prices starting at B$50 a day (£20/US$30), or B$300 (£115/US$175) a week.

Motorbike rental is much more informal, usually offered by Malaysian guesthouses and shops in more touristy areas. Officially, you must be over 21 and have an appropriate driving licence, though it's unlikely you'll have to show the latter; you'll probably need to leave your passport as a deposit, however. Wearing helmets is compulsory. The cost of rental varies from RM20 to RM30 per day, while bicycles can be rented for around RM4 a day. For information on bike rental in Singapore, see p.540.

RULES OF THE ROAD AND OTHER MATTERS

Malaysia, Singapore and Brunei follow the UK system of **driving on the left**. Most road signs are recognizable, and wearing seat belts in the front is compulsory. One confusing habit that Malaysian drivers have adopted is that they flash their headlights when they are claiming the right of way, not the other way around, as is common practice in the West.

On highways, the speed limit is 110kph, and 90kph on trunk roads, while in built-up areas it's 50kph; you'd be wise to stick religiously to these limits, since speed traps are commonplace mandatory fines are a hefty RM200. There are

A DRIVING VOCABULARY

Utara	North
Selatan	South
Barat	West
Timur	East
Awas	Caution
Ikut Kiri/Kanan	Keep left/right
Kurangkan Laju	Slow down
Jalan Sehala	One way
Lencongan	Detour
Berhenti	Stop
Beri Laluan	Give way
Had Laju . . ./jam	Speed limit . . . /per hour
Dilarang Memotong	No overtaking
Dilarang Melatak Kereta	No parking
Lebuhraya	Expressway/highway

plenty of garages throughout Malaysia, Singapore and Brunei; in any case, the rental agency will supply you with emergency numbers to call in the event of a breakdown.

Fuel is readily available in Malaysia. It's worth noting that it costs considerably more in Singapore due to its higher taxes on petrol.

CITY TRANSPORT

Most **Malaysian** cities and towns have some kind of bus service; details are given in the text wherever appropriate. Fares are always very cheap even if some of the bus networks – in places like KL and Georgetown – initially appear absolutely unfathomable to visitors. In KL, there are also the Komuter train and LRT (Light Rail Train) systems (see p.86). It's usually easier to jump in a taxi, sometimes the only way to reach certain local sights. Taxis are always metered, but meters not always used, despite this being illegal. Taxi drivers in KL often refuse to go to certain destinations, especially if the traffic is likely to be heavy or if it is raining. Drivers don't always speak English, so if you need to head to a complicated address, it's not a bad idea to have it written down on a piece of paper.

Trishaws (bicycle rickshaws), seating two people, are seen less and less these days, made redundant by the chaotic traffic systems in most towns. But they're still very much part of the tourist scene in places like Melaka, Penang, Kota Bharu and Singapore. Taking a trishaw tour can be a useful, atmospheric introduction to the town and the drivers often provide interesting, anecdotal information.

In most cases, trishaws aren't much cheaper than taking a taxi – bargain hard to fix the price in advance. You can expect to pay a minimum of RM3 for a short journey, while chartering by the hour can cost as much as RM25. Tours usually cost around RM25 for two for an hour's ride. Singapore also has trishaws, as well as other methods of getting around see p.537 for all the details.

ACCOMMODATION

While accommodation in Malaysia and Singapore is not the cheapest in Southeast Asia, in most places you can still get pretty good deals on simple rooms: in Malaysia, double rooms for under RM30 (£6/US$9) are common; under S$25 (£10/US$15) in Singapore. East Malaysia is more expensive, particularly in Sabah where you'll often pay RM40–50 (£7–9/US$11–13.50) for a very ordinary place.

The very cheapest form of accommodation is in a **dormitory bed** at a guesthouse, backpacker hostel or lodge, but these generally only exist in the more obvious tourist spots – Singapore, Kuala Lumpur, Georgetown, Kota Bharu and Cherating. At the other end of the scale, the region's luxury **hotels** offer a level of comfort and style to rank with any in the world. Prices in some of these, relatively speaking, have gone down since the economic recession of 1997, with many hotels offering competitive promotions; this is particularly true of Malaysia where, for example, an en-suite room with balcony, or attached personal garden, plus breakfast, can go for as little as RM120 (£25/US$35).

At the budget end of the market you'll have to share a bathroom, which in most cases will feature a shower and either a squat or Western-style toilet. Instead of showers, older places, or those in rural areas, sometimes have a *mandi* – a large basin of cold water which you throw over yourself with a bucket or ladle; it's very bad form to get soap in the basin or, worse still, get in it yourself. While **air-conditioning** is standard in the smarter hotels, some at the budget end also have air-con rooms which cost a little more than their regular ones.

Room rates remain relatively stable throughout the year, rising slightly during the major holiday periods – Christmas, Easter, Chinese New Year and Hari Raya. It's always worth bargaining during the monsoon lull on the east coast of the Peninsula (Nov–Feb), or if you're staying for a couple of weeks in one place. When asking for a room, note that a **single** room usually means it will contain one double bed, while a **double** has a double bed or two single beds, a **triple** three, and so on, making most rooms economical for families and groups; baby cots are usually available only in more expensive places.

In popular resorts, you'll often be accosted by people at bus or train stations advertising rooms: it's rarely worth going with them (especially since it's then hard to turn down the room if you don't like it), although they might be useful in securing you a room in the peak holiday season, saving you a lot of fruitless trudging around.

GUESTHOUSES, HOMESTAYS AND HOSTELS

The mainstay of the travellers' scene in Malaysia and Singapore are the **guesthouses**, located in popular tourist areas and usually good places to meet other people and pick up information. They can range from simple beachside A-frame huts to modern multistorey apartment buildings complete with a TV and video room. Their advantage for the single traveller on a tight budget is that almost all offer **dormitory beds**, which can cost as little as RM7–8 a night (or S$9 in Singapore). There are always basic double rooms available, too, usually with a fan and possibly a mosquito net, and averaging RM20 (S$20). Fierce competition on the Malaysian east coast means that prices there occasionally drop as low as RM15 for a double room, though this is somewhat offset by the pricier huts and chalets on the islands in the south, where you'll be hard pushed to find anything for under RM25.

In certain places – Kota Bharu especially – **homestay** programmes are available, whereby you stay with a Malaysian family, paying for your bed and board. The facilities are modest, and although some people find staying with a family too restrictive, it can be a good way of sampling Malay home cooking and culture. Local tourist offices have details of participants in the scheme.

Official **youth hostels** in Malaysia and Singapore are often hopelessly far-flung and no cheaper than dorms and rooms in the guest-houses – the rare exceptions are noted in the text. As a rule, it's not worth becoming an HI member just for the trip to Malaysia or Singapore, though if you're travelling further afield it might pay for itself eventually. Each major town generally also has both a **YMCA** and a **YWCA**. Like the youth hostels, these are rarely conveniently located, though their facilities are better than those at the youth hostels. However, at RM40 a night, the YMCA and YWCA are poor value compared to the budget hotels.

HOTELS

The cheapest **hotels** in Malaysia and Singapore are usually Chinese-run and cater for a predominantly local clientele. These places are generally clean and well kept and there's never any need to book in advance: just go to the next place around the corner if your first choice is full. Ordinary rooms (around RM25 a night, or S$30 in Singapore) are usually divided from one another by thin partitions and contain a washbasin, table and ceiling fan, though never a mosquito net; mattresses are usually rock hard. In the better places – often old converted mansions – you may also be treated to beautifully polished wooden floors and antique furniture. You'll often have the choice of air-con rooms as well, though the noisy rattle may not seem worth the extra RM10 or so. Showers and toilets (squat-style almost everywhere) are shared and can be pretty basic. Another consideration is the noise level, which can be very considerable since most places are on main streets. A word of **warning**: most of the hotels at the cheaper end of the scale also function as brothels, and so you should pick and choose carefully, particularly if you're a woman travelling alone. Those which are described using the Malay term *rumah persinggahan* usually double as brothels.

If you can't stand the noise in the cheaper places, then the **mid-range hotels** are your only alternative in most towns, though they're rarely better value than a well-kept budget place. The big difference is in the comfort of the mattress – nearly always sprung – and getting your own Western-style bathroom. Prices range from RM40–100 (S$50–150 in Singapore), for which expense you can expect a carpeted room with air-con and TV, and, towards the upper end of the range, a telephone and refrigerator. In these places, too, a genuine distinction is made between single rooms and doubles.

Also in the mid-range category are **government resthouses** (*rumah rehat*), which once provided accommodation for visiting colonial officials, though a lot of the old buildings have been replaced by more modern ones. Their

---

ACCOMMODATION PRICE CODES

All the accommodation in this book has been price-coded according to the following scale:

In Malaysia

① RM20 and under	④ RM61–80	⑦ RM161–220
② RM21–40	⑤ RM81–110	⑧ RM221–360
③ RM41–60	⑥ RM111–160	⑨ RM361 and above

In Singapore and Brunei

① Under $25	④ $61–100	⑦ $201–300
② $25–40	⑤ $101–150	⑧ $301–400
③ $41–60	⑥ $151–200	⑨ $401 and above

The price codes denote the **cheapest available room** with a double bed. Some guesthouses provide dormitory beds, for which the dollar price is given. In the case of luxury hotels (category ⑤ and above), the price codes have been calculated to include taxes. Breakfast isn't usually included in the price, unless otherwise stated.

facilities, which range from antiquated to modern, are generally excellent value: the rooms are large and well equipped, boasting a separate lounge area in many cases and private bathrooms always. Each resthouse has its own restaurant as well. In many towns the resthouses have been replaced by *Seri Malaysia* hotels, which offer a uniformly good standard of accommodation for around RM100 per night, including breakfast.

Moving to the top of the scale, the **high-class hotels** are as comfortable as you might expect, many with state-of-the-art facilities. Recently, the trend in Malaysia has been to reflect local traditions with the incorporation of kampung-style architecture – low-level timber structures with saddle-shaped roofs and open-sided public areas; hotels with such features still have all the usual trappings though, such as swimming pools, air conditioning and business facilities. While prices can be as reasonable as RM120 per room (S$150 in Singapore), rates in popular destinations such as Penang can rocket to RM300 and above – though this is still relatively good value compared to hotels of an equivalent standard in London or New York. Having said that, famous hotels, like the *Raffles* in Singapore, can virtually charge what they like. Don't forget that the price quoted by the hotel rarely includes the compulsory ten percent **service charge** and five percent **government tax** (four percent in Singapore), often signified by "++" after the price. It is always cheaper to stay at top hotels if you can do so as part of a pre-booked package – ask your travel agent if you want to stay at a specific hotel.

LONGHOUSES

The most atmospheric places to stay in Malaysia are the wood-and-bamboo stilted **longhouses**, found only on the rivers of **Sarawak** and **Sabah**. The traditional dwellings of many indigenous groups, longhouses can be home to dozens of families, and usually consist of three elevated sections reached by a simple ladder. A long, open veranda is used for jobs like drying rice and washing clothes, behind which is a longroom where the families eat, dance, talk and play music and games; further in are the private quarters of each family, usually just one room with an open fire for

cooking. Large mats are stored in the rafters and brought down to sleep or sit on. Of course, each tribe has its idiosyncratic variations on this basic pattern. Traditionally-built longhouses are fast disappearing though, and most contemporary examples are built of more durable material like stone and hardwoods, and furnished with corrugated-iron roofs.

Increasingly, the most practical way to stay at longhouses is as part of an organized **tour**, inevitably more a commercialized experience than visiting independently. However, it's still possible to travel along the rivers and, with only a minimal command of Malay at your disposal, be directed to communities off the beaten track which seldom see visitors. The best time of year to experience Sarawakian longhouse life outside of a package trip is during the *gawai* harvest festival in early June (see p.389). Visiting groups usually get a room to themselves in the longhouse, though during a festival the place may be so crowded that you end up sleeping sardine-fashion in the long room, and even out on the veranda.

Traditionally, there's no charge to stay in a longhouse, though it is good manners to bring **gifts** such as exercise books and pens and pencils for children, or to give a donation of, say, RM10 per visitor. Once there, you can participate in many activities including weaving, cooking, using a blowpipe, fishing, helping in the agricultural plots, and perhaps going out on a wild-boar hunt. For more details, including a rundown of longhouse etiquette, see p.367.

CAMPING

Despite the rural nature of most of Malaysia, there are few official opportunities for **camping**, perhaps because guesthouses and hotels are so reasonable. Where there are campsites, they charge around RM10 per person per night, and facilities are very basic. If you go trekking in the more remote regions, for example in Endau-Rompin National Park, camping is about your only option; note that equipment is rarely included in the advertised price of an organized trip. In Singapore, camping is confined to Pulau Ubin (see p.585); there are no official campsites in Brunei.

EATING AND DRINKING

One of the best reasons to come to Malaysia and Singapore (even Brunei, to a lesser extent) is for the food. The countries' cuisines are inspired by the heritage of their three main communities, Malay, Chinese and Indian. From the ubiquitous hawker stalls to the restaurants in world-class hotels, the standard of cooking is extremely high and food everywhere is remarkably good value.

Basic noodle- or rice-based meals at a stall rarely come to more than a few ringgit or Singapore dollars, and even a full meal with drinks in a reputable restaurant should rarely run to more than RM40 or S$30 a head – though if you develop a taste for delicacies such as shark's-fin or bird's-nest soup, the sky is the limit. The most renowned culinary centres are Singapore, Georgetown, KL, Melaka and Kota Bharu, although other towns, like Johor Bahru, Ipoh, Kuching and Sibu all have their own distinctive dishes too.

VEGETARIANS AND VEGANS

Vegetarians will find specialist Chinese and Indian restaurants in larger towns and cities; details are given in the text. Otherwise, things can be tricky, particularly in the more remote areas: the Chinese barely class chicken and pork as meat, and use meat stock as the basis for some dishes. It's wise to say "I only eat vegetables" (in Malay: *saya hanya makan sayuran*) and steel yourself for a diet of vegetables and rice.

Vegans really have their work cut out: tell your waiter, "I do not eat dairy products or meat" (*Saya tidak makan yang di perbuat dari susu atau daging*) and keep your fingers crossed.

THE CUISINES

As well as mainstream dishes from the principal **ethnic cuisines** – Malay, Chinese and Indian – hawker stalls, cafés and restaurants throughout the region serve up a variety of regional dishes that reflect the pattern of immigration over the last five hundred years. A hybrid cuisine known as **Nonya** evolved from the mixed-race marriages of early Chinese immigrants and local Malays; it's found in Singapore, and in the former Straits Settlement towns in Malaysia like Georgetown and Melaka. Even the indigenous Malay cuisine mixes various elements from other Asian cuisines. The most familiar Chinese cooking style is Cantonese, but all over Malaysia and Singapore you can also sample Szechuan, Hokkien, Beijing and other regional Chinese specialities. Indian food splits into Northern, Southern or Muslim styles of cooking. Below are accounts of the different cuisines, while for a rundown of the most popular dishes, turn to the food glossary on p.50.

MALAY FOOD

Surprisingly perhaps, good **Malay** cuisine can be hard to find, with the best cooking often confined to the home. On the positive side, the Malay restaurants that do exist are of a universally high standard, presenting dishes with a loving attention to detail. The cuisine is based on rice, often enriched with *santan* (coconut milk) which is served with a dizzying variety of curries, and *sambal*, a condiment comprising pounded chillies blended with *belacan* (shrimp paste), onions and garlic. Other spices which characterize Malay cuisine include ginger and *galangal* (a ginger-like root), coriander, lemon grass and lime leaves. The most famous **dish** is *satay* – virtually Malaysia's national dish – which is skewers of barbecued meat (chicken, mutton or beef) dipped in spicy peanut sauce.

The classic way to sample Malay curries is to eat *nasi campur*, a buffet (usually served at lunchtime) of steamed rice supplemented by any of up to two dozen accompanying dishes, including *lembu* (beef), *kangkong* (a variety of greens), fried chicken, fish steaks, curry sauce and various vegetables. Other popular dishes include *nasi goreng* (mixed fried rice with meat, seafood and vegetables) and *rendang*. Pork, of course, is taboo to all Muslims, but has been married with Malay cooking in Nonya dishes (see below). For **breakfast**, the most popular Malay dish is *nasi lemak*, rice cooked in coconut milk and served with *sambal ikan bilis* (tiny crisp-fried anchovies in hot chilli paste), fried peanuts and slices of fried or hard-boiled egg.

Much of the diet of the indigenous groups living in settled communities in **East Malaysia** tends to revolve around standard Malay and Chinese dishes. But in the remoter regions, or at festival times, you may have an opportunity to sample indigenous cuisine. In Sabah's Klias Peninsula and in **Brunei**, villagers still produce *ambuyat*, a glue-like, sago-starch porridge that's dipped in sauce; or there's the Murut speciality of *jaruk* – raw wild boar, fermented in a bamboo tube, and definitely an acquired taste. Most famous of Sabah's dishes is *hinava*, or raw fish pickled in lime juice. In Sarawak, you're most likely to eat with the Iban or Kelabit, sampling wild boar with jungle ferns and sticky rice.

NONYA FOOD

The earliest Chinese immigrants settled in the Straits Settlements of Melaka, Penang and Singapore and intermarried with local Malays. The descendants of these unions – the Peranakans or Straits Chinese – evolved their own particular culture and cuisine, called **Nonya**, from the name given to women of families (men were called Babas). There's more information on Peranakan culture on p.314.

Typical Nonya **dishes** incorporate elements and ingredients from Chinese, Indonesian and Thai cooking, the end product tending to be spicier than Chinese food. Chicken, fish and seafood form the backbone of the cuisine, and unlike Malay food, pork is used. Noodles (*mee*) flavoured with chillies, and rich curries made from rice flour and coconut cream, are common. A popular dish is *laksa*, noodles in spicy coconut soup served with seafood and finely chopped beansprouts, lemon grass, pineapple, pepper, lime leaves and chilli; *asam laksa* is the version served in Penang, its fish stock giving it a sharper taste. Other popular Nonya dishes include *ayam buah keluak*, chicken cooked with Indonesian "black nuts"; and *otak-otak*, fish mashed with coconut milk and chilli paste and steamed in a banana leaf.

CHINESE FOOD

Chinese food dominates in Singapore and Malaysia, with perhaps only the cooking in Hong Kong reaching a higher standard – fish and seafood is nearly always outstanding, with prawns, crab, squid and a variety of fish on offer almost everywhere. Noodles, too, are ubiquitous, and come in wonderful variations – thin, flat, round, served in soup (wet) or fried (dry).

The dominant style of Chinese cookery, at least in terms of restaurant numbers, is **Cantonese** – as it is in most foreign countries, echoing the pattern of immigration from southern China – but later groups of settlers from **other regions** of China spread Foochow, Hokkien, Hainanese, Teochow and Szechuan dishes throughout Peninsular Malaysia, East Malaysia and Singapore. Of these, Hokkien and Teochow are dominant, especially in Singapore where Hokkien fried *mee* (noodles with pork, prawn and vegetables) and *char kuey teow* (spicy flat noodles mixed with meat, fish and egg) are available almost everywhere. The classic Cantonese lunch is dim sum (literally "to touch the heart"), comprising a variety of steamed and fried dumplings and other titbits served in bamboo baskets in cafés and restaurants. Other popular lunch dishes are Hainan chicken rice (not surprisingly, rice cooked in chicken stock and topped with tender steamed or fried chicken) or rice topped with *char siew* (roast pork); while standard dishes available everywhere include chicken in chilli or with cashew nuts; buttered prawns, or prawns served with a sweet and sour sauce; spare ribs; and mixed vegetables with tofu (beancurd) and beansprouts. For something a little more unusual, try a **steamboat**, a Chinese-style fondue filled with boiling stock in which you cook meat, fish, shellfish, eggs and vegetables; or a **claypot** – meat, fish or shellfish cooked over a fire in an earthenware pot.

INDIAN FOOD

In the same way as the Chinese, immigrants from North and South **India** brought their own cuisines with them, which vary in emphasis and ingredients, though all utilize *daal* (lentils), chutneys, yogurts and sweet or sour *lassis* (yogurt drinks). North Indian food tends to rely more on meat, especially mutton and chicken (neither North nor South Indians eat beef), and uses breads – *naan*, *chapatis*, *parathas* and *rotis* – rather than rice, to great effect. The most famous style of North Indian cooking is *tandoori* – named after the clay oven in which the food is cooked; you'll commonly come across *tandoori* chicken marinated in yogurt and spices and then baked. A favourite **breakfast** is *roti canai* (pancake and *daal*) or *roti kaya* (pancake or bun with an egg-and-coconut based jam).

Southern Indian (and Sri Lankan) food tends to be spicier and more reliant on vegetables. Its staple is the *dosai* (pancake), often served at breakfast time as a *masala dosai*, stuffed with onions, vegetables and chutney, and washed down with *teh tarik*, a sweet, frothy milky tea. Indian Muslims serve the similar *murtabak*, a grilled *roti* pancake with egg, onion and minced meat.

Many South Indian cafés turn to serving *daun pisang* (literally, banana leaf) at lunchtime, usually a vegetarian meal where rice is served on banana leaves and small, replenishable heaps of various vegetable curries are placed alongside; in some places, meat and fish side dishes are on offer, too. It's normal to eat a banana-leaf meal with your right hand, though restaurants will always have cutlery if you can't manage. As with the other immigrant cuisines, the Indian food available in Malaysia and Singapore has adapted to Malay tastes and to the availability of ingredients over the years: banana-leaf curry, for example, is more widely available in Malaysia and Singapore than in India, while another Malay/Indian staple, *mee goreng* – fried egg noodles with spices and chillies – isn't known at all in India.

HAWKER STALLS

To eat inexpensively in Malaysia or Singapore you go to **hawker stalls**, traditionally simple wooden stalls on the roadside, with a few stools to sit at. In Singapore, Kuala Lumpur and some other major cities, the trend is to corral hawker stalls in neat, often air-conditioned food centres where you can pick different dishes from a variety of stalls, but in most of Malaysia the old-style stalls still dominate the streets.

Wherever you find the stalls, you don't have to worry too much about **hygiene**: most are scrupulously clean, with the food cooked instantly in front of you. Avoid dishes that look as if they've been standing around for a while, or have been

reheated, and you should be fine. The standard of cooking at hawker stalls is high and they are very popular; politicians and pop stars crowd in with the locals to eat at the cramped tables.

Most hawker stalls serve standard Malay **noodle** and **rice dishes**, satay and, in many places, more obscure regional delicacies. The influence of the region's immigrants also means you'll encounter Chinese noodle and seafood dishes, Indian specialities and Indonesian food. At modern food centres, particularly in Singapore, you'll increasingly come across Western food like burgers, and steak and eggs, or even Japanese and Korean food. Hawker centres usually have a hot and cold drinks stall on hand; in Singapore and most Malaysian cities, you'll nearly always be able to get a **beer**, too.

Hawker stalls don't have menus, though most have signs in English detailing their specialities; otherwise you order by pointing at anything you like the look of. You don't have to sit close to the stall you're patronizing: find a free table, and the vendor will track you down when your food is ready. You generally pay for your meal when it's brought to your table, though you're sometimes asked to pay when you order.

Many hawker stalls are closed at breakfast time, as Malays tend to eat before they go to work, and Chinese and Indians head for the coffee houses and cafés. That said, you should be able to track down an early starter knocking out Asian breakfasts. Most outdoor stalls open instead at around 10am, usually offering the day's *nasi campur* selection; prices are determined by the number of dishes you choose on top of your rice. Hawker stalls usually close well before midnight; any open after this time will be limited to fried noodles and soups.

KEDAI KOPIS

Few streets exist without a **kedai kopi**, or **coffee shop**, usually run by Chinese or Indians. Most open at 8am or 9am, though some – especially the Chinese-owned ones, which offer early-morning tea and dim sum – are up and running at dawn; closing times vary from 6pm to midnight. Basic Chinese coffee shops serve noodle and rice dishes all day, and feature a decent selection of cakes and cookies. The culinary standard is never spectacularly high, but you're unlikely to spend more than small change for a filling one-plate meal. Some cafés are a little more adventurous

and serve full meals of meat, seafood and vegetables, for which you'll pay from around
RM5/S$5 per person; Malay-run cafés, where you
can find them, usually serve a midday spread of
nasi campur dishes. Indian cafés tend to be a bit
livelier and – especially in the Indian quarters of
Singapore, Kuala Lumpur, Georgetown and
Melaka – decidedly theatrical. Here you can
watch the Muslim *mamak* men at work, making
the frothy *teh tarik* (tea) by pouring liquid from a
height from one vessel into another, and pounding
and moulding the *roti* into an oily, bubble-filled
shape.

It's worth noting that the Chinese-run *kedai
kopis* are often the only places you'll be able to
get a beer in the evening; this is especially true in
towns along Malaysia's largely Muslim east
coast.

RESTAURANTS

On the whole, proper **restaurants** are either
places you go to be seen or to savour particular
delicacies found nowhere else, like **fish-head
curry** (a famous Singaporean dish), Chinese specialities like **shark's-fin dishes** and **bird's-nest
soup**, and high-quality seafood. In many restaurants, the food is not necessarily superior to that
served at a good café or hawker stall – you're just
paying the (often considerable) extra for air-con
and tablecloths. One reason to splash out, though,
is to experience a **cultural show** of music and
dance, often performed in larger restaurants in
the main cities in Singapore, several of the
large Chinese seafood restaurants put on displays. Some of the best shows are detailed in the
text.

Both Malaysia and Singapore do have a tradition of **haute cuisine**, often available in the
top-notch hotels. All the best hotel restaurants
in Kuala Lumpur, Singapore and Georgetown
boast well-known chefs, drawing in the punters
with well-received French, Thai and Japanese
food as well as more local delicacies.

Unless you're in a Muslim restaurant, or anywhere in Brunei, you'll be able to wash down your
meal with a glass of cold **beer**; wine is less
common, though smarter establishments will normally retain a modest choice. Few **desserts** feature on Southeast Asian restaurant menus, but
the region's bounty of tropical **fruit** more than
compensates: the glossary on p.53 lists some of
the less familiar fruits you may come across.

Tipping is not expected; bills arrive complete
with service charge and (in Malaysia and
Singapore) government tax. In the main, restaurants are open from 11.30am to 2.30pm and from
6 to 10.30pm. Making yourself understood is
rarely a problem, nor is negotiating a menu: many
are written in English, especially in Singapore.

DRINKING

Tap water is safe to drink in Malaysia and
Singapore, though it's wise to stick to bottled
water, widely available for around $2 a litre,
when travelling in rural areas. Using ice for
drinks is generally fine, too, making the huge
variety of **fresh fruit drinks**, available in hawker
centres and street corners, even more pleasant;
always specify that you want them without
sugar, unless you like your fruit juice heavily
laced with syrup. Sugar-cane mangles can be
found on many street corners, producing a
watery, sweet drink that's very cloying yet still
manages to be invigorating. The usual range of
soft drinks is available everywhere for around
RM1.20 a can/carton, with the F&N and Yeo
companies providing more unusual flavours, and
Pokka making cans of decent fruit juices. Cartons
of fruit-juice drinks, though overly sweet, can be
handy for journeys, again costing about RM1;
soya milk in cartons or freshly made at hawker
stalls is another popular local choice.

Tea and coffee are as much national drinks as
they are in the West. You'll often find that sweet
condensed milk is added unless you ask for it
without (*teh-o* is tea without milk, *kopi-o* for coffee). If you don't like the often overbrewed tea or
coffee, most cafés have Milo, the ubiquitous
chocolate drink.

ALCOHOLIC DRINKS

In Malaysia and Singapore, despite the Muslim
influence, alcohol is available in bars, restaurants, Chinese *kedai kopis* and supermarkets.
Only in Brunei (officially a dry state) is **alcohol**
banned, though non-Muslim visitors may bring a
small quantity into the country for their own consumption (see p.22).

Anchor and Tiger **beer** (lager) are locally produced and are probably the best choice, though
you can also get other Western beers, as well as
the Chinese Tsingtao and a variety of stouts,
including Guinness and the Singaporean ABC,
which is truly horrible (it's best drunk mixed with

FOOD AND DRINK GLOSSARY

Many menus, especially in Singapore, are written in English, but it's worth noting that transliterated spellings are not standardized throughout Malaysia, Singapore and Brunei – you may well see some of the following dishes written in a variety of ways; we've used the most widely accepted spellings. For a full rundown of the various cuisines available in the three countries, see pp.46–48.

NOODLES (*MEE*) AND NOODLE DISHES

Bee hoon	Thin rice noodles, like vermicelli; *mee fun* is similar.	Laksa	Noodles, beansprouts, fish-cakes and prawns in a spicy coconut soup.
Char kuey teow	The fried version of *kuey teow*, featuring any combination of prawns, Chinese sausage, fishcake, egg, vegetables and chilli.	Mee	Standard round yellow noodles that look like spaghetti, made from wheat flour.
Foochow noodles	Steamed and served in soy and oyster sauce with spring onions and dried fish.	Mee goreng	Indian or Malay fried noodles.
		Mee rebus	Yellow noodles in a spicy gravy, garnished with bean-sprouts, egg and fried onion.
Hokkien fried mee	Yellow noodles fried with pieces of pork, prawn and vegetables; a variant in KL has the noodles cooked in soy sauce with tempeh.	Mee suah	Noodles served dry and crispy.
		Sar hor fun	Flat rice noodles served in a chicken-stock soup, to which prawns, fried shallots and beansprouts are added; a speciality in Ipoh.
Kang puan mee	A rich Sibu speciality – noodles cooked in lard.	Wan ton mee	Roast pork, noodles and vegetables served in a light soup containing dumplings.
Kuey teow	Flat noodles, comparable to Italian tagliatelle; *hor fun* is similar.		

RICE (*NASI*) DISHES

Biriyani	Saffron-flavoured rice cooked with chicken, beef or fish; a North Indian speciality.		chicken broth, and chilli and ginger sauce.
		Lemang	Glutinous rice stuffed into lengths of bamboo.
Claypot	Rice topped with meat (as diverse as chicken and turtle), cooked in an earthenware pot over a fire to create a smoky taste.	Nasi campur	Rice served with an array of meat, fish and vegetable dishes.
		Nasi goreng	Fried rice with diced meat and vegetables.
		Nasi kunyit	Rice cooked in turmeric; a side dish.
Daun pisang	Malay term for banana-leaf curry, a southern Indian meal with chutneys and curries, served on a mound of rice, and presented on a banana leaf with *popadums*.	Nasi kerabu	Purple, green or blue rice with a dash of vegetables, seaweed and grated coconut; a Kota Bharu speciality.
		Nasi lemak	A Malay classic: *ikan bilis* (fried anchovies), cucum-ber, peanuts and fried or hard-boiled egg slices served on coconut rice.
Hainan chicken rice	Singapore's unofficial national dish: steamed or boiled chicken slices on rice cooked in chicken stock, and served with	Nasi puteh	Plain boiled rice.

MEAT, FISH AND BASICS

Ayam	Chicken	*Kambing*	Mutton	*Sup*	Soup
Babi	Pork	*Kepiting*	Crab	*Tahu*	Tofu (beancurd)
Daging	Beef	*Sayur*	Vegetable	*Telor*	Egg
Ikan	Fish	*Sotong*	Squid	*Udang*	Prawn

GENERAL TERMS

Asam	Sour	*Istimewa*	Special (as in	*Makan*	Food
Garam	Salt		"today's	*Manis*	Sweet
Goreng	Fried		special")	*Minum*	Drink
Gula	Sugar	*Kari*	Curry	*Pedas*	Spicy

OTHER SPECIALITIES

Ambal	Swamp plant eaten as vegetable in Sarawak.
Ayam goreng	Malay-style fried chicken.
Ayam percik	Barbecued chicken with a creamy coconut sauce; a Kota Bharu speciality.
Bak kut teh	Literally "pork bone tea", a Chinese dish of pork ribs in soy sauce, ginger, herbs and spices.
Char siew pow	Cantonese steamed bun stuffed with roast pork in a sweet sauce.
Chye tow kueh	Also known as "carrot cake", this is actually an omelette made with white radish and spring onions.
Congee	Rice porridge, cooked in lots of water and eaten with slices of meat and fish; sometimes listed on menus as "porridge".
Coto makassar	A meat broth boosted with chunks of rice cake.
Dim sum	Chinese titbits – dumplings, rolls, chicken's feet – steamed or fried and served in bamboo baskets.
Dosai	Southern Indian pancake, made from ground rice and lentils, and served with *daal* (lentils) and spicy dips.
Fish-head curry	The head of a red snapper (usually), cooked in a spicy curry sauce with tomatoes and okra; a contender for the title of Singapore's most famous dish.
Gado gado	Malay/Indonesian salad of lightly cooked vegetables, boiled egg, slices of rice cake and a crunchy peanut sauce.
Ikan bilis	Deep-fried anchovies.
Kai pow	Similar to *char siew pow*, but contains chicken and boiled egg.
Kerupuk	Prawn or fish crackers.
Kongbian	Chinese-style bagels, found only in Sibu.
Midin	Stir fried jungle fern, native to Sarawak.
Murtabak	Thick Indian pancake, stuffed with onion, egg and chicken or mutton.
Utak-otak	Fish mashed with coconut milk and chilli paste and steamed in a banana leaf; a Nonya dish.
Popiah	Chinese spring rolls, filled with peanuts, egg, beanshoots, vegetables and a sweet sauce; sometimes known as *Lumpia*.
Rendang	Dry, highly spiced coconut curry with beef, chicken or mutton.
Rojak	Indian fritters dipped in chilli and peanut sauce; the Chinese version is a salad of greens, beansprouts, pineapple and cucumber in a peanut-and-prawn-paste sauce.
Roti canai	Light, layered Indian pancake served with a thin curry sauce or *daal*; sometimes called *roti pratha*.

continued overleaf

continued from previous page

Roti john	Simple Indian dish of egg, onion and spicy tomato sauce spread on bread and heated.		or fish and other titbits dunked into a steaming broth until cooked.
Satay	Marinated pieces of meat, skewered on small sticks and cooked over charcoal; served with peanut sauce, cucumber and *ketupat* (rice cake).	*Ubi kaya tumis* *Umai*	Braised tapioca leaves Raw fish salad, mixed with shallots and lime, found in East Malaysia and Brunei.
Sop kambing	Spicy Indian mutton soup.	*Umbut kelapa masak lemak*	Young coconut shoots
Steamboat	Chinese equivalent of the Swiss fondue: raw vegetables, meat	*Yam basket*	Sarawak speciality: meat, vegetables and soya bean-curd in a fried yam pie crust.

DESSERTS

Bubor cha cha	Sweetened coconut milk with pieces of sweet potato, yam and tapioca balls.	*Es kachang*	Shaved ice with red beans, cubes of jelly, sweetcorn, rose syrup and evaporated milk.
Cendol	Coconut milk, palm sugar syrup and pea-flour noodles poured over shaved ice.	*Pisang goreng* *Pisang murtabak*	Fried banana fritters. Banana pancake.

DRINKS

Air minum	Water.	*Kopi susu*	Coffee with milk.
Bandung	A sweet drink, bright pink in colour, made with rose essence and a little milk.	*Lassi*	Sweet or sour yogurt drink of Indian origin.
		Teh	Tea.
		Teh-o	Black tea.
Bir	Beer.	*Teh susu*	Tea with milk.
Jus	Fruit juice.	*Teh tarik*	Sweet, milky tea, poured
Kopi	Coffee.		between two cups to
Kopi-o	Black coffee.		produce a frothy drink.

a Tiger beer, which is what you'll see many people doing).

Locally produced **whisky** and **rum** are cheap enough, too, though they're pretty rough stuff and can well do with mixing with Coke. The **brandy**, which is what the local Chinese drink, tends to be better. In the more upmarket restaurants, you can get cocktails and imported **wine**, though the latter is pretty expensive. Only on Pulau Langkawi and Sabah's Pulau Labuan, both duty-free islands, can wine be bought from the supermarkets at prices roughly equivalent to the West (approximately RM20 for the least expensive bottle). In the longhouses of Sabah and Sarawak, you might be invited to sample *tuak*, a rice wine made by most families, that's about the same strength as beer.

WHERE TO DRINK

In **Malaysia**, there is a thriving **bar scene** in KL (mainly in the Golden Triangle and Bangsar) and its modern suburb, Petaling Jaya, popular with fashionable youths and yuppies, as well as the East Malaysian state capitals, Kuching and Kota Kinabalu. Other towns have less of a scene, though in most of the places popular with Western tourists, you'll be able to get a beer in something approaching a bar – otherwise, go to a Chinese *kedai kopi* for a bottle of beer. Fierce competition ensures **happy hours** (usually daily 5–7pm) are a regular feature in most bars, bringing the beer down to around RM5 a glass, though spirits still remain pricey; look out for "all-night" discounts that appear from time to time. While there are some bars which open all day

(11am–11pm), most tend to double as clubs, opening in the evenings until 3 or 4am.

In **Singapore**, bars are much the same, although the variety is even wider, ranging from those run on an English pub theme, featuring occasional guest beers from the UK, through to early evening karaoke bars (see p.603 for the details). The more glitzy places often introduce a cover charge (around S$8–25) from 10pm onwards at weekends. Bars open from 7pm to midnight, though some also cater for the lunchtime crowd by offering bargain meals.

TROPICAL FRUIT

The more familiar fruits available in Malaysia and Singapore include forty varieties of banana, known locally as *pisang*; coconut (*kelapa*); seven varieties of mango; three types of pineapple (*nanas*); and watermelon (*tembikai*).

Chempedak This smaller version of the *nangka* (see jackfruit below) is normally deep-fried, enabling the seed, which tastes like new potato, to be eaten too.

Ciku Looks like an apple; varies from yellow to pinkish brown when ripe, with a soft, pulpy flesh.

Durian Malaysia and Singapore's most popular fruit has a greeny-yellow, spiky exterior and grows to the size of a soccer ball from March to May, June to August, and November to February. It has thick, yellow-white flesh and an incredibly pungent odour that's been likened to a mixture of mature cheese and caramel.

Guava Has a green, textured skin and flesh with five times the vitamin C content of orange juice.

Jackfruit This large, pear-shaped fruit, also known as *nangka*, grows up to 50cm long and has a greeny-yellow exterior with sweet flesh inside.

Langsat together with its sister fruit, the *duku*, this looks like a small, round potato, with juicy white flesh which can be anything from sweet to sour.

Longgan Similar to the lychee, this has juicy white flesh and brown seeds.

Mangosteen Available from June to August and November to January, this has a sweet though slightly acidic flavour. Its smooth rind deepens to a distinctive crimson colour when ripe.

Markisa Known in the West as passion fruit, this has purple-brown dimpled skin with a rich flavour; it's a frequent ingredient in drinks.

Papaya Better known as *betik*, this has milky orange-coloured flesh which is a rich source of vitamins A and C.

Pomelo Limau bali, as this is also known, is the largest of all the citrus fruits; it looks rather like a grapefruit, though it is slightly drier and has less flavour.

Rambutan The bright-red rambutan's soft, spiny exterior has given it its name – *rambut* means "hair" in Malay. Usually about the size of a golf ball, it has a white, opaque fruit of delicate flavour, similar to a lychee.

Salak Teardrop-shaped, the *salak* has a skin like a snake's and a bitter taste.

Star fruit Also known as *carambola*, this waxy, pale-green fruit, with a star-shaped cross-section, is said to be good for high blood pressure, the yellower the fruit, the sweeter its flesh.

Zirzat Inside the bumpy, muddy green skin of this fruit is smooth white flesh like blancmange, hence its other name, custard apple. It's also known as soursop (Margaret Brooke, wife of Sarawak's second rajah, Charles, described it as "tasting like cotton wool dipped in vinegar and sugar").

MAIL AND TELECOMMUNICATIONS

The communications network in Malaysia and Singapore is generally fast and efficient, though some of the smaller offshore islands still have no phone network. Mobile phones are in evidence everywhere, and in many remote areas, this can be the only way of keeping in touch.

Mail can be sent to you in Malaysia, Singapore and Brunei care of the **poste restante**/general delivery section of the local GPO (see below); when picking up mail, be sure to have the staff check under first names as well as family names – misfiling of letters is common.

POSTAL SERVICES

Malaysia has a well-organized postal service, with overseas mail taking four to seven days to reach its destination. Postcards to anywhere in the world require a 50 sen stamp, while aerogrammes cost a uniform 50 sen; you can buy stamps in post offices. Packages are expensive to send, with surface/sea mail taking around two months to Europe, longer to the USA, and even airmail taking a few weeks. There's usually a shop near the post office which will wrap your parcel for $5 or so. It's worth noting that if you leave your letter or package **unsealed**, the postage will be cheaper. Each Malaysian town has a **General Post Office** (GPO) with a **poste restante/general delivery** section, where mail will be held for two months. If you're having mail sent there, make sure your surname is in capitals or underlined, and that the letter is addressed as follows: name, Poste Restante, GPO, town or city, state (optional). GPOs will also forward mail (for one month), free of charge, if you fill in the appropriate form. Usual post office **opening hours** are Monday to Saturday 8am–6pm (except for the states on the east coast of the Peninsula, where Friday is closing day).

In **Singapore**, the GPO, housing the poste restante counter, is beside Paya Lebar MRT station; see p.612 for more details and opening hours. There are other post offices across the island, usually open Monday to Friday 8.30am–5pm and Saturday 8.30am–1pm, though postal services are available until 9pm at the Comcentre on Killiney Road (Mon–Fri). Singapore's postal system is predictably efficient, with letters and cards reaching some international destinations within three days. Stamps are available at post offices (some have vending machines operating out of hours), and at some stationers and hotels. Airmail letters to Europe and the US start at 75¢, aerogrammes to all destinations cost 35¢ and postcards cost 30¢. You'll find fax and telex facilities in all major post offices, too.

Post offices in **Brunei** are open Monday to Thursday and Saturday 7.45am–4.30pm, and on Friday, 8–11am and 2–4pm; see p.517 for details of the GPO. Some hotels can also provide basic postal facilities. Postcards to anywhere in the world cost 30¢, aerogrammes 45¢; overseas letters cost 90¢ for every 10g.

TELEPHONES

For dialling to and from the region, see the box opposite for all the relevant **dialling code** information. Note that Singapore has no **area codes**; both Malaysia and Brunei do, and they are included in the telephone numbers given throughout the book – omit them if dialling locally. It's also worth pointing out that many businesses in Malaysia and Singapore have **mobile-phone numbers** – usually prefixed ☎011 or 010 – these are very expensive to call. It's possible to use your BT or AT&T **chargecard** in both Malaysia and Singapore.

PHONING ABROAD

From the UK: dial your international access code followed by ☎0060 (Malaysia), ☎00 65 (Singapore) or ☎00 673 (Brunei) + area code minus first 0 (except Singapore) + number

From the US: dial your international access code, then ☎0060 (Malaysia), ☎0065 (Singapore), or ☎00673 (Brunei) + area code minus first 0 (except Singapore) + number

FROM MALAYSIA

Dial ☎00 + IDD country code (see below) + area code minus first 0 + subscriber number. To call Singapore though, simply dial the code ☎02, followed by the number.

FROM SINGAPORE

Dial ☎001 + IDD country code (see below) + area code minus first 0 + subscriber number. To call Malaysia though, simply dial ☎020, then the Malaysian area code followed by the number.

FROM BRUNEI

Dial ☎01 + IDD country code (see below) + area code minus first 0 + subscriber number

IDD CODES

Australia ☎61	Ireland ☎353	UK ☎44
Canada ☎1	New Zealand ☎64	USA ☎1

TIME

Malaysia, Singapore and Brunei are 8 hours ahead of GMT, 16 hours ahead of US Pacific Standard Time, 13 ahead of Eastern Standard Time, and 2 hours behind Sydney.

MALAYSIA

There are **public telephone** boxes in most towns in Malaysia; local calls cost just 10 sen for an unlimited time. For long-distance calls, it makes sense to use a **cardphone**, which are as common as coin-operated phones. There are three companies operating cardphones: the ubiquitous Uniphone, whose yellow phones tend to be the most expensive; the government-run Telekom, the most widespread and the best choice; and Cityphone, whose phones are green and are found mainly in the bigger cities. Phonecards, which come in denominations of RM5, RM10, RM20 and RM50, can be purchased from Shell and Petronas service stations, most 7-Eleven outlets, newsagents and some grocers. Before inserting the card, press button *2 and the instructions will appear in English. If your card runs out during the call, press * when you hear the tones to eject the card, and you can insert a new card without losing the connection.

Cardphones which can be used to make international calls carry an international logo on the phone booth. Although there is an international direct-dial (IDD) facility from most phone boxes, you cannot make **collect** (reverse-charge) **calls** from them. For these (and for long-distance calls) it's best to go to a **Telekom** office, located in most towns (and detailed in the text throughout), where – if you haven't called collect – you pay the cashier after your call. Telekom offices are generally only open during normal office hours, though there are 24-hour offices in KL, Penang and Kota Kinabalu.

In KL, Penang and Kota Kinabalu there are also **Home Country Direct** phones – press the appropriate button and you'll be connected with your home operator, who can either arrange a collect call, or debit you; if you're paying, settle your bill with the cashier after the call.

SINGAPORE

Local calls from private phones in Singapore cost next to nothing; calls from public phones cost 10¢ for three minutes, with the exception of Changi Airport's courtesy phones, which are free. Singapore has **no area codes. Cardphones** are taking over from payphones in Singapore: cards, available from the **Comcentre** (see p.612) and post offices, as well as 7-Elevens, stationers and bookshops, come in denominations starting from $2. **International calls** can be made 24 hours from all public cardphones. Some cardphones also take credit cards and some are equipped with **Home Country Direct** phones (see p.55). IDD calls made from hotel rooms in Singapore carry no surcharge. For directory enquiries, dial ☎100 and for IDD information call ☎100 or ☎1607, or ☎104 for international enquiries.

BRUNEI

Local calls from phone boxes in **Brunei** cost 10¢, and are free if made from private phones. **International** (IDD) calls can be made through hotels, in booths at the Telekom office in the capital, or from cardphones in shopping centres and other public places. Phonecards start at $10, and can be bought from the Telekom office and post offices.

THE MEDIA

Malaysia has three daily national English-language newspapers, another which comes out in the afternoon, and a weekly tabloid, all of which are indirectly owned by the government. The *New Straits Times* – sister to Singapore's *Straits Times*, but to all intents a separate company – is a thick broadsheet with blatantly government-slanted political news, as well as wide arts coverage. The *Business Times* covers finance throughout Southeast Asia, while the *Star* is a news-focused tabloid. The afternoon *Malay Mail* has an extensive "what's on" section; the daily tabloid, the *Sun*, is strong on populist columns about all things Malaysian and has an excellent weekly listings magazine – *Time Out* – on Thursdays. All four daily papers have Sunday editions as well. There are also Chinese-, Tamil- and Malay-language newspapers and a variety of weekly and monthly English-language magazines, the best of which include *Aliran Monthly*, which treats economic and political issues from a less centralized, more independent perspective; the weekly listings magazine *Day & Night*; and the monthly style/features magazine *Men's Review*.

As well as dailies in Chinese, Malay and Tamil, **Singapore** has two morning English-language newspapers, the *Straits Times*, a decent broadsheet with good coverage of international events, and the *Business Times*, dealing mainly with commercial and financial news. In addition, an amusingly tame tabloid, the *New Paper*, hits the streets every afternoon.

TV AND RADIO

Two of **Malaysia**'s three **television channels**, RTM1 and RTM2, are government-owned; they broadcast in Malay, with some material in Chinese, Tamil and English. The third station, TV3, is run commercially and shows English-language news and documentaries, Chinese kung fu, and Tamil, British and American films and soaps. In KL there is also another commercial station, Metrovision. The country has one satellite TV service, Astro, with about forty channels carrying movies, documentaries and the like.

In **Singapore**, the Television Corporation of Singapore (TCS) screens programmes in English, Chinese, Malay and Tamil. Channel 5 and Channel News Asia feature the most English-language programmes, Channel 8 specializes in Chinese soap operas, and the Central channel features English-language movies and documentaries. For sport from around the globe, check out the Sports City channel. Most Singaporean TV sets also receive Malaysia's RTM1, RTM2 and TV3 channels; similarly, in southern Malaysia it's possible to pick up Singaporean TV and radio.

In **Brunei**, Radio and Television Brunei (RTB) broadcasts daily on a single channel; many of its programmes are imported, and there's English-language news at 7pm each evening.

The six main Malaysian **radio stations** are also government-run, and include one devoted to pop music, and others broadcasting in Malay, Chinese and Tamil. The BBC World Service can be received on shortwave (in Johor, you might be able to pick it up on FM), as can Voice of America.

In **Singapore**, the Radio Corporation of Singapore (RCS) broadcasts several English-language radio shows daily: Gold (90.5FM), an information and music channel; Heart (91.3FM), offering music and "infotainment"; Symphony FM (92.4FM), featuring classical music; Perfect 10 (98.7FM), playing pop music; and Class (95FM), playing middle of the road hits. BBC World

Service can be picked up 24 hours a day on 88.9FM. There are also daily broadcasts in Chinese (95.8FM), Malay (94.2FM) and Tamil (96.8FM). For programme listings, check in the daily newspapers, or in *8 Days* magazine.

In **Brunei**, RTB broadcasts two channels a day on the medium-wave and FM bands – one in Malay, the other in English and Chinese. More surprisingly, London's Capital Radio can be received across the state.

POLICE AND EMERGENCIES

If you lose something in Malaysia, Singapore or Brunei, you're more likely to have someone running after you with it than running away. Nevertheless, you shouldn't become complacent – muggings have been known to occur and theft from dormitories by other tourists is a common complaint.

Most people carry their passport, traveller's cheques and other valuables in a concealed money belt, and guesthouses and hotels will often have a safety deposit box. Always keep a separate record of the numbers of your traveller's cheques, together with a note of which ones you've cashed. It's probably worth taking a photocopy of the relevant pages of your passport, too, in case it's lost or stolen. In the more remote parts of Sarawak or Sabah there is little crime, and you needn't worry unduly about carrying cash – in fact, the lack of banks means that you'll probably have to carry more than you might otherwise.

It's worth repeating here that it is very unwise to have anything to do with illegal **drugs** of any description in Malaysia and Singapore. If you are arrested for drugs offences you can expect no mercy from the authorities (see box, p.22) and little help from your consular representatives.

A plus for women travellers is that **sexual harassment** in Malaysia and Singapore is minimal, and certainly no more than you might encounter at home – the level of contact rarely goes beyond the odd whistle or shy giggles. Irritating though it can be, you have to expect some attention both as a foreigner and as a woman, but it's often down to no more than pure curiosity and your novelty value.

MALAYSIA

If you do need to report a crime in Malaysia, head for the nearest police station (marked on the maps and included in the text), where there'll invariably be someone who speaks English; you'll need a copy of the police report for insurance purposes. In many major tourist spots, there are specific **tourist police stations** which are geared up to problems faced by foreign travellers. The police are generally more aloof than in the West, dressed in blue trousers and white short-sleeved shirts, and armed with small handguns. While you're likely to be excused any minor misdemeanour as a foreigner, it pays to be deferential if caught on the wrong side of the law.

In the predominantly **Muslim** east-coast states of Kelantan and Terengganu, restrictions on contact between people of the opposite sex (such as the offence of "close proximity") and eating in

---

EMERGENCIES

In an emergency, dial the following numbers:

Malaysia
Police/Ambulance ☎999
Fire Brigade ☎994

Singapore
Police ☎999
Fire Brigade/Ambulance ☎995

Brunei
Police ☎993
Ambulance ☎991
Fire Brigade ☎995

public during daylight hours in the Ramadan month apply to Muslims only, and are customary rather than legal in nature. However, it's courteous to observe restrictions like this where possible; there's advice throughout the *Guide* on how to avoid giving offence. Lastly, if you're **driving**, watch out for police speed traps – if you're caught speeding there's a spot fine of RM200.

SINGAPORE

Singapore is known locally as a "fine city". There's a fine of $500 for smoking in public places such as cinemas, trains, lifts, air-conditioned restaurants and shopping malls, and one of $50 for "jaywalking" – crossing a main road within 50m of a designated pedestrian crossing or bridge. Littering carries a $1000 fine, with offend-ers now issued Corrective Work Orders and forced to do litter-picking duty, while eating or drinking on the MRT could cost you $500. Other fines include those for urinating in lifts (legend has it that some lifts are fitted with urine detectors), not flushing a public toilet and chewing gum (which is outlawed in Singapore). It's worth bearing all these offences in mind, since foreigners are not exempt from the various Singaporean punish-ments – as the American Michael Fay discovered early in 1994, when he was given four strokes of the cane for vandalism.

Singapore's **police**, who wear dark-blue uni-forms, keep a fairly low profile, but are polite and helpful when approached. For details of the main police station, and other emergency information, check the relevant sections of "Listings", p.610.

PEOPLES

Largely because of their pivotal position on the maritime trade routes between the Middle East, India and China, the present-day countries of Malaysia, Singapore and Brunei have always been a cultural melting-pot. During the first millennium Malays arrived from Sumatra and Indians from India and Sri Lanka, while later the Chinese migrated from mainland China and Hainan island. But all these traders and settlers arrived to find that the region already con-tained a gamut of indigenous tribes, thought to have migrated here around 50,000 years ago from the Philippines, which was then connected by a land bridge to Borneo and Southeast Asia. Indeed, the indigenous tribes which still exist on the Peninsula are known as the *Orang Asli*, Malay for "the original people".

First people they may have been, but the descendants of the various indigenous groups now form a small minority of the overall **popula-tions** of the three countries. Over the last 150 years a massive influx of Chinese and Indian immigrants, escaping poverty, war and revolution, has swelled the population of **Malaysia**, which now stands at nearly 23 million: just under half are Malays, while the Chinese make up a quarter of the population, the Indians seven percent, and the various indigenous groups just over a tenth.

Brunei's population of around 320,000 is heavily dominated by Malays, with minorities of Chinese, Indians and indigenous peoples. In **Singapore**, there were only tiny numbers of indi-genes left on the island by the time of the arrival of Raffles. They have no modern-day presence in the state and more than three-quarters of the 3.8-million strong population are of Chinese extrac-tion, while around 14 percent are Malay and 7 percent Indian.

THE MALAYS

The **Malays**, a Mongoloid people believed to have originated from the meeting of Central Asians with Pacific islanders, first moved to the west coast of the Malay Peninsula from Sumatra in early times. Known as Orang Laut (sea people), they sustained an economy built around fishing, boat-building and, in some communities, piracy. It was the growth in power of the Malay sultanates from the fifteenth century onwards (see p.619) – coinciding with the arrival of Islam – that estab-lished Malays as a force to be reckoned within the Malay Peninsula and in Borneo. They devel-oped an aristocratic tradition, courtly rituals and a social hierarchy (for more on which, see p.305) which have an influence even today. The rulers of the Malaysian states still wield immense social and economic power, reflected in the sharing of the appointment of the *Yang Dipertuan Agong*, a pre-eminent sultan nominated on a five-year cycle. Although it's a purely ceremonial position, the *agong* is seen as the ultimate guardian of Malay Muslim culture and, despite recent legislation to reduce his powers, is still considered to be above the law. The situation is even more pronounced in **Brunei**, to which many Muslim Malay traders fled after the fall of Melaka to the Portuguese in 1511. There, the sultan is still the supreme ruler (as his descendants have been, on and off, for over 500 years), his powers verging on the autocratic.

Even though Malays have been Muslims since the fifteenth century, the region as a whole is not **fundamentalist** in character. Only in Brunei is alcohol banned, for instance, and while fundamentalist groups do hold sway in the eastern states of Kelantan and Terengganu, their influence is rarely oppressive.

The main contemporary change for Malays in Malaysia was the introduction of the **bumiputra** policy – a Malay word meaning "sons of the soil" – initiated after independence to separate those inhabitants of the country who had cultural affinities indigenous to the region from those who originated from outside. The policy was designed to make it easier for the Malays, the Orang Asli of the Peninsula, and the various Malay-related indigenous groups in Sarawak and Sabah, to compete in economic and educational fields against the Chinese and Indians, who – since the large-scale immigration of the nineteenth century – had traditionally tended to be the higher achievers.

These days, the *bumiputra* are offered certain **privileges**, mostly financial or status-enhancing, not available to the non-*bumiputra*. In practice, these privileges are only fully extended to Muslim Malays; Malaysian companies are supposed to employ a Malay at a senior level and all companies must have at least a 51-percent Malay shareholder profile, although the rapid development of the economy in recent years has led to a relaxing of such rules. Also, Malays get discounts on buying houses and find it much easier to get loans from the banks. As a consequence, Malays tend to take the top positions in government, state-owned companies and prestigious private firms.

Although tensions between Malays and the Chinese have led occasionally to unrest (the worst example being the race riots of 1969), the overall effect of stimulating Malay opportunities, mostly at the expense of the Chinese, seems to have been positive. Some critics have likened the *bumiputra* policy to a form of apartheid, but as long as the modern Malaysian economic miracle continues to enrich the whole community, those excluded from the policy rarely complain in public. The situation is slightly different in **Singapore**, where the policy doesn't hold sway: despite being greatly outnumbered by their Chinese compatriots, Singapore's Malay community appears content to stay south of the causeway and enjoy the state's higher standard of living.

THE CHINESE AND STRAITS CHINESE

Chinese traders began visiting the region in the seventh century, but it was in Melaka in the fifteenth century that the first significant community established itself. However, the ancestors of the majority of Chinese now living in Peninsular Malaysia emigrated from southern China in the nineteenth century to work in the burgeoning tin-mining industry. In Sarawak, Foochow, Teochew and Hokkien Chinese from southeastern China played an important part in opening up the interior, establishing pepper and rubber plantations along Batang Rajang; while in Sabah, Hakka Chinese labourers were recruited by the British North Borneo Chartered Company to plant rubber, and many stayed on, forming the core of the Chinese business community there.

Although many Chinese in the Peninsula came as labourers, they graduated quickly to shopkeeping and business ventures, both in established towns like Melaka and fast-expanding centres like KL, Penang and Kuching. Chinatowns developed throughout the region, even in Malay strongholds like Kota Bharu and Kuala Terengganu, while **Chinese traditions**, religious festivities, theatre and music became an integral part of a wider Malayan, and later Malaysian, multiracial culture. On the political level, the Malaysian Chinese are well represented in parliament and occupy around a quarter of the current ministerial positions. By way of contrast, **Chinese Bruneians** are not automatically classed as citizens and suffer a fair amount of discrimination at the hands of the majority Malay population.

Singapore's nineteenth-century trade boom drew large numbers of Cantonese, Teochew, Hokkein and Hakka Chinese traders and labourers, who quickly established a Chinatown on the south bank of the Singapore river. Today, the Chinese account for 77 percent of the state's population and are the most economically successful racial group in Singapore. As the proportion of Singaporean Chinese born on the island increases, the government's efforts to cultivate a feeling of Singaporean national identity are beginning to show signs of working, especially among the younger generation. Consequently, the main difference between the Chinese in Singapore and those in Malaysia is that Singapore's Chinese majority prefers to think of itself simply as Singaporean. Nevertheless, as in Malaysia, they still display their traditional work ethic and spurn none of their cultural heritage.

One of the few examples of regional intermarrying is displayed in the **Peranakan** or "Straits-born Chinese" heritage of Melaka, Singapore and, to a lesser extent, Penang. When male Chinese immigrants settled in these places from the sixteenth century onwards to work as miners or commercial entrepreneurs, they often married local Malay women, whose male offspring were termed "Baba" and the females "Nonya". **Baba-Nonya** society, as it became known, adapted elements from both cultures to create its own traditions: the descendants of these sixteenth-century liaisons have a unique culinary and architectural style (for more on which see p.314). Although Baba-Nonyas dress as Malays (the men in stiff-collared tunics and *songkets* and the women in sarongs and fitted, long-sleeved blouses), their Malay is a distinct dialect, and most follow Chinese Confucianism as their religion. Nowadays though, the cultural idiosyncracies of the Straits Chinese have largely been assimilated into the ways of Singapore and Malaysia as a whole, meaning that you'll need to visit museums to see evidence of them.

THE INDIANS

The second-largest non-*bumiputra* group in Malaysia, the **Indians**, first arrived as traders more than two thousand years ago, although few settled and it wasn't until the early fifteenth century that a small community of Indians (from present-day Tamil Nadu and Sri Lanka) was based in Melaka. But, like the majority of Chinese, the first large wave of Indians – Tamil labourers – arrived in the nineteenth century as indentured workers, to build the roads and railways and to work on the European-run rubber estates. But an embryonic entrepreneurial class from North India soon fol-

lowed and set up businesses in Penang and Singapore; these merchants and traders, most most of whom were Muslim, found it easier to assimilate themselves within the existing Malay community than the Hindu Tamils did.

Although Indians comprise only 10 percent of Malaysia's population (7 percent in Singapore) their impact is felt everywhere. The Hindu festival of Thaipusam (see p.122) is celebrated annually at KL's Batu Caves by upwards of a million people (with a smaller, but still significant celebration in Singapore); the festival of Deepavali is a national holiday; and Indians are increasingly competing with Malays in the arts, and dominate certain professional areas like medicine and law. And then, of course, there is the area of food – very few Malaysians these days could do without a daily dose of *roti canai*, so much so that this North Indian snack has been virtually appropriated by Malay and Chinese cafés and hawkers.

Even today in Malaysia, many Tamils work on private plantations and are unable to reap many of the benefits of the country's economic success. The Indians' political voice has also traditionally been weak, although there are signs that a younger generation of political leaders from the two Indian-dominated political parties, the Malaysian Indian Congress and the Indian Progressive Front, are asserting the community's needs more effectively.

INDIGENOUS PEOPLES

The **Orang Asli** – the indigenous peoples of Peninsular Malaysia – mostly belong to three distinct groups, within which various tribes are related by geography, language or physiological features.

The largest of the groups is the **Senoi** (the Asli word for person), who number about 40,000. They live in the large, still predominantly forested interior, within the states of Perak, Pahang and Kelantan, and divide into two main tribes, the Semiar and the Temiar, which still live a traditional lifestyle, following animist customs in their marriage ceremonies and burial rites. On the whole they follow the practice of shifting cultivation (a regular rotation of jungle-clearance and crop-planting), although government resettlement drives have successfully persuaded many to settle and farm just one area.

The **Semang** (or Negritos), of whom there are around 2000, live in the northern areas of the Peninsula. They comprise six distinct, if small, tribes, related to each other in appearance – they are mostly dark-skinned and curly haired – and share a traditional nomadic, hunter-gatherer lifestyle. However, most Semang nowadays live in settled communities and work within the cash economy, either as labourers or selling jungle produce in markets. Perhaps the most frequently seen Semang tribe are the Batek, who live in and around Taman Negara.

The third group, the so-called **Aboriginal Malays**, live in an area roughly south of the Kuala Lumpur–Kuantan road. Some of the tribes in this category, like the Jakun who live around Tasek Chini and the Semelais of Tasek Bera, have vigorously retained their animist religion and artistic traditions despite living in permanent villages near Malay communities and working within the regular economy. These are among the easiest of the Orang Asli to approach, since some have obtained employment in the two lakes' tourist industries; others are craftspeople selling their wares from stalls beside the water. See p.244 for more details.

These three main groupings do not represent all the Orang Asli tribes in Malaysia. One, the Lanoh in Perak, are sometimes regarded as Negritos, but their language is closer to that of the Temiar. Another group, the semi-nomadic Che Wong, of whom just a few hundred still survive on the slopes of Gunung Benom in central Pahang, are still dependent on foraging to survive and live in temporary huts made from bamboo and rattan. Two more groups, the Jah Hut of Pahang and the Mah Meri of Selangor, are particularly fine carvers, and it's possible to buy their sculptures at regional craft shops.

The tribes of Tasek Chini and Tasek Bera apart, it's difficult to visit most Orang Asli communities. Many live way off the beaten track and can only be reached if you go on a tour (some operators do visit Orang Asli settlements in Tasek Bera or Endau Rompin National Park). It's most unlikely that visitors would ever chance upon a remote Orang Asli village, though you will sometimes pass tribe members in the national parks or on inaccessible roads in eastern Perak, Pahang and Kelantan. To learn more about the disappearing Asli culture, the best stop is KL's Orang Asli Museum (see p.123).

In direct contrast to the Peninsula, indigenous groups make up a substantial chunk of the population in Sarawak, which is what attracts many visitors there in the first place – see the Sarawak chapter, p.352, for all the details. Although the Chinese comprise 29 percent of the state's population and the Malays and Indians around 24 percent together, the remaining 47 percent are made up of various indigenous **Dyak** groups – a word derived from the Malay for "upcountry".

The largest Dyak groups are the Iban, Bidayuh, Melanau, Kayan, Kenyah, Kelabit and Penan tribes, all of which have distinct cultures, although most have certain things in common, including a lifestyle predominantly based outside towns. Many live in **longhouses** (see p.367) along the rivers or on the sides of hills in the mountainous interior, and maintain a proud cultural legacy which draws on animist religion (see p.63 for more on this), arts and crafts production, jungle skills and a rich tradition of **festivals**. The *ngajat*, a dance traditionally performed by warriors on their return from battle, is now more commonly performed in the longhouses, albeit in a milder, truncated form, often for tourists. Spectacular costumes featuring large feathers are worn by the dancers who, arranged in a circle, perform athletic leaps to indicate their virility.

The **Iban**, a stocky, rugged people, make up nearly one-third of Sarawak's population. Originating hundreds of miles south of present-day Sarawak, in the Kapuas valley in Kalimantan, the Iban migrated north in the sixteenth century, coming into conflict over the next two hundred years with the Kayan and Kenyah tribes and, later, the British. Nowadays, Iban longhouse communities are found in the Batang Ai river system in the southwest, and along the Rajang, Katibas and Baleh rivers in the interior – though tribe members tend to migrate to Kuching and Miri, looking for work. These communities are quite accessible, their inhabitants always hospitable and keen to illustrate aspects of their culture like traditional dance, music, textile-weaving, blow-piping, fishing and games. For the Iban, the planting and cultivation of rice – their staple crop – is intimately connected with human existence, a relationship which underpins their animist beliefs. In their time, the Iban were infamous head-hunters – some longhouses are still decorated with authentic shrunken heads. These days, though, the tradition of head-hunting has been replaced by that of *bejalai*, or "journey", whereby a young man leaves the community to prove himself in the outside world – returning to their longhouses with television sets, generators and outboard motors, rather than heads. For more details about the Iban, see p.388.

The most southern of Sarawak's indigenous groups are the **Bidayuh** (see p.385), who – unlike most Dyak groups – traditionally lived away from the rivers, building their longhouse on the sides of hills. Culturally, they are similar to the Iban, although in temperament they are much milder and less gregarious, keeping themselves to themselves in their inaccessible homes on Sarawak's mountainous southern border with Kalimantan.

The **Melanau** are a coastal people, living north of Kuching in a region dominated by mangrove swamps. Many Melanau, however, now live in towns, preferring the kampung-style houses of the Malays to the elegant longhouses of the past. They are expert fishermen and cultivate sago as an alternative to rice. Many Melanau died in the battles that ensued when the Iban first migrated northwards, and the survival of their communities owes much to the first White Rajah, James Brooke, who protected them in the nineteenth century. He had a soft spot for the Melanau, thinking them the most attractive of the state's ethnic peoples and employing many as boat-builders, labourers and domestic servants.

The **Kelabit** people live on the highland plateau which separates north Sarawak from Kalimantan. Like the Iban, they live in longhouses and maintain a traditional lifestyle, but differ from some of the other groups in that they are Christian; they were converted just after World War II, during which the highlands had been used by British and Australian forces to launch attacks on the occupying Japanese. The highlands were totally inaccessible before the airstrip at Bario was built; now the area has become popular for hikers, since many longhouses which welcome visitors lie within a few days' walk of Bario (see p.437 for more).

The last main group is the semi-nomadic **Penan**, who live in the upper Rajang and Limbang areas of Sarawak in temporary lean-tos or small huts. They rely, like some of the Orang Asli groups in the Peninsula, on hunting and gathering and collecting jungle produce for sale in local markets. They also have the lightest skin of all the ethnic groups of Sarawak, largely because they live within the shade of the forest, rather than on the rivers and in clearings. In recent years the state government has tried to resettle the Penan in small villages, a controversial policy not entirely unconnected with the advance of logging in traditional Penan land, which has caused opposition from the Penan themselves and criticism from

international groups. Some tour operators now have itineraries which include visiting Penan communities in the Baram river basin and in the primary jungle that slopes away from the Kelabit Highlands.

Most of the other groups in Sarawak fall into the catch-all ethnic classification of **Orang Ulu** (people of the interior), who inhabit the more remote inland parts of the state, further north than the Iban, along the upper Rajang, Balui and Linau rivers. The most numerous, the **Kayan** and the **Kenyah**, are closely related and in the past often teamed up to defend their lands from the invading Iban. But they also have much in common with their traditional enemy, since they are longhouse-dwellers, animists and shifting cultivators. The main difference is the more hierarchical social structure of their communities, each of which has one leader, a *penghulu*, who has immense influence over the other inhabitants of the longhouse. Nowadays, many Kayan and Kenyah are Christians – converted after contact with missionaries following World War II – and their longhouses are among the most prosperous in Sarawak. Like the Iban, they maintain a tradition of *berjelai*, and the return of the youths from their wanderings is always an excuse for a big party, at which visitors from abroad or from other longhouses are always welcome. There's more information on both the Kenyah and Kayan on p.404.

Sabah has a population of around 1.6 million, made up of more than thirty distinct racial groups, between them speaking over eighty different dialects. Most populous of these groups are the **Dusun**, who account for around a third of Sabah's population. Traditionally agriculturists (the word *Dusun* means "orchard"), the Dusun are divided into subgroups which inhabit the western coastal plains and the interior of the state. These days they are known generically as **Kadazan/Dusun**, although strictly speaking "Kadazan" refers only to the Dusun of Penampang. Other branches of the Dusun include the **Lotud** of Tuaran and the **Rungus** of the Kudat Peninsula, whose convex longhouses are all that remain of the Dusun's longhouse tradition. Although most Dusun are now Christians, remnants of their animist past are still evident in their culture, most obviously in the harvest festival, or *pesta kaamatan*, when their *bobohizan*s, or priestesses, perform rituals to honour the *bambaazon*, or rice spirit. In the *samazau* dance – almost the national dance of East Malaysia – the costumes worn are authentically Kadazan. Two rows of men and women dance facing each other in a slow, rhythmic movement, flapping their arms to the pulse of the drum, their hand gestures mimicking the flight of birds. Not to be outdone, the women of the Kwijau community have their own dance, the *buloh*, which features high jumping steps to the percussive sounds of the gong and bamboo.

The mainly Muslim **Bajau** tribe drifted over from the southern Philippines some two hundred years ago, and now constitute Sabah's second largest ethnic group, accounting for around 10 percent of the population. Their penchant for piracy quickly earned them the sobriquet "Sea Gypsies", though nowadays they are agriculturalists and fishermen, noted for their horsemanship and their rearing of buffalo. The Bajau live in the northwest of Sabah and occasionally appear on horseback at Kota Belud's market (see p.437).

Sabah's third sizeable tribe is the **Murut**, which inhabits the area between Keningau and the Sarawak border, in the southwest. Their name means "hill people", though they prefer to be known by their individual tribal names, such as Timugon, Tagal and Nabai. The Murut farm rice and cassava by a system of shifting cultivation and, at times, still hunt using blowpipes and poison darts. Though their head-hunting days are over, they retain other cultural traditions, such as the construction of brightly adorned grave huts to house the graves and belongings of the dead. Another tradition that continues is the consumption at ceremonies of *tapai* or rice wine, drawn from a ceremonial jar using bamboo straws. Although the Murut now eschew longhouse life, many villages retain a ceremonial hall, complete with a *lansaran*, or bamboo trampoline, for festive dances and games.

RELIGION, TEMPLES AND SOCIAL CONVENTIONS

Three great religions – Islam, Buddhism and Hinduism – are represented in Malaysia and Singapore, and they play a vital role in the everyday lives of the population. Indeed, some religious festivals, like Muslim Hari Raya and Hindu Thaipusam, have been elevated to such stature that they are among the main cultural events in the regional calendar.

In Malaysia, **Islam** is a significant force, given that virtually all Malays, who comprise about half the population, are Muslim; in Singapore – where three-quarters of the population are Chinese – **Buddhism** is the main religion. There's a smaller, but no less significant, **Hindu** Indian presence in both countries, while the other chief belief system is **animism**, followed by many of the indigenous ethnic peoples of Malaysia – including the Orang Asli in the Peninsula and the various Dyak groups in Sarawak. However, the main tribal group in Sabah, the Kadazan, is **Christian**, as are the Kelabit in Sarawak, though Christianity is otherwise a minority religion in much of Malaysia and Singapore, practised primarily by the Eurasian community. The other main feature of religion in the region is that both Islam and Buddhism in Malaysia and Singapore are syncretic adaptations of the religions as practised

elsewhere, partly due to the influence of animist elements which over the centuries have been integrated from indigenous beliefs.

It's not uncommon to see the **temples** of different creeds happily existing side by side, each providing a social as well as a religious focal point for the corresponding community; in the early days, the temple formed an essential support network for newcomers to Malaysia and Singapore. Architectural traditions mean that the Chinese and Indian temples, built out of brick, have long outlasted the timber Malay mosque, making them the oldest structures you're likely to see in the region.

Although Malaysians and Singaporeans in general are hospitable, friendly and tolerant of visitors, it helps to know about the region's customs and to try to abide by the main rules of **etiquette**. Most are related to tenets of the various religions, though in East Malaysia – especially during stays in a longhouse – you're exposed to more subtle customs to do with status and social behaviour.

ANIMISM

The first principle of **animism** is that everything in nature has a soul or spirit (*semangat*), which inhabits mountains, trees, rocks and lakes, and has to be mollified as it controls the forces of nature. Although many of Malaysia's indigenous groups are now nominally Christian or Muslim, many of their old beliefs and ceremonies still survive. Birds, especially the **hornbill**, are of particular significance to the Iban and the Kelabit peoples in Sarawak. Many Kelabit depend upon the arrival of migrating flocks to decide when to plant their rice crop, while Iban hunters still interpret sightings of the hornbill and other birds as good or bad omens. In the Iban male rite-of-passage ceremony, a headdress made of hornbill feathers adorns the young man's head.

For the Orang Asli groups in the interior of the Peninsula, most of their remaining animist beliefs centre on healing and funereal ceremonies. A sick person, particularly a child, is believed to be invaded by a bad spirit, and drums are played and incantations performed to persuade the spirit to depart. The death of a member of the family is followed by a complex process of burial and reburial – a procedure which, hopefully, ensures an easy passage for the person's spirit.

An important link between the animism still practised by the tribal groups and Islam is provided by the **bomoh** (medicine man), who can still be found in Malay villages and some towns, performing tasks like calling on the elements to bring rain during droughts or preventing rain from ruining an important ceremony. A central part of the *bomoh*'s trade is recitation, often of sections of the Koran, while – like his Orang Asli counterparts – he uses various healing techniques, including herbs, localized burning to parts of the body and chants to cure or ease pain and disease. Although there are still quite a few *bomoh* in Malaysia, they are a vanishing breed, largely because there are fewer younger men willing to continue the tradition and the Muslim establishment frowns on the practice.

ISLAM

The first firm foothold **Islam** made in Malaysia was the conversion of Paramesvara, the ruler of Melaka, in the early fifteenth century. The commercial success of Melaka accelerated the process of Islamicization and, one after another, the powerful Malay court rulers took to Islam, adopting the title sultan ("ruler"), either because of sincere doctrinal conversion or because they took a shrewd view of the practical advantages to be gained by embracing the new faith. On a wider

cultural level, too, Islam had great attractions – its revolutionary concepts of equality in subordination to Allah freed people from the feudal Hindu caste system which had previously dominated parts of the region.

With the fall of Melaka in 1511, the migration of Muslim merchants to Brunei strengthened the hold of Islam in the region. The first wave of Islamic missionaries were mostly **Sufis**, the mystical and generally more liberal wing of Islam. Sufi Islam integrated some animist elements and Hindu beliefs: the tradition of pluralist deity worship which is central to Hinduism continued, and accounts for the strong historical and cultural importance of **festivals** like Deepavali and Thaipusam, where powerful deities are commemorated.

However, in the early nineteenth century the dominance of Sufism declined when a more puritanical Islamic branch, the **Wahabi**, captured Mecca. The return to the Koran's basic teachings became identified with a more militant approach, leading to several *jihad*s (holy wars) in Kedah, Kelantan and Terengganu against the Malay rulers' Siamese overlords and, subsequently, the British. The British colonial period inevitably drew Christian missionaries to the region, but they had more success in Borneo than on the Peninsula. Indeed, the British, in a bid to avoid further unrest among the Malays, were restrained in their evangelical efforts and Islam continued to prosper.

Islam in Malaysia today is a mixture of Sufi and Wahabi elements and as such is relatively liberal. Although most Muslim women wear traditional costume, especially headscarves, very few adopt the veil. Some taboos, like not drinking alcohol, are ignored by a number of Malays (though public consumption of alcohol is banned in Brunei). There are stricter, more fundamentalist Muslims – in Kelantan and Terengganu the local government is dominated by them – but in general Islam here has a modern outlook, blending a vibrant, practising faith with a business-minded approach.

The most important point of the Islamic year is **Ramadan**, the ninth month of the Muslim lunar calendar, when the majority of Muslims fast from the break of dawn to dusk, and also abstain from drinking and smoking. The reason for the fast is to intensify awareness of the plight of the poor and to identify with the hungry. During Ramadan many hawker stalls sell cakes and fruit, and families often break their fast at the stalls, although the most orthodox Muslim families tend to eat privately during this period. The end of Ramadan is marked by the two-day national holiday, **Hari Raya Puasa**, at which point the fast stops and the festivities begin. By tradition, royal palaces (*istanas*) are open over the holiday – usually the only days in the year when they are – and Malay families invite friends and business associates into their houses for food and refreshments.

VISITING A MOSQUE

While only a proportion of the faithful attend the **mosque** every day, on Friday – the Muslim day of prayer – Malays converge on their nearest mosque (*masjid*), with all employers providing an extended three-hour lunch break to provide time for prayers, lunch and the attendant socializing. In Malaysia, every town, village and hamlet has a mosque, with loudspeakers strapped to the minaret to call the faithful to prayer. The capital city of each state is the site of the *Masjid Negeri*, the state mosque, always more grandiose than its humble regional counterparts – an ostentatious statement of Islam's significance to the Malay people. Designs reflect religious conservatism, and you'll rarely see contemporary mosques varying from the standard square building topped by onion domes and minaret – though there were some notable flirtations with obscure geometrics and fibreglass in the 1960s. Only in Melaka state, where Malaysia's oldest mosques are located, does the architecture become more interesting, revealing unusual **Sumatran influences**.

Once at the mosque, the men wash their hands, feet and faces three times in the outer chambers, before entering the prayer hall to recite sections of the **Koran**. After this initial period, an **Imam** will lead prayers and, on occasions, deliver a sermon, where the teachings of Allah will be applied to a contemporary context. Women cannot enter the main prayer hall during prayers and must congregate in a chamber to the side of the hall. Visitors are welcome at certain times (it's always worth checking first with the local tourist office) and must wear acceptable clothing – long trousers and shirt for men, and a long cloak and headdress, which is provided by most mosques, for women. No non-Muslim is allowed to enter a mosque during prayer time or go into the prayer hall at any time, although it's possible to stand just outside and look in.

HINDUISM

Hinduism arrived in Malaysia long before Islam, brought by Indian traders more than a thousand years ago. Its central tenet is the belief that life is a series of rebirths and reincarnations that eventually leads to spiritual release. An individual's progress is determined by *karma*, very much a law of cause and effect, where negative decisions and actions slow up the process of upward reincarnation and positive ones accelerate it. A whole variety of **deities** are worshipped, which on the surface makes Hinduism appear complex; however, a loose understanding of the *Vedas* – the religion's holy books – is enough for the characters and roles of the main gods to become apparent. The deities you'll come across most often are the three manifestations of the faith's supreme divine being: Brahma the Creator, Vishnu the Preserver and Shiva the Destroyer.

The earliest Hindu **archeological remains** are in Kedah (see p.191) and date from the tenth century, although the temples found here indicate a synthesis of Hindu and Buddhist imagery. Although almost all of the region's Hindu past has been obliterated, elements live on in the popular arts like *wayang kulit* (shadow plays), where sacred texts like the *Ramayana* (see below) form the basis of the stories.

There was a Hindu **revival** in the late nineteenth century when immigrants from Southern India arrived to work on the Malaysian rubber and oil-palm plantations and built temples to house popular idols. The Hindu celebration of Rama's victory – the central theme of the epic *Ramayana* – in time became the national holiday of **Deepavali** (the festival of lights), reflecting the Malaysian policy of religious tolerance, while another Hindu festival, **Thaipusam**, when Lord Subramaniam and elephant-headed Ganesh, the sons of Shiva, are worshipped, has become the single largest religious gathering in the region.

Visitors are welcome in Malaysia's and Singapore's Hindu **temples**, and are expected to remove their shoes before entering. Step over the threshold and you enter a veritable Disneyland of colourful gods and fanciful creatures. The style is typically Dravidian (South Indian), as befits the largely Tamil population, with a soaring *gopuram*, or entrance tower, teeming with sculptures and a central courtyard leading to an inner sanctum to the presiding deity. In the temple precinct, there are always busy scenes – incense burning, the application of sandalwood paste to the forehead, and the *puja* (ritualistic act of worship). However, as most Hindu temples are run by voluntary staff, it's often impossible to find anyone to give you a guided tour of the temples' abundant carvings and sculptures.

CHINESE RELIGIONS

Most visitors will be more aware of the region's **Chinese** religious celebrations than of the Muslim or Hindu ones, largely because the festivals themselves are particularly welcoming of tourists and are often exciting. Most are organized by *kongsis*, or clan houses, which are the cornerstone of all immigrant Chinese communities in Malaysia and Singapore and traditionally provided housing, employment and a social structure for the newly arrived (see p.178).

Chinese religion shares animist beliefs with the ethnic groups. Chinese pioneers, while opening out the rivers of Sarawak for trade, could understand the beliefs and practices (except the head-hunting!) of the Iban and Melanau tribesmen they were dealing with, partly because they could identify with the animist ideas that were a driving force in their own lives. Malaysian and Singaporean Chinese usually consider themselves either **Buddhist**, **Taoist** or **Confucianist**, although in practice they are often a mixture of all three. These different strands in Chinese religion ostensibly lean in very different directions: Confucianism began as a philosophy based on piety, loyalty, humanitarianism and familial devotion, and has transmuted into a set of principles that permeate every aspect of Chinese life; Taoism places animism within a philosophy which propounds unity with nature as its chief tenet; and Buddhism is primarily concerned with the attainment of a state of personal enlightenment, *nirvana*. But in practice, the combination of the three comprises a system of belief which is first and foremost pragmatic. The Chinese use their religion to ease their passage through life, whether in the spheres of work or family, while temples double as social centres, where people meet and exchange views.

CHINESE TEMPLES

The rules of geomancy, or *feng shui* (wind and water), are rigorously applied to the construction of Chinese **temples**, so that the building is placed in such a geographical position as to render it free from evil influences. Visitors wishing to cross the threshold of a temple have to step over a kerb that's intended to trip up evil spirits, and walk through doors painted with fearsome door gods; fronting the doors are two stone lions, whose roars provide yet another defence. Larger temples typically consist of a front entrance hall opening onto a walled-in courtyard, beyond which is the hall of worship, where joss (luck) sticks are burned below images of the deities. Temples are normally constructed around a framework of huge, lacquered timber beams, adorned with intricately carved warriors, animals and flowers. More figures are moulded onto outer walls, which are dotted with octagonal, hexagonal or round grille-worked windows. The most important and striking element of a Chinese temple is its **roof** – a grand, multitiered affair, with low, overhanging eaves, the ridges alive with auspicious creatures such as dragons and phoenixes and, less often, with miniature scenes from traditional Chinese life and legend. *Feng shui* comes into play again inside the temple, with auspicious room numbers and sizes, colour and sequence of construction. Elsewhere in the temple grounds, you'll see sizeable ovens, stuffed constantly with paper money, prayer books and other offerings; or a pagoda – a tall, thin tower thought to keep out evil spirits.

Chinese temples play an important part in Chinese community life and many have weekly musical and theatrical performances, which can be enjoyed by visitors as well as locals. Most temples are open from early morning to early evening; devotees go in when they like, to make offerings or to pray – there are no set prayer times. Visitors are welcome and all the larger temples have janitors who will show you round, although only a few speak good English.

SOCIAL CONVENTIONS AND ETIQUETTE

The main rules when **entering a home** are: always take your shoes off; dress modestly in a Muslim household – for women that means below-knee-length skirts or shorts, a bra and sleeved T-shirts, for men, long trousers; never help yourself to food without first being offered it; and if eating with your hands or chopsticks, avoid using your left hand, which in Islamic culture is considered unclean. Taking a small present to someone's home, like flowers, fruit or chocolates, is always appreciated. When travelling to longhouse communities in East Malaysia, or to Orang Asli villages in the Peninsula, it's a good idea to bring some little **gifts**, and notebooks and pens for the children will come in useful. For the finer points of longhouse etiquette, see p.367.

In most respects Malaysia and Brunei are not particularly strict Muslim societies, but certain public acts which are quite acceptable in most non-Muslim countries are looked down upon here. Among these are kissing or cuddling, arguing, raising one's voice, pointing, or drinking in public. Other, more subtle, points of etiquette include not touching the head of a Malaysian, Muslim or otherwise, as the head is considered sacred in Eastern culture; and not shaking hands unless the host has offered theirs.

Women in Muslim Malaysia and Brunei have in recent years upped their public profile enormously, but this has not been reflected in a revolution in dress – in both cities and rural areas, Muslim women still dress in long, brightly coloured skirts and headscarves, covering all traces of their limbs, hair and neck (even schoolgirls are clothed this way); when it comes to prayers, they usually enter a mosque by a separate entrance and worship from behind a screen. Non-Muslim women may be forbidden to enter mosques altogether in a few cases, though other places allow women inside provided they wear a long cloak (supplied at the door).

It's advisable for tourists to dress **modestly** in conservative and rural areas by covering legs and upper arms, though headscarves are not necessary for women; in such areas you should also think twice about stripping off and swimming outside earmarked resorts (Muslim women go into the water fully clothed). Male and female visitors alike should be especially sensitive to such issues in Kelantan and Terengganu, whose state governments are controlled by the Islamist party PAS; new policies in both states encourage the separation of the population along gender lines, with separate checkouts for men and women in some stores.

FESTIVALS

With so many ethnic groups and religions represented in Malaysia, Singapore and Brunei, you'll be unlucky if your trip doesn't coincide with some sort of festival, either secular or religious. Religious celebrations range from exuberant, family-oriented pageants to blood-curdlingly gory displays of devotion. Secular events might comprise a carnival with a cast of thousands, or just a local market with a few cultural demonstrations laid on. If you're keen to see a major religious festival, it's best to make for a town or city where there is a large population of the particular ethnic group involved – all the relevant details are given in the list of festivals and events below, and are backed up by special accounts throughout the text.

If you're particularly interested in specifically **Malay festivities**, it's worth noting that in the northeastern Malaysian towns of Kota Bharu and Kuala Terengganu, cultural centres have been established as a platform for traditional Malay pastimes and sports – there's more information in the "East Coast" chapter, p.249. **Chinese religious festivals** – in particular, the Festival of Hungry Ghosts – are the best times to catch a free performance of a Chinese opera, or *wayang*, in which characters act out classic Chinese legends, accompanied by crashing cymbals, clanging gongs and stylized singing.

A FESTIVAL AND EVENTS CALENDAR

JANUARY–FEBRUARY

Perlis Bird Singing Competition Bird-lovers and bird-owners from Malaysia and beyond gather at Kangar to hear the region's most melodious songbirds do battle (early Jan).

Thaiponggal A Tamil thanksgiving festival marking the end of the rainy season and the onset of spring; offerings of food are made at Hindu temples such as Singapore's Sri Srinivasa Perumal Temple on Serangoon Rd (mid-Jan).

Procession of Kwong Teck Choon Ong Scores of cultural troupes perform lion dances and operas, and process around Kuching to honour this Chinese deity (Jan).

Chinese New Year Chinese communities spring spectacularly to life, to welcome in the new year. Old debts are settled, friends and relatives visited, and red envelopes (*hong bao*) containing money are given to children; Chinese operas and lion-and dragon-dance troupes perform in the streets, while ad hoc markets sell sausages and waxed ducks, pussy willow, chrysanthemums and mandarin oranges. Colourful parades of stilt-walkers, lion dancers and floats along Singapore's Orchard Road and through the major towns and cities of west-coast Malaysia celebrate the *Chingay* holiday, part of the new year festivities (Jan–Feb).

Chap Goh Mei The fifteenth and climactic day of the Chinese New Year period, and a time for more feasting and firecrackers; women who throw an orange into the sea at this time are supposed to be granted a good husband; the day is known as *Guan Hsiao Chieh* in Sarawak (Feb).

Thaipusam Entranced Hindu penitents carry elaborate steel arches (*kavadi*), attached to their skin by hooks and skewers, to honour Lord Subriaman. The biggest processions are at Kuala Lumpur's Batu Caves and from the Sri Srinivasa Perumal Temple to the Chettiar Hindu Temple in Singapore (Jan/Feb).

Birthday of the Monkey God To celebrate the birthday of one of the most popular deities in the Chinese pantheon, mediums possessed by the Monkey God's spirit pierce themselves with skewers; elsewhere street operas and puppet shows are performed. Make for Singapore's Monkey God Temple on Seng Poh Rd, or look out for ad hoc canopies erected near Chinese temples (Feb & Sept).

Regatta Lipa-Lipa *Lipa Lipa* – elegant square-rigged fishing boats – race at Semporna, on Sabah's east coast (Feb).

Brunei National Day The sultan and 35,000 other Bruneians watch parades and fireworks at the Sultan Hassanal Bolkiah National Stadium, just outside Bandar Seri Begawan; the rest watch on TV (Feb 23).

MARCH–MAY

Hari Raya Haji An auspicious day for Muslims, who gather at mosques to honour those who have completed the hajj, or pilgrimage to Mecca; goats are sacrificed, and their meat given to the needy. Known as *Hari Raya Aidiladha* in Brunei and sometimes in Malaysia and Singapore too (early March in 2001, late Feb in 2002, mid-Feb in 2003).

Le Tour de Langkawi A ten-day international bicycle race which, despite its name, covers most of Peninsular Malaysia before finishing in Langkawi (March).

Easter Candlelit processions held on Good Friday at Christian churches like St Peter's in Melaka and St Joseph's in Singapore (March/April).

Qing Ming Ancestral graves are cleaned and restored, and offerings made by Chinese families at the beginning of the third lunar month – signals the beginning of spring and a new farming year (April).

Singapore Film Festival Annual bash showcasing the sorts of movies that would otherwise never muscle their way into the local cinemas' Arnie- and kung-fu-dominated programmes (April/May).

Vesak Day Saffron-robed monks chant prayers at packed Buddhist temples, and devotees release caged birds to commemorate the Buddha's birth, enlightenment and the attainment of Nirvana (May).

Pesta Kaamatan Celebrated in the villages of Sabah's west coast and interior, the harvest festival of the **Kadazan/Dusun** people features a ceremony of thanksgiving by a *bobohizan* (high priestess), followed by lavish festivities; the festival culminates in a major celebration in Kota Kinabalu (May).

Birthday of the Third Prince Entranced mediums cut themselves with swords to honour the birthday of the Buddhist child god Ne Zha; their blood is wiped on much sought-after paper charms. It's a ritual observed at various Chinese temples throughout the region (May).

Sabah Fest A week of events in Kota Kinabalu, offering a chance to experience Sabah's food, handicrafts, dance and music (late May).

Brunei Armed Forces Day The formation of Brunei's armed forces is celebrated with parades and displays on the padang (May 31).

JUNE–AUGUST

Yang di-Pertuan Agong's Birthday Festivities are held in KL to celebrate the birthday of Malaysia's pre-eminent sultan (June 4).

Malaysia International Kite Festival A showcase of kite-flying and design, held at Tumpat in Kelantan (June).

Gawai Dayak Sarawak's Iban and Bidayuh peoples celebrate the end of harvesting with extravagant longhouse feasts. Aim to be in an Iban longhouse on the Rajang river or in the Batang Ai river system, or on dry land around Serian or Bau. (June).

Singapore Festival of the Arts Annual celebration of world dance, music, drama and art, utilizing venues around the state (June).

Feast of Saint Peter Melaka's Eurasian community decorate their boats to honour the patron saint of fishermen (June 24).

Dragon Boat Festival Rowing boats, bearing a dragon's head and tail, race in Penang, Melaka, Singapore and Kota Kinabalu, to commemorate a Chinese scholar who drowned himself in protest against political corruption (June/July).

Singapore Food Festival The whole island goes into an eating frenzy for a month, with outlets from hawker stalls to hotel restaurants staging events, tastings and special menus (July).

His Majesty the Sultan of Brunei's Birthday Celebrations Starting with a speech by the sultan on the Padang, celebrations continue for two weeks with parades, lantern processions, traditional sports competitions and fireworks – see local press for details (July 15).

Pesta Rumbia The uses of the *rumbia*, or sago palm, in handicrafts, housing, food and traditional medicines are demonstrated by the villagers of Kuala Penyu, in Sabah (late July).

Kelantan Cultural Week Kelantan citizens celebrate their heritage through cultural performances and handicraft demonstrations; particularly good in Kota Bharu (July–Aug).

Flower Festival Based in the Cameron Highlands, with a display of floral arrangements and a competition for the best flower-covered float (Aug).

Sarawak Extravaganza Kuching hosts a month of arts and crafts shows, street parades, food fairs and traditional games, all celebrating the culture of Sarawak (Aug).

Singapore National Day Singapore's independence is celebrated with a huge show at the National Stadium, featuring military parades and fireworks (Aug 9).

Malaysia National Day Parades in KL, Kuching and Kota Kinabalu to mark the formation of the state of Malaysia (Aug 31).

Festival of the Hungry Ghosts *Yue Lan*, held to appease the souls of the dead released from Purgatory during the seventh lunar month, when Chinese street operas are held, and joss sticks, red candles and paper money burnt outside Chinese homes (late Aug).

SEPTEMBER–DECEMBER

Malaysia Fest Fifteen-day festival in Kuala Lumpur, showcasing the best of Malaysian food, handicrafts and culture (Sept).

Moon Cake Festival Also known as the Mid-Autumn Festival (held on the 15th day of the 8th moon), when Chinese people eat and exchange moon cakes (made from sesame and lotus seeds and sometimes stuffed with a duck egg) to honour the fall of the Mongol Empire, plotted, so legend has it, by means of messages secreted in cakes. After dark, children parade with gaily coloured lanterns. Chinatowns are the obvious places to view the parades, but Singapore's Chinese Gardens and Kuching's Reservoir Park also have particularly good displays (Sept).

Navarathiri Hindu temples devote nine nights to classical dance and music in honour of the consorts of the Hindu gods, Shiva, Vishnu and Brahman; one reliable venue is Singapore's Chettiar Temple (Sept–Oct).

Thimithi Hindu firewalking ceremony in which devotees prove the strength of their faith by running across a pit of hot coals; best seen at the Sri Mariamman Temple in Singapore (Sept–Nov).

Festival of the Nine Emperor Gods The nine-day sojourn on earth of the Nine Emperor Gods – thought to bring good health and longevity – is celebrated in Singapore at the Kiu Ong Yah Temple (Upper Serangoon Rd) by Chinese operas and mediums cavorting in the streets (Oct).

Pilgrimage to Kusu Island Locals visit Singapore's Kusu Island in their thousands to pray for good luck and fertility at the Tua Pekong Temple and the island's Muslim shrine (Oct/Nov).

Kota Belud Tamu Besar Sabah's biggest annual market, attended by Bajau tribesmen on horseback, features cultural performances and handicraft demonstrations (Oct/Nov).

continued overleaf

continued from previous page

Deepavali Hindu festival celebrating the victory of Light over Dark: oil lamps are lit outside homes to attract Lakshmi, the Goddess of Prosperity, and prayers are offered at all temples (Oct/Nov).

Ramadan Muslims spend the ninth month of the Islamic calendar fasting in the daytime, and breaking their fasts nightly with delicious Malay sweetmeats served at stalls outside mosques (begins late Nov in 2000, mid-Nov in 2001, early Nov in 2002, late Oct in 2003).

Hari Raya Puasa The end of Ramadan, which Muslims celebrate by feasting, and by visiting family and friends; this is the only time the region's royal palaces are open to the public, including Brunei's, where the holiday is known as *Hari Raya Aidilfitri* (late Dec in 2000, mid-Dec in 2001, early Dec in 2002, late Nov in 2003).

Christmas Shopping centres in major cities compete to create the most spectacular Christmas decorations (Dec 25).

Bear in mind that the major festival periods may play havoc with even the best-planned travel itineraries. Over Ramadan in particular, transport networks and hotel capacity are stretched to their limits, as countless Muslims engage in *balik kampung* – the return to one's home village; Chinese New Year wreaks similar havoc. Some, but by no means all, festivals are also public holidays (when everything closes); check the lists in the box, opposite, for those.

Most of the festivals have **no fixed dates**, but change annually according to the lunar calendar; the Islamic calendar shifts forward relative to the Gregorian calendar by about ten days each year, so that, for example, a Muslim festival which happens in mid-April one year will be nearer the beginning of April the following year. We've listed rough timings, but for specific dates each year it's a good idea to check with the local tourist office.

OPENING HOURS AND PUBLIC HOLIDAYS

Specific opening hours are given throughout the text, but check below for the general opening hours of businesses and offices in Malaysia, Singapore and Brunei. It's worth noting that in Malaysia's more devout Muslim states, Friday – not Sunday – is the day of rest. Businesses and offices close after lunch on Thursday to accommodate this, while government offices in Brunei close on Fridays *and* Sundays.

Singapore and Malaysia share several common **public holidays**, as well as each having their own. Transport becomes a headache on these days, though you're only likely to be really inconvenienced around Chinese New Year (Jan–Feb) and the month of Ramadan (Nov/Dec), when hotels are bursting at the seams and restaurants, banks and shops all close. Local tourist offices can tell you exactly which dates these holidays fall upon annually. In Malaysia, a further complication is that some public holidays vary from state to state, depending on each state's religious make-up.

We've listed, in the box opposite, only the most widely celebrated holidays; in addition, countless localized **state holidays** mark the birthdays of sultans and governors. Don't be surprised to turn up somewhere and find everything closed for the day.

MALAYSIA

In **Malaysia**, **shops** are open daily 9.30am–7pm and shopping centres typically open daily 10am–9pm. **Government offices** tend to work Monday to Thursday 8am–12.45pm & 2–4.15pm, Friday 8am–12.15pm & 2.45–4.15pm, Saturday 8am–12.45pm; however, in the states of Kedah, Kelantan and Terengannu, on Thursday the hours are 8am–12.45pm, with offices closing on Friday and opening on Sunday. Banks open Monday to Friday 10am–3pm and Saturday 9.30am–1.30pm; as with government offices, Thursday is a half-day and Friday a holiday in the states of Kedah, Kelantan and Terengganu. It's impossible to give general opening hours for temples, mosques and museums – check the text for specific hours, given where appropriate.

PUBLIC HOLIDAYS

We've not listed exact dates for Muslim holidays as they move forward each year by ten or eleven days relative to the Julian calendar. For an explanation of the festivities associated with some of the holidays below, see box, pp.68–70.

SINGAPORE

January 1: New Year's Day
January/February: Chinese New Year (2 days)
February/March: Hari Raya Haji
March/April: Good Friday
May 1: Labour Day

May: Vesak Day
August 9: National Day
November: Deepavali
December: Hari Raya Puasa
December 25: Christmas Day

MALAYSIA

January 1: New Year's Day
January/February: Chinese New Year (2 days)
February/March: Hari Raya Haji
February: Thaipusam
March/April: Maal Hijrah (the Muslim New Year)
May 1: Labour Day
May: Pesta Kaamatan (Sabah only)

May/June: Birthday of the Prophet Mohammed
June: Gawai Dayak (Sarawak only)
June 4: Yang di-Pertuan Agong's birthday
August 31: National Day
November: Deepavali
December: Hari Raya Puasa
December 25: Christmas Day

BRUNEI

January 1: New Year's Day
January/February: Chinese New Year
February/March: Hari Raya Haji
February 23: National Day
March/April: First Day of Hijrah
May/June: Birthday of the Prophet Mohammed
June 1: Armed Forces' Day

July 15: Sultan's Birthday
October: Israk Mikraj
November: First day of Ramadan
November/December: Anniversary of Revelation of the Koran
December: Hari Raya Aidilfitri
December 25: Christmas Day

SINGAPORE AND BRUNEI

In Singapore, **shopping centres** open daily 10am–10pm; **banks** are sure to open at least Monday to Friday 10am–3pm, Saturday 11am–1pm and sometimes longer; while **offices** generally work Monday to Friday 8.30am–5pm and sometimes on Saturday mornings. In general, Chinese **temples** open daily from 7am to around 6pm, Hindu temples from 6am to noon and 5 to 9pm and **mosques** from 8am to 1pm; specific opening hours for all temples and museums are given in the text.

Government offices in **Brunei** open 7.45am–12.15pm & 1.30–4.30pm, except Friday and Sunday; **shopping centres** daily 10am–10pm; and **banks** Monday to Friday 9am–3pm and Saturday 9–11am.

SHOPPING AND SOUVENIRS

Southeast Asia offers real shopping bargains, with electrical equipment, cameras, clothes, fabrics, tapes and CDs all selling at competitive prices. What's more, the region's ethnic diversity means you'll be spoilt for choice when it comes to souvenirs and handicrafts.

Unless you're in a department store, prices are negotiable, so be prepared to haggle. If you're planning to buy something pricey – a camera, say, or a stereo – it's a good idea to pay a visit to a fixed-price store and arm yourself with the correct retail price; this way, you'll know if you're being ripped off. Asking for the "best price" is always a good start to negotiations; from there, it's a question of technique, but be realistic – shopkeepers will soon lose interest if you offer an unreasonably low price. Moving towards the door of the shop often pays dividends – it's surprising how often you'll be called back. If you do buy any electrical goods, make sure you get an international **guarantee**, and that it is endorsed by the shop.

Throughout the *Guide*, good buys and bargains are picked out and there are features on the best things to buy in specific regions. Malaysian pastimes throw up some interesting purchases: *wayang kulit* (shadow play) puppets, portraying characters from Hindu legend, are attractive and light to carry; equally colourful but completely impractical if you have to carry them around are the Malaysian kites, which can be several metres long. There's a round-up below of the other main souvenir items you might want to bring back. For specific details of shopping and **shops in Singapore**, see p.609.

In East Malaysia, the craft shops of Kota Kinabalu in **Sabah** have a wide variety of ethnic handicrafts native to the state. Most colourful of these are the *tudong duang*, a multicoloured food cover that looks more like a conical hat, and the painstakingly elaborate, beaded necklaces of the Runggus tribe. Also available are the bamboo, rattan and bark haversacks that locals use in the fields. For more unusual mementos, look out for the sumpitan, a type of blowpipe, or the sompoton, a musical instrument consisting of eight bamboo pipes inserted into a gourd, which sounds like a harmonica. Kota Kinabalu's stalls and markets also sell Indonesian and Filipino products, some of which is worth a look, such as mats and wooden sculptures of animals and birds.

Sarawak's peoples also produce a wide range of handicrafts using raw materials from the forest, with designs that are inspired by animist beliefs. In longhouses, you may see blowpipes and tools being made. If you travel deep into the forested interior you might get a chance to meet the semi-nomadic Penan peoples, who are experts at firing metal and making parangs (long knives). Kuching is also renowned for its **pottery**; ceramic vases and bowls designed with Iban and Bidayuh native designs. If you travel a few miles out of town you can visit the pottery factories where craftsmen use traditional methods (see p.372).

FABRICS

The art of producing **batik** cloth originated in Indonesia, but today batik is available across Southeast Asia and supports a thriving industry in Malaysia. To make batik, hot wax is applied to a piece of cloth with either a pen or a copper stamp; when the cloth is dyed, the wax resists the dye and a pattern appears, a process that can be repeated many times to build up colours. Batik is used to create shirts, skirts, bags and hats, as well as traditional sarongs – rectangular lengths of cloth wrapped around the waist and legs to form a sort of skirt worn by both males and females. These start at around RM15 and are more expensive, depending on how complex and colourful the design is. In some of the Malaysian east-coast towns, little cottage industries have sprung up enabling tourists to make their own batik clothes; we've given details where relevant.

The exquisite style of fabric known as **songket** is a big step up in price from batik; made by hand-weaving gold and silver thread into plain cloth, songket is used to make sarongs, headscarves and the like. Expect to pay at least RM100 for a sarong-length of cloth, and RM300–400 for the most decorative pieces. The other thing you'll be able to buy in Indian enclaves everywhere is primary-coloured silk **sarees** – look in Little India in Singapore and the Chow Kit and Lebuh India enclaves in Kuala Lumpur for the best bargains. Prices start at around $50.

Unique to Sarawak is **pua kumbu** (in Iban, "blanket"), a textile whose complex designs are created using the *ikat* method of weaving (see p.389 for more details). The cloth is best picked up in the bazaar towns or longhouses along the state's many rivers.

METALWORK AND WOODCARVING

Of the wealth of metalwork on offer, **silverware** from Kelantan is among the finest and most intricately designed; it's commonly used to make earrings, brooches and pendants, as well as more substantial pieces. Selangor state is renowned for its **pewter** – a refined blend of tin, antimony and copper, which makes elegant vases, tankards and ornaments. Prices for pewter are fixed throughout Malaysia. Over in Brunei, the speciality is **brassware** – cannons, kettles (called kiri) and gongs – decorated with elaborate Islamic motifs. Brunei brassware, however, is substantially more expensive than similarly sized Malaysian pewter articles.

Natural resources from the forest have traditionally been put to good use, with rattan, cane, wicker and bamboo used to make baskets, bird cages, mats, hats and shoulder bags. **Woodcarving** skills, once employed to decorate the palaces and public buildings of the early sultans, are today used to make less exotic articles such as mirror frames. However, it's still possible to see one of the dynamic **statues** created by the Orang Asli tribes at cultural shows and festivals in Kuala Lumpur and Kuantan. As animists, Orang Asli artists draw upon the natural world – animals, trees, fish, as well as more abstract elements like fire and water – for their imagery. Of particular interest are the **carvings** of the Mah Meri of Selangor, which are improvisations on the theme of *moyang*, literally "ancestor", which is the generic name for all spirit images. Dozens of moyang, each representing a different spirit, are incorporated into the Meri's beliefs and inspire the wooden-face sculptures which they carve. Also popular are topeng, or face masks. Look out too, for the exquisite woodcarving made by Sarawak's indigenous tribespeoples, much of it representing slender rice-gods; you'll find this work sold along Kuching's waterfront.

OUTDOOR PURSUITS

With some of the oldest tropical rainforest in the world and countless beaches and islands, trekking, snorkelling and scuba diving are common pursuits in Malaysia, while Singapore is only a short step away from these diversions. The more established resorts on the islands of Penang, Langkawi and Tioman offer more elaborate sports such as jet skiing and paragliding, while Cherating (the budget-travellers' centre on the east coast), with its exposed, windy bay, is a hot spot for windsurfers. Although all these places and activities are covered in more detail in the relevant chapters, below are some pointers to consider.

If you intend to take up any of these pursuits, check that your **travel-insurance** policy covers you. For details of any problems you might encounter out in the Malaysian wilds, see "Health" (p.23).

SNORKELLING, DIVING AND WINDSURFING

The crystal-clear waters of Malaysia and its abundance of tropical fish and coral make **snorkelling** and **diving** a must for any underwater enthusiast. This is particularly true of Sabah's Pulau Sipadan and the Peninsula's east coast, where islands like Perhentian, Redang, Kapas and Tioman are turning their natural resources into a lucrative business. Pulau Tioman offers the most choice for schools and dive sites – though some damage has already been caused to the coral reefs by over-eager visitors. However tempting the coral looks, don't remove it as a souvenir: this can cause irreparable damage to the reefs and upset the delicate underwater ecosystem.

Most beachside guesthouses have snorkelling **equipment** for rent (though flippers are rare) and rates are very reasonable at RM15–20 per day – check before you set out that the mask makes a secure seal against your face. Dive shops offer **courses** ranging from a five-day beginner's open-water course, typically around RM500, right through to the dive-master certificate, a fourteen-day course costing about RM1200. Make sure that the shop is registered with **PADI** (Professional Association of Diving Instructors); it's also a good idea to ascertain the size of the group, and that the instructor speaks good English. All equipment and tuition should be included in the price: it's worth checking the condition of the gear before signing on the dotted line.

Windsurfing has yet to take off in all but the most expensive resorts in Malaysia, with the notable exception of Cherating (p.283). Its large, open bay and shallow waters provide near-perfect conditions for the sport, and a few local entrepreneurs are catching on by renting out equipment – usually for around RM15 per hour – but don't expect expert coaching.

TREKKING

The majority of **treks**, either on the Malay Peninsula or in Sarawak and Sabah, require some forethought and preparation. As well as the fierce sun, the tropical climate can unleash torrential rain without any warning, which rapidly affects the condition of trails or the height of a river – what started out as a ten-hour trip can end up taking twice as long. That said, the time of year is not a hugely significant factor when planning a trek. Although the rainy season (Nov–Feb) undoubtedly slows your progress on some of the trails, conditions are less humid then, and the parks and adventure tours not oversubscribed.

Most visitors trek in the large **national parks** to experience the remaining primary jungle and rainforest at first hand. Treks in the parks often require that you go in a group with a guide, although it's quite possible to go to most parks on your own and then join a group once there. Costs and conditions vary among the parks; each park account in the *Guide* contains full practical and trekking details. For inexperienced trekkers, Taman Negara (see p.212) is probably the best place to start, boasting the greatest variety of walks, while Bako National Park (see p.379) in southwest Sarawak offers fairly easy, day-long hikes amidst spectacular scenery. For the more experienced, other parks in Sarawak, especially Gunung Mulu (see p.428), should offer sufficient challenges for most tastes; the largely inaccessible Endau Rompin park (see p.348) in the south of Peninsular Malaysia is for serious expedition fiends only. Mount Kinabalu Park (see p.475) in Sabah is in a class of its own, the hike to the top of the mountain a demanding but highly rewarding combination of trekking and climbing. **Tour operators** in your home country (see the various "Getting There" sections), and those based in Kuala Lumpur (p.119), Kuching (p.375), Miri

---

CHECK LIST OF TREKKING EQUIPMENT

The check list below assumes you'll be staying in hostels and lodges. This may not always be possible and if you plan to camp, you'll need more equipment, not least your own tent (since most tours don't include camping equipment).

ESSENTIALS	**CLOTHING AND FOOTWEAR**	**OTHER USEFUL ITEMS**
Backpack	Shirts/T-shirts	Plastic bag
Sleeping bag	Trousers	(to rainproof your pack)
Mosquito net	Skirt/dress	Candles
Water bottle	(mid-calf length is best)	Emergency snack food
Toiletries and toilet paper	Woolly sweater	Spare bootlaces
Torch	Gloves	Sewing kit
Pocket knife	Rainproof plastic coat or poncho	Small towel
Sunglasses (UV protective)	Cotton hat with brim	Soap powder
Sun block and lip balm	Jacket	Insulation mat
Insect repellent	Trekking boots	Large mug and spoon
Compass	Cotton and woollen socks	Basic first-aid kit

(p.419) and Kota Kinabalu (p.456), are the best places for more information on conditions and options in the parks – Malaysia's tourist offices aren't much help, although there is a national parks section at MATIC in KL.

Basic **clothing** and **equipment** for all treks, be they three hours or ten days, should comprise loose, cotton long trousers and long-sleeved shirts which protect against sun and sharp thorns; good hiking boots (preferably canvas ones which dry out quickly) with thick socks; hats which shield both the front and the back of the head from the sun; and as small and comfortable a rucksack as you can get by with. There's a trekking equipment check list in the box, opposite, which should see you through most of the treks you're likely to undertake in Malaysia.

For many people, the ubiquitous **leech** – whose bite is not actually harmful or painful – is the most irritating aspect to jungle trekking. When there's been a heavy rainfall, you can rely upon the leeches to come out. Always tuck your trousers into your socks and tie your boot laces tight. The best anti-leech socks are made from calico; you can buy these for around RM10 a pair from the Malaysian Nature Society, 17 Jalan Tanjung, SO 13/2 Seri Damansara, KL (☎03/632 9422 or 635 8773, *www.mns.org.my*). If you find the leeches are getting through, the best remedy is to soak the outside of your socks and your boots in insect repellent, or dampen tobacco and apply it in between your socks and shoes. It's best to get into the habit of checking your feet and legs every twenty minutes or so for leeches.

DIRECTORY

AIRPORT TAXES From Malaysia, an airport tax of RM5 is levied on all domestic flights and on flights to Brunei or Singapore, and RM40 on international flights. Singapore charges a S$15 airport tax on all international flights. In both these countries these costs are usually included in the ticket. For Brunei, a charge of B$5 is payable on flights to Malaysia and Singapore and B$12 to other destinations.

CHILDREN The general levels of hygiene in Malaysia, Singapore and Brunei make travelling with children a viable prospect. Asian attitudes towards the young are far more tolerant than they are in the West; indeed children inevitably attract a great deal of attention, too, which can be both tiring and stressful for the child. Remember that children dehydrate much more quickly than adults, particularly if they have diarrhoea, so keep up their fluid intake. Everything you might need is readily available, with the exception of fresh milk – though even this can be found in supermarkets. Disposable nappies and powdered milk are easy to find, and bland Chinese soups and rice dishes are ideal for systems unaccustomed to spicy food. The biggest problem is likely to be in the evening, for only the smartest hotels have a baby-sitting service, though every restaurant or *kedai kopi* will have a high chair. Only upmarket hotels will provide baby cots, though others may be able to rustle something up if given advance warning. However, rooms in the cheaper hotels usually come with an extra bed (see "Accommodation", p.43), for little extra cost. Children under 12 get into most attractions for half-price, and even at the most basic resorts, there'll be a children's playground.

CONTRACEPTIVES Oral contraceptives are available from all pharmacists in Malaysia,

Singapore and Brunei, as are spermicidal gels. Condoms are also widely obtainable and pharmacies plentiful.

DUTY-FREE GOODS Duty-free products in Singapore include electronic and electrical goods, cosmetics, cameras, clocks, watches, jewellery, precious stones and metals. Malaysia has no duty on cameras, watches, cosmetics or electronic goods; in addition, perfumes, cigarettes and liquor are duty-free. Pulau Labuan and Pulau Langkawi are both duty-free islands, though neither has a particularly impressive range of products.

ELECTRICITY Mains voltage in Malaysia, Singapore and Brunei is 220 volts, so any equipment which uses 110 volts will need a converter. In all three countries, the plugs have three square prongs like British ones. If your appliance has a different type of plug, take an adapter.

GAY AND LESBIAN LIFE There is a thriving gay scene in KL (see p.114); though homosexuality is officially outlawed in Singapore, a discreet scene does exist. More information on gay life in Malaysia, Singapore and Brunei can be found on the Internet at *www.utopia-asia.com*

LAUNDRY Most towns will have a public launderette, where clothes can be washed cheaply. Only rarely do you do the wash yourself; it's more likely that you leave the clothes there and pick them up later that day or the following day. In addition, an increasing number of budget hostels have washing machines available for guests for a small charge, or offer a laundry service for around RM10/S$8. Small sachets of soap powder (75 sen) are readily available from general stores if you prefer to hand-wash. Dry-cleaning services are less common, though any hotel of a decent standard will be able to oblige.

TIME DIFFERENCES Malaysia, Singapore and Brunei are 8 hours ahead of GMT, 16 hours ahead of US Pacific Standard Time, 13 ahead of Eastern Standard Time, and 2 hours behind Sydney.

WORKING Unless you've got a prearranged job and a work permit, opportunities for working in Malaysia and Singapore are few and far between. Helping hands are often required in guesthouses; the wages you'll get for these jobs are low, but board and lodging are often included. Work is also occasionally available teaching in language schools, though you're far more likely to secure employment if you have a TEFL (Teaching English as a Foreign Language) qualification, or at least some experience in the field. With the construction boom in Malaysia and the push to develop industries linked to new technology, opportunities are also available to those with engineering and computing skills.

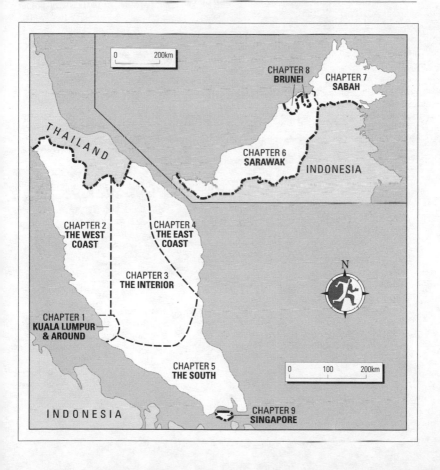

CHAPTER ONE

KUALA LUMPUR AND AROUND

Kuala Lumpur is the youngest of Southeast Asia's capitals and, these days, the most economically successful after Singapore. A safe and sociable place, the city has a real buzz to it, and enough interesting monuments to keep visitors busy for a week at least. The ethnic and cultural mix of Malays, Chinese and Indians makes itself felt throughout: in conversations on the street, in the variety of food for sale, in the good manners, patience and insouciance shown to visitors, and in the sheer number of mosques, Buddhist temples and Hindu shrines. Another of KL's most noticeable features is its adoption of a particularly Asian alliance of the old and the new. It's not unusual to see youths heading for the mosques on Friday in traditional clothes, then, prayers duly completed, darting into the nearest cybercafé.

Having survived a sharp economic recession in the late 1990s, Kuala Lumpur has bounced back with renewed vigour. The city's **nightlife** is one sign of this recovery: KL is one of the most exciting places in Southeast Asia to go out, with a wide variety of restaurants, bars, cafés and hip nightclubs to suit most predilections and pockets.

Despite the building boom of recent times, Kuala Lumpur still has a fair amount of greenery, and the wider expanses of Templer Park and the modern hill station of the Genting Highlands are both only an hour's bus ride away, in the ancient state of **Selangor**, which surrounds the federal territory of the capital. Also just outside the city, the rugged limestone Batu Caves, on KL's northern boundary, contain the country's most sacred Hindu shrine, focus of a wild celebration during the annual Thaipusam religious festival. Other sites within easy reach of the city include the Orang Asli Museum, showcasing the lifestyle and culture of the Peninsula's indigenous peoples; and the Forest Research Institute of Malaysia, with a treetop canopy walkway for a quick taste of the rainforest. Venturing west from KL down the valley of the Klang river brings you to the new town of Shah Alam, with its splendid mosque. Northwest of the Klang rivermouth is the picturesque Kuala Selangor, the premier attraction of the area being the pulsating fireflies of nearby Kampung Kuantan.

ACCOMMODATION PRICE CODES

Throughout the Malaysia chapters we've used the following **price codes** to denote the cost of the cheapest available room for two people. Single occupancy should cost about twenty percent less than double, though it's only mid-range and top-tier hotels that are likely to offer such discounts. Some guesthouses provide dormitory beds, for which the ringgit price is given.

① RM20 and under	④ RM61–80	⑦ RM161–220
② RM21–40	⑤ RM81–110	⑧ RM221–360
③ RM41–60	⑥ RM111–160	⑨ RM361 and above

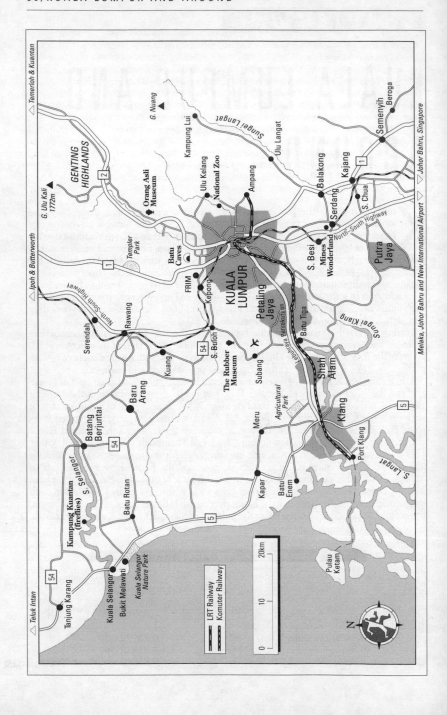

KUALA LUMPUR

Founded in the mid-nineteenth century, **KUALA LUMPUR**, or **KL** as it's known to residents and visitors alike, is a city where signs of economic growth abound – it's almost impossible to walk through town without taking detours around vast cavities full of construction equipment, while city maps are out of date before the ink's dry. It helps that anything goes here, because the city has never had a coherent style. The first grand buildings around Merdeka Square, dating from the 1880s, were eccentric mishmashes themselves, the result of British engineers and architects bringing together a zestful conglomeration of Moorish, Moghul, Malay and Victorian elements. Today, those colonial buildings that remain rub shoulders with chic, modern banks designed to look like traditional Malay houses; other buildings have an extravagant, futuristic look that wouldn't be out of place in Hong Kong or New York. Indeed, in architectural terms, KL now leads rather than follows – it possesses the tallest building in the world at time of writing, the Petronas Twin Towers, and the grandest communications tower in the Menara KL. You'll often notice a peculiarly Islamic aesthetic at work, not just in the celebrated Twin Towers, which consciously echo minarets, but also in buildings like the Maybank and the Dayabumi Complex, which fuse the modern with the traditional.

At regular times of the day and evening, the sound of the muezzin's call to prayer, *Allahu Akbar*, drifts across from the minarets of the three main mosques, while at Friday lunchtime especially, you can't but notice the thousands of white-robed men converging on the mosques to fulfil their religious duties. That said, to the extent that Kuala Lumpur is an **Islamic** city, it's among the world's most liberal examples, one where dress codes are tempered by Malay patterned headscarves, and residents are as likely to be seen wielding cellular phones as they are clutching the Koran.

A trip around the city centre reveals its multicultural nature. The standard itinerary includes the colonial core around **Merdeka Square** and the enclaves of **Chinatown** and **Little India**, followed by a trip either north up Jalan Tunku Abdul Rahman to the warren of plankboard passages known as **Chow Kit Market**, or south to the **Muzium Negara** (National Museum). Now new attractions like the **Islamic Museum**, and a trio of cultural edifices, including the **National Theatre**, can be added to the must-see list. Heading at random in almost any direction is just as rewarding, not least for the contact this brings with KL street life, one major facet of which are its numerous, boisterous **markets**, the entrances to some of which – like the wet fish market in between Jalan Tun H.S. Lee and Jalan Petaling – you'd miss if you blinked at the wrong moment. And everywhere are hawker stalls with food of every shape and description, as well as soya milk, fresh fruit and juice stalls – the latter a necessity, since KL's **humidity** can fell even the most hardened tropical traveller.

Some visitors are disappointed by KL; untrammelled development has given the city more than its share of featureless buildings, follies and failures, terrible traffic snarl-ups and visible, urban poverty. You'll soon become aware, too, of the pollution, which on some days hangs above KL in malevolent clouds. Thankfully, it's easy to escape to the gentle sanctuary of the **Lake Gardens** and **Lake Titiwangsa**, on the city's outskirts. At the very least, KL's busy vibrancy can be enjoyed for a few days before you head further afield.

Some history

Kuala Lumpur (the name means "muddy estuary" in Malay) was founded in 1857 when the chief of Selangor State, Rajah Abdullah, sent a party of Chinese prospectors to explore the area around the confluence of the Klang and Gombak rivers. The aim was to find extractable deposits of **tin** – a metal that had already brought great wealth to the northern town of Ipoh. Although many of them died from malaria as they hacked through the dense, swampy jungle, the pioneers had their reward in the discovery of rich deposits 6km from the confluence, near **Ampang**, which grew into a staging post for Chinese labourers who arrived to work in the mines. The first Chinese *towkays* (merchants) set up two secret societies in Ampang, and fierce competition between them for the economic spoils soon developed. This boiled over into angry confrontations between rivals, effectively restraining until the 1870s the growth of Ampang, the initial centre of KL. The arrival of an influential Chinese merchant, **Yap Ah Loy** – who had a fearsome reputation as a secret-society boss in mainland China – helped unify the divergent groups. Ah Loy's career was a symbol of the Eldorado lifestyle of KL's early years. Starting out as a minor gangster, he became a local hero when he organized the protests in the Negeri Sembilan miners' rebellion of the mid-1860s (see p.295), on the back of which he invested in gambling dens and tin. By the time Ah Loy was 30 he had become KL's *Kapitan Cina*, or Chinese headman. But the precarious rule of the pioneers was swept rudely aside during the settling of the Selangor Civil War (see p.126) through British gunboat diplomacy, and in 1880 the British Resident of Selangor State, **Frank Swettenham**, took command. KL became the state capital and, in 1896, capital of the Federated Malay States.

Until the 1880s, KL was little more than a shantytown of wooden huts precariously positioned on the edge of the river bank. Reaching the settlement was a tough job in itself. Small steamers could get within 30km of the town along Sungei Klang, but the rest of the trip was either by shallow boat or through the roadless jungle. Getting to the tin mines was even worse. In his memoirs, *Footprints in Malaya*, Swettenham remembered it being ". . . a twelve-hour effort and very strenuous and unpleasant at that, for there was no discernible path and much of the distance we travelled up to our waist in water. Torn by thorns, poisoned by leech bites and stung by scores of blood-sucking insects, the struggle was one long misery." And yet people were drawn to the town like bees to honey. Early British investors, Malay farmers, Chinese *towkays* and workers – and, in the first years of the twentieth century, Indians from Tamil Nadu – all arrived in the search for something better, whether the work was in the tin mines, on surrounding rubber estates or, later, on roads and railway construction.

Swettenham demolished most of KL's wooden huts and imported **British architects** from India to design solid, grand edifices, suitable for a new capital. He faced an initial setback in 1881 when fire destroyed all the buildings; rebuilding was slow, and sanitary conditions the following year were described by the governor as "pestilential". Nevertheless, by 1887 the city had five hundred brick buildings, and eight times that number by the early 1900s. The population, which grew from four thousand to forty thousand in the 1880s, was predominantly Chinese, and was further swollen by the arrival of the Tamils. The seeds of KL's staggering modern growth had been sown.

Development continued steadily in the first quarter of the twentieth century. Catastrophic floods in 1926 inspired a major engineering project which straightened the course of Sungei Klang, confining it within reinforced, raised banks and successfully preventing future flooding. By the time the **Japanese invaded** in December 1941, overrunning the British army's positions with devastating speed, the commercial zone around Chinatown had grown to eclipse the original colonial area, and the *towkays*, enriched by the rubber boom, were already installed in opulent townhouses along today's Jalan Tunku Abdul Rahman and Jalan Ampang. Although the Japanese bombed the city, they missed their main targets; little physical damage occurred beyond a general looting of stores and the blowing up of bridges by the retreating British army. But the invasion had a radical psychological impact on each of the ethnic communities in the city. The Japanese, while inflicting terrible repression on their historic enemies, the Chinese – at least five thousand were killed in the first few weeks of the invasion alone – ingratiated themselves with some Malays, by suggesting loyalty to the occupiers would be rewarded with independence after the war. The Indians also suffered, with thousands sent to Burma to build the infamous railway; very few of them survived.

At the end of the war, following the **Japanese surrender** in September 1945, the British were once more in charge in the capital, but found they couldn't pick up where they had left off. Nationalist demands had replaced the Malays' former acceptance of the colonizers, while for some of the Chinese population, identification with Mao's revolution in 1949 led to a desire to see Malaya become a communist state. The following period of unrest (1948–60), which stopped just short of civil war, became known as the **Emergency**. Although very few incidents occurred in KL itself during the period – the guerrillas were aware that they couldn't actually take the capital – the atmosphere in the city remained tense. The look of the city changed, too, during this postwar period, with the nineteenth-century buildings which had dominated KL – the Sultan Abdul Samad Building, the Railway Station and other government offices – gradually being overshadowed by a plethora of **modern developments**.

Malaysian independence – **Merdeka** – finally came in 1957, but tensions between the Malays and the Chinese later spilled over into the 1969 **race riots** in the city. As a consequence, Tunku Abdul Rahman, the first prime minister, was forced to set an agenda for development which aimed to give all Malaysia's ethnic groups an equal slice of the economic cake. Interracial hostilities have been transformed in the last thirty years, galvanized into an all-hands-on-deck approach to quicken the pace of economic progress. Through the 1990s the Klang Valley, which runs west from KL to Klang through Petaling Jaya and Shah Alam, became a thriving industrial zone, feeding the manufacturing sectors of this expansion. The next project which will dramatically change the look of the city and the surrounding area – one that won't be finished until 2020 – is the **Multimedia Super Corridor** (MSC). Stretching 60km from Kuala Lumpur City Centre, the new development which houses the Twin Towers, south to the new airport, the MSC includes two futuristic small cities, the "paperless" **Putrajaya**, which will be the new seat of government, and Cyberjaya, a centre for hi-tech industry.

Arrival and information

KL is at the hub of Malaysia's transport systems. It has a new, architecturally spectacular and hugely efficient international airport, while buses from all over Peninsular Malaysia converge on one of the city's four bus stations. The train station doubles as a tourist sight, a magnificent building fusing Moorish architectural flourishes with British colonial design. The **city centre** itself is quite small, bordered by the Chow Kit district to the north, the Golden Triangle to the east, Brickfields to the south and the Lake Gardens to the west.

By air

The new, ultramodern **Kuala Lumpur International Airport** (KLIA) is at Sepang, 72km south of the centre. The arrivals hall contains offices of all the major car rental firms, and there are money exchange outlets here, too. Airport coaches (daily 6am–midnight; every 30min; 90min; RM25) leave from the bus station on Level 1; follow the clearly marked signs from Arrivals at Level 4 to the escalators down to the bus concourse. The bus service will drop you directly at your accommodation. Alternatively, from the same concourse, take the local bus to Nilai train station (daily 6.30am–10pm; every 30min; 40min; RM1.50) and change onto the Komuter train line (daily 6.30am–10.30pm; every 15min; 1hr; RM4.70) which terminates at KL train station. Tickets for both the airport bus and local bus can be bought from the counter in the concourse. Taxis into the centre cost around RM65 – buy a coupon at the Taxi

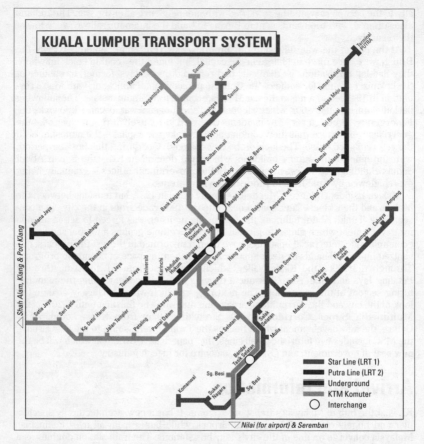

KUALA LUMPUR TRANSPORT SYSTEM

Star Line (LRT 1)
Putra Line (LRT 2)
Underground
KTM Komuter
○ Interchange

△ Shah Alam, Klang & Port Klang

▽ Nilai (for airport) & Seremban

counter in the arrivals hall; avoid the taxi touts, who may charge upwards of RM140, and have been known to demand payment in US, rather than Malaysian, dollars.

The old international airport at **Subang**, 30km west of the centre, is to be phased out by 2002, when the ERT (an express rail link) from KLIA to the capital opens. Until then, some domestic and international flights will continue to arrive at Subang, namely Malaysia Airlines' services within Peninsular Malaysia, Air Asia's flights from Taiwan, Berjaya Air's services from Malaysian islands, and Pelangi flights from Indonesia. Bus #47 (daily 6am–9pm; every 30min; 40min; RM1.60; buy tickets on board) leaves from outside the Terminal 1 departure hall. The bus drops you at either KL's Railway Station or the Klang Bus Station. Taxis from Subang to the centre cost around RM40 – buy a coupon from the desk in the arrivals hall.

By train, bus and taxi

Kuala Lumpur's striking **train station** (see p.96) is on Jalan Sultan Hishamuddin, from where Chinatown is ten minutes' walk north (follow the covered walkway starting outside the east side of the station and finishing across from Central Market); the National Art Gallery is opposite and the Muzium Negara another ten minutes' walk further south.

There's a good information kiosk (daily 8am–8pm) in the station concourse, with lists of hotels and train timetables. Hotels near the Putra World Trade Centre can be reached by Komuter train, while those in the Golden Triangle area are accessible by bus or taxi.

Most long-distance buses arrive at the giant **Pudu Raya bus station**, an island of concrete in the middle of Jalan Pudu, just to the east of Chinatown. Though it looks chaotic, it's actually quite an efficient place, with hundreds of buses setting off day and night from here for most of the main destinations on the Peninsula. The buses draw into ground-floor bays, while the ticket offices are on the floor above, along with dozens of stalls selling food, and a left-luggage office. **Long-distance taxis** also arrive at Pudu Raya, on the second floor. The Plaza Rakyat station, used by KL's LRT metro trains see p.86), is next to the station, and Chinatown hotels are within walking distance of here; for the Golden Triangle, take bus #29, which goes to the Lot 10 Shopping Centre.

Some buses from the east coast end up instead at **Putra bus station**, a smaller, more modern terminus to the northwest of the city centre, just beside the Putra World Trade

MOVING ON FROM KL

BY AIR

Until the new high-speed rail link from the city to **KLIA airport** opens in 2002, the easiest way to get there is to call a taxi from your hotel (RM65 to the airport); taxis flagged down on the street tend not to want to go out that far. Most of the larger hostels can help arrange transport to the airport for around the same price; you can also use the airport coach service – call them on ☎03/653 3154, preferably giving a day's notice, to ensure being picked up from your hotel in good time. Alternatively, take the Seremban-bound Komuter train from platform 3B of the Railway Station, get off at Nilai, then change onto the local airport bus from directly outside the station. If your flight leaves from **Subang**, go to the Klang bus station and catch the twice-hourly service there.

BY TRAIN

You must book, preferably at least three days in advance, for the **night sleeper** to Singapore or Butterworth; booking isn't necessary for most other routes. Most of the large hotels can book train tickets for you, but the tourist offices can't. To get a taxi from the Railway Station, you prepay the fare to your destination at the desk by the east exit, near Platform 4.

BY BUS OR LONG-DISTANCE TAXI

Most **long-distance buses** and taxis leave from inside **Pudu Raya bus station**. At the main entrance there's a Tourist Police Office and, close by, an **information counter** (☎03/230 0145) where you can find out which bays cover your destination and when they are scheduled to leave. Buses also operate from outside the terminus (you can't miss people touting these services); most of these leave only when full, which can take a while. **Long-distance taxi** journeys – to destinations like Penang, Melaka and Kuantan – are a good deal, seldom much more than twice the price of the bus; again the drivers wait for a full car-load before departing.

For east-coast (Kota Bharu) buses, go to the Putra bus station (☎03/442 9530), by the Putra World Trade Centre; for services west of KL in Selangor State (Port Klang and Shah Alam), the Klang bus station on Jalan Sultan Mohammed (☎03/337 338); and for the east coast and interior, including Kuala Lipis and Gua Musang, the Pekeliling bus station on Jalan Raja Laut (☎03/442 1256).

BY FERRY

Ferries to Tanjung Balai in Sumatra depart from Port Klang, 38km southwest of KL (see p.130), reachable by Komuter train from the Klang bus station on Jalan Sultan Mohammed.

Centre. This is handy for the budget hotels on Jalan Raja Laut and in the Chow Kit area, but it's quite a way from Chinatown, 2km to the south. To head downtown from the bus station, cross Jalan Tun Ismail and use the PWTC LRT station.

Services from Kuantan and from the interior stop at **Pekeliling bus station**, at the northern end of Jalan Raja Laut, about 700m beyond the northern end of Jalan Tuanku Abdul Rahman; from Pekeliling, you can head into the centre from the Tun Razak LRT stop opposite, across Jalan Tun Razak. The **Klang bus station**, at the south end of Jalan Sultan Mohammed, near Central Market, is used by Klang Valley buses to and from Port Klang, Klang, Shah Alam and Kuala Selangor; just to the north is an LRT stop, Pasar Seni.

Information and maps

KL has lots of **tourist information centres**, each of which hands out free **maps** and leaflets. The biggest is **MATIC** (Malaysian Tourist Information Complex) at 109 Jalan Ampang (daily 9am–9pm; ☎03/264 3929), close to the junction with Jalan Sultan Ismail; you can get here on bus #23, #24a, #176 or #182 from Jalan Hang Lekir in Chinatown. Housed in a beautiful old colonial building that was originally a tin *towkay*'s house, the main desk hands out various free city maps and brochures, as well as holding details of accommodation in KL and throughout the country; another desk takes bookings for Taman Negara National Park (see p.212). Cultural shows are held weekly (days vary) on the first floor, where there is also a very good exhibition of traditional musical instruments.

The **KL Visitors' Centre** (Mon–Fri & Sun 8am–5pm, Sat 8am–12.45pm; ☎03/274 6063), located directly outside the train station's west entrance, has a greater abundance of leaflets; its staff are more knowledgeable and helpful, and can help you with finding and booking accommodation. Here you can pick up the excellent *KL Sightseeing* map and bus-route details. For **listings** of events in the city, check the weekly magazine *Day and Night*, the "Time Out" section in Thursday's edition of the *Sun* newspaper, and the "Metro" section in the tabloid *Malay Mail*.

City transport

Most of the city centre – the Colonial District, Chinatown and Little India – is easy to cover on foot, though pedestrians should take care as neither cars nor motorbikes can be trusted to stop at traffic lights or pedestrian crossings. Avoid the temptation to try to walk everywhere, because in time you'll become exhausted by the combined effects of humidity and traffic fumes. When you can, either take the **LRT** metro, jump on a **bus** – avoiding if possible the rush-hour periods (8–10am & 4.30–6.30pm) – or take a **taxi**; these, although plentiful and fairly inexpensive, can be tricky to flag down during peak periods, and during the frequent downpours of rain. To get to sights outside the city, you'll need to drive, or use the modern **Komuter train** system, which serves the Klang valley, or get buses, which are useful for attractions like Kuala Selangor and the Batu Caves.

A new transport hub was being built in KL's centre at time of writing. To be finished in 2002, the KL Sentral station, as it's known, will be served by Komuter trains and one of the two LRT lines; it will also be the terminus for a new express train service out to KLIA.

Light Rail Transit

The latest attempt to ease KL's chronic traffic problems is the **Light Rail Transit (LRT)** system, a metro network comprising two, mostly elevated, lines. LRT1 – also known as

Star – runs from Ampang in the east of the centre through the Masjid Jamek hub to Sentul Timur in the north of town and Sri Petaling to the south. LRT2, or Putra as it's also called, has the longest stretch of fully automated metro in the world, running from west of the centre to northeast, intersecting with the Star line at Masjid Jamek. The lines are easy to spot in the city centre since trains run on raised concrete ramps above the main roads. Trains on both systems operate every 5–15 minutes from 6am to midnight; they're fast and efficient, though during rush hour they often get full. Fares start at 70 sen for journeys between, say PWTC and Hang Tuah, on the Star line, or between KLCC and Bangsar on the Putra line. You buy your tickets from the office outside each station, and pass them through an electronic gate to get to the platforms. On LRT1, you can use stored-value tickets (either RM20, RM50 or RM100) which are returned to you at the gate, with the remaining amount on the ticket displayed on the machine. These cards will also be good for the PRT (see p.88) when it opens. Cards called Touch & Go can be used on LRT2 and also work on Cityliner buses (see below) (RM20 and RM50). A map and booklet on the system can be picked up from each station.

Buses

KL's **bus** services are comprehensive, quick and inexpensive. For visitors, the downside is that they're quite difficult to fathom, because none of the local city services starts from fixed depots; you just go to bus stops which sometimes list the numbers of buses which pass by.

KL city **buses** run every few minutes from 6am to 11pm daily. Fares start from 90 sen on the larger, municipal-owned Intrakota buses and 60 sen on the privately-run Cityliner services, and go up to just above RM2; for example you pay around RM2.20 to go to the Batu Caves, just outside KL. Buses operated by Intrakota have no conductor, so you pay the driver – you'll need to have the exact change. The key pick-up points are the east side of Central Market, on Jalan Hang Kasturi; the Jalan Sultan Mohammed terminus (opposite Klang bus station), 100m south of the market; the Kota Raya plaza on Jalan Cheng Lock; and Lebuh Ampang, the northern continuation of Jalan Hang Kasturi.

The integrated bus and train card, Touch & Go, is valid on City Liner buses and LRT2, and can be bought from stations on this route. Intrakota buses also have a Fare Card, though this doesn't cover the LRT and isn't worthwhile unless you're staying in KL for a month or more.

Komuter trains

Main-line **Komuter** trains run along two lines – one from Rawang to Seremban (change at Nilai for a bus to KLIA), the other from Sentul to Port Klang. Both connect at the central KL stations of Putra, Bank Negara and Kuala Lumpur Railway Station. The trains are modern and run smoothly at thirty-minute intervals, with extra services during the early-morning and evening rush hours. Tickets, which start at RM1, can be purchased from the stations and automatic machines at the stops. There are various saver passes for periods of one week up to one year, but the best value for the visitor is the RM5 day-ticket (valid Mon–Fri after 9.30am) for unlimited travel on the network. Komuter trains really come into their own for travelling to and from Shah Alam, Klang and Port Klang.

Taxis

Taxi fares start at RM1.50 and rise 30 sen for every kilometre travelled; you'll seldom pay more than RM10 for any journey within the city. Remember to check if the driver has put his meter on when you get into the vehicle. However, as KL's traffic is so congested, it's often faster to get out and walk.

Although the majority of taxi drivers know the city well, some don't speak English, and so it's best to have your destination written down if it has a complicated address, or have a map handy. There are numerous taxi ranks around the city, usually situated beside bus stops; it's a good idea to wait on the correct side of the road for the direction you want to go in since taxi drivers often refuse to turn their cab round. Alternatively you can simply flag one down and jump in – bashful visitors will usually be overlooked in the melee. To call a cab, use Comfort Radio Taxi Service (☎03/733 0507); Koteksi (☎03/781 5352) or Radio Teksi (☎03/442 0848); you'll be charged an extra RM1 for the booking.

Monorail (PRT)

Construction of the **Monorail** or PRT, a sixteen-kilometre elevated-rail system serving the city and dovetailing with the two LRT networks, is underway, although no date has been set for its completion. Trains will run from Kampung Pasir, southwest of the centre, to Jalan Tun Razak at the northern edges of the city, meeting LRT1 at Sultan Ismail station and LRT2 at Hang Tuah. The biggest gain from the PRT will be its traversal of the city's main shopping areas, especially Jalan Sultan Ismail, one of KL's most crowded central arteries.

Accommodation

There's a wide range of **accommodation** available in KL, at very reasonable prices; rates have gone down, if anything, in recent years, as the city emerges from a period of economic depression. Most travellers head for the hotels and backpackers' hostels of **Chinatown**, though **Little India** has now become a decent alternative for budget and mid-range places to stay. A few inexpensive places lie close to the Pudu Raya bus station and around **Jalan Pudu**. The first-class hotels, many of which are worth checking out for their excellent deals and promotions, are situated a couple of kilometres further east, in the **Golden Triangle**. West and north of Little India and Chinatown, the hotels along the two-kilometre stretch of **Jalan Tuanku Abdul Rahman** (or Jalan TAR, as it's usually called) include some of the sleaziest and most infamous in town.

In busy periods – July, August, November and December – it's advisable to make advance bookings at budget hotels and backpackers' hostels. You don't need to book at mid-range or top-tier hotels.

Chinatown

The following hotels, hostels and lodges are marked on the map on p.99.

Backpackers Travellers Inn, second floor, 60 Jalan Sultan (☎03/238 2473, fax 202 1855). Centrally located, on the eastern edge of Chinatown, this popular place has small, clean single and double rooms, some with air-con, and dorms. The *pièce de résistance* is the roof bar, which stays open half the night at weekends; here you can get affordable beers and enjoy the small sound system playing international grooves. Manager Stevie runs a small travel agency, Backpackers Transport, which offers city and Kuala Kuantan Fireflies tours as well as an airport shuttle service. ②, dorm beds RM15.

Backpackers Travellers Lodge, first floor, 158 Jalan Tun H.S. Lee (☎03/201 0889, fax 238 1128). Second operation for Stevie's family, run by brother Vincent and his friendly staff. A range of clean rooms, some with air-con, as well as four-bed options and dorms. Videos are shown every night and there's Internet access on three terminals (RM10 an hour). Always busy, so it's best to book ahead. Recommended. ②, dorm beds RM8.

City Inn, 11 Jalan Sultan (☎03/238 9190, fax 441 9864). Mid-range modern hotel. Its small, spotless, air-conditioned rooms are en suite. ④.

Furama, Kompleks Selangor, Jalan Sultan (☎03/230 1777, fax 230 2110). A modern hotel with air-con and small but comfortable, well-equipped rooms. ⑤.

Leng Nam, 165 Jalan Tun H.S. Lee (☎03/230 1489). Beside the Sri Maha Mariamman Temple, and close to Chinatown's most picturesque street, Jalan Petaling, this traditional Chinese-run hotel has a great atmosphere. Small rooms come with two large beds; toilets and shower are shared. ②.

Lok Ann, 113a Jalan Petaling (☎03/238 9544). Tidy hotel, offering rather charmless en-suite rooms with air-con and TV. Better value than others at the same price. ③.

Malaya, Jalan Hang Lekir (☎03/232 7722, fax 230 0980). One of the most expensive hotels in Chinatown, but excellent value for the price. The deluxe rooms have all the trimmings, and the café is renowned. Price includes breakfast. ⑤.

Mandarin, 2–8 Jalan Sultan (☎03/230 3000, fax 230 4363). Chinatown's largest hotel, boasting a coffee house, 24hr room service, a gym and even a hair salon. Rooms are spacious with full facilities. ④.

Sun Kong, 210 Jalan Tun H.S. Lee (☎03/230 2308). Run by a friendly family, this is one of the cheapest and smallest Chinese-run hotels in the area, with a shrine in the hall and dark polished-wood floors; the rooms, though small and spartan, are clean. ②.

Swiss Inn, 62 Jalan Sultan (☎03/232 3333, fax 201 6699). Comfortable, modern hotel in the heart of Chinatown, complete with a terrace overlooking Jalan Petaling and a café that does cheap breakfasts. ⑤.

Travellers Moon Lodge, 36b Jalan Silang (☎03/230 6601). Just south of Jalan Tun Perak, this popular lodge includes a rather cramped dorm, small two- and three-bed rooms and a roof terrace. The management is friendly; there's a fine collection of maps, pamphlets and books for guests to peruse. ②, dorm beds RM9.

YWCA, 12 Jalan Hang Jebat (☎03/230 1623, fax 201 7753). This delightful hostel – safely away from the noise of Chinatown – only rents its clean, comfortable singles and doubles to women, mixed couples and families. With the added advantage of a lovely sitting room, it's a great deal if you qualify. ②.

Wan Kow, 16 Jalan Sultan (☎03/238 2909). The rather unpromising entrance leads to an airy lobby and box rooms. Cheap and clean. ②.

Near the train station

The following places to stay, other than the *YMCA*, are marked on the map on pp.92–93.

The Heritage Station Hotel, Kuala Lumpur Railway Station, Jalan Sultan Hishamuddin (☎03/273 4522, fax 273 5588). Ideal if you've an early-morning train to catch. The lobby and rickety but antique lift still retains some of the atmosphere of an erstwhile era when it was KL's premier colonial hotel. Though a little worn, the rooms are as atmospheric as the rest of the place. Excellent value. ④.

Kuala Lumpur International Youth Hostel, 21 Jalan Kampung Attap (☎03/273 6870, fax 274 1115). From the train station, follow Jalan Sultan Sulaiman around to the Police Co-op building and then turn right down Jalan Kampung Attap. The hostel is at the end of the block in a very quiet location. The rooms are all dorms with four, six or ten beds; there's also a café and a laundry service. It doesn't have the same buzz as similar places in Chinatown, though. Dorm beds RM8.

Travellers Station, KL Railway Station, Jalan Sultan Hishamuddin (☎03/272 2237, station1@tm.net.my). Superb, spacious, switched-on backpackers' place with Internet access, washing machines and loads of information on other parts of Malaysia and Southeast Asia in general. Owner Indy does a night tour which takes in Chinese and Indian temples and clubs. ①, dorm beds RM8.

YWCA, 95 Jalan Padang Belia, Brickfields (☎03/274 1439, fax 274 0559). Recently refurbished, this hostel has clean, snug, double rooms and – ideal for groups – four-bed rooms (RM75). They also have a small library and a gym. ④.

North of the centre: Little India, Chow Kit Market and the World Trade Centre

The following hotels, hostels and lodges are marked on the maps on p.92 and p.104.

Champagne, 141 Lorong Bunus, off Jalan Masjid India (☎03/293 2422). This hotel, popular with the Indian business types, shares the same management as the *Chamtan*, but isn't as good, with smaller rooms. ③.

Chamtan, 62 Jalan Masjid India (☎03/293 2422). Sister hotel to the *Champagne*, with slightly better rooms, boasting TVs and attached bathrooms. ③.

City Villa KL, 69 Jalan Haji Hussein (☎03/292 6077, fax 292 7734). This long-established hotel has good, small rooms with bath and air-con. Its location near Chow Kit Market makes it noisy early in the morning, though its handiness for the market's splendid *roti canai* stalls is some compensation. ⑤.

Coliseum, 98 Jalan TAR (☎03/292 6270). KL's most famous old-style hotel. It can be a bit noisy, but oozes atmosphere; its bar even has cowboy-saloon-style doors. The restaurant serves great steaks with gravy. ②.

Empire, 48b Jalan Masjid India (☎03/293 6890). Cheaper than the better-known *Champagne* and *Chamtan*, this is a good deal; rooms have air-con and TV, and there are discounts for longer stays. ③.

Kowloon, 142 Jalan TAR (☎03/293 4246, fax 292 6548). The rooms are small, though modern and well-kept, with TV and air-con. Its coffee house, open to non-residents, serves excellent cakes and cappuccinos. ④.

The Legend, Putra Place, 100 Jalan Putra (☎03/442 9888, fax 441 1030). One of KL's most luxurious hotels, with comfortable rooms and an excellent range of restaurants, some of which have fantastic views across the city. It's next door to a shopping centre, The Mall, and also handy for the Putra World Trade Centre across the road. ⑧.

Palace, 40 Jalan Masjid India (☎03/298 6122, fax 469 6868. Top-of-the-range, excellent-value air-con hotel, but rooms are small despite all mod cons. ④.

Tivoli, 136 Jalan TAR (☎03/292 4108). Another low-budget place overlooking the traffic-clogged Jalan TAR. Clean rooms with shared showers and toilets. ②.

Around Pudu Raya

The following hotels, hostels and lodges are marked on the map on p.103.

Katari, 38 Jalan Pudu (☎03/201 7777, fax 201 7911). Bang opposite the bus station, this new, upmarket business hotel has a coffee house and small, clean rooms with the usual facilities. ④.

Kawana Tourist Inn, 68 Jalan Pudu Lama (☎03/238 6714, fax 230 2120). Neat, small rooms in a modern, rather bare place, but extremely good value and only ten minutes' walk from the bus station. ②.

KL City Lodge, 16 Jalan Pudu (☎03/230 5275, fax 201 3725). Has dorms and air-con rooms; useful extras include Internet access, a laundry service and free lockers. Avoid the rooms which overlook busy Jalan Pudu. ③; dorm beds RM12.

Pudu Raya, fourth floor, Pudu Raya bus station (☎03/232 1000, fax 230 5567). In a noisy and unattractive location, though convenient for travellers arriving late or leaving town very early. The small rooms are good, with en-suite bathrooms and air-con. ④.

The Golden Triangle

The following hotels, hostels and lodges are marked on the map on p.103.

Bonanza (☎03/245 8457), 72 Jalan Bukit Bintang. The only budget place in this upmarket part of town. Small rooms and dorms. ②, dorm beds RM20.

Concorde, 2 Jalan Sultan Ismail (☎03/244 2200, fax 244 1628). The trendiest of the area's hotels, housing the *Hard Rock Café* and fashionable boutiques. It has large rooms with full facilities, and a small business centre offering, among other services, Internet access. The price includes an all-you-can-eat breakfast and airport pick-up if required. ⑧.

Equatorial, Jalan Sultan Ismail, opposite the MAS building (☎03/261 7777, fax 261 9020). Vast three-hundred-room hotel with an enormous swimming pool, shops, Internet access and some good restaurants and cafés. ⑦.

Federal, 35 Jalan Bukit Bintang (☎03/248 9166, fax 248 2877). Used mostly by locals, this rather staid old hotel has large, comfortable rooms and a revolving rooftop restaurant. Also offers Internet access. ⑥.

Istana, 73 Jalan Raja Chulan (☎03/244 1445, fax 249 5500). From the moment you walk into its glittering lobby you know you're in one of KL's best hotels. The rooms are of a high standard, the decor is palace-like and there's a swimming pool. Also here is a booking office for *Taman Negara National Park Resort* (see p.212), run by the same group as the hotel. Price includes breakfast. ⑦.

The Lodge, Jalan Sultan Ismail (☎03/242 0122, fax 241 6819). Outstanding value at this motel-style place, which boasts a swimming pool and an outdoor restaurant. ④.

Malaysia, 67 Jalan Bukit Bintang (☎03/242 8033). Atmospheric, old-style Chinese-run place with good-sized rooms. ⑤.

Park Royal, Jalan Imbi, cnr of Jalan Sultan Ismail (☎03/242 5588, fax 241 4281). In an undistinguished modern building, it has larger-than-average rooms, and Internet access. ⑦.

The Regent, 160 Jalan Bukit Bintang (☎03/241 8000, fax 245 7732). A prestigious hotel, with a large swimming pool, massive rooms and luxurious suites. ⑧.

The Renaissance, 130 Jalan Ampang (☎03/262 2233, fax 263 1122). One of the city's latest luxury hotels, sharing facilities – including a swimming pool, gym and restaurants – with the adjacent *New World Hotel*, which is slightly cheaper. Also has Internet access. ⑧.

The Shuttle Inn, 112b Jalan Bukit Bintang (☎03/245 0828). The cheapest of the mid-range hotels in the area, located right by the main shopping complexes. Small, clean, air-con rooms, with attached bathrooms. A good option for sampling KL's nightlife or mall culture while avoiding crammed buses and taxi fares. ③.

The City

The city centre is easy to walk around, with the Central Market the best spot from which to get your bearings. Across Sungei Klang, due west of the market, and 200m north, lies the Colonial Quarter centred on **Merdeka Square**. Just south of here, along Jalan Sultan Hishamuddin, are the chief focal points for the city's Muslim community: the **Masjid Negara** (National Mosque) and the new **Islamic Arts Museum**; nearby are the landmark train station and the **Muzium Negara** (National Museum). East of Central Market are the city's two main traditional commercial districts, **Chinatown** and **Little India**. One of the most prominent (and busiest) of KL's central streets, Jalan Tunku Abdul Rahman (or Jalan TAR), runs due north from Merdeka Square for 2km to **Chow Kit Market**. Closer in, west of the square, are the **Lake Gardens**, the city's green lungs.

Just east of Chinatown, the congested **Jalan Tun Perak** leads to the Pudu Raya bus station and onwards to the **Golden Triangle**, the fashionable consumer sector around three main roads – Jalan Bukit Bintang, Jalan Imbi and Jalan Sultan Ismail. Where most of the city's development is taking place, the district contains most of the city's expensive hotels, nightlife spots, modern malls, and the lofty Menara KL and **Petronas Towers**. At the northern edge is **Jalan Ampang**, one of the first streets to be developed as a residential area for rich tin *towkays* and colonial administrators at the start of the twentieth century.

All these areas, and most of KL's sights, lie within the **Jalan Tun Razak**, which runs round the city's northern edge; popular spots just outside in the suburbs include **Lake Titiwangsa** and the important Chinese **Thean Hou Temple**. Along the road itself are a trio of fabulous new buildings – the Art Gallery, National Theatre and National Library.

The Colonial Quarter

The small **Colonial Quarter** (see map on p.99), which developed around the confluence of the Gombak and Klang rivers in the 1880s, is unlike any other area of KL, its eccentric fusion of building styles at extreme odds with the rest of the city. The district is centred on the beautifully tended, 200-metre-long **Merdeka Square** on the west bank of the Klang. Both English cricket ground and Malay *padang* (field), it's now the most famous stretch of green in Malaysia, as it was here that Malayan independence – referred to as *merdeka* (freedom) – was proclaimed on August 31, 1957.

On the western side of the square, the **Royal Selangor Club** was the British elite's favourite watering hole. Colonial wags used to refer to the low, black-and-white mock-Tudor building as "the Spotted Dog" in memory of the club mascot, a Dalmatian, which a former member used to tie up at the steps. Dating from 1890, the club looks and feels like a bastion of male tradition, but now admits women members; it's not open to the public, though. To the north, the Anglican **St Mary's Church** (1894), usually open in the daytime, welcomed the city's European inhabitants every Sunday before they repaired to the club.

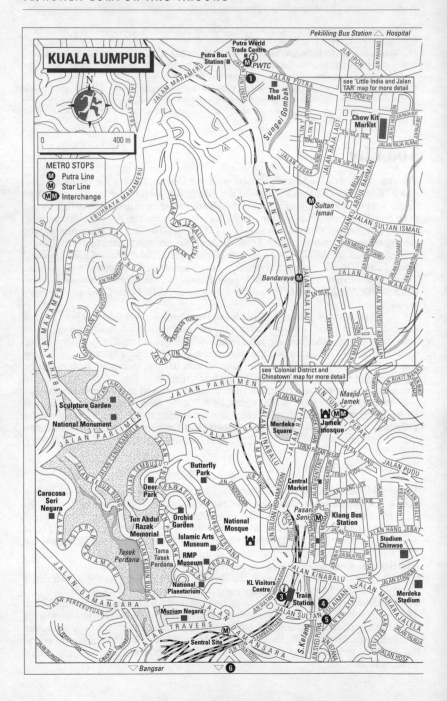

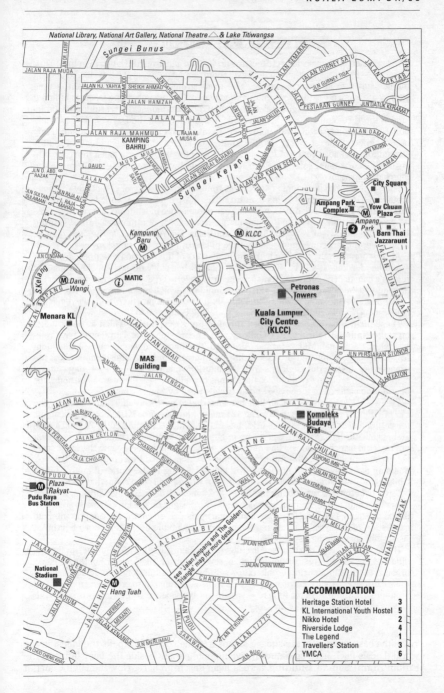

National Library, National Art Gallery, National Theatre △ & Lake Titiwangsa

Sungei Bunus

JALAN RAJA MUDA
JLN DR LATIFF
JALAN HJ. YAHYA SHEIKH AHMAD
JALAN HAMZAH
JALAN RAJA UDA
JALAN RAJA MAHMUD
KAMPING BAHRU
JALAN RAJA MUDA MUSA
DAUD
JLN TD ABD RAZAK
JLN SULTAN SULAIMAN
JLN RAJA AU
RAJA MAHADI
JALAN SUNGAI BAHARU

Sungei Kelang

JALAN SEMARAK
JALAN GURNEY SATU
JLN GURNEY TIGA
PESIARAN GURNEY
JLN DATUK KERAMAT
JALAN DAMAI
JLN MURNI
JALAN AMAN

JALAN TUN RAZAK

City Square
Ampang Park Complex
Yow Chuan Plaza
Ampang Park
Barn Thai Jazzaraunt

Kampung Baru Ⓜ
JLN CENDANA
Ⓜ KLCC

Ⓜ Dang Wangi
ⓘ MATIC
JALAN AMPANG

Ⓜ Menara KL

JALAN SULTAN ISMAIL
JLN PUNCAK
MAS Building
JALAN TENGAH

Petronas Towers

Kuala Lumpur City Centre (KLCC)

JALAN KIA PENG

JALAN RAJA CHULAN
JLN BUKIT CEYLON
JALAN CEYLON
JLN PERSIARAN RAJA CHULAN

JALAN CONLAY
Kompleks Budaya Kraf
JALAN RAJA CHULAN

Plaza Rakyat Ⓜ
Pudu Raya Bus Station

JALAN BUKIT BINTANG
JALAN SULTAN
LORONG IMBI
JALAN IMBI

National Stadium
Ⓜ Hang Tuah

see Jalan Ampang and The Golden Triangle map for more detail

CHANGKAT TAMBI DOLLA
JALAN CHAN WING

ACCOMMODATION

Heritage Station Hotel	3
KL International Youth Hostel	5
Nikko Hotel	2
Riverside Lodge	4
The Legend	1
Travellers' Station	3
YMCA	6

KL'S NEW ARCHITECTURE

The explosion of giant-scale **architecture** projects in and around KL began in the 1970s, when KL's first construction boom gave room for inventive architects to expand on themes suited to its tropical climate. The many ground-breaking projects of the time explored, among other ideas, whether climate should be the governing factor in building design, or if cultural or religious elements should be paramount. The resulting KL buildings of the 1970s and 1980s – the Maybank, Tabung Haji and the Dayabumi – saw traditional elements interacting with innovative architectural expressions, often to strikingly original effect. Some architects looked to the past and combined the archetypal saddle-shaped Minangkabau roof and Islamic arches with the latest functionalist thinking; others have incorporated solar panelling for power, and water concourses to regulate the internal temperature.

The architect who best demonstrates the contemporary fusing of essentially religious motifs with new design is **Hijas Kasturi**. His most impressive work is perhaps the **Maybank Building** (see p.101), where the predominance of white denotes purity, while its great height, sleekness and grandeur are reminiscent of a minaret. In his **Tabung Haji**, at the intersection of Jalan Ampang and Jalan Tun Abdul Razak, the five columns supporting the structure represent the five pillars of Islam, the single tower unity with God; appropriately, the building is the headquarters of the Islamic Bank of Malaysia.

Another leading architect, **Ken Yeang**, has as his chief design consideration the region's climate. His **Menara Measiniaga** skyscraper – on the way to the old airport at Subang – is the latest in a string of tropical buildings which make maximum use of natural light and ventilation: inside, plants spiral up its walls (a practice often called vertical landscaping), while energy-efficient solar panelling is integral to the design.

These themes have been developed through the 1990s, during which a trio of buildings, the **National Library**, **Art Gallery** and **Theatre**, on Jalan Tun Razak, have reinterpreted traditional Malay forms. Although the library, designed by Shamsuddin Mohammed, is dominated by a gleaming roof covered in large blue-ceramic tiles, the grandeur of the exterior contrasts with the interior's incorporation of everyday cultural symbols, with sculpture that utilizes the shapes of traditional earthenware pots, and walls bearing the patterns of the *songket* headscarves worn by Malay women.

Two world-class skyscrapers and an awe-inspiring airport were finished in time for the 1998 Commonwealth games in KL. The 421-metre-high **Menara KL** telecommunications tower, the fourth highest in the world, has external motifs dominated by Arabic scripts and Islamic designs. Visitors can go up in an elevator to an observation deck and look out over the fast-changing skyline of the city. Hot on its high heels came the most spectacular new building of all – American architect Cesar Pelli's **Petronas Twin Towers**. Standing at just over 450m high, it is the tallest building in the world (though China's Chongqing Tower, under construction at time of writing, will soon claim that honour). Its tapered twin towers, resembling minarets, are joined 41 floors up by a bridge, forming something akin to a megalithic gateway, while the designs on the interior walls are a profusion of squares and circles symbolizing harmony and strength. Here is the ultimate expression of Malaysia's intention to stand at the economic heart of modern Southeast Asia, while maintaining its traditions and faith.

The next phase is in the hands of architects like Zaini Zainul, who continues in the tradition of East-meets-West design which is revolutionizing the look of Southeast Asian urban areas and influencing architecture worldwide. Commissioned to design parts of the paperless cyber-city Putrajaya (see p.132), he is setting out to create an environment – on an island in a man-made lake – which will be pleasant to live and work in, with echoes of European eco-friendly cities.

On the eastern edge of the square stands a 95-metre-high flagpole, the tallest in the world. Locals flock here on Saturday evenings to parade beside the fairy lights of the **Sultan Abdul Samad Building**, across Jalan Raja from here. Now the High Court, it has a two-storey grey-and-red brick facade dominated by a forty-metre-high clock tower, and curved colonnades topped with impressive copper cupolas; the building isn't open to the public.

Designed by Anthony Norman (also responsible for St Mary's) and finished in 1897 (making it contemporary with the Railway Station; see p.96), the Sultan Abdul Samad Building was among the earliest of the capital's **Moorish-style buildings**, a cluster of which are to be found around here. What they all had in common was an eclectic and rather eccentric interpretation of Islamic style which drew on Spanish, Moorish, Venetian, Mogul and North Indian sources. Picturesque fantasies predominate, featuring onion domes, cupolas, colonnades, arched windows and wedding-cake plaster work. One man is largely responsible for this original urban fabric – Charles Edwin Spooner, the State Engineer in the 1890s. Under his guidance, architect A.C.A. Norman came up with an initial design for the Sultan Abdul Samad Building – in the Neoclassical Renaissance style, which was then the general standard for government buildings in the Straits Settlement Crown Colonies of Singapore, Malacca and Penang, as well as elsewhere throughout the British Empire. But Spooner argued that the symbols of the Federated Malay States, a protectorate rather than a colony, should reflect the Islamic sensibilities of the traditional Malay rulers. So a more "Eastern" design was eventually used, though not one based on traditional Malay timber buildings but imported from colonial India. Other buildings which followed in this mould, all designed by Norman, include the Post Office (now the Federal Courts), the Public Works Department and the High Court.

To the north stands the black-domed old **City Hall**, and to the south the **National Museum of History** (daily 9am–6pm; free). Once the workplace of former British prime minister John Major in his days as a banker, this cream-coloured building, also in a Moorish style, on the corner of Jalan Raja was converted in 1996 from government offices into a museum. It provides an informative romp, which can be covered in half an hour, through the main points of the nation's history, spanning everything from the geological formation of the Malay Peninsula to Prime Minister Mahathir's Vision 2020 programme, which aims for Malaysia to achieve full industrialized status by that year. On the opposite corner is the original Public Works Department, which has striped brickwork and keyhole archways. These days the building houses **Infokraft** (daily 9am–5pm; free), a contemporary crafts and textiles gallery whose displays can be purchased by visitors.

Jalan Sultan Hishamuddin and around

As you head south of Merdeka Square, along Jalan Sultan Hishamuddin, you pass the gleaming 35-storey **Dayabumi Complex** on your left. Built in the 1980s, it was the first modern building in KL to incorporate Islamic principles in its design. Malay architect Nik Mohammed took modern mosque architecture as his model and produced a skyscraper whose high-vaulted entrance arches and glistening white open-fretwork has become characteristic of progressive Malaysian city architecture (see box, opposite).

The modern **General Post Office** is next door, while a couple of hundred metres further down, on the opposite side of Jalan Sultan Hishamuddin, stands the seventy-metre-high minaret and geometric latticework of the **Masjid Negara**, the National Mosque (daily 9am–6pm except Fri 2.45–6pm), which opened in 1965. It's an impressive building, with sweeping rectangles of white marble bisected by pools of water, and a grand hall which can accommodate up to ten thousand worshippers. In the prayer hall, size gives way to decorative prowess, the dome adorned with eighteen points signifying the five pillars of Islam and the thirteen states of Malaysia. To enter as a visitor (which you can only do in-between prayers), you need to be properly dressed: robes can be borrowed (free) from the desk at the mosque entrance.

The Museum of Islamic Arts

West of the mosque, on Jalan Lembah Perdana, is the new, ultramodern **Museum of Islamic Arts** (Tues–Sun 10am–6pm; RM8), one of the world's first museums to dedicate itself completely to the arts of the Muslim world. This fascinating collection of textiles, metalwork, miniature paintings, ceramics and rare manuscripts is a must-see, for the experience of being in the large, open-plan building with its gleaming marble floors as much as the displays. The bulk of the exhibits are on the second and third floors. The latter's calligraphy section contains hand-written sections of the Koran, constituting the "fine art" collection here; dating back 1000 years in some cases, they're often intricate and beautiful. It is on this floor too where you can best view the museum's inverted dome – it actually bulges downwards – at ceiling level, its intricate designs finished by master craftsmen from Uzbekistan and Iran, as well as detailed models of many of the world's most impressive and important mosques. The roof offers a lovely view over KL; the museum also houses a good café and shop selling postcards, batik and household objects bearing Islamic motifs.

The RMP Museum

Just west of the Islamic Arts Museum, along Jalan Perdana, is the **RMP Museum** (10am–6pm, Fri 10am–2pm & 3–6pm; free), covering the vivid history of the Malaysian police force. Inside, among the photographs are some fascinating images (*c.* 1900), including a rural shot of British officers and their local charges on patrol on buffaloes. The museum also has a variety of weapons confiscated from the communists during the Emergency, including a vicious assortment of *parangs* and a curved, bladed implement known as the Sarawak axe. A Cessna plane stands guard outside, along with a few armoured cars and cannon used by the Japanese when they invaded Kelantan in 1941.

The Railway Station

Back on Jalan Sultan Hishamuddin, the 1911 **Railway Station** lies some 300m south of the mosque. Not KL's original train station, which stood on a site close to Merdeka Square, the current construction, probably the city's most famous building, was built on a grand scale by a British architect, A.B. Hubbock, who took over from Anthony Norman (see p.95) after the latter was compulsorily retired in 1903 on grounds of inefficiency. Hubbock had previously lived in India and been inspired by North Indian Islamic architecture, something reflected in the station, which could have come straight out of the *Arabian Nights*, meshing spires, minarets and arches with a hardy iron roof. For the best views, turn left onto Jalan Kinabalu, from whose bridge you can appreciate the station's seven minarets, positioned between two thirty-metre-high domes, in their full glory. It's an incongruous sight, with the futuristic Dayabumi and other skyscrapers dominating the skyline behind.

Muzium Negara and south to Brickfields

Continuing about 1500m beyond the station, to the end of Jalan Sultan Hishamuddin and then southwest along Jalan Damansara, brings you to the **Muzium Negara**, Malaysia's National Museum (daily 9am–6pm; RM1). Built in 1963, it has a sweeping roof, characteristic of Sumatran Minangkabau architecture, and an exit (paradoxically at the end of the building facing the road) flanked by Italianate mosaics showing scenes from Malaysia's history and culture. Much of the museum's original collection was destroyed by World War II bombing, but the extensive ethnographic and archeological exhibits on display here are still impressive.

The museum's entrance is at the back of the building, past the reproduction of the Pinitu Malim archway, from a Malay fort in Kedah. The **ground floor** is mostly taken up with tacky life-size dioramas depicting various aspects of traditional Malaysian life, from the prosaic activities of the Malay kampung (village) – fishing, farming and weaving – to the pomp and ritual of a wedding and a Malay circumcision ceremony. At the end of the room, a cross-section of a Melaka *Baba* house is revealed, loaded with mahogany furniture, intricate carpets and ornaments made from silver, brass and gold. Also on the ground floor are *wayang kulit* (shadow play) displays, which show how the wooden puppets used in this ancient artistic tradition differ in design and colour depending on their provenance.

On the **upper floor**, a large but uninspiring section of stuffed birds and animals needn't detain you long, certainly not if you're waylaid by the much more impressive collection of weapons, including a large number of *kris* daggers (see p.274), *parang*s (machetes), swords and miniature cannons. Finally, there's a fabulous section on traditional musical instruments: the *serunai*, a reed flute with a multicoloured end; the *rebab*, a kind of fiddle played with the instrument held upright, its base in the musician's lap; numerous two-metre-long Kelantanese drums and smaller *rebana* drums; and Chinese lutes, gongs and flutes. Malay instruments are still in common use at festivals and ceremonies, while traditional Chinese music in Malaysia – virtually extinct at independence – has now been partially revived. If you're interested in hearing the music produced by these instruments, check out the venues listed on p.116.

Brickfields

Located 2km south of the city centre on either side of Jalan Tun Sambanthan, the **Brickfields** district was first settled by Tamils employed to build the railways, and named after the brickyards which lined the railway tracks. The main street runs along the back of the original rail line and many of the buildings, *c*.1900, still remain. However, all this will change as Brickfields finds itself at the centre of the **Sentral**, the new station and business district due to be finished in 2002; high-speed trains linking the KLIA to the centre of the city will terminate here. Brickfields is a good place to come to eat (see p.112), and also worth a trip to visit its Temple of Fine Arts (daily 11am–9pm; free) at 116 Jalan Berhala. This lovely sanctuary of Indian culture features monthly concerts and special events during Hindu festivals, as well as traditional Indian music and dance lessons most evenings. It also has a café serving Tamil food. Behind the *YMCA* here (see p.89) is one of KL's best secondhand bookshops, Skoob Books (see p.117). To get to Brickfields, take bus #5 from Klang bus station (90 sen).

West of Merdeka Square: the Lake Gardens

Once at the National Museum, you're only a short walk from the **Lake Gardens** (daily 9am–6pm), one square kilometre of close-cropped lawns, gardens and hills originally laid out in the 1890s by the British state treasurer to Malaya, Alfred Venning, though much of the spectacular landscaping has been completed within the last 25 years. Spread around a lake (Tasek Perdana), the park incorporates a number of sights – the National Monument, the Butterfly House and Bird Park, Orchid and Hibiscus Gardens, the National Planetarium and the colonial mansions of the former Governor of the Malay States – while just beyond, on the northern edge, is Malaysia's Parliament House.

There are a number of routes to the gardens. From the Muzium Negara, you can take the footbridge across Jalan Damansara which leads to the entrance of the National Planetarium. Alternatively, head west along Jalan Bangsar for about 100m, looking out for the small pathway leading into a tunnel at the junction with Jalan Kebun Bunga. This takes you to the southern edge of the gardens, from where it's a good twenty-minute walk along the lake and up the hill to the bird park and flower gardens. Approaching from the National Mosque or the Islamic Arts Museum, it's best to use Jalan Perdana. From the Kota Raya bus stop, on Jalan Cheng Lock in Chinatown, you can take bus #22 to the gardens' main entrance, on Jalan Parlimen.

In the gardens

Opposite the main entrance, off Jalan Parlimen, is a great bronze sculpture designed by Felix de Weldon, better known for his work on the Iwo Jima Memorial in Washington DC. The fifteen-metre-high shiny slab was constructed in 1966 to commemorate the nation's heroes, yet strangely the seven military figures protruding from it appear to be European rather than from any of the various Malaysian ethnic groups who fought in World War II and during the Emergency (see p.83). Reached by a path leading up from the car park, the monument stands surrounded by a moat with fountains and ornamental pewter water lilies – a tranquil spot. Back at the car park, looking down on Jalan Parlimen, is the **Taman ASEAN sculpture garden**, to which neighbouring countries have contributed abstract works in marble, iron, wood and bamboo.

The **Butterfly House** (daily 9am–5pm; RM5) – five minutes' walk south of the National Monument – holds a diverse collection of butterflies (dead and alive). More likely to hold your attention, though, is the excellent **Bird Park** (daily 9am–6pm; RM3), modelled on Singapore's Jurong Bird Park (see p.588); retrace your steps from the Butterfly House to Jalan Cenderawasih and turn left uphill, following the road for 200m to the Bird Park entrance. Within, walkways loop around streams and pools taking in the enclosures of indigenous species such as hornbills, the Brahminy Kite and the Hawk Eagle, and specimens of the largest pheasant in the world, the Argus Pheasant. Just to the north of the Bird Park are the **Orchid** and **Hibiscus Gardens** (daily 9am–6pm; Sat & Sun RM1, otherwise free), where hundreds of plants are grown and sold; the hibiscus section especially provides a wonderful assault on the eye.

The main road through the gardens then weaves down past a field of deer, to the **Tun Abdul Razak Memorial**, a house built for the second Malaysian prime minister, who is commemorated by a collection of memorabilia inside, while his motorboat and golf trolley are ceremonially positioned outside. From here, you're only twenty minutes from the southern entrance (for access to the Muzium Negara). Beyond is the **lake** itself, which takes nearly an hour to walk around; on the lake's eastern shore you can rent boats and pedalos (RM5 gets you 30min on either) and buy food and drink from a number of stalls.

On a hill to the east of the lake is the **National Planetarium** (Tues–Sun 10am–7pm; RM1), housed in a building strongly reminiscent of a mosque, with a blue-domed roof, minaret tower and fountains cascading water along an imposing stairway. Aside from the usual shows, some in English, detailing the constellations, there are static displays illuminating the Islamic origins of astronomy as well as Malaysia's modern-day thrust for the stars via various satellite launches. For an extra RM6, you can enter the Space Theatre and watch one film from a daily changing programme of wide-screen IMAX movies. Those with cast-iron stomachs may also care to experience zero gravity in the Shuttle Spaceball (RM1), where the would-be astronaut is spun in three directions within a man-sized gyroscope – to the amusement of all onlookers. The viewing gallery on the fourth floor provides a panoramic view of Kuala Lumpur's skyline and the surrounding Lake Gardens.

Up a winding hill road to the west of the lake stands KL's most exclusive hotel, **Caracosa Seri Negara** (☎03/282 1888). This former colonial residence of the British Governor of the Malay States comprises two elegant whitewashed mansions – the "Caracosa", built in 1904 for Sir Frank Swettenham; and the "Seri Negara", formerly called the "Kings House", which was used for guests. The buildings were only returned to the Malaysian government in 1987, and in 1989, after a visit by Queen Elizabeth II, became a hotel. The hotel has since played host to virtually all visiting heads of state, but is also open to the public for lunch, dinner and a high tea (daily 3.30–6pm; around RM30). All the suites, costing over a thousand ringgit per night, come with their own butler, who meets guests at the airport and is on hand during their entire stay.

East of Merdeka Square: Jamek Mosque and Central Market

East of Merdeka Square, Lebuh Pasar Besar includes KL's busiest bridge, connecting the Colonial Quarter with the more frenetic life of the old commercial district on the east side of the Klang river. Just north of the bridge, on a promontory at the confluence

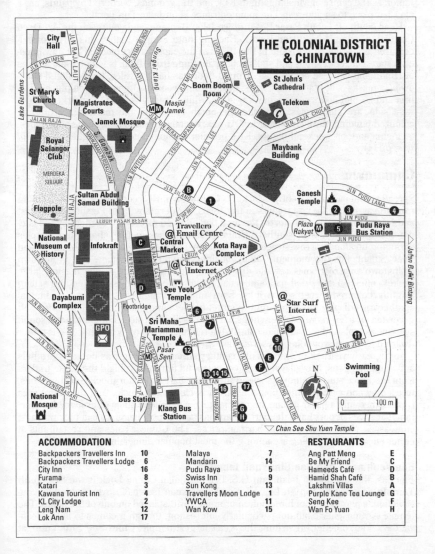

THE COLONIAL DISTRICT & CHINATOWN

ACCOMMODATION				RESTAURANTS	
Backpackers Travellers Inn	10	Malaya	7	Ang Patt Meng	E
Backpackers Travellers Lodge	6	Mandarin	14	Be My Friend	C
City Inn	16	Pudu Raya	5	Hameeds Café	D
Furama	8	Swiss Inn	9	Hamid Shah Café	B
Katari	3	Sun Kong	13	Lakshmi Villas	A
Kawana Tourist Inn	4	Travellers Moon Lodge	1	Purple Kane Tea Lounge	G
KL City Lodge	2	Wan Kow	11	Seng Kee	F
Leng Nam	12	YWCA	11	Wan Fo Yuan	H
Lok Ann	17	Wan Kow	15		

of the Klang and Gombak rivers, is KL's most attractive devotional building, the **Jamek Mosque** (open to visitors in between prayer times; free). It's a site replete with significance, since it was here – on a section of dry land carved out from the enveloping forest – that tin prospectors from Klang established a base in the 1850s, which soon turned into a boom town. The mosque, part of the second great period of expansion in KL, was completed in 1909 by the British architect A.B. Hubbock (see p.96), and incorporates features he had copied from Mogul mosques in North India – pink brick walls and arched colonnades, topped by oval cupolas and squat minarets. There's an intimacy here that isn't obvious at the much larger national mosque (which replaced the Jamek as the centre of Muslim faith in KL), and the grounds, bordered by palms, are a pleasant place to sit and rest. The main entrance is on Jalan Tun Perak.

Head south off Lebuh Pasar Besar down Jalan Benteng, and you reach the Art Deco **Central Market** (daily 9am–10pm). Backing onto Sungei Klang, this large pastel-coloured brick hangar was built in the 1920s as the capital's wet market, but now houses restaurants, craft shops and stalls selling anything from T-shirts to porcelain statues of Hindu and Chinese deities. The ground floor has batik textiles, hand-painted shadow-play masks, silk scarfs, hats, bags, baskets and wooden Orang Asli sculptures. The first and second floors contain hawker stalls, while directly outside the market, on the west side, are more cafés. Opposite the northern end of the market is a brightly coloured building, the Central Market **Annex**, containing some funky gift shops, cafés, a cinema and, on weekend nights, KL's premier predominately gay nightclub, *Liquid* (see p.114).

Chinatown

Spreading out east from Central Market is **Chinatown**, KL's commercial kernel, dating from the arrival of the first traders in the 1860s. Bordered by Jalan Petaling to the east and Jalan Tun Perak to the north, the area had adopted its current borders by the late-nineteenth century, with southern-Chinese shophouses, coffee shops and temples springing up along narrow streets such as Jalan Tun H.S. Lee (formerly Main St) and Jalan Sultan. For the moment, family businesses still predominate – a stroll down Chinatown's narrow lanes reveals dilapidated shops and Chinese pharmacies, large baskets of cured and dried meats alternating with the ranks of street vendors selling brightly coloured sweet soft drinks, soya milk and cigarette lighters. Traditional apothecaries display medicines on the street corners and quaint tea houses offer rich green tea for a few ringgit. Other shops here are as likely to stock computers and sound systems as tools and pots and pans, and what remains of the early architecture is rather dwarfed by the surrounding skyscrapers.

In the early years of the nineteenth century, **Jalan Petaling** was home to brothels and gambling dens. Nowadays, dozens of colourful umbrellas shield the street traders from the fierce sun, and tourists spend their time bargaining for mock Gucci watches, bric-a-brac and clothes. After 6pm the street is closed to vehicles and the entire area transformed into a pasar malam (night market), where food stalls offer *loong kee* (rectangular slices of pork) and deep-fried bananas, and expert hagglers can pick up bags, sunglasses, clothes and crafts at bargain prices. The Chinese cafés and restaurants at either end of Jalan Petaling are among the most popular dinnertime places in KL.

See Yeoh and Chan See Shu Yuen temples

Just past the junction of Jalan Tun H.S. Lee and Jalan Cheng Lock is the **See Yeoh Temple**, founded by Yap Ah Loy, KL's early headman (see p.82), who funded its construction; a photograph of him is often prominently displayed on one of the altars. The temple is atmospheric but not particularly interesting, though it comes to life on festival days. You're better off visiting the area's largest temple, **Chan See Shu Yuen**, at the very southern end of Jalan Petaling. The main deity here is Chong Wah, a Sung-dynasty emperor. The inner shrine is covered in scenes of lions, dragons and mythical creatures battling with warriors. Statues representing the temples' three deities stand behind a glass wall, with a mural of a brilliant-yellow sun above them. From outside, you can see the intricately carved roof, its images depicting more monumental events in Chinese history and mythology, and decorating the edge of the pavilion are blue-ceramic vases and small statues of peasants – the guardians of the temple – armed with poles crowned with lanterns.

Sri Maha Mariamman Temple

Oddly perhaps, KL's main Hindu shrine, the **Sri Maha Mariamman** temple, is also located in the heart of Chinatown, on Jalan Tun H.S. Lee, between the two main Buddhist temples. The earliest temple on this site was built in 1873 by Tamil immigrants and named after the Hindu deity, Mariamman, whose intercession was sought to provide protection against sickness and "unholy incidents". In the case of the Tamils, who had arrived to build the railways or work on the plantations, they needed all the solace they could find from the appalling rigours of their working life.

Significant renovation of the temple took place in the 1960s when sculptors from India were commissioned to design idols to adorn the five tiers of the gate tower – these now shine with gold embellishments, precious stones and exquisite Spanish and Italian tiles. Above the gate is a hectic profusion of Hindu gods, frozen in dozens of scenes from the *Ramayana*. Outside the pyramid-shaped entrance, garland-makers sell their wares, and sweetmeats and other delicacies are often available from nearby hawkers, making for a colourful scene most times of day.

During the Hindu **Thaipusam** festival, the temple's golden chariot is paraded through the streets on its route to the Batu Caves, on the northern edge of the city (see p.122). For the rest of the year, the chariot is kept in a large room in the temple; you can view it by asking an attendant to unlock the door.

The temple is always open to the public and is free to visit, although you may want to contribute a ringgit or so towards its upkeep. Visitors must leave their shoes at a rack situated to the left of the entrance and pay 10 sen to pick them up when leaving.

Chinatown's eastern edge

Chinatown's main west–east thoroughfares, Jalan Tun Perak and Jalan Cheng Lock (the latter the route of the original rail line through KL) converge at the Pudu Raya roundabout, just off which stands the **Malay Banking (Maybank) Building**. Built in the late 1980s by Hijas Kasturi, it's a structure typical of the new KL, designed with Islamic principles in mind (see p.94). Unlike many of the other modern skyscrapers here, there's actually a reason to venture inside – to visit either the small art gallery or the **Numismatic Museum** (Mon–Sat 10am–6pm; free), both on the main lobby floor. The latter is an unusually interesting collection, arranged in chronological fashion, starting with pre-coinage artefacts once used for transactions in Southeast Asia – tin ingots, gold dust and bars of silver or, for what the caption describes as "ordinary people", cowrie shells, rice and beads. Coins were gradually introduced into the region along with the arrival of the various colonizing powers; early sixteenth-century Portuguese coins on display are delicately engraved with miniatures of the Malay Peninsula and tiny kites billowing in the air. The first mass-produced coins, issued by the East India Company (see p.622), bore the company's coat of arms – a practice echoed later by timber and rubber companies, who until the late eighteenth century minted tokens to pay their expanding labour pool. The very first notes were produced by a private bank in 1694, although the first official notes were only issued at the end of the nineteenth century, by the British. During the Japanese invasion, the occupying administration produced its own notes which, after the Japanese surrender, the British diligently collected and stamped "not legal tender" and "specimen only".

Across the Pudu Raya roundabout from the Maybank, the bus station inhabits an oblong island in the wide road; also here is Plaza Rakyat LRT stop. North of here, a little street, Jalan Pudu Lama, is the location of KL's second most important Hindu shrine, the **Court Hill Ganesh Temple** (daily 9am–6pm; free), a small and often crowded place, with dozens of stalls outside selling garlands, incense, sweetmeats and charms. This was a favoured stop for visitors on their way to KL's original law courts, once sited nearby. Supplicants prayed to the chief deity, Lord Ganesh, who specializes in the removal of all obstacles to prosperity, peace and success.

Menara KL, Jalan Ampang and the Golden Triangle

Back at the Maybank building, Jalan Raja Chulan leads northeast past the Neoclassical-fronted headquarters of the state telephone company. The area north of the western stretch of the road is dominated by Bukit Nanas, on which stands the **Menara Kuala Lumpur** communications tower (daily 10am–10pm; RM8). To get here from Central Market, take bus #6a or #6b to the southern end of Jalan P. Ramlee, then walk up Jalan Punchak towards the tower, a short, steep hike. The tower, standing at 421 metres, is the tallest in Asia and the fourth tallest in the world. It's a striking addition to the KL skyline, nearly a match for the nearby Petronas Towers (see below), and is the best lookout from which to piece together the disparate parts of the city and its surroundings.

Designed in the shape of the *gasing*, or Malaysian spinning top, the Menara has become a popular tourist attraction. The foyer has the usual souvenir shops as well as a moneychanger, a post-office counter, a *McDonald's* serving a special Menara version of the Big Mac (four burgers in a bun), and a video room screening an informative film about the tower's construction. The entrance to the high-speed lifts is decorated with ornate tiles and mirrors, courtesy of craftsmen from Isfahan in Iran. The viewing gallery is on Level One, at the base of the bulbous portion at the tower's top. Immediately above it is *Seri Angkasa*, a revolving buffet-style restaurant which has to qualify as the city's most glittering dinner-date destination (see p.111).

Running along the northern side of Bukit Nanas, **Jalan Ampang** swings east out of the city. South of the section of the road between Jalan Sultan Ismail and Jalan Tun Razak lies the Kuala Lumpur City Centre (KLCC) development, whose centrepiece, the **Petronas Twin Towers**, is – at time of writing – the tallest building in the world (the Chongqing tower, under construction in China, will be taller). The entire site, once that of the Selangor Turf Club, was designed as a testimony to Malaysia's booming economic power. The towers house the offices of the national petroleum company, Petronas, several other multinational companies, and the Suria shopping mall. Critics already sneer that one of the towers is leaning (an unlikely story), but the gleaming multifaceted facade of this twenty-first-century complex is undeniably impressive. The **Podium** at the base of the towers contains the Petronas Concert Hall, the home of the National Orchestra, Dewan Filharmonik; an interactive Petroscience education centre; an art gallery containing the largest private collection in Malaysia; and a public library. At the back is a large public park, lake and garden.

The architecture along Jalan Ampang jumps back a hundred years as you head outwards. Mansions were built here with profits from the tin industry by Chinese *towkays* and British businessmen and administrators, whose architectural inspiration ranged from Islam to Art Deco. One mansion is now the tourist information office, MATIC, at no. 109 (see p.86), while a little further along on the same side of the road, another became *Le Coq D'Or* restaurant (p.111), supposedly built by one tin baron to impress another, who had refused to let his daughter marry him because he had once been too

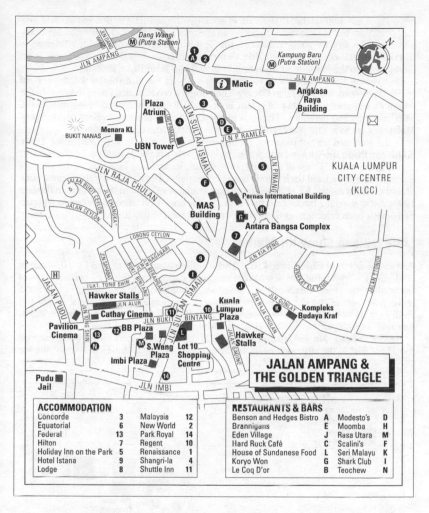

JALAN AMPANG & THE GOLDEN TRIANGLE

ACCOMMODATION				RESTAURANTS & BARS			
Concorde	3	Malaysia	12	Benson and Hedges Bistro	A	Modesto's	D
Equatorial	6	New World	2	Brannigans	E	Moomba	H
Federal	13	Park Royal	14	Eden Village	J	Rasa Utara	M
Hilton	7	Regent	10	Hard Rock Café	C	Scalini's	F
Holiday Inn on the Park	5	Renaissance	1	House of Sundanese Food	L	Seri Malayu	K
Hotel Istana	9	Shangri-la	4	Koryo Won	G	Shark Club	I
Lodge	8	Shuttle Inn	11	Le Coq D'or	B	Teochew	N

poor. Some of the surviving period residences along Jalan Ampang are now foreign embassies and high commissions, although others further east along Jalan Ampang were pulled down in the 1980s to make way for more modern developments, like the Ampang Shopping Complex, Yuan Chuan Plaza and City Square, all at the junction with Jalan Tun Razak, around 3km from the centre. Buses #23, #24, #173, #186 and #176 from opposite the Oriental Bank on Jalan Hang Lekir, come out this way, to the junction of Jalan Ampang and Jalan Tun Razak.

The Golden Triangle

The grid of roads south of Jalan Ampang – with Jalan Sultan Ismail and Jalan Bukit Bintang at its heart – comprises what locals refer to as the **Golden Triangle**, the nightlife and entertainment focus of the city. Here, among the hotels, shopping malls, neon signs and nightclubs, thousands of smartly dressed KL youths, expats and visitors drift from bar to club to shop, taking in the arts and handicraft stalls and food centres along the way. By public transport, the best way to get into the Golden Triangle is to take bus #29 or #60 from outside Central Market, or bus #30 or #40 from Jalan Gereja, east to the junction of Jalan Sultan Ismail and Jalan Bukit Bintang.

One reason for visiting the area during the day is the **Kompleks Budaya Kraf** (daily 10am–6pm; free) on Jalan Conlay. The complex contains two floors devoted to the country's wide range of arts and crafts, including silver-, pewter- and brassware, batik, woodcarvings and ceramics. This is a good opportunity to see excellent examples of Malaysia's crafts in one place, and to do some serious souvenir shopping.

In the southern part of the area, on the corner of Jalan Pudu and Jalan Hang Tuah, is the old **Pudu Jail**, its outside walls covered with what's claimed to be the longest mural in the world. The wall painting, of lush jungles and lazy beaches, is the work of the prisoners, who used their hands to apply the paint. The site is now the largest slice of real estate in central KL still awaiting commercial development. For a time in the late 1990s it was used for large-scale raves; the prisoners – who weren't invited to the parties – have been relocated to Sungei Buloh, 30km west of the city.

Little India to Chow Kit Market

Just to the north of Chinatown, **Little India** – the commercial centre for KL's Indian community – lies on the site of a Malay kampung dating from the very earliest days of the settlement. Much smaller than Chinatown, though equally fascinating, Little India is the main area in the city for buying silk goods, especially saris, *songket*s, scarfs and skull caps, as well as handmade jewellery. Along its lanes also lie some of the very best hawkers' stalls in the city, selling delicious Malay and Indian food (see p.109).

Head into **Jalan Masjid India** from Jalan Melayu, and it's soon clear you've entered the Tamil part of the city, with *poori* and samosa vendors and cloth salesmen vying for

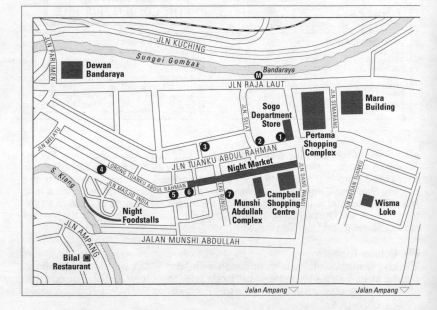

positions on the crowded streets outside the cafés and hotels. At the end of the street, ten minutes' walk north, Lorong Bunus leads off to the west to a small market, where you'll see **garland-makers** busy at their craft. There's a nightly pasar malam here, a good place to eat tandoori chicken and other Indian and Malay dishes. Also to the west off Jalan Masjid India, tucked away on the long, narrow Lorong Tuanku Abdul Razak, lies another night market selling clothes and a melange of odds and sods. The further into the market you go, the more you feel like you're in India – and you'll be in the company of very few tourists too.

Along Jalan TAR

KL's largest day market, Chow Kit, is 2km north of Little India, along **Jalan Tunku Abdul Rahman** (or **Jalan TAR** as it's always known). The street – named after the first prime minister of independent Malaysia – is at its most interesting at its extremities, so having dawdled around the southern end, head west to Jalan Raja Laut, where virtually any bus will take you north to Chow Kit (Jalan TAR carries southbound traffic only – an unsuccessful attempt at easing the city's chronic traffic congestion).

Along Jalan TAR, just east of the Bandaraya LRT stop, is the plain facade of the **Coliseum Hotel**, where the British owners of the rubber plantations once met to drink tumblers of whisky and water and eat steak. It's still one of KL's most characterful places, serving up hearty if overpriced meals (see p.110) and ice-cold beers; the adjacent Coliseum Cinema puts on a strict diet of kung-fu films, and Indian and Malay romances and dramas. On Saturday nights the section of Jalan TAR south of Jalan Dang Wangi becomes a **pasar malam** (6–11pm), KL's longest and busiest street market, strongest on food, soft drinks and kitchenware, and also selling clothes and toys.

Another five minutes' walk north from the Coliseum, down narrow Jalan Medan Tuanku, **Wisma Loke** (Mon–Fri 10am–6.30pm, Sat 10am–5pm) is a beautiful colonial

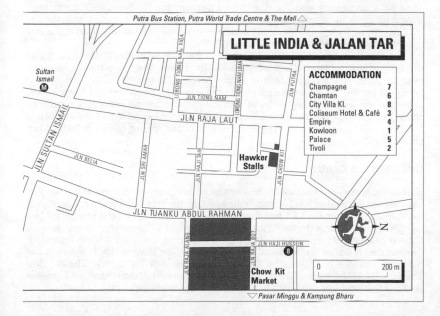

building. Once the home of Loke Yew, a Chinese business baron, it's now an antique and handicraft gallery, also known as the Artequarium (daily 9am–6pm). The display pieces – sandalwood and mahogany furniture, pewter and ceramic pots and jars – are rather overpriced, but looking them over gives you an excuse to poke around the white two-storey building, taking in the sumptuous interior with its ornate ceiling, blue floor tiles and exotic pillars.

Chow Kit Market

At the northern end of Jalan TAR, the entrance to **Chow Kit Market** (daily 9am–5pm) is announced by a gaggle of stalls crowding the pavements – the best place in KL to buy cheap secondhand clothes. Heading here up Jalan Raja Laut by bus, you should get off at Jalan Haji Taib and walk east for five minutes, crossing Jalan TAR to the market entrance. Inside you pass a warren of stalls selling colourful Islamic textiles and fabrics on one side, and delicious Malay takeaway fare – excellent *roti canai*, *teh tarek* and high-quality *nasi campur* – on the other. Soon you're amid the city's largest raw produce market, precariously traversing plankways leading past stalls laden with meat, fish, vegetables, spices, tofu and fruit. You'll be pressed to buy worms – for eating – squirming in baskets, while crabs and lobsters crawl around in near-empty tubs of water. In addition to food there are shoes, cassettes and fabrics on sale. This all adds up to one of the most interesting places in KL to spend your day, though more lurid accounts in some newspapers suggest it's also the haunt of pickpockets and drug addicts; the police regularly trawl the area in the early morning for illegal aliens (usually Indonesians) supposedly orchestrating nefarious activities.

Kampung Bahru

Ten minutes' walk east of Chow Kit Market along Jalan Raja Alang is **Kampung Bahru**, the oldest Malay residential area in KL, founded in 1899. From the Putra LRT line's Kampung Bahru stop, the district is a pleasant one-kilometre walk north, over Sungei Klang. At the junction of Jalan Raja Alang and Jalan Raja Abdullah stands the district's **mosque**, built in 1924, a strong concrete structure at odds with most of the surrounding traditional Malay wooden houses.

Continuing along Jalan Raja Alang, at the junction with Jalan Raja Muda Musa, a narrow twist of lebuhs houses the Sunday market, the **Pasar Minggu**, actually a Saturday evening event, running from 6pm to 1am. There's a thoroughly Malay atmosphere here, and poking around turns up a number of jewellery, handicraft and fabric shops, alongside the usual hawker stalls. In particular, there are two excellent handicraft shops located where the main, narrow market street branches off from Jalan Raja Muda Musa, as well as a number of stalls which sell batik and *songket* fabrics at knockdown prices.

Out from the centre

KL's urban sprawl is infamous. Main drags south like Jalan Syed Putra and Jalan Tun Sambanthan are choked solid at rush hour although the volume of traffic has lightened to some degree since the LRT and Komuter transport systems kicked into gear. Most visitors take one look at the traffic and decide to stay put within the city centre until it's time to move on. It's worth venturing into the suburbs, though, for some rewarding destinations, not least the **National Art Gallery** on the main orbital highway at the northern extreme if KL, nearby **Lake Titiwangsa** and the terrific **Thean Hou Temple**, just to the south of the city. A little way southwest of the centre, the **Bangsar** area is a fashionable suburb with bars, cafés and ice-cream parlours.

The National Art Gallery and Lake Titiwangsa

One of a trio of new, beautifully designed sloping tropical buildings along Jalan Tun Razak, the orbital highway north of the centre, the **National Art Gallery** (daily 10am–6pm; free) stands at the junction with Jalan Temerloh. Its collection is decent enough, though not thoroughly representative given the dynamism prevalent in Malaysian art. The ground floor is given over to temporary exhibitions, usually of painting, sculpture or photography from Malaysia and other Southeast Asian countries, with the permanent collection occupying the first and second floors. If you were hoping to expand your knowledge of Malaysian artists here, you'll be disappointed by the poorly annotated collection, which provides only the artists' names and dates of the works. There are some good examples of colourful and exciting work, especially in the landscapes and portraits offering historical insights into another, more rural Malaysia, where the making of handicrafts and playing of music, depicted in these images, predominate. But the most outstanding work is of a much darker hue: Ooi Kooi Hin's *It's So Quiet* features a woman screaming in a room of corpses. On the brighter side, Lucy Liew's exuberant work *Colours Of Hornbills* captures the wonders of nature beautifully.

Set in a small park close off Jalan Pahang, 300m north of the Art Gallery, the oval-shaped **Lake Titiwangsa** is usually swamped with locals who come to the boathouse on the western side of the lake, ten minutes' walk from the main road here, to rent boats (RM5 an hour) for getting out onto the water. There are concrete walkways through the landscaped park, but most people don't do anything too energetic. The best thing by far is to head for one of the numerous hawker stalls nearby, though many people eat at the *Nelayan Titiwangsa Restaurant* (see p.112), on the lake's northwestern edge.

To get to the lake, catch buses #172, #169 or #170 from Lebuh Ampang on the northern edge of Chinatown; ask for the lake stop, and you'll be dropped off at Tawakal Hospital on Jalan Pahang. Walk north along here for ten minutes then turn right onto Jalan Kuantan – the lake is 100m up on the left.

Thean Hou Temple

KL's huge and colourful Buddhist **Thean Hou Temple** (daily 9am–6pm; free), completed in 1987, is located on a hilltop 3km south of the city centre, between a sacred bodhi tree and a 100-year-old Buddhist shrine. The temple is always busy, with busloads of tourists descending for the marvellous views north over the city and south to the satellite town of Petaling Jaya (see p.128). It's also the most popular place in KL for Chinese marriages, and has its own registry office on the first floor of the temple complex.

The main focus of excitement is the pagoda, in whose inner temple stands the shrine to Thean Hou's main deity, Kuan Yin, the Goddess of Mercy, who – legend has it – appears on earth in a variety of forms and can be identified by the precious dew flask which she always holds. The decor is as ornate as you'd expect, with a ceiling whose intricate patterns contain hundreds of green lanterns. In the centre of the line of sculpted deities sits Thean Hou, with Kuan Yin to her right, in front of whom visitors gather to burn offerings of joss sticks and paper money.

The easiest way to get here is by bus #27 or #52 from Klang bus station, getting off at Wisma Belia on Jalan Syed Putra (tell the driver you want to be let off at the temple). From here, the temple is five minutes' walk east up a steep hill on the right.

Bangsar

Three kilometres west of Brickfields is the **Bangsar** district. Until the early 1990s, the small grid of streets around Jalan Bangsar was a quiet, middle-class residential area with a few good cafés and a popular pasar malam. Nowadays, it's the trendiest area in KL to eat and drink in the evening, with dozens of excellent restaurants, busy bars and two hawkers' areas (see map, overleaf). The beauty of Bangsar is that there are so

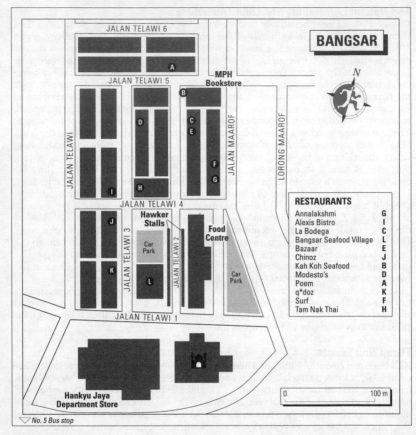

JALAN TELAWI 6

BANGSAR

JALAN TELAWI 5

MPH Bookstore

N

JALAN TELAWI

JALAN MAAROF

LORONG MAAROF

JALAN TELAWI 4

Hawker Stalls

JALAN TELAWI 3

Car Park

JALAN TELAWI 2

Food Centre

Car Park

RESTAURANTS	
Annalakshmi	G
Alexis Bistro	I
La Bodega	C
Bangsar Seafood Village	L
Bazaar	E
Chinoz	J
Kah Koh Seafood	B
Modesto's	D
Poem	A
q*doz	K
Surf	F
Tam Nak Thai	H

JALAN TELAWI 1

Hankyu Jaya Department Store

0   100 m

▽ No. 5 Bus stop

many places to go within easy walking distance of one another, including several good bookshops and a couple of Internet cafés. The pasar malam, still held every Saturday, is one of the best in the Klang Valley area, selling fresh food, hardware, kitchenware and clothing. The easiest way to get here is to take bus #5 from the Jalan Sultan Mohammed terminus (see p.87); the last bus back to the centre goes at around 11pm (a taxi to the centre should cost no more than RM5).

Eating

KL boasts an extraordinary number of hawker stalls, coffee shops and restaurants, many of which are very cheap and offer a high standard of cooking. The vast majority of eating places serve **Malay**, **Chinese** or **Indian food**, though international cuisine is becoming more popular, with Italian, Japanese, Thai, Korean, and Western fast-food outlets ever present.

Locals make little distinction between eating at inexpensive **hawker stalls** and pricier **restaurants** – the quality of food at a stall is usually just as good, and the regional dishes many of them offer aren't available in the restaurants. To try certain dishes, however, like sharks'-fin soup and bird's-nest soup, you'll need to dine out at one of the big hotels. Though most Malay restaurants in KL serve only a limited range of dishes, finding good Chinese or Tamil and North Indian food is much easier – try cafés and restaurants in Chinatown and Little India. In the latter especially, the cafés and hawkers do a manic trade, offering up excellent curries served on banana leaves, *murtabak*, *dosai* and *roti*.

Hawker stalls

Traditionally, **hawker stalls** were open-air affairs, and many of these still line the traffic-choked roads in little enclaves throughout the city. Increasingly, however, stalls are found grouped together in food courts inside buildings such as shopping malls; the food is usually no more expensive than outside, but the surroundings are often air-conditioned and less cramped.

Indoor

Unless specified, indoor hawker stalls tend to open between 10am and 10pm daily; a few Muslim-run stalls close on Fridays.

Ampang Shopping Complex, at the junction of Jalan Ampang and Jalan Tun Razak. The food court in this hi-tech mall offers a mix of international and Asian fare, designed to please Ampang's middle classes.

Central Market, first and second floors, Jalan Hang Kasturi. Best are the superb Malay stalls on the first floor, where plates of *nasi campur* cost just RM2.

Jalan Sultan Ismail Behind the *Hilton*, near the junction with Jalan Raja Chulan. The stalls here open late morning for *nasi campur*, Malay salad (*ulam*), Chinese noodles, Indian and Malay curries and fried fish. There are also fresh juice and beer vendors here.

Jalan Telawi Tiga Food Centre, Jalan Telawi Tiga, Bangsar. Compared to the glittery surroundings, this is a rather plain building, but the food is great, with outstanding Indian tandoori stalls. Take any Bangsar bus from the Jalan Sultan Mohammed stop just south of Central Market.

Medan Hang Tuah, basement and fourth floor, *The Mall*, Jalan Putra. Dozens of stalls here sell everything from burgers to Chinese steamboats. In the basement is a mix of Chinese noodle dishes and Malay *nasi* options.

Pudu Raya bus station, first floor, Jalan Pudu. A dozen stalls in busy, hot surroundings, serving a mix of Chinese, Malay and Indian *nasi*, *roti* and noodles. This place keeps longer hours than many, and a few stalls are open all night.

Semua House, basement, junction of Jalan Melayu and Jalan Masjid India. Very popular and crowded lunchtime spot, where you can opt for a fabulous *nasi campur*, or an equally good banana-leaf curry washed down with tea, juice or *lassi*.

Sungei Wang Plaza Hawker Centre, on the fourth floor of this mall, 500m from the southern end of Jalan Sultan Ismail. A crowded food centre selling Malay and Chinese fast food.

Outdoor

Some outdoor stalls open early, providing a nourishing breakfast for people on their way to work, while others don't kick off until 6pm or 7pm, but then stay open until 2am (even later in the Golden Triangle).

Chow Kit Market, Jalan Sultan. At the top end of Chow Kit Market there are some wonderful *roti canai* and *nasi campur* stalls. Daily 8am–7pm.

Dayabumi Complex, Jalan Raja Laut. This collection of stalls, in a courtyard next to the Dayabumi skyscraper, is good for light lunches and fruit juices.

Jalan Alur, Golden Triangle. A wide street with lots of Chinese cafés which put tables out into the street after dark. If you like fried chicken wings, this is the best place to go in KL. Open from 7pm.

Jalan Masjid India, Little India. There are dozens of excellent food stalls, both Indian and Malay, along the main street. Although lunchtime is when the number of stalls open is at its peak, there's still plenty to eat until 11pm.

Jalan Telawi Tiga, Bangsar. Behind the *Jalan Telawi Tiga Food Centre* (see overleaf) are a dozen or so excellent stalls including Korean, North Indian tandoori and Malay. Take any Bangsar bus from Jalan Sultan Mohamed, near Central Market. Open from 6pm.

Jalan Thambapillai, off Jalan Tun Sambanthan, Brickfields. A cluster of predominantly Chinese cafés, though *Sri Vani's Corner* – just beside the *YMCA* – is renowned as the best tandoori hawker in KL. Plenty of buses from Klang station pass by the area. Stalls open 6pm; closed Mon.

Jalan Tun H.S. Lee and Jalan Petaling market. Essentially a wet-fish (and meat and veg) market occupying an area between these two streets, this place also has some great Chinese noodle stalls in this warren of plankways reached via narrow openings halfway down either street. Open early morning till 6pm. Look out also for a couple of Chinese stalls on Lorong Petaling, which is the first lane running parallel to Jalan Petaling on the eastern side. These open at around 7pm and are superb for favourites like Hokkien *mee*.

Restaurants and cafés

All the **restaurants and cafés** listed below are open daily from 11am or noon until midnight, unless otherwise stated. Most restaurants stay open throughout the year, though note that most Malay restaurants close during Ramadan, opening instead after sunset, and staying open until midnight. Most places are closed during the two-day Hari Raya festivals. **Phone numbers** are given below where it's necessary to reserve a table in advance.

It's difficult to be precise about **prices** at KL restaurants, save to say that you'll generally spend more than at a hawker stall, but rarely have to fork out more than RM30 per person. That said, even in top-class restaurants it's possible to sit down and just order a plate of noodles; the reviews give an idea of how much you can generally expect to pay for an decent meal. It's worth looking out for eat-all-you-want buffets and special deals at the top hotels (see the "Time Out" section of Thursday's edition of the *Sun* and the weekly *Day & Night* magazine for details).

Central KL

Ang Patt Meng Café, 97 Jalan Petaling, Chinatown. There are many cheap Chinese cafés like this, serving morning noodles and, after midday, *nasi campur* with meat, fish and vegetable dishes.

Be My Friend Café, Central Market Annex. Sandwiches, salads, jacket potatoes and beer in stylish surroundings. Good terrace from which to watch the comings and goings around the market. On Friday and Saturday nights it metamorphoses into the terrace for the vibrant house-music club, *Liquid*.

Bilal Restaurant, 33 Jalan Ampang. At the western, city-centre, end of Jalan Ampang, this is one of KL's most revered North Indian restaurants, particularly popular for its chicken and mutton curries and *naan*s. Prices are reasonable, at about RM20 for two people.

Coliseum Café, 98 Jalan TAR. Colonial hotel-restaurant famous for it's shuffling service and sizzling steaks; also offers chicken, fish, salads, and Chinese dishes. Steak meals are overpriced at around RM30 per person.

Hameeds Café, ground floor, Central Market. Superb, busy, North Indian and Malay café, serving tandoori chicken, curries and rice dishes. Open when the market's open – a good air-conditioned spot for *roti* in the morning and fish-head curry later on.

Hamid Shah Café, 30 Jalan Silang, Chinatown. Excellent, busy, café for Malay and North Indian curries and *roti*. Very good value at around RM10–12 for two people. Daily 8am–6pm.

Kenanga Seafood Restaurant, first floor, MARA Building, Jalan Raja Laut. Malay restaurant noted for its squid, crab and prawn dishes – from around RM20 a head.

Lakshmi Villas, Lebuh Ampang, Little India. On the edge of Chinatown, this is the best South Indian café in KL. The ground floor serves various *dosais*; the first floor specialises in banana-leaf curries. A bargain at around RM6 for two people. Closes at 7pm.

Old China Café, 11 Jalan Balai Polis, off Jalan Petaling. Legendary Chinatown place, serving traditional Nonya cuisine in a genteel setting – the antiques around the place give the impression you're eating in an opulent Chinese parlour. Pricey, but worth the extra expense.

Purple Cane Tea Lounge, Lebuh Sultan, Chinatown. This third-floor place offers a good opportunity to learn about different types of tea and try sticky Chinese sweets. It also runs a shop, stocking all manner of infusions, on the corner of Lebuh Sultan and Jalan Sultan.

Santa's Restoran, 7 Jalan Tun H.S. Lee, at the street's northern end. This lively place has delicious chapatis and curries – RM5 gets you a chapati, rice and a choice of curries.

Seng Kee Restaurant, 100 Jalan Petaling, Chinatown. Frenetically busy restaurant with great prawn and duck dishes, at around RM25 for two people.

Wan Fo Yuan Vegetarian Restaurant, Lebuh Sultan, Chinatown. The area's best-known vegetarian restaurant, serving excellent tofu and vegetable dishes.

Golden Triangle

Benson & Hedges Bistro, in the *Embassy* hotel, Jalan Ampang. Fifty metres east of junction with Jalan Sultan Ismail. Popular European-style café with a lively atmosphere; specializes in pasta, sandwiches, coffees and pastries. Around RM30 for two people.

Eden Village, 260 Jalan Raja Chulan (☎03/241 4027). Popular family restaurant, with dozens of types of fish cooked Cantonese style. A meal for two costs around RM80.

Golden Phoenix, at the *Hotel Equatorial*, Jalan Sultan Ismail (☎03/261 7777). Top-of-the-range Chinese restaurant specializing in exotic seafood dishes; expect to spend over RM30 a head.

Hard Rock Café, *Concorde Hotel*, 2 Jalan Sultan Ismail. The usual burgers, steaks and salad for around RM20 a head (drinks extra), accompanied by loud music and pop and rock artefacts.

House Of Sundanese Food, L2, ground floor, Lot 10, Jalan Bukit Bintang (☎03/248 7323). Excellent Indonesian restaurant with reasonable prices. House specialities include dishes like *gado-gado* and beef *rendang*.

Koryo-Won, Antara Bangsa Complex, 37 Jalan Sultan Ismail (☎03/242 0425). Next to the *Hilton*. This top Korean restaurant specializes in spicy meat and fish dishes. Expensive, but makes a nice change.

Le Coq d'Or, 121 Jalan Ampang (☎03/242 9732). Housed in a converted tin *towkay*'s mansion, full of atmosphere, it's worth visiting just for a drink on the veranda if you don't want to eat. The French, Malay and Chinese dishes aren't at all bad, though, and shouldn't set you back more than RM40 a head. Dress smartish.

The Lodge, cnr of Jalan Raja Chulan and Jalan Sultan Ismail. This outdoor restaurant, part of the *Lodge* hotel, is popular with foreigners and Malaysians alike for its excellent and affordable steaks and grilled fish.

Modesto's, Jalan Perak, just off Jalan P. Ramlee (☎03/248 9924). This sprawling pizza-and-pasta joint also has a lively bar.

Moomba, UOA Centre, 19 Jalan Pinang (☎03/262 8226). Passable effort at cutting-edge Australian cuisine – barramundi fillets, mud crabs, baby lamingtons for dessert – in a split-level space. Expect to pay around RM25 a head.

Rasa Utara, BB Plaza, Jalan Bukit Bintang. A northern Malay menu characterizes this busy restaurant; try the *ayam percik*. Moderately priced.

Scalini's, 19 Jalan Sultan Ismail (☎03/245 3211). The most stylish Italian restaurant in town, on a hill up above the traffic of the Golden Triangle. Alfresco dining is an option, as is a drink at the long wooden bar. Around RM40 a head.

Seri Angkasa, Menara KL (☎03/208 5055). Revolving restaurant which serves excellent lunches, high teas and dinner buffets atop KL's landmark communications tower. Breathtaking views guaranteed. Smart dress (no shorts and sandals) essential for dinner, which costs around RM55 a head.

Shang Palace, *Shangri-La Hotel*, Jalan Sultan Ismail (☎03/241 6572). One of the most popular places in KL for *dim sum*; dinner, too, is highly regarded but not cheap.

Soho's, first floor, Wisma Peladang. Next to Lot 10, Jalan Bukit Bintang. Upmarket Italian place, specializing in Tuscan cuisine, for KL sophisticates. Among the best fare on offer are its imaginative salads. Around RM50 for two people.

The Taj, *Federal Hotel*, Jalan Bukit Bintang (☎03/248 9166). Award-winning top-of-the-range Indian restaurant famous for its *naans*, *lassi* and chicken tandoori.

Teochew Restaurant, 272 Jalan Pudu. Well-known and extremely busy Chinese restaurant, noted especially for its high-quality *dim sum* (served daytime only) at around RM50 for two people.

North of the centre

Cili Padi Thai Restaurant, second floor, The Mall, Jalan Putra. To get here, take the LRT to the PWTC stop. Excellent, moderately priced Thai restaurant, good on Bangkok-style cuisine, including elaborate chicken and seafood dishes.

Hoshigaoka Restaurant, The Mall, Jalan Putra. Superb Japanese food at reasonable prices – sushi is around RM6 a portion and set meals start from RM12. There's a more central branch at Lot 10 Shopping Centre, Jalan Bukit Bintang, in the Golden Triangle.

Museum Restaurant, *The Legend Hotel*, 100 Jalan Putra (☎03/442 9888). Award-winning Chinese restaurant serving Cantonese and Teochew cuisine amid beautifully displayed antiques and paintings. Also worth checking out is the same hotel's Japanese *Gen* restaurant, which does good-value set lunches.

Nelayan Titiwangsa Restaurant, Jalan Kuantan, off Jalan Pahang, Lake Titiwangsa (☎03/422 8600). Take bus #172, #169 or #170 from Lebuh Ampang, and get off at the Tawakul Hospital on Jalan Pahang, from where Jalan Kuantan is a ten-minute walk north; the restaurant is beside the entrance to the lake. Built on a floating platform, this seafood restaurant serves Malay and Chinese dishes. Though meals here are overpriced, at around RM50 for two, the price includes a show of traditional Malay song and dance.

Bangsar

For a map of Bangsar, see p.108.

Alexis Bistro, 29 Jalan Telawi Tiga (☎03/284 2880). Big helpings of designer food for the cappuccino set, and lots of magazines to read if you want to pass some time. You can eat well here for around RM25 per head.

Annalakshmi, 46 Jalan Maarof (☎03/282 3799). Most people opt for the as-much-as-you-can-eat buffet, with delicious vegetable curries, *daal* and pastries at this excellent South Indian vegetarian restaurant. It's a fine place and reasonably priced at around RM20 a head.

Bangsar Seafood Village, Jalan Telawi Tiga. Over-expensive seafood specialist, attractively located in a large garden.

Bazaar, 18 Jalan Telawi Dua (☎03/282 4492). Turkish cuisine in a restaurant that successfully captures a Mediterranean feel. Around RM20 a head.

Chinoz, 43 Jalan Telawi Tiga (☎03/283 1231). A mix of Eastern and Western dishes, including gourmet sandwiches. A little on the expensive side (around RM30 per head) for what it does.

Kah Koh Seafood, junction of Jalan Telawi Lima and Jalan Telawi Dua. Cramped corner place with about the best Chinese food in the whole KL area. Their cashew chicken and chilli chicken are quite out of this world.

La Bodega, 16 Jalan Telawi Dua. Spanish-style tapas bar with excellent food, including good paella, and a youthful clientele. Around RM20 for two people.

Modesto's, 12a Jalan Telawi Tiga. Bangsar outlet of the pasta and pizza joint in Jalan Perak. There's a pool table and seats outside for watching the passing parade.

Poem, 38a Jalan Telawi Lima (☎03/284 1977). Cool, stylish cybercafé, with several terminals on which to surf the Internet (RM6 for 30min). The set dinner is RM20, with cheaper snacks and drinks available.

q*doz, 57 Jalan Telawi Tiga (☎03/284 3699). Perhaps Bangsar's most stylish restaurant, with adventurous dishes and a good selection of wine. Not cheap but worth splashing out on.

Surf, 54 Jalan Maarof. The interior waterfall at this cybercafé provides a tranquil atmosphere in which to plug in to the information highway (RM15 per hour). Western food and beer available.

Tam Nak Thai, 27 Jalan Telawi Tiga. One of a chain of Thai restaurants popular with locals. Offers vegetarian and spicy *tom yam* dishes at reasonable prices.

Brickfields

To get here, head to the Jalan Sultan Mohammed terminus and take bus #5, which takes you down Jalan Tun Sambanthan, Brickfields' main street.

Ghandi, Jalan Thunbapillai. Recommended Indian vegetarian restaurant that also sells Indian spices and other groceries.

Ikan Bakar, Jalan Thunbapillai. Specializes in seafood – you choose your fish from a tank and can watch it being cooked at the pavement kitchen. The barbecued stingray in banana leaves is delicious. The fish are priced by weight, so you may want to check how much your selection will cost before finalizing your order.

Puteri Restaurant, 146 Jalan Tun Sambanthan. One of a number of good North Indian cafés in Brickfields, with fine *roti canai* and curries.

Sri Devi Restaurant, Jalan Travers. Brickfields' best, selling excellent banana leaf curries from midday onwards and wonderful *dosai*s all day. Extremely cheap.

Drinking and nightlife

KL has a growing number of excellent bars and fashionable clubs and discos, mostly in the Golden Triangle and Bangsar districts. The **bars** here, often called pubs (a hangover from the British colonial presence), are a draw not just for British and Australian expats but also for well-heeled Malaysians. Beer is relatively expensive throughout KL – usually RM6–7 a glass – but many places have "happy hours", when the price drops by a couple of dollars. Most bars are open throughout the day from noon onwards, and close at midnight; karaoke bars – for which the seemingly insatiable appetite shows no sign of abating in KL – tend to open from 9pm to 1 or 2am, and don't have a cover charge. Many of the larger places feature live music, usually covers of Western and Malay hits performed by Indonesian or Filipino bands.

The music played in KL's **clubs** is mostly US and British house music, with mainstream international soul tracks and Malay hits putting in an appearance, and techno and drum-and-bass increasing in popularity. Most clubs have "ladies' nights" during the week, when entrance is free for women. KL now also has its own **rave** scene, with frequent large-scale one-off events boasting international DJs. Both clubs and rave venues usually open at around 9pm, though nothing much tends to happen before midnight; the clubs generally close at 3am, although raves and an increasing number of clubs run through until morning. Entrance charges are high, around RM20 for clubs and more for raves. Club **listings** can be found in the daily "Metro" section of the *Star* newspaper and in the events section in the *Malay Mail*; the monthly *ETC* magazine, available at newsagents, lists the larger events. Leaflets given out in Central Market and in the Golden Triangle's shopping malls (notably BB Plaza) advertise new clubs and bars with DJs. For some background on the Malaysian pop and traditional music scenes, see p.64.

KL is a **safe** city at night as well as during the day, with few offensive drunks or any threatening drug-related activity to be seen. It's easy to get around by **taxi** during the small hours (call for a taxi if you can't find one in the streets – it usually arrives promptly); you seldom pay more than RM10 to travel from the heart of town back out to the suburbs.

Bars and pubs

Brannigans, Lorong Perak, just off Jalan P. Ramlee. Unsubtle two-floor bar and disco, popular with the expat crowd. There's a RM10 cover charge at weekends. Mon–Fri 5pm–2am, Sat & Sun 5pm–3am.

Bull's Head, Central Market, Jalan Benteng. A very busy bar, popular with expats, tourists and business people alike. Closes at midnight.

Coliseum Hotel, 98 Jalan TAR. Always busy, the *Coliseum* bar has a rich history and relaxed atmosphere. The work of Malaysia's foremost cartoonist, Lat, is displayed on the walls. Daily 10am–10pm.

Echo Jazz Bar, Jalan Telawi 2, Bangsar. KL's trendiest bar for cold beer, cocktails and conversation in a comfortable setting. The evening begins with jazz on record, with DJs playing house later on. Daily 6pm–2am.

Lai-Lai Karaoke Lounge, Sungei Wang Plaza, Jalan Sultan Ismail, Golden Triangle. Close to the junction with Jalan Bukit Bintang, this is KL's best karaoke bar.

Modesto's, Jalan Perak, just off Jalan P. Ramlee. As well as having a restaurant (see p.111), this place has a busy bar with table-top football, pool and darts.

The Pub, *Shangri-La Hotel*, Jalan Sultan Ismail. In KL's most opulent hotel, this is better than most hotel bars, with a good atmosphere. Open to residents and non-residents alike.

Riverbank, Central Market, Jalan Benteng. Well-placed bar, opposite the river, with occasional live music. It's also handy for the cultural performances at the nearby bandstand.

Ronnie Q's, 32 Jalan Telawi Dua, Bangsar. You'll love this long-established bar if you're into watching reruns of soccer matches on small portable TV screens and rubbing shoulders with KL's older expat businessmen.

Discos and clubs

Backroom/Sparks, 8 Lorong P. Ramlee, off Jalan P. Ramlee. Behind the *Shangri-La Hotel*. KL's largest dance-music club, *Backroom*, features top international DJs playing global house, techno and drum 'n' bass, as well as the best of the home-grown talent, who play mostly US house. In another vast room here is *Sparks*, the premier Cantonese techno club in KL, with hundreds of Chinese Malaysians going crazy to 160bpm Hong Kong hits. Worth visiting just for the extraordinary contrast between the two. RM30 admission covers both places and pays for one free drink. Thurs–Sat 10pm–6am.

Baze-2, Yow Chuan Plaza, near the intersection of Jalan Tun Razak and Jalan Ampang. Busy discotheque frequented by KL's more well-heeled night hawks; soul, reggae and house music is on offer. Wed–Sat 8pm–3am.

The Embassy, Jalan Ampang, near the intersection with Jalan Tun Razak. Long-standing discotheque attracting a 30- and 40-something set. RM20. Fri & Sat 10pm–4am.

The Jump, 241 Jalan Tun Razak. Restaurant/bar with a fun discotheque. Ladies' night is Wednesday, with free entrance and free drinks for women.

Gay KL

KL has a decent **gay and lesbian** scene, with a number of bars, clubs and gay-friendly cafés. In addition to the venues listed below, *Backroom* (see above) is another popular gay hangout.

Blue Moon, *Hotel Equatorial*, Jalan Sultan Ismail. Opposite the MAS Building. This gay-friendly bar, popular with KL's gay crowd, is the only place in town where you'll hear Malaysian golden oldies from the 1950s, French schmaltz and Malaysia's most famous singer, the golden-voiced baritone, P. Ramlee. Daily 7pm–midnight.

Boom Boom Room, 11 Lebuh Ampang. A gay disco hangout, where the vocal end of house music reigns and a twice-nightly drag show create a winning combination.

Liquid, Central Market Annexe. *The* KL dance-music success story and one of the best house clubs anywhere, with a mostly young, gay clientele in a perfect little venue with a terrace overlooking Sungei Klang and the General Post Office. Uplifting house and Euro-trance are the order of the night, cocktails and cold beers on the terrace the perfect chill-out option. RM10. Fri & Sat 10pm–3am.

Entertainment and art

KL's cultural scene, though still relatively small for its size, is growing rapidly. The recent opening of the **National Theatre** (☎03/245 2525), on Jalan Tun Razak, gives the National Theatre Company and the National Symphony Orchestra a spacious, modern home. Performances here include classical music, national and international theatre, and dance. KL also has some excellent **fringe theatre companies**, including the Five Arts Centre, Straits Theatre Company and Instant Café. Look in the listings sections of the *New Straits Times, Malay Mail,* the *Star* and the *Sun* for details of performances, as none of these groups are based in a particular venue. For general entertainment **list-**

ings, check the weekly magazine *Day & Night*, the "Time Out" section in Thursday's edition of the *Sun* newspaper, and the "Metro" section in the tabloid *Malay Mail*, which has the most comprehensive details of concerts, films, plays, clubs and art exhibitions.

Art and sculpture

KL is developing a strong **visual arts** scene, with numerous, mostly private, galleries, listed below, stocked with new work and visiting exhibitions, notably from Southeast Asian countries. Banks and oil companies – such as the state-owned Petronas, which runs the gallery in Petronas Twin Towers – sponsor art and sculpture in KL; in the case of the Maybank's pioneering ground-floor gallery, this has led to dozens of Malay (and increasingly Indian and Chinese Malaysian) artists selling their work and gaining international reputations. One young artist, H.H. Lim, now lives in Rome where he is building a big reputation. Working in mixed media, he creates installations which incorporate painting, sculpture, video and performance; his work can be seen in the Maybank Gallery. Another brilliant young artist is Sylvia Lee Goh from Penang. Her exotic oil paintings are rich in colour, detail and texture, often reflecting her Baba-Nonya background; a number of her works can be seen at the Galeri Petronas. The older generation of Malaysian artists include colourful abstract painters like Ismael Latiff, S. Chandhiran and Tajuddin Ismail, and more naturalistic artists whose work reflects everyday life: Rahmat Ramli, Maamor Jantan and Sani Mohammed Dom; some of these are represented in the Maybank Gallery. **Sculpture** in public places is also a growth area; among the impressive works in the city are Lee Kiew Sing's *Vision 2020* outside the Public Bank on Jalan Raja Laut, and Syed Ahmad Jamal's iron and marble figures at the UNBC Building on Jalan Kuching.

Art Folio, second floor, City Square, 182 Jalan Tun Razak. Stacks of watercolours, oil paintings and ceramics, at high prices.

Art House, second floor, Wisma Stephens, Jalan Raja Chulan, Golden Triangle. Specializes in Chinese brush paintings and ceramics.

Collectors' Focus, Lot T, 137, third floor, City Square, 182 Jalan Tun Razak.. A good place to check out affordable works of art.

Galeri Petronas, Petronas Twin Towers, KLCC. Large space with excellent temporary exhibitions, often on naturalistic themes such as the rainforest or the oceans.

Impression Arts, first floor, Wisma Stephens, Jalan Raja Chulan, Golden Triangle. Another commercial outlet for KL's artistic talent.

Maybank Gallery, ground floor, Maybank Building, Pudu Raya roundabout. KL's most influential art gallery, with shows that change monthly – the best place to gain an insight into contemporary Malaysian art.

National Art Gallery, Jalan Tun Razak. The first-floor gallery is of rather mixed quality, but the second-floor displays on ASEAN artists are well worth a look, as is the beautiful building, the interior of which resembles the Guggenheim in New York.

Cinemas

Cinema is popular in KL, and of more interest to visitors now that there is a trend away from single-screen cinemas showing Malay, Cantonese or Tamil films towards cineplexes, which show more commercial international films – US and Indian blockbusters are the most popular among the locals. Some of these films are dubbed into Malay, but the Western ones are usually kept in the mother tongue. Listings for cinemas appear in the papers given above; tickets at all cinemas cost around RM10–15.

Central Market Cineplex, third floor, Central Market Annex (☎03/230 8548). Three screens which show mainly US movies.

Cineplex, Mid Valley Mega Mall, Bangsar. Multiscreen complex showing Western films.

Coliseum, Jalan TAR, next to the *Coliseum Hotel* (☎03/292 5995). Shows the latest Cantonese and Taiwanese blockbusters.

Federal, Jalan Raja Laut, at cnr of Jalan Sultan Ismail (☎03/442 5041). Specializes in Malay cinema, which ranges from corny romances to historical epics.

Film Net Café, the Stonor Centre, 3 Jalan Persiaran Stonor (☎03/241 5323). About 500m southeast of the Petronas towers. Excellent art-house cinema, usually showing two quality international movies each night at 7.30pm and 9-10pm.

President, Sungei Wang Plaza, 500m from the southern end of Jalan Sultan Ismail (☎03/248 0084). Screens English-language films, usually a few months behind US and European release. There are several other cinemas within this shopping complex.

Rex, Jalan Sultan (☎03/238 3021). Single screen in the heart of Chinatown, showing a mixture of local and US movies.

Cultural shows, dance and traditional music

Though the contemporary dance scene is very much in its infancy, traditional dance can be seen at the **cultural shows** put on by some restaurants (you need to be dining there to watch) and other venues, though what's on offer is often lame and inauthentic. The only time you can be guaranteed seeing traditional dance and music is during public holidays and festivals, such as Chinese New Year and the Yang Dipertuan Agong's birthday (see p.71); performances, though usually free, are never in regular venues, so ask at the KL Visitors Centre for details.

Malaysian Tourist Information Complex (MATIC), 109 Jalan Ampang (☎03/243 4929). Costumed shows are held occasionally on the first floor in the afternoons, and sometimes in the gardens outside, too.

Nelayan Titiwangsa Restaurant, Jalan Kuantan, off Jalan Pahang, Lake Titiwangsa. Atmospheric location overlooking the lake, though featuring a rather tame song-and-dance troupe.

Sri Melayu, Jalan Conlay, behind the *KL Hilton.* The traditional Malay-style house, delicious buffet meals and enthusiastic performers make this the best option for an all-round cultural evening out, with Chinese, Indian and Malay dance on offer.

Temple of Fine Arts, 116 Jalan Berhala, Brickfields (☎03/274 3709). Arts organization which was set up to preserve Tamil Hindu culture by promoting dance, theatre, folk, classical music and craft-making. Now it has expanded its scope – in early 2000 *Swan Lake* was performed there. Probably the best place in KL to see traditional Indian dance; it prides itself on being the bastion of dance forms like Bharata Natyam, Odissi, Manipuri, Kathakali and tribal folk styles.

Live music

Concerts featuring Malay pop stars or visiting big names from other Southeast Asian countries (and further afield) take place at large venues like the Merdeka Stadium and the Civic Centre in Petaling Jaya (see p.128). These events are always over by 11pm to ensure that everybody can get home easily by public transport. Tickets start at around RM20 and can be bought from the venue itself or through a ticket agency; the easiest one to find is the *Horizon Music Centre* (☎03/274 6778) on the ground floor of Central Market.

Barn Thai, 370 Jalan Tun Razak (☎03/244 6699), just south of the junction with Jalan Ampang. Ampark Park LRT. Bar with nightly live jazz performed by local outfits.

Hard Rock Café, *Concorde Hotel,* 2 Jalan Sultan Ismail. Features well-known local rock bands. Gets absolutely packed on Friday and Saturday nights – you don't have to eat if you've come to see the band, but you will have to pay a cover charge (RM20). Daily 11am–midnight.

Merdeka Stadium, Jalan Stadium. Stages occasional large concerts, mostly of visiting Western rock acts, ballad singers and (a must-see) Malay heavy-metal bands – look for posters around town.

Markets and shopping

KL is a seven-days-a-week city as far as **shopping** is concerned. The malls are open from 10am to 10pm and shops from 9am to 6pm. Malls are the places for KL's youth and yuppies to go, and are especially busy on Saturday and Sunday. For tourists and older locals, the premier browsing locations are the **pasar malams** (night markets), where goods of all sorts are sold at competitive prices, bargains are easy to come by and the atmosphere is always gregarious, almost like a festival.

There are some decent outlets for **handicrafts** in the city, though it's usually better to pick them up in rural areas where they tend to be made, as the range of items on offer is wider there, and you're also more likely to pick up a bargain. That said, a visit to the Royal Selangor Pewter Factory (see below) near KL shows the scale and sophistication of the pewter production, and provides an opportunity to buy items at lower prices than in the shops. You can also pick up batik products in the city, including textiles, bags, belts and hats, as well as carvings, artwork and sculpture – check the list of shops below for the best deals.

Markets

Central Market, Jalan Hang Kasturi, Chinatown. See p.100. Daily 9am–10pm.

Chow Kit, Jalan Haji Hussein, off Jalan TAR. See p.106. Daily 9am–5pm.

Jalan Petaling, Chinatown. See p.100. Daily 9am–10pm.

Jalan TAR. See p.105. Sat 7pm–midnight.

Merdeka Stadium, Jalan Stadium. KL's only regular flea market selling antiques to secondhand clothes. Fri & Sat 4pm–midnight.

Pasar Minggu, Jalan Raja Muda Musa, Kampung Bharu. See p.106 for details. Sat 6pm–1am.

Pudu Market, bordered by Jalan Yew, Jalan Pasar and Jalan Pudu, 2km southeast of the centre. A massive market selling mostly food. Mon–Sat 8am–4pm.

Batiks, pewter and handicrafts

Aked Ibu Kota, Jalan TAR, opposite the *Coliseum*. On KL's busiest main street, this shopping centre sells local handicrafts, including batiks.

Central Market, Jalan Hang Kasturi. Here you can buy batik clothing and handicrafts, including bags, caps, kites and masks, some of which you'll be able to watch being made by the craftsmen on site.

Chin Li, 13 Jalan Sultan Mohammed. Stocks a wide range of painting, sculptures and finely made furniture at steep prices.

Dai-Ichi Arts and Crafts, 122 mezzanine floor, *Park Royal Hotel*, near the southern end of Jalan Sultan Ismail. An impressive collection of highly priced pewter products.

Infokraft, cnr of Jalan Sultan Hishamuddin and Lebuh Pasar Besar. Stocks a decent range of crafts from government-sponsored manufacturers – they aren't cheap, though.

Jalan Masjid India, Little India. Excellent for saris and other colourful Indian fabrics. Also religious paraphernalia, metalwork and handicrafts from the Middle East, Indonesia and north Asia.

Kompleks Budaya Kraf, Jalan Conlay, near the junction with Jalan Raja Chulan. All of Malaysia's crafts under one roof, beside the museum.

Royal Selangor Pewter Factory, 4 Jalan Usahawan, Sentul, 4km northeast of the centre. Take bus #167 or #169 from Lebuh Ampang. Here you can see how pewter is made. Mon–Fri 9am–6pm, Sat 9am–noon.

Wisma Batek, Jalan Tun Perak, close to the junction with Jalan Benteng. Offers a wide selection of shirts, sarongs, blouses, trousers, bags and local drawings and paintings, at prices cheaper than in the Central Market.

Books and CDs

For bookshops, see also "Listings", overleaf.

Skoob Books, 88 Jalan Padang Belia, Brickfields. Behind the *YMCA*; take bus #5 from the Jalan Sultan Mohammed terminus to Jalan Tun Sambanthan. One of KL's best secondhand bookshops, this place also features an art gallery, performance space and café.

Tower Records, BB Plaza, Jalan Bukit Bintang. The main outlet to buy music of all sorts, including Malaysian pop.

Yaohan, first and second floors of The Mall, Jalan Putra. PWTC LRT. This Japanese department store incorporates the best bookshop in the city.

Shopping malls

BB Plaza, cnr of Jalan Bukit Bintang and Jalan Sultan Ismail, Golden Triangle. The mall with the most frequent price reductions in town; excellent deals on cameras, electronic equipment and shoes. Also has trendy boutiques galore.

Imbi Plaza, cnr of Jalan Imbi and Jalan Sultan Ismail, Golden Triangle. Specializes in computers, with hardware and software on sale.

Lot 10 Shopping Centre, junction of Jalan Bukit Bintang and Jalan Sultan Ismail, Golden Triangle. Young KL's most exclusive shopping venue, specializing in designer clothes, sportswear and music. Contains an outlet of the Japanese department store Isetan.

The Mall, Jalan Putra. Besides the massive food centre in the basement and on the fourth floor, the main attraction here is the Japanese department store, Yaohan, with a wide range of designer clothing.

Metrojaya, City Square, Jalan Tun Razak. Malaysia's most popular chain store (from which the building takes its name) takes pride of place here, with brand-name clothing at reasonable prices.

Star Hill, cnr of Jalan Bukit Bintang and Jalan Gading. The cutting edge of KL shopping and the place to hang out with the latest beautiful people, shopping at upmarket Western clothes stores.

Wisma Stephens, Jalan Raja Chulan, Golden Triangle. A complex which includes bars, a couple of art galleries, music stores, clothes shops and cafés.

Yow Chuan Plaza, junction of Jalan Tun Razak and Jalan Ampang. Specializes in fairly commercial arts and crafts, including some batik and various artefacts.

Listings

Airlines The offices of most airlines are in and around the Golden Triangle. Major airlines include: Aeroflot, ground floor, 1 Jalan Perak (☎03/261 3331); American Airlines, Angkasa Raya Building, 123 Jalan Ampang (☎03/242 4311); Bangladesh Airlines, Subang Airport (☎03/248 3765); British Airways, Wisma Merlin, Jalan Sultan Ismail (☎03/242 6177); Cathay Pacific, UBN Tower, 10 Jalan P. Ramlee (☎03/238 3377); China Airlines, Level 3, Amoda Building, 22 Jalan Imbi (☎03/242 7344); Delta Air Lines, UBN Tower, 10 Jalan P. Ramlee (☎03/291 5490); Garuda, first floor, Angkasa Raya Building, 123 Jalan Ampang (☎03/262 2811); Japan Airlines, twentieth floor, Jalan Ampang, Menara Lion (☎03/261 1728); KLM, Shop 7, ground floor, President House, Jalan Sultan Ismail (☎03/242 7011); MAS, MAS Building, Jalan Sultan Ismail (☎03/261 0555); Pelangi Air, c/o MAS (☎03/262 4448); Qantas, UBN Tower, 10 Jalan P. Ramlee (☎03/238 9133); Royal Brunei, first floor, Wisma Merlin, Jalan Sultan Ismail (☎03/230 7166); Singapore Airlines, Wisma SIA, 2 Jalan Dang Wangi (☎03/292 3122); Thai International, Kuwasa Building, 5 Jalan Raja Laut (☎03/293 7100); United Airlines, MAS Building, Jalan Sultan Ismail (☎03/261 1433).

Banks and exchange Main offices are: Bank Bumiputra, Jalan Melaka; Bank of America, first floor, Wisma Stephens, Jalan Raja Chulan; Chase Manhattan, first floor, Pernas International Building, Jalan Sultan Ismail; Hongkong Bank, 2 Lebuh Ampang; Maybank, 100 Jalan Tun Perak; Standard Chartered Bank, 2 Jalan Ampang; United Malayan Banking Corporation, UMBC Building, Jalan Sultan Sulaiman, south of the train station. Almost all of these banks change money (Mon–Fri 10am–4pm, Sat 9am–12.30pm), but you get better rates from official money-changers, of which there are scores in the main city areas; the kiosk below the General Post Office, on Jalan Sultan Hishamuddin, gives good rates. A bank which doesn't charge commission on American Express traveller's cheques is Pacific Bank, junction of Jalan Hang Lekir and Jalan Hang Kasturi. This makes their exchange rate as good as, if not better than, those at money-changers.

Bookshops For English-language books try Berita Book Centre, Bukit Bintang Plaza; Minerva Book Store, 114 Jalan TAR; MPH, Jalan Telawi Lima, Bangsar and at BB Plaza, Jalan Bukit Bintang;

Times Books, first floor, Yow Chuan Plaza, junction of Jalan Ampang and Jalan Tun Razak; Yaohan Book Store, second floor, The Mall, Jalan Putra.

Buses Transnasional can be contacted on ☎03/238 4670.

Car rental All main companies have offices at the airport; or contact Avis, 40 Jalan Sultan Ismail (☎03/241 7144); Budget, 29 Jalan Yap Kwan Seng (☎03/242 5166); Hertz, International Complex, Jalan Sultan Ismail (☎03/243 3433); National Car Rental, ninth floor, Menara Bausted, 69 Jalan Raja Chulan (☎03/248 0522).

Embassies and consulates Australia: Menara Baustead, 69 Jalan Raja Chulan (☎03/246 5555); Brunei: 113 Jalan U Thant (☎03/261 2820); Canada: seventh floor, Osk Plaza, 172 Jalan Ampang (☎03/261 2000); China: 229 Jalan Ampang (☎03/242 8495); Indonesia: 233 Jalan Tun Razak (☎03/984 2011); Japan: 11 Persiaran Stonor (☎03/242 7044); Laos: 108 Jalan Damai (☎03/248 3895); Netherlands: 4 Jalan Mesra, off Jalan Damai (☎03/248 5151); New Zealand: 193 Jalan Tun Razak (☎03/238 2533); Philippines: 1 Changkat Kia Peng (☎03/248 4233); Thailand: 206 Jalan Ampang (☎03/248 8333); UK: 185 Jalan Ampang (☎03/248 2122); US: 376 Jalan Tun Razak (☎03/216 5000); Vietnam: 4 Persiaran Stonor (☎03/248 4036).

Emergencies Dial ☎999 for ambulance, police or fire. For the Tourist Police Unit call ☎03/241 5522 or 241 5243.

Hospitals and clinics General Hospital, Jalan Pahang (☎03/292 1044); Pantai, Jalan Pantai, off Jalan Bangsar, Bangsar (☎03/282 5077); Tung Shin Hospital, Jalan Pudu (☎03/232 1655). There are 24hr casualty wards at all of the above.

Internet access *Adamz Cyber Café*; Lot 2, Central Market Annex; *Cheng Lock Internet*, Jalan Cheng Lock, Chinatown; *Dataran Cyber Café*, ground floor, Medan Mara Building, Jalan Raja Laut; *Easy Access*, 146a Jalan Bukit Bintang; Golden Date Internet Zone, first floor, City One Plaza, Jalan Musha Abdullah; *Masterworld Surfnet Café*, first floor, 23, Jalan Petaling; *Poem*, 38a Jalan Telawi 5; *Star Surf*, 105 Jalan Sultan (opposite Rex Cinema); *Surf*, 54 Jalan Maarof, Bangsar; *Traveller's E Mail Centre*, Room 6, third floor, Wisma Kwong Siew, 147 Jalan Tun H.S. Lee. The going rate is around RM5 an hour.

Laundry Most hotels, guesthouses and lodges will do your laundry for you for a few dollars.

Left-luggage office At Pudu Raya bus station, Jalan Pudu (daily 8am–10pm; RM2 per item).

Police The Chinatown police station is at the southern end of Jalan Tun H.S. Lee (☎03/232 5044). The main Tourist Police station, where you must report stolen property and claim your insurance form, is on Jalan Hang Tuah (☎03/230 2222 ext 259), opposite the old Pudu Jail.

Post office The General Post Office is on Jalan Sultan Hishamuddin, opposite Central Market (Mon–Fri 8am–4pm, Sat 8am–2pm); poste restante/general delivery mail comes here.

Sports Bowling at Federal Bowl, *Federal Hotel*, Jalan Bukit Bintang (daily 10am–11pm; RM10). Golf at Kelab Golf Negara, Subang, near the airport (green fees RM60–100). There are public swimming pools in Chinatown, near Chinwoo Stadium, off Jalan Hang Jebat (daily 10am–12.50pm & 3–8pm) and at Bangsar Sports Complex, Jalan Bangsar, Bangsar (daily 8am–10pm; RM8 adults, RM4 children), where there are also squash, tennis and badminton courts. Most large hotels have swimming pools, open to residents only. You can play tennis at Kelanga Sports Complex, Jalan Padan Belia, Brickfields (daily 8am–10pm; RM12 an hour).

Taxis Comfort Radio Taxi Service (☎03/733 0507); Koteksi (☎03/781 5352); Radio Teksi (☎03/442 0848).

Telephone offices The cheapest places to make international calls are the Telekom Malaysia offices dotted around the city. The largest is the one in Wisma Jothi, Jalan Gereja. Making calls from the major hotels costs at least fifty percent more.

Tour operators The tour operators listed here are all able to organize tailor-made adventure trips across Malaysia: Angel Tours, lower-ground floor, City Tower, Jalan Alur (☎03/241 7018); Asian Overland Services, 35 Jalan Sultan Sulaiman (☎03/292 5637); Borneo Travel, Lot 36–37, The Arcade, *Hotel Equatorial*, Jalan Sultan Ismail (☎03/261 2130); Fairwind Travel, Lot T, Sungei Wang Plaza, Jalan Sultan Ismail (☎03/248 6920); Insight Travel, ninth floor, Plaza MBF, Jalan Ampang (☎03/261 2488).

Trains The information kiosk in the Railway Station has up-to-date timetables; call ☎03/274 7443 or 273 8000 for information and reservations.

Travel agents Backpackers Transport, Backpackers Travellers Inn, 60 Jalan Sultan (☎012/638 8382); Reliance Travel, third floor, Sungei Wang Plaza, Jalan Sultan Ismail (☎03/248 6022); STA, fifth floor, Magnum Plaza, 128 Jalan Pudu (☎03/248 9800); Tina Travel, 30 Jalan Mamarda, Ampang Point (☎03/457 8877).

Visa extensions Immigration Office, third floor, Jalan Pantai Bahru, off Jalan Damansara (Mon–Fri 9am–4.30pm; ☎03/757 8155).

AROUND KUALA LUMPUR

The most obvious attractions around the capital (see map on p.80) are to the **north**, where limestone peaks rise up out of the forest and the roads narrow as you pass through small kampungs. There is dramatic scenery as close as 13km from the city, where the Hindu shrine at the **Batu Caves** attracts enough visitors to make it one of Malaysia's main tourist attractions. Nearby, the **Forest Institute of Malaysia** and **Templer Park** encompass the nearest portion of primary rainforest to the capital. To the northeast of KL, about 30km from the city, the much-hyped **Genting Highlands** is the least inspiring of the country's hill stations. Northwest from KL is the attractive town of **Kuala Selangor**, which has a Nature Park where you can stay in lovely jungle huts; nearby, at **Kuala Kuantan**, there's a wonderful attraction, the nightly dance of its **fireflies**.

Beyond the suburbs to the southwest of KL is **Petaling Jaya**, which though a sizeable city in itself, is only a short – at least outside rush hour – bus or taxi ride away from KL. A little further out is the new town of **Shah Alam**, with its magnificent mosque, the biggest in Southeast Asia. You can combine a visit here with one to the neighbouring **agricultural park**, an interesting blend of environmentalism, education and commercial good sense. Continuing west, you reach Malaysia's first capital, **Klang**, whose old centre retains a warehouse now turned into a fascinating tin museum, and also contains one of the country's most atmospheric mosques. Another appealing day-trip is to the quaint Chinese fishing village of **Pulau Ketam**, an hour's ferry ride from the coastal town of Port Klang.

The main reason for travelling south is to take a look at **Putrajaya** and **Cyberjaya**, two new towns at the heart of Prime Minister Mahathir's ambitious Multimedia Corridor scheme, which aims to create an information-technology industrial zone stretching from downtown Kuala Lumpur out to KLIA. Though far from being finished, the towns promise dynamic new architecture, including the vast, gothic brickwork of the new Parliament building. Public transport out here was minimal at time of writing (one useful service is the Transnasional bus from KL's Pudu Raya bus station), but increasingly KL tour operators are organizing trips around the vast building site.

The Zoo

One of the easiest sights to visit just outside KL is the **Zoo Negara**, Malaysia's national zoo (daily 9am–6pm; RM6), beyond Jalan Tun Razak on Jalan Ulu Klang, 14km northeast of the city centre; buses #17 and #174 run here regularly from Lebuh Ampang (40min; RM2.20). Set in large grounds, the zoo needs at least three hours to see everything, unless you take advantage of the shuttle bus (RM1) which drops you off at the main attractions, such as the tiger and lion enclosures. The zoo is particularly strong on indigenous species including the *musang* fox, civet, tiger, bearded pig and rhino. There is also an exceptional collection of **snakes**, including the Sumatran pit viper and the Indian rock python. However, several of the cages and fenced areas are almost devoid of vegetation, and many of the animals look cramped and ill at ease, an exception being the two smooth-coated otters who have their own little island and appear to adore the attention they get. At the back of the zoo proper is an **aquarium**, which, although rather dark, is worth venturing into to catch a glimpse of various coral-reef fish.

FRIM, Batu Caves and Templer Park

Malaysia's **Forest Research Institute** (FRIM), **Templer Park** and – one of the most popular attractions around KL – **Batu Caves**, lie to the north of the capital, off Jalan Kuching and its continuation, **Route 1**. Their proximity to this road makes it feasible to visit all three on one day if you're driving; note that you need to pass through one toll point (60 sen) on Jalan Kuching, about 2km out of the city. With a car, it's also feasible to continue northeast from the caves to the Orang Asli Museum (see p.123) and Genting Highlands (see p.124). Inconveniently if you're using public transport, it's largely impossible to go from one sight to the next without returning to the centre, though you can use buses to get from Batu Caves to Templer Park and vice versa (see p.212).

The Forest Research Institute

If you can't make it out to Taman Negara and its forest-canopy walkway (see p.212), you can instead stroll through the treetops at the **Forest Research Institute of Malaysia** (FRIM) (daily 8am–6.30pm; ☎03/635 9578). The canopy walkway here, which takes about twenty minutes to traverse, provides a unique view of KL's skyscrapers through the trees. Within the fifteen-square-kilometre area of the park are several trails that are also worth trying. You should prepare as you would for any other jungle trek: bring along plenty of drinking water and insect repellent, and wear laced shoes. For those who wish to learn more about Malaysia's ecological heritage, there's also a museum, which contains details of the institute's research; an arboretum; as well as an eclectic range of wood-based antiques and implements, including an intricately carved boat, treasure chests and a four-poster bed.

To reach FRIM by **bus** from KL, take #148 from Jalan Hang Kasturi in Chinatown; (1hr; RM1.60). By **car**, continue north from the Jalan Kuching toll point for about 4km, watching for signposts for Middle Ring Road 2, which you take west; after another 4km you'll see FRIM signposted on your right.

Batu Caves

Long before you reach the entrance to the **Batu Caves**, you'll see them ahead: small, black holes in the vast limestone thumbs which comprise a ridge of hills 13km north of the city centre. In 1891, ten years after the caves were noticed by the American explorer William Hornaby, local Indian dignitaries convinced the British colonial authorities that the caves were ideal places in which to worship (probably because their spectacular geography was thought reminiscent of the sacred Himalayas). Soon ever-increasing numbers of devotees were visiting the caves to pray at the shrine established here to Lord Muruga, better known as **Lord Subramaniam**; later the temple complex was expanded to include a shrine to the elephant-headed deity **Ganesh**. Today the caves and shrines are surrounded by the full panoply of religious commercialism, with shops selling Hindu idols, pamphlets, bracelets, postcards and cassettes. The caves are incredibly popular, and always packed with visitors, but the numbers most days are nothing compared to the hundreds of thousands of devotees who descend here during the annual three-day **Thaipusam festival** (see box, overleaf).

The caves

To the left of the brick staircase leading up to the main Temple Cave, a small path leads off to the so-called **art gallery cave** (daily 8.30am–7pm; RM1), which contains dozens of striking multicoloured statues of deities, portraying scenes from the Hindu scriptures. As well as these psychedelic dioramas – including a naked goddess astride a five-headed snake, flanked by figures with goats' heads carrying farming implements – flamboyant murals line the damp walls of the cave depicting jungle settings, mythic battles and abstract designs.

At the top of the main staircase, there's a clear view through to the **Subramaniam Swamy Temple** (daily 8am–7pm), set deep in a cave around 100m high and 80m long, the cave walls lined with idols representing the six lives of Lord Subramaniam. The temple, illuminated by shafts of light from gaps in the cave ceiling high above, has an entranced guarded by two statues, their index fingers pointing upwards towards the light. Within the temple, devoted to Lord Subramaniam and another deity, Rama, a dome is densely sculpted with more scenes from the scriptures. In a chamber at the back of the temple is a statue of Rama, who watches over the well-being of all immigrants, adorned with silver jewellery and a silk sarong. If you want to look closely at this inner sanctum, the temple staff will mark a small red dot on your forehead, giving you a spiritual right to enter.

Practicalities

You can reach the caves on **bus** #11 from Central Market (hourly; 40min; RM2.20). On the way, the bus passes **Pak Ali's House** (daily 9am–6pm; RM3), a good example of a

---

THAIPUSAM AT THE BATU CAVES

The most important festival in the Malaysian Hindu calendar (along with Deepavali), **Thaipusam** honours the Hindu deity Lord Subramaniam. Originally a Tamil festival from Southern India, it's a day of penance and celebration, held during full moon in the month of "Thai" (between January 15 and February 15), when huge crowds arrive at the Batu Caves. What was originally intended to be a day of penance for past sins has now become a major tourist attraction, with both Malaysians and foreigners flocking to the festival every year.

The start of Thaipusam is marked by the departure at dawn, from KL's Sri Maha Mariamman Temple, of a golden chariot bearing a statue of Subramaniam. Thousands of devotees follow on foot as it makes its seven-hour procession to the caves. Once there, the statue is placed in a tent before being carried up to the temple cave by devotees. As part of their penance – and in a trance-like state – the devotees carry numerous types of *kavadi* ("burdens" in Tamil), the most popular being milk jugs decorated with peacock feathers placed on top of the head, which are connected to the penitents' flesh by hooks. Others wear wooden frames with sharp spikes protruding from them which are carried on the back and hooked into the skin; trident-shaped skewers are placed through some devotees' tongues and cheeks. This rather grisly procession – which now only occurs in Malaysia, Singapore and Thailand – has its origins in India, where most of Lord Subramaniam's temples were sited on high ridges which devotees would walk up, carrying heavy pitchers or pots to honour the deity. At Batu, the 272-step climb up to the main chamber expresses the idea that you cannot reach God without expending effort.

Once in the temple cave, the devotees participate in ceremonies and rituals to Subramanian and Ganesh, finishing with a celebration for Rama, when milk from the *kavadi* vessel can be spilt as an offering; incense and camphor are burned as the bearers unload their devotional burdens. The festival takes many hours to complete, in an atmosphere so highly charged that police are needed to line the stairs and protect onlookers from the entranced *kavadi*-bearers and their instruments of self-flagellation.

Extra buses (#98) run to the caves during Thaipusam. It's advisable to get there early (say 7am) for a good view of the proceedings. Although there are numerous cafés at the caves, you should also take plenty of water and snacks with you, as the size of the crowd is horrendous.

traditional Malay stilt house, common in Kuala Lumpur in the early years of the twentieth century. It was built in 1917 using timber hewn from the nearby jungle, its veranda, stairs and roof carved with opulent shapes and ornate designs. You may wish to get off the bus, have a quick look inside and continue on to the caves on the next bus; the last bus back to KL leaves the caves around 5.30pm. To **drive** to the caves, continue north from the Jalan Kuching toll point for about 6km, leaving the road (which continues into Route 1) at the Batu Caves exit, which is clearly signposted; the caves, which you can now see in the distance, are only 1–2km away from here.

There are two canteens in the compound below the caves. Open daily from 8am to 5pm, they sell drinks and Malay **food**.

Templer Park

Opened in the 1950s, and named after Sir Gerald Templer (the last of Malaya's British High Commissioners), **Templer Park** (daily 8am–6pm; free) is the closest you'll get to primary **rainforest** if you haven't got time to visit the state parks in the interior. The park is at its busiest at weekends, when visitors arrive from the capital, but you don't need to make too much of an effort to escape the crowds.

Templer covers over a square kilometre of primary forest, dominated by a belt of limestone outcrops set in a valley, cutting through the hills for 5km. A narrow road winds from the entrance to an artificial lake, 300m to the east, before shrinking to a narrow path, which snakes up into the forest. This trail leads back and forth across the shallow, five-metre-wide Sungei Templer, reaching a dramatic waterfall after an hour's walk. From here you can follow the riverside path through primary jungle for another hour or so, but you'll have to return by the same route. An alternative is to leave the main path on a trail to the left of the waterfall, from where a one-hour trek hugs the edge of the hillside and later meets the concrete road near the park entrance. Other paths snake up into the forested hills and pass natural swimming lagoons and waterfalls. The park's highest point is **Bukit Takun** (350m), in its northern corner, rising on the western side of the river; the trail peters out at the base of the hill, though. Few animals are now to be seen in the park, as what is left of the jungle here is surrounded by development, which has frightened off much of the wildlife.

Practicalities
Buses #38 and #43 both come here from KL's Pudu Raya bus station; the trip takes fifty minutes and costs around RM1.50. Alternatively, you can combine visiting the park with a trip to the Batu Caves, from where you catch the #11 back out to Route 1 and then wait for a bus to the park. By **car**, you continue north up Route 1 beyond the Batu Caves exit for about 7km; the park is clearly signposted on your right.

There's nowhere at the park to buy refreshments, so you may wish to bring your own food and drink. The park authorities permit **camping**, a rewarding experience as long as you're prepared to rough it – there isn't an official campsite, or any toilets, washing or cooking facilities.

The Orang Asli Museum

Like Templer Park (see above), the **Orang Asli Museum** (Mon–Thurs & Sun 9am–5.30pm; free), run by the government-sponsored Centre for Orang Asli Affairs, holds a certain interest if this is as far into rural Malaysia as you're going to get. Located about 20km northeast of KL as the crow flies (a fact which makes it a possible stopping-off point en route to Genting Highlands; see overleaf), the museum provides a fine illustration of the cultural richness and demographic variety of the Orang Asli (Malay for "original people") – Malaysia's indigenous inhabitants (see Basics, p.60). The foyer of the unobtrusive timber building contains a large map of west Malaysia, showing the distribution of the Orang Asli groups. The information makes clear that the Orang Asli are found, in varying numbers, in just about every part the peninsula, which may well surprise visitors who often see little sign of them during their travels. Many of the Orang Asli maintain a virtually pre-industrial **lifestyle** – some still rely on blowpipes for hunting – and pursue their traditional occupations in some isolation, hunting and gathering in the fast-depleting forests, fishing along the increasingly polluted Johor coastline, or carving their extraordinary handicrafts. This separation is believed to be partly deliberate on their part: the Orang Asli see that their culture is under threat, and that too much close contact with modern Malaysia is likely to do them more harm than good.

The museum also contains descriptions of the various groups of Orang Asli, and collections of the tools of their trade – from fishing nets and traps to guns and blowpipes. At the far end of the museum's main room are photographs of Orang Asli militia commandeered by the Malay and British military to fight the Communist guerrillas in the 1950s (see p.209), while other displays describe the changes forced on the Orang Asli over the past thirty years – some positive, like the eradication of serious disease and the development of health and school networks, others less encouraging, like the erosion of the family system as young men drift off to look for seasonal work.

Particularly interesting, hidden in an annexe to the rear of the building, are examples of traditional handicrafts, including the **head carvings** made by the Mah Meri tribe from the swampy region on the borders of Selangor and Negeri Sembilan, and the Jah Hut from the slopes of Gunung Benom in central Pehang. The carvings, around 50cm high, show stylized, fierce facial expressions, and are fashioned from a particularly strong, heavy hardwood. They still have religious significance – the most common image used, the animist deity Moyang, represents the spirit of the ancestors – and are prevalent in current religious ceremonies, when similar masks are worn during dances honouring a pantheon of gods. The Orang Asli's **animist religion** is influenced by early Hindu beliefs, and the carvings here show similarities with those of some Hindu deities.

Practicalities

Bus #174 leaves Lebuh Ampang in KL every thirty minutes for the fifty-minute trip here along the old Gombak road. When you get off the bus (ask the driver to tell you when you've arrived, as it's not obvious), cross to the other side of the road – there are two run-down shops opposite the bus stop – and head 50m further up, where a narrow, steep side road leads to the museum. On the return trip, you wait outside the shops for the bus. By **car**, head up Jalan Kuching/Route 1 from KL, and about 3km beyond the toll point (see p.121), watch for signs for Jalan Gombak, which heads east. You carry on along Jalan Gombak for about 10km, when you'll see the museum on your right. From here, it's quite feasible to continue on to Genting Highlands (see below for details).

Genting Highlands

Of the three hill stations located on the western side of the Banjaran Titwangsa mountain range, north of KL, the **Genting Highlands** (Genting is Chinese for "on top of the clouds") is the odd one out. Whereas Fraser's Hill (see p.230) and the Cameron Highlands (see p.135) are places for short treks, visits to waterfalls and colonial tranquillity, Genting – 30km northeast of the city as the crow flies – can be stress-inducing in the extreme. Although the highlands themselves are eminently attractive – something that's obvious from the journey there, as the bus zigzags its way gingerly up the road 2000m above sea level – upon arrival you're deposited at a brain-numbingly noisy, concrete resort, perched on top of the hill, where the focus of attention is a quadrangle of high-rise hotels, with shopping arcades and restaurants. An exclusive golf course is the main "green" recreation the hill station has to offer, besides horse riding, and you'd be hard pushed to find any trails reaching out from the hotels. Before the late 1970s, when the development began, the whole area was covered in forest, but now Malaysians flock here from the city in their thousands to frequent the only casino in the country and to spoil their families in the fast-food outlets, swimming pools and amusement park.

On the way up to the top, the bus passes the Awana Golf Club and Country Resort on the right; to the left a **cable car** (Mon 12.15–8.30pm, Tues–Sun 8.30am–9.30pm; every 20min; RM5) offers an alternative and precipitous journey up the remaining few kilometres to the resort hotel at the top. You can either get off the bus at the Skywaystation cable terminus, to travel the eleven-minute, four-kilometre cable ride up the side of the mountain, or chug on up into the bowels of the eighteen-storey *Genting Highlands Resort Hotel* (☎03/211 1118; ⑥), where one-armed bandits and arcade games vie for your attention. Two floors above is the **casino** (open 24hr; minimum age 21), where the chips start at RM10. Outside, 20m from the concrete forecourt which is usually full of exhaust-belching buses, there's a **swimming pool** and a small area set aside for picnicking. The other hotels are the *Awana Towers* (☎03/211 3015; ⑥) and the *Theme Park Hotel* (☎03/262 2666, fax 211 3535; ⑨); there is no budget accommodation here. All of these establishments have overpriced **restaurants**..

You can get here on the Genting **bus** (hourly 8am–7pm; 1hr; RM5) from Pudu Raya bus station (tickets from booth 43). Getting a seat on a return bus can be difficult (it's not possible to reserve seats), and often involves competing for space with a crowd of young Malaysians – get to the stop at the *Genting Highlands Resort Hotel* early. You can also get here in a shared taxi from the second floor at Pudu Raya (RM10 per person or RM40 per taxi). By **car**, you can follow the route for the Orang Asli museum, heading south once there for a couple of kilometres until you reach Route 2, which you take northeast; the uphill turning for the resort is clearly signposted to your left after about 12km.

To Kuala Selangor

Northwest of KL, much of the land has been given over to one of Malaysia's most lucrative resources, oil palm – the plantations hereabouts stretch for dozens of kilometres. It's ironic, then, that Selangor's former days as a major rubber-producing area are remembered in the **Rubber Museum**, near Sungei Buloh, a third of the way to **Kuala Selangor** on the coast. The latter town is itself an attractive, if neglected, place, mostly visited nowadays for the nearby attractions, the Kuala Selangor Nature Park, and the area's top draw, Kualal Kuantan's luminous **fireflies**.

To get to Kuala Selangor, take Jalan Kuching out of the city, passing through the toll point (60 sen) after 2km. Continue north from the Jalan Kuching toll point for about 4km, watching for signs for Middle Ring Road 2, which you take west for around 5km. Take the exit signposted for Sungei Buloh; this gets you on to Route 54, on which you head northwest for about 50km until you reach Batang Berjuntai, by the Selangor river. The last part of the journey involves heading west along a minor road, parallel to the river, to its mouth, passing Kampung Kuantan (see p.127) along the way, followed by a short sprint up the coastal Route 5.

The Rubber Museum

The Malaysian rubber story began in 1877 with an Englishman, Henry Wickham, who collected sixty thousand seeds from Brazil and took them to Kew Gardens in London, where they were germinated. Of these, 22 were sent to Singapore and nine to Kuala

Kangsar, where they were planted in the garden of the Resident, Hugh Low. By the 1930s, thousands of square kilometres were under rubber cultivation, and Malaya's rubber industry had dwarfed that of Brazil. You can trace the development of the industry in the city's **Rubber Museum** (Mon–Thurs 8.30am–12.30pm & 2–4pm, Fri & Sat 8.30am–noon; RM1), in the grounds of the Rubber Research Institute, just over 20km northwest of KL as the crow flies, south of a kampung called Sungei Buloh. Inside the museum, photographs, diagrams and drawings record in great detail various changes in the technology of rubber production, from manual distillation techniques to large-scale automation. More intriguing is the information on the lives of the tens of thousands of immigrants – mostly Tamil Indians and Teochew Chinese – who worked on the vast estates, clearing malarial swamps for plantation.

Practicalities

From KL, catch **bus** #144 or #145 from stands 21–23 at Pudu Raya bus station (every 40min; 70min); ask for the Rubber Research Institute (RRI) and you'll be dropped at the gates. By **car**, you can get here by heading west along Middle Ring Road 2; leave the road by going south along Jalan Sungei Buloh (don't head west, as that takes you on to Route 54 for Kuala Selangor). The turning for the museum is on your right after a few minutes' drive, about 5km before (north of) the old Subang airport. Very few people make the effort to visit the museum (mainly because it's so far out); when you get here you may need to pick up the keys from the manager, who lives in the adjacent bungalow.

Kuala Selangor and around

The former strategic royal town of **KUALA SELANGOR** lies 67km northwest of KL, on the banks of Sungei Selangor. Today, the town is no more than one main street of two-storey concrete buildings and is really only worth a stop if you're on your way to the nearby nature park (see below) or Kampung Kuantan (see opposite). All that remains of Kuala Selangor's more glorious past are the remnants of two forts overlooking the town, the largest of which, **Fort Altingberg** (daily 9am–4.30pm; free), recalls a period in Malaysian history when this part of the country changed hands, bloodily, on several occasions. Originally called Fort Melawati, Altingberg was built by local people during the reign of Sultan Ibrahim of Selangor in the eighteenth century, and was later captured by the Dutch (who renamed it) as part of an attempt to wrestle the tin trade from the sultans. The fortress was partly destroyed during local skirmishes in the Selangor Civil War (1867–73). Within its grounds is a cannon, reputed to be from the Dutch era, and a rock used for executions. Bukit Melawati, the hill on which the fort is based, also has a lighthouse and a resthouse built during the British colonial period. On Saturdays the road from the town up to the fort is closed to traffic and all visitors ascend by way of a trolley car (RM5).

Kuala Selangor is reached from KL on the hourly **bus** #141 from bay 23 at Pudu Raya bus station; the ninety-minute trip costs around RM4. The bus drops you at the **bus station** along the main road into town, about 2km from the centre, conveniently near the nature park. From here, it's easy to get a local bus into town. The only **hotel** here is *Hotel Kuala Selangor*, 88 Main St (☎03/889 2709; ②), an airy place with clean, good-sized rooms and large ceiling fans. A good way to see the fireflies at Kuala Kuantan and take in the fort and the Nature Park on one trip is to take the half-day **tour** here from KL, run by Backpackers Transport (☎012/638 8382; RM100).

Kuala Selangor Nature Park

Two kilometres from Kuala Selangor by road – although its edges lie directly below the fort – is the **Kuala Selangor Nature Park** (daily 8am–7pm), opened in 1987. Among

---

FIREFLIES

Known locally as *kelip kelip*, **fireflies** aren't really flies, but six-millimetre-long **beetles** which belong to the Lampyridae family and are found in the region stretching from India to the Philippines and Papua New Guinea. Their rhythmic flashing is becoming an increasingly rare sight, as the beetles' natural habit – **mangrove swamps** – is hacked back for development. During the day, the fireflies rest on blades of grass behind the mangroves; after sunset they move to the mangrove trees to feed on nectar from the leaves and attract mates with their synchronized flashing, at a rate of three per second. All the male fireflies flash within one-thirtieth of a second of each other (scientists are still trying to work out exactly why); the females also produce a bright light, but don't flash in the same flamboyant way as the males. It's important for visitors to remain quiet when watching the firefly display and not to take flash photographs, as such behaviour scares the insects away.

---

the different habitats in this reclaimed mangrove swamp are mud flats, lakes and a small patch of forest; together, they are host to around 150 species of birds, with thirty more passing along the coastline annually. The only site in Malaysia where the spoonbill sandpiper has been sighted, the park is also home to silver-leaf monkeys, which live in the forest; and a variety of crabs and fish, which live along the coast in the mangroves. There are several clearly marked **trails** in the park, the longest 2km in length. Along it you'll find hides where you can unobtrusively watch the birdlife and the monkeys at play.

It's easy to get to the park from Kuala Selangor's bus station: simply walk a short distance towards town, and take the first left, Jalan Klinik, by the petrol station; the park entrance is 200m along from here. You can also get here on the **buses** which run up Route 5 **from Klang**; ask to be let off at the park, and you'll be dropped at the petrol station from where you walk up Jalan Klinik. **Accommodation** in the park ranges from sturdy A-frame huts (①) to small three-bed chalets (RM40 per person); either type can be booked at the park itself or in advance (daily 9am–5pm; ☎03/889 2294). Weekends are always busy, but during the week you stand a good chance of getting a bed on the day. As there's nowhere to get food in the park, you may want to bring your own provisions, especially if you're staying, or eat in Kuala Selangor.

Kampung Kuantan

Most people who make the trip to Kuala Selangor come to see the **fireflies**, which glow spectacularly in the early evening along the banks of the narrow Sungei Selangor, 8km inland of Kuala Selangor itself, at a small village called **KAMPUNG KUANTAN**. One kilometre down a well-marked road from the village is **Firefly Park Resort**, a new development which incorporates chalet-style accommodation and a café. The resort jetty is the main place to get on sampans (daily 7.45–10.30pm; RM10 per person, minimum of two passengers; bookings on ☎03/889 1208), small motor boats which hold four to six people. The boats purr almost noiselessly upriver for forty minutes, enough time for the passengers to observe the extraordinary fireflies, which have developed a striking synchronized flashing pattern (see box, above). The best time to view the flies is on a dry night between 8pm and 10pm, after which time they will have found a mate and stopped glowing.

There's no public transport to Kampung Kuantan. Renting a long-distance **taxi** here from KL's Pudu Raya bus station costs around RM100 for the return trip (RM30 from Kuala Selangor). The resort has **accommodation** in pricey riverside four-bed chalets (around RM40 per person). A couple of kilometres back towards Kuala Selangor is a small fishing village, Pasir Penambang, with riverside restaurants, an excellent place to stop for seafood dishes. Try the *New River View* at no. 1 Jalan Besar (the village's main street) for its speciality squid.

West of KL: the Klang Valley

Three hundred years before KL was founded, the **Klang Valley** was one of the most important regions in Malaysia, with Selangor's sultans based at the royal town of **Klang**. In the late nineteenth century, with the discovery of new tin deposits further inland, Klang lost its importance, but the valley remained ripe for development as KL expanded rapidly. The first road linking Klang to KL wasn't built until the 1920s – previously all goods were carried along a narrow horse track or went by river – but a decade later the rail line between the two towns came into existence, and today it serves as a commuter line. The Federal Highway (also called Lebuhraya Persekutuan or Route 2), is the main artery of the region today, cutting west from the capital to the coast. En route it passes through Petaling Jaya, a satellite town of KL, noted for its restaurants and bars; Shah Alam, the state capital of Selangor; and Klang, Selangor's former capital, with an interesting tin-mining museum. At the end of the Klang valley is **Port Klang**, where there are ferries to the offshore island of Pulau Ketam, and to the Indonesian island of Sumatra.

Petaling Jaya and around

Known locally as PJ, **PETALING JAYA** lies 12km southwest of the centre of KL, at the start of the Klang Valley. Originally conceived as an overspill suburb for the city, PJ provided low-cost, modern housing for those who flocked to KL to find work in the 1970s, when the Malaysian economy began to expand rapidly. Now PJ is virtually a separate, sprawling city, encompassing a manufacturing base rooted in electronics, computers and textiles. PJ also attracts KL's cash-rich middle class, who come to eat in its swanky restaurants and sample the nightlife as an alternative to suburban Bangsar.

The town is split into 25 planned sections, the main ones being "State", "Damansara Utama", "Bandar Utama" and the Orwellian "Section 2" (or SS2). **State** is the closest thing PJ has to a municipal centre, and boasts an enormous Civic Centre which stages large-scale concerts and exhibitions. **SS2** is probably the most interesting section for foreign visitors, with its terrific pasar malam (nightly 6pm–midnight) held in and around a massive square known locally as "glutton square". Here, you'll find hawkers selling *satukeping* – delicious pancakes layered with brown sauce and shredded vegetables. **Bandar Utama** is home to Malaysia's largest shopping mall, 1 Utama, which includes a mammoth food court, offering Japanese, Vietnamese and Western cuisine, alongside Malaysian favourites. Later at night, the focus shifts to **Damansara Utama**, a massive rectangular area bounded by four roads, along which are dozens of restaurants and nightclubs, which stay open until 4am over the weekend.

Practicalities

From KL, **buses** #28, #30, #33 and #35 from Klang bus station (every 10min; 20min), run to State in PJ, where you change for buses to other sections of town. PJ's main **eating** area is based around the hawker stalls at SS2, offering a mixture of food including burgers, pizza and Korean food, and plenty of Chinese and Malay noodle and rice dishes too. For specific restaurants, try *Out of Africa* – decorated with stuffed wildlife trophies – at 1 Jalan Sultan, close to the Petaling Jaya *Hilton*. Other good restaurants are found in Damansara Utama, where most of the **nightlife** is too. The PJ Civic Centre at Jalan Penchala in State (☎03/757 1211) is a state-of-the-art venue which puts on some big-name rock and classical concerts, musicals and exhibitions.

If you need to get back to KL late at night or in the small hours, expect to pay around RM15 for a taxi back to the capital.

Shah Alam

About 5km west of PJ, the purpose-built town of **SHAH ALAM** was designated as the state capital of Selangor in 1982. Much of its ultramodern centre is generally devoid of interest, the exception being the stunning **Sultan Salahuddin Abdul Aziz Shah Mosque** (Thurs–Sat 10am–noon & 2–4pm). Completed in 1988 at a cost of RM162 million, this is the largest mosque in Southeast Asia, a vast complex incorporating massive blue-marble pillars and set in an expanse of shining concrete and glistening water – the prayer hall alone holds sixteen thousand people. The 92-metre-high dome, designed by computer, has a striking blue-and-white design, its main panels emblazoned with Koranic inscriptions. The dome is porous – when rain falls between the joints of the outer panels, it's collected in a special channel, flows into a storage tank and is pumped up into one of the four minarets. Worshippers taking their ablutions before prayers trigger the flow of water from the tank by breaking a photoelectric beam.

To visit the mosque, women must wear a *tudong* (plain headscarf) and a long dress (with long sleeves) or trousers, and men long-sleeved shirts and long trousers. Take the Cityliner #206 or #222 Shah Alam buses from KL's Klang bus station (every 30min); you'll need to ask the driver to let you off at the mosque, though most services will drop you right outside. The Komuter train also stops at Shah Alam, though you'll have to catch a bus or a taxi from the station to the mosque.

The Agricultural Park

Three kilometres west of Shah Alam, the **Bukit Cahaya Sri Alam Agricultural Park** presents traditional Malaysian agrarian activities in a beautiful natural setting (Tues–Sun 8.30am–6pm; RM2). It's aimed particularly at school groups, but isn't a bad day out if you're interested in tropical horticulture and agro-forestry. Four roads fan out from the park headquarters, where you can pick up a map and brochures describing the park activities. The road going northeast leads to a dam and a freshwater fish-breeding centre, passing a rice field, an aviary and mushroom, spice and orchid gardens en route. Along the road that heads north from the HQ are a campsite and another dam, from where there is a short, well-signposted pathway into primary jungle. Other roads lead to food stalls, an open-air theatre, an insect house, a tropical-fruits plantation, and even a small Orang Asli village – whose inhabitants no longer pursue a traditional lifestyle.

Regular **buses** from Shah Alam (daily 8am–6pm; every 30min) head to the park; there are also hourly buses from KL's Klang bus station – either the #222 or #338 (1hr 20min; around RM4). The buses drops you within sight of the park entrance, with the headquarters a further ten-minutes' walk beyond. You leave the park either by getting the #222 or #338 bus from the main road, or catching the (less regular) Shah Alam town bus, which leaves from next to the park HQ and runs to the PNKS Complex in Shah Alam, from where the #206 or #222 run on to KL.

Klang

The Federal Highway, running the length of the Klang Valley, comes to an end in **KLANG**, 30km southwest of KL. As erstwhile royal seat and historic capital of Selangor State, Klang is hundreds of years older than KL, and from the early sixteenth century onwards was at the centre of one of the most important tin-producing areas in Malaysia, its development inextricably bound up with the gradual expansion of tin production. But in this was sown the seeds of its own decline; it was from Klang that the expedition up Sungei Klang to seek new tin deposits was organized, the success of which led to the founding of Kuala Lumpur in the 1850s. In 1880, KL superseded Klang as state capital, and the old river port ceased to have any political or ceremonial importance.

Although still a bustling, commercial centre, whose main industry is fishing, Klang's historic buildings – the tin museum, the mosque, the government offices and the old istana (palace) – reflect a more dignified, graceful past, where the call to prayer dictated the pace of life. Most of these buildings are found in the compact **old quarter** of town – to get here from the bus station, follow the main road left from the station and cross the bridge over Sungei Klang. (If you arrive by train, you'll already be on this side of the river and within the old district itself.) Immediately below you, on your right after you've crossed the bridge from the new town, is the Gedung Rajah Abdullah, an old tin warehouse built in 1856 by Rajah Abdullah, the Sultan of Selangor's son, both as a home and storehouse for the tin he owned; it was at Abdullah's prompting that the pioneers rafted up Sungei Klang in 1857 to look for new sources of tin. The building is now the **Gedung Abdullah Museum** (daily 9am–4pm except Fri noon–2.45pm; free), devoted to the history of tin mining here. As well as an extensive photographic record and hourly video show detailing the history of tin and the town, the museum contains examples of tin currency, including tortoise-shaped ingots, and various pieces of tin-production equipment.

You can only visit the magnificent nineteenth-century **istana** during the two-day Hari Raya Puasa festival (at the end of Ramadan), but the walk up the road there, past well-tended plants, trees and flowerbeds offers a ravishing prospect, with the main golden spire of the palace gleaming in the background. To reach the istana, follow Jalan Besar, which runs under the bridge opposite the museum, deeper into the old part of Klang. The road passes well-maintained Chinese terraced shops and cafés before reaching the main street, Jalan Istana, which leads to the istana, another 200m to the north. If you return the way you came and take the first right onto Jalan Kota Raja past the padang, you'll reach Klang's mosque, the intimate and atmospheric **Masjid Sultan Suleiman**, ten minutes' walk further on, with seven yellow domes and grey-stone outer walls. Here, low, arched entrances set into the walls lead into narrow passages where the worshippers sit and read the Koran; the inner prayer room has stained-glass windows. The mosque is open to visitors in-between prayers.

Practicalities

The Komuter train runs at least every thirty minutes to Klang from KL's main station (RM3.60 one way); hourly **buses** – the #51, #58 or #225 – from Klang bus station in KL take over an hour to reach Klang. There are also hourly services (RM4) from Klang's bus station heading north on Route 5 to Kuala Selangor and its nature park (see p.126). For **food**, there are several fine restaurants built on stilts over the river.

Port Klang and around

Eight kilometres west of Klang is **PORT KLANG**, from where ferries run to Sumatra and to Pulau Ketam, a quaint Chinese fishing village, on the most westerly of the Malaysian islands opposite the port. Port Klang itself has little of interest, but if you are there in the third week of November, around the beginning of the rainy season, watch out for the Raja Muda Regatta, a competition pitting top yachts against the elements.

The Komuter train from Klang (journey time 15min) stops directly opposite the main jetty; bus passengers disembark 100m further along the road from here. The jetty is where comfortable air-conditioned boats leave for **Tanjung Balai** in Sumatra (6 weekly at 11am; 3hr 30min; RM150 plus RM15 departure tax). To travel on these boats, you need a prearranged visa for Tanjung Balai (RM75), which you can get from the Indonesian Embassy in KL (see p.119). Arriving from Sumatra, you can get to KL on the Komuter train (hourly; 7am–10pm); the Customs building near the Pulau Ketam jetty has facilities for changing money. Conveniently opposite the bus stop is a **café**, the *Sri Thankashmi Villas*, serving *masala dosai*.

Pulau Ketam

An hour's ferry ride (daily 7am–8pm; every 30min; from the pier 50m west of Tanjung Balai jetty) from Port Klang through the mangrove swamps is the fishing village of **PULAU KETAM** (the name means "Crab Island"), a Chinese stronghold since three fishermen established a community here at the beginning of the twentieth century. Today, it is most appealing for its clapboard houses built on stilts, its lack of cars, and its restaurants, which serve delicious seafood.

Bicycles can be rented at the *Sea Lion Villa Lodge*, next to the jetty, for RM3 an hour, but everything on the island is within easy walking distance. The Hock Leng Keng **temple** at the end of Jalan Merdeka – the main shopping street with old painted movie banners strung across it to provide shade – is worth checking out, as is the local Chinese Association hall, the balcony of which provides a pleasant view across the village. Rather less pleasant is the pollution in the water around the houses, all too apparent at low tide.

It's possible to **stay** on the island at the *Sea Lion Villa Lodge* (☎03/351 4121; ②) and the *Pulau Ketam Lodge* (☎03/351 4200; ②) on Jalan Merdeka, although there is little to do in the evening. The reasonably priced seafood is worth sampling though; not surprisingly, the speciality is crab, best eaten at the *Kuai Lok Hian* restaurant by the jetty (around RM13), where the sea breeze will keep you cool as you watch the fishing boats plough up and down the estuaries between the islands.

South of KL

The area south of KL used to be dominated by a vast collection of rubber plantations. Today, while some plantations – of oil palm – still exist, a significant chunk of the land has been cleared for development. Already completed is the **Mines Wonderland**, a theme park popular with local families, but this project pales beside the 750-square-kilometre **Multimedia Super Corridor** (MSC; *www.mdc.com.my*), which will stretch from the Petronas Twin Towers in downtown KL to the international airport 60km south. Aimed to be completed by 2020 (when the country intends to have achieved full industrial-nation status), the MSC will, according to Malaysian Prime Minister Dr Mahathir, be "a new paradigm for creating value in the information age". He wants the MSC to rewrite the way business is done in his part of the world, foreseeing a time when component manufacturing can be done in China on machines programmed in Japan with software written in India and finance from banks in East Malaysia. The idea is not to take on and beat the West, but to encourage foreign companies to use the MSC as a marketing gateway to Asia. Dr Mahathir's super-hi-tech vision has some notable supporters, with the likes of Bill Gates on the project's advisory panel.

Within this zone, two cities, **Putrajaya** and **Cyberjaya**, are under construction, as is a computer-network infrastructure it's hoped will surpass the best in the world. Until the two cities start functioning as living communities (it's planned for the inhabitants and enterprises to be in place around 2003), the main reason for visiting is out of curiosity, though Malaysians are already coming to Putrajaya in their droves, if only to use its fabulous **mosque**, already completed, or climb up the nearby lookout tower to gaze over the area, which is still being landscaped.

Mines Wonderland

En route to Putrajaya, you can experience one of the strangest sensations in sultry Malaysia at the **Mines Wonderland** in Sungei Besi (daily 4–11pm; RM18). Once the lake at the world's largest open-cast tin mine, here you can experience a mini-world covered in machine-generated snow in the "Snow House". After dark, there are various laser and light shows, plus some mildly thrilling fire-eating and snake-wrestling displays.

You can get here by **driving** south out of KL on the North–South Highway; leave the road near Serdang – the exit for the park is clearly signposted. It's also possible to reach the complex on **bus** #110 from KL's Pudu Raya bus station.

Putrajaya and Cyberjaya

At time of writing, a few buildings in **PUTRAJAYA**, the city which will be Malaysia's new, paperless, seat of government, are in use – some government buildings, the mosque and a couple of swish hotels. Living accommodation for government employees, shops and a public transport network are all to come.

The first thing you notice upon turning into the wide avenue leading towards the city are the lampposts, shaped like vast spiders with bulbous heads. After about 1km, you see the **Taman Wetland Putrajaya** on the right. The car park here has an information board giving a short explanation on the ecology of the parkland, which leads away from the lake to the left. Beside the car park, the forty-metre-high tower offers a good view of the Putrajaya site. Travelling the last 2km to the city's centre, the scale of its architecture becomes apparent. Nearly all government departments are in the process of moving here, and the immense red-brick **Parliament Building**, the first to be finished, is visible on the right as you arrive at the inner orbital road. All the main buildings in Putrajaya will line this inner circle; accommodation, shops and other amenities will lie on the outer orbital road network.

Behind the Parliament is an artificial **lake**. On the other side of the lake is a set of large, low, white buildings, comprising Prime Minister Mahathir's retirement residence. Immediately to the left of the Parliament building is the **mosque**. Inspired by the Sheikh Omar Mosque in Baghdad, it can hold up to eight thousand people in its main hall and two thousand in the women's prayer hall. Its minaret, 116m high, has a cross-section in the shape of an eight-pointed star; the dome is made of fibreglass, decorated with mosaic tiles from Tehran.

At time of writing, **CYBERJAYA** (*www.cyberjaya-msc.com*), 10km southwest of Putrajaya, was in the early stages of being built; there is, however, a hotel already open for business, *Cyber View Lodge* (*www.cyberview-lodge.com.my*; ⑦). In time, it's hoped Cyberjaya will become Malaysia's powerhouse of hi-tech industry and electronic commerce; indeed, it's the site of the Multimedia University, which is already training the country's brave new futurists.

Practicalities

Until public transport to both cities is up and running, the best way to get to both cities is by **car**: take the North–South Highway south out of the city, leaving the road at the Kajang exit (50 sen toll to do so), about 30km from KL. It's important to exit west from the highway, not east (which takes you to Kajang itself); continue west along the road, signposted to Uniten, for about 4km to reach the entrance road to Putrajaya on your left (south). You can also visit on a half-day **tour** with Backpackers Transport in KL (☎012/638 8382; RM80).

travel details

Trains

Kuala Lumpur to: Alor Setar (1 daily; 10hr); Butterworth (3 daily; 7hr); Gemas (4 daily; 4hr); Ipoh (3 daily; 3hr 30min); Klang (every 30min; 1hr); Nilai (every 30min, 50min); Port Klang (every 30min; 1hr 15min); Singapore (3 daily; 6hr 30min); Tapah Road (3 daily; 2hr).

Buses

Kuala Lumpur

Pudu Raya station to:

Alor Setar (4 daily; 9hr); Butterworth (13 daily; 7hr); Cameron Highlands (4 daily; 4hr 30min); Fraser's Hill (hourly; 4hr); Genting Highlands (hourly; 1hr); Ipoh (every 30min; 4hr); Johor Bahru (18 daily; 6hr); Kuala Kedah (6 daily; 8hr); Kuala Perlis (3 daily; 9hr); Lumut (9 daily; 4hr); Melaka (every 30min; 2hr); Mentakab (every 30min; 2hr 30min); Mersing (1 daily; 8hr); Muar (10 daily; 3hr); Penang (6 daily; 8hr); Seremban (9 daily; 1hr); Singapore (7 daily; 7hr); Tanjong Bidara (3 daily, 2hr); Taiping (11 daily; 5hr).

Pekeliling station to:

Jerantut (4 daily; 3hr 30min); Kuala Kubu Bharu (8 daily; 2hr); Kuala Lipis (4 daily; 4hr).

Putra station to:

Kemaman (3 daily; 6hr); Kota Bharu (9 daily; 10hr); Kuala Terengganu (6 daily; 7hr); Kuantan (8 daily; 5hr); Temerloh (hourly; 3hr).

Istana Hotel to:

Kuala Tembeling jetty (for Taman Negara; 1 daily, 4hr).

Ferries

Port Klang to: Pulau Ketam (every 30min; 1hr).

Flights

Kuala Lumpur to: Alor Setar (4 daily; 50min); Bandar Seri Begawan (1 daily; 2hr 20min); Ipoh (2 daily; 35min); Johor Bahru (7 daily; 45min); Kota Bharu (6 daily; 50min); Kota Kinabalu (10 daily; 2hr 30min); Kuala Terengganu (4 daily; 45min); Kuantan (4 daily; 40min); Kuching (9 daily; 1hr 45min); Labuan (1 daily; 2hr 25min); Langkawi (4 daily; 55min); Miri (2 daily; 2hr 15min), Penang (12 daily; 45min); Sibu (1 daily; 2hr); Singapore (11 daily; 55min).

CHAPTER TWO

THE WEST COAST

The **west coast** of the Peninsular Malaysia, from Kuala Lumpur north to the Thai
border, is the most industrialized and densely populated – not to mention cosmopolitan – part of the whole country. Its considerable natural resources have
long brought eager traders and entrepreneurs here, but it was the demand for the
region's tin in the late nineteenth century that spearheaded Malaysia's phenomenal
economic rise. Immigrant workers, most of whom settled in the region for good,
bestowed a permanent legacy here – the predominantly Chinese towns that punctuate
the route north. Perak State – once boasting the richest single tin field in the world – and
its capital, the old tin-boom city of Ipoh, are still littered with reminders of the recent
industrial past. But even when the light industry surrounding Malaysia's other major
commodity, rubber, took over from the dying tin trade in the 1950s, the essentially agricultural nature of much of the region wasn't quite obliterated. The states of **Kedah** and
Perlis, the latter tucked into the northern border, share the distinction of being the historical *jelapang padi*, or "rice bowl", of Malaysia, where rich, emerald-green paddy fields
and jutting limestone outcrops form the Peninsula's most dramatic scenery.

This is the area in which the **British** held most sway, attracted by the political prestige of controlling such a strategic trading region. Although the British had claimed
administrative authority since 1826 through the Straits Settlements (which included
Singapore and Melaka as well as Penang), it was the establishment here of the
Federated Malay States of Perak, Pahang, Selangor and Negeri Sembilan fifty years
later that extended colonial rule to the whole Peninsula.

Most visitors are too intent on the beckoning delights of Thailand to bother stopping
at anything other than the major destinations. But nowhere are the rural delights of the
country more apparent than at the **hill stations** north of the capital, designed as cool
retreats for colonial administrators. The largest of these, the **Cameron Highlands**,
some 150km north of KL, is one of the country's most significant tourist spots, a justi-
fiably popular mountain retreat with opportunities for forest treks and indulgence in the
traditional British comforts of crackling log fires and cream teas.

Due west of here, tiny **Pulau Pangkor**, though not as idyllic as the islands of the
Peninsula's east coast, is an increasingly visited resort, with the best beaches in the
area. However, the fastest development is on its far northern rival, **Pulau Langkawi**,
the largest island in the glittering and largely unpopulated Langkawi archipelago. Most

travellers wisely give the port of **Butterworth** a wide berth, just using it for access to the island of **Penang**, whose vibrant capital, **Georgetown**, combines modern shopping malls with ancient Chinese shophouses.

These main destinations aside, there's a whole host of intriguing and undervisited places off the beaten track, such as **Ipoh**, 200km northwest of Kuala Lumpur, which has elegant colonial buildings and mansions at every turn, and its northern neighbour the royal town of **Kuala Kangsar**, a quiet place of architectural interest. The route north also passes through the old mining town of **Taiping**, whose small hill station, **Maxwell Hill**, is now fading gently into insignificance. The state capital of Kedah is **Alor Setar**, the last major town before the border (and the last significant stop other than Pulau Langkawi). Long a stamping ground for successions of invaders, the region still reveals a Thai influence in its cuisine, although Alor Setar itself is a staunch Muslim stronghold. From here it's a short hop via any of the **border towns** – Kuala Perlis, Kangar and Arau – into Thailand itself.

Because of its economic importance, the west coast has a well-developed transport infrastructure. The pristine **North–South Highway**, pleasantly free of heavy traffic north of KL, virtually shadows the already adequate **Route 1**, and runs from Malaysia's northern border at Bukit Kayu Hitam all the way to Singapore. The **train line**, which runs more or less parallel to these roads, is used less, though its border crossing at Padang Besar facilitates easy connections with Hat Yai, the transport crossroads of southern Thailand. Both roads and the train line pass through all the major towns – Ipoh, Taiping, Butterworth and Alor Setar – with **express buses** providing the fastest and most frequent way of travelling between the major towns, and **local buses** serving the hills and the coast.

Cameron Highlands

Amid the lofty peaks of **Banjaran Titiwangsa**, the Peninsula's main mountain range, the various outposts of the **CAMERON HIGHLANDS** (at an average altitude of 1800m) form Malaysia's most extensive hill station. The place took its name from William Cameron, a government surveyor who stumbled across it in 1885 during a mapping expedition. Cameron actually failed to mark his find on a map, and it wasn't until the 1920s that the location was officially confirmed. When he visited in 1925, Sir George Maxwell, a senior civil servant, saw the same potential for a hill station here as he'd seen at Fraser's Hill (see p.230). Others, too, were quick to see the benefits of the region, and early tea planters were followed by Chinese vegetable farmers and wealthy landowners in search of a weekend retreat; the ensuing spate of development culminated in today's hotels and luxury apartments.

Despite seventy years of tourism, William Cameron's early, glowing descriptions of the plateau's gentle contours and dramatic peaks still apply. Although tall condominiums occasionally punctuate the landscape, a quintessential English character remains, the rolling green fields dotted with country cottages, farms and a golf course. While weekenders flock here in their thousands, it's not difficult to avoid the crowds as most are content to enjoy the views from their hotels. The vast plateau and surrounding hills and forests are ideal for **walking**, and the climate is cool; leisure activities here tend to be rather wholesome and simple, with the emphasis on fresh air and early nights – in fact, there's precious little else to do here, particularly in the evenings when **eating** provides just about the sole diversion. The Highlands' colonial past means you can round off a day of walking with an English cream tea, followed by dinner incorporating the local speciality, the steamboat (see p.47).

The highlands encompass three small towns: **Ringlet**, a rich agricultural area and site of the famous tea plantations; 13km beyond and 300m higher, **Tanah Rata**, the

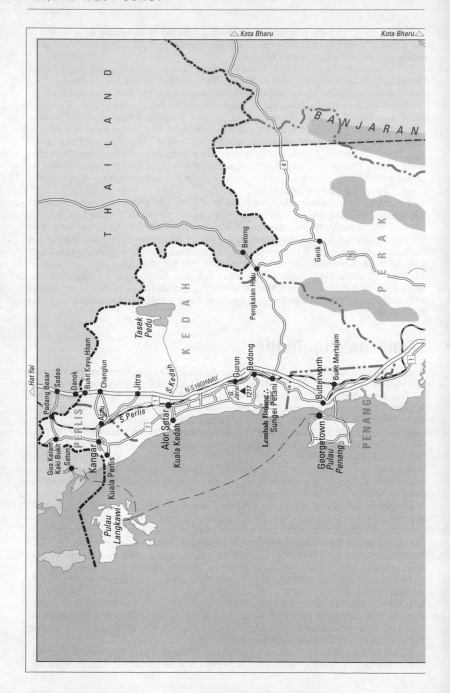

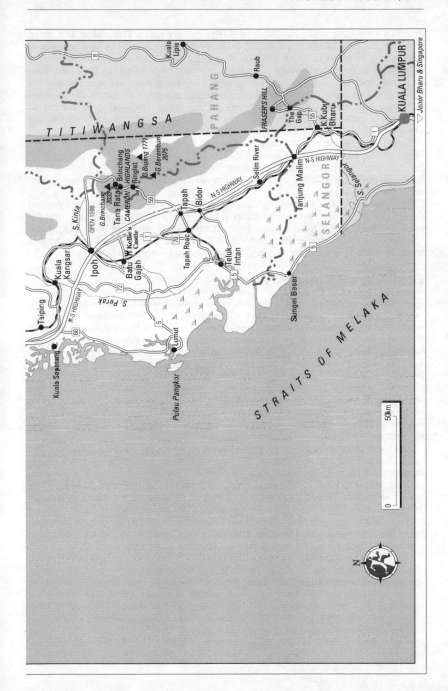

principal settlement of the highlands; and 5km further north, **Brinchang**, renowned for its farms, most of which are located to the north of the town. The best **accommodation** is to be found in Tanah Rata and Brinchang; the towns are also convenient for tours of the farms and tea estates, since many operators will collect you from your hotel or guesthouse. You could also try renting one of the **bungalows** and **apartments** dotted around the region, particularly if you're travelling in a group or plan to stay for some time. Accommodation **prices** soar at peak holiday times – book ahead if you can to ensure a place – when you can expect the price of an ordinary room to double; it's always worth bargaining out of season.

Tours of the whole region, which take around three hours, can be arranged by any of the hostels and depart at 8.45am and 1.45pm daily (typical cost RM15). Though a bit "whistle-stop" in character, they do at least cover all the main sights and destinations, including the Boh tea plantation, butterfly farm and Sam Poh temple, in one swoop. The inevitable shopping stop at the end is mercifully low-key.

The **weather** in the Cameron Highlands is as British as the countryside, and you can expect rainstorms even in the dry season. It makes sense to avoid the area during the monsoon itself, and at major holiday times (Christmas, Easter and Hari Raya) if you want to avoid the crowds. Temperatures drop dramatically at night – whatever the season – so you'll need socks and warm clothes, as well as waterproofs.

En route to the highlands: Tapah

The road and rail routes north from KL towards the Cameron Highlands pass through pale-green splashes of endless **rubber plantations**. It's a fairly monotonous stretch, but for the 350-kilometre **Banjaran Titiwangsa** range, which rises up away to the east. The main jumping-off point for the Cameron Highlands is **TAPAH**, about 40km to the southwest along Route 59. Hardly more than a crossroads, Tapah is easily reached from KL, 125km to the south, or Ipoh, 45km to the north, using the North–South Highway or Route 1. If you're driving up from KL and have time to spare, a more idiosyncratic route here than using the main highways is to follow the coastal Route 5, running through low-lying marshland almost all the way to **Teluk Intan**, 157km northwest of the capital. Here you can stop off at the leaning pagoda-like clock tower and grab a bowl of noodles, before taking the minor back roads to Bidor, 14km south of Tapah, to connect with the North–South Highway and Route 1.

The north–south Jalan Besar is Tapah's main street, west off which run Jalan Raja and Jalan Stesen. Local bus services use the **bus station** on Jalan Raja; there are hourly departures from here to Tanah Rata (8.15am–6.15pm; 2hr). Express bus services, including those to Hat Yai in Thailand, only stop briefly in Tapah (either at the local bus station or on Jalan Besar); ticket agencies for these services, such as the Kah Mee, 10 Jalan Raja (☎05/412 973), opposite the bus station; or *Caspian* – which is also a restaurant – nearby on the main road; can either tell you where to catch your bus, or more than likely flag it down for you. The **train station**, called "Tapah Road", where trains from destinations up and down the west coast arrive, is a few kilometres west of town; it's easy enough to get from the station into town by taxi (RM7) or the hourly local bus (90 sen).

You're unlikely to need to stay in Tapah, though it has some very reasonable **hotels**, of which the cheapest is the *Hotel Bunga Raya*, 6 Jalan Besar (☎05/401 1436; ①), on the corner with Jalan Raja; it's basic and clean, and all its rooms are en suite. Two other options are two minutes' walk away on Jalan Stesen. The good-value *Timuran*, 23 Jalan Stesen (☎05/401 1092, fax 401 2570; ②) has spotless rooms, some with air-con, and there's also a busy restaurant downstairs. A slightly more comfortable place is just opposite, the *NH Hotel*, 24 Jalan Stesen (☎ & fax 05/401 7188; ③), with carpeted, en-suite rooms and TVs. There are a number of cheap, nondescript Indian and Chinese **restaurants** dotted around town.

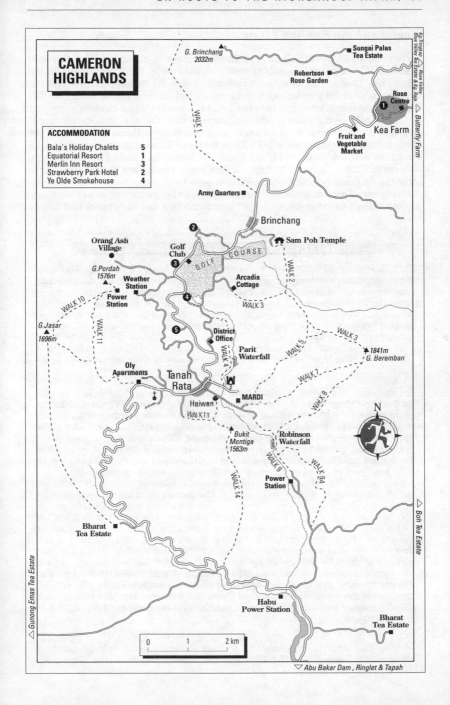

CAMERON HIGHLANDS

ACCOMMODATION

Bala's Holiday Chalets	5
Equatorial Resort	1
Merlin Inn Resort	3
Strawberry Park Hotel	2
Ye Olde Smokehouse	4

Ringlet and the Boh Tea Estate

There's not much to **RINGLET**, the first settlement you reach in the Cameron Highlands. The area to the north of town is dominated by the immense Sultan Abu Bakar Dam, its glittering blue water contrasting with the deep green of the forest. There are several **tea plantations** in the area, of which the best known is the **Boh Tea Estate** (Tues–Sun 11am–3pm), 8km northeast of town. Here you can take a free tour on which you'll see the whole production process – from the picking to the packing of the tea, which you cannot do at the estate's more frequented **Palas** division (☎05/496 1146), north of Brinchang (see p.147). There are buses from Ringlet to Habu – the junction for the Boh Tea Estate – daily at 6.30am, 11.30am, 3.15pm and 5.15pm, with return journeys at 7.20am, 12.20pm, 3.45pm and 6pm. From Tanah Rata, the quickest way to get to the tea estate is to take a taxi (RM10 one-way).

Buses from Tapah stop on the main road in Ringlet before moving on to Tanah Rata. It's easy enough to get to Ringlet from Tanah Rata, since there are buses four times a

---

WALKING IN THE CAMERON HIGHLANDS

The Cameron Highlands feature a number of **walks** of varying difficulty. While the forest sometimes obscures the view, the trails here take in some of the most spectacular scenery in Malaysia, encompassing textured greenery and misty mountain peaks. Some of the walks are no more than casual strolls, while others veer off into what seems like the wild unknown, giving a sense of isolation rarely encountered in lowland Malaysia. Despite the presence of large mammals in the deep forest, such as honey bears and monkeys, you're unlikely to come across much wildlife on the trails, perhaps the odd wild pig or squirrel. Fortunately the **flora** at all times of the year is prolific, including ferns, pitcher plants and orchids amongst the tremendous canopy of trees.

Unfortunately, the trails are often badly signposted and maintained, though there are various sketch **maps** on sale in town (RM1) and at many of the hotels. Despite their apparent vagueness, they do make some sort of sense on the ground, although some of the trails marked no longer exist. The *Cameronian Inn* and *Father's Guest House* are good contacts for trail information and hiring guides. There used to be more official trails but many were closed during the 1970s due to the supposed threat of Communist guerrillas hanging out in the undergrowth. Even now, if you want to attempt any **unofficial routes**, a guide is essential and you must also obtain a permit from the District Office (see "Listings", p.144), which is tricky and expensive.

However, the **official trails**, detailed below (and marked on the map on p.139) are varied enough for most tastes and energies. The timings given are for one-way walks for people with an average level of fitness. You should always inform someone, preferably at your hotel, where you are going and what time you expect to be back. On longer hikes, take warm clothing, water, a torch and a cigarette lighter or matches for basic survival should you get lost. If someone doesn't return from a hike and you suspect they may be in **trouble**, inform the District Office immediately. It's not a fanciful notion that the hills and forests are dangerous – mudslides, for example, are not uncommon in some spots. The most notorious incident to date concerns the American silk entrepreneur Jim Thompson, who came on holiday here in Easter 1967 and disappeared in the forest. The services of Orang Asli trackers, dogs and even mystics failed to provide any clue to his fate – a warning to present-day trekkers of the hazards of jungle life.

Walk 1 (1hr) A short but tough walk, starting just north of Brinchang, up a rarely used and unmaintained track by the army quarters. You can either return the way you came or by walking east along the sealed access road back to the main

day starting 8.30am, with the last service at 1.30pm. While there are **places to stay** in town, including one deluxe hotel, the *Lakehouse* (☎05/495 6152, fax 495 6213; ⑨), this is a somewhat isolated place to base yourself.

Tanah Rata

The tidy town of **TANAH RATA** is the highlands' main development, a genteel place festooned with hotels, white-balustraded buildings, flowers and parks. It comprises little more than one street (officially called Jalan Pasar, but usually just known as "Main Road"), which is where you'll find most of the hotels, banks and other services, as well as some of the best restaurants in the Cameron Highlands, all lined up in a half-kilometre stretch. Since the street also serves as the main thoroughfare to the rest of the region, it suffers from the constant honking of departing buses during the day, but at night becomes the centre of the Cameron Highlands' social life, with restaurant tables spilling out onto the pavement.

road, passing turnings for the Rose Garden (see p.147) and Sungei Palas Tea Estate en route (see p.147).

Walk 2 (1hr 30min) Begins just before the Sam Poh Temple below Brinchang – it's not clearly marked, and is often a bit of a scramble; you'll need to be reasonably fit and well prepared. The route undulates severely and eventually merges with Walk 3.

Walk 3 (2hr 30min) Starts at *Arcadia Cottage* to the southeast of the golf course, crossing streams and climbing quite steeply to reach the peak of Gunung Beremban (1841m). Moderately arduous.

Walk 4 (20min) Paved in stretches, this starts south of the golf course and goes past Parit Waterfall, leading on to a watchtower with good views over Brinchang. The last stop is the Forest Department HQ from where a sealed path leads back to the main road.

Walk 5 (1hr) Branches off from Walk 3 and ends up at the Malaysian Agriculture Research and Development Institute (MARDI). It's an easy walk through peaceful woodland, after which you can cut back up the road to Tanah Rata.

Walk 6 The official numbering system falls down here: there are two Walk 6's. Most people call the two-and-a-half-hour route from the summit of Gunung Jasar, along a ridge to the Bharat tea estate, Walk 6. The alternative Walk 6 (1km) runs a short way from the Parit waterfall to join Walk 5.

Walk 7 (2hr) Starts near MARDI and climbs steeply to Gunung Beremban; an

arduous and very overgrown hike best recommended as a descent route from Walk 3.

Walk 8 (3hr) Another route to Gunung Beremban, a tough approach from Robinson Waterfall; more taxing than Walk 7.

Walks 9 and 9A (1hr) The descent from Robinson Waterfall to the power station is reasonably steep and strenuous; the station caretaker will let you through to the road to Boh. Walk 9A, less steep than Walk 9, branches off from the main route to emerge in a vegetable farm on the Boh road.

Walks 10 and 11 (2hr–2hr 30min) Walk 10 starts just behind the *Oly Apartments* and involves a fairly strenuous climb to Gunung Jasar (1696m). The only problem is that the end of the route, at Gunung Perdah, is now blocked by a power station – you'll have to return the way you came or go along the less challenging (and slightly shorter) Walk 11, which bypasses the summit.

Walk 12 Now replaced by a road to the power station.

Walk 13 (1hr) Its starting point is a halfhour's walk southwest of the *Cameronian Holiday Inn* in Tanah Rata; eventually merges with Walk 14.

Walk 14 (3hr) A tricky and initially steep route via Bukit Mentiga (1563m), with great views. It begins at Haiwan (a veterinary centre) and continues south, becoming very hard to pick out until it joins the road 8km from Tanah Rata. It's best not to do this one alone.

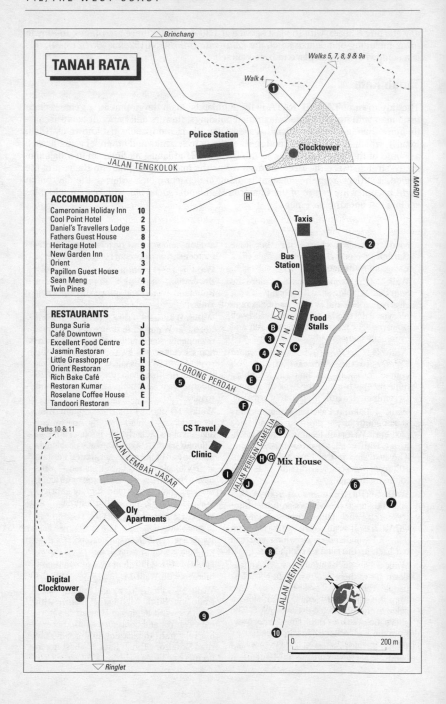

TANAH RATA

Brinchang

Walks 5, 7, 8, 9 & 9a

Walk 4

1

Police Station

Clocktower

JALAN TENGKOLOK

MARDI

H

Taxis

2

Bus Station

ACCOMMODATION
Cameronian Holiday Inn	10
Cool Point Hotel	2
Daniel's Travellers Lodge	5
Fathers Guest House	8
Heritage Hotel	9
New Garden Inn	1
Orient	3
Papillon Guest House	7
Sean Meng	4
Twin Pines	6

A

Food Stalls

B

3

MAIN ROAD

C

4

D

RESTAURANTS
Bunga Suria	J
Café Downtown	D
Excellent Food Centre	C
Jasmin Restoran	F
Little Grasshopper	H
Orient Restoran	B
Rich Bake Café	G
Restoran Kumar	A
Roselane Coffee House	E
Tandoori Restoran	I

E

5

LORONG PERDAH

F

Paths 10 & 11

G

JALAN LEMBAH JASAR

CS Travel

JALAN PERISAN CAMELLIA

Clinic

H @ Mix House

I

6

J

7

Oly Apartments

8

Digital Clocktower

JALAN MENTIGI

N

9

10

0   200 m

Ringlet

All the local and long-distance **buses** go only as far as Tanah Rata; to move further on to Brinchang and other destinations you'll have to change here. The **bus station** is about halfway along the main road, and Tanah Rata's **taxi rank** is just a little further north. At the far end of town, past the hospital and the police station, the road bends round to the west to continue on to Brinchang.

Tanah Rata is an ideal base to explore the Cameron Highlands, with many **walks** starting nearby (see box, p.140); a couple of waterfalls, a mosque and three reasonably high mountain peaks are all within hiking distance. Several of the walks pass through, or close to, the **Malaysian Agriculture Research and Development Institute** (MARDI; ☎05/491 1255) a couple of kilometres east of town, which is open for tours by appointment, though it's rather dry for anyone other than a specialist. This is the location for the annual **Flower Festival** held most years in August, when colourful floats compete for prizes.

Accommodation

Budget lodging is of a good standard in Tanah Rata, with even the simplest **hostels** offering hot showers and higher levels of service and cleanliness for the price than in many other parts of the Peninsula. Many of the budget places have touts at the bus station waiting to escort you. **Hotels** tend to double in price during high season and at weekends as you'd expect; the prices we've indicated below are for weekday stays. Some places also have working fireplaces, which can make no end of difference to an otherwise uninspiring hotel. The places strung along the main road can be a bit noisy; for a quieter stay you'll have to pay the higher prices charged at the comfortable hotels out on the Brinchang road, or rent one of the **apartments** or cottages in the locality. These are advertised in shop windows in Tanah Rata – rates quoted are usually per day, and a residential cook or caretaker can often be hired at an additional cost. Try the *Golf View Villa*, a six-room bungalow for RM360 (☎05/491 1624); the *Lutheran Bungalow*, which sleeps twenty at RM25 a head (☎05/491 1584); *Rose Cottage*, which has two rooms and costs RM230 (☎05/491 1173); or *Country Lodge*, which sleeps six people for RM270 (☎05/491 1811). All the accommodation below is marked on either the Tanah Rata map or the main map of the highlands.

Cameronian Inn, 16 Jalan Mentigi (☎05/491 1327, fax 491 4966). Friendly, clean and well-informed place, with Internet access and a library. There's a small dorm and some double rooms. Organized treks set off from here at 9.30am most mornings, with non-guests welcome at no charge. ②, dorm beds RM6.

Cool Point, just off the main road behind the Shell station (☎05/491 4914, fax 491 4070). A new hotel in a quiet location; its rooms, though large, tend to be dark and damp. ⑥.

Daniel's Travellers Lodge, 9 Lorong Perdah (☎05/491 5823, fax 491 5828). One huge attic dorm and some doubles. There's a good communal sitting area and café with comfy chairs and pumping music – less pleasant at night when you're trying to sleep. ②, dorm beds RM6.

Father's Guest House (☎05/491 2484, fax 491 5484, *fathersonline@hotmail.com*). The best of the budget places, set on a quiet hill in the outskirts. There are doubles in a stone house and dorm beds in tunnel-like aluminium outhouses. They also have a large collection of books, a few Internet terminals and very friendly, well-travelled staff. ②, dorm beds RM7.

Heritage, Jalan Gereja (☎05/491 3888, fax 491 5666). Set on a hill near the approach road from Ringlet, this comfortable hotel, the most upmarket in Tanah Rata, has several posh restaurants. ⑧.

New Garden Inn, 42 Jalan Masjid (☎05/491 5170, fax 491 5169). A little less expensive, and not as smart as the *Cool Point*. The doubles are clean, though the furniture's rather worn. Only worth the asking price on weekdays, when it's half-rate. ⑥.

Orient, 38 Main Rd (☎05/491 1633). Very good value, with thoughtfully furnished, airy rooms, although it can be noisy during holiday periods. ③.

Papillon Guest House, 8 Jalan Mentigi (☎05/491 5942). Head out to the *Twin Pines*, then follow the road to reach this friendly, clean hostel. The dorms are a bit cramped and there aren't too many facilities, apart from a pleasant lounge. ②, dorm beds RM10.

Seah Meng, 39 Main Rd (☎05/491 1618). Clean, well-kept rooms, very similar to the *Orient*'s next door; one of the best-value hotels. ②.

Twin Pines, 2 Jalan Mentigi (☎05/491 2169). Set back from the road, this blue-roofed building has small doubles, an attractive patio garden and books full of travellers' tips. There are also dorms, a café and online facilities. ①, dorm beds RM6.

ON THE BRINCHANG ROAD

Bala's Holiday Chalets (☎05/491 1660, fax 491 4500). A kilometre or so towards Brinchang, this English-style country house has rooms and dormitories, as well as a lounge and two dining rooms, a real fire and beautiful gardens. A great spot for afternoon tea. ②, dorm beds RM10.

Merlin Inn Resort (☎05/491 1211, fax 491 1178). More promising from the outside than inside. Standard, bland rooms, some overlooking the golf course, and a pool/snooker room. ⑥.

Strawberry Park (☎05/491 1166, fax 491 1949). A high-class hotel in a superb location at the top of a hill, which makes it rather inaccessible, though a hotel minibus leaves on request. There's an indoor swimming pool. ⑧.

Ye Olde Smokehouse (☎05/491 1215, fax 491 1214). Midway along the Tanah Rata–Brinchang road. Twelve suites, most with four-poster beds, just on the tasteful side of kitsch. Leaded windows and wooden beams belie the fact that this country pub is only about 65 years old. ⑨.

Eating and drinking

There are a number of places in Tanah Rata offering Western dishes, particularly pepper steak, but nothing especially imaginative. Much cheaper than the restaurants, and often more satisfying, are the Malay **food stalls** along the main road. Open in the evening, they serve satay, *tom yam* (spicy Thai soup) and the usual rice and noodle combinations, for about RM2 per dish.

Bunga Suria, Jalan Perisan Camellia. A haven for vegetarians as well as meat eaters, this is the best South Indian restaurant in Tana Rata.

Café Downtown, 41 Main Rd. Good spot for breakfast and lunch. Does tasty pastries and cakes as well as set meals of noodles and rice.

Excellent Food Centre, on the main road opposite the post office. Lives up to its name with a large, inexpensive menu of Western and Asian dishes – it's great for breakfast. Open during the day only. In the adjacent *Fresh Milk Corner*, you can get wonderful shakes and *lassis*.

Jasmine Restoran, 45 Main Rd. With *rijstafel* set meals, it's popular with German and Dutch travellers. The evening karaoke sessions can get a bit rowdy.

Little Grasshopper, 57b Perisran Camellia 3. On the second floor above the new shophouses. Excellent-value steamboats, starting at just RM6, served by friendly staff in a tasteful setting. Also has traditional Chinese tea.

Orient Restoran, 38 Main Rd. Standard Chinese food in the restaurant below the hotel. The set meals are reasonable value, as are the steamboats.

Restoran Kumar, Main Rd. Along with *Thanam* next door, the *Kumar* specializes in claypot rice.

Rich Bake Café, Main Rd. Bright, jazzy spot which sometimes has live music; serves good pancakes.

Roselane Coffee House, 44 Main Rd. The various set menus and low-price meat grills here make up for the twee decor.

Tandoori Restoran, Main Rd. Tasty, good-value Indian food, including *naan* breads and tandoori dishes. The food can take time to arrive.

Ye Olde Smokehouse (☎05/491 1215). The hotel's restaurant offers intimate surroundings for a romantic splash-out. Their traditional English menu features a choice of roast meat dinners for around RM70, and other dishes starting at RM20; afternoon tea is RM11. You'll need to book in advance.

Listings

Banks There is a branch of HSBC on the main road, north of the post office, and a Maybank on the southern branch of Lorong Perdah.

District office 39007 Tanah Rata (Mon–Fri 8am–1pm & 3–4.30pm; ☎05/491 1105, fax 491 1843). Contact them immediately if you suspect someone has got lost on a walk. Also call here to obtain permits for unofficial trails.

Hospital Main Rd, opposite the park (☎05/491 1966). There's also a clinic at 48 Main Rd (8.30am–12.30pm, 2–5.30pm & 8–10pm). Ring doorbell after clinic hours in emergencies.

Internet access Mix House Net, 76b Jalan Perisan Camellia.

Laundry *Highlands Laundry*, Main Rd (☎05/491 1820) is reasonably priced, and most hostels also offer this service.

Police station Main Rd, opposite the *New Garden Inn* (☎05/491 1222).

Post office Main Rd (☎05/491 1051); pick up poste restante/general delivery mail here.

Service station There are service stations in both Tanah Rata and Brinchang.

Sport Cameron Highlands Golf Club (☎05/491 1126) has an eighteen-hole course (RM45 for a half-day, RM60 at weekends, half-price after 4pm, equipment rental extra); there's a strict dress code. Tennis courts at the golf club (RM4 per hr for court, RM5 for racket).

Taxi rank Main Rd (☎05/491 1234).

Travel agent CS Travel, Main Rd (☎05/491 1200), is an agent for express bus tickets from Tapah to all major destinations.

Brinchang and around

After Tanah Rata, **BRINCHANG**, 5km or so further north, seems rather scruffy. Sprawling around a central square and the main road – called Main Road (or Jalan Besar) – through town, it lacks the charm of its neighbour, though it has a saving grace, the lively **night market** which opens at about 4pm on Saturdays and holidays. In the holiday periods, you may have to resort to Brinchang as an alternative to Tanah Rata in order to find a room – not a disaster, since Walks 1–3 (see box, p.140) are easily approached from here, and reaching the **farms** and **tea estates** to the north (see over leaf) is quicker from here too. A more challenging alternative to the local trails is to hike to the summit of **Gunung Brinchang** (2032m), the highest peak in Malaysia accessible by road. This takes two to three hours from Brinchang and although the road there is sealed, it's an extremely steep and exhausting climb. On a clear day though, the views back down the broad valley are wonderful. You can also walk to the **Sam Poh Temple**, 1km southeast of Brinchang, a gaudy modern place with a monastery which was built in 1965.

Practicalities

Buses leave Tanah Rata for Brinchang and Kampung Raja (the furthest point north here that's served by public transport) every hour or so between 6.40am and 6pm, arriving at the **bus station** just south of the square. A **taxi** from Tanah Rata to Brinchang costs around RM4.

ACCOMMODATION

Most of the **hotels** in Brinchang line the east and west sides of the central square, and although the numbering system leaves much to be desired, you shouldn't have too much difficulty locating them. When you do, you'll find them uniformly overpriced.

BRINCHANG

N

Restaurant Sakaya
Hong Kong Restaurant

Central Market

Stalls

P

MAIN ROAD

ACCOMMODATION
Equatorial Resort	1
Golden Star	6
Green Garden	2
Kowloon	8
Parkland	9
Pines & Roses	5
Rafflesia Inn	7
Rosa Passedena	4
Silverstar	3

0   50 m

▽ *Tanah Rata*

Brinchang sees very little of the backpacker scene and consequently there's next to no budget accommodation. The standard high-season price hikes apply.

Brinchang, 36 Main Rd (☎05/491 1755, fax 491 1246). Good-sized rooms with colour TV and phone (RM95).

Equatorial Resort, Kea Farm (☎05/496 1777, fax 496 1333, *info@cam.equatorial.com*). Luxury resort, about 2km north of Brinchang, near the Rose Centre (see opposite). Has modern rooms that are very good value. With residents getting meal vouchers – redeemable in the hotel's restaurants – to the value of half of the standard room rate, this is a real bargain. The hotel's towers are perched precariously on the edge of the mountain with lovely views; facilities include a cinema complex and gym. ⑦.

Golden Star Hotel, 26 Main Rd (☎05/491 2233). The next best choice after the *Silverstar* for an inexpensive night's sleep; the rooms are nothing special, but they're clean and looked after. ③.

Green Garden, Lot 13, Main Rd (☎05/491 5824, fax 491 5824). On the northwest corner of the square, this has clean rooms with well-equipped bathrooms. They're overpriced for what you get, though. ⑤.

Kowloon, 34–35 Main Rd (☎05/491 1366, fax 491 1803). Small, comfortable rooms with TVs and bathrooms – good value by Brinchang's standards. ⑤.

Parkland, 45 Main Rd (☎05/491 1299, fax 491 1803). Run by the same management as the *Kowloon*. The rooms are a little larger and better furnished. ⑤.

Pines and Roses (☎05/491 2203). Friendly service and simple, clean, carpeted doubles leading off a dark corridor. Good value. ⑤.

Rafflesia Inn, Lot 30, Main Rd (☎ & fax 05/491 2859). This new backpacker operation is the only real budget accommodation in town. It has a comfy TV lounge, but the dorm beds are a bit hard. ②, dorm beds RM10.

Rosa Passadena, 1 Bandar Baru Brinchang (☎05/491 2288, fax 491 2688, *rosapsch@tm.net.my*). Large, modern, professionally run hotel; the small but cosy rooms come with minibars and hot tubs, but everything is a little better at the *Equatorial*. ⑦.

Silverstar, 10 Main Rd (☎05/491 1387). Fifteen basic, fair-sized rooms with *mandi*s (where you empty a bucket of water over yourself to wash). One of the few places in Brinchang where you won't pay over the odds for clean sheets and a place to sleep. ②.

EATING AND DRINKING

As well as the Malay **food stalls** in the central square, the following cafés and restaurants are worth a try.

Hong Kong, Main Rd, west side of square. This posh-looking place serves the usual Chinese dishes and steamboats.

Kowloon, 34–35 Main Rd. Smart, efficient restaurant with prices to match. The dishes from the very large Chinese menu are worth the extra cost.

Parkland, 45 Main Rd. Part of the hotel, this pleasant, airy restaurant has good views over town but is fairly pricey for the bland, international cuisine it serves.

Restoran Sakaya, Main Rd. Near the *Hong Kong*, this inexpensive Chinese eating house does buffet lunches, costing from RM3 for three dishes, including rice.

North of Brinchang

All over the Cameron Highlands – but especially north of Brinchang – you'll pass small sheds or greenhouses by the roadside, selling cabbages, leeks, cauliflowers, mushrooms and strawberries. These are the produce of the area's various fruit and vegetable **farms**, where narrow plots are cut out of the sheer hillsides to increase the surface area for planting, forming giant steps all the way up the slopes. However, such ingenious terrace farming poses a problem for the transportation of the harvested crop, since the paths between the terraces are only wide enough for one nimble-footed person. This has been solved by the introduction of a **cable system**, initially operated by brute force but now powered by diesel engine, which hoists the large baskets of vegetables from the terraces to trucks waiting by the roadside high above, from where they are taken to market – over forty percent of the produce is for export to Singapore, Brunei and Hong Kong.

A couple of more specific targets might entice you out into the countryside north of Brinchang. You could easily pass on the **Butterfly Farm** (daily 8am–6pm; RM3), 5km to the north at Kea Farm, where butterflies fly among the flowers and ponds; the Kampung Raja bus from Brinchang passes outside. Better is the **Robertson Rose Garden** (daily 10am–4pm; free), a visit to which is rewarded by superb views of the sculpted sweep of the surrounding hills; it's 2km to the northwest of Brinchang on the way to the Sungai Palas Tea Estate. Rose bushes aside, the shop here sells honey and cordials, as well as attractive dried-flower arrangements. Flower lovers are also well served by **Rose Valley** (daily 8am–6pm; RM3), which has over 450 varieties of roses on display as well as many other blooms, most on covered terraces; it's on the road to **Kampung Tringkap**. The **Rose Centre** at Kea Farm is similar (daily 8am–6pm; RM3), but spread over a larger area with a spectacular view of the surrounding valleys from its summit, crowned in surreal fashion by a colourful Mother-Hubbard-like boot. The sculptures here, of which the boot is one, were created by Burmese craftsmen and do a lot to liven up a potentially dull attraction.

THE SUNGAI PALAS TEA ESTATE

Set high in the hills north of Brinchang, the **Sungai Palas Tea Estate** (Tues–Sun 8.30am–3pm, tours roughly every 10min; free) doesn't attract crowds of people. Despite the romantic imagery used on tea packaging, handpicking – though the best method for producing the highest quality tea – is now far too labour-intensive to be economical. Instead, the Tamil, Bangladeshi and Malay workers who live on the estates pick the small, green leaves with shears. Once in the factory, the full baskets are emptied into large wire vats where the leaves are withered by alternate blasts of hot and cold air for sixteen to eighteen hours; this removes around fifty percent of their moisture. They are then sifted of dust and impurities and rolled by ancient, bulky machines. This breaks up the leaves and releases the moisture for the all-important process of **fermentation**, when they begin to emit their distinctive, pungent smell. Following ninety minutes' grinding in another machine, the soggy mass is fired at 90°C – in what is effectively a spin-dryer – to halt the fermentation process, and the tea turns black. After being sorted into grades, the tea matures for three to six months before being packaged and transported to market.

How much you glean of this process from your guide is dependent on your hearing, as the noise in parts of the factory is so deafening that all sound save the roar of the dryers is obliterated. Some areas of the building are also made extremely dusty by the tea impurities, so take a handkerchief to cover your mouth and nose. There's a pleasant **café** and garden on the premises where you can enjoy a drink of tea before or after the tour.

You can head to the tea estate by **bus** from Brinchang's bus station at 9.30am, 11.45am, 1.45pm and 4.15pm. To return, you can walk to the main road (20min) and wait for one of the municipal buses which go to Brinchang from Kampung Raja, or one of the tea-estate buses which return at 1.45pm and 4.15pm; it is also possible to walk the 6km or so back to Brinchang, though the hilliness of the route may be enough to put you off.

Ipoh and around

Eighty kilometres north of Tapah in the Kinta Valley is **IPOH**, the state capital of Perak and third-biggest city in Malaysia. It grew rich on the tin trade, which transformed it within the space of forty years from a tiny kampung in a landscape dominated by dramatic limestone outcrops to a sprawling boomtown. Now a metropolis of over half a million people, Ipoh (the name comes from that of the *upas* tree which thrived in the area, and whose sap was used by the Orang Asli for arrow-head poison) is a far cry from the original village on this site. Perak had been renowned for its rich tin deposits since the sixteenth century, which made it vulnerable to attempts from rival chiefs to seize the throne and thus gain control of the lucrative tin trade. However, it wasn't until the discovery of a major field in 1880 that Ipoh's fortunes turned; before long it became a prime destination for pioneers, merchants and fortune-seekers from all over the world, and a cosmopolitan city, something reflected in the broad mix of cultures today. To accommodate the rapidly increasing population, between 1905 and 1914 the city expanded across Sungei Kinta into a "new town" area, its economic good fortune reflected in a multitude of **colonial buildings** and Chinese **mansions**. Despite the later decline in demand for tin, when Malaysia turned to oil to resurrect its hopes of prosperity, the export of tin is the fifth largest earner of foreign currency in the country, and Ipoh is still a major player in Malaysia's meteoric rise to the top of the Southeast Asian economic league table.

Yet despite its historical significance and present-day administrative importance, Ipoh is a disappointment to many visitors – the colonial parts of Georgetown (see p.169), for example, are far more interesting. In fact, the main reason people stop is to visit Ipoh's outlying attractions – the Chinese cave temples of **Sam Poh Tong** and **Perak Tong**, the anachronistic ruin of **Kellie's Castle** and the unique development at the **Tambun Hot Springs**. To do these justice, though, you're likely to have to spend at least one night in the city.

Arrival, information and accommodation

The **layout** of central Ipoh is reasonably straightforward, since the roads more or less form a grid system. What *is* confusing is that some of the old colonial **street names** have been changed in favour of something more Islamic, though the street signs haven't always caught up; hence, Jalan C.M. Yusuf instead of Jalan Chamberlain, Jalan Mustapha Al-Bakri for Jalan Clare and Jalan Bandar Timar for Jalan Leech. In practice, people recognize either name. The muddy and lethargic **Sungei Kinta** cuts the centre of Ipoh neatly in two; most of the hotels are situated east of the river, while the **old town** is on the opposite side between the two major thoroughfares, Jalan Sultan Idris Shah and Jalan Sultan Iskander.

Both the North–South Highway and Route 1 pass through Ipoh, which is also a major stop for express buses and trains between Butterworth and KL. The **train station** is on Jalan Panglima Bukit Gantang Wahab (more simply Jalan Panglima), west of the old town. Just south of the train station, at the junction of Jalan Tun Abdul Razak and Jalan Panglima, is the **local bus station**, opposite which is a **taxi stand**; **express buses** operate from behind a bank of ticket booths across the road. Local buses from **Lumut** (the departure point for Pulau Pangkor; see p.153) use a separate forecourt, beside a row of shops, a little further along Jalan Tun Abdul Razak. The Sultan Azlan Shah **airport** is 15km from the city; a taxi into the centre costs about RM10.

The **tourist office** is in the State Economic Planning Unit, close to the train station on Jalan Tun Sambanthan (Mon–Thurs 8am–1pm & 2–4.30pm, Fri & Sat 8am–12.15pm & 2.45–4.30pm, closed first and third Sat of every month; ☎05/241 2959, fax 241 2958); besides assistance on Ipoh, it can provide information on travel throughout Perak State. The local Tourist Association office is at the rather inconveniently sited *Royal Casuarina* hotel, 18 Jalan Gopeng, at the eastern end of town (same hours as above; ☎05/255 5555 ext 8123).

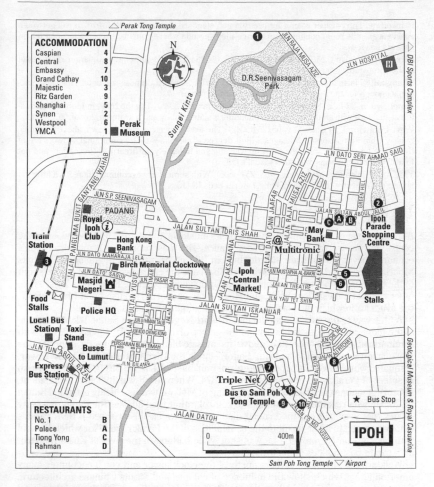

Accommodation

Most of the **places to stay** in Ipoh are found east of the river, around Jalan C.M. Yusuf and Jalan Mustapha Al-Bakri; the latter has a more seedy feel, though it's generally much quieter. The best-known place in town is the elegant *Majestic*, on the third floor of the train station.

Caspian, 6–10 Jalan Jubilee (☎05/242 3327). The purple and sky-blue building isn't hard to spot. Good rooms with air-con and hot water. ④.

Central, 20–26 Jalan Ali Pitchay (☎05/242 4777, fax 242 4555). All the rooms come with TV, balcony and bathrooms. Excellent value, and first choice in the mid-range category. ③.

Embassy, Jalan C.M. Yusuf (☎05/254 9496). The best budget place if you want your own bathroom. All rooms are clean and have hot water. ②.

Grand Cathay, 92–94 Jalan C.M. Yusuf (☎05/241 9685). The rooms here are spick-and-span, if basic. ②.

Majestic, third floor of the train station, set back a little from Jalan Panglima (☎05/255 5605, fax 255 3393). Its recent renovation recaptures the fine colonial style which made this place so sought after in its prime. The cheaper rooms are pretty much standard, but an extra RM30 or so will get you a spacious en-suite room opening onto a huge tiled veranda where you'll be served afternoon tea on wicker chairs. ⑥.

Ritz Garden, Jalan C.M. Yusuf (☎05/254 7777, fax 254 5222). Better-equipped, larger rooms than at the comparably priced *Caspian*. ④.

Shanghai, 85 Jalan Mustapha Al-Bakri (☎05/241 2070). Standard Chinese-run hotel, clean and functional enough for the money. Also has some air-con rooms. ②.

Hotel Syuen, 88 Jalan Sultan Jalil (☎05/253 8889, fax 253 3335). The top hotel in Ipoh. Of international standard with all the trimmings, including a stately lobby and a swimming pool. ⑧.

West Pool Hotel, 74 Clare St (☎05/254 5042). The least expensive place in town, above a furiously busy Chinese restaurant. Manages a high degree of cleanliness. The communal showers are of the *mandi* type. There are a few signs up warning you to leave your firearms at reception, and not to drill holes in the walls, but otherwise it's OK. ①.

YMCA, 211 Jalan Raja Musa Aziz (☎05/254 0809). With some dorm accommodation, it's a little too far out of the centre to be convenient. ③, dorm beds RM15.

The City

Although most of Ipoh's attractions are on its outskirts, there are a few diversions in the centre that are worth at least a cursory glance. The most prominent reminder of Ipoh's economic heyday is the **train station**, built in 1917 at the height of the tin boom. With its Moorish turrets and domes, and a veranda that runs the entire two-hundred-metre length of the building, it's a typical example of the British conception of "East meets West". Like other colonial train stations in KL and Hong Kong, it sported a plush hotel (the *Majestic*; see overleaf) in which the planters, traders and administrators sank cocktails.

A little way to the east, the modernist **Masjid Negeri** on Jalan Sultan Iskandar is one of the more conspicuous landmarks in the centre of town, all tacky 1960s cladding, with a minaret that rises over 40m above its mosaic-tiled domes. Directly opposite the mosque, on the parallel Jalan Dato' Sagor, stands the **Birch Memorial Clock Tower**, a square, white tower incorporating a portrait bust of J.W.W. Birch, the first British Resident of Perak, who was murdered in 1874. When Birch was installed as Resident, his abrupt manner and lack of understanding of Malay customs quickly offended Sultan Abdullah, who resented his attempts to control rather than advise (the Pangkor Treaty earlier that year laid out the crucial distinction between the two; see p.160). Birch's manner proved to be an insult to the sensibilities of the Perak royalty for which he paid with his life – on November 2 he was shot while bathing in the river at Kuala Kangsar, on a trip to post notices of his own reforms.

Walk around any of the streets north of the clock tower and you'll encounter many other buildings which show the influence of colonial and Straits Chinese architecture, the most impressive of which is the white-stucco **Hong Kong Bank** on Jalan Dato' Maharaja Lela, with its Corinthian columns and unusual pillared tower. Turning right from the bank into Jalan Sultan Yusuf, you're on the outskirts of **Chinatown**, of equal architectural note, although many of the pastel-coloured nineteenth-century shophouses along the streets to the east are looking rather tatty nowadays.

The **Perak Museum** (daily 9am–5pm; free) is housed in an elegant, former tin miner's mansion, only a short walk north from the station. Covering two floors, the museum has evocative photos of Ipoh's glory days during the tin boom, but otherwise the displays lack imagination.

Ipoh's **Geological Museum** (Mon–Thurs 8am–1pm & 2–4.30pm, Sat 8am–12.45pm, closed first and third Sat of every month; free), on Jalan Sultan Azlan Shah on the far eastern outskirts of the city (RM5 by taxi from the centre), does its best to make tin seem interesting, but other than granting a perfunctory insight into what made the city rich, the only achievement here is comprehensiveness – over six hundred samples of minerals and an array of fossils and precious stones are displayed.

Eating and drinking

At lunchtime, regional specialities are available at most Chinese **restaurants** and **cafés** in Ipoh, including *sar hor fun* (see p.50). The *Grand Cathay* restaurant on Jalan C.M. Yusuf is very popular with Chinese locals; on the same road is the *Rahman*, an extremely friendly Indian restaurant. Around Jalan Bandar Timar in the old town are several Chinese cafés, the oldest and best known of which is the *Kedai Kopi Kong Heng* (lunchtime only). Jalan Sultan Abdul Jalil and the surrounding streets are a good bet for Chinese food in general, with the *Palace* restaurant in the *Excelsior* hotel worth the modest splurge, and less expensive options like the *Kedai Kopi Tiong Yong* just round the corner on Jalan Raja Ekram. There are also several **bakeries** in town serving lovely fresh bread and pastries; try the *Noor Jahan* on Jalan Raja Ekram.

Many of Ipoh's restaurants close in the evenings, so you may have to resort to the **hawker stalls**, some of which lie near the train station and at the top of Jalan C.M. Yusuf. The best stalls, however, are at the southern end of Jalan Greenhill, east of the Shanghai hotel, where nearly a hundred stay open well into the night, serving just about anything you care to name. On Jalan Sultan Abdul Jalil you'll also find some very good-quality Indian stalls, and the *No.1* banana-leaf-curry house.

Listings

Airlines MAS, Lot 108, Bangunan Seri Kinta, Jalan Sultan Idris Shah (☎05/241 4155).

Airport ☎05/312 2459 for flight information.

Banks Maybank and Bank Bumiputra are on Jalan Sultan Idris Shah; there's an Oriental Bank on Jalan Yang Kalsom.

Buses Tickets for Lumut buses can be bought from Perak Roadways, under the advertising hoardings on Jalan Tun Abdul Razak, opposite the express bus station.

Car rental Avis (☎05/313 6586) and Budget (☎05/313 4558) both have offices at the airport.

Cinemas There is one on the fourth floor of the IPOH Parade shopping complex, Jalan Sultan Abdul Jalil, just east of the *Syuen* hotel.

Hospital On Jalan Hospital (☎05/254 1835).

Internet access MultiTronic, 133 Jalan Sultan Idris Shah (☎05/254 4893); Triple Net, 41 Jalan C.M. Yusuf (☎05/254 4725).

Police The station is on Jalan Panglima (☎05/253 5522).

Post office The GPO is practically next door to the train station, on Jalan Panglima.

Taxis There's a taxi stand at the bus station. To phone for a cab, call Nam Taxi (☎05/241 2189).

Trains ☎05/254 0481 for information.

Travel agents HWA Y/K Tours and Travel, 23 Jalan Che Tak (☎05/250 4060); and K&C Travel & Tours, 250 Jalan Sultan Iskandar (☎05/250 6999) both sell airline tickets.

Visa extensions The Immigration office is at Level 2, Bangunan Serikinta, Jalan Sultan Idris Shah (Mon–Thurs 8am–1pm & 2–4.30pm, Fri 8am–12.15pm & 2.45–4.30pm; ☎05/254 9316). Note that they stop accepting applications an hour before they close for the day.

Around Ipoh

Much of Ipoh's striking surroundings have been marred by unsightly manufacturing industries. Nevertheless, it's not long before you escape the industrialization and find yourself in the heart of extensive rubber plantations, typical of so much of this part of the country. To the north and south of Ipoh are craggy **limestone peaks**; those nearest to the city are riddled with caves where Ipoh's immigrant workers established **Buddhist temples**, now popular pilgrimage centres, particularly during the Chinese New Year celebrations.

The Perak Tong and Sam Poh Tong temples

The **Perak Tong Temple** (daily 8am–6pm; free), 6km north of Ipoh, is the more impressive of the two Chinese cave temples just outside the city, situated in dramatic surroundings and doubling as a centre for Chinese art; to get here, take the #141 Kuala Kangsar bus from the local bus station (20min). The gaudiness of the temple's exterior – bright red-and-yellow pavilions flanked by feathery willows and lotus ponds – gives you no hint of the eerie atmosphere inside, where darkened cavern upon cavern honeycombs up into the rock formation. The huge first chamber is dominated by a fifteen-metre-high golden statue of the Buddha, plump and smiling, with two startled-looking companions on either side, dancing and playing instruments. A massive bell, believed to be more than a century old, fills the chamber with booming echoes from time to time – it's rung by visiting devotees to draw attention to the donation they've just offered. Walking past the bell into the next chamber, as your eyes become more accustomed to the gloom, you'll notice the decorated walls, covered with complex calligraphy and delicate flower paintings. Towards the back of this musty hollow, a steep flight of 385 crudely fashioned steps climbs up and out of the cave to a sort of balcony, with views of great limestone outcrops and ugly factory buildings.

The **Sam Poh Tong Temple** (daily 8am–4.30pm; free), just south of the city, is also a popular place of pilgrimage for Chinese Buddhists. Built into a rock face, the huge limestone caverns open towards the rear to give more impressive views over the surrounding suburbs and hills. Unfortunately, the upkeep of the temple leaves a lot to be desired; the place is covered with litter and graffiti. There's an expensive bar nearby and a good Chinese vegetarian restaurant. A visit to the temple makes an easy half-day trip: catch the green "Kinta" bus #66 or #73 (to Kangar) from the local bus station, or from the roundabout near the *Embassy* hotel; it's a ten-minute journey.

Kellie's Castle

If you only have time for one trip from Ipoh, make it to **Kellie's Castle**, a mansion situated in the Kinta Kelas Rubber Estate, 12km south of Ipoh. It stands as a symbol of the prosperity achieved by many an enterprising foreigner who saw the potential of the rubber market in the early 1900s. The mansion, with a weighty rectangular tower and apricot-coloured bricks, was to have been the second home of William Kellie Smith, a Scottish entrepreneur, who settled here in order to make his fortune. Designed with splendour in mind, there were even plans for a lift to be installed, the first in Malaysia. However, during the mansion's construction in the 1920s, an epidemic of Spanish influenza broke out, killing many of the Tamil workers. In an act of appeasement, Smith had a Hindu temple built near the house; among the deities represented on the temple roof is a figure dressed in a white suit and pith helmet, presumably Smith himself. While work resumed on the "castle", Smith left on a trip to England in 1925; however, he fell ill and died in Portugal. The crumbling, warren-like remains, set in lush, hilly countryside, are now covered in graffiti dating back to 1941, recording the passage of tourists over the years.

Getting to the castle from Ipoh is best done by taxi (about RM20 one way, or RM30 return including a wait while you look around). Less straightforwardly, you can take bus #36 or #37 from the local bus station to Batu Gajah (departures every 1hr 20min or so; 30min), from where you can walk the remaining 4km on the A8 road (clearly signposted), or catch bus #67, which passes the castle fairly frequently, or take a taxi from the main road (around RM4).

Tambun Hot Springs

At the **Tambun Hot Springs** (Tues–Sun 8am–9pm; RM3), 8km northeast of Ipoh, you can indulge in hot, mineral-rich soaks in the two thermal swimming pools, one cooler than the other, which are fed by hot springs – no mean feat of engineering, as the enthusiastic owner will probably tell you. All around you, steaming slimy water breaks through the surface of the earth; you can even crawl into the corner of a nearby limestone cave for a natural sauna (not for the claustrophobic). Another of the surrounding caves, once inhabited by Japanese monks, was later home to Japanese soldiers hiding out during World War II; they left painted characters on some of the cave walls. Unfortunately, a new pools complex is being constructed near the caves, and the building work – a real eyesore – hampers access to the pools; as a consequence, you're likely to have the place more or less to yourself.

To reach the hot springs, take the "Rambutan" bus from Ipoh's local bus station for about thirty minutes until you see the signpost for "Resort Air Panas", off to the right of the main road; the springs are a further kilometre down a dirt track through the construction site.

Pulau Pangkor

With some of the best beaches to be found on this side of the Malay Peninsula, **PULAU PANGKOR** is one of the west coast's more appealing islands. It's also one of the most accessible, lying just a forty-minute ferry ride from the port of **Lumut** (see p.155). This fact has turned Pangkor into an increasingly popular weekend resort, with an airport and three international-standard hotels, while the adjacent, privately owned island of Pangkor Laut, just off the southwest coast of Pulau Pangkor, is home to one of Malaysia's most exclusive resorts. These facilities are disproportionate to Pangkor's small size and at odds with its quiet, almost genteel, atmosphere. The inhabitants still live largely by fishing and boat-building rather than tourism – although development around Teluk Nipah looks set to tip the balance. For all its tranquillity, Pulau Pangkor played an important part in the development of modern Malaysia, witnessing the signing of the ground-breaking **Pangkor Treaty** of 1874, which led to the creation of the Residential System (see box, p.160), thus furthering the notion of indirect British rule.

Most of the thriving local villages lie in a string along the island's east coast, while tourist accommodation and the best beaches are on the west side. The interior is mountainous and densely forested, inaccessible but for a few tiny trails and one main road that connects the two coasts, but there's plenty to occupy you around the rim, from superb stretches of sand to historical sites, including a seventeenth-century Dutch fort and several temples.

It's well worth remembering that **Thaipusam** is celebrated roughly a month late here, falling on the full moon in mid-February or early March. The unmissably gruesome spectacle of Hindu religious fervour goes on for two days, the processions starting out on the beach at Pasir Bogak, and ending up at the Sri Pathirakaliaman temple on the island's east coast.

Travel practicalities

Pangkor **airport** (☎05/685 4516), to the north of the island, is served by daily flights from Singapore (RM220 one way) and Kuala Lumpur (RM150 one way). The passenger-only **express ferries** from Lumut (see p.155) to Pulau Pangkor run approximately every half-hour (daily 6.45am–8pm; RM2 one way; 40min), calling at Kampung Sungei Pinang Kecil before reaching the main jetty at Pangkor Town. You can catch a catamaran from the same jetty for an extra ringgit, which will get you to the island in half the time. In addition, seven boats a day, run by Pan Silver (☎05/683 5541; RM8 return), run from Lumut jetty to a jetty 1km east of the *Pan Pacific Resort* (a shuttle bus runs between the latter jetty and the hotel).

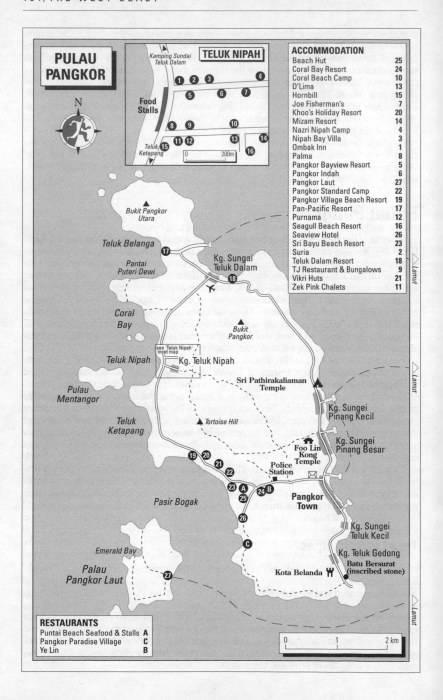

PULAU PANGKOR

N

TELUK NIPAH

Kamping Sundai
Teluk Dalam

Food
Stalls

Teluk
Ketapang

0   200m

ACCOMMODATION

Beach Hut	25
Coral Bay Resort	24
Coral Beach Camp	10
D'Lima	13
Hornbill	15
Joe Fisherman's	7
Khoo's Holiday Resort	20
Mizam Resort	14
Nazri Nipah Camp	4
Nipah Bay Villa	3
Ombak Inn	1
Palma	8
Pangkor Bayview Resort	5
Pangkor Indah	6
Pangkor Laut	27
Pangkor Standard Camp	22
Pangkor Village Beach Resort	19
Pan-Pacific Resort	17
Purnama	12
Seagull Beach Resort	16
Seaview Hotel	26
Sri Bayu Beach Resort	23
Suria	2
Teluk Dalam Resort	18
TJ Restaurant & Bungalows	9
Vikri Huts	21
Zek Pink Chalets	11

△ Lamut

Bukit Pangkor
Utara

Teluk Belanga

Pantai
Puteri Dewi

Coral
Bay

Teluk Nipah

Pulau
Mentangor

Teluk
Ketapang

Kg. Sungai
Teluk Dalam

see 'Teluk Nipah'
inset map

Kg. Teluk Nipah

Bukit
Pangkor

Sri Pathirakaliaman
Temple

△ Lamut

Kg. Sungei
Pinang Kecil

Tortoise Hill

Kg. Sungei
Pinang Besar

Foo Lin
Kong
Temple

Police
Station

Pasir Bogak

Pangkor
Town

Kg. Sungei
Teluk Kecil

Emerald Bay

Palau
Pangkor Laut

Kg. Teluk Gedong
Batu Bersurat
(inscribed stone)

Kota Belanda

△ Lamut

RESTAURANTS

Puntai Beach Seafood & Stalls	A
Pangkor Paradise Village	C
Ye Lin	B

0   1   2 km

Pulau Pangkor has a sealed **road** of varying quality forming a loop that takes in much of the island's circumference, avoiding the mountainous interior and cutting inland only between Pangkor Town, where the ferry docks, and the tourist developments at Pasir Bogak, 2km away on the west coast. **Renting a motorbike** or **pushbike** in Pangkor Town or from a hotel or guesthouse on the west coast costs around RM30 and RM10 per day respectively; the *Pangkor Standard Camp* has a good selection. As Pulau Pangkor is only 3km by 9km, a trip around the island is easily accomplished in a day. You could see all the sights by motorbike in about five hours, stopping en route for lunch – add another few hours if you're on a bicycle. Otherwise the only other means of transport are the shared **minibus taxis** (RM4 from Pangkor Town to Pasir Bogak, RM10 to Teluk Nipah and RM24–30 for a round-island trip), and the **local buses**, which run hourly between 8am and 6pm from Pangkor Town to Pasir Bogak. It's only a couple of kilometres from Pangkor Town across to the west coast, but there's no shade along the way.

En route to Pulau Pangkor: Lumut

Although it's possible to fly to Pangkor, most people cross to the island by ferry (see box, p.153) from the quiet mainland coastal town of **LUMUT**, about 80km southwest of Ipoh. There are bus services there from Ipoh roughly every hour (journey time 90min; RM4) and a daily direct bus from Tapah (2hr; RM9), although the latter originates in Kuala Lumpur and is often full when it reaches Tapah. Once a relatively obscure fishing village, Lumut has since become the main base of the Royal Malaysian Navy, whose towering apartment buildings dominate the coastline from the sea. In an attempt to cash in on the success of Pulau Pangkor, Lumut too has seen its own spate of development, though this is still low-key. The town manages to retain its charm, with multicoloured fishing boats bobbing about in the tiny marina, and stores specializing in the shell and coral handicrafts for which Lumut is famed locally.

Lumut's **bus station**, on the road out to Ipoh, is a minute's walk south of the jetty where the boats to Pangkor depart; all boat tickets can be bought at the jetty itself. If you need to **change money**, it's better to do so in Lumut, as it can be hard to change traveller's cheques in Pangkor Town; most of Lumut's several moneychangers and banks are on Jalan Sultan Idris Shah. Walking north from the bus station takes you to a filling station at the junction with both the shore road (Jalan Iskandar Shah/Jalan Titi Panjang) and another inland road (Jalan Sultan Idris Shah), which leads off to your left. There's a **tourist office** (Mon–Sat 9am–5pm; ☎ & fax 05/683 4057) on Jalan Sultan Idris Shah, just past the petrol pumps. Further down the same street are two **places to stay**. The *Orient Star* (☎05/683 4199, fax 683 4223; ⑧) at the very end of the road, is the top spot in town, very pleasantly situated on the beach. Along the same road is the *Galaxy Inn* (☎05/683 8731, fax 683 8723; ③), the quietest of the mid-range choices. Similarly equipped, with good en-suite air-conditioned rooms, are the *Indah*, 208 Jalan Iskandar Shah (☎05/683 5064; ③), a little way northwest along the waterfront from the jetty, offering the best views; and the closest to the bus station, the *Harbour View*, Jalan Titi Panjang (☎05/683 7888, fax 683 7088; ③) – to get there, walk to the service station, and turn right onto the shore road. Just past the *Harbour View* is Lumut's least expensive option, the clean and basic *Phin Lum Hooi*, 93 Jalan Titi Panjang (☎05/683 5641; ②).

Pangkor Town and around

The ferry from Lumut drops you at the jetty in **PANGKOR TOWN**, the island's principal settlement, whose few dusty streets feature *kedai kopi*s graced with Nonya marble-topped tables and antique clocks. The best part of the town by far is the lively port, where the early-morning catch – the *ikan bilis* (anchovies) are particularly renowned – is packed into boxes of crushed ice to be despatched to the mainland.

Other than to stretch your legs once you've got off the ferry, there's very little reason to stop long; minibus taxis to the beaches on the other side of the island leave from the jetty. There's a branch of Maybank with an ATM in Pangkor Town, just to your left as you come ashore from the jetty. The town has a couple of **places to stay**: the *Chuan Fu*, 60 Main Rd (☎ & fax 05/685 1123; ①) is the best choice, with rooms ranging from basic doubles to en-suite affairs with air conditioning; its communal rear balcony overlooking the water adds character. Nearer the jetty, *Hotel Min Lian* at no. 1a (☎05/685 1294; ③) charges a good deal more and delivers less. Around the *Chuan Fu* are a number of Chinese **restaurants** and the island's only **cybercafé** – the *Fisherman* (☎019/565 1123); its rates are much lower than at the beachside hostels, and there's also much less of a queue.

South to Teluk Gedong

Following the coastal road south out of town, after 1500m you come to pretty **KAMPUNG TELUK GEDONG**, a gathering of traditional wooden stilted houses named after the bay in which they are cradled. Here, set back from the road on the right, is the **Kota Belanda**, or Dutch Fort, originally built in 1670 to store tin supplies from Perak and keep a check on piracy in the Straits, but destroyed in 1690 by the Malays, who were discontent with Dutch rule. The fort was rebuilt in 1743 but only remained in use for a further five years, when the Dutch finally withdrew after being subject to several more attacks. The abandoned site was left to decay, and the disappointing half-built structure that you see today is, unbelievably, a recent reconstruction.

A few metres further along the road, on the left, lies the **Batu Bersurat**, a huge boulder under a canopy. On the rock, the year 1743 is inscribed beside a drawing which – with the use of some imagination – depicts a tiger mauling a child, a grisly memorial to a Dutch child who disappeared while playing nearby. A more plausible account of the incident is that the infant was kidnapped by the Malays, in retribution for the continuing Dutch presence.

West to Pasir Bogak

A two-kilometre road connects the east and west coasts of Pulau Pangkor, terminating in the west at the holiday village of **PASIR BOGAK**, the biggest and most upmarket development on the island. That said, if you've come to Pangkor for the beaches (and most people do), you'll be disappointed by what's on offer here. A narrow strip of grubby sand, the beach is virtually nonexistent when the tide is high, a fact that seems to have escaped the notice of the chalet owners, who continue to renovate and upgrade their accommodation to cater for the weekend trade.

It's only worth staying on Pasir Bogak if you're after luxury **accommodation**; the mid-range and budget places lack character compared to their rivals in Teluk Nipah. Only a few of the **chalets** front the beach itself; most line the road that continues north along the west coast, but even so, they're all reasonably close to the sea. It's worth shopping around – some places are grossly overpriced, and rates can rocket everywhere at weekends. All the hotels here have **restaurants** attached, with the exception of *Pangkor Standard Camp*, which does, however, have the basic *Pangkor Restaurant* right behind it. By far the best-value food is at *Ye Lin*, which offers huge plates of excellent Chinese food; it's slightly away from the principal cluster, back on the road to Pangkor Town. The finest views can be had at the *Pangkor Paradise Village* up a dirt track to the south of the main strip, whose beachfront restaurant – on stilts over the water – is great for a beer at sunset. Back in the thick of things, there are some food stalls clustered around the inexpensive *Pantai Beach Seafood Restaurant*, on the seafront just north of the *Standard Camp*. Otherwise, the food here – like the accommodation – is generally overpriced.

Beach Hut, Pasir Bogak (☎ & fax 05/685 1159). Friendly, mid-range collection of pleasant beachfront chalets and simple double rooms. ③.

Coral Bay Resort, Pasir Bogak (☎05/685 5111, fax 685 5666). The *Sri Bayu*'s competion for top dollar. This concrete high-rise has the best rooms on the beach, at a reasonable rate, but lacks charm. ⑤.

Khoo's Holiday Resort, Pasir Bogak (☎05/685 2190, fax 685 1164). Large complex of tasteful doubles perched on the hillside. The views are fantastic, there are air-con options and the rate includes breakfast. Recommended. ②.

Pangkor Standard Camp, Pasir Bogak (☎05/685 1878). The best deal for those on a budget, with clean A-frames sleeping three at a squeeze. You'll find better chalets elsewhere though ①.

Pangkor Village Beach Resort, Pasir Bogak (☎05/685 2227, fax 685 3787). Has a wide choice of slightly tatty accommodation on one of the most pleasant patches of beach. Only the dorm (RM25) is worth the money; the A-frames (②) are overpriced, as are the luxury chalets (⑥).

Sea View, Pasir Bogak (☎05/685 1605, fax 685 1970). Large, standard beachside hotel with doubles and pleasant chalets (⑥). The management organizes a range of treks and boat trips. ⑤.

Sri Bayu Beach Resort, Pasir Bogak (☎05/685 1929, fax 685 1050). By far the most characterful outfit on the beach. The carved-wood and antique-strewn lobby leads onto a well-landscaped garden and chalets. The rooms themselves though, while comfortable enough, aren't quite up to the whopping price tag. ⑧.

Vikri Huts, Pasir Bogak (☎05/685 4258). Run-down A-frame huts on a large patch of flat ground. Poorer quality accommodation than at the *Standard Camp*, though a little closer to the beach. ②

Teluk Ketapang and Teluk Nipah

Much better beaches than those at Pasir Bogak are to be found about 2km further north at **TELUK KETAPANG** (aptly, "Turtle Bay"), which has been known to harbour the increasingly rare giant **leatherback turtle**. The creatures swim thousands of miles to lay their eggs on Malaysia's beaches, normally favouring the Peninsula's eastern coast (see p.280), though there are a few sightings here between May and September. Otherwise, take the opportunity to stretch out on white-sand beaches – edged by palm trees – which are slightly less crowded than Pasir Bogak's, and much wider and cleaner.

There's no accommodation at Teluk Ketapang; you'll have to make do with either staying in Pasir Bogak or, better, continuing north a couple more kilometres to **TELUK NIPAH**, which has become the traveller's hangout, and where there are some splendid beaches. Of these, **Coral Bay** is the best – a perfect cove with crystal-clear sea and smooth, white sand, backed by dense jungle climbing steeply to Bukit Pangkor, one of the island's three peaks. The bay is inaccessible by road; to reach it, you have to climb over the rocks at the northern end of Teluk Nipah – watch the tide or you might have to swim back. This is the best spot on the island for snorkelling, and most of the hostels here rent out masks and snorkels for about RM10 a day.

Much of the recent development on Pangkor has focused on Teluk Nipah because of its beaches. There are new places opening all the time, but the atmosphere is still quiet and informal. Room rates can double at weekends or halve if you're a good bargainer. Standards within each price category tend to be pretty much uniform, so having decided how much you want to pay, you're best off choosing a place by atmosphere and location. There are **food stalls** lined up along the beach in between the two roads into the kampung, and a few restaurants further up. Most popular however, and something of a social hub, is *TJ Restoran* a little way up the first (southmost) road leading inland. **Internet access** is available at *Nipah Bay Villa* and *Purnama Beach Resort*, which have one terminal each (RM20 an hour), open to non-residents.

Accommodation

All the accommodation listed below is marked on the Teluk Nipah inset map on p.154.

Coral Beach Camp (☎05/685 2711, fax 685 2796). Simple, double chalets with shower in a small, well-kept garden. There are some A-frames at half the cost. ②.

D'lima (☎05/685 2494). Opposite *Coral Beach Camp* and very similar. Cold-water double chalets with *atap* roofs – a reasonable budget choice. ②.

Hornbill (☎05/685 2005, fax 685 2006). The first place reached on the coast road from Teluk Ketapang. The rooms all boast wooden floors, balconies and a view of the beach. You can, however, get your own similarly equipped chalet at one of the inland places for less. ⑥.

Joe Fisherman Village (☎05/685 2389). One of the first establishments here, and still the back-packer's spiritual home on Pangkor. With A-frames (①), chalets (②) and a small but very friendly café, this is as homely as it gets. Recommended.

Mizam Resort (☎ & fax 05/685 3359). The last stop along the road in from Teluk Ketapang. Though run by friendly people, it's overpriced and a long walk from the beach. ④.

Nazri Nipah Camp (☎05/685 2014). Laid-back traveller place with a dorm (RM10), some A-frames (RM20) and chalets (②), and kitchen facilities; the chalets have their own showers. Can provide lots of advice on water sports and treks. Recommended.

Nipah Bay Villa (☎05/685 2198, fax 685 2386). One of the best choices if you want air-con, satellite TV and hot water. ⑥.

Ombak Inn (☎05/685 1638). Low-key cluster of very basic A-frames (RM20) and chalets (RM30). Both the rooms and the garden have gone to seed a long time ago, but they're not unpleasant.

Palma Beach Resort (☎05/685 3693, fax 685 4431). Well-designed, sturdy chalets with air-con, TVs and an efficient management. A good mid-range choice. ⑤.

Pangkor Bayview Resort (☎05/685 3540, fax 685 1308). Near the beach, opposite the *Ombak Inn*. The spacious chalets here are en suite and have air-con and TV. A good choice if you want to spend a little more than the average. ⑤.

Pangkor Indah Beach Resort (☎05/685 2107). Pleasant, wooden chalets with bathrooms and air-con. ④.

Purnama Beach Resort (☎05/685 3530, *pbr2000@tm.net.my*). Package-deal development with a good range of accommodation, ranging from comfortable dorms (RM20) to plush chalets (④).

Seagull Beach Resort (☎05/685 2878, fax 685 2857). Set a long way back from the beach, this place has very basic rooms, not en suite, as well as rooms with bathroom and air-con, though its prices are pretty high for what's on offer. ③.

Suria Beach Resort (☎05/685 3922). Smart hotel rooms with air-con and TV; no chalets though. ③.

TJ Restoran and Bungalows (☎05/685 3477). The best-value accommodation here, boasting double chalets with showers, at half the prices elsewhere. The management is very friendly and doesn't hike the price up too much at peak times. Their café is a good deal too, with tables named after different countries. Recommended. ①.

Zek Pink Beach Chalets (☎ & fax 05/685 3529). Close to the coast road, these pink-painted chalets with all mod cons live up to their name; even the furniture is in rosy shades. ⑤.

The north coast

The road cuts inland from Teluk Nipah and crosses to the northeastern tip of the island, where it branches off west to the high-class *Pan Pacific Resort* (☎05/685 1091, fax 685 2390; ⑧), situated in secluded **TELUK BELANGA**. You can get here directly by ferry from Lumut, though unless you're staying at the resort you'll be charged RM40 (collected at the entrance gate) to use the beach, for which price they include a snack. The beach fee covers the sports facilities here – except for the golf course – and use of the beach itself, Pantai Puteri Dewi ("Beach of the Beautiful Princess"), a fine stretch of crunchy white sand.

Doubling back to the junction with the main road, you'll pass the airport and come to the pleasant *Teluk Dalam Resort* (☎05/685 5000, fax 685 4000; ⑧), large chalets set around a quiet bay, with a couple of restaurants. After continuing up the steep hill and craggy headland for 3km, you descend into the first bay on the east coast. There's not much to see on this side of the island until you reach the **Sri Pathirakaliaman** Hindu temple, overlooking the sea. Only worth a cursory glance, it lies just north of **Kampung Sungei Pinang Kecil**, little more than a few straggling dwellings by the roadside, and the first stop for the ferry from Lumut; and 1km north of the more substantial **KAMPUNG SUNGEI PINANG BESAR**. In the latter, down a small turning to the west, you'll find the **Foo Lin Kong** temple, a cross between a place of worship and a theme park. Inside the dim, rather spooky room that houses the shrine are some authentic-looking shrunken heads designed to ward off evil spirits, and a few incongruous Guinness bottles acting as offerings. Surrounding the temple itself is a miniature Great Wall of China spreading up the hillside, a small children's playground and a dismal zoo. Pangkor Town is just 1km or so south from here along the main road.

Other islands: Pulau Pangkor Laut and Pulau Sembilan

Some of the Pulau Pangkor hotels arrange **fishing and snorkelling day-trips** to the small islands around (about RM15 per person). No accommodation is available except on **PULAU PANGKOR LAUT** to the southwest, a privately owned island which is the exclusive domain of the **Pangkor Laut Resort** (☎05/699 1100, fax 699 1200; ⑨). With its sympathetically designed accommodation and top-class restaurants, this luxurious resort is well worth visiting for Emerald Bay alone, whose superb sand and waters make it one of the most beautiful beaches in Malaysia. There are eight daily ferries to the island, run by the resort itself; strictly, they are for the use of residents only, although you can use them for a day-trip to the hotel pool or restaurant.

   PULAU SEMBILAN, an archipelago of nine islands two hours south by boat from Pulau Pangkor, is the setting for an annual **fishing safari**, a competitive event held in conjunction with the lavishly celebrated Lumut Pesta Laut, a popular festival that takes place in Lumut every August. Only one island in the clump, Pulau Lalang, has fresh water and accessible beaches, and at present there is nowhere to stay. You can charter a boat there from Lumut jetty or Pasir Bogak for around RM300.

Kuala Kangsar

While Ipoh (see p.147) is the state administrative capital of Perak, **KUALA KANGSAR** – 50km to the northwest – is its royal town, home to the Sultans of Perak since the fifteenth century, with monuments to match. Built at a grandiose sweep of Sungei Perak,

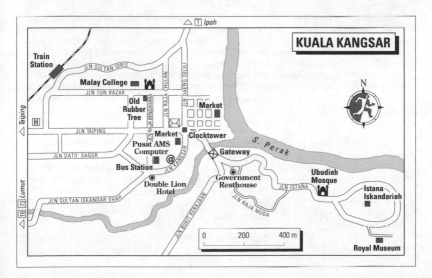

THE RESIDENTIAL SYSTEM

Late in 1873, Raja Abdullah of Perak invited the new Governor of the Straits Settlements, Andrew Clarke, to appoint a **Resident** (colonial officer) to Perak, in exchange for Abdullah being recognized as the Sultan of Perak instead of his rival, the intractable Sultan Ismail. This held some appeal for the British, whose involvement in Malay affairs had hitherto been unofficial, and who were eager to foster stability and facilitate economic progress in the region. So on January 20, 1874, the **Pangkor Treaty** was signed by Clarke and Abdullah; the idea was that the Resident – each state would have its own – would play an advisory role in Malay affairs of state in return for taking a sympathetic attitude to Malay customs and rituals.

It is doubtful that the Malays had any idea of the long-term consequences of the treaty, whose original version indicated that the decision-making process would be collective, much like the Malays' own courts; more significantly, the distinction between the political and the religious was from the start a nonsensical concept for the Malays, for whom all action was dictated by the laws of Islam. The interpretation of the newly created post was in the hands of **Hugh Low** (1824–1905), one of the early Residents, whose jurisdiction of Perak (1877–89) was based in Kuala Kangsar. The personable Low lived modestly by British standards in the Residency building (no longer extant) and, with his two pet chimpanzees for company, kept open house during his ten-hour working day. Low's adroit linguistic skills won him favour with the local chiefs, with whom he could soon converse fluently, and whose practices he quickly understood. Having spent nearly thirty years in Borneo, Low had become great friends with Charles and James Brooke (see p.356), and sought to emulate their relatively benign system of government.

The approval of the Malay nobility – by no means guaranteed, as the Birch incident shows (see p.624) – was vital to the success of the Residency scheme, and was secured principally by compensating them for the income they had lost from taxes and property. This suited the sultans well, who not only obtained financial security for themselves by virtue of their healthy stipends, but also got protection from other rivals. As time went on, lesser figures were given positions within the bureaucracy, thus weaving the Malays into the fabric of the administration, of which the cornerstone was the **State Council**. Although the sultan was its ceremonial head, the Resident chose the constituent members and set the political agenda, in consultation with his deputies – the District Officers – and the Governor.

The increasing power of central government soon began to diminish the consultative side of the Resident's role, and by the 1890s fewer and fewer meetings of the council were being held. Even in religious matters, the goal posts were often moved to suit British purposes. Furthermore, there were few Residents as talented and sympathetic as Hugh Low and so, predictably, the involvement of the British in Malay affairs became less to instruct their subjects in new forms of government and more to affirm British status. Sultan Abdullah, bent on acquiring local power and status, thereby inadvertently provided a foot in the door for the British, an act which ultimately led to their full political intervention in the Peninsula.

it's a neat, attractive town of green parks and flowers, little visited by tourists – another reason to make time for at least a couple of hours' stopover between Ipoh and Taiping (see p.162). Nineteenth-century accounts of Kuala Kangsar rhapsodized about its situation: Ambrose B. Rathborne wrote in his *Camping and Tramping in Malaya* (1883) that it had "one of the prettiest views in the Straits . . . overlooking Sungei Perak, up whose beautiful valley an uninterrupted view is obtained". Rathborne camped and tramped his way through the jungle on an elephant, the only way to reach Kuala Kangsar at the time.

With the planting of nine **rubber-tree** seedlings here at the beginning of Hugh Low's Residency in 1877 (see box, above), Kuala Kangsar was in at the start of colonial

Malaya's most important industry (one of the original trees survives in a compound next to the District Office). Despite the town's one-time importance as an administrative centre, not much has survived from that period, but a clutch of monuments on the outskirts of town provides a snapshot of Kuala Kangsar's royal and religious importance for the Malays.

Several places of interest are within easy walking distance of the town centre. Heading east from the clock tower in the centre of town, follow Jalan Istana as it curves around the fast-moving river, passing through the ornamental gateway that straddles the street. After about 2km, as you begin to notice the gentle gradient of Bukit Chandan, you'll reach the **Ubudiah Mosque**, whose large, gold, onion domes soar skywards; non-Muslims should ask permission before entering. Disproportionately tall, it looks like Islam's answer to Cinderella's castle. Its construction, in 1917, was interrupted several times, most dramatically when two elephants belonging to Sultan Idris rampaged all over the imported Italian marble floor.

A five-minute walk onward up the same road brings you to the imposing white marble **Istana Iskandariah**, the sultan's ultramodern official palace. It's closed to the public, though a stroll round to the left of the huge gates gives a good view down the river. There is no crown in the sultan's regalia, a fact explained by an early legend associated with Sungei Perak: a former prince was caught in a severe storm while sailing on the river. Throwing his crown overboard to calm the waves, he saved the sinking ship – but not his headgear. Since that day, new Sultans have been enthroned to the sound of drumming rather than by being crowned.

Close by, off to the left as you circle the palace to rejoin the road, the **Royal Museum** (Mon–Thurs, Sat & Sun 9.30am–5pm, Fri 9.30am–12.15pm & 3–5pm; free) is of greater architectural significance. This former royal residence, the erstwhile Istana Kenangan, is a traditional stilted wooden structure, apparently – so the local guides say – built without the use of a single nail, with intricate friezes and geometric-patterned wall panels. Inside, the museum displays a collection of royal artefacts (medals, costumes and so on), although its photographs of past and present royalty in Perak are of more interest.

Back in town, the most evocative memory of colonial days is provided by the **Malay College** on Jalan Tun Razak, its elegant columns and porticoes visible as you approach the centre from the train station. Founded in January 1905, it was conceived by British administrators as a training ground for the sons of Malay nobility, an "Eton of the East", where discipline and tradition was more English than in England – although the schoolboys were required to wear formal Malay dress. The success of many of the college's pupils in finding good jobs in the newly created Malay Administrative Service left parents clamouring for places for their offspring, and started a craze for English education elsewhere in the country.

Practicalities

Kuala Kangsar lies on Route 1 and on the main west-coast train line. The **train station** is on the northwestern outskirts of town, a twenty-minute walk from the clock tower in the centre of town. Buses from Ipoh, Butterworth and Taiping pull up at the **bus station** at the bottom of Jalan Raja Bendahara, close to the river. There are a couple of **places to stay**: the *Double Lion* at 74 Jalan Kangsar (☎05/776 1010; ②), just south of the bus station, has simple rooms without bathrooms, though it was under renovation at time of writing and is set for a price rise after the work is completed in 2001. A quieter, pricier option is the Government Rest House or *Rumah Rehat Seri Temengong* (☎05/776 3872; ④), along Jalan Istana; half a kilometre southeast of the clock tower on the way to the Ubudiah Mosque, it has lashings of colonial atmosphere and a stately riverside location. You can access the **Internet** at Pusat AMS Computer, second floor, 86 Jalan Kangsar (☎05/777 6320), which is close to most of the town's **restaurants**.

Taiping and Maxwell Hill

Set against the backdrop of the mist-laden Bintang hills, **TAIPING** – like so many places in Perak – has its origins in the discovery of tin here in the first decades of the nineteenth century. As a mining centre, overrun by enthusiastic prospectors, it had an unsurprisingly turbulent early history. Originally known as Larut, the town was torn apart in 1871 by violent wars between various Chinese secret societies, whose members had come to work in the mines. A truce was finally declared in 1874, after British intervention as a result of the Pangkor Treaty, and the town was – somewhat hopefully – renamed Taiping, meaning "everlasting peace" – which, incidentally, makes it the only sizeable town in Malaysia today with a Chinese name.

Despite these shaky beginnings, Taiping began to thrive. Its growing prosperity helped fund many firsts at a time when Kuala Lumpur was barely on the map: the first railway in the country (built to facilitate the export of the tin, connecting Taiping with the coastal port of Fort Weld, now called Kuala Sepetang); the first English-language school in 1878; the first museum in 1883; and the first English-language newspaper (the *Perak Pioneer*) in 1894. With the establishment of the nearby hill station of **Maxwell Hill** (now Bukit Larut; see p.165) as a retreat for its administrators, Taiping was firmly at the forefront of the colonial development of the Federated Malay States. For years, tin was its life force, mined and traded by a population that was largely Chinese, and superstitious: the mere presence of a European close to a tin mine was disliked and resented. Ambrose B. Rathborne noted that "No greater offence can be given to a gang of miners than by descending their mine with boots on and an umbrella opened overhead, as it is popularly supposed that such a proceeding is an insult to the presiding spirits, who, out of revenge will make the tin ore disappear." Geology was the actual reason for the eventual depletion of the tin deposits, with the declining market for tin in later years taking an additional toll on the wealth of the town. Nowadays, bypassed by the North–South Highway and replaced in administrative importance by Ipoh, Taiping is declining gracefully, its tattered two-storey shop fronts indicative of the run-down atmosphere that pervades the town. Although the main reason people visit is to relax at Maxwell Hill, allow yourself at least half a day to explore the sights of Taiping – the **gardens**, **Perak Museum** and the fine buildings which line the wide roads.

The Town and around

Taiping is easily walkable, and since the central streets are laid out on a grid system, there's no problem finding your way around. The four main streets, which run parallel to each other, are Jalan Taming Sari, Jalan Pasar, Jalan Kota and Jalan Panggung Wayang. Up Jalan Pasar are the **padang** and the sparkling-white **District Office**, which marks the northern limit of the Chinese district. The gardens – Taman Tasik – spread to the northeast of here, close to the foot of Maxwell Hill, with the museum a little to the northwest; on the opposite side of town, on its southwestern outskirts, are three **temples** for the Hindu, Chinese and Muslim communities respectively.

A wander around the shop-lined streets surrounding Taiping's **central market** – you see wizened *towkay*s lurking at the rear of musty shophouses and dingy *kedai kopi*s – does little to detract from its reputation as a murky old mining town, though Taiping's numerous, lively night markets (see p.164) bring welcome splashes of colour and life. North of here up Jalan Taming Sari is **All Saints' Church**, founded in 1887. The oldest church in Malaysia, it cuts a forlorn figure these days: termites are slowly destroying the wooden structure, and there's talk of completely demolishing and rebuilding the church to "preserve" it for future generations. In some ways, the tiny churchyard

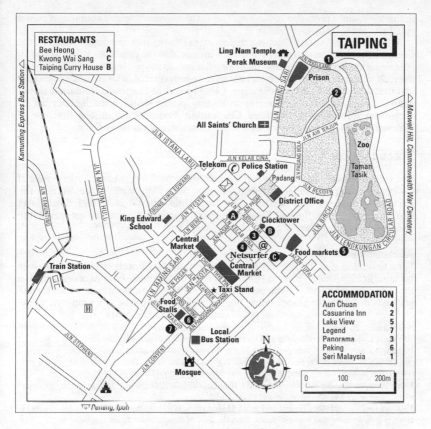

is more interesting, containing the graves of the earliest British and Australian settlers, many of whom died at an unusually early age; others, after many years of service to the Malay states, failed to obtain a pension to allow them to return home.

Another hundred metres further on, the **Perak Museum** (daily 9.30am–5pm; closed Fri noon–2.45pm; free), housed in a cool and spacious colonial building, boasted as many as thirteen thousand exhibits when it opened in 1883. It's often billed as the best museum in Malaysia, an accolade that's difficult to understand. Even the collection of stuffed rare snakes fails to excite much interest, although there is an extensive collection of ancient weapons and Orang Asli implements and ornaments. Next door to the museum, the **Ling Nam Temple** is one of Taiping's main Chinese centres of worship, while opposite the museum is a **prison**, built in 1885 and subsequently used by the Japanese during World War II – today it's where most of the executions of Malaysia's drug offenders are carried out.

Backtracking down Jalan Taming Sari takes you to the padang, from where it's a ten-minute stroll east to **Taman Tasik**, the extensive lake gardens which are landscaped around two former tin-mining pools. At the height of the industry's success, large areas of countryside were being laid waste, creating unsightly muddy heaps and stagnant pools. In Taiping, at least, the Resident retained a colonial sense of propriety and turned this area into a park in 1880. It's still immaculately kept, with a gazebo, freshwater fish in the lakes, and a profusion of flowers. There's also a nine-hole golf course and even a small zoo (daily 10am–6pm; RM2).

A few minutes' walk to the northeast of the park, past the lotus pond, is the **Commonwealth War Cemetery**, a serene memorial to the casualties of World War II, containing the graves of 866 men, many of whom could not be identified. Split in two by the road to Maxwell Hill, the cemetery is all too neatly divided, with Indians on one side and British and Australians on the other. Close by are the **Burmese Pools**, a series of natural rock pools that are not nearly as inviting as they sound. A much better bet for a cool dip are the more traditional **Coronation Pools** (RM1), just at the base of Maxwell Hill, where the chlorine-free water comes straight from the hills.

Practicalities

The **train station** is on Jalan Stesyen behind the hospital, just over a kilometre west of the centre of Taiping. An inconvenient 7km taxi ride (RM5) north of the centre is the Kamunting **express bus station**. The **local bus station** is further down Jalan Panggong Wayang on the left. There are several places where you can use **email**, the cheapest being the large *Net Surfer*, 36–38 Jalan Tupai (☎05/805 9596).

Accommodation

For a town of its size, Taiping has a remarkable number of **hotels**, which is just as well because in high season it often has to cater for the overspill from Maxwell Hill. For those on a tight budget, or who prefer a bit more action, the town rather than the hill station is definitely the place to stay. One or two of the places here are old-style wooden Chinese houses with shutters, full of character but rather grotty.

Aun Chuan, 25 Jalan Kota, on junction with Jalan Halaman Pasar (☎05/807 5322). The least expensive option, above *KFC* – it's clean and spacious, with wooden floors and en-suite rooms. ②.

Casuarina Inn, Taman Tasik (☎05/804 1339). Stands on the site of the former official quarters of the British Resident in Perak State, overlooking the lake gardens. The rooms are huge, if a little musty; the helpful management know all there is to know about the local sights. ④.

Lake View, 1a Circular Rd (☎05/805 4181). Right by the lake, this friendly but basic hotel has good views. The nearby karaoke bar can get noisy. ②.

Legend Inn, cnr of Jalan Convent and Jalan Masjid (☎05/806 0000, fax 806 6666). The best hotel in town, a little smarter and less expensive than the *Seri Malaysia*, but without the view. ⑤.

Panorama, 61–79 Jalan Kota (☎05/808 4111, fax 808 4129). A pleasant, reasonably priced and centrally located hotel with nice bathrooms. ④.

Peking, 2 Jalan Idris Taiping (☎05/807 2975). A real gem of a traditional Chinese wooden house with carvings and coloured glass. The clean, simple rooms have air-con and cold showers; for a very modest surcharge (RM5), you can have hot water too. Great value. ②.

Seri Malaysia, Taman Tasik (☎05/806 9502, fax 806 9495). Well-equipped rooms with air-con and kettles for making tea and coffee. The top lakeside hotel. ⑤.

Eating and drinking

The most atmospheric meals to be had in town are those at Taiping's numerous **food markets**. The largest is along Jalan Chung Thye Phin (Cross St), while the eastern side of the food market on Jalan Tupai is great for ice-cream sundaes and fruit salads, as well as all manner of main courses. Opposite the *Peking* hotel on Jalan Idris Taiping is another large row of stalls, where you can get a burger or seafood. There's a good Chinese restaurant, *Kwong Wai Sang*, on Jalan Panggung Wayang, and an Indian place – *Taiping Curry House* – near the clock tower on Jalan Tupai. The *Bee Hong* vegetarian Chinese restaurant, on Jalan Pasar near the junction with Jalan Kelab Cina, has some great beancurd concoctions.

Maxwell Hill (Bukit Larut)

MAXWELL HILL – 12km northeast of Taiping – is Malaysia's smallest (and oldest) hill station, named after the first Assistant Resident of Perak, George Maxwell. Here, at approximately 1035m above sea level, the climate is wonderfully cool, and on a clear day there are spectacular views down to the west coast. Unfortunately its status as reputedly the wettest place in Malaysia, with 5m of rainfall annually, also means that it's frequently too cloudy at the top to see much at all. Nevertheless, the air of colonial nostalgia makes Maxwell Hill well worth visiting. There are a few tame forest **walks** here too, but you'll have to use your initiative if you want to depart from the road, as they're not marked. The climb to The Cottage – a stone bungalow built in the 1880s for British officialdom – leads through groves of evergreens and the largest variety of flowers in the country, to the only accessible **summit**. Protect yourself against leeches, which can be a problem in the forest, by wearing long trousers, and socks and shoes, not sandals.

The narrow road up to the hill station twists and turns round some terrifying bends and is only accessible by government Land Rover; private vehicles are not allowed up. The service (hourly 8am–5pm; 35min; RM2 one way) begins at the foot of the hill, ten minutes' walk from the lake gardens in Taiping. If you're only making a day-trip, it's especially advisable to **book your seat** there in advance (either in person at the booking office where the service begins, or by calling ☎05/807 7243), otherwise at busy times you could find yourself hanging around waiting for a space. Book the return journey up at the hill station itself, in the booth by the *Rumah Beringin Resthouse*.

Many people prefer to **walk** up from Taiping instead, which takes from two-and-a-half to three hours; the marked path starts at the Land Rover pick-up point. You'll need to be quite fit, but this way you get more time to take in the views and can still make it down again by early evening. About midway to the summit is the Tea Garden House, little more than a shelter now, and once part of an extensive tea estate. It's an ideal place to stop for a rest, as the view at this point is superb, with the town of Taiping and the mirror-like waters of the gardens visible below.

Practicalities

The choice for **accommodation** on Maxwell Hill is between resthouses and bungalows. Standards are pretty uniform, with most places offering hot water, kitchen facilities and spacious rooms. As there's only room for a total of 53 people, you'll need to **book** in advance at the office at the foot of the hill, where you book the Land Rovers (☎05/807 7241). Bungalow prices are for the whole building (sleeping six), while the resthouses rent out individual rooms. **Food** is available at each of the resthouses, while at the bungalows, the caretaker can arrange for food to be prepared for you, or you can do your own cooking – buy your provisions in Taiping.

The Land Rover stops right next to the *Rumah Beringin* (RM150) bungalow, not quite as quiet as the other places (as day-trippers often come here for a couple of hours before heading back down). All the other places to stay are dotted around the hills within a mile of the drop-off point, and the driver will take you to your door if you ask. A one-hundred-metre walk downhill from the stop are the basic rooms of the *Rehat Bukit Larut* resthouse (①); a minute's walk up from here brings you to the *Rumah Anykasa* (RM150). A quarter of a mile uphill from the Land Rover stop, there's a junction to the left of which are the *Rumah Cendana* (RM100), *Rumah Tempinis* (RM100), and the VIP-class *Sri Kayangan* (RM200) bungalows, all spaced well away from each other; taking a right leads after about 400m to the *Rumah Rehat Gunung Hijau* resthouse, which is the most secluded up here (①).

Penang

North of Taiping, towards the coast, the landscape becomes increasingly flat and arid as the road eases away from the backbone of mountains that dominate the western seaboard. Sitting 94km north of Taiping is the dusty, industrial port town of **Butterworth**, part of **PENANG**, a confusing amalgam of state and island. Everything of interest in Penang State is on **Pulau Pinang** ("Betel Nut Island" in Malay) – a large island, 285 square kilometres in area, upon which the first British settlement on the Malay Peninsula was sited. The confusion gets worse, as the island's city, (Malaysia's

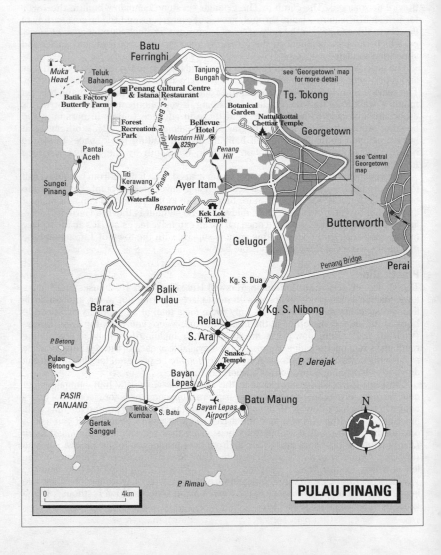

second largest), the likeable **Georgetown**, is also often referred to as "Penang". A fast-moving, go-ahead place, Georgetown has a reputation as a duty-free shopping mecca that accords with its history as a trading port. Despite the gigantic high-rise KOMTAR building – visible even from the mainland – epitomizing its commercial development, Georgetown has sacrificed few of its traditional buildings and customs to modernity. In its Chinatown, one of Malaysia's most vibrant, faded two-storey shophouses and ornate temples predominate, legacies of the massive influx of immigrants attracted here by the early establishment of a colonial port. Hot on their heels were the Indian merchants, bringing with them spices, cloths and religious customs, nowhere more evident in the city than during the annual festival of Thaipusam (see p.68). To the northwest of the town centre, huge mansions and elegant gardens bear witness to the rewards reaped by early entrepreneurs. Georgetown also has some of the country's best British colonial architecture in the area surrounding crumbling Fort Cornwallis, the island's oldest building.

While Georgetown is likely to be your base during a stay on Pulau Penang, most visitors make day-trips out, traditionally to the beaches at **Batu Ferringhi** and the much quieter **Tanjung Bungah** along the north coast. No longer the hippie hangout of the 1970s, this stretch is now mostly five-star resort territory, though some budget places nestle between the plush high-rises. Although pollution and overdevelopment have taken their inevitable toll, the beaches themselves aren't bad and the nightlife keeps most people happy. The beaches, however, are not the only reason to come to Penang: there are enough markets, temples and historic buildings in the busy Georgetown streets to occupy at least a couple of days, and journeys to the south and west of the island reveal a startlingly rural and mountainous interior, with a population that retains many of its traditions and industries. There are also about thirty hiking trails around the island, well described in *Nature Trails of Penang Island*, published by the Malaysian Nature Society.

The island is the focus of several important **festivals** and events throughout the year, starting with Thaipusam in February. Perhaps the best known of the rest is the Penang Bridge Run held in May, when thousands of competitors hurtle across the bridge to Butterworth at dawn as part of a half-marathon. June is also a busy month, witnessing the International Dragonboat Race, the Equestrian Carnival and, on the northern coast, a beach volleyball tournament. In July, Georgetown's flower festival and Grand Parade provide colour, while the Cultural Festival provides a showcase for Penang's Malays, Chinese and Indians.

Some history

Pulau Pinang was ruled by the **sultans of Kedah** until the late eighteenth century. In the wake of years of harassment by Kedah's enemies, the sultan, Mohammed J'wa Mu'Azzam Shah II, was prepared to afford trade facilities to any nation that would provide him with military protection. Enter **Francis Light** in 1771, a ship's captain of the European trading company of Jourdain, Sullivan and de Souza, who was in search of a regional trading base for both his company and the East India Company. According to contemporary accounts, Captain Light was a charming man, well trained in the art of diplomacy, and it was not long before the Sultan had housed the captain in his fort at Kuala Kedah, conferring upon him the honorary title of "Deva Raja" (God-king) and taking him into his confidence.

Light knew that the East India Company wanted to obtain a strategic port in the region to facilitate its trade with China, and as a refuge from its enemies in the Bay of Bengal. In forwarding the Sultan's offer of the island of Penang to the Company, Light drew particular attention to its safe harbour, and to the opportunities for local commerce. In 1772 the Company sent its own agent, Edward Moncton, to negotiate with the

Sultan, but the talks soon broke down. It was another twelve years before agreement was reached, spurred on by the accession of a new sultan, Abdullah, and the East India Company's mounting concern that other countries were gaining a regional foothold – the French, at war with Britain, had acquired port facilities in northern Sumatra, having already made a pact with Burma, and the Dutch were consolidating their position in the Straits of Melaka.

In accordance with an agreement arranged by Light, the Company was to pay Sultan Abdullah RM30,000 a year. Unfortunately for the Sultan, the Company's new governor-general Charles Cornwallis firmly stated that he could not be party to the Sultan's disputes with the other Malay princes, or promise to protect him from the Burmese or Siamese. This rather pulled the rug from under Light's feet because it was on the basis of these promises that the Sultan had ceded the island of Penang in the first place. Undeterred, Light decided to conceal the facts from both parties, and on his own initiative formally **established a port** at Penang on August 11, 1786. For the next five years Light adopted stalling tactics with the Sultan, assuring him that the matter of protection was being referred to authorities in London. The Sultan eventually began to suspect that the company had reneged on the agreement, and attempted to drive the British out of Penang by force, but the effort failed; the subsequent settlement imposed by the British allowed the Sultan an annual payment of only RM6000, and no role in the future government of the island.

So it was that Penang, then inhabited by less than a hundred indigenous fishermen, became the **first British settlement** in the Malay Peninsula. Densely forested, the island was open to settlers to claim as much land as they could clear – in somewhat debonair mood, Light encouraged the razing of the jungle by firing coins from a cannon into the undergrowth. After an initial, late-eighteenth-century influx of mainly Chinese immigrants, attracted by the possibilities of new commerce, Penang quickly became a major colonial administrative centre – within two years, four hundred acres were under cultivation and the population had reached ten thousand. Francis Light was made superintendent and declared the island a free port, renaming it "Prince of Wales Island" after the British heir apparent, whose birthday fell the day after the founding of the island. Georgetown, named – unsurprisingly – after the British king at that time, George III, has retained its colonial name even though the island's name has reverted to Penang.

For a time, all looked rosy for Penang, with Georgetown proclaimed as capital of the newly established **Straits Settlements** (incorporating Melaka and Singapore) in 1826. But the founding of Singapore in 1819 was the beginning of the end for Georgetown, and as the new colony overtook its predecessor in every respect (replacing it as capital of the Straits Settlements in 1832), Penang's fortunes rapidly began to wane. In retrospect, this had one beneficial effect: with Georgetown stuck in the economic doldrums for a century or more, there was no significant development within the city, and consequently many of its colonial and early Chinese buildings survive to this day. Although Penang was occupied by the Japanese during World War II, the strategic significance of Singapore once more proved to be Penang's saving grace, and there was little or no bomb damage to Penang island.

Butterworth

Realistically, the only reason to spend any time at all in **BUTTERWORTH**, 370km from KL, is to sort out your transport to Penang island – which can usually be done within half an hour of arrival. The **bus station, port complex, long-distance-taxi stand** and **train station** are all next door to each other, lying right on the quayside, so you shouldn't have to venture any further. Although Butterworth is on a branch of the main north–south rail line, only one of the daily trains on the route doesn't pass through

Butterworth. This stops instead at the nearby station of Bukit Mertajam, from where Butterworth is a short bus or local train ride to the northwest.

There are plenty of **places to stay**, although the decent hotels are a fair way from the port; none of the nearby options are particularly appealing. From the bus station, walking northeast along the main road for a minute or so brings you to the rock-bottom grime of the *Pak Tai Hotel*, on your left (☎04/331 7059; ②); the sign for it is faded and so can be hard to spot. Keep walking and the road curves to your left past a huge intersection and a Hong Leong Bank; on the other side of the road, near a Maybank, is the overpriced *Sin Tong Ah* (☎04/323 9679; ③), though it's clean and comfortable with air-con. Otherwise, the *Ambassadress* (☎04/344 2788; ③) is just one of many places along Jalan Bagan Luar, the main road running out of Butterworth; facilities are better here, but it's more than walking distance from the terminals. The stalls on the top floor of the bus terminal are the best **eating** options, staying open well into the night.

The 24-hour passenger and **car-ferry service to Georgetown** takes fifteen minutes (passengers 60 sen return, cars RM1 return); from the top floor of the bus station, you can walk over the signposted causeway to the ferry ticketing booths. The **Penang Bridge**, the longest in Asia at 13km, crosses from just south of Butterworth – turn west off Route 1, 5km south of Butterworth, for the bridge – to the east coast of the island, 8km south of Georgetown (a toll of RM7 is payable only on the journey out from the mainland); if you are coming over by **long-distance taxi** from any point on the Peninsula, check whether or not the toll is included in the fare.

Georgetown

Visiting **GEORGETOWN** in 1879, stalwart Victorian traveller Isabella Bird called it "a brilliant place under a brilliant sky", a simple statement on which it's hard to improve – Malaysia's most fascinating city retains more of its cultural history than virtually anywhere else in the country. Fort Cornwallis, St George's Church and the many buildings on and around Lebuh Pantai all survive from the earliest colonial days, and the communities of Chinatown and Little India have contributed some fine temples. Later Thai and Burmese arrivals left their mark on the city, but its predominant feature are the rows of peeling two-storey **Chinese shophouses**, their shutters painted in pastel colours, with bright-red Chinese lettering covering their colonnades and cheerfully designed awnings to shield the goods from the glaring sun. While the confusion of rickshaws, buses, lorries and scooters make parts of Georgetown as frenetic and polluted as most other places in the region, life in the slow lane has changed very little over the years. The rituals of worship, eating out at a roadside stall, the running of the family business, have all continued with little concern for Georgetown's contemporary technological development. It may no longer be a sleepy backwater – most of the island's one-million strong population now lives here – but the city's soul is firmly rooted in the past.

Strategically sited Georgetown is no stranger to visitors, since ships from all over the world have been docking at present-day Swettenham Pier since Francis Light first established his port here in 1786. Over the years, not surprisingly, it acquired a rather dubious reputation for backstreet dives frequented by boisterous sailors on shore leave. Where once ships' chandlers and supply merchants ran thriving businesses, modern-day maritime trade is of an entirely different nature: neon-lit bars and dingy brothels help to boost the spirits of foreign navy crews who make regular forays around the city's streets. There's been a gradual change though, especially since the late 1970s, when foreign tourists first descended upon Penang in significant numbers. Nowadays, parts of downtown Georgetown sparkle with the state-of-the-art hotels and air-con shopping malls familiar to much of modern Malaysia. But perhaps more than any other place in the country Georgetown is a magnet for budget travellers – the city is some-

Copthorn Hotel

JLN TANJUNG BUNGAH

TANJUNG BUNGAH

JLN LEMBAH PERMAI

TANJUNG TOKONG

GEORGETOWN

N

Batu Ferringhi

Botanical Gardens

Midlands Park Centre

PULAU TIKUS

Nattukkottai Chettiar Temple

Adventist Hospital

Dharmmikarama Burmese Temple

Wat Chayamangkalaram

Royal Thai Consulate

E&O Hotel

see 'Central Georgetown' map

Fort Cornwallis

General Hospital

JLN BURMA

Golf Course

Komtar Centre

Kek Lok Si Temple

Penang Hill Funicular Railway

Masjid Negeri

Stadium

Butterworth

0   1   2km

▽ University, Penang Bridge

thing of a hangout, a place not only to renew Thai visas, but to relax and observe street life from a pavement café – in between trips to the beach.

Arrival, information and transport

Passenger and car **ferries from Butterworth** dock at the centrally located terminal on **Pengkalan Weld** in Georgetown; those **from Medan** (Indonesia) and **Langkawi** (see p.195) dock at **Swettenham Pier**, a few hundred metres north along the dockside. Arriving at either the express-bus station or taxi stand also puts you at the eastern edge of Georgetown, just a short walk from the hotels and major amenities. The Penang Bridge brings **drivers** into the island on Jalan Udini, 8km south of Georgetown on the east coast. Driving into the city is not for the traffic-shy, though the major routes are well signposted. It's easiest to park in the KOMTAR building on Jalan Penang, which is within easy walking distance of the hotel area. The **airport**, at Bayan Lepas on the southeastern tip of the island, handles flights from Singapore, KL, Kuching and Kota Kinabalu, among other destinations (see opposite). Yellow bus #83 (roughly hourly, 6am–9pm; RM1.45) takes about 45 minutes to run into Georgetown, stopping at the KOMTAR building and subsequently at the Pengkalan Weld ferry terminal; a taxi into the city costs around RM26 – buy a coupon beforehand from inside the terminal building.

On arrival, the most convenient tourist office is the **Penang Tourist Centre** (Mon–Thurs 8.30am–1pm & 2–4.30pm, Fri 8.30am–12.30pm & 2.30–4.30pm, Sat 8.30am–1pm; ☎04/261 6663), on the ground floor of the Penang Port Commission building on Jalan Tun Syed Sheh Barakbah; they produce an excellent island and city **map** (RM1). A couple of doors down at no. 10 is **Tourism Malaysia** (Mon–Thurs 8am–12.45pm & 2–5pm, Fri 8am–12.15pm & 2.45–4.15pm, Sat 8am–1pm, closed first and third Sat of every month; ☎04/262 0066), which is more helpful. Best of all is the **Tourist Information Centre** (daily 10am–6pm; ☎04/261 4461) on the third floor of the KOMTAR building, which is really clued up on local information and can also arrange half-day tours of the city (from around RM30), not a bad way to see Penang if your time is limited.

PUBLIC TRANSPORT
The city is fairly small – you could walk from Pengkalan Weld to the top of the main street, Lebuh Chulia, in about twenty minutes – and so it's best to **get around** on foot;

MOVING ON FROM PENANG ISLAND

Most journeys from Penang Island involve changing in Butterworth, where you can pick up long-distance buses and trains to destinations in the Peninsula and on to Hat Yai, Surat Thami and Bangkok in Thailand.

BY AIR
Among the direct international **flights** from Georgetown are services to **Medan** in Sumatra, **Bangkok** and **Phuket** in Thailand, and **Singapore**. To get to Bayan Lepas International Airport, take yellow bus #83 (hourly on the hour 6am–9pm; 45min; RM1.45) from Pengkalan Weld or the KOMTAR building.

BY FERRY
The 24-hour passenger and car **ferry** from the Pengkalan Weld terminal is free on the leg to **Butterworth** (daily 6am–midnight every 20min; midnight–6am hourly). Express ferries to **Medan** and **Langkawi** depart twice daily from Swettenham Pier. Tickets for either route can be purchased in advance from the office next to the Penang Tourist Association and from the tourist information office at the KOMTAR building. Tickets for Langkawi are also sold by the Kuala Perlis–Langkawi Ferry Service (☎04/262 5630) and Langkawi Ferry Service (☎04/264 2088), both at the Penang Port Commission building; the travel agencies on Lebuh Chulia will also book tickets for you.

BY BUS AND TRAIN
The nearest **train station** is in Butterworth (information on ☎04/323 7962); there is a booking office in the Pengkalan Weld ferry terminal where you can reserve tickets to anywhere on the Peninsula. Although some **buses** depart from the KOMTAR building for destinations on the Peninsula (including KL, Kota Bharu, Kuala Terengganu and the Cameron Highlands), they can get busy, so book ahead at SIA Tours & Travel, 35 Pengkalan Weld (☎04/262 2951); in any case, there are more services from the terminal at Butterworth. The travel agencies on Lebuh Chulia can reserve seats on buses from Butterworth, though services from there are so numerous that you can just turn up without booking beforehand.

BY TAXI
Taxis from the Pengkalan Weld ferry terminal charge about RM40 per vehicle to **Butterworth** station. Long-distance taxis depart from several hostels (such as the *New China* on Lebuh Leith) to **Hat Yai** in Thailand (RM200 for up to four passengers).

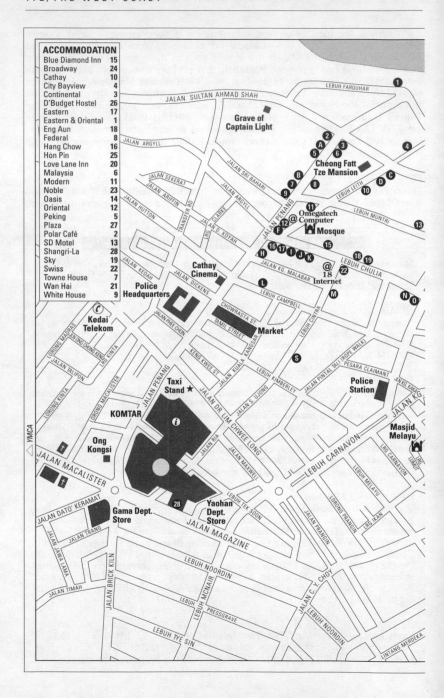

ACCOMMODATION

Blue Diamond Inn	15
Broadway	24
Cathay	10
City Bayview	4
Continental	3
D'Budget Hostel	26
Eastern	17
Eastern & Oriental	1
Eng Aun	18
Federal	8
Hang Chow	16
Hon Pin	25
Love Lane Inn	20
Malaysia	6
Modern	11
Noble	23
Oasis	14
Oriental	12
Peking	5
Plaza	27
Polar Café	2
SD Motel	13
Shangri-La	28
Sky	19
Swiss	22
Towne House	7
Wan Hai	21
White House	9

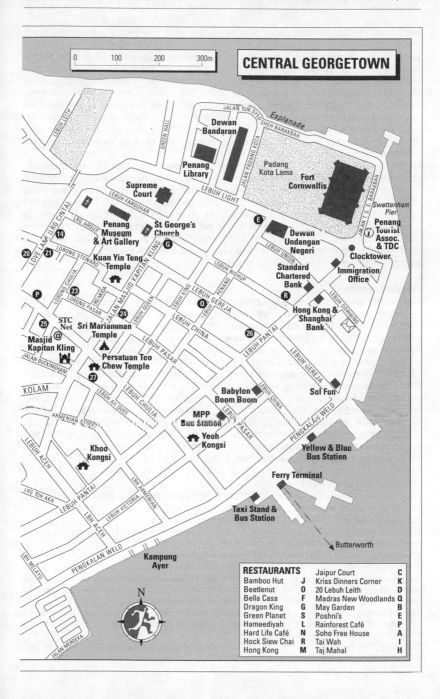

CENTRAL GEORGETOWN

0 100 200 300m

Esplanade

JALAN TUN SYED SHEH BARAKBAH

GREEN HALL

Dewan
Bandaran

Penang
Library

JALAN PADANG KOTA

Padang
Kota Lama

Fort
Cornwallis

JALAN T S S BARAKBAH

Swettenham
Pier

Penang
Tourist
Assoc.
& TDC

Supreme
Court

LEBUH FARQUHAR

LEBUH LIGHT

Penang
Museum
& Art Gallery

St George's
Church

LRG CINTAI

LRG ARGUS

LOVE LANE

14

Kuan Yin Teng
Temple

LORONG STEWARD

20 21

LORONG CHULIA

E

Dewan
Undangan
Negeri

Clocktower

Immigration
Office

LEBUH UNION

LEBUH BISHOP

LEBUH KING

LEBUH QUEEN

LEBUH PENANG

Standard
Chartered
Bank

R

Hong Kong &
Shanghai
Bank

P

23

LORONG PASAR

LORONG JPK MODA

JALAN MASJID KAPITAN KLING

LEBUH GEREJA

STC
Net

25

24

Sri Mariamman
Temple

Q

LEBUH CHINA

LEBUH DOWNING

Masjid
Kapitan Kling

JALAN BUCKINGHAM

26

LEBUH PANTAI

LEBUH GEREJA

Persatuan Teo
Chew Temple

27

LEBUH PASAR

KOLAM

LEBUH AST QUEE

LEBUH CHULIA

ARMENIAN STREET

Babylon
Boom Boom

LEBUH CHINA

Sol Fun

LEBUH ACEH

MPP
Bus Station

Yeoh
Kongsi

PENGKALAN WELD

Yellow & Blue
Bus Station

LRG TOH AKA

LEBUH PANTAI

Khoo
Kongsi

LBH ARMENIAN

LBH VICTORIA

Ferry Terminal

LBH ACEH

Taxi Stand &
Bus Station

PENGKALAN WELD

Butterworth

LBH MELAYU

Kampung
Ayer

JALAN MERDEKA

N

RESTAURANTS			
Bamboo Hut	J	Jaipur Court	C
Beetlenut	O	Kriss Dinners Corner	K
Bella Casa	F	20 Lebuh Leith	D
Dragon King	G	Madras New Woodlands	Q
Green Planet	S	May Garden	B
Hameediyah	L	Poshni's	E
Hard Life Café	N	Rainforest Café	P
Hock Siew Chai	R	Soho Free House	A
Hong Kong	M	Tai Wah	I
		Taj Mahal	H

you'll miss most of the interesting alleyways otherwise. For longer journeys in town, and for travelling around the island, you'll need to master the excellent **bus service**. Red-and-white **Transit Link** buses – the most common of the lot – run on most routes through the island and around the city from a station on Lebuh Victoria, a block north of Pengkalan Weld. Leaving from the station next to the ferry terminal on Pengkalan Weld, blue buses service the north of the island, and yellow buses the south and west. There are also a number of minibuses operating and a few buses run by the small Sri Negara company; we've given details of useful services in the text. All buses stop on Jalan Ria, by the KOMTAR Building. **Fares** are rarely more than a ringgit and services are frequent, though by 8pm in the evening they become more sporadic and stop completely at 10pm.

The traditional way of seeing the city is by **rickshaw**; drivers tout for custom outside the major hotels and all along Lebuh Chulia. Negotiate the price in advance; a ride from the ferry terminal at Pengkalan Weld to the northern end of Lebuh Chulia costs around RM3. There are **taxi** stands by the ferry terminal and on Jalan Dr. Lim Chwee Long, off Jalan Penang. Drivers rarely use their meters, so agree the fare in advance – a trip across town runs to about RM5, while a ride out to the airport or Batu Ferringhi costs RM20. To book a taxi in advance, call Jade Auto (☎04/226 3015), C.T. Taxis (☎04/229 9467) or J.R.I. Taxis (☎04/229 0501). For **bike or car rental** – particularly useful if you plan to see the rest of the island – see p.184.

Accommodation

Despite the profusion of hotels and guesthouses, Georgetown is one of the few places in the whole country where you might experience difficulty in finding **accommodation**, particularly at the budget end of the scale. Arrive early in the day or book ahead by phone or you may face a great deal of traipsing around (or have to rely on one of the rickshaw drivers – they are usually able to find rooms, for a commission). The budget places, mostly on and around **Lebuh Chulia**, are usually within ramshackle wooden-shuttered mansions, often with porticoes and elegant internal staircases. Most have **dorm beds** as well as rooms, and offer other useful services, such as selling bus tickets to Thailand and obtaining Thai visas. The two official **youth hostels** are a long way from the city centre: the *YMCA* is at 211 Jalan Macalister, 4km west from the KOMTAR building (☎04/229 2349; ②), and the *YWCA* at 8 Jalan Mesjid Negeri (☎04/828 1855; ②).

In Georgetown's mid-range places – mostly in the same noisy area – you're often just paying for air-con and more modern furniture. Top-of-the-range hotels are more or less all located on **Jalan Penang** and **Lebuh Farquhar**, west of the centre.

ALONG LEBUH CHULIA

The numbering scheme on Lebuh Chulia is reckoned from its eastern end – house numbers increase westwards along the street.

Blue Diamond, 422 Lebuh Chulia (☎04/261 4117). Behind the modern frontage is a long inner courtyard and a grand staircase. The large, scruffy rooms are en suite, and have luxurious sprung mattresses; there's also a dorm and a friendly café. ②, dorm beds RM8.

Eastern, 509 Lebuh Chulia (☎04/261 4597). Small, clean rooms with fan or air-con and saloon-style wooden doors. More solidly built than most. ②.

Eng Aun, 380 Lebuh Chulia (☎04/261 2333). Standard Chinese-run place which seems to draw in more of the traveller crowd than it deserves. It's noisy at night, and the fact you don't get your own key makes the dorm more trouble than it's worth. ②, dorm beds RM8.

Hang Chow, 511 Lebuh Chulia (☎04/261 0810). Scruffy but clean with some rustic charm. A very few ringgit more will get you your own shower; a few of the rooms have air-con. There's a simple Chinese restaurant downstairs. ②.

Honping, 273b Lebuh Chulia (☎04/262 5243). Hotel rooms above the *Co Co Island* restaurant, with air-con and hot tubs. Functional, but a little untidy. ③.

Sky, 348 Lebuh Chulia (☎04/262 2323). Basic and a little dingy. The rooms with air-con are good value; the rest of the rooms have fans. ②.

Swiss, 431 Lebuh Chulia (☎04/262 0133). A large, bland but functional hostel that sees a lot of the traveller crowd. Set back from the road, with parking and an airy café, this is a little better than the *Eng Aun* opposite. ②.

AROUND LEBUH CHULIA

Broadway Hostel, 35f Jalan Masjid Kapitan Kling (☎04/262 8550, fax 261 9525). Very clean, with sparsely furnished en-suite rooms, a dorm and friendly Indian management. ②, dorm beds RM7.

Cathay, 15 Lebuh Leith (☎04/262 6271, fax 263 9300). Stylish colonial mansion dating from 1910. The cool greys of the decor, spacious rooms and courtyard fountain make for a tranquil environment. ④.

D'Budget Hostel, 9 Lebuh Gereja (☎04/263 4794). The long corridors are a little claustrophobic, but the dorms and rooms are clean, well kept and secure. Shared bathroom with hot showers and Western-style toilets, and notice board. ②, dorm beds RM7.

Love Lane Inn, 54 Lorong Cinta (☎019/471 8409, *ocean008@hotmail.com*). Spartan and clean, but rather sterile. Dorms (RM10) and very simple, inexpensive doubles. ①.

Modern, 179c Lebuh Muntri (☎04/263 5424). On the corner of Lebuh Leith, this basic hotel is friendly enough, but seems to be falling apart. The top-floor rooms have balconies. ①.

Noble, 36 Lorong Pasar (☎04/261 2372). Tucked away on a small side street, with friendly management. The en-suite rooms are a good deal, and so fill up faster than the rooms with fans. ①.

Oasis Hotel, 23 Lorong Cinta (☎04/261 6778). The best of the budget places, its clean rooms and dorm set in an attractive stone house with a shady, tranquil garden. Also has communal hot showers and a friendly atmosphere. Recommended. ①, dorm beds RM8.

Plaza Hostel, 32 Lebuh Ah Quee (☎04/263 0560, *plazahostel@hotmail.com*). Besides its simple rooms, this place also has the best dorm in Georgetown, with a balcony, sitting area, washing facilities and lockers. There's a good café, Internet access, travel books, a good notice board and well-informed staff. ②, dorm beds RM8.

S.D. Motel, 24 Lebuh Muntri (☎04/264 3743, *sdmotel@penangnet.com*). Bare, though clean, rooms and an air-con dorm with communal hot showers. The staff are knowledgeable and can offer useful advice as regards travel in and around Penang. ②, dorm beds RM13.

Wan Hai, 35 Lorong Cinta (☎04/261 6853). The rooms and dorm are a little dingy, partly compensated for by the roof terrace, availability of bikes for rent and the very inexpensive rates. ①, dorm beds RM8.

ALONG JALAN PENANG AND ELSEWHERE

City Bayview, 25a Lebuh Farquhar (☎04/263 3161, fax 263 4124). Modern high-rise place close to the sea, with its own pool and fantastic views over the bay and town from the rooftop revolving restaurant. Good value. ⑥.

Continental, 5 Jalan Penang (☎04/263 6388, fax 263 8718, *hotelconti@po.jaring.my*). The rooms are comfortable and have air-con, though they're overpriced unless there's a promotion deal going. ⑤.

Federal, 39 Jalan Penang (☎04/263 4179). Grubby, but the rooms are well equipped for the price. The rooms are en suite, with hot water and TV. ②.

Hotel Malaysia, 7 Jalan Penang (☎04/263 3311, *hotelmal@tm.net.my*). Modern hotel next door to, and almost identical to, the *Continental*. ⑤.

Oriental, 105 Jalan Penang (☎04/263 4211, fax 263 5395). Good-value mid-range hotel with helpful, professional staff and comfortable, en-suite doubles. ④.

Peking, 50a Jalan Penang (☎04/263 6191). Large, clean rooms in this moderately priced but bland hotel. ③.

Polar Café, 48a Jalan Penang (☎04/262 2054, fax 262 9611). Comfortable rooms, sprung mattresses and inclusive continental breakfast make this a good choice – the only drawback is the singalong bar at the front, which can keep you awake till the small hours. ②.

Shangri-La, Magazine Rd (☎04/262 2622, fax 262 6526). The most luxurious hotel in Georgetown, conveniently placed next to the KOMTAR building. All the facilities you would expect for a place of its price. ⑨.

Towne House, 70 Jalan Penang (☎04/263 8621, fax 262 3541). Plush and well-appointed rooms at a reasonable rate. A little smarter and less expensive than the *Oriental*. ③.

White House, 72 Jalan Penang (☎04/263 2385). Very clean, large rooms, with hot showers and optional air-con, for half what you'd pay elsewhere. The rooms with fans only are amongst the best-value accommodation in Georgetown, and can fill up early. Recommended. ②.

The city centre

The main area of interest in Georgetown is the central square-kilometre or so bordered by Jalan Penang, Jalan Magazine and the sharply curving coast. The most prominent, if not most aesthetically pleasing, landmark is the Komplex Tun Abdul Razak (or KOM-TAR), a huge high-rise of shops and offices towering over the western corner of the city centre. The whole of this area could effectively be termed **Chinatown**, since the entire centre of Georgetown is dominated by shuttered two-storey shophouses and a liberal scattering of *kongsis* (clan associations) that have stood here in various forms since the late eighteenth century. In the thick of it is tiny **Little India**, between Lebuh King and Lebuh Queen, while the remnants of the city's **colonial** past – Fort Cornwallis, St George's Church and the building housing the Penang Museum – are all clustered relatively close together at the eastern end of town, not far from Swettenham Docks. For a reminder of Penang's past economic success, typified by millionaire's row and the *Eastern and Oriental (E&O) Hotel*, the area around **Jalan Penang**, west of the central area, is worth exploring.

FORT CORNWALLIS AND THE WATERFRONT

The site of **Fort Cornwallis** (daily 8.30am–7pm; RM1) on the northeastern tip of Pulau Pinang marks the spot where the British fleet, under Captain Francis Light, disembarked on July 16, 1786. A fort fronting the blustery north channel was hastily thrown up to provide barracks for Light and his men, and was named after Lord Charles Cornwallis, Governor-General of India. The present structure dates from around twenty years after, but for all its significance little remains to excite the senses, just peeling walls and the seventeenth-century **Sri Rambai cannon**, sited in the northwest corner of the citadel. Presented to the Sultan of Johor by the Dutch, this was confiscated by the British in 1871 during their attack on Selangor – they loaded 29 guns, including the cannon, onto the steamer *Sri Rambai* and upon reaching Penang, threw it overboard; it remained submerged for almost a decade. According to local legend, the cannon refused to leave the seabed during the subsequent salvage operation and only floated to the surface when Tunku Qudin, the former Viceroy of Selangor, tied a rope to it and ordered it to rise. Since then it's been considered a living entity with mystical powers; the local belief is that barren women can conceive by laying flowers on its barrel.

STREET NAMES IN GEORGETOWN

The most confusing thing about finding your way around Georgetown is understanding the **street names**, which all used to reflect the city's colonial past; however, the current political climate encourages either a Malay translation of an existing name – Penang Road has become Jalan Penang, Penang Street is Lebuh Penang, Weld Quay has become Pengkalan Weld, and Beach Street is now Lebuh Pantai – or complete renaming. This would be relatively straightforward were it not for the fact that the new names have not always been popularly accepted – Lorong Cinta, for example, is almost universally known as Love Lane – and even on official maps you'll sometimes see either name used. The most awkward of the new names is Jalan Mesjid Kapitan Kling for the erstwhile Pitt Street, which more often than not is referred to simply as Lebuh Pitt.

M. WINCH/AXIOM

Petronas Twin Towers, KL

JERRY DENNIS

Sultan Abdul Samad building, KL

JIM HOLMES/AXIOM

Tropical downpour, KL

CHARLES DE LEDESMA

Islamic Art Museum, KL

JIM HOLMES/AXIOM

SIMON RICHMOND

Batu Caves, KL

Pulau Ketam, off Port Klang

Kek Lok Si Temple, Penang

Sri Mariamman Temple, Georgetown, Penang

Thaipusam, Penang

Georgetown, Penang

Canopy walkway, Taman Negara

Inside the fort, there's a replica of a traditional Malay house, a craft shop and, close to the cannon, a claustrophobic underground bunker detailing the history of Penang – unimaginatively presented, but informative. An open-air auditorium hosts local music and dance festivals – keep an eye on the local press for details of shows.

The large expanse of green that borders the fort, the **Padang Kota Lama**, was once the favourite promenade of the island's colonial administrators and thronged with rickshaws and carriages. On the south side, opposite the grand sweep of the **Esplanade**, was a bandstand where Filipino groups played to strolling passers-by. Now used for sports and other public events, the padang is bordered by some superb examples of Anglo-Victorian architecture: the **Dewan Undangan Negeri** (State Legislative Building) with its weighty portico and ornate gables, and the **Dewan Bandaran** (town hall), of equal aesthetic if not political merit, the city's affairs now being conducted from the KOMTAR building.

Turning left past the food stalls outside the fort brings you to the Moorish-style **clock tower** at the junction of Lebuh Light and Lebuh Pantai. Presented to the town in 1897 to mark Queen Victoria's Diamond Jubilee, it is sixty feet (20m) high, each foot representing a year of her reign. Turn to the right here and you're at the top of one of Georgetown's oldest streets, **Lebuh Pantai**, the heart of the business district. This narrow and congested road once fronted the beach – its swaying palms were the first sight of the island for anyone approaching from the mainland. The street is a far cry from today, with scores of moneylenders squeezed cheek-by-jowl between the imposing bank and government buildings, not to mention the constant buzz of motor scooters. Gracefully lining an otherwise ill-proportioned street are some of Georgetown's best colonial buildings, including the Standard Chartered Bank and the Hong Kong Bank, the heavy pillars of the former forming an elegant archway.

A left turn down any of the adjoining streets leads to the **waterfront**, but there's little of interest here except the passage of the lumbering yellow ferries to and from Butterworth. The ferry terminal is also known as "Clan Piers", since each of the jetties is named after a different Chinese clan (see overleaf). Much is made of the quaint lifestyle of the inhabitants of **Kampung Ayer**, a settlement built on stilts close to the ferry terminal. The unsanitary and semi-derelict properties here are home to the hundreds of harbour workers and their families, who are unable to move elsewhere because of the high cost of land.

ST GEORGE'S CHURCH TO LEBUH CHULIA

On the western side of Lebuh Pantai you're in Chinatown again. A leisurely five-minute stroll from here, through Lebuh Chulia or down any of the parallel side streets to the north, brings you to Jalan Masjid Kapitan Kling (or Lebuh Pitt), one of the city's main thoroughfares. Near its northern end, opposite the junction with Lebuh Bishop, is the Anglican **St George's Church** (Tues–Sat 8.30am–12.30pm & 1.30–4.30pm, Sun 8.30am–4.30pm). One of the oldest buildings in Penang, and as simple and unpretentious as anything built in the Greek style in Asia can be, it was constructed in 1817–19 by the East India Company using convict labour; its cool, pastel-blue interior must have been a welcome retreat from the heat for the new congregation. In 1886, on the centenary of the founding of Penang, a memorial to Francis Light was built in front of the church in the form of a Greek temple – Victoriana at its most eclectic.

Next to the church, on Lebuh Farquhar (which takes its name from a former lieutenant-governor of the settlement), is the **Penang Museum and Art Gallery** (daily except Fri 9am–5pm; free), housed in a building dating from 1821 that was first used as a school. It has an excellent collection of memorabilia: rickshaws, press cuttings, faded black-and-white photographs of early Penang's Chinese millionaires and a panoramic photograph of Georgetown taken in the 1870s – note just how many buildings still survive. The art gallery upstairs, a bit hit-and-miss, displays temporary exhibitions of contemporary paintings and photographs.

A few minutes' walk south of St George's Church along Jalan Masjid Kapitan Kling, the **Kuan Yin Teng Temple** is dedicated to the Buddhist Goddess of Mercy. While not the finest example of a *kongsi* (that honour goes to the Khoo Kongsi; see below), it can claim the title of the oldest Chinese temple in Penang. Originally constructed in 1800, it was completely ravaged during World War II; what you see today, including the massive roof dominated by two guardian dragons, is a restoration.

The area east of here, enclosed by the parallel roads of Lebuh King and Lebuh Queen, forms Georgetown's compact **Little India** district. Surrounded on all sides by Chinatown, it's a vibrant, self-contained community comprising sari and incense shops, banana-leaf-curry houses, and the towering **Sri Mariamman Temple** (open daily from early morning to late evening) on the corner of Lebuh Queen and Lebuh Chulia. A typical example of Hindu architecture, the lofty entrance tower teems with brightly coloured sculptures of gods and swans, as well as hundreds of pigeons who make this their home; the inner sanctum has a nine-metre-high dome, with statues of forty other deities and lions. At times, the compound becomes quite frenetic with the activities of the devotees of the main deity, Mariamman. Within a few metres of here, across Lebuh Chulia, the **Persatuan Teochew Temple** features fearsome guardians painted on the insides of the temple doors.

Lebuh Chulia itself – the central artery of Chinatown – was where the southern Indian immigrants chose to establish their earliest businesses (*chulia* being the Tamil word for "merchant"), and the Indian shops here still deal in textiles. But the area (like much of central Georgetown) looks predominantly Chinese, its shophouses and arcades selling everything from antiques and bamboo furniture to books, photographic services and foreign holidays.

MASJID MELAYU AND THE KHOO KONGSI

Back on Jalan Masjid Kapitan Kling, follow the road along for 300m south from the junction with Lebuh Chulia, past lines of jewellery stores, each one guarded by a sleepy octogenarian armed guard. You'll soon see the **Masjid Melayu** ahead, tucked away on Lebuh Acheh; the oldest mosque in Penang, it has an Egyptian-style minaret, its sole unusual feature.

Across Lebuh Acheh, in a secluded square on an alleyway connecting Jalan Masjid Kapitan Kling and Lebuh Pantai, stands the **Khoo Kongsi**, *kongsi* being the Hokkien term for "clan-house", a building in which Chinese families gather to worship their ancestors. In Penang, the *kongsi*s were originally formed to provide mutual help and protection for nineteenth-century immigrants, who naturally tended to band together in clans according to the district from which they came. At one time this led to rivalry and often violence between the different Chinese communities (see box, opposite), though these days the *kongsi*s have reverted to their supportive role, helping with the education of members' children, settling disputes between clan members or advancing loans. Consequently, they are an important means of preserving solidarity, although traditionally women have been excluded from many of the functions and are rarely represented in the hierarchy.

Many of the *kongsi*s in Penang are well over a hundred years old, excellent examples of traditional Chinese architecture. There is generally a spacious courtyard in front of the clan-house, opposite which is a stage for theatrical performances, and two halls in the main building itself, one for the shrine of the clan deity, the other for the display of the ancestral tablets (the equivalent of gravestones). Completed in 1894, the Khoo Kongsi (closed for renovations at time of writing) was an ambitious and extensive project with a roof styled in the manner of a grand palace; it took eight years to complete but was immediately gutted in a mysterious fire. Suspecting sabotage, the clan mem-

THE PENANG RIOTS

Chinese immigrants in Penang brought their traditions with them, including the establishment of **triads** (secret societies), branches of organizations that had evolved in China during the eighteenth century as a means of overthrowing Manchu rule. Once in Penang, the societies provided mutual aid and protection for the Chinese community, their position later bolstered by alliances with Malay religious groups originally established to assist members with funerals and marriages.

As the societies grew in wealth and power, gang warfare and extortion rackets became commonplace. The newly appointed governor-general, Sir Harry Ord, and his inefficient police force (largely composed of non-Chinese) proved ineffective in preventing the increasing turmoil. In 1867, matters came to a head in the series of events known subsequently as the **Penang Riots**. For nine days Georgetown was shaken by fighting between the Tua Peh Kong society, supported by the Malay Red Flag, and the Ghee Hin, allied with the Malay White Flag. Police intervention resulted in a temporary truce, but a major clash seemed inevitable when, on August 1, 1867, the headman of the Tua Peh Kong falsely charged the Ghee Hin and the White Flag societies with stealing cloth belonging to Tua Peh Kong dyers. All hell broke loose and fighting raged around Armenian, Church and Chulia streets. Barricades were erected around the Khoo Kongsi, where much of the fiercest fighting took place, and you can still find bullet holes in the surrounding shops and houses. The authorities were powerless to act, since the battery of artillery normally stationed at Fort Cornwallis had just left for Rangoon and relief forces had not yet arrived. Countless arrests were made, but the police soon had to release many from custody as there was no more room for them in the overflowing jails.

The fighting was eventually quelled by *sepoys* (Indian troops) brought in from Singapore by the governor-general, but by then hundreds had been killed and scores of houses burned. As compensation for the devastation suffered by the city, a penalty of RM5000 was levied on each of the secret societies, some of which was later used to finance the building of four police stations to deal with future trouble.

bers rebuilt the house on a lesser scale, making the excuse that the previous design had been too noble to house the ancestral tablets of ordinary mortals. The resulting structure, meticulously crafted by experts from China, has a saddle-shaped roof that reputedly weighs 25 tonnes. Its central hall is dark with heavy, intricately carved beams and pillars and bulky mother-of-pearl inlaid furniture; an Art Deco grandfather clock stands somewhat incongruously in the corner. Behind this is a separate chamber, with delicate black-and-white line drawings depicting scenes of courtly life. The hall on the left is a richly decorated shrine to Tua Peh Kong, the god of prosperity; the right-hand hall contains the gilded ancestral tablets. Connecting all three halls is a balcony minutely decorated in bas-relief, whose carvings depict episodes from folk tales – even the bars on the windows have been carved into bamboo sticks.

AROUND JALAN PENANG

Jalan Penang, 500m west of St George's Church, separates the traditional commercial district from the residential quarter further to the west, an elegant part of town formerly frequented by colonial types.

At the far northern end of the road, on Lebuh Farquhar, stands the legendary **Eastern & Oriental Hotel** (closed for renovation until 2001), once part of the Sarkies brothers' select chain of colonial retreats (as was the *Raffles* in Singapore; see p.55). Rudyard Kipling and Somerset Maugham both stayed here, taking tiffin on the terrace and enjoying the cooling sea breeze. About five minutes' walk west along Lebuh Farquhar, the road merges with sea-facing Jalan Sultan Ahmad Shah, across which you'll find the overgrown churchyard where Francis Light is buried. Further along, the huge stylish mansions set back from the road in acres of manicured lawn give the road its nickname – "millionaires' row" – and though the preposterous costs of upkeep have seen several of the houses fall into disrepair, the road remains a reminder of the ostentatious wealth of colonial Penang.

Backtracking along Jalan Sultan Ahmad Shah, five minutes' walk east brings you to Lebuh Leith, on the corner of which is the stunning **Cheong Fatt Tze Mansion**, whose outer walls are painted in a striking rich blue. It's the best example of nineteenth-century Chinese architecture in Penang, built by Thio Thiaw Siat, a Cantonese businessman. The elaborate ceremonial halls, bedrooms and libraries, separated by cobbled courtyards, small gardens and heavy wooden doors, have been restored; sadly, much of the house's furniture and antiques disappeared long ago, but there is a plan to replace these with faithful reproductions. The inside of the mansion can only be seen on a guided tour (daily except Tues & Thurs at 11am; 1hr; RM10).

Back on Jalan Penang, don't let the sophisticated shopfronts put you off bargaining a little, a necessity in the cramped tourist **market** 500m southwest of the Cheong Fatt Tze Mansion, opposite the police station. This market is the place to pick up leather goods – particularly bags and wallets. Just a little further south is the ordered calm of the KOMTAR building, the nucleus of Penang's business and government administration, comprising five levels of air-conditioned shops, offices and fast-food joints, topped by a gigantic circular tower – a handy landmark.

Out from the centre

Worth exploring are several sights on the western and northern **outskirts** of Georgetown, most of which provide a welcome break from the frenetic city. In particular, trips to Ayer Itam and Penang Hill are a cool alternative to heading for the northern beaches for the day. Buses run to all the destinations below from the station on Lebuh Victoria; you can also pick them up at the station at the KOMTAR building on Jalan Ria.

THREE TEMPLES AND THE BOTANICAL GARDENS

A fifteen-minute bus ride (Transitlink #202, #212, minibus #31, #31a, #88, #88a or blue bus #93) towards Batu Ferringhi brings you to **Wat Chayamangkalaram** on Lorong Burma, a Thai temple painted in yellow and blue and flanked by two statues, whose fierce grimaces and weighty swords are designed to ward off unwanted visitors. Inside, a 33-metre-long statue of the Reclining Buddha is surrounded by other, elaborately decorated Buddha images covered with gold leaf. The **Dharmmikarama Burmese Temple** across the road is less spectacular, although the white-stone elephants at the entrance are attractive and the temple's two stupas are lit to good effect at night. Both temples are open between sunrise and sunset (free).

Further west on Jalan Kebun Bunga is the **Nattukkottai Chettiar Temple**, a seven-kilometre bus ride from the city centre on the hourly Transitlink #7. Sri Negara's bus #137 will also take you there; ask to be dropped off at the waterfall hotel, from where the temple is a five-minute walk north. This is the focus of the Hindu Thaipusam festival in February, in honour of Lord Subramanian, when thousands of devotees walk through the streets bearing *kavadi*s (sacred yokes) fixed to their bodies by hooks and spikes spearing their flesh. The biggest such event in Malaysia is at Kuala Lumpur's Batu Caves (see p.121); the festivities here in Georgetown are a similar blend of hypnotic frenzy and celebration. At other times of the year, you're free to concentrate on the temple itself, in which an unusual wooden colonnaded walkway with exquisite pictorial tiles leads up to the inner sanctum, where a life-sized solid-silver peacock – the birds crop up throughout the temple – bows its head to the deity, Lord Subramanian.

Just five more minutes further up Jalan Kebun Bunga (formerly Waterfall Rd) from the temple lie the **Botanical Gardens** (daily 7am–7pm; free) in a lush valley, a good place to escape the city and enjoy some fresh air. Unfortunately, the waterfall that gives the road its name has been cordoned off, and can't be easily seen from a distance either.

AYER ITAM AND THE KEK LOK SI TEMPLE

A thirty-minute bus ride west (take Transitlink #1, #101, #130, #351, #361, yellow bus #85 or minibus #21), **Ayer Itam** is an appealing wooded hilly area (almost 250m above sea level), spread around the **Ayer Itam Dam**, built in the early 1960s. Despite its 550-million-litre capacity, the dam is rather dwarfed by the vertiginous surroundings, through which several short trails snake. If you're looking for a stroll outside the city, you'll do better at Penang Hill (see below), although you might come on up to the dam after visiting the nearby Kek Lok Si Temple, a couple of kilometres back down the road.

As you approach Ayer Itam, the sprawling, fairy-tale complex of **Kek Lok Si Temple** (open morning to late evening; free) makes an intriguing sight, the tips of its colourful towers peeking cheekily through the treetops. Supposedly the largest Buddhist temple in Malaysia, it's a serious place of worship as well as being a major tourist spot, with fantastic shrines and pagodas, linked by hundreds of steps, and bedecked with flags, lanterns and statues. The entrance to the complex is approached through a line of trinket stalls, their awnings forming a tunnel stretching a few hundred metres uphill. The "Million Buddhas Precious Pagoda", the most prominent feature of the compound, has a tower of simple Chinese saddle-shaped caves and more elaborate Thai arched windows, topped by a golden Burmese *stupa*. It costs RM2 to climb the 193 steps to the top, where there is a great view of Georgetown and the bay.

PENANG HILL

Just on the outskirts of Georgetown is the small hill station of **Penang Hill** (Bukit Bendera), an 821-metre-high dome of tropical forest due west of the city. Once the retreat for the colony's wealthiest administrators, nowadays it's a popular weekend excursion for the locals. The cooler climate up here benefits flowering trees and shrubs, and there are several gentle, well-marked walks through areas whose names (Tiger Hill, Strawberry Hill) conjure up colonial days. You can also walk from here down to the Botanical Gardens, a steep descent which takes about an hour.

To get to the hill, take Transitlink #1, #101, #130, #351, #361, yellow bus #85 or minibus #21 to the terminus and then either walk the remaining fifteen minutes or take the Transitlink #8 which terminates at the base of Penang Hill. The last bit of the journey is made by **funicular railway** (daily 6.30am–9.15pm, Sat until 11.45pm; every 30min; 30min; RM4 return), which deposits you at the top, where there's a post office, police station, a few food stalls and a hotel, the *Bellevue* (☎04/829 9500, fax 829 2052; ⑤). The hotel terrace affords a superb view of Georgetown; a drink or a meal here is perfect at sunset when the city's lights flicker on in the distance.

Eating

Georgetown's status as Malaysia's second city means there is no shortage of cafés and restaurants. Surprisingly however, it's only really standard Malay, Chinese and Indian food which is significantly represented, though a few places serve seafood, North Indian and Nonya specialities. **Hawker stalls** dish out the cheapest meals and are located either in permanent sites, in which case they're open all day and evening, or by the roadsides and down alleyways (these stalls spring up at meal times only). In addition, a roving **pasar malam** (night market), with stalls selling all manner of food, is held every two weeks at various venues around town (near the stadium is a favourite) – any of the tourist offices will have the details.

Of the **cafés** (usually open 8am–11pm), the ubiquitous Chinese *kedai kopi*s serve reliable rice and noodle standards, with many also specializing in fine Hainan chicken rice. The other local favourite is Penang *laksa*, noodles in thick fish soup, garnished with vegetables, pineapple and *belacan* (shrimp paste). The Indian *kedai kopi*s around Jalan Penang and Little India offer *murtabak*s, *roti*s and *biriyani*s as well as a bewildering array of curries; none serve alcohol. The main travellers' hangouts are dotted on or around Lebuh Chulia, often little more than hole-in-the-wall joints serving Western breakfasts, banana pancakes and milkshakes, each for less than a couple of dollars. These tend to open from around 9am to 5pm (the exceptions are noted below). For **Western fast food**, the KOMTAR building on Jalan Penang (10am–10pm) has a *KFC*, a *McDonald's* and a *Pizza Hut*.

Jalan Penang is home to a handful of more upmarket **restaurants**, mainly specializing in seafood; for high-class Western, Malay, Japanese or Chinese food you should head to the top hotels, whose set meals sometimes work out quite reasonably and provide a good opportunity to sample more unusual dishes, often with some sort of cultural entertainment thrown in; you only need to book in advance on Saturday night. Note that during **Ramadan**, Muslim-run places open only after sunset and can be very busy coping with the demand from Penang's hungry Muslims.

HAWKER STALLS

Chinatown, Lebuh Kimberley and Lebuh Cintra. Open late into the night, this place does every sort of noodle and rice dish, each for just a few ringgit.

Food Court, KOMTAR building. On the ground floor and on the roof. The atmosphere's a little sterile, but there's a good range of Chinese, Malay and Indian food.

Jalan Tun Syed Shah Barakah, near Fort Cornwallis, at the west end of the esplanade. Most of the stalls serve Chinese food, though a few do Malay fare. The fruit juices here are particularly fine.

Midlands Park Centre, Jalan Sultan Ahmed Shah. The *One-Stop International Food Garden* on the sixth floor has the full range of Eastern and Western cuisine with self-service and service sections. Most dishes are around RM6. Take any bus heading for Batu Ferringhi from the KOMTAR building.

CAFÉS

Bamboo Hut, Lebuh Chulia. Good for all-day breakfasts and Indian dishes. Also has great milkshakes, served in bamboo cups.

Green Planet, 63 Lebuh Cintra. Roomy and comfortable, with tasteful rattan and bamboo decor, this café serves international veggie food (falafel, waffles, pizza), with some ingredients organically grown, and wonderful baguettes and wholemeal bread. Open 9.30am–3pm & 6pm–midnight.

Hard Life Café, 363 Lebuh Chulia. Bob Marley and co plastered across the walls and the sound system make this a laid-back spot for drinks, snacks and beers. They also run the *Reggae Club* further up the street.

Kriss Dinners Corner, Lebuh Chulia. Tasty, good-value buffet of Chinese and Malay food. Shows films and football in the evenings.

Rainforest Café, 294a Lebuh Chulia. Run by the same management as the *Green Planet*, with a similar set up. Aside from wholesome food, it also has an Internet terminal.

Taj Mahal, Jalan Penang. Near the junction with Lebuh Chulia, this busy and very inexpensive North Indian eatery is popular with the locals; it often stays open until 1am.

Tai Wah, Lebuh Chulia. At the eastern end, near Jalan Penang, this late-night café has passable food. It also has a lively bar in the evenings.

RESTAURANTS

Beetlenuts, Lebuh Chulia. For Tex-Mex cuisine and beers; the decor includes a carved-up Volkswagon.

Bella Casa, cnr of Jalan Penang and Lebuh Chulia. A good range of Italian food. Around RM30 a head.

Dragon King, 99 Lebuh Bishop. Upmarket restaurant that specializes in Nonya cuisine – try any of the *asam* fish dishes. Expensive, and service can be slow.

Hameediyah, 164 Lebuh Campbell. They'll try and haul you in from the street if you look remotely interested. Let them: the place has great Indian food at reasonable prices, around RM4 a head for a full meal.

Hock Siew Chai, Lebuh Bishop. Good-value vegetarian Chinese food.

Hong Kong, 29 Lebuh Cintra. Although this looks like any number of *kedai kopi*s in the area, the food is of much better quality than usual, a fact reflected in the prices. There's an extensive Chinese menu with "specials" at RM6–8 per main dish; the portions are huge.

Jaipur Court, 11 Lebuh Leith. Very good-value Indian cuisine in an attractive old colonial building with some outdoor seating.

Kashmir, basement of *Oriental Hotel*, 105 Jalan Penang. Very popular chic North Indian restaurant; you'll need to book at weekends. Relatively expensive – RM7 or more per dish.

Kong Lung, 11A Lebuh Leith. Good-value Japanese restaurant that shares premises with the *20 Leith St* pub. You can choose to eat outside or beside the sushi bar, from where you can watch the chef at work. Around RM20 a head.

Madras New Woodlands, 60 Lebuh Penang. Excellent Southern Indian cuisine at bargain prices. *Thalis* – spicy dishes with crispy pancakes – for lunch cost RM4.

May Garden, 70 Jalan Penang. Plush but affordable Cantonese restaurant with excellent food. Very popular with the crowd from the nearby high-rise hotels.

Poshni's, 3–5 Lebuh Light. Neat and clean Thai restaurant with fiery dishes for around RM4.

Revolving Restaurant, fourteenth floor, *City Bayview Hotel*, Lebuh Farquhar. Serves Western and Oriental dishes, with a colourful all-you-can-eat buffet (RM26). Daily 9am–11pm; buffet Mon–Fri noon–2.30pm; Sat & Sun noon–3pm.

Sky Café, 348 Lebuh Chulia. Very popular with the locals, this is one of the few places in town serving Chinese/Malay food until late (11.30pm). Fish-head *bee hoon* (a hot rice-vermicelli dish) is a speciality.

Soho Free House, Jalan Penang. Next to the *Polar Café*, this pub looks as if it's been transported straight from England, with authentic fish and chips, pies and draught Guinness.

Drinking, nightlife and entertainment

Most of Georgetown's **bars** are comfortable places in which to hang out – some of the best are detailed below. With the periodic arrival of the Malaysian navy, though, a good many turn into rowdy meat markets, and a place that may have been fine the night before can become unpleasant for women visitors, so choose carefully. Usual opening hours are 6pm–2am; occasional **happy hours** (usually 6–8pm) make the cost of beer more reasonable. In Georgetown's **discos**, which stay open until the early hours (a cover charge of around RM10 usually applies), you're unlikely to hear the latest Western club sounds; indeed several seem to be in the grip of the drag-show craze that has swept down from Thailand. Other entertainment is thin on the ground: the Cathay (Jalan Penang) and Rex (Jalan Burma) **cinemas** show recent releases of English-language movies; check the *New Straits Times* for details of screenings and other Penang listings. There's no cultural centre in Penang, so it's up to the five-star hotels both in town and at Batu Ferringhi to put on traditional shows; these are expensive as you have to pay for a meal in order to watch one.

Babylon Boom Boom, Lebuh China Ghaut. Gay and straight disco and café, whose main attraction is the twice-nightly drag-cabaret performance, which would give some Vegas shows a run for their money. Good fun.

Carmen Inn, basement, *City Bayview*, 25a Lebuh Farquhar. One of the better of the hotel clubs, it concentrates on Sixties and Seventies sounds.

Cheers, 22 Jalan Argyll. A little dingy, and not much like its American counterpart, though friendly enough, with a happy hour (6–8.45pm).

Flint's Club, cnr of Lebuh Geraja and Pengkalan Weld. DJs and live bands in a trendy bar. The RM20 cover charge includes the cost of your first drink.

Hong Kong Bar, 371 Lebuh Chulia. Tiny, long-established serviceman's bar with none-too-recent hits on the jukebox and a stupefyingly sexist visitors' book.

Hotlips, cnr of Jalan Penang and Jalan Sultan Ahmed Shah. A tasteless pair of giant red lips glows like a beacon outside this tacky club, with disco sounds and karaoke. Daily 8pm–2am.

Polar Café, 48a Jalan Penang. Family-run singalong bar with organist and jukebox, bright lights and TV. A hamburger stall operates outside at night.

Rock World, in a yard off Lebuh Campbell, west of the junction with Lebuh Cintra. A spangle of neon, featuring the local would-be Bon Jovis every weekend. Very 1980s.

Sol Fun, Pengkalan Weld. Techno makes it to Penang at this gay disco in a converted warehouse. There's also a nightly "Funky Divas" show and a cinema in case you get bored with the music.

Tai Wah, Lebuh Chulia. This daytime café turns into a lively bar in the evening, with the cheapest beer in town. The resident Tom Waits impersonator provides a musical diversion until the small hours.

20 Lebuh Leith. This renovated 1930s Straits-style mansion, littered with film memorabilia, has a large video screen, plenty of tables in the beer garden and a decent teriyaki bistro. A little pricey, it is at least reasonably novel.

Listings

Airlines Cathay Pacific, Menara PSCI, Jalan Sultan Ahmed Shah (☎05/226 0411); Malaysia Airlines, ground floor, KOMTAR building, Jalan Penang (☎04/262 0011); Singapore Airlines, Wisma Penang Gardens, Jalan Sultan Ahmed Shah (☎04/226 3201); Thai International, Wisma Central, Jalan Macalister (☎04/226 6000).

Airport ☎04/643 0373 for flight information.

American Express c/o Mayflower Tours, 274 Lebuh Victoria (Mon–Fri 8.30am–5.30pm, Sat 8.30am–1pm; ☎04/262 8198, fax 261 9024). Credit card and traveller's cheque holders can use the office as a poste restante/general delivery address.

Banks and exchange Major banks (Mon–Fri 10am–3pm, Sat 9.30–11.30am) are along Lebuh Pantai, including Standard Chartered and the Hong Kong Bank, but since they charge a hefty commission, the licensed moneychangers on Lebuh Pantai, Lebuh Chulia and Jalan Masjid Kapitan Kling (daily 8.30am–6pm) are preferable – they charge no commission and their rates are often better.

Bike rental Outlets on Lebuh Chulia rent out motorbikes (RM20 a day) and bicycles (RM8 a day).

Bookshops United Books Ltd, Jalan Penang, has a large selection of English-language books. There are several bookshops in the KOMTAR building, including Popular Books on the second floor. Times Books in the nearby Lifestyle department store also has a good selection. In addition, there are a few secondhand bookshops on Lebuh Chulia, the best of which is H.S. Sam Bookstore at no. 144, near the junction with Lebuh Queen.

Car rental Avis, at the airport (☎04/643 9633); Hertz, 38 Lebuh Farquhar (☎04/263 5914) and at the airport (☎04/643 0208); National, at the airport (☎04/643 4205).

Consulates Australia, c/o Denis Mark Lee, 1c Lorong Hutton (☎05/263 3320); Indonesia: 467 Jalan Burma (☎04/227 4686); Thailand: 1 Jalan Tunku Abdul Rahman (☎04/226 9484); UK: Standard Chartered Bank Chambers, Lebuh Pantai (☎04/262 5333). There is no representation here for citizens of the USA, Canada, Ireland or New Zealand – KL has the nearest offices (see p.119).

Hospitals Adventist Hospital, Jalan Burma (☎04/226 1133; to get there, take blue bus #93 or minibus #26, #31 or #88 or Transitlink #202 or #212); General Hospital, Jalan Utama (☎04/229 3333; Sri Negara bus #136 or #137).

Internet access As well as a few places in the KOMTAR building, you'll find no shortage of Internet terminals in and around Lebuh Chulia. The *18 Internet Café*, 18 Lebuh Cintra (☎04/264 4902), has the best equipment, but you'll have to pay for a minimum of one hour. *STC Net Café*, 221 Lebuh Chulia (☎ & fax 04/264 3378, *stc_net@hotmail.com*) is friendlier and charges by the minute. Omega Tech Computer, 48 Leith St (☎04/264 3804), is also a good option.

Pharmacy There are several along Jalan Penang (10am–6pm).

Police The police headquarters is on Jalan Penang; in emergencies call ☎999.

Post office The General Post Office is on Lebuh Downing (Mon–Fri 8.30am–5pm, Sat 8.30am–4pm). The efficient poste restante/general delivery office is here; a parcel-wrapping service is available at book and stationery shops on Lebuh Chulia.

Sport You can play golf at Bukit Jambul Country Club, 2 Jalan Bukit Jambul (☎04/644 2255; green fees RM100 Mon–Fri, RM150 Sat & Sun), or the Penang Turf Club Golf (☎04/226 6701; green fees RM84). There's racing at the Penang Turf Club, Jalan Batu Gantung (☎04/226 6701) – see the local paper for fixtures. You can swim at the Pertama Sports Complex, Paya Terubong, near Ayer Itam (9–11am & 4–9pm; RM4).

Telephone offices Calls within Penang made from public telephone booths cost a flat rate of 10 sen and can be dialled direct. For international calls you can buy a phonecard or use the Telekom office at the GPO on Lebuh Downing, open 24 hours.

Travel agents Try MSL Travel in the *Angora Hotel*, 202 Jalan Macalister for student and youth travel. There are a large number of other agencies along Lebuh Chulia.

Visa extensions Pejabat Imigresen, Lebuh Pantai, on the cnr of Lebuh Light (☎04/261 5122). For on-the-spot visa renewals.

The northern coast

The narrow strip, about 15km in length, along Pulau Penang's **north coast** has been aggressively marketed since the early days of package tourism, and even more so in recent years with the growth in popularity of the condominiums that are being built here, particularly among Japanese holiday-makers. Worryingly, the area is still being developed, with huge apartment buildings springing up all over the place, often sold before they've even been completed.

Hemmed in by the densely forested interior, this stretch of coast is punctuated by a series of bays and beaches, linked by a twisting road lined with resort hotels which advertise themselves as being part of the "Pearl of the Orient". However, the filthy ocean rather detracts from this image, and there's nothing here to touch the east coast of the peninsula, though the sand is crunchy, golden and relatively clean. There are three main developments strung out along the northern coast: Tanjung Bungah, Batu Ferringhi and Teluk Bahang. The first two have arisen purely to serve the needs of tourism rather than growing out of local demand; this is particularly obvious at **Tanjung Bungah**, where you wonder if there are any locals at all. Occupied for the most part by a string of deluxe resorts, **Batu Ferringhi** is the biggest of the three, and has gone a fair way towards establishing a community and spirit of its own, while **Teluk Bahang**, with just one modern hotel, is the only place to maintain its fishing-village roots. If you want to stay at any of the beaches, it's wise to ring the hotels and guesthouses first to check on space, especially during Christmas, Easter and Hari Raya.

Tanjung Bungah

TANJUNG BUNGAH, 12km and twenty minutes' bus ride (blue buses #93, minibuses #26, #31, #31a, #88, #88a or Transitlink #202) from the KOMTAR building, is really the nearest decent beach to Georgetown. That said, it comprises a largely uncoordinated string of properties, and its beach is not as good as the one further west, just before the bus station on the way to Batu Ferringhi. There's little in the way of budget **accommodation** here, the best option being the fairly isolated *Seaview Hotel* (☎04/896 2582; ③), which has a tolerable beach; it's further out towards Batu Ferringhi up some steps on the south side of the road. Of the upmarket options, the *Copthorn*, Jalan Tanjung Bungah (☎04/890 3303, fax 890 3333; ⑥) offers the best deals, with breakfast included in the price. For **eating**, you're pretty much restricted to the hotels; the *Seaview* serves fairly inexpensive food. The upmarket hotels along here offer a variety of food – at five-star prices.

Batu Ferringhi

BATU FERRINGHI ("Foreigner's Rock"), a ten-minute bus ride further west on Transitlink #202 or Transitlink air-con #93 (but not the standard #93), took its name from the foreigners who hung out here in the early 1970s, when the island's waters really were jewel-like. Although it is almost unrecognizable from its hippie heyday, for most visitors it still provides the right mix of relaxation and excitement – the beach during the day, shopping and eating in the evening, and drinking at night in the bars and discos.

Orientation is very simple: the road runs more or less straight along the coast for 3km, along which all the hotels and restaurants are lined up side by side. The centre, such as it is, lies between two bridges a couple of kilometres apart and has a Telekom office, post office and police station, opposite which are a mosque and a clinic; the bus from Georgetown stops here, and will take you wherever you want along the main road if you ask. Avis has an office in Batu Ferringhi (π04/881 1522). There's an **Internet** café, *Internet Fax* (π04/881 2094, fax 881 2096), at the end of the short road leading inland from the police station. The **beach** is remarkably clean, and every major hotel has a pool. During the day the trinket stalls, tailors' shops and street hawkers remain fairly unobtrusive, but when the sun goes down the road comes alive with brightly lit stalls selling batik, T-shirts and fake designer watches.

ACCOMMODATION

Towards the western end of Batu Ferringhi there's a small enclave of **budget guesthouses** facing the beach, reached by the road next to the *Guan Guan Café*. The standards tend to be lower than in Georgetown and the prices higher; the budget places all seem to have the option of air-con rooms, pitched at about twice what you'd pay in town. Independent travellers don't get particularly good deals in the expensive hotels, most of whose business is with tour groups, but it's definitely worth enquiring about discounts, as there always seems to be a special offer going at one of them.

Ah Beng (π04/881 1036). One of the nicest guesthouses, this is a serene, family-run place with polished-wood floors, a communal balcony overlooking the sea, and a washing machine. ②.

Ali's (π04/881 1316, *alisgues@tm.net.my*). Very popular, with a relaxing open-air café and garden, and a pleasant wooden veranda, this is the best budget place on the beach. The rooms are a touch better than similarly priced ones elsewhere. Recommended. ②.

Baba's (π04/881 1686). A spotless and friendly guesthouse. The rooms with fans are relatively inexpensive, but – as ever – you'll pay over the odds for air-con. ②.

Bayview Beach Resort (π04/881 2123, fax 881 2140, *bbr@po.jaring.my*). This is grander than most, with a ballroom and glass lifts, but no more expensive than some of its neighbours. ⑦.

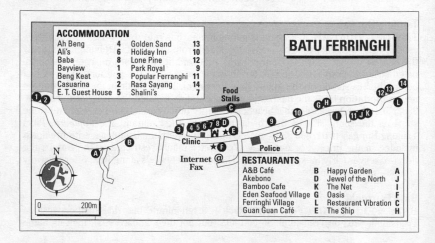

BATU FERRINGHI

ACCOMMODATION

Ah Beng	4	Golden Sand	13	
Ali's	6	Holiday Inn	10	
Baba	8	Lone Pine	12	
Bayview	1	Park Royal	9	
Beng Keat	3	Popular Ferranghi	11	
Casuarina	2	Rasa Sayang	14	
E. T. Guest House	5	Shalini's	7	

Food Stalls

Clinic

Internet @ Fax

Police

RESTAURANTS

A&B Café	B	Happy Garden	A
Akebono	D	Jewel of the North	J
Bamboo Cafe	K	The Net	I
Eden Seafood Village	G	Oasis	F
Ferringhi Village	L	Restaurant Vibration	C
Guan Guan Café	E	The Ship	H

N

0   200m

Beng Keat Guest House (☎ & fax 04/881 1987). Set away from the beach, this has clean, comfortable rooms with showers, plus a garden and a small kitchen for self-catering. It lacks the character of the waterfront places, but the rooms themselves are the best deal on the strip. ②.

Casuarina Beach (☎04/811 1711, fax 881 2155, *caspen@tm.net.my*). At the western end of the beach. An intimate, low-rise, open-plan hotel of international standard. ⑧.

ET Guest House (☎04/881 1553). Friendly and clean, run by the same family that runs *Baba's*. Some rooms have air-con, though these are a little overpriced. ②.

Golden Sands Resort (☎04/881 1911, fax 881 1880, *gsh@shangri-la.com*). The active social programme here, and the pool, make it one of the liveliest of the upmarket places. ⑧.

Holiday Inn (☎04/881 1601, fax 881 1389, *hirp@tm.net.my*). Another clone, with high standards and some great views of the sea. ⑦.

Lone Pine (☎04/881 1511, fax 881 1282). Modernist low-rise with an elegant beachside lawn and pool. Less palatial than some, but with a gentle charm and high standards. ⑦.

Park Royal (☎04/881 1133, fax 881 2233). Long-standing favourite with the Japanese. The rooms are large and grand, and there's a good pool and an Indonesian restaurant. ⑧.

Popular Ferringhi Motel and Restaurant (☎04/881 3333, fax 881 3494). Hidden behind a row of restaurants, set back from the beach, this new place has incomparably better air-con rooms than the beachfront backpackers' places. ④.

Rasa Sayang (☎04/881 1811, fax 881 1984, *rsr@shangri-la.com*). This classy hotel makes the biggest concession to traditional Malay architecture here, boasting Minangkabau-style roofs. Costs fifty percent more than the other grand hotels. ⑧.

Shalini's (☎04/881 1859). Standard, clean rooms with or without air-con. You can get better value elsewhere on the strip, though. ②.

EATING AND DRINKING

There are some budget **restaurants** in Batu Ferringhi, but most places cater for the overspill from the large hotels, all of which have several restaurants of their own. By the beach are some cheap food stalls, including the elaborate *Rastafarian Café*. There are also some fine seafood restaurants, and a few interesting Malay places. The roadside **stalls** (evenings only) by the *Guan Guan Café* sell inexpensive local food, or try *A&B Café*, by the western bridge, for tasty banana-leaf curries.

Akebono. By the *Guan Guan Café*, this large Japanese restaurant has good-value set lunches at RM12.

Bamboo Café. Serves inexpensive and very tasty Malay food, cooked by the septugenarian *bomoh* (medicine man) Papa Din.

Eden Seafood Village. The boast at this huge beachfront place is "Anything that swims, we cook it". A cultural show accompanies the meal. Far from cheap, at around RM20 a dish.

Ferringhi Village. This bright and bustling place at the eastern end of the beach serves a good range of Chinese food, seafood and steaks.

Guan Guan Café. By the beach, just behind the food stalls. Moderately priced, with a wide selection of Malay and Western snacks.

Happy Garden. At the western end of the main strip, this is set just off the road in a colourful garden. Serves cheapish Chinese and Western food.

Jewel of the North. Very tasty North Indian food at around RM15 per dish.

The Net. Banana-leaf curries from 10.30am–2.30pm, as well as other South Indian meals lunchtime and evenings. Inexpensive.

Oasis. Centrally located on the main road, this place does Malay dishes from as little as RM2.

Restaurant Vibration. Beachfront snacks and drinks, accompanied by an endless loop of Bob Marley tracks.

Ship. Next door to the *Eden Seafood Village* is this unmissable, huge black boat with sails and rigging, serving steak at RM25 a head.

Teluk Bahang

Five kilometres west of Batu Ferringhi, the small fishing kampung of **TELUK BAHANG** is the place to come to escape the development. Towards the western end of the village, the long spindly pier, with its multitude of fishing boats, is the focus of daily life. The small path which disappears into the forest beyond the pier is the start of a two-hour trek west to the lighthouse at **Muka Head**, a rocky headland where the beaches are better than the ones at Teluk Bahang itself; however, since the big hotels run boat trips out there, it's unlikely that you'll have the sands to yourself. Just to the south, 200m up the road into the interior, is a **batik factory**, really more of a shop (though you can watch the cloth being turned out) with prices hiked up for the folk on the bus tours; a little further south are the Butterfly Farm and Forest Recreation Park (see opposite).

PRACTICALITIES

Accommodation here is somewhat limited. The very friendly *Rama's Guest House* (☎04/885 1179; ①) is the cheapest place, a hippie homestay that survived the 1970s, with some basic dorm beds (RM8) as well as rooms; take the north (beachward) turn at the Teluk Bahang roundabout and it's about 20m down the road on the right. Further along the beach is the *Fisherman's Village* (no phone; ①), with simple rooms in a family home. *Miss Loh's* (①), another survivor from hippie times, is a better choice, a longhouse and garden in the kampung a little back from the sea. To get there, turn left at the roundabout and carry on for about 100m, past the batik factory and mosque; after the telecom tower, turn right, cross the bridge and you'll see the hostel on your left. You can book a room at the Kwong Tuck Hing shop, also run by Miss Loh, on the main road. At the other end of the scale, the beautifully decorated *Penang Mutiara*, on the eastern end of the shore road (☎04/885 2828, fax 885 2829; ⑧) has a good range of restaurants, water sports and a better beach than its rivals in Batu Ferringhi, though it's considerably more expensive than most places there. The last option is the sterile *Hotbay* (☎04/885 7323; ③) between the *Mutiara* and the roundabout; its grubby rooms are hardly worth considering.

Tanjung Bungah's real attraction is its plethora of inexpensive **places to eat** on the little stretch of main road, including an excellent seafood restaurant (open 6–10pm) called the *End of the World*, just by the pier; among its specialities are huge, fresh prawns. Set in a park incorporating traditional buildings from the nation's states, the *Istana Malay Theatre Restaurant* (☎04/885 1175) features a nightly traditional dance show at 8.30pm; dinner here will set you back at least RM45 a head.

The rest of the island

Given that all the accommodation on Penang island is either in Georgetown, near the airport or on the north coast, seeing the **rest of the island** generally means making day-trips (unless you want to stay the night in one of the airport hotels). Public transport takes in most of the points of interest picked out below; indeed, it's possible to do a circuitous day-trip by bus: yellow buses #66 and #352 head southwest from Georgetown via Jelutong to Balik Pulau, from where yellow bus #76 (4 daily) continues to Teluk Bahang; here you can change to blue bus #93, which heads east through Batu Ferringhi and back to Georgetown. Make sure you leave Georgetown by 8 or 9am in order to complete your trip the same day. However, getting around by bus rather misses the point, which is to get away from the main road and explore the jungle, beaches and kampungs at leisure. It's much better to **rent a motorbike**, or even a **bicycle**, from one of the outlets on Lebuh Chulia – the bus circuit already mentioned is a seventy-kilometre round trip, so you have to be fairly fit to accomplish it using pedal-power, especially since some parts of the road are very steep. Once clear of the outskirts of Georgetown the traffic eases up; the interior is blissfully free of traffic, though it can get busy along the northern and eastern shore roads.

South from Georgetown to Gertak Senggul

The road south from Pengkalan Weld in Georgetown heads past the university to the **Snake Temple**, 12km from the city (and reachable on yellow bus #66). This is a major attraction for bus-tour parties (and their video cameras), and the usual souvenir and food stalls clutter up the otherwise impressive entrance which is guarded by two stone lions, the doors featuring brightly painted warrior gods. The temple was founded in memory of Chor Soo King, a monk who arrived from China over a hundred years ago and gained local fame as a healer. His statue sits in the main square in front of the temple, clothed in red and yellow. Inside, draped lazily over parts of the altar, are a handful of poisonous green snakes, which – legend has it – mysteriously appeared upon completion of the temple in 1850 and have made the temple their refuge ever since. They're fairly lethargic (apparently drugged by incense) and most have been doctored – it's considered safe enough to have your photograph taken with the snakes curled over you.

Continuing south, the road leads past the airport at Bayan Lepas to **Batu Maung**, 7km from the Snake Temple. There's not much here except pretty coastal scenery and an expensive Chinese seafood restaurant. Though there isn't much point in doing so, you can reach Batu Maung directly on yellow bus #68 or #96, or minibus #27 or Transitlink #303, all of which leave from Georgetown's KOMTAR building. Backtrack a couple of kilometres to Bayan Lepas and carry on west for 3km along the main road to reach **Teluk Kumbar**, where the sea looks particularly uninviting and the beach, though reasonable, gets very crowded at weekends. West of here, the four-kilometre stretch of road along the south coast towards **Gertak Sanggul** is one of the most attractive parts of the island, gently winding and tree-lined, with the odd tantalizing glimpse of glittering ocean. The road ends at a scenic bay where you can watch the local fishing boats at work. It's possible to reach Gertak Sanggul directly from Georgetown on yellow bus #67 or #80 from the KOMTAR building.

North to Teluk Bahang

Just to the east of Teluk Kumbar, the road north winds steeply up to the village of **Barat**, where you have the choice of heading northeast to **Balik Pulau** or southwest to **Pulau Betong**. Neither are particularly enthralling, though there's something attractive in the quiet pace of life and the friendliness of the local people. Balik Pulau is probably the better choice, simply because of the string of good cafés along the main road.

The road northeast from here takes you back to Georgetown via Ayer Itam; heading northwest, after about 5km you can take a short westward detour off the main road to reach **Sungei Pinang** and **Pantai Acheh**, Chinese fishing villages built along a narrow and largely stagnant river. If you don't mind feeling conspicuous – and can stand the pervasive rotting-fish smell – they are good places to watch the fishermen painstakingly maintaining their wooden boats.

Back on the main road, the route climbs very steeply as it winds round the jungle-clad hillside, offering the occasional view over the flat, forested plain which stretches toward the sea. A couple of kilometres from the turning for Sungei Pinang are the disappointing **Titi Kerawang Waterfalls**, outside the rainy season little more than a dismal, rubbish-strewn trickle; however, they're worth a stop to buy fresh fruit from the roadside stalls.

The road then levels and straightens out before reaching the **Forest Recreation Park** (Tues–Sun 9am–5pm; free) on the east side of the road. The museum here (RM1) introduces visitors to the different types of forest on Penang, and there are several well-marked forest trails and a children's playground nearby. Further along the road to Teluk Bahang is the **Butterfly Farm** (Mon–Fri 9am–5pm, Sat, Sun & holidays 9am–6pm; RM4, RM1 charge for cameras). This is home to all manner of creepy-crawlies, including frogs, snakes, stick insects and scorpions, as well as four thousand butterflies of around 120 species, and is well worth a visit. The **batik factory** (see p.188), less than 1km from the park, is an uninspiring end to the island circuit; within sight, around 200m away, is the roundabout at Teluk Bahang (see p.187). A right turn here brings you onto the northern coastal road, 20km or so from Georgetown.

Sungei Petani and around

From Butterworth, the train line and highways run north, into the state of **Kedah** and through the small town of Sungei Petani, 35km away. Few people stop here, but those who do are drawn by two fairly specialist attractions: the **archeological remains** at Lembah Bujang (Bujang Valley) 10km further northwest; and Gunung Jerai (Kedah Peak), 9km north of the valley.

The Town

SUNGEI PETANI is the nearest point from which to reach both the Bujang Valley and Kedah Peak. A clock tower dominates Jalan Ibrahim, the main north–south road through town; from here, a side road directly to the east leads to the **train station**. One block south of the clock tower, another side road branching east (Jalan Kuala Ketil) crosses over the tracks and leads to the **express bus stop** – little more than a yard and some food stalls. A further block south is the junction with Jalan Petri, which continues west past the local bus station, taxi stand and budget hotels.

If you plan to visit both Lembah Bujang and Gunung Jerai in one day, you'll need to stay overnight at one of Sungei Petani's **hotels**, all of which are close to the centre. West along Jalan Petri from the local bus station, at no. 7 is the *Duta* (☎04/421 2040; ②), which also happens to be the best value in town, with large, clean en-suite rooms

---

A SHORT HISTORY OF KEDAH

Kedah's history is a sad catalogue of invasion and subjugation, mainly by the Thais, lasting more or less up until the beginning of the twentieth century. The state has long been noted for its independent spirit: an eleventh-century Chola-dynasty tablet inscription mentions "Kadaram [Kedah] of fierce strength". By the thirteenth century, Kedah was already asserting its own economic superiority over the Srivijaya empire (see p.618) by sending ships to India to trade jungle products for such exotic goods as Arabian glass and Chinese porcelain. Despite becoming a vassal state of **Ayuthaya** – the mighty Thai kingdom – during the mid-seventeenth century, Kedah still managed to express its defiance. For decades, the Malay states had been left to get on with their own affairs, provided they sent monetary tributes to Thailand from time to time. But when, in 1645, the Kedah ruler was summoned to appear at the Thai court in person – an unprecedented request – he refused point-blank, claiming that it was beneath the dignity of a sultan to prostrate himself before another ruler. In a climb-down, the king of Ayuthaya sent a statue of himself to Kedah, instructing the court, rather hopefully, to pay homage to it twice a day. At the beginning of the nineteenth century, Kedah's relationship with its Thai conquerors degenerated into a *jihad*, or holy war, led by Sultan Ahmad. The strength of religious feeling frightened the Bangkok government, who deposed Ahmad, but in 1842 the British, anxious to see peace in the region and realizing the strength of Ahmad's hold over his people, forced the sultan's reinstatement. Even this gesture had little effect on stubborn Kedah: as recently as the beginning of the twentieth century, when Kedah was transferred by the Thais to British control, it adamantly refused to become part of the Federated Malay States.

and friendly, well-informed staff. Satellite TV, air-con and hot showers await you at the *Seri Malaysia*, 21 Jalan Pasar (☎04/423 6524, fax 423 4106; ④) just two minutes' walk north of the express bus stand. For **food**, there's a very popular Chinese **restaurant** at the *Lucky Hotel*, and a small but lively night market one block north of Jalan Dewa – the street leading north from the local bus station.

Lembah Bujang

Lying between Gunung Jerai to the north and the Sungei Muda to the south, **Lembah Bujang** is the site of some of Malaysia's most important archeological discoveries. Much of the country's history before 1400 AD had been somewhat sketchily pieced together from unreliable, often contradictory contemporaneous accounts, until the discovery in the Bujang Valley, in the early nineteenth century, of "the relics of a Hindoo colony". This important find by Colonel James Low, a member of the Madras Army stationed at Penang and keen amateur archeologist, gave credence to the prevailing theory that Hinduism was the dominant ideology in early Malaya. However, early-twentieth-century excavations have revealed fifty or so **Buddhist temples** (known as *candis*) in the Bujang basin, creating controversy in academic circles which continues today.

Candi Bukit Batu Pahat, one of the tenth-century temples now reconstructed on the Lembah Bujang site, embodies the styles of not only Mahayana Buddhism but also the cults of Shiva and Vishnu. The fact that India – the birthplace of Hinduism and Buddhism – has no direct equivalent of this architecture signifies that the religions must have been adapted to the local culture, creating a modified theology, so the argument goes.

Since excavations are still taking place, most of the site is off-limits to the public, but you can visit the **archeological museum** (daily 9am–5pm; free), which displays photographs of some of the finds *in situ*, as well as a number of relocated stone pillars, pots and jewels. The historical information is fairly turgidly written and there are precious few contextual comments on the artefacts, though. Behind the museum, eight *candis* (including Candi Bukit Batu Pahat) have been reconstructed using original materials. With the whole project still in its infancy, transport to the site isn't straightforward. From Sungei Petani, take a local bus to the small village of Bedong, 8km north; here you'll see a signpost for the museum. Another, rather infrequent, bus from Bedong takes you most of the final 15km west, dropping you on the main road, from where the museum is a two-kilometre walk away. A taxi is a better bet; chartering one from Bedong should only cost RM10 one-way.

Gunung Jerai

Dominating the landscape, **Gunung Jerai** (1200m) is a massive limestone outcrop 9km north of Lembah Bujang as the crow flies. It's the highest peak in Kedah, and on clear days offers panoramic views over the rolling rice fields stretching up to Perlis in the north, and along the coastline from Penang to Langkawi. Gunung Jerai is replete with history and legend; tales abound of the infamous **Raja Bersiong** ("the king with fangs") who once held court over the ancient kingdom of Langkasuka, and archeological digs here have revealed the existence of a water temple (Candi Telaga Sembilan) which many believe was the private pool of Raja Bersiong. A few hours is enough to stroll around the **Sungei Teroi Forest Recreation Park** halfway up the mountain, with its rare orchids and animals, the latter including the lesser mouse deer and the long-tailed macaque, for which the conservation area is renowned. At the top of the path leading to the recreation park is a **Museum of Forestry** (daily 9am–3pm; free), of limited interest.

The jumping-off point for Gunung Jerai is just north of the town of **Gurun**, on Route 1. Local bus #2 from Sungei Petani (every 30min; 30min) drops you at the bottom of the mountain, from where you can walk up to the summit (a gentle two-hour climb) or get one of the **jeeps** that make the journey up every 45 minutes (daily 8.30am–5pm; RM5 return). While it would be stretching things to call the settlement on the peak a "hill station" (there was no colonial tradition here), a pleasant overnight stay can be had at its one hotel, the *Peranginan Gunung Jerai* (☎04/423 4345; ④), which has a restaurant as well as comfortable chalets – the owners provide tents for those who prefer sleeping alfresco (RM30).

Alor Setar and around

The last major stop before the Thai border, **ALOR SETAR**, the tiny state capital of Kedah, is a city keen to preserve its heritage, a fact attested to by its many royal buildings and museums. Something of Kedah's past (see box, p.190) is also evidenced by the many Thais still living in Alor Setar today, worshipping in the splendidly restored Thai temple and running businesses and restaurants. For all that, Alor Setar is one of most Malay towns you'll find on the west coast, sustained in part by the predominance of Islam which, throughout the years in which Kedah was subject to external domination, played an important part in the maintenance of traditional Malay values. It has also been the hometown of two of Malaysia's prime ministers: Tunku Abdul Rahman and Mahathir Mohammed.

Located on Route 1 and the main west-coast train line, Alor Setar is something of a **transport hub**, with useful connections to Thailand; it's also served by buses for Kuala Kedah, where the ferries to Pulau Langkawi (see p.195) set sail.

The Town

Sungei Kedah runs along the western and southern outskirts of Alor Setar. The main sights are located in the west of the town around the padang, which has a large modern fountain at its centre. The area just to the west is dominated by **Masjid Zahir**, its Moorish architecture highlighted at night by thousands of tiny lights. Facing the mosque, the elegant **Istana Balai Besar** (Royal Audience Hall) – the principal official building during the eighteenth century – stands serene amid the roaring traffic. The present two-storey, open-colonnaded structure dates back only to 1904, when the original hall was rebuilt to host the marriages of Sultan Abdul Hamid's five eldest children. So grand was the refurbishment and so lavish the ceremony that the state was nearly bankrupted.

Just behind the Balai Besar, the old royal palace now serves as the **Muzium Di Raja** (daily 10am–5pm; Fri closed noon–2.30pm; free), an excellent way of preserving this dainty little 1930s building. The museum has its fair share of eulogistic memorabilia – medals and fond recollections of the current sultan's salad days – and some of the rooms have been kept exactly as they were used by the sultan and his family.

Across the way stands a curious octagonal tower, the **Balai Nobat**, housing the sacred instruments of the royal orchestra; unfortunately, the tower and its contents are not open for public view. Played only during royal ceremonies – inaugurations, weddings and funerals – the collection consists of three ornate silver drums, a gong, a long trumpet and a double-reeded instrument similar to the oboe, which combine to produce the haunting strains of *nobat* music (the name derives from a Persian word for a very large kettle drum, played in Malay royal palaces). Since the instruments are regarded as the most treasured part of the sultan's regalia, so the musicians themselves are given a special title, *Orang Kalur*, relating to the time when they were also keepers of the royal records. The Kedah Nobat, the oldest and most famous of these

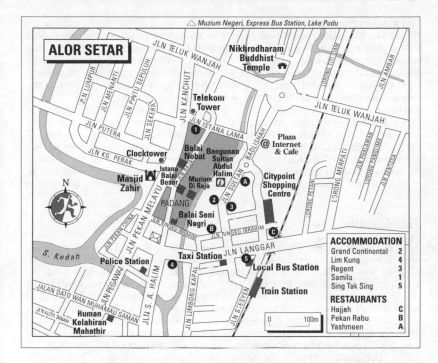

ALOR SETAR

JLN TELUK WANJAH

JLN LUMPUR
JLN MENANTI
JLN PINTU SEPULUH
JLN SEKERA
JLN KANCHUT

Nikhrodharam Buddhist Temple ♨

Telekom Tower

JLN TELUK WANJAH

JLN CITY SIAM

JLN AMBAR

JLN PUTERA

JLN ISTANA LAMA

JLN KG. PERAK

Clocktower

Balai Nobat

Bangunan Sultan Abdul Halim ℹ

Plaza @ Internet & Cafe

JLN BADLISHAH

Masjid Zahir ☪

Istana
Balai Besar

Muzium Di Raja ℹ

Citypoint Shopping Centre Ⓐ

LORONG MERPATI
JLN PHALAWAN
LORONG PANGLIMA
JLN SENTOSA

N

PADANG

Balai Seni Negri Ⓑ

LORONG PEKAN

JLN PEKAN CHINA
JLN PEKAN MELAYU
JLN TUNKU IBRAHIM

JLN TUNGKU IBRAHIM

Ⓒ

S. Kedah

Police Station

JLN S. A. HALIM

Taxi Station

JLN LANGGAR

Local Bus Station

JALAN DATO WAN MUHAMAD SAMAN
JLN PEGAWA
JLN NAUTA PANAH

Rumah Kelahiran Mahathir

JLN LIMBONG KAPAL
JLN S. ESTEN

Train Station

ACCOMMODATION
Grand Continental 2
Lim Kung 4
Regent 3
Samila 1
Sing Tak Sing 5

RESTAURANTS
Hajjah C
Pekan Rabu B
Yashmeen A

0   100m

ensembles, played at the installation of independent Malaysia's first constitutional monarch in 1947.

Just north of the padang on Jalan Kanchut is the **Telekom Tower** (daily 10am–10pm), the most modern sight in Alor Setar. A mini-version of the one in KL, it has a fast-food restaurant and viewing gallery. Walk east from here along Jalan Telok Wanjah and you'll see the **Nikhrodharam Buddhist Temple**, just beside the roundabout. The building of this glittering temple complex, decorated with many colourful statues, mosaics and paintings, began in the 1950s and was only finished in 1995. A match for many in Thailand, it's testimony to the continuing influence of Thai culture in the city.

On the padang's south side, the grandiose, white-stucco **Balai Seni Negeri** (same hours as Muzium Di Raja) is an art gallery displaying largely uninspiring and derivative works showing the influence of traditional Malay culture on contemporary artists – rural scenes abound, as you might expect. South of the padang, across the Sungei Kedah, is **Rumah Kelahiran Mahathir** (Tues–Sun 10am–5pm; Fri closed noon–3pm; free), 18 Lorong Kilang Ais, the birthplace and family home of Dr Mahathir Mohammed. Reached by heading west along Jalan Dato Wan Muhammad Saman, it's now a museum, documenting the life of the local doctor who became the most powerful Malaysian prime minister of modern times.

For a glimpse of contemporary culture, head for the **Pekan Rabu**, a daily market running from morning to midnight. Situated in a large building on Jalan Tunku Ibrahim, it comprises a large collection of stalls selling everything from handicrafts to local farm produce, a good place to sample traditional Kedah food like the "dodol durian", a sweet cake made from the notoriously pungent durian fruit (see p.53).

The Muzium Negeri

Hop on bus #31 heading north from Jalan Raja, adjacent to the padang, and after about 1500m you'll pass the **Muzium Negeri** (Tues–Sun 10am–6pm, Fri closed noon–3pm; closed Mon except public and school holidays 10am–6pm; free) on Jalan Lebuhraya Darulaman. It contains some background information on the archeological finds at Lembah Bujang (see p.191), but the exhibits fail to ignite much interest, except for the delicate silver tree close to the entrance, known as the *bunga mas dan perak* ("the gold and silver flowers"). The name refers to a practice, established in the seventeenth century, of honouring the ruling government of Thailand by a triennial presentation of two small trees of gold and silver, about 1m in height, meticulously detailed even down to the birds nesting in their branches. The cost of these ornaments was estimated at over a thousand Spanish dollars, no mean sum for those times. While the tradition was seen by Ayuthaya as a recognition of its suzerainty, Kedah rulers considered the gift a show of goodwill and friendship – characteristically refusing to acknowledge their vassal status.

Practicalities

Alor Setar's huge Sharap Perdana **express bus station**, 6km north of the centre, is used by long-distance services; it's well connected to the city by municipal buses (60 sen) and taxis (RM7). The **local bus station** on Jalan Langgar is where to catch the #106 to Kuala Kedah for the Langkawi ferry, and is also the departure point for the service to Kangar, from where there's a connecting service to the Langkawi ferry jetty at Kuala Perlis. The **train** station, unsurprisingly on Jalan Stesyen, is just a minute's walk south of the local bus station. Alor Setar is a principal station on the west coast route and a place to pick up the express train to Hat Yai and Bangkok, strangely though, the train doesn't stop here on the return leg. The domestic **airport** (MAS office ☎04/721 1186), 11km north of town, is accessible by the hourly "Kepala Batas" bus from the express bus station, or by taxi (around RM10).

The State Tourist Office (Tues–Thurs, Sat & Sun 8am–4.15pm, second and fourth Thurs each month 8am–12.45pm; closed first and third Sat of every month; ☎04/730 1957) is in the State Secretariat Building (Bangunan Sultan Abdul Halim) on Jalan Sultan Badlishah. Most of the major **banks** are on Jalan Raja.

Accommodation

The **budget hotels** are close to the local bus station along Jalan Langgar. Furthest away from the station, but by far the best value, is the *Lim Kung* (☎04/732 8353; ①), whose exceptionally friendly manager takes pride in his large wooden house which boasts simple, clean rooms; the communal showers are up to the same standard. The *Sing Tak Sing Hotel*, right above the bus station (☎04/732 5482; ②), is a slightly seedy, cavernous alternative, some of whose rooms have air-con. There are two excellent mid-range options, the better of the two being the *Hotel Regent*, 1536g Jalan Sultan Badlishah (☎04/731 1900, fax 731 1291; ③), whose exterior and interior both look a lot more expensive than it is. For slightly larger rooms, try the comfortable *Hotel Samila*, 27 Jalan Kanchut, just north of the padang (☎04/731 8888, fax 732 2344; ④), whose rates include breakfast. Most of the top-class hotels are inconveniently situated on the outskirts of town, a notable exception being the landmark *Grand Continental*, 134–141 Jalan Sultan Badlishah (☎04/733 5917, fax 733 5161; ⑤), with cosy rooms.

Eating

You'd do well to sample some **Thai cuisine** while in town – try *Hajjah*, opposite Citypoint on Jalan Tungku Ibrahim, for Thai seafood. One of the best-value places is the

Yashmeen, on Jalan Sultan Badlishah, which serves excellent and filling Indian food. For a variety of dishes under one roof head for the Pekan Rabu market, and try the restaurant at the *Samila* which, like the hotel, is good value, serving Western cuisine. Of the many **cybercafés** in the Citypoint shopping centre, *MCC Internet* on the third floor is the cheapest (☎04/732 4439). Further north on Jalan Sultan Badlishah, the *Plaza Internet & Café* (☎04/734 4358) stays open until about midnight.

Pulau Langkawi

Situated 30km off the coast, at the very northwestern tip of the Peninsula, is a cluster of 104 tropical islands known collectively as **LANGKAWI**. The archipelago's beauty has fostered many traditional stories, so much so that Langkawi has become known as the "Islands of Legends". In true Malay fashion, almost every major landmark here has a myth associated with it, each story ruthlessly hijacked by the tourist authorities to promote the islands. Most are little more than tiny, deserted, scrub-clad rocks jutting out of the sea; only three are inhabited, including the largest of the group, **Pulau Langkawi**, once a haven for pirates, now a sought-after refuge for wealthy tourists. With the encouragement of its biggest fan, Dr Mahathir, who once worked here as a doctor, Pulau Langkawi has in recent years seen unparalleled development, enhanced by its duty-free status, making it Malaysia's premier island retreat. Some of the country's most luxurious hotels are here, and a new airport has been built to cope with the increasing number of visitors. Langkawi is not a budget destination: to appreciate all the islands have to offer, you need to spend quite a bit of money, though you could scrape by on RM60 a day if all you do is sit on the beach.

It's perhaps because of Pulau Langkawi's size (around 500 square kilometres) that its interior is much cultivated even now, with most of the inhabitants still living a traditional way of life. Consequently, its natural attractions – a mountainous interior, white sands, limestone outcrops and lush vegetation – have remained relatively unspoiled despite development along its shores. The island's charms consist largely of lazing around on beaches and enjoying the sunshine, although you can also visit the ancient **Makam Mahsuri** (the tomb of a legendary woman; see p.198), various splendid waterfalls and the **Telaga Air Panas** hot springs.

The principal town on the island is **Kuah**, a boom town of hotels and shops in the southeast of the island, where you'll find most of the duty-free bargains. The main tourist development has taken place around two bays on the western side of the island, at **Pantai Tengah** and **Pantai Cenang**. The former is by far the more commercialized, although there is some budget accommodation available on both beaches. More recent building work has taken place at two beaches on the north coast, **Pantai Datai** and **Tanjung Rhu**, where accommodation is limited to top-class resorts.

There is basically one circular route around the island, with the other main road cutting the island in two, connecting north and south; various minor roads are well surfaced and signposted. **Public transport** around the island is limited to **taxis**, the bus companies having gone out of business due to the increasingly upmarket island clientele relying on their resorts' private coaches. A trip from the Kuah jetty to Pantai Cenang costs RM14, while a three-hour taxi tour of the island runs to around RM50 per vehicle. Many of the chalets and motels offer **motorbike rental** for around RM35 per day or **bicycles** for RM15. It takes at least a full day to see everything, with plenty of places to stop for a bite to eat and a fuel top-up (one tank should last you all day though). On neighbouring Pulau Singa Besar and Pulau Payar, designated **wildlife and marine parks** provide a little extra interest. You can also dive and snorkel off some of the archipelago's other, uninhabited islands, though the only way to do this is by taking an expensive day-trip, organized either by the Pulau Langkawi tourist office or one of the hotels.

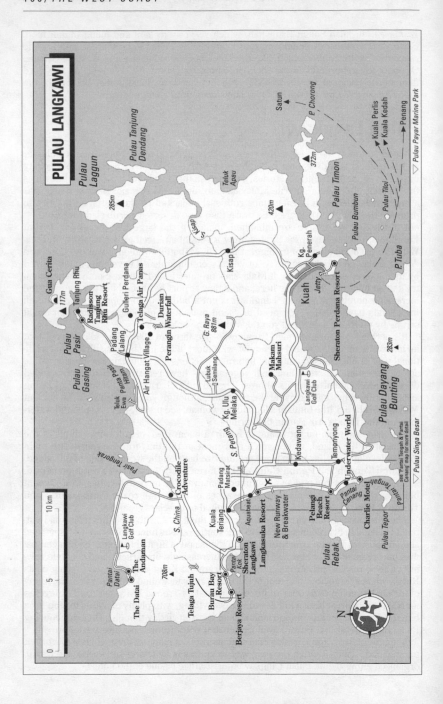

PULAU LANGKAWI

0 5 10 km

Pantai Datai
The Datai
The Andaman
Langkawi Golf Club
708m
S. China
Telaga Tujuh
Burau Bay Resort
Berjaya Resort
Pantai Kok
Sheraton Langkawi
Langkasuka Resort
Kuala Teriang
Aquabeat
Padang Matsirat
S. Petang
New Runway & Breakwater
Pelangi Beach Resort
Charlie Motel
Pantai Cenang
Underwater World
Pantai Tengah
see 'Pantai Tengah & Pantai Cenang' map for more detail

Pulau Rebak
Pulau Tepor
Pasir Tengorak

Crocodile Adventure
Kg. Ulu Melaka
Lubuk Semilang
Air Hangat Village
Durian Perangin Waterfall
Telaga Air Panas
Guleri Perdana
Padang Lalang
Radisson Tanjung Rhu Resort
Tanjung Rhu
Gua Cerita
117m

Pulau Pasir
Pulau Gasing
Teluk Panta Pasir Ewa
Hitam

Pulau Laggun
285m
Pulau Tanjung Dendang

S. Kisap
Kisap
G. Raya 881m
Makam Mahsuri
Langkawi Golf Club
Kedawang
Temonyong

420m
Teluk Apau

Kg. Penerah
Kuah
Jetty
Sheraton Perdana Resort
Palau Timon
Pulau Bumbun
P. Tuba
283m
Pulau Dayang Bunting

372m
Satun
P. Chorong
Kuala Perlis
Kuala Kedah
Penang
Pulau Tilai
▷ Pulau Payar Marine Park

▷ Pulau Singa Besar

N

Getting to Langkawi

All transport from the mainland heads to Pulau Langkawi. The island is most commonly reached from **Kuala Perlis** (see p.205), adjacent to the Thai border, from where there are **fast boats** every day (hourly; 45min; RM13 one way). **Ferries** also operate nine times daily from **Kuala Kedah** (7am–7pm; 1hr 15min; RM15 one way), 51km to the south, just 8km from Alor Setar (see p.194); there's no need to book tickets in advance. Both services run to the Kuah jetty on the southeastern tip of the island, about five minutes' drive from Kuah itself. Two direct passenger boats sail here **from Georgetown** (daily 5pm & 5.30pm; 2hr 30min; RM35 one way), docking at Kuah jetty. There are also ferry services **from Thailand**: three times daily from Satun, on the border (1hr 30min; RM19) – the ferries dock at the Kuah jetty. There are domestic **flights** to Pulau Langkawi from KL, Georgetown and Ipoh, and international services from Singapore and Kansai Airport in Japan.

Kuah

Lining a large sweep of bay in the southeastern corner of the island, **KUAH**, with a population of thirteen thousand, is easily the largest town on Langkawi. The town has been greatly developed in recent years, with a new ferry terminal, hotels and shopping complexes popping up all along the bay. Land has been reclaimed, marooning the whitewashed **Masjid Al-Hana** – a mosque which used to dominate the waterfront – behind a car park. Beside the ferry terminal is **Dataran Lang** (Eagle Square), graced by an enormous sculpture of an eagle (Langkawi means "red eagle"). Next to the square is **Lagenda Langkawi Dalan Taman** (daily 9am–9pm; RM5), a theme park based around the legends of the islands, its twenty hectares of landscaped gardens punctuated by more giant sculptures. There are vantage points over the bay and surroundings, but no shade or place to buy refreshments. Most of the hotels and shopping complexes are further around the bay.

Practicalities

Ferries run to the jetty on the southeastern tip of the island, about five minutes' drive from Kuah itself. A taxi from the jetty into Kuah costs around RM4 (you can get one at half the price if you walk a little way onto the main road). The **airport** (☎04/955 1311) is 20km west of Kuah, near Pantai Cenang; a taxi to any of the western beaches or Kuah costs less than RM16.

The Langkawi **tourist office** (daily except Fri 9am–5pm; ☎04/966 7789, fax 966 7889) located on Jalan Persiaran Putera (the route into Kuah from the jetty) next to the mosque, is very helpful; there's also an information booth at the airport (same times as main tourist office). Kuah is not an unattractive place, but despite the multitude of hotels it's not somewhere you're likely to want to stay. As well as the numerous duty-free shops along the main road, selling everything from hooch to handbags, you'll find the **post office** (daily except Fri 9am–5pm), **police station** (☎04/966 6222) and **hospital** (☎04/966 3333) close to each other. Behind the MAYA shopping complex, also on the main road, are three parallel streets where all the **banks** (virtually the only places to change money on the island) and the **Telekom centre** are located. There's an MAS office (☎04/966 6622) in the Tabung Haji building.

ACCOMMODATION

Kuah is even less budget oriented than the rest of Langkawi and, apart from a few exceptions, you could be in for a pretty dismal night's sleep unless you spend big money.

Asia, 3a and 4a Jalan Persiaran Putera (☎04/966 6216). Has unpleasant, grimy, overpriced doubles. ③.
Beringin Beach Resort, Pantai Dato' Syed Omar (☎04/966 6966, fax 966 7970). Leaving the jetty, turn left and head up the road for 200m or so; this brings you to a right turning from where the hotel

is a signposted kilometre away. The best-value place in Kuah, in a quiet and secluded spot on a mangrove beach, it has neat, well-equipped cabins with TVs, air-con and hot showers at a very good price. ③.

City Bayview, Jalan Pandak Mayah 1 (☎04/966 1818, fax 966 3888, *cbvlgk@tm.net.my*). Carry on past the turning for the *JB Motel* to this huge place, which has comfortable doubles. ⑤.

Hotel Central, 33 Jalan Persiaran Putera (☎04/966 8585, fax 966 7385). On the main road from the jetty, keeping the sea to your left, head northwest for 400m, past the giant *Lada Complex*, to get to this high-rise place, with clean, modern rooms. ④.

Hotel Langkawi, 6–8 Pekan Kuah (☎04/966 6248, fax 965 2874). Just northwest of the *Asia*. The clean doubles with communal facilities are worth the money; the air-con rooms with hot showers are a little overpriced, though better than the ones at the nearby *Asia* and *Putra*. ②.

JB Motel, 19 Jalan Pandak Maya 4 (☎04/966 8545). A few minutes' walk further in the same direction as the *Langkawi*. Take the large side road leading inland (Jalan Pandak Maya 1) after you pass the food stalls; on the second right past the Maybank you'll find the motel, in the middle of a row of shops parallel to the shore road. A little smarter than the *Langkawi*, this place has spotless en-suite doubles; there's no hot water though. ③.

Putra, 3 Jalan Persiaran Putra (☎& fax 04/966 2145). Just 100m northwest of the mosque and tourist information, this place has small, musty rooms. ②.

Sheraton Perdana Resort, Jalan Pantai Dato' Syed Omar (☎04/966 2020, fax 966 6414). Two kilometres southeast down the main road from the ferry terminal. Set in landscaped grounds, with a private beach, sports facilities and several swimming pools, this hotel commands a spectacular view of island-dotted Langkawi Bay. ⑧.

Tiara Langkawi, Persiaran Mutiara (☎04/966 2566, fax 966 2600). Half a kilometre from the junction with Jalan Pandak Maya 1 along the seafront, taking the left fork at the bizarre clock-sculpture will bring you to this peach-coloured, fairy-tale castle complex. The fairy-tale ends upon entry however; the rooms are very ordinary and twice the price of the *City Bayview*'s. ⑧.

EATING

Kuah has numerous eating places of various standards, from the **hawker stalls** – past the post office heading towards the jetty – to the pricier seafood **restaurants** on the seafront, like *Prawn Village*, next to the *Asia* hotel. Despite the ready availability of fresh fish, these places are fairly expensive, each dish setting you back at least RM8 – there are better places elsewhere on the island. There's an **Internet café**, *I.T. Base*, at 6–7 Banguan Chempaka (☎ & fax 04/966 2218), on the corner of the main road and Jalan Pandak Maya 1.

To the west coast: Pantai Tengah

Taking the main road west out of Kuah, just past the Langkawi Golf Club, about 10km from town, you see a signpost for **Makam Mahsuri** (the tomb of Mahsuri; daily 10am–6pm; RM2). In **Kampung Mawat**, a couple of kilometres off the main road west of Kuah, the tomb is enshrined in Langkawi's most famous legend, which tells of a young woman named Mahsuri, born over two hundred years ago. Her beauty was such that it inspired a vengeful accusation of adultery from a spurned suitor – or, as some versions have it, a jealous mother-in-law – while her husband was away fighting the invading Siamese. Mahsuri protested her innocence but was found guilty by the village elders, who sentenced her to death. She was tied to a stake, and as the ceremonial dagger was plunged into her, began to bleed white blood, a sign that proved her innocence. With her dying breath, Mahsuri muttered a curse on Langkawi's prosperity, to last seven generations – judging by the island's increasing income in recent years, this must be starting to wear off. The white-marble tomb stands alone in a shady garden; also here is a reconstruction of a traditional Malay house.

Back on the main road, heading west, you come after a further 8km to a junction from where the first of the island's western beaches, **PANTAI TENGAH**, 6km away, is clearly signposted. The beach is a quiet spot, and the sand itself isn't at all bad, but the secluded nature of the bay here means that the water isn't renewed by the tide and so is murky. There are also jellyfish here, so take local advice before you swim.

By the junction with Jalan Pantai Tengah are a few shops and restaurants – the only place on either west-coast beach that attracts locals. There's also an **Internet café** here, *Elite Style Computer* (☎04/955 9376) which stays open until about 1am.

Accommodation

Accommodation is a little sparser here than on Pantai Cenang, and likewise the beach is less crowded. There are a few low-key places and some bigger resorts on the main road.

Charlie Motel (☎04/955 1200, fax 955 1316). A little tatty, this beachfront place is passable, but the standard air-con rooms are less private than the *Tanjung Malie's*. ④.

Green Hill Beach Motel (☎019/449 9935). Slightly more expensive than its neighbours, this collection of basic bungalows with fan or air-con is the scrubbiest of the budget options. ②.

Langkawi Holiday Villa (☎04/955 1701, fax 955 1504). The top spot on the beach, very grand with a spa and a choice of restaurants, including Italian and Japanese. It's not quite as exclusive as more secluded resorts in the same price bracket elsewhere on the island. Has a good range of water sports open to non-guests. ⑧.

Langkawi Village Resort (☎04/955 1511, fax 955 1531, *lvr@pd.jaring.my*). Very pleasant, unpretentious kampung-style resort. The accommodation is in well-designed, two-storey chalets with all the trimmings – air-con, satellite TV, hot water and good beds. ⑦.

Sugary Sands Motel (☎04/955 3473). Another beach-hut operation with standard

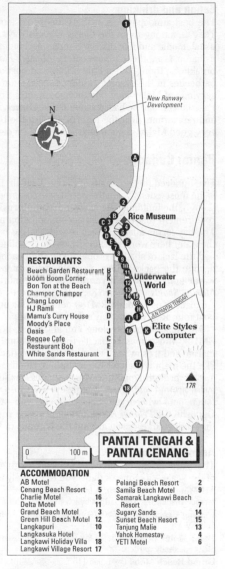

RESTAURANTS

Beach Garden Restaurant	B
Boom Boom Corner	K
Bon Ton at the Beach	A
Champor Champor	F
Chang Loon	H
HJ Ramli	G
Mamu's Curry House	D
Moody's Place	I
Oasis	J
Reggae Cafe	C
Restaurant Bob	E
White Sands Restaurant	L

PANTAI TENGAH & PANTAI CENANG

0   100 m

ACCOMMODATION

AB Motel	8	Pelangi Beach Resort	2
Cenang Beach Resort	5	Samila Beach Motel	9
Charlie Motel	16	Semarak Langkawi Beach	
Delta Motel	11	Resort	7
Grand Beach Motel	3	Sugary Sands	14
Green Hill Beach Motel	12	Sunset Beach Resort	15
Langkapuri	10	Tanjung Malie	13
Langkasuka Hotel	1	Yahok Homestay	4
Langkawi Holiday Villa	18	YETI Motel	6
Langkawi Village Resort	17		

or air-conditioned rooms. Not as good as the *Tanjung Malie*, but a passable second choice. ②.

Sunset Beach Resort (☎04/955 1751). A huge jump in quality and price. This unpretentious and friendly cluster of sturdy chalets amongst shady trees makes an intimate alternative to the big resorts. ⑤.

Tanjung Malie (☎ & fax 04/955 1891). The best of the budget places on Tengah, its comfortable chalets, with fans or air-con, set in a garden. ②.

Eating and drinking

The best atmosphere is at the Chinese restaurants by the junction with Jalan Pantai Tengah, among them the *Chang Loon*, always busy, offering fresh fish as well as the usual noodle and rice dishes. Simpler and quieter is *HJ Ramli* opposite, which, despite its name, is another Chinese eatery. *Moody's Place* on the junction serves good Western breakfasts, though it's a little pricey and portions are small. *Charlie's* does beachfront barbecues in the evening, while *Oasis*, also on the beach, has the best **bar**, as well as servings of Malay food. Further south, still along the shore road, there's inexpensive Pakistani food to be had at *Boom Boom Corner*, and a whole row of more expensive bars and restaurants near the resorts. One of the best is the *White Sands Restaurant*, with very good Malay seafood at around RM17 a dish.

Pantai Cenang

Five hundred metres north of Pantai Tengah, the development at **PANTAI CENANG** is the most extensive on the island, with cramped chalet sites side by side. By and large though, the buildings themselves are unobtrusive, mainly because of the government's requirement that beachfront accommodation not exceed the height of a coconut tree. The bay forms a large sweep of wide, white beach with crisp, sugary sand, but again the water here won't win any prizes for cleanliness. Less dedicated sun-worshippers will find the lack of shade a problem, but the beach's sheer length and breadth means that, despite the package-tour clientele, it never gets too crowded. Plenty of places offer **water sports** and **boat rental**, one of the more organized centres being the *Langkawi Marine Sports* (☎04/955 1389). Its prices are negotiable and vary with the time of year – expect to pay around RM180 per boat (for up to eight people) for a round-the-island boat tour, RM110 for a day's fishing or RM25 for ten minutes' waterskiing.

The main attraction along Pantai Cenang is **Underwater World** (daily 10am–6pm; RM12), whose boast is that it's the largest aquarium in Asia, housing over five thousand marine and freshwater fish. Although the attached duty-free shopping complex seems like the main reason for the operation, the fish are well presented, the highlight being a walk-through aquarium where sharks, turtles and hundreds of other sea creatures swim around and above boggle-eyed visitors in a transparent tunnel. There's also a touch pool where you can get feely with starfish, sea slugs and sea cucumbers. Opposite the *Pelangi Beach Resort* is a **rice museum** (10am–6pm; RM2) with its own mini-golf course, based around the legends of Langkawi.

Accommodation

There are dozens of **places to stay**, although not many good options at the budget end of the scale – if money's tight, you're unlikely to be able to afford a sea view.

AB Motel (☎04/955 1300). A friendly and attractive development with gardens, hammocks and a terrace restaurant. The budget beach huts are a little nicer than at its competitors. ②.

Cenang Beach Resort (☎04/955 1395). A quiet outfit with small bungalows; all come with air-con and TV. ④.

Delta Motel (☎04/955 2253, fax 953 1307). Pleasant and inexpensive wooden chalets in a well-planned, shady garden. ②.

Grand Beach Motel (☎04/955 1457, fax 955 3846). A rare budget place on the northern end of the beach. Clean bungalows with fans or air-con, at a low price. ②.

Langkapuri Beach Resort (☎04/955 1202, fax 955 1959). A range of sturdy brick chalets on a leafy patch of beach. The rooms have air-con and hot showers. Friendly staff. ⑤.

Pelangi Beach Resort (☎04/955 1001, fax 955 1122). Pantai Cenang's finest accommodation, an impressive five-star, two-storey timber development which echoes traditional Malay architecture. ⑧.

Samila Beach Resort (☎04/955 7530, *samila77@hotmail.com*). Plain chalets with showers and the option of air-con. ③.

Semarak Langkawi Beach Resort (☎04/955 1377, fax 955 1159). A large outfit with spacious, well-maintained chalets. The standard rooms are OK, but the *Langkapuri* offers better value. ④.

Yahok Homestay (☎04/955 8120)). Smaller than the nearby *Yeti*, with something of a reggae theme, as the music and decor bear out. All four rooms are en suite. A good choice. ③.

Yeti Beach Motel (☎017/477 1678). A laid-back spot, set back from the road on the landward side. The very simple, clean cabins with communal showers are priced as low as you'll find on Langkawi, and the staff are friendly. ③.

Eating and drinking

Most of the big resorts have attached **restaurants**, where the emphasis is on Westernized local dishes. The *Delta* is good value, but doesn't serve alcohol; the *Semarak Langkawi* has a pleasant, if slightly expensive, terrace restaurant; the *AB Motel* is better value. The *Beach Garden Resort Bistro* is a pretty beachside operation catering to the tastes of German visitors, as do many of the places along the beach; you'll also find pizzas, pasta and beer here. On the opposite side of the road is the excellent, but pricey *Champor Champor*. Meaning "mix mix", this small bar and restaurant, in a leafy, secluded spot, combines Western and Oriental influence to successful effect: meals are around RM20 a head. For top-notch food, head for the *Pelangi Beach Resort* – eating at its excellent Chinese or Thai restaurants will set you back around RM50 a head. At the other end of the spectrum, the *Reggae Bar* is a lively spot, with drinks, music and chicken wings aplenty, right on the beach – bring your guitar. Nearby, *Mamu's Curry House* has some very good Indian seafood while *Restaurant Bob* serves *roti*s and a tasty budget Malay fare at night, as well as the mysterious "power soup" (the ingredients are confidential of course). A few **Internet** terminals are available at both branches of The Shop, which sells general provisions; one of its stores is near the *AB Motel*, the other opposite *Mamu's Curry House*.

North to Pantai Kok

Immediately north of the *Pelangi Beach Resort*, major development of the airport and surroundings is afoot. The extension of the runway into the bay has effectively ruined what beach there was, and the long-term plan is to turn this area into yet another golf course. The now defunct thousand room *Delima Resort* further up the coast is eloquent testimony to development run amok – it had to be abandoned when the chalets starting falling to pieces because of shoddy workmanship.

Heading north, skirting around the airport, a right turn brings you to the **Padang Matsirat** (literally, "Field of Burnt Rice"). Shortly after Mahsuri's death (see p.198), the Siamese conquered Kedah and prepared to attack Langkawi. The island's inhabitants set fire to their staple crop and poisoned their wells in order to halt the advance of the invaders, and to this day, so the legend goes, traces of burnt rice resurface in the area after a heavy downfall of rain.

Just past the *Sheraton* complex is **PANTAI KOK**, which lies on the far western stretch of Langkawi. It's the best beach on the island, a large sweep of powdery white sand with relatively clear and shallow water – quieter and more secluded than Cenang, more intimate in feel, and with little to do in the evening except look up at the stars. In addition, you're also only 2km from the splendid falls at Telaga Tujuh, just to the north (see overleaf).

Practicalities

Unfortunately, the budget **accommodation** on the beach has been bulldozed to make way for a golf course, so the big resorts are the only option for now. Further up the coast is the *Langkasuka Resort* (☎04/955 6888, fax 955 5888, *langresort@po.jaring.my*; ⑥), a luxurious place on a lovely beach, with promotional discounts of up to fifty percent. A couple of kilometres uphill along the coast road, north from the turning for Padang Matsirat, is the *Sheraton Langkawi* (☎04/955 1901, fax 955 1968, *www.sheraton.com*; ⑨) perched on a clifftop. Its chalets, set in a slightly crowded garden, are luxurious enough, but you feel the place isn't quite up to the asking price.

A kilometre or so west of Pantai Kok is the *Burau Bay Resort* (☎04/959 1061, fax 959 1172, *sales-mktg.pbl@meritus-hotels.com*; ⑦). Its metallic and plastic chalets are a little tacky, though they have TV and air-con. At the western end of the beach, the *Berjaya Langkawi Beach and Spa Resort* (☎04/959 1888, fax 959 1886, *www.berjayaresorts.com.my*; ⑧) is more luxurious; the decor is a little kitsch, but the Japanese massages, facials and forest spa are its real attraction.

On the shore road north of Pantai Cenang, the **restaurant**-cum-trendy-crafts-shop, *Bon Ton at the Beach* (☎04/955 3643), has survived the development of the area; it's worth visiting for its well-presented local food and home-made cakes, and for the seven traditional kampung houses that stand beside it.

Telaga Tujuh

The road west of the turnoff to the *Berjaya Resort* leads to a car park, from where a dirt track heads up to the island's most wonderful natural attraction, **Telaga Tujuh** (literally, "Seven Pools"), a cascading freshwater stream that has pounded large recesses into the rock, forming several pools down a slope. During the rainy season, the slipperiness of the moss covering the rock in between the pools enables you to slide rapidly from one pool to another, before the fast-flowing water disappears over the cliff to form the ninety-metre **waterfall** you can see from below – it's only the depth of the water in the last pool that prevents you from shooting off the end too. This being Langkawi, there's an associated legend, suggesting the spot is the playground of mountain fairies. They're believed to have left behind a special kind of lime and the *sintuk* (a climbing plant with enormous pods), which grow around these pools; the locals use them as a hair wash, which is thought to rinse away bad luck.

The walk to the pools from the turning near the *Burau Bay Resort* takes about 45 minutes, the last stage of which involves a steep two-hundred-metre climb up from the inevitable cluster of souvenir stalls at the base of the hill. Look out for the long-tailed macaques that bound around the trail; they are playful, but can be vicious if provoked. If you're lucky, you may spot a cream-coloured giant squirrel (famed in these parts) scampering up the tree trunks, or great hornbills hanging out in the treetops; the latter, with their huge, hooked orange beak and cackle-like call, are the most distinctive of all Malaysian birds.

Along the road to the falls, just before you reach the base of the hill, the *Seven Wells Motel and Seafood Restaurant* (☎04/959 3842; ②), has a few double rooms, with showers; it's located on a quiet spot near the stream. The motel serves good **food** too, which is fortunate – it's the only place to eat here that isn't an expensive resort restaurant.

Datai

From Pantai Kok, the main road north heads to Pulau Langkawi's **north coast**. On the way you'll pass **Crocodile Adventure** (daily 9am–6pm; RM7), which has daily "man versus crocodile" shows at 11.15am and 2.45pm. Ten kilometres further on, you'll reach a new road off to the left which leads a further 12km to **DATAI**, the site of Langkawi's newest resort development. En route, the road curves and climbs to reveal a couple of secluded coves from where you can see several Thai islands in the distance; the sea at this point is a clear jewel-like blue. Just before you reach the resort area there's more development close to the top-notch Datai Bay Golf Club.

In the short time that the *Datai* (☎04/959 2500, fax 959 2600, *datai@ghmhotels.com*; ⑨) has been open, it has already become one of Malaysia's most exclusive resorts. Volcanic rock and wood have been used here to stunning effect, creating architecture in tune with the forest surroundings. The views across the bay to Thailand are stunning, as is the price. Under the same management is the *Andaman* (☎04/959 1088, fax 959 1168, *anda@po.jaring.my*; ⑧), which shares the beach at Datai Bay. These are two of the most attractive hotels to be found on either coast, the *Andaman* the grander (Nelson Mandela and Prime Minister Mahathir have been among its guests in recent years). Both are set well away from the road and have a non-motorized water-sport policy, making them surprisingly quiet for such large operations. To reach either of these resorts by taxi, you'll pay around RM25 from the airport, and RM40 from the jetty at Kuah.

Tanjung Rhu and Durian Perangin falls

Backtracking from Datai, further round the north coast, past Teluk Ewa, a couple of reasonable stretches of undeveloped beach look inviting, but the otherwise panoramic view from here is marred by an unsightly factory belching out large clouds of concrete dust. A little further on is **Pantai Pasir Hitam** ("Black Sand Beach"), where the cliff drops down away from the road to the black sands.

Five kilometres further east, the road intersects with the main north–south route across the island at the village of **Padang Lalang**. Turn left, and a couple of kilometres through some swampy land brings you to **TANJUNG RHU**, also known as "Casuarina Beach" because of the profusion of these trees here. The only development here is the *Radisson Tanjung Rhu Resort* (☎04/959 1033, fax 959 1899; ⑨). A close second to the *Andaman* and *Datai* resorts but not quite as tasteful or secluded, it's nevertheless a very classy outfit which receives its fair share of visiting dignitaries. Outside on the approach road, past the sign that warns "Alcohol is the root of all evil", are some food and drink stalls – which don't sell beer. Although the sand here is a bit gritty, the sea, sheltered by the curve of the bay, is unusually tranquil, almost like a lagoon. The tide goes out far enough for you to walk out to the nearby islands of **PULAU PASIR** and **PULAU GASING**, perfect for a bit of secluded sunbathing. On a promontory accessible only by boat from Tanjung Rhu (RM80), you'll find the isolated **Gua Cerita** (Cave of Tales), facing the Thai coastline. Despite the profusion of bat droppings, it's worth having a close look inside the cave, as you can make out ancient lettering on the walls – verses of the Koran.

Back at the crossroads, it's another 2km east to the site of **Telaga Air Panas** ("Hot Springs"), reputedly formed during a quarrel between the island's two leading families over a rejected offer of marriage. Household items were flung about in the fight: the spot where gravy splashed from the pots became known as Kuah ("gravy"), and here, where the jugs of boiling water landed, hot springs spouted. There's not much to see and what there is has been subsumed within the **Air Hangat Village** (daily 10am–6pm; RM4), which encompasses the hot springs and an arts pavilion, designed in traditional Malay kampung style; demonstrations of folk and classical dance, kick boxing and *silat* are put on here at various times of the day. There is also an expensive restaurant that puts on a cultural show every evening, inevitably catering to tour groups.

Next along the road is the **Galleri Perdana** (Tues–Sun 10am–5pm; RM2), which contains over ten thousand state gifts and awards presented to Prime Minister Dr Mahathir – there are plans afoot to create a prime-ministerial art gallery on the island too. Further on is the turnoff for **Durian Perangin**, a waterfall reached along a difficult and rocky path, and fairly disappointing unless you happen to catch it during the wet season when the water level is high. Shortly after this, the road curves to the south for the remaining 10km to Kuah.

Other Langkawi islands

Expensive **day-trips** to some of the nearer islands to Pulau Langkawi are organized by various hotels at Pantai Tengah or Pantai Cenang and by a couple of firms. These excursions are fine if you're into diving, snorkelling and fishing, but otherwise provide little incentive to leave the main island. It's also possible to get to some islands independently, taking the island-hopping boat which visits – among others – Pulau Singa Besar and Pulau Dayang Bunting (see below); it leaves from the Marble Beach jetty, two minutes' walk southeast of the Kuah jetty (daily at 9am & 2.30pm; RM45); the tourist office in Kuah has details of the current route.

Mountainous **Pulau Tuba**, 5km south of Langkawi, is the only other island with accommodation – just the one option, the *Sunrise Beach Resort* (☎04/966 9752, *putri51@hotmail.com*; ④), with its own swimming pool. There's barely enough space around the rim of the island for the dirt track which encircles it, though it does take in some deserted beaches. It's awkward to get to Tuba – a matter of hanging round the Marble Beach jetty until someone offers to take you across in one of the small speedboats; a return trip costs RM6.

Pulau Dayang Bunting (literally, "Island of the Pregnant Maiden") is the second largest island in the archipelago, about fifteen minutes' boat ride from Marble Beach jetty. It's the exception to the rule in having at least a couple of specific points of interest, but you'll have to visit on a day-trip as there's nowhere to stay. Here, **Tasik Dayang Bunting**, a large and tranquil freshwater lake, is reputed to have magical properties believed to make barren women fertile. The area is overwhelmed by massive, densely forested limestone outcrops, at their most dramatic around the **Gua Langsir** ("Cave of the Banshee"), a towering 91-metre-high cave on the island's west coast, which is said to be haunted – probably because of the sounds of the thousands of bats which live inside. The island-hopping boat drops you at a jetty near the lake before continuing to the cave, 8km to the north.

Langkawi's most recent attempt at green tourism is realized on **Pulau Singa Besar**, a wildlife sanctuary 3km off the southern tip of Pantai Tengah and also a stop for the island-hopping boat. The organized day-trip includes the services of a guide, since for obvious reasons you're not allowed to roam around at will. Monkeys, mouse deer, iguanas and peacocks are among the wildlife to have been freed on the island, although how many animals you actually see is inevitably a matter of luck.

Pulau Payar's Marine Park has great schools of tropical fish, and south of the island, 13km west of the Peninsula, lies a coral garden supporting the largest number of coral species in the country. A few companies organize day-trips to the marine park; those run by Langkawi Coral, which has an office at Kuah Ferry Terminal (☎04/966 7318), are the most expensive at RM220 per person, but the price includes hotel pick-ups, lunch, the use of their reef-viewing platform and all snorkelling equipment; Island and Sun at Simping 3, Pantai Tengah (☎ & fax 04/955 7166) has the cheapest trip, done in small speedboats (RM150; doesn't include hotel transfers). No accommodation is available; to **camp** you must first obtain permission from the Fisheries Department at Alor Setar (☎04/732 5573).

North to the Thai border

The tiny state of **Perlis** – at 800 square kilometres the smallest in Malaysia – lies at the northwestern tip of the Peninsula, bordering Thailand. Together with neighbouring Kedah, it's traditionally been viewed as the country's agricultural heartland, something reflected in the landscape which is dominated by lustrous, bright-green paddy fields. There's no special reason to stop here; most people pass quickly through the state's dull towns on their way to Thailand. Although both main roads and the train line cut inland to the border, it's easy enough to catch local buses out to the coastal villages covered below.

Kuala Perlis

Though it's the second largest settlement in the state, the little town of **KUALA PERLIS**, 45km north of Alor Setar, has only two streets. Boats from Langkawi and from Satun in Thailand dock here; buses drop you at an unmarked stand adjacent to the jetty, from where a wooden footbridge connects with the older, more interesting part of town, a ramshackle collection of buildings on stilts. Though you can reserve tickets at the Kuala Perlis–Langkawi Ferry Service's jetty office (☎04/985 4494), but it's just as easy to turn up and board, with hourly departures throughout the day.

There are two **banks** in the main part of town, near the jetty. The town also has a couple of **hotels**. With the water on your left, walk into town and turn right opposite the covered market. You'll come to the grimy and overpriced *Pens Hotels* (☎04/985 4122, fax 985 4131; ④), which has some air-con rooms. A better idea is to keep walking down the main road for about 500m until you reach the outskirts of town; opposite the mosque is a right turn from where the *Asia Hotel*, 18 Taman Sentosa (☎04/985 5392; ②) is signposted. It's a more modest affair than the *Pens*, but a lot cleaner, with a better-than-average Chinese restaurant downstairs.

You can reach Satun in **Thailand** directly from Kuala Perlis: small boats from Langkawi stop here en route, leaving from the jetty when they are full (30min; RM4); at weekends you'll be charged an additional RM1 for the immigration officers' overtime payment. For details of land crossings into Thailand, see box below.

Kangar, Arau and Kaki Bukit

Buses from Kuala Perlis run 12km north to **KANGAR**, the state capital, another unremarkable modern town. The centrally located **express bus station** is where you change onto buses for the border. The nearest **train station** is 10km to the east at **ARAU**, the least interesting of all Malaysia's royal towns – its Royal Palace (closed to the public) on the main road looks like little more than a comfortable mansion. The town is only really handy for the daily train to Hat Yai and Bangkok (which doesn't stop here on the return journey), and there are less convenient daily connections to Butterworth, Alor Setar, Sungei Petani, Taiping, Ipoh, Tapah Road and Kuala Lumpur.

With your own transport, and time to kill before crossing the border, you could visit **Gua Kelam Kaki Bukit** (literally, "a cave of darkness at the foot of a hill"), a 370-

---

CROSSING INTO THAILAND

The two **border crossings** are at the villages of Padang Besar and, further southeast, Bukit Kayu Hitam. The **train** comes to a halt at **Padang Besar**, where a very long platform connects the Malaysian service with its Thai counterpart. You don't change trains here, although you must get off and go through customs at the station. Frequent **bus** services from Kangar's local bus station (a kilometre north of the express terminus) drop you on the road at the border, which is open from 6am to 10pm. The first train gets to Padang Besar at 7.40am, the last at 4.20pm, while buses run regularly throughout the day. The **North–South Highway** runs to the border at **Bukit Kayu Hitam**, from where it is about a five-hundred-metre walk to Danok on the Thai side; the opening times here are the same.

There are regular bus connections from both border crossings to **Hat Yai**, southern Thailand's transportation hub, 60km away. The train passes through here, too, on its way north to Bangkok.

metre-long limestone cave once part of a working tin mine; it lies in a valley about 25km north of Kangar up Route 1. The stream that runs through the cavern was once used to carry away excavated tin ore to the processing plant near the cave's entrance. Access through the cave is by way of a suspended wooden walkway, also used by locals – and their motorbikes – as a means of getting to the other side of the valley, though for visitors the walkway's attraction is that it allows them to look down into the former mine. The town of **Kaki Bukit**, 1km south of the cave, is easily reached by bus from Kangar.

travel details

Trains

Alor Setar to: Arau (2 daily; 45min); Bangkok (Thailand; daily; 18hr 15min); Butterworth (daily; 2hr 45min); Hat Yai (Thailand; daily; 2hr 20min); Ipoh (daily; 4hr 30min); Kuala Lumpur (daily; 8hr 50min); Padang Besar (2 daily; 1hr 15min); Sungei Petani (2 daily; 50min–1hr 10min); Taiping (daily; 3hr); Tapah Road (daily; 5hr 40min).

Butterworth to: Alor Setar (1 daily; 1hr 40min); Bangkok (Thailand; daily; 19hr 55min); Hat Yai (Thailand; daily; 4hr); Ipoh (2/3 daily; 2hr 55min); Kuala Kangsar (2/3 daily; 2hr); Kuala Lumpur (2/3 daily; 7hr); Sungei Petani (2 daily; 1hr 30min); Taiping (2/3 daily; 1hr 30min); Tapah Road (2/3 daily; 4hr 50min).

Ipoh to: Butterworth (3 daily; 3hr 25min–5hr 10min); Kuala Kangsar (4 daily; 1hr–1hr 30min); Kuala Lumpur (4 daily; 4hr 15min); Taiping (3 daily; 1hr 40min–2hr 30min); Tapah Road (3 daily; 1hr).

Kuala Kangsar to: Butterworth (2/3 daily; 2hr 30min); Ipoh (3 daily; 1hr); Kuala Lumpur (3 daily; 4hr 30min); Taiping (5 daily; 40min–1hr); Tapah Road (3 daily; 2hr).

Padang Besar to: Alor Setar (2 daily; 3hr 25min); Bangkok (Thailand; daily; 17hr 15min); Butterworth (daily; 2hr 40min); Hat Yai (Thailand; 2 daily; 1hr 20min); Ipoh (daily; 8hr); Kuala Lumpur (daily; 12hr 15min); Sungei Petani (2 daily; 1hr 40min–4hr 15min); Taiping (daily; 6hr 30min); Tapah Road (daily; 9hr).

Taiping to: Alor Setar (daily; 3hr 30min); Butterworth (4 daily; 1hr 50min–2hr 40min); Ipoh (4 daily; 1hr 25min–2hr 10min); Kuala Kangsar (4 daily; 30min–1hr); Kuala Lumpur (4 daily; 5hr 40min); Padang Besar (daily; 4hr 45min); Sungei Petani (daily; 2hr 45min); Tapah Road (4 daily; 2hr 20min–4hr).

Tapah Road to: Alor Setar (daily; 7hr); Butterworth (3 daily; 4hr 20min–6hr 20min); Ipoh (3 daily; 1hr 10min); Kuala Kangsar (4 daily; 1hr 50min–2hr 45min); Kuala Lumpur (4 daily; 3hr 20min–3hr 50min); Padang Besar (2 daily; 8hr 10min); Sungei Petani (daily; 6hr); Taiping (3 daily; 2hr 30min–3hr 40min).

Buses

Alor Setar to: Butterworth (every 45min; 30min); Hat Yai (Thailand; hourly; 3hr); Ipoh (3 daily; 3hr); Johor Bahru (2 daily; 16hr); Kota Bharu (2 daily; 8–9hr); Kuala Lumpur (2 daily; 5hr); Kuala Perlis (hourly; 1hr 30min); Kuala Terengganu (2 daily; 8hr); Kuantan (2 daily; 9hr 30min).

Butterworth to: Alor Setar (every 45min; 30min); Bangkok (Thailand; 2 daily; 18hr); Hat Yai (Thailand; 2 daily; 3hr 30min); Ipoh (hourly; 3hr); Kota Bharu (2 daily; 6hr); Kuala Lumpur (at least 15 daily; 4hr 30min); Kuala Perlis (hourly; 3hr 45min); Kuala Terengganu (1 daily; 8hr); Kuantan (2 daily; 9hr); Lumut (8 daily; 3hr); Melaka (1 daily; 6–7hr); Seremban (1 daily; 6hr); Singapore (at least 1 daily; 16hr); Sungei Petani (hourly; 1hr); Taiping (14 daily; 2hr 15min).

Ipoh to: Alor Setar (3 daily; 3hr); Butterworth (hourly; 3hr); Kangar (2 daily; 4hr); Kuala Kangsar (every 45min; 1hr); Kuala Lumpur (every 30min–1hr; 3hr); Kuala Terengganu (2 daily; 11hr); Kuantan (2 daily; 8hr); Lumut (every 30min–1hr; 1hr 30min); Melaka (1 daily; 5hr); Penang (hourly; 3hr); Singapore (4 daily; 10–11hr); Tapah (hourly; 1hr).

Lumut to: Butterworth (4 daily; 4hr); Ipoh (every 30min–1hr; 1hr 30min); Kuala Lumpur (8 daily; 5hr 30min); Kuantan (5 daily; 9hr 30min); Taiping (every 30min; 1hr 10min); Tapah (2 daily; 2hr).

Tapah to: Butterworth (2 daily; 4hr 30min); Hat Yai (Thailand; daily; 10hr); Ipoh (hourly; 1hr); Kuala Lumpur (at least 10 daily; 2hr); Kuala Terengganu (daily; 6hr); Kuantan (2 daily; 6hr); Lumut (1 daily; 2hr); Melaka (1 daily; 3hr 30min); Singapore (2 daily; 10hr).

Ferries

Butterworth to: Georgetown (every 20min–1hr, 24hr service; 20min).

Georgetown to: Butterworth (every 20min–1hr, 24hr service; 15min); Langkawi (2 daily; 2hr 30min); Medan (Indonesia; daily; 4hr).

Kuala Kedah to: Langkawi (9 daily; 1hr 15min).

Kuala Perlis to: Langkawi (hourly; 45min); Satun (Thailand; 3 daily; 30min).

Langkawi to: Kuala Kedah (8 daily; 1hr 15min); Kuala Perlis (hourly; 45min); Penang (2 daily; 2hr 30min); Satun (Thailand; 3 daily; 1hr 30min).

Flights

Georgetown to: Johor Bahru (1 daily direct and at least 2 daily via KL; 1hr 5min–3hr 35min); Kota Kinabalu (at least 3 daily via KL; 3hr 10min–5hr 10min); Kuala Lumpur (at least 12 daily; 45min); Kuching (at least 5 daily via KL; 3hr 30min–9hr 55min depending on transit time); Langkawi (at least 2 daily; 30min); Medan (Indonesia; at least 1 daily; 20min).

Ipoh to: Johor Bahru (at least 2 daily via KL; 2hr 55min); Kuala Lumpur (at least 2 daily; 35min).

Langkawi to: Kuala Lumpur (at least 5 daily; 55min); Penang (at least 2 daily; 30min).

CHAPTER THREE

THE INTERIOR

The **interior** states of Pahang and Kelantan were the last regions of Peninsular Malaysia to excite the interest of the British colonial authorities. Until the 1880s the Bendahara (Prince) of Pahang, Wan Ahmed, ran his southern central state as a private fiefdom, unvisited by outsiders except for a hundred or so Chinese and European gold prospectors who had established contacts with a few remote Malay villages and **Orang Asli** settlements. When explorer and colonial administrator Sir Hugh Clifford visited, he noted that the region "did not boast a mile of road and . . . was smothered in deep, damp forest, threaded across a network of streams and rivers . . . flecked here and there by little splashes of sunlight." What Clifford also noted – indeed the reason for his visit – was that Pahang was "wonderfully rich in minerals". Wan Ahmed gave the British mining and planting rights, in exchange for military protection against the incursions of the Siamese and Kelantanese.

First to arrive were British officials, followed by tin and gold prospectors, then by investors in rubber and other plantation enterprises. The new arrivals initially used the rivers to get around, though the larger companies soon began to clear tracks – the forerunners of today's roads – into the valleys and along the mountain ridges. Development was made much easier when the jungle railway opened in the 1920s (see p.230). Slowly, small towns like **Temerloh**, **Raub** and **Kuala Lipis** grew in size and importance, while new settlements like Gua Musang were established to cater for the influx of Chinese merchants and workers.

Since the 1980s, when the only highway into the interior (Route 8 from Bentong to Kota Bharu) was finished, the impact of the **timber, rubber and palm-oil industries** cannot be underestimated. The whole region, though still not entirely accessible (there are still corners whose "utter remoteness from mankind" has changed little since Clifford's day), has been transformed. Much of the primeval landscape, hitherto the preserve of Orang Asli, a few Malays and the odd Chinese trader, has been rapidly tamed, providing economic incentives for people from both east and west coasts to move into these areas. This encroachment has had a huge effect on the indigenous tribes of the interior. Since the late 1950s the greater part of the Orang Asli have opted out of their traditional lifestyle; now it's probable that only a few hundred truly nomadic tribespeople remain, and even those have been tainted by economic progress. Orang Asli expert, Iskandar Carey, wrote in the 1970s that "there are groups of Senoi in the deep jungle who have never seen a road,

THE EMERGENCY AND THE ORANG ASLI

During the **Emergency** years (1948–60), ethnic Chinese Communist guerrillas – many originally members of the Malayan Communist Party – built camps deep in the forested interior from which to operate against both British and Malayan forces. At the peak of the conflict, around ten thousand guerrillas were hiding out in dozens of camouflaged jungle camps. For a long time they milked a support network of Chinese-dominated towns and villages in the interior, in many cases cowing the inhabitants into submission by means of public executions – although in some areas many of the poor rural workers identified with the insurgents' struggle to wrest the ownership of the large rubber plantations away from the British. It was only when the government successfully planted informers that the security services started to get wind of guerrilla operations.

The effect of the conflict on the way of life of the **Sakai** – the Orang Asli groups who inhabit areas north of the Kuantan Highway (Route 2), as far as Kuala Krai in Kelantan – was dramatic. All but the most remote tribes were subject to intimidation and brutality, from guerrillas on one side and government forces on the other. In effect, the Orang Asli's centuries-old invisibility had ended. The population of Malaysia was now aware of their presence, and the government of their strategic importance.

The Orang Asli had no choice but to grow food and act as porters for the guerrillas, as well as – most important of all – provide intelligence, warning them of the approach of the enemy. Meanwhile, government forces built eleven jungle forts, some near the towns of Raub and Tanjung Malim. In near desperation they implemented a disastrous policy – soon abandoned – of removing Orang Asli from the jungle and relocating them in new **model villages** near Raub and Gua Musang, which were no more than dressed-up prison camps. Thousands were placed behind barbed wire and hundreds died in captivity before the government dismantled the camps. By then, not surprisingly, active support for the insurgents among the Orang Asli had risen – though allegiances were switched to the security forces when the guerrillas' fortunes waned and their defeat became inevitable.

Government attempts to control the Orang Asli during the Emergency led inexorably to the imposition upon them of a framework of laws, social strategies and programmes – ranging from providing basic health and education facilities to subjecting the Orang Asli to Islamic proselytising – during the 1960s and 1970s. In recent years Asli activists and legal experts have begun to contest a number of these government-sponsored initiatives. The issue of **land rights** is now considered by a growing number of people to be the most urgent affecting the Orang Asli. According to one commentator, Lim Heng Seng, "the Asli find themselves virtually squatters on state land", and as long as the problem of legal entitlement to land remains unresolved, encroachment on Asli land will continue. Land is everything to the Orang Asli – in the Semiar language, land is called *nerng-rik*, which means "country". Life has changed very rapidly for most Orang Asli since the Emergency years, and what is seen as progress for many other Malaysians could be a cultural trap closing in on the indigenous people.

although they are familiar with helicopters, a word for which has been incorporated into their language." The Centre of Orang Asli Affairs in KL co-ordinates a variety of policies, including health and educational drives, initiatives which, though inevitably diluting the purity of Asli culture, have lifted the Orang Asli's standard of living and begun the process of integrating them into mainstream, multiracial Malay culture.

Banjaran Titiwangsa (Main Range) forms the western boundary of the interior; to its east is an H-shaped range of steep, sandstone mountains with knife-edge ridges and luxuriant valleys where small towns and kampungs nestle. The rivers which flow from these mountains – Pahang, Tembeling, Lebir, Nenggiri and Galas – provide the northern interior's indigenous peoples, the Negritos and Senoi, with their main means of transport. Visitors, too, can travel by boat to perhaps the most stunning of all Peninsular Malaysia's delights, **Taman Negara** – the country's first national park, straddling the

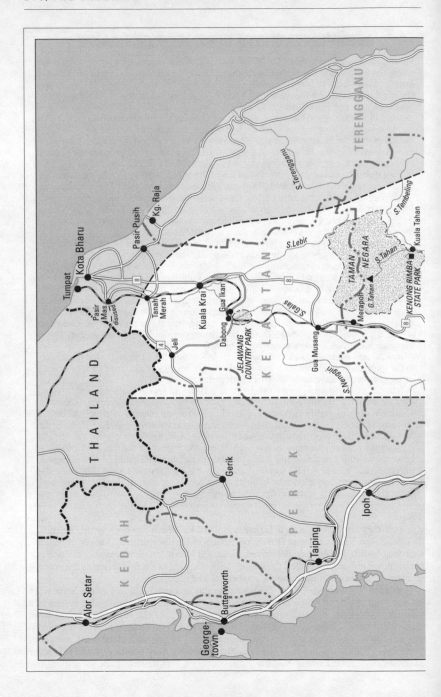

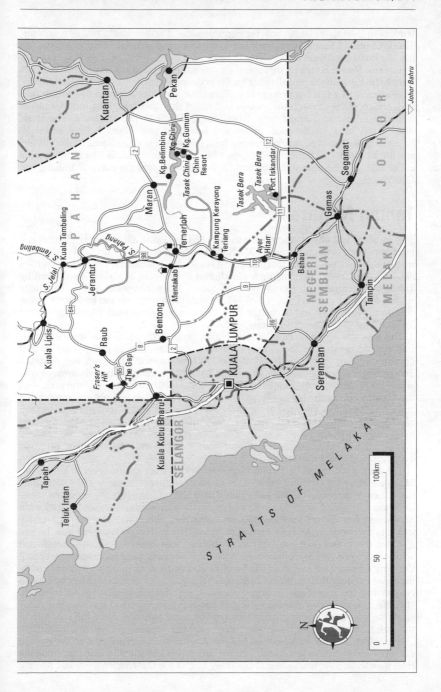

borders of Pahang, Kelantan and Terengganu states. Further south, two lake systems, **Tasek Chini** and **Tasek Bera**, are home to the Jakun and Semelai – Orang Asli who still live in a quasi-traditional way.

The new **Route 8** cuts up through the interior; the **drive** takes around twelve hours from KL to Kota Bharu (not allowing for the occasional landslide or rock fall). However, unless you're in a real hurry to get to either coast, consider a trip on the **jungle railway**, which winds through the valleys and round the sandstone hills from Gemas in Negeri Sembilan to Tumpat, near Kota Bharu, 500km to the northeast. The train, which runs at a snail's pace, is seldom less than two hours behind schedule. Nevertheless, it's a great way of meeting local people and seeing remote Malay villages and the interior's spectacular landscapes, with stops at **Kuala Lipis** (the former capital of Pahang), at the **Kenong Rimba** and **Jelawang** parks, and the **caves** at Dabong and Gua Musang.

Taman Negara

Two hundred and fifty kilometres northeast of KL is Peninsular Malaysia's largest and most important protected area, **TAMAN NEGARA** (literally "the national park"; for a map of the area, see p.225). Spread over 4343 square kilometres, the park comprises dense lowland forest, higher-altitude cloudforest (enveloping its highest peak, **Gunung Tahan**), numerous hills, Orang Asli settlements, hides, campsites and a chic jungle retreat. From the streams which snake down from the mountains and feed fierce waterfalls, to the lush flora and fauna, the park experience (as the tourist brochures never tire of telling you) is second to none.

The area was first protected by state legislation in 1925, when 1300 square kilometres was designated as the Gunung Tahan Game Reserve; thirteen years later it became the King George V National Park. At independence, the park was renamed Taman Negara and extended to its current boundaries. In 1991, the Malaysian Parks and Wildlife Department decided it would be best to split the running of the park, with the department continuing to oversee its ecological management, but accommodation and eating facilities privatized at the three main sites – Tahan, Trenggan and Keniam. Since then there has been substantial **redevelopment** by the Singapore-based *Pernas* hotel chain: at Kuala Tahan a massive cash injection has financed over one hundred deluxe chalets, with smaller, less obtrusive developments taking place at Kuala Trenggan and Kuala Keniam.

The park itself forms by far the largest undivided tract of rainforest in Peninsular Malaysia; indeed it contains some of the **oldest rainforest** in the world – older than the Congo or Amazon – which has evolved over 130 million years. Although for many the chance of seeing sizeable mammals, especially **elephants**, is one of the park's big draws, very few visitors have any success unless they either make a three- or four-day trek into the forest, or journey upriver to remote Kuala Keniam and head into the jungle from there. But stay overnight in the **hides** – tree houses positioned beside salt licks – and you'll often spot mouse deer, tapir and *seladang* (wild ox), especially during the rainy season. That said, it's quite possible to spend a week in the park and see nothing more exciting than a mound of elephant dung, armies of ants and leeches, and a colourful shape – perhaps an argus pheasant – bashing through the undergrowth. **Birdlife**, at least, is ever present – the park has over three hundred species – and many are quite easy to spot with good binoculars and some patience. For a full rundown of the park habitats and species on view, see the wildlife account in Contexts, p.637.

Every **trek** into the forest has its fascinations. For those unfamiliar with the tropical rainforest environment, just listening to the bird, insect and animal sounds, smelling the rich, intoxicating air, marvelling at the sheer size of the dipterocarp trees and peering into the **rainforest canopy** is bound to be a memorable experience. There's a myriad of entrancing sights: flowering lianas, giant bamboo stands with fungi which glow in the dark and chattering **macaque monkeys** rattling across the treetops. A few dozen nomadic Batek Orang Asli, a subgroup of the Negritos, remain in the area; most are hunters and gatherers (the park authorities generally turn a blind eye to their hunting game here), though some work at the *Taman Negara Resort*, the park headquarters. You may pass the Asli's vine and forest-brush shelters, built to stand only for a few days before the inhabitants move on again – but you'll seldom see the people themselves.

The undoubted success of the Taman Negara – over sixty thousand people a year now visit the park – brings its own problems. According to some Malaysian environmentalists, the increasing number of visitors is having an impact on the park's ecosystem: the popular trail to Gunung Tahan is suffering accelerated **erosion** due to the large number of hikers; furthermore, some of them leave rubbish on the route, littering a formerly pristine environment. Also of concern is the effect on the biological food chain of the gradual migration of large mammals from the noisy Kuala Tahan area around the resort.

The best time to **visit** the park is between February and October, during the so-called dry season, although it still rains most days even then; at other times of year, there can be restrictions on the trails and boat trips. Those who want a tranquil, at-one-with-nature experience may well not take to the village of **Kuala Tahan** (the settlement just across the river from the park headquarters; see p.216) and would be better advised to stay upstream at **Nusa Camp** (see p.219), which is smaller and more basic, though not nearly as convenient. Alternatively head straight for the upriver camps at **Kuala Keniam** and **Kuala Trenggan**, or camp at one of the twelve designated sites dotted around the park.

Routes to the park

The vast majority of visitors take a bus to **Tembeling jetty** (see p.216), from where it's a three-hour boat trip (there are two departures of motorized sampans daily at 9am and 2pm, though the second departure is at 2.30pm on Fri) up Sungei Tembeling to the park headquarters at **Kuala Tahan**; details of the boat journey are given on p.216. The **jungle railway** (see p.230) makes two stops in the vicinity of the jetty, the closer of which is at **Kuala Tembeling** (tell the guard if you want to get out here as it's an unscheduled stop), a half-hour walk from the jetty (there's no public transport from here to the jetty). Nor is there accommodation at Kuala Tembeling – those who arrive too late to catch the boats stay the night in **Jerantut** (see overleaf), also served by the train. It's possible to **drive** to Jerantut via the road which leads north off Route 2 east of Mentakab (see overleaf), or via Route 64, which heads east off Route 8 (see p.229); however, the road from Jerantut to Kuala Tahan isn't fully surfaced, and shouldn't be attempted in wet conditions without a four-wheel-drive. Onward routes from Jerantut to the park are covered fully on p.215.

Though the times we list for the jungle railway were correct at time of writing, it's particularly important on this route to check the latest details, including the times of connecting trains, with KTMB (☎03/273 8000, fax 273 6527, *passenger@ktmb.com.my*) before you travel.

From KL

A shuttle **bus** to the Tembeling jetty (daily departures at 8am; RM25) leaves from KL's *Istana Hotel* (see p.90), where there's also a **booking office** for the *Taman Negara Resort*. You don't need to be staying at the resort to use this bus (tickets for which can be bought from many of the hostels in KL), which arrives at the jetty in time for the 2pm boat departures. You can also take a bus to Jerantut (RM9) from KL's Pekeliling station (see p.86), which leaves six times a day for the three-hour trip. The 7am and 8am buses from KL get you to Jerantut in time to catch the 11am bus (around RM3) to the jetty, leaving you with a long wait for the 2pm boats. For more details on how to reach the park via Jerantut, see below.

There are no scheduled **flights** into the park, though Kris Air (☎03/746 5210) operates irregular services between KL and the **Sungei Tiang airstrip** (RM190 return), from where Kuala Tahan is a further thirty minutes north by boat (around RM80).

BY JUNGLE TRAIN VIA MENTAKAB OR GEMAS
Though slow in comparison with the shuttle bus from KL, the **jungle railway** is the most atmospheric way to get to the Tembeling jetty for Taman Negara. The most common approach to the jungle train from KL is to take a bus to **MENTAKAB**, a small town on the Kuantan Highway (Route 2), less than 100km east of KL and about 100km south of Kuala Tahan. Buses run to Mentakab twice an hour from KL's Pudu Raya terminus; the trip takes two-and-a-half hours. Once in Mentakab, head for the train station by walking south from the bus station onto the main road, Jalan Temerloh, and bearing left for 50m to a big junction; you then turn right, go another 200m and watch for a narrow road on your right, signed to the train station – a fifteen-minute walk.

Although it's unlikely you'll want to stay in Mentakab if you're heading north, you might need to heading south, as one of the four daily southbound trains here arrives at 10.12pm, another around 1.30am. There are numerous budget **hotels** on Jalan Temerloh, of which the cleanest is the *London Café and Hotel*, 71 Jalan Temerloh (☎09/277 1119; ②), which has neat, basic doubles with attached bathrooms. A few doors away on a side street leading south is the *Hotel Hoover*, 25 Jalan Moh Hee Kiang (☎09/277 1622; ①) which has smaller doubles than the *London*, but reduces prices a little for single occupancy (unlike the *London*). A little closer to the bus station is the *Hotel Mentakab*, 60 Jalan Temerloh (☎09/277 1275; ②), an ugly concrete block with dingy corridors but reasonable, clean, large rooms on a par with the *Hoover*. For food, there are a few decent *kedai kopi*s near the bus station.

Those who prefer to do as much of their journey by train as possible can catch a train from KL south to **Gemas** to connect with the 2.20am jungle train, which gets to Jerantut at 5.30am and Kuala Tembeling thirty minutes later. This leaves plenty of time to walk the 2km west to the jetty for the 9am boats – there are unlikely to be any taxis as this is a very remote stop. The total fare for the train trip from KL to Kuala Tembeling is around RM12.

From the east coast
From **Kota Bharu** (see p.253), you can catch one of the three daily trains from **Wakaf Bharu**, 7km away (see p.262); these take about five hours to reach Kuala Tembeling and a further half-hour to get to Jerantut. The 8.10am departure should get you to Kuala Tembeling in time for the 2pm boats to Kuala Tahan; if the train is more than about half an hour late though, you'll miss the connection and have to spend the night in Jerantut. The 3.50pm from Wakaf Bharu arrives at Jerantut at around 9.25pm, the 7.25pm at 12.40am. **From Kuantan**, two daily buses (8am & noon; RM12) go straight to Jerantut, or there's an hourly service to Temerloh (see p.246), where you change for Jerantut (usually within the hour).

Jerantut
A small, busy town, **JERANTUT** has one major street, Jalan Besar, lined with Chinese cafés and houses. From the **bus station**, where the buses arrive from KL and Kuantan, it's a five-minute walk south to Jalan Besar and the centre of town; the **train station** is off Jalan Besar, just behind *Hotel Sri Emas*.

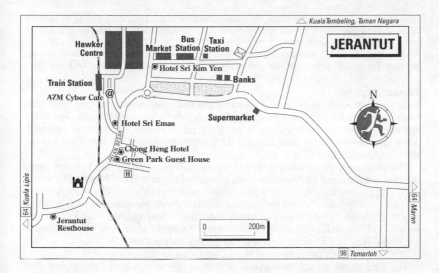

Shared taxis (RM16 per vehicle) and local buses (40min; RM1.20) leave for the **Tembeling jetty** from the bus station; take the 7am bus to be at the jetty in time for the morning boats, or the 11am bus to catch the afternoon boats. Many hostels, the *Sri Emas* and *Green Park* in particular, also organize **minibuses** (daily at 8.30am; 30min; RM4) from Jerantut to the jetty.

You can **bypass the jetty** altogether and take the bus tours (RM23) organized by the management of the *Jerantut Resthouse* and *Sri Emas Hotel*. These leaves Jerantut daily around 7am and include visits to cocoa, oil-palm and rubber plantations on the way to Kuala Tahan, where the tours arrive around 10.30am. These trips are a much faster way to reach the park than using the boats (and cost only a little more), though you miss out on some nice scenery if you do the journey by road.

ACCOMMODATION AND EATING

Jerantut has plenty of good-value **accommodation** and **places to eat**. There are the usual Chinese cafés dotted along the main street, but all are eclipsed by the mighty hawker centre between the train and bus stations, containing stalls and some small restaurants serving Thai, Malay and Chinese food; they're usually open until 3am. Near the train station itself, you'll find Jerantut's only **cybercafé** – the AZM, 4 Jalan Stesen Kertapi, though several of the **places to stay** listed also offer Internet access.

Chong Heng Hotel (Travellers' Inn), 24 Jalan Besar (☎09/266 3693; (RM15)). South of the *Sri Emas*, on the opposite side of the road. The friendliest place in town, it has spotless, inexpensive rooms, a café and an Internet terminal. ①.

Green Park Guest House, Lot 34, Jalan Besar (☎09/266 3884, *greentn@tm.net.my*). There's a dorm and some basic doubles. The owner, Azam Rahman, is a trekking guide who gives a nightly talk on Taman Negara at 8.00pm, and can arrange all manner of trips to the park. ①, dorm beds RM8.

Hotel Sri Emas (☎09/266 4499, fax 266 4801), in the middle of town, at the junction of Jalan Besar and the road which leads to the train station. A large, well-run operation with a wealth of information on Taman Negara. There's a dorm (RM7), some very inexpensive doubles and air-con rooms. In addition, there's a communal hot shower and Internet access. The friendly and helpful managers organize minibuses to the park and give talks at 8.30pm nightly on what you can do in Taman Negara; you can attend these sessions even if you're not staying at the hotel. The downside however, is that you might feel you're staying in a travel agency. ①.

Jerantut Resthouse (☎09/266 6200). One kilometre west of the train station on Jalan Besar. A large, rambling place boasting comfortable dorms and twin-bed chalets with bathrooms at a bewildering range of prices. Good value. ②, dorm beds RM10.

Sri Kim Yen, Lot 1751, Jalan Diwangsa (☎09/266 2168). Conveniently, but noisily, located near the bus stop. The en-suite air-con doubles with bathrooms are better value than at the *Sri Emas*. ②.

Tembeling jetty

From the **Tembeling jetty**, motorized **sampans** make two mass departures to Taman Negara (daily at 9am & 2pm, though Fri afternoon departure is at 2.30pm; 3hr; RM19 one way). Tickets for the boats can be bought at places to stay in Jerantut or on board. A few **speedboats** for the park HQ also depart from the jetty at the same times as the sampans (45min; RM30).

The sheer number of boats departing for the park from Tembeling jetty has made the area something of a mini-bazaar, with a hundred or more visitors waiting for a connection at any one time. At the jetty are a handicraft shop (daily 9am–6pm), three rather expensive cafés (same hours) selling *nasi campur*, noodles and snacks and, up some nearby steps, the *Taman Negara Resort* **ticket office**, where you must buy a park entry permit (RM1) as well as a licence (RM5) if you're taking a camera into the park. To the left of the jetty is a kiosk where you can book accommodation at *Nusa Camp* (see p.219). Boats to both the resort and Nusa Camp leave at the same time.

The sixty-kilometre trip to the park begins on the wide Sungei Pahang, but after 300m or so the sampans branch off into the narrower **Sungei Tembeling**. At first, you'll see huts high up on the bank beside small pepper orchards and oil-palm plantations, but soon the moss-draped trees reach down to the water, the forest canopy thickens, and a dab of brown leaves or a sporadic outbreak of red flowers interrupts the various shades of green. Occasionally white-horned cows and buffalo can be seen wallowing in the water, and birds dart across the bows of the sampan, swooping into the trees. The sampans run to two separate points: the *Taman Negara Resort* – the park headquarters – at Kuala Tahan, and *Nusa Camp*, a private campsite 2km further northeast, outside the park boundary on the east side of Sungei Tembeling.

The park: arrival, information and transport

The park entrance is at the village of **KUALA TAHAN**, situated at the confluence of the Tahan and Tembeling rivers. Arriving **by boat**, after disembarking at the jetty you climb the steps to the *Taman Negara Resort* office, where you sign in. Arriving in Kuala Tahan **by road**, you'll need to get across the river to reach the park office – just wait for one of the "umbrella boats", which go back and forth across the river all day (see opposite An excellent site and park **map** is available at the office for no charge – and if you are staying in a resort chalet, you'll also get a glossy brochure giving details about the park and listing the on-site facilities. The information desk in the office deals with queries from all park visitors, regardless of where you're staying.

Most of the **chalets** lie east of the *Taman Negara Resort* office; there's also accommodation in the village itself. Just along the path which runs through the chalets, there's the **hostel**, a small library and annexe – where slide shows about the park take place every day at 8.45pm. The **library** (daily 9am–11pm) has a diverse selection of geographical journals and accounts of the park; the slide show gives an entertaining, if out-of-date, rundown of the park's main features. Behind the office is the official **Parks and Wildlife Department** headquarters and a **shop**, selling basic provisions. The path beside the shops leads up some steps to the **campsite**, where another office rents out everything you'll need for trekking and camping, including backpacks and lightweight jungle boots. You can also store your luggage at this office (RM1 per day).

LEAVING THE PARK

Most people **leave the park** the way they came, by boat down Sungei Tembeling – book your seat at the resort office or at any of Kuala Tahan's floating restaurants, unless you're staying at *Nusa Camp*, which has its own Tembeling jetty-bound boat. You can also take the **minibus** back to Jerantut from Kuala Tahan – it's best to make a booking at the *Teresek View* (see p.219), or at the floating *Family Restaurant*.

For the more adventurous, there are two **treks** which lead out of the park. One route heads upstream on Sungei Tembeling and then branches off east into the jungle through Terengganu State; the other leaves the Gunung Tahan trail at the Padang and heads west out of the park to Merapoh in Kelantan, a village which is accessible by jungle railway and Route 8.

THE TERENGGANU ROUTE
To reach **Terengganu State** you'll need to take the sampan up Sungei Tembeling to the start of the trail at Kampung Besar, on the east bank of the river (around RM70; 4hr). You should hire a guide (around RM100) up to the beginning of the trail (or at least make sure that the boatman knows where to drop you), and bring camping gear and food for two days. After around four-hours' walk on the trail from Kampung Besar, there's a site where you can make camp, and the next day continue west for another six hours until you reach a laterite road. Going east on this road, you'll arrive at a small kampung, where you can camp overnight, and the next day get a bus out to the south–north Highway 14 (Kuantan to Kuala Terengganu).

THE KELANTAN ROUTE
The route to **Kelantan** is reached from the Gunung Tahan trail – you will need a guide to get you onto the trail, which runs west-northwest before joining a four-wheel-drive track to **Merapoh**, two day's walk from the Tahan trail's Padang Camp (see p.226).

Transport
Transport around the park is by sampan, which come in varying sizes depending on the depth of the river. The smaller, lighter craft run along the shallow tributaries like Sungei Tahan and Sungei Tenor, with the more powerful boats used to reach Trenggan and Keniam upriver on Sungei Tembeling. "Umbrella boats" (50 sen) shuttle across the river all day from any one of the floating restaurants on the banks of the village side of the river, opposite the resort entrance.

To **rent a boat** either ask the staff at the *Taman Negara Resort* parks and wildlife office (next to the minimart), who will arrange a trip on your behalf, or – the less expensive option – speak to the boatmen at the jetty, and sort out a price with them. Sampan hire is on a per boat basis (seating four) and prices depend upon the distance travelled. An RM80 one-way fare, for example, will get you as far as the upriver sites such as Kuala Keniam, or to Lata Berkoh on Sungei Tahan. When renting a sampan to the upriver sites, remember to book your return trip at the same time, since the boatmen only operate out of Kuala Tahan and Nusa Camp.

Accommodation and eating

Visitors can **stay** either within the park – at the *Taman Negara Resort, Nusa Camp* or one of several smaller sites – or in Kuala Tahan itself.

THE TAMAN NEGARA RESORT
Accommodation at the *Taman Negara Resort* can be pre-booked in KL, either at MATIC (Malaysian Tourist Information Complex, 109 Jalan Ampang; daily 9am–9pm; ☎03/264

KUALA TAHAN & TAMAN NEGARA RESORT

ACCOMMODATION

Agoh's Chalets	6
Durian	9
Ekotan	5
Tahan	8
Teresek View	7
Liana	3
Riverview	4
Resort Hostel	1
Resort Chalets	2

RESTAURANTS

Family Restaurant	C
Tahan Restaurant	B
Teresek Restaurant	A

Equipment hire & left luggage

Parks and Wildlife Office Shop Library

Interpretative Centre for Slide Show

Sungei Tahan

i Taman Negara Resort Office

Main jetty

Sungei Tembeling

Floating Restaurants

Shop

S. Tembeling

Park Lodge Internet Terminals

0   100m

N

▷ *Bukit Teresek, Canopy Walkway & Tahan Tide*

▽ *Jerantut*

3929) or in the *Hotel Istana* office, Lot 6, second floor, 73 Jalan Raja Chulan (☎03/245 5585, fax 245 5430); alternatively, call the resort direct (☎09/266 3500, fax 266 1500). It's best to book around two weeks in advance of your trip if possible, though if you're planning to camp it isn't necessary to reserve beforehand. The two-storey, two-bedroom **bungalows** are the height of luxury (RM600), with a balcony, a bathroom with a hot shower and a kitchen. Next down in price, the hundred-plus twin-bed **chalets** with bathroom (⑦) are also highly impressive, if a little institutional-looking from the outside, with fiercer aircon than in most expensive hotels. There's no point staying at the hundred-bed **hostel** however: the huge dormitory charges a ridiculous RM40 a head, at least double what you'd pay across the river in the village. Lastly, there is the **campsite** (RM2 per person per day), 300m from the resort office, which looks directly onto the jungle (campers are advised not to leave any food outside their tents otherwise the monkeys will get it). You can rent tents from RM8 a night from the camping shop at the campsite itself.

There are two **places to eat** here. The *Tahan Restaurant* (daily 8am–11pm) charges around RM40 a head, but the buffet is good and worth a splurge. Cheaper, but much more basic, is the *Teresek Cafeteria* (daily 8am–9pm) which serves fried noodles and mixed rice, with free hot water; bring your own tea or coffee.

KUALA TAHAN

The increasing popularity of Taman Negara as a holiday destination has led to a fair bit of development in recent years at Kuala Tahan, and there's a variety of **places to stay**. For **food**, all the floating restaurants here, beside the shingle beach, do set meals of Chinese and Malay food, as well as simple snacks like omelettes, for around RM9 – the best range of dishes is at the *Family Restaurant*, which also organizes tours around the park.

Agoh's Chalets, 35 Taman Chempaka, Jalan Aman (☎ & fax 09/296 7006). Has some very bare doubles in large cottages, with fan and shower; a dorm; and some absurdly priced, cold, brick family rooms sleeping four (RM100). ②, dorm beds RM12.

Durian Chalet (☎09/266 8940, *aafzal@mailcity.com*). To get here, walk east past the *Tahan Guest House*, turn left, go past the mosque and continue on for five minutes. This is the place to get away from it all, a few colourfully painted bamboo weave chalets in a durian garden: peaceful, friendly, and inexpensive. ②.

Ekotan Chalets (☎09/266 9897). Behind the *Riverview*, this is the only mid-range option worth considering, with comfortable – though slightly overpriced – air-con chalets (⑤). There's a dorm (RM15) with comfy bunks, clean sheets and mosquito nets, and another dorm with air-con (RM20).

Liana (☎09/266 9322). This barracks-style corridor of four-bed dorms is lacking in much maintenance and charm, but it's inexpensive and the management are a friendly lot. Dorm beds RM10.

Tahan Guest House (☎09/266 7752). A two-storey building with four-bed dorms on the ground floor and doubles with shower above. It's quieter than the *Teresek*, but the terrace of rooms isn't as private. ②, dorm beds RM10.

Tembeling Riverview Hostel and Chalets (☎ & fax 09/266 6766). The best budget place here, this is an attractive complex of thatched, timber chalets and a café in a garden, with nice river views. The doubles with shower are good value and the two dormitories are the best around by a long shot. ②, dorm beds RM10–12 depending on size of room.

Teresek View Motel (☎09/266 9177, *del_tum@yahoo.com*). The first place you come to as you head up the hill on the east side of town. Has a bit of everything accommodation-wise, as well as restaurant and shop. The four-bed dorms are basic, though you do get mosquito nets; also on offer are rather flimsy chalets with hot water and fan (③), and some poky, brick A-frames with bathrooms (②). Dorm beds RM10.

NUSA CAMP

Far smaller than the resort, **Nusa Camp** is 2km further upstream on the east bank of Sungei Tembeling, outside the park proper. Boats from Tembeling jetty will take you straight there, stopping briefly at Kuala Tahan first. Although accommodation and food here are a little cheaper than at the resort, the disadvantage of staying here is that you are dependent on the sampans to ferry you over the river to the park proper, or down to Kuala Tahan. The costs of these trips does add up, as the boatmen charge around RM5 each way. There aren't any official hikes starting from here, though you can walk to the **Abai waterfall**, on the same side of the river about an hour from the camp, or up the nearby peak of **Gunung Warisan**, two hours' hike from Nusa.

To stay here, it's best to book your **accommodation** in advance at MATIC (☎03/262 7982, fax 262 7682) in KL, or at SPKG Tours (☎09/266 3360, fax 266 4309) in Jerantut, or at the office by the jetty at Kuala Tembeling (☎09/266 3043). The most expensive accommodation here is in the twin-bed "Malay Houses" (⑥), with attached bathrooms; despite the price, the facilities are a lot more basic than the chalets at the resort. The tiny **tepee**-like pyramid buildings (③) have an external toilet and shower; the four-bed dorm rooms cost about RM11 a night. Nusa Camp has one small **cafeteria** (daily 8am–10pm) which does cheap set meals.

OTHER SITES

Accommodation is also available at lodges, hides and campsites throughout the park; these are covered in more detail in the accounts on pp.220–228. The **lodges** upriver at **Kuala Trenggan** (10 beds; RM100) and **Kuala Keniam** (10 beds, RM110), an hour and two hours respectively from Kuala Tahan by sampan, are built along the same lines as the chalets at Kuala Tahan, although they're less luxurious. They should be booked in advance if you're planning to go straight there from the Tembeling jetty; otherwise leave booking until you arrive in Kuala Tahan. There isn't an official campsite at either of these places, though you can pitch your own tents. Along Sungei Keniam in the remote northeast of the park is *Perkai Lodge* (RM15), run by the Parks and Wildlife Department. It's very basic, with just eight beds, and you don't need to book – though you will need to take your own bedding. Trenggan has a **cafeteria**, although stocks of food are usually low unless a group is expected, when a boatful of provisions will be brought in from Kuala Tahan. Staying at *Perkai Lodge*, you have to bring your own food, which you can cook on the rudimentary barbecue at the back of the lodge.

There's an RM5 charge to stay overnight in the various **hides** (see box below) dotted around the park; you have to reserve a place at the resort office in Kuala Tahan as each can only accommodate four to six people. Although you don't need to reserve a spot at any of the twelve **campsites**, check with the Parks and Wildlife Department office as to which are actually open, since they're rotated to avoid overuse. All the campsites, with the exception of the one at Kuala Tahan, have no facilities whatsoever – you'll even have to take your own bottled water.

Inside the park

Essential places to visit close to the resort include the steep hike up nearby **Bukit Teresek**; the **canopy walkway**, where you can observe jungle life close up; and **Gua Telinga**, a large limestone cave. These places and activities are among the most frequented in the park because of their proximity to Kuala Tahan (indeed you could do all three quite feasibly in a day); with three days to spare, your itinerary could also include a guid-

---

THE HIDES

Spending a night in one of the park's six **hides** (known as *bumbun*s) doesn't guarantee sightings of large mammals, especially in the dry season when the **salt licks** – where plant-eating animals come to supplement their mineral intake – are often so waterless that there's little reason for deer, tapir, elephant, leopard or *seladang* (wild ox) to visit. But it's an experience you're unlikely to forget. Not only are the hides at the very roughest end of the accommodation scale – the mattresses are sometimes sodden and not without the odd flea, there's a simple chemical toilet and no washing or cooking facilities – but you're deep in the jungle with only a torch (an indispensable item) for illumination.

It's best to go in a group and take turns keeping watch, listening hard and occasionally shining the **torch** at the salt lick – if an animal is present its eyes will reflect brightly in the torch beam. Many people leave scraps of food below the hide, although environmentalists disapprove since this interferes with the animals' naturally balanced diet. As well as a torch, take rain gear, hat and sleeping bag, and all the food and drink you will need – and bring all your rubbish back for proper disposal at the resort. You have to book your bunk in the hide at the wildlife office, next to the supermarket in the resort. For a full rundown of the wildlife you might see from the hides, turn to Contexts, p.637.

There are four hides north of the *Taman Negara Resort* and two to the south. Of the northern ones, the closest is the seven-bed **Bumbun Tahan** which is situated just south of the junction with the Bukit Teresek trail. However, much more promising are the seven-bed **Bumbun Tabing**, on the east bank of Sungei Tahan (see "Bukit Teresek", p.222, for directions), and the seven-bed **Bumbun Cegar Anjing**, an hour further and slightly to the south, on the west bank of Sungei Tahan, beside the old airstrip. It is reached by fording the river, but in the wet season is only accessible by boat as the river's too powerful to wade across. The most distant hide to the north of the resort is the six-bed **Bumbun Kumbang**, an eleven-kilometre walk from Kuala Tahan, which, because of its remote location, is the best place to catch sight of animals. Recent boat access to Kuala Terenggan (45min) however means that you now only have to hike for 45min after being dropped off to reach the hide. As visitor numbers increase, animals are likely to move further away.

To the south, there's the six-bed **Bumbun Belau** on the Gua Telinga trail, and beyond the cave, the seven-bed **Bumbun Yong**, at either of which there's only a small chance of spotting wildlife as the hides are quite close both to the traffic on Sungei Tembeling and the resort's vast electricity generator – the combination of these noises has frightened most animals away.

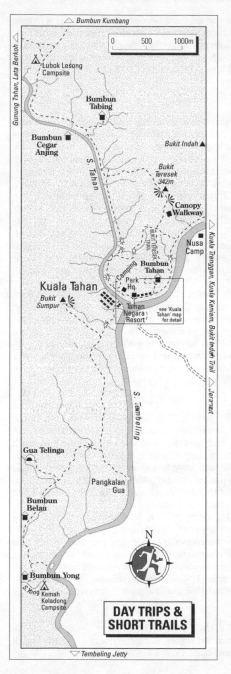

△ Bumbun Kumbang

0   500   1000m

Gunung Tahan, Lata Berkoh

△ Lubok Lesong
Campsite

Bumbun
Tabing ■

Bumbun ■
Cegar
Anjing

Bukit Indah ▲

S. Tahan

Bukit
Teresek
342m ▲

Canopy
■ Walkway

BUKIT TERESEK TRAIL

Nusa
Camp

Kuala Trenggan, Kuala Keniam, Bukit Indah Trail   △ Jerantut

Camping

Bumbun
Tahan ■

Kuala Tahan

Park
Hq.

Bukit ▲
Sumpur

Taman
Negara
Resort

see 'Kuala
Tahan' map
for detail

S. Tembeling

Gua Telinga ■

Pangkalan
Gua

Bumbun ■
Belau

N

Bumbun Yong ■

S. Yong   △ Kemah
Keladong
Campsite

**DAY TRIPS &
SHORT TRAILS**

▽ Tembeling Jetty

ed forest walk, or a night in one of several **hides** (see box, opposite). These are positioned deep in the jungle overlooking salt licks, where you can spy animals drinking the brackish water.

To get into truly undisturbed forest you really need to stay for a week or more. On a week's visit, for example, you could start with the thirty-kilometre **Rentis Tenor trail**, a lasso-shaped trek leading west from Kuala Tahan to Gua Telinga, then northwest into deep forest to the campsite at Sungei Tenor, where you stay in a small clearing beside a river. Back at base, you could hire a boat (RM140 for four persons) to take you upriver to Kuala Keniam, visit *Perkai Lodge*, walk along the wild **Keniam trail** (where elephants are sometimes spotted), and spend the night in a hide at Kumbang before taking a sampan from Kuala Trenggan back to park headquarters. Unless the park is very busy, you're unlikely to see more than a handful of people on these trails.

The most adventurous activity of all is the seven-day, 55-kilometre **trek to Gunung Tahan**; for this you must plan to be in the park at least nine days, and all groups have to be accompanied by a guide from the Parks and Wildlife Department. The trail involves **crossing Sungei Tahan** numerous times – quite a challenge if the waters have been swollen by rain – and some **steep climbing** towards the end. One of the chief thrills of the route is that it passes through various types of terrain, from lowland jungle to cloudforest, before reaching the 2187-metre summit.

The account of the park below is divided into three sections: day-trips that you can make from Kuala Tahan, longer trails – the Rentis Tenor and Gunung Tahan – which require a certain commitment, and trips made from the upriver sites at Trenggan and Keniam. For some treks you'll require specific equipment and resources, which are detailed where appropriate. None of the trails themselves, however, require any special skills, nor do they demand anything beyond an average level of fitness. Whether you're going on a day-hike or a longer trail, you should **inform park staff** first, so they know where you are if you get into any difficulty – despite the trails being well marked, people do sometimes hurt themselves tripping over tree roots or lose their way. There's a map showing the area around Kuala Tahan on p.221, and a map of the whole park on p.225.

Day-trips

From Kuala Tahan, there are various **day-trips** involving **trail walking, river and waterfall excursions** and **hide visits**. T-shirts, long trousers and strong sports shoes (although hiking boots are better) are adequate, and you should always have a hat for protection from the sun, mosquito repellent and water to hand. It's a good idea to take **binoculars** to get the best possible look at birds from the jungle floor, while a **magnifying glass** can open up a whole new world of insects and leaf and bark formations.

The *Lia* floating restaurant in Kuala Tahan operates **rubber-tubing trips** (2.30pm; 2hr; RM25) that are very good fun: a boat takes you upriver towards Trenggan and lets you coast all the way down over five gentle rapids. It's still a relaxing way to see the jungle, despite the increased amount of boat traffic these days. Similar in concept, though far less interesting, are their "rapids shooting" trips, essentially a boat trip to Trenggan lodge and back with the motors on all the time; these will leave you wishing you'd hung onto your RM25. The resort can organize rafting trips down the Tahan river (RM35), though it isn't exactly white water.

The **night jungle walks** (9.30pm; 1hr 30min; RM15; bookings and departures from the resort reception) are fun if you like insects and fauna – the informative guides take groups of about ten on a spooky hike, pointing out the odd scorpion, luminous fungus and medicinal plant. You should return just in time for the last boat back to Kuala Tahan, though it's worth asking your guide beforehand to make sure of this. On the so-called **night safaris** (RM25), booked at the same desk or at the floating restaurants, you're very unlikely to spot many elephants and tigers from a jeep, but you'll see a lot of startled buffaloes.

BUKIT TERESEK

Although undoubtedly the most heavily used trail in the park, the route to **Bukit Teresek** (which also leads on to Bukit Indah; see below) is an excellent starter, and enables you to acclimatize to the heat and humidity. You start by following the path which weaves between the chalets east of the resort office, beyond which a trail heads northeast away from the river. It's wide and easy to follow, hitting **primary jungle** almost immediately; most of the tree types for around 500m along the way have been labelled. After around twenty minutes the trail divides, straight on to Bukit Teresek and left for the Tabing hide (see box, p.220) and Bukit Indah.

The climb up **Bukit Teresek** – a 342-metre hill – is best negotiated early in the morning, before 8am, while it's still relatively cool. Along the trail you might hear **gibbons** or **hill squirrels** in the trees; the **monkeys** are relentless pursuers of any type of food, so keep it out of sight. It takes about one hour at an even pace to reach the top, where there's a shelter set on exposed sandstone. The views from here north over the valley to Gunung Tahan and Gunung Perlis (1279m) are marvellous. Back at the base of the hill, the canopy walkway is just 300m to the north along a clearly marked, springy path crisscrossed by slippery tree roots.

THE BUKIT INDAH TRAIL AND THE CANOPY WALKWAY

About thirty minutes' walk northeast from the resort, along the riverside **Bukit Indah trail**, is the **canopy walkway** (daily 11am–3pm, except Fri 9am–2.45pm; RM5). At any one time only a small group of people can gain access to the walkway, so you're often likely to have to wait at the start. Taking around thirty minutes to negotiate, the walkway is a 450-metre swaying bridge made from aluminium ladders bound by rope, supported at twenty- to sixty-metre intervals by 250-year-old tualang trees. Set 30m above the ground, it's reached by climbing a sturdy wooden tower; you return to terra firma by another wooden stairwell at the end of the third section. Once you've got used to the walkway's swaying, it's a pleasurable experience taking in the fine views of Sungei Tembeling and observing the insect life and tree parasites which abound at this height. Geckos, cicadas, crickets and grasshoppers hop and fly about, often landing on the walkway before leaping back onto a branch or leaf. Other species usually visible include the grey-**banded leaf monkey**, with a call that sounds like a rattling tin can, and the white-eyed **dusky leaf monkey**, with its deep, nasal "ha-haw" cry; both lope about in groups of six to eight.

Past the canopy the route divides, with one branch leading north and slightly uphill to the Tabing hide, another 1km further on. The other goes northeast, heading marginally downhill and cutting back towards Sungei Tembeling along the lovely **Bukit Indah trail**. Initially, this follows the riverbank, and you're bound to see monkeys, plenty of bird life, squirrels, shrews, a multitude of insects and (if it's early or late in the day) perhaps tapir or wild ox (*seladang*). The path to Bukit Indah itself leaves the main riverside trail (which continues to Kuala Trenggan, 6km away) and climbs at a slight gradient for 200m; the top of the hill offers a lovely view over Sungei Tembeling. It's a three-kilometre, three-hour return trip from the resort office.

GUA TELINGA AND KEMAH KELADONG

Another major trail leads south alongside the river, with branches off to the limestone outcrop of Gua Telinga, the Belau and Yong hides, and the campsite at Kemah Keladong.

From the jetty by the *Tahan* restaurant, take a sampan across Sungei Tahan. On the other side, follow the trail through a small kampung (where some of the resort and Park and Wildlife Department staff live) into the trees and dense foliage. The undulating trail heads across some steep spurs, traverses magnificent lowland rainforest before it descends to the flat land of the river terrace along Sungei Tembeling. The forest here has a quite different appearance from that on the hill slopes, partly the effect of flooding, notably that of 1926 which devastated extensive areas of forest around Kuala Tahan. After 3km, you follow the sign north for a further 200m to reach **Gua Telinga**. The limestone cave looks small and unassuming, but it's deceptively deep – something you only really discover when you slide through it. Although in theory it's possible to follow a guide rope through the eighty-metre cave, in practice only small adults or children will be able to tug themselves through the narrow cavities. Be warned – most people will have to crawl along dark narrow passages in places, and negotiate areas of deep, squishy guano. Thousands of tiny roundleaf and fruit bats reside in the cave, as well as giant toads, black-striped frogs and whip spiders (which aren't poisonous). You're most likely to see the roundleaf bats, so called because of the shape of the "leaves" of skin around their nostrils, which help direct the sound signals transmitted to assist the bat in navigation.

From Gua Telinga, it's another 1km to the Belau hide through beautiful tall forest, and another kilometre to that at Yong (for both, see box on p.220), where the trail divides, north to Kemah Rentis (see p.227) and southeast to the tranquil **Keladong campsite**, 500m further on, on the terraced bank of Sungei Yong. With an early start, it's quite possible to reach this point, have a swim in the river, and get back to the resort before dusk, but bring at least a litre of water per person and a packed lunch.

LATA BERKOH

Most people visit the "roaring rapids" of **Lata Berkoh** by boat, as it's an eight-kilometre, three-hour trip on foot. You could, however, walk the trail there and arrange for a boat to pick you up for the return journey, getting the best of both worlds.

Sampans to the rapids leave from the jetty at Kuala Tahan (around RM80 per boat-load of four; 30min), heading upstream on Sungei Tahan, the busiest of the park's tributaries. The jetty at the other end is just 100m from the rudimentary *Berkoh Lodge*, a small building set back from the river in a clearing. If you're intending to sleep here, first check on space with the Parks and Wildlife Department office in Kuala Tahan, and bring your own bedding and food – mattresses and a barbecue frame are provided. On the opposite bank is the Melantai **campsite** (see also "The Gunung Tahan trail" below); you can ford the river to reach this most of the year, but in the rainy season you'll have to use the trail which runs from the *Taman Negara Resort*.

The **waterfall** itself is 50m north of the lodge. There's a deep pool for swimming, and the rocks overlooking the swirling water are ideal for a picnic. If you ask the boatman to cut his engine, you'll improve your chances of hearing the sounds of the forest, and of seeing kingfishers with their yellow-and-red wings and white beaks, large grey-and-green fish eagles, multicoloured *bulbul* birds and, on the rocks, camouflaged monitor lizards.

The **trail** from the resort to Lata Berkoh starts at the campsite and leads through dense rainforest, past the turning for the Tabing hide to the east. After around 3km you reach the campsite at **Lubok Lesong**, just to the left of which there's a broad, pebbled beach leading down to a deep pool in Sungei Tahan. The route to the waterfall veers west from the main trail around thirty minutes' walk beyond the campsite, crossing gullies and steep ridges before reaching the river, which must be forded. The final part of the trail runs north along the west side of Sungei Tahan before reaching the falls.

Longer trails

The two main long trails in the park are the eight-day trek to **Gunung Tahan** and back, and the four-day, circular **Rentis Tenor** trail, which reaches the beautiful Sungei Tenor before dipping back east. For either, you'll need loose-fitting, lightweight cotton clothing with long sleeves, long trousers to keep insects at bay, a raincoat or waterproof poncho, and a litre bottle of water (plus water-purifying equipment or tablets). Also take a tent, a powerful torch, cooking equipment and a compass, all of which can be rented from the resorts' camping shop, where you can also buy a map and spare batteries; check with your guide or the resort office as to how much food you'll need to take. For Gunung Tahan you also need a sleeping bag for the two nights spent at a high-altitude camp. To keep out the leeches – a serious problem after heavy rain – wear walking boots or sports shoes, with your trousers tucked into heavy-duty socks, and spray on insect repellent liberally every hour or so. The Orang Asli approach is to go barefoot and flick off the leeches as they begin to bite, but this requires an advanced jungle temperament.

Perhaps the most important advice on all long-distance trails is to know your limitations and not run out of time. Slipping and sliding along in the dark is no fun and can be dangerous – it's easy to fall at night and impossible to spot snakes or other forest-floor creatures which might be on the path.

THE GUNUNG TAHAN TRAIL

The 55-kilometre trek to Peninsular Malaysia's highest peak, **Gunung Tahan** (2187m), is the highlight of any adventurous visitor's stay in Taman Negara – but you have to allow at least nine days to accomplish it: seven to complete the trek and one day either side to get in and out of the park. Although in peak season hundreds of people trudge along the trail every week, the sense of individual achievement after fording Sungei Tahan dozens of times, hauling yourself up and down innumerable hills and camping out every night – let alone the final, arduous ascent – is supreme. Not for nothing do successful hikers proudly display their "I climbed Gunung Tahan" T-shirts.

To the indigenous inhabitants of the region, the Batek Orang Asli, Gunung Tahan is the **Forbidden Mountain**; in their folklore the summit is the home of a vast monkey,

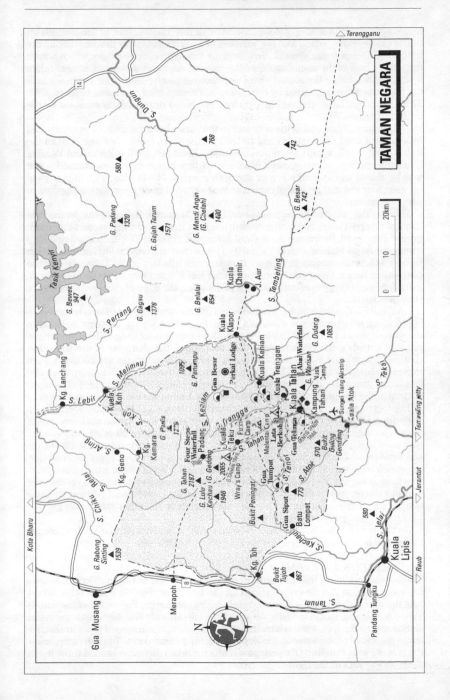

who stands guard over magic stones. Because of this, they venture to the foothills on hunting expeditions, to find wild pig, monkey or squirrel, but rarely head further up the mountain. To reach the summit, you have to follow precarious ridges which weave around the back of the mountain, since the most obvious approach from Sungei Tahan would involve scaling the almost sheer one-thousand-metre-high Teku gorge – which the first expedition, organized by the Sultan of Pahang, tried and failed to do in 1863. The summit was finally reached in 1905 by a combined British–Malay team led by the explorer Leonard Wray.

The Gunung Tahan trail is the only one in the park where you must be accompanied by a **guide** (hiring one costs around RM500 for the seven days), although in truth the trail is easy to follow with a compass and map. Head first for the Parks and Wildlife Department office, where you can discover if a trek has already been planned – you may be able to join up with a group, and split the cost. Most trekkers go in groups of between four and ten; groups of twelve or more have to take two guides, according to park regulations.

The first day involves an easy six-hour walk to **Melantai**, the campsite on the east bank of Sungei Tahan, across the river from Lata Berkoh. On the second day more ground is covered, the route taking eight hours and crossing 27 hills, including a long trudge up Bukit Malang ("unlucky hill"). This section culminates at **Gunung Rajah** (576m), before descending to **Sungei Puteh**, a tiny tributary of the Tahan. Before the campsite at **Kuala Teku** you'll ford the Tahan half a dozen times – if the river's high, extra time and energy is spent following paths along the edge of the river, crossing at shallower spots.

On the third day you climb from 168m to 1100m in seven hours of steady, unrelenting trekking which takes you up onto a ridge. Prominent among the large trees along the ridge is *seraya*, with a reddish-brown trunk, as well as oaks and conifers, but the *seraya* thin out when the ridge turns to the west. Here, the character of the landscape changes dramatically to montane oak forest where elephant tracks are common. Park experts believe that elephants live around this point, where the forest is more open and less dense than lower down, but still rich enough in foliage to provide food. The night is spent at the Gunung Tahan base camp, **Wray's Camp**, named after Leonard Wray.

The fourth day's trek takes six hours of hard climbing along steep gullies, ending up at **Padang Camp**, on the Tangga Lima Belas ridge, sited on a plateau sheltered by tall trees. The summit is now only two-and-a-half hours away, through open, hilly ground with knee-high plants, exposed rocks, and peaty streams, which support thick shrubs and small trees. Weather conditions up the mountain can't be relied upon: the moss forest, which ranges from 1500m to 2000m, is often shrouded in cloud, which can be present even at the top. The trail follows a ridge into the moss forest and soon reaches the **summit** where, provided it's clear, there's a stupendous view, around 50km in all directions. It's a pristine environment: pitcher plants, orchids and other rare plants grow in the crevices and gullies of the summit.

On the return trip, the fifth night is spent back at the Padang, the sixth at Sungei Puteh, and by the end of day seven you're back at Kuala Tahan.

TO FOUR-STEPS WATERFALL
The seven-day (50km) trail to **Four-Steps Waterfall**, east of Gunung Tahan, follows the same route as that described above for the first three days. At Kuala Teku, hikers take the right fork instead, which after eight hours of following the course of the Sungei Tahan reaches the foot of the falls. Although the falls are only 30m high, their gorgeous setting makes the trek worthwhile: flat stones by the path are a good point to rest, listen to the sound of the water and look out for birds and monkeys. You can camp below the falls at **Pasir Panjang** (Panjang pass), which can be reached in around three hours along a clear path to the right of the falls.

THE RENTIS TENOR TRAIL
The other major long-distance trail is the four-day, thirty-kilometre, circular **Rentis Tenor**, which leads south to Sungei Yong, then northwest to the campsite at Kemah Rentis and southeast back to Kuala Tahan. The initial route is the same as that to Gua Telinga (see p.223), bearing north at the Yong hide (2hr from the resort), before following the course of Sungei Yong and reaching the campsite at **Kemah Yong**, just under 10km from the resort. Two hundred metres south of the campsite a side trail leads off to the left to **Bukit Guling Gendang** (570m), a steep, ninety-minute climb best undertaken in the morning, after a good night's rest. From the top, there's a lovely view north to Gunung Tahan, west to Gua Siput and beyond that to Bukit Penyengat (713m), the highest limestone outcrop in Peninsular Malaysia. Towards the summit the terrain changes from lowland tropical to montane forest, where tall conifer trees allow light to penetrate to the forest floor and **squirrels** predominate, with the black giant and cream giant the main species. Both are as big as the domestic cat, their call varying from a grunt to a machine-gun burst of small squeaks.

On day three the main trail continues on into the upper catchment of Sungei Yong, then over a low saddle into the catchment of Sungei Rentis. The path narrows through thick forest alongside the river, crossing it several times, until it joins **Sungei Tenor** three hours later. Here there is a remote and beautiful clearing, **Kemah Rentis**, beside the river, where you camp. It's a fifteen-kilometre hike back to the resort from here; some trekkers go easy and spend a fourth night at **Kemah Lameh** (4km from Kemah Rentis) or the **Lubok Lesong** campsite (8km from Kemah Rentis) on Sungei Tahan.

As for the trail itself from Sungei Tenor, follow the river downstream through undulating terrain to the rapids at **Lata Keitiah** (which takes around 1hr), beyond which another tributary stream, Sungei Lameh, enters the Tenor. You're now in lowland open forest where walking is fairly easy; after four hours the trail leads to **Bumbun Cegar Anjing** (another possible overnight stop) from where it's 3km back to the resort.

Trenggan, Keniam and Perkai lodges

The **upriver lodges** are excellent bases for exploring less visited parts of the park. The boat journey here along the rapid-studded **Sungei Tembeling** is exciting, while the lodges are set in tranquil surroundings, various hikes into which take in visits to caves, and bird-watching and fishing areas.

The lodge at **KUALA TRENGGAN**, 11km upstream from *Taman Negara Resort*, can be reached either by boat, which takes less than an hour, or by one of two trails, which take between six and eight hours. The shorter and more direct trail (9km) runs alongside Sungei Tembeling on a well-trodden, lowland forest path which can be quite hard going; the easier inland route (12km) runs north past the campsite at Lubok Lesong, bearing right into dense forest where elephant tracks may be seen, and then crosses the narrow Sungei Trenggan 500m to the north, to reach the lodge. The **river trip** costs around RM80 per boat; on the way, look out for water buffalo on the east bank of the river. **Trenggan Lodge** itself (10 beds; RM100) – a collection of wooden chalets – is partially hidden by forest on a bend in the river; there's a small café in the largest chalet, an elevated building with a veranda.

A further 20km north along Sungei Tembeling is **KUALA KENIAM** (2hr from the resort; RM140 per boat), where there's a ten-bed lodge (RM110; must be booked as a whole) and a campsite. From here, you could hike the three-kilometre **Perkai trail** along Sungei Perkai (which cuts away from Sungei Tembeling, 200m north of the lodge). The trail, which runs roughly parallel to the river, leads to *Perkai Lodge*, a popular spot for fishing and bird-spotting; in places it's possible to leave the main path and find a way down to the water. This far from Kuala Tahan, the region is rich in wildlife, including banded and dusky leaf monkeys, long-tailed macaques and white-handed gibbons, all of which are relatively easy to spot, especially with binoculars. As for big mammals, elephants certainly roam in these parts and park staff say there are tigers too, though there hasn't been a sighting for several years. Smaller animals like tapirs, civets and deer are best seen at night or early in the morning.

The trail ends at a small clearing on the river's edge, where **Perkai Lodge**, with its eight bunk beds, stands. The lodge doesn't have any resident staff (unlike the ones at Trenggan and Keniam), so you must bring food, drink and bedding if you intend to stay; it does, however, have a barbecue area and some crockery out the back. Though very few people use the lodge, you still need to book with the wildlife office at the resort.

THE KENIAM–TRENGGAN TRAIL

After Gunung Tahan, the thirteen-kilometre **Keniam–Trenggan trail** is the great highlight of the park, combining the possibility of seeing elephants with visits to three caves, one of which is big enough for an army to camp in. It's generally a full day's hike, but in dry conditions can be covered in around six hours. Some people take two days instead, pitching a tent either in one of the caves or on a stretch of clear ground near a stream – there aren't any designated campsites in this remote corner of the park. The trail is a tough one, with innumerable streams to wade through, hills to circumvent, and trees blocking the path.

The trail cuts southwest from *Keniam* lodge along a narrow, winding path through dense forest dominated by huge *meranti* trees with red-brown fissured bark. It's two hours before you enter limestone-cave country, first reaching **Gua Luas** which, though it doesn't have a large internal cavity, is impressive nonetheless. One hundred metres south is **Gua Daun Menari** (Cave of the Dancing Leaves), which does have a large chamber through which the wind blows leaves and other jungle debris. Climb up the side of the cave and you'll see small dark holes leading into the cave chamber where, in the pitch darkness, thousands of roundleaf bats live.

To regain the main trail, go back 50m towards Gua Luas and look for an indistinct path on the left; follow this for another 30m, at which point you should see the main trail ahead. Bear left here – the third cave, **Kepayang Besar**, is around ten minutes' walk further on. This has a very large chamber at the eastern side of the outcrop which is easy to enter and an excellent place to put up a tent. The fourth cave, **Kepayang Kecil**, is the last limestone outcrop on the trail. Here, a line of figs drops a curtain of roots down the rock, behind which lies a small chamber, with a slightly larger one to the right, containing stalactites and stalagmites.

After passing Kepayang Kecil you're about halfway along the trail, but there are plenty more streams to cross, with armies of ants, flies and leeches. The trail is illuminated in places by patches of sunlight highlighting tropical fungi on the trees and plants, though you're soon back in the gloom again. Parts of the path are wide and easy to follow, while other sections are far narrower, passing through tunnels of bamboo. The final two hours comprise more boggy crossings as the trail descends slightly to the Trenggan valley, arriving at *Trenggan Lodge*.

From KL northeast to Kuala Krai

Two routes cut across the interior from KL to the northeast coast: the jungle railway and Route 8. The main points of interest are **Fraser's Hill**, 100km northeast of KL; **Kuala Lipis**, the former tin-mining town and erstwhile capital of Pahang, 170km northeast of KL; the state park at **Kenong Rimba**; the caves at **Gua Musang**; and **Jelawang park**. But the chief reason for making the trip to the northeast coast is to spend time in the forests and sandstone hills of this region, an environment removed from the economic expansion of the west coast and the beach-dominated muggy east coast.

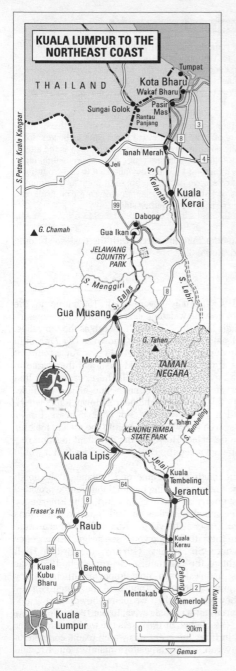

In this lush and rugged region, **Senoi** Orang Asli still lead semi-nomadic lives along inaccessible river basins and in the wide catchment area of the ponderous **jungle railway** (see box, overleaf). The lifestyles of the two main groups, the Temiar and the Semiar, revolve around a combination of shifting cultivation (where there is still enough accessible land left for this to be feasible), the trading of forest products, fishing and animal trapping. The **Temiar** are mountain dwellers, though the Temiar of southern Kelantan sometimes raft timber down Sungei Kelantan to **Kuala Krai**, selling the wood on to Chinese middlemen. Although the Temiar are increasingly exploiting the forest for timber, their logging practices are marginal compared to those of the State Forestry Department. The **Semiar**, in contrast, prefer to live in lowland jungle or flat open country, and there are several Semiar communities close to Merapoh in southern Kelantan.

By road from KL, there are two ways to connect with Route 8. The first involves taking **Route 2** past the Genting Highlands and turning north at Bentong, where Route 8 begins. The second, **Route 55**, leaves Route 1 at the Kuala Kubu Bharu turning and heads northeast past Fraser's Hill, joining Route 8 at Raub. As you proceed further eastwards, the scenery gets ever more spectacular, the road following ridges along the sides of large hills, with small plantations and forests below. Kampungs become fewer and so do the cars.

Further northeast, about 20km south of Kuala Lipis, Route 64 leads east off Route 8 for Jerantut and Taman Negara (see p.212). Beyond Kuala Lipis, **Route 8** heads due north, running parallel with the railway for 100km until it bears east at Gua Musang, meeting the railway again 80km further on at Kuala Krai. The final section of Route 8, onwards

THE JUNGLE RAILWAY

It took indentured Tamil workers eight years to built the five-hundred-kilometre **jungle railway** from Gemas, southeast of KL, to Tumpat on the northeast coast. The line has been in full operation since 1931 (the first section from Gemas to Kuala Lipis was opened in 1920) and much of its rolling stock has not been upgraded since. Initially it was used exclusively for freight – first for tin and rubber, and later for oil palm, before a passenger service opened in 1938.

Originally known as the "Golden Blowpipe", the train is best avoided if you want to cross the interior quickly – it takes fourteen hours to get from Gemas to Kota Bharu, five hours longer than by bus. But as a way of **encountering rural life** it can't be beaten: for the Malays, Tamils and Orang Asli who live in these remote areas, the railway is the only alternative to walking. On the train, your fellow passengers range from cheroot-smoking old men in sarongs to fast-talking women hauling kids, poultry and rice to and from the nearest market. The ancient carriages are always packed to bursting point as the trains rumble through the isolated kampungs of Pahang and Kelantan, crossing iron bridges over wide rivers, with craggy mountains rearing up on either side.

to Kota Bharu on the northeast coast (see p.252), intersects with the east–west Route 4, and later the Kuala Terengganu road, Route 3.

Fraser's Hill

The development at **FRASER'S HILL** (actually seven hills), 1500m up in the Titiwangsa mountain range, was built to provide welcome relief for the British expatriate community from the humidity of Kuala Lumpur, 75km to the south as the crow flies. The seven hills which comprise the hill station were originally known as *Ulu Tras*, until the arrival in the 1890s of a solitary British pioneer, called James Fraser. An accountant by profession, he travelled to Australia at the peak of its gold rush and then came to Malaya. Although gold wasn't found in any quantity in the hills here, Fraser did find plentiful **tin** deposits. The tin was excavated by Chinese miners and hauled by mule, along a perilous hill route down through thick jungle, to the nearest town, Raub, where Fraser set up a camp and a gambling den for his workers. But after 25 years, Fraser mysteriously disappeared, and when a search party trekked up into the area to look for him in 1917, the camp and mines were deserted. However, the excellent location recommended itself to the party, who soon convinced the British authorities that it would make a perfect **hill station**.

Fraser Hill was never as popular as the much larger Cameron Highlands to the north (see p.135), and feels remote even today. The surrounding mountainous jungle provided perfect cover for some of the communist guerrillas' secret camps during the Emergency in the 1950s (see p.209), from where they launched strikes on British-owned plantations and neighbouring towns. If you head to Fraser's Hill via the Kuala Kubu Bharu route (see opposite), halfway up the road from there to the Gap you'll see a sign, "Emergency Historical Site", marking the spot where **Sir Henry Gurney**, the British High Commissioner for Malaya at the height of the communist insurgency in 1951, was ambushed and killed. The guerrillas hadn't known how important their quarry was; their aim had been only to steal guns, ammunition and food, but when Gurney strode towards them demanding that they put down their weapons, they opened fire.

With the end of the Emergency, the area saw a partial revival in the 1960s. The annual Fraser's Hill International Bird Race, established in 1988, sets the tone for the rather reserved atmosphere here today. Held in June, the event – in which teams compete to sight as many species of birds as they can – attracts visitors mainly from KL, and tourists who don't have the time to visit the state parks. Although it's possible to come here on a day-trip from KL, it's preferable to stay the night at one of the hotels or lodges around the hill station.

Routes via Kuala Kubu Bharu and Raub

To get to Fraser's Hill **from KL**, you need to catch the Kuala Kubu Bharu bus from bay 21 at Pudu Raya bus station (hourly; RM3.80). Aim to leave KL by 9am so as to get to the attractive small town of **Kuala Kubu Bharu**, 50km northeast of KL and 30km from Fraser's Hill, in time to have a quick look round at the sleepy streets and wooden houses before the Fraser's Hill bus leaves at noon. There are two other direct buses there from the town, one at 8am, the other at 2pm; all these services take about an hour to reach Fraser's Hill, usually pausing at the start of **the Gap**, the narrow, twisting one-way road which leads up the final 8km to Fraser's Hill (traffic flow along it changes direction every 40min). If you miss the last direct bus, you'll need to charter a taxi up from the taxi rank at the Kuala Kubu Bharu bus station (RM40). Alternatively, catch the Raub-bound bus (daily at 2.30pm, though it's usually late) and disembark at the junction with the Gap, where there's a resthouse (see below), from where you walk up.

Arriving on buses **from the interior**, which come via Raub, about 30km to the east, you also get off at the junction with the Gap, from where you can either walk up or, if you've arrived early in the day, wait for a bus from Kuala Kubu Bharu at the hotel here, *The Gap Rest House* (☎09/362 2227; ③). Though its colonial-style building is in need of some repair, it has elegant rooms, great views and a fine dining room – not a bad place to stay the night. **RAUB** itself, a gold-mining town which acquired a reputation in the 1950s as one of the main areas sympathetic to the communist guerrillas, is worth a brief stop on your way here or as you head on northeast to Kuala Lipis (see p.234). Overlooking the padang is the two-storey **resthouse**, with clean double rooms (☎09/355 5230; ③) and the 1910 Courthouse and District Office. The bus station is adjacent to the town's main street, where there are several elegant Chinese shophouses.

The hill station and trails

A small row of shops and a clock tower is all that marks the "centre" of the hill station, a small, flattish area surrounded by densely wooded hills, with named trails snaking off on all sides. None of the trails takes more than two hours to cover, so you can walk them all within a couple of days; bear in mind that in wet weather you need to take the standard precautions against leeches (see p.75). The Fraser's Hill Development Corporation was responsible for naming each of the trails, and plans more in the future. They're not always clearly marked, but you're unlikely to get lost. Though the vegetation here isn't primary jungle, and so few mammals are to be seen, Fraser's Hill is particularly renowned for its **birdlife** – look out for flycatchers, woodpeckers and hornbills. There's a more comprehensive account of the region's flora and fauna in the "Wildlife" section of Contexts, p.639.

The two main routes which loop around the hills start along Jalan Genting, which leads north from the clock tower. Along here is the WWF-sponsored **Nature Education Centre** (Wed–Sun 9.30am–5.30pm; ☎09/362 2517, *www.fhnec.cjb.net*), which organizes bird-watching, night walks and seminars on local flora and fauna. Follow Jalan Genting north as it winds up a beautiful hill, and after about ten minutes' walk you come to a fork, just beyond the children's playground. Turn right and you soon reach the *Temerloh Bungalows* (see p.233), from where you can continue along Jalan Lady Maxwell to the Bishop's House, the start of the Bishop's Trail. This uphill route joins the Maxwell trail and takes about an hour, before running into Jalan Kuari. For a longer walk, turn left at the fork after the children's playground and go past *Ye Olde Smokehouse Hotel* to reach the **Jeriau Waterfall**, around 4km (1hr) from the clock

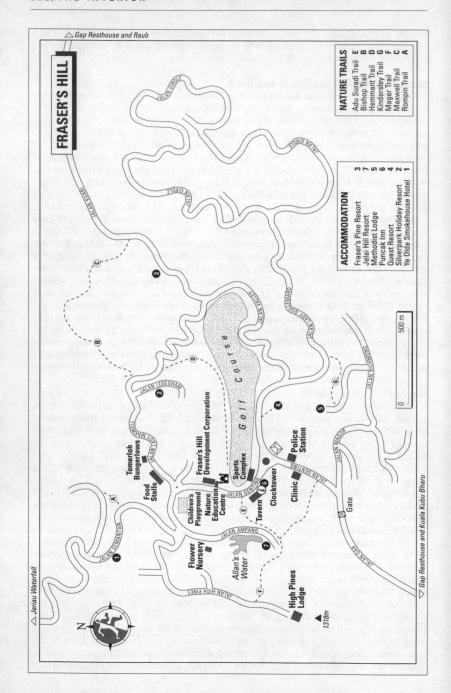

△ Gap Resthouse and Raub

FRASER'S HILL

△ Jeriau Waterfall

▽ Gap Resthouse and Kuala Kubu Bharu

NATURE TRAILS

Adu Suradi Trail	E
Bishop Trail	B
Hemmant Trail	D
Kindersley Trail	G
Mager Trail	F
Maxwell Trail	C
Rompin Trail	A

ACCOMMODATION

Fraser's Pine Resort	3
Jelai Hill Resort	7
Methodist Lodge	5
Puncak Inn	6
Quest Resort	4
Silverpark Holiday Resort	2
Ye Olde Smokehouse Hotel	1

0   500 m

Golf Course

Temerloh Bungerlows

Food Stalls

Fraser's Hill Development Corporation

Sports Complex

Children's Playground

Nature Education Centre

Tavern

Clocktower

Police Station

Clinic

Gate

Flower Nursery

Allan's Water

High Pines Lodge

1318m

JALAN GIROLE

JALAN GIROLE

JALAN GIROLE

JALAN GIROLE

JALAN TUDIH

JALAN GENTING

JALAN LEMARO

JALAN VALLEY

JALAN LEDEGHAM

JALAN MAXWELL

JALAN LADY

JALAN GENTING

JALAN MAGOR

JALAN RICHMOND

JALAN AMPANG

JALAN HIGH PINES

JALAN SEMANTAN

JALAN PAH

N

tower. Next to the waterfall is a concrete-lined swimming area – the water is freezing cold – and tables for picnicking. If you follow the narrow road opposite the turnoff to *Ye Olde Smokehouse Hotel*, you soon reach a flower nursery, and beyond that a small **lake** where you can rent rowing boats (RM4 for 15min).

Probably the most scenic route is to head west from the *Jelai Hill Resort* along the Mager trail to *High Pines Lodge*, which weaves along the side of a hill buzzing with cicadas and flying beetles. After around thirty minutes the trail drops down Jalan High Pines leading to the lodge, which is a good vantage point for bird-spotting.

Another good walk starts at the information office: take Jalan Lady Guillemard east until it joins the loop road, Jalan Girdle. This leads to the most remote section of the hill station, bordering **Ulu Tramin Forest Reserve**, with private bungalows hidden down driveways. Completing the circle, all the way round and back to the information office, takes around ninety minutes.

Practicalities

Right by the clock tower is the Fraser's Hill **information office** (daily 8am–7pm; ☎09/362 2201), where you can pick up a reliable **map** with all the accommodation marked (30 sen), **rent bicycles** (RM4 per hr) and check on the availability of accommodation. Green fees for the nine-hole golf course east of Jalan Genting are RM30 a day during the week and RM40 at the weekend, with an RM15 charge for renting clubs. Outside the *Quest Resort* (see below) is a small branch of Maybank where you can **change money. Buses** to Kuala Kubu Bharu leave at 10am and 4pm; if you're heading east, take the earlier Kuala Kubu bus and ask to be dropped at the Gap, where you can wait at the resthouse for the 3.30pm bus to Kuala Lipis, via Raub.

All the hotels listed below have **restaurants**. Cheaper, good-quality options for eating are the small row of cafés opposite the clock tower, which sell *rotis*, rice and noodle dishes, and the food stalls at the northern end of Jalan Genting. The best place for a **drink** is *The Tavern*, opposite the Sports Centre. In addition to the **accommodation** listed, there are **bungalows** dotted around in the hills, which you can rent from the Fraser's Hill Development Corporation (☎09/362 2248, fax 362 2273), up Jalan Genting past the mosque.

Fraser's Pine Resort, Jalan Kuari (☎09/362 2122, fax 783 6108). One of the largest developments in the area, unobtrusively positioned in a valley between two hills. As well as rooms, the resort rents out apartments during the week. Accommodation is in modern, apartment-style units with kitchens. ⑦.

Jelai Highlands Resort, Jalan Ampang (☎09/362 2600, fax 362 2600). Basic doubles set in a scenic garden. The rooms are a shade smarter than you'd get at the *Quest*. ⑤.

Methodist Lodge (☎09/362 2236, KL office ☎03/232 0477). Around thirty minutes' walk south of the information office, along first Jalan Mager, and then Jalan Richmond, off which a turning leads north to the lodge. Alternatively, you can get here by taking the Kindersley Trail going uphill, west off Jalan Lady Guillemard; the view is breathtaking. Has large, if plain, double rooms with bathrooms and spacious communal areas. ④.

Puncak Inn, Jalan Genting (☎09/362 2055). The cheapest place here, centrally located opposite the clock tower. The basic rooms are badly maintained and not worth the asking price, though. ③.

Quest Resort, Jalan Lady Guillemard (☎09/362 2300, fax 362 2284, *quest@tm.net.my*). An ugly concrete block on the hill above the information office. Some of its rooms have the saving grace of a pleasant view across the golf course, but all are overpriced and musty. ⑤.

Silverpark Holiday Resort, Jalan Ledegham (☎09/362 2888, fax 362 2887). A complex of whitewashed, red-roofed towers. The large suite rooms are marginally smaller than the *Pine Resort*'s. Make sure you get a room with an outward facing view or you may feel like you've moved into a posh housing estate. ⑦.

Ye Olde Smokehouse, Jalan Semantan (☎09/362 2226, fax 362 2035). One of the quietest and most characterful lodgings, with a faded colonial elegance and catering for a wealthy clientele, this small place is designed along the lines of an English Tudor country cottage. The sumptuous, country-style rooms have four-poster beds and a full English breakfast is available. Recommended. ⑧.

Kuala Lipis

It's hard to believe that **KUALA LIPIS**, about 100km northeast of Fraser's Hill by road, was the state capital of Pahang from 1898 to 1955. Today, it's a sleepy, inconsequential place of only seven thousand people, situated at the confluence of Sungei Lipis and Sungei Jelai (a tributary of the Pahang), dwarfed by steep hills and surrounded by forest and plantations. There's none of the tin-mining fervour which characterized the town's peak years (1910–30), although the recent revival of gold mining in the area is causing a mini-boom in the local economy. Kuala Lipis still has frontier-town charm; each Friday night the bus station disappears under a hundred pasar malam stalls, when rural Malays and Semiar tribespeople bring their produce here by train from as far afield as Kuala Krai and on boats from upriver.

Kuala Lipis started life as a small riverside settlement in the early nineteenth century; the population grew from a few dozen to around two thousand by the 1890s. By then it was a **trading centre** for *gaharu* (a fragrant aloe wood used to make joss sticks) and other jungle products, collected by the Semiar and traded with Chinese *towkays*. Until the first road was built from Kuala Lumpur in the 1890s – allowing the 170-kilometre journey here from the capital to be made by bullock cart – the river was the only means of transport; the trip from Singapore by ship and then sampan upriver took over two weeks. Nevertheless, because of its central geographical position and early importance as a transit point on Sungei Pahang for locally mined tin, Kuala Lipis was where the colonial government set up its state administrative headquarters. However the tin deposits soon evaporated and the fabled gold never materialized. The rise of Kuantan

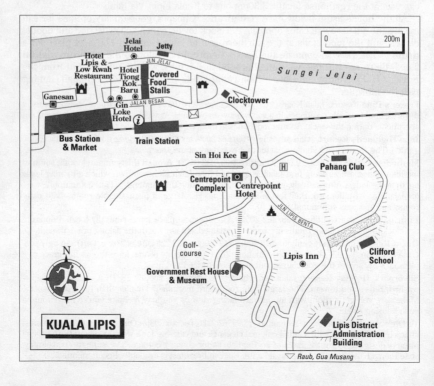

marginalized Kuala Lipis, which slipped into genteel obscurity; today there are a disproportionately large number of fine period buildings for a town whose main street is only 400m long. Nearby Kenong Rimba State Park (see p.237) is the main reason most travellers stop here, promising rainforest hikes without the crowds which frequent nearby Taman Negara.

The Town

Heading left from the train station takes you down narrow Jalan Besar past a jumble of Chinese shophouses incorporating busy bars, general-purpose shops and the town's hotels. Each Friday, the buses are moved from the **market** area, next to the bus station, and the whole district is transformed into a vibrant pasar malam, when everybody in town turns out. Stalls here sell everything from fruits, river fish and pet birds to cleaning utensils and digital watches; hawkers prepare massive trays of cooked noodles, seafood, pies, deep-fried prawn cakes and superb cornmeal puddings. To cap it all, while you eat you'll be approached by peddlers pushing all manner of charms and miracle cures.

Pahang's most famous Resident, Hugh Clifford, lived on Bukit Residen, a 400 metre-high hill overlooking the town. His former house – a graceful one-storey colonial building – is now the *Government Rest House* (see overleaf), with a **museum** detailing the town's cultural history. The exhibits – mostly bric-a-brac – originally belonged to British and Malay colonial civil servants and include oblong brass boxes for betel leaf, coconut oil lamps and embroidered sashes. The photographs are more interesting, with one showing the resthouse at the time of the great flood of 1926, when the level of the flood waters was recorded on the outside wall. In the drawing-room to the right of the main entrance is a collection of spears, *parung*s and *kris* daggers (see p.274) with highly ornate handles; ceramic vases, cups and plates. Upstairs are more photographs – of Pahang's royal family – and the grand bedroom, with its marvellous views over the town and beyond to Kenong Rimba and Taman Negara parks. To walk up to the *Rest House*, turn right from the train station along Jalan Besar and right again at the roundabout, 100m on. Follow the road to its left marked "To the Golf Course"; after 50m take the path along the western flank of the golf course to a flight of concrete steps overgrown with weeds, which lead up through the trees – this is the most direct way up to the top of the hill. If you're driving, head south down Jalan Lipis Benta and take the right up the hill after you pass the *Lipis Inn*.

On the hill opposite stands the town's largest colonial structure, the **Lipis District Administration Building**, around ten minutes' walk from the train station. Dating from 1919, it's been beautifully maintained, and now serves as the local law court. The other central hill, Bukit Lipis, also has two period buildings: the Pahang Club (1867) with its distinctive sloping roof, and Clifford School (1913). Now fallen into disrepair (the once tended gardens have now been almost reclaimed by the jungle), the **Pahang Club** is every bit the archetypal colonial club in the tropics. It was the first building constructed by the British in the town, later serving as a temporary residence for Hugh Clifford. The occasional large function is still held in the main room with its dark mahogany floor, though most of the action these days takes place in the musty, tobacco-stained bar, through the hall to the right. The Pahang Club has only kept afloat by opening its doors to anyone who can pay the RM100 annual membership, while visitors to the area are welcome in the club for dinner (RM10 a steak) or drinks (the bar closes when the last customer has left). The billiard room is also still in use, and there's an indoor badminton court and tennis court attached to the club; ask at reception if you want to book the facilities.

Directly below the Pahang Club, the **Clifford School** was built in 1913, part-funded by Hugh Clifford, and maintained as the first multiracial private school in Malaysia, admitting both British and Chinese boys. A grandiose group of buildings painted deep crimson, with a long, low veranda beneath a magnificent grey-tiled roof, the school is perhaps the most famous in Malaysia – one of a select group where the country's leaders and royalty are educated.

Practicalities

Both **train and bus stations** are very central, close to the town's inexpensive hotels, and a fifteen-minute walk from the *Government Rest House*. The **jetty** – from where boats leave on Saturdays for Kenong Rimba State Park – lies 50m northeast of the market on Jalan Jelai. The official **tourist office** (☎09/312 5032, Mon–Fri 9am–5pm, Sat 9am–1pm) is just outside the station; nearby is another (☎09/312 3277), a private concern tucked away on the left of the train station exit, opposite the ticket booth. Its owner Hassan Tuah provides an informative map of the town and a colourful brochure on nearby Kenong Rimba State Park, with details of his own tour to the park. You can access the **Internet** at Best Modern Computing (☎09/312 3355) on Level 3 of the Centrepoint shopping complex, and there's a terminal at the *Hotel Lipis*.

ACCOMMODATION

There aren't many **places to stay** at the top end of the market, though there are a couple of budget hotels, the majority of which lie along Jalan Besar between the train and bus stations.

Centrepoint (☎09/312 2688, fax 312 2699). On Level 5 of the Centrepoint shopping complex. whose rooms compare with the *Lipis Inn*'s and cost a good deal less – the trade-off, of course, is living above a concrete shopping centre. ④.

Gin Loke, 64 Jalan Besar (☎09/312 1388). This friendly place has well-scrubbed, if basic, rooms with shared toilets and showers; the seating area upstairs has some attractive Chinese antiques. ①.

Government Rest House, Jalan Bukit Residen (☎09/312 7284). See p.235 for directions. The most atmospheric place to stay, amid stately surrounds, it has twenty en-suite bedrooms, all with air-con or fan. Though the furniture is a bit old, all the rooms are large and clean. ②.

Hotel Jelai, 44 Jalan Jelai (☎09/312 1192). Though lacking the atmosphere of a family-run guesthouse, it's quiet and has attractive views of the Sungei Jelai. The basic rooms are as good as anything you'll find on Jalan Besar and the air-con rooms with TV are the only ones in the centre of town worth the money. ②.

Hotel Lipis, 63 Jalan Besar (☎09/312 3142). Run by Appu, a trekking guide (it's also known as *Appu's Guest House*), this brightly painted place has a spotless dorm, Internet facilities and a range of rooms with shared showers. ①, dorm beds RM7.

The Lipis Inn, 1 Komplek Taipan, Jalan Benta Lipis (☎09/312 5888). A run-of-the-mill high-rise place, with small rooms. It's only worth its rates during promotions, when the TV- and air-con equipped en-suite rooms almost halve in price. ⑤.

Hotel Tiong Kok Baru, 69 Jalan Besar (☎09/312 2044). Above a restaurant, this small, friendly and efficient place has rooms cleaner than most operating theatres, though some are mere wooden partitions. ①.

EATING AND DRINKING

There's a smattering of below-average Chinese **cafés** on Jalan Besar, but better by far is the lively *Sin Hoi Kee*, just by the roundabout on Jalan Lipis. The covered road linking Jalan Besar and Jalan Jelai has some good, inexpensive **stalls** and there's an Indian banana-leaf curry house – the *Genesan* – at the extreme west end of Jalan Besar opposite the bus station. Excellent seafood can be had at the *Low Kwan* **restaurant** underneath the *Hotel Lipis*, but you could end up paying RM40 for one dish. The *Rest House* has a restaurant (Mon–Sat 8–10am, noon–2pm & 8.30–11pm) specializing in traditional Pahang dishes like river trout in durian sauce and chicken in coconut and lemon grass. They don't serve alcohol here; for a beer, head for one of the noisy **bars** on Jalan Besar.

Kenong Rimba State Park

KENONG RIMBA STATE PARK is one of the best reasons to travel the jungle train into the interior and, if coupled with a visit to Kuala Lipis, makes for a nicely varied three- to five-day stop-off en route from KL to Kota Bharu. Rimba's main attraction is that it offers a compact version of the Taman Negara experience – jungle trails, riverside camping, mammal-spotting and **excellent bird-watching** – at much reduced prices and without the hype which characterizes the larger park on its northeastern border. One-tenth of the size of Taman Negara, Kenong Rimba stretches over 128 square kilometres of the **Kenong Valley**, east of Banjaran Titiwangsa. It's dotted with limestone hills, which are riddled with caves of varying sizes, and crossed by trails which snake along the forest floor. The park is also a promising place to spot **big mammals**, many of which have been driven away from Taman Negara by the increase in tourism, and have ventured across into Rimba. That said, it's still unlikely you'll catch sight of a tiger or elephant, although there's certainly more of a chance here than in Taman Negara.

As Rimba is small, you can see most of its main sights within four days. You could check out the caves for a day, spend another trekking to the waterfall, and two or three days walking back via the Batek Orang Asli village. If you only have time for a brief visit to the park, you could make straight for the waterfall and camp there for a night, leaving the park by the same route the next day.

You'll need to hire a recognized **guide** to visit the park. Harry Tan at the *Gin Loke* hotel can put you in touch with the best of the local guides; you could also try either of the information offices or Appu at the *Hotel Lipis*. Guide fees are RM45 a day and include food, use of cooking utensils and rental of ground and cover sheets. Entry permits, which your guide will buy at the park office, cost RM1.

No special **equipment** is needed, besides a water bottle (always carry at least one litre of water with you on the trails), something to sleep under, and ground sheets to sleep on (the last two are provided by the guide, though you may have to ask). You'll have to bring your own blanket if you want one, but it never really gets cold in the park. Lots of mosquito repellent is also worth having on hand; in addition, you may want to bring a gift to the village (cigarettes and T-shirts seem to be preferred).

Practicalities

The easiest way to get to the park is to travel **from Kuala Lipis** on Saturday, when a sampan (RM16) leaves the Jalan Jelai jetty at 2pm (returning people to their kampungs from the pasar malam), arriving at the **Tanjung Kiara jetty**, ninety minutes' walk from the park, at around 4pm. On other days of the week, you can charter a sampan directly from Kuala Lipis, at around RM70 per boat. However, it's cheaper to take the 6.30am jungle train to **Batu Sembilan** (30min; RM1), just a few stops to the south of Kuala Lipis, where you walk left (east) along a narrow road 50m to the jetty on Sungei Jelai. Here, sampans take you on the thirty-minute trip downstream (RM20 per person), turning left into Sungei Kenong to reach the Tanjung Kiara jetty.

From the jetty, it's a thirty-minute walk on a wide road through the rather spread-out **Kampung Dusun**, past the path leading to the first of the park's caves (see p.239), and a small store on the right, to a bridge where the park proper begins. After a further hour along a narrow path through lowland forest, you reach the **park headquarters** at **GUNUNG KESONG**, in a clearing beside Sungei Kesong, where twelve chalets and the park office are situated. To use the **chalets**, which are two-bed en-suite wooden affairs (④), it's advisable to book in advance at the official tourist office in Kuala Lipis. The **campsite**, where it only costs RM4 to put up your tent, is close to the chalets; there are toilets and showers on site but no cooking facilities. Some campers use Kesong as a base and then head further into the park to camp, often at the Kenong campsite, four

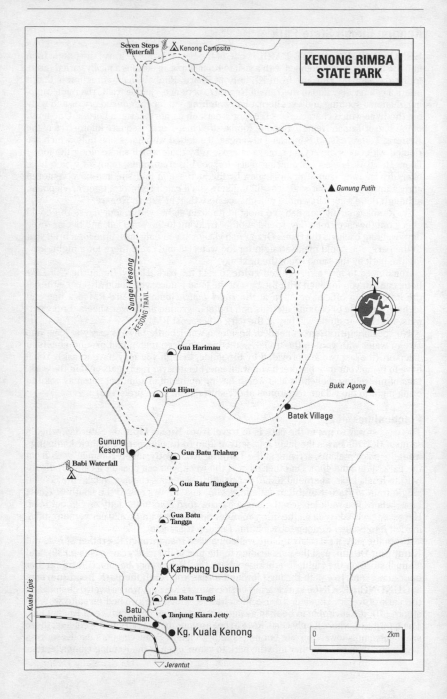

hours' walk away in the north of the park (see below). It's best to bring your own food as **eating** options are very limited at Gunung Kesong; occasionally there are some *roti* stalls, but usually there's nothing.

The caves

The first of the six **caves** in Rimba is outside the park proper, close to the Tanjung Kiara jetty. About ten minutes' walk from the jetty along the road, look out for a path on your left which leads west to **Gua Batu Tinggi**, a small cave just big enough to clamber into. Inside, there's a surprising variety of plant life, including orchids and fig trees. There's a waterfall 100m further along the trail, an excellent place for swimming.

Gua Batu Tangga (Cave of Rock Steps) is a twenty-minute walk direct from the camp at Gunung Kesong, though you can also get there from the Batu Tinggi cave by returning along the trail leading to it and crossing the road, following the path to the left of a house – a sign points to the cave, which lies twenty minutes' walk further on. Shaped like an inverted wok, the large limestone cave has a wide, deep chamber, in whose northwest corner a row of rocks forms ledges or steps, which give the cave its name. The cave is sometimes occupied by elephants – the trail through it narrows between rocks rubbed smooth over time, probably by the passage of the great creatures – but you're more likely to catch sight of mouse deer or porcupine scurrying away. Two smaller caves, **Gua Batu Tangkup** and **Gua Batu Telahup**, are just a few hundred metres beyond Tangga on the same trail.

Two more caves lie close to the park headquarters: **Gua Hijau** (Green Cave), just five minutes' walk east over two bridges, is home to thousands of bats, while **Gua Harimau** (Tiger Cave), a little further along on the right, is scarcely more than an overhang and reputedly the lair of tigers.

The trails

The main trail in the park, the nine-kilometre Kesong trail, leads north from the headquarters to **Seven Steps Waterfall** (4hr). If you don't want simply to retrace your steps on the return trip, there's an alternative route which runs back to the southeast and passes close to the Batek village.

From park headquarters, the trail to the waterfall runs along Sungei Kesong in lowland forest, through which little sunlight penetrates. Over the years, the Batek have cleared portions of forest around this trail for agricultural purposes; this could account for the jungle's impenetrability, as secondary forest tends to grow back more thickly than primary. The trail crosses several bridges; 250m before the waterfall you cross Sungei Kesong for the final time to reach the Kenong **campsite**. From here, you're very close to the waterfall, the trail continuing through high forest to a set of rapids, with jungle closing in all around. There's nowhere to rest except on the boulders where, close to the edge of the river, you can sit and listen to the loud hiss of the water dropping over the nearby falls.

Returning on the southeastern loop of the trail takes longer – around 12 hours if you're stopping to see the sights – and is harder going as it traverses small hills – Gunung Putih (884m) is the largest – and follows a less well-defined path. Three hours after Gunung Putih you pass close to a **Batek village**, where someone may invite you to their hut or display some wares to sell or trade. Although this isn't an official campsite, you can ask to pitch a tent near the huts, especially if you decide to climb **Bukit Agong** (1800m), a stiff ascent which takes around two hours each way from the village; there isn't a clearly marked path however. Returning to the park headquarters from the village takes around another four hours; you'll need to continue along the southeastern loop part of the trail (there is no direct path to the headquarters from Bukit Agong), which connects with the trail from the jetty at a point a little way north of Kampung Dusun.

Gua Musang

Back on Route 8 and the train route, the jungle landscape changes near Merapoh, 80km north of Kuala Lipis, where it's dominated by large, round sandstone hills. From Merapoh, it's another hour or so to **GUA MUSANG**. The largest town in the interior of **Kelantan**, it's a largely unappealing place which expanded fast over the last decade as logging money flowed in, accelerated by the arrival of Route 8, which has made remote tracts of forest accessible to the timber saws. Most of the timber merchants, and their employees, are Chinese, and there's a distinct frontier spirit here, typical of many towns in rural Malaysia. Gua Musang positively churns with Toyota Land Cruisers and motorbikes, its cheap hotels and cafés full of people making business deals day and night. At weekends, dozens of young Chinese promenade up and down the two-street town, flocking to karaoke bars or to kung-fu movies at the only cinema.

The main reason tourists stop is to visit the **caves** that riddle the mass of limestone above the town. Both the caves and the town are named after a small creature, the *musang*, which looks like a civet and used to live up in the caves; it's now almost extinct. To get to the caves, cross the railway track at the station and walk through the tiny, cramped kampung in the shadow of the rock behind the station. Here you'll have to ask one of the villagers to guide you (it's usual to pay around RM10 for this); it is possible to reach the caves on your own, but the trail – which is directly at the back of the huts – is difficult to negotiate after rain, when it's likely to be extremely slippery. Wear strong shoes and take a torch to use inside the cave.

Once you've climbed almost vertically up 20m of rock face you'll see a narrow ledge; turn left and edge carefully along until you see a long slit in the rock which leads into a cave – you'll need to be fairly thin to negotiate this. The inside of the cave is enormous, 60m long and 30m high in places, and well lit by sunlight from holes above. The main cave leads to lesser ones, which have rock formations jutting out from the walls and ceilings. The only way out is by the same route, which you'll need to take very carefully, especially the near-vertical descent off the ledge and back down to the kampung.

Practicalities

There are four trains a day from Kuala Lipis north to Gua Musang, the first leaving at 4.30am, arriving just after 6am; the last at 3.30pm, arriving at 5.10pm; departures south are at 5am and 12.30pm. The **train station**, situated directly below the limestone rock, is at the eastern end of the town's main street, Jalan Besar, where a few of the **hotels** are located. The cheap Chinese-run *Hotel Merling* (①), on the right-hand-side of the street as you leave the station, has the least expensive rooms in town and is passable, though pretty basic. Only a few ringgit more will get you a clean room with fan at the *Gunung Emas* (☎09/912 4373; ①), a little further along on the same side of the road. A bit further up on the opposite side of Jalan Besar is

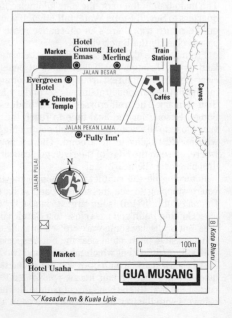

the *Evergreen Hotel* (☎09/912 2273; ③), with the *Hotel Usaha* (☎09/917 4003, 912 4002; ③) 400m on from it, after the road swings left and becomes Jalan Pulai. Both offer comfortable air-con en-suite rooms with hot water; the *Usaha*'s are a little larger. The *Kedesar Inn*'s (☎09/912 1229, fax 912 2131; ③) musty doubles and large shabby chalets (⑥) aren't recommended, though it does however have a few bunk rooms sleeping four (RM35 per room), which have their own bathrooms. A far better choice overall is the *Fully Inn*, 75 Jalan Pekan Lama (☎09/912 3311, fax 912 3322; ⑥), a smart place near the train station, with a good restaurant, luxurious rooms and good-value promotional prices.

Gua Musang is not particularly renowned for its food, but the stalls near the station cook good *nasi campur*, and the Chinese **cafés** on Jalan Besar serve hearty meals. *Restoran Haji Sulaiman*, below the *Hotel Usaha*, is also a good bet, busy well into the night serving Chinese and Malay food.

Dabong and around

If you take the train north from Gua Musang, the next stop is 50km away at **DABONG**, a quintessentially Kelantanese Malay village, sited on Sungei Galas and surrounded by flat-topped limestone peaks and dark-green forest. The simple, wooden kampung huts here are slowly being outnumbered by brick and concrete constructions. It's not an uninteresting place to pass the time: timber-stilted houses peep out from between banana trees, and a few sampans ply the huge brown river. The main reason for getting out of the train here is to visit **Gua Ikan**, a deep cave 3km to the southwest, or – more excitingly – the **Jelawang Country Park**, on a mountain further south. Though Route 8 splits away from the train line at Gua Musang, rejoining it some 80km northeast at Kuala Krai, you can drive to Dabong by turning west off Route 8 about 50km south of Kuala Krai.

There is only one **place to stay** in Dabong itself, a government resthouse, the *Rumah Rehat Dabong* (☎09/744 0725; ②) which is a bit grimy and dilapidated. To reach it, walk out of the train station along the main road towards the river (west) and turn left after 100m, just past the schoolhouse; the resthouse is the yellow building 50m further on your right. A far better idea, however, is to stay in the Jelawang Country Park itself (see below). There are a few **food stalls** near the train station, but not much in the town itself.

Gua Ikan

The caves at **Gua Ikan** – distinguished by a stream running through a wide cavity – are a little way south of Dabong. To get there on foot, cross the railway track heading away from the village, turn right (south), and walk for 4km along a wide, paved road; alternatively, ask at the train station about getting a minibus taxi (RM10 return per person, including a wait at the cave). The limestone caves are clearly signposted off to the right of the road, set in a small, unmaintained park. In the main cave, 40m long and 20m high, a small river runs along the cave floor; you can follow its course provided you've brought a torch and waterproof boots (the rocks are too slippery to go barefoot). This leads out to the other side of the cave to a small rock-enclosed area, a lovely spot to rest and listen to the birds and monkeys.

Jelawang Country Park

The **Jelawang Country Park** has much in common with the better-known Kenong Rimba. It offers the possibility of seeing **large mammals** and **rare birds**, as well as boasting Peninsular Malaysia's highest waterfall, **Lata Jeri**. The pool below is a reasonably pleasant spot at which to soak aching feet.

You'll require a guide (hire one at the *Perdana Stong Hill Resort*; see below) to strike out on one of the local **trails**. The three-hour **Seven Waterfalls** hike takes you circuitously up the west side of the waterfall to the top of Gunung Stong (where the campsite, see below, is located), then heads down the east side; the uphill part of the trek takes around ninety minutes and is fairly gruelling, involving some sheer, muddy sections, though rocks at the side of the trail allow you to rest and look back over the forest. The **Elephant Trek**, the longer of the two official trails here, follows the main path up the mountain for two hours to the top of Gunung Stong, before winding along the ridge and crossing over onto neighbouring Gunung Ayan. Although it's possible to return to the waterfall campsite the same day on this trek, it's preferable to camp for the night at a clearing along the trail, near a small stream – you'll need some warm clothing and a sleeping bag. People have seen elephants here, and there's a high chance of encountering **tapir**, **monkey** and **deer** in the early morning or early evening.

PRACTICALITIES

To continue to Jelawang **from Dabong**'s train station, walk west along the road leading directly out of the station towards the river, until you get to a T-junction where you turn left and take the first right, after a mosque, down some concrete steps. Here there's a jetty, where a sampan takes you across Sungei Galas to the other bank (RM1). It's then a four-kilometre taxi ride (you might have to wait half an hour for a vehicle; RM3) northeast to Kampung Jelawang, nestling under **Gunung Stong** (1421m) directly ahead – you can actually see the cascade of Lata Jeri from the road.

Coming here independently from the **northeast coast**, you need to leave Kota Bharu by 9am, taking bus #5 from the local bus station for the ninety-minute journey to **Kuala Krai** (RM4). From there, you head to Dabong either by train or boat; see opposite for details; if you arrive by boat, walk up the steps, turn right and carry on past the mosque to the other jetty, from where you get the sampan across Sungei Glass. It's not a bad idea to arrive on one of the **tours** here, promoted fairly vigorously in Kota Bharu (see p.260) as the "Jelawang Jungle Trail"; travel agencies and guesthouses there can arrange trips, which are not bad value at around RM30 per day.

The most convenient place to ask the taxi driver to drop you is the *Perdana Stong Hill Resort* (☎ & fax 09/747 6100; ④), an attractive collection of luxury chalets with expensive dorm beds (RM25), restaurant and park information. It's a lot more pleasant here than at the resthouse in Dabong, and is also the place to hire a guide (RM60 a day) for the trails. The resort is well signposted from Jelawang and located right at the foot of Gunung Stong, two and a half kilometres further on. The *Baha Adventure Camp*, snugly sited beside the waterfall amid large trees, has inexpensive and basic chalets (RM10) and sites to pitch tents (RM3). There are two chemical toilets close by, but no showers, so most visitors make good use of the waterfall's small rock pools instead.

On to Kuala Krai and the northeast coast

Moving on from Dabong, there's a choice of transport: a **boat** from the upstream jetty (Thurs–Sat 2pm; RM5) runs as far as **Kuala Krai**, a journey which takes ninety minutes, as does the daily **train** service (northbound at 5am, 7am, 7.45am, 2.30pm & 5.30pm, southbound at 6.55am, 10.45am, 4.45pm, 8.30pm and 10.15pm). The train ride is splendid, chugging along valley floors where trees and plants almost envelop the track, and then climbing steeply to cross long, metal bridges over a network of rivers. Along the way the train passes through seven tunnels; when the minimal lighting malfunctions, the swaying carriages are plunged into darkness. The few stations along the way are hardly more than lean-tos; if there is anywhere left in the Malay Peninsula that is truly remote, it's here. Obscure little settlements, squeezed into the dense green cloak of jungle, have Senoi Orang Asli names like Renok, Kemubu and Pahi, from where local people board the train with their massive bundles of goods.

On the final section of the jungle railway – the 75km from Kuala Krai to Tumpat on the northeast coast (the towns in the northern half of this route are covered on pp.252–262) – the geography changes from mountainous, river-gashed jungle to rubber, pepper and palm-oil plantations. This is also **cattle country**, where cows are a constant problem for train drivers, as they graze along the railway sidings, often straying onto the track. The trains usually travel slowly enough to avoid hitting the cows, but occasionally there's a collision. Along the route, villages become more numerous and the train swells with Malay traders and saree-clad Indian women heading for Kota Bharu (see p.252). The penultimate stop is Wakaf Bharu (see p.262), 7km from Kota Bharu, with the end of the line at Tumpat, another thirty minutes northwest of Wakaf Bharu.

Kuala Krai

The only town of any size between Gua Musang and Kota Bharu, **KUALA KRAI**, on the east bank of the 200-metre-wide Sungei Kelantan, is a busy commercial centre serving inland Kelantan. Once, great barges laden with goods were floated from here down to the coast, but nowadays most of the local traffic is confined either to Route 8, which runs close to the town centre, or to the jungle railway which passes south of the town. But despite Krai's regional importance, the pace of life here is slow, and there's very little going on through the baking hours of the early afternoon.

The centre consists of the east–west street, Jalan Sultan Yahya Petra, and the north–south Jalan Ah Sang, where you'll find most hotels and services. About the only distraction is to take a walk up to the Mini Zoo and the Museum (daily 9am–12.30pm & 2–5pm; RM1 entry to each), ten minutes out of town on a well-marked road. The **zoo** is eminently missable, a sad array of ill-kept and unkempt animals. Further up the hill in a large Malay house, the **museum** commands a fine view of the town. Besides the ubiquitous stuffed animals, there are photographs of town dignitaries, markets, street life and Orang Asli in traditional dress. Other exhibits include a church organ whose chair is decorated with intricate Kelantanese symbols, various musical instruments, and a large wall-hanging displaying the Kelantan royal family tree.

PRACTICALITIES

The train station is at the eastern end of Jalan Ah Sang, with the **bus station** a hundred metres or so west along the road. Another few minutes' walk west takes you to the opposite end of the high street, from where the **jetty** is a minute's walk left, through an archway near the police station. Trains leave north at 7.57am, 9.23am and 7pm for the two-hour trip to Wakaf Bharu (the stop for Kota Bharu), and at 5am, 9am, 3.30pm, 7.45pm and 9.25pm for the trip south to Dabong and Gua Musang. Buses north to Kota Bharu leave every thirty minutes from 6.30am to 6pm (around RM5), and there are also services to Gua Musang (around RM3) every hour, and one daily to KL at 10.30am (around RM25).

Boats to Dabong leave at 10.05am, and usually also at 2pm daily except Friday (1hr 30min; RM5), for the journey down Sungei Kelantan into Sungei Galas. There's no need to book, but get to the jetty at least fifteen minutes before departure. The jetty consists of a leaky bamboo raft connected to the riverbank by a single, bowed plank – not practical if you're carrying any luggage.

For **accommodation**, there's *Hotel Krai*, 190 Jalan Ah Sang (☎09/966 6301; ②), which has basic, clean rooms with fans, shared toilets and shower. It's better than the *Joomui Hotel* opposite on 189 Jalan Ah Sang (①), whose shutters and red-tiled roof make it seem more romantic than its run-down interior actually is. There are good Muslim **cafés** on the high street and near the bus station, where tasty *nasi campur* and *roti canai* are served until about 9pm. Further along Jalan Ah Sang are a few busy Chinese **hawker centres**, serving seafood dishes, including Kelantese specialities like river trout and perch. At the other end of town, on the approach from Route 8 along Jalan Sultan Yahya Petra, just past the zoo and museum, there's a line of **satay stalls**. For **Internet access**, there are a couple of computer stores on the south side of the road between the train and bus stations.

Tasek Chini and Tasek Bera

The main interest in the southern part of the interior, below the KL–Kuantan road (Route 2), lies in its two lake systems, **Tasek Chini** and **Tasek Bera**, beautiful areas where Orang Asli groups live and work. Chini is much smaller and more developed than Bera, with a small resort and a large village at its northern end, offering inexpensive accommodation and the chance to buy excellent handicrafts. The larger lake system at Bera, surrounded by dense forests, is sparsely populated and has fewer facilities for visitors, but is even more stunning and wilder than Chini. Access to Tasek Bera is via **Temerloh**, the main town on Route 2, which is of slight interest but has reasonable hotels and places to eat, while Chini can be reached from Temerloh or Kuantan. Both areas require a taxi, your own transport, or a lot of bus and boat hopping.

The **Jakun** Orang Asli around Tasek Chini live in settled communities, occasionally doing seasonal work. At more remote Tasek Bera, the **Semelai** cultivate vegetables, tapioca, rice and other crops and collect forest products for a living. There are **crocodiles** in the lake here, and the Semelai believe their ancestors concluded a pact with the mythic supreme crocodile of the lake, forging a relationship of mutual respect. The Semelai live on the edge of the jet-black lake in elevated houses built of wood, tree bark and *atap* leaves; their sturdy boats are made from hollowed-out tree trunks, although these days they tend to buy them from the Malays, rather than making them themselves. Along Tasek Bera's seemingly endless passages through the rushes, a loud and eerie sound emanates from the *berbeling* – crude windmills made of bamboo which help the Semelai find their way through the swamps.

Tasek Chini

Spanning an area of around twenty square kilometres, **Tasek Chini** is a conglomerate of twelve connecting lakes of varying sizes. The lakes have given rise to a plethora of **myths and legends**, which is hardly surprising given their serene beauty. The waters here are a deep green, almost black, though from June to September their surface is brightened by shimmering pink-and-white **lotus blossoms**. According to the creation legend of the indigenous Jakun, they were planting crops one day when an old woman with a walking stick appeared and said that the group should have sought her permission before clearing the land. But she allowed them to stay, and to legitimize their right she stabbed her stick into the centre of the clearing and told them never to pull it out. Years later, during a particularly ferocious rainstorm, a tribe member accidentally pulled out the stick, leaving a huge hole which immediately filled with water, creating the lake. Another legend tells of an ancient city which, when threatened with external attack, was flooded by its inhabitants using a system of aqueducts, with the intention of draining it later. Curious Malaysian scientists have embarked upon several research projects over the years, but nothing associated with these stories has ever been found. Some Jakun believe a serpent – or *naga* – guards the lakes, but it has remained as elusive as the lost city.

All the lakes in the system can be explored by hiring a boat, either from the *Chini Resort* in the south (see opposite), or nearby **Kampung Gumum**, a Jakun Orang Asli village of sixty village-style huts (see p.246). During the summer months, the *Chini*

Resort attracts enough visitors to support a small-scale tourist industry, including a growing number of Orang Asli **carvers** who live and display their work here.

Boat trips and trails

Of the **boat trips** you can make here, the shortest (costing around RM30) is to the Orang Asli **show village**, only twenty minutes away from the *Chini Resort*. The village consists largely of one traditional house, built of bamboo and *atap* leaves by the Jakun, and elevated on wooden stilts, but most of the people actually live in Gumum. Better are the two-hour trips west and south to **Laut Melai**, the lake where the lotuses are most plentiful, and to **Laut Babi**, the biggest lake in the system. If the water is low, clumps of spiky *pentenas* grass can be seen protruding from the water, and gulls often swoop down to pluck fish from the water. In May, the few resident Chini turtles lay their eggs – the boatmen may know where to find them.

The most popular **trail** is the one leading along the side of Tasek Chini, from the resort to Kampung Gumum, a two-kilometre trip. The path can be hard to follow after heavy rain, and may involve wading through water. A longer, four-hour trail from the resort goes to a **campsite** at **Laut Terembau**, the path weaving in and out of mangroves, oil-palm plantations and forest. The trail continues beyond the camp and after 5km leads to a secondary road; travel east along this for 20km and you arrive at the Segamat–Kuantan road (Route 12).

Practicalities

From KL, catch the hourly KL–Kuantan bus (3hr; RM10) from either Pekeliling or Pudu Raya bus station to the small town of **Maran**, 180km east of KL on Route 2. You'll have to take a taxi to **Kampung Belimbing** (RM20), then on Sungei Pahang. From Belimbing jetty, close to the road, you'll have to rent two boats, one to take you upriver to the new dam near the mouth of Sungei Chini (RM10), and from there another (RM50) south across the lake itself to the resort, or the hostels at nearby Kampung Gumum. Along the way, lianas cloak the giant trees leaning across the narrow river; the boat may well pass a group of Jakun fishermen pulling up their nets.

From Kuantan – the easiest option is to take a taxi or tour – contact the Kuantan tourist office (☎09/513 3020), which can arrange return transport and boats from RM150 for two people. It's quite possible to tour the lake and return to Kuantan on the same day. The other way to get to Chini from Kuantan is to take bus #121 (5 daily, with first bus at 8am; RM5) to **Felda Chini**, an uninteresting village set in a monotonous landscape of oil palms 16km southeast of the lake. The bus takes ninety minutes to reach the kampung, from where you will have to take a ride on the back of a motorbike (around RM20) or hitch a lift to cover the sixteen kilometres to Kampung Gumum or *Chini Resort*. If you're booked to stay at the resort, you could try asking them to collect you – call them from the public phone at Felda Chini. The bus back to Kuantan from Felda Chini leaves at 5pm. Tours of Tasek Chini can also be arranged in **Cherating** (see p.283) at several of the hotels and the Travel Post, a self-styled travel agency in the kampung's main street.

Most boats take you to the jetty below **Chini Resort** (☎09/477 8037, fax 477 8036), a quiet development tucked into the forest on the edge of the main lake, and the only place with a range of accommodation. It can get very busy at weekends when large groups often make block-bookings, so it's best to go in the week – during the wet season (October to January) you may have the place to yourself. The five small **dormitories** have ten beds in each (RM15), while the nine two-bed **chalets** (③) can also be equipped with extra mattresses for around RM20 extra per person. There's a **café**, which serves meals throughout the day, a **restaurant** (noon–2pm & 7–11pm) and a **ranger's camp** where you can rent inexpensive tents, calor-gas stoves and sleeping bags.

Five minutes by boat (RM5) east of the *Chini Resort* is **KAMPUNG GUMUM**, with a small store and three **places to stay**. In front of the jetty, the *Kijang Mas Chalets* (②) are probably the plushest accommodation you'll find hereabouts; the chalets are clean and have good views of the lake. Behind them you'll find *Chalet Kampung Gumum* (②), a similar outfit minus the view; both have small **restaurants**. A road just to the north leads to *Rajan Jones House*, a very simple, friendly affair, where RM17 will get you a dorm bed, dinner and breakfast; a well at the bottom of the garden provides the only means of washing. Jones organizes treks round the lake and, when not in the "house", is likely to be found in the shop he owns on the lakeshore.

If you wish to use the **campsite** at Laut Terembau, bring food and water with you, as the site is merely a clearing and doesn't have any facilities. There's also a campsite on the west side of the lake system at **Palau Babi**, and another where Sungei Chini divides off from Sungei Pahang at the top of the lake complex, not far from Belimbing; both campsites can only be reached by hiring a boat from the resort.

Tasek Bera

The most extensive lake system in Malaysia, **TASEK BERA** is much larger and far less developed than Chini. Tasek Bera's warren of channels lead from one lake to another through waterways where *nemkung rasau*, a sharp, high grass with a sticky yellow fruit, grows with abandon, and reeds sprout from the water. The main lake, in the northern part of the system, is over 16km wide and incredibly beautiful, its peat-edged watercourse and peat-floored bed rendering the waters jet black in places. At the edges, the Semelai Orang Asli's centuries-old practice of shifting cultivation has helped create a forest of great diversity, in which large trees have been thinned and a wide variety of edible plants, such as pepper and root vegetables, have been sown. Apart from the Semelai, the only visitors the lake has seen in recent years are staff from Pahang's Fisheries Department, who come to take samples of the water and fish to ensure the Orang Asli aren't using chemicals or poisons to boost their catch. There's not a great deal to do at the lake beyond renting a boat for **rides** around the channels – the local Parks and Wildlife Department is planning a headquarters within the lake system, which will include visitor facilities. The quality of its management will be a test of Malaysia's environmental credentials, since Tasek Bera was declared the country's first "wetland of international importance" in 1995.

A Semelai hut belonging to a local guide, Sham Sudin, marks one point on Tasek Bera where **boats** can be rented; Sudin, who speaks some English and can answer questions on local flora and fauna, charges RM100 for a two- to three-hour trip around the lake. It's possible to stay in the family home for RM10 a night, including meals. The best way to find Sudin is to enquire at the shop on the hill just before the bridge over Sungei Bera. Alternatively, you could stay at the new *Persona Lake Resort*, Tanjung Kuin 28300 Bera (☎011/951172; ⑤), which has dorms for RM30 and well-furnished chalets, though you may feel it spoils the remote feel of the lakeside. The resort has a booking office at Temerloh, next to the bus station (Mon–Sat 9am–4.30pm; ☎09/296 8280) and also offers boat rental.

Access from Temerloh

The most convenient way to reach the main lake is from **TEMERLOH**, a town on Route 2, the best option being to hire a taxi from there (around RM60 per day). Otherwise, the closest you can get by public transport is by taking a bus (3 daily) via Kampung Kerayong to Felda Tementi on Route 10, from where you'll have to take a taxi or hitch to the jetty on the main lake's north shore. The track there through oil-palm plantations sees quite a lot of traffic, including plantation staff vans and motorbikes belonging to the Semelai (who charge around RM10 to take you to the lakeside).

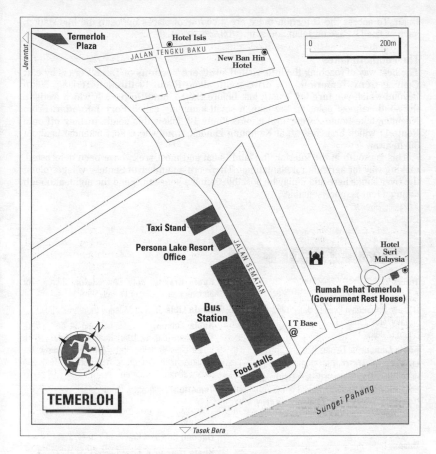

Termerloh Plaza
Hotel Isis
New Ban Hin Hotel
JALAN TENGKU BAKU
Jerantut
0   200m
Taxi Stand
Persona Lake Resort Office
JALAN SEMATAN
Hotel Seri Malaysia
Rumah Rehat Temerloh (Government Rest House)
Dus Station
I T Base @
N
Food stalls
TEMERLOH
Sungei Pahang
▽ Tasek Bera

The *Persona Lake Resort* office at Temerloh's bus station can provide information on getting to the lake. The best day to arrive is Tuesday, if only because that's when a pasar malam is set up on Jalan Tengku Baku. There's also a market every Sunday morning by the river, close to the bus station.

You may need to spend the night at Temerloh on your way to Tasek Bera. Fortunately, **accommodation** is easy enough to find. The budget places, run-down though functional enough, are all on or very near to Jalan Tengku Baku, west of the bus station. The best bet here is the *Hotel Isis*, 12 Jalan Tengku Baku (☎09/296 3136; ①), which has waterless doubles with fan and a few en-suite rooms with air-con. If the *Isis* is full, try the *New Ban Hin Hotel* (☎09/296 2331; ①), which has a variety of rooms with or without air-con and shower, though it's not as clean. On the northern approach road, just past the roundabout, are the *Seri Malaysia Hotel*, 37092 Jalan Hamzah (☎09/296 5788, fax 296 5711; ⑤) and, right next door, *Rumah Rehat Temerloh* (the government resthouse) 28000 Jalan Hamzah (☎09/296 3218, fax 296 3431; ④); the latter's rooms are larger and better equipped, with TV, fridge, air-con and hot water.

For **eating** in the evening the only option is the Malay hawker centre next to the bus station, though there are some good Indian **cafés** open during the day on Jalan Tengku

Baku. To access the **Internet**, there are a couple of places opposite the bus station, such as the IT Base on Jalan Sematan (☎09/296 3273).

The southern lakes

The best way of reaching the little-visited **southern sections** of Tasek Bera is by **car**. Coming **from Temerloh**, you drive south along Route 10 through Teriang, 30km beyond which you turn left (east), just before Bahau, onto **Route 11**, which leads to the southernmost point on the lake, a small kampung called **Fort Iskandar**. From Kuantan, take Route 2 west until it joins Route 12; follow this south, turning off onto Route 11 which branches off at Kampung Landak, from where Fort Iskandar is about 30km away.

This far south in the interior, the land is flat and most areas have been deforested, making way for agricultural plantations. There are a number of Semelai villages along the river banks here and it may be possible to find a house to spend the night, although taking a tent is more sensible.

travel details

Trains

Gemas to: Gua Musang (1 daily; 11hr); Jerantut (1 daily; 3hr); Kuala Lipis (2 daily; 8hr); Mentakab (1 daily; 4hr); Tumpat (1 daily; 13hr 20min); Wakaf Bharu (2 daily; 14hr 30min).

Kuala Lumpur to: Gemas (5 daily; 3hr).

Wakaf Bharu to: Dabong (2 daily; 3hr); Gemas (2 daily; 13hr); Gua Musang (2 daily; 6hr); Jerantut (2 daily; 10hr 30min); Kuala Krai (3 daily; 2hr); Kuala Lipis (2 daily; 9hr); Kuala Tembeling (2 daily; 10hr); Mentakab (2 daily; 12hr 30min).

Buses

Gua Musang to: Kuala Krai (hourly; 3hr).

Jerantut to: Kuala Lipis (hourly; 1hr 30min); Kuala Tahan (1 daily; 2hr 30min); Tembeling jetty (3 daily; 40min).

Kuala Krai to: Kota Bharu (every 30min; 2hr 30min); Kuala Lumpur (1 daily; 8hr).

Kuala Lipis to: Gua Musang (hourly; 2hr).

Kuala Lumpur to: Gua Musang (4 daily; 6hr); Kota Bharu (6 daily; 10hr); Kuala Krai (4 daily; 8hr); Kuala Lipis (6 daily; 3hr); Mentakab (hourly; 1hr 15min); Raub (10 daily; 1hr 30min); Temerloh (every 30min; 1hr 30min).

Temerloh to: Jerantut (hourly; 1hr).

Ferries

Dabong to: Kuala Krai (1 or 2 daily; 2hr).

Kuala Lipis to: Kenong Rimba (Sat at 2pm; 3hr).

Tembeling jetty to: Taman Negara (daily at 9am & 2pm except Fri at 2.30pm; 3hr).

CHAPTER FOUR

THE EAST COAST

The four-hundred-kilometre stretch from the northeastern corner of the Peninsula to Kuantan, roughly halfway down the east coast, displays a quite different cultural legacy to the more populous, industrialized western seaboard. For hundreds of years, the Malay rulers of the northern states of **Kelantan** and **Terengganu** were vassals of the Thai kingdom of **Ayuthaya**, suffering repeated invasions as well as the unruly squabbles of their own princes. Nevertheless, the relationship forged with the Thais allowed the Malays a great deal of autonomy which, together with the adoption of Islam in the seventeenth century, gave the region a strong sense of identity and independence. Remaining free of British control until 1909, the region escaped the economic and social changes that rocked the western Malay Peninsula during the nineteenth century. Cut off by the mountainous, jungle interior from technological advances taking place in the Federated Malay States (see p.624), Kelantan, Terengganu and **Pahang** retained their largely rural character. While immigrants poured into the tin and rubber towns of the west, the east remained underdeveloped and, as a result, still lacks the ethnic diversity of the rest of the country. The recent discovery of oil off the shores of Terengganu has dramatically increased the standard of living for some east-coast residents, whose per capita income was previously well below the national average. But for the most part, the economy – one of the poorest in the federation – is still based on small-scale sea and river fishing, and rice farming.

Since the 1950s, Parti Islam SeMalaysia (the Pan-Malayan Islamic Party, or **PAS** for short) has dominated local **politics** in Kelantan, with the party in control of the state ever since their landslide victory in the 1990 elections. Their green-and-white flags flew over Terengganu as well in 1999, when PAS wiped out the ruling party UMNO in state elections. Appealing to the growing number of Malays who find little of value in what they see as the money-motivated policies of Dr Mahathir Mohamed, PAS has sought to run both states along more religious lines, introducing separate check-outs at supermarkets for men and women, revoking many bar licences and even banning karaoke. The austere lifestyles of the PAS party leaders contrast noticeably with those of the "UMNO-putras", and the appeal for a back-to-basics society based on the Koran is strong, especially among the poor and disadvantaged. The party newspaper – *Harakah* – is about the only place in the country you'll see the government criticized in print.

ACCOMMODATION PRICE CODES

Throughout the Malaysia chapters we've used the following **price codes** to denote the cost of the cheapest available room for two people. Single occupancy should cost about twenty percent less than double, though it's only mid-range and top-tier hotels that are likely to offer such discounts. Some guesthouses provide dormitory beds, for which the ringgit price is given.

① RM20 and under	④ RM61–80	⑦ RM161–220
② RM21–40	⑤ RM81–110	⑧ RM221–360
③ RM41–60	⑥ RM111–160	⑨ RM361 and above

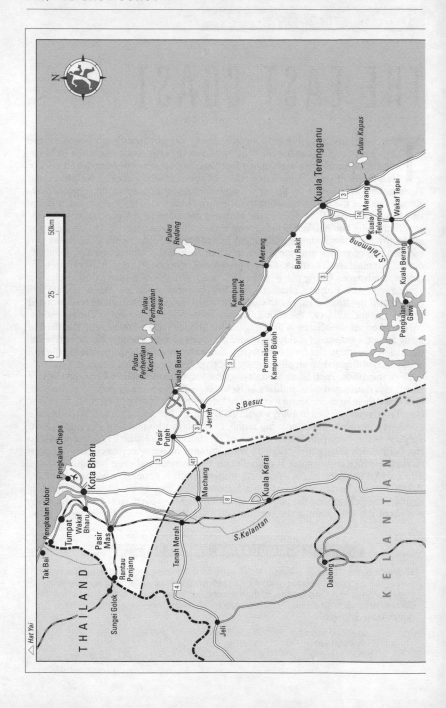

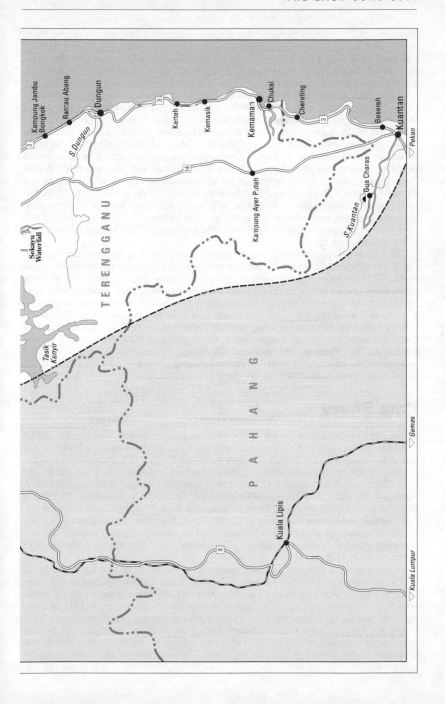

However, PAS's coalition partners, the Chinese-dominated Democratic Action Party (DAP), and many westernized, urban Malays fear their existing freedoms may be impinged upon should the Islamists come to national power. PAS is trying to allay these fears by adopting a broad, business-friendly approach, aimed at showing they are capable of running a modern state; for now, you still find beer in any Chinese-run bar, and see bikini-clad, as well as fully veiled, women on the beach right alongside each other.

For the visitor, the east coast provides a welcome contrast to the entrepreneurial west coast. The casuarina-fringed beaches and coral reefs on three of the most beautiful islands in the South China Sea, **Pulau Perhentian**, **Pulau Redang** and **Pulau Kapas**, are the greatest attraction here, and two of the three main cities also have some appeal. In **Kota Bharu**, the last major town before the Thai border, the inhabitants still practise ancient Malay crafts such as kite-making and top-spinning; **Kuala Terengganu**, 160km to the south, is an up-and-coming oil-rich town with an old Chinese quarter and a traditional boat-building industry. Both are infinitely preferable to the urban disaster that is **Kuantan**, which you may find hard to avoid passing through, since it is connected to the nation's capital by Route 2, the congested and perilous road which runs across the Peninsula (and which boasts the highest accident rate in the whole country).

The islands off the east coast – in the stretch from Kota Bharu to Kuantan – are virtually out of bounds between November and February because of the annual **monsoon**; the heavy rains and sea swell are too great to allow boats to reach any of them. Since there are no rail links (apart from the jungle railway from Tumpat, near Kota Bharu, into the interior), travel throughout the region is limited to the relatively traffic-free Route 3, hugging the coast, and Route 14 a little way inland, which links Kuala Terengganu with Kuantan, running virtually parallel to Route 3. It's the coastal road that's the more interesting, connecting a whole string of blissfully laid-back fishing kampungs like **Merang**, **Marang** and **Cherating**. In addition, between May and September, the beaches surrounding **Rantau Abang** are one of only five places in the world where giant leatherback turtles come to nest.

Kota Bharu

At the very northeastern corner of the Peninsula, close to the Thai border, **KOTA BHARU** is the capital of Kelantan State, still the most "Malay" region in Malaysia and one of the country's most important cultural centres. Despite this, some people find the city's initial appearance something of a disappointment. It doesn't take long, though, for Kota Bharu's charm to work, and many people stay much longer than they planned. A showcase for skills and customs little practised elsewhere in Malaysia, the town is proud of its traditions, nurtured by its **Gelanggang Seni** (Cultural Centre) and the various **cottage industries** that thrive in its hinterland. There are regular festivals – if you arrive in September after the rice harvest you'll be treated to celebrations in the surrounding villages. During the month of **Ramadan** (see p.70), strongly Muslim Kota Bharu virtually shuts up shop.

Isolation not only fostered a unique culture here – so much so that a traveller in the 1820s noted distinct differences between the dialect and dances of Kelantan and those of the rest of the Malay Peninsula – but also allowed Kota Bharu greater political autonomy than other state capitals. The railway only arrived in the region in 1931, skirting the state capital – the journey to Kuala Lumpur prior to that time involved thirteen ferry crossings. Kelantan's embrace of **Islam** helped preserve its isolation, and its long coastline encouraged trading contacts with the Arab world, enabling a free flow of new ideas and customs from as early as the 1600s. Travel to Mecca was common by the nineteenth century and, unlike the rest of the country, Kelantan's legal system operated according to Islamic law – an important factor in the maintenance of national pride under Thai overlordship. Kota Bharu's most famous son of the time, **To' Kenali**, a renowned *ulama* or religious teacher, spent some years studying in Cairo. He returned to his home town to establish *pondok*s – "hut schools" next to the mosque – in order to spread Islamic doctrine throughout the state. The current equivalent of this is the reliance of PAS (see p.249) on Muslim schools to spread its message in the villages.

Kota Bharu is one of only three towns and cities in Malaysia (together with Kuala Terengganu and Dungun) to have a Malay majority. This is evident the minute you enter the town – Malay women are dressed more circumspectly than elsewhere, and attending the mosque is a prominent feature of the day. Even so, while Kota Bharu isn't a place to sport beach wear, and foreign women sometimes complain about feeling uncomfortable here, there's a relaxed air about the town which belies its political conservatism and mitigates its male-dominated outlook.

While you might well be drawn away from the centre by the opportunity to witness the various trades at first hand – kite and top construction, batik-printing and weaving – this shouldn't distract you from Kota Bharu's **historical buildings**, sited around Padang Merdeka, or its fine markets. Using the town as your base, you can also head out to the local **beaches** and to the temples in the surrounding countryside, on the Thai border.

Arrival, information and transport

Long-distance **buses** arrive at one of the two bus stations, inconveniently situated on the southern outskirts of Kota Bharu: the state bus company, SKMK, operates from the **Langgar bus station** on Jalan Pasir Puteh, as does the MARA company, which runs buses here from KL and Singapore; other companies use the larger **Jalan Hamzah bus station**. There are only unofficial taxis at the stations, charging up to RM15 for the two-kilometre drive to the centre at night; the daytime charge is around RM4. The **local bus station**, where you'll arrive if coming from Kuala Terengganu, is on Jalan Padang Garong; SKMK also operates some services from here, notably to Wakaf Bharu (see p.262) and Kuala Besut (see p.264), and has an information counter (daily 8am–9pm, closed Fri 12.45–2pm). The **long-distance taxi** stand is behind the local bus station,

---

CROSSING THE BORDER INTO THAILAND

From Kota Bharu, you can cross the Thai border at two designated crossings, one inland, the other at the mouth of the Golok river. Both of the **border posts** are open daily between 6am and 6pm – remember that Thai time is one hour behind Malaysian time. **Visas** for Thailand can be obtained from the consulate in Kota Bharu (see "Listings", p.259).

The coastal access point is at **Pengkalan Kubor**, 20km northwest of Kota Bharu, which connects with the small town of Tak Bai on the Thai side. Take bus #27 or #43 from the local bus station for the thirty-minute journey (RM1.70), then the car ferry (50 sen).

More convenient, however, is the land crossing at **Rantau Panjang**, 30km southwest of Kota Bharu. Bus #29 departs from the local bus station in Kota Bharu every thirty minutes (6.45am–6.30pm; RM2.60) for the 45-minute trip there, or you can take a shared taxi from Kota Bharu for RM3.50 per person. Once at Rantau Panjang, it's a short walk across the border to Sungei Golok on the Thai side. Trains depart from there at noon and 3pm for the 23-hour trip to Bangkok via Hat Yai and Surat Thani. Buses to Bangkok leave at 9am and 12.30pm; buses to Hat Yai take four hours. Train information can be checked with the State Railway of Thailand in Sungei Golok (☎073/611162), although they're unlikely to accept a seat reservation over the phone. If you want to be sure of a seat, book your tickets at the *Town Guesthouse* (see p.256).

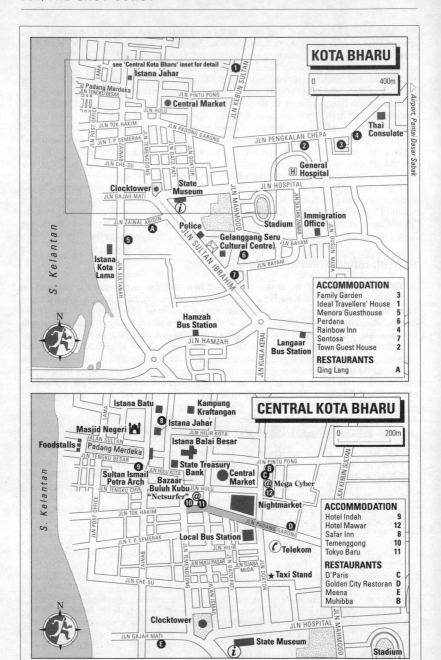

KOTA BHARU

0   400m

Airport, Pantai Dasar Sabak

see 'Central Kota Bharu' inset for detail

Istana Jahar

Padang Merdeka

JLN TENGKU BESAR

JLN PINTU PONG

Central Market

JLN HULU

JLN TOK HAKIM

JLN PADONG GARONG

JLN T. P. SEMERAK

JLN ZAINAL

JLN CHE-SU

JLN DATO PATI

JLN TEMENGGONG

JLN DOKTOR

JLN KEBUN SULTAN

JLN PENGKALAN CHEPA

Thai Consulate

General Hospital

JLN HOSPITAL

JLN MAHMOOD

Clocktower

State Museum

JLN GAJAH MATI

JLN ZAINAL ABIDIN

Police

JLN SULTAN IBRAHIM

JLN SULTANAH

Istana Kota Lama

Gelanggang Seru Cultural Centre

Stadium

JLN SULTAN ZAINAB

JLN DUSUN MUDA

Immigration Office

JLN BAYAM

JLN BAYAM

Hamzah Bus Station

JLN HAMZAH

JLN KUALA KRAI

Langaar Bus Station

S. Kelantan

N

ACCOMMODATION

Family Garden   3
Ideal Travellers' House   1
Menora Guesthouse   5
Perdana   6
Rainbow Inn   4
Sentosa   7
Town Guest House   2

RESTAURANTS

Qing Lang   A

CENTRAL KOTA BHARU

0   200m

Istana Batu

Kampung Kraftangan

LAMA

Masjid Negeri

Istana Jahar

JLN HILIR KOTA

Jalan Sultan

Foodstalls

Padang Merdeka

Istana Balai Besar

JLN PINTU PONG

JLN KEBUN SULTAN

JLN TENGKU BESAR

State Treasury Bank

Central Market

Mega Cyber

Sultan Ismail Petra Arch

JLN HULU KOTA

JLN TENGKU CHIK

Bazaar Buluh Kubu

JLN HULU

Nightmarket

JLN TOK HAKIM

"Netsurfer"

JLN PADONG GARONG

JLN POST OFFICE

JLN T. P. SEMERAK

Local Bus Station

ZAINAB

JLN TEMENGGONG

JLN HILIR

JLN DATO PATI

JLN HULU PASAR

JLN SUARA MUDA

JLN DOKTOR

Telekom

Taxi Stand

JLN CHE-SU

JALAN ISMAIL

S. Kelantan

N

Clocktower

JLN GAJAH MATI

JLN HOSPITAL

JLN MAHMOOD

State Museum

Stadium

ACCOMMODATION

Hotel Indah   9
Hotel Mawar   12
Safar Inn   8
Temenggong   10
Tokyo Baru   11

RESTAURANTS

D'Paris   C
Golden City Restoran   D
Meena   E
Muhibba   B

on Jalan Doktor. Served by flights from KL and Georgetown, the local **airport** is 9km northeast of the centre, from where a taxi into town costs RM15 – buy a coupon from the taxi counter in the airport.

The nearest **train station** to Kota Bharu is 7km to the west at Wakaf Bharu, the penultimate stop on the jungle railway (see p.230) through the interior from Gemas. From here it's a twenty-minute ride into town on bus #19 or #27 – they run to and from the local bus station.

The **Tourist Information Centre** (Mon–Thurs & Sun 8am–1pm & 2–4.45pm; ☎09/748 5534, fax 748 6652), close to the clock tower on Jalan Sultan Ibrahim, is very helpful; **tours** of various local craft workshops, cookery courses, homestays (see below) and trips to Jelawang Country Park (see p.241) can be booked here.

Although most of the sights in Kota Bharu are within easy walking distance of each other, you may want to opt for a **trishaw**. Trishaws can be found along the roads around the bus station and night market, and the normal fare for a ten-minute journey is RM5 – make sure you agree the price beforehand. For longer journeys, a **taxi** is more convenient; they operate from the stand, also used by the long-distance taxis, behind the local bus station on Jalan Doktor. You can also hire a taxi for sightseeing; the rate is roughly RM30 per hour.

Accommodation

Competition between the many **guesthouses** in Kota Bharu ensures some of the cheapest (if basic) accommodation in Malaysia can be found here, with the rates often including breakfast also. Some places let you do your own cooking, although given the low cost of eating out, this hardly seems worthwhile. All guesthouses have dorms as well as ordinary rooms, unless otherwise stated; common rooms, TV and laundry facilities are standard, while a few places offer batik workshops (where you can watch the cloth being dyed and even create your own patterns), bike rental and cultural tours. In contrast, the budget **hotels** are poor value, often dirty, noisy and located in seedy areas. However, you'll find quite a few mid-range bargains, and while luxury options are very limited, the choice is wider if you stay out of town at one of the beach resorts (see "Around Kota Bharu", p.260).

An alternative option is the **homestay programme** run by Roselan Hanafiah at the Tourist Information Centre (see above). This offers the chance to stay with a family, often expert in a particular craft; the cost is RM220 per person including all meals, with a minimum of two people staying for two nights.

Family Garden, 4945d Lorong Islah Lama (☎09/747 5763). Near the Thai consulate, this homely place includes free breakfast and transport to the long-distance bus stations in the price. The rooms are small, with shared bathrooms. ①.

Ideal Travellers' House, 3954f Jalan Kebun Sultan (☎09/744 2246). Friendly, full of character and quiet despite its very central location, this budget hostel with a peaceful beer garden and dorm is the most pleasant retreat you'll find in Kota Bharu. The simple singles and doubles come with or without bathrooms. ①, dorm beds RM6.

Indah, 236b Jalan Tengku Besar (☎09/748 5081, fax 748 2788). Reasonably priced, old-fashioned air-con rooms with good views over the river and padang, though not significantly better than the more inexpensive *Tokyo Baru*. ③.

Mawar, Jalan Parit Dalam (☎09/744 8888, fax 747 6666). Has a Baroque lobby, all gilt, wood and mirrors; small but comfortable rooms; and its own café. Situated right by the pasar malam. ⑥.

Menora Guest House, 3338d Jalan Sultanah Zainab (☎09/748 1669). Delightful guesthouse with large, brightly painted rooms, some of which are en suite. The roof garden has a river view and the café is very popular. ①, dorm beds RM6.

Perdana, Jalan Mahmood (☎09/748 5000, fax 744 7621). Despite looking like a concrete monstrosity from the outside, this hotel offers good value, boasting a swimming pool, squash courts, gym, in-house movies and spacious en-suite rooms with modern furnishings. ⑧.

Rainbow Inn, 4423a Jalan Pengkalan Chepa (☎09/743 4936). A few large, clean rooms in a 100-year-old wooden house about 1km east of the centre. Laid-back and friendly, with a garden, batik workshop, dorms and bikes for rent. ①, dorm beds RM6.

Safar Inn, Jalan Hilir Kota (☎09/747 8000, fax 747 9000). Close to all the cultural sights and set in an attractive villa, though the rooms themselves aren't quite up to the price. ⑤.

Sentosa, 3180a Jalan Sultan Ibrahim (☎09/744 3200). Close to the Cultural Centre, this friendly hotel, a little overpriced for what it offers, has clean, airy rooms, though no lounge or bar. ③.

Temenggong Hotel, Jalan Tok Hakim 15000 (☎09/748 3481, 744 1481). Professionally run, spotless place in the centre. The modern rooms complete with bathtub, fridge, TV and air-con are of a standard you'd expect to pay a good deal more for. ④.

Tokyo Baru, 3945 Jalan Tok Hakim (☎09/744 4511, fax 744 9488). Close to the pasar malam, with a welcoming management. The simple, clean doubles with fan or air-con are good value; rooms on the top floor have great balconies overlooking the town centre. ②.

Town Guest House, 286 Jalan Pengkalan Chepa (☎ & fax 09/748 3207). A warm and welcoming family-run guesthouse, with a communal lounge, rooftop café and Internet facilities. Recommended. ①.

The Town

The centre of Kota Bharu, hugging the eastern bank of Sungei Kelantan, is based on a grid pattern, its busy roundabout sporting a curious pink rocket-like clock tower marking the junction of the town's three major roads, Jalan Hospital, Jalan Sultan Ibrahim and Jalan Temenggong. The area surrounding the clock tower is where you'll find most of the shops, banks and offices, while around Jalan Padang Garong, a few blocks to the north, are Kota Bharu's **markets**. Further north still, close to the river, the quiet oasis of **Padang Merdeka** marks Kota Bharu's historical centre, a compact square of fascinating buildings. The **State Museum** and the **Gelanggang Seni** (Cultural Centre), south of the clock tower, document Kota Bharu's cultural inheritance. Most of these sights are within easy walking distance of each other, and quite feasibly visited in one day.

Around Padang Merdeka

The small **Padang Merdeka**, to the north of the centre, is the town's historical heart. Despite its grand title – Independence Square – it's not much more than a grassy patch of land, on which the British displayed the body of the defeated Tok Janggut (Father Long Beard), a peasant spiritual leader who spearheaded a revolt against the colonial system of land taxes and tenancy regulations in 1915, one of the few specifically anti-colonial incidents to occur on the east coast.

The padang is bordered on its northern side by the white **Masjid Negeri**, known as *Serambi Mekah* – "Veranda of Mecca" – because of its prominent role in the spread of Islam throughout Kelantan. Dominating the eastern end of the square, the immense **Sultan Ismail Petra Arch** is a recent timber building commemorating the declaration of Kota Bharu as a cultural town; beyond lies a pedestrianized area and the royal palaces. Half-hidden behind high walls and entrance gates, the single-storey **Istana Balai Besar**, built in 1844, contains the Throne Room and State Legislative Assembly; now used primarily for ceremonial functions, it is closed to the public. To the right of its gates is the former Kelantan **State Treasury Bank** – its presence gave the square its unofficial name of "Padang Bank". An unobtrusive stone bunker no more than two metres high, it remained in use until well into the twentieth century.

Adjacent to the former treasury, the **Istana Jahar** (daily except Fri 8.30am–4.45pm; RM2) houses the Royal Customs Museum. Although not the oldest building in the square – it was constructed in 1887 – it is certainly the most traditional in style, with a timber portico and highly polished decorative panels adorning the exterior. The building takes its name from the *jahar* tree (also called "flame of the forest" thanks to its burnt-orange flowers), a specimen of which was planted outside in the courtyard by Sultan Mohammed IV. In 1911, he ordered extensive renovations to the palace, adding an Italian marble floor, which cools the interior, and a wrought-iron spiral staircase. The ground floor of the palace is given over to a display of exquisite textiles – intricate henna-coloured *ikat* weaving and lustrous *songket*s – together with samples of the ornate gold jewellery belonging to the Royal Family. Upstairs you'll see life-size reconstructions of various traditional royal ceremonies, from weddings to circumcisions. In the childbirth ritual, the mother is made to sit over a hot stove, supposedly to encourage the delivery of the afterbirth. Behind the istana is a **Weapons Gallery** (RM1), with an impressive collection of spears, daggers and *kris*, and traditional clothing.

As you leave the museum, turn the corner to your left and after a few metres you'll see the sky-blue **Istana Batu** (daily 8am–4.45pm, closed Fri; RM2), an incongruous 1930s villa built as the sultan's residence. One of the first concrete constructions in the state (its name means "stone palace"), it's now the Kelantan Royal Museum, with the rooms left in their original state. Portraits of the ruler and his family survey the vast amounts of English crockery and glassware which crowd the dining-room table – kitsch and cluttered beyond belief. Still, it's worth a half-hour wander, from reception rooms to scullery, if only for comparison with the relatively humble standards of previous rulers.

Directly opposite, another large pedestrianized square is the site of the **Kampung Kraftangan** (daily except Fri 8am–4.45pm), or "Handicraft Village", mainly a collection of gift shops and a café. The Handicraft Museum (daily except Fri 8am–4.45pm; RM1) occupies one of several authentic timber houses in the compound, though it displays a disappointingly limited range of crafts.

The markets

To the south, away from Padang Merdeka, are two of the most vibrant markets in Malaysia. The **Central Market** (daily 8am–6pm), in an octagonal warehouse, is the focus of the town, buzzing with stalls selling produce of all kinds, from meat and fresh vegetables to cooking pots and batik sarongs. Virtually all the stall-holders are female, the coloured headscarves of their traditional Muslim dress augmenting the vivid display. The scene is best viewed from the third floor, with the yellow perspex roof casting a soft light over the geometric piles of vegetables below. Look out for the local fish-cracker speciality, *keropok batang*, greyish brown and flat in its raw state, but delicious fried and dipped in chilli sauce.

One block to the south, hundreds of brightly lit food stalls set up each evening in a car park, forming a **night market** of epic proportions. Besides offering a gastronomic experience (see "Eating", overleaf), this performs a social function, too, as it's the place to catch up on all the local gossip.

The State Museum and the Gelanggang Seni

Situated on the corner of Jalan Hospital and Jalan Sultan Ibrahim, the **State Museum** (Thurs–Sat 8am–4.45pm; RM2) houses an odd collection – romantic rural Malay paintings and lots of earthenware pots. Better is the collection of musical instruments on the first floor, among which is the *kertok*, a large coconut with its top sliced off and a piece of wood fastened across the opening to form a sounding board. Decorated with colourful pennants and hit with a cloth beater, it's one of the percussion instruments peculiar to Kelantan. To see these in action, visit the **Gelanggang Seni**, Kota Bharu's Cultural Centre, on Jalan Mahmood, about 200m southeast of the museum; it's reached via either Jalan Sultan Ibrahim or Jalan Hospital. Free performances here (March–Oct Mon, Wed & Sat except during Ramadan; check details with the Tourist Information Centre, p.255) feature many of the traditional pastimes of Kelantan (see box, overleaf) – using *gasing* (spinning tops) and *rebana* (giant drums); on Wednesday evenings there

TRADITIONAL PASTIMES IN KELANTAN

Gasing uri or **top-spinning** is one of the most vigorous of the sports played in the state and, with none of the childish connotations it has in the West, is taken very seriously, requiring a great deal of strength and dexterity. There are two types of competition: the straightforward spin, in which the winner is simply the one whose top spins the longest – the record time in Kelantan is 1 hour 47 minutes – and the striking match, whereby one top has to knock out the other. The launching process is the same, however: a long length of rope is tightly wound around the top, the loose end of the rope fastened to a tree trunk, and the top is flung from shoulder-height rather like a shot put – no mean feat when you consider that it weighs about 5kg. The spinner then has to rely on the nimble fingers of his partner, the "scooper", to transfer the top from its landing place to the arena where its progress is judged. Competition is fierce, particularly in the knockout game, which takes place in an atmosphere almost like a boxing match; try to see it in a local village if you can – the Tourist Information Centre can tell you where a competition is being held (usually in Sept).

Kite-flying (*wau ubi*) is a hugely popular activity, so much so that the emblem for the national airline, MAS, features the *wau bulan*, or "moon kite", the most common of all the designs. Originally regarded as a means of contacting the gods, the kites are highly decorated for the deities' benefit. The contest in which a kite-flyer had to cut the string of an opponent's kite was banned some time ago since it caused so many heated disputes – quite apart from the fact that the strings, which contained ground glass to make them sharp, were also highly dangerous. Nowadays, competitions are a much more muted affair, with participants being judged purely on their kite-handling skills and the altitude achieved.

The playing of *rebana* – **giant drums** – might not seem like a sport, but once you witness the energy required to produce the thunderous roll on these massive instruments, you'll begin to understand why it's classified as such. The brightly coloured drums have a diameter of over 1m, weigh 100kg, and are decorated with bamboo sticks that fan out from the rim like the spokes of a bicycle wheel. During a festival held here every July, a competition is held to determine the most skilful group of players. Each team comprises six players who play different-sized drums nonstop for around thirty minutes, maintaining fast and complex rhythms using a combination of hands and sticks – the winner is the group with the most consistent and harmonious technique. The spectacle, conducted in the traditional costume of tunic, *songket* and headdress, is best seen outdoors.

are *wayung kulit* (shadow play) performances. The traditional shows on Saturday nights – unique to Kelantan – are derived from nineteenth-century court entertainments and strongly influenced by Thai culture; they combine singing, dancing, romance and comedy. A visit to the centre is still the easiest way to see many of the arts that are dying out elsewhere in Malaysia, and the standard here is consistently high.

Eating

Easily the most exciting place to eat at is Kota Bharu's **night market** (daily 6.30pm–midnight; closed for evening prayers 7.30–8pm), with an amazing variety of food – although vegetarians could find themselves limited to vegetable *murtabak*s. If you ask, you'll get a spoon and fork; otherwise use the jug of water and roll of tissue on each table to clean your hands before and after – and eat with your right hand only. Try the local speciality *ayam percik* (barbecued chicken with a creamy coconut sauce) or the delicious *nasi kerabu* (purple, green or blue rice with a dash of vegetables, seaweed and grated coconut), and finish with a filling *pisang murtabak* (banana pancake), and you won't have parted with much more than RM5. The town's **restaurants** are a let-down after the night market; many close in the evenings in the face of such stiff competition. Note that the only places which serve alcohol are the Chinese *kedai kopi*s.

D'Paris, Jalan Doktor. Passable attempt at a European café, serving freshly baked pastries, sandwiches and cappuccinos.

Golden City Restoran, Jalan Padang Garong. Lively and brightly lit *kedai kopi* serving standard Chinese food. Try the *wan tan mee* or *curry mee*, spicy noodle dishes for around RM3.

Golden Jade Seafood Restoran, *Hotel Perdana*, Jalan Mahmood. A pricey outlet lacking in atmosphere, although the Shanghai and Cantonese dishes are recommended. Around RM15 per dish.

Meena, Jalan Gajah Mati. Inexpensive banana-leaf curries as well as *thosai*s, and other South Indian sundries, popular with Malays and Indians alike.

Muhibba, Jalan Pintu Pong. Above a good bakery, this place does a buffet of Chinese vegetarian food (RM7).

Pata Seafood Restoran, *Hotel Indah*, 236b Jalan Tengku Besar. Wide-ranging menu including crab and prawns from RM2.50–4 per dish.

Qing Lang, Jalan Zainal Abidin. An air-con Chinese vegetarian place. Around RM3 per dish.

Listings

Airlines MAS, Komplek Yakin, Jalan Gajah Mati (☎09/737 4000).

Airport Sultan Ismail Petra Airport, 9km northeast of town, is served by domestic flights only. Flight information on ☎09/743 7000.

Banks and exchange Bank Bumiputra, Jalan Kebu Sultan; Hong Kong Bank, Jalan Padang Garong; Standard Chartered Bank, Jalan Tok Hakim.

Bookshops Johan Bookshop on Jalan Padang Garong has a small selection of English-language books; Central Bookstore on Jalan Temenggong, by the clock tower, offers more choice, as does Muda Osman, Jalan Tengku Chik, west of Central Market.

Buses The SKMK information counter (daily 8am–9pm, Fri 8am–12.45pm & 2–9pm; ☎09/744 0114) at the local bus station provides information on local and long distance services, including a timetable. For information on services run by the other companies, you'll need to head to their respective stations: SKMK buses and MARA services to KL and Singapore depart from the Langgar bus station on Jalan Pasir Puteh, while other firms use the station on Jalan Hamzah.

Car rental Avis, *Hotel Perdana* lobby (☎09/748 5000). Hawk and Budget have kiosks at the airport.

Hospital The General Hospital is on Jalan Hospital (☎09/748 5533).

Internet access It's not hard to find an Internet café in Kota Bharu; most are clustered around the Central Market. Good choices are *Net Surfer Café* on Jalan Hulu and *Mega Cyber*, Jalan Parit Dalam.

Left luggage At the bus station on Jalan Hamzah (daily 8am–10pm).

Police Headquarters on Jalan Sultan Ibrahim (☎09/748 5522).

Post office The GPO is on Jalan Sultan Ibrahim (Mon–Thurs & Sun 8am–4.30pm; ☎09/748 4033). Efficient poste restante/general delivery at counter 20.

Shopping Kota Bharu offers a vast range of home-produced items in several modern multistorey shopping complexes. The Bazaar Bulu Kubu on Jalan Hulu, south of Padang Merdeka, houses a cinema, as well as souvenirs and handicrafts. Syarikat Kraftangan at Kampung Kraftangan (see overleaf) has higher prices compared to other markets, but its kites, weaving and puppets are of better quality too. The shops along Jalan Sultanah Zainab are good for antiques and silverware.

Taxis The long-distance taxi stand is on Jalan Doktor (☎09/744 7104), behind the local bus station; fares (per person) are around RM15 to Kuala Terengganu, RM30 to Kuantan and RM40 to KL.

Telephones The Telekom centre is on Jalan Doktor (daily 8am–4.30pm).

Thai visas From the Royal Thai Consulate, 4426 Jalan Pengkalan Chepa (☎09/748 2545; Mon–Thurs & Sun 9am–noon & 2–3.30pm). Two-month tourist visas (RM33) are issued within 24hr. Many nationalities can get a one-month visa stamped in at the border; ask at the consulate if you're unsure of whether you need to apply in advance for a visa.

Trains From the station at Wakaf Bharu (information ☎09/749 6986), services run south on the jungle railway to Kuala Lipis and the interior. For details of the train route into Thailand from the border, see p.253.

Travel agent Boustead Travel, 2833 Jalan Temenggong (☎09/744 9952). The management of the *Menora Guest House* (see p.255) also does tours to Jelawang Country Park (see p.241).

Visa extensions On-the-spot visa extensions at the Immigration Department, second floor, Wisma Persekutuan, Jalan Bayan (daily 8am–4pm except Thurs 8am–12.45pm; ☎09/748 2120).

Around Kota Bharu

While there's plenty in Kota Bharu itself to keep you occupied for at least a couple of days, the surrounding areas offer relaxation at the **beaches** to the north and east of town, and a look at the **cottage industries** producing local crafts. The area north of town towards the border is unsurprisingly Thai in character, boasting a few **temples** dotted among the emerald-green rice paddies.

The **beaches** around town are popular with the locals, often becoming crowded at weekends, although the conservative attitudes within the state are not, on the whole, conducive to relaxed sunbathing (though you can see a few locals, especially Chinese, in Western swimwear). Compared to what's on offer further south, the sands here are nothing special; the wistfully romantic names of the beaches are often better than the beaches themselves.

Pantai Cahaya Bulan

As every guidebook tells you, Kota Bharu's best-known and most-visited beach is more commonly known as Pantai Cinta Berahi, the "Beach of Passionate Love", though the Muslim government has officially changed its name to the less suggestive **Pantai Cahaya Bulan** (PCB for short), or "Moonlight Beach".

On the way to PCB is the **Tokong Mek Chinese Temple**, about 6km outside Kota Bharu to the left of the main road. It's a peaceful little temple, with some unusually dramatic wall reliefs featuring tigers and dragons.

About 100m inland from the beach itself, off the main road, is the signposted **Taman Buaya**, a crocodile farm (RM2), where the entrance fee covers the "House of Mirrors", a small zoo, a snake farm and, of course, sight of the lolling crocodiles.

CRAFT WORKSHOPS

The **workshops** lining the road from the town to the beach let you see master craftsmen at work, with an opportunity to buy at the end of each demonstration; most workshops are open daily from 9am to 5pm. Batik-printing and weaving are the commonest **crafts** in Malaysia, and most of the workshops here will allow you to experiment with the techniques and create your own designs. The making of the **gasing** (spinning top) – resembling a discus except for a short steel spike inserted in one side – is an art. The process of carefully selecting the wood, which must be delicately planed and shaped, together with the precise balancing of the metal spike, can take anything up to three weeks. An intricate **wau** (kite), typically about 1.5m long by 2m across, takes around two weeks to complete, the decorations being unique to each craftsman, although tradition dictates leaf patterns and a pair of birds as the principal elements in the design. The most unusual aspect of the kite's structure is the long projection above its head, supporting a large bow that hums when the kite is flying, the musical quality of which can be judged in competition. **Kampung Penambang** is particularly good for *songket* weaving and batik, while **Kampung Kijang** specializes in kite-making; both villages are barely beyond the town suburbs.

PRACTICALITIES

Eleven kilometres north of town, Pantai Cahaya Bulan is a thirty-minute ride on **bus** #10 from outside the Central Market. The bus passes through Kampung Penambang and Kampung Kijang, and also right by the short side road for the temple.

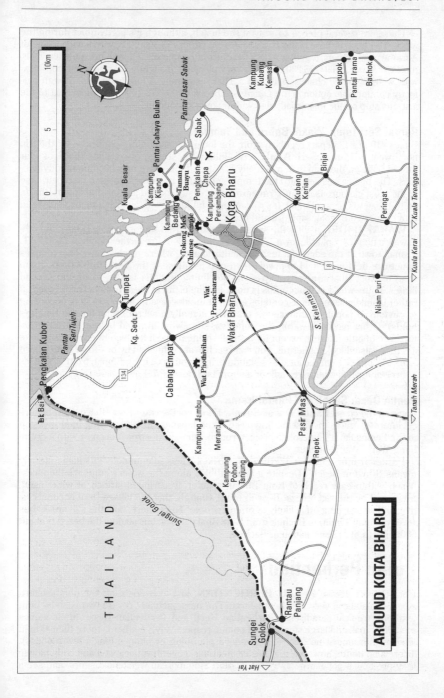

AROUND KOTA BHARU

There are several **places to stay** at the beach, although it's pretty quiet during the week. The best of these is the *Perdana Resort* (☎09/773 3000; ⑦), with a wide range of A-frames and chalets, together with a beachfront restaurant. Though not quite as plush, the *PCB Resort* (☎09/773 2307; ⑥) is a very pleasant, if slightly old-fashioned, complex, with well-appointed chalets, pool and a Thai restaurant. A less luxurious, though perfectly comfortable option is the *Longhouse Beach* (☎09/773 1090; ③), right next to the last bus stop on the main road, also with its own restaurant.

Pantai Seri Tujuh, Wakaf Bahru and Tumpat

Buses #19 or #43 depart regularly from the local bus station in Kota Bharu for the trip northwest to **Pantai Seri Tujuh**, a two-kilometre stretch of coastline that looks far more idyllic on the map than it actually is – its lagoons have now become muddy puddles. The bus passes several Thai temples en route, in various states of disrepair. One of the most glamorous is **Wat Pracacinaram**, easily spotted just outside Wakaf Bharu, on the road to Cabang Empat. It's a brand new building, with an elaborate triple-layered roof decorated in gold, sapphire and red.

WAKAF BAHRU itself is the site of the nearest train station to Kota Bharu, but otherwise a nondescript little town. The end of the line is 12km further north at **TUMPAT**, a small town at the edge of a lush agricultural area, where tumbledown Thai temples punctuate field upon field of jewel-green rice paddies. At the **Wat Pothivihan**, 15km west of Kota Bharu, a forty-metre-long Reclining Buddha is said to be the second largest in the world (although this is not a unique claim in these parts). The colossal, if rather insipid, plaster statue contains ashes of the deceased, laid to rest here according to custom (a popular rumour says that it is actually a secret cache for the temple's funds). Other pavilions within the complex, somewhat dwarfed by the central structure, are of little interest, except for a small shrine to the left which honours a statue of a rather wasted-looking hermit. You can reach Wat Pothivihan by bus from Kota Bharu – the #19 or #27 from the local bus station brings you to Cabang Empat, from where it's a three-and-a-half-kilometre walk or a short taxi ride (RM5) away.

Pantai Dasar Sabak and Pantai Irama

Back on the coast, **Pantai Dasar Sabak**, 13km northeast of Kota Bharu, is of historical interest – it was the first landing place of the Japanese in 1941, during their invasion of the Peninsula. It's a desolate place, a rough, windswept stretch of coast with a crumbling World War II bunker.

Pantai Irama, a further 12km south, strikes a less solemn note – its name literally means "Rhythm Beach". Despite a little rubbish along the water's edge, it's the nicest beach within easy reach of Kota Bharu, a quiet, tree-fringed stretch of white sand, freshened by the sea breeze. Bear in mind, though, that the village here is conservative, and so stripping off is likely to offend people. To get here, take the #23 or #39 bus (every 30min; 45min) to Bachok from Kota Bharu's local bus station; the beach is about 500m north of the bus station at Bachok.

Pulau Perhentian

Until the late 1980s, **PULAU PERHENTIAN**, just over 20km off the northeastern coast, remained a very well-kept secret. The name actually covers two islands, both textbook tropical paradises – Perhentian Kecil and Perhentian Besar (their names meaning small and large stopping-off points, respectively); neither is more than 4km in length, with almost no electricity, modern plumbing or phones (bar a few mobiles). There's no doubt, however, that the Perhentians' cover has been well and truly blown: they are now a popular getaway for KL and Singaporean weekend visitors, and see a

SNORKELLING AND DIVING AROUND THE PERHENTIANS

Outside the monsoon, the **snorkelling** conditions around the Perhentians are superb: the currents are gentle, and visibility is up to 20m, although the seasonal sea lice can be a problem, inflicting an unpleasant but harmless sting not unlike that of a jelly fish. A foray around the rocks at the ends of most bays turns up a teeming array of brightly coloured fish and live coral; you'll also get a chance to spot turtles. Don't break any of the coral off – it's razor-sharp, and you'd also be damaging the subaqua ecosystem. You'd also do well to drop nothing at all overboard and suggest that your guide does the same. Snorkelling equipment can be rented from most chalets, while snorkelling trips around either island to undeveloped coves cost around RM30 per person – your accommodation can either rent you a boat or tell you where to join one of these trips. Asking the organizers of such trips about their environmental policy before you sign up with them is one of the best ways to encourage good practice around the reefs.

For the more adventurous still, there are several operations on both islands running **diving courses**; there are some spectacular dive sites a short boat ride offshore. Prices are pretty much uniform; most chalets offer a single dive for qualified divers for around RM85, an open-water course for RM750, and an advanced course for RM550.

regular stream of backpackers. Nevertheless, the low-budget chalet accommodation here hasn't been forced out by upmarket resorts, as has happened on some of Malaysia's other islands; big-money investment has so far been put off by the lack of any kind of infrastructure (though gone are the days when you had to draw up the well water for your daily shower). However, new chalets are springing up all the time, and there is talk of relocating Kampung Pasir Hantu on Perhentian Kecil to the mainland to make way for development. In the meantime, although the islanders say that the place has changed beyond belief in recent years, life on Pulau Perhentian remains delightful, with flying foxes, monkeys and lizards for company.

Perhentian Besar caters more to the resort-oriented crowd while Kecil gets most of the backpacker scene. The interiors of both islands consist of largely inaccessible, tree-covered rocky hills, although a few paths offer some challenging **walks** through the jungle. A **fishing trip** with local fishermen (easily arranged at your accommodation for around RM30 per person) offers a chance to see the way of life that sustains most islanders – bear in mind, though, that the swell of the water, combined with the smell of the landed fish, can make you queasy. The sea here also offers opportunities for snorkelling and diving; see box, above.

Facilities at the islands' chalets are fairly basic, though a few of the simplest A-frames still use hurricane lamps instead of electric lighting. The water supply on Besar is from the mains; on Kecil it comes from storage tanks. Almost all the chalet establishments have their own **restaurant** – you don't have to be a resident to eat at them. The food mostly comprises infinite but monotonous variations on rice and noodles with fish or chicken; you can also get snack foods such as toast, omelettes and banana pancakes. Neither island boasts a raging nightlife, so you'll probably be tucked up in bed by 10pm. Indeed, with the victory of the Islamist PAS party in the 1999 Terengganu state elections, the situation as regards **alcohol** on the islands is up for review and likely to take a turn towards the temperate. Officially, at time of writing, you can drink in your hotel room, but not in a restaurant, and only non-Muslim-run shops are allowed to sell you booze. The actual situation however, is rather different, with many places on the islands selling alcohol, particularly in high season; the local people are Muslim, but seem to have no objection to you bringing your own drink from the mainland.

The harsh east-coast **monsoon** means that the boats which head to the islands from the coastal town of Kuala Besut (see overleaf) operate a regular service only between

ACCOMMODATION

Abdul's	23	Fauna	26	Paradise	17
Aur Beach	10	Flora	25	Pasir Panjang	6
Cempaka	7	IBI's	22	Perhentian Island Resort	15
Coco Hut	20	Impeani	14	Petani	13
Cozy Chalets	19	Mama's Place	18	Rajawali	9
Coral View	16	Mata Hari	5	Samudra	28
D'Lagoon	1	Mira's Place	12	Seahorse Chalets	21
East West	8	Moonlight Chalets	2	Sunset View	11
Everfresh	24	Panorama	4	Symphony	3
				Wanderer	27

PULAU PERHENTIAN

▽ *Kuala Besut*

March and October; at other times of year services are much reduced, so much so that you may have to wait two or three days for a boat. Be warned that during peak season, in August, the accommodation at the popular Long Beach fills up, making some hostels less than idyllic, especially as some places can suffer from a shortage of fresh water (the dry season lasts from June to August).

En route to the Perhentians: Kuala Besut

The departure point for Pulau Perhentian is the ragged little town of **KUALA BESUT**, 45km south of Kota Bharu, off the coastal Route 3. It's reached by bus #3, which leaves Kota Bharu's local bus station every fifteen minutes throughout the day for the hour's ride to Pasir Puteh, from where bus #96 (every 30min) makes the remaining half-hour journey to Kuala Besut. It's simpler to take a shared taxi there (RM5), which can be organized by most guesthouses in Kota Bharu.

There are no banks in Kuala Besut, or on the islands, so **change money** before you arrive. The *kedai kopi*s will exchange cash only, at a lousy rate. There's always a chance that unfavourable weather conditions may force you to spend the night in town; one of the better **places to stay** is the *Coco Hut Chalet* (☎09/696 2085; ①), a clean, simple place with small rooms and communal showers. If you're feeling flush, try the *Primula Besut Beach Resort* (☎09/695 6311, fax 695 6322; ⑤), a white, concrete complex a couple of kilometres further south; you'll have to take a taxi there.

Boats to and around the Perhentians

Slow, unsophisticated fishing **boats** depart for the Perhentians from the Kuala Besut quayside, just behind the bus station. The journey takes an hour and a half – morning departures are preferable, since the weather tends to be more reliable then. In season (March–Oct), services operate roughly every two hours between 9am and 5pm; at other times there are just two or three departures a day depending on the weather. Tickets cost RM20 one way and can be bought from one of the offices near the quayside or on the boat; avoid getting a return as the boat companies rarely honour one another's tickets – despite claiming to do so – and it's not possible to predict which company you'll be using for the return leg. Perhentian Ferry Travel and Tours (☎09/691 6979) and Bonanza Express (☎09/691 0290) are among the few reputable boat companies. Ferries run by Pelangi, and those from the *Perhentian Island Resort*, are to be avoided at all costs, the latter having been known to charge double the advertised fare once out at sea. A few fast boats at the jetty also sail for the Perhentians, taking half an hour to get there (RM30 one way). All boats drop you at the bay of your choice – at those bays without a jetty (such as Coral Bay), reaching the shore entails a bit of wading.

Most chalet operations have small **speedboats** for getting around or between the islands, the standard price for any trip being RM10.

Perhentian Kecil

On the southeastern corner of **PERHENTIAN KECIL** is the island's only village, **KAMPUNG PASIR HANTU**, with its only jetty, police station, school and clinic – but the littered beach and scruffy houses don't encourage you to linger. The west-facing coves, such as **Coral Bay**, have the advantage of views of sunsets – a major event in the Perhentian day – and good snorkelling in their sheltered waters; that said, the best snorkelling here is to be had at the cove where *D'Lagoon* is located, on the far north east of the island (see overleaf). East-facing **Long Beach** has been the target of most development on Kecil, not surprisingly, since it boasts a wide stretch of uncluttered, glistening-white beach, with deep, soft sand. However, it's more exposed to the elements, a fact which forces many of the chalets here to close from the end of October to April, when the huge surf keeps the boats away. Throughout the rest of the season, the water's pretty tame and shallow at low tide, giving easy access to the coral-like rocks at either end of Long Beach. Below we list **accommodation** on both west- and east-facing shores; *DJ's*, a **restaurant** on Coral Bay, and the *Moonlight Chalets* are popular spots for dinner.

Western-shore accommodation, including Coral Bay

Aur Beach (no phone). Basic but popular chalets with showers. ③.

Impeiani (☎012/928 5080). The most upmarket spot on the island, though not quite up to the standard of some of the places on Perhentian Besar. The large hotel-style rooms with air-con are connected by attractive walkways through the jungle; there's a good restaurant, too. ⑦.

Mira's Place (☎011/976603). Located on its own sandy bay, a 25min walk south of Coral Bay, this popular cluster of rustic chalets has a communal TV and radio. Recommended. ①.

Petani (☎019/881 2444). Fifteen minutes around the headland from *Mira's Place,* this is a rough 45min trek from Coral Bay, so it's best to get a speedboat here from a nearby beach. Much cheaper than the *Impeiani*, with which it shares the superb beach, this has clean, well-built chalets with shower. ④.

Rajawali (☎010/980 5244). High up on the rocky headland, this chalet operation takes mainly package bookings. ①.

Sunset View (☎012/938 8083). Slightly overpriced though smartly furnished en-suite chalets, well placed on the southern end of the bay. ④.

Eastern-shore accommodation, including Long Beach

Cempaka (☎010/985 3729). A mishmash of basic A-frames without electricity (RM30), and double chalets with shower (③). There are also some less expensive doubles in a longhouse. ②.

D'Lagoon (no phone). Set in a tiny and isolated cove a kilometre from Long Beach, at the very northeastern tip of the island, with tents, rooms and chalets. From here, you can clamber across the narrow neck of the island to the turtle-spotting beach on the other side (though the best place to see turtles is on Perhentian Besar – see below). ②.

East West (no phone). Scrubby, basic A-frames on a steep hill. Though the accommodation is grimy, it does at least have lovely views. ①.

Mata Hari (☎019/956 8726). Simple but well-designed chalets in a garden, complete with mosquito nets, hammocks and a good restaurant. Recommended. ②.

Moonlight Chalets (☎010/982 8135). A wide range of good-value chalets set at the northern end of the beach, ranging from basic A-frames without electricity to en-suite doubles. This is also the best place on the island for food; the café does wild "special shakes" containing mashed up Mars Bars and M&Ms, and the upstairs restaurant has a good view across the beach. ①/②.

Panorama (☎010/984 1181). Set back from the beach in the shady jungle with some basic cabins (②), and a few plusher ones (④). Has a good restaurant, with Western and local dishes, though the setting is not quite up to the *Mata Hari*'s next door.

Pasir Panjang Chalets (☎010/985 3589). Strange, half-brick, half-wooden rooms with shower and air-con. Well furnished but considerably overpriced. ⑥.

Symphony (no phone). Hurricane lamps, thatched roofs and very friendly staff who try hard to please. Its A-frames are set in a sandy garden, and there's a communal shower block. Recommended. ①.

Perhentian Besar

The best place on the islands for **turtle-watching** is undoubtedly Three Coves Bay on the north coast of Perhentian Besar. A stunning conglomeration of three beaches, separated from the main area of accommodation by rocky outcrops and reachable only by speedboat, it provides a secluded haven between May and September for green and hawksbill turtles to come ashore and lay their eggs (see also "Rantau Abang", p.281).

The western shore

The bulk of the **accommodation** on the island is on its western half; there's a lot to choose from, so it shouldn't be too difficult to find somewhere suitable if your first option is full, though bear in mind that there isn't much at the low end of the scale. The beach improves as you go further south and the atmosphere is slightly more sedate than at Long Beach.

Many of the chalets have **cafés**; it's worth splashing out for the hearty pizzas (RM12) at the *Seahorse Chalets*, just behind the Seahorse Dive Shop. *IBI*'s on the main beach has a popular **restaurant**, and for something more upmarket, the decor and view at *Coral View* get the thumbs up over the *Perhentian Island Resort* restaurant. Continuing south from *Abdul's*, a set of wooden steps traverses the rocky outcrop to a beach café serving breakfasts, snacks and set meals (RM6–8). Expensive **Internet** facilities (RM20–25 an hour) can be found at *Coral View*, *IBI's* and *Seahorse Café*.

Abdul's (☎010/983 7303). Fronting one of the best strips of beach, with some basic rooms in a longhouse as well as some costlier ones with shower. This is one of the best places at the lower end of the price spectrum. ①.

Coco Hut (☎019/910 5019). Somewhat characterless A-frames, with attached showers, on the beachfront. ②.

Coral View (☎ & fax 010/903 0943). Located on a rocky outcrop, the tastefully designed and very well-furnished chalets are the best accommodation on either island. Ranging from hotel style en-suite rooms with air-con, minibar and hot water (⑧), to good doubles with shower (⑤), this should be your first choice if you're splashing out. The restaurant, overlooking two bays, is also worth the outlay, offering tasty chicken and beef dishes.

Cozy Chalets (☎09/697 7703). Built on a headland which separates the beach north and south, this has smart, carpeted chalets built two by two up on the rocks. There's also a scenic restaurant. ③.

IBI's (☎010/910 6244). Large, clean but slightly ramshackle chalets set on an excellent beach in semidetached pairs, sharing a bathroom. There's a book exchange, a good restaurant and email facilities, though the rooms themselves are not quite as good as those at *Abdul's*. ②.

Mama's Place (☎010/981 3359). Pastel-coloured chalets, some by the beach, with cheaper ones behind. Rather regimented, this large operation, the only inexpensive option north of *Cozy Chalets*, has decent doubles. ②/③.

Paradise Chalets (☎010/981 0930). Similar to *Mama's Place* next door, this has double chalets that are functional enough, though a little expensive for what you get and rather crudely laid out. ③.

Perhentian Island Resort (☎013/244 8530, fax 03/243 4984). The *Coral View* apart, this is the only place on the island with air-con; though there's a wide range of rooms available here, they're bare and overpriced by comparison. There is, however, a pool and a wide range of water-sports facilities; this is also the best spot on the island for guests and non-guests alike to snorkel. The lovely beach fronting the resort does *not* belong to them, despite what the signs here would have you believe. ⑧.

Seahorse Chalets (no phone). Thatched A-frames set back from the beach, with shared bathrooms, an Internet terminal and a good restaurant. ①.

Flora Bay

The steep trail (45min in total) across to **Flora Bay**, on the southern side of the island, begins just past the second jetty south of *Abdul's*, behind some private villas intended for visiting politicians. You can also get here using a trail (30min) which starts behind the *Perhentian Island Resort*, via the waterworks.

Everfresh (☎09/697 7620). Laid-back place at the end of Flora Bay – you get one of their attractive bungalows on stilts to yourself. ②.

Fauna (☎010/985 6843). The chalets here all face the beach and are set in a neat garden. ②.

Flora Bay (☎011/726 6011). Smart A-frame huts, ranging from basic doubles with shower to family rooms. ②.

Samudra Beach Chalets (☎010/983 4929). Pleasant bungalows and smaller, less expensive A-frames, all en suite. ②.

Wanderer (no phone). A pleasant little encampment of ramshackle A-frames in one of the quietest spots hereabouts. ②.

Merang and Pulau Redang

There's absolutely nothing to do in **MERANG** (not to be confused with Marang, 57km further down the coast) – and that's its attraction. A tiny coastal kampung 120km south of Kota Bharu, Merang began to attract foreign travellers in the 1970s. The only places to stay were in the homes of the villagers and soon this became the very reason people wanted to come here – to get away from bland and impersonal hotels. During the 1980s a few enterprising locals turned this into a more formal arrangement, with the introduction of **homestays**. Unfortunately, at the time of writing, none were in operation, the reason for this perhaps linked with the development of **Pulau Redang**, to the nothwest, as a major resort. However, Merang is still beautifully tranquil and, for the time being, the fishing community remains virtually unchanged by its visitors.

The kampung at Merang is clustered around a small T-junction close to the beach, whose rough yellow sand slopes steeply down to the sea. It's a reasonable place to swim, though there's more litter the closer you get to the village; a jetty has been built beside Merang's lighthouse, ruining what used to be the best spot for swimming (ironically, the harbour is already silting up, making rebuilding in the future necessary). To the north of the main village, dominating this sweep of bay, a large mound serves as an ideal lookout across the blustery coastline – Pulau Bidong, a former refugee camp for Vietnamese boat people, and Pulau Redang are clearly visible from here. Just before the start of Ramadan (see p.70), the beach sometimes becomes the focus of a local festival, when visitors are invited to join in the traditional games and music. For the rest of the year, fishing forms the mainstay of village life – if you get up early enough (around 6am), you'll see the fishermen returning with the day's catch.

Practicalities

Without your own transport, Merang is unfortunately not a convenient stopover en route to or from Kota Bharu and the Perhentian Islands. Coming from the north, take any bus bound for Kuala Terangganu as far as **Permaisuri**, just before Kampung Buloh on Route 3. From here, taxis (RM15 per car) or a regular minibus service (known as an econovan; RM6) go on to Merang, a further 33km away. From Kuala Terengganu, a direct bus leaves for Merang from the local bus station (8 daily; first bus at 8.30am). Otherwise you can catch a bus as far as **Batu Rakit**, one of a string of pretty coastal kampungs, from where you may be able to hitch a lift for the remaining 16km to Merang; it's safer to take a taxi (RM25) all the way from Kuala Terengganu if you want to be sure of not getting stuck. Returning to Kuala Terengganu is easier, since econovans (RM5) wait at the jetty to meet visitors and workers returning from Pulau Redang. Four buses a day to Kuala Besut (see p.264) pass along the main shore road heading north, and you can flag one down anywhere.

Among **places to stay**, the *Kenbara Resort* (☎ & fax 09/653 1770; ②) is a friendly, spotless establishment fifteen minutes' walk from the jetty, right by the beach. It has cooking facilities – handy as there are few dining-out options in Merang – and a small dorm (RM10). The management arranges all-day snorkelling trips to Redang (RM80 per person or RM350 per boatload of eight). Further north, towards the jetty, is the *Merang Inn Village Resort* (☎ & fax 09/653 1435; ②), which has standard and air-con chalets set back from the road, and a small restaurant. At the opposite (southern) end of town is the tasteful and luxurious *Aryani* (☎09/653 2111, fax 653 1007; ⑨), where for a mere RM1055 you can sleep in a hundred-year-old traditional Malay house – the "Redang Suite" as it's called – built on stilts, and swim in a pool that looks like the stage set for a Hollywood musical. The house, which formerly belonged to a Terengganu Sultan, was moved here piece by piece.

There are no **restaurants** apart from those at the hotels; however, there are two basic *kedai kopi*s, with cheaper, tastier fare than the restaurants, at the junction and on the seafront, and two or three provision stores for other snacks. Every Sunday, there's a pasar malam where the stalls serve cooked seafood on the main road.

Pulau Redang

Northeast of Merang lies **PULAU REDANG**, just 5km by 8km in size, in the north of which an area has been set aside for recreational purposes, allowing for some easy forest walks between the two rocky hills that run the length of the island. However, the island's chief attraction is that it's surrounded by the latest of Malaysia's government-designated **marine parks**, designed to minimize the damage to the spectacular coral reefs. The sea here boasts abundant marine life, sustained by the **coral reef** which thrives in the mangrove-sheltered waters of the Sungei Redang estuary. In the mid-1970s, the reef suffered a large-scale attack of the coral-eating "crown of thorns" starfish; barely had the reef recovered when agricultural development and the building of a road to the upper reaches of the river in the late 1980s deposited silt and caused more massive damage to the coral. Happily, coral reefs have remarkable properties of self-renewal, and their preservation is helped by the regulation of certain activities, such as spear-fishing, trawling and water sports, in their vicinity. The best snorkelling is off the southern coast around the islets of Pulau Pinang and Pulau Ekor Tibu, while **scuba diving** is best around Redang's northeastern region. Among the most common fish are batfish, angel fish, box fish and butterfly fish, which feed off the many anemone, sponges and bivalves to be found around the rocks.

Despite winning Tourism Malaysia's "Best Tourist Attraction" award in 1994/95, Redang is a big disappointment if you're looking for an unspoilt island paradise. In recent years, Redang has been extensively redeveloped by the *Berjaya* luxury-hotel group: forests have been felled and hillsides levelled to make way for a golf course, new roads and a freshwater pipeline from the mainland. A new village is being built inland for the two-thousand-strong fishing community which lives on stilted houses in the estuary. The local government wants them to be relocated so a new jetty and more resort developments can be built, but the villagers, who were shifted once before from the nearby Pulau Pinang (not to be confused with Penang island), were understandably reluctant to move at time of writing. However, with pollution from the village visibly killing off the fragile reef in the estuary, the rights and wrongs of the issue are by no means clear cut.

Practicalities

The island's two *Berjaya* resorts run a daily Merang–Redang **ferry** (1hr; RM80 return), leaving the mainland at 10am, 2pm and 6pm, and returning at 8am, noon and 4pm. It's also possible to charter boats out to the island from the Merang jetty from around RM40 one way; ask about this in Merang at the *Kenbara* and *Merang Inn Village Resort* (see opposite).

For **accommodation**, though there are several hotel and dive operations along the southeast side of the island, the main focus of tourist activity are the two *Berjaya* operations: the *Beach Resort* (☎09/697 1111, fax 697 3899; ②), which has the sandy bay at Teluk Dalam in the north all to itself, and the *Golf and Spa Resort* (☎09/697 3988, fax 697 3899; ⑦) overlooking the old fishing village. Apart from a couple of campsites within walking distance of the fishing village, the rest of the accommodation is located around the beach at Pasir Panjang, on the east side of the island. The most pleasant place to stay is the *Coral Redang Island Resort* (☎09/623 6200, 623 6300; ⑦), with its own pool, restaurant and dive centre; the cheapest place on the island is the *Redang Lagoon* (☎09/827 2116; ⑥), where the room rate includes meals. There's also a small dormitory here for RM20 a night, which represents the only budget accommodation on Redang, so if you're not prepared to pay for an alternative, make sure to book ahead here. Other options include the *Redang Beach Resort* (☎09/623 8188, fax 623 0225; ⑥), *Redang Bay* (☎09/620 3200, fax 624 2048; ⑤) and *Redang Pelangi Resort* (☎09/622 3158, fax 623 5202; ⑨). All places to stay on the island have offices in Kuala Terengganu (ask the Tourist Information Centre there for details; see p.271), where packages costing from around RM320 per person for two nights, inclusive of meals and transport, are available; you can also book a package at the *Ping Anchorage Travellers' Homestay* in Kuala Terengganu, who offer two nights at the *Redang Pelangi Resort* for RM275 per person, including meals and boat transfers. On Pulau Pinang, the *Marine Park Centre* (☎011/971125) has a campsite and some facilities for visitors.

Kuala Terengganu and around

As you approach **KUALA TERENGGANU** from the north, a huge hillside sign in Malay and Arabic reads "God Save Terengganu" – or as locals wryly remark, "God Save the Oil". The discovery of **oil** in the South China Sea, just off the coast here, has undoubtedly been the main factor in Terengganu State's recent prosperity, and evidence of the new wealth is immediately apparent as you enter Kuala Terengganu, the state capital, where high-rise office buildings and banks jostle for position in the busy commercial sector.

THE TERENGGANU PEASANTS' REVOLT

In the first three decades of the twentieth century, major changes were being wrought on the **Terengganu peasantry**. The introduction by the Malay rulers of the system of *cap kurnia*, or royal gifts of land, created a new class of absentee landlords, and reduced farmers who had previously been able to sell or mortgage their land to the status of mere tenant cultivators. Furthermore, the installation of the **British Advisory system** in 1910 sought to consolidate colonial power by imposing new land taxes, a costly registration of births, deaths and marriages, and permits for everyday things like collecting wood to repair houses.

These ploys were greatly resented by the peasantry, whose response was expressed primarily in religious terms – the deterioration of their living conditions signalled to the faithful the imminent coming of the Imam Mahdi who would restore tradition and true faith. Consequently, their actions were directed against all *kafir* (unbelievers), including the Malay rulers who were seen to be in collusion with the colonists.

The campaign of resistance began in 1922 with a series of anti-tax protests, organized by the village *imam*s and spearheaded by two charismatic *ulama*s (Islamic scholars), **Sayyid Sagap** and **Haji Drahman**. As the peasants' courage and militancy increased, so relations with the government deteriorated, until one incident in April 1928 triggered a **full-scale revolt**. A group of around five hundred armed men angrily confronted three British officials investigating an illegal tree-felling near Tergat, deep in the Terengganu interior. This was an attempt to provoke the British into defending their interests; however, Sultan Sulaiman himself travelled upstream to hear the crowd's grievances, which he duly promised to consider. The resulting legislation was a compromise that failed to satisfy the peasantry, who decided on a major assault on Kuala Terengganu. Moving upriver, they first captured the District Office at Kuala Berang and then proceeded to Kuala Telemong, where they were to join forces with a local band. But the rendezvous never happened: impatient to capitalize on previous successes, the gang at Kuala Telemong, a motley crew by comparison with the well-armed band at Kuala Berang, decided to attack the government installation alone, walking straight into the line of fire. Many of their leaders, who had previously been considered invulnerable, were killed, taking the wind out of the sails of the deeply disillusioned peasants.

However, it was the behaviour of the two *ulama*s that dealt the most powerful blow to the rebellion. Sayyid Sagap denied that he had ever been involved, claiming to be a loyal subject of the sultan; luckily for him, he had remained too far in the background to be successfully implicated. On hearing about the Kuala Telemong shooting, Haji Drahman fled to Patani, although he eventually returned voluntarily to face trial. Malay and British officials alike not only feared him personally but realized that he was too influential a figure to imprison, and so persuaded him to call off the hostilities in return for comfortable exile to Mecca and a healthy stipend from the government to keep him there. The peasants, having had their collective will broken, were not only deserted by their leaders but then subject to the unfettered and strangling effects of British bureaucracy.

As recently as the early 1970s though, Kuala Terengganu, 160km south of Kota Bharu, was little more than an oversized fishing village that just happened to be the seat of the sultan, whose descendants established themselves here in the early eighteenth century. The town was involved in a certain amount of trade, with neighbouring states and countries particularly interested in its local crafts – boat-building, *songket*-weaving and brassware – but economic development was slow, and what wealth there was accrued only to the rulers. A short-lived **peasants' revolt** in 1928 (see box, opposite) resulted from the imposition of new taxes on an already overburdened populace. It was the only rebellion in the Peninsula to be led by religious leaders, taking on the character of a *jihad* (holy struggle) against infidels, and one of the few involving the normally passive peasantry.

Today, even in these nouveau riche times for Kuala Terengganu, the outward trappings of modernity have not changed the essence of this tiny Muslim metropolis, sited in what is still a conservative, strongly Islamic state. For the casual visitor, there's plenty that appeals, from the istana and Chinatown district, to the lively market and waterfront. The **Istana Tengku Long Museum** is one of the best cultural complexes in Malaysia, and well worth a visit. Using the city as a base, you can also venture inland to **Tasek Kenyir** and the **Sekayu Waterfall**, to experience something of the outdoor life for which the state's interior is renowned. Handicraft skills thrive in the area around the town, such as **Pulau Duyong**, in the estuary of Sungei Terengganu.

Arrival, information and accommodation

The **express bus station** is at the northern end of town, on Jalan Sultan Zainal Abidin. The **airport**, served by flights from KL, is 13km northeast of the centre, from where a taxi into town costs RM15–20; the city bus marked "Kem Seberang Takir" picks up from the road directly outside the airport and runs to the **local bus station** in Jalan Masjid Abidin, just south of which is the **taxi stand**. Once in the centre, you can easily get around on foot.

The **Tourism Malaysia Office** (Mon–Wed, Sat & Sun 8am–12.45pm & 2–4.15pm, Thurs 8am–1pm, closed first & third Sat of every month; ☎09/622 1433) is situated south of the centre in Jalan S. Omar, on the fifth floor of the Menara Yayasan Islam Terengganu building. The rather better **Tourist Information Centre** (daily 8am–5pm ☎09/622 1553) is more centrally located near the GPO on Jalan Sultan Zainal Abidin. Both can be reached from the centre on foot.

Accommodation

There isn't a great deal of choice, or quality, when it comes to **hotels** in Kuala Terengganu – the cheap ones around the local bus station are downright seedy and unwelcoming. Fortunately, there are two good **hostels** and another inexpensive place on Pulau Duyong, *Awi's Yellow House* (see p.275), which should suit those who prefer to stay away from the action.

Kenangan, 65 Jalan Sultan Ismail (☎09/622 2688, fax 626 4535). A little run-down and musty, though kitted out with air-con and TV; the family rooms have bathtubs and would be great value if they were spring-cleaned. ②.

KT Mutiara, 67 Jalan Sultan Ismail (☎09/622 2655, fax 623 6895). Small, neat, spotless rooms with air-con. A touch overpriced for what's on offer, but much cleaner than the *Kenangan* next door. ④.

Motel Desa, Bukit Pak Api (☎09/622 3033, fax 622 3863). Set in quiet gardens on a hill overlooking town, 1500m from the centre, this place boasts well-appointed rooms and a swimming pool. ④.

Ping Anchorage Travellers' Homestay, 77a Jalan Dato' Isaac (☎09/626 2020, fax 626 2022, *patrvl@tm.net.my*). Budget hostel with excellent information boards, laundry facilities and a helpful travel agency, which organizes trips to Pulau Redang (see p.268). The rooms and dorm are very basic, though clean, and there's a seating area on the roof. ②, dorm beds RM6.

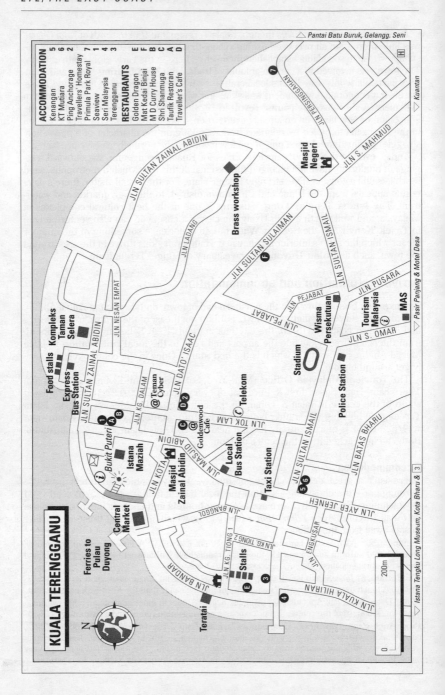

KUALA TERENGGANU

ACCOMMODATION
Kenangan	5
KT Mutiara	6
Ping Anchorage	2
Travellers' Homestay	7
Primula Park Royal	1
Seaview	4
Seri Malaysia	3
Terengganu	3

RESTAURANTS
Golden Dragon	E
Mat Kedai Binjai	F
M D Curry House	B
Shri Shanmuga	C
Taufik Restoran	A
Traveller's Cafe	D

Pantai Batu Buruk, Gelangg. Seni

Kuantan

Pasir Panjang & Motel Desa

Istana Tengku Long Museum, Kota Bharu & 3

JLN PERSINGGAHAN

JLN S. MAHMUD

Masjid Negeri

JLN SULTAN ZAINAL ABIDIN

Brass workshop

JLN LADANG

JLN SULTAN SULAIMAN

JLN NESAN EMPAT

JLN SULTAN ISMAIL

JLN PUSARA

JLN PEJABAT

JLN PEJABAT

Wisma Persekutuan

Tourism Malaysia

JLN S. OMAR

MAS

Stadium

Police Station

Kompleks Taman Selera

Food stalls

Express Bus Station

JLN SULTAN ZAINAL ABIDIN

JLN KG. DALAM

@ Teman Cyber

JLN DATO' ISAAC

Telekom

JLN TOK LAM

Bukit Puteri

A B

JLN KG. DALAM

D 2

@ C

@ Goldenwood Cafe

Local Bus Station

JLN BATAS BHARU

Istana Maziah

JLN MASJID ABIDIN

Masjid Zainal Abidin

JLN KOTA

Taxi Station

JLN SULTAN ISMAIL

5 6

JLN AYER JERNEH

Central Market

JLN BANGGOL

JLN BANDAR

JLN KG. TIONG 1

JLN KG. TIONG 2

Stalls

E

3

JLN ENGKUSAR

JLN KUALA HILIRAN

Teratai

4

Ferries to Pulau Duyong

N

0   200m

Primula Park Royal, Jalan Persinggahan (☎09/622 2100, fax 623 3360, *primul@tm.net.my*). Luxury, reasonably priced hotel complete with swimming pool. It's about 1500m walk east of the express bus station; a taxi from town should cost around RM3. ⑧.

Seaview, 18a Jalan Masjid Abidin (☎09/622 1911, fax 622 3048). With helpful staff, this place has very clean air-con rooms, though they're a little sparsely furnished for the asking price. ③.

Seri Malaysia, Jalan Hiliran (☎09/623 6454, fax 623 8344). An upmarket hotel, part of a national chain, set on the river. Rates include breakfast. ⑤.

Terengganu, 12 Jalan Sultan Ismail (☎09/622 2900, fax 622 2906). Close to the jetty, with spacious rooms and comfortable fittings; slightly shabbier than the *Seaview*, but half the price. ②.

The City and around

Connected to Route 3 by a large, modern bridge, the centre of Kuala Terengganu is located within a compact promontory at the mouth of the wide, fast-flowing Sungei Terengganu. The main artery through the commercial sector is Jalan Sultan Ismail, where you'll find the banks and government offices, while the **old town**, to the north-west of the centre, spreads back from Jalan Bandar and the waterfront. The various crafts for which the town is renowned are all practised in **workshops** on the outskirts, and there are regular buses to most from the local bus station. The **Gelanggang Seni** (Cultural Centre) and the **Istana Tengku Long Museum** reflect the state's cultural heritage, while just across the estuary, **Pulau Duyong** is the last place in Malaysia where a unique boat-building technique is still practised.

The old town

The neat and precise **Istana Maziah** (closed to the public) is one of Kuala Terengganu's few historic monuments, set back from the sea in manicured gardens on Jalan Sultan Zainal Abidin. Now used only for official royal functions, it's reminiscent of a French chateau, with a steeply inclined red-tile roof and tall, shuttered windows.

Further west along the pedestrianized promenade, **Bukit Puteri** (literally "Princess Hill"; daily 9am–5.45pm; RM1), rises high above the town. Relics of its time as a stronghold during the early nineteenth century – when the sultans Mohammed and Umar were fighting each other for the Terengganu throne – include a fort, supposedly built using honey to bind the bricks, and several cannons imported from Spain and Portugal. The hill is a popular spot, always crawling with school children; the lighthouse at the top is still in use.

Turn to your left after you've descended the steps from Bukit Puteri to walk along **Jalan Bandar**, the continuation of Jalan Sultan Zainal Abidin. The dusty, narrow street forms the centre of **Chinatown**, its decaying shophouses providing a sharp contrast to the highrises of the modern city. Efforts are being made to revitalize the area, and there are some excellent shops here, such as Teratai, no. 151, selling local arts and crafts. Close to the junction with Jalan Kota is Kuala Terengganu's **Central Market** (daily 6am–6pm), a modern multistorey building which backs onto the river and oozes vitality and prosperity. Upstairs, above the crowded and claustrophobic wet market, is the best place to search out batik, *songket*s and brassware. Further south from the market, along Jalan Bandar, is the remainder of Chinatown; east from the market, at the far end of Jalan Kota, is the **Masjid Zainal Abidin**, an unremarkable modern structure built in 1972 on the site of the original nineteenth-century wooden mosque.

Gelanggang Seni and the craft centres

At the far southeastern end of town, a two-kilometre walk or trishaw ride from the centre, is the **Gelanggang Seni**, a modern cultural complex facing the town's beach, Pantai Batu Buruk. The centre hosts performances (Fri & Sat 5–7pm except during

THE KRIS

The **kris** occupies a treasured position in Malay culture, a symbol of manhood and honour believed to harbour protective spirits. Traditionally, all young men crossing the barrier of puberty receive one, which remains with them for the rest of their lives, tucked into the folds of a sarong; for an enemy to relieve someone of a *kris* is tantamount to stripping him of his virility.

The weapon itself is intended to deliver a horizontal thrust rather than the more usual downward stab. When a sultan executed a treacherous subject, he did so by sliding a long *kris* through his windpipe, just above the collar bone, thereby inflicting a swift – though bloody – death. The distinguishing feature of the dagger is the hilt, shaped like the butt of a gun to facilitate a sure grip. The hilt can be used to inflict a damaging blow to the head in combat, especially if there isn't time to unsheath the weapon.

The daggers can be highly decorative: the iron blade is often embellished with fingerprint patterns or the body of a snake, while the hilt can be made from ivory, wood or metal; the designs are usually based on the theme of a bird's head.

Ramadan; free) of traditional dances and *silat* (see p.642) by amateur groups – check with the tourist office for current details.

Of perhaps greater interest – certainly if you're looking to buy souvenirs – are the various arts and crafts centres scattered around town. Terengganu artisans have long been known for their **brassware**, working in an alloy called "white brass", unique to the state. Formerly the preserve of the sultans, white brass – a brass containing at least forty-percent zinc, with added nickel to make the colour less yellow – is now used to make decorative articles such as candlesticks and large gourd-shaped vases. The small **workshop** (daily 8.30am–6pm) on Jalan Ladang, close to the Tourism Malaysia office, uses the traditional "lost-wax" technique, whereby a wax maquette is covered with clay, then placed in a kiln to fire the clay and melt the wax, leaving a mould into which to pour the molten brass. When the metal hardens, the clay is chipped off and the metal surface is polished and decorated.

The *mengkuang* style of **weaving** is practised in Terengganu: using the long thin leaves of pandanus trees, similar to those of bulrushes, women fashion delicate but functional items like bags, floor mats and fans. Ky Enterprises, about 3km due south of the centre on Jalan Panji Alam, is a good place to watch the process; take minibus #12, #13c, #15 or #26 (15min; 60sen) there from the local bus station.

There are several other craft workshops in neighbouring Pasir Panjang, about 500m west of Jalan Panji Alam. Perhaps the most famous is that belonging to Abu Bakar bin Mohammed Amin, a **kris** maker on Lorong Saga (call to make an appointment; ☎09/622 7968). Here you can watch the two-edged dagger and its wooden sheath (for more on the *kris*, see box, above) being decorated with fine artwork, a process which, together with the forging, can take several weeks to complete. To get to the workshops, take minibus #12 (60 sen) from the local bus station and get off at the sign marked "Sekolah Kebangsaan Psr. Panjang".

Pulau Duyong

Accessible by a five-minute ferry ride (60 sen) from the jetty near central market, **Pulau Duyong** is the largest of the islets dotting the Terengganu estuary. This community is famous for its **boat-building**, an old skill that has developed into a commercial enterprise. In the island's dry docks, old-fashioned deep-sea fishing boats line up alongside state-of-the-art luxury yachts – but whatever the price tag, the construction method is the same. The craftsmen work from memory rather than from set plans, building the hull using strong hardwood pegs to fasten the planks, then applying special sealant derived from swampland trees, which is resistant to rot. Unusually, the frame is fitted afterwards, giving the whole structure strength and flexibility. There's not much to do on Pulau Duyong other than stroll up and down the seafront, passing from workshop to workshop, though the village here is pleasant, with a myriad of brightly painted wooden houses.

There's one **place to stay** here, *Awi's Yellow House* (☎ & fax 09/624 7363; ①/②), a delightful timber complex of huts and walkways built on stilts over the water. It offers a variety of accommodation from basic huts to a spacious dorm (RM6), complete with mosquito nets. If you arrive by boat, follow the river south as closely as possible; you'll see *Awi's* on the west bank about 500m from the rivermouth (the place is known to all the locals so you can always ask directions if needed). From the bus station, ask for minibus #16 or #20 (60 sen) or take a taxi (RM5), and get off at the base of the Sultan Mahmud Bridge, from where *Awi's* is a short walk. Buses across the bridge are infrequent, and the ferries stop running at around 6pm, so *Awi's* is not an ideal base, but it has its own cooking facilities and is beautifully peaceful.

The Istana Tengku Long Museum

The new **Istana Tengku Long Museum** (daily 9am–5pm, Fri closed noon–3pm; RM5), 3km west of the town centre in an idyllic site by the wide Sungei Terengganu, is among Malaysia's most exciting cultural complexes. The main building, **Bangunan Utama**, houses displays of exquisite fabrics at ground level, while the second floor has displays on various crafts, and the third details the history of Terengganu. In the attached building to the left is the **Petronas Oil Gallery**, and behind this the **Islamic Gallery**, with fine examples of Koranic calligraphy. Beside the river are two examples of the **sailing boats** for which Kuala Terengganu is famed – unique combinations, which you can climb into, of European ships and Chinese junks. A small **Maritime Museum** is close by, as is an excellent outdoor gallery of smaller, beautifully decorated fishing boats.

The landscaped gardens feature imposing modern interpretations of the triple-roofed houses common to the area (see box, below, for more on traditional architec-

---

MALAY DOMESTIC ARCHITECTURE

The **traditional Malay house**, raised on stilts to afford protection from floods and wild animals, is now found only in rural areas, with the best examples being in the states of Kelantan and Terengganu. This simple, airy "kampung architecture" style, with its emphasis on timber, is being adopted by many new hotels and public buildings to evoke a more informal atmosphere and emphasize Malay traditions, often to award-winning success.

As these traditional houses are made of wood, you won't see any over 200 years old – weather and termites take their toll. The walls of these houses have many windows to let in the maximum amount of light and air, and are often embellished with elaborate carvings. Inside, a large, rectangular room acts as the principal family area and as a reception room for guests, with bedrooms and storerooms behind, while the kitchen is connected to the main part of the house by an open courtyard. The roof is covered by *atap* (palm thatch), though these days tiles or corrugated iron are just as common.

Regional variations in these village houses are most pronounced in the state of Negeri Sembilan, between KL and Melaka, whose Minangkabau settlers from Sumatra brought with them their distinctive saddle-shaped roofs – sweeping, curved structures called "buffalo horns". The states of Kelantan and Terengganu share cultural influences with their Thai neighbours to the north in their gables and tiled roofs, with fewer windows and more headroom, while those in Melaka are characterized by a decorative, tiled stairway leading up to an open-sided veranda.

ture). Also within the grounds are ancient timber palaces which have been rebuilt, the supreme example being the **Istana Tengku Long**, originally built in 1888 entirely without nails (to Malays, these signify death, because of their use in coffins). Like the majority of traditional east-coast houses, the hardwood rectangular building has a high, pointed roof and a pair of slightly curved wooden gables at either end. Each gable is fitted with twenty gilded screens, intricately carved with verses from the Koran and designed to not only admit air but also provide protection from driving rain.

The museum is easily reached by a twenty-minute journey on the Losong-bound minibus (50 sen), which departs regularly from the local bus station, passing through some attractive kampungs – on the way, look out for the traditional high-gabled stilted houses. There are plans to run a ferry from the jetty close to the central market – enquire at the Tourist Information Centre for details.

Eating

There are excellent **food stalls** just south of Jalan Kampung Tiong 1 serving the usual Malay dishes (11.30am–midnight; some stalls closed Fri). By comparison restaurants are poor value, although there are one or two notable exceptions.

Mat Kedai Binjai, Jalan Sultan Sulaiman. You'll find tasty Malay fare in this busy, inexpensive roadside café.

M.D. Curry House, 19c Jalan Tok Lam. Some of the best South Indian *thali*s you'll find in Malaysia, with excellent, eat-as-much-as-you-like vegetarian and meat curries slapped down on your banana leaf. Outstanding and inexpensive (around RM5).

Restoran Golden Dragon, Jalan Bandar. Always packed with locals, this large Chinese *kedai kopi* has a wide range of dishes.

Shri Shanmuga, Jalan Tok Lam, by the junction with Jalan Dato' Isaac. Another good banana-leaf curry place.

Taufik Restoran, Jalan Masjid Abidin. A popular Indian place serving *murtabak*s and curry dishes, from RM2. Closed in the evening.

Travellers Café, Jalan Dato' Isaac. Western café food with some local dishes thrown in. One of the few places in the vicinity where you'll get a beer with your meal.

Listings

Airlines The MAS office is at 13 Jalan Sultan Omar (☎09/624 5618).

Airport Sultan Mohammed Airport is 13km northeast of town; flight information on ☎09/666 4500.

Banks and exchange Standard Chartered, UMBC and Maybank are all on Jalan Sultan Ismail.

Buses There are regular buses from Kuala Terengganu to cities and major towns on the Peninsula. Local buses go every 30min to Marang (7am–6pm; RM1) and to Dungun and Rantau Abang (7.30am–6pm; RM2).

Hospital The state hospital is off Jalan Sultan Mahmud on Jalan Peranginan (☎09/623 3333), 1km southeast of the centre.

Internet There are many Internet cafés on the western side of Jalan Tok Lam, all very good value at about RM3 an hour, among them the *Goldenwood Café* at no. 59 (☎09/626 5282), just south of the junction with Jalan Dato' Isaac.

Left luggage This service is available at the express bus station on Jalan Sultan Zainal Abidin and at the local bus station on Jalan Masjid Abidin (both RM1 a day).

Police The main police station is on Jalan Sultan Ismail (☎09/622 2222).

Post office The GPO (for poste restante/general delivery) is on Jalan Sultan Zainal Abidin.

Telephones There's a Telekom office on Jalan Sultan Ismail (8.30am–4.15pm).

Travel agents Ping Anchorage Travel and Tours, 77a Jalan Dato' Isaac (☎09/622 0851), is efficient and can provide useful information on visiting Pulau Redang (see p.268) and Pulau Kapas (see p.279), as well as sights around the town. The Tourist Information Centre on Jalan Sultan Zainal Abidin has information on visiting most local places, including Tasek Kenyir and Sekayu Waterfall (see below, and can also recommend travel agencies.

Visa extensions The Wisma Persekutuan office on Jalan Pejabat issues on-the-spot-visa extensions (Mon–Wed & Sat 8.00am–4.15pm, Thurs 8.30am–1pm).

Around Kuala Terengganu

You can make excursions from Kuala Terengganu to **Tasek Kenyir**, a lake formed by the construction of a vast hydroelectric dam, and to the **Sekayu Waterfall**. There are also organized trips (around RM300 for three days) to **Pulau Redang**, 45km off the Terengganu coast, where there's a stunning marine park. With the exception of Sekayu, these places are protected areas and so have to be seen on visits arranged by local travel agents (see "Listings", above), which makes exploring them not only expensive but also rather regimented.

Tasek Kenyir

A lake of some 360 square kilometres, with 340 islands, **Tasek Kenyir** was created in 1985 when the Kenyir hydroelectric dam across Sungei Terengganu was completed. Currently being developed as an alternative gateway to Taman Negara, it was once an area of lush jungle – partially submerged trees still jut out of the clear waters. In fact, the rotting trunks have contributed to the reduction in oxygen levels in the water, causing fish to look for food elsewhere. Though Malaysia's largest hydroelectric dam may not seem a promising place for a "back-to-nature" experience, tours here take in the many nearby waterfalls with plunge pools for swimming, as well as the limestone Bewah Caves, deep in the hills that surround the lake.

Two types of **accommodation** are available at Tasek Kenyir: upmarket floating chalets built over the water, with full facilities, or more basic houseboats; the latter are cheaper and provide better access to the lake. Typical packages for a one-night stay cost from RM160 per person in a houseboat and RM190 in a floating chalet, including bus transfer from Kuala Terengganu, meals and a guided tour. There's currently no budget accommodation, though you can camp if you have your own gear. You can also come here on a day-trip from Kuala Terengganu for RM100, including lunch and snacks; contact *Uncle John's Resort* (☎09/622 9360, fax 622 9569) for details.

Sekayu Waterfall

If you can't face parting with the money for an organized trip to Tasek Kenyir, then a trip to **Sekayu Waterfall**, reachable by public transport, is a good compromise – you can take a peek at the dam on the way. The falls are part of a government park complex, known as **Hutan Lipur Sekayu** (daily 9am–6pm; RM1); it's a busy weekend picnic spot, even if the environment here has been somewhat tamed, with rustic shelters, a bird park, mini-zoo and an "all-you-can-eat" fruit farm.

To get here from Kuala Terengganu, take a local bus to Kuala Berang (45min; RM2), and after taking a look at the dam, take a taxi for the fifteen-minute drive to the park (RM20 oneway). Don't forget to arrange a pick-up time with your driver as there is no taxi stand at the park. The *Ping Anchorage* (see p.271) in Kuala Terengganu can arrange a day-trip here, costing around RM40 for four people.

It's possible to **stay** at the park: there are a number of **chalets** (RM50) and a **resthouse** – the *Sekayu*, with clean, if slightly musty, en-suite doubles (③) – which must be booked in advance at the Forest Department in Kuala Berang (☎09/681 1259); you can also reserve a chalet at the *Sekayu Eco Adventure Resort* (☎09/625 2754; ②).

Marang and Pulau Kapas

Times are changing in **MARANG**, a tiny coastal village 17km south of Kuala Terengganu. Its conservative residents have long been used to the steady trickle of foreign visitors, drawn to the place by the promise of "old Malaysia", as well as the delights of nearby **Pulau Kapas**, 6km offshore. But the village, home to a handful of guesthouses and batik shops as well as local traders, and nicknamed "Cowboy Town" because of its dusty one-horse feel, is having a face-lift. Some of the ramshackle wooden shops and houses that lined the road have been demolished and replaced by a car park; a new jetty complex and walkways have also been built. While visitors might bemoan Marang's loss of character, local people welcome the improved safety and san-

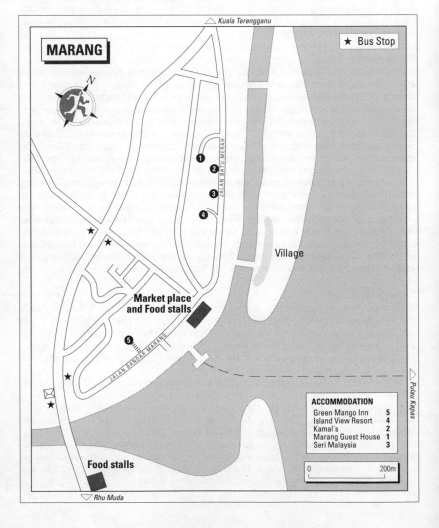

MARANG

★ Bus Stop

△ Kuala Terengganu

N

Village

Market place and Food stalls

JALAN BATU MERAH

JALAN BANDAR MARANG

▷ Pulau Kapas

Food stalls

ACCOMMODATION

Green Mango Inn	5
Island View Resort	4
Kamal's	2
Marang Guest House	1
Seri Malaysia	3

0   200m

▽ Rhu Muda

itation that the new buildings bring. Shades of the old Marang linger in the sleepy backwater to the north of the main street, with coconut trees by a lovely clear lagoon, and colourful fishing boats. There are long empty stretches of beach here, and 2km further to the south at **Rhu Muda**.

Practicalities

Any Dungun- or Rhu Muda-bound **bus** (every 30min) from Kuala Terengganu will drop you on the main road at Marang, from where a five-minute walk down one of the roads off to the left brings you into the centre. Although the northern end – the one nearer the town – of Rhu Muda is easy enough to walk to, you can also pick up a bus there on the main road.

There are no banks in Marang, though there is a police station and post office just before the bridge at the south end of the village. The **jetty** for boats to and from Pulau Kapas is just off the main street; the **ferry companies** have their offices on the main road, all offering the same deal of RM15 for a return trip, but arrangements can just as easily be made through most of the guesthouses here. Sailings are dependent on the tide, since the harbour is very shallow – mid-morning is the usual departure time. During the monsoon months (Nov–Feb), Pulau Kapas is completely inaccessible.

ACCOMMODATION AND EATING

Unless you have your own transport, **staying at Rhu Muda** puts you out on a limb, for although there are a whole string of beach resorts, there's not the same sense of community that there is in Marang itself. About the best of the cheaper accommodation is the *Angullia Beach House Resort* (☎09/618 1322; ②), 2km south of Marang, a spacious grassy compound with variously priced chalets, all with their own verandas. Better, but much pricier, is the award-winning *Marang Resort and Safaris* (☎09/618 2588, fax 618 2334; ⑦), 8km south of Marang, where traditional huts sit in the mangroves between the river and the sea. The deluxe chalets really are just that, with VCRs and outside sunken baths. All the resorts have their own **restaurants**.

Among places to stay **in Marang**, listed below, most guesthouses have budget chalets and their own **restaurants**, serving Western food. The food stalls near the market are worth checking out, particularly *Din Canai*, which does *roti canai*. **Internet** facilities are available at Cyber Kit just seawards of the traffic lights.

Green Mango Inn, A71 Bandar, Marang (☎09/618 2040). The most atmospheric place by far – a real traveller's hangout with books, chess sets and LP's nailed to the walls as decoration. There's a dorm (RM6), and some A-frame doubles, not en suite. ①, dorm beds RM6.

Island View Resort, Lot 1506 Kampung Paya, Marang (☎09/618 2006). A mishmash of different chalets, and terraces of rooms; the air-con ones are good value. ①/②.

Kamal's, 1b Pelancongan, Marang (☎09/618 2181). An established place, with clean chalets and a café-bar; it closes during the monsoon season (Nov–Jan). ①.

Marang Guest House (☎09/618 1976). Above *Kamal's*. Fresh, comfortable cabins and some A-frames set on a hill, with a good restaurant and excellent views over the ocean. ①/③.

Seri Malaysia, Lot 3964 Kampung Paya (☎09/618 2889, fax 618 1285). The most upmarket accommodation here: comfortable, en-suite rooms with breakfast included. Good value. ④.

Pulau Kapas and Pulau Gemia

A thirty-minute ride by fishing boat from Marang takes you to **PULAU KAPAS**, less than 2km in length and one of the nicest islands on the east coast. Most of the guesthouses in Marang can arrange transport (RM15 return) out to the island, which can easily be visited in a day. It's a fine spot, with coves on the western side of the island accessible only by sea or by clambering over rocks – you'll be rewarded by excellent sands and aquamarine waters. Access to the remote eastern side is via a track that leads back from the jetty, taking around 45 minutes, the sheer cliffs which plummet to the water's edge making for a tense but dramatic walk. Like many of its neighbours, Kapas is a designated marine park, the best snorkelling being around rocky **Pulau Gemia**, just off the northwestern shore of Pulau Kapas, while the northernmost cove is ideal for **turtle-spotting** (see below).

Practicalities

All **accommodation** on Pulau Kapas, listed below, is at the two western coves that directly face the mainland. On Pulau Gemia, there's the *Gem Isles Resort* (☎ & fax 09/624 5109), a well-designed place with all the chalets built on stilts at the water's edge. It can be booked only as part of a package deal, starting at RM170 for a two-day stay for two, including a night's accommodation in a double room and all meals.

Beauty Island (☎011/971958). Ramshackle chalets with attached showers, a long way from the beach. ②.

Kapas Island Resort (☎09/623 6110). Exclusive Malay-style chalets, with a swimming pool and extensive water-sports facilities. ⑤.

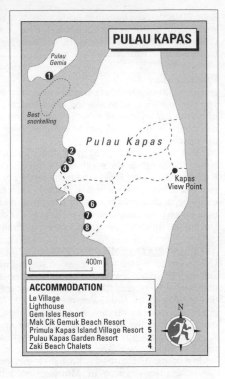

ACCOMMODATION

Le Village	7
Lighthouse	8
Gem Isles Resort	1
Mak Cik Gemuk Beach Resort	3
Primula Kapas Island Village Resort	5
Pulau Kapas Garden Resort	2
Zaki Beach Chalets	4

Le Village (☎09/624 6090). Has a delightful beachside restaurant and well-designed chalets. ⑤.

Lighthouse (☎09/618 1529; ②) At the far end of the bay, this is an attractive building of dark, polished timber, with some budget dorm beds (RM10) – with only a *mandi* for washing (using well-water), though, it's a touch overpriced. ②.

Mak Cik Gemuk Beach Resort (☎010/984 0972). There's a variety of double rooms here, some without shower (②), others with (③), though they're all a little cramped and shabby.

Pulau Kapas Garden Resort (☎010/984 1686, fax 624 5162). This welcoming place is worth checking out, with comfortable, neat rooms and breakfast included; it also has a beachside restaurant and a resident diving instructor – courses start from RM950. ③.

Zaki Beach Chalet (☎010/619 5258). The best value on Pulau Kapas, this laid-back place is set in a shady grove, with comfortable A-frames (its cheaper rooms near the generator are very noisy, though). The restaurant here is definitely the place to be in the evenings. ②.

Rantau Abang

South of Marang, the coastal Route 3 passes through numerous fishing kampungs before reaching the village of **RANTAU ABANG**. Although no more than a collection of guesthouses strung out at regular intervals along a couple of kilometres of dusty road, the village, 43km from Marang, has made its name as one of a handful of places in the world where the increasingly rare **giant leatherback turtle** comes to lay its eggs, returning year after year between May and September to the same beaches (see box, opposite). While other species, including hawksbill, Olive Ridley and green turtles, are also to be found in these parts, it is the sight of the huge, ponderous leatherbacks, with their unusual coat of black, rubbery skin, lumbering up the beach, that is the real attraction. Outside the egg-laying season, the long, unspoilt beach is a tranquil place to hang out for a day or two.

MARINE TURTLES

Among **giant leatherback turtles**, only the female – measuring 150cm in length and weighing 400kg on average – comes ashore, on the very beach where she herself hatched. She heaves herself out of the water at night with her enormous front flippers until she reaches dry sand; she then uses her rear flippers to make digging movements, creating a narrow hole 50–80cm deep in which she deposits up to a hundred eggs. The turtle then covers the hole with her hind flippers, while disguising the whole nest site by churning up more sand with the front ones. It is this action which causes the turtle to wheeze and shed tears in order to remove the kicked-up sand from her eyes and nose – although a more romantic explanation has it that the creature is grieving for her lost eggs.

Although a single turtle never lays eggs in consecutive seasons, it can nest three or four times within the same season at two-weekly intervals. The eggs incubate for fifty or sixty days, the temperature of the sand influencing the sex of the **hatchlings** – warm sand produces more females, cooler sand favours males. The hatchlings, no more than a hand-span in length, then crawl to the surface of the sand, leaving their broken shells at the bottom of the pit. The first few hours of a hatchling's life are particularly hazardous, for if it doesn't get destroyed by larvae or fungi in the sand, it can be picked off by crabs, birds and other predators before even reaching the sea. Usually emerging under the cover of night, hatchlings seem to know in which direction the sea lies (even if it can't be seen from where they hatched – it's this element of the turtle's behaviour that most baffles scientists), and propel themselves rapidly towards the water's edge using their outsize flippers. While it was once thought that they headed towards the lightest area in their vision (other sources of light such as torches were known to disturb their progress), other studies showed that the hatchlings were also moving away from the land's higher horizon. In so doing, it is thought that the turtles somehow memorize the beach on their scuttle towards the water, which in later life enables females to relocate the place where they hatched. Once in the water, turtles swim in the direction from which the waves are coming, as if guided by a magnetic sense of direction. Years later, when mature, the turtles, swimming in waters as far away as South America, somehow manage to find their way back to nest on the coast of Terengganu, which nobody really understands.

While the survival of the striking leatherback turtle is an emotive cause for concern, all **marine turtles** – green, black, Olive Ridley, Kemp's Ridley, hawksbill, loggerhead – are at risk. Harmful fishing methods, such as the use of trawl nets, are responsible for the deaths of more than 100,000 marine turtles each year – a figure that explains the dramatic reduction in turtles nesting on the Terengganu coast, from 10,155 in 1956 to a mere 27 in 1995. This figure rose slightly in 1996, but experts reckon there are as few as six turtles laying eggs on the beach here. With a survival rate of only fifty percent among hatchlings, this is bound to have drastic consequences for the survival of the species: current estimates reckon on a figure of between 70,000 and 75,000 females left in the world.

In Southeast Asia in particular, the turtles have a predator far more menacing than any in the wild – human beings. While Muslims in Malaysia eschew turtle meat, which is forbidden by their religious law, neighbouring nations such as Indonesia and the Philippines have traditionally relied on the turtle as an important source of nutrition. More worrying was the deliberate slaughter of turtles for their shells – each worth around RM400 – which were fashioned into ornaments, such as bowls and earrings, primarily for the Japanese market. Until 1992, when a ban was enforced, Japan imported twenty tons of hawksbill shells annually for this purpose, which represented the killing over 30,000 turtles.

Turtle-watching was once something of a sport, with tourists riding the creatures for the sake of a good photograph – behaviour that, not surprisingly, was scaring the turtles away. Nowadays, there are specific places where the public is allowed to watch the nesting turtles; observers are asked to keep at least 5m away and refrain from making noise and using torches, camera flashes and fires (unfortunately, not everyone follows these rules). In order to protect the turtles, the guesthouses will arrange for you to be woken during the night if one is sighted, for a fee of RM3. By the time you arrive, the eggs will have been taken away by rangers, for safety.

The state government, with the support of the Worldwide Fund for Nature, has now set aside the coastline 10km either side of Rantau Abang as a **sanctuary** for nesting turtles; specific nesting areas have been established on the beach, fenced off from curious human beings. Also off-limits are the **hatcheries** set up to protect the eggs from theft or damage; the eggs are dug up immediately after the turtle has laid them and reburied in sealed-off sections of the beach, surrounded by a wire pen tagged with a date marker. When the hatchlings have broken out of their shells, they are released at the top of the beach (4–6am), and their scurry to the sea is supervised to ensure their safe progress. Despite these measures, the real damage to marine turtles is being inflicted elsewhere (see box, overleaf).

The **Turtle Information Centre** (May–Aug daily 8am–12.45pm, 2–6pm & 8–11pm, except Fri 9am–noon & 3–11pm; Sept–April Mon–Wed & Sat 8am–12.45pm & 2–4pm, Thurs 8am–12.45pm; free), to the north of the central strip where most of the accommodation is found, is informative and interesting, with a video and other displays relating to the turtles.

Practicalities

Local buses from Kuala Terengganu and Marang run every thirty minutes (7.30am–6pm; 1hr) to Rantau Abang. Coming by express bus from the south, you have to change at Dungun, 13km away (see opposite), from where you can easily get a local bus for the remainder of the journey. Buses drop you on the main road, at the R&R Plaza, just a short walk from all the accommodation and the Turtle Information Centre.

There are surprisingly few **accommodation** options, all of them close to the beach. Prices double when the turtles are in town (May–Sept); the price codes in this section refer to the **high-season rate**. *Dahimah's Guest House* (☎09/845 2843; ①–③), 1km south of the information centre at the far southern end of the strip, is extremely good value, with very comfortable rooms and chalets around a central courtyard, ranging from doubles with fan to riverside air-con family rooms. Though a little run-down, the friendly, long-established *Awang's* (☎ & fax 09/844 3500; ②), handily located near the Turtle Information Centre, has much more of a backpackers' feel; it offers a variety of simple rooms as well as some overpriced air-con chalets. Next door, *Ismail's* (☎019/983 6202; ①) is very basic and not as clean; it can be the only option available in high season, though.

All guesthouses have their own **restaurants** (closed Nov–Jan), serving the usual traveller-oriented fare – omelettes, fried rice and noodles with vegetables or chicken. In addition, there are **food stalls** near *Awang's*, and the excellent *Kedai Makan Rantau Abang*, 750m further south, a cheerful local eating house offering substantial rice and noodle dishes. For midnight snacks while turtle-watching, try the 24-hour café at the modern R&R Plaza – a mall on the main road opposite the information centre – with a wide-ranging menu featuring Western and Malay dishes.

South to Cherating

The route south from Rantau Abang is a further indictment of the rampant development that has accompanied Terengganu's economic success, peppered with ugly oil refineries and huge residential complexes for their workers built with little or no regard for the local environment. This rapid industrialization hasn't deterred the growth of tourism however, as illustrated by the success of the award-winning *Tanjung Jara Beach Hotel* (☎09/844 1801; ⑨), a luxury resort in the style of a Malay palace, 8km south of Rantau Abang. This is easily the most attractive of the resorts along this stretch, though the sight of the offshore rigs in these parts may be off-putting for sun-seekers. It's only when you reach the secluded bay of Cherating that the scenery takes a distinct upturn.

Dungun to Chukai

The backwater town of **KUALA DUNGUN**, a further 5km south of Tanjung Jara, is predominantly Chinese, with a handful of shophouses and a weekly night market each Thursday; there's no reason to spend much time here, though. The **local bus station** (for services to Rantau Abang) is on the west side of the padang, while express buses (to KL and Singapore) arrive and depart from outside the hospital on Route 3 itself – tickets can be purchased from either the *A.A.* or *Aziz* restaurants on the main road.

The *Sri Dunun Hotel*, 135k Jalan Tambun (☎09/848 1881; ①) is the best **place to stay**, with very inexpensive, spotless doubles with shower and some air-con rooms for not much more. *Kasaya*, 223–227 Jalan Tambun (☎09/848 1704; ②) is another good option, with clean, en-suite rooms. Both are very near the bus station, from where you walk east across the padang to reach Jalan Tambun, into which you turn left. However, with local buses leaving every thirty minutes to Rantau Abang (25min) en route to KL (2hr) and every thirty minutes to Kemaman (2hr), you probably won't need to spend the night here.

South of Dungun, the highway swerves suddenly inland, bypassing a small promontory, before rejoining the coast at **Paka**, a small fishing village now dwarfed by the immense power plant just to the south. This marks the beginning of a dreary string of developments, including Kerteh and Kemasik, that are best passed through swiftly. **Kemaman**, an untidy, sprawling town halfway between Dungun and Kuantan – and barely distinguishable from its neighbour, **Chukai** – is significant only in that it's here that you'll have to change buses to reach any of the small kampungs along the road to Kuantan, including Cherating.

Cherating

The fast-expanding travellers' hangout of **CHERATING**, 47km north of Kuantan, hugs the northern end of a windswept bay, protected by the shelter of a rocky cliff. Although most of the locals have long since moved to a small village further south, the settlement still tries to reflect kampung life by offering simple chalets and homestays at a modest charge to visitors. Ramshackle stilted huts nestle in palm groves, while a handful of beach bars lead the gentle carousing well into the night. The sum total of Cherating's billing as a "cultural village" seems to be the opportunity to learn batik-printing – though even this seems to be a thinly disguised front for marketing off-the-peg clothes at inflated prices. However, Cherating is a good place in which to unwind and enjoy a nightlife that comes as close as the east coast gets to raging.

With a reliable sea breeze, Cherating is ideal for **windsurfing** (Nov–Feb is the best time), and some of the beach bars and chalets here rent out equipment from RM15 an hour. If that's a bit too active for your liking, try a brisk walk west along the **beach** to where the rippling tide makes fascinating patterns on the sand. Sungei Cherating, whose brown waters run into the bay here, is really only passable at low tide, effectively cutting off the route further west. Clambering over the rocks at the eastern end of the bay brings you to a tiny secluded cove, though the beach here isn't as good as that

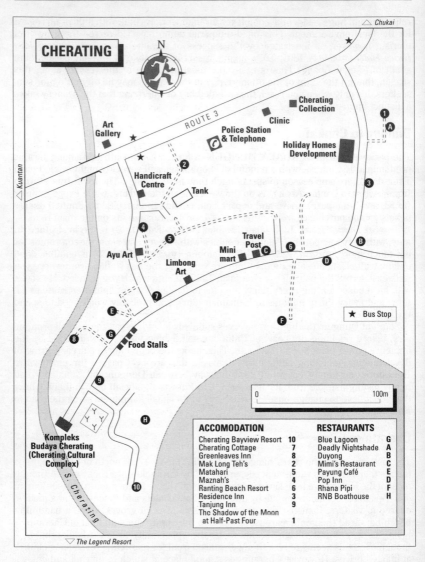

belonging to the exclusive *Club Med* over the next outcrop. Low tide is less of a problem here than in the main part of the bay, where you'll have to walk out at least 200m on soft, wet sand to reach the sea, and still further to get deep enough to swim.

Practicalities

Any express or local bus travelling Route 3 between Kuala Terengganu and Kuantan will drop you off at Cherating, but make sure you state your destination to the driver. Two rough tracks – the one nearer the bridge is the more direct – lead from the road down into the main part of the village, about five minutes' walk away. Chalets shaded by tall, gently swaying palm trees are dotted along both tracks, increasing in density when you reach the main drag, a tiny surfaced road that runs roughly parallel to the beach. This is where you'll find most of the restaurants and bars, as well as the provisions stores. Also here is Travel Post (☎09/581 9825), a tiny travel agency where you can book bus tickets around Malaysia and to Singapore, tours to Gua Charas (see p.291) and Tasek Chini (p.244), as well as local river and snorkelling trips (RM15 including equipment). They also have six **Internet** terminals (RM5 an hour) and can change foreign currency.

ACCOMMODATION

Cherating has no shortage of **places to stay**, and new accommodation is springing up all the time. The best places are listed below and marked on the map opposite; some didn't have phones at the time of writing. Bear in mind that prices often rise by fifty percent at weekends and on public holidays.

Cherating Bayview Resort, Lot 367 Kampung Cherating Lama (☎09/581 9248, fax 581 9415, *miorzub@tm.net.my*). Though situated on a lovely beach, the overpriced chalets here don't compare with those at the *Residence Inn*. (⑥).

Cherating Cottage (☎09/581 9273, fax 581 9279, *cottage1@tm.net.my*). A sturdily built bar and restaurant surrounded by chalets for every budget, from RM10 dorms to air-conditioned en-suite rooms. The basic chalets come with bathrooms, some with hot water. There's also an Internet terminal. ①–③.

Greenleaves Inn (☎ & fax 09/581 9825). A New Age den in the jungle – every loft, veranda and cabin here was crafted and painted by Iggy, an artist from KL. The simple, kitsch chalets are located next to the river; the communal area sees the odd DJ in high season. ②.

Mak Long Teh's (☎09/581 9290). Set back from the main road, this is a ramshackle, though functional, collection of huts on stilts. Conveniently, it offers home cooking in a warm family environment. ①.

Matahari (☎09/581 9835). Just north of *Cherating Cottage*. Spacious, sturdy chalets, each with a fridge and large veranda, as well as a separate communal area with a TV room, cooking facilities and a batik studio. ①.

Ranting Beach Resort (☎09/581 9068) Attractive, though slightly overpriced, chalets surrounding an airy restaurant. Also has a wide range of rooms. ②.

Residence Inn (☎09/581 9333, fax 581 9252). The most upmarket place within the village itself, this establishment boasts large, very well-equipped rooms ranged around a pleasant swimming pool and lobby area. It's excellent value if you avoid the twenty percent weekend and public holiday surcharge. ④.

Shadow of the Moon at Half-Past Four (☎09/581 9186). Well-designed timber chalets with attached bathroom, hot water and hand-crafted furniture tucked away in a beautiful wooded area; there's a dorm, too. The *Deadly Nightshade* bar and lounge are the real attraction (see below). ②, dorm beds RM10.

Tanjung Inn (☎09/581 9081). A scenic, landscaped garden, set around a lake with an attractive range of chalets and family rooms. (RM20, RM45).

EATING AND DRINKING

Eating is the main focus of nightlife in Cherating, and unusually for Muslim parts of Malaysia, there are many lively **bars**. Most chalet operations have their own **restaurants** – with monotonously similar menus. The evening **food stalls** on the road through the village offer Malay standards like *nasi lemak*, *rojak ayam* and *cendol*. For breakfast, the *roti canai* stall just past the Travel Post can't be beat. The places we've listed are marked on the map opposite.

Blue Lagoon. Busy bar and restaurant whose Chinese-based menu attracts the expat crowd from the oil refineries up the coast; averages RM8 per dish.

Deadly Nightshade, at the *Shadow of the Moon at Half-Past Four*. One of the most imaginatively designed bars you'll come across in all of Malaysia. Fairy lights, piles of books, chess sets and home-made furniture add to the atmosphere. There are excellent set meals for around RM7, and on Thurs & Fri, banana-leaf curries and barbecues.

Duyong. Good, inexpensive Chinese food with a beach view.

Mimi's Restaurant. Decent, cheap North Indian curries and Western food.

Payung Café. Good-value Italian food, in a riverside setting. Also open for breakfast and lunch, with Western dishes like goulash.

Pop Inn. Pub-style steak house on the beach, also serving snacks. Stays open late; has the odd live band and DJ.

Rhana Pipi. On the beach opposite the *Ranting Beach Resort*, this laid-back bar keeps late hours and also serves decent Western food.

RNB Boat House. Right on the seafront, this place serves home-made Mexican, Chinese and Malay fare, specializing in prawns.

Kuantan and around

It's virtually inevitable that you'll pass through **KUANTAN** at some stage, since it's the region's transport hub, lying at the junction of Routes 2 (which runs across the Peninsula from KL), 3 (the coastal highway) and 14 (which starts at Kuala Terengganu, running south inland of Route 3). The brash state capital of **Pahang**, sprawling out from a thriving commercial centre, Kuantan's situation on a promontory north of the Sungei Kuantan estuary means that traffic up the east coast used to face a significant diversion inland before reaching the town, a factor which many consider has played its part in its failure to capture business from Singapore. This has changed with the completion of a new bridge connecting the centre of Kuantan directly to the southern Route 3 – though this has done little to alleviate traffic congestion. Land prices in the vicinity of the bridge have soared, however, fuelled by developers keen to take advantage of the improved transport links; this is leading to the eviction of traditional communities no longer able to meet the inflated rents.

While there's little to capture your imagination in the dull, concrete buildings of the town centre – aside from the magnificent **Masjid Negeri** – the fishing communities to the south of town make an interesting diversion. The beach satellites of **Teluk Chempedak** and **Beserah** just to the north are more pleasant places to stay than the centre itself, and those with more time to spare should not miss out on **Gua Charas**, a limestone cave temple within easy reach of the town. The trip here is worth it for the stunning setting alone – dramatic outcrops in virtually deserted plantation country.

Arrival, information and accommodation

The **local bus station** is on Jalan Besar, beside Sungei Kuantan; the **express bus station** is on Jalan Stadium, in front of the Darulmakmur stadium. **Taxis** can be found between Jalan Besar and Jalan Mahkota, whereas long-distance taxis arrive at the express bus station. A taxi to the centre from the **airport**, 15km east of town, costs RM20.

Jalan Besar, running close by Sungei Kuantan and leading into Jalan Telok Sisek, is home to most of the budget hotels and restaurants, while, one block behind, Jalan Mahkota (which continues into Jalan Haji Abdul Aziz beyond the junction with Jalan Bank) is where you'll find the GPO, Telekom office and police station. The **Tourist Information Centre** (Mon–Fri 9am–5pm, Sat 9am–1pm; ☎09/513 3026), in a large glass-and-wood booth at the end of Jalan Mahkota facing the playing fields, can help you out with accommodation in and around Kuantan, and also organizes day-trips to the surrounding areas.

Accommodation

Kuantan has no shortage of **hotels**, though many of the basic Chinese-run boarding houses at the bottom end of the market are poor value; those in the middle range are much better.

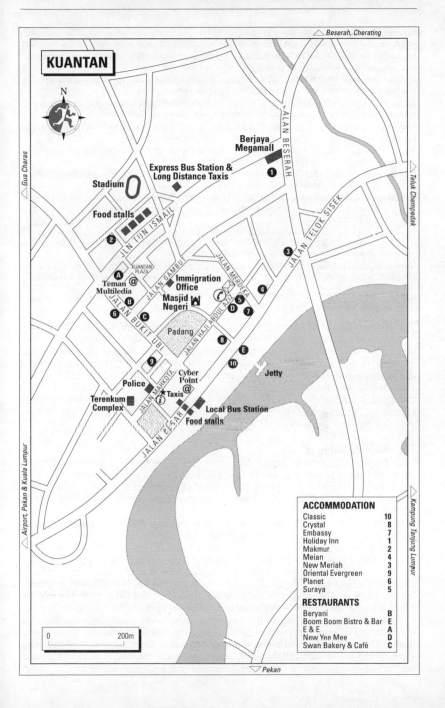

KUANTAN

N

Beserah, Cherating

Gua Charas

JALAN BESERAH

Teluk Chempedak

Berjaya Megamall

Express Bus Station & Long Distance Taxis

Stadium

Food stalls

JLN TUN ISMAIL

JALAN GAMBUT

JALAN MERDEKA

JALAN TELOK SISEK

KUANTAN PLAZA

Teman Multiledia

Immigration Office

Masjid Negeri

JALAN BUKIT UBI

JALAN HAJI ABDUL AZIZ

Padang

JALAN MAHKOTA

Police

Cyber Point

Taxis

Terenkum Complex

Jetty

JALAN BESAR

Local Bus Station

Food stalls

Airport, Pekan & Kuala Lumpur

Kampung Tanjung Lumpur

0   200m

Pekan

ACCOMMODATION

Classic	10
Crystal	8
Embassy	7
Holiday Inn	1
Makmur	2
Meian	4
New Meriah	3
Oriental Evergreen	9
Planet	6
Suraya	5

RESTAURANTS

Beryani	B
Boom Boom Bistro & Bar	E
E & E	A
New Yee Mee	D
Swan Bakery & Café	C

Classic, 7 Jalan Besar (☎09/555 4599, fax 513 4141). One of the best-value hotels in town, with large, well-lit rooms, a café, huge bathrooms with actual bathtubs and great views of the river. ③.

Embassy, 60 Jalan Teluk Sisek (☎09/552 7486). Clean Chinese-run hotel with large, good-value doubles, (no singles though); all rooms have attached bathrooms. ①.

Holiday Inn, Jalan Beserah (☎09/555 5899, fax 552 2016, *hikua@tm.net.my*). Kuantan's newest luxury four-star, boasting a swimming pool and a *dim sum* restaurant. ⑥.

Krystal, 59–61a Jalan Mahkota (☎09/552/6577). A close second to the *Oriental Evergreen*, this well-managed hotel has small, clean, partitioned rooms, with or without bathrooms. ②.

Makmur, 1 Lorong Pasar Baru (☎09/514 1363, fax 514 2870). Clean option with a range of rooms; handy for the express bus station, supermarkets and local food stalls. ②.

Meian, 78 Jalan Teluk Sisek (☎09/552 0949). Basic and spotless, with a communal hot shower for the simplest rooms; this is the best of the cheap places here. ①.

New Meriah, 142–144 Jalan Teluk Sisek (☎09/552 5433). The large, carpeted rooms, though slightly dingy, have shower and bathtub; a good choice. ②.

Oriental Evergreen, 157 Jalan Haji Abdul Rahman (☎09/513 0168, fax 513 0368). Tucked down a side street off the main road, this quiet hotel, with air-con en-suite rooms is more comfortable than its run-down surrounds suggest. ②.

Planet, 77 Jalan Bukit Ubi (☎09/513 9852). With the lowest priced singles in Kuantan, this is an efficiently run, wooden partitioned, Chinese-run hotel. It's reasonably clean, but basic to the point of being a little grim. You can do better elsewhere for doubles. ①.

Suraya, 55 Jalan Haji Abdul Aziz (☎09/555 4266, fax 555 4028). Tasteful, subtly lit rooms and a health club make this a slightly better choice than the *Classic*; the views here aren't as good though. ③.

The town centre

The commercial part of Kuantan is relatively small, clustered around Jalan Besar, Jalan Mahkota and Jalan Tun Ismail. While most of the town's urban architecture is distinctly unmemorable, its one real sight, the enormous **Masjid Negeri** on frenetic Jalan Mahkota, is stunning. Built in 1991, its pastel exterior (green for Islam, blue for peace and white for purity) is more reminiscent of a huge birthday cake than a place of worship. Despite its conventional design – a sturdy square prayer hall with a looming central dome and minarets at all four corners – it's one of the most impressive modern mosques in Malaysia, particularly at dusk when the plaintive call to prayer and the stunning lighting combine to magical effect.

The riverside villages

Most people's priority is to escape the centre of Kuantan by making the short hop to the south bank of the river by bus or long-tailed boat from a jetty northeast of the local bus station – though these services have dwindled since the completion of the bridge. In the communities of Kampung Tanjung Lumpur, Kampung Cempaka and Peramu you'll find plenty of peace and quiet.

Reached by bus from the local bus station, **Kampung Tanjung Lumpur**, about a kilometre east of the centre, is an impoverished fishing community consisting mainly of illegal Indonesian immigrants, to whom the authorities have long turned a blind eye. The rocketing land prices however are forcing families to relocate. Still, it's a good place to visit for seafood restaurants. **Peramu**, a couple of kilometres up the road, and also reached by bus from the local bus station, is changing more visibly, with new housing and the recent installation of mains water. It also boasts a lively afternoon market, a long line of stalls a few minutes' walk away from the riverside.

The coastline to the south of the town is in many ways more appealing than the beach at Teluk Chempedak (see p.290) to the north, not least because it is still relatively undeveloped. The beach at **Kampung Cempaka**, about 3km south of Kampung Tanjung Lumpur, is particularly good, a wide sweeping expanse of sand and shallow sea, whose currents are a whole lot safer than the buffeting waves further north.

Though it's close enough to town for a day-trip, a good alternative is to stay here at the *Sanubari Beach Resort* (☎09/534 1537; ⑤), a delightful, family-run operation with comfortable chalets, a swimming pool and excellent cuisine. To get here, take a bus to Peramu, followed by an exhilarating ride pillion on a motorbike-taxi (RM5) for the remaining 6km.

Eating and drinking

Kuantan's **restaurants** win no gastronomic awards; note that many of them close in the evening. The **food stalls** near the mosque on Jalan Mahkota behind the Ocean Shopping Complex on Jalan Tun Ismail are the best bet, and those by the river behind the bus station. A couple of Western-style **bars** have recently opened in the centre of town, catering to young, affluent Malaysians and expats, though Teluk Chempedak (see overleaf) is generally a livelier place for an evening out.

Berjaya Megamall, cnr of Jalan Tun Ismail and Jalan Beserah. Within this shopping centre is the best of Kuantan's food courts, with Malay, Chinese and Indian stalls.

Boom Boom Bistro and Bar, Jalan Teluk Sisek. A yellow-and-blue-painted prewar bungalow, formerly a 1920s gentleman's club and a Japanese interrogation centre during the World War II, now serves Mexican and American food, beers and other drinks to Kuantan's smart set. There's a quieter attached coffee shop for meals during the day.

New Yee Mee, Jalan Haji Abdul Aziz. Large, busy, budget Chinese restaurant with a very wide-ranging menu.

Restoran Beryani, Jalan Bukit Ubi. One of the few North Indian restaurants in town. Inexpensive.

Restoran E & E, 219 Jalan Tun Ismail. Interesting Malay versions of Western food in an air-con lounge. Steaks in cashew sauce, pizzas and Cantonese spaghetti are served up with varying levels of culinary success; portions are small.

Swan Bakery Café, Jalan Bukit Ubi. Large air-conditioned café serving cakes and Western and Chinese food.

Listings

Airlines MAS, 7 ground floor, Wisma Bolasepak Pahang, on Jalan Gambut, close to the junction with Jalan Bukit Ubi (☎09/515 7055).

Airport The Sultan Ahmad Shah airport is 15km west of town; flight information on ☎09/538 1291.

Banks OCBC and UMBC are on Jalan Teluk Sisek. Standard Chartered Bank, Maybank and Hong Kong Bank are all situated around the intersection of Jalan Besar and Jalan Bank. There is also a large Maybank on Jalan Haji Abdul Aziz near the mosque.

Buses Express services run from the station on Jalan Stadium to most points on the Peninsula, including services (hourly 8am–5pm) to Temerloh (for Tasek Chini and Tasek Bera), Kuala Lipis (2 daily) and Jerantut (for Taman Negara; 4 daily).

Car rental Avis, 102 Jalan Teluk Sisek (☎09/523666); National, 49 Jalan Telok Sisek (☎09/552 3666).

Cinemas Golden Screen Cinemas Multiplex (☎09/508 8038) on the top floor of Berjaya Megamall shows some English-language movies.

Internet access Good choices include Cyberpoint, third floor, 152 Jalan Besar, opposite the local bus station (☎09/513 7685); Teman Multi Media, B20, ground floor, Lorong Tun Ismail 1 (☎09/514 5733); and Surfers Paradise, Premiun Lanes, level 4, Kuantan Plaza (☎09/515 0888). The last of these is the most expensive, but it's open until 1am.

Post and communications The GPO, with poste restante, is on Jalan Haji Abdul Aziz; the Telekom office is next door (daily 9am–4.15pm).

Shopping The biggest complex is the Berjaya Megamall on the cnr of Jalan Tun Ismail and Jalan Beserah, near the *Holiday Inn*.

Taxis The long-distance taxi stand is above the express bus station (☎09/513 4478); fares per person are RM20 to Kuala Terengganu, RM25 to KL, RM25 to Mersing and RM35 to JB.

Visa extensions The immigration office is on the first floor, Wisma Persekutuan, Jalan Gambut (Mon–Fri 9am–4.15pm; ☎09/521373).

Teluk Chempedak

TELUK CHEMPEDAK, around 5km east of Kuantan, is a leafy suburb of wide roads and grand houses. Sitting on the tip of the promontory, the beaches here have spawned a small collection of resort hotels and pricey trinket shops, all eager to capitalize on the urban disaster that is Kuantan, and edging out all but the most tenacious of the budget hostels. The narrow, sloping beach north of the promontory has a pleasant cliff walk at its northern end, even if the sea here – churned up by the constant wind into a grey broth – is less than inviting.

Bus #39 runs regularly from outside the mosque on Jalan Mahkota to Teluk Chempedak – the last bus is around 9.30pm. The bus stops at the beach on the eastern side of the promontory; most of the **hotels** are off to the right as you face the sea, while a number of restaurants and snack bars face the sea to the left. The nicest place to stay is the *Hyatt* (☎09/566 1234, fax 567 7577, *hyatt_kuantan@hrktn.com.my*; ⑧), whose kampung-style covered walkways and restaurants are pleasantly freshened by the sea breeze; it has a couple of swimming pools and some good restaurants. The quaint *Hotel Kuantan* (☎09/568 0026; ③–⑤), opposite the *Hyatt*, is somewhat chaotic in appearance but oozes charm, with spotless tiled rooms and an efficient, friendly management. There are fewer places on the western side of the promontory: the government-run *Rumah Rehat* (☎09/567 4414; ④) isn't bad, with large, clean rooms.

The **places to eat** in Teluk Chempedak, on the busier eastern side, are considerably more inspiring than in Kuantan. The *Hyatt* has several restaurants, including a pizzeria, but you'll pay at least RM20 a dish here. Facing the beach at the far end of the row of shops are some basic **food stalls** with good *rojak*, while a few doors up, the *Massafalah* and *Abdulla* restaurants serve good seafood and steamboats for around RM12 a head. Cheaper is the *Sri Pantai ABC Seafood Restaurant*, over the road from the *Hyatt* & *Kuantan* hotels.

Beserah

Ten kilometres north of Kuantan on the road to Kuala Terengganu, the small village of **BESERAH** is famous for its salted fish and *keropok* (fish crackers). Here, fishermen still haul the day's catch to the processing areas by buffalo cart – a mode of transport that is becoming increasingly rare in techno-conscious Malaysia. Although it functions as yet another "cultural village" for Kuantan's tourists, its few handicraft workshops looking remarkably like souvenir outlets, Beserah is on the whole an unassuming place.

A few **guesthouses** have popped up in Beserah, making it a convenient and altogether more pleasant place to stay than Kuantan, particularly since buses (60 sen) from the local bus station ply the route regularly from 7am to 6pm; coming here from Kuantan, you get off at the "Pantai Beserah" sign on the right. If you follow the road further out for about 25m, past the sign round to the left, you'll find the friendly, IYHF-affiliated *Belia Perkasa* (☎09/544 8178, fax 544 8179), with cheap dorm beds (RM8). The *Beserah Guesthouse* (☎09/555203, fax 552831; ②) is about 100m further on, past the post office, an old-fashioned wooden boarding house facing a grey-sand beach, with strict house rules and shabby rooms. Considerably more laid-back is *La Chaumiere* (☎09/544 7662; ①); you get here by turning right instead of left at the "Pantai Beserah" sign and walking for 1km. The price includes breakfast and, if convenient, the helpful owner will collect you from Kuantan for RM10. Further up the main road, a sign on the left points you to *Jaafar's Guest House* (no phone; ①), about 500m down a well-marked trail. Tranquil woodland is the setting for this, the longest-established homestay in the area, a relaxed family home where the price includes breakfast, dinner and free tea. **Places to eat** are rather thin on the ground, though the guesthouses generally offer evening meals and there's a pasar malam, with stalls selling seafood and the usual rice and noodle dishes, on Mondays, by the Mobil station.

Gua Charas

If you have any time to spare in Kuantan, you should visit **Gua Charas**, a cave temple 25km northwest of Kuantan, built into one of the great limestone outcrops surrounding the town. It can be seen as a leisurely day-trip: bus #48 from the local bus station departs every hour for the thirty-minute journey to the village of Panching; look to the right about halfway along the route for the well-kept Chinese cemetery on the hillside. At Panching, a sign to the caves points you down a four-kilometre track through overgrown rubber plantations and rows upon rows of palm-oil trees – agricultural legacies responsible for the large numbers of Tamils living in the area, descendants of the indentured workers brought from Southern India in the nineteenth century. It's a long, hot walk to the cave, so take plenty of water with you.

Once you've reached the outcrop and paid your RM1 donation, you're faced with a steep climb to the Thai Buddhist **cave temple** itself. About halfway up, a rudimentary path strikes off to the right, leading to the entrance of the main cave. Descending into the eerie darkness is not for the faint-hearted, even though the damp mud path is dimly lit by fluorescent tubes. Inside the vast, echoing cavern, with its algae-stained vaulted roof and squeaking bats, illuminated shrines gleam from gloomy corners, guiding you to the main shrine deep in the cave, where a nine-metre sleeping Buddha is almost dwarfed by its giant surroundings. Back through the cave, steps lead to another, lighter hollow. It's nothing special, but if you go as far as you can to the back, the wall opens out to give a superb view of the surrounding countryside, stubby oil palms in regimented rows stretching towards the horizon.

Pekan

Just 45km south of Kuantan lies the unassuming royal town of **PEKAN**, whose name means "small town". The state capital of Pahang until 1898, Pekan has a sleepy complacency which gives the impression that nothing much has happened here for a very long time. Its neat and sober streets are lined with palaces, some modest, some vulgar – all products of the state's rapid turnover of sultans – and a handful of colonial buildings in varying states of decay.

At the edge of the tiny commercial sector, Jalan Tengku Ahmad faces the languid riverfront. Down the street, past a row of shophouses dating from the beginning of the twentieth century and shaded by huge rain trees, is the **Muzium Sultan Abu Bakar** (daily 9.30am–5pm, closed Fri 12.15–2.45pm; RM1), the State Museum of Pahang. It's housed in a well-proportioned Straits colonial building that has been used for various purposes down the years: as the sultan's istana, as the centre of British administration, and as the headquarters of the Japanese army during the occupation. Today it houses a collection which includes splendid Chinese ceramics salvaged from the wreck of a junk in the South China Sea, and an impressive display of royal regalia in the new east wing.

Further west along Jalan Tengku Ahmad is the unusual **Masjid Abdullah**, built during the reign of Sultan Abdullah (1917–32). No longer used for active worship, this Art Deco structure, whose blue domes look more Turkish than Southeast Asian, is now

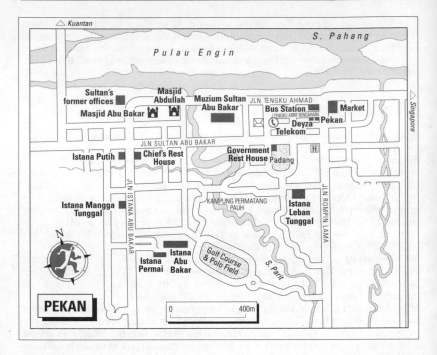

home to the Pusat Dakwah Islamiah, the state centre for the administration of religious affairs. Next door, the current mosque, **Masjid Abu Bakar**, is more conventional, with gold, bulbous domes.

Round the corner at the end of the road, past the unremarkable former offices of the sultan, is a crossroads. An archway built to resemble elephants' tusks marks your way ahead to the royal quarter of the town, past the fresh, white **Istana Putih** on the corner. Opposite, the **Chief's Resthouse** of 1929 seems rather bereft, its wooden terraces gradually decaying; just south of here is the sky-blue **Istana Mangga Tunggal**, and the **Istana Permai** (closed to the public), a tiny blue-roofed subsidiary palace that is home to the Regent of Pahang. Here you'll also see the rectangular facade of the **Istana Abu Bakar**, the palace currently occupied by the royal family, its garish opulence untypical of the buildings in Pekan; the expansive grounds are now a royal golf course and polo ground.

North of the nearby sports field, a narrow winding lane brings you into **Kampung Permatang Pauh**, the secluded village area of Pekan with simple wooden houses built on stilts. A ten-minute walk across Sungei Parit leads to the most impressive of Pekan's royal buildings, the **Istana Leban Tunggal** – a refined wooden structure fronted by a pillared portico, with an unusual symmetrical hexagonal tower.

Practicalities

From Kuantan, Pekan is a 45-minute journey on bus #31, which leaves every 45 minutes from the local bus station. If you're coming from the south, just ask your bus driver to drop you off in town – all buses pass through Pekan on their way to Kuantan. If you want to head south, it's better to backtrack to Kuantan to pick up one of the many express buses from there, as the local services here are infrequent.

Places to stay in town are limited, and with regular connections to Kuantan, you shouldn't need to spend the night here. The best place is the *Government Resthouse* (☎09/422 1240; ③), on the corner of the padang, where the rooms and bathrooms are vast, and the service good. Close to the bus station is the *Deyza*, 102a Jalan Tengku Arrif Bendahara (☎09/422 3690; ①), which is basic but clean – the *Pekan* next door is a little run-down, though bearable for a night. The choice of **restaurants** is grim, the best being the couple of Indian places along Jalan Tengku Arrif Bendahara; the food stalls near the bus station are very uninspiring.

travel details

Trains

Kota Bharu to: Gemas (3 daily; 9hr 30min–12hr 50min); Jerantut (2 daily, 6.20am and 8.20am; 5hr); Kuala Lipis (1 daily; 4hr 15min–5hr 20min), Kuala Tembeling (1 daily, 6.20am; 4hr 40min); Singapore (1 daily; 13hr).

Buses

Kota Bharu to: Alor Setar (2 daily; 8hr); Butterworth (2 daily; 8hr); Johor Bahru (1 daily; 10hr); Kuala Lumpur (2 daily; 8hr); Kuala Terengganu (5 daily; 4hr); Kuantan (5 daily; 6hr); Melaka (1 daily; 10hr). For details of buses into Thailand, see p.253.

Kuala Terengganu to: Alor Setar (2 daily; 9hr 30min); Butterworth (2 daily; 9–10hr); Ipoh (1 daily; 11hr); Johor Bahru (2 daily; 10hr); Kota Bharu (5 daily; 4hr); Kuala Lumpur (2 daily; 8–9hr); Kuantan (6 daily; 4hr), Marang (every 30min; 30min); Melaka (3 daily; 7hr); Mersing (2 daily; 6hr); Rantau Abang (every 30min; 1hr).

Kuantan to: Alor Setar (4 daily; 8hr); Butterworth (5 daily, 5hr); Ipoh (4 daily; 6hr); Johor Bahru (4 daily; 7hr); Kota Bharu (5 daily; 6hr); Kuala Lipis (1 daily; 6hr); Kuala Lumpur (hourly; 6hr); Kuala Terengganu (6 daily; 4hr); Melaka (1 daily; 6hr); Mersing (4 daily; 4hr); Singapore (3 daily; 7hr); Temerloh (hourly; 3hr).

Flights

Kota Bharu to: Kuala Lumpur (at least 5 daily; 50min); Penang (at least 3 daily via KL, 4hr–5hr 40min).

Kuala Terengganu to: Kuala Lumpur (at least 4 daily; 45min).

Kuantan to: Kuala Lumpur (at least 4 daily; 40min); Singapore (2 weekly; 50min).

CHAPTER FIVE

THE SOUTH

T he south of the Malay Peninsula, below Kuala Lumpur and Kuantan, has some of
the most historically and culturally significant towns in the country. In the fifteenth century, the foundation of the west-coast city of **Melaka** led to a Malay
"golden age" under the Muslim Melaka Sultanate, during which period the concept of *Melayu* (Malayness), still current in Malaysia, was established. For all its influence, the sultanate was surprisingly short-lived, its fall in the early sixteenth century to
the Portuguese marking the start of centuries of colonial interference in Malaysia. The
Dutch and British followed the Portuguese in Melaka; indeed, British colonial rule was
an essential part of the eighteenth- and nineteenth-century development of the country.
The colonial inheritance is one of the main reasons people come to Melaka; among its
other attractions is the unique culture of the Peranakan community, also called Baba-
Nonya, the society that resulted from the intermarriage of early Chinese immigrant
traders and Malay women.

Just two hours by bus from KL, Melaka, in the centre of a small state of the same
name, makes a logical starting point for exploring the south. While its sights will keep
you absorbed for several days, other local destinations make good day-trips: the easy-
going towns of **Muar** and **Segamat**, **Pulau Besar**, and the coastal villages of **Tanjung
Bidara** and **Tanjung Kling**. Between KL and Melaka, the region that's now the state
of Negeri Sembilan is where the intrepid **Minangkabau** tribes from Sumatra settled,
making their mark in the spectacular architecture of **Seremban** and **Sri Menanti**, both
just over an hour south of the capital.

At the tip of the Peninsula, the town of **Johor Bahru** (or JB) dates back only to 1855,
its origins in the establishment of a settlement, Tanjung Puteri, across the Johor Straits
from Singapore. Visitors tend to travel the east or west coasts, from KL and Kuantan to
JB, avoiding the mountainous interior where the road network is poor. Along with the
train line, the North–South Highway connects KL with Singapore via the west coast; its
counterpart, the narrow Route 3 on the east coast, is a good deal more varied, winding
for 300km through oil-palm country and past luxuriant beaches. Most people head for
the active little seaport of **Mersing** in order to reach **Pulau Tioman** and the other
islands of the **Seribuat archipelago** – a draw for divers and snorkellers as well as
those who simply like the idea of sandy beaches and transparent waters. Increasingly,

visitors are also getting off the beaten track to see the primeval **Endau Rompin National Park**, the southernmost tropical rainforest in the Peninsula. It's a worthy and more rugged alternative to the much-visited Taman Negara further north.

Seremban and Sri Menanti

The Minangkabau tribes from Sumatra established themselves in the Malay state of **Negeri Sembilan**, whose modern-day capital is the town of **Seremban**, 67km south of Kuala Lumpur. The cultural heart of the state though, is the royal town of **Sri Menanti**, 30km east of Seremban. Centres of **Minangkabau** civilization (see box, p.300) since the early years of the Melaka Sultanate, both towns showcase traditional Minangkabau architecture, typified by distinctive, saddle-shaped roofs.

The modern state of Negeri Sembilan is based on an old confederacy of nine districts (hence its name – *sembilan* being Malay for "nine"), whose early origins are uncertain. By the middle of the nineteenth century, British control over the area and its thriving **tin trade** was virtually complete, with colonial authority administered from Sungei Ujong (today's Seremban). Wars between rival Malay and Minangkabau groups for control over the mining and transportation of tin were commonplace, most notably between the Dato' Kelana, the chief of Sungei Ujung, and the Dato' Bandar, who controlled the middle part of Sungei Linggi, further to the south.

The heavy influx of Chinese immigrants – who numbered about half the total population of Negeri Sembilan by the time of the first official census in 1891 – only had the effect of prolonging the feuds, since their secret societies, or triads, attempted to manipulate the situation to gain local influence. The most significant figure to emerge from this period was **Yap Ah Loy**, a charismatic leader who helped orchestrate clan rivalry through a series of violent skirmishes, one of which resulted in the sacking of Sri Menanti. He later moved to the newly established tin-mining town of Kuala Lumpur, where he quickly became an influential figure (see p.82). In an attempt to control a situation that was rapidly sliding out of control, the British Governor Jervois installed Abu Bakar of Johor as overlord, a man not only respected by the Malays but also apparently sympathetic to the colonists' aims. However, two prominent British officials, Frank Swettenham (later Resident in Selangor at the time of KL's early meteoric expansion) and Frederick Weld, weren't convinced about Abu Bakar's loyalty and bypassed his authority with the use of local British officials. Learning from their mistakes in Perak, where the hurried appointment of a British advisor had caused local uproar (see p.150), the British adopted a cautious approach. A treaty was eventually signed in 1895, narrowing the divide between the British colonial authorities and the Minangkabaus that had been the cause of so much strife.

Seremban

An hour south of the capital, **SEREMBAN** is a bustling town in whose commercial centre decorative Chinese shophouses sit alongside faceless concrete structures; further out, imposing colonial mansions line its streets. However, by far the best reason to come to Seremban is to visit the **Taman Seni Budaya Negeri** (State Arts & Culture Park; Tues, Wed, Sat & Sun 10am–6pm, Thurs 8.15am–1pm, Fri 10am–12.15pm & 2.45–6pm; free), 3km northwest of the centre, close to the North–South Highway. The state's museum and cultural centre is the best introduction that you could have to the principles of Minangkabau architecture: the new museum building is of traditional construction, and the grounds contain three original timber houses, reconstructed in the 1950s. The first of these, the **Istana Ampang Tinggi**, built forty years before the palace at Sri Menanti (see p.299), was

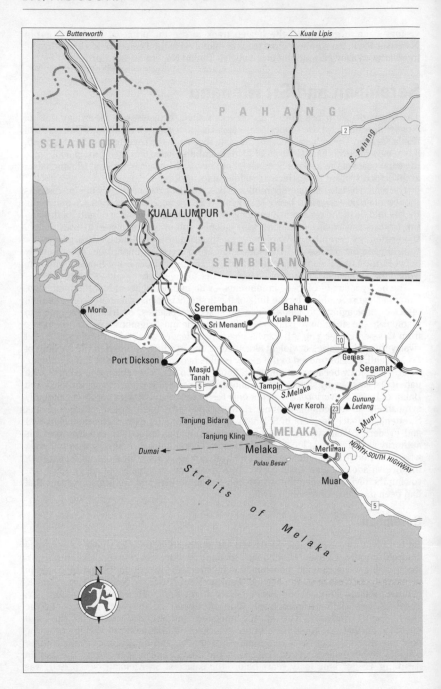

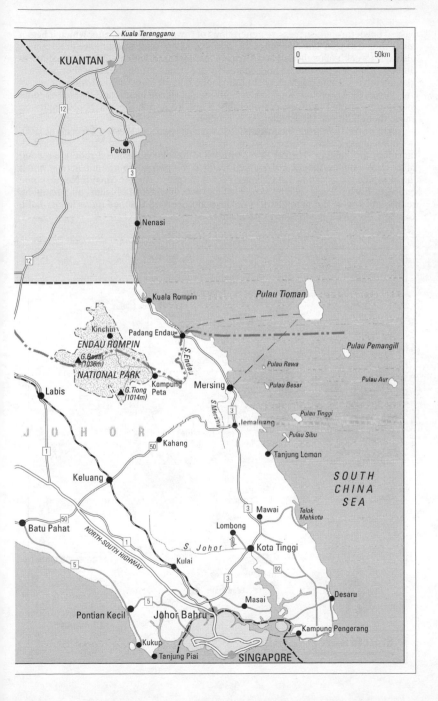

passed down through successive generations of royalty until 1930, after which it began to fall into disrepair. The interior of the veranda, where male guests were entertained, displays a wealth of exuberant and intricate leaf carvings, with a pair of unusual heavy timber doors. The two other houses nearby are similar, though less elaborate, their gloomy interiors only relieved by shutters in the narrow front rooms. Inside the museum proper, the lower floor contains an exhibition of village handicrafts, as well as some moth-eaten stuffed animals; considerably more lively are the old photographs on show, though little of the labelling is in English.

North of the river from the bus and taxi stations, past the **Wesley Church** of 1920, is the business district where most of the hotels, restaurants and banks are located, including the hulking Oriental Bank with its Minangkabau-inspired roof. East along Jalan Dato' Sheikh Ahmad, a right turn leads to the recreation ground, across which the nine pillars supporting the scalloped roof of the grey concrete **Masjid Negeri** come into view. Each pillar, topped by a crescent and star, symbols of Muslim enlightenment, represents one of the nine districts of the state. Beyond this lies the artificial **Lake Garden**, the focus of Seremban's parkland area.

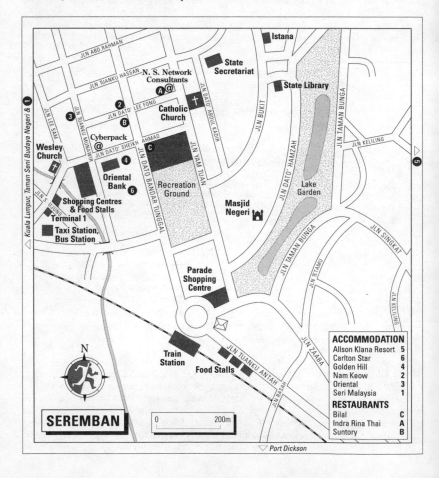

Head north along Jalan Dato' Hamzah and after a ten-minute walk you'll see the white-stucco, Neoclassical **State Library** – once the centre of colonial administration – with its graceful columns and portico. Past the black-and-gilt wrought-iron gates of the istana (closed to the public), a left turn leads to the current **State Secretariat** which reflects the Minangkabau tradition. Its hillside position ensures that the layered, buffalo-horn roof is one of the first sights you see in town.

Practicalities

Seremban has regular train connections with Kuala Lumpur and is linked with both Melaka and KL by express buses. The **bus station** and **taxi rank** are about five minutes' walk from the town across the river, while the **train station** is just to the south of the centre.

The town has a chronic shortage of decent, inexpensive **hotels** (indeed, many of the cheaper ones are brothels); the places we've listed below are all above board. There's no shortage of **places to eat**, however. The *Bilal* at 100 Jalan Dato' Bandar Tunggal serves reliable Indian dishes; the nearby *Suntory* restaurant (10am–10pm), on the same road, has a reasonably priced, wide-ranging Chinese menu and an air-con lounge. Good Thai food is available at *Restoran Indra Rina Thai*, 4 Jalan Dato' Lee Fong Yee. There are **food stalls** along Jalan Tuanku Munawir and close to the train station; any of the bakeries on Jalan Dato' Sheikh Ahmad is a good spot for breakfast.

Seremban is well supplied with **Internet** cafés; two of the best are N.S. Network Consultants, 13 Jalan Dato' Lee Fong Yee (open 24hr) near the *Restoran Indra Rina Thai*, and Cyberpack (daily 10.30am–midnight) on Jalan Dato' Sheikh Ahmad. There are a few more in the giant Terminal One shopping centre (next to the bus station) which also has a **cinema** on the top floor.

ACCOMMODATION

Allson Klana Resort, Jalan Penghulu Cantik (☎06/762 9600). Set 500m east of the lake gardens, this is the top spot in Seremban, with everything you'd expect from a high-class hotel, including a gym and restaurant. ⑨.

Golden Hill, 42 Jalan Dato' Sheikh Ahmad (☎06/763 5760). The double rooms at this centrally located hotel all have air-con; however, the place is a bit dingy and the staff are unhelpful. ②.

Hotel Carlton Star, 47 Jalan Dato' Sheikh Ahmad (☎06/762 5336, fax 762 0040). Slightly cheaper than the *Nam Keow* and better overall. The rooms are nothing special, but they're neat and clean by Seremban standards. ④.

Nam Keow, 61–62 Jalan Dato' Bandar Tunggal (☎06/763 5578). Reasonably clean en-suite rooms, larger than those at the *Oriental*, but run-down and triple the price. ④.

Oriental, 11 Jalan Tuanku Munawir (☎06/763 0119). Easily visible on your left as you walk up from the railway and bus stations. Its spartan rooms are clean and well ventilated – the best budget place here by far. ②.

Seri Malaysia, Jalan Sungai Ujung (☎06/764 4181, fax 764 4179). One kilometre away from the bus station, on the road to the State Museum. If you're after luxury this is a good bet, with large, nicely furnished rooms; breakfast is included in the price. ⑤.

Sri Menanti

Thirty kilometres east of Seremban lies the former royal capital of Negeri Sembilan **SRI MENANTI**, its palaces, ancient and modern, set in lush, mountainous landscape. The only reason to visit this little town, however, is to see a jewel of Minangkabau architecture, the **Istana Lama** (Mon–Wed & Sat 10am–6pm, Thurs 8.30am–1pm): a timber palace set in geometric gardens, it was the seat of the Minangkabau rulers, whose migration to the Malay Peninsula began in the fifteenth century during the early years of the Melaka Sultanate. The sacking of Sri Menanti during the Sungei Ujong tin wars

THE MINANGKABAU

The old adat, *ancient heritage,*
Neither rots in the rain,
Nor cracks in the sun.

Old Minangkabau proverb.

The **Minangkabau** people, whose cultural heartland is in mountainous west of central Sumatra (Indonesia), established a community in Malaysia in the early fifteenth century. As they had no written language until the arrival of Islam, their **origins** are somewhat sketchy; their own oral accounts trace their ancestry to Alexander the Great, while the *Sejarah Melayu* (see p.616) talks of a mysterious leader, Nila Pahlawan, who was pronounced king of the Palembang natives by a man who was magically transformed from the spittle of an ox. Oxen feature prominently, too, in the legend surrounding the origins of the name "Minangkabau". Their original home in Sumatra under attack from the Javanese, the native people agreed to a contest whereby the outcome of a battle fought between a tiger (representing the Javanese) and a buffalo (representing the locals) would determine who controlled the land. Against all the odds, the buffalo killed the tiger, and henceforth the inhabitants called themselves Minangkabau, meaning "the victorious buffalo".

In early times the Minangkabau were ruled in Sumatra by their own overlords or *rajas*, though political centralization never really rivalled the role of the strongly autonomous *nagari* (Sumatran for village). Each *nagari* consisted of numerous **matrilineal clans** (*suku*), each of which took the name of the mother and lived in the *adat* house, the ancestral home. The *adat* household was also in control of ancestral property which was passed down the maternal line. The *sumando* (husband) stayed in his wife's house at night but was a constituent member of his mother's house, where most of his day was spent. But although the idea that the house and clan name belonged to the woman remained uppermost, and women dominated the domestic sphere, political and ceremonial power was in the hands of men; it was the *mamak* (mother's brother) who took responsibility for the continued prosperity of the lineage (he was the administrative figurehead and the authority for the proper distribution of ancestral property).

While population growth and land shortage encouraged **migration**, it was the *sumando*'s lack of ties to his wife's family, and his traditional role as an entrepreneur, that facilitated his wanderlust. The society encouraged a man's desire to further his fame, fortune and knowledge, and, when Islam became more established, this was achieved by undertaking religious studies under famous teachers or visits to Mecca.

When and why the Minangkabaus initially emigrated to what is now **Negeri Sembilan** in Malaysia is uncertain. Their subsequent history is closely bound up with that of Melaka and Johor, with the Minangkabau frequently called upon to supplement the armies of ambitious Malay princes and sultans. Little is known of their interaction with the native Malay population, although evidence of intermarriage with the region's predominant tribal group, the Sakai, indicates acceptance by the Malays of the matrilineal system. What is certain is that the Minangkabaus were a political force to be reckoned with. Their dominance in domestic affairs was aided by their reputation for supernatural powers, rumours of which were so widespread that the early eighteenth-century trader Alexander Hamilton noted, "Malays consider the Minangkabau to have the character of great sorcerers, who by their spells can tame wild tigers and make them carry them whither they order on their backs."

Although migration remained standard practice, after the mid-nineteenth century the drift was towards urban centres, and communal living in the *adat* house became relatively rare. In the twentieth century, two important adaptations to the matrilineal system were documented: the tendency for families from the various clans to migrate rather than just the husband; and a change in the hereditary customs, whereby individually earned property can be given to a son, becoming ancestral property only in the next generation. Today, the Minangkabau are very much integrated with the Malays, and their dialect is almost indistinguishable from standard *Bahasa Melayu*.

destroyed the original palace; the four-storey version that stands here now was designed and built in 1902 by two Malay master craftsmen who, as the tradition dictates, used no nails or screws in its construction. Until 1931, the palace was used as a royal residence, with the ground floor functioning as a reception area, the second as family quarters, and the third as the sultan's private apartments. The tower, once used as the treasury and royal archives, can only be reached by ladder from the sultan's private rooms and is not open to the public. At its apex is a forked projection of a type known as "open scissors", now very rarely seen (though it's reproduced in the roof of the Muzium Negara in Kuala Lumpur; see p.96).

The whole rectangular building is raised nearly 2m off the ground by 99 pillars, 26 of which have been carved in low relief with complex foliated designs. Though the main doors and windows are plain, a long external veranda is covered with a design of leaves and branches known as *awan larat*, or "driving clouds". Above the front porch is the most elaborate decoration, a pair of fantastic creatures with lions' heads, horses' legs and long feathery tails; its style suggests that the craftsmen responsible were Chinese.

Inside, the Istana Lama is of little or no decorative interest. The palace now houses the lacklustre **Muzium Di Raja** (Tues, Wed, Sat & Sun 10am–12.45pm & 2–6pm, Thurs 8am–12.45pm, Fri 10am–12.15pm & 2.45–6pm; free), a rather stuffy commemoration of local royalty, its reconstructed state rooms bedecked in yellow (the royal colour) lacking atmosphere. There are old costumes, ceremonial *krises*, golfing memorabilia and photographs of past sultans and British administrators, all of which fail to excite.

Reaching Sri Menanti is relatively straightforward. From Seremban, take a United **bus** for the 45-minute journey to Kuala Pilah. There, you can either wait for an infrequent local bus to Sri Menanti, or take a shared taxi, a ten-minute ride costing no more than RM4 per person. You'll be dropped at a dilapidated row of shops, not far from a small mosque – walk past this and you'll spot the Istana Lama. Don't be misled by the sign for the Istana Besar, the rather imposing current royal palace, topped by a startling blue roof.

Port Dickson and Tanjung Bidara

The rather dismal strip of the **coast** stretching south of the capital to Melaka is a major draw for KL weekenders who, attracted by the populous resort of **PORT DICKSON**, turn a blind eye to its polluted sea. It's hard to see why the town, 34km southwest of Seremban, is so popular: it's not much more than a few shops and banks. Port Dickson's beach, stretching as far as the Cape Rachado (Tanjung Tuan) lighthouse, 16km to the south, is marred by passing oil tankers, sludgy brown sand, dishwater-grey sea and an enormous sewage pipe spilling out into the north of the bay. Yet it attracts a growing number of regular weekenders, to whom the town is affectionately known as PD. Whatever the reason for the town's popularity, its hoteliers are rubbing their hands with glee. To cope with the increasing demand, new hotels and condominiums are constantly springing up along the length of the coastline – most of the developers involved have, sensibly, built swimming pools too.

Regular bus connections with KL ensure ease of access to all points along this stretch of coast. The coastal road, Route 5, branches west off the North–South Highway south of KL and reaches the west coast at Morib; a little tortuous in places, the road at least makes for a more varied journey than travelling the monotonous highway.

Practicalities

Buses from KL stop at the **bus station** in the commercial part of town. The best **places to stay**, listed overleaf, are strung out along Jalan Pantai (part of Route 5), which runs south of Port Dickson. Locations along the road are usually specified according to milestones – the number of the mile you're currently in is usually painted on lampposts along the way, prefaced by *batu* (stone). It's easy enough to hop on any Melaka-bound bus until you reach the hotel of your choice; coming from Melaka, you can get off the buses at any point on the coastal road before reaching town.

Most chalets and hotels have their own **restaurants**, and many other eating places line the road, of which the nicest is the Muslim *Pantai Ria*, near the seven-mile marker; it specializes in seafood and Chinese cuisine at around RM8 a dish. The food court just north of the *Regency* is also worth a visit for its range of foods and pleasant outdoor seating. With the inexpensive places to stay – few enough amongst the big resorts – mostly found at the four- and five-mile markers, **food stalls** nearby offer everything from burgers to freshly caught fish.

ACCOMMODATION

Asrama Belia (☎06/647 2188). Behind a row of shops and restaurants, north of the Petronas service station at the four-mile marker. Affiliated to the IYHF (as the only sign attests), this comfortable place has cooking facilities, clean, newly renovated chalets (③) and dorms (RM10).

Bayu Beach Resort (☎06/647 3703, fax 647 2507). Halfway between the fourth and fifth mile marker. A pleasant complex of apartments offering very good-value deals for parties of four. To either side of the resort lies the best beach for a long way. ⑦.

Kong Ming (☎06/662 5683). At the eight-mile marker, right by the beach near the Sri Pena building, this is basic but bearable, with clean, sparsely furnished rooms. ②.

Ming Court Vista (☎06/662 5244). Located near the seven-mile marker, just south of the Shell service station, this is one of the longest-established upmarket resorts, but doesn't match up to the *Regency*. Closed for renovations at the time of writing. ⑥.

Moon Chalets (☎06/640 6944). At the seven-mile marker, the small, plush chalets here are well away from the road in a quiet, leafy setting. ④.

Regency (☎06/647 4090, fax 647 4792). PD's most upmarket hotel, located near the five-mile marker. Built in striking Minangkabau style, it has facilities for water sports and tennis, along with a popular Thai restaurant. Good value. ⑦.

Rotary Sunshine Camp (☎06/647 3798). On a hill south of the three-mile marker. The cheapest accommodation in PD, a cheerful turquoise- and yellow-painted complex of basic chalets, with only dorm beds available (RM6).

Tanjung Bidara

In between Port Dickson and Melaka lie the beach satellites of Tanjung Bidara and Tanjung Kling (see p.320). South from PD, Route 5 follows the coast closely for about 20km before heading inland to a junction at the town of Masjid Tanah. The small beachside village of **TANJUNG BIDARA** is a short detour through lush paddy fields off Route 5 (take bus #47 from Masjid Tanah) – the beach is much better than those at Port Dickson and Tanjung Kling. There are two fine **places to stay**: the *Tanjung Bidara Beach Resort* (☎06/542990; ⑤), with pleasant rooms, family chalets and a pool; and the *Bidara Beach Lodge* (☎06/543340; ②) a little further south, a quiet, delightful guesthouse with cosy en-suite rooms.

Melaka and around

Happy is a nation that has no history.

Anon.

When Penang was known only for its oysters and Singapore was just a fishing village, **MELAKA** (formerly "Malacca") had already achieved worldwide fame. Under the auspices of the Melaka Sultanate, founded in the early fifteenth century, political and cultural

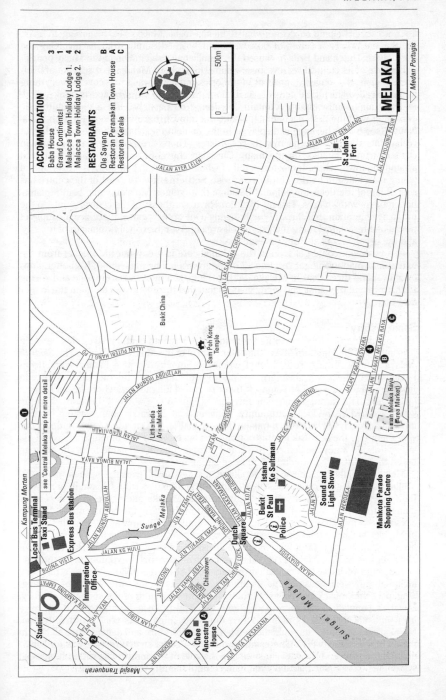

MELAKA

ACCOMMODATION
Baba House 3
Grand Continental 1
Malacca Town Holiday Lodge 1. 4
Malacca Town Holiday Lodge 2. 2

RESTAURANTS
Ole Sayang B
Restoran Peranakan Town House A
Restoran Kerala C

0   500m

St John's Fort
Bukit China
Sam Poh Kong Temple

JALAN BUKIT SENJUANG
JALAN AYER LELEH
JALAN LAKSAMANA CHENG HO
JALAN HUJUNG PASIR
JALAN PARAMESWARA
JALAN TAKAR MELAKA RAYA

Taman Melaka Raya
(Area Market)

see Central Melaka map for more detail

JALAN MUNSHI ABDULLAH
Little India Area Market
JALAN BENDAHARA
JALAN KEE ANN
JALAN BUNGA RAYA
JALAN MUNSHI ABDULLAH
JALAN KG HULU

JALAN PUTERI HANG LI PO

Sungei Melaka

Kampung Morten
Local Bus Terminal
Taxi Stand
Express Bus station
Immigration Office
Stadium
Buona Vista

JLN KAMPUNG EMPAT
JLN HANG TUAN
JLN TOLONG
JALAN KUBU
JLN TENGKERA
JALAN HANG JEBAT
JALAN TUN TAN CHENG LOCK
JALAN TUKANG EMAS
JALAN KG PAYAT

Chinatown
Chee Ancestral House

Dutch Square
Bukit St Paul
Istana Ke Sultanan
Police
Sound and Light Show
Mahkota Parade Shopping Centre

JALAN KOTA
JALAN LAKSAMANA
JALAN GEREJA
JALAN KOTA
JALAN CHAN KOON CHENG
JALAN MERDEKA
JALAN QUAYSIDE
JLN KOTA LAKSAMANA

Sungei Melaka

Medan Portugis

Masjid Tranquerah

life flourished, helping to define what it means to be Malay. Yet, beginning in 1511, Melaka was where a series of takeovers and botched administrations involving the Portuguese, Dutch and British, caused the humiliating subjugation of the Malay people.

Because of its cultural legacy, there's something about Melaka that smacks of over-preservation, all too easily apparent in the brick-red paint wash that covers everything in the so-called "historical centre". At its core, the **Dutch Square** sports a fake wind-mill and nineteenth-century fountain, bordering on pastiche. For a more authentic encounter with the past, it's better to strike out into **Chinatown**, where the rich Baba-Nonya (see p.314) heritage is displayed in the opulent merchants' houses and elegant restaurants that line the narrow thoroughfares. There are reminders of the human costs of empire building in the many Christian churches and graveyards scattered around the town, where tombstones tell of whole families struck down by fever and of young men killed in battle. The **Portuguese Settlement** to the east of the centre has something of the decaying colonial heritage that typifies Melaka, while land reclama-tion in the new town area, **Taman Melaka Raya**, southeast of the centre, points to the urban regeneration that the city badly needs. Out of the centre, there are a couple of places of interest, including the green-belt area of **Ayer Keroh**, 14km north of the city, and the beach resort at **Pulau Besar**.

At a push you could get around the colonial core in a day (an RM5 ticket from the tourist information will get you into all of the town's public museums). It's better, how-ever, to spend three days in Melaka, taking things at a more leisurely pace and seeing Chinatown and the outskirts. Many visitors find that the city grows on them the longer they stay.

Some history

The foundation of Melaka had its roots in the fourteenth-century struggles between Java and the Thai kingdom of Ayuthaya for control of the Malay Peninsula. The *Sejarah Melayu* (Malay Annals) records that when the Sumatran prince Paramesvara (from Palembang in the Srivijaya empire; see p.618) could no longer tolerate subservience to Java, he fled to the island of Temasek (later renamed Singapore), where he set himself up as ruler. The Javanese subsequently forced him to flee north to Bertam where he was welcomed by the local community. While his son, Iskandar Shah, was out hunting near modern-day Melaka Hill, a mouse deer turned on the pursuing hunting dogs, dri-ving them into the sea. Taking this courageous act to be a good omen, Shah asked his father to build a new settlement there and, in searching for a name for it, he remem-bered the *melaka* tree, which he had been sitting under.

Melaka rapidly became a cosmopolitan market town, **trading spices** from the Moluccas in the eastern Indonesian archipelago and textiles from Gujarat in northwest India; a levy exacted on all imported goods made Melaka one of the wealthiest king-doms in the world. With the adoption of **Islam** in the early fifteenth century, Melaka consolidated its influence; it was said that to become a Muslim was to enter the society of Melaka Malays. Melaka's meteoric rise was initially assisted by its powerful neigh-bours, Ayuthaya and Java, who made good use of its trading facilities. But they soon had a serious rival, as Melaka started a campaign of **territorial expansion**. By the time of the reign of its last ruler, Sultan Mahmud Shah (1488–1530), Melaka's territory included the west coast of the Peninsula as far as Perak, the whole of Pahang, Singapore and most of east-coast Sumatra. By the beginning of the sixteenth century, Melaka's population had increased to one hundred thousand, and it would not have been unusual to count as many as two thousand ships in its port. **Culturally**, too, Melaka was supreme – its sophisticated language, literature and dances were all bench-marks in the Malay world. The establishment of a court structure (see box on p.305) defined the nature of the Melaka state and the role of the individuals within it, a social system which remained virtually unchanged until the nineteenth century.

Sungei Palas Tea Estate, Cameron Highlands

Wall sculpture in the Rose Centre, Cameron Highlands

Fishermen off the east coast

View of beach, Beserah, Terengganu

JERRY DENNIS

MARTIN STOLWORTHY/AXIOM

Drum Festival, Kota Bharu

Food hawkers at night market, Kota Bharu

Kite Festival, Tumpat

Dragon head carving, Melaka

Christ Church with national flag, Melaka

MALAY COURT STRUCTURES

One of the most outstanding achievements of the Melaka Sultanate was to create a **court structure**, setting a pattern of government that was to last for the next five hundred years, and whose most prominent figures are still reflected in the street names of most towns in the country. At the top of the hierarchy was the **sultan** who, by virtue of his ancestry (which could be traced back to the mighty empire of Srivijaya), embodied the mystique which set Melaka apart from its rivals. He was far from being an autocratic tyrant: a form of social contract evolved whereby the ruler could expect undying loyalty from his subjects in return for a fair and wise dispensation of justice (this was the crux of the confrontation between Hang Tuah and Hang Jebat; see box, p.311). Nor were sultans remote ceremonial figures; many supervised the planting of new crops, for instance, or wandered freely in the streets among the people, a style of behaviour that may explain the relative humility of the palaces they occupied.

Below the ruler was a clutch of **ministers**, who undertook the day-to-day administration of government. The most important of these was the **Bendahara**, who dealt with disputes among traders and among the Malays themselves. In effect, he was the public face of the regime, wielding a great deal of power, backed by his closest subordinate, the **Penghulu Bendahari**, who supervised the *syahbandar*s (harbour masters) and the sultan's domestic staff. Potential Bendaharas were trained at the office of the **Temenggung**, who was responsible for law and order, working in close partnership with the **Laksamana**, the military commander, whose strongest armed force was the navy. Wide-ranging consultation regarding new measures took place in a **council of nobles**, who had earned their titles either through land ownership or from blood ties with royalty. Little is known of the **common people** of Melaka, though it is certain that they had no part in the decision-making process; the *Sejarah Melayu* (see p.616) nevertheless speaks of them with some respect: "Subjects are like roots and the ruler is like the tree; without roots the tree cannot stand upright."

To reinforce the status of the royal family, the colour yellow was only allowed to be used by royalty and no one but the ruler was permitted to wear gold – unless it was a royal gift. In addition, commoners could not have pillars or enclosed verandas in their houses, or windows and reception rooms in their boats. Despite these methods of distinction, threats to the throne were commonplace – particularly from the Bendahara.

But a sea change was occurring in Europe which was to end Melaka's supremacy. The **Portuguese** were seeking to establish links in Asia by dominating key ports in the region and, led by Alfonso de Albuquerque, **conquered Melaka** in 1511. Eight hundred officers were left to administer the new colony; although subject to constant attack, the Portuguese – or "white Bengalis" as they were known by the Malays – maintained their hold on Melaka for the next 130 years, introducing Catholicism to the region through the efforts of **St Francis Xavier**, the "Apostle of the East". Little tangible evidence of the Portuguese remains in Melaka today (bar the Eurasian community to the east of town), a reflection of the fairly tenuous nature of their rule, which relied on the internal squabbles of local leaders to dissolve any threats to the Portuguese position.

However, the formation of the Vereenigde Oostindische Compagnie (VOC), or **Dutch East India Company**, in 1602 spelled the end of the Portuguese. Having already founded Batavia (modern-day Jakarta), the VOC set its sights on Melaka, for the saying was, "Whoever controls Melaka has his hands on the throat of Venice". The ascendancy of Johor, an enemy of the Portuguese, gave the Dutch a natural ally, but although they made several attempts on Melaka from 1606 onwards, it wasn't until January 14, 1641, after a five-month siege, that they finally captured the city.

Where the Portuguese had tried to impose rule on the Malays, the Dutch sought to integrate them, finding them useful on matters of etiquette when negotiating with other

Malay rulers. The Protestant Dutch made half-hearted attempts at religious conversion, including translating the Bible into Malay, but on the whole their attitude to the Catholic Melakans was tolerant. Chinese immigrants were drawn to the city in large numbers, often becoming more successful in business than their European rulers; many of the Chinese married Malay women, creating a new racial mix known as **Peranakan** or Baba-Nonya (see box, p.314). However, the settlement never really expanded in the way the VOC had hoped. High taxes drove merchants away to more profitable ports like the newly founded Penang, and the Dutch relied ever more on force to maintain their position in the Straits – which lost them the respect of their Malay subjects. A ditty put about by their British rivals at that time had it that, "In matters of commerce, the fault of the Dutch/Is offering too little and asking too much".

The superior maritime skills and commercial adroitness of the British East India Company (EIC) provided serious competition for the control of Melaka. Weakened by French threats on their posts in the Indies, the Dutch were not prepared to put up a fight and handed Melaka over to the British on August 15, 1795, initially on the understanding that the EIC was to act as a caretaker administration until such time as the Dutch were able to resume control. For a while Melaka flew two flags and little seemed to have changed: the language, the legal system and even some of the officials remained the same as before. But the EIC was determined upon the supremacy of Penang, and against the advice of the resident, **William Farquhar**, ordered the destruction of Melaka's magnificent fort to deter future settlers. In fact, the whole population of Melaka would have been forcibly moved to Penang had it not been for Thomas Stamford Raffles, convalescing there at the time, who managed to impress upon the London office the impracticality – not to mention the cruelty – of such a measure.

Despite the liberalizing of trade by Farquhar, the colony continued to decline, and with the establishment of the free-trade port of Singapore in 1819, looked set to disintegrate. British administrators – just thirty in number, though this rose slowly to around 330 by 1931 – attempted to revitalize Melaka, introducing progressive agricultural and mining concerns, while the **Chinese** continued to flock to the town, taking over former Dutch mansions. However, investment in new hospitals, schools and a railway did little to improve Melaka's spiralling deficit. It wasn't until a Chinese entrepreneur, Tan Chey Yan, began to plant **rubber** that Melaka's problems were alleviated for a time; the industry boomed during the early years of the twentieth century. After World War I, though, even this commodity faced mixed fortunes – when the **Japanese occupied** Melaka in 1942, they found a town exhausted by the interwar depression.

Modern-day developments, such as the **land reclamation** in Taman Melaka Raya and the reorganization of the chaotic road network, are still working to reverse Melaka's long-term decline. Whatever damage was wrought during its centuries of colonial mismanagement, nothing can take away the enduring influence of Melaka's creation of a Malay language, court system and royal lineage – a powerful legacy established in a mere hundred years that was to permanently affect development in the Peninsula.

Arrival, information and transport

Both bus stations are located on the northern outskirts of the city, off Jalan Hang Tuah. In a tiny square by the river is the chaotic **express bus station**, just south of the **taxi stand**. The **local bus station** operates services to/from most destinations within the conurbation, as well as Singapore. From either, it's just a ten-minute walk to the town centre. Many of the streets are very narrow and the one-way system is awkward, so **drivers** should park their cars at the first possible opportunity and get around the city by bus, trishaw or taxi.

Many people arrive by **ferry** on the four-hour daily service from Dumai in Sumatra, which docks at the Shah Bandar jetty near Jalan Quayside, within easy walking distance

MOVING ON FROM MELAKA

BY AIR

From Batu Berendam Airport, which caters only for small aircraft, Pelangi Air (☎06/282 2648) runs a service to both Singapore (RM150 one way) and Ipoh (RM120 one way) from Monday to Saturday, and there are Tuesday and Saturday flights to Pekan Baru (RM145) and Medan (RM258), both in Sumatra. For tickets, contact MAS, on the first floor of the *City Bayview Hotel*, Jalan Bendahara (☎06/283 5722); or *Atlas Travel*, 5 Jalan Hang Jebat (☎06/282 0777).

BY BUS

There are frequent departures from the express bus station to KL, Ipoh, Butterworth, Alor Setar and other points on the Peninsula; most express services to Singapore leave from the local bus station. There's rarely any need to book in advance; just turn up before departure and buy a ticket from one of the booths at the bus station.

BY FERRY

Two companies combine to offer a daily service to Dumai in Sumatra (2hr; RM80 one way): Madai Shipping at 321a Jalan Tun Ali (☎06/284 0671), near the bus station, and Tunas Rupat at 17a Jalan Merdeka (☎06/283 2506).

BY TRAIN

From Tampin train station (☎06/411 1034), a regular luxury train service, the Peninsular Line, runs to Singapore. There are regular buses to Tampin from the local bus station.

of both the historical centre and the budget hostel area. Melaka's **airport**, Batu Berendam, is 9km north of the city and handles Pelangi Air services from Singapore, Ipoh, Kuantan, Langkawi, Tioman and Pekan Baru in Sumatra. The no. 56 bus from the airport into the centre is irregular, so it's best to take a taxi into town (around RM10). There's no **train station** in Melaka itself, the nearest being at Tampin, 38km away; buses from there drop you at the local bus station.

The very helpful **Tourist Information Centre** is on Jalan Kota (Mon–Thurs & Sat 8.45am–5pm, Fri 8.45am–12.15pm & 2.45–5pm, Sun 9am–5pm; ☎06/283 6538), 400m from the Shah Bandar jetty; they supply, among other information, free English-language leaflets detailing events in the city, and also sell a **museum ticket** (RM5) which allows entry to all of Melaka's state-run museums on the day (though not the privately run Baba-Nonya museum; see p.314). The information board outside displays the times of the river trips to Kampung Morten (see p.313).

City transport

Most of the places of interest are located within the compact historical centre, and so are best visited **on foot**. For longer journeys, **taxis** or **trishaws** are the best bet, both costing roughly the same (though trishaw drivers are more difficult to negotiate with); a sightseeing tour by trishaw, covering all the major sights including Medan Portugis, costs from RM25 per hour for two people. You should be able to get a trishaw around the Dutch Square and outside the Mahkota Parade Shopping Centre. Taxis are quite hard to find on the street, but you can always get one from the taxi stand. A trip from the bus station to the centre costs around RM7.

The **town bus service** has several useful routes for visitors, departing the local bus station: #17 runs to Taman Melaka Raya and Medan Portugis (50 sen to either), and #19 out to Ayer Keroh (RM1.20). **Car rental** outlets are given in "Listings" on p.319.

Accommodation

Melaka has a huge selection of **hotels**, although prices are a little higher than in other Malaysian towns. Most in the lower price bracket are located in the noisiest areas, around the bus stations or main shopping streets. Standards are generally high though, compared to those in KL or Georgetown. In the Taman Melaka Raya area (from the local bus station, you can get bus #17 there; a taxi or trishaw there costs RM5) there's a rapidly growing number of budget **hostels**, all offering broadly the same facilities; touts often wait at the local bus station.

Baba House, 125 Jalan Tun Tan Cheng Lock (☎06/281 1216, fax 281 1217). These beautifully restored Peranakan houses have been turned into an atmospheric hotel, though the lobby area is better than the rooms themselves, which are a little small. ⑤.

Chong Hoe, 26 Jalan Tukong Emas (☎06/282 6102). A well-looked-after hotel in Chinatown offering smallish rooms with air-con and shower, though the location, opposite the mosque, can be noisy. ②.

Eastern Heritage, 8 Jalan Bukit China (☎06/283 3026). One of the best budget hostels in Melaka, set in an imaginatively decorated house that makes the best of its original architectural features. The dorms and rooms are spotless, and there are nice touches such as a plunge pool and a batik workshop. The sole drawback is that there's only one bathroom. ②, dorm beds RM6.

Grand Continental, 20 Jalan Tun Sri Lanang (☎06/284 0048, fax 284 8125). Efficient though rather characterless hotel that's very reasonably priced, its facilities including a pool and coffee house. ⑥.

Heeren House, 1 Jalan Tun Tan Cheng Lock (☎06/281 4241, fax 281 4239). An ideal location in Chinatown and tasteful rooms – some with four-poster beds – make this the best choice for a small, upmarket hotel. Prices, which include breakfast, are slightly higher at weekends. ⑥.

Hotel Equatorial, Jalan Bandar Hilir (☎06/628 28333, fax 282 9333). With brightly decorated rooms boasting a wide range of restaurants, this comes a close second to the *Renaissance* in terms of grandeur. Recommended. ⑥.

Majestic, 188 Jalan Bunga Raya (☎06/282 2367). A fading colonial hotel tucked away from the traffic, with musty but clean air-con rooms, antediluvian bathrooms and Raj-like service in the bar. Good value overall. ②.

Malacca, 27a Jalan Munshi Abdullah (☎06/282 2252). Housed in an elegant old building, this hotel boasts large rooms full of substantial old wooden furniture. The noisy road is a drawback, though it's otherwise good value. ②.

Malacca Town Holiday Lodge, 148b Jalan Taman Melaka Raya 1 (☎06/284 8830). Above the large *Kingdom* restaurant. Run by the Lee family, who now have another guesthouse west of the bus station, this is a friendly place, a shade less expensive than its partner establishment. There's a choice of rooms, with or without attached showers. ①.

Malacca Town Holiday Lodge 2, 52a Kampong Empat (☎06/284 6905). Occupying the three floors of the Wine and Spirit Association building, this slightly tired-looking hostel's rooms are all named after famous brands of liquor. Apart from being in a quiet area, there's some antique Chinese furniture to add to the atmosphere, plus bicycle rental (RM10 a day) and a wide choice of rooms. ②.

May Chiang, 59 Jalan Munshi Abdullah (☎06/282 2101). Modest hotel with small, clean rooms which, though not quite as nice as the *Malacca*'s, are double-glazed and therefore quieter. ②.

Renaissance Melaka, Jalan Bendahara (☎06/284 8888, fax 284 9269). The town's major luxury hotel, with an imposing lobby – complete with huge chandeliers – and elegant, well-furnished rooms. ⑨.

Robin's Nest and Robin's Nest II, 205b and 202 Jalan Melaka Raya (☎06/282 9142). These two friendly, family-run hostels, practically next to each other, have dorms and small rooms. There are hot showers, kitchen facilities and pleasant lounges with videos to watch. ①, dorm beds RM8.

Sunny's Inn, 270a Jalan Taman Melaka Raya (☎06/283 7990). As pleasant a hostel as you'll find in Malaysia, with Japanese-style sanded floorboards, a roof terrace and a raised lounge area complete with books and board games. There are dorms and a wide range of rooms, including ordinary doubles with fans and air-con en-suite rooms, all great value. The small sign makes it hard to spot. ①, dorm beds RM8.

Traveller's Lodge, 214b Jalan Melaka Raya (☎06/281 4793). Small and homely family-run hostel, with cable TV, a cosy lounge and roof garden. ①, dorms RM7.

The City

The centre of Melaka is split in two by the murky **Sungei Melaka**, the western bank of which is occupied by **Chinatown** and, 2km to the north, **Kampung Morten**, a small collection of stilted houses. On the eastern side of the river lies the colonial core – the main area of interest – with **Bukit St Paul** at its centre, encircled by Jalan Kota. Southeast of here is a section of reclaimed land known as **Taman Melaka Raya**, a new town that's home to a giant shopping centre and many of the budget hotels, restaurants and bars. There are a few sights further east of the centre, a little too far flung to be comfortably covered on foot: **Medan Portugis** (Portuguese Square), **St John's Fort** and **Bukit China**, the last of these being the Chinese community's ancestral burial ground. Town bus #17 runs regularly to Medan Portugis 3km from town, from where St John's Fort is only about a kilometre's walk; you can take a taxi or trishaw from the latter to Bukit China (around RM6).

Central Melaka's historic buildings are denoted as such by being painted a uniform brick-red. Intended to symbolize the red laterite from which many of Melaka's original structures were constructed, this practice has, sadly, destroyed the individual character of each building. That said, it has at least meant that the area has been kept in reasonable condition.

The Istana to Muzium Rakyat

On Jalan Kota, the **Istana Ke Sultanan** (daily 9am–6pm, closed Fri 12.15–2.45pm; RM2), in the geographical centre of town, has played an equally central role in Malaysian history. The imposing dark-timber palace, in neatly manicured gardens, is a contemporary reconstruction, based on a description in the *Sejarah Melayu*, of the original fifteenth-century istana. In the best Malay architectural tradition, its multilayered, sharply sloping roofs contain no nails. It was here that the administrative duties of the state were carried out, and also where the sultan resided when in the city (for the most part he lived further upriver at Bertam, safe from possible attacks on Melaka). Inside – remove your shoes to ascend the wide staircase to the verandaed first floor – is a cultural museum which houses a rather tired display of life-sized re-creations of scenes from Malay court life, including the epic duel of Melaka's most famous warriors, Hang Tuah and Hang Jebat (see box, p.311), as well as costumes and local crafts. The building alone, though, is worth the entrance fee.

At the time of their conquest of Melaka, the Portuguese used the forced labour of fifteen hundred slaves to construct the mighty **A Famosa** fort. All that's left of it today is a single gate, the crumbling whitewashed **Porta de Santiago**, just to the right as you leave the palace museum. The hillside site was chosen not only for its strategic position but also because it was where the Sultan's istana was located – its replacement by the Portuguese stronghold a firm reminder of who was now in charge. Square in plan, with walls nearly 3m thick, the fort had as its most striking feature the keep in the northwestern corner, which loomed 40m and four storeys high over the rest of the garrison. This was no mean feat of engineering, even if the design of the fort as a whole was considered old-fashioned by contemporary European observers. When it defeated the Portuguese in 1641, the Dutch East India Company used the fort as its headquarters, later modifying it, adding the company crest and the date 1670 to the Porta de Santiago – features which are just about distinguishable today.

The fort stood steadfast for 296 years and probably would have survived, were it not for the arrival of the British in 1795. With their decision to relocate to Penang, orders were given in 1807 to destroy the fort in case it was later used against them. The task of demolition fell to Resident William Farquhar, who reluctantly set about the task with gangs of labourers armed with spades and pickaxes. Failing to make an impression on its solid bulk, he resorted to gunpowder, blowing sky-high pieces that were "as large as

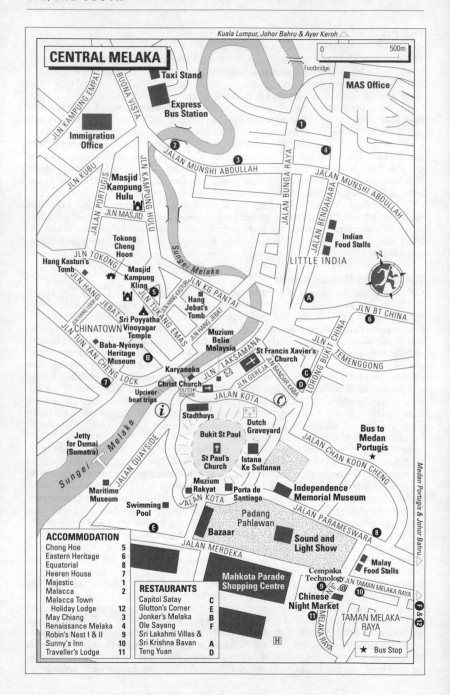

Kuala Lumpur, Johor Bahru & Ayer Keroh △

CENTRAL MELAKA

0   500m

Footbridge

Taxi Stand

Express
Bus Station

MAS Office

JLN KAMPUNG EMPAT

BUONA VISTA

❶

❷

JLN KUBU

**Immigration
Office**

JALAN MUNSHI ABDULLAH

❸

JLN KAMPUNG HULU

JALAN PORTUGIS

JALAN BUNGA RAYA

JALAN BENDAHARA

JALAN MUNSHI ABDULLAH

❹

**Masjid
Kampung
Hulu**

JLN MASJID

Indian
Food Stalls

**Tokong
Cheng
Hoon**

Sungei Melaka

LITTLE INDIA

N

Hang Kasturi's
Tomb

JLN TOKONG

JLN HANG JEBAT

**Masjid
Kampung
Kling**

JLN KG PANTAI

❺

JLN HANG KASTURI

Hang
Jebat's
Tomb

JALAN BT CHINA

❻

JLN HANG LEKIR

**Sri Poyyatha
Vinoyagar
Temple**

JLN TUKANG EMAS

JLN HANG JEBAT

**Muzium
Belia
Malaysia**

JLN BUKIT CHINA

CHINATOWN

JLN TUN TAN CHENG LOCK

**Baba-Nyonya
Heritage
Museum**

Ⓑ

Ⓐ

St Francis Xavier's
Church

LORONG BUKIT CHINA

JLN TEMENGGONG

❼

Karyaneka

JLN LAKSAMANA

Ⓒ

JLN GEREJA

JLN BANDAR KABA

Ⓓ

Christ Church

DUTCH
SQUARE

JALAN KOTA

Ⓒ

Upriver
boat trips

ⓘ

Stadthuys

Ⓒ

Dutch
Graveyard

**Bus to
Medan
Portugis**
★

Jetty
for Dumai
(Sumatra)

Bukit St Paul

JALAN QUAYSIDE

JALAN CHAN KOON CHENG

Sungei Melaka

**St Paul's
Church**

Istana
Ke Sultanan

Muzium
Rakyat

Porta de
Santiago

**Independence
Memorial Museum**

**Maritime
Museum**

Swimming
Pool

JALAN KOTA

JALAN PARAMESWARA

❽

Ⓔ

Padang
Pahlawan

Bazaar

**Sound
and
Light Show**

**Malay
Food Stalls**

ACCOMMODATION

Chong Hoe	5
Eastern Heritage	6
Equatorial	8
Heeren House	7
Majestic	1
Malacca	2
Malacca Town Holiday Lodge	12
May Chiang	3
Renaissance Melaka	4
Robin's Nest I & II	9
Sunny's Inn	10
Traveller's Lodge	11

JALAN MERDEKA

**Mahkota Parade
Shopping Centre**

Cempaka
Technology

❾

JLN TAMAN MELAKA RAYA

❿

**Chinese
Night Market**

❶❶

MELAKA RAYA

**TAMAN MELAKA
RAYA**

Ⓗ

★ Bus Stop

RESTAURANTS

Capitol Satay	C
Glutton's Corner	E
Jonker's Melaka	B
Ole Sayang	F
Sri Lakshmi Villas &
Sri Krishna Bavan	A
Teng Yuan	D

Medan Portugis & Johor Bahru △

F & 12

HANG TUAH AND HANG JEBAT

If any ruler puts a single one of his subjects to shame, that shall be a sign that his kingdom will be destroyed by Almighty God. Similarly it has been granted by Almighty God to Malay subjects that they shall never be disloyal or treacherous to their rulers, even if their rulers behave evilly or inflict injustice on them.

From the *Sejarah Melayu*

Recounted in the seventeenth-century epic *Hikayat Hang Tuah*, the tale of the duel between **Hang Tuah** and **Hang Jebat** symbolizes the conflict between absolute loyalty to the sovereign and the love of a friend. These two characters, together with Hang Kasturi, Hang Lekir and Hang Lekiu, formed a band known as "The Five Companions" (because of their close relationship since birth), and were highly trained in the martial arts. When they saved the life of the Bendahara Paduka Raja, the highest official in the Malay court, Sultan Mansur Shah was so impressed by their skill that he appointed them court attendants. Hang Tuah rapidly became the Sultan's favourite and was honoured with a beautiful *kris*, **Taming Sari**, which was said to have supernatural powers. This overt favouritism rankled with other long-serving officials who, in the absence from court of the rest of the companions, conspired to cast a slur on Hang Tuah's reputation by spreading the rumour that he had seduced one of the sultan's consorts. On hearing the accusation, the sultan was so enraged that he ordered the immediate execution of Hang Tuah. But the Bendahara, knowing the charge to be false, hid Hang Tuah to repay his debt to him, reporting back to the sultan that the deed had been carried out.

When Hang Jebat returned to the palace, he was shocked to discover Hang Tuah's supposed death and rampaged through Melaka, killing everyone in sight as retribution for the life of his treasured friend. The sultan, in fear of his own life, soon began to regret his decision, at which point the Bendahara revealed the truth and Hang Tuah was brought back to protect the sultan from Hang Jebat's fury and to exact justice for the murders committed. Hang Tuah wrestled hard with his conscience before deciding that the sultan had the absolute right to dispose of his subjects how he wished. So, with a heavy heart, Hang Tuah drew his *kris* against Hang Jebat and, after a protracted fight, killed him, a much-recounted tale whose moral – of deference to the sovereign – is seen by some as setting the seal on the Malay system of government.

elephants and even some as large as houses". Sultan Munshi Abdullah said that the fort "was the pride of Melaka and after its destruction the place lost its glory, like a woman bereaved of her husband, the lustre gone from her face".

Turning your back on the gate, and facing **Padang Pahlawan** (Warrior's Field), a large open green that forms the centre of the downtown area, you'll see the **Independence Memorial Museum** (Tues–Thurs, Sat & Sun 9am–6pm, Fri 9am–noon & 3–6pm; free – closed for renovations at the time of writing). Built in 1912, this elegant mansion of classic white stucco, with two golden onion domes on either side of its portico, formerly housed the colonial **Malacca Club**, whose most famous guest was the novelist Somerset Maugham. This is where he was told the tale which was the basis of his short story *Footprints in the Jungle*, in which both the Club and Melaka itself (which he calls Tanah Merah) feature prominently. The museum depicts the fascinating events surrounding the run-up to independence in 1957, but unfortunately it's poorly laid out, and the sequence is hard to follow.

MUZIUM RAKYAT

Skirting west round the base of the hill from Porta de Santiago brings you to the **Muzium Rakyat** (People's Museum; daily 9am–6pm; Fri closed 12.15–2.45pm; RM1.50) on Jalan Kota. Its ground and first floors house exhibits showing the development and successes of Melaka during the last decade – fine if you're into housing policy and the structure of local government. The third floor contains the much more interesting – and at times gruesome – **Museum of Enduring Beauty** (covered by Muzium Rakyat ticket). Taking "endure" in the sense of "to suffer", the exhibits show how people have always sought to alter their appearance, no matter how painful the process might be: head deformation, dental mutilations, tattooing, scarification and foot-binding are just some of the "beautifying" processes on display. For some light relief, the top floor here has a display of **kites** from Malaysia and around the world.

Bukit St Paul

If you double back through the Porta de Santiago and climb up the steps behind, past the trinket and picture sellers, you reach **Bukit St Paul**. An alternative route from Jalan Kota, near the Muzium Rakyat, is up a steep set of steps near a renovated Dutch building, the proposed site of the Islamic and Martial Arts Museum (as yet still at the planning stage). On the summit stands the shell – roofless, desolate and smothered in ferns – of **St Paul's Church**, a ruin for almost as long as it was a functioning church. Constructed in 1521 by the Portuguese, who named it "Our Lady of the Mount", the church was visited by the Jesuit missionary **St Francis Xavier** between 1545 and 1552. On his death in 1553 his body was brought here for burial – a brass plaque on the south wall of the chancel marks the spot where he was laid. A grisly story surrounds the exhumation of the saint's body in 1554 for its transfer to its final resting place in Goa in India. In response to a request for his canonization, the Vatican demanded his right arm which, when severed from his body – which allegedly showed very few signs of decay after nine months of burial – appeared to drip blood. A related tale concerns the marble statue of St Francis that has stood in front of the church since 1952: on the morning following its consecration ceremony, a large casuarina tree was found to have fallen on the statue, severing the right arm.

The Dutch Calvinists changed the denomination of the church when they took over in 1641, renaming it St Paul's Church, and it remained in use for a further 112 years until the construction of Christ Church at the foot of the hill (see opposite). The British found St Paul's more useful for military than for religious purposes, storing their gunpowder here during successive wars, and building the lighthouse that guards the church's entrance. The tombstones that lie against the interior walls, together with those further down the hill in the **graveyard** itself, are worth studying. Being the only major port in the Straits until the nineteenth century, Melaka received many visitors, some of whom were buried here (including Bishop Peter of Japan, who was a missionary in Melaka in 1598), as well as large numbers of Portuguese, Dutch and British notables, whose epitaphs have long been partly obscured by lichen. In the graveyard on the slopes below, note the tomb of the Velge family, five members of which died within twenty days of one another during the diphtheria epidemic of 1756.

Dutch Square and around

A winding path beside St Paul's Church brings you down into the so-called **Dutch Square**, one of the oldest surviving parts of Melaka, although two of its main features date from much later times; the Victorian marble fountain was built in 1904 to commemorate Queen Victoria's Diamond Jubilee, the clock tower erected in 1886 in honour of Tan Beng Swee, a rich Chinese merchant.

Presiding over the entire south side of the square is the sturdy **Stadthuys**, now housing the **Museum of Ethnography** (Mon & Wed–Sun 9am–6pm, Fri closed 12.15–2.45pm; RM2). The simple, robust structure – more accurately a collection of buildings dating from between 1660 and 1700 – was used as a town hall throughout the whole period of Dutch and British administration. Although the long wing of warehouses projecting to the east is the oldest of the buildings here, recent renovations have revealed the remains of a Portuguese well and drainage system, suggesting that this was not the first development on the site. The wide, monumental interior stair-cases, together with the high windows that run the length of the Stadthuys, are typical of seventeenth-century Dutch municipal buildings, though they are less suited to the tropical climate than European winters. Look out of the back windows onto the white-washed, mould-encrusted houses that line the courtyard, and you could be in a Vermeer scene. The museum itself displays an array of Malay and Chinese ceramics and weaponry, though there's also a reconstruction of a seventeenth-century Dutch dining room. The rooms upstairs have endless paintings giving a blow-by-blow account of Melakan history, and old photographs showing how little the town has changed over the last hundred years.

Turn to the right as you leave the Stadthuys and you can't miss **Christ Church** (Tues–Sun 9am–5pm; free), also facing the fountain. Built in 1753 to commemorate the centenary of the Dutch occupation of Melaka, its simple design, with neither aisles nor chancel, is typically Dutch; its porch and vestry were nineteenth-century afterthoughts. The cool, whitewashed interior has decorative fanlights high up on the walls; there are elaborate, 200-year-old hand-carved pews, and the roof has heavy timber beams, each cut from a single tree. The plaques on the walls tell a sorry tale of early deaths in epi-demics, and a wooden plaque to the rear of the western wall of the church commemo-rates local planters who were killed in World War II.

East of the church, along Jalan Kota, lie the overgrown remains of the **Dutch Graveyard**. This was first used in the late seventeenth century, when the VOC was still in control (hence the name), though British graves easily outnumber those of their pre-decessors. The tall column towards the centre of the tiny cemetery is a memorial to two of the many officers killed in the Naning War in 1831, a costly attempt to include the nearby Naning region as part of Melaka's territory under the new Straits Settlements.

North to St Peter's Church

Back at Christ Church, head north up Jalan Laksamana, moving quickly past the **Muzium Belia Malaysia** (daily 9am–6pm, closed Fri 12.30–2.45pm; RM1.50) – replete with pictures of smiling, wholesome youths shaking hands with Dr Mahathir. The road leads to **St Francis Xavier's Church**, a twin towered nineteenth-century neo-Gothic structure. Further up from here, skirting the busy junction with Jalan Temenggong and taking Jalan Bendahara directly ahead, you're in the centre of Melaka's tumble-down **Little India**, a rather desultory line of incense and saree shops, interspersed with a few eating houses. After about five minutes' walk, you come to a sizeable crossroads with Jalan Munshi Abdullah, beyond which is **St Peter's Church**, set back from the road on the right. The oldest Roman Catholic church in Malaysia, built by a Dutch convert in 1710 as a gift to the Portuguese Catholics, it has an unusual barrel-vaulted ceiling. The church really comes into its own at Easter as the centre of the Catholic community's celebrations.

The river and docks

If you feel like a rest from pavement pounding, take one of the **boat trips** up Sungei Melaka. These leave from the small jetty behind the Tourist Information Centre (hourly from 10am–2pm, depending on the tide; 45min; RM7); buy your tickets at the office, or on the boat itself. The trip takes you past "Little Amsterdam", the old Dutch quarter of red-roofed godowns, which backs directly onto the water. Look out for the slothful mon-itor lizards that hang out on either side of the bank, soaking up the sun, and the local fishermen who line the route, mending boats and nets. The boat turns round without stopping at Kampung Morten (see p.316), opposite which, on the east bank, you can just make out a few columns and a crumbling aisle – all that remains of the late-sixteenth-century Portuguese church of St Lawrence – poking out from beneath the undergrowth. On the return journey, you're taken beyond the jetty to the **docks** along Jalan Quayside, crowded with low-slung Sumatran boats bringing in charcoal and timber which they trade for rice; these heavy wooden craft are still sailed without the aid of a compass or charts. The best time to catch the activity at the docks is around 4.30pm, when the multicoloured fishing boats leave for the night's work. From here, you can also see the new **Maritime Museum** (daily 9am–9pm, closed Fri 12.15–2.45pm; RM2) on the quayside, housed in a towering replica of the Portuguese cargo ship, the *Flor De La Mar*, which sank in Melaka's harbour in the sixteenth century. Inside its hull, lots of model ships and paintings chart Melaka's maritime history from the time of the Malay Sultanate to the arrival of the British in the eighteenth century. Across the road, another section of the museum houses a drab display about the Malaysian navy and, much more interestingly, some of the recovered items from the wreck of the *Diana*, which sank in the Straits of Melaka while on route to Madras in 1817. The salvage operation, which began in 1993, eventually yielded eighteen tons of chinaware.

Chinatown and Masjid Tranquerah

Melaka owed a great deal of its nineteenth-century economic recovery to its Chinese community: it was one Tan Chey Yan who first planted rubber here, and a certain Tan Kim Seng who established a steamer company early on, which later became the basis of the great Straits Steam Ship Company, providing regular communication between different parts of the colony. Most of these early entrepreneurs settled in what became known as **Chinatown**, across Sungei Melaka from the colonial district. Turn left after the bridge by the Tourist Information Centre, then take the first right to follow the one-way system, and you come to **Jalan Tun Tan Cheng Lock**, fondly known as "Millionaires Row". The elegant townhouses that line the narrow road are the ancestral homes of the **Baba-Nonya** community (see box, below), descendants of the original Chinese pioneers who married local Malay women – it is said that Chinese women of high class were reluctant to emigrate. The wealthiest and most successful of these merchants built long, narrow-fronted houses, and minimized the "window tax" by incorporating several internal courtyards, designed also for ventilation and the collection of rainwater.

At nos. 48–50, the **Baba-Nonya Heritage Museum** (daily 10am–12.30pm & 2–4.30pm; RM8; not covered by all-day Melaka museum ticket) is an amalgam of three

---

THE BABA-NONYAS

Tales of Melaka's burgeoning success brought vast numbers of merchants and entrepreneurs to its shores, eager to benefit from the city's status and wealth. The Chinese, in particular, came to the Malay Peninsula in droves, to escape Manchu rule – a trend that began in the sixteenth century, but continued well into the nineteenth. Many Chinese married Malay women; descendants of these marriages were known as **Peranakan** or sometimes "Straits-born Chinese". While their European counterparts were content to while away their time until retirement, when they could return home, the expatriate Chinese merchants had no such option, becoming the principal wealth-generators of the thriving city. The **Babas** (male Sino-Malays) were unashamed of flaunting their new-found prosperity in the lavish townhouses which they appropriated from the Dutch, transforming these homes into veritable palaces filled with Italian marble, mother-of-pearl inlay blackwood furniture, hand-painted tiles and Victorian lamps. The women, known as **Nonyas** (sometimes spelt Nyonya), held sway in the domestic realm and were responsible for Peranakan society's most lasting legacy – the **cuisine**. Taking the best of both Malay and Chinese traditions, its dishes rely heavily on sour sauces and coconut milk; its eating etiquette is Malay – using fingers, not chopsticks.

adjacent houses belonging to one family, and an excellent example of the Chinese Palladian style. Typically connected by a common covered footway, decorated with hand-painted tiles, each front entrance has an outer swing door of elaborately carved teak, while a heavier internal door provides extra security at night. Two red lanterns, one bearing the household name, the other messages of good luck, hang either side of the doorway, framed by heavy Greco-Roman columns. But the upper level of the building is the most eye-catching: a canopy of Chinese tiles over the porch frames the shuttered windows, almost Venetian in character, their glass protected by intricate wrought-iron grilles, with eaves and fascias covered in painted floral designs. Inside, the homes are filled with gold-leaf fittings, blackwood furniture inlaid with mother-of-pearl, delicately carved lacquer screens and Victorian chandeliers.

Further up the road, at no. 107, the **Restoran Peranakan Town House** is another former mansion, now a restaurant specializing in Nonya cuisine (see "Eating", p.318). Beyond, at no. 117, you can't fail to notice the **Chee Ancestral House**, an imperious Dutch building of pale-green stucco topped by a gold dome, and home to one of Melaka's wealthiest families, who made their fortune from tapioca and rubber. Continuing northwest from here, up Jalan Tengkera, you pass through Melaka's suburbs of stylish Peranakan mansions and come to the **Masjid Tranquerah**, about 2km from the town centre on the right. A pagoda-like Melakan mosque dating from the eighteenth century, it's where Sultan Hussein, who ceded Singapore to Stamford Raffles in 1819, is buried. You can also get here from the local bus station on bus #51, which continues on to Tanjung Kling (see p.320).

Back in Chinatown, Jalan Hang Jebat – formerly named "Jonkers Street" or "Junk Street" – runs parallel to Jalan Tun Tan Cheng Lock. Melaka's **antiques** centre (see "Shopping", p.318), it's worth a wander even if you don't intend to buy. Crammed between the Chinese temples and shophouses here is the small, whitewashed tomb of **Hang Kasturi**, one of the "Five Companions" (see box, p.311). A short way east up Jalan Tokong is **Tokong Cheng Hoon** (Merciful Cloud Temple, under renovation at the time of writing), reputed to be the oldest Chinese temple in the country – though several others would dispute the title. Dedicated to the Goddess of Mercy, the main prayer hall has a heavy saddled roof and oppressive dark-timber beams, reminiscent of its counterpart in Georgetown (see p.178). Smaller chambers devoted to ancestor worship are filled with small tablets bearing a photograph of the deceased and strewn with wads of fake money and papier-mâché models of luxury items, symbolizing creature comforts for the dead. The temple authorities here act as the trustees for Bukit China, the ancestral burial ground to the northeast of town (see overleaf).

A little further down is the 1748 **Masjid Kampung Kling**, displaying an unusual blend of styles: the minaret looks like a pagoda, there are English and Portuguese glazed tiles, and a Victorian chandelier hangs over a pulpit carved with Hindu and Chinese designs. Next door, the Hindu **Sri Pogyatha Vinoyagar Temple** also has a minaret, decorated with red cows, but its gloomy interior is disappointing. From the temple, head north for Jalan Kampung Hulu and its **Masjid Kampung Hulu**, thought to be the oldest mosque in Malaysia. Constructed around 1728 in typical Melakan style, it's a solid-looking structure, surmounted by a bell-shaped roof with green Chinese tiles and, again, has more than a hint of pagoda in its minaret. Such architecture has its origins in Sumatra, perhaps brought over by the Minangkabaus (see box, p.300) who settled in nearby Negeri Sembilan.

From here, an alternative route back to the centre of town is to walk south down Jalan Kampung Hulu as it follows the river and merges into Jalan Kampung Pantai. At the junction with Jalan Hang Kasturi, a couple of minutes further on, you can pause for a moment at **Hang Jebat's Tomb**, another tiny mausoleum to one of the great warriors of the Malay "golden age".

Kampung Morten

The village of **Kampung Morten**, named after the British District Officer who donated RM10,000 to buy the land, is a surprising find in the heart of the city. It's easiest to explore this community on foot: take the footbridge down a small path off Jalan Bunga Raya, one of the principal roads leading north out of town (you can also reach the village by heading east from the local bus station). The wooden stilted houses here are distinctively Melakan, with their long, rectangular living rooms and kitchens, and narrow verandas approached by ornamental steps. On the left as you cross the footbridge, the **Villa Sentosa** (daily 9am–5pm; voluntary donation), with its miniature kampung house and mini-lighthouse, is a 70-year-old family home that now functions as a museum. The warm and welcoming family will gladly show you artefacts and heirlooms handed down by the old patriarch, Tuan Haji Hashim Hadi Abdul Ghani, who died at the age of 98.

Medan Portugis and St John's Fort

The road east of Jalan Taman Melaka Raya leads, after about 3km, to Melaka's Portuguese Settlement; turn right into Jalan Albuquerque, clearly signposted off the main road, and you enter its heart. You can also get here on bus #17 or #25 from Jalan Parameswara, just outside Jalan Taman Melaka Raya.

In 1933, the colonial administration, prompted by increasing levels of poverty and the depletion of the Portuguese community (which was barely any larger than the two thousand recorded in the first census in 1871), established this village on the historic site of their original community. Today you're likely to recognize the descendants of the original Portuguese settlers only by hearing their language, **Kristao**, a unique blend of Malay and old Portuguese, or by seeing their surnames – Fernandez, Rodriguez and Dominguez all feature as street names.

Medan Portugis (Portuguese Square), at the end of the road, is European to the hilt – you could be forgiven for thinking that its whitewashed edifice, worn by the salty winds, was a remnant from colonial times. Through the archway, the souvenir shop and tourist-oriented restaurants surrounding the central courtyard soon make it clear that this is a purpose-built "relic", dating only from 1985. That said, the square, cooled by the sea breeze, is a good place for a quiet beer at sunset, and the local restaurateurs make an effort to conjure up a Portuguese atmosphere, though the food is Malay in character. A three day **fiesta** – the feast of St Pedro – is held in the square, commencing on June 29 every year, with traditional Portuguese food, live music and dancing.

Heading back into town, you can make a brief detour to **St John's Fort**, up Bukit Senjuang. The fort, a relic of the Dutch occupation, is not terribly exciting, somewhat dwarfed by the adjacent water tower, but does offer good views over the town and the Straits of Melaka.

Bukit China

Northeast of the colonial heart of Melaka is **Bukit China**, the ancestral burial ground of the town's Chinese community, indeed the oldest and largest such graveyard outside China. Although Chinese contacts with the Malay Peninsula probably began in the first century BC, it wasn't until the Ming Emperor Yung-Lo sent his envoy Admiral Cheng Ho here in 1409 that commercial relations with Melaka were formally established, according the burgeoning settlement with vassal status. At the foot of the hill, at the eastern end of Jalan Temenggong is the **Sam Poh Kong**, a working temple dedicated to Cheng Ho, upon whom the title of "Sam Poh" or "Three Jewels" was conferred in 1431. Accounts of the time are vague about the arrival of the first Chinese settlers, though the *Sejarah Melayu* recounts that on the marriage of Sultan Mansur Shah (1458–77) to the daughter of the Emperor, Princess Hang Liu, the five hundred nobles accompanying her stayed to set up home on Bukit China. It was supposedly these early pioneers who dug the well behind the temple; also known as the **Sultan's Well**, it has been of such importance to the local inhabitants as a source of fresh water that successive invading armies all sought to poison it. The Dutch enclosed it in a protecting wall, the ruins of which still remain.

At the top of Bukit China, horseshoe-shaped **graves** stretch as far as the eye can see. On the way up, you'll pass one of the oldest graves in the cemetery, belonging to Lee Kup who died in 1688. He was the first Chinese *kapitan*, a mediatory position created by the VOC (see p.621), which made it possible for them to rule the various ethnic communities. His successor was Captain Li, whose grave on the other side of the cemetery is the subject of local myth: a fortune teller, asked to advise on the location and construction of the grave, prophesied that if it were to be dug three feet deep, Li's son would benefit; any deeper and all profit would go to his son-in-law. Whether by accident or design, the grave was made three-and-a-half feet deep, and the son-in-law, Chan Lak Koa, went on to found the elaborate Tokong Cheng Hoon (see p.315) as an expression of gratitude for his prosperity.

In the 1980s the burial ground was the subject of a bitter legal battle between its trustees and the civil authorities. Competing plans to develop the area into a cultural and sports centre provoked a claim by the government for a RM2 million bill for rent arrears, stating that the exemption over the previous centuries had been a "clerical error". This outraged the Chinese community who flatly refused to pay. The controversy was only settled in the early 1990s when the decision was made to develop Melaka's waterfront area instead. Today, Bukit China is more an inner-city park than burial ground, where you're likely to encounter locals jogging, practising martial arts or simply admiring the view.

Eating

Surprisingly, there are very few quality restaurants in the centre of town – in fact, aside from a few places in Chinatown, it's hard to find much open at night. Instead, **Taman Melaka Raya** is fast becoming the favoured food centre, featuring Chinese, Nonya, Malay, Indian and seafood restaurants. Budget meals are not as common as elsewhere in Malaysia – even the city's principal **food stalls** on Jalan Merdeka, known as "Gluttons' Corner", are overpriced; it's far better to try the stalls just off Jalan Parameswara. Sampling **Nonya cuisine** is a must at some stage in your stay, though it is generally more expensive than other types of food. The emphasis is on spicy dishes, using sour herbs like tamarind, tempered by sweeter, creamy coconut milk; some specialities are mentioned below. By contrast, the city's few remaining **Portuguese** restaurants are generally disappointing, pricier still and tourist-oriented (a notable exception is *Heeren House*; see overleaf).

Usual restaurant **opening hours** are daily 9am–11pm, unless otherwise stated; phone numbers are given where it's necessary to book (usually only on Sat nights).

Capitol Satay, Jalan Bukit China. Experience the Melaka version of fondue – *satay celup* – at this lively café, where you take your pick of assorted fish, meat and vegetables skewered on sticks and cook them in a spicy peanut sauce before eating. Each stick is around 40 sen; you'd be hard pressed to spend more than RM5 per person.

Chinese night market, Taman Melaka Raya. A blur of chopping cleavers and furiously boiling woks make for great entertainment while you sample from the many stalls. Dishes can be made to order if you can make yourself understood. Very inexpensive, it's open 24hr.

Gluttons' Corner, Jalan Merdeka. More a collection of permanent restaurants than food stalls, the city's highest-profile eating area also has high prices and impersonal service. One of the better places is *Bunga Raya*, whose local seafood is popular with the locals. A full meal at any of the restaurants costs at least RM12 a head.

Heeren House, 1 Jalan Tun Tan Cheng Lock. This stylish air-conditioned café and gift shop, beneath the hotel, offers Nonya lunches at weekends for RM15 and very reasonably priced local Portuguese fare. Daily 8am–6pm.

Jalan Bendahara Indian food stalls. *Roti canai* and other South Indian favourites are served here from early morning till well into the night.

Jalan Merdeka/Jalan Parameswara Malay food stalls. Quick, tasty fare can be had from these stalls along the road linking Jalan Merdeka with Jalan Parameswara, south of the *Equatorial* hotel.

Jonkers Melaka, 17 Jalan Hang Jebat. In a beautiful Peranakan house, this café is also a gift shop and art gallery. Good for vegetarians – set meals, including Nonya cuisine, start at RM16. There are home-made desserts too. Daily 10am–5pm.

Long Feng Chinese Restaurant, *Renaissance Melaka Hotel*, Jalan Bendahara. Excellent Cantonese and Szechuan dishes in a classy setting. It's not cheap – around RM25 per dish.

Mahkota Parade/Parkson Grand, Jalan Merdeka. The Merdeka Grand shopping mall has a decent air-conditioned food court with dishes for around RM5, while the adjacent mall, the Parkson Grand, has a full range of Western fast-food outlets and a supermarket.

Ole Sayang, 198–199 Jalan Taman Melaka Raya (☎06/283 4384). A moderately priced Nonya restaurant with re-created Peranakan decor. Try the beef *goreng lada*, in a rich soya-based sauce, or the *ayam lemak pulut*, a spicy, creamy chicken dish; both cost around RM7. Open 11.30am–2.30pm & 6–9.30pm, closed Wed.

Restoran D'Nolasco, Medan Portugis. A Mediterranean atmosphere accompanies the oriental food, such as crabs in tomato and chilli sauce with soy. Around RM20 a head.

Restoran Kerala, 668 Jalan Taman Melaka Raya. Cheap and cheerful South Indian food in a sparkling clean establishment. Excellent banana-leaf curries as well as tandoori set meals, each for about RM5.

Restoran Peranakan Town House, 107 Jalan Tun Tan Cheng Lock (☎06/284 5001). Marble tables with white-lace tablecloths, and a reasonably priced Nonya menu in a picture-book Chinatown setting. Try spicy *rendang* dishes (RM8) or claypot *ayam* (RM9). Lunch only.

Restoran Teng Yuan, cnr of Lorong Bukit China and Jalan Banda Kaba. Vegetarian Chinese restaurant with a buffet of inexpensive tofu and bean dishes.

Sri Lakshmi Villas, 2 Jalan Bendahara. Both this and *Sri Krishna Bavan* next door have reliable South Indian *thali*s with as many top-ups as you can eat for RM4 a go. Good for vegetarians.

Nightlife and entertainment

At night, while the centre of town is dead – except for the discos in the top hotels – **Taman Melaka Raya** comes alive. There's no shortage of karaoke bars (usually 8pm–2am), though both these and the discos are expensive and somewhat lacking in character. For a straightforward drink at a reasonable price, you're better off eschewing the Western-style bars in favour of one of the grotty Chinese bottle shops in the centre of town.

   Mahkota Parade includes a 24-lane bowling alley, an amusement arcade and a three-screen cineplex. Otherwise the only source of entertainment is the nightly **Sound and Light Show** on Padang Pahlawan (closed for renovations at the time of writing). A must for fans of high drama ("Something is rotten in the state of Melaka" intones the soundtrack), it drags a bit at an hour in length, but provides a one-stop introduction to the city's history. The buildings are well lit and the sound system is used imaginatively; take lots of mosquito repellent. Shows are in English (daily 9.30pm, 8.30pm during Ramadan; RM10) and you can buy tickets from the booths at each end of the padang.

Shopping

Melaka is famed for its **antiques**, and there are many specialist outlets along Jalan Hang Jebat and Jalan Tun Tan Cheng Lock; you can find anything from Nonya tableware to HMV gramophones in the musty shop interiors. Prices are usually fixed, although it doesn't hurt to bargain. If the item you're thinking of buying is a genuine antique (many shops fill their windows with colourful but inauthentic clutter), then check that it can be exported legally and fill in an official clearance form; the dealer should provide you with this. Jalan Bunga Raya and Jalan Munshi Abdullah comprise the modern shopping centre, where you'll find a variety of Western and local goods.

Abdul Co, 79 Jalan Hang Jebat. A good place for china and glass.

Dragon House, 65 Jalan Hang Jebat. The best value for old coins and banknotes, with helpful staff.

Jehan Chan Art Gallery, 10 Jalan Tun Tan Cheng Lock (☎06/286 1615). Jehan Chan, a former teacher, has achieved considerable fame nationally for his paintings in watercolour and oil. They can be viewed and purchased at his small gallery.

Koo Fatt Hong, 92 Jalan Tun Tan Cheng Lock. Specialists in "Asia Spiritual and Buddha images" – various deities carved in stone and wood.

Orang Utan, 59 Lorong Hang Jebat. Here, local artist Charles Chan sells his paintings, and T-shirts printed with witty cartoons and sayings.

Parkson Grand, Jalan Merdeka. A huge air-con department store, connected to the Mahkota Parade Shopping Mall; fast food and a supermarket in the basement.

Ringo, 12 Jalan Hang Jebat. British bikes and old biker artefacts, as well as unusual toys; pricey.

Tribal Arts Gallery, 10 Jalan Hang Rebat. Specialists in Sarawakian crafts, including woodwork and weaving.

Wah Aik, 92 Jalan Hang Jebat. Renowned for making silk shoes for bound feet. With foot binding no longer practised, the shoes are now lined up in the window as souvenirs, at a mere RM75 per pair.

Listings

Airlines MAS ☎06/283 5722; Pelangi Air ☎06/317 4175.

Banks and exchange Bank Bumiputra, Jalan Kota; Hong Kong Bank, 1a Jalan Kota; Overseas Chinese Banking Corporation, Jalan Hang Jebat. Often more convenient, with rates as good as the banks', are the moneychangers, including Malaccan Souvenir House and Trading, 22 Jalan Tokong, and Sultan Enterprise, 31 Jalan Laksamana. Maybank, accepting most debit and credit cards, has ATMs opposite the Hong Kong Bank on Jalan Kota.

Bookshops Estee Book Exchange, Jalan Taman Melaka Raya, has a good selection of English-language classics and other fiction; Lim Bros, 20 Jalan Laksamana, has books on the Malaysian economy and politics, as well as colonial memoirs and expensive travel guides. MPH, on the ground floor of Mahkota Parade, also has an excellent range of books, as does Tai Khuang upstairs on the second level.

Car rental Avis, 124 Jalan Munshi Abdullah (☎06/284 6710, fax 284 6918).

Cinema The Cineplex in Mahkota Parade shows English-language films; check in the newspapers for what's on when.

Hospital The Straits Hospital is at 37 Jalan Parameswara (☎06/283 5336).

Internet access You can get online at the Cempaka Technology Shop at 155 Jalan Melaka Raya or the Internet Booth Café, 3a Jalan Kota Laksamana (☎06/281 3266).

Police The Tourist Police office (☎06/282 2222) on Jalan Kota is open 24hr.

Post office The GPO is inconveniently situated on the way to Ayer Keroh on Jalan Bukit Baru – take town bus #19. A minor branch on Jalan Laksamana sells stamps and aerograms.

Sport The Merlin Melaka sports centre on Jalan Munshi Abdullah offers ten-pin bowling, snooker, squash and roller skating.

Swimming There's a public swimming pool on Jalan Kota (daily 10am–1pm, 2–4.15pm & 6–8pm; RM1.80).

Telephones The Telekom building is on Jalan Chan Koon Cheng (daily 8am–5pm). The quietest and most efficient place to make international calls, though, is the Cempaka Technology Shop at 155 Jalan Taman Melaka Raya.

Travel agents Try Atlas Travel at 5 Jalan Hang Jebat (☎06/282 0777) for plane tickets.

Visa extensions Visas can be extended on the spot at the immigration office on the second floor of the Bangunan Persekutuan, Jalan Hang Tuah (☎06/282 4958).

Around Melaka

While there's more than enough to keep you occupied in Melaka itself, you may well fancy a break from sightseeing for more relaxed pleasures, using the city as a base. Nearby lie the resorts at **Pulau Besar** and **Tanjung Kling**, while for rural pursuits, head up to **Ayer Keroh**, with its recreation parks.

Ayer Keroh

Fourteen kilometres north of the centre, **AYER KEROH** – despite its position adjacent to the North–South Highway – is a leafy recreational area that provides a pleasant alternative to staying in the city itself. Town buses #19 and #105 run here every thirty minutes from Melaka's local bus station.

The major attractions are all within a few hundred metres or so of one another. Apart from the **Hutan Rekreasi** (daily 7am–6pm; free), an area of woodland set aside for walking and picnicking, all the attractions – the **Taman Buaya** (Crocodile Park; Mon–Fri 9am–6pm, Sat & Sun 9.30am–7pm; RM4); the **Melaka Zoo** (Mon–Fri 9am–6pm, Sat & Sun 9.30am–6.30pm; RM3), purportedly the oldest and second largest in the country; and the **Taman Rama Rama** (Butterfly Park; daily 8.30am–5.30pm; RM5), with its walk-through aviary and small marine centre – are somewhat contrived. The only display that demands more than fleeting attention is the **Taman Mini Malaysia** and **Mini ASEAN** (Mon–Fri 10am–6pm, Sat & Sun 9.30am–6.30pm; RM5), a large park fifteen minutes' walk north of the Crocodile Park, with full-sized reconstructions of typical houses from all thirteen Malay states and the other members of the Association of South East Asian Nations, an economic alliance of the region's states. The specially constructed timber buildings are frequently used as sets for Malaysian films and soap operas, and cultural shows featuring local music and dance are staged at the park's open-air arena – ask at the ticket office for details.

The area around the lake, just off the main road, is where you'll find most of the **places to stay**, limited exclusively to upmarket resort accommodation. The best of the bunch is the *Paradise Malacca Village Resort* (☎06/232 3600, fax 232 5955; ⑥), a sprawling complex which partly uses traditional timber and rattan decor, with comfortable rooms around the swimming pools. Next door, *D'Village Resort* (☎06/232 8000; ⑤) is the least attractive option, with blue-roofed chalets crammed together, though it does have the cheapest rooms. **Places to eat** are more or less limited to those in the resorts, save for a few tourist-oriented food stalls at the main attractions.

Tanjung Kling

The village and beach resort of **TANJUNG KLING** ("kling" being a term – now considered derogatory – for the Tamil immigrants who first populated this village) lies on Route 5, around 9km west of Melaka and 18km southeast of the turnoff to Tanjung Bidara (see p.302). New developments are popping up all around this area, despite the fact that the dingy beach is less than inviting, and the village itself lacks amenities.

A right turn at the mosque, following the signpost to the Malacca Club, brings you to **Makam Hang Tuah**, the grave of the famous fifteenth-century warrior (see box, p.311). It was formerly known locally only as *Makam Tua* or "Old Grave" in order to conceal its presence from the Portuguese, who went about destroying all buildings connected with the Melaka Sultanate on their takeover in 1511.

There's a string of small resorts back on the main road, of which the most appealing is the homely *Shah's Beach Resort* (☎06/315 3121, fax 315 2088; ⑤). Its intriguingly designed wooden chalets incorporate elements of Portuguese architecture, as well as genuine antique furniture; the facilities here include an open-air *atap*-roofed restaurant, tennis courts and a pool. Next door, in stark contrast, the *Riviera Bay Resort* (☎06/315

1111, fax 315 3333; ⑧) is an enormous complex with an arched entrance, boasting large, comfortable rooms. It also has a decent range of restaurants and – fortunately – a good pool, since the beach is narrow and litter-strewn. The hotel's "leisure club", open to non-residents, offers windsurfing, tennis and squash.

Pulau Besar

Long before it was turned into an exclusive beach resort, **PULAU BESAR** (literally, Big Island, though it covers just sixteen square kilometres), about 5km off the coast of Melaka, was known as the burial ground of passing Muslim traders and missionaries, tales of whom live on in distorted local legends. Although vigorously promoted by the tourist authorities, its historic sites consist of little more than a few ancient graves, several wells, and remnants of the Japanese occupation, such as a bunker and dynamite store. However, the island's beaches and hilly scenery are pleasant enough, and its compact size makes it easy to stroll around in a day.

Pulau Besar is easily reached by **ferry** (RM11 return), departing from the Anjung Batu jetty in Melaka (6 daily starting 8.30am, last boat 6.30pm). You can also get there by fishing boat from the **Pengkalan Pernu jetty** in Umbai (on request; RM8 return for a group of 12, otherwise RM50 to hire whole boat one way), 6km southeast of Melaka (bus #2; 20min). You might want to stay overnight in the luxury *Pandanusa Resort* (☎06/281 5939; ⑥), the only available indoor **accommodation** on the island. For the more budget conscious, there's the campsite (☎06/281 8007, fax 281 5941; RM20 per person including tent rental) next to the resort. As for **eating**, there are a couple of local *kedai kopi*s serving rice and noodle dishes, and there's a pricey restaurant at the resort itself.

Gunung Ledang and Segamat

Inland from Melaka, east of the North–South Highway, a maze of minor roads covers the sparsely populated lowland, the only feature on the horizon being the conical **Gunung Ledang**. Further inland still, you'll meet up with the sweep of Route 1, connecting a string of lifeless towns, of which the least dull is **Segamat**.

Gemas, 25km northwest of Segamat, is a grubby little place whose merit is its importance to the train network – it's the southern terminus of the so-called "jungle railway", and so is where you'll have to change if you want to venture into the interior by train (see p.230). Transport connections throughout inland Johor are uncomplicated, with a good network of buses serving all destinations.

Gunung Ledang

Formerly called Mount Ophir by the British, **Gunung Ledang** (1276m), the highest mountain in the state of Johor, is believed by the animist Orang Asli to be inhabited by spirits. The best-known legend associated with Gunung Ledang concerns the betrothal of Sultan Mansur Shah to the mountain's beautiful fairy princess. A lengthy list of requirements was presented to the sultan, on fulfilment of which the princess would consent to marry him; while the sultan was not daunted by such items as trays of mosquito hearts and a vat of tears, he drew the line at a cup of his son's blood, and withdrew his proposal.

Gunung Ledang features a **waterfall** – an impressive cataract after the rains, but disappointing in dry season – and challenging **treks**, though the latter are restricted to experienced climbers with their own camping equipment. Once you're past the hotel and clutter of food and souvenir stalls at the approach to the waterfall, the surroundings gradually become more leafy and refreshing, leading to the start of the trail to the summit. A series of rapids, which the main path follows closely, form natural pools, ideal for a cooling dip, though the water is a bit murky in places. Reaching the water-fall's source, a 45-minute hike, requires stamina.

Practicalities

To drive here, turn off the North–South Highway at Tangkak, from where you take Route 23 northeast, passing **Sagil** after 11km. After a further 3km, you'll see the water-fall clearly signposted ("Air Terjun") off the road, from which point it's 1500m to the beginning of the rapids. The mountain is easily reached by any Segamat-bound express bus from Melaka – though the driver may tell you to get off in Sagil, the best place to leave the bus is at the stop a couple of kilometres beyond, signposted "Gunung Ledang Resort"; from here, you simply take the turning opposite.

You pay the RM1 entrance fee at the *Gunung Ledang Resort*, a combination of hotel and park administration offices (☎06/977 2888, fax 977 3555; ⑥), with comfortable, en-suite **rooms**. Also here is the Kem Rimba adventure camp, which includes an obstacle course, adjoined by thirty "jungle huts" – unfurnished metal shacks – where you can stay for RM50 a night (closed for renovation at time of writing). If you're on a tight bud-get, the best way to see the mountain is to **camp** at one of the many sites along the trail; the resort charges a nominal RM3 a week per person for this, and there's inexpensive **food** to be had at the market stalls outside the gate. There are various **packages** on offer that combine a stay at the resort with expeditions up the mountain, from around RM150 – contact the resort or the national rail company KTM (☎03/272 7267, fax 273 6527) for details.

Segamat

While there's no real reason to continue on to **SEGAMAT**, about 40km northeast of Gunong Ledang (and 130km east of Seremban along Route 1), it's not an unpleasant town; if you have the convenience of your own transport, stop here for a drink and a wander around the grassy padang. It's bordered by some elegant old colonial buildings such as the **Sekolah Tinggi**, formerly the English High School, as well as the District Office and an ill-proportioned Catholic church. The more modern, anonymous com-mercial centre is more than 1km to the south.

The **bus station** is centrally located on the main road, Jalan Genuang. Not far away is the **train station** on Jalan Stesen, from where Jalan Genuang is a short walk east. There's no tourist office, though it's easy enough to find **accommodation** hereabouts: the basic *Tai Ah* (☎07/931 1709; ②) is next to the bus station; over the road is the spick-and-span, though sterile, *Pine Classic Inn*, 30 Jalan Genuang (☎07/932 3009, fax 932 3011; ③); and the *Segamat Inn* (☎07/931 1401; ②) is in the UMNO building next to the GPO on Jalan Awang. Also good value is the *Hotel Mandarin*, 99–101 Jalan Genuang (☎07/931 1393; ③), a little less expensive and better furnished than the *Pine Classic*. Most of the town's **restaurants** are also on Jalan Genuang, but don't expect anything special.

From Melaka to Johor Bahru

The journey from Melaka southeast along **Route 5** to Johor Bahru (see p.325) covers a distance of 206km, the first 45km of which – to the Malay town of **Muar** – is through verdant countryside dotted with neatly kept timber stilted houses with double roofs. These houses, in some of the prettiest kampungs in Malaysia, are especially numerous along Route 5 and, with time to spare en route between Melaka and Muar, you could stop to visit one of them, the striking **Penghulu's House**; heading south, you find it to your right, just off the main road 2km south of the village of **Merlimau**. The house, built in 1894 for a local chieftain, has elaborate woodcarvings adorning the veranda and eaves, and the front steps are covered in colourful Art Nouveau hand-painted tiles. It's still inhabited by the chieftain's descendants, who will show you around. Further south, the towns of **Batu Pahat** and **Pontian Kecil** are of scant interest (the former, slightly inland, has a reputation as a red-light resort for Singaporeans). If you do want to stop anywhere else before Johor Bahru and Singapore, aim for **Kukup**, right at the southern end of the west coast, and terrific for seafood.

To get to Johor Bahru in a hurry, skip the scenery of Route 5 and use the **North–South Highway** instead. From Melaka, you can head north to the highway via Ayer Keroh (see p.320); it's also straightforward to join the highway from Muar (take the Bukit Pasir road for about 20km) and Batu Pahat (take Route 50 northeast off Route 5).

Muar

The old port town of **MUAR** – also known as Bandar Maharani – exudes an elegance and calm that attracts surprisingly few tourists. Legend has it that Paremesvara, the fifteenth-century founder of Melaka, fled here from Singapore to establish his kingdom on the southern bank of Sungei Muar, before being persuaded to choose Melaka. Although rejected by the Sumatran prince, Muar later became an important port in the Johor empire (see p.621), as well as a centre for *ghazal* music (see p.642) – and the place whose dialect is considered the purest Bahasa Malaysia in the Peninsula.

Today, Muar's commercial centre looks like any other, with Chinese shophouses and *kedai kopis* lining its parallel streets, Jalan Maharani, Jalan Abdullah and Jalan Meriam. But if you turn right out of the bus station on Jalan Maharani, following the river as the road turns into Jalan Petri, you'll see an altogether different part of town. Under the shade of huge rain trees, Muar's Neoclassical colonial buildings – the **Custom House** and **Government Offices** (Bangunan Sultan Abu Bakar) on your right, and the **District Police Office** and **Courthouse** on your left – still have an air of confidence and prosperity from the town's days as a British administrative centre. The graceful **Masjid Jamek** successfully combines Western and Moorish styles of architecture.

Practicalities

Bus #2 runs frequently here from Melaka's local bus station, taking less than ninety minutes to arrive in Muar at the **bus station** on Jalan Maharani. There are plenty of reasonable **hotels**, a selection of which appears below. Aside from **eating** houses in the commercial centre of town, none of which can be particularly recommended, the *Medan Selera* near the bridge on Jalan Maharani serves Malay snacks, while the *Classic Hotel* has a good ground-floor restaurant with great Chinese food – to get there, head down Jalan Sulaiman, which leads away from the river from a point about 100m southwest of the bridge, and turn left into Jalan Ali. Otherwise, you could try the *Heritage Garden*, a mid-range Chinese restaurant on Jalan Bakri, the road leading east from the bridge.

Kingdom, 158 Jalan Meriam (☎06/952 1921). Walk southeast away from the river along Jalan Sulaiman and take the second left onto Jalan Meriam. This clean, inexpensive Chinese-run hotel has simple but functional attached bathrooms. ③.

Riverview, 29 Jalan Bentayan (☎06/951 3313, fax 951 8139). Walk along Jalan Maharani from the bus stop, keeping the river on your left, and turn right onto Jalan Bentayan. Has large, comfortable rooms with decent attached bathrooms. ④.

Rumah Persinggahan Tanjong Emas, Jalan Sultanah (☎06/952 7744, fax 953 7933). A ten-minute taxi ride away from the town centre in a countryside setting. This place has the quietest, most upmarket accommodation in town, with huge rooms complete with TV and telephone, a children's play area, as well as some family chalets. ③.

Town View Hotel, 60 Jalan Sisi (☎06/951 1788, fax 953 7236). Jalan Sisi leads off from the water-front, a short walk northeast of the bus stop. Under the same management as the *Riverview*, this place is a little smarter, with comfortable en-suite rooms with TV. ④.

Batu Pahat and Pontian Kecil

Heading south, Route 5 hugs the palm-fringed coast as far as **BATU PAHAT** (also called Bandar Penggaram), where the Art Deco **Masjid Jamek** and Straits Chinese **Chamber of Commerce** are the only buildings of note. The town has a reputation as a venue for "dirty weekends", though a more noteworthy association is with a couple of important political events. The governing party, UMNO, initially a coalition of orga-nizations opposed to the British-inspired Malayan Union, had its origins here in 1946. Years later, during the constitutional crisis of 1983, Prime Minister Dr Mahathir held a mass rally in the town to protest against the position taken by the sultans, urging the people to assert their constitutional rights and elect him. The choice of Batu Pahat as the venue for this conscience-stirring symbolized Dr Mahathir's desire to remind the rulers of UMNO's role in reversing their original acquiescence with the Malayan Union many years before (see p.626).

Batu Pahat is a convenient point to cut across to the **east coast**: Route 50 links the town with Mersing, 140km away (see p.331). To the south of Batu Pahat lies plantation country – the crop in this case being pineapples, piled high on roadside stalls in sea-son, filling the air with their sweet smell. The next place of any consequence is the unassuming town of **PONTIAN KECIL**, 70km southeast of Batu Pahat, where you can stop off for a cup of tea or lunch at the cutesy, old-world *Resthouse* (☎06/951 6655; ②), on the seafront just up from the bus station (from where there are regular services to JB).

Kukup

The signs flanking the roadside at **KUKUP** feature giant king prawns shown waving their tentacles – in eager expectation, no doubt, at the money you're about to part with. This small fishing community, just 19km south along Route 95 from Pontian Kecil, has opened its doors to the Singapore package-tour trade, whose clients come to see the ancient, stilted houses built over the murky river and to sample Kukup's real attraction, the **seafood**: the town's single tumbledown street is packed with restaurants. Tours usually include an appetite-inducing trip to the offshore **kelong**, a huge fish trap with rickety wooden platforms. The nets cast from here float on their moorings rather than being anchored to the sea bed. The agency right by the jetty or any of the restaurants can sell you a ticket for the 45-minute tour (RM5).

Practicalities

There's a dearth of transport from Pontian Kecil to Kukup, so you're better off catch-ing a **taxi** between the two for around RM4 per person. There are at least half a dozen places to **eat**, from the enormous *Makanan Laut*, closest to the jetty, where you can see the food being prepared in a vast array of woks, to the more modest *Restoran Zaiton Hussin* immediately opposite, where the emphasis is on Malay rather than Chinese-style seafood. Expect to pay RM13 for fish, RM12 for prawns and RM6 for mussels.

A kilometre back towards Pontian Kecil from Kukup, you'll see a turnoff for **Tanjung Piai**. A gradually narrowing road through lush tropical fruit plantations takes you to the "southernmost tip of the mainland Asia continent" as the advertising for the *Tanjung Piai Resort* (☎ & fax 07/696 9000; ③) puts it. This string of large wooden chalets, on concrete pylons at the edge of the mangrove swamps, commands a dramatic vista of the ships coming to and from Singapore, clearly visible on the horizon; there's also a seafood restaurant and friendly management. Apart from eating, there's little to do here other than chill out, perhaps watch the fireflies at night and enjoy the view.

Kukup is a little-known exit point from Malaysia to Tanjung Balai in **Indonesia**, a 45-minute ferry ride from the jetty (daily at 11am and 3pm, except Fri no service, Sun 3pm only; RM45 one way). The problem with **arriving** in Kukup from Indonesia is that onward travel connections are sketchy – you'll have to catch a ferry onward from Kukup to Pontian Kecil. You don't need to arrange a visa in advance for this trip.

Johor Bahru

The southernmost Malaysian city of any size, **JOHOR BAHRU** – or simply **JB** – is the main gateway into **Singapore**, linked to the city-state by a 1056-metre **causeway** carrying a road, a railway, and the pipes through which Singapore imports its fresh water. Around fifty thousand people a day travel across the causeway (the recently built **second crossing** from Geylang Patah, 20km west of JB, to Tuas in Singapore is much less used because of its high tolls), and the ensuing traffic, noise and smog affects most of unsightly downtown Johor Bahru. The town has long had to tolerate unflattering comparisons with squeaky-clean Singapore, for which it has served as a red-light haunt for many years, but things do at last seem to be changing. The past two decades have seen the state of Johor – of which JB is the capital – become one of the three sides of an economic "Growth Triangle", together with Singapore and Batam island in the Indonesian Riau archipelago. Confronted by mounting production costs in their own country, Singaporean investors have flooded across the causeway to take advantage of low labour costs, and JB has prospered accordingly. Today, the air of decay which hangs over much of downtown JB is slowly being dispelled, as the manufacturing boom finances new international hotels and ever-more dazzling shopping malls. Development is particularly evident among the arcades of **Taman Century Estate**, a couple of kilometres north of the city centre along the Tebrau Highway; another recent project is the huge duty-free complex and ferry terminal a couple of kilometres east of the city centre.

Despite these improvements, JB remains ill equipped to win the hearts of visitors. By day, it's a hectic city whose only real attraction is the royal **Istana Besar**; by night, its main streets are lit by the neon lights of its hostess bars and nightclubs. If you've arrived from Singapore, there's little here to keep you from making the quick getaway up the North–South Highway to the considerable attractions of Melaka (see p.302) and Kuala Lumpur (see p.79).

Historically though, JB stands with Melaka as one of the most important sites in the country. Chased out of its seat of power by the Portuguese in 1511, the Melakan court decamped to the Riau archipelago, south of modern-day Singapore, before upping sticks again in the 1530s and shifting to the upper reaches of the Johor river. A century of uncertainty followed for the infant kingdom of Johor, with persistent offensives by both the Portuguese and the Acehnese of northern Sumatra, forcing the court to shift its capital regularly. Stability was finally achieved by courting the friendship of the Dutch in the 1640s; the rest of the seventeenth century saw the kingdom of Johor blossom into a thriving trading **entrepôt**. By the end of the century, though, the rule of the wayward and tyrannical Sultan Mahmud had halted Johor's pre-eminence among the Malay kingdoms, and piracy was causing a decline in trade. In 1699, Sultan Mahmud was killed by his own nobles and, with the Melaka-Johor dynasty finally finished, successive power struggles crippled the kingdom.

Bugis immigrants to Johor, escaping the civil wars in their native Sulawesi, eventually eclipsed the power of the sultans (see p.622), and though the Bugis were finally chased out by the Dutch in 1784, the kingdom was now a shadow of its former self. The

Johor-Riau empire – and the Malay world – was split in two, with the Melaka Straits forming the dividing line following the Anglo-Dutch treaty of 1824 (see p.623). As links with the court in Riau faded, Sultan Ibrahim assumed power, amassing a fortune based upon hefty profits culled from plantations in Johor. The process was continued by his son Abu Bakar, named Sultan of Johor in 1885 and widely regarded as the father of modern Johor; it was he who, in 1866, named the new port across the Johor Straits *Johor Bahru*, or "New Johor".

Arrival, information and accommodation

The Larkin **bus station** is on Jalan Geruda, 3km away from the centre of JB; the **train station** is to the east of the city centre, off Jalan Tun Abdul Razak. Flights to JB land at **Senai airport**, 25km north of the city, from where a regular bus service (RM1.40) runs to the bus station; alternatively, you can get a taxi to the city for about RM25. Heading out to the airport, there's a shuttle bus (RM4) from outside the Tourist Information Centre, which connects with all major MAS flights. The MAS office is at Level 1, Menara Pelangi, Jalan Kuning Taman Pelangi (☎07/334 1001). **Ferries** from Tanjung Pinang and Pulau Batam – both in Indonesia – arrive at the terminal in the Bebas Cukai shopping centre, 2km east of the causeway; tickets for these services can be booked at Sriwani Tours and Travel (☎07/221 1677).

The main **Tourism Information Centre** (JOTIC) (Mon–Fri 8am–4.15pm, Sat 8am–12.45pm, Sun 10am–4pm; ☎07/222 3392) is on Jalan Air Molek; there's also an office on the causeway (Mon–Fri 8am–4.15pm, Sat 8am–12.45pm, Sun 10am–4pm; ☎07/222 3591). There are **moneychangers** in the main shopping centres, or try Maybank, 11 Jalan Selat Tebrau; Bank Bumiputra, 51 Jalan Segget; Hong Kong Bank, 1 Jalan Bukit Timbalan; or OCBC, Jalan Ibrahim. A brace of cashpoints can be found on the south side of the Merlin Tower. To get **online**, try the *Pussat Internet Café* on the second floor of the Kotaraya shopping centre or the *ABC Café* (open 24hr), next to the *Hawaii Hotel* on Jalan Meldrum. You can **rent a car** by contacting either Avis, at the *Tropical Inn* (☎07/223 7971); Hertz, 1 Jalan Trus (☎07/223 7520); Mayflower Car Hire, second floor, Wisma Tan Cheng, Jalan Tun Abdul Razak (☎07/241 1400); or National, 50b Bangunan Felda, Jalan Segget (☎07/223 0503).

TRAVEL BETWEEN JB AND SINGAPORE

Two frequent **bus services** run between JB and Singapore throughout the day from Larkin station: the air-con Singapore–JB Express (daily 6.30am–1.30pm; every 10min; RM2.20) is the more comfortable, though the #170 is cheaper (RM1.20) and runs every ten minutes from 6am to 11.30pm. It's also possible to board buses to Singapore at the causeway terminal, which is much closer to the centre of JB than the bus station. There's also an MAS bus service (RM10) from JB's Senai airport to Singapore's *Novotel Orchid* – buses connect with all major departures and arrivals. The buses drop passengers outside the **immigration** checkpoints at each end of the causeway; retain your bus ticket as you'll need it for the onward journey. Once you're through immigration (the formalities take about ten minutes to complete), you continue into Singapore on any bus of the same type as the one that you took to the causeway, though not necessarily on the very same vehicle.

The **train** journey to Singapore costs RM8 for a second-class seat; you have to be cleared by Malaysian immigration on board, and then again by the Singapore authorities at the Woodlands checkpoint in the north of the island. **Taxis** between Singapore and JB departing from the KOMTAR building car park cost RM6–7 per person, and leave only when they are full.

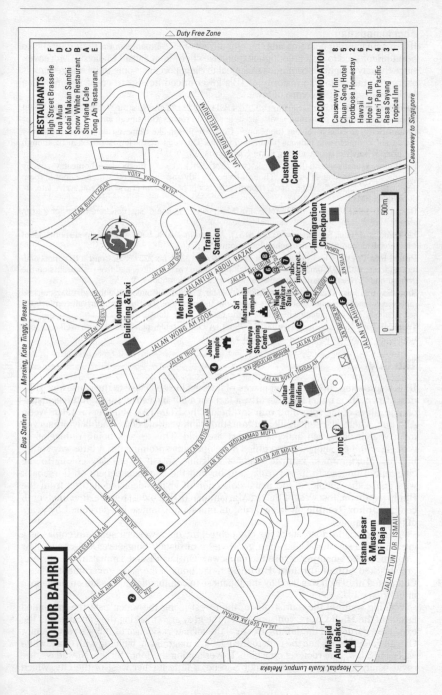

JOHOR BAHRU

RESTAURANTS

High Street Brasserie F
Hua Mua D
Kedai Makan Santini C
Snow White Restaurant B
Storyland Cafe A
Tong Ah Restaurant E

ACCOMMODATION

Causeway Inn 8
Chuan Seng Hotel 5
Footloose Homestay 2
Hawaii 6
Hotel Le Tian 7
Puteri Pan Pacific 4
Rasa Sayang 3
Tropical Inn 1

Accommodation

JB's manufacturing boom means the city attracts more businessmen than tourists, so **hotel** prices tend to be a little higher than elsewhere in mainland Malaysia. Moreover, since the city's nightlife continues to appeal to Singaporeans, some of its budget hotels charge by the hour. The majority of JB's lower-priced hotels are on or around Jalan Meldrum, right in the centre of town.

Causeway Inn, 6a–f Jalan Meldrum (☎07/224 8811, fax 224 8820). Near the waterfront, this decent hotel is the best in its price range, with sizeable en-suite rooms with air-con and TV. ④.

Chuan Seng, 35 Jalan Meldrum (no phone). Concrete prison-like Chinese-run hotel above a busy restaurant, complete with hideous partitioned rooms. The beds are the lowest-priced in JB, though the place is only worth considering if the *Footloose* is full. ②.

Footloose Homestay, 4h Jalan Ismail (☎07/224 2881). A very inexpensive homestay run by Brenda, a friendly Scottish woman. Though basic, it's tidy and characterful, with one double room and one small dorm. It's best to book, though efforts will be made to fit you in if you arrive late. ②, dorm beds RM14.

Hawaii, 21 Jalan Meldrum (☎07/224 0633). Moth-eaten linen and bare concrete make for a grim atmosphere, but the rooms are reasonably clean. ②.

Le Tian, 2a–d, Jalan Siu Nam (☎07/224 8151). An unremarkable hotel with cramped rooms, all of which have air-con and small attached bathrooms. ③.

Puteri Pan Pacific, The Kotaraya, Jalan Trus (☎07/223 3333, fax 223 6622). Central JB's most opulent address, with 500 sumptuous rooms including huge corner suites, and five restaurants on the ground floor. Prices halve during the seemingly random promotions. ⑧.

Rasa Sayang, Jalan Datok Dalam (☎07/224 8600, fax 224 8612). Comfortable though characterless mid-priced hotel in a quiet spot a short walk from the centre of JB. The rooms are all comfortable but smallish. The rate includes breakfast at the hotel's coffee house. ④.

Tropical Inn, 15 Jalan Gereja (☎07/224 7888). A comfortable, plush hotel, with well-equipped rooms, decent restaurants, a coffee bar and a gym. ⑤.

The City

JB is a sprawling city, with most places of interest located close to the causeway. Hilly **downtown JB** is undeniably scruffy, a fact born out by a stroll through the claustrophobic alleys of the sprawling **market**, below the KOMTAR building on Jalan Wong Ah Fook, where machetes, silk and "one-thousand-year-old eggs" (actually preserved for a year in lime, ash and tea leaves) are sold. This area is being redeveloped, though, with new shopping and office developments sprouting up. A little way south, the **Sri Mariamman Temple** lends a welcome splash of primary colour to the cityscape. Underneath its *gopuram*, and beyond the two gatekeepers on horseback who guard the temple, is the usual collection of vividly depicted figures from the Hindu pantheon. Just west of the Sri Mariamman is JB's oldest temple, the nineteenth century **Johor Temple** on Jalan Trus, its murals of Chinese life darkened by years of incense smoke.

After the cramped streets of the city centre, the open western **seafront** comes as a great relief. From here, there are good views of distant Singapore, and of the slow snake of traffic labouring across the causeway. On Jalan Bukit Timbalan, the austere, grey-bricked **Sultan Ibrahim Building** today houses the state government offices. Completed in 1940, it was used by the Japanese to command their assault on Singapore in February 1942.

Walking south of the tourist office, then west along the water, past the garlanded facade of the **High Court**, you soon reach the grey arch marking the entrance into the expansive gardens of the **Istana Besar** – the former residence of Johor's royal family. Ornate golden lamps line the path to the istana, a magnificent building with chalk-white walls and a low, blue roof, set on a hillock overlooking the Johor Straits. Nowadays, the royal family lives in the Istana Bukit Serene, a little further west of the city, which

---

THE SULTANS AND THE LAW

The antics of the British Royal Family are nothing compared to what some of the nine royal families in Malaysia get up to. Nepotism, meddling in state politics and flagrant breaches of their exemption from import duties are among their lesser misdemeanours, which generally go unreported in the circumspect local press. But the most notorious of them all is Johor's Sultan Iskandar Ibni Al-Marhum Sultan Ismail – along with his son, the Tunku Ibrahim Ismail. The former is alleged to have beaten his golf caddy to death in the Cameron Highlands after the unfortunate man made the mistake of laughing at a bad shot. Tunku Ibrahim, for his part, was convicted of shooting dead a man in a JB nightclub, though the prince was immediately pardoned because of who his father was. Such behaviour had long incensed Prime Minister Dr Mahathir, who was itching to bring the lawless royals into line. He got his chance in 1993 when yet another beating incident involving the Sultan of Johor was brought up in the federal parliament along with 23 other similar assaults since 1972. As a result, the federal parliament voted in the Constitutional Amendment Bill, removing the sultans' personal immunity from prosecution. Naturally, the royal families were not too happy about this, but following a stand-off with Mahathir, they agreed to a compromise – no ruler would be taken to court without the Attorney General's approval. To underline his victory against the sultans, Mahathir introduced another constitutional amendment in 1994, to the effect that the sultans could only act on the advice of the government. Despite this, the Sultan of Johor retains considerable influence in the state and is the only one of the Malay royals to have a private army.

---

means that the Istana Besar is open to the public. To the right of the building is the ticket booth of the **Museum Di Raja Abu Bakar** (daily 9am–5pm, last entry 4pm; RM18, children RM8). The bulk of the pieces on show here are gifts from foreign dignitaries, including exquisite ceramics from Japan, crystal from France and furniture from England, as well as Southeast Asian items like stuffed tigers, ornate daggers and an umbrella stand crafted from an elephant's foot.

Further west, the four rounded towers of the **Masjid Abu Bakar** make it the most elegant building in town. Completed in 1900, the mosque can accommodate two thousand worshippers; as at the istana, Sultan Abu Bakar himself laid the first stone, though he died before the mosque was completed.

Eating

There are scores of **restaurants** in JB, serving everything from Pakistani to Japanese dishes. The liveliest place to eat is the large **night market**, across the footbridge from the train station and beside the Indian Temple. A smaller night market takes place on the waterfront in front of the General Hospital on Jalan Skudai; it's about 500m west of the Abu Bakar mosque.

High Street Brasserie, 60 Jalan Ibrahim. Pleasant café serving Chinese and Malay meals and snacks. Daily 8am–10pm.

Jaws 5 Restaurant, *Straits View Hotel*, 1d Jalan Skudai. Open-air restaurant with backdrop of traditional Malay houses; its inexpensive menu includes fish and shark's-fin dishes. Daily 11.30am–midnight.

Kedai Makan Santini, 39 Jalan Trus. A bona fide South Indian eatery where your food is slapped down in front of you on a banana leaf and you eat with your hands. Excellent, inexpensive vegetarian and meat dishes. Daily 6.30am–10pm.

Kotoraya Shopping Centre, Jalan Trus. On the top floor, there are several Western fast-food outlets and a good range of hawker stalls which stay open till 8.30pm.

Restoran Hua Mui, 131 Jalan Trus. Western and Chinese dishes are on the menu in this two-floored restaurant. Daily 7am–9.30pm.

Selasih Restaurant, in the *Puteri Pan Pacific* hotel, The Kotaraya, Jalan Trus. Serves tasty dishes from all thirteen states in Malaysia. A meal costs RM30–40 per head; the cheaper set lunches are worth checking out. Daily 11.30am–3pm & 6.30–11pm.

Snow White Restaurant, 9a and 11a Jalan Siu Nam. Affordable, open-sided restaurant up above the thrum of JB's traffic; specializes in Cantonese seafood and steamboats, though it also serves Malay food. Daily 11am–2am.

Storyland Café, Jalan Seyed Mohd Mufti. Pleasant, Western-style café with pastries, good sandwiches and European meals. Also has a tranquil reading area. Daily 8am–6pm, Sat until 3pm.

Tong Ah Restaurant, 14 Jalan Ibrahim. No-frills *nasi padang* restaurant, decorated with a few aged cigarette posters. Daily 7am–8pm.

Warong Saga, 5 Jalan Mahmudiah. This amiable restaurant serves cheap Chinese staples; its decor is a mixture of portraits of Malay royalty, seven-inch vinyl singles and coolie hats. Daily 7am–7pm.

Up the east coast from JB

Without the patronage of neighbouring Singapore, the area around Johor Bahru would have quietly nodded off into a peaceful slumber. Not that it's exactly a thrilling region even now: places like the desultory seaside resort of **Desaru** on the **east coast** have flourished, one suspects, more for their geographical than their aesthetic merits. Most people heading east beat a hasty path along Route 3 to Mersing, neglecting to stop even at **Kota Tinggi**, whose waterfall constitutes the region's most enduring sight.

Kota Tinggi and around

KOTA TINGGI, 40km northeast of JB, clings to the wide and fast-flowing Sungei Johor. Although the town's not worth a visit in its own right, you may want to stop at the **waterfall** (daily 8am–6pm; RM2) at **LOMBONG**, 15km northwest. Of the two falls here, the pool at the bottom of the farther one is the bigger and the better for swimming; deep and unobstructed by boulders. If you remain on land, you'll still be soaked by the fine spray given off by the pounding water. There's chalet accommodation and a couple of restaurants here (see below).

About 90km north of Kota Tinggi up Route 3 lies the port of Mersing (see opposite), from where boats depart for Pulau Tioman (see p.334). Another minor diversion can be found about 15km northeast of Kota Tinggi en route to Mersing: the road east off Route 3 here leads past the forgotten royal mausoleums, at **Mawai**, of previous Johor sultans, to the uninspiring resort bay of **Teluk Mahkota**, amid bleak and desolate marshland. If you choose instead to head southeast from Kota Tinggi, you come to the resort of Desaru (see opposite), 50km away.

Practicalities

Buses (RM5) from JB's Larkin bus station run every twenty minutes on the one-hour trip to Kota Tinggi, stopping at the centrally situated **bus station**, which caters for both express and local services. Bus #41 leaves hourly from Kota Tinggi (daily 7am–7pm; RM2), winding up through rubber-plantation country to the entrance to the waterfall.

Several decent **hotels** are located around Kota Tinggi's bus station. The modern and spotless *Sin May Chun*, 26 Jalan Tambatan (☎07/883 3573; ②), offers the best value; the *Bunga Raya* further along at 12 Jalan Jaafar (☎07/883 3023; ①) is also well kept. Top of the line is the *Hotel Seri Kota*, 47–49 Jalan Jaafar (☎07/883 8111, fax 883 8115; ③), with comfortable, well-maintained air-con doubles and nice bathrooms. All three are close to each other, a two-minute walk southwest from the bus stand. Seafood is a speciality in the town, with a number of flashy **restaurants** close to the river, including the *Sin Mei Lee* and the *Mui Tou*. This is the place to try out crab, lobster and prawns – prices are surprisingly reasonable at around RM6–8 per dish.

You can stay by the Lombong **falls** in the air-con chalets of the *Kota Tinggi Waterfalls Resort* (☎07/883 6222, fax 883 1146; ⑥). Despite the unattractive concrete buildings, the rooms are modern and the setting is wonderful, with jungle creepers trailing down to the tumultuous water. The Chinese *Restoran Air Terjun*, just by the entrance, has a good menu, though the resort's restaurant has the best view of the falls.

Desaru

As beaches go, **DESARU**, 50km southeast of Kota Tinggi, isn't that bad, with its sheltered, casuarina-fringed bay. It's the nearest major resort to Singapore, though there are better places further up the coast, and the wide, well-kept but rather soulless streets here don't inspire lengthy stays.

With the road route here from JB covering nearly 100km (via Kota Tinggi, then southeast along Route 92), most visitors from Singapore come by sea from Changi Point (see box, p.534), arriving at the Malaysian port of **Kampung Pengerang**. Shuttle buses make the 45-minute journey from the port to Desaru itself. From JB, the PGB company runs bus #5 here (hourly; 2hr; RM5), and there are also local connections from Kota Tinggi.

The five **places to stay**, listed below, are all strung in a row along the beach. All have **restaurants**, predominantly Chinese and Japanese, where a very average meal costs a bare minimum of RM15 a head. Be warned that room rates rise by about fifty percent on Saturdays and Sundays.

Desaru Holiday Chalet (☎07/822 1211, fax 822 1937). Next to the *Desaru Leisure Camp*, 1km from the *Perdana* and *Impean*, it has large and comfortable cabins set on the beach. ⑤.

Desaru Impean Resort (☎07/838 9911, fax 838 9922). At the northern end of the beach, this is the largest of the hotels here, modern though rather kitsch, with a miniature railway and theme park; the rooms are very well kitted out however. ⑧.

Desaru Leisure Camp (☎07/822 1205, fax 822 2666). A kilometre or so beyond the *Desaru Perdana*. This overpriced, rather sorry place – the only option if you're avoiding the rates charged at the big hotels – has tents (RM40), spartan, box-like rooms and slightly better "mini huts" (RM40) ③.

Desaru Perdana Beach Resort (☎07/822 2222, fax 822 2223). A little less grand than the *Desaru Impean* next door, but more tasteful. ⑧.

Golden Beach Hotel (☎07/822 1101, fax 822 1480). At the southeastern end of the strip, this is passable, its swimming pool and golf course offering some compensation for the small, rather uninspiring rooms. ⑥.

Mersing and around

The fishing port of **MERSING**, 130km north of Johor Bahru, lies on the languid Sungei Mersing. You're unlikely to stay more than one night in this bustling and industrious little town, which is the main gateway to **Pulau Tioman** and the smaller islands of the Seribuat archipelago. Hotels, restaurants and travel agencies have sprung up to cater for the seasonal flood of tourists – it pays to work out exactly what you want to do before arriving in Mersing, or you may be swamped by the touts that hang around the jetty.

Mersing is grouped around two main streets, Jalan Abu Bakar and Jalan Ismail, fanning out from a roundabout on Route 3. The town's Chinese and Indian temples, just south of the roundabout, are unremarkable; the only real sight is the square **Masjid Jamek**, on a nearby hilltop, its cool, pastel-green tiled dome and minaret lit to spectacular effect at night, when it appears to hang in the sky. In the centre of town, by a mini-roundabout on Jalan Abu Bakar, is a historic Chinese **shophouse**, built by a Mersing pioneer named Poh Keh, its veranda and floral wall motifs a little too prettily renovated.

Practicalities

The **jetty** is about ten minutes' walk east along Jalan Abu Bakar from the roundabout – for details of getting to the islands, see opposite. **Express buses** from Singapore, JB or Kuantan drop you off just before the roundabout, and at the R&R Plaza near the jetty. On Jalan Sulaiman, close to the river bank, is the **local bus station** used by services from Kota Tinggi, Endau and elsewhere. The **Mersing Tourist Information Centre** (METIC, Mon–Fri 8am–12.45pm & 2–6.30pm, Sat 8am–12.30pm; ☎07/799 5212) is in a new building on Jalan Abu Bakar, with helpful staff who offer impartial advice on the many different island deals. The **post office** is further southwest along the opposite side of the street. Mersing is well supplied with **cybercafés**, the best being Cyberworld at 36 Jalan Abu Bakar. You can **change money** at the Maybank or Bank Bumiputra on Jalan Ismail.

It can be problematic **leaving Mersing** by bus, as few services originate here, so there can be a scramble for seats in the peak season. Express-bus tickets can be bought in advance from *Restoran Malaysia* and R&R Plaza. You may experience problems buying a ticket at the former – if so the staff at METIC will help you. Buses out of Mersing depart from the R&R Plaza near the jetty.

MERSING

0 100 200m

Pulau Tioman

Jetty

R & R Plaza
(buses to Singapore
and Kuantan)

JLN DATO ONN

S. Mersing

Car
Park

METIC

Stadium

Local
Bus
Station

Market

JLN HUSNI

JLN IBRAHIM

JLN SULTANAH

JLN SULAIMAN

Cyberworld

Food Stalls

JLN ABU BAKAR

Shophouse

Supermarket

JLN ISMAIL

Masjid
Jamek

Kuantan, Pekan, Kuala Rompin, Endau

JLN MD ALI

Government Rest House

N

ACCOMMODATION

Country	5
Embassy	6
Kali's Guest House	1
Omar's Backpacker's Inn	3
Sarina Inn	8
Seri Malaysia	7
Sheikh Backpackers	4
Teluk Iskandar Inn	9
Timotel	2

RESTAURANTS

Al Arif	E
Restoran Ee Lo	B
Restoran Malaysia	C
Restoran Seafood Chinese	D
Zam Zam	A

Singapore, Johor Bahru

GETTING TO THE ISLANDS

Mersing is the main departure point for Tioman and the other islands of the Seribuat Archipelago (for details of departures from Tanjong Gemuk, see overleaf). At the jetty there's a secure **car park** (RM7 per day) and a cluster of agency booths representing various islands, boats and resorts, known collectively as the **Tourist Centre**. For impartial information you're better off going to METIC (see opposite). It's sensible to change money in Mersing before you head out to the islands, as the exchange rates there are lousy.

Thirteen companies operate **express boats to Tioman**; the journey takes two hours or less, depending on the tide. Inside the nearby R&R Plaza – a collection of restaurants, moneychangers and more resort offices – you'll find a large signboard giving details of the day's sailings, including departure times and the name of the company operating each service – the last departure is normally no later than about 4pm, depending on the tide. Once you've found out which company operates the boat you want to catch, buy your ticket from the corresponding booth (RM25 for the one-way trip, though Mersing travel agents may offer discounts if you buy an open-return ticket). You can also take a speed boat to any part of Tioman (90min; RM30 per person one way) from the same jetty. As with the ferries, you can buy a ticket at the jetty or at a travel agent.

To get to the **other islands**, it's better to book in advance at the office representing that particular island (all the offices are based around the jetty), or at one of the many **travel agencies** in town (mostly found along Jalan Abu Bakar and, to a lesser degree, Jalan Ismail), since boat services are less regular and accommodation more at a premium. Another possibility is taking one of the day-trips, organized by Mersing's *Omar's Backpackers' Hostel*, which go to three or four of the small, mostly uninhabited islands between Tioman and the coast; see p.345 for details.

ACCOMMODATION

There's no shortage of low-budget **hotels** in Mersing. To get to either of the two places to the north of town, take the half-hourly local bus or a taxi (RM3).

Country, 11 Jalan Sulaiman (☎07/799 1799). Near the bus station, this hotel is more upmarket than its price suggests; the rooms have bathrooms and balconies, though the furniture is a little old. ②.

Embassy, 2 Jalan Ismail (☎07/799 3545). Clean and comfortable, this relatively quiet and well run place has two or three beds to a room, in addition to ordinary doubles, some with air-con. The rooms with fans are the best-value budget doubles in town. ①/②.

Kali's Guesthouse (☎07/799 3613). A charming place by the sea, 2km north of town, with a peaceful garden and a choice of A-frames, chalets or dearer cottages. Phone them to be picked up from town, or take the Padang Endau-bound bus. ②/③.

Omar's Backpackers' Hostel, Jalan Abu Bakar (☎07/799 5096). Opposite the GPO, this friendly hostel has clean dorm beds and double rooms. Omar himself is very useful for local information and runs island-hopping tours (see p.345). ①, dorm beds RM8.

Sarina Inn, Lot 956, Jalan Sekakap (☎07/799 6012). Four kilometres south of the centre; to get there, turn left off Jalan Ismail before the hospital and keep the sea to your left along the shore road. A small, family-run affair by the sea, it has great views and three comfortable doubles. ③.

Seri Malaysia, Jalan Ismail (☎07/799 1876, fax 799 1886). Opposite the hospital, a ten-minute walk from the jetty. Part of the nationwide chain of reasonably priced quality hotels. Rates include breakfast; it's worth asking about promotional rates which can lower the price by a third in low season. ⑤.

Sheikh Backpackers, 1b Jalan Abu Bakar (☎07/799 3764, *starmj@tm.net.my*). Simple and friendly hostel with inexpensive dorms. The management can arrange trips to Endau Rompin National Park (see p.348). Dorm beds RM8.

Teluk Iskandar Inn, 1456 Jalan Sekakap (☎07/799 6037, *krisma14@tm.net.my*). A few doors south of the *Sarina Inn*, the *Iskandar* is even more pleasant, with several well-constructed wooden chalets, all en suite, and a comfortable communal sitting area. They're priced according to the quality of their sea views. ③–⑤.

Timotel, 839 Jalan Endau (☎07/799 5888, fax 799 5333). Despite its unpleasant facade, this new hotel, on the main road, is in fact the plushest place in town, with huge double beds and breakfast included in the rate; there's also an attached karaoke pub and a good restaurant. ⑤.

EATING
Mersing is a great place for **eating**, with seafood topping the menu. The **food stalls** near the roundabout are particularly good – try the satay and the banana fritters.

Al Arif, Jalan Ismail. Opposite the Parkson Ria supermarket, this Indian café serves good-quality food, though it's a little overpriced.

Golden Dragon, *Embassy Hotel*, 2 Jalan Ismail. Has the widest-ranging Chinese and seafood menu in town, though it's a touch more expensive than some. Averages RM8 per dish.

Restoran Ee Lo, Jalan Dato' Md. Ali, on the Jalan Abu Bakar mini-roundabout. A variety of Chinese and Malay dishes, as well as a limited range of seafood. Inexpensive.

Restoran Seafood Chinese, Jalan Ismail. One of the best seafood (and air-con) restaurants in town, with a good selection of crab, prawn and mussel dishes at around RM10 each.

Zam Zam, Jalan Abu Bakar. Always busy, this place serves tasty Indian food, including great *roti canai*. Good for vegetarians.

North of Mersing
About 35km north of Mersing along Route 3, past **Kampung Air Papan** (reputed to have the best beach in the locality), is the village of **Padang Endau**, on the Johor side of the Sungei Endau. Across the bridge, in Pahang state, 3km from the village centre, is the **Tanjung Gemuk ferry terminal**, from where there are daily services to Tioman at 9am and 2pm (RM25 one way; ☎07/794 2053). The journey is slightly faster than from Mersing, taking just over an hour to reach the *Berjaya Tioman Beach Resort*, the first stop on the island. The jetty consists of a largely empty development of shops and a *Seri Malaysia Hotel* (☎09/413 2725, fax 413 2732; ④), which organizes trips into the Endau Rompin National Park (see p.348). Heading further north up Route 3 brings you eventually to the former state capital of Pahang, Pekan (see p.291), served by hourly buses from Mersing.

Pulau Tioman

Shaped like a giant apostrophe in the South China Sea, **PULAU TIOMAN**, 30km east of Mersing, has long been one of Malaysia's most popular holiday islands. Thirty-eight kilometres in length and nineteen kilometres at its widest point, it is the largest of the 64 volcanic islands that form the **Seribuat archipelago**. According to legend, the origins of Pulau Tioman lie in the flight of a dragon princess on her way to China. She fell in love with the surrounding waters and decided to settle here permanently by transforming her body into an island. First mention of the island in official records dates back to 1403, when a Chinese trading expedition to Southeast Asia and Mecca found Tioman, with its abundant supplies of fresh water, a handy stopping place. Shipping charts called it Zhumaskan, though local inhabitants believe the island to be named after the *tiong* (Hill Mynah bird) that is commonly found here.

Ever since the 1970s, when Tioman was voted one of the ten most beautiful islands in the world by *Time* magazine, crowds have been flocking to its palm-fringed shores, in search of the mythical Bali H'ai (for which it was the chosen film location in the Hollywood musical, *South Pacific*). But thirty years is a long time in tourism. Where slow fishing vessels used to ply the seas for the arduous five-hour journey to Tioman, noisy express boats now complete the trip in less than two hours. These services, and the several daily flights from Singapore and other parts of the Peninsula, have helped destroy the sense of romantic isolation that once made the island so popular. Those

SNORKELLING AND DIVING AROUND PULAU TIOMAN

With such abundant **marine life** in waters around Tioman, it's unlikely that you'll want to be island-bound the whole time. Many of the nearby islets provide excellent opportunities for **snorkelling**, and most of the chalet operations offer **day-trips** for the purpose, costing around RM25 (excluding equipment). Many **dive centres** on Tioman offer the range of PADI certificates, from an intensive four-day "Open Water" course which includes three days of theory and seven to nine dives (around RM750), through to the fourteen-day "Dive Master" (RM1200); check that qualified English-speaking instructors are employed, and that the cost includes all the necessary equipment. For the already qualified, two dives cost RM160 per person. Of the dive shops, B&J's in Air Batang is the best established (☎09/419 5555). Another, environmentally oriented outfit – Anemone Divers – has just opened up near *Nazri's II* on Air Batang.

It's worth sparing a thought for the environmental impact of the various snorkelling and diving trips. Ask to be moored rather than anchored, make sure there's a no litter into the sea policy from the boat operators before paying for your trip (cigarette butts are a major nuisance), wear a T-shirt rather than sun block and never touch any of the corals.

Most of the best dive sites are around **Pulau Tulai**, a large island about 6km off the northwestern coast of Tioman, though spots close to the *Berjaya Tioman Beach Resort* and off the southern coast are also good; the calm, deep waters of **Monkey Bay** are ideal for beginners. Some of the most rewarding dive sites include:

Golden Reef (typical depth 10–20m). Fifteen minutes off the northwestern coast; rocks provide a breeding ground for marine life, as well as producing many soft corals.

Pulau Chebeh (15–25m). In the northwestern waters, this is a massive volcanic labyrinth of caves and channels. Napoleon fish, trigger fish and turtles are present in abundance.

Pulau Labas (5–15m). South of Pulau Tulai, tunnels and caves provide a home for puffer fish, moray eels and corals such as fan and sweet-lip nudibranch.

Pulau Renggis (5–13m). Directly opposite the *Berjaya Tioman*, this sheltered spot is suitable for training and night dives. Good for spotting barracuda, stingray,

angel fish and buffalo fish, as well as two resident, harmless black-tip sharks.

Tiger Reef (10–25m). Southwest of Pulau Tulai, and deservedly the most popular site, with yellow-tail snappers, trevally and tuna, spectacular soft coral and gorgonian fans.

Tokong Magicienne (10–25m). Due north of Pulau Tioman, this colourful, sponge-layered coral pinnacle is a feeding station for larger fish – silver snappers, golden-striped trevally, jacks and gropers.

Tokong Malang (5–15m). Just off the southeastern tip of Pulau Tulai, this shallow reef traversed by sand channels is full of sponges. Watch out for barracuda, large cuttlefish, yellow-spotted stingray and leopard shark.

in search of unspoilt beaches will also be disappointed (though there are some superb exceptions); damage has also been inflicted on the surrounding coral and marine life. However, Pulau Tioman displays a remarkable resilience, and to fail to visit it is to miss out – the greater part of the island has still not lost its intimate, village atmosphere.

As you approach, Tioman's mountains loom above you, shrouded in cloud; the two peculiar granite pinnacles of Bukit Nenek Semukut on the southern part of the island are known as *chula naga* (dragon's horns). The sheer size and inaccessibility of its mountainous spine has preserved its most valuable asset – the dense **jungle**; you can go **wildlife-spotting** on its few easy hikes, which afford a high chance of seeing mouse deer, tree snakes, flying lemur, long-tailed macaques and monitor lizards, some upwards of six feet long. There are also plenty of opportunities for **outdoor activities**, particularly diving (see box) and water sports. Look out for the clusters of greater

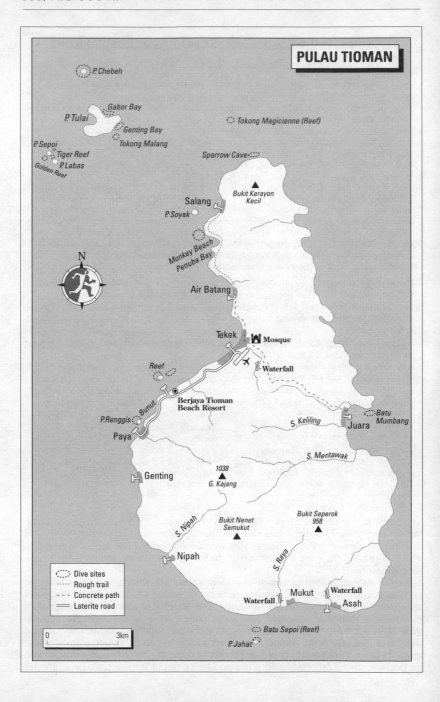

PULAU TIOMAN

P. Chebeh

Gabor Bay
P. Tulai
Genting Bay
Tokong Magicienne (Reef)
Tokong Malang

P. Sepoi
Tiger Reef
P. Labas
Golden Reef

Sparrow Cave

Bukit Kerayon
Kecil

Salang
P. Soyak

Monkey Beach
Penuba Bay

Air Batang

Tekek ▓ Mosque

Reef

Waterfall

Bunut

Berjaya Tioman
Beach Resort

P. Renggis
Paya

S. Keliling
Juara
Batu
Mumbang

S. Mentawak

Genting

1038
▲
G. Kajang

Bukit Nenet
Semukut
▲

Bukit Seperok
958
▲

S. Nipah

S. Raya

Nipah

Waterfall
Mukut
Waterfall
Asah
Waterfall

Dive sites
Rough trail
Concrete path
Laterite road

0   3km

Batu Sepoi (Reef)
P. Jahat

frigate birds that gather on the surrounding islands and rocks; occasionally you'll even see Christmas Island frigate birds, which breed only on the island after which they are named, more than 2000km south of Tioman. The island's ridge of mountains culminates in an impressive cluster of peaks in the south, of which the highest, **Gunung Kajang** (1038m), is inaccessible to all but the most experienced and well-equipped climbers.

Like the rest of the Peninsula's east coast, Tioman is affected by the **monsoon** between November and February, when the whole island winds down dramatically, many places closing. July and August are the busiest months, when prices increase and accommodation is best booked in advance. Even in the dry season, it rains almost daily here; cloud seems to hang permanently around the island's mountainous ridge.

Accommodation possibilities here range from the island's one international-standard resort, through to chalet developments and simple beachfront A-frames – the latter being gradually edged out by identical, tin-roofed box chalets. The standard and pricing of each type of accommodation – A-frames, box chalets with shower, air-con chalets – hardly varies from place to place on the same beach, so it's a good idea to pick your spot according to atmosphere and view as much as anything else. Most of the places to stay on Tioman are along the west coast, with the largest concentration of popular budget establishments being in the bay of **Air Batang** just north of the island's grotty main village, **Tekek**. The east coast's sole settlement, **Juara**, is very quiet – you'll easily find a place to stay here or in Air Batang for under RM20 per head. **Genting** and **Salang** are smaller, slightly more upmarket resorts though both have budget outlets, while **Paya** and **Nipah**, together with **Mukut** on the island's southern coast, are just opening up to tourism. Long gone are the days when you had to resort to a hurricane lamp at night – everywhere has an electricity supply now, albeit from a local generator. Nightlife has still to take off, however, though beer is available everywhere on the island.

Arrival and information

Arriving by express boat or speedboat **from Mersing** (see p.333 for details of services), it's important to decide in advance which bay or village you want to stay in, since the express boats generally make drops only at the major resorts of Genting, Paya, Tekek, Air Batang and Salang (in that order). There are only occasional express boats from Mersing to Juara on the east coast, though you could get a speedboat here. The two daily ferries here **from Tanjong Gemuk** (see p.334) stop first at the *Berjaya Tioman Beach Resort*. **From Singapore**, there's a daily catamaran service (see p.335), which runs directly to the *Berjaya Tioman Beach Resort*. The **Tourist Information Centre** (daily 7.30–11.30am & 2–4.30pm), situated right beside the jetty at Air Batang, can help with boat tickets or day-trips.

Arriving **by air**, you land at the airstrip in Tekek, from where there's a half-hourly shuttle bus to the *Berjaya Tioman Beach Resort*, 2km to the south. To reach the other beaches, you can get a sea bus (see below) from the nearby Tekek jetty, or rent a boat – or walk.

Getting around the island

The road between Tekek and the *Berjaya Tioman Beach Resort*, used by the airport bus, is the only one on the island wide enough for vehicles other than motorbikes. A two-metre-wide concrete path, used by motorbikes and walkers, runs north from Tekek to the headland marking the end of the beach, a twenty-minute walk; the path commences again on the other side of the rocks for the length of Air Batang. The network of **trails** is limited, though crossing the island has been made a lot easier by the building of cement steps beginning around ten minutes' walk north from Tekek jetty and running intermittently as far as Juara (see p.342 for details of the route). Less obvious

LEAVING TIOMAN

Although many of the travel agencies in Mersing may try to sell you an open-return boat ticket to Tioman, tickets are readily available from outlets at any of the bays on the island. **Express boats** all leave at around 7 or 8am daily, making their pick-ups from each jetty. Slower boats usually leave before noon, picking up from every bay – check with your chalet-owner. The ferry to Tanjung Gemuk (11am and 4pm) leaves from the *Berjaya Tioman Beach Resort*, as does a fast catamaran to Singapore (1.30pm; 4hr 30min). There are also **flights** to Kuala Lumpur (4 daily; RM146), Singapore (daily; RM192) and Kuantan (daily; RM84) with Berjaya Air (☎03/244 1718), Pelangi Air (☎03/746 3000 or ☎02/336 6777) and Tradewinds (☎02/225 4488). You can make reservations for Berjaya Air and Pelangi Air at the *Berjaya Tioman Beach Resort* (☎09/414 1000).

trails connect Genting with Paya, and Air Batang with Penuba Bay, Monkey Beach and Salang – details are given in the respective sections.

Transport around the shore of the island is problematic these days, as **sea bus** services – boats plying a fixed route with designated stops – have been greatly reduced. The sea bus from Juara operates only outside monsoon, calling at Salang, Air Batang, Tekek, and – two hours after setting off – the *Berjaya Tioman Beach Resort*; it then heads back and does the same stops in reverse. There is one departure a day at 3pm (though it can be a bit hit-and-miss – some days it doesn't run at all), the fare from Juara to Tekek being RM10. If you don't want to walk back, you could hire a small boat, though this is very expensive: a five-seater will set you back RM200 for this journey. Lastly, you could also hop onto one of the **round-the-island boat trips** (RM55) which run from the various chalets, but they tend to only spend an hour or so in each spot.

Since so much of the west coast is paved, **bicycle rental** – at RM4 an hour from several outlets in Tekek and Air Batang – seems a sensible option, but you can't go far without having to carry the bike over the headlands at some point.

Tekek

The sprawling village of **TEKEK**, the main settlement on the island, isn't really a place you'd want to stay for long. Years of over-development have been followed by a bust, and much of the seafront is now run-down or fenced off. The incessant stream of chugging ferries, the roar of aeroplanes and the churning of concrete mixers all combine to make Tekek the least inspiring part of Tioman.

The shabby central beach has yet to get a face-lift, and the whole area suffers from an unpleasant litter problem, though things start to get better well south of the main jetty where, apart from a few high-end resorts, the shore is relatively unspoilt. For a break from the beach, pop into the **Tioman Island Museum** (daily 9.30am–5pm; RM1) on the first floor of the airstrip's terminal complex. Apart from displaying some twelfth- to fourteenth-century Chinese ceramics, which were lost overboard from early trading vessels, it also outlines the facts and myths concerning the island. North of the main jetty, at the very end of the bay, is the government-sponsored **Marine Centre**, its hefty concrete jetty and dazzlingly blue roofs making it hard to miss. Set up to protect the coral and marine life around the island, and to patrol the fishing taking place in its waters, the centre also contains an aquarium and displays of coral (daily 9.30am–4.30pm; free).

Practicalities

You'll find **moneychangers** in the new terminal complex next to the airstrip and, a ten-minute walk south of the main jetty, the police station and a post office. Most of the

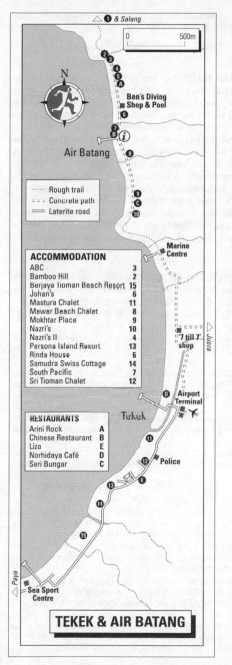

ACCOMMODATION

ABC	3
Bamboo Hill	2
Berjaya Tioman Beach Resort	15
Johan's	6
Mastura Chalet	11
Mawar Beach Chalet	8
Mokhtar Place	9
Nazri's	10
Nazri's II	4
Persona Island Resort	13
Rinda House	5
Samudra Swiss Cottage	14
South Pacific	7
Sri Tioman Chalet	12

RESTAURANTS

Arini Rock	A
Chinese Restaurant	B
Liza	E
Norhidaya Café	D
Seri Bungar	C

TEKEK & AIR BATANG

places to eat are attached to the chalet operations; the best are those with beachside settings, such as *Sri Tioman Chalets*. One of Tekek's nicest **restaurants**, *Liza*, is at the far southern end of the bay, with a wide-ranging menu specializing in seafood and Western snacks – it's popularity has pushed the prices up to around RM20 a meal, though. A rickety bridge crosses a small, stagnant lagoon just past the airstrip, over which you'll find *Norhidayah Café*, serving snacks, fried rice and noodles; it's also good for sunset drinks.

There's lots of **places to stay** in Tekek, though most are dilapidated and located next to piles of rubbish and the ever-present building materials. However, the high-end options well south of the main beach can be a good choice, especially the *Berjaya Tioman Beach Resort*, the only place of an international standard here. With Air Batang (see overleaf) just a little way north, though, it's hard to see why anyone would want to stay in Tekek proper.

Berjaya Tioman Beach Resort (☎09/419 1000, fax 419 1718). A village-sized complex 1500m south of Tekek, with everything from double rooms to deluxe apartments; other facilities include two pools, tennis courts, horse riding, water sports and a golf course. Occasional promotions offer good value. ⑧.

Mastura Chalet (☎09/715283). Simple wooden chalets set back from the beach in a built-up area. It's bearable for a night, though pretty unappealing. They also run a diving school. ②.

Persona Island Resort (☎ & fax 09/414 6213). Set back from the beach, next to the post office. A pleasant, upmarket operation with sturdy hotel-style rooms and an airy restaurant set around a courtyard. The management offer island-hopping tours to more remote parts of the archipelago. ⑤.

Samudra Swiss Cottage (☎09/419 1843). Just north of the *Berjaya Tioman* resort, in a shady jungle setting, this has a beach that's among the best in Tekek, as well as a dive shop and small restaurant. Its bamboo-weave huts, set in a garden, are good value. ②.

Sri Tioman Chalets (☎011/224 2829). Good atmosphere and value, with a reasonable seafood restaurant and chalets set on the beach north of the *Persona*. ②.

Air Batang and Penuba Bay

Despite its ever-increasing popularity, **AIR BATANG**, 2km north of Tekek from jetty to jetty, is still one of the best areas on Tioman, competing with Juara for the budget market. Larger than Salang or Juara, far less developed than Tekek and well connected by boat services, Air Batang, or ABC as it's often called, is a happy medium as far as many visitors are concerned; what development there is here tends to be relatively tasteful and low-key.

A jetty divides the bay roughly in half; the beach is better at the southern end of the bay, close to the promontory, though the shallow northern end is safer for children. The cement path that runs the length of the beach is interrupted by little wooden bridges over streams, overhung with greenery. A fifteen-minute **trail** leads over the headland to the north which, after an initial scramble, flattens out into an easy walk, ending up at **Penuba Bay**. This secluded cove is littered with dead coral right up to the sea's edge, which makes it hard to swim comfortably, though the snorkelling is good; many people prefer the peace and quiet here to the beach at Air Batang. From Penuba Bay, it's an hour's walk to Monkey Beach, beyond which is Salang (see opposite).

Accommodation

As you get off the boat, a signpost helpfully lists the direction of the numerous **places to stay** in the bay. All but the most basic A-frames have fans and their own bathrooms, and mosquito nets are usually provided. Anything costing more than about RM50 a night should have a hot shower. **Internet** facilities are available at *ABC*, *Nazri's II* and *Bamboo Hill*, but they're uniformly expensive (around RM20 an hour).

ABC (☎09/419 1154). At the far northern end of the bay, and therefore a little quieter than most, this long-established operation is still among the best in Air Batang. The pretty chalets are set in a well-tended garden with its own freshwater stream. ①.

Bamboo Chalets (☎09/419 1339, fax 419 1326, *bamboosu@tm.net.my*). Beautiful wooden chalets on stilts, perched on the northern headland of Air Batang, with stunning views. The rooms are well equipped, with fridges, mosquito screens and bedside lamps. Excellent value – the best accommodation on Air Batang. ③.

Johan's (☎09/419 1359, *jjohan@goplay.com*). A good choice, with well-spaced standard chalets and new, larger ones up the hill on a pleasant lawn. There's also a dorm (RM10); some rooms have air-con. ②.

Mawar Beach Chalet (☎09/419 1153). Though well run, the chalets here, arranged in a long line facing the beach, seem rather uniform and dull. There's a restaurant and resident monitor lizard, though. ②.

Mokhtar's Place (☎09/419 1148). South of the jetty, this place is more comfortable than most, though the chalets are a little close together and face inwards, rather than out to sea. ②.

Nazri's II (☎09/419 1375, *cabnora@tm.net.my*). Located at the northern end of Air Batang, this elaborate outfit boasts large, air-con cottages set in spacious grounds, as well as some ordinary, cheaper chalets at the back. The lively restaurant offers good food, though it's a little pricey. ②–④.

Nazri's Place (☎09/419 1329, *bungur@tm.net.my*). At the southern end of the bay, this has the best bit of beach on the strip. Besides offering the same range of rooms as the affiliated *Nazri's II*, it also has six very inexpensive A-frames with shared bathrooms. ②–④.

Penuba Chalets (☎011/952963). The only accommodation at Penuba Bay, with a quieter beach than at Air Batang. If you stay here, you're committed to eating here every night, too, unless you fancy a scramble over the headland in the dark. Its chalets, on stilts and high up on the rocks, have fantastic views out to sea. ②–⑤.

Rinda House (☎09/419 1157). A good spot in a neat, shaded setting at the northern end of Air Batang, perfect for lying in one of their hammocks and watching the sun go down. One of the friendliest and lowest-priced hostels on Tioman, with simple, clean huts and shared facilities. ①.

South Pacific (no phone). Close to the jetty. Clean chalets with attached bathrooms, some right on the beach. ①.

Eating, drinking and nightlife

Air Batang keeps its **nightlife** low-key, unlike Salang (see below), which can get rowdy during the season. Most of the chalets have their own **restaurants**, open to non-residents. Menus, which tend to reflect Western tastes, have fish as a staple feature.

ABC. Good-quality food – chicken and fish dishes average RM10 – and fresh fruit juices. The informal bar and good sound system mean this friendly joint is always rocking.

Arini Rock. Some of the best budget-priced Malay and Western food on the island.

Chinese Restaurant. Right by the jetty, this imaginatively named place serves authentic, though pricey, Cantonese cuisine.

Nazri's II. The food is slightly more expensive than elsewhere – chicken-in-a-basket or burgers average RM8. Its balcony is great for a sunset beer, and the atmosphere seems to be lively right the way into monsoon.

Nazri's Place. Does a very hearty breakfast for RM8.50 and lots of Western-style food for lunch and dinner (around RM10 a dish). Good location on the beach.

Seri Bungur Restoran. Serves traditional Malay food; you won't need to part with more than about RM7 per person.

Salang and Monkey Beach

Just over 4km north of Air Batang, **SALANG** is a quieter, less developed bay with a better beach. Nevertheless, there has been a lot of development recently and the string of hostels stretches pretty much the whole length of the seafront. Though most accommodation here costs a shade more than at Air Batang, there are still lots of budget choices. The southern end of the beach is the more scenic, while swimming is a bit of an ordeal at the northern end, where sharp rocks and coral make the water difficult to approach. Just off the southern headland is a small island, Pulau Soyak, with a pretty reef for snorkelling.

A rough trail takes you over the headland to the south for the 45-minute scramble to **Monkey Beach**. There are few monkeys around these days, but the well-hidden cove is more than adequate compensation. It's a popular spot for trainee divers because of its clear, calm waters, and you may want to base yourself here to take advantage of the two good **dive schools**, Dive Asia and Ben's Diving Centre, both of which run daily courses (RM725–1200), with instruction in English and German.

▽ *Monkey Beach*

ACCOMMODATION	
Khalid's Place	4
Nadia's Salang Bay Resort	5
Salang Beach Resort	2
Salang Huts	1
Salang Indah	3
Zaid's	6

RESTAURANTS	
Nora's Café	C
Salang Dream	B
Sunset Boulevard	A

Practicalities

On the right (south) as you leave the jetty are a little cluster of budget **places to stay**, listed overleaf. You can get **online** at the *Salang Beach Resort* and *Salang Huts* if you can stomach the hefty charge (around RM20 an hour). There is a two-level choice when it comes to **eating**: the expensive restaurants at *Salang Dream* and *Salang Beach Resort*, where the emphasis is on Malay cuisine and seafood at around RM10 per dish, and the more informal *Zaid's* and *Nora's Café*, serving excellent Western and Malay dishes for no more than RM3. For **nightlife**, there are several choices: *Four S Bar*, a candlelit bar with a good range of beers, the *Dive Bar* next to Ben's Diving Centre and the more upmarket *Sunset Boulevard*, which has the best views of the bay.

ACCOMMODATION

Khalid's Place (☎09/419 5317, fax 419 5421). With friendly management, this place is set back from the beach in landscaped gardens. Some of the rooms have air-con. ③.

Nora's Café (no phone). A friendly family operation, whose well-kept chalets (RM35) with bathroom, fan and mosquito nets make them the best value here, set behind the little lagoon where the local monitor lizards are getting on to alligator size.

Salang Beach Resort (☎09/419 5019, *salangsayang@hotmail.com*). The *Salang Sayang Resort*, as this place is also known, has upmarket pretensions, with comfortable, hillside chalets (③) and more expensive sea-facing ones. There are also some family rooms. ⑤.

Salang Huts (☎09/419 5027). The chalets here at the far end of the bay are considerably quieter than others along the stretch, though they overlook unattractive piles of rocks and there's no beach to speak of. ②.

Salang Indah (☎09/419 5015, fax 419 5024). The largest outfit, towards the centre of the bay, has well-appointed chalets to suit every budget, from run-of-the-mill sea-facing box rooms to two-storey family chalets with air-con and hot shower (RM180); they also arrange a range of snorkelling and diving trips. ②.

Zaid's (☎09/415 9020). The best place to stay, with attractive hillside chalets and lower-priced ones on the beach. There's also an air-con longhouse that would suit a family. ③.

Juara

As Tioman's western shore becomes more and more developed, many people are making their way to **JUARA**, the only settlement on the east coast. Life is simpler here; the locals speak less English and are much more conservative than elsewhere on the island (officially, alcohol isn't served in Juara). Although Juara's seclusion may have saved it so far from the excesses all too apparent on the west coast, new chalets are already springing up. For the time being, however, Juara is refreshingly free from the buzz of speedboats and motorbikes, while its lovely wide sweep of beach is far cleaner and less crowded than anywhere on the other side. The constant sea breeze means that fans aren't necessary, though the downside to this is that the water is always choppy, and the bay, facing out to the open sea, is the most susceptible on the island to bad weather.

JUARA

△ Tekek

RESTAURANTS	
Ali Putra	A
Beach Café	B
Bushman's	D
Happy Café	C

Jetty

Juara Mutiara Shop

ACCOMMODATION	
Atan's	2
Basir	4
Juara Bay Resort	7
Mezanie Chalet	8
Mutiara	3
Paradise Point	1
Rainbow	6
Sunrise	5

N

0   200m

▽ South Bay & ⑧

Practicalities

There's only one daily **sea bus** to the kampung from the west coast – if you miss it, the journey to this isolated bay must be made on foot through the jungle, a steep trek that takes just under two hours from Tekek, not counting rest stops. The start of the trail (a five-minute walk from the airstrip) is easy enough to identify, since it's the only concrete path that heads off in that direction, passing the local mosque before hitting virgin jungle after about fifteen minutes. There's no danger of losing your way: cement steps climb steeply through the greenery, tapering off into a smooth, downhill path once you're over the ridge. Here there are unusual blue ferns, and some of the rarer trees are labelled. After 45 minutes, there's a **waterfall**, where it's forbidden to bathe – it supplies Tekek with water. From this spot, it's another hour or so to Juara village, which consists of two bays; the path emerges at the northern one, opposite the **jetty**.

ACCOMMODATION

Most of the **accommodation** (and restaurants) are on the northern bay, within a five-minute walk of the jetty. Although the southern bay does have a few chalets, to get to the nearest restaurants from here you'll face a long scramble over the rocks or a dark walk along the concrete path that runs behind all the developments.

Among the places to stay, *Paradise Point* (①) is the only one north of the jetty, about 200m away along the beach; it has the cheapest chalets here, with attached bathrooms. *Atan's* (②), just south of the jetty and the path, boasts two interesting, two-storey guesthouses, rather like Swiss chalets. The biggest operation here, though, is *Mutiara* (☎ & fax 07/799 4833; ①–③), with a wide variety of rooms and prices – these are also the people to see if you want to arrange a boat trip for fishing or snorkelling. They have more chalets behind their shop, a little way north along the beach. A little further south, *Basir* has good sea-facing chalets (②), and some cheaper huts as well, while at the southern end of the strip, *Sunrise* (①) and *Rainbow* (①) have characterful, painted A-frames right on the beach.

As you follow the path round to the even quieter southern bay, you'll pass the turning for the *Juara Bay Resort* (closed and looking unlikely to reopen at the time of writing), at the southern edge of the northern bay. The beach here is even better than that on the northern bay, and there are several cheap places to stay, including *Mezanie Chalet* (☎09/547 8445; ②), which boasts clean huts and its own restaurant.

EATING

While there's less choice for **eating** than on the west coast, portions here tend, on the whole, to be larger, and the menus more imaginative. The restaurant at *Paradise Point* does good *rotis* as well as unusual dishes, such as fish with peanut sauce and fried rice with coconut, averaging around RM5. Two simple places, *Ali Putra* and *Beach Café*, nestle side by side at the jetty; both have a huge range of local and Western dishes. South of the jetty, *Happy Café* is always busy, has good music and is one of the few places here to eat ice cream among other things, while the restaurant at *Sunrise* is open for breakfast and lunch only, offering muesli, home-baked bread and cakes, as well as the usual rice and noodle fare. At night, try *Bushman's*, a shack next to *Sunrise*, and the only place serving alcohol at Juara.

Asah and Mukut

South of Juara are the deserted remains of the village at **ASAH**; you can get here on the round-the-island boat trip (see p.338), or take a sea taxi from Genting (RM60 per person), the nearest point of access. These days, the only signs of life are the trails of litter left by day-trippers dropping by to visit the famous **waterfall**, the setting for the *Happy Talk* sequence from the film version of *South Pacific*. A fifteen-minute walk from the ramshackle jetty, the twenty-metre-high cascade is barely recognizable as the one in the film, though certainly photogenic enough. Though the deep-plunge pool at the foot of the waterfall provides a refreshing dip, there's not much else to detain you in

Asah, except for the stunning view of the dramatic, insurmountable twin peaks of **Bukit Nenek Semukut**.

Mukut

It's far better to spend time at nearby **MUKUT**, a tiny fishing village just five minutes from Asah by sea taxi, in the shadow of granite outcrops. Shrouded by dense forest, and connected to the outside world by a solitary cardphone, it's a wonderfully peaceful and friendly spot to unwind, though be warned that this is still a conservative place, unused to Western sunbathing habits.

Having paid handsomely to get here, you'll probably want to make it worth your while by staying for some time. The nicest position is occupied by *Chalets Park* (③), with secluded chalets shaded by trees. The accommodation at *Sri Tanjung Chalets* (②), at the far western end of the cove, overlooks a patch of beach – book at the house in the village where the name is painted on a tyre. **Places to eat** are few and basic; the *Sri Sentosa* is a bit on the dingy side, though popular with the locals, while the views from *Mukut Coral Resort* and the *7-Eleven* café just by the jetty make up for their lack of variety.

South of Tekek: Paya, Genting and Nipah

The western beaches south of Tekek are rarely frequented by foreign tourists, though they're popular with local holiday-makers. There also seems to be more of a sense of local kampung life here, despite the concrete resorts. Just 5km south of Tekek, the understated developments at **PAYA**, in contrast to those at Genting a little further south, seem relatively peaceful. Once again, package tours are the norm, and individual travellers turning up at this narrow stretch of pristine beach will find their options somewhat limited. **Jungle walks** are worth exploring here, as the greenery is at its most lush, despite the minor inroads made by the resorts. The thirty-minute trail north to Bunut ends up at a fantastic, deserted beach. From here it's a hot 45-minute walk through the golf course back to the *Berjaya Tioman Beach Resort* and a further half-hour to Tekek. You can even walk between Paya and Genting, a tough, overgrown and at times steep trek taking about an hour from jetty to jetty.

The only budget **accommodation** in Paya is at the rustic *Paya Holiday* (☎011/716196; ②), right in the centre of the small bay; it's barely furnished, but quite serviceable. A little further to the north, the *Paya Beach Resort* (☎07/799 1432, fax 799 1436; ⑤) has shoddily built, though comfortable, chalets, and offers sea sports and snooker. By far the best operation is the *Paya Tioman Resort* (☎011/324121; ④), set back in the woodland, with an open-air restaurant and barbecue facilities.

Genting

Usually the first stop for boats from the mainland, **GENTING**, at the western extremity of the island, hardly offers a heartening welcome, being an ugly blot on the landscape. The settlement, its cramped developments catering largely for Singaporean tour groups, is awash with discos and karaoke bars. Except during weekends and holidays (when prices rise by about fifty percent), it has a rather gloomy feel.

The southern end of the beach is the best, which is also where most of the low-budget **accommodation** is situated. There's little to choose between *Genting Jaya* (☎07/799 4811; ②) and the many more similar, unnamed places nearby, all offering wooden bedrooms. At the far northern end of the concrete path, the *Sea Star Beach Resort* (☎011/718334; ②) is not bad for the price, though *Sun Beach* (☎07/799 4918; ③), the largest enterprise just north of the jetty, has the widest variety of rooms and a large balcony restaurant. Places to eat are generally limited to big, open-plan **restaurants** attached to the resorts; the emphasis is on catering for large numbers rather than providing interesting, quality meals. Prices are predictably inflated, though the *Yonghwa Restaurant* in front of the jetty has more moderately priced dishes on its Chinese-based menu.

Nipah

For almost total isolation, head to **NIPAH** on Tioman's southwest coast. Comprising a clean, empty beach of coarse, yellow sand, and a landlocked lagoon, it has no village to speak of, though there is a Dive Centre and canoeing. You might be lucky enough to get a ferry from the mainland to drop you here since there's an adequate jetty, but it's more likely that you'll have to come by sea taxi from Genting, costing around RM30 per person.

There's only one **place to stay**: the *Nipah Resort* (☎011/764184; ②), offering basic chalets and more expensive A-frames, as well as a nicely designed restaurant; the food can get a little monotonous though. The air-con longhouse, *Nipah Paradise*, at the far end, caters only for pre-booked packages from Singapore.

The other Seribuat islands

Though Pulau Tioman is the best known and most visited of the 64 volcanic islands which form the **SERIBUAT ARCHIPELAGO**, there are a handful of other accessible islands whose beaches and opportunities for seclusion outstrip those of their larger rival. For archetypal azure waters and table-salt sand, four in particular stand out: Pulau Besar, Pulau Tinggi, Pulau Sibu and Pulau Rawa – though none of them are particularly geared to a tight budget. All the islands are designated **marine parks** and, like Tioman, belong to the state of Pahang, unlike their port of access, Mersing, which lies in Johor.

Pulau Rawa is only a 75-minute boat ride (RM40 day return) from Mersing, making it close enough to be visited on a day-trip from there, though you'll need to charter a boat specially for the purpose. Although the island's sugary sands and transparent waters get rave reviews, the sandflies (see box, below) are unavoidable, and you're not allowed to bring your own food and drink. There's only one **place to stay** on the island, the deluxe *Rawa Safaris Island Resort* (☎07/799 1204, fax 799 3848; ⑤–⑧), where there are cheap *atap*-roofed A-frames as well as comfortable, well-equipped chalets with air-con and proper bathrooms, and every facility for water sports. Try to book a couple of days in advance, especially at weekends.

Omar's Backpackers' Hostel in Mersing (see p.333) offers a one-day **island-hopping trip** aboard the *Black Sausage*, its traditional Malay fishing boat, the only cheap way of seeing several islands at the same time. The trips (Feb–Nov at 10am; 7hr) take in either three islands to the south of Mersing (Pulau Hujung, Tengah and Besar) or four to the north (Pulau Harimau, Mensirip, Gual and Rawa). The use of snorkelling equipment,

---

SANDFLIES

Sandflies can be a real problem on all of the Seribuat islands, though reputedly Juara, on the east coast of Tioman, is the worst place, especially in summer. These little pests, looking like tiny fruit flies, with black bodies and white wings, suck blood and so cause an extremely itchy lump, which can sometimes become a nasty blister if scratched. The effectiveness of various treatments and deterrents is much debated; the general feeling is that short of dousing yourself all over with insect repellent or hiding out in the sea all day long, there's not much you can do to avoid the insects, although using suntan oil rather than lotion or cream is supposed to help. Urine (your own) is among the more esoteric remedies for the itching. The closest thing to a consensus, though, seems to be that Tiger Balm, available at any chemist, can reduce the maddening itch and help you get a night's sleep before you claw your skin off.

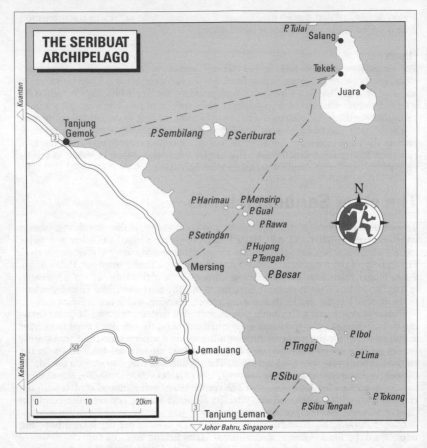

together with a packed lunch and boat transport from one splendid coral reef to another, are included in the price (RM65).

Pulau Besar

The long and narrow **PULAU BESAR**, 4km by 1km in size, is also known as Pulau Babi Besar, or "Big Pig Island". Just over an hour's ride from Mersing by ferry (1 daily around noon; RM30 return), it's one of the most developed islands, with a variety of resorts and chalets, but despite this, you're still likely to have the place to yourself outside the main holiday periods.

Topped by two peaks, Bukit Atap Zink (225m) and Bukit Berot (275m), the island is crossed by three relatively easy **trails**: a ten-minute stroll from behind the *Hillside Chalet Island Resort* at the northern end of the island brings you to the Beach of Passionate Love, while an hour's walk starting either from behind the central jetty or from just beyond the *Nirvana Resort* leads to secluded bays. The island is claimed to be sheltered from the worst of the monsoon, but there's a strong undertow and constant sea breeze even in the dry season.

Accommodation and eating

With one exception, the **resorts** are all located at intervals on the west-facing beach, the best on the island. Top among them is the *Radin Island Resort* (☎07/799 4152, fax 799 1413; ⑥), more or less in the middle of the bay, with superbly designed chalets. The only budget-oriented place is a set of four A-frames (②) right by the sea, not far from the *Radin Island* – ask at the small shop by the phone and post box. The *Nirvana Resort* (☎07/799 5979, fax 799 5978; ⑤), at the far southern end of the bay, has its own jetty and the best bit of beach on the island; its clapboard buildings look a bit motley at first sight, but they're quite comfortable inside. Next door is *Suntam Island Resort* (☎07/799 4995; ②), with simple, homely chalets set apart from one another in a well-tended flower garden. Right at the far northern end of the island, the exclusive *Hillside Chalet Island Resort* (☎07/799 4831; ⑥) has an isolated setting, a good thirty-minute walk from the rest of the developments. Its beach isn't that special, but the chalets are comfortable, arranged in flourishing green gardens; breakfast is included in the rate.

All the places to stay have their own **restaurants**, open to non-residents; the one at the *Hillside* is the most expensive at around RM30 per head. The *Radin* has an elegant open-air restaurant designed to catch the sea breezes, while *Suntam Island Resort* serves reasonable meals, such as *nasi goreng* for around RM4.

Pulau Tinggi

One of the largest islands of the group, **PULAU TINGGI**, a two-hour boat ride from Mersing (RM50 return), is also the most distinctive, with its towering dormant volcanic peak sticking up like a giant upturned funnel (*tinggi* means "tall" or "high"). The mountain can be climbed, an arduous four-hour trip, though you need a local guide as the route can be quite dangerous. A gentler excursion is to the **waterfall**, pretty disappointing outside the rainy season, about thirty minutes over the headland along a well-worn path – but with a splendid beach a little way downstream.

Accommodation is limited to a few resorts. *Nadia's Inn* (☎011/799 5582; ②–⑧) has good chalets to suit every budget, as well as a bar and a good swimming pool. The friendly *Tinggi Island Resort* (☎011/762217; ⑥), on a hillside overlooking the beach, is a little less plush, but has good water sports facilities. You can eat at both of the resorts for about RM15 per person a meal, and at the food stalls by the jetty, which serve *nasi goreng*.

Pulau Sibu

Closest to the mainland, **PULAU SIBU** is the most popular of the islands after Tioman. Though it's also the least scenically interesting, the huge monitor lizards and the butterflies here make up for the lack of mountains and jungle. The island's narrow waist can be crossed in only a few minutes, revealing a double bay known as Twin Beach. Like the rest of the islands, Sibu boasts fine beaches, though the sand is yellower and the current more turbulent here than at some others; most of the coves have good offshore coral.

Practicalities

The majority of the resorts on Sibu operate their own boats from **Tanjung Leman**, a tiny mainland coastal village clearly signposted off Route 3, about 30km south of Mersing. These boats, which take an hour to reach the island, need to be arranged in advance, apart from the *Black Pudding*, a daily boat run by the *O&H Kampung Huts* (see overleaf). Secure parking is available at the jetty for RM7 per day.

Tanjung Leman is awkward to get to without your own transport. If you're taking *O&H's* boat, a free bus ride from Mersing is included – if not you pay RM10 for the journey. A taxi to the village from Johor Bahru or Mersing costs around RM60, but since there is no stand at Tanjung Leman, you must arrange to be picked up when you return.

ACCOMMODATION AND EATING

Halfway along Sibu's eastern coast, *O&H Kampung Huts* (☎011/354322; ①–③) is a friendly and relaxed set-up of A-frames and some dearer, though still fairly basic, chalets; it's the best place to stay on the island if you're on a budget. Also on the eastern side, the *Sea Gypsy Village Resort* (☎07/222 8642, fax 238 7305; ⑥) is much more exclusive, aiming for the diving market, with all-inclusive packages costing around RM400 per night for two people. It's a tasteful place, with simple chalets and an attractive lounge and dining area. For something unusual, try *Rimba Resort* (☎011/711528; ⑦), on the north coast, whose simply furnished, cosy two-bed cottages have an African theme and whose communal areas are scattered with floor cushions; they offer a package including boat transfers and all meals. *Sibu Island Cabanas* (☎07/331 1920; ⑥) is one of the lower-priced options – its chalets are shabby, though its stretch of beach is good. Head back from the *Cabanas*, over the small ridge in the centre of the island, to get to *Twin Beach Resort* (☎03/948 8966; ③), the only place with views of both sunrises and sunsets; its A-frames and pricier chalets are run-down, but then you can also camp here for free.

Eating on Pulau Sibu is a pleasure. The *O&H* has excellent fish and chicken curries with rice, vegetables and salad, as well as Western dishes, at around RM15 for a full meal. *Sea Gypsy* also offers great cuisine, including grilled fish, though for residents only. The restaurant at *Twin Beach* specializes in Chinese food at reasonable prices.

Endau Rompin National Park

One of the few remaining areas of lowland tropical rainforest left in Peninsular Malaysia, the **ENDAU ROMPIN NATIONAL PARK** covers approximately 870 square kilometres – about one and a half times the area of Singapore. Despite being valued by conservationists for the richness of both **flora and fauna** (see box, opposite), the area was the site of damaging logging in the 1970s, and it wasn't until its designation as a national park in 1989 that adequate protective measures were finally put in place. This dense, lush habitat has nurtured several species new to science, including at least three trees, eight herbs and two mosses, documented by the Malaysian Nature Society during its 1985–86 expedition, which itself helped to establish the need for a properly controlled park here. There's plenty on offer for the less specialized nature-lover, from gentle **trekking** to more strenuous mountain-climbing and **rafting**; although gradually becoming accustomed to tourists, Endau Rompin still has a long way to go before it suffers the overuse that afflicts Taman Negara, and for the time being at least, its trails remain refreshingly untrampled.

Surrounding the headwaters of the lengthy Sungei Endau and sitting astride the Johor–Pahang state border, the region was shaped by volcanic eruptions more than 150 million years ago. The force of the explosions sent up huge clouds of ash, creating the quartz crystal ignimbrite that's still very much in evidence along the park's trails and rivers, its glassy shards glinting in the light. Endau Rompin's steeply sloped mountains level out into sandstone plateaux, and the park is watered by three **river systems** based around the main tributaries of Sungei Marong, Sungei Jasin and Sungei Endau, reaching out to the south and east. At the confluence of the latter two rivers, at the eastern end of the park, lies Endau Rompin's base camp at **Kuala Jasin**. Although the park's boundaries lie some distance beyond the rivers, it is only in these river valleys that you can roam freely. The aboriginal people of the area are commonly referred to by the

FLORA AND FAUNA IN ENDAU ROMPIN

There are at least seven species of **hornbill** (see box on p.435) in the park, which are hard to miss, particularly in flight, when their oversized, white-tipped wings counterbalance their enormous curved orange bills. Early in the morning, the hooting of the male **gibbon** joins the dawn chorus of insects, cuckoos and babblers. This is the time of day when the wildlife is most active; by noon all the action has died down. The late afternoon cool heralds a second burst of activity, and is a particularly good time for bird-watching, and at night, owls, frogs, rats and pythons are about. If you're on a tour with a guide (see overleaf), you've a better chance of spotting tiger or elephant **footprints**, though wild pigs, mouse deer and colourful toads are far more usual sightings. The park is also the habitat of the increasingly rare **Sumatran rhinoceros**, though this hides out in the far western area of the park, off-limits to visitors.

At the upper levels of the jungle, **epiphytes** are common: non-parasitic plants which take advantage of their position on tree branches to get the light they need for photosynthesis. Massive palms are found here too, but it's mostly orchids and ferns that flourish. Lower down in the forest shade, moths and spiders camouflage themselves among the greyish brown lichen that covers the barks, and squirrels and lizards scurry up and down. Much closer to eye level, where most of the light is cut out by the virtually impenetrable canopy, are **birds** like babblers and woodpeckers. You'll also see **tree frogs**, whose expanded disc-like toes and finger tips, sticky with mucus, help them cling to leaves and branches. The forest floor is mostly covered by **ferns and mosses**, as well as tree seedlings struggling to find sunlight from a chink in the canopy.

generic term **Orang Ulu**, meaning "upriver people" – their lives revolve around the rivers (you can still see them using dugouts made from a single tree trunk and canoes made of lengths of bark sewn together with twine). In recent years, these nomadic peoples, traditionally collectors of forest products such as resins, rattan and camphor wood, have become more settled, living in permanent villages such as Kampung Peta, accessible only by an old logging track two hours' drive from the nearest tarmac road.

Acquiring a permit for the park can require a certain degree of determination, and given that conditions inside the park are fairly primitive, it's best to book yourself on a tour; see "Practicalities", overleaf, for thorough information on visiting the park.

Hikes and trails

Near base camp, the **Janing Barat plateau** (710m) can be reached by a relatively easy four-hour trail which leads southeast from Kuala Jasin. Topped by a giant sandstone slab, the outcrop marks an abrupt change from the lush growth of wild ginger, characterized by its bright crimson flowers, and the ever-present betel-nut palm, in favour of tough fan palms above. On the ridge of the mountain, at around 450m, is a boggy, waterlogged area, producing a small patch of heath forest, though it is in the taller forest that most of the wild animals can be found – look out for the occasional group of pigs, or a solitary tapir chewing at the bark of the trees.

Each river boasts a major **waterfall**, the best of which is along Sungei Jasin, southwest of base camp. Two routes lead from the base camp to the head of the river, where the spectacular **Buaya Sangkut** cascades in a forty-metre torrent, almost as wide as it is high. A track along the northern bank leads directly to the falls, a six-hour hike across the multiple ridges of Bukit Segongong (765m). An Orang Ulu legend tells of an old crocodile who lived in the pools above the waterfall, and one day got stuck between some rocks, its body transforming itself into the white-water rapids – the translation of the waterfall's name in fact means "trapped crocodile". A longer, less-defined trail branches off south, about ten minutes' walk out of base camp, crossing Sungei Jasin to reach the estuary, Kuala Marong, about 45 minutes later. From here, you can head east along Sungei Marong as far as Kuala Bunuh Sawa (2hr), or continue along Sungei Jasin to the **Upeh Guling** waterfall, ten minutes further on. Although initially less impressive than Buayu Sangkut, it has one striking feature, the collection of deep potholes just upstream of the falls. Here, the river's steep sides have been eroded by the water into smooth, natural bathtubs – a good place to soothe aching feet. Following the river closely for a further two hours brings you to **Batu Hampar** waterfall, where you can either pitch tent, or continue the additional three hours to Buaya Sangkut.

Practicalities

The best time to visit Endau Rompin is between February and October, while the paths and dry and the rivers calm. During the monsoon, however, the park is completely inaccessible, since many of its waterways are swollen and the trails are too boggy to use. Further information on current conditions in the park can be obtained from the tourist office in Kuantan (see p.286). Take loose-fitting, lightweight cotton clothing that dries quickly – even in the dry season you're bound to get wet from crossing rivers – and helps to protect you from scratches and bites. Waterproofs will come in handy, and you'll need tons of insect repellent – and a lighter to burn off leeches.

There are two **road routes** to the park. From **Rompin** in Pahang, there's a paved road 26km to Selanding, followed by a dirt road for the remaining 24km to Kinchin which is on the park boundary. From the **south**, you need to approach on **Route 50**: at the signpost for the Kahang oil-palm mill, 5km east of Kahang, turn north and continue for 48km along logging tracks (passable in an ordinary car unless it's very wet) until you reach the Orang Asli settlement of Kampung Peta, the site of the Visitor Control Centre; here you leave your car and register with the park rangers. (To reach Route 50 from Mersing, take Route 3 south as far as Jemaluang, where you head west along Route 50 for a further 42km until you reach the turning for the park.) From the Visitor Control Centre, it's another 15km to the base camp at Kuala Jasin, taking close to three hours on foot, though by boat it takes just 45 minutes (departures on request; RM10 per person). **By boat**, you can reach the park by making a trip upriver from **Endau**, 33km north of Mersing – a six-hour trip on a motorboat as far as Kampung Peta, costing around RM200 one way.

Though you can enter the park from either Johor or Pahang, only the former requires visitors to pay for a **permit** to enter the park. This costs RM20 and is available on the spot from Johor State Economic Unit, Level 2, Bangunan Sultan Ibrahim, Johor Bahru (Mon–Fri 8am–4.15pm, Sat 8am–12.45pm; ☎07/223 7471, fax 223 7472); you'll need a photocopy of your passport and three photos. However charges don't stop there if you enter via Johor: once inside the park it costs RM40 per person per day to visit the Upeh Guling waterfalls, Kuala Marong or the Janing Barat plateau, and RM35 for the Buayu Sangkut waterfalls. You'll also be charged an extra RM10 to use your camera, and Johor law requires you to hire a guide (RM30 a day). None of these charges apply if you enter the park from Pahang: with a free entry permit from the district office on the high street in Rompin (☎09/414 5205), you're at liberty to enter the park alone.

Both the Johor and Pahang authorities and the Malaysian Nature Society advise you to book an **organized tour** through a travel agency, which will spare you the hassle of arranging permits and travel. Packages organized by the *Seri Malaysia* (see p.334) start at RM90 (minimum four people) for a day-trip into the park and run to RM200, which includes a night at the hotel and camping out in the park itself at **Jeram Gerugul**. This compares to RM440 for the four-day/three-night trip organized by Wilderness Experience (☎03/717 8221) based in Petaling Jaya. Other tour operators who can arrange trips into the park include *Memories Holiday Resort* (☎03/245 0746) in Kuala Lumpur, New Asia Holiday Tours and Travel (☎07/233 7392) in Johor Bahru, and Giamso Travel (☎07/799 2253) in Mersing. Ask at the Visitor Control Centre at Kampung Peta for advice on arranging a **rafting** trip; rafting down the peaty Sungei Endau is a possibility, with short stretches of stony bed and relatively sluggish flow interspersed by white-water rapids and huge boulders. After the river merges with Sungei Kinchin, the flow becomes slower and the scenery generally less exciting.

Accommodation and eating

There are basic A-frame huts at the Visitor Control Centre in Kampung Peta (③). Although new chalets are planned, for now the only facilities within the park itself are at the designated **camping grounds** at the Upeh Guling, Batu Hampar and Buaya Sangkut waterfalls, which cost RM10 per person per night. If you're on a tour, your guide cooks **food** for you, though it's worth taking energy-giving snacks as well. If you're not on a tour, you'll have to fend for yourself – remember that carrying cooking pots in addition to the rest of your gear can get very tiring in dense jungle.

travel details

Trains

Gemas to: Kuala Lumpur (5 daily; 3hr 40min–4hr 15min).

Johor Bahru to: Gemas (5/6 daily; 3–5hr); Kuala Lipis (2 daily; 7hr); Kuala Lumpur (3 daily; 5hr 40min); Seremban (3 daily; 4hr 20min); Singapore (6 daily; 25min); Tumpat (1 daily; 12hr).

Segamat to: Kuala Lumpur (5 daily; 3hr 35min–5hr 10min).

Seremban to: Gemas (3 daily; 2hr); Johor Bahru (3 daily; 5–7hr); Kuala Lumpur (5 daily; 2hr); Singapore (3 daily; 6hr).

Buses

Johor Bahru to: Alor Setar (2 daily; 12hr); Butterworth (at least 2 daily; 12hr); Ipoh (2 daily; 8hr); Kota Bahru (1 daily; 12hr); Kuala Lumpur (hourly; 5hr); Kuala Terengganu (2 daily; 10hr); Kuantan (5 daily; 6hr); Melaka (6 daily; 3hr); Mersing (at least 3 daily; 2hr 30min); Singapore (every 10min; 1hr).

Melaka to: Alor Setar (6 daily; 12hr); Butterworth (14 daily; 9hr); Ipoh (14 daily; 4hr); Johor Bahru (6 daily; 3hr); Kota Bharu (3 daily; 13hr); Kuala Lumpur (hourly; 2hr); Kuala Terengganu (3 daily; 9hr); Kuantan (1 daily; 5hr); Mersing (2 daily; 5hr); Singapore (9 daily; 5hr).

Mersing to: Johor Bahru (at least 3 daily; 2hr 30min); Kluang (every 45min; 2hr); Kuala Lumpur (5 daily; 7hr); Kuantan (5 daily; 3hr 30min); Melaka (2 daily; 5hr); Singapore (4 daily; 3hr 30min).

Seremban to: Butterworth (4 daily; 9hr); Ipoh (2 daily; 5hr); Johor Bahru (2 daily; 3hr); Kota Bharu (4 daily; 10hr); Kuala Lumpur (every 45min; 1hr); Mersing (2 daily; 5hr).

Ferries

Melaka to: Dumai (Sumatra; 2 daily; 2hr).

Mersing to: Pulau Desar (1 daily, 1hr 10min); Pulau Rawa (1 daily; 1hr 20min); Pulau Sibu (1 daily; 2hr); Pulau Tinggi (1 daily; 2hr); Pulau Tioman (at least 2 daily; 2–5hr).

Pulau Tioman to: Singapore (daily; 4hr 30min).

Flights

Johor Bahru to: Ipoh (at least 2 daily via KL; 2hr 15min–7hr 15min); Kota Kinabalu (at least 6 daily; 2hr 20min); Kuala Lumpur (at least 6 daily; 45min); Kuching (4 daily; 1hr 25min); Langkawi (1 daily; 2hr 20min); Penang (at least 5 daily via KL; 2hr 30min; and one direct; 1hr 5min).

Melaka to: Ipoh (6 weekly; 50min); Medan (2 weekly; 1hr); Pekan Baru (2 weekly; 30min); Singapore (6 weekly; 55min).

Pulau Tioman to: Kuala Lumpur (4 daily; 45min); Kuantan (1 daily; 45min); Singapore (1 daily; 30min).

CHAPTER SIX

SARAWAK

Six hundred kilometres across the South China Sea from Peninsular Malaysia, the two East Malaysian states of Sarawak and Sabah occupy the northwest flank of the island of Borneo (the rest of which, save the enclave of Brunei, is Kalimantan, part of Indonesia). **SARAWAK** is the larger of the two states, and a more different place to Peninsular Malaysia is hard to imagine. Clear rivers spill down the jungle-covered mountains to become wide, muddy arteries nearer the sea, while the surviving rainforest, highland plateaux and river communities combine to form one of the most complex and diverse ecosystems on earth. Monkeys, deer and lizards abound, although **deforestation**, caused by both the logging industry and indigenous farming, has had a serious effect on mammals like the orang-utan and proboscis monkey, which are now endangered species. Ironically, even Sarawak's official state emblem, the eccentric-looking hornbill, is at risk – the bird's beak has been used for centuries by indigenous tribespeople to carve images from the natural and supernatural worlds. Sarawak has its fair share, too, of **national parks**, including the mountainous Gunung Mulu and the cave-riddled Niah.

The most convincing reason for hopping across the sea to Sarawak, however, is for its culture – visitors can't fail to make contact with its **indigenous peoples**. Making up around half the state's population, they fall into groups known historically either as Land Dyaks (who live up in the hills – the Bidayuh are an example), Sea Dyaks (such as the Iban and Melanau, who dwell along river valleys) or Orang Ulu (like the Kenyah, Kelabit and Kayan, who live along rivers in the remote parts of the interior). The indigenous peoples have for centuries lived in massive **longhouses**, visits to which are the highlight of most trips to Sarawak. Though very few authentically constructed wooden beauties have survived – nowadays, most longhouses are functional, though still snug, concrete buildings with electricity supplies – and few of the inhabitants wear traditional dress, this takes nothing away from the enjoyment of being among these people; their warmth, hospitality and humour remain legendary despite the passing of many traditions. The best time to visit is during the festival period in June when harvest and fertility rituals (and sometimes also marriage ceremonies) are enacted, involving much dancing, singing and storytelling, the participants wearing traditional garments and sometimes centuries-old heirlooms. Unfortunately, the number of longhouses is decreasing, and communities are moving into more conventional kampung-style housing. Such changes reflect the fact that government policies and economic changes have conspired to make moving away from traditional lands (and accommodation) more appealing to native peoples. But although many of the younger men and women head for the cities and towns for work, a good many also return to the longhouses or kampungs at weekends and at festival times.

Tour operators based in Kuching and Miri now pay certain longhouses an annual stipend in exchange for bringing in foreign travellers, sums which pay for structural renovations, and travel and education costs for the longhouse children. Though it's possible for independent visitors to get to upriver longhouses on a local longboat, it's as well to note that some longhouses are preoccupied with the arrangements they've entered into with tour companies, and so it's best to aim for relatively unvisited longhouses, such as those in the **Batang Ai** area, east of Kuching near the Kalimantan border. That said, the one time when all longhouses throw open their doors to visitors is at festival time.

Resistance to logging concessions, once the main area of controversy, is now dying down as timber production itself is scaled down (as a result both of international pressure and the development of alternative, more sustainable, monocultures such as oil palm). Consequently, the question of **land rights** has become paramount over the last few years. In recent years, a **transmigration project** has resulted in over ten thousand Orang Ulu peoples being displaced from their ancestral homes along the Balui river in the inaccessible centre of the state. The reason for this was the intended building of a massive hydroelectric dam at **Bakun** although, incredibly, the plan has now been scotched – only after the tribes had moved. Now relocated to a bleak, riverless plain hours by four-wheel-drive from their former homes, these people are campaigning for a reversal of the policy – or at least proper compensation – and enlisting legal advice from international human-rights organizations. There's more on indigenous rights and the politics of logging on pp.633–636.

Most people start their exploration of Sarawak in the capital **Kuching**, in the southwest. A beautiful city, it's the starting point for visiting Iban longhouse communities on the Ai, Lemanak and Skrang rivers to the east, and the Bidayuh dwellings around Bau and Penrissen to the south. Kuching is also a base for seeing nearby **Bako National Park**, often underestimated by travellers, yet one of Asia's most perfect small nature parks. Although Sarawak is not noted for its **beaches**, there are excellent ones in Bako and further along the state's southwestern seaboard, accessible from the capital by bus and boat.

A four-hour boat ride north of Kuching, the city of **Sibu** marks the start of the popular route along **Batang Rajang**, Sarawak's longest river (*batang* means "big river" or "river system"). Most people stop at the upriver town of **Kapit**, using it as a base to visit longhouses along the Katibas and Baleh tributaries. More adventurous souls continue up the main river to **Belaga**, a remote interior settlement fronting this picturesque upper section of the Rajang, which acts as a magnet for tribal peoples from a vast hinterland.

The road route north from Sibu, now completely sealed, makes for a fast, comfortable trip. You pass near the backwater retreat of **Mukah** and through the town of **Bintulu** before reaching **Niah National Park**, with its vast cave system and accessible forest hikes. On its way north to the Brunei border, the road passes through **Miri**, a busy, vibrant town built on oil money, and noted for its sensational fish restaurants.

Northeast of here, tons of hardwood logs – the fruit of the state's aggressive policy of deforestation – are floated down the **Batang Baram** from forests upstream. Express boats go upriver via **Marudi**, where a proud fort overlooks the majestic river, and onwards to **Gunung Mulu National Park**. Sarawak's chief natural attraction, Mulu features astonishing limestone **pinnacles** and numerous extraordinary caves and passageways under its three mountains. A favourite route is to fly here in a Twin Otter plane from Miri. You can also fly from Miri and Marudi to **Bario** in the northeastern **Kelabit Highlands**, a forested plateau from where you can visit Kelabit longhouses and encounter some of the few remaining semi-nomadic Penan.

Some history

Sarawak's first inhabitants were cave-dwelling **hunter-gatherers** who lived here forty thousand years ago. Evidence of the existence of early humans was discovered in 1958 at Niah Caves, by a team from the Sarawak Museum headed by its curator, Tom Harrisson. The various tribes lived fairly isolated lives and there was little contact with the wider world until the first trading boats from Sumatra and Java arrived in the sixth century AD, exchanging cloth and pottery for jungle produce. These merchants were mainly Hindus, some of whom subsequently settled in Sarawak, while a larger group of

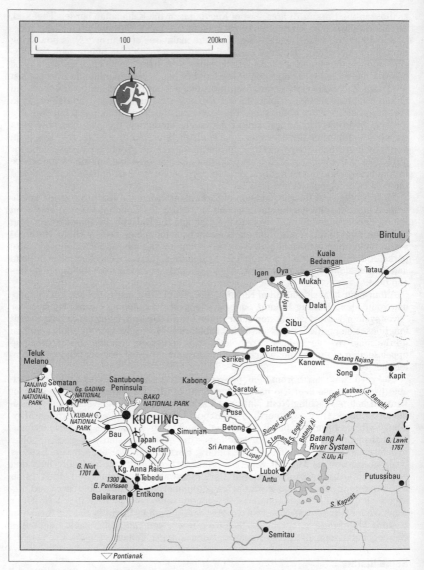

Muslim Malays from Java and Sumatra founded the city of Vijayapura in northern Borneo, close to Brunei, in the eleventh century.

As the Srivijaya empire collapsed at the end of the thirteenth century, so regional trading patterns changed and **Chinese merchants** became dominant, bartering beads and porcelain with the coastal Melanau people for bezoar stones (from the gall bladders of monkeys) and birds' nests, both considered aphrodisiacs by the Chinese. In time, the traders were forced to deal with the rising power of the Malay sultans, who by the fif-

teenth century controlled the northwest of Borneo. Paramount was the **Sultan of Brunei**, at the height of whose power even the indigenous peoples of Sarawak, based on the coast and in the headwaters of the large rivers in the southwest, were being taxed heavily. Meanwhile, Sarawak was attracting interest in Europe. Pigafetta, the chronicler of Magellan's voyage in the sixteenth century, described meeting Sea Dyak groups near Brunei Bay, while in the seventeenth century the **Dutch** and **English** established short-lived trading posts near Kuching in order to extract pepper and other spices.

SARAWAK PRACTICALITIES

Flights from Peninsular Malaysia to Sarawak can be quite expensive, and accommodation and travel within the state cost a little more than on the mainland. However, food and (soft) drinks are always a bargain, and ethnic artefacts bought along the way are usually good value too. Note that Sarawak has different rules on **entry permits** to the rest of Malaysia; see p.20.

GETTING THERE

Flights to Kuching are the most straightforward way into Sarawak; the prices that we've listed are approximate one-way fares unless otherwise stated. From **Kuala Lumpur**'s new airport, there are scheduled services with MAS (at least 10 daily; RM260, or RM180 for a night flight) and charter flights with Transmile (5 weekly; RM170); Air Asia flights to Kuching use the old Subang Airport (around 10 weekly; RM260). There are MAS flights from **Johor Bahru** (RM170), **Singapore** (RM230), **Kota Kinabalu** in Sabah (RM230) and the Kalimantan city of **Pontianak** (RM280); from Brunei, Royal Brunei flies to Kuching from **Bandar Seri Begawan** (around RM250). There are also MAS flights **to Miri**, in the north of the state, from KL (RM420) and Kota Kinabalu (RM100).

The main **overland** route into Sarawak is by bus **from Kuala Belait** in Brunei to Miri, a very straightforward crossing involving a ferry across the Belait river; see p.524 for all the details. The other main crossing is via **Sipitang** in Sabah (see p.472) to Lawas, by local bus or the daily Lawas Express which originates in Sabah's capital Kota Kinabalu (see p.450). From Indonesian Kalimantan, there are remote border crossings to villages in the northeastern Kelabit Highlands (see p.436). More straightforward is the overland route, with daily buses leaving from **Pontianak** and crossing from Entikong to Tebedu in southwest Sarawak, around 100km south of Kuching. There are daily **boat** services **from Brunei** to Lawas and Limbang, the two far northern divisions of Sarawak – see p.510.

GETTING AROUND

Boats – the main mode of transport – nearly always run to a reliable timetable, and come in three main types: seagoing **launches**, which ply the busy stretch from Kuching to Sarikei, at the mouth of Batang Rajang; express **boats**, which shoot up and down the main rivers; and smaller **longboats**, which provide transport along the tributaries.

Occasionally it may be necessary to **rent a longboat**, particularly for travel along the more remote tributaries, though this can be prohibitively expensive if you aren't travelling as part of a group: it's common to pay in excess of RM100 a day per person for a boat ride to visit the more distant longhouses. In addition, although the distances travelled

---

With the eventual decline in power of the Brunei sultanate, the region became impossible to administrate. At the beginning of the eighteenth century civil war erupted as a result of feuding between various local sultans, while piracy threatened to destroy what was left of the trade in spices, animals and minerals. In addition, the indigenous groups' predilection for **head-hunting** had led to a number of deaths among the traders and the sultan's officials, and violent territorial confrontations involving the more powerful ethnic groups were increasing.

Matters were at their most explosive when the Englishman **James Brooke** took an interest in the area. Born in India, Brooke joined the Indian army and, after being wounded in the First Anglo-Burmese War, was sent to his family home in Devon to convalesce. Returning to the East, he arrived in a Singapore in the 1830s, where he learned of the Sultan of Brunei's troubles in Sarawak. The sultan's uncle, Hashim, had recruited Dyak workers to mine high-grade antimony ore in a valley of the Sarawak river (near present-day Kuching), but conditions were intolerable and the Dyaks, with the support

from one longhouse to another are often not great (around 5km on average), travelling upstream against the current, in shallow waters and through rapids can be hard going. You may have to get out of the boat and help pull it over the rocks; bear in mind also that the cost of diesel gets greater the further away from towns you go.

In northern Sarawak, an essential way of getting around is by MAS-operated **Twin Otter planes**, seating around eighteen people. These tiny aircraft service a great many remote communities, most significantly Bario in the Kelabit Highlands and Gunung Mulu National Park. It's best to book a week or two in advance for both legs of your journey, as the planes can fill up fast. The standard baggage allowance on these planes is only 10 kilos per person, with excess baggage charged at around RM1.30 per kilo.

In some areas, you'll need a **permit** before you can visit, though it's usually a straightforward matter to obtain one; details are given in the text.

ACCOMMODATION

Most towns in Sarawak have mid-range hotels, lodging houses and cut-price *rumah tumpangan* (the local term for guesthouses); the only places with top-class **hotels** are Kuching, Miri, Bintulu, Sibu and Gunung Mulu National Park. Budget travellers aren't as well catered for as in Peninsular Malaysia or Sabah, though many of the Chinese-run hotels offer clean, functional rooms for as little as RM18 a night, as well as dorms. Don't expect to save funds by **camping**: there are no campsites and locals seldom, if ever, sleep out in the open – to do so would at the very least invite much curiosity, and at worst attract unfriendly wildlife.

Unfortunately, **longhouses** which are relatively accessible and open to receiving visitors are now mostly the preserve of tour operators. Areas which still offer travellers the chance of just turning up at longhouses unannounced include along Sungei Katibas, a tributary of the Batang Rajang; and the Kelabit Highlands, an upcountry region. Both regions take some time to visit and are quite expensive to get to. Independent visitors to longhouses aren't usually expected to pay for their lodging, but gifts are greatly appreciated. For information on how longhouses are laid out, and more details on arranging a visit to one, see p.367. The best occasions to see traditional costumes and festivities is the Iban *Gawai Dayak* period (see p.389) and the Bidayuh *Gawai Padi* (see p.383).

Throughout the Malaysia chapters we've used the following **price codes** to denote the cost of the cheapest available room for two people. Single occupancy should cost less than double, though it's only mid-range and top-tier hotels that are likely to offer such discounts. Some guesthouses provide dormitory beds, for which the ringgit price is given.

① RM20 and under	④ RM61–80	⑦ RM161–220
② RM21–40	⑤ RM81–110	⑧ RM221–360
③ RM41–60	⑥ RM111–160	⑨ RM361 and above

of local Malays, rebelled. Brooke – having chartered a schooner in Singapore and gathered together a small but well-armed force – quelled the rebellion and, as a reward, demanded sovereignty over the area around Kuching. The sultan had little choice but to relinquish control of the difficult territory and in 1841 Brooke was installed as the first **White Rajah** of Sarawak, launching a dynastic rule which lasted for a century.

Brooke signed treaties with the sultan and tolerated the business dealings of the Chinese, though his initial concern was to stamp out piracy and pacify the warring tribal groups. He built a network of **forts** to strengthen his rule, and sent officials into the malarial swamps and mountainous interior to make contact with the Orang Ulu. Displaying an early environmental awareness, Brooke also opposed calls from British- and Singapore-based businessmen to exploit the region commercially which, he believed, would have been to the detriment of the ethnic groups, whom he found fascinating. In the 1840s he wrote, "Sarawak belongs to all her peoples and not to us. It is for them we labour, not for ourselves." Despite these laudable words, Brooke's administration was not without its troubles. In one incident his men killed dozens of Dyaks, who were part of a pirate fleet, while in 1857 Hakka Chinese **gold-miners**, based in the settlement of Bau on the Sarawak river, opposed Brooke's attempts to eliminate their trade in opium and suppress their secret societies. They attacked Kuching and killed a number of officials – Brooke got away by the skin of his teeth. His nephew, **Charles Brooke**, assembled a massive force of warrior Dyaks and followed the miners; in the ensuing battle over a thousand Chinese were killed.

The acquisition of territory from the Sultan of Brunei continued throughout Charles Brooke's administration, which began in 1863. River valleys – known as **divisions** – were bought for a few thousand pounds, the Dyaks living there either persuaded to enter into deals or crushed if they resisted. Elsewhere, Brooke set the warrior Iban against the Kayan, whose stronghold was in the central and northern interior, and by 1905 his fiefdom encompassed almost all of the land traditionally occupied by the coastal Malays, as well as that of the Sea Dyaks along the rivers and the Land Dyaks in the mountains. Brunei itself had shrunk so much it was now surrounded on all three sides by Brooke's Sarawak.

During the 1890s Charles Brooke encouraged Chinese **immigration** into the area around Sibu and along the Rajang river, where pepper, and later rubber, farms were established. Bazaars were set up and traders travelled the rivers bartering with the ethnic groups. Charles Brooke thought that these few intrepid Chinese traders – mostly poor men forever in debt to the *towkay*s (merchants) in the towns who had advanced them goods on credit – might undermine the indigenous way of life, so he banned them from staying in longhouses and insisted they report regularly to his officials.

The third and last rajah, **Vyner Brooke**, consolidated the gains of his father, Charles, but was less concerned with indigenous matters, although the new constitution, which he proposed in 1941, would have helped to bring the sub-colonial backwater of Sarawak into the twentieth century. The **Japanese invasion**, however, effectively put an end to his control. Brooke escaped, but most of his officials were interned and some subsequently executed. With the Japanese surrender in 1945, Australian forces temporarily ran the state; Vyner returned the next year and ceded Sarawak to the British government. Many Malays opposed this, believing that **British rule** was a backward step; their protest reached its peak in 1949 when the British governor was murdered. With Malaysian independence in 1957, attempts were made to include Sarawak, Sabah and Brunei in the **Malaysian Federation**, inaugurated in 1963, with Brunei exiting at the last minute. Sarawak's inclusion in the federation was opposed by Indonesia, and skirmishes broke out along the Sarawak–Kalimantan border, with Indonesia arming communist guerrillas inside Sarawak, who opposed both British and Malay rule. During this insurgency, known as the **Konfrontasi**, the small Sarawak army needed to call upon British military aid to help defend the bazaar towns in the interior; the conflict continued for three years, but was eventually put down by Malaysian troops aided by the British.

Throughout the 1960s and 1970s reconstruction programmes strengthened regional communities and provided housing, resources and jobs. These days, Sarawak is a predominantly peaceful, multiracial state, though social tensions have been triggered by the government's economic strategy, initially concerned with the environmental impact of the **timber industry**. Over the last few years, however, the question of land rights has become paramount (see box, p.403).

Sarawak has long battled with Kuala Lumpur over the issue of national funding and political loyalties. Politics in the state is certainly complex, with much horse-trading involving the Iban-dominated **Sarawak National Party** (SNAP) and various Muslim-led parties (Muslims constitute less than a third of the state's population). During SNAP's period of power in the state, many felt that central government funding was inadequate and that Sarawak was being overlooked; federal policies led to an erosion of their power base. In a revealing twist, Dayak and Orang Ulu politicians have in recent years changed sides and tied their flags to the Barison Nasional mast, invariably taking the longhouse constituencies with them. The staggering results of 1999's national elections speak for themselves: for the first time, opposition parties won no seats in Sarawak. It does seem to be the case that the state's coffers are now fuller than ever before, making development – whether it be in the form of new hospitals, roads or better equipped schools – quicker and easier to bring on stream.

THE SOUTHWEST

The most densely populated part of the state, **southwest Sarawak** supports around one and a half million people. It's also the only part of the state to be well served by road, a reflection of its long-standing trading importance. Malays from Sumatra and Java first arrived 1300 years ago, Chinese traders have been visiting the region since the eighth century, while Iban tribes migrated here from the Kapuas river basin in present-day Kalimantan around three hundred years ago, supplanting the original Bidayuh population. A second wave of Chinese immigrants settled here in the eighteenth century, initially to mine gold and antimony, the latter then in great demand in Europe for use in medicines and dyes. Later, when the bottom dropped out of the antimony market, the Chinese switched their endeavours to growing pepper and rubber.

Set upriver from the swamp-ridden coastline, **Kuching** is likely to be visited as a starting point for the more adventurous travelling to be done beyond Sibu, four hours away by boat. But the city and surroundings contain enough to occupy a couple of weeks' sightseeing. Kuching's **Sarawak Museum** holds the state's best collection of ethnic artefacts, antique ceramics, brassware and natural-history exhibits, while easy day-trips include visits to the **Gunung Gading** and **Kubah parks**, **Matang Wildlife Centre** and **Jong's Crocodile Farm**, all to the south, and the **Sarawak Cultural Village**, on Santubong Peninsula to the north. You'll need more time for **Bako National Park** – at least a couple of days – as you will to visit the **Bidayuh communities** near the Kalimantan border or the languid coastal village of **Sematan** to the west. Visiting the Iban longhouses around the **Skrang, Ai and Lemanak rivers**, east of the capital, is more complicated altogether, though the trip is rewarded by the warm reception.

Kuching

With its many period attractions and modern, energetic atmospheric, **KUCHING** is one of the most pleasant cities in Malaysia. You could be mistaken for thinking that the city still runs to a nineteenth-century clock – some of its colonial architecture, like the restored courthouse and Astana (the local spelling of "istana"), still serve their original purpose. In the heart of the old town, the commercial district is a warren of crowded lanes in which Kuching's **Chinese** community run cafés, hotels, general stores and laundries. Main Bazaar, the city's oldest street, sports the remains of its original **godowns** – now converted into shops – overlooking Sungei Sarawak, Kuching's main supply route since the city's earliest days. What's really unique about Kuching, though, is its **atmosphere**, at once both exciting and laid-back; vibrant and mellow: a town where no one's ever too busy to introduce themselves and ask you where you're from. This is largely because the city has always been an ethnic melting pot – never truer than today – where travellers have always been made welcome. The city's 250,000 inhabitants are divided between Chinese, Malays, Indians and the various Dyak and Orang Ulu groups (mainly Iban and Bidayuh, but also Melanau, Kayan and Kenyah); the Chinese are the largest group, followed by the Iban.

In 1841, James Brooke came up the river, arriving at a village, known as Sarawak, which lay on a small stream called Sungei Mata Kuching (cat's eye), adjoining the main river; it seems likely that the stream's name was shortened by Brooke and came to refer to the fast-expanding settlement. However, a much-repeated tale has it that the first rajah pointed to the village and asked its name. The locals, thinking Brooke was pointing to a cat, replied – reasonably enough – "*kucing*" (cat). Either way, it wasn't until 1872 that Charles Brooke officially changed the settlement's name from Sarawak to Kuching.

Until the 1920s, the capital was largely confined to the south bank of Sungei Sarawak, stretching only from the Chinese heartland around Jalan Temple, east of today's centre, to the Malay kampung around the mosque to the west. On the north bank, activity revolved around the fort and a few dozen houses reserved for British officials. It was the prewar **rubber boom** which financed the town's expansion: Jalan Padungan, an elegant tree-lined avenue, 1km east of the centre, became the smart place in which to live and work. The kampung areas increased in size, too, as the population was swollen by the arrival of a new bureaucracy of Malay civil servants, as well as by Dyaks from the interior and immigrants from Hokkien province in mainland China looking for work. The city escaped serious destruction during World War II, since Japanese bombing raids were mainly intent on destroying the oil wells in the north of Sarawak – the few bombs that were dropped on Kuching missed the military base at Fort Margherita and set fire to a fuel store.

Since independence, business has boomed, and though many of the impressive nineteenth-century buildings have been restored, others have been destroyed to make way for new roads and office developments. However, the planners cast a sympathetic eye over perhaps the most important part of Kuching. Following large-scale renovation, a pedestrianized riverside area, referred to as the **waterfront**, once again integrates the city with the waters to which it owes its growth. The city is culturally exciting too; its **Sarawak Museum**, with its lovely ceramic jars once so popular with longhouse communities, is one of the finest in Malaysia, and whenever there's an auspicious date in the Chinese calender, the **Chinese temple** is a frenzy of celebration and activity.

Arrival, information and transport

Kuching's **airport** is 11km south of the city; conveniently, the arrivals hall contains a currency exchange (daily 8am–8pm). To reach the city centre, take either a taxi (buy coupons from a booth outside the arrivals hall; RM16.50) or the #12a bus, which runs from directly outside the terminal to the bus station on Lebuh Jawa (daily 7am–6pm; every 40min; 30min; 90 sen), one of several stations in the centre (see "Day-trips" p.375). The **long-distance bus station**, where buses frequently arrive from all main towns in Sarawak and from Pontianak in Kalimantan, is at Jalan Penrissen, 5km south of town, from where Sarawak Transport Company buses #3 and #3a (daily 6.30am–6pm; every 30min; 50 sen) run to Lebuh Jawa; a taxi into town from Jalan Penrissen costs RM10. **Boats** from Sibu and Sarikei dock at the Bintawa wharf (also known as the Express Association wharf), 5km east of the city centre in the suburb of Pending. You can walk down to the main road, 100m away, and catch bus #17 or #19 into the centre (daily 6am–11pm; every 30min; 30min; 60 sen); these buses run along Main Bazaar before reaching the bus station at Jalan Masjid.

Information
There is a small **Sarawak Tourist Association** (STA) desk in the airport (daily 8am–5pm; ☎082/456266), but their main office is next to the Sarawak Steamship Building on Main Bazaar, at the junction with Jalan Tun Haji Openg (Mon–Thurs 8.30am–12.45pm & 2–4.15pm, Fri 8.30–11.30am & 2.30–4.45pm, Sat 8am–12.45pm;

MOVING ON FROM KUCHING

BY AIR

Take a taxi or the #12a bus from the station on Lebuh Jawa out to the airport (flight enquiries on ☎082/457373). Apart from flights to Singapore, Brunei and other cities in Malaysia (see p.442 for details), there are services to Pontianak (RM170) in Indonesian Kalimantan.

BY BOAT

Express Bahagia, 50 Jalan Padungan (☎082/421948), runs daily direct services to **Sarikei** (RM29) and **Sibu** (RM33), departing at 12.30pm from Bintawa wharf. There's no need to book in advance; simply turn up half an hour before the boat departs and buy your tickets at the jetty.

BY BUS

Long-distance **buses** to points north in Sarawak, and southwards to Kalimantan, depart from the Jalan Penrissen bus station. Larger express-bus companies operating out of the Jalan Penrissen terminal include Biaramas Express (☎082/452139); PB Express (☎082/461277), whose downtown agent is Natural Colour, in Lebuh Khoo Hun Yeng's Electra House; and Borneo Highway Express (☎082/619689), tickets for whose services are available at Yong Ngee Loong, 43 Jalan Gambir (☎082/243794). The green-and-yellow buses of the Sarawak Transport Company depart from the western end of Lebuh Jawa for Anna Rais, Serian, Sri Aman and Lubok Antu. For details of departures to sights in the vicinity of Kuching, see p.375.

☎082/240620). This has plenty of maps (including free city maps), bus timetables, hotel listings and dozens of glossy leaflets on everything from weaving to tattooing. For a detailed map of Sarawak state, ask for the "Periplus" Sarawak map at one of the city's specialist booksellers (see p.374). There's another tourist office, the Sarawak Tourism Board's **Visitor Information Centre** (Mon–Thurs 8am–2.15pm, Fri 8am–4.45pm, Sat 8am–12.45pm; ☎082/410942), on Jalan Mosque overlooking the Padang. Besides giving general information, it contains the booking desk of the National Parks and Wildlife Office, which issues overnight-stay **permits** for Bako National Park (call ☎082/248088 for booking enquiries).

For comprehensive listings of hotels and restaurants in and around the city, pick up a copy of Mike Reed and Wayne Tarman's excellent, free *Official Kuching Guide*, available in all city hotel lobbies; the booklet also gives insights into visiting longhouses. The English-language *Borneo Post*, available at all newsagents, only contains a small section on cultural events in the state.

City transport

You can **walk** around much of downtown Kuching with ease and so will have little use for the city buses. A few of the local bus routes are handy, including the Chin Lian Long company's blue-and-white buses which trundle out from Jalan Mosque to the Indonesian consulate, the immigration office and Bintawa wharf.

The main **taxi rank** is at the western end of Jalan Gambier. You can usually flag down a taxi in front of the plush hotels along Jalan Tunku Abdul Rahman; avoid going into any of the hotel concourses, however, as the fixed prices charged by the taxis are a lot steeper when the pick-up point is a hotel. You should always negotiate the price before starting the trip – often the "fixed rate" lowers after a bit of haggling; getting across the city from, say, the *Holiday Inn Kuching* to Lebuh Jawa shouldn't cost more than RM6. Note that fares increase significantly after midnight.

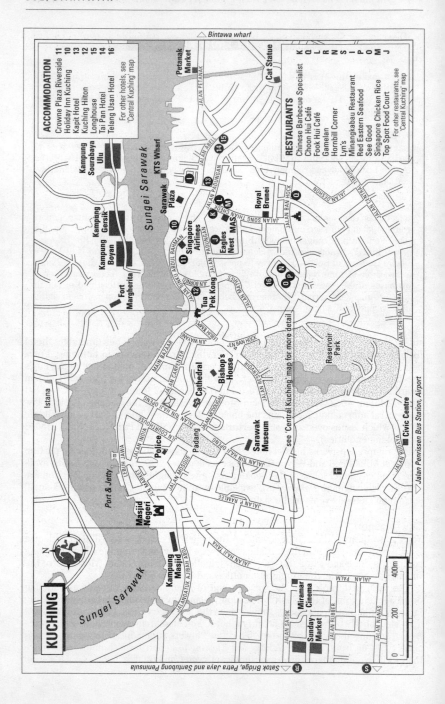

KUCHING

ACCOMMODATION
Crowne Plaza Riverside 11
Holiday Inn Kuching 10
Kapit Hotel 13
Kuching Hilton 12
Longhouse 15
Tai Pan Hotel 14
Telang Usan Hotel 16
For other hotels, see
'Central Kuching' map

RESTAURANTS
Chinese Barbecue Specialist K
Choon Hui Café L
Fook Hui Café R
Gamelan N
Hornbill Corner S
Lyn's I
Minangkabau Restaurant P
Red Eastern Seafood O
See Good M
Singapore Chicken Rice J
Top Spot Food Court
For other restaurants, see
'Central Kuching' map

Diesel-powered **tambang** boats (daily 6am–10pm; every 15min; 20 sen) depart from the jetty opposite the courthouse on the waterfront, crossing Sungei Sarawak to reach Fort Margherita in the northern part of Kuching. The boat trip only takes a few minutes. Should you wish to cruise the river at greater leisure, you can rent your own *tambang* for around RM20 per hour.

Accommodation

Finding inexpensive **accommodation** in Kuching isn't easy – be prepared to pay around RM30 for a double room if the budget places are full. There are quite a number of reliable mid-range lodging houses in the Jalan Green Hill area, a five-minute walk southeast from Main Bazaar and the waterfront. At the top end of the scale, most of the expensive hotels have great views over the river, as well as swimming pools and 24-hour service. If you want to stay on the coast, head for the Santubong Peninsula (see p.377). All the hotels below are marked on either the map of greater Kuching opposite or central Kuching overleaf.

Anglican Rest House, Jalan McDougall (☎082/240188). Kuching's best deal is set in the gardens of the Anglican Cathedral. It's often full (particularly in August), so call to book ahead. The main two-storey, wooden colonial building has comfortable, twin-bed rooms with high ceilings and shared bathrooms, and there are also two self-contained apartments with bedroom, veranda and bathroom. The resthouse has had a few security problems, so don't leave valuables unattended. ②.

Arif, Jalan Haji Taha (☎082/241211). Snug and friendly place, handily positioned for the night market. A variety of rooms are available, with fan, air-con and bath. ②.

B&B Inn, first floor, 30–31 Jalan Tabuan (☎082/237366). Kuching's only backpacker-oriented address has dorms, a handful of bare but tidy private rooms sharing common facilities, and a toast-and-tea breakfast thrown in for good measure. ②, dorm beds RM14.

Borneo, 30 Jalan Tabuan (☎082/244122). Comfortable hotel – Kuching's oldest – whose lovely rooms have polished wooden floors, air-con, bath or shower, and TV. ④.

Crowne Plaza Riverside, Jalan Tunku Abdul Rahman (☎082/247777, *www.holidayinn-sarawak.com/hik.html*). One of Kuching's priciest and most opulent hotels, this ten-floor marble extravaganza offers all the comforts and amenities you could wish for: several classy restaurants and bars, full sporting facilities, a business centre and an adjoining shopping complex. The views from the river-facing rooms are breathtaking. ⑦.

Fata Hotel, Junction of Lobuh Temple and Jalan McDougall (☎082/248111). In an excellent location, a few metres from Reservoir Park. The small rooms have air-con, showers and TV. ③.

Holiday Inn Kuching, Jalan Tunku Abdul Rahman (☎082/423111, fax 426169, *www.holidayinn-sarawak.com/hik.html*). Overlooking the river, with some of the rooms (for an extra RM20) looking directly out onto the fort on the opposite bank. There's a pool, restaurant and bookshop. ⑦.

Kapit Hotel, 59 Jalan Padungan (☎082/420961). Away from the centre and popular with a Malaysian business clientele. Rooms have air-con, shower and TV. ②.

Kuching, 6 Jalan Temple (☎082/413985). About the best budget option if the *B&B Inn* is full. That said, it's very basic, with one shower and toilet on each floor; each room has a fan and sink. ①.

Kuching Hilton, Jalan Tunku Abdul Rahman (☎082/248200). Another top-class hotel, whose front rooms have a great view of the river. There's a pool and a mouthwatering range of food and drink outlets. ⑦.

Longhouse, Jalan Abell (☎082/419333). East of the centre, this hotel is frequented mainly by visiting business people. Rooms have air-con, shower and TV. ②.

Mandarin, 6 Jalan Green Hill (☎082/418269). One of the most promising places in the area. Full facilities – air-con, shower, toilet and TV – but most of the rooms are rather small. ③.

Merdeka Palace Hotel, Jalan Tun Abang Haji Openg (☎082/258000, *www.jaring.my/mpalace*). This excellent place boasts large rooms with air-con, TV and elegant bathrooms, and a fine restaurant. The rooms at the front overlook the Padang; there are sometimes reductions on rooms at the back. ⑤.

Orchid Inn, 2 Jalan Green Hill (☎082/411417). Like the *Mandarin*, this is fairly comfortable and close to some excellent cafés; it has particularly friendly staff. ③.

Tai Pan, 93 Jalan Padungan (☎082/417363). Cosy, family-run place, situated on a lane just off the main street. The rooms, though small, have air-con, shower and TV. ②.

Telang Usan, Jalan Ban Hock (☎082/415588, fax 425316, *tusan@po.jaring.my*). This gem of a hotel has superb art by the late Kenyah artist Tusan Padan adorning the walls. A meeting point for most of Kuching's cognoscenti and all Orang Ulu people living in or visiting the city, it boasts an excellent restaurant and bar too. Recommended. ④.

The City

The central area of the city, sandwiched between Jalan Courthouse to the west, Jalan Wayang to the east and Reservoir Park to the south, is usually referred to as **colonial Kuching**. The courthouse, the post office and the Sarawak Museum are the most impressive buildings here, with the museum itself the city's most absorbing attraction; if you exclude the museum, the buildings will occupy only an hour or two of your time. Set within this small area is **Chinatown**, which incorporates the main shopping streets – Main Bazaar and Jalan Carpenter. To the east of Jalan Wayang lie Jalan Green Hill, Jalan Tunku Abdul Rahman and Jalan Padungan, the principal hotel districts. The area around Jalan Tunku Abdul Rahman is gradually becoming the new town centre, with

bars, pubs and plazas galore. Further south from the old town's narrow, busy streets – yet only fifteen minutes' walk from the river – is **Reservoir Park**; while bordering the colonial area, on the western edge of the centre, is Jalan India, another shopping hot spot and home, as the name suggests, to several of the city's best Indian restaurants. A short hop further west is the state **mosque** and main Malay residential area, dominated by detached kampung-style dwellings with sloping roofs, intricate carvings around the windows and elevated verandas. Southwest of here, Satok bridge leads to Kuching new town and the timber museum, while north, across the river, is **Fort Margherita** – now the Police Museum – and the **Astana**, still the residence of Sarawak's head of state.

The courthouse and the waterfront

The most obvious place to start is at the square, white **courthouse**, on the south bank at the junction of Main Bazaar and Jalan Tun Haji Openg. Built in 1874, and sporting impressive Romanesque columns and a balcony, the courthouse is fronted by the **Charles Brooke Memorial**, a six-metre-high granite obelisk erected in 1924, at whose four corners are stone figures representing the four largest ethnic groups in Sarawak: the Chinese, Dyaks, Malays and Orang Ulu. Today the four-room court still holds sessions to which the public are admitted (Mon–Thurs 10am–noon); it's worth going inside the main court chamber in any case to see the ceiling and wall **murals**, the traditional designs painted by artists from various tribal groups. These vividly coloured paintings contain scenes from longhouse life: a woman weaving *pua kumba* cloth on her loom, men hunting with blowpipes, and celebrations after the rice harvest.

When, in the 1830s, the rebellious Chinese gold-miners who nearly ended James Brooke's tenuous rule ran amok through the streets of Kuching, they razed the riverside wooden fort that used to stand directly north of the courthouse. The miners were sentenced to death across the road, and the site of the fort was redeveloped. Today, all that remains is the single-turreted **Square Tower**. It's one element of the recent restoration and reclamation which created Kuching's delightful **waterfront**, stretching almost a kilometre from the Jalan Gambier markets in the west, past the Tower, as far east as the *Holiday Inn*. The waterfront has quickly become *the* place to see and be seen in the evening, its manicured lawns enlivened by sculptures and seating areas. Several of the godowns (warehouses) that once fronted onto the river were sacrificed during the development, but two fine buildings – the lovingly restored Sarawak Steamship Building, and the former Chinese General Chamber of Commerce (see p.369) – have survived. Early-morning strollers here will see elderly Sarawakians going about their daily t'ai chi routines.

South to Bishop's House

Just south of the courthouse, the **Round Tower** was originally built as a dispensary in the 1880s, its austere dimensions explained by the fact that it was designed to double as a fort in an emergency. Directly opposite, across Jalan Tun Haji Openg, is the absurdly grand **post office**, whose massive ornamental columns, semicircular arches and decorative friezes were outmoded almost as soon as they were completed in 1931. Continuing south, skirt the well-groomed grassland known as **Padang Merdeka**, turn east onto Jalan McDougall and you'll see the modern Anglican **Cathedral**. A walk through its grounds leads to the oldest consecrated plot in Borneo, the European **cemetery**. An unassuming plot of land, and very easily missed, it nevertheless manages to conjure up the ghosts of old Kuching. Of the few stones still legible, one recalls Charles James Fox and Henry Steel, "officers of the Sarawak Government, who were treacherously murdered at Kanowit" in 1859. "Justice", the stone reassures us, "was done". A few steps further east stands another Kuching landmark, the large, two-storey wooden **Bishop's House**, built in 1849, making it the oldest surviving building in the city.

The Sarawak Museum

Back at the padang, head a little way south to reach Kuching's prime tourist attraction, the **Sarawak Museum** (daily except public holidays; free). Its main building, built in the 1890s (the largest colonial structure in Kuching), is set back from the road in love-ly gardens; another wing, opened in 1983, lies on the west side of Jalan Tun Haji Openg (it's connected to the main building by the bridge over the road). Recently closed for renovations, the newer building should be open again, perhaps with admission charges, by the time you read this.

It was Charles Brooke who conceived the idea of a museum in Kuching, prompted by the nineteenth-century naturalist Alfred Russell Wallace, the latter spending two years in Sarawak in the 1850s; Wallace's natural-history exhibits now form the basis of the collection on show in the main building. The museum's best-known curator was **Tom Harrisson** (1911–76), whose discovery of a 39,000-year-old skull in the caves at Niah in 1957 prompted a radical reappraisal of the origins of early man in Southeast Asia. Under the museum's auspices, Harrisson frequently visited remote Orang Ulu tribes, bringing back the ceremonial artefacts that comprise some of the museum's greatest assets, on display in the new wing.

THE MAIN BUILDING

There's an information desk at the main entrance, beyond which is the **natural science** section, whose varied exhibits include a massive hairball from a crocodile's stomach and fairly pedestrian displays highlighting the diverse range of plant, animal and bird species in Borneo. The **ethnographic** section on the upper floor is of an altogether different standard, despite the occasionally vague labelling. Here you can walk into an authentic wooden Iban longhouse (for more on longhouses, see box, opposite) and climb up into the rafters of the *sadau* (loft), which is used to store bamboo fish baskets, ironwork and sleeping mats; you're also free to finger the intricately glazed, sturdy Chinese ceramic jars and fine woven *pua kumbu* cloth. The Penan hut here is a much simpler affair, constructed of bamboo and rattan, within which are blowpipes and *parang*s (machetes), animal hides, coconut husks used as drinking vessels, and hardy back-baskets, made from the pandanus palm and the *bemban* reed. At the other end of the floor, there's a collection of fearsome Iban war totems, and woodcarvings from the Kayan and Kenyah ethnic groups who live in the headwaters of the Rajang, Baram and Balui rivers. One carving – a ten-metre-high ceremonial pole made of hardwood – sports a pattern of grimacing heads and kneeling bodies stretching up in supplication. Towering above all of this, on one of the walls, is a massive mural of images from long-house life: sowing and reaping rice, hunting, fishing, dancing and playing music. Cabinets lining the walls close by showcase **musical instruments** used by the various tribes: the Bidayuh's heavy copper gongs, Iban drums and the Kayan *sape*, a stringed instrument looking a little like a lute. Also, keep an eye out for the small collection of Iban *palangs* – two-centimetre-long rhinoceros-bone penis pins – which were once a popular method of re-energizing a wilting love life in the longhouse: inserted horizontally through the foreskin by the longhouse "doctor", in case you were wondering.

THE NEW WING

Across the road, in the new wing, there's an unparalleled collection of antique ceramics and brassware, prehistoric relics and early trading goods. In the main room upstairs, going anticlockwise, you come first to the **prehistoric artefacts**, including ceramic fragments found at Tom Harrisson's Niah and Santubong excavation sites – in particular remnants of plain, globular Neolithic vessels used in funerary rites. Early **Chinese ceramics**, exchanged by Chinese traders for spices, rattan and tropical birds, are well represented, too. Typical of the Song Dynasty is the dish decorated with carved lotus petals, and there's also a vase in the shape of two joined fishes with one

LONGHOUSES

In the nineteenth century, observers described Sarawak's **longhouses** as being up to 1km long and sometimes having many more than one hundred doors – the maximum number found today. Traditionally, longhouses were erected by rivers – the main means of transport for Sea Dyaks and Orang Ulu groups, though the predominant Land Dyak group, the Bidayuh, built their dwellings away from rivers, up in the hills.

Most longhouses were made from timber laced up with bamboo and rattan cord, and needed rebuilding every 20 to 30 years, when these organic materials rotted. A communal **veranda** (*tuai*) in front ran parallel to the **private apartment** (*bilek*) at the back, where the families ate, slept and kept their artefacts and possessions, some of which (like ceramic jars) can be centuries old. On the veranda the inhabitants socialized, dried rice, wove baskets and textiles, and greeted visitors. The older longhouses would have this veranda above the ground for security, and you would reach it by a near-vertical ladder; underneath the longhouse, pigs and chickens would rummage around, eating the various bits of debris thrown from above.

Nowadays longhouses are made with more long-lasting materials like concrete, for the floors and walls, and corrugated iron for the roofs. Most modern ones have the veranda as the ground floor and the animals kept behind the house, as in a Malay kampung. As in the old days, outlying huts, set away from the main house, are used to store grain.

While most **visits** to longhouses are made on organized tours these days, it's not uncommon for foreigners to be invited personally after they've struck up friendships with the locals. A good spot to meet members of Sarawak's indigenous communities is Kuching's *De Tavern* (see p.373); sometimes, however, even conversations with locals at riverside jetties can result in invitations. If you visit a longhouse independently, you aren't usually expected to pay for your stay. However, gifts of any sort are most welcome – from basic food supplies like meat, salt and sugar (or a financial contribution towards food) to Western clothes and cassettes; gifts of toys are guaranteed to endear you to the kids. The gifts should be given to the chief to distribute, as you are supposed to socialize with the chief's family first – unless you're there on the invitation of one of the other inhabitants, in which case you can present the gifts to your host. Should you turn up totally on spec, ask to meet the *tuai rumah* (headman); under no circumstances should you waltz up the stairs and into a longhouse uninvited. There's usually someone around who speaks some English, often the local teacher. Among other points of longhouse **etiquette**: shake hands with everybody who wants to shake yours but don't touch the locals anywhere else (for example, don't tousle the hair of the children). You can, however, eat as much as you want, without worrying if you seem to be eating the family's entire supply of food – it is the custom to stuff visitors, whether foreigners or next-door neighbours, and there's usually more food in reserve. You should also accept the offer to swim in the river – everybody goes, usually in small groups, for a wash at the start of the day and at dusk – but be careful not to reveal your anatomy; wear a sarong or shorts.

mouth. The Tang and Yuan Dynasty wares show a qualitative step forward – look for the beautiful blue-and-white glazed teapot decorated with a pair of dragons whose heads form the spout, tails the handle and legs the feet. Later fifteenth-century wares – the products of larger, more complex kilns – are more elaborate still. There are wonderful examples of work adorned with sprig moulding; one dish is decorated with a four-clawed dragon pursuing a flaming pearl.

From the tenth century onwards, Borneo's tribal groups traded rhinoceros horn, ivory and spices for Chinese ceramics, most notably colourful **storage jars**, which became closely linked to tribal customs and beliefs (see box, overleaf). Many of the hundreds of jars here are magnificent objects, in brown, black and vivid-green glazes, with dragon-emblazoned motifs. One spectacular giant is almost a metre high, coloured blue and white, and adorned with scenes of real and mythical Chinese life, incorporating the

The status and wealth of members of Sarawak's indigenous tribes depended on how many **ceramic jars** they possessed. Ranging in size from tiny, elegantly detailed bowls to much larger vessels, over a metre in height, the jars were used for a range of purposes including storage, brewing rice wine and making payments – dowries and fines for adultery and divorce settlements. The most valuable jars were only used for ceremonies like the *Gawai Kenyalang* (the rite of passage for a mature, prosperous man, involving the recitation of stories by the longhouse bard); or for funerary purposes: when a member of northern Sarawak's Berawan died, the corpse was packed into a jar in a squatting position. As decomposition took place, the liquid from the body was drained away through a bamboo pipe, leaving the individual's bones or clothing, which would subsequently be removed, placed in a canister and hoisted on to an ossuary above the river bank. It's said that the jars can also be used to foretell the future, and can summon spirits through the sounds they emit when struck.

intricate detail of plant petals, houses and epic landscapes. Contemporary ceramics that you find on sale in Kuching take their influence from these early jars, with skilled Chinese potters – mainly immigrants from Canton province – adopting the traditional decorative patterns of the ethnic groups, in animist images of birds, plants and fish.

The other major section is devoted to an exquisite **brassware** collection. Many of these superbly wrought cannons and kettles were crafted in Brunei and, again, through exchange with traders and merchants, many found their way into interior longhouses, where they were traditionally used to store wealth and as currency. Both kettles and cannons are strikingly ornate, adorned with miniature animals; in the case of the dragon cannons, the creature comprises the very body of the object.

From the Sarawak Museum to Reservoir Park

Behind the new wing of the museum, the **Islamic Museum** (daily except public holidays, 9am–6pm; free) is housed in the Madrasah Melayu Building, a former religious school, painted in brilliant white and with a cool tiled interior. The museum's seven galleries represent diverse aspects of Islamic culture, from architecture to weaponry, history to coinage, and textiles to prayer.

Back across the road at the Sarawak Museum's main building, a path through the sloping garden leads to the **Heroes Memorial** (commemorating the dead of World War II and the Konfrontasi (see p.358) – less than five minutes' walk away. You'll pass the **Kuching Aquarium** (daily 9am–6pm; free) on the way, which contains a small collection of marine life, including turtles from Sipadan in Sabah (see p.496). Following the path past the memorial takes you to the corner of the museum gardens and out onto narrow Jalan Reservoir, across which lies **Reservoir Park**, a beautiful, if artificial, tropical environment with many resident bird species and wildlife. Quiet during the day, it perks up in late afternoon; there's a café (daily 8am–4.30pm), a drinks kiosk, boats for rent, a playground and stretching frames for workout enthusiasts. The other road bordering the park, Lorong Park, leads up to the **Civic Centre** on Jalan Budaya, an ultramodern building with a **planetarium** (Tues only) and space for temporary exhibitions. The Sarawak Tourist Association office can provide information on current events here, though most visitors come for the restaurant on the top floor which has a **viewing platform** offering fine views over the city and – on a good day, as far as Kalimantan.

Chinatown and further east

Back at Jalan Tun Haji Openg, the grid of streets running eastwards to the main Chinese temple, Tua Pek Kong, constitutes Kuching's **Chinatown**. On busy Main

Bazaar and, one block south, on Jalan Carpenter, there are numerous cafés, restaurants, laundries and stores operating out of renovated two-storey shophouses, built by Hokkien and Teochew immigrants who arrived in the 1890s. The shophouses were originally divided into three sections: the front room was where the merchant conducted business and stored his goods (salt, flour, jungle products collected by indigenous peoples, and salted fish caught and prepared by Malay fishermen), the back room was the family quarters, and the loft was where the business partners would sleep. As part of the renewal of the waterfront, all these shophouses have now been spruced up, and the classy antique stores given a new lick of paint.

Sandwiched between the western ends of Jalan Tunku Abdul Rahman and Jalan Padungan, overlooking the river, stands **Tua Pek Kong**, the oldest (it was built in 1876) Taoist temple in Sarawak; in accordance with Chinese tradition, its position was carefully divined through geomancy. Plenty of people drop by during the day to pay their respects to the temple deity, Tua Pek Kong, who is much in demand in this dynamic city. Supplicants burn paper money and joss sticks, and pray for good fortune. The temple maintains an immensely busy cultural life, especially during Chinese New Year, when it plays host to theatrical and musical performances.

Tua Pek Kong may have been taking care of all matters spiritual in the Chinese community, but matters temporal were long the domain of the squat, cream-coloured edifice below on the waterfront, once the Chinese General Chamber of Commerce. The building now houses the **Chinese History Museum** (daily except Fri 9am–6pm; free), which makes use of paintings, black-and-white photographs and a modest selection of artefacts to chart the arrival and subsequent integration of Sarawak's Chinese community.

Jalan Tunku Abdul Rahman heads east from the Tua Pek Kong, past several of the swankier hotels and the Sarawak Plaza. Also leading east from the temple, a little way south of Jalan Tunku Abdul Rahman, is **Jalan Padungan**, which runs eastwards out to the edge of the city. The 1500-metre walk along this tree-lined avenue takes you past some splendidly ornate shophouses (whose elaborate decor was paid for by the rubber boom of the 1930s). At its eastern end, you can't fail to spot the **cat statue**, a 1.5-metre-high white-plaster effigy, her paw raised in welcome. Created by local artist Yong Kee Yet as a nod to the supposed derivation of the city's name, it's a popular spot for family photos.

North across Sungei Sarawak

The first buildings erected on the north side of the river were small dwellings, part of a Malay kampung. Following the arrival of the British in Kuching, Charles Brooke had two of the city's most important buildings constructed here. **Boats** cross from a number of waterfront jetties, including the one opposite the courthouse on Main Bazaar (daily 6am–10pm; every 15min; 20 sen). Once across the river, you can follow a marked path towards the **Astana**, built by Charles Brooke in 1869 and still the official home of Sarawak's governor. An elegant, stately building with a distinctive shingle roof, it's set in a long, sloping garden with an excellent view of the courthouse on the opposite bank. Various pieces of Brooke memorabilia and other relics are kept in one of the rooms, but unfortunately you can only visit the Astana on two days of the year, over the Hari Raya Puasa holiday at the end of Ramadan (see p.70).

Along the river bank, 1km to the east, is **Fort Margherita**; retrace your steps back to the jetty and you can follow a marked path there. The first fort built on this site was James Brooke's most important defensive installation, commanding the view along Sungei Sarawak. However, the fort was burned to the ground in 1857 by rebel Chinese gold-miners and was rebuilt by Charles Brooke in 1879, who named it after his wife. It is the finest example of the Brookes' system of fortifications, and renovations have ensured that it looks much as it did in the nineteenth century. There are around twenty other river forts of humbler construction throughout Sarawak, strategically placed to repel pirates and Dyak or Kayan war parties. Looking for all the world like a defensive English castle, Fort Margherita is the only one of the forts open to the public; the grounds and interior now house a **Police Museum** (Tues–Sun 10am–6pm; free, though take your passport as you need to have identification to gain entry). Outside the central keep stand old cannons and other pieces of artillery, while inside there is a solid collection of swords, guns and uniforms. There's even a reconstructed opium den, and exhibits on illegal games and drugs, while photographs recall the communist insurgency and Konfrontasi (see p.358).

From the fort, it's easy to thread your way eastwards and down to the Malay kampungs over which it stands guard: **Kampung Boyan** shades into **Kampung Gersik**, which in turn is assimilated by **Kampung Sourabaya Ulu**. All three feature wonderful clapboard stilthouses, some in cheery pastel blues and greens, others gloriously dilapidated, teetering on knock-kneed stilts and accessed by bowed promenades. From this side of the fort, boats will deposit you near the *Crowne Plaza Riverside Hotel* on the east side of the city centre.

From Jalan Gambier to Jalan Satok

Back at the waterfront on the south bank, heading west from Main Bazaar brings you onto Jalan Gambier, fronting which is the **cargo port** – less important than it once was, though still a fascinating place. In the late afternoon you'll see cargo boats from West Kalimantan unloading tons of tropical fruits to be sold in the nearby **markets**. One block back on Jalan Market, there's a series of open-air food stalls which are very much the focal point for the port workers, who tuck into noodle soups and stir fries, *roti canai* and dhal throughout the day. East of here a handsome arch leads into **Jalan India**, the busiest pedestrian thoroughfare in Kuching and the best place in the city to buy shoes and cheap clothing. The street is named after the Indian coolies who arrived in the early part of the twentieth century to work at the docks; at no. 37, a dim passageway leads to the oldest of the Indian community's mosques, dating back to the mid-nineteenth century.

About 100m west of the Jalan Market food stalls is the **Masjid Negara** (9am–3pm; closed Fri), standing on a steep hill, its gold cupolas glinting in the dying sun at evening prayers. There's been a mosque on this site for around two hundred years, though this one only dates from the 1960s. Male visitors must wear long trousers and women skirts and a headscarf (this is provided by the mosque at the entrance). From here, following the curve of the river southwest for 300m or so along Jalan Datuk Ajibah Abol, you reach the Malay enclave of **Kampung Masjid**. The area retains many well-preserved family houses, built at the start of the twentieth century by well-to-do government officials, and boasting traditional features such as floor-level windows fronted by carved railings.

To the south of Kampung Masjid is the wide, traffic-clogged **Jalan Satok**. At its junction with Jalan Palm, opposite the Miramar Cinema, lies the site of Kuching's **Sunday market**, which actually kicks off on Saturday afternoon; it continues until about midnight, picks up again at 7am on Sunday and finally ends around noon. Buses #4a and #4b get you there from the Matang Transport Company bus station on Jalan P. Ramlee, or from outside the post office, in five minutes. This is the place for picking up supplies of everything from rabbits to knives; other stalls sell satay, curry pie, sweets and *lycheesank*, a soft drink – Iban in origin – made with puréed beans, rice pellets, sugar and lychees. Amid the congested confusion, look out for the alley where Dyaks sell fruit, vegetables and handicrafts – a good place to pick up inexpensive baskets and textiles.

Petra Jaya

Across Satok bridge, southwest of the centre, the road careers round to the northern part of Kuching and the new town, known as **Petra Jaya**. This is an ugly area, devoid of any real interest and, compared to the older parts of Kuching, apparently devoid of life, too. Still, it's where you'll find two contrasting museums.

The appropriately log-shaped **Timber Museum** (Mon–Thurs 8.30am–4pm, Fri 8.30–11.30am & 2.30–4.30pm, Sat 8am–12.30pm; free) is next to the stadium on Jalan Wisma Sumbar Alam, which is the main thoroughfare in Petra Jaya; bus #8 runs here from the Matang Transport Company terminal. Built in 1985 for the express purpose of putting across the timber industry's point of view in the increasingly acrimonious debate on tropical deforestation, the museum does its job well, with informative displays and exhibits, and plenty of facts and figures about tree types and the economic case for logging. Hardly surprisingly, the other side of the argument – the devastation of land which has been farmed for generations by the tribal groups – isn't addressed. The rationale that economic development must come before all other considerations fails to address the simple fact that most of the timber-related wealth either goes into the pockets of big business tycoons, or is siphoned off in state taxes to the national government. The displays even suggest that the Dyaks, who have lost much of their customary land through deforestation, have ultimately gained as they now live in less remote areas with health and education facilities nearby. But many ethnic groups, who have recently set up representative committees, would say the forests are their livelihood: remove the forests and tribal culture eventually withers and dies.

There's some light relief in the **Cat Museum** (Tues–Sun 9am–5pm; free) in Petra Jaya's DBKU Building, visible from just about all over Kuching. Claiming to be the only such museum in the world, the exhibits take as their starting point the supposed derivation of the city's name from the Malay word for "cat" – which means photos of cats from around the world, *Garfield* comic strips, feline-related art and folklore that's strictly for cat freaks. To get here, take bus #2b from the Petra Jaya bus company's terminus, near Jalan Market.

Eating and nightlife

Kuching is a great city for **food**, with a lot of conspicuous spending fuelling a competitive scene where new places are opening – or shutting – almost every week. Local **specialities** such as wild boar and deer sometimes crop up on Chinese menus; seafood favourites include steamed pomfret fish and *umai*. The jungle fern vegetables, *midin* and *paku*, are available throughout the city, and delicious rubbery little vegetables, *ambal* (sometimes called "bamboo clam" and known locally as "monkeys' penises"), are a wild delicacy, collected amongst the mangrove swamps lining the coast and rivers. In addition, Kuching has its own versions of *kuey teow* (thick rice noodles, with meat and vegetables in gravy), and *laksa*, the latter often slurped down by Sarawakians for breakfast, though some prefer *kolok mee*, an oily, tasty dish featuring dry noodles.

With such a rich range of dishes to sample, it's worth noting that many of the **cafés** and **hawker stalls**, especially those along Jalan Carpenter, close at around 7pm; even the top **restaurants** close early, with last orders at around 10pm. However, Kuching's **nightlife** has, in recent years, begun to take off, with bars and discos attracting varied crowds most nights of the week, until 3 or 4am.

Food centres and hawker stalls

Gerai Anekarasa Hawker Centre, Jalan Satok, under the bridge; you can take any Petra Jaya bus there. Famous for its barbecued chicken and steaks; a whole chicken plus rice and vegetables only costs around RM10 for two here.

Jalan Carpenter Hawkers, Jalan Carpenter. Opposite the Chinese temple, this compact centre has a range of dishes including excellent *laksa*. Popular with Kuching's young Chinese.

Jalan Market open-air market. Massive hawker centre that's very cheap and popular with locals for basic rice, noodle and curry dishes; a handful of stalls sell seafood and beer into the early hours.

Petanak Market, Jalan Petanak. West of the *Longhouse Hotel*, this early-morning market has a food centre that kicks off at 5am, making it an excellent option at the end of a very late night out; all regional cuisines are represented.

Top Spot Food Court, sixth floor, Taman Keret, Jalan Padungan. Set above a car park, the stalls in this open-sided food court offer everything from seafood to satay, and claypot to steak; all benefit from a fine view out over the city.

Restaurants and cafés

Chin Heng Café, 5 Jalan Green Hill. Taxi drivers' haven and local café for those who stay in the nearby inns. Breakfast is served until 11am, after which delicious chilled beans, sweet and sours, and stir fries appear for around RM3 a portion. Run by a very friendly family.

Chinese Barbecue Specialist, Jalan Padungan. Takeaway meals of barbecued duck, chicken and back cuts of pork are hacked up unceremoniously and laid on rice at the front of this bustling, rough and ready shophouse; a Cantonese kitchen with a sitting area operates out the back.

Choon Hui Café, Jalan Ban Hock. Storming *laksa* and filling *kolok mee* make this plain coffee shop, near Kuching's Hindu temple, a huge breakfast-time hit with locals.

City Tower, Civic Centre, Jalan Budaya. The decent Chinese food at this plush restaurant is outshone by the marvellous city views. Around RM50 for two people.

Denis' Place, 80 Main Bazaar. Western-style café-bar with superb international cuisine, coffee and pastries.

Fook Hui, Jalan Padungan. Famed coffee shop whose reputation depends, in part, on its *ha kau* pork dumplings.

Gamelan, Wisma Gaya, off Jalan Simpang Tiga (☎082/410026). This Indonesian restaurant is a real treat and well worth the RM5 taxi ride to get you there. *Ikan asam pedas* (hot and sour fish) is a particularly tasty option.

Hornbill Corner, Jalan Ban Hock. Excellent outdoor seafood restaurant well known for steamboat where you grill stingray and marinated meats on a barbecue plate yourself.

Jubilee Restoran, 49 Jalan India. Excellent Malay restaurant set amid busy textile stores. The *kacang goreng* (peanuts in fish paste), *sayur* (green beans in chilli and lemon) and *tahu* (bean-curd) are particularly tasty house specials – or simply make do with a *roti canai* or a *murtabak*. Full meals from RM8 for two.

Lyn's, 10, Lot 62, Lorong 4, Jalan Nanas (☎082/234934). Tandoori specialist, a short taxi ride from the town centre, but worth seeking out for its excellent North Indian menu. Closed Sun.

Madinah, 47 Jalan India. Dependable (mainly) Malay food, next door to the *Jubilee*; the beef *rendang* is particularly good, as is the fish curry.

Meisan Restoran, ground floor, *Holiday Inn Kuching*, Jalan Tunku Abdul Rahman. Spicy Szechuan food. Although the Sunday-lunchtime *dim sum* is reasonably priced, evening meals are expensive, at RM50 for two including beer, but worth splashing out for.

Minangkabau, 168 Jalan Chan Chin Ann. Excellent Indonesian restaurant with a tasty range of dishes specializing in chilli-hot fish curries and beef *rendang*, all for the very reasonable cost of around RM10–15 for two.

Nam Sen, 17 Jalan Market. Highly cool old coffee shop, complete with varnished chairs, marble tables and "No spitting" signs. Popular with boiler-suited workers from the nearby docks and handy for snatching an early-morning coffee or noodle soup before catching a bus.

National Islamic Café, Jalan Carpenter. Serves halal food, curries and unleavened bread from mid-morning until around 9pm. Very popular with visitors and inexpensive at RM3–4 a head.

Red Eastern Seafood, Jalan Ban Hock. Cracking steamboat place which also offers fruit and ice cream. One of a gaggle of popular seafood restaurants around Ban Hock.

River Café, Main Bazaar. Breezy waterfront café serving quite divine *popiah*, and a challenging *laksa*.

See Good, Jalan Ban Hock (in front of the *Telang Usan* hotel and beside the *Hornbill*). Don't be fooled by this seafood eating-house's inauspicious surrounds: standards of cooking are very high, and the owners friendly. Slipper lobster in pepper, bamboo clams, steamed pomfret, *ambal* and *midin* make for a fine dinner. This place also has the best range of wines of any restaurant in Kuching (and, arguably, across Sarawak). Two can eat heartily for RM60, including beer. Evenings only; closed on the fourteenth and eighteenth of every month.

Singapore Chicken Rice, Jalan Song Thian Cheok. Tasty fast food Southeast Asian style; ignore the tacky decor.

Steakhouse, *Kuching Hilton*, Jalan Tunku Abdul Rahman. One of Kuching's best-kept secrets, a tremendous international restaurant run by an Italian chef. All-you-can-eat buffet at lunch or a three-course meal in the evening for under RM50.

Tiger Garden Coffee Shop, Jalan Green Hill. Serves the best Chinese dumplings in town and great for other Chinese staples, too – RM3 a head, including coffee or tea.

Bars and nightclubs

Ang Café Bar and Club 11, ground floor, Riverbank Suites, Jalan Tunku Abdul Rahman. Pleasant café and bar overlooking the river. *Club 11* gets popular with locals from 8pm onwards.

De Tavern, Jalan Borneo. Facing the *Hilton* car park. A convivial Kayan-run watering-hole whose owner-manager is happy to pour a free glass of *tuak* for first-time visitors.

Dulit Terrace and Tuak Bar, *Telang Usan Hotel*, Jalan Ban Hock. Mellow bar at the front of Kuching's most pleasing hotel where you can develop a taste for *tuak* or sample excellent Kenyah home cooking. It's a meeting place for local journalists, tour leaders and visiting Kenyah.

Eagles' Nest, 20 Jalan Bukit Mata Kuching. Trendy Kuching hangout where you can dance to an up-to-date soundtrack of Sarawakian hits and international soul and house tracks, or shoot pool with the local experts. Stays open late.

Hornbill's Corner, Jalan Ban Hock. Just 100m from the *Telang Usan* hotel. Watching televised soccer matches, including UK games beamed down by satellite, is the prime activity at this great bar and restaurant.

Peppers, *Kuching Hilton*. The city's biggest club, with a house and techno dance floor downstairs and karaoke lounge upstairs.

The Royalist, Jalan Borneo. Directly above *De Tavern*. This English-style pub, with Brooke memorabilia, attracts a friendly set of locals and expatriates.

Shopping

Kuching is the best place in Sarawak to buy just about anything, especially tribal textiles and handicrafts. Most of the **handicraft** and **antique** shops are along Main Bazaar, Jalan Temple and Jalan Wayang. Kuching is well known for its locally produced Chinese pottery, whose decoration bears local Dyak influences. There are some ceramics stalls on the road to the airport, but it's better to visit the **potteries** (daily 8am–noon & 2–6pm) themselves, where you can walk around and watch the potters in action at the wheel and firing kilns; each pottery also has a shop on site. They're clustered together on Jalan Penrissen, 8km from town – take Sarawak Transport Company bus #3, #3a, #9a or #9b from Lebuh Jawa.

Arts of Asia, 68 Main Bazaar. One of the most comprehensive private galleries in town, it sells naturalistic paintings and sculpture, which tend to be expensive.

Atelier Galley, 104 Main Bazaar. Collection of handicrafts, *objet d'art*, furniture and antiques.

Borneo Adventure, 55 Main Bazaar. This shop, run by the tour operator of the same name, has the best postcards you can buy in Sarawak, including some excellent nature and ethnographic images.

Eeze Trading, just east of the *Holiday Inn Kuching* on Jalan Tunku Abdul Rahman. Souvenirs for the person who has everything – it's the only shop in the city selling dried insects.

Galeri M, at the *Hilton* hotel and Main Bazaar. Besides beadwork, hornbill carvings and Sarawakian antiques, you can find a massive range of contemporary local art here.

Ngee Tai Pottery Factory, eighth mile, Jalan Penrissen. Located on the right-hand side of the road as you head out of town, this is probably the best of the potteries here. The master potter, Ng Hua

Ann, shows visitors a wide range of ceramic wares ranging from huge pots to small souvenir items such as coffee mugs and flower vases.

Sarakraf, 14 Main Bazaar. Decent stock of baskets, textiles and ironwork.

Sarawak Batik Art Shop, 1 Jalan Temple. A fine collection of Iban *pua kumbu* textiles (see p.389).

Sarawak House, 67 Main Bazaar. Flashy and expensive but usually worth a look for textiles and longhouse artefacts.

Sarawak Plaza, Jalan Tunku Abdul Rahman, close to the *Holiday Inn Kuching*. This mall is the major focus for Western products – fashion accessories, shirts and shoes, and dance-music cassettes. The handicraft store has a good range of bags, T-shirts and ethnic jewellery. Perhaps the most useful stop is the pharmacy on the first floor.

Sing Ching Loon, 57 Main Bazaar. The handicrafts and antiques here are pricey, though it's good for a browse.

Tan Brothers, Jalan Padungan, close to the junction with Jalan Mathies. Baskets, carvings and bags.

Telang Usan, Jalan Ban Hock. The shop in the hotel lobby sells superb Penan and Orang Ulu crafts.

Yeo Hing Chuan, 46 Main Bazaar. Interesting carvings and other handicrafts; a quality thirty-centimetre carved hardwood figure costs about RM400.

Listings

Airlines MAS, Lot 215, Jalan Song Thian Cheok (☎082/246622); Merpati, c/o Sin Hwa Travel Service, 8 Lebuh Temple (☎082/246688); Royal Brunei Airlines, first floor, Rugayah Bldg, Jalan Song Thian Cheok (☎082/243344); Singapore Airlines, Wisma Bukit Maja Kuching, Jalan Tunku Abdul Rahman (☎082/247777).

Airport Flight enquiries on ☎082/457373.

Banks and exchange Hong Kong Bank, 2 Jalan Tun Haji Openg; Overseas Union Bank, junction of Main Bazaar and Jalan Tun Haji Openg; Standard Chartered, Wisma Bukit Maja Kuching, Jalan Tunku Abdul Rahman. There are moneychangers at the airport (daily 8am–8pm) and in the city: Majid & Sons, 45 Jalan India, and Mohamad Yahia & Sons, in the basement of the Sarawak Plaza on Jalan Abell; both offer good rates.

Bookshops Bells Bookshop, third floor, Sarawak Plaza, and Mohamad Yahia & Sons, with branches in the *Holiday Inn* and the basement of the Sarawak Plaza; offer the best range of books in Sarawak, and also stock the best maps of the state; in addition, they sell the English-language *Borneo Post*, which features international news and a small section on events in the state. Sky Book Store, 57 Jalan Padungan, and Star Books, 30 Main Bazaar, are good for geographical, cultural and anthropological material.

Car rental Mayflower Car Rental, fourth floor, Bangunan Satok, Jalan Satok (☎082/410110); Pronto Car Rental, first floor, 98 Jalan Padungan (☎082/236889).

Consulates Indonesia, 111 Jalan Tun Haji Openg (Mon–Thurs 8.30am–noon & 2–4pm; ☎082/241734); New Zealand (☎082/482177); UK c/o British Council, Bangunan WSK (☎082/256044).

Hospitals Sarawak General Hospital, Jalan Ong Kee Hui (☎082/257555), charges RM1 for A & E consultations. For private treatment, go to Norman Medical Centre, Jalan Tun Datuk Patinggi (☎082/440055).

Internet access Cyber City, Taman Sri Sarawak, off Jalan Borneo (daily 10am–10pm; ☎082/257555).

Laundry All Clean Services, 175g Jalan Chan Chin Ann (☎082/243524); Mr Dobi, Jalan Chan Chin Ann (next block along from *Pizza Hut*), daily 8am–7.30pm.

Pharmacy Apex Pharmacy, Electra House, Lebuh Power (☎082/246011), and second floor, Sarawak Plaza, Jalan Tunku Abdul Rahman; UMH, Jalan Song Thian Cheok (opposite MAS).

Police Central Police Station, opposite Pandang Merdeka (☎082/241222). Come here to report stolen and lost property.

Post office The main post office is on Jalan Tun Haji Openg (Mon–Sat 8am–6pm, Sun 10am–1pm); post restante/general delivery can be collected here – take your passport.

TOUR OPERATORS IN KUCHING

The standard of the **tours** on and around the Ai, Lemanak and Skrang rivers, 300km east of Kuching, is high. The Iban **longhouses** here are vibrant, fascinating places, and always welcoming. It's worth shopping around to see who's offering the best deal, as some companies are now charging below the hitherto standard fee of RM100 per person per day.

Asian Overland, 286a first floor, Westwood Park, Jalan Tubuan (☎082/251163). Good longhouse trips in the Kuching vicinity and on the Batang Ai river system (see p.386 for details). Also arranges trips further afield to Mulu National Park and on the "Head-hunters Trail" from Mulu to Lawas.

Borneo Adventure, 55 Main Bazaar (☎082/245175). Award-winning operation running excellent trips throughout Sarawak and Sabah, including some splendid treks around the Kelabit Highlands. Its jungle lodge (◎), a longhouse-style hotel set beside the Ulu Ai longhouse of Nanga Sumpa, is a triumph of ecotourism.

Borneo Transverse, 16 Jalan Green Hill (☎082/257784). Excellent, veteran outfit which offers, amongst others, a unique tour to an Iban longhouse on the Lemanak

river which has recently been built to authentic specifications.

CPH Travel Agencies, 70 Jalan Padungan (☎082/243708). Sarawak's longest-established operator, with good contacts in the native communities.

Interworld, 161 Jalan Temple (☎082/252344). Organizes expeditions up the Skrang and Batang Ai rivers, plus Niah and Mulu adventures.

Telang Usan Transportation, second floor, 127a Bangunan Kelolong, Jalan Nagor (☎082/254787). Kenyah-run operation with excellent connections in the Baram region to the north of the state; it's the only operator offering trips to the longhouses around Long San on Batang Baram.

Tropical Adventure, 17 Main Bazaar (☎082/413088). Adventures on offer here include trekking around Bario, exploring Mulu and trips to Iban longhouses.

Swimming There's a pool at MBKS Bldg, Jalan Pending (Mon–Fri 2.30–9pm, Sat 6.45–8.45pm, Sun 9.30am–9pm; ☎082/426915); RM2 adults, RM1 children. Closed on public holidays.

Telephones International calls can be made at the Telekom office, Jalan Batu Lintang (Mon–Fri 8am–6am, Sat 8am–noon), from most public cardphones, and from all major hotels.

Visa extensions Head to the Immigration Office, first floor, Bangunan Sultan Iskander, Jalan Simpang Tiga (Mon–Fri 8am–noon & 2–4.30pm; ☎082/245661); take Chin Lian Long bus #11. Get there by 3.30pm to have your application processed on the day.

Day-trips around Kuching

The area **around Kuching** is well served by road, and at least a week's worth of interesting excursions can be made by bus or car without the trouble of hiring guides and porters. Within an hour's bus ride of the city are Kubah National Park, Matang Wildlife Centre and the villages, beaches and resorts on Santubong Peninsula. Some people stay out at one of the peninsula's luxury hotels, near to which is the Sarawak Cultural Village, a showpiece community where model longhouses are staffed by guides from each of the ethnic groups.

Three Kuching **bus** companies operate useful services within the area. From the western end of Lebuh Jawa, Sarawak Transport Company (STC) buses depart for Bau and Lundu to the west, and Jong's Crocodile Farm to the east. To head north to Damai, Santubong and Bako, use Petra Jaya Transport buses, which leave from below the open-air market on Jalan Market. Finally, for Matang and Kubah, take Matang Transport Company buses from the northern end of Jalan P. Ramlee.

Jong's Crocodile Farm

Jong's Crocodile Farm (daily 9am–5pm; RM5), 29km south of Kuching on the Serian Highway, is hardly an essential trip since, apart from at feeding times (daily 9am & 3pm), there isn't a great deal to see. But it's worth a quick look in, especially if you haven't got time to head upriver into Sarawak's interior, where you might have a more authentic, heart-stopping meeting with a crocodile. On the farm, various types of crocodiles (an endangered species in Sarawak) are bred on the premises; some are killed at a tender age and their skins sold. Just to keep you on your toes, the farm features some grisly photographic reminders that people are frequently attacked by crocodiles; one photo shows a dead croc whose stomach has been cut open, revealing an assortment of masticated animals. To get to the farm, take STC bus #3 or #3a to Siruban village (4 daily; 40min; RM2.30).

Kubah National Park

Located just 20km west of Kuching, the dipterocarp forest of **Kubah National Park** (RM3 fee, no permit needed) offers a pleasing and manageable day-trip out of Kuching; It's possible to get an early bus there (Matang Transport Company #11; hourly from 6.30 to 9.30am then every two hours until 4.50pm; RM1.65), have a vigorous hike and then get to Matang Wildlife Centre for the afternoon, returning to Kuching on the last bus (around 4.30pm from Matang Polytechnic). Situated on a sandstone plateau, this small park contains crystal-clear streams, waterfalls created out of hardened limestone and a wide selection of palms and orchids. Indeed Kubah is considered one of the richest sites for palm species in the world: ninety-five types have been found there, including coconut, sago and many rattans, with 18 of these species endemic to the region (among Sarawak's other parks, only Gunung Mulu has more types of native palm).

Three modest mountains – **Selang**, **Sendok** and **Serapi** – emerge out of the lush forest; they're crisscrossed by trails, waterfalls and streams. Staff at park headquarters will point you in the direction of Kubah's marked hikes, among them the three-hour **Ulu Raya Trail**, a good walk to catch sight of the palms; the **Waterfall Trail**, a ninety-minute uphill hike to impressive, split-level falls; and the **Bukit Selang Trail**, less than an hour's walk from headquarters and boasting some grand views. Kubah's best views, however, are from the three-hour **Gunung Serapi (Summit) Trail** – from the mountain's summit, you can see Kuching and much of southwestern Sarawak. The **Rayu Trail**, leads, after three hours, to the Matang Wildlife Centre. There's **accommodation** (RM40 for a bed in the resthouse; RM20 for a hostel bed) but no canteen or places to eat nearby, so bring your own provisions. Kuching's Visitor Information Centre (see p.361) handles bookings.

The Matang Wildlife Centre

The recently-opened **Matang Wildlife Centre** (RM3 entrance), 12km north of Kuba, is the place to go if you want to see orang-utans, who are kept here in large pens containing trees and other structures to climb. There's also accommodation and walking trails, as well as large enclosed areas of rainforest and spacious cages for numerous endangered wildlife species. Unfortunately public transport stops a little way short of the centre: take the #11 from outside Kubah parkgive bus to Matang from centre of Kuching; the bus terminates at Matang Polytechnic, from where you can walk or hitch-hike the remaining 5km to the centre. Getting a lift is actually very easy to do, as almost all the traffic along the road is going to the centre, mostly either staff or fellow visitors. When leaving the centre, it's worth asking others for a ride to the Polytechnic, Kubah or back into Kuching.

At the centre's headquarters just across Sungei Rayu, you'll find the **Interpretation Centre** on the right. A lot of thinking has gone into its exhibits, which provide a thorough grounding in endangered species in the state and throughout Malaysia; one exhibit is simply a mirror, which you stand in front of to read its caption: "What is the greatest danger to wildlife in Sarawak?" The photographs are excellent and the exhibits packed with facts; the section on orang-utans mentions that these human-like creatures are revered by local people because it's believed they showed humans the way to give birth naturally in the early days.

Behind here there's a **café** which provides basic rice and noodle lunches from 11am to 5pm. A path leads beside this through dense forest up to the enclosures (allow one hour to get round them all). The walk around the enclosures takes you past crocodiles; two aviaries which include hornbills, mynahs and pheasants; civets, sun bears and orang-utans. From a viewing platform you can watch the orang-utans up close as they rest and feed (feeding times are at 9am and 3pm).

Four other, short **trails** meander away from the café. Two lead to small waterfalls, one is circular and passes most of the enclosures, and the last, the Rayu trail, leads to Kubah Park (see opposite). Returning to the headquarters, you pass the **campsite** (RM4) and the other **accommodation** (chalets ②; dorm beds RM10). As with Kubah, it's better, though not essential, to book your accommodation in advance at the Visitors Information Centre in Kuching.

Santubong Peninsula

Located 25km north of Kuching and bordered by the Sarawak river to the south, the **Santubong Peninsula** (also called the Damai Peninsula) is dominated by the 810-metre Gunung Santubong. Once the site of a major eighth-century trading settlement, the peninsula is a region full of strangely shaped rocks within patches of secondary forest. Stretches of the river and coastline are being rapidly developed as a retreat for tourists and city-weary locals, with the *Holiday Inn Resort Damai Lagoon* and the *Holiday Inn Resort Damai Beach* setting the pace. Thankfully, these top-notch resorts haven't diluted the experience of sitting on the peninsula's golden sand, watching a spectacular sunset with Sarawak's lush green hills to one side and boats and small islands flashes of colour on the other side. Most people, other than *Holiday Inn* residents, come out to the peninsula to explore the riverside villages of Buntal and Santubong, or to visit the informative and entertaining **Sarawak Cultural Village**, a collection of traditionally built dwellings which showcases the lifestyles of the state's indigenous peoples.

Buntal, Kampung Santubong and the resorts

From Kuching's Petra Jaya bus company terminus (see p.375), the #2b bus (daily 6.40am–6pm; every 40min) makes the forty-minute trip through housing developments and small rubber and pepper plantations, leaving the main road and running along the edge of the river to **Buntal**. This quiet riverside kampung, bordered by forest, is famed in these parts for its **seafood restaurants**, which stand on stilts in the seaside shallows; *Lim Hok An* is the pick of the bunch. There's a small beach, too, and the locals offer short boat trips along Sungei Sarawak.

From Buntal, the bus returns to the main road and weaves up the lower reaches of Gunung Santubong, before turning east down a narrow road for 2km to **KAMPUNG SANTUBONG**, a very pretty place, set on an inlet with fishing boats hauled up onto the beach. Two Chinese cafés, *Son Hong* and the *Santubong*, whip up tasty stir-fry and rice dishes, and one of the houses opposite the *Santubong* takes lodgers (①); very few tourists actually stay on the peninsula unless it's at one of the resorts up the road (see below). There are some interesting **rock carvings** near Santubong – head back along the Kuching road for 200m and turn left just before the six-kilometre sign. Thirty metres down the track you'll see a path running between two rocks leading to some curiously carved boulders, one featuring a prone human figure; the other forms are hard to decipher. An exact dating hasn't been made, although archeologists think the images could be around a thousand years old.

The bus continues from Santubong for another 5km and, after winding further up the densely forested mountain road, dips down to the *Holiday Inn Resort Damai Beach* (☎082/846999, *www.holidayinn-sarawak.com/hirdb.html*; ⑧, promotional discounts often available), a mini-resort nestling in a natural hollow at the end of the road. Boasting a swimming pool and tennis courts alongside a private palm-fringed beach, it also has a fleet of vans to take you anywhere – at a price, though the #2b bus stops right outside the hotel gates. The splendid *Holiday Inn Resort Damai Lagoon* (☎082/846900, *www.holidayinn-sarawak.com/hirdl.html*; ⑧) out-swanks its counterpart. Sculpted around a magnificent, lagoon-style swimming pool with sunken bar, this compact resort boasts its own private cove, a range of good restaurants, plus health centre, sauna, jacuzzi and water-sports facilities.

The **trail** that loops from the *Santubong Mountain Trek* restaurant (a few minutes' walk back along the road to Kuching) around to the entrance of the Cultural Village (see below) makes for a pleasant ninety-minute forest stroll. The restaurant is also the starting point for the much more demanding **Gunung Santubong Trek** (RM1), for whose final ascent you need to rely upon ropes and rope ladders; however, you don't need a guide, as the trail is well marked. Allow at least three hours for your ascent, plus a couple more to return to sea level.

Sarawak Cultural Village

Beside the entrance to the *Holiday Inn Resort Damai Beach* is the **Sarawak Cultural Village** (daily 9am–5.30pm; stage shows at 11.30am & 4.30pm; adults RM45). It comprises seven authentically built traditional dwellings which stand in a dramatic setting, the sea to one side, a lake in the middle of the site and jungle escarpment of Gunung Santubong looming behind. As well as Iban, Orang Ulu and Bidayuh longhouses, there's a Malay townhouse, a Chinese farmhouse, a Melanau "tall house" (*rumah tinggi*) and a Penan jungle settlement.

When it was opened in the early 1990s, the village was a kind of theme park for the state's varied ethnic groups, though today the set-piece houses and facilities feel like a real community. The village is not just a functioning affair by day: some of the approachable people you come across in the houses, most notably the Iban and Bidayuh, live in them all the time, although the other groups come in by day and actually live elsewhere. In the daytime, there are demonstrations of weaving, cooking and instrument-playing, along with more idiosyncratic pursuits like top-spinning (in the Malay townhouse), blow-pipe-drilling (in the Penan settlement) and sago-processing (at the Melanau tall house); the **shows** put on twice daily are, however, rather too touristy, and some visitors have complained at their trivialization of ancient forest skills – the Penan segment, for instance, has a man moving in slow motion, mimicking the practice of hunting with a blowpipe and aiming it at the audience, before turning his sharp-shooting to balloons dangling from the roof of the auditorium. Nevertheless, as an overview of the costumes, traditions and daily lives of Sarawak's peoples, the cultural village is a valuable experience (especially if you've not got time to explore Sarawak's river systems), one which has garnered several tourist-industry awards. A particularly good time to visit is August, when the village hosts a festival of world music (see box, opposite).

THE RAINFOREST MUSIC FESTIVAL

Held annually at the Sarawak Cultural Village since 1998, the **Rainforest Music Festival** (day-tickets around RM20; see *www.rainforestmusic-borneo.com* or contact the Sarawak Tourist Board, ☎082/423 600, for the latest information) takes place in August, with seminars and workshops in the afternoons, and an outdoor stage providing the setting for the main performances in the evenings. While a variety of Western artistes have performed here, the festival is especially worthwhile for the opportunity it affords to watch performers from various parts of Malaysia, some rarely seen outside their own communities. At the very first festival, for example, Mak Minah, a Temuan Orang Asli singer from the Peninsula, brought the house down with her powerful voice; East Malaysian artistes you're likely to see here every year include the Sape Ulu Quartet (the *sape* being a traditional bamboo lute) from the upriver district of Belaga, in the wild centre of the state; and Usun Apau, a Penan vocal group that sings *sinui* (ancestral) tunes. The event is made all the more appealing by its atmospheric setting, as Heidi Munan, author of the section on Malaysian music in "Contexts", p.641, describes: "Musicians and audience move from one Damai longhouse to the next for concerts, workshops, flute-offs, drum-outs and sing-ins. Gongs and drums pulse from the dimly lit spaces into the jungle darkness (above, Gunung Santubong looms mightily), and the rhythmic stomp of many feet reverberates through the sturdy old structure. A female voice holds the floor, praising the deeds of famous ancestors in a skilfully improvised drink song. Then hornbill dancers troop on . . ."

Bako National Park

Though no further away from Kuching than the Santubong Peninsula, **BAKO NATIONAL PARK** – a two-hour bus and boat journey northeast of the city – is too much of a gem to try to pack into one or even two days. The park's ecology, wildlife, views and atmosphere make it feel more like a place which time forgot, where monkeys swing from trees to the roofs of the dilapidated hostel buildings, and beaches that are among the best in Sarawak can be reached on short hikes.

Bako is Sarawak's oldest national park, occupying the northern section of the Muara Tebas Peninsula at the mouth of Sungei Bako. The area was once part of a forest reserve – a region set aside for timber growing and extraction – but in 1957 was made a national park, fully protected from exploitation. Although relatively small, Bako is spectacular in its own way: its steep rocky cliffs, punctuated by deep bays and lovely sandy beaches, are thrillingly different from the rest of the predominantly flat and muddy Sarawak coastline. The peninsula is composed of sandstone which, over the years, has been worn down to produce delicate pink iron patterns on cliff faces, honeycomb weathering and contorted rock arches rising from the sea. Access to some of the beaches is difficult, requiring tricky descents down nearly vertical paths. Above, the forest contains various species of wildlife, and rivers and waterfalls for bathing. The hike to the highest point, **Bukit Gondol** (260m), offering a wide view over the park to the South China Sea, is among the most popular of the trails which crisscross Bako.

Practicalities

A **permit** is required to visit the park. Day-trippers can arrange theirs in Kampung Bako; those who want to stay in the park need to go to the Parks and Wildlife Department desk at the Visitor Information Centre in Kuching (see p.361), where they can pick up their permits and reserve accommodation, a process which only takes a few minutes. Once you're at the park, it's generally a straightforward business to extend your stay if you want to.

To **get to the park**, take the Petra Jaya #6 bus (hourly; RM3.80 return) from the open-air market beside Electra House. The buses run to the jetty at **Kampung Bako**, where you have to rent a **longboat** for the thirty-minute cruise to the park headquarters (RM30 per boat; each takes up to 10 people). By car from Kuching, the 37-kilometre journey takes around forty minutes, and there's a car park at Kampung Bako where you can leave your vehicle safely. There's rarely a delay in catching a longboat at the kampung, unless a large tour group is being relayed out to the park, and even then the wait is only around an hour.

Once at the **park headquarters**, you pay the park fee (RM3) and sign in. The ranger then gives you an informative **map** of the park and takes you to your accommodation. You may want an hour to look around the excellent displays and exhibits at the headquarters; these identify the flora and fauna in the park as well as describing in detail the park's history and unique characteristics.

Accommodation and eating

At the park headquarters, various types of **accommodation** have been built along the edge of the forest, divided from the beach 50m away by a row of coconut trees. Although seldom full during the week, Bako tends to get very busy at weekends and bank holidays. For budget travellers the **hostel** is good value (dorm beds RM11), with a fully equipped shared kitchen. Going up the scale, there's also a range of **lodges** (③), all of which provide bed linen, fridge and cooking facilities. Some hikers prefer to **camp** on the trails – tents can be rented from the headquarters for RM4, although it's doesn't cost much more to stay at the hostel.

The **café** at the park headquarters is very simple, with a daily menu of rice with vegetables, meat or fish and egg dishes, all at budget prices. The park **shop** has a limited range of goods but can keep you supplied with tinned provisions, rice, fruit and a few vegetables, so there's no need to lug food out from Kuching.

Around the park

Given the easy access from Kuching and cheap accommodation within the park, many people stay a few days longer than planned at Bako, taking picnics to one of the seven **beaches**, relaxing at the park headquarters itself, or going slow on the trails to observe the flora and fauna. In all, you'll come across seven different types of **vegetation**, including peat bog, scrub and mangrove; most of the sixteen trails run through an attractive mixture of primary dipterocarp forest and *kerangas* (in Iban, "poor soil"), a sparser type of forest characterized by much thinner tree cover, stubbier plants and more open pathways. On top of the low hill on the Lintang trail, the strange landscape of Padang Baut is covered in rock plates, where, among the shrubs, you'll find **pitcher plants**, whose deep, mouth-shaped lids open to trap water and insects which are then digested in the soupy liquid. On the cliffs, delicate plants cling to vertical rock faces or manage to eke out an existence in little pockets of soil, while closer to the headquarters the coastline is thick with mangrove trees.

One of the great pluses of Bako is the near-certainty that you will see **wildlife**, either while lazing at the chalets or out on the trails. Monkeys are always lurking around on the lookout for food, so it's important to keep the kitchen and dormitory doors locked. Even the rare flying lemur has been sighted swinging from the trees around the park headquarters. Although the best time to see wildlife on the trails is undoubtedly in the early morning and dusk – the rare proboscis monkey as well as macaque and silver-leaf monkeys will make sure they are heard if not easily seen – even in the raw heat of the day, animal activity is usually assured. Snakes, wild boar, giant monitor lizards, squirrels,

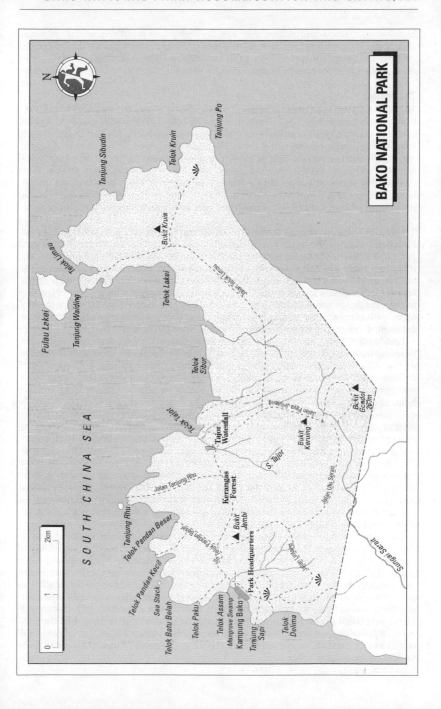

BAKO NATIONAL PARK

N

SOUTH CHINA SEA

Tanjung Sibudin

Tanjung Po

Telok Kruin

Bukit Kruin

Telok Lakei

Jalan Telok Limau

Telok Limau

Pulau Lakei

Tanjung Waiding

Telok Sibur

Telok Tajor

Bukit Gondol
267m

Jalan Paya Jir-Tubang

Tajor
Waterfall

Bukit
Keruing

S. Tajor

Kerangas
Forest

Jalan Tanjung Rhu

Telok Tanjung Rhu

Telok Pandan Besar

Jalan Pandan Besar

Bukit
Jambi

Jalan Ulu Serait

Telok Pandan Kecil

Sea Stack

Telok Batu Belah

Telok Paku

Telok Assam

Mangrove Swamp

Kampung Bako

Park Headquarters

Jalan Lintang

Tanjung
Sapi

Telok
Delima

Sungai Serait

0   1   2km

bearded pigs, otters and mouse deer can be sighted, especially if you're quiet and observant. The park headquarters and the open paths in the *kerangas* are the best places for **bird-watching**: 150 species have been recorded in Bako, including two rare species of hornbills (for more on which, see p.435).

The trails

The park map you receive when you first sign in clearly shows the **trails**, which all start from park headquarters. The sixteen trails are all colour-coded, with splashes of paint, denoting the trail, clearly marked every 20m on trees and rocks. It's best to get an early start, taking much-needed rests at the strategically positioned viewpoint huts along the way. You'll need to carry a litre of water per person (you can safely refill your bottle from the streams), a light rainproof jacket, mosquito repellent and sun screen. Wear comfortable shoes with a good grip (there's no need for heavy-duty walking boots), light clothing like a T-shirt and shorts, and take a sun hat. Don't forget your swimming gear either, as cool streams cut across the trails, and beaches and waterfalls are never far away.

Probably the most popular trail is the 3.5-kilometre hike to **Tajor Waterfall**, a hike lasting around two and a half hours, though it can easily be done in ninety minutes if you don't linger too long for rests or plant study. The initial half-hour climb from the jetty, on a steep and circuitous path up the forested cliff is the hardest section. At the top you move swiftly through scrub and into *kerangas* – a section without much shade, where pitcher plants are profuse. The path leads to a simple wooden hut with a fine prospect of the peninsula. Moving on, you return to sun-shielded forest, where the dry, sandy path gives way to a muddy trail through peat bog, leading eventually to the waterfall itself, a lovely spot for swimming and eating your picnic.

Leaving the Tajor hut at the wooden hut and viewpoint, a path descends west to two beautiful **beaches**, Telok Pandan Kecil and Telok Pandan Besar, each around a thirty-minute hike from the viewpoint, with Kecil in particular involving a steep, rugged descent down sandstone rocks to reach the refreshingly clean water. During the week you'll probably be the only person at either. The other two beaches at Bako – Teluk Sibur and Limau – are much harder to reach, but enjoyable once you've got there. To find **Teluk Sibur** beach, continue past Tajor Waterfall, following the main trail for around forty minutes, before turning west on the black-and-red trail. The demanding descent to the beach takes anything from twenty minutes to an hour to accomplish. You'll have to drop down the cliff face using creepers and roots to help you, and your troubles aren't over when you reach the bottom either, since you're then in a mangrove swamp and must tread carefully so as not to lose your footing among the stones. After wading across a shallow stream you reach the beach – the longest on the peninsula and, not surprisingly, seldom visited. It is at once stunningly beautiful and desolate – a perfect spot for swimming, picnicking and daydreaming; watch out, though, for sand-flies, which have a small but irritating bite.

The hike to **Teluk Limau**, estimated at seven hours, can be done in five at a push. The terrain alternates between swampland and scrub, giving an exhilirating variety of environments on one trail, and provides fabulous views round the whole peninsula. It's not really feasible to get to the beach, which marks the most northerly point in the park, and return the same day; either bring a tent and food and camp on the beach – as perfect a spot to lay your head as you will ever find – or arrange with park headquarters for a boat to pick you up for the trip back, which costs around RM200. Once out at Limau you could detour on the way back along the marked trail to **Kruin**, at the eastern end of the park – an area where you're very likely to spot wildlife. There is a secluded freshwater pond on the way and, from the top of the nearby hill, a grand view of the park's eastern edges.

Far western Sarawak

Far western Sarawak has not really been on the tourist trail until now. But there is much to gain from the few days it would take to visit **Gunung Gading National Park**, located just north of the small town of Lundu, the lovely beach village of **Sematan**, and perhaps get a fishing boat to Sarawak's newest national park, **Tanjung Datu**, further west along the coast.

Bau

STC #2 buses (RM3) depart from Kuching's Lebuh Jawa throughout the day, pulling into the nondescript market town of **BAU** an hour later. Nineteenth-century prospectors were drawn here by the gold that veined the surrounding countryside, but drab modern-day Bau doesn't live up to its romantic past. The largest and best of the caves around Bau is the **Fairy Cave**, 10km south of town. Tour agents in Kuching arrange adventure caving here, but as long as you pack a torch, you can take a taxi from Bau and have a wander through the cave yourself. It's also worth visiting Bau around *Gawai Padi* time, in June, when Bidayuh communities in and around the town celebrate the festival throughout the month. The festival is centred around seven shamanistic rituals in which the Bidayuhs give thanks to the Rice Goddess for an abundant harvest. The final ritual is a celebration involving the whole community and comprises singing and dancing (generally to recorded music – the use of the traditional *sape* and drums appears to be a dying art among the Bidayuh). Everyone is welcome to the celebrations, which differ slightly from village to village.

Lundu and the Gunung Gading National Park

The #2b STC bus leaves Kuching for **LUNDU** via Batu Kawa at 8am, 11.15am, 12.30pm, 2.15pm and 4pm (RM7.80), clattering through a landscape which gradually transforms from plantation into forest, with jungle-clad hills close by. A dozy and enchanting up-country place reaching out from the banks of Sungei Lundu, the town comprises a few blocks of shophouses, a large, new two-storey market and some government buildings. On the signposted road out towards the park lie attractive kampung houses within lush gardens where pineapples and papaya and mango trees compete for space. If you're merely waiting for an onward connection, take a walk around the small **market**, where you can buy fresh fruit, or go into one of the busy *kedai kopi*s, selling excellent *roti canai* and *nasi campur* throughout the day, bordering the town square; the *Jouee* serves excellent noodles. There are a couple of **places to stay**: the *Lundu Gading Hotel*, Lot 174, Jalan Lundu and the *Cheng Hak Boarding House*, 51 Jalan Bazaar (☎082/735018; ②) nearby.

Beyond the entrance for Gunung Gading National Park (see below), the road from Lundu continues northward until it reaches the coast, some 8km later, at **Pandan Beach**, which you can reach on the same bus that heads to the park. Considered by many locals to be the best in the area, Pandan is a half-kilometre-long stretch of white sand near a beachfront kampung; a little way out to the east, the shorter **Siar Beach** is another pleasing spot. Neither have any eating or accommodation facilities.

Gunung Gading National Park

From Lundu's central bus terminal, the regular STC #17 "Pandan" bus (daily 8am–4pm; every 2hr; 40 sen) covers the 2km up the road north of town to the headquarters of **Gunung Gading National Park**. The protected area, which mostly clings to the sides of four small mountains, was used solely as a conservation zone for the parasitic **Rafflesia** (see p.460) plant until it received full national park status in 1994. The emphasis is still on conservation, however, with visitors only allowed to view the spectacular plant, with its enormous blooms, from plankways that stop anyone treading on the brown young buds. If you call the park headquarters (☎082/735714) first thing in the morning, you can ask the warden what chance there is of viewing one that day, and when you arrive, a ranger will lead you out to the plant – one in bloom, if you are really in luck.

Besides Gunung Gading itself, the park has three other mountains, **Perigi**, **Lundu**, and **Sebuloh**. It's possible to climb both Gading and Perigi on the colour-coded **trails** that trace the forest. Both are full-on hikes, not to be undertaken lightly; the first is a seven-hour round trip, the second an eight-hour trip. Both can be done as day-trips but the most enterprising approach with the former is to camp on the summit. From there you can follow a trail back to Batu Bakubu, a former communist camp during the insurgency. For lesser mortals, the two-hour round trip offered by the **Waterfall Trail** is a more sedate alternative. Waterfall 7, where it ends, offers good, refreshing swimming.

Visitors **register** on arrival at the park (RM3 entry). **Accommodation** in the park takes the form of a hostel (dorm beds RM10) and chalets (②); there's a high chance that during the week there'll be empty beds, though you can book at the Visitor Information Centre in Kuching, who can also advise on whether any *Rafflesia* are in bloom.

Sematan and Tanjung Datu National Park

Some 25km northwest of Lundu, the few quiet shophouses of **SEMATAN** are located at the end of the road from Kuching, about 100km west of the state capital. **Buses** (RM2.50) head to Sematan from Lundu at 10am, 2pm and 3.30pm, returning at 11am, 3.30pm and 4.30pm. The town's long, mostly deserted **beach** has reasonably clean yellow sand with coconut palms – but be aware that sandflies (see p.345) are notoriously bad here, and the water is shallow. A coastal track runs for several miles northwest of Sematan; an hour's walk from town is rugged **Cape Belinsah**, where there's nothing to do but clamber around on the rocks. Already listed as a conservation zone, the area may soon be gazetted as a national park: enquire at the Visitor Information Centre in Kuching for the current state of play. For **accommodation** in Sematan, there's only the *Sematan Hotel* (☎082/711162; ②) on Sematan Bazaar, a friendly place with small, clean rooms. Two or three Chinese **cafés** in the village serve hot meals; the local crabs are particularly tasty.

As well as laid-back beaches, Sematan also has several local **trails**, starting from the wood just a couple of minutes across the bay, 200m away. Ask one of the boatmen hanging around the small central jetty to take you over – it should only cost a few dollars. Once across the water, the boatman can point out the start of a circular trail which runs through plantations and a tiny kampung, before winding around to join the road on which the bus comes in. All in all, it's a two-hour trip. Another excursion from Sematan is **TELUK MELANO**, a fishing village sitting in a beautiful bay. This is only possible in the dry season (April–Sept), as the rest of the time the seas are too high for boats to safely negotiate. There are two ways to get there, by speedboat (RM250 to hire, maximum six passengers) or by local fishing boat (around RM20 per person; the boats normally arrive at around 10am daily at Sematan jetty); the trip takes around two hours. Teluk Melano is a pretty place, home to around 40 families who live in traditional wooden Malay houses scattered around the bay. It's possible to stay with one of these families via the Sarawak Fishing Villages Homestay Programme, a community project set up by the Malaysian Fisheries Board; call the Sarawak Tourist Board (☎082/423600) for details.

Tanjung Datu National Park

Further along the coast is **Tanjung Datu National Park**, ten minutes away by boat from Teluk Melano (boats leave when full; 10min; RM20). Situated in a mountainous region around a coastal spur where the peaks tower above, the park has swift, clean rivers and isolated, dazzling beaches, rather like those at Bako (see p.379). The main reasons to head this far out, however, are to explore the park's small coral shore, where pristine coral is easy to view in the shallow sea, and simply to spend some hours on the beautiful isolated beaches, close to the border with Kalimantan. The reef is only a short distance from the shore; further out there are a number of artificial reefs, begun in 1986, which have now started to take shape, with marine life establishing itself alongside. There are no visitor facilities as yet at the park, though once at Teluk Melano a visit is quite feasible and worth the effort.

Anna Rais and south to the border

One hundred kilometres south of Kuching, up in the mountains straddling the border with Kalimantan, lies **ANNA RAIS**, the largest Bidayuh settlement in the area. Here the two remaining traditional **Bidayuh longhouses** offer a fascinating insight into the culture of the only remaining Land Dyaks in Sarawak still living a semi-authentic lifestyle.

Unlike other ethnic groups, the Bidayuh built their multi-levelled, elevated longhouses at the bases of hills rather than on rivers and, as a consequence, endured violent attacks during the nineteenth century from other more aggressive groups, especially the Iban. But the Bidayuh weren't exactly passive victims: traditional communities always had a **head-house**, where the heads of their enemies were kept and which served as a focus for male activities and rituals. Although quite an introverted group, the Bidayuh in Anna Rais welcome sympathetic visitors as much as the more demonstrative Iban or Kelabit. The community is used to visitors so everybody is greeted warmly at any time of year. For more on longhouses, see box, p.367.

From Kuching's Lebuh Jawa, STC bus #9 (daily 6.40am–5.55pm; every 30min; 2hr) heads to Anna Rais. When visitors arrive, they are greeted by locals at the car park and escorted around the settlement, which consists of two longhouses on either side of a river, Sungei Penrissen, and many separate dwellings. The best time to go is at the weekend when the women are finished with their farming duties, the children are in from school and the wage-earners back from working in the oil-palm plantations or in Kuching. As you wander around, you'll be offered food and drink, possibly even betel nut – a traditional way of making someone welcome – to chew, and invited to watch and participate in craft demonstrations. Most visitors stay a couple of hours, returning to Kuching the same day. Alternatively, ask at the longhouse if you can sleep in the community hall at **KAMPUNG ABANG**, a ten-minute drive beyond Anna Rais, and a useful overnight stop if you want to trek up nearby Gunung Penrissen (see below) the next day. South of Abang, an upmarket development, provisionally called the *Borneo Highlands Resort*, was under construction at time of writing; it will feature a golf course with spectacular views, as well as pricey chalets. The Visitor Information Centre in Kuching (see p.361) can update you on this.

Gunung Penrissen

The most accessible of the mountains on the Sarawak/Kalimantan border is the spectacular 1300-metre **Gunung Penrissen**, located a few kilometres from and directly south of Anna Rais. The Penrissen hike involves tough walking along narrow paths and crossing fast-flowing streams which descend from the source of Sungei Sarawak; vertical ladders help you on the last section. As the trails aren't easy to follow, you must hire a guide in Anna Rais (expect to pay around RM100 for a group of up to five people). Although the ascent and descent of Penrissen can be done in one hard day, you may prefer to set up camp at the foot of the summit, so bring a tent and food. Gunung Penrissen was strategically important in the 1950s border skirmishes between the Malaysian and Indonesian armies, and there's still a Malaysian **military post** close to the summit, from where you can gaze over the rainforest into Kalimantan to the south and east, and to the South China Sea over the forests to the north.

Serian and the border crossing

Some 20km southeast of Anna Rais is the **border crossing** at **Tebedu**, 120km from Kuching. Buses to Tebedu leave from **Serian**, a workaday town on the main Kuching–Sri Aman road, although most people get the through coaches from Kuching to Pontianak which leave hourly until 12.30pm (RM34.50). If you're not on the through coach then make sure you get to Tebedu in time to catch one of the local buses which go to the Indonesian town of **Entikong** and on to Pontianak; these stop running in the early afternoon. Tebedu is little more than an administrative centre, with a couple of dispiriting hotels. The border crossing at Entikong opens from 6am–6pm; no visa is needed.

Sri Aman and Batang Ai National Park

Although Sibu – and the longhouses of the Batang Rajang – is only four hours by boat from Kuching, the most popular destination for **longhouse visits** from Kuching is the area around **Batang Ai National Park**, a six-hour, 200km journey east of the city. Most of the half-dozen longhouses that are frequently visited are on the Lemanak and Skrang rivers, just over an hour by longboat from the sizeable town of **Sri Aman**, 150km southeast of Kuching.

Sri Aman

SRI AMAN is the second biggest town in southwest Sarawak and the administrative capital of this part of the state. It sits near the mouth of the Sungei Lupar, whose lower reaches are over 1500m wide, though the river narrows dramatically further up the flat alluvial plain. Just before Sri Aman, a small island in the river obstructs the flow of the incoming tide, producing the town's renowned tidal bore: at regular intervals – only once or twice a year – when enough water has accumulated, a billowing wave rushes by with some force; longboats are hauled up onto the muddy bank and large vessels head for midstream in an attempt to ride the bore as evenly as possible. At its most impressive, the bore rolls up like a mini-tidal wave, rocking boats and splashing the new Chinese temple which is set back from the pier. Somerset Maugham was caught by the wave in 1929 and nearly drowned, a tale he recounted in "Yellow Streak" in his *Borneo Tales*.

The busy town itself has a central defensive fort, **Fort Alice**, built by Charles Brooke in 1864 and thus predating Fort Margherita in Kuching. More compact than the one in the capital, the fort (now a government office and not open to the public) has turrets, a courtyard and, oddly, a drawbridge. Charles Brooke based himself in this region for many years, heading a small force which repelled the advances of pirates and intervened in the upriver conflicts between warring Iban factions.

Practicalities

Sri Aman is reached either by STC **bus** from Lebuh Jawa (daily at 7.30am, 9.30am, noon, 3pm & 7.30pm; RM15), or on the Biramas Express (daily at 1pm; RM15) from the Jalan Penrissen terminal; the journey takes three or four hours. There are several **hotels**: the *Champion Inn*, 1248 Main Bazaar (☎083/320140; ②), is the most central, with small, comfortable rooms; and *Hoover Hotel*, 139 Jalan Club (☎083/321985; ③), the best in town, with larger rooms than the *Champion Inn*. You can **eat** at the *Hoover*'s café, or at *Chuan Hong*, a Chinese *kedai kopi* in the centre of town at no. 1, Jalan Council.

Batang Ai National Park

Open since 1991, **Batang Ai National Park**, dominated by a lake created as part of a hydroelectricity project, is home to orang-utan, gibbon and hornbills, among other wildlife. The main reason people come here, however, is to use the lake as a jumping-off point to visit the **Iban** longhouses lining the narrow Skrang, Lemanak, Ai and Engkari rivers, which feed the lake. A gregarious, highly hospitable people, the Iban make any trip an enjoyable time for visitors, whether they be from a longhouse upstream or from outside Sarawak. Just going fishing, eating delicious fish and jungle vegetables, and sitting on the longhouse veranda makes for a memorable experience. Iban culture is especially vibrant in these parts, and a particularly worthwhile time to visit is during the harvest festival, or *Gawai Dayak,* in June, where traditional dress is encouraged and age-old rituals enacted including wedding, christening and circumcision ceremonies. For more on the Iban and their customs, see the box overleaf.

Practicalities

The Kuching-based **tour operators** listed on p.375 offer longhouse trips to Batang Ai lasting two to five days (RM130–300). For travellers on a short stay, tours like this are ideal, but check that the size of the group doesn't exceed six to eight people as things can get a bit congested. An expensive option – but worth every sen – is to go on Borneo Adventure's trip to its longhouse hotel (⑥) close to the lake or the the luxurious *Hilton Batang Ai Resort* (☎082/248200, fax 428984; ⑨) on the banks of the reservoir, one of Sarawak's new breed of quirky, out-station resorts. Travelling with Borneo Transverse allows you to visit a longhouse on Sungei Lemanak which, although something of an experiment, is an exciting development for upriver Iban communities, its construction largely financed by the tour company and the Sarawak government. Thirty families at Serubah longhouse – which has now collapsed – opted to move to this new home, a longhouse built according to traditional design principles, with *belian* (ironwood) shingles for the roof (instead of the corrugated iron used extensively today), softwood from the *unkubung* tree for the walls and floors (instead of concrete) and bamboo for the elevated veranda (largely non-existent in many modern constructions). The families who live here enjoy receiving and hosting regular visits from tourists; however, a small number of families from the original longhouse preferred to move to a modern longhouse nearby, where they wouldn't have their lives under tourist scrutiny.

The **Skrang** is reached by taking a Betong bus from Sri Aman, and getting off just short of Entabau, at the Pais jetty. Of all the tributaries in this region, the Skrang is the most touristy, and you may find that longhouses won't take you in unless you've booked through the operator which has "adopted" them. To reach either the **Lemanak**, or the **Batang Ai** and its tributaries you'll need to take an STC bus from Sri Aman southeast to **LUBOK ANTU**, 50km away. Here, you'll need to ask for the local shuttle (RM1.50) down to the **Batang Ai reservoir jetty**, about 10km to the northeast, in order to explore the tributaries of the Batang Ai. This is not a very regular service, and if you get to Lubok Antu late, you'll have need of the decent rooms at the *Kelingkang Inn* (☎083/584331; ②) and of meals served up beside the bus station in the *Oriental Café*.

SIBU AND THE RAJANG BASIN

At the very heart of Sarawak lies the 560-kilometre-long **Batang Rajang**, Malaysia's longest river. Already 200m across at the inland bazaar town of Kapit, by the time the

THE IBAN

The **Iban** – one of the ethnic groups categorized as Sea Dyaks – comprise nearly one-third of the population of Sarawak, making them easily the most numerous of Sarawak's indigenous peoples. They originated in the Kapuas river basin of west Kalimantan, on the other side of the mountains which separate Kalimantan and Sarawak, but having outgrown their lands they migrated to the Lupar river in southwest Sarawak in the early sixteenth century. Once in Sarawak, the Iban clashed with the coastal Melanau, and by the eighteenth century they had moved up the Rajang into the interior, into areas that were traditionally Kayan. Inevitably, great battles were waged between these two powerful groups, with one contemporary source recording seeing "a mass of boats drifting along the stream, while the Dyaks were spearing and stabbing each other; decapitated trunks and heads without bodies, scattered about in ghastly profusion."

The practice of **head-hunting** became established during the Iban migrations; the more heads in a longhouse, the more it would be feared by outsiders and so be less likely to be attacked. It generally didn't matter how the head was taken or to whom it belonged – though revenge occasionally played a part. An account in the *Sarawak Gazette* in 1909 – just when Charles Brooke hoped his policy of stopping head-hunting was at last becoming effective – reported that:

> *Justly are the Dyaks called head-hunters, for during the whole of their life, from early youth till their death, all their thoughts are fixed on the hunting of heads. The women, in their cruelty and blood-thirstiness, are the cause. At every festival the old trophies are taken from the fireplace and carried through the house by the women who sing a monotonous song in honour of the hero who cut off the head, and in derision of the poor victims whose skulls are carried around. Everywhere, the infernal chorus, "Bring us more of them", is heard.*

Although conflict between the various ethnic groups stopped as migration itself slowed down, heads were still being taken as recently as the 1960s during the Konfrontasi skirmishes, when Indonesian army units came up against Iban fighters in the Malaysian army.

Along with the Melanau, the Iban are the most "modernized" of Sarawak's ethnic groups. Around twenty percent live in towns – mostly Kuching, Sri Aman and Sibu – and these days work in most sectors of the state's economy, from handicrafts to manufacturing. Indeed, many Iban hold positions of power – from their ranks some of Sarawak's most well-known politicians have been drawn. Even the bulk of the rural Iban, the vast majority of whom still live in longhouses, undertake seasonal work in the rubber and oil industries, and it is no small irony that **logging** – the business which has most devastated their own customary lands – has provided much plentiful and lucrative work. This process has led to some longhouses becoming occasional homes, with many families living where their work is for much of the year. Traditionally, young men would also leave the longhouse to go on *bejalai*, joining warring parties; nowadays though, youths on *bejalai* are more likely to be found trying to get work at Sibu's docks or Kuching's oil-palm plantations – the idea being for a young man to establish his independence before he can get married.

Rajang reaches the busy port of Sibu it is eight times as wide. As you approach along the coast from Kuching, your initial impressions of the Rajang are of a wide, dirty channel, used to transport logs from the interior of the state to the outside world. Around ninety minutes upriver from the coast, the major port of **Sibu** is the headquarters of the timber cartels, although the focus of forestry development has now shifted further up into the interior as much of the lower reaches of the Rajang have already been denuded of valuable timber. The river is the highway not just for timber, but for all the region's different ethnic groups, from Sibu's prosperous Chinese

Unlike most of Sarawak's other ethnic groups, the Iban are a very egalitarian people – the longhouse *tuai* (headman) is more of a figurehead than someone who wields power. Women in the community have different duties to men; they never go hunting or work in logging, but are great weavers; indeed, it's an Iban woman's weaving prowess that determines her status in the community. The women are most renowned for their beautiful **pua kumbu** (blanket or coverlet) work, a cloth of intricate design and colour. The *pua kumbu* once played an integral part in Iban rituals, when they were hung up prominently during harvest festivals and weddings, or used to cover structures containing charms and offerings to the gods. And, when head-hunting was still a much-valued tradition, the women would wear the *pua kumbu* to receive the "prize" brought home by their menfolk. The cloth is generally made by using the *ikat* technique, which involves binding, tying and then dyeing the material so as to build up complex patterns.

Of all the customs maintained by the Iban, perhaps the most singular is their style of **tattooing**, which is not just a form of ornamentation, but also an indication of personal wealth and other achievements. Many designs are used, from a simple circular outline for the shoulder, chest or outer side of the wrists, to more elaborate designs (dogs, scorpions or dragons) for the inner and outer surfaces of the thigh. The two most important locations for tattoos are considered to be the hand and the throat. A tattoo on the hand indicates that you have "taken a head" – some elders still have these – while one on the throat means that you are a fully mature man, with wealth, possessions, land and family. Tattooing is usually carried out by an experienced artist, either a longhouse resident or a travelling tattooist who arrives just prior to the festival season. A carved design on a block of wood is smeared with ink and pressed to the skin, the resulting outline then punctured with needles dipped in dark ink, made from a mixture of sugar-cane juice, water and soot. For the actual tattooing a hammer-like instrument is used that has two or three needles protruding from its head. These are dipped in ink, the hammer placed against the skin and hit repeatedly with a wooden block, after which rice is smeared over the inflamed area to prevent infection.

The Iban are extremely gregarious and love an opportunity to throw a **party**, drinking *tuak*, eating heaps of meat and fish and cracking jokes (the Iban lexicon is rich with double entendres). The games visitors find themselves playing when visiting the Iban are often designed to get as many laughs at their expense as possible. The best time to visit is the first two days of June, when the **Gawai Dayak** (harvest festival) gets into swing – but the end of May and most of June take the form of a summer holiday; a time for relaxing, hunting, craft-making and merrymaking. It is also the season to hold celebrations and rituals like weddings, christenings and circumcisions; many Iban who live in the cities return over this period. Another festival, the *Gawai Antu* (festival for the departed souls), is sometimes celebrated in November or December; it's the Iban equivalent of the Christian All Souls' Day or the Taoist Hungry Ghost Festival. The *Gawai Antu* is both an acknowledgement of the deep rituals which still imbue Iban culture and an opportunity to hold a vast party with unlimited eating and drinking. To find out where and when one is being held, ask around at tourist offices in Kuching or Sri Aman. Each longhouse hosts at least one open weekend during a *gawai* when visitors are welcome, though it's customary to bring **gifts**. For more on longhouses and what to do when you visit, see p.367.

traders to the Penans, former hunter-gatherers, whose lands are far upriver. In many ways, it's changed little since the nineteenth century, when Chinese and Malay adventurers took boats from Sibu wharf to **Kapit**, before heading up the Rajang to the frontier settlement of **Belaga** to trade with the nomadic Penan. This is a world of isolated colonial forts, longboat trips and thriving Iban and Kayan communities, people living on the cusp of the traditional and modern worlds; guides in Kapit and Belaga can lead you on jungle treks to **Kayan longhouses** or visits to **Penan** communities. In between Sibu and Kapit, the little town of **Song** is a jumping-off point for **Iban**

longhouses along the Katibas tributary of the Rajang; there are also Iban longhouses along the Baleh tributary, east of Kapit.

A little history

For centuries, the Rajang was rife with tribal conflict. In the fifteenth century, when the Malay sultanates were at their height, Malays living in the estuaries of southern Sarawak pushed the immigrant Iban up the rivers towards present-day Sibu. This antagonized the indigenous people of those regions, especially the Baleh and upper Rajang Kayan, and throughout the seventeenth and eighteenth centuries they and the Iban fought amongst themselves for territory and heads. Occasionally, when they felt threatened, the Malays and the Iban would form an uneasy alliance to attack inland Kayan tribes and carry out piratical raids on passing Indonesian and Chinese ships.

With the arrival of the British, it was clear that no serious opening up of the interior could go ahead until the region was made relatively safe – which meant controlling the land and subjugating, or displacing, many of the indigenous inhabitants. To this end, James Brooke (see p.356) bought a section of Batang Rajang from the Sultan of Brunei in 1853, while his successor, Charles, asserted his authority over the Iban and Kayan tribes, and encouraged **Chinese pioneers** to move into the interior. Some of the more intrepid among these started to trade upriver with the Iban and, with support from the Malay business community and Brooke officials, built settlements at Kanowit and Sibu in the late nineteenth century, hacking out farms in the jungle, on which, with varying degrees of success, they grew rice, vegetables, pepper and rubber. Indeed, Sibu's early growth was largely financed by the proceeds of rubber cultivation. But the pioneers faced numerous disputes with the Iban who, having come here after being pushed out of their river valleys by the Malays, resented the Chinese for clearing and growing crops on land the Iban believed now belonged to them.

The traders among the pioneers would spend a month or more plying the tributaries, leaving cloth, salt and shotgun cartridges on credit with the Dyaks and then returning to pick up **jungle produce** in exchange, like birds' nests, camphor, beeswax, honey and bezoar stones. But it was a risky life for these pioneers, especially when faced with an Iban tribesman whose only way out of a credit impasse was to do away with the trader. Most of the traders lived on their *atap*-roofed boats, never leaving them, even while doing business with the Iban. Some, however, learned the tribal languages and customs and, although banned from doing so by Brooke, spent nights in the longhouses; a few even took Dyak wives.

Sibu

Sixty kilometres upriver from the South China Sea lies **SIBU**, Sarawak's second largest city and the state's biggest port. It seethes with activity, most of the action taking place on the long jetties with their separate bays for passenger boats, commercial craft and logging barges. Most of the local population are Foochow Chinese (the town is known locally as New Foochow); indeed, the town's remarkable modern growth is largely attributed to these industrious and enterprising immigrants. Sibu, unlike Kuching or Miri, never retained a large contingent of Brooke officials, which means its Chinese character has never really been diluted. Following the success of the early rubber plantations, manufacturing industries (largely textiles and consumer items) were established here, while later, after independence, Chinese businessmen moved into the lucrative trade in **timber**. But it wasn't all unimpeded expansion: in 1928 the Chinese godowns along the wharf and many of the cramped lodging houses and cafés were destroyed by fire; the town was devastated again in World War II by advancing Japanese forces, who occupied it for three years, during which time much of the Chinese population was forced into slave labour.

There is still a wild edge to Sibu: the traders are louder and more persuasive, the locals more assertively friendly compared to Kuching folk. Everywhere are signs of the timber cartels' wealth: multistorey commercial buildings sit on the outskirts of town, and there are brand new Toyota pick ups on the streets. The town's most striking land mark is the towering, seven-storey pagoda, next to the temple, north of which is the old **Chinatown**, its warren of narrow streets home to most of the cheap hotels, the hawker stalls and the cramped fish, meat and vegetable markets. Beyond simply soaking up the town's vibrant atmosphere, there's little for visitors to do in Sibu, though you'll want to check out the massive, bustling pasar malam and the small museum on the edge of town, which focuses on the Chinese migration and the displaced ethnic communities. Most people come here as it's the first stage of an expedition upriver – though don't be surprised if you end up feeling sorry to leave.

Arrival, information and accommodation

Flights from Kuching, Bintulu and Miri arrive at the **airport**, 25km east of the city centre. Make your way out of the tiny terminal and on to the main road, where there is a bus stop for the #3a into town (daily 7am–6pm; every 40min); the taxi drivers at the airport will tell you not to bother with the bus, and then charge you RM20 for the journey into the centre. The #3a bus takes you to the **bus and taxi station** on Jalan Khoo Peng Loong, 200m west of Chinatown, where several of the city's budget hotels are located; the station is also where the long-distance buses from Bintulu and points north arrive.

Travelling by boat from Sarikei or Kuching, you dock at the **upriver boat wharf**, 100m northwest of the bus terminal. This is where you come to catch the express boat

---

MOVING ON FROM SIBU

BY AIR
From Sibu's airport, there are numerous daily flights to Kuching (RM72 one way), Bintulu (RM64 one way), Miri (RM112 one way) and Kota Kinabalu (RM180 one way). Bus #3a runs out to the airport (RM2) from the foot of the esplanade, on Jalan Maju.

BY BOAT
Upriver express departures to Kanowit (RM7), Song (RM12) and Kapit (RM15) leave at least hourly until mid-afternoon from Sibu's upriver wharf. Destinations are displayed on signs in the windows of all boats, and cardboard "clocks" at the jetty show their estimated departure times. Only the first two departures carry on to Belaga, and even then only if the water of the Pelagus Rapids (p.400) is deep enough. From the downriver wharf, Concorde Marine, 1 Jalan Bank (☎084/331593) runs a daily direct service to Kuching at 8.15am, while Express Bahagia, 20a Jalan Tukang Besi (☎084/319228), runs another daily service there, via Sarikei, at 11.30am.

BY BUS
There are departures to Kuching, Mukah, Bintulu and Miri through the day – book through one of the several bus companies scattered along Jalan Khoo Peng Loong and Jalan Maju, among them locally based Lanang Rd Co, 6 Jalan Maju (☎084/314527); there are also a couple of daily connections to Kalimantan.

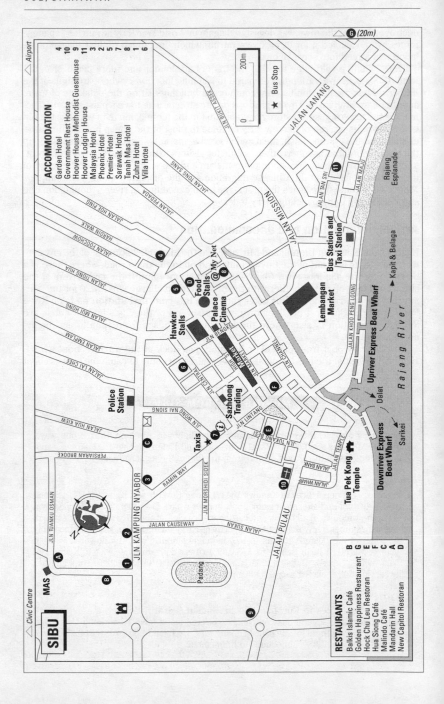

SIBU

ACCOMMODATION

Garden Hotel	4
Government Rest House	10
Hoover House Methodist Guesthouse	9
Hoover Lodging House	11
Malaysia Hotel	3
Phoenix Hotel	2
Premier Hotel	5
Sarawak Hotel	7
Tanah Mas Hotel	8
Zuhra Hotel	1
Villa Hotel	6

RESTAURANTS

Balkis Islamic Café	B
Golden Happiness Restaurant	G
Hock Chu Leu Restoran	E
Hua Siong Café	F
Malindo Café	C
Mandarin Hall	A
New Capitol Restoran	D

on to Kapit and Belaga, while for **downriver boats** – the ones arriving from Kapit and heading to Sarikei – there's another jetty, 100m further northwest, just beside the Chinese temple. For more **departure details**, see the relevant sections in "Listings", p.395.

Sibu's **Visitor Information Centre** is at 32 Jalan Cross (☎084/340980), beside the *Sarawak Hotel* and off Ramin Way. Here you can get tourist leaflets, a list of accommodation and a **map** of greater Sibu.

Accommodation

It is fairly easy to find **accommodation** in Sibu; with most places to stay located within a ten-minute walk of the jetty. Prices are cheaper than in Kuching, though the standard of the rooms is not quite as high.

Garden, 1 Jalan Hoe Ping (☎084/317888). Likeable forty-room hotel just a stone's throw from the city centre, with a coffee shop and business centre. Recommended. ③.

Government Rest House, Jalan Pulau (☎084/330406). Fifteen minutes' walk from the wharf in a large colonial building at the far end of Jalan Pulau. The rooms, all doubles, are comfortable, and some overlook a tranquil garden at the back. ②.

Hoover House Methodist Guesthouse, Jalan Pulau (☎084/332973). Set back from the street in a car park, this place has excellent, spotless rooms with bathroom attached, plus some with communal bathrooms. The best deal in town. ②.

Hoover Lodging House, 34 Jalan Tan Sri (☎084/334490). Unobtrusively positioned in a cramped side street close to the bus station, and surprisingly clean for this price bracket. The cheapest rooms are tiny, with fans and shared facilities, but paying a little more secures you an en-suite room. ①.

Malaysia, Jalan Kampung Nyabor (☎084/332299). A popular, though fairly shabby place, located on a busy main road, with small rooms, shared toilet and shower; it's family-run and friendly. ②.

Phoenix, Jalan Ki Peng, off Jalan Kampung Nyabor (☎084/313877). Smart and friendly, this is one of the best upmarket hotels, with spacious modern rooms, some with baths and TV. ④.

Premier, Jalan Kampung Nyabor (☎084/323222). Sumptuous hotel – you can tell by the chill of the air-con as you approach the doorway. The rooms are spacious and smartly decorated. ⑦.

Sarawak, 34 Jalan Cross (☎084/333455). Offers large, tastefully decorated rooms equipped with TV, air-con and shower. ②.

Tanah Mas, Lorong Bengkel (☎084/333188). Another decent, central hotel in the *Premier* mould. There's a vast lobby and large, air-con rooms. ⑥.

Villa Hotel, 2 Jalan Central (☎084/337833). Always busy, this Chinese-run first-floor place is clean and friendly, with small rooms and communal bathrooms. ②.

Zuhra, Jalan Kampung Nyabor (☎084/310711). This quality hotel has smallish, modern rooms with air-con, TV and shower. ③.

The Town

For a century or more, Batang Rajang has been Sibu's commercial and industrial lifeline. Along the **wharf**, on Jalan Khoo Peng Loong, plankways lead to several points where boats dock, while the stalls lining the road sell basic provisions for river journeys. At the western edge of the harbour is the **Rajang Esplanade**, a small park built in 1987 on reclaimed land. It's a popular place to sit and enjoy the evening breeze, and occasionally cultural events, too, like traditional dancing and Chinese firework displays.

Head to the western end of Jalan Khoo Peng Loong, past the upriver boat wharf, and south along Jalan Channel to reach Jalan Temple and the **Tua Pek Kong Temple**. There was a small, wooden temple on this site as early as 1870, though soon afterwards it was rebuilt on a much grander scale, with a tiled roof, stone block floor and decorative fixtures imported from China. Two large concrete lions guard the entrance, while the fifteen-metre-wide main chamber is always busy with people paying respects to the deity, Tua Pek Kong, a prominent Confucian scholar. The statue of Tua Pek Kong, to the left of the front entrance, is the most important image in the temple and survived both the fire of 1928 and Japanese bombardment. Elsewhere, the roof and columns are decorated with traditional statues of dragons and birds, while emblazoned on the temple wall to the left of the entrance are murals depicting the signs of the Chinese zodiac. For a small donation, the caretaker will tell you the story of the temple and give you a brief rundown on the significance of these and other images. In 1987 the rear section of the temple was replaced by the RM1.5-million, seven-storey **pagoda**, from the top of which there's a splendid view of the Rajang snaking away below.

Across the way, in the network of streets around Jalan Market, Jalan Channel and Jalan Central, is **Chinatown**, with its plethora of hardware shops, newspaper stalls, rowdy cafés, textile wholesalers, cassette sellers, food and fruit-juice vendors and hotels. The central artery, **Jalan Market**, is the hub of possibly the most vibrant pasar malam in Sarawak (nightly from dusk until 10pm): at sunset, hundreds of stalls are set up, offering a wide variety of foods (see below).

On the southwestern edge of the old town, across Jalan Channel, the daily **Lembangan Market** – not quite as large as the pasar malam – opens before dawn and closes around 5pm. Many of the hawkers here are Iban from nearby longhouses, selling anything from edible delicacies like flying fox, squirrel, snake, turtle, snail, jungle ferns and exotic fruits; to rattan baskets, beadwork, charm bracelets and leather belts.

The Civic Centre

On the outskirts of Sibu, the one place worth visiting is the modern **Civic Centre**, 2km north of the centre, which contains a small but high-quality collection in its **Cultural Exhibition Hall** (Tues–Sun 10.30am–5.30pm; free) on the ground floor. To get there, take the Jalan Tun Abang Haji Openg bus #3 from the bus terminal and ask for the Civic Centre. In a series of display chambers, the hall details the varied peoples of the Rajang by means of well-chosen photographs, artefacts and paraphernalia. Among the costumes, backpacks and instruments in the Orang Ulu chamber, look out for some evocative old snaps of headmen, and an amazing photograph of a peace-making ceremony between Kayan and Iban tribespeople on November 16, 1924, at which representatives from both tribes killed pigs to authenticate their truce. There are more atmospheric pictures – of tattooing and cock-fighting – in the adjacent Iban chamber, plus a scale model of an Iban longhouse that was made using bark, ironwood and bamboo. The mocked-up Malay wedding room falls somewhere short of interesting, but the Chinese display makes a good stab at charting the history of the Foochow migration to the region (a bust of Wong Nai Siong, the Methodist minister who led the original pioneers, takes centre stage), alongside records of the numerous cultural associations which were the immigrants' first port of call when they arrived. In exchange for voluntary labour, the associations would find the new arrivals paid work and lodgings and induct them into the business and cultural life of the city.

Eating

Throughout town there are Chinese **cafés** selling Sibu's most famous dish, Foochow noodles – steamed and then served in a soy and oyster sauce with spring onions and dried fish. Other local favourites include *midin* (a type of wild fern), *kang puan mee* (noodles cooked in lard) and *kong bian* (oriental bagels, sprinkled with sesame seed). Prawn and crab are of a high quality and, in season, tropical fruit like star fruit, rambutan and guava are available from market stalls. Although Sibu has some fine air-con **restaurants**, most people prefer to be outside when the weather's good; even the well-off opt to eat at **hawker stalls**. Busiest in the morning are those at the Lembangan Market, while in the evening everyone congregates at the pasar malam in the town centre, which serves up, besides *dim sum* and snacks, specific Sibu delicacies like stuffed dumplings, grilled fish in shrimp sauce and chicken wings in peanut oil, chillies and garlic, as well as a range of offal and pig's and duck's heads. The pasar malam's only drawback is that there's nowhere to sit and eat the piping-hot delicacies you've bought – most people wander down to the esplanade to eat. Also popular are the stalls in the block on Jalan Bengkel, west of the *Premier Hotel*, and those in the two-storey, circular building just to the south, where the stalls specialize in Malay food – crisp green beans with soy sauce and ginger, and curried chicken and beef dishes – with plenty of tables protected from the elements.

Most cafés are **open** throughout the day, from around 7am to 8pm, with the Chinese coffee houses staying open until around midnight. Restaurants open from around 11am until 11pm.

Cafés and restaurants

Balkis Islamic Café, 69 Jalan Osman. Very good North Indian staples like *roti canai, murtabak* and curries. It's near the MAS office and post office and costs around RM3 a head. Open 7am–8pm.

Golden Happiness Restaurant, Jalan Chengal. On two levels, this Foochow restaurant is always packed to the rafters, thanks to such culinary delights as frogs' legs coated in cashews, venison with ginger and sublime Foochow noodles.

Hock Chu Leu Restoran, 28 Jalan Tukang Besi. Well-known Foochow restaurant with great baked fish and fresh vegetables. Around RM25 for two, including beer.

Hua Siong Café, Jalan Market. Busy place popular with locals, near the market and jetty. Great for drinking beer or tea, and eating basic Chinese fare, while you watch frenetic Sibu go by.

Malindo Café, 20 Jalan Kampung Nyabor. Tasty, spicy Indonesian food – the stuffed crab is both particularly good and cheap, at RM4–5 a head.

Mandarin Hall, Wisma See Hua, Jalan Tuanku Osman. Excellent Foochow restaurant that turns its hand to breakfast each morning, when stalls serving *bubor cha cha, dim sum, laksa* and *kang puan mee* do a roaring trade in the dining room.

New Capitol Restoran, Jalan Workshop. Specializing in seafood, this Cantonese restaurant is expensive, though worth the splurge: it costs RM25–30 a head, including drinks.

Peppers Café, *Tanah Mas Hotel*, Jalan Kampung Nyabor. Its wide-ranging menu – from Western dishes to Malay fish curries – is very popular with Sibu business people. Not cheap, at around RM40 for two.

Listings

Airlines The MAS office is at 61 Jalan Tunku Osman (☎084/326166).

Airport For flight information call ☎084/307082.

Banks Bumiputra, Lot 6 & 7, Jalan Kampung Nyabor; Public Bank, 2–6 Jalan Tunku Osman.

Handicrafts Chai Chiang Store, 5 Jalan Central, for woodcarvings, beadwork, bamboo and rattan baskets, and mats; prices are cheaper than in Kuching. There are also stalls selling basketware where Jalan Channel hits the wharf. There are several ceramics factories close to Sibu: buses leave every hour from Jalan Khoo Peng Loong to Toh Brothers, Jalan Ulu Oya.

Hospital Jalan Oya (☎084/343333).

Internet access My Net, in the quadrangle behind the *Tanah Mas* hotel; Forever Link Computers, second floor, Wisma Sanyan, Jalan Morshidi Sidek.

Laundry Dobi Sibu, 5g Jalan Bindang.

Police Jalan Kampung Nyabor (☎084/336144).

Post office The main office is on Jalan Kampung Nyabor (Mon–Fri 8am–6pm, Sat 8am–noon).

Taxis Sibu Taxis ☎084/320773.

Tour operators Ibrahim Tourist Guide, 1 Jalan Bengkel (☎084/318987), runs an overnight tour to an Iban longhouse close to Sibu; it's good value at around RM200 for two people. Frankie Ting at Sazhong Trading (Mon–Sat 8am–4.40pm; ☎084/336017), 4 Jalan Central, organizes a similar trip to nearby Rumah Sawai, and tours of Iban longhouses along Sungei Mujong, near Kapit.

Up the Rajang: Kanowit, Song and Sungei Katibas

From Sibu, express boats head up the Rajang, stopping first at **Kanowit**, after which they head upriver to **Kapit**, a three-hour journey from Sibu; other boats stop at **Song**, from where it's possible to explore **Sungei Katibas** (see opposite). As the river narrows imperceptibly, small Iban boats can be seen hugging the sides of the river to get as far away as possible from the swell that the fast boats create. Timber yards and wood-reprocessing plants – a frequent sight on the stretch from Sarikei to Sibu – become less frequent as you head upriver, and the weight and mass of the jungle on either side becomes more apparent.

Boats to Song leave Sibu at 7.30am, 12.15pm and 1pm (RM12); those to Kapit leave hourly (daily 5.30am–2.30pm; RM15), with the first two services going beyond Kapit – water levels permitting – right the way to the upper reaches of the Rajang and Belaga. You can't book in advance – seats are on a strictly first-come, first-served basis – so always arrive at least fifteen minutes early to get a seat, and then nip off to buy any provisions you require for the journey.

Kanowit

An hour from Sibu, the boat reaches the sleepy settlement of **KANOWIT**. The only real reason to get out here is to see **Fort Emma**, one of the first defensive structures built by James Brooke. It's just a couple of hundred metres to the west of the jetty in front of the town's two hotels (see below) – en route you'll pass the lurid-green mosque and a gaily flowered waterfront park. Built in 1859 of timber and bamboo, the fort took its name from James's beloved sister, its presence intended to inhibit the numerous raids by the local Iban on the remaining Rajang Melanau tribes. However, soon after the fort was built it was overrun by an Iban warring party; future attacks were only repulsed by stationing a platoon here, mostly comprising Iban and Malays in the pay of Brooke's officials. Up until the Japanese occupation, Fort Emma was the nerve centre of the entire district, but with the passing of colonial rule the building fell into disuse as there were no more pirates to repulse, head-hunters to pursue, or rebellious Chinese miners to suppress. Despite years of neglect, the fort, perched on raised ground, is still impressive.

Practicalities

The two **hotels**, both on the waterfront Jalan Kubu, are the *Kanowit Air Con* (☎084/752155; ②) which, despite its name, only has air conditioning in some of its rooms; and the *Harbour View Inn* (☎084/753188; ②), whose rooms can be noisy in the early morning due to its proximity to the jetty. There are also a few waterfront **cafés**, serving basic Chinese rice dishes and the odd Malay dish.

Song and Sungei Katibas

Three boats a day from Sibu carry on to **SONG**, another hour upstream, at the head of one of the Rajang's major tributaries, Sungei Katibas, which winds and narrows south towards the mountainous border region with Kalimantan. There's not much to Song, which is little more than a few blocks of waterfront shophouses (some of them 1920s wooden affairs, their shutters painted in cheery blues and greens), a jetty, a small Chinese temple and two waterfront hotels: the *Capital Hotel* (☎084/777252; ①), with small, stuffy rooms and shared bathrooms; and much smarter *Katibas Inn* (☎084/777323; ②). Along the riverside are the usual Chinese stores, plus several coffee shops knocking out simple noodle dishes. In addition, stalls on the upper floor of the market facing the *Capital* serve *nasi lemak* and other Malay staples; you have to head up to the nearby *Happy Garden Seafood Restaurant* for a meal of any sophistication. Song does have a helpful **guide**, Richard Kho, who can arrange visits to Iban longhouses on the Katibas (see below); staff at the *Capital* can tell you how to contact him.

Sungei Katibas

To explore **Sungei Katibas**, you need to catch the passenger longboat which leaves Song twice each morning; departure times vary, so ask at the jetty. On the Katibas are several Iban longhouses worth visiting, including the large community at the junction of the Katibas and one of its own small tributaries, Sungei Bangkit. It takes between two and three hours to reach **Nanga Bangkit**, which comprises an impressive fifty-door longhouse and a dozen smaller dwellings on the opposite bank. This is the boat's final port of call, so most of your fellow passengers will get off here, and one is bound to invite you to visit. The longhouse women are excellent weavers, and you can buy a wall hanging or thin rug here, often straight from its maker, for around RM300. There are another twelve or so Iban longhouses along the banks of the river, each with its own rice fields, which cling to the inclines.

You can rent a boat to travel further up Sungei Bangkit; negotiate the fare before you start the trip – going to Rumah Guyang, Sungei Bangkit's next longhouse, should cost around RM80 each way. However, you might prefer to tag along with a smaller longboat which heads that way daily; these passenger boats push on from Nanga Bangkit as far as **Nanga Engkuah**, an Iban community with three sizeable longhouses an hour further south. To access the border region from here – say, to reach idyllic **Rumah Api**, at the end of the river – requires chartering a vessel in Nanga Engkuah (an expensive business at around RM300 each way).

Despite their proximity to big-town Sibu, the river communities still hold their customs dear. Along the banks of the Katibas and the Bangkit you may catch sight of small **burial houses** set back on the banks. For a good 100m either side of the burial spots, the jungle is left undisturbed; these areas are strictly out of bounds to locals from neighbouring longhouses and other visitors. The surrounding areas also remain uncultivated out of respect to the ancestors.

Kapit and around

KAPIT – around three hours east of Sibu – is a fast-growing town with a frontier atmosphere, a riverside bazaar in the middle of thick jungle being made more accessible by the day. It started life as a remote settlement for a small community of British officials and Chinese *towkay*s trading with the region's indigenous population, but these days, the signs of rapid expansion are everywhere: machine parts and provisions are unloaded from the tops of the express boats, local landowners drive around in Toyotas, picking up workers to clear land or build houses, and new municipal buildings are fast changing the character of the town. There is still a strong native presence; the fruit sellers are much more forthright here than in Sibu or Kuching because (for the time being at least) this is still their territory. The timber and oil-palm industries employ native workers from distant longhouses on short-term contracts, and the bright lights of Kapit are where they come to spend their wages – karaoke lounges, snooker halls and brothels are all much in evidence.

Although most travellers stay just one night, waiting for boats either way along the **Rajang** or for connecting longboats along **Sungei Baleh**, it's easy to get to like Kapit. Though the place is little more than a few streets cleared out of the luxuriant forest, there are lots of good cafés in which to while away the time, and a decent museum.

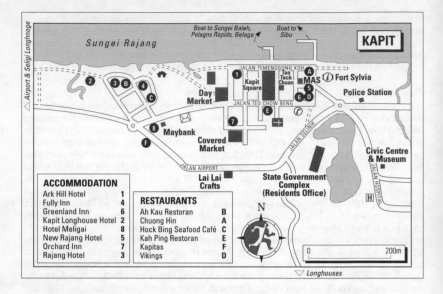

Kapit is also a good place to organize trips to nearby the Pelagus Rapids and to local Iban communities, with regular minivans heading out to the largest Iban longhouse in the area, Rumah Seligi.

The Town

Close to the jetty is Kapit's main landmark, **Fort Sylvia**. Renamed after Vyner Brooke's wife in 1925, it was built in 1880 in an attempt to prevent the warring Iban attacking smaller and more peaceable groups such as the upriver Ukit and Bukitan. The fort also served to limit Iban migration along the nearby Sungei Baleh, and confine them to the section of the Rajang below Kapit. Its most famous administrator was **Domingo de Rozario** who, born in the Astana kitchen in Kuching, was the son of James Brookes' Portuguese chef. De Rozario's memoirs record that life in Kapit was pleasant and that he got on well with the natives, but he found it most troublesome when dealing with "cases of heads taken on raids". For many years the fort housed administrative offices, though it was being converted into the home of the local tourist office at time of writing.

Along Kapit's oldest riverside street, **Jalan Temenggong Koh**, the rows of simple shophouses which once nestled between patches of jungle are now giving way to stores and cafés housed in concrete buildings, which can better withstand the deluges of rain that regularly occur here. The **jetties** are always a hive of activity, too, with dozens of longboats bobbing up and down and scores of people with bulky bundles of goods making their way back and forth between the express boats and smaller craft. Merchants, timber employers and visitors watch the goings-on from marble-topped tables in the *Chuong Hin Café*, opposite the jetty.

Kapit's main square – simply called **Kapit Square** – is surrounded by shops selling everything from noodles to rope. The walk westwards along Jalan Temenggong, which forms the square's northern edge, leads to the **day market** where tribespeople rail at you until you buy a cluster of tropical fruit, and other traders point out boxes of wriggling eels and shrimps. Occasionally frogs, turtles, birds and monkeys are sold. There are textile and shoe stalls upstairs in the main building; the stalls in front of the market sell great fast food – prawn cakes, *pau* (Chinese buns), curry puffs and sweet pastries. The best place in town to buy ethnic artefacts is Lai Lai Crafts on Jalan Airport, which has an excellent collection of rugs, sarongs, baskets, *pua kumbu* textiles, woodcarvings, beads and ceramics.

Back from the jetty, near the pond, is the **Civic Museum** (Mon–Fri 2–4.30pm; free), which has a collection of interesting exhibits on the tribes in the Rajang basin, including a well-constructed longhouse and a mural painted by local Iban; the sketches and watercolours of Kapit, Belaga and Song on display, by Timothy Chua, portray a life which is slowly disappearing. The museum also describes the lives of the Hokkien traders who were early pioneers in the region.

Practicalities

Express **boats** dock at the town jetty, from where it is a few minutes' walk to anywhere in town. At time of writing, preparations were underway to move the **tourist office** to Fort Sylvia itself. Three **banks** can change traveller's cheques: the Maybank, beside the *Hotel Meligai*; MBF, beside the *Kapit Longhouse Hotel*; and Bank Simpanan Nasional on the riverfront. **Internet access** is available in the town library on Jalan Selinik (Mon–Fri 9am–4.30pm, Sat 9am–12.30pm).

To travel beyond Kapit you need a **permit**, available from the Resident's Office (Mon–Fri 8am–12.30pm & 2.15–4.15pm) on the first floor of the State Government Complex, 100m north of the jetty on Jalan Selinik. Take your passport with you; the process takes around twenty minutes to complete.

Accommodation

Ark Hill, 10 Jalan Penghulu Geridong (☎084/796168). One block west of Kapit Square, this has small, clean rooms, including air-con and shower. RM45.

Fully Inn, Jalan Temenggong Koh (☎084/797366). Eighteen neat and tidy rooms; some with views over the river, a few with tiny balconies. ②.

Greenland Inn, Jalan Teo Chow Beng (☎084/796388). The rooms here are small and clean, and some offer good views over the Rajang. All rooms have air-con and attached bathroom. ④.

Kapit Longhouse Hotel, 21 Jalan Berjaya (☎084/796415). Although a bit grubby, it's second only to the *Rajang* as regards popularity with travellers. The rooms are small, with chugging fans; bathrooms are shared. ②.

Meligai, Jalan Airport (☎084/796817). The only upmarket hotel in town which is full of brash businessmen. There is a good restaurant here, and the large rooms have full facilities. ③.

New Rajang Inn, 104 Jalan Teo Chow Beng (☎084/796600). Small rooms which are all fully equipped with air-con, shower and TV. ②.

Orchard Inn, 64 Jalan Airport (☎084/796325). Rooms with air-con, shower and TV. ③.

Rajang, 28 Jalan Temenggong Koh, New Bazaar (☎084/796709). One of Sarawak's best-known travellers' hotels, where the guys at reception strum guitars and have sing-songs during siesta. The large rooms, many overlooking the river, have efficient fans and good bathrooms. ①.

Eating

Kapit is a fine place to **eat**, which is just as well, as it's one town where you may spend a lot of time just sitting around waiting for river connections. The food from the **hawker** stalls and **markets** is great, as is the fare in some of the sit-down **restaurants**.

Ah Kau Restoran, Jalan Berjaya. Specializes in local recipes: wild boar, steamed fish, jungle vegetables, and as much rice as you can eat, with beer, at RM25 for two.

Chuong Hin, Jalan Temenggong Koh. This café is the top place here for breakfasts: savoury cakes, curry puffs and hard-boiled eggs. The staff are fantastically surly with travellers for some unknown reason, but there's no better place to watch the comings and goings at the wharf.

Covered Market, south of Kapit Square. A dozen separate stalls serving Chinese, Malay and Dyak dishes. *Gerai Islam* sells *roti canai* and various noodle dishes with local vegetables, seafood and meat. The optimum time to eat here is between noon and 3pm, though it's open until 9pm.

Day Market stalls, Jalan Teo Chow Beng. Sarawak fast food like curry puffs, prawn cakes, corn-meal cake and tofu buns. Open 7am–5pm.

Hock Bing Seafood Café, west of the temple. With some pavement tables, this bustling café serves the best prawn, wild-boar and fern dishes in Kapit. Friendly, atmospheric and excellent value at around RM20 for two people, including beer.

Kah Ping Restoran, Jalan Teo Chow Beng. A good spot to watch Kapit life go by; the best options here are the Chinese noodle and rice dishes.

Kapitas, west end of Jalan Airport. This bar serves good chicken, rice and noodles, along with Tiger beer on draught.

Vikings, eastern end of Jalan Teo Chow Beng. It had to come to Kapit: Western fast food including fried chicken, french fries and hamburgers, all at local prices.

Up the Rajang from Kapit

Worthwhile trips can be made from Kapit to **Seligi longhouse** (although this doesn't compare with visiting the more traditional Iban communities along Sungei Baleh; see opposite) and the spectacular **Pelagus Rapids**, an hour upriver from the town.

The best guide in Kapit is the fully licensed Tan Teck Chuan, 11 Jalan Tan Sit Leong, Kapit Square; ☎084/796352, fax 796655), a *towkay* and explorer who knows Sungei Baleh and its tributaries very well. He organizes one- and two-night tours to longhouses (a two-day, one-night trip for two costs RM300), has good contacts with Iban *tuai*s and, given a month's notice, can organize a major six-day excursion to visit a very isolated **Penan** community northeast of the upper Baleh. As only a handful of tour groups make it out here each year, these Penan aren't in the habit of churning out tribal dances for outsiders; instead, visitors get to join in with whatever the community usually does – eating, chatting, making animal traps and perhaps going on a night hunt. Other four-day trips Mr Tan organizes include visits to a **Kayan** longhouse, Long Singut, on Sungei Baleh, and three-day trips along the Baleh's Gaat and Mujong tributaries to visit **Iban** communities. The latter still perform the *mering* ceremony for welcoming strangers, in which the *tuai* sings a song before blessing offerings of welcome like eggs, tobacco and rice cakes; the visitors copy his actions, after which everyone sits down and informal conversation, tea-drinking and eating can commence.

Seligi longhouse

Ten kilometres west of Kapit is **Rumah Seligi**, for which minivans leave from Jalan Airport about twice an hour. The best time to visit is the early evening, when the Iban have returned from farming in the nearby fields or from other jobs in Kapit. A sizeable proportion of the community is living outside the area at any one time, either on *bejalai* (see p.389), or simply to make better money in the timber yards upriver or on oil-palm estates. The forty-door longhouse uses a combination of new and traditional materials; the softwood structure has been modernized over the years with concrete supports and a corrugated-iron roof. The community are used to visitors so there is no need to go as part of a tour or with a guide, or to ask to see the headman when you arrive. You will be shown around and may be asked to participate in activities ranging from drinking *tuak* to weaving.

Pelagus Rapids

An hour upriver of Kapit lie the churning waters of the **Pelagus Rapids**, an 800-metre-long, deceptively shallow stretch of the Rajang where large, submerged stones make your through passage treacherous. According to local belief, the rapids' seven sections represent the seven segments of an enormous serpent which was chopped up and float-ed downriver by villagers to the north. It's only in the last ten years that running the rapids has become safe, thanks to the latest express boats which have reinforced steel hulls and immense thrust.

Tucked in between the rapids and the jungle-covered Bukit Pelagus behind is the *Pelagus Rapids Resort* (☎084/799050; ④), a beautiful longhouse-shaped hideaway whose exquisite double rooms, with attached bathroom and a veranda, look out either over the beautiful stretch of river or west over the swimming pool towards the profuse, jungle-hugging hills. Its riverfront dining room is exemplary, serving three meals a day, the menu running to exotic local dishes like *pangsoh* (chicken baked in bamboo) and various exotic takes on steamed fish.

The resort's resident guide, Nyaring Bandar, leads day-trips (RM100) to the Iban longhouse nearby where he was raised, as well as a fascinating two-hour boat trip to visit a Punan community (a small subgroup of the Orang Ulu); on the latter, you can see *Klirieng* burial poles of elaborate design with a dug-out chamber on top for storing the bones of aristocrats. It's rare to see these poles nowadays as the practice was discon-tinued many years ago. Also on offer are night-time hikes into the surrounding rain-forest and two rewarding day-treks (guide not required), one following a trail which runs directly up the hill behind the resort to an old forest track and back down towards the river (3hr round trip), the other meandering along a path which runs beside the river, coming back the way you came.

Most people get to the resort by calling them in advance to arrange a speedboat from Kapit (RM45 return). Express boats to and from Belaga can use the landing bay 300m along the river from the resort's jetty, but you'll need to arrange for the resort's boat to drop you at this bay as there's no path there from the resort.

Sungei Baleh

Sungei Baleh branches off from the Rajang 10km east of Kapit, at the point where the main river twists north towards the Pelagus Rapids (see above). Several boats leave Kapit for Sungei Baleh between 7am and noon. Some ply only the 20km to **NANGA BALEH** (90min; RM8), a large, modern longhouse, where there is also a logging camp; some push on to the junction with the Gaat tributary, two and a half hours from Kapit (RM10); while others follow the shorter stretch to the Sungei Mujong junction (1hr; RM6) – a large tributary closer to Kapit. The site of another logging camp, Putai, about 100km east of Kapit as the crow flies, is as far upriver as the express boats can manage; further upriver longboats are used.

Some of the most authentic **Iban longhouses** in the Baleh region are on Sungei Gaat, and can be reached by renting a longboat or by tagging along with one of the locally owned boats heading up the tributaries. The longhouse wharves at the junctions of the Baleh and these smaller rivers are the places to ask for advice on how to travel further, and to find out which longhouses are good to visit; almost anyone who invites you to their home will be trustworthy. **Renting longboats** to take you along the tribu-taries is expensive at around RM100 per day, but the boats are at least easy to come by in good weather, when quite a number traverse the upper reaches of the rivers, head-ing to longhouses which (for the moment) lie just beyond the boundaries of the logging zone.

Wherever you head, the **scenery** is magnificent – the land is covered in dense jungle, with the mountains on the Sarawak–Kalimantan border, 50km to the south, peeping out of the morning mist. Occasionally you'll hear sounds of conversation, ham-mering and splashing as you round a corner and catch sight of an Iban family pulling their bamboo fish traps out of the water, or cooking their catch over an open fire. The river brims with fish, while the surrounding forest supports deer, buffalo and wild boar.

Here, you're within sight of the remote peak, **Batu Tiban**, reached by explorer Redmond O' Hanlon, and described in his book *Into The Heart Of Borneo* (see p.647).

To Belaga and beyond

In the nineteenth century, the 150-kilometre trip from Kapit to **Belaga**, on the furthest reaches of the Rajang, took two weeks in a longboat, a treacherous trip which involved negotiating rapids and dodging Iban raids on longhouses which belonged to the original inhabitants of the **upper Rajang**, the **Kenyah** and the **Kayan**. After Charles Brooke purchased the region from the Sultan of Brunei in 1853, a small bazaar was built in Belaga, and Chinese pioneers arrived to trade with both the Kayan and the nomadic **Punan** and **Penan**, who roamed over a wide swath of the forest. The British presence in this region was tiny – officials would occasionally brave the trip from Kapit, but no fort was built this far up the river.

These days the trip takes up to six hours, depending on the river level. Occasionally the boat companies cancel departures: if the water level is very low, the Pelagus Rapids can be particularly hazardous, but if the level is high, the Rajang becomes a raging torrent. However, if the conditions are right, it's an excellent trip. Logging camps are scarcer in this stretch of the river, and as you near the centre of Sarawak, wispy clouds cloak the hills and the screech of rainforest monkeys and birds can be heard.

Longhouses are dotted along the river bank. As far as **Long Pila**, ninety minutes from Kapit, the people are all Iban, though between here and Belaga there are many other tribes, including the Ukit, Bukitan, Tanjong and Sekapan. Before the 1860s the Kayan were numerous here, too, but when they protected the killers of two government officials, Charles Brooke led a punitive expedition against them, driving them back to the Belaga river, upstream of Belaga itself.

Belaga

Though **BELAGA**, which lies 40km west of the confluence of the Rajang and Sungei Balui, is as remote as you can get in the Sarawak interior, it's not uncharted territory by any means. As early as 1900, Chinese *towkays* had opened up Belaga to trade and were supplying the tribespeople with kerosene, cooking oil and cartridges, in exchange for beadwork and mats, beeswax, ebony and tree gums. In recent years logging roads have snaked their way over the interior and so there is now a road – used by a few four-wheel-drives – from Belaga to Tubau, where it's possible to get an express boat to Bintulu. Until the **Bakun Dam** (see box, opposite) diversion tunnel made river travel beyond Belaga impossible, visitors would use Belaga as a jumping-off point for visits to longhouses along Balui. Now the express boats go no further than Bakun logging camp, which holds no appeal at all. But even without the opportunity to travel northeast, Belaga is still an enchanting place to visit; it still has the widest ethnic mix of any bazaar town in Sarawak.

Having said that, there's nothing particular to do in Belaga itself except watch the comings and goings. Sometimes the Penan arrive to sell things – their uniquely carved knives can be picked up here for a third of the price you would pay in Sibu. A seasonal appearance is also made by the **wild-honey collectors** from Kalimantan, who arrive in March and again in September to trade their jungle produce for supplies. Other faces on Belaga's small network of streets include Kayan and Kenyah (see box, p.404), with their fantastic tattoos and elongated ear lobes, wandering through the bazaar and eating wild boar and fried ferns in the Chinese cafés.

Belaga is fairly compact, comprising the market, some shops selling provisions, a few nondescript houses and, beyond, a small track snaking towards the formidably dense

THE BAKUN DAM

The go-ahead for the controversial **hydroelectric dam** at **Bakun** was given by Malaysian Prime Minister Dr Mahathir in 1993. The 205-metre-high, concrete-faced dam, one hour upstream on Batang Rajang from Belaga, was meant to have generated 2400 megawatts of electricity, supplying all of Sarawak's electricity and even some of Peninsular Malaysia's as well; politicians even talked of selling excess power to Indonesia. But the human impact of the project was immense. As it was intended to flood seven hundred square kilometres of rainforest, including indigenous agricultural lands and many thriving longhouse communities, in order to build the dam, nearly ten thousand people were relocated: almost all of the largest Kayan and Kenyah longhouse communities – who were never consulted about the plan – were **moved to Asap**, two hours' drive north along the logging roads from Belaga. Only small groups of families held on at the most isolated of the longhouses along Sungei Balui.

However, in 1997, during the region's economic crisis (see p.631), the scheme was shelved, just one of a series of mega-projects proposed in the early 1990s which subsequently hit the rocks. A new company has since proposed a 500-megawatt hydroelectric power station to revive the project. The initial stage of its construction, a **diversion tunnel** at the confluence of the Balui and the Rajang, has already been built, making it impossible for express boats to manoeuvre through.

The communities at Asap have received **compensation**, but their representatives continue to argue that the sums agreed upon have not been nearly enough. There are now fears that while all groups are finding it hard going at Asap, the smaller groups, like the Ukit, will find it particularly tough to adapt to the harsher conditions there, and the remaining traditional elements of their culture will disappear. Many of the resettled people want to return, but there are no plans to let them do this, the government saying that as they have already received compensation, the land has in effect been bought from them.

forest, a few hundred metres away. South and adjacent to the river, a small path weaves through pepper gardens and past wooden, stilted houses, to a school; twenty minutes' walk along, there's a pretty kampung where the Kejaman (a small ethnic group related to the Kayan, and now almost extinct) burial pole that's on display outside the Sarawak Museum in Kuching was found in the early years of the twentieth century. Just beyond the kampung and before the playing field, as you look out over the river you see a Kayan *salong* or **burial tomb** on the opposite bank; it's a small wooden construction with a multicoloured wooden sculpture sporting the image of a face. It's taboo for anyone other than the dead person's family to go within 100m of the tomb. As the Kayan prefer to build their longhouses along tributaries, yet position *salong*s on the main rivers, the tombs were often all you could see along the river for many kilometres when it was possible to travel along Sungei Balui.

Practicalities

Belaga's three **hotels** all offer similar rooms, which are of quite a high standard considering how isolated the town is. The *Hotel Belaga*, 14 Main Bazaar (☎086/461244; ②), is the favourite – the rooms have bathroom and fan. Owner Andrew Tiong and his family run a **café** downstairs, which is the best place to eat in town. The *Bee Lian Inn*, 11 Main Bazaar (☎086/461416; ②), and *Hotel Sing Soon Huat*, 27 New Bazaar (☎086/461257; ②), are the alternatives, both with small, basic rooms.

Belaga's only registered **guide**, John Bampa (☎086/461218), is an excellent person to get in touch with as he has sound contacts with most of the accessible Kayan and Kenyah longhouses along the upper Rajang. He can also organize longboats for trips along the Rajang and its narrow tributaries between Belaga and Bakun.

On to Asap and Tubau

From Belaga, it's possible to get to Tubau, where an express boat can be picked up to Bintulu (see p.407). Though marginally cheaper – and a lot quicker – than returning to Sibu and getting a bus from there to Bintulu, the **Belagu–Tubau route** entails following an atrocious logging track through a deforested area. Four-wheel-drives make the trip a few times each week, but you can only find out when the next one is going once you're in Belaga itself; registered guide John Bampa (see overleaf) or the owner of the *Belaga Hotel* should be able to find out when a vehicle is making the trip. The journey takes three hours and costs RM50 per passenger, or RM200 to charter a vehicle.

After around two hours' drive north up the Belagu–Tubau track, another logging track leads off to the east to **ASAP**, where the people from Sungei Balui have been resettled (see box, overleaf). Asap couldn't be more unlike their previous homes though – it's on a denuded plain, featuring just one – very puny – river, Sungei Asap. If you want to visit Asap (although it has no sights to speak of), it's best to go to Tubau first and then charter another vehicle (RM50 per person, or RM200 to charter vehicle) for the two-hour trip there. Upon arriving, ask to be let off at the school, where you may find English-language teacher Usat Ibut; he will arrange lodging for you (there are no hotels in Asap) and introduce you to his Kenyah family, who live in one of the fifteen longhouse complexes here. However, don't expect the vibrant communal atmosphere of the longhouses around Kuching or Kapit; Ibut will tell you that the Kenyah and Kayan people are not satisfied with conditions at Asap. He will point to the lack of public transport (it costs RM50 one way to get to Tubau, the nearest town, by Land Cruiser, whereas a bus would cost much less), and tell you how the fields where they cultivate their crops can be as much as two hours' walk away, unlike their plots on Sungei Balui

---

THE KAYAN AND KENYAH

The **Kayan** and the **Kenyah** are the most numerous and powerful of the Orang Ulu groups who have been living for centuries in the upper Rajang, and along Sungei Balui and its tributaries. The Kayan are the more numerous, at around forty thousand, while the Kenyah population is around ten thousand (though there are substantially more Kenyah over the mountains in Kalimantan). Both groups migrated from East Kalimantan into Sarawak approximately 600 years ago, although during the nineteenth century, when Iban migration led to clashes between the groups, they were pushed back to the lands they occupy today.

The Kayan and the Kenyah have a lot in common: their language, with Malay–Polynesian roots, is completely different to those of the other groups, and they have a well-defined social hierarchy (unlike the Iban or Penan). Traditionally, the **social order** was topped by the *tuai rumah* (chief) of the longhouse, followed by a group of three or four lesser aristocrats or *payin*, lay families and slaves (slavery no longer exists).

Both groups take great pride in the construction of their **longhouses**, which are very impressive. Tom Harrisson, of the Sarawak Museum, learned of a longhouse on the upper Balui which was nearly one kilometre long, and across the border in Kalimantan, it's possible to visit a longhouse, in the Kenyah town of Long Nawang, that's as high as a three-storey building and hundreds of metres long.

Artistic expression plays an important role in longhouse culture, the Kayan especially maintaining a wide range of **musical traditions** including the lute-like *sape*, which is used to accompany long voice epics. **Textiles** are woven by traditional techniques in the upriver longhouses, and Kayan and Kenyah **woodcarvings**, which are among the most spectacular in Southeast Asia, are produced both for sale and for ceremonial uses.

Potent **rice wine** is still drunk by some Kayan, although nearly all the communities have now converted to Christianity, as a result of which alcohol is less in evidence.

which were far closer to the longhouse. Despite the understandable catalogue of grievances, Asap is a community making the most of difficult conditions: they make sure
that all visitors receive Sarawak's famous hospitality no matter how tough their own
lives have become.

Once comprising just a jetty and a few shops catering for employees of the logging
companies, **TUBAU** has developed into a little town. Ask to be let off at the **KTS jetty**,
used by all the **express boats**, including services down Sungei Kemena to Bintulu
(hourly from 7am to 2am; 2hr 40min; RM18). There are no hotels, though locals can
point you towards a lodging house used by workers awaiting the early boat to Bintulu.

THE COAST FROM SIBU TO LAWAS

The route along the western flank of Sarawak from Sibu towards the Bruneian border
is one of the most travelled in the state. Although dense mangrove swamp deprives the
150km of inland road linking Sibu with Bintulu of a clear view of the South China Sea,
a lone chink in the vegetation yields access to the charming and peaceful Melanau
backwater of **Mukah**, which is perfect for a few days' relaxation. Further northeast, the
Sibu–Brunei road offers diversions into some of Sarawak's – indeed Malaysia's – best
national parks. **Similajau National Park**, 20km northeast of the industrial town of
Bintulu, is a long thin strip of beach and forest; **Lambir Hills National Park**, further
up the main highway, 30km south of Miri, is more established, and scientific reports
have suggested that its species of vegetation are more numerous than anywhere else
so far studied across the globe. However these places are just preparation for Sarawak's
most famous park, **Niah National Park**, halfway between Bintulu and Miri. Noted for
its formidable **limestone caves** – the mouth of the main cave is the largest in the world
– the park was put on the map in the mid-1950s when the curator of the Sarawak
Museum, Tom Harrisson, discovered human remains and rock graffiti inside the caves;
subsequent work suggests that Southeast Asia's earliest inhabitants were living in
Sarawak as long as forty thousand years ago.

Northeast of Niah, it's another two hours to **Miri**, which, like Sibu, is a predominantly Chinese town and an important administrative centre – though there the similarities end. The region developed commercially much later than southwestern
Sarawak, with Miri's rapid expansion stimulated by the discovery of massive oil
reserves in the vicinity. Over the last twenty years Bintulu has grown to rival Miri, specializing in the tapping of abundant pockets of natural gas on its doorstep. Both towns
have a smaller percentage of indigenous inhabitants than Sarawak's other main settlements, and although some Iban and Melanau live in the area, there are very few longhouses to visit. You need to pass through Miri en route to Batang Baram for flights and
river trips to Marudi and Gunung Mulu park, or to catch a flight to the Kelabit
Highlands (for all of which see "The Northern Interior", p.423).

From Miri, the road runs along the coast to Kuala Baram (the mouth of the Baram
river) and on to Kuala Belait and the **Brunei border**. East of here, tucked into the folds
of Brunei, are two peculiar "divisions" of Sarawak: finger-shaped **Limbang**, and **Lawas**,
the most northerly strip of Sarawak, stretching north to meet Sabah.

Mukah

Should racing up and down the waterways of the Rajang Basin leave you temporarily
too exhausted to countenance the walking trails and sapping heat of Sarawak's northerly national parks, a couple of days' easy living in laid-back **MUKAH** is sure to provide
the perfect tonic. The town is accessed by a poor track that strikes north from

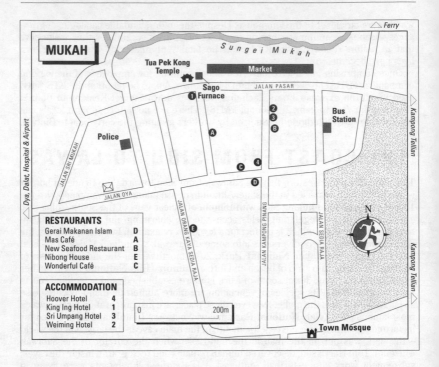

MUKAH

Tua Pek Kong Temple

Market

Sago Furnace

JALAN PASAR

Bus Station

Police

Ferry

S u n g e i   M u k a h

Oya, Dalat, Hospital & Airport

JALAN SRI MUKAH

JALAN OYA

JALAN ORANG KAYA SEDIA RAJA

JALAN KAMPONG PINANG

JALAN SEDIA RAJA

Kampong Tellian

Kampong Tellian

N

RESTAURANTS
Gerai Makanan Islam	D
Mas Café	A
New Seafood Restaurant	B
Nibong House	E
Wonderful Café	C

ACCOMMODATION
Hoover Hotel	4
King Ing Hotel	1
Sri Umpang Hotel	3
Weiming Hotel	2

0   200m

Town Mosque

Sarawak's main highway, passing oil palms, sago and ship-shape longhouses before veering west along the coast.

Mukah is a charmingly sleepy seaside bolt hole in a traditionally Melanau-dominated area. Indeed, as you approach town, you'll see an impressive **mosque** to your left, its spiked roof themed upon the conical hat traditionally worn by the Melanau. Half a kilometre north of here is the **old town**, a simple grid of streets running roughly east–west along the south bank of **Sungei Mukah**, and containing new shophouses and older, more charismatic wooden versions, some brightened by striped screens. Sights are few and far between in downtown Mukah: the best the town can offer is the garish, river-facing **Tua Pek Kong Temple**, from whose veranda you can view the river's stilt houses and boats. The bearded Tua Pek Kong, patron saint of businessmen, sits at the head of the temple's main hall, while on its walls are finely painted murals of Buddhist and Taoist deities, among them the Monkey God, as well as Kuan Yin and – bottom on the right on the right-hand wall – the patron saint of beggars, Ji Gong, who you'll recognize by his dishevelled clothing and the bottle he clutches. Just east of the temple, there's a weathered old **smokestack** that testifies to Mukah's colonial sago trade.

There's a gem of a water village, **Kampung Tellian**, just 3km from town. Straddling Sungei Tellian, which at its wider points is clogged with jolly blue fishing boats, the village is a veritable spaghetti junction of winding paths, precarious crisscrossing boardwalks and bridges. The friendly Melanau residents of its many stilt houses still wring a living from processing sago the traditional way – by pulverizing the pith in large troughs and squeezing the pulp through a sieve, then leaving it to dry.

Practicalities

Mukah's **bus station** lies on the eastern edge of the old town. From here, there are daily buses for Sibu and Bintulu. The **airport**, served by Kuching flights, is 3km west of town, and best reached in one of the taxis that buzz around town (RM6); tickets for outbound flights can be purchased at MAS, on the waterfront at 6 Jalan Pasar.

All the **accommodation** in Mukah itself is to be found in the old town. The *Hoover Hotel*, on Jalan Oya (☎084/871251; RM30), is Mukah's cheapest **hotel**, its grubby rooms redeemed by the characterful old wooden shophouse which contains it. On Main Bazaar, the *Sri Umpang* (☎084/871888; ③) is far more appealing, with tidy air-con rooms and attached bathrooms; the *Weiming Hotel* (☎084/872278; ②), directly across the road, and the *King Ing Hotel* (☎084/871400; ②), on Jalan Boyan opposite the temple, run it a close second. A strip of beach a few kilometres southwest of town contains a lovely, small hotel, the *Mukah Kaul Resort* (☎084/873933, fax 873762; ③), with its own beach; it can be reached on hourly buses (RM1.50) from the bus station.

Mukah's best **restaurant**, the *Nibong House*, a five-minute walk from the old town, represents your best chance of sampling the area's speciality, *umai*. Other options are more workaday: for Malay food, there's the *Gerai Makanan Islam*, opposite the *Hoover*, or the *Wonderful Café and Bakery*, further down the road. The *Mas Café*, around the corner, is clean and inviting, and does good *laksa* and *nasi campur*, while the tidy *New Seafood Café*, beside the *Sri Umpang*, does passable *kuey teow*.

Bintulu and Similajau National Park

BINTULU is at the centre of Sarawak's fastest growing industrial area. Up until 25 years ago, the settlement was little more than a convenient resting point on the route from Sibu to Miri, but when large **natural gas** reserves were discovered offshore in the 1960s, speedy expansion began. Since then Bintulu has followed in Miri's footsteps as a primary resources boom town, a far cry from the town's origins. The name Bintulu is, in fact, derived from the Malay *Menta Ulau* – "the place for gathering heads"; before Bintulu was bought by Charles Brooke from the Sultan of Brunei in 1853, Melanau pirates preyed on the local coast, attacking passing ships and decapitating their crews.

Modern Bintulu is very ordinary, a flat, compact rectangle of streets bordered by the airfield to the east and Sungei Kemena to the west, with nothing much of interest in between. But inexpensive accommodation is easy to find, the restaurants are excellent and the markets sell local delicacies like fresh fish grilled with *belacan* (shrimp paste). Although most people just stay overnight to await a bus connection to Niah National Park, longer stays allow **Taman Tumbina Park** (see p.410), just north of the centre, and nearby **Similajau National Park** (p.411) to be taken in.

Arrival and accommodation

The **airport**, incredibly, is right in the town centre, within 100m of most of the hotels and restaurants. The **long-distance bus station** is 5km out of town at Medan Jaya, from where you can get into the centre on local bus #29 (70 sen) or by taxi (RM10). At the northern end of the centre, on Lebuh Raya Abang Galau, is the **local bus station**, right by the Kemena river. The town's main **taxi rank** is on Main Bazaar. Boats for trips up Sungei Kemena to Tubau dock at the **main jetty**, a short way south of the taxi rank. There is no tourist office, although some leaflets on the town can be picked up from the **Bintulu Development Authority**, on Jalan Sommerville (Mon–Fri 8.30am–4.30pm; ☎086/332011).

MOVING ON FROM BINTULU

BY AIR
Bintulu is served by MAS **flights** to Kuching (RM120), Sibu (RM65), Miri (RM70) and Kota Kinabalu (RM125).

BY BUS
Dozens of long-distance **buses** run the arterial routes from Bintulu, including Suria Bus Company (☎086/335489) air-con services to Miri via Batu Niah (for Niah National Park; RM18). Many other bus companies operate here, meaning that there are at least ten daily departures for Kuching (RM52), eight to Sibu (RM17) and several to Miri (RM18). In addition, Borneo Highway Express (☎086/339855) runs a daily 5.30pm service to Pontianak (RM87) in Kalimantan.

BY BOAT
There are five daily express **boats** (around RM16) to Tubau, 60km east.

Accommodation

There's quite a wide range of **accommodation** in Bintulu, though the only real budget choices are the *rumah tumpangan*s down by the river, basic lodging houses with dormitory-style rooms catering for timber-camp workers and oil-company employees. They're often full, and there have been complaints from solo women travellers about conditions and behaviour in several of them; the places we've listed below are all a grade up and much nicer.

Capital, Jalan Keppel (☎086/331167). This is a popular travellers' hotel: cheap, basic and noisy. The shared bathrooms have *mandi*s – bucket-over-the-head showers. ②.

City Inn, 149 Jalan Masjid (☎086/337711, fax 336529). The rooms here are small but do come with air-con, TV and shower; after dark, the din from the nearby *La Bamba* karaoke joint can make sleeping difficult. ②

Fata Inn, 113 Jalan Masjid (☎086/332998). Amiable staff and pleasant air-con rooms with attached bathrooms make the *Fata* an appealing choice; ask for a room with hot water. ③.

Hoover, Jalan Abang Galau (☎086/337166). Smart but overpriced rooms equipped with air-con and shower. ④.

Kemena Inn, 78 Jalan Keppel (☎086/331533). This is a popular place, with decent rooms, run by a friendly family. A good first choice. ②.

King's Inn, Jalan Masjid (☎086/337337). Modern, clean and cool rooms with all the usual facilities. ③.

National Inn, Jalan Abang Galau (☎086/337222). Small rooms with ferociously cold air-con. ③.

Plaza, Jalan Abang Galau (☎086/335111). The top end of the hotel spectrum, with a swimming pool, and large modern rooms with full facilities; their brochure has the audacity to boast airport shuttles. ④.

Royal, 10 Jalan Padada (☎086/332166). Lent an air of some distinction by its varnished-wood trimmings, the *Royal* offers considerable privacy and comfort. ③.

The Town and around

Bintulu's main commercial streets, **Main Bazaar** and **Jalan Keppel** (the latter named after an early British official who did a long stint here), are lined with cafés spilling over with boisterous beer-drinkers, while the stores overflow with shoes, clothes and electrical equipment. A couple of blocks to the west of the commercial hub, Main Bazaar passes the **Kuan Yin Tong**, a less impressive Chinese temple than those in Kuching or Sibu; it's a rallying point for the town's Hokkien-descended population in the evening. Fifty metres west of here across Main Bazaar is the **day market** – two large,

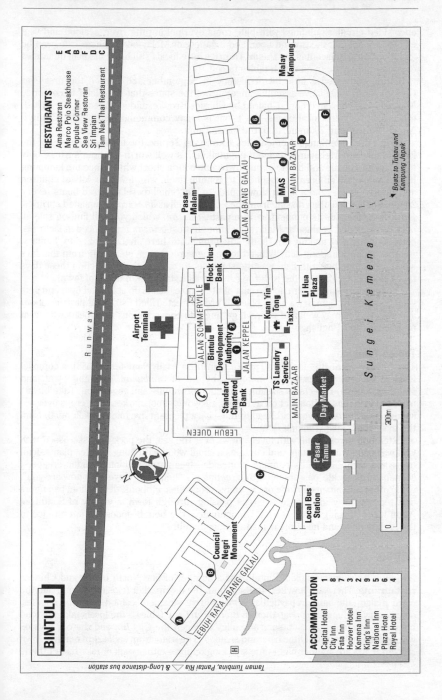

BINTULU

RESTAURANTS
Ama Restoran — E
Marco Po'o Steakhouse — A
Popular Corner — B
Sea View Restoran — F
Sri Impian — D
Tam Nak Thai Restaurant — C

ACCOMMODATION
Capital Hotel — 1
City Inn — 8
Fata Inn — 7
Hoover Hotel — 3
Kemena Inn — 2
King's Inn — 9
National Inn — 5
Plaza Hotel — 6
Royal Hotel — 4

Runway

Airport Terminal

Pasar Malam

Hock Hua Bank

JALAN SOMMERVILLE

Bintulu Development Authority

JALAN KEPPEL

Kuan Yin Tong

Li Hua Plaza

Taxis

Standard Chartered Bank

TS Laundry Service

LEBUH QUEEN

MAIN BAZAAR

Day Market

Pasar Tamu

Local Bus Station

Council Negri Monument

LEBUH RAYA ARANG GALAU

Taman Tumbina, Pantai Ria & Long-distance bus station

JALAN ABANG GALAU

MAS

MAIN BAZAAR

Malay Kampung

Sungei Kemena

Boats to Tubau and Kampung Jepak

300m

open-sided circular buildings with blue roofs overlooking the river; seafood and vegetables are sold on the ground floor, and a variety of Malay and Chinese cafés can be found upstairs. Adjacent is the **Pasar Tamu**, where locals still bring in small quantities of goods and lay them on rough tables to sell.

Bintulu witnessed a little bit of history in September 1867, when the first ever Council Negri (legislative assembly meeting) of the states that were later to comprise Malaysia was convened here. Chaired by Charles Brooke, and attended by five British officers and sixteen local chiefs, the event is today commemorated by the **Council Negri Monument**, 200m north of the Pasar Tamu.

Across the wide Sungei Kemena lies **Kampung Jepak**, the traditional home of the local Malay and Melanau-descended population. It's well worth the hour's trip, if only to escape the hustle and bustle of the town centre for a short while, since the kampung has a completely different atmosphere to Bintulu itself, with few cars, lots of children and elderly people, and a much slower pace of life. Small diesel-powered boats (every 20min; RM1) make the crossing from the jetty. As well as its *cencaluk* or salted shrimps, Jepak is famous for its pungent shrimp paste, *belacan*, which you will find on sale all over Sarawak and Peninsular Malaysia; although most *belacan* is produced in factories, cottage industries making the stuff still proliferate here in December to January. Another major kampung activity used to be sago-processing, stemming from the days when sago, together with fish, was the staple food (most of the production these days takes place in factories at the Kidurong Industrial Estate, 20km north of town).

The town's **pasar malam**, to the east of the centre, starts up at around 6pm and gets very crowded by 9pm. It's a great place to browse, eat grilled fish, meat pastries, *umai* and sweets; you may well find yourself getting into conversations with locals who want to practise their English.

Taman Tumbina

Two kilometres north of town is **Taman Tumbina** (daily 9am–6pm; RM3), a compact tropical recreation area, whose name (a hybrid of *tumbuhan*, meaning plant, and *binatang*, animal) reflects its sizeable collection of wildlife and vegetation. Take bus #1 from the local bus station, get off at the Sing Kwong supermarket, then cross over the roundabout in front of you and head uphill – it's a pleasant five-minute walk north from the main road, Jalan Tanjung Batu.

Extending across a hill with lovely views over the sea, the park is crisscrossed with walkways and wooden steps and contains a small wood with bougainvillea plants, fruit trees and ferns, its paths running alongside streams and dipping under creepers. Mynah birds tackle passers-by with greetings – "hello, goodbye and how-are-you"; while other inhabitants include orang-utans, crocodiles, gibbons, deer, a lion, two tigers donated several years ago by a circus passing through town, a variety of Southeast Asian birds, flamingos and ducks. Unfortunately the **beach** opposite the entrance to the park is dirty and no effort is made to maintain it.

Eating

Although no culinary capital, Bintulu has a number of fine North Indian and Chinese **restaurants**. There are **hawker stalls** at both the day market (closing at 2pm) and the pasar malam, the latter in particular serving great steamed seafood, stir-fried noodles, *umai*, satay and *pisang goreng*, though there aren't any tables – the locals take the food home to eat. Tables are set along the alley between the *City Inn* and the *Sri Impian*, where you can buy night-time beer and seafood. The waterfront stalls 2km north of town at **Pantai Ria** are another night-time snacking option – either walk or take bus #1 there.

Ama Restoran, Jalan Keppel. This place has excellent curries, and is particularly busy at lunchtime.

Marco Polo Steakhouse, Lebuh Raya Abang Galau. This upmarket steakhouse has an in-house band which makes conversation impossible, though at least they're better than the karaoke which starts up later in the evening.

Popular Corner, Lebuh Raya Abang Galau. Several outlets under one roof, selling claypot dishes, seafood, chicken rice and juices; out front is a capacious forecourt where you can choose to sit.

Sea View Restoran, 254 Esplanade. An atmospheric Chinese café, pleasantly positioned overlooking Sungei Kemena and away from the traffic. The food is of a high standard; meals go for around RM15 a head, including beer.

Sri Impian, Jalan Keppel. Offers an expansive spread of Malay food. There's also an in-house *murtabak* and *roti canai* stall.

Tam Nak Thai Restaurant, off Lebuh Raya Abang Galau. Curries, tom yam soups and all the other Thai classics, served in a pleasing dining room.

Listings

Airlines MAS is at 129 Jalan Masjid (☎086/331554).
Airport Call ☎086/331963 for flight information.
Banks Standard Chartered, 89 Jalan Keppel; Hock Hua Bank, Jalan Keppel.
Hospital Lebuh Raya Abang Galau (☎086/331455).
Laundry Teo Soon, 48 Main Bazaar; same-day service costs around RM5.
Pharmacy There are two directly opposite the main jetty.
Police Branch on Jalan Sommerville (☎086/331129).
Post office Main office on Jalan Tun Razak (☎086/332375).
Telephone Telekom office at the western end of Jalan Sommerville (Mon–Sat 8.30am–4.30pm).
Tour operators Similajau Adventure Tours, lobby, *Plaza Hotel* (☎086/331552) will arrange hiking trips to the nearby national parks, plus boat excursions along Sungei Kemena.
Visa extensions The Immigration Department (☎086/312211) is on Jalan Tun Razak.

Similajau National Park

Twenty kilometres northeast along the coast from Bintulu, the **Similajau National Park** might well persuade you to stop in the region a bit longer. The seventy-square-kilometre park has a lot in common with Bako, near Kuching, with its long, unspoiled sandy beaches broken only by rocky headlands and freshwater streams. Beach walks and short hikes are possible here, either along the 30km of coastline or following the trails which run alongside small rivers winding into the forest, their source in the undulating hills which rise only a few hundred metres from the beach. Shrubs grow on the cliff faces, pitcher plants can be found in the ridges and orchids hang from the trees and rocks. Two dozen or so species of mammal have been recorded in the park, including gibbons and long-tailed macaques, mouse deer, wild boar, porcupines, civets and squirrels. The monkeys are quite friendly but sightings of anything else are quite rare unless you're very patient. Saltwater crocodiles are found occasionally wallowing in some of the rivers, especially after rain – one good reason for not swimming in the river close to the park centre – and there have even been sightings of dolphins and porpoises out in the waves.

The trails

By far the greatest attractions are the beaches, on which turtles occasionally nest in April and May. The two-and-a-half-hour walk north to the two **turtle beaches** starts from the park headquarters, the first stage involving crossing Sungei Likau in a motorized longboat. The trail ascends into the forest and soon reaches the turning to the **Viewpoint Trail** which, some forty minutes from the headquarters, delivers superb views of the South China Sea. Meanwhile the main trail follows the coastline to the turtle beaches, an hour beyond which is **Golden Beach**, noted for its fine sand. Walk north along Golden Beach for ten minutes, and you reach the trail which runs inland along the side of Sungei Sebubong. Although the park offers a boat trip from the headquarters to this point, it's much more enjoyable to walk – the route into the forest is especially gratifying after the heat and lack of shade on the open beach. After fifteen minutes the trail reaches **Kolam Sebubong**, a freshwater pool whose waters are stained a remarkable ruby red by harmless tannin from the nearby peat swamp.

The other worthwhile trail leads to the **Selansur Rapids**. Follow the Turtle Beach trail for one hour and look for a marked trail which heads into the forest parallel to a small river, Sungei Kabalak. It passes through forests of sparse *kerangas* and towering dipterocarps before climbing the sides of hills, where you'll hear monkeys high up in the trees and the omnipresent chainsaw-like call of the cicadas. After around ninety minutes you reach the rapids, a pleasant place to rest and take a dip.

Though the trails aren't particularly arduous, it's as well to **wear** light boots, a long-sleeved shirt and long trousers, as well as a hat to protect against the sun. It's also useful to have a water bottle, although the river water is quite drinkable.

Practicalities

You can get here by renting a **speedboat** (RM250 per day, for up to eight passengers) from Bintulu's main jetty. The boats arrive at the park headquarters on the jetty, the starting point for the short trail north to the beach. You can also get to Similajau by **road:** leave the trunk road to Batu Niah (see opposite) after 15km and bear left along the road to a small kampung, Kuala Likau, which is at the entrance to the park. A taxi from town shouldn't cost more than RM40.

Accommodation at the park (☎086/391284) ranges from chalets with rooms (②) and cooking facilities, to the hostel (①, dorm beds RM5) and the **campsite**, where rented tents cost only RM3. The park headquarters has a **canteen** that serves simple rice and noodle dishes, and an **information centre** (daily 8am–5pm), with a small display on the local flora and fauna.

Niah National Park

NIAH NATIONAL PARK, 131km northeast of Bintulu, consists of 31 square kilometres of lowland forest and limestone massifs, the highest of these being the cave-riddled **Gunung Subis**, rising to nearly 400m. A visit to the park is a highly rewarding experience – in less than a day you can explore a **cave** that's among the world's largest, see prehistoric rock paintings in the remarkable Painted Cave, and hike along trails through primary forest. Although the region wasn't designated a National Park until 1975, it has been a National Historic Monument since 1958, when Tom Harrisson discovered evidence that early man had been using Niah as a cemetery. In the outer area of the present park, deep excavations revealed **human remains**, including skulls which dated back forty thousand years and artefacts like flake stone tools, sandstone pounders, mortars, bone points and shell ornaments – the first evidence that people had lived in Southeast Asia that long ago.

Practicalities

Roughly halfway between Bintulu and Miri, the park is 11km off the main road close to the small town of **Batu Niah**, which you can reach by regular Syarikat Bas Suria ser-

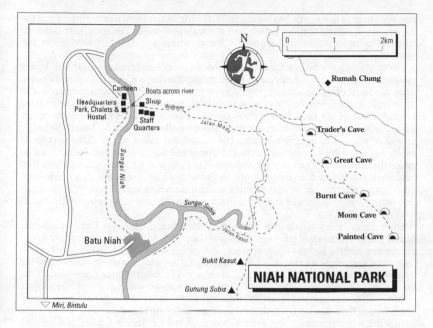

Miri, Bintulu

vices from either Bintulu (see p.407) or Miri (see p.415). Batu Niah has **accommodation** – the best place is the *Niah Cave Inn* (☎085/737333; ③) – and a few average Chinese cafés.

The caves are 4km north of Batu Niah, and reached either by a pleasant thirty-minute walk along the forest path or by **longboat** (daily 8am–4pm; RM10) or taxi (RM10) from town. The path from Batu Niah leads straight to the **park headquarters** (RM3 entry fee), which is beautifully located on the western bank of Sungei Niah, with the forest deep and thick on the other side of the river. The **hostel** here has salubrious rooms sleeping up to four (a bed costs RM10.50, or you can rent an entire room for RM42). Otherwise, you might splash out on one of the smart **chalets** (RM94 for four people) constructed beside the park headquarters. You'll only need to book accommodation in advance (at the Parks and Wildlife Department offices in Bintulu or Miri) if you intend to visit at weekends, when the park is at its busiest.

Just by the park headquarters is a **shop** (daily 7am–10pm) where you can buy basic foodstuffs, and a **canteen** (daily 7.30am–10pm) which has a limited range of dishes, such as stir fries, noodles and omelettes, at very reasonable prices. The new **Interpretation Centre**, beside the park headquarters, has a good display on the history of the caves, as well as geological and archeological information.

The caves and trails

The **caves** are a thirty-minute walk from the park headquarters. You begin by crossing the narrow Sungei Niah by sampan, then head east on the only trail into the park, which strikes off from beside a general store that stocks chocolate, drinks, batteries and torches. The trail follows a wooden walkway through dense rainforest where you are likely to see monkeys, hornbills, bird-wing butterflies, tree squirrels and flying lizards. A clearly marked path leaves the walkway on the left after forty minutes, running to an Iban dwelling, **Rumah Chang**, where you can buy soft drinks and snacks.

Further along the main walkway, a rock- and creeper-encrusted jungle wall looms up ahead and the path takes you up through the **Trader's Cave** (so called because early nest-gatherers would congregate here to sell their harvests to merchants) to the mind-blowing, 60m by 250m west mouth of the **Great Cave**. Crude steps have been dug out of the rock for the final ascent. From within the immense, draughty darkness the disembodied voices of **bird's-nest collectors** can be heard above the squeal of masses of bats. Made from the congealed saliva of the three species of swiftlet which breed here, the nests are perceived as an aphrodisiac and used to make the famous bird's-nest soup; the collectors can just be made out on top of thin beanstalk poles which snake up from the cave floor. A few years ago there were grave concerns that lax official scrutiny of their activities would lead to the exhaustion of the fragile stocks of swiftlet nests; now though, the situation is regarded as having stabilized.

Once inside, the walkway continues on to the Painted Cave, via **Burnt Cave** and **Moon Cave**. The smell of guano intensifies as the path leads around extraordinary rock formations, and the sounds – of your voice, of dripping water, of bat-chatter and the nest-collectors' scraping – are magnified considerably. As the walkway worms deeper into the darkness, the light through the cave mouth ebbs and artificial lighting takes over. As the planks are often slippery with guano, it's best to wear shoes with a grip and take a torch.

After thirty minutes you reach the **Painted Cave**, in which early Sarawak communities buried their dead in **boat-shaped coffins**, or "death ships", arranged around the cave walls; when Harrisson first entered, the cave had partially collapsed, and the contents were spilled all around. Subsequent dating proved that the caves had been used as a cemetery for tens of thousands of years. One of these wooden coffins is still perched on an incline, as though beached after a monumental journey, its contents long since removed to the Sarawak Museum for safekeeping.

Despite the light streaming from an opening at the far end of the cave, it's hard to distinguish the **wall paintings** that give the cave its name (especially as they are now fenced off), but they stretch from the dark right-hand corner behind the coffin – a thirty-metre-long tableau depicting boats on a journey, the figures apparently either jumping on and off, or dancing. This image fits various Borneo mythologies where the dead undergo water-bound challenges on their way to the afterlife. The markings, although crude, can be made out, but the brown paint strokes are now extremely faded.

The only way back to the entrance is by the route you came – try to be there at dusk to see the swiftlets return and the bats swarm out for the night. Even if you miss this, there's plenty to keep you occupied on the march back, including fireflies and luminous fungi visible from the walkway – switch off your torch and let your eyes accustom themselves to the dark.

There are two **trails** in the park which, after the claustrophobic darkness of the caves, offer a much-needed breath of fresh air. The first, **Jalan Madu**, splits off to the right from the plank walkway around 800m from the park headquarters and cuts first east, then south, across a peat swamp forest, where you see wild orchids, mushrooms and pandanus. The trail crosses Sungei Subis and then follows its south bank to its confluence with Sungei Niah, from where you'll have to hail a passing boat to cross over to Batu Niah (RM1). The other, more spectacular trail is that to **Bukit Kasut**, the clearly marked path winding through *kerangas* forest, round the foothills of Bukit Kasut and up to the summit – a hard one-hour slog, at the end of which there's a view both of the impenetrable forest canopy and Batu Niah.

Miri and Lambir Hills National Park

With a population of 200,000 and rising, **MIRI** is certainly a boom town, and, despite historic links with Western businesses – specifically the oil producer Shell – and a significant expatriate community, it retains a strong Chinese character. Some of **MIRI's** earliest inhabitants were pioneering Chinese merchants who set up shops to trade with the Kayan longhouses to the northeast along Batang Baram. But Miri remained a tiny, unimportant settlement up until the time oil was discovered in 1882, though it wasn't until 1910 that the black gold was drilled in any quantity. Since then, over six hundred wells have been drilled in the Miri area, onshore and offshore, and the main refineries are just 5km up the coast at Lutong. Miri is congested with traffic, but after a week or two spent trekking in wild northeastern Sarawak, you may well think favourably of the place. On the way there from Niah, you pass **Lambir Hills National Park** (see p.419), about 50km to the north and 32km south of Miri. Perfect for a day-trip out of the city, with some pleasant trails, it's particularly popular with Miri locals at weekends.

Arrival, information and accommodation

Miri's **airport** is 8km west of the town centre. Bus #9 (daily 6.15am–8pm; every 45min; RM1) runs from outside the terminal to the **local bus station**, located next to the town's original shopping centre, Wisma Pelita. It's a five-minute walk from this bus station east to Jalan China and the old town. The **long-distance bus station** is 4km southeast of the centre, from where regular buses run to the local bus station; a taxi into the centre costs around RM6.

Next to the local bus station, the **Visitor Information Centre** (☎085/434181) at 452 Jalan Melayu has maps and leaflets, and is also the place to go if you need to book accommodation at the local national parks or to obtain a **permit** to visit Marudi on the Batang Baram, or the Kelabit Highlands.

Accommodation

Miri has lots of regular **hotels** and some guesthouses with dorm beds, though we don't list the latter as they are really basic and none too clean.

Brooke Inn, 14 Jalan Brooke (☎085/412881). Quiet, clean hotel whose cosy rooms have TV, air-con and smartly tiled bathrooms; should you find yourself at a loose end, the friendly reception staff

---

MOVING ON FROM MIRI

BY AIR

There are daily flights from Miri to several destinations, chiefly Kota Kinabalu (RM104), Kuching (RM165), Sibu (RM115), Marudi (RM30), Gunung Mulu (RM70), Bario (RM70), Bintulu (RM69), Pontianak (RM300) and Kuala Lumpur (RM422). Hourly #9 buses (RM2) head to the airport from the town bus station.

BY BUS

All buses leave from the long-distance bus station. Suria Bus Company (☎085/412173) serves Bintulu and other locations south, including Kuching and Pontianak; Miri Transport (☎085/418655) goes to Lambir Hills; Miri Belait Transport (☎085/419129) heads to Limbang daily at 7am (RM26) and Kuala Belait in Brunei (around RM12); the last departure from Kuala Belait to Bandar Seri Begawan is at around 3.30pm, so set off early if you want to get to the Brunei capital the same day.

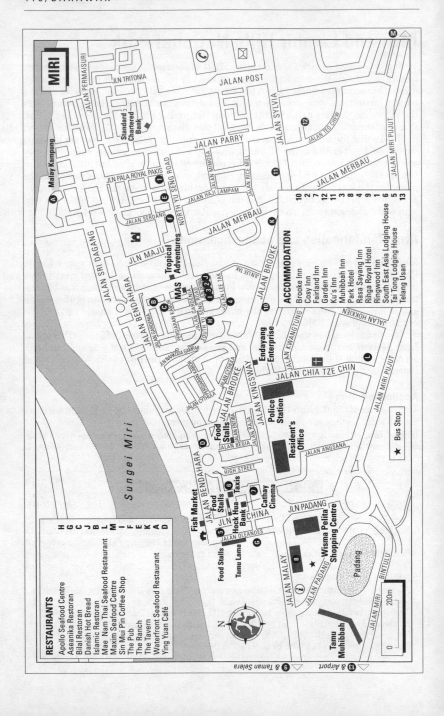

MIRI

RESTAURANTS

Apollo Seafood Centre	H
Aseanika Restoran	G
Bilal Restoran	C
Danish Hot Bread	J
Islamic Restoran	B
Mae Nam Thai Seafood Restaurant	L
Maxim Seafood Centre	M
Sin Mui Pin Coffee Shop	I
The Pub	F
The Ranch	E
The Tavern	K
Waterfront Seafood Restaurant	A
Ying Yuan Café	D

ACCOMMODATION

Brooke Inn	10
Cosy Inn	2
Fairland Inn	7
Garden Inn	12
Ku's Inn	11
Muhibbah Inn	3
Park Hotel	8
Rasa Sayang Inn	4
Rihga Royal Hotel	9
Ringwood Inn	1
South East Asia Lodging House	6
Tai Tong Lodging House	5
Telang Usan	13

will pipe up to your room your choice of movie from the local video shop. Excellent location too. Recommended. ②.

Cosy Inn, South Yu Seng Rd (☎085/415522). Well positioned close to the MAS office and a string of excellent Indian cafés. The rooms, though small, all have air-con, TV and bathroom. ③.

Fairland Inn, Jalan Raja, at Raja Square (☎085/413981). Excellent hotel with a perfect roof for drying laundry on. Clean, well-equipped rooms, and friendly and helpful staff. ②.

Garden Inn, Lot 290, Jalan Teo Chew (☎085/419822). This is a quiet hotel, family-run and hence very hospitable, with small rooms in the middle of the new town. Family rooms are available for RM80. ③.

Ku's Inn, 3 Jalan Sylvia (☎085/413733). Located on a busy street, the rooms are cosy, with air-con and shower. ③.

Muhibbah Inn, Lot 548, South Yu Seng Rd (☎412003). Uncharismatic but clean rooms, the least expensive of which are box-like, with shared bathrooms along the corridor. ②.

Park, Jalan Malay (☎085/414555). With so many other mid-range hotels in town, the *Park* has felt the pinch recently, and its heavily discounted rooms, with air-con and TV, are a snip. ③.

Rasa Sayang Inn, Lot 566, Jalan Lee Tak (☎085/413880). Located in a quiet spot with small rooms and full facilities. Comfortable, and a pleasant place to stay. ②.

Rihga Royal, Jalan Temenggong Datuk Oyong Lawai (☎085/421121, fax 425057). Bus #1 comes here, although people who can afford to stay here can also afford a taxi. Unimpeachable resort-style hotel that also prides itself on its excellent business facilities; within its manicured grounds is a giant swimming pool, fitness centre and full range of restaurants and bars. An all-you-can-eat breakfast is included in the price. ⑥.

Ringwood Inn, Lot 826, North Yu Seng Rd (☎085/415888). Upmarket place which is popular with business people. The rooms are large with full facilities – air-con, showers and TV. Good value. ⑤.

South East Asia Lodging House, Raja Square (☎085/416921). This is very cheap (and a little sleazy), with dorm beds and shared facilities. ①.

Tai Tong Lodging House, Jalan China (jetty end). Situated in the old part of town, it has men-only dorms, and more expensive private rooms. ②, dorm beds RM8.

Telang Usan, Block 1, 2.5km Jalan Airport (☎085/411433). Reachable on airport bus #9. The rooms here are spacious, with air-con and TV, and the breakfasts are of the traditional Kayan variety – fresh tropical fruit. ④.

The Town and around

The **old town** around Jalan China was once the commercial hub of Miri and, packed as it is with cafés and shops, is still the most enjoyable area to wander around. There's a **wet fish market** at the north end of Jalan China, next to which is the **Chinese temple**, a simple red-and-yellow building whose bottle-green roof is patrolled by fearsome dragons. From its small, river-facing forecourt where devotees burn joss sticks and paper money, you can watch the boats being unloaded at the fish market next door. The wide road running parallel to the river, **Jalan Bendahara**, is the simplest route into the new town area, at the western end of the centre; if you push on east, past the central **mosque**, you'll pass the old Malay kampung, between Jalan Bendahara and the river. It's now a nondescript commercial area, with the houses mostly converted into shops and offices.

Directly south of the bus station is the padang, on whose edge lies **Tamu Muhibbah** (daily 6am–2pm), the town's jungle-produce market, where Orang Ulu come downriver to sell rattan mats, tropical fruits, rice wine and even jungle animals. Just east of the bus station is the first of Miri's shopping malls to be constructed, **Wisma Pelita**; the shops in Miri are in fact some of the best in Sarawak (see "Listings", overleaf).

Taman Selera, 4km west of town, has a tranquil beach one kilometre long; it's a fine place to watch the sun go down, eat satay and drink beer from the hawker stalls. Buses #1, #5 and #11 (40 sen) head out here from the bus station.

Eating, drinking and nightlife

You can hardly go wrong for **food** in Miri, although the *Apollo*, *Maxim's* and *Bilal* are a cut above the other **restaurants** for value and quality. As for stalls, the ones next to the

Cathay Cinema on Jalan China are known for their delicious *laksa* and *congee* (Chinese rice porridge); at night you can dine at the stalls in the market at the junction of Jalan Entiba and Jalan Begia. For cream cakes, head to the *Danish Hot Bread* bakery, on South Yu Seng Road next to the *Cosy Inn*. We list some of the city's best restaurants and cafés below.

Along North Yu Seng Road in the new town are two of the rowdiest watering-holes in Sarawak, including *The Ranch* and *The Pub* – rock-music-playing, hard-drinking **bars** where expatriate oil personnel and other Europeans meet. The *Tavern*, a little way south in the *Pacific Orient Hotel*, is a shade more upmarket. Keep an eye out for the Filipino bands that often play live around town.

Apollo Seafood Centre, 4 South Yu Seng Rd. Very popular with expatriates and visitors alike. The grilled stingray and pineapple rice is exquisite, although eating here is not cheap at around RM40 for two, including beer.

Aseanika Restoran, Jalan Melayu. Malay café serving excellent *roti*s and curries. Closed during Ramadan.

Bilal Restoran, Lot 250, Persiaran Kabor. Superb Indian food: *roti*s, *naan*, *murtabak*, and outstanding tandoori chicken, a giant-sized portion of any of which costs around RM6.

Islamic Restoran, 233 Jalan Maju. Around the corner from the *Bilal*, this decent place specializes in spiced Malay dishes.

Mae Nam Thai Restaurant, *Dynasty Hotel*, Jalan Miri Pujut. Authentic Thai cuisine at around RM20 a head for a filling meal.

Maxim Seafood Centre, Lot 342, Blk 7, Jalan Miri Pujut. Although it's a bit of a trek to get there (take a taxi), *Maxim's* is Miri's most popular restaurant, serving a superb array of grilled fish with *belacan,* and delicious vegetable dishes with chilli, herbs and garlic. It costs roughly RM40 for two, including beer.

Sin Mui Pin Coffee Shop, 5 South Yu Seng Rd. A high-quality fish restaurant, with a vibrant atmosphere. The stingray is excellent – order your rice and vegetables from the people at the back. Get here before 8pm to avoid a long wait.

Tanjong Seaview, Taman Selera beach. This food centre, very popular with young Miri couples and families, offers superb satay at low prices.

Waterfront Seafood Restaurant, Jalan Pala Roya Pakis. Overlooking Sungei Miri and the shambolic Malay kampung, and set above the hubbub of downtown Miri, the *Waterfront* cooks up dependably delicious seafood.

Ying Yuan Café, Lot 55, Jalan Bendahara. Busy Chinese café noted for its *nasi campur*, which includes prawns, chicken, baby sweet corn and okra: cheap, filling and delicious.

Listings

Airlines MAS is on South Yu Seng Rd (☎085/414144).

Airport For flight enquiries call ☎085/414242.

Banks and exchange Standard Chartered, Jalan Merpati; Bank Bumiputra, Jalan Bendahara (11am–3pm only). There is a moneychanger in the Magnum 4-digit shop at 12 Jalan China.

Car rental Mega Services, 3, Lorong 1, Sungei Krokop (☎085/427436).

Hospital Miri's General Hospital is on the airport road (☎085/420033).

Internet access *WWW Café*, Lot 943, Jalan Post (back of Imperial Mall); *Fantasy Net Café,* first floor, Bendarlan Plaza, Jalan Bendarlan.

Laundry There are no downtown laundries, so ask at your hotel reception.

Pharmacy There's one on the first floor, Wisma Pelita Tunku, Jalan Padang.

Police headquarters On Jalan King (☎085/433677).

Post office On Jalan Post.

Shopping Pelita Book Centre on the first floor of Wisma Pelita has a wide selection of English-language books on Sarawak culture and geography; Longhouse Handicraft Centre, on the top floor, sells rattan bags, *pua kumbu* textiles, wooden carvings, jars, hats and beads. At Syarikat Unique Arts and Handicrafts Centre, Lot 2994, Jalan Airport, 4km out of Miri, native crafts can be bought at lower prices than in town.

Taxis Miri Taxis (☎085/432277).

Telephones The Telekom office is on Jalan Post (daily 7.30am–10pm).

Tour operators Endayang Enterprise, second floor, Judson Clinic, 171a Jalan Brooke (☎085/438740, fax 661927), does trips to Mulu; Borneo Adventures, ninth floor, Wisma Pelita (☎085/414935), a branch of the excellent Kuching operation, manages trips out to any of northern Sarawak's attractions, and has excellent guides in the Kelabit Highlands. Tropical Adventures, ground floor, *Mega Hotel*, Jalan Merbau (☎082/419337), specializes in treks to the Baram, Gunung Mulu Park and the Kelabit Highlands; expect to pay at least RM600 for two people to go on a five- or six-day trek. Seridan Mulu, ground floor, *Righa Royal* (☎085/414300) runs trips into the little-visited Loagan Bunut National Park – a superb place for bird-watching – as well as Mulu. Their five-day trip incorporating both parks, a night in a longhouse and a visit to Marudi is excellent value at RM300 per person.

Visa extensions The immigration office is at Jalan Kipas (Room 3; Mon–Fri 8am–noon & 2–4.15pm).

Lambir Hills National Park

The contours of the region comprising the **Lambir Hills National Park** (daily 9am–5pm; RM3) were formed sixty million years ago, when a vast area of sedimentary rock was laid down, stretching from present-day western Sarawak to Sabah. There is limestone and clay at lower levels, and sandstone and shale closer to the surface. Subsequent upheavals created the hills and the rich soil substrata, and gave rise to the local rainforest, with its distinctive vegetation types. Mixed dipterocarp forest makes up over half the area with the vast hardwood trees – *meranti, kapur* and *keruing* – creating deep shadows on the forest floor; the *kerangas* forest, with its peat soils, low-lying vegetation and smaller trees, is lighter and drier.

Fourteen well-marked **trails** crisscross the south part of the park, several leading to **waterfalls**. The longest trail – the four-hour trek to the summit of **Bukit Lambir** – is tough but rewarding, with a wonderful view across the park, the sounds of insects and birds echoing below. The trail cuts across deceptively steep hills, where gnarled roots are often the only helping hand up an almost vertical incline – you may well catch sight of monkeys, lizards or snakes on the trail.

To reach the three **Latak waterfalls**, 1500m from park headquarters, follow the trail marked "Latak", which branches off north from the Bukit Lambir trail. The furthest of the falls (Latak itself) is the best, its 25-metre cascade feeding an alluring pool, but given its proximity to park headquarters, it is inevitably overrun at the weekends. There are more spectacular falls further afield, past Latak; it takes two and a half hours to reach the **Pantu** and **Pancur** waterfalls – watch for the narrow paths which lead down to the rivers from the main Bukit Lambir trail. These are fine places to stop and eat, and take a deliciously cool swim. The most remote waterfall, **Tengkorong**, is a further thirty minutes' walk from Pancur.

Practicalities

Approaching from Niah National Park, you can take the Batu Niah–Miri **bus** which takes ninety minutes (RM2.40); ask for the Lambir Hills stop. Buses leave Miri's bus station every thirty minutes (daily 6.30am–4.30pm) for the forty-minute trip to the park (RM1.20) – any bus bound for Batu Niah, Bakong or Bekenu will do. It's a simple matter to get here by **car**, with the park signposted off the main Bintulu–Miri road.

Accommodation at the park is limited, so it's best to book in advance at Miri's Visitor Information Centre (see p.415). The two options are the **chalets** (②), which have cooking facilities, and the **campsite** (RM4 per tent per night). Both are close to the road, next to the **park headquarters** – where you pay your entry fee and obtain park **maps** – and the **canteen** (daily 8am–7pm). If you intend to go on the longer trails, bring hiking boots, water bottle, torch, sun hat and insect repellent.

North of Miri: the border with Brunei

The trip by **road** from Sarawak **to Brunei** is quite straightforward, though heading on **to Sabah** can take up to two days from Miri; many people prefer to get a flight to Kota Kinabalu. The only advantage – and not a particularly compelling one at that – of the land and sea route is that you can visit the territorial divisions of **Limbang** and **Lawas**, which contrast greatly with the land around Miri as they are sparsely populated by an ethnic mix of Iban, Murut, Berawan and Kelabit. This is a difficult area to get around, though, as there are few boats and no roads.

The trunk road north of Miri runs a few kilometres in from the coast to **Kuala Baram**, 30km away, a small town situated at the mouth of Batang Baram. After crossing the river by ferry (daily 6am–8pm; every 20min; free), you soon arrive at the Bruneian **border** town of Kuala Belait (see p.524), another 6km further on.

You can travel on public transport from Miri to Kuala Belait and on to the capital, Bandar Seri Begawan; the price of the Miri Belait Transport Company ticket (RM2.50) covers the bus journey and ferry crossing. At Kuala Belait, a Bruneian bus runs to Seria, for connections to Bandar Seri Begawan. The last bus from Seria to the Brunei capital leaves at around 3.30pm.

Limbang

Just to the south of Bandar Seri Begawan is **Limbang**, a strip of Sarawak roughly 30km wide and 50km deep, sandwiched between the two parts of Brunei. It's an inaccessible and thus seldom-visited district, though travel here is possible along Sungei Limbang, which snakes into the interior from the mangrove-cloaked coast, and provides access to Gunung Mulu National Park by an adventurous river trip along Sungei Medalam (see p.430). For centuries, Limbang Town was a trading centre run by Malays, who bartered the jungle produce collected by the Berawan, Kelabit, Besayak and Murut peoples with fellow Malay and Chinese merchants. Although the White Rajahs never actually bought Limbang from the Sultan of Brunei, as they did the areas to the south, Charles Brooke occupied the region in 1890, following demonstrations by the ethnic groups against the increasingly decadent rule of the sultan. However, Brooke's main reason for interceding was to acquire as large a slice of what was left of Brunei as possible, before his Sabah-based rivals in the British North Borneo Chartered Company overran it.

Limbang Town

The only building of note in the division's only settlement, **LIMBANG TOWN**, is the riverbank **fort**, the most northerly of Charles Brooke's defensive structures. Constructed in 1897, it was renovated in 1966 when much of the woodwork was replaced by more durable materials like concrete and *belian* (ironwood). The fort was originally designed to serve as an administrative centre, but was instead used to monitor native insurgency in the early years of the twentieth century. The rest of the small town is composed of a few streets set back from the river; the main street, Jalan Bangsiol, leads to the **market**, which is at its busiest on Friday when fruit, animals and vegetables are brought in from the forest to be sold.

PRACTICALITIES

The **airport** is 2km south of the town; a **taxi** into the centre (there are no buses on this route) costs around RM6. The **jetty** used by boats from Labuan in Sabah and from Brunei is behind the fort on Jalan Bangsiol; the daily Lawas boat uses the jetty 400m north of the old town. The **bus station** is five minutes' walk along Jalan Banking from the

Labuan/Brunei jetty. **Internet access** is available at *Media Cybercafé*, second floor, Limbang Plaza, close to the bus station.

Two **boats** leave at 6.30am and 7.30am for Labuan (RM20), and there are also hourly departures to Brunei (RM15) until 6pm. The daily Lawas boat (7.30am; RM20) uses the jetty 400m north of the old town. Five daily **buses** to Nanga Medamit – from where you can reach Gunung Mulu National Park (see p.428) – leave from the bus station, the first leaving at 5.30am; the trip takes around ninety minutes. The Lawas Express bus leaves at 8.30am, running to the border with the Bruneian district of Temburong and onto Lawas (RM15). There are daily **flights** to and from Miri and Lawas, which cost around RM25; Willing Travel on Jalan Bangsiol is the local ticket agent.

The cheapest **accommodation** in town is the inappropriately named *Royal Hotel* (☎085/215690; ①) on Jalan Tarap, where all rooms share facilities. The *Muhibbah Inn* (☎085/212488; ③) on nearby Jalan Banking also has a number of economical rooms, and represents far better value than the neighbouring *Metro Hotel* (☎085/211133; ③), where you'll have to pay RM20 extra for the luxury of a window. At the *Royal Park Hotel* (☎085/212155; ③), opposite the Lawas jetty some 400m north of the old town, the well-presented rooms afford decent value.

The hawker **stalls** on the breezy first floor of the market offer the most affordable **food** in town, as well as good views of the water village across the river. There are more stalls in the covered building south of the bus station, and still more on the open ground below Jalan Merdeka. The pick of Limbang's **restaurants** are the friendly Malay joints, the *Mesra* and the *Selera Muhibbah*, both good for *roti*s and *biriyani*s; the *Fortune Restaurant*, serving quality Chinese food; and the plain *Ming Seng Coffee Shop*, with a smaller range of Chinese fare.

Lawas

Boxed in between Brunei's sparsely inhabited Temburong District and Sabah is Sarawak's most northwesterly district, **Lawas**. Bought by Charles Brooke from the

Sultan of Brunei in 1905, the division is a little larger than Limbang, and has more coast-line. From its origins as a remote bazaar and trading centre for Berawan, Kelabit and Chinese pioneers, **LAWAS TOWN** – the only settlement of any size in the area – has grown into a bustling centre on Sungei Lawas, becoming prosperous from its timber industry. Above the river is a large new market which is the town's main focal point, selling tropical fruits and vegetables, and with several food stalls upstairs. On the other side of the street is another produce market situated underneath a massive *ara*, a trop-ical hardwood tree, providing much-needed shade for the traders. Saturdays are busiest at both markets, when traders from Sabah sometimes arrive to sell clothes and textiles. The only other diversion in town is the Chinese **temple** five minutes north of the market, on Jalan Bunga Teratai, remarkable only for the unusual fact that a large portion of it is open to the elements.

North of town, Jalan Punang leads, after around 7km, to **Punang** itself, the site of a reasonably attractive beach – minibuses (RM2) make the trip from the bus station.

Practicalities

Lawas **airport** is around 3km south of town – a bus usually meets the daily flights from Kota Kinabalu, Limbang, Bario and Ba Kelalan in the Kelabit Highlands. The MAS agent is Eng Huat Travel Agency, on Jalan Law Siew Ann (☎085/285570). **Boats** arrive and depart from the jetty beside the old mosque, 400m east of the town: the *Pertama Lawas* leaves daily for Brunei (7.30am; RM20) and there are also boats to Sabah's Pulau Labuan (daily at 7.30am; RM20) and to Limbang (daily at 9am; RM20). Tickets are sold at the jetty just before departure. The **bus station** is in the centre of town, 50m north of the markets.

Buses leave the station daily at 7am and 1.30pm for Brunei's Temburong District (1hr 30min; RM10), heading on to Kota Kinabalu in Sabah (5hr 30min, RM22). The other way out of Lawas is by **Land Cruiser** (4 daily between 7.30am and 3.30pm; RM40), which leave from the parking space in front of the *Mee Yan Hotel* to the low-land Kelabit settlement of Ba Kelalan (see p.442), 90km south, where you can hike to Bario in the Kelabit Highlands. Most of the six-hour trip is on unpaved logging roads; the only other stop on the bone-wrenching journey is Long Samado, another logging bazaar. It's worth noting that Sarawak has different rules on entry permits to the rest of Malaysia, which means that when you leave the state for another part of the country, you must have a valid permit to stay in Malaysia generally – you can extend your exist-ing permit, or apply for a new one, at the Immigration Department in Kuching, Miri or Bintulu; see p.20.

The *Soon Seng Lodging House* at 18 Jalan Dato Taie (☎085/285490; ①), ten minutes' walk north from the bus station, is the town's most inexpensive **place to stay**, with tiny, dusty, poky rooms and communal bathrooms. Higher up the scale are the *Mega Inn*, 1 Jalan Muhibbah (☎085/283888; ③), right in the centre of town, beside where the Land Cruisers to Long Samado gather, and the *Million Inn*, down the road at no. 5 (☎085/285088; ③); both have modern air-con, en-suite rooms, though they can be noisy in the mornings. Your most opulent option is *Hotel Perdana*, 365 Jalan Punang (☎085/285888; ⑤), a vast establishment fifteen minutes' walk north out of town.

For inexpensive **food**, try the upper floor of the market, with the usual selection of Malay and Chinese stalls. There's no menu at the tidy *Soon Yeng* **restaurant** below the hotel of the same name, but the Chinese food there is good. Otherwise, most of the best eating places cluster around the *Mee Yan Hotel*. Across the road from it is the Malay *Restoran Hj Narudin Bin Matusop*, while one block away in the other direction, the *Bee Hiong* restaurant specializes in *dim sum*. The *Mee Yan*'s next-door neighbour, the *Ho Peng*, is by far the best Chinese coffee shop in town, though, serving up sensa-tional noodle dishes.

THE NORTHERN INTERIOR

The **northern interior**, loosely defined as the watershed of **Batang Baram** – the wide river to the northeast of Miri – incorporates both the wildest, most untouched areas of Sarawak, and the most environmentally degraded. At the northernmost point of the White Rajahs' reach (and almost completely ignored by the Sultan of Brunei) the Baram had a number of Brooke fortifications, but the tribal groups living along the river's reaches were largely left to their own devices. More recently though, Baram was the first part of Sarawak to be heavily logged, and timber yards now line the river for 50km from **Kuala Baram** to **Marudi**, the largest town in the region, and for 20km to the east. The scale of the industry can be judged by the number of timber rafts which float down the wide, silt-clogged river. Although the state government is cutting back production statewide, the previously inaccessible parts of the northern interior – the northernmost edges of the Kayan and Kenyah ancestral lands on either side of the upper Baram – are being opened up to logging, with trucks weighed down with hardwoods passing along the well-maintained logging roads every twenty minutes or so. Despite the very obvious environmental problems of the region, many of the **longhouses** in this beautiful part of the state have gained economically by the timber economy. It is now much quicker and cheaper to get from upriver longhouses to downriver depots and on to Marudi than ever before, and longhouse residents can find work on their doorstep with the timber cartels. But soil erosion as a result of the deforestation has damaged their lands, water catchments are murky and often unfit for drinking, and the food supply – either forest game or from agricultural land – is diminishing. The Penan are the worst affected because, as hunters and gatherers, they rely solely on the forest for survival. Nevertheless, because of the perceived economic gains in the region, resistance to the logging has largely evaporated.

Despite the despoliation, the northern interior holds many of Sarawak's most renowned natural delights. One of Batang Baram's tributaries, **Sungei Tutoh**, branches off east to **Gunung Mulu National Park**, which contains the famous limestone pinnacles and many impressive cave systems. Further east still, straddling the border with Kalimantan and only accessible by plane, lies the magnificent **Kelabit Highlands**, a lush, sparsely populated mountain plateau, whose pleasing climate and low humidity makes it the best place in the state for long treks in the rainforest. Modern longhouse communities like **Long San** on the Baram are quite easy to visit thanks to a well-maintained logging track which connects it to the little bazaar town of **Lapok**, 90km to the northwest as the crow flies. Accessible by bus from Miri, Lapok lies near the **Loagan Bunut National Park**, its lake home to a large population of tropical birdlife.

Travel in the region is very efficient, due to the excellent rural air service and reliable river boats. In a ten-day trip you can, for example, visit Gunung Mulu, the Kelabit Highlands, the bazaar town of Marudi, and a Kenyah longhouse on Sungei Tutoh, a tributary of the Baram. However, it is difficult to get a seat on some of MAS's Twin Otter flights, particularly to Mulu and Bario from Miri and Marudi, so it's advisable to book weeks in advance if you can.

Marudi and around

On Batang Baram 80km southeast of Miri, **MARUDI** is the only sizeable bazaar town in the whole Baram watershed, supplying the interior with consumer items, from outboard engines to plastic buckets. Marudi's **jetty**, where dozens of express boats and larger vessels crowd the water, is the centre of the community; stalls and cafés here do a brisk trade as the boats disgorge those who come to visit or barter. Timber magnates in jeans and dark glasses drive by in brand new Toyota vans, while groups of young men wait for temporary labour in the timber camps, processing yards and nearby rubber estates.

Marudi was acquired from the Sultan of Brunei by Charles Brooke in 1882. He renamed it Claudetown, after the first official sent by James Brooke to administer the area. Charles Brooke encouraged Iban tribespeople from the middle Rajang to migrate here, to act as a bulwark against Kayan war parties who, at their peak in the mid-nineteenth century, amassed up to three thousand warriors on expeditions downriver in search of human trophies.

The town is dominated by two features, the jetty and the hilltop **Fort Hose**, which is reached by taking Jalan Fort from the main Bazaar Square, west of the jetty, to the top of the hill. Built in 1901, the fort was named after the best known of Sarawak's Residents, the naturalist Charles Hose; its ironwood tiles are still in perfect condition, as are the ceremonial brass cannons at the front. The fort is now a government office, though part of it houses a **Penan handicraft centre** (Mon–Fri 9am–2pm), selling baskets, metalwork and textiles. Five minutes further along the hilltop road is the old Resident's house, which, though sturdy and quite habitable, is abandoned and beginning to become tatty in the tropical climate.

Practicalities

It only takes a few minutes to walk from Marudi's **airport** into town, although **taxis** usually meet the morning flights from Gunung Mulu, Bario and Miri. The boat **jetty**, where boats arrive from Kuala Baram and Long Lama, is north of the centre and only five minutes' walk from the main hotel, the massive *Grand* (☎085/755711; ②). Just off the airport road, Jalan Cinema, it provides far and away the best **accommodation** in town, with clean, quiet rooms; its reception has details of Gunung Mulu tours and visits to longhouses. The *Alisan*, on Jalan Queen, off Jalan Cinema (☎085/755971; ③), is a very good deal, too, with large, clean rooms, boasting air-con, TV and sizeable bathrooms. Other options include the *Hotel Zola*, a stone's throw from the jetty on Jalan Cinema (☎085/755311; ②), and the *Victoria Hotel*, Lot 961, Bazaar Square (☎085/756067; ②), which has good views over the river.

There are two excellent **restaurants**. The Indian *Restoran Koperselara*, just past the *Alisan* hotel on Jalan Cinema, sells *roti canai*, curries and refreshing *teh tarek*; a full meal here costs around RM4. With outdoor tables, *Boon Kee Restoran*, set behind the main street in Jalan Newshop, is a great place for dinner; a favourite meal here is sweet and sour prawns, greens in garlic, with rice – all for around RM15 a head, including beer. Otherwise, a couple of cafés beside the jetty and on the square do adequate rice and noodle dishes.

River trips from Marudi

The upriver Baram express boat (daily at 8.30am, 10am & 2.30pm; RM15) goes as far as the settlement of **Long Lama**, 80km southeast, returning to Marudi at 6.45am and 10am. It's possible to stay the night at the longhouse here, but there's nothing to see or do at this small settlement.

Another daily departure from Marudi is the Tinjar Express (8am) along the **Sungei Tinjar** (a tributary of the Baram), which takes two hours to reach the Kayan longhouse at **Long Teru**, most of whose inhabitants work in a timber camp. The only boat along the Tutoh river (another of the Baram's tributaries) leaves Marudi at noon for **Long Terawan**, where there's a connection for Gunung Mulu National Park. Although most people travel this route specifically to go to the park, on the way you pass a number of traditional Kayan longhouses which are worth visiting. An hour from Marudi along the Tutoh, you reach the periphery of the loggers' activities; from here on, the river is clear, the jungle closing in around the river banks. Finally, the boat (hourly 7am–3pm; RM12) west from Marudi to **Kuala Baram** (see p.420) takes three hours, with numerous buses waiting at the other end for onward travel to Miri or Brunei.

Loagan Bunut National Park

Northern Sarawak's newest national park, **LOAGAN BUNUT**, is an ornithologist's paradise – there's little else to do but go boating round Bunut lake and watch the many species of **birds**, including heron, bittern, stork-billed kingfishers, egrets and hornbills. The 100-square-kilometre park, comprising the compact lake and surrounding forest, remains a well-kept secret, even though it's been open since 1991; however, Miri's Parks and Wildlife Department is building a road down to the lake's edges, which will make access to the park from Miri far simpler than it currently is. The undisturbed forest around the lake promises fine hikes, and accommodation chalets, a hostel and a café are being constructed to cater for the expected increase in the number of people visiting. These facilities – the access road, trails and accommodation – are all due to open some time in 2001.

Tucked away on the upper reaches of **Sungei Teru**, a tributary of Sungei Tinjar, Loagan Bunut is no ordinary lake. In the dry-spell months of February, May and June the water level drops drastically, and it's then that a peculiar form of fishing, which the local **Berawan** people call *selambau*, is carried out. Just prior to the whole lake becoming one expanse of dry cracked mud, the *ikan baung* and *ikan bawan* which haven't escaped down the lake's two watercourses are scooped up into giant spoon-shaped wooden frames in a spectacular action; fish even jump into the boats in a lame attempt at escaping their fate. For birds, these months are a perfect time to feed too, and in May and June the surrounding peat-swamp forest supports breeding colonies of many avian species, particularly darters, egrets and herons.

The lake

If you arrive here by longboat along Sungei Bunut (see overleaf for details of routes to the park), it's immediately clear – even before you reach the lake proper – how proluse the region's birdlife is, with herons and kingfishers swooping across the narrow river, calling out in flight. Ten minutes into the boat journey, look out for a Berawan **burial pole** which rises up from the ground on the left-hand bank; on a platform 5m up, an ossuary jar can just be seen.

One hundred metres further on, the Bunut flows into the lake proper. Initially the lake can appear huge, its edges hard to detect as the sunlight is often hazy; however, it's only around 500m in width and 1km in length. On the lake are a number of rafts with small cabins built on them, housing Berawan fishermen. Around these homes lie an intricate network of fishing plots, with underwater nets and lines tied to stakes pushed into the lake bed; boats move slowly and carefully around here so as not to get entangled with them. At the southeast corner of the lake is the privately run lodge (see overleaf).

The best times to drift by boat across the lake are **early morning** and **dusk** when the birds are at their most active. It's then that you may well see the lumbering gait of a **hornbill** (see p.435) and hear its characteristic, guttural squawk. You can also go **fishing** along Sungei Teru, just east of the lodge, when the river is high. A short **trail** leads from the back of the lodge into the dense jungle; however, the trail very soon becomes hard to follow and it's best not to venture any further without Meran, the lodge owner, as guide. Beyond these activities there is little to do in the park; most visitors adapt to Berawan ways quickly and simply relax, taking in the tranquillity of this beautiful spot which remains a sanctuary of calm in Sarawak's frenzy of development.

Practicalities

To get to Loagan Bunut by public transport, take the Lapok bus (every two hours from 7am until 3pm; 2hr 30min; RM15) from the long-distance bus station in Miri (see p.415). The bus terminates in **LAPOK**, a small bazaar town at the junction of Sungei Tinjar and Sungei Teru, 80km south of Miri; on the main street, where the bus drops you, there are a few **cafés** offering simple meals and drinks. To get here from Marudi, get the daily 8am boat to Lapok via Long Lama (3hr; RM15). Buy any provisions you need in Lapok, as there are no shops in the park; also bring mosquito repellent, as the mosquitoes at the lake are particularly voracious. From Lapok, the last bus back to Miri leaves at 4pm, though it's possible to head further east along logging tracks to Long San (see below), a route regularly covered by four-wheel-drives. Until the tarred road down to the park is completed, the remainder of the journey involves being driven 6km along a logging track to Sungei Bunut, followed by a fifteen-minute longboat trip to the park. You need to arrange in advance for the driver to collect you in Lapok (RM40); call Bunut's private **lodge** (☎011/292164; ③), at the edge of the lake, to do so. The lodge is a six-bedroom, bamboo-lined building elevated on stilts, with an open veranda out front; the rooms here are clean, if spartan, and have mosquito nets. Meals at the lodge are cooked by Meran on a simple gas stove or barbecued on the veranda. It's possible to book accommodation at the lodge independently, although given the difficulties of reaching the park, you may want to consider visiting on an organized **tour**. Seridan Mulu, a tour operator in Miri (see p.419), does day-trips and a three-day, two-night trip (RM500) here, the latter giving ample time to explore the lake and its environs.

Long San and around

LONG SAN, 250km southeast of Miri, is the largest **Kenyah** community on the Baram. Although there are a dozen or more longhouse communities on the river, Long San is the only small town, with a variety of dwellings including a large, modern longhouse, shops, an art gallery and a prominent Catholic Church.

It was just fifty years ago that Long San was established by the Kenyah, who moved here from Long Tikan, 20km upstream, when the agricultural lands there became exhausted.Though not a repository of traditional rituals and beliefs, the Kenyah here are a strong, unified, mostly forward-looking community who are keen to develop a small, manageable tourist industry. Largely not bothered that the rainforest is being stripped around them, they are only too pleased not to be any longer isolated from mainstream social and economic development. As well as vastly improved links with other towns (five years ago it took three days to get to Marudi by longboat; now Lapok is just three hours away by four-wheel-drive and Marudi is an easy boat ride from there), they now have a good clinic and an excellent school.

The region around Long San constitutes another compelling reason to travel so far upcountry. Only a few minutes away by longboat is the historic bazaar of **Long Akah**, its shell of a fort somehow highly atmospheric, as if colonial soldiers had only just left. Also nearby, a settled **Penan** community offers an insight into the world of Borneo's last hunter-gatherers.

The Town

Long San can shock those who believe Sarawak's indigenous peoples live either just in longhouses or have exchanged traditional life for the modernity and anonymity of the city. In fact, Long San is a busy, thriving community where you are just as likely to hear house music blasting from a window as watch an old-timer deliver a long prose poem at a night's revelry.

The village, with around a thousand people, has two distinct sections, one on each side of a small river, Sungei San, a tributary of Batang Baram. The older part is centred around a forty-door **longhouse** featuring an open-plan ground level onto which the private rooms open (which compensates for the lack of a first-floor veranda), and creature comforts like TV, refrigerators and radios. The longhouse's first door belongs to Kenyah businessman Datuk (Senator) Stephen Wan Ullock, probably the most influential Kenyah in Sarawak today. The front room of his spacious apartment is decorated by work from Tusau Padan, the great Kenyah artist. Five minutes' walk away over the bridge is the new part of town, dominated by the Catholic mission with its staggeringly impressive new **church**, completed in 1998, as well as a schoolhouse and shopfronts surrounding a well-tended padang. The church is probably the only one in the world to be decorated with Kenyah wooden carvings and designs, inspired by Padan's work. Ask the mission head, Brother Albert, to show you around the inside.

Practicalities

Until the planned airstrip is built in around 2002, the only way to get to Long San is by four-wheel-drive, either from Miri or Lapok. Contact Long San councillor Anthony Lawai (☎085/417985) or the manager of Miri's *Hotel Telang Usan*, Jau Eeng (☎085/411433), to arrange a time and place to be picked up. The trip from Miri takes between five and six hours and costs RM70 per passenger, or RM280 to charter the vehicle one way. Alternatively, you can get the Miri–Lapok bus (see opposite) and arrange to be picked up from Lapok (RM50 per passenger). The two-hour trip from Lapok to Long San is along well-maintained logging roads passing tracks down to Long Lama and Long Silat, other Kayan longhouse communities, on the way.

There is just one place to stay at Long San, at Lawai's **guesthouse** (RM10 a night; RM20 a day for three meals), an attractive wooden building 40m from the silt-heavy Baram river. Opposite is Lawai's shop where you can buy snacks, essential items, cold beer and local firewater. Lawai, who speaks excellent English, takes responsibility for visitors and shows them around.

Around Long San

Anthony Lawai organizes a fascinating **day-trip** (RM150 per person) taking in a nearby **Kayan longhouse**, a **Penan community**, and **Long Akah** and its **fort**, finishing with a swim in the rapids upstream. It's also possible to visit isolated longhouses further afield, though this is expensive – around RM200 per day per person – given the high costs of buying diesel upriver. The best places to make for are **Long Mekaba**; a Kayan longhouse two hours upriver, where resident musicians play the lute-like *sape* and traditional dances are sometimes performed; and **Long Moh** and **Long Pallai** (4–5hr away by boat) where the accoutrements of longhouse life – firewood, chickens, pigs and longboats – are still housed underneath the traditional *belian* building.

The road from Lapok continues beyond the turning for Long San, heading east for another 100km as far as **Lio Matoh** (see p.441), where it's possible to trek to Bario in the Kelabit Highlands. It is possible to charter a four-wheel-drive from Long San to Lio Matoh (RM280).

Long Liam and Long Beku

Twenty minutes down Batang Baram from Long San is the thirty-door Kayan longhouse of **LONG LIAM**. Along the way, the longboat passes *laran* trees whose large white flowers drop into the water and are eaten by the fish which the Kenyah and Kayan net. The longhouse, of 160 people, is 40 years old; its inhabitants, many of whom originally came from Sungei Akah, near Long Akah (see overleaf), grow rice, tapioca, maize and sweet corn in fields close by Long Liam. Their diet is supplemented with wild fruits from the jungle, and *kuman babi*, wild pig, which is plentiful in the forest. The only other building of note here is a small school staffed by three teachers giving lessons in Malay and Kayan.

Another two hours along the river is the **Penan** community at **LONG BEKU**. The 180 or so Penan here – who are extremely poor in stark contrast to the nearby Kayan and Kenyah – have been in the area for fifty years, using Beku as a base while they hunt wild boar and cut sago. Some members of the community derive an income from making *parang*s (machetes), and you may well see them smelting the iron, then slotting the blade into a wooden handle before sharpening it on a lathe.

Long Akah

In the nineteenth century, **LONG AKAH** was a vital trading post supplying the whole of the upriver region. Sarawak's Resident was once based here, and the **fort** permanently garrisoned. Its pretty little cottages with their well-tended gardens were used by colonial officers and civil servants on missions into the territory. Now, Long Akah is decaying, the superb *belian* shingle roof of the vast barn-like centrepiece building – the former storehouse – seemingly collapsing a little more with every tropical storm. Still, the place is redolent of history; to walk along its overgrown concrete path alongside white, wooden bungalows is to revisit a tropical outpost of Empire. Nowadays employees of Sarawak's Agricultural Department reside here, supplying farmers with pesticides, fertilizers and seeds.

Accessible now only by a five-minute river trip is Long Akah's once impressive **fort**, overlooking a spur on Batang Baram. Now dilapidated, this spacious building started life as the furthest outpost of the Brookes's security apparatus. Unless funds are put aside to preserve this magnificent, whitewashed wooden structure – where you can wander around and pick up mementos of a bygone age, if you are so inclined – the place will soon collapse.

Gunung Mulu National Park

Located deep in the rainforest, **GUNUNG MULU NATIONAL PARK** is Sarawak's premier national park and largest conservation area, featuring over 20,000 animal species and 3500 plant species. Until 1992, when commercial flights began to cover the route, Gunung Mulu was accessible only by a full-day trip from Marudi along the Baram, Tutoh and Melinau rivers, but the region has been a magnet for explorers and scientists since the 1930s. Quite apart from the park's primary rainforest, which is characterized by clear rivers and high-altitude vegetation, there are three mountains dominated by dramatically eroded features, including dozens of fifty-metre-high razor-sharp limestone spikes – known as the **pinnacles** – on Gunung Api; there's also the largest limestone **cave system** in the world, much of which is still being explored. The two major hikes, to the pinnacles and to the summit of **Gunung Mulu**, are daunting, but the reward is stupendous views of the rainforest, stretching as far as Brunei.

Most of the world's limestone landscapes have been modified by glaciation within the last two million years. Mulu predates this period considerably (the region was formed over twenty million years ago) and has been weathered by a combination of rainfall, rivers and high temperatures, but never by ice. The caves, which penetrate deep into the mountains, were created by running water and are very ancient: the oldest formed around five million years ago, the youngest during the last fifty thousand years. The surface water driving down the slopes of Mulu has eroded vast amounts of material, shaping the landscape outside, as well as carving cave passages within, dividing the great chunks of limestone into separate mountains.

Modern **explorers** have been coming to Mulu for nigh on a century and a half, starting in the 1850s with Spenser St John, who wrote inspiringly about the region in his book *Life in the Forests of the Far East*, though he didn't reach the summit of Gunung Mulu. A more successful bid was launched in 1932 when the South Pole explorer Lord Shackleton got to the top during a research trip organized by Tom Harrisson, who would later become the curator of the Sarawak Museum. After his successful ascent, Shackleton wrote that:

> *Although it was steep, the going during the first day or two was comparatively good, for the forest still consisted of big timber rising to a height of over one hundred feet. But it grew colder and soon we entered at around four thousand feet that extraordinary phenomenon, the moss forest. Sometimes we found ourselves plunging deeper and deeper, not knowing whether we were walking on the top of the wood or on the forest floor and occasionally having to cut tunnels through the squelching moss.*

In 1976, a Royal Geographical Society expedition put forward a quite overwhelming case for designating the region a national park, based on studies of the flora, fauna, caves, rivers and overall tourist potential. Over 250km of the caves have now been explored, yet experts believe this is only around thirty percent of the total.

Practicalities

Most visitors come to Mulu on a **tour** (see "Kuching", p.375; "Miri", p.419 and "Kuala Lumpur", p.119, for addresses of tour operators), the advantage over an independent visit being that most of the incidental costs, including boat travel to and from the park and the hiring of guides (mandatory for the treks and cave visits) are included in the price. The **minimum costs** per group for a guide and the various activities are as follows: for the **pinnacles** (2 nights/3 days) around RM110; **Mulu summit** (3 nights/3 days) around RM260; **adventure caving**: RM80 for Sarawak Chamber; RM20 for Deer Cave and Lang's Cave; and RM40 for Clearwater Cave and Wind Cave. The charge for a porter is RM25 for one day and night.

It's also possible to visit the park **independently**, arriving unannounced and booking into the park hostel or finding spare beds at the tour-operators' lodges. Visiting the park this way, preferably in a group of two to four people, you should end up paying less than on a tour, but allow yourself an extra day at the beginning of the visit to discuss options and prices with one of the guides based at the park headquarters or the nearby lodges. Try to avoid arriving at the weekend or on a public holiday when the park is at its busiest.

Whether you're here independently or as part of a group, at some point you'll probably have to shell out for **boat travel** within the park. For a group of up to four people, prices range from RM80 for the trip to Clearwater Cave, up to RM250 for the journey to Kuala Birar, en route to the pinnacles; once at the park though, it's possible to hitch rides along **Sungei Melinau**, the main thoroughfare through the park, connecting the airport with the headquarters, the caves and the main trails. It's worth asking at the tour-operators' lodges as to what cheaper options are available; the operators often have their own boats whose prices undercut the official transport. However, prices where guides are obligatory – like the pinnacles climb and the Mulu trek – are non-negotiable.

Equipment

Among the **equipment** you'll need are a large plastic water bottle, comfortable walking shoes with a good tread, sun hat and swimming gear, a poncho/rain sheet, torch, mosquito repellent, headache pills, salt solution, ointment for bites, and a basic first-aid kit. On the trails it's best to wear light clothing – shorts and T-shirts – rather than fully cover the body; this way, if the conditions are wet, it'll be easier to see any leeches that might be clinging to you. For the pinnacles, Gunung Mulu and Head-hunter's Trail, bring long trousers and long-sleeved shirts for the dusk insect assault, and for the occasional cool nights. A thin mat is also useful on the trails.

Routes to the park

There are **flights** to Mulu from Miri (3 daily; RM70) and Marudi (2 weekly; RM40). The runway here is due to be expanded in 2001, opening it to use by Fokker planes, which have up to fifty seats (compared to the Twin Otter's eighteen); until then, it's best to book two or more weeks ahead, as flights can be very full.

Reaching Mulu by **boat from Miri** involves four separate stages and takes all day, but is a pleasant trip nonetheless. The first step is to take an early bus (6am; RM2.20) or taxi (RM20) to Kuala Baram, at the mouth of Batang Baram, which takes thirty minutes. From there, take the hourly express boat upriver to Marudi (RM18) – you'll need to catch the 7am or 8am to be in time to connect with the noon express to Long Terawan (RM20). When the river is low, this latter may only go as far as Long Panai (RM12), from where you can take a longboat (RM10) to Long Terawan. Soon after leaving Marudi the boat turns into the narrow Sungei Tutoh and the scenery changes from lines of timber yards to thick forest, with occasional settlements stretching down to the bank. It takes about three hours to reach Long Terawan, where there'll be a shared **longboat** (RM35 per person) to take you on the final two-hour trip, down Sungei Tutoh and into its tributary, Sungei Melinau, to the park. It's along the Melinau that the scenery really becomes breathtaking, the multiple greens of the forest deepening in the early-evening light, the peaks of Gunung Mulu and Api peeping through a whirl of mist. The return trip requires getting up at 5am to get the boat to Long Terawan in time for the next stage on to Marudi. Give the Berawan boatmen at Mulu headquarters ample warning (two days) that you want to be on that early morning ride.

It's also possible to enter the park by boat from the north, setting off **from Nanga Medamit** and travelling up the Sungei Medalam, a tributary of the Limbang. Along the way, you pass Iban longhouses at Melaban and Bala, as well as the rangers' lodge at Mentawai. On this route, expect to pay around RM100 for the two-hour trip to **Kuala Terikan**, from where you can hike into the park, overnighting at a longhouse, Rumah Bala Lesong. For details of getting to Nanga Medamit from Limbang Town, see p.421; for information on leaving the park by this route, see p.434.

Arrival, accommodation and eating

The **airstrip** is 2km east of park headquarters, and longboats (RM5) meet the planes to take you to the headquarters or wherever you've arranged to stay. Longboats from Long Terawan stop at the park headquarters and continue to the lodges. Upon arrival at the **park headquarters** (daily 7am–9pm; no phone) you must sign in and pay your park fees (RM3 per person; RM5 for a camera permit; RM10 for a video camera). If you have arranged to sleep at one of the tour-group lodges a few hundred metres upstream, then the longboat will take you there after a brief stop at the headquarters. The park's office has surprisingly little information on Mulu, but the lodges themselves are better equipped: some have books on the caves, and their visitors' books make for fascinating reading.

Accommodation and eating

Next to the park headquarters you'll find various **places to stay**, ranging from a hostel with dorm beds (RM11) and cooking facilities, through to chalets (④/⑤) of various shapes and sizes. The park's last word in comfort and sophistication, the *Royal Mulu*

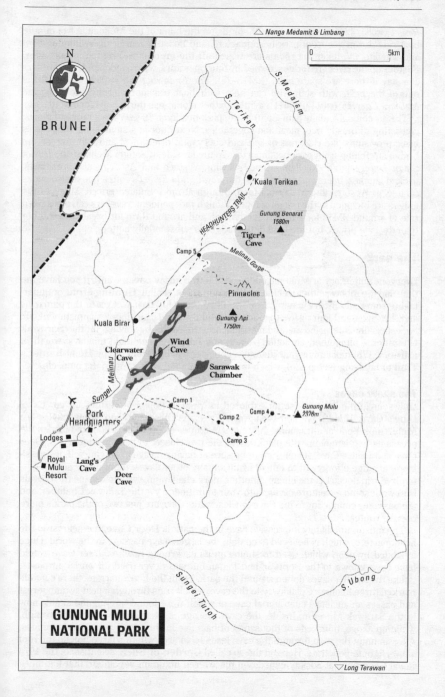

Nanga Medamit & Limbang

0   5km

BRUNEI

N

S. Terikan

S. Medalam

Kuala Terikan

HEADHUNTER'S TRAIL

Gunung Benarat
1580m

Tiger's
Cave

Camp 5

Melinau Gorge

Pinnacles

Kuala Birar

Gunung Api
1750m

Clearwater
Cave

Wind
Cave

Sungei Melinau

Sarawak
Chamber

Camp 1

Park
Headquarters

Camp 2

Camp 4

Gunung Mulu
2376m

Lodges

Camp 3

Royal
Mulu
Resort

Lang's
Cave

Deer
Cave

Sungei Tutoh

S. Ubong

**GUNUNG MULU
NATIONAL PARK**

Long Terawan

Resort (☎085/421122, fax 421088; ⑦) stands on the bank of the Melinau, a five-minute boat ride downriver from park headquarters, and boasts a sun deck, swimming pool and satellite TV. Its smart rooms are raised off the ground on wooden promenades. Further up the river are **lodges**, owned by tour operators, where independent travellers can stay if there are spare beds (RM15–25). The *Endayang Inn* (☎085/438740; ②) is one of the best, with staff who can help with boat transport around the park; the *Melinau Canteen* (☎011/291641), a little further along, has dorm beds for RM10.

The air-con **café** (daily 8am–8pm) at the park headquarters serves a range of meals, consisting of mostly rice, meat and vegetables. Next door is a small shop which sells basic provisions like rice, tins of fish and curry, and dried meat and fish. Across the bridge stretching from park headquarters to the far side of Sungei Melinau, the *Buyun Sipan Lounge* is an excellent venue, serving Western and Asian meals, breakfasts, packed lunches, beers and cold drinks; the *Royal Mulu Resort*'s coffee house also cooks up decent Western and Malaysian food, though at more inflated prices. Meals at the lodges are included in the prices of tours, though independent travellers can pay a fixed rate of around RM12 for a three-course meal, and around RM6 for breakfast – higher than the café prices, but the food in the lodges is substantially better.

The park

Everyone's itinerary at Mulu includes a visit to the **show caves** – and, if you have the time and the money, either trekking to the **pinnacles**, scaling **Gunung Mulu** or under-taking some **adventure caving**. You will need three full days to trek to the pinnacles and the caves, and four or five to reach the Mulu summit. Sticklers for punishment will be especially interested in ending their trip to Mulu by caving in the **Sarawak Chamber** – altogether, an action-packed and fairly unforgettable ten-days' worth of activities. When planning your itinerary, consider leaving Mulu by the **Head-hunter's Trail** to Limbang (see p.420), which is easily combined with a trip to the pinnacles.

The show caves

Only four of the 25 caves so far explored in Mulu are open to visitors – Deer Cave, Lang's Cave, Wind Cave and Clearwater Cave. As these so-called **show caves** are Mulu's most popular attractions, they can sometimes get quite crowded, and there's the occasional log jam along the plankway to the two closest to park headquarters, Deer Cave and Lang's Cave. If you want to be sure of having a cave all to yourself, it's possible to arrange a foray out to one of Mulu's many other caves, though this sort of customized trip doesn't come cheap. Another more challenging way to escape the crowds is to work some adventure caving into your tour itinerary – the Sarawak Chamber, and the passages connecting Wind Cave to Clearwater Cave are just two of the park's more popular routes.

The most immediately impressive cave in the park is **Deer Cave**, the nearest to the headquarters, which is believed to contain the largest cave passage in the world. Once inhabited by deer, which used to shelter in its cavernous reaches, Deer Cave would have been known to the Berawan and Penan but was never used for burial purposes, unlike the smaller caves dotted around the park. From the headquarters, there's a well-marked three-kilometre plankway to the cave, which runs through a peat-swamp forest and passes an ancient Penan burial cave in which were found fragmented skulls, now in the Sarawak Museum. Inside, the cave passage is over 2km long and 174m high, while up above, hundreds of thousands of bats live in the cave's nooks and crannies. After an hour, the path through the cave leads to an area where a large hole in the roof allows light to penetrate. Here, in the so-called **Garden of Eden**, scientists of the 1976 Royal Geographical Society expedition discovered luxuriant vegetation that had been undisturbed for centuries; the leader, Robin Hanbury-Tenison, noted that "even the fish were tame and gathered in shoals around a hand dipped in the water". It's an incredible spot: plants battle for the light, birds and insects celebrate the warm air, giant ferns grow in clusters around rocks and families of grey leaf monkeys scuttle about unafraid. The best – and the busiest – time to visit Deer Cave is in the late afternoon: wait around the cave entrance at dusk and you'll see vast swarms of bats streaming out of the cave into the darkening skies, off in search of food. Close to the Deer Cave entrance is the entrance to **Lang's Cave** (named after the local guide who first found it), the smallest of the show caves; it still merits a look, if only to gaze at its weird and wonderful rock formations, especially the curtain stalactites and coral-like growths – helictites – that grip its curved walls.

Probing some 107km through Mulu's substratum, **Clearwater Cave**, thought to be the longest in Southeast Asia, is reached by a fifteen-minute longboat journey (RM80) along Sungei Melinau from the park headquarters. The longboats moor at a small jungle pool, after which the cave is named, at the base of the two-hundred-step climb to the cave mouth. Discovered in 1988, the cave tunnels here weave deep into the mountain; ordinary visitors can only explore the small section close to the entrance, where lighting has been installed along a walkway leading 300m on to **Young Lady's Cave**, which ends abruptly in a fifty-metre-deep pothole. Deep inside the main body of the cave is the subterranean **Clearwater River**, which flows through a five-kilometre passage reaching heights and widths of as much as 90m. En route to Clearwater Cave, most visitors halt at the comparatively small **Wind Cave**, which contains a great variety of golden, contorted rock shapes, stalactites and stalagmites, best seen in the subtly illuminated King's Room. It's another five minutes from Wind Cave to Clearwater Cave, either by boat or via the walkway joining them; the alternative is to adventure-cave between them, an exhausting and muddy five-hour trip involving lots of wading and swimming in the icy Clearwater River. Wind Cave and Clearwater Cave can be combined with a trip to or from the pinnacles.

The pinnacles

Five million years ago a constant splatter of raindrops dissolved Gunung Api's limestone and carved out the **pinnacles** – 50m high, with the sharpness of samurai swords – from a solid block of rock. The erosion is still continuing and the entire region is pockmarked with deep shafts penetrating far into the heart of the mountain: one-third of Gunung Api has already been washed away and in perhaps another ten million years the whole of it will disappear. Getting a good view of the pinnacles requires a demanding **ascent** up the south face of Gunung Api to a ridge 1200m up the mountain. Once there, it's impossible not to be overawed by the sheer size and grandeur of the pinnacles, especially when the setting sun causes them to cast shadows far across the tops of the trees growing on the soil caught in the crevices near their base.

From the park headquarters, the first part of the trip to the pinnacles is an hour-long journey by longboat upstream along Sungei Melinau; you may have to help pull the boat through the rapids if the water level is very low. After landing at Kuala Birar, there's a two-and-a-half-hour trek through lowland forest to reach **Camp 5**, where there's a large hut for sleeping and cooking facilities, partially protected by a rocky overhang. Here, you're close to the Melinau gorge, with nearby **Gunung Api** (1750m) and **Gunung Benarat** (1580m) casting long shadows across it in the fading afternoon light. Also here is a bridge straddling the river; the path which disappears into the jungle on the other side is the first stage of the Head-hunter's Trail (see overleaf). Most pinnacle climbers stay two nights at Camp 5, embarking on the climb of Gunung Api the next morning and staying a second night upon returning that evening.

Only a few metres from Camp 5, another track leads to the south face of the mountain where it disappears among tree roots and slippery limestone debris. It's vital to bring a litre of water per person at the very least, as there's none on the trail, which takes about seven hours there and back; carry little else with you – wear light clothing and a hat, and bring a snack – or you'll be too weighed down. (Indeed, tour operators are being economical with the truth when they describe the climb as "moderate" – to the less than fully fit, climbing to the pinnacles can be extraordinarily taxing.) The trail is honeycombed with holes and passages through which rainwater immediately disappears. After two hours' climb, including rests, a striking vista opens up: the rainforest stretches below as far as the eye can see, and wispy clouds drift along your line of vision. The climb gets tougher as you scramble between the rocks, and the high trees give way to **moss forest**, where pitcher plants feed on insects, and ants and squirrels dart in and out among the roots of trees.

The last thirty minutes of the climb is almost a sheer vertical manoeuvre. Ladders, thick pegs and ropes help you on this final ascent; just when your limbs are finally giving way, you arrive at the top of the **ridge** which overlooks the pinnacles. The ridge is itself a pinnacle, although sited across a ravine from the main cluster, and if you tap the rocks around you, they reverberate because of the large holes in the limestone underneath. The vegetation here is sparse, but includes the balsam plant with pale pink flowers, and pitcher plants. After taking in the stunning sight of the dozens of fifty-metre-high grey-limestone shapes, jutting out from their perch in an unreachable hollow on the side of the mountain, it's time for the return slog, which takes three to four hours (longer when the route is particularly slippery).

Walks from Camp 5

Once back at the camp, most people rest, swim, eat and sleep, preferring to start the return trip to park headquarters the following day; it's possible to stay longer and explore the area, however. A path (2hr round trip) from the camp follows the river further upstream and ends below the **Melinau gorge**, where two vertical walls of rock rise 100m above the river, which emerges from a crevice. There's nowhere other than slippery rocks to rest and admire this beautiful spot before you return to Camp 5.

Another short trail from Camp 5 leads to the base of **Gunung Benarat** and to the lower shaft of **Tiger's Cave**, a return trip of around three hours. Once across the bridge, turn left to get on to the so-called **Head-hunter's Trail**, from which the trail to the cave branches off after about a kilometre. A third, much longer option is to follow the Head-hunter's Trail all the way out of the park to **Limbang**, a route supposedly traced by Kayan war parties in days gone by. Once across the bridge you turn left and walk along a wide trail passing a large rock, Batu Rikan (around 4km). From here the trail is clearly marked to **Kuala Terikan**, two hours (5km) away, a small Berawan settlement on the banks of Sungei Terikan, where you'll find basic hut accommodation. The trail continues for three hours to Sungei Medalam, where you can stay at an Iban longhouse, Rumah Bala Lesong. The next day, you take a longboat (RM200 to charter whole boat, RM50 per passenger; 2hr) to Nanga Medamit, where buses go to Limbang Town (see p.420), arriving in the late afternoon. This is a particularly good route for those wanting to get to Brunei from Mulu, as boats run frequently from Limbang to Bandar.

Gunung Mulu

The route to the summit of **Gunung Mulu** (2376m) was first discovered in the 1920s by Tama Nilong, a Berawan rhinoceros-hunter. Earlier explorers hadn't been able to find a way around the huge surrounding cliffs, but Nilong discovered the Southwest ridge trail by following rhinoceros tracks, enabling Lord Shackleton in 1932 to become the first mountaineer to reach the summit. It's a more straightforward climb these days, though much of the route is very steep; any reasonably fit person can complete it.

HORNBILLS

Hornbills are those bizarre, almost prehistoric-looking, inhabitants of tropical forests, whose presence (or absence) is an important ecological indicator of the health of the forest. You should have little difficulty in identifying hornbills: they are large, black-and-white birds with disproportionately huge bills (often bent downwards), topped with an ornamental **casque** – a generally hollow structure attached to the upper mandible. The function of the casque is unknown, though it's thought it may play a role in attracting a mate and in courtship ceremonies. In addition to this, the birds have a long tail and broad wings which produce a loud whooshing sound as they glide and flap across the forest canopy.

Hornbills are heavily dependent upon large forest trees for **nesting**, using natural tree cavities as nest sites. The female seals herself into the cavity by plastering up the entrance to the nest hole with a combination of mud, tree bark and wood dust. This prevents snakes, civets, squirrels and other potential predators from raiding the nest. She spends up to three months here, totally dependent on the male bird to provide her and her offspring with a diet of fruit (mainly figs), insects and small forest animals by means of a narrow slit in the plaster wall. When the young bird (there's only one per brood) is old enough to fly, the female breaks open the mud wall to emerge back into the forest. Given the hornbill's nesting habits, it is essential that large, undisturbed, good-quality tracts of forest are retained in order to secure their future. Sadly, hornbill populations in many parts of Asia have declined or been driven to the point of extinction by human encroachment, overhunting and deforestation.

Ten of the world's 46 species of hornbill are found in Malaysia, many of them endangered or present only in small, isolated populations. Two of the most commonly seen species are the pied hornbill and the black hornbill. The **pied hornbill** can be identified by its white abdomen and tail, and white wingtips in flight. Apparently more tolerant of forest degradation than other species, it's the smallest hornbill you're likely to see, reaching 75cm in length. Outside breeding season, it gathers in noisy flocks which are generally heard well before they are seen. The **black hornbill** is only slightly larger and black, save for the white tips of the outer tail feathers (some individuals also show a white patch behind the eye). Amonger the larger species of hornbill found in Malaysia are the **helmeted hornbill** and the **rhinoceros hornbill**, both over 120cm in length, mainly black, with white tails and bellies. The rhinoceros hornbill has a bright orange rhino-horn-shaped casque (hence the name), whereas the helmeted hornbill has a bright red head, neck and helmet-shaped casque. The call of the helmeted hornbill is a remarkable series of "took" notes which start off slowly and then accelerate to reach a ringing crescendo of cackles.

Good places to spot hornbills in Malaysia are Gunung Mulu National Park, Taman Negara, Fraser's Hill, Langkawi, Sabah's Danum Valley, and Mount Kinabalu National Park.

The first stage is from park headquarters to **Camp 3**, an easy three-hour walk on a flat trail which crosses from the park's prevalent limestone plain to the sandstone terrain of Gunung Mulu. En route, **hornbills** (see box, above) fly low over the jungle canopy and, if you watch the trail carefully, you may see wild-boar and mouse-deer tracks. The first night is at the open hut at Camp 3, which has cooking facilities. Day two comprises a hard, ten-hour, uphill slog; there are two resting places on the way where you have time to wash your tired limbs in small rock pools. From here onwards you're in a moss forest, small openings revealing lovely views of the park. The next part of the trail is along Nilong's **southwest ridge**, a series of small hills negotiated by a narrow, twisting path. When the rain has been heavy, there are lots of little swamps to negotiate, one known as "Rhino's Lake" because it was here that what was thought to be the last rhinoceros in the area was shot in the 1950s. It can be cool at **Camp 4**'s hut, 1800m up, so you'll need a sleeping bag.

Most climbers set off well before dawn for the hard ninety-minute trek from Camp 4 to the **summit**, if possible timing their arrival to coincide with sunrise. At dawn itself, the forest wakes up, the insect and bird chorus reverberating in the thin, high-altitude air. After an hour's climb you pass an overgrown helicopter pad. On the final stretch there are big clumps of pitcher plants, though it's easy to miss them as by this point you are hauling yourself up by ropes onto the cold, windswept, craggy peak. From here, the view is exhilarating, looking down on Gunung Api and, on a clear day, far across the forest to Brunei Bay. Sungei Melinau can also just be made out, a pencil-thin wavy light-brown line, bisecting the deep-green density of the forest carpet.

It's just possible to do the **return leg** from the summit to park headquarters in one day, omitting another night at Camp 4; this trip takes around twelve hours. The red-and-white marks on the trees marking the trail are easy to see, so you shouldn't lose your way in fading light.

The Kelabit Highlands

Along the border with Kalimantan and 100km southeast of Gunung Mulu, the long, high plateau of the **Kelabit Highlands** has been the home of the Kelabit people for hundreds of years. Western explorers had no idea of the existence of this self-sufficient mountain community until the beginning of the twentieth century, when Brooke officials made a few brief visits. But the Highlands were (literally) not put on the map until World War II, when British and Australian commandos, led by Major Tom Harrisson (who later became curator of the Sarawak Museum in Kuching; see p.366), used a number of Kelabit settlements as bases for waging a guerrilla war against the occupying Japanese forces. After parachuting into the forest, Harrisson and his team were taken to the largest longhouse in the area, in the village of **Bario**, to meet the chief, with whose help Harrisson set out to contact the region's other ethnic groups. Within twelve months, Harrisson was in a position to convince Allied Command in Manila that the tribes were thirsty for retaliation against their occupiers.

Before Harrisson's men built the airstrip at Bario, trekking over the inhospitable terrain was the only way to get here – it took two weeks from Marudi to the west, which, according to early accounts, required hacking through moss forests and circumnavigating sharp limestone hills and savage gorges. It was another seven days through similar conditions to the furthest navigable point on Batang Baram, **Lio Matoh**, just off the edge of the plateau. After the war, missionaries arrived and converted the animist Kelabit to Christianity, with the consequence that many of their traditions, like burial rituals and the promiscuous parties called *iraus* (where Chinese jars full of rice wine were consumed) disappeared. What's more, the magnificent Kelabit **megaliths** associated with these traditions were soon swallowed by the jungle: the dolmens, along with urns, rock carvings and ossuaries used in funereal processes, were all lost to the elements. Among the carvings, those of human faces celebrated feats of valour, like a successful head-hunting expedition, and birds were also popular images – a motif that still survives in the bead- and craftwork of neighbouring ethnic groups. Now the three most populous Kelabit settlements – Bario, Long Lellang to the southwest and Ba Kelalan to the north – have a daily air service in MAS Twin Otter planes, giving the highland people the chance of daily contact with the world beyond, and curious tourists the opportunity to visit them with relative ease.

For all the recent contact, the highlands remain a gloriously unspoiled region, with dazzlingly vivid flora, abundant game and a cool refreshing climate. Not surprisingly, these factors have made it a popular target for walkers, attracted by jungle **treks** and the prospect of encountering friendly local people, many of whom live in sturdy **longhouses** (a visit to which is an unmissable part of any trip here) surrounded by their livestock, fruit trees and wet paddy fields. The Kelabit aren't as concerned as the Iban or Kayan with formality; when you turn up at a longhouse and attract the attention of an adult inhabitant, you're inevitably invited in, soon after which the chief will arrive and take charge, urging you to eat with his family and (probably) insisting that you stay in his rooms. If you're here to stay with prior acquaintances, no harm is done by turning the chief down and staying with them. Your arrival will usually be an excuse for a mini-party, with much laughing, joking and cross-cultural leg-pulling (there's often someone who can speak some English). Swimming in the river below the longhouse is a delight, and if a hunter offers to take you on a night trek – go.

From Miri, a number of excellent **tours**, which include trekking and visits to longhouses are available; see p.419 for details. However, you can also travel to the highlands independently, then hire a guide in Bario (some of the trails don't even require guides).

Bario and around

The central settlement of **BARIO** is approximately 15km west of the border with Indonesian Kalimantan, and a few days' hard hike from Long Lellang to the south or Ba Kelalan to the north. It's a small but widely dispersed community, set among the plateau's rolling hills, surrounded by rice fields and comprising six distinct settlements – Ullong Pallang, Bario Assal, Padang Pasir, Arur Dalan, Pa Ramapuh and Pa Derong. Although Bario's new airfield is now 2km away to the east, **Padang Pasir**, the site of the former landing strip (now a buffalo pasture), is still the closest the place gets to a "centre", its small cluster of buildings containing a lodging house, a handful of dwellings and a new block of shops. With no telephones and next to no motorized vehi-

cles, the pace of life could hardly be slower, with only arriving planes disturbing the tranquillity.

Practicalities

The daily **flights** from Miri and Marudi bring in pieces of machinery, food, household and agricultural utensils as well as visitors. The planes don't land when the weather's bad so you may well get stuck in Bario – bring enough funds to stay a day or two longer than you intended, as there are no banks. Trying to get on the flight from Miri in the first place can be hard, as Bario people tend to book ahead and the flights fill up quickly: if you can't get a seat, ask to be put on the reserve list and call back the day before you want to fly. It's best not to head here on a Friday or Saturday, when the Kelabit in Miri go home for the weekend. The MAS office (daily 10am–noon) is just above a lodging house, *Tarawe's* (see below).

Bario only has two **places to stay**. One hundred metres north of the old airfield is *Tarawe's*, a relaxed lodging house (②) run by John Tarawe and his English wife Karen Hedderman. It has four rooms with three beds in each, and mats for occasions when large groups arrive. Inexpensive, hearty meals are available here, including wild boar, ferns in garlic, rice and other seasonal dishes (around RM10), and breakfasts of noodles and eggs (around RM5). There are two **cafés** in Padang Pasir which sell soft drinks, noodles, cakes and rice dishes in the daytime.

To explore the highlands without fear of getting lost, it's worth hiring one of the several **guides** in Bario; you can contact them by making enquiries at *Tarawe's*. The usual rate to hire one is around RM60 a day, but bear in mind that if you take the guide part of the way along a one-way trip, you'll be expected to pay for his return to Bario. Should you reach a longhouse unaided, you can always hire one of the locals as a guide to highlight the local attractions.

Among guides in Bario, Jamah Riboh (he can be contacted in Miri on ☎085/657013 – there are few phones in the highlands at present), a former high-school teacher, specializes in close-to-the-land excursions, including a short one to Pa Umor, the closest longhouse to Bario, and a scenic six-day trek through primary forest to Long Lelland on the upper reaches of Batang Baram, from where it's possible to fly back to Miri. After estimating the fitness of those in the group, Jamah sets the pace accordingly. Whenever possible, his trips involve gathering wild vegetables, catching fish and cooking, Kelabit-style, on the campfire.

Day-trips from Bario

A good way to acclimatize to the high-altitude conditions is to embark on short treks from Bario – the walk to the longhouse at Pa Umor is especially rewarding. Follow the track past *Tarawe's* for thirty minutes, then turn down a narrow path to the right, and after about an hour you'll reach **Pa Umor**, a modern longhouse, where someone's bound to invite you in. From here the path leads past the fork to the Kalimantan frontier post at Lembudud (six hours away) and over a precarious bridge, past remnants of an earlier longhouse, into a lovely copse, from where there are fine views of the lush highlands. Watch out for a right fork along a buffalo track, which leads into a thick, aromatic forest. At the end of this path is one of only two functioning **salt licks** on the highlands. Extracting fine, grey salt from the muddy water at the bottom of the small well is a traditional Kelabit industry which goes back centuries, though with imported salt readily available, it's seldom practised nowadays. The salt is then cooked and dried, and heaved back on the narrow trail to the longhouses.

Two other longhouses, **Pa Ukat** and **Pa Lungan**, lie further along the main track. Ignore the right turn to Pa Umor and keep walking; it takes around forty minutes to get to Pa Ukat, and Pa Lungan is three hours further along the winding road. Both are pleasant, easy walks, but you should make an early start if you're heading to the latter as there's little shade along the way.

A twenty-minute stroll west of Bario, along the road adjacent to the airstrip, leads to one of the larger longhouses in the area, hilltop **Ullong Pallang**. The residents' grand-parents decamped here from Pa Main (see below) during the Konfrontasi.

South of Bario

The Kelabit longhouses of **Ramudu**, **Pa Dalih** and **Long Dano**, where it's possible to stay, can be linked up in the **Bario Loop**, a demanding four- or five-day trek through secondary forest that starts and finishes on the old airstrip at Padang Pasir (see p.437). From Ramudu, it's possible to continue for the gruelling six- to eight-day trip south on the **Harrisson trail** to the Baram river settlement of **Lio Matoh**, which is as far as the long arm of the logging companies has reached so far.

The Bario loop

Tracing the **Bario Loop** is the perfect way to experience the natural beauty and see the attractive longhouses of the Kelabit Highlands. The clockwise loop we've described takes you in a vague oval through the settlements of Kampung Baru, Long Dano, Pa Dalih, Ramudu and Pa Berang. All walkers stop over in Long Dano, Ramudu and Pa Berang, and many also spend a fourth night at Pa Dalih. Some sections of the journey (Long Dano–Pa Dalit, for instance) are easier to follow than others, and longhouse residents do occasionally report seeing unaccompanied tourists popping out of the jungle. Nevertheless it's wise to hire a guide in Bario (see opposite): the cost shouldn't be more than RM400, including a RM10–20 courtesy charge at each longhouse to cover food and lodging. Comfortable shoes with a good grip are essential, as are waterproofs and a light pack.

The first leg is the nine-hour slog from Bario to Long Dano. The initial route is across the airfield and along a wide, stream-side track to the longhouse settlement of **Kampung Baru**, which appears some 45 minutes later. One kilometre beyond the settlement, you follow a path to the left over a wobbly steel-and-bamboo bridge, which leads onto a narrow, undulating buffalo path. If it's been raining, mud will have collected in troughs along the route. The path weaves up and down the sides of the hills and occasionally drops into the mud pools which provide bathing holes for the buffalo, the most valuable livestock of the Kelabit. There are several resting places en route; you'll see Kelabit families carrying produce back and forth to Bario, including genera-tors and rolls of wire to bring electricity to isolated longhouses. Four or five hours out of Kampung Baru, you'll pass through the area where the longhouse of **Pa Main** used to stand, until its residents relocated to the Bario settlements of Pa Ramapuh and Ullong Pallang during the uncertain times of the Konfrontasi. Your guide should be able to lead you to the hillside site of the British Army outpost that oversaw Pa Main, where empty shell canisters and other such detritus remain to this day.

LONG DANO

From here, another three hours' walking brings you to the Kelabit longhouse com-munity of **Long Dano**, which nestles in fields beside a small brook, with the forest crowding in around. Visitors spend most of their time on the communal bamboo veranda, from where you can see tiny apartments, one for each family. Below the veranda are storerooms for the stocks of rice, other grains and fried fish. A Christian community, Long Dano incorporates a Methodist church and even a tiny shop. The settlement is surrounded by tended fields, the river nearby is full of fish and game is abundant. Jobs like rice harvesting, mat-making and textile-weaving are dictated by the time of year – the rice-growing cycle starts in August with the clearing and planting of the fields, and the crop is harvested in February. After the hard labour required in processing the rice, the Kelabit women turn their attention to crafts and the men to hunting or fishing, going on trips to other longhouses or to big towns like Miri and Marudi. Some Long Dano Kelabit leave to work in Miri or in the logging industry, but most return for the *irau*s which centre on massive feasts of wild boar, crackers, rice and traditional games. The conversion to Christianity since the war has meant that rice wine has been banned – there are copious jugs of lemonade and chocolate drinks instead.

PA DALIH

The track from Long Dano to **Pa Dalih** is in very good condition, and the journey takes just two hours. It's tempting to push on to Ramudu, but since this next leg is arguably the most exacting of the loop, you might want to catch your breath before the rigours of the five-hour hike. Comprising three longhouses, a school and a football field, Pa Dalih is a springboard to several highland adventures, among them the half-day hike to see the village's huge stone drums, once used as caskets for the dead. You could also try the two-day, one-night round-trip to **Pa Dit waterfall**, and the full-on trek east to **Long Layu** and **Lembudud**, over the Kalimantan border.

RAMUDU

The journey from Pa Dalih to **Ramudu** kicks off by skirting Pa Dalih's paddy fields. Shortly after you emerge into buffalo pasture, where to your left is a large rock in whose carved niches the remains of the village's dead were once left in jars; one collapsed example is still apparent. Four or five hours of steep ups and downs follow, before you reach the ten-door Ramudu longhouse, set behind groves of pineapple trees and sugar cane, vegetable gardens and a grassy airstrip. The people of Ramudu are famed for their skilfully woven rattan baskets, worn on the back, and they may have a surplus of stock which you can buy. They also make deliciously moreish *gula tapur*, or sugar-cane candy. Ten minutes before you reach Ramudu is a **carved boulder** with intriguing representations of a face, a buffalo and a human figure. Paran Belaan is the man to speak to if you intend to push south, off the Bario loop, to Long Beruang and beyond.

PA BERANG AND BACK TO BARIO

Pa Berang is seven and a half hours away from Ramudu, along a path that sets off past Ramudu's rice-mill shed and across a hanging bridge spanning Sungei Kelapang. The trail follows the Kelapang for an hour, then plunges into the forest for several hours of crisscrossing the Batang river, finally reaching Pa Berang after a last couple of hours' splashing through swampland. The settlement is home to eight Penan families, who live in somewhat poorer conditions than those enjoyed by the residents of the loop's other longhouses. Food isn't forthcoming here, so you'll need to have brought rice and tinned food with you from Bario, which you'll be able to prepare in the kitchen of the chief, Tama Simun. Tama doubles as village pastor, and his banging on a bamboo chime each morning at 5am, to call the village together for some vociferous hymn-singing, provides trekkers with a jarring morning call. Tama doesn't speak English, though the local teacher, Balang Ibun, does.

The last section of the loop, which takes between four and five hours, threads around a few gentle slopes and crosses a half-sunk bridge over Sungei Drapur, before coming to a lengthy stretch of swamp forest that becomes a quagmire in the rainy season. The going is made fractionally easier by the lengths of bamboo that locals have laid along portions of the path, but you'll still be glad to surface in the pastures that border on Bario's old runway.

Further south: Lio Matoh

From Ramudu, a southerly trail runs right the way down to the head of Batang Baram, at Lio Matoh. The trail follows the watershed of Sungei Kelapung, taking a full day to reach the jungle shelter at **Long Okan**, which hasn't any facilities, so you'll need a light blanket for sleeping. The next day it's four more hours along a hard, hilly trail to **Long Beruang**, a large Penan settlement whose inhabitants are semi-nomadic, preferring sago-collecting and hunting to the settled rice-growing of the Kelabit. It's worth having a few little gifts, like food or tobacco, at hand.

A day's walk on from Long Beruang gets you to the longhouse at **Long Banga**, from where it's a two-hour walk downhill off the plateau to the timber camp and longhouse at **Lio Matoh**, the most easterly settlement on Batang Baram. For the Kelabit especially, this is a thriving, busy community in contrast with the jungle longhouses up the track. From Lio Matoh, small longboats sometimes travel downriver – it's a question of asking around and negotiating a price; to go just to Long San (see p.426), two days away by boat, will cost around RM500. To continue from Long San, take a four-wheel-drive vehicle to Lapok (RM50), where an express boat can be picked up to Marudi (RM15), or go through to Miri (RM70).

North of Bario

The last of the main trails from Bario is the four-day trail due north through the villages of Pa Lungan and Pa Rupai to the large Kelabit village of **Ba Kelalan**, which has an airstrip, from where it's possible to travel overland to Lawas (see p.421). You can make side trips to climb **Bukit Batu Lawi** (2039m) or **Gunung Murud** (2438m), the twin peaks of the former making it the most impressive mountain in the area. The Kelabit traditionally believed Batu Lawi had an evil spirit and so never went near it; although animist beliefs don't play much part in Kelabit life these days, climbers will still have difficulty finding a local prepared to act as a guide to Lawi. The lower peak can be climbed without equipment, but the other sheer-sided peak requires proper gear – it was only scaled for the first time in 1986. Gunung Murud is the highest mountain in Sarawak, an extremely hard climb and only accessible to highly experienced mountaineers.

To Ba Kelalan via Pa Lungan

The time required for this difficult trek depends on fitness: although a Kelabit could pull it off in ten hours, it's best to allow three days – this is some of the richest, thickest forest in Borneo.

The route from Bario heads past the longhouse at Pa Ukat (see p.438): watch out for the **trailside boulder** a few kilometres along the trail, on which human faces are carved, the only known example of funerary art remaining in the highlands. After about eight hours you reach **Pa Lungan**, which consists of detached family units around a large rectangular field for pigs and buffalo. Visitors stay in the longhouse, usually in the chief's quarters.

On the second day, it takes around four hours to get to the abandoned village of **Long Rapung**. On the way, before the forest closes in around you, look out for Gunung Murud on your left, if it's not shrouded in mist. A small shelter still exists at Long Rapung, which is nothing more than just an intersection of paths and a place to rest – you could spend the night here, allowing for a less strenuous third day. Otherwise, press on to **Pa Rupai**, four to five hours away on a hard narrow trail infamous for its leeches. A long downward slope passes through irrigated rice fields to the village. You're now in Kalimantan, although there are no signs to prove it.

It takes two more hours before the village of **Long Medan** comes into sight; here you can rent a motorcycle to the town of Long Nawang in Kalimantan and fly onto

Tarakan (provided you have a visa). The last stage of the trail to Ba Kelalan curves out of Long Medan and climbs a short, steep hill – this point marks the frontier with Kalimantan. You then walk alongside rice fields to the army outpost outside Ba Kelalan where you need to show your passport.

Ba Kelalan is smaller and more compact than Bario, comprised of single dwellings, a large longhouse and a few shops selling basic provisions. As in Bario, the airport is right in the centre of town, with the main street running parallel. There's a small **hotel**, the *Green Valley Inn* (②) and two coffee shops. **Flights** leave mid-morning to Lawas, or else you can trek north to Buduk Aru for two hours, where a Land Rover travels the logging road, taking four dusty (or mud-splattered) hours to reach Lawas. Along much of the road the signs of deforestation are only too apparent: wide gashes in the forest open out the scenery and piles of timber await collection.

travel details

Buses

Batu Niah to: Bintulu (4 daily; 2–3hr); Miri (8 daily; 2–3hr).

Bintulu to: Batu Niah (8 daily; 2–3hr); Sarikei (4 daily; 4hr); Sibu (4 daily; 4hr).

Kuching to: Anna Rais (every 30min; 2hr); Bako (12 daily; 1hr); Damai beach (every 40min; 1hr); Lundu (4 daily; 2hr); Pontianak (Indonesia; 6 daily; 8–10hr); Sarikei (3 daily; 5–6hr); Serian (1 daily; 1hr); Sri Aman (3 daily; 3hr); Tebedu (1 daily; 10hr).

Limbang to: Lawas (1 daily; 4hr 30min); Miri (1 daily; 5hr); Nanga Medamit (5 daily; 90min).

Miri to: Batu Niah (4 daily; 2–3hr); Bintulu (4 daily; 3hr); Kuala Baram (every 15min; 45min); Kuala Belait (6 daily; 3hr); Lambir Hills (every 30min; 40min).

Mukah to: Bintulu (2 daily; 1hr 15min).

Sarikei to: Bintulu (4 daily; 4hr); Kuching (3 daily; 5–6hr).

Sibu to: Bintulu (4 daily; 4hr); Mukah (1 daily; 2hr 30min).

Boats

Belaga to: Kapit (2 daily; 4hr).

Bintulu to: Tubau (5 daily; 2–3hr).

Kapit to: Belaga (2 daily; 4–5hr); Mujong (1 daily; 2hr); Nanga Baleh (2 daily; 1hr 30min); Sungei Gaat (1 daily; 2hr).

Kuala Baram to: Marudi (7 daily; 3hr)

Kuching to: Sarikei (1 daily; 2–3hr); Sibu (1 daily; 4hr).

Limbang to: Bandar Seri Begawan (10 daily; 30min); Labuan (2 daily; 1–2hr); Lawas (1 daily; 30min).

Long Lama to: Marudi (3 daily; 3hr).

Marudi to: Kuala Baram (7 daily; 2–3hr); Lapok (1 daily; 2hr); Long Lama (3 daily; 3hr).

Sarikei to: Kuching (2 daily; 2–3hr); Sibu (2 daily; 1–2hr).

Sibu to: Kapit (9 daily; 3–4hr); Kuching (2 weekly; 14hr).

Tubau to: Bintulu (5 daily; 3hr).

Flights

Bario to: Marudi (1 daily; 50min); Miri (1 daily; 1hr 15min).

Bintulu to: Kota Kinabalu (2 daily; 1hr 15min); Kuching (5 daily; 1hr); Miri (3 daily; 35min); Sibu (3 daily; 1hr).

Kuala Lumpur to: Kuching (at least 10 daily; 1hr 40min).

Kuching to: Bandar Seri Begawan (3 weekly; 1hr 10min); Bintulu (5 daily; 1hr); Johor Bahru (3 daily; 1hr 20min); Kota Kinabalu (5 daily; 2hr 20min); Kuala Lumpur (9 daily; 1hr 40min); Miri (5 daily; 1hr); Pontianak (Indonesia; 4 weekly; 1hr);

Sibu (2 daily; 40min); Singapore (2 daily; 1hr 20min).

Limbang to: Lawas (5 weekly; 20min); Miri (1 daily; 40min).

Marudi to: Bario (1 daily; 50min); Miri (2 daily; 20min).

Miri to: Bario (1 daily; 1hr 15min); Bintulu (3 daily; 35min); Gunung Mulu (2 daily; 35min); Kota Kinabalu (4 daily; 40min); Kuala Lumpur (2 daily; 24hr 30min); Kuching (5 daily; 1hr); Lapok (5 daily; 2hr 30min); Lawas (2 daily; 45min); Limbang (1 daily; 40min); Long Lellang (1 weekly; 1hr 10min); Marudi (2 daily; 20min); Pontianak (Indonesia; 4 weekly; 2hr 30min); Sibu (4 daily; 1hr).

Sibu to: Bintulu (3 daily; 35min); Kota Kinabalu (2 daily; 1hr 40min); Kuching (10 daily; 40min); Miri (3 daily; 1hr).

CHAPTER SEVEN

SABAH

U ntil European powers began to gain a foothold here in the nineteenth century, **SABAH**, at the northern tip of Borneo, was inhabited by tribal peoples who had only minimal contact with the outside world, so that their costumes, traditions and languages were unique. But since joining the Malaysian Federation at its foundation in 1963, Sabah has undergone rapid, if patchy, modernization, its various peoples largely exchanging an identification with indigenous ways for a collective Malaysian identity which has led to the erosion of many traditions. As the state's cultural landscape has changed, so has its environment; the **logging** industry has decimated vast portions of the state's natural forests, the cleared regions often used to plant thousands of acres of oil palm, a monoculture which has little truck with ecological diversity. Sabah's urban centres are hardly attractive or historically rich places either: World War II bombs and hurried urban redevelopment have conspired to produce a capital city and a chain of towns almost devoid of architectural worth, while a lack of funding from Kuala Lumpur – a situation that's only recently begun to improve – has left the state's infrastructure and economy in a state of disrepair.

Thankfully, this bleak picture neglects the natural riches on parade in a fertile region, whose name – according to some sources – goes back to biblical times and means "the land below the wind" (Sabah's 72,500 square kilometres falling just south of the typhoon belt). Within the state are a variety of **terrains**, from wild, swampy, mangrove-tangled coastal areas, through the dazzling greens of paddy fields and rainforests to the dizzy heights of the Crocker Mountain Range – home to the highest mountain peak between the Himalayas and New Guinea, Mount Kinabalu. The eastern part of Sabah encompasses some fabulous areas for spotting **wildlife**; at Sungei Kinabatangan – soon to be a protected area – you can see forest-dwelling proboscis monkeys, orang-utans, bearded pigs, elephants and hornbills, and on Pulau Selingan, there are turtles who swim ashore to lay their eggs.

More than eighty dialects are spoken by Sabah's ethnic groups, which number over thirty, though with traditional costumes increasingly losing out to T-shirts and shorts, it would take an anthropologist to distinguish one tribe from another. The peoples of the **Kadazan/Dusun** tribes constitute the largest indigenous racial group, along with the **Murut** of the southwest, and Sabah's so-called "sea gypsies", the **Bajau**. More recently, Sabah has seen a huge influx of Filipino and Indonesian immigrants, particularly on its east coast. One of the few annual events when indigenous culture is celebrated is the Sabah Fest, a week-long celebration, held in May, that's the climax of *Pesta Kaamatan*, the Kadazan/Dusun harvest festival. It's always worth visiting one of the **tamus**, or market fairs, held in towns and villages across the state, usually weekly. The *tamu* has long been an important social focal point of tribal life in Sabah, and each draws crowds of people from the surrounding region, who come to catch up with local goings-on as much as to buy and sell produce.

Its inaccessibility and the expense of visiting, relative to the rest of Malaysia, make Sabah a place to visit with a specific purpose in mind, the classic reason being to climb 4101-metre Mount Kinabalu in the northwest. Most trips start in the capital **Kota Kinabalu**, from where Sabah's main road heads south to **Beaufort**, the point at which the state's only railway heads into the rural **interior**, its route taking advantage of the

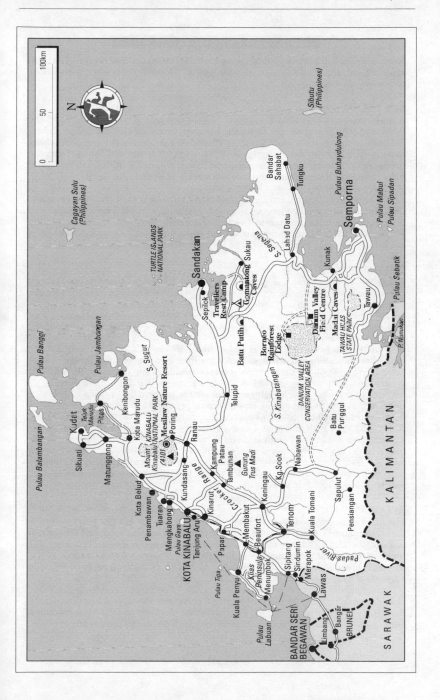

SABAH PRACTICALITIES

Sabah is 600km and a pricey air ticket away from the Peninsula, while several of its highlights will cut large chunks out of your **budget**, so it's worth doing some sums before committing yourself to a visit here.

GETTING THERE

Kota Kinabalu (KK) is almost certain to be your first port of call in Sabah. From the Peninsula, MAS flies there out of **Kuala Lumpur** (from RM440) and **Johor Bahru** (RM350), with some non-stop services. There are also departures out of **Kuching** (around RM230), with direct flights every day except Tuesday and Friday. From the Brunei capital **Bandar Seri Begawan**, Royal Brunei flies to KK (RM117) daily. Finally, from Tarakan in **Kalimantan**, there are two weekly MAS flights to Tawau (RM210) in the southeast of Sabah.

Daily **boats** from **Brunei**, and from **Lawas** and **Limbang** in northern Sarawak, run to Pulau Labuan, from where there are regular connections with KK. There's a daily ferry from northeastern **Kalimantan** to Tawau and a weekly ferry from Zamboanga in the **Philippines** to Sandakan. The only **overland route** into Sabah is from Lawas which is a short bus ride away from the border at Merapok; see p.422 for more.

GETTING AROUND

Unless you rent your own transport in KK (see p.457), or can afford to take internal flights, you'll rely almost exclusively upon buses, minibuses and Land Cruisers for getting around. Unfortunately, Sabah has the poorest **roads** on average in Malaysia – around a quarter of all roads aren't sealed and many are little more than dirt tracks. That said, most roads between towns are fine; it's mainly in rural areas that the roads could do with much improvement.

By far the most common form of public transport on both local and long-distance routes are the **minibuses**, whose drivers have their own way of doing things – either going the straightest way between two points at breakneck speed or languidly following a circuitous path, picking up and dropping customers off. There have been some attempts to get these vehicles outlawed, but for the moment they remain a necessary evil. The roomier, though usually slower, **buses** generally leave early in the morning; they're worth catching for trips between the main towns – say from KK to Kudat, Sandakan, Lahud Datu or Tawau. **Land Cruisers** – outsize jeeps – are the most comfortable means of travel, though appreciably more expensive than minibuses or other buses. Sabah is also crisscrossed by a good **plane** network, with daily flights between Kota Kinabalu, Sandakan, Tawau and other places. There's no equivalent in Sabah to Sarawak's express boats, and you'll have to rent your own **boat** – usually a substantial outlay – if you're intent on a river trip.

ACCOMMODATION

The range of **accommodation** in Sabah has improved in the last few years, with new backpacker hostels, beach resorts and jungle campsites popping up around the state; in addition, there's a plethora of mid-price, functional Chinese-run hotels. There's less of a **longhouse** scene in Sabah than there is in Sarawak, though it's quite feasible to stay overnight in one of the small longhouses around Sapulut, or on the Kudat Peninsula. The etiquette of longhouse visits is the same as in Sarawak – see p.367 for details.

Throughout the Malaysia chapters we've used the following **price codes** to denote the cheapest available room for two people. Single occupancy should cost less than double, though it's only mid-range and top-tier hotels that are likely to offer such discounts. Some guesthouses provide dormitory beds, for which the ringgit price is given.

① RM20 and under	④ RM61–80	⑦ RM161–220
② RM21–40	⑤ RM81–110	⑧ RM221–360
③ RM41–60	⑥ RM111–160	⑨ RM361 and above

swath cut through the Crocker Mountain Range by the broad Sungei Padas. The train line terminates midway between the towns of **Tenom** and **Keningau**, to the southwest of which is Murut territory, isolated enough to allow a taste of the adventures that travelling in Sabah once entailed; a short way north, Kadazan/Dusuns tend the patchwork of paddy fields that quilts **Tambunan Plain**.

North of Kota Kinabalu, the main road strays into **Bajau** country before turning eastwards through lowland dipterocarp forest and the awesome granite shelves of **Mount Kinabalu**. The mountain is a joy, its challenging but manageable slopes tailor-made for very fit amateur climbers; on clear days the jagged summit offers staggering views of Sabah's west coast below, though it's often cloudy at the top. Further north are the beaches and coconut groves of **Kudat**, where the few remaining **longhouses** of the Rungus tribe can be visited.

The towns of the eastern seaboard are rather ramshackle affairs, but possess a kind of frontier charm. Nevertheless, **Sandakan**, a busy community built with timber money, is a major draw, largely as it's the main base for visiting the offshore **Turtle Islands Park**, where you can often spot turtles and, in season, watch them laying their eggs. Indeed, if wildlife is your main reason for coming to Sabah, you'll doubtless be keen to visit the nearby **Sepilok Orang-utan Rehabilitation Centre**, as well as the lower reaches of **Sungei Kinabatangan**, which support groups of proboscis monkeys, orang-utans and elephants. Further south, the **Danum Valley Conservation Area** has embarked on a programme of ecotourism, its *Borneo Rainforest Lodge* offering visitors a luxurious environment from which to enjoy the jungle. Of more specialized interest is **Pulau Sipadan**, just off Semporna on the southeastern coast. Sabah's only oceanic island (it's not part of the Bornean continental shelf), Sipadan offers superb diving, with some expensive packages on offer, though recent moves to market the other islands in the chain have improved access to the archipelago generally. With its muddy sea, nearby **Pulau Mabul** is rated as one of the world's top muck dives.

Some history

Little is known of Sabah's **early history**, though archeological finds in limestone caves in the east of the state indicate that the northern tip of Borneo has been inhabited for well over ten thousand years. Chinese merchants were trading with local settlements by 700 AD, and by the fourteenth century, the tract of land now known as Sabah came under the sway of the sultans of Brunei and Sulu, though its isolated communities of hunter-gatherers would generally have been unaware of this fact. Europe's superpowers first arrived in 1521, when the ships of the Portuguese navigator Ferdinand Magellan stopped off at Brunei and later sailed northwards. But it was to be nearly 250 years before any colonial settlement occurred, when – in 1763 – one Captain Cowley established a short-lived trading post on Pulau Balambangan, an island north of Kudat, on behalf of the British East India Company. Further colonial involvement came in 1846, when Pulau Labuan (at the mouth of Brunei Bay) was ceded to the British by the Sultan of Brunei. In 1878 the Austrian, **Baron von Overbeck** – with the financial backing of British businessman Alfred Dent – agreed to pay the Sultan an annuity of US$15,000 to cede northern Borneo to him. Shortly afterwards a further annual payment of US$5000 was negotiated with the Sultan of Sulu, who also laid claim to the region. Von Overbeck hastened to England to finalize matters and in 1881 the **British North Borneo Chartered Company** was registered, with full sovereignty over northern Borneo. Shortly afterwards, von Overbeck sold his shares to Dent.

With the company up and running, the first steps were taken towards making the territory pay its way: rubber, tobacco and, after 1885, timber, were commercially harvested. By 1905 a **railway** linked the coastal town of Jesselton (later called Kota Kinabalu) with the resource-rich interior. When the company introduced taxes the locals were understandably ill pleased and native resistance followed – **Mat Salleh**, the son of a

Bajau chief, and his followers sacked the company's settlement on Pulau Gaya in 1897. Another uprising, in **Rundum** in 1915, resulted in the slaughter of hundreds of Murut tribespeople by British forces.

No other major disturbances troubled the Chartered Company until New Year's Day, 1942, when the Japanese Imperial forces invaded Pulau Labuan; less than three weeks later Sandakan fell. The years of **World War II** were devastating ones for Japanese-occupied Sabah, which was bombed by Allied forces eager to neutralize its harbours. By the time of the Japanese surrender on September 9, 1945, next to nothing of Jesselton and Sandakan remained standing. Even worse were the hardships that the captured Allied troops and civilians endured – culminating in the Death March of September 1944, when 2400 POWs made a forced march from Sandakan to Ranau, 170km west as the crow flies. Only six men, all Australians, survived.

Unable to finance the rebuilding of North Borneo, the Chartered Company sold the territory to the British Crown in 1946, and Jesselton was declared the new capital of the **Crown Colony of North Borneo**. However, within fifteen years, plans had been laid for an independent federation consisting of Malaya, Singapore, Sarawak, North Borneo and Brunei. Although Brunei pulled out at the last minute, the **Federation** was still pro-claimed at midnight on September 15, 1963, with North Borneo quickly being renamed Sabah. Objecting to the inclusion of Sarawak and Sabah in the Federation, Indonesia's president Sukarno initiated his anti-Malaysian Konfrontasi policy (see p.629), and spo-radic skirmishes broke out along the Sabah–Kalimantan border for the next three years. The decade that followed saw Sabah's **timber industry**, begun in the nineteenth century, reach its destructive peak (for more on this issue, see p.633).

It's only very recently that relations with Kuala Lumpur, strained since the mid-1980s, have taken a turn for the better. Sabah toed the Barisan Nasional line until 1985, but then the opposition **Parti Bersatu Sabah** (PBS), led by the Christian Joseph Pairin Kitingan, was returned to office in the state elections – the first time a non-Muslim had attained power in a Malaysian state. Subsequently, the people of Sabah complained of minimal funding of their state's infrastructure and a corresponding loss of foreign investment – and of blatant pro-Muslim propaganda on the part of central government, which ran as far as offering Christians cash incentives to convert to Islam. Anti-federal feelings were worsened by the fact that 95 percent of the profits from Sabah's flourishing crude oil exports were being siphoned off to KL. Pairin hold power in the 1994 **state elections**, but then the tables were turned when first three, and then many more of his assemblymen defected to the opposition. In the 1999 elections, the trend towards local BN-aligned parties holding power in East Malaysia was further con-solidated – now few seats remain in PBS's hands.

Kota Kinabalu and around

Since 1946, Sabah's seat of government has been based at **KOTA KINABALU**, halfway up the state's western seaboard. KK (as it's universally known) certainly isn't one of the world's magical cities, World War II bombing having all but robbed it of charismatic buildings, and first impressions are of a grim concrete sprawl. But KK still manages to charm visitors with the friendliness of its citizens; the lively buzz which characterizes its bars, cafés and markets; and its proximity to a clutch of idyllic islands.

Modern-day Kota Kinabalu can trace its history back to 1882, the year the British North Borneo Chartered Company first established an outpost on nearby **Pulau Gaya**. After this was burned down by followers of the Bajau rebel, Mat Salleh, in 1897, the Company chose a mainland site for a new town which was known to locals as *Api Api*, or "Fire, Fire". One explanation for the name was that it referred to the firing of the original settlement; another, that it reflected the abundance of fireflies inhabiting its swamps. Renamed **Jesselton**, after Sir Charles Jessel, the vice-chairman of the Chartered Company, the town prospered. By 1905, the Trans-Borneo Railway reached from Jesselton to Beaufort, meaning that for the first time, rubber could be transported efficiently from the interior to the coast.

The Japanese invasion of North Borneo in 1942 marked the start of three and a half years of **military occupation**: of old Jesselton, only the Atkinson Clock Tower and the post office (today's tourist office) survived the resulting Allied bombing. However, progress since the war has been startling and today, with a population well above 200,000, Kota Kinabalu (meaning simply Kinabalu City, the change of name having taken place in 1967) has a busy seaport once more.

Most of downtown KK was reclaimed from the sea during the twentieth century – so ruthlessly in some places that pockets of stilt houses have been left stranded in stagnant lakes. On the resulting new patches of land, large complexes of interconnecting concrete buildings – the Sinsuran and Segama complexes and Asia City are three – have been constructed, their ground floors taken up by shops, restaurants and businesses, the upper floors turned into apartments. In addition, the Sutera Harbour project – still not finished – is expected to add another shopping centre, some big-name hotels, a marina and a bus station to the waterfront. The city has a limited number of sights, the best of which are its **markets** and the **State Museum**, while south of the centre a series of kampungs provide a glimpse into the region's relatively recent tribal past. But KK's highlight is, without doubt, offshore **Tunku Abdul Rahman Park**, whose five unspoilt islands (including Pulau Gaya), are just a short trip away by boat from the city centre.

Arrival, information and transport

KK's **airport** is 6km south of the centre. Six yellow-and-red Luen Thung Company buses a day head into town from the airport (first bus approximately 6.30am, last bus 5.30pm; 65 sen), stopping opposite the GPO on Jalan Tun Razak. From the airport, you can also catch a minibus into town (RM1–1.50) from the main road (a five-minute stroll from the airport terminal), or take a taxi, for which you need to buy a RM12 coupon in the arrivals hall.

Trains from Tenom and Beaufort pull in close to the airport at **Tanjung Aru Station**, located 5km south beside Jalan Kepayan, the main road to points south of KK; you'll have no trouble catching a bus heading into town. **Long-distance buses** from Sandakan and elsewhere congregate along Jalan Tunku Abdul Rahman, from where it's no more than a ten-minute walk to any of KK's central hotels. **Ferries** to and from Labuan dock in front of the *Hyatt Hotel* on Jalan Tun Fuad Stephens.

Information
The **Sabah Tourism Promotion Corporation** (STPC; Mon–Fri 8am–5pm, Sat 8am–2pm; ☎088/212121, *www.jaring.my/sabah*) is in the old GPO at 51 Jalan Gaya; ask for the excellent tourist **map** of KK available free here. **Tourism Malaysia** (Mon–Fri 8.30am–4.30pm, Sat 8.30am–12.30pm; ☎088/211732), across Jalan Gaya in the EON CMG Building, is also fully stocked with leaflets on Sabah, and can likewise answer questions about Peninsular Malaysia or Sarawak. It also has a small, well-stocked shop selling attractive handicrafts. For information about the environment and ecology of Sabah's National Parks, visit the **Sabah Parks** office (Mon–Fri 8.30am–noon, Sat 8.30am–noon; ☎088/211881), which faces the South China Sea at Block K of the Sinsuran Complex, Jalan Tun Fuad Stephens.

What's on information is in relatively short supply in KK, though details of cultural events can be found in any of Sabah's English-language newspapers – the *Borneo Mail*, *Sabah Times*, *Morning Post* and *Daily Express*. Otherwise, the **notice boards** at the

---

MOVING ON FROM KK

BY AIR

From KK's **airport** there are regular flights to Sarawak, Brunei, the mainland and Singapore, as well as services to Manila, Taipei and Hong Kong. Six buses a day run to the airport from opposite the GPO (first bus 6.30am); otherwise take a Putatan- or Petagas-bound minibus from behind the Centrepoint shopping centre, but check with the driver that he's going all the way to the airport.

BY BUS

Long-distance buses for points north, south and east of KK leave from the open land along Jalan Tunku Abdul Rahman in the centre of town. These buses, heading to main destinations like **Sandakan**, **Kudat** and **Tawau**, regularly ply Sabah's bumpy roads, but it's advisable – especially if you're going to the east coast – to get to the depot by 7.30am, as a fleet of buses leave around that time and the journey can take up a large part of the day. This terminus is also the departure point for the daily **Lawas Express** (1pm) to Lawas in Sarawak and the 7.15am direct bus to Mount Kinabalu Park.

BY TRAIN

Although there is a rail link from KK to Beaufort, with one train a day leaving from Tanjung Aru, the bus gets you there twice as quickly as the train. The stretch of line between Beaufort and Tenom (see p.467) is the most picturesque part of the Sabah train system.

BY FERRY

There are five daily services to Pulau Labuan (RM28), the first leaving at 7.15am and the last at 1.30am. All tickets are sold at the jetty and it's worth booking ahead if you plan to travel at the weekend or over a holiday. Alternatively, you could drop by at Rezeki Murni (☎088/236834), Lot 3, first floor, Block D, Kompleks Segama.

Trekkers Lodge and *Jack's B&B* (see p.452) are valuable sources of information on matters as diverse as boats to Indonesia and good hawker stalls.

City transport

The city centre is compact enough to traverse on foot in half an hour. **Taxis** are inexpensive – it costs no more than RM5–6 to travel right across the city centre. There are taxi ranks outside the *Hyatt Hotel* on Jalan Datuk Salleh Sulong; at the GPO, on Jalan Tun Razak; along Jalan Perpaduan (close to the spot used by the long-distance buses); and at Centrepoint shopping centre on Lebuh Raya Pantai Baru. See "Listings", p.457, for taxi booking numbers.

Taking a **bus** is more complicated, since there's no central station in KK. **Minibuses** for the suburbs and the airport leave when full from the bare ground north of the Centrepoint shopping centre. The bus stop opposite the GPO on Jalan Tun Razak is the starting point for **scheduled buses** travelling through KK's suburbs – as far as Tuaran in the north and Penampang in the south. Marginally cheaper (and much safer) than minibuses, these leave at set times, empty or full, but take longer to reach their destinations and are far scarcer than the ubiquitous, smaller minibuses.

Accommodation

Facilities for backpackers have improved significantly in recent years, with a number of **hostels** now up and running in the centre, and more on the outskirts. The bulk of the

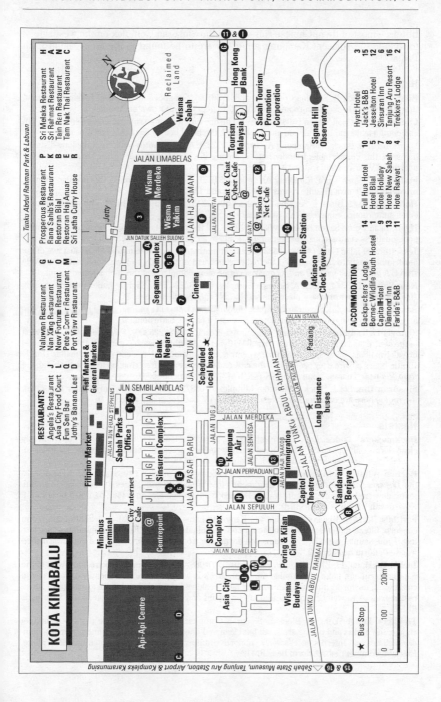

hotels – most of them Chinese-run – are in the Sinsuran Complex on the west side of town, and the adjacent Kampung Air; a few are to be found in the area around Jalan Pantai.

Hotels

Bilal, Lot 1, Block B, Segama Complex (☎088/256709). Set above an excellent Indian restaurant, this place offers basic, clean rooms; an extra RM5 gets you your own bathroom. ②.

Capital, 23 Jalan Haji Saman (☎088/231999). The one hundred or so rooms here are spacious, light and comfortable and have air-con and TV, though the hotel boasts few other amenities. ④.

Diamond Inn, Block 37, Kampung Air (☎088/213222). A few minutes' walk from the long-distance bus stop, this comfortable, friendly hotel is among the best places in its price bracket, its rooms boasting TV, air-con and fridge. ③.

Full Hua, 14 Jalan Tugu, Kampung Air (☎088/234950). Superbly positioned, this popular, friendly, place has small, neat en-suite rooms with air-con and TV. ③.

Holiday, Lot 1/2, Block F, Segama Complex (☎088/213116). A friendly hotel, with nicely decorated en-suite rooms, complete with TV and air-con. ③.

Hyatt, Jalan Datuk Salleh Sulong (☎088/221234). All the comforts you might imagine – swimming pool, business centre, choice of restaurants – and in a central location. ⑥.

Jesselton, 69 Jalan Gaya (☎088/223333). Lady Mountbatten and Muhammad Ali are just two of the illustrious guests to have sampled the old-world charm of this, KK's oldest hotel, set on a lovely street. A good Western grill and a convivial coffee shop complement the sophisticated rooms. ⑦.

New Sabah, Lot 3/4, Block A, Segama Complex (☎088/224590). Slightly tattier than the nearby *Holiday*, this rather ordinary place has serviceable rooms, all en suite. ③.

Rakyat, Lot 3, Block I, Sinsuran Complex (☎088/222715). Its nine rooms offer a modicum of comfort; a few extra ringgit secure you air-con, TV and a private bathroom. ③.

Shangri-La Tanjung Aru Resort, Tanjung Aru Beach (☎088/225800). Five kilometres southwest of the centre; a taxi here from town costs RM10. Set in delightful seaside gardens, this luxury hotel boasts two pools, water-sports and fitness centres, several food outlets – and prices to match. Hourly shuttle buses ensure easy access into the city, and there are also free runs up to its sister-hotel, the *Rasa Ria* near Tuaran, 35km from KK (see p.473). Recommended. ⑨.

Sinsuran Inn, Lot 1, Block I, Sinsuran Complex (☎088/211158). Though only simply decorated, the rooms here are capacious and clean, and have TV, bathroom and air-con. ③.

Hostels

Backpackers' Lodge, Lot 25, Lorong Dewan, Australia Place (☎088/261495). New, spotlessly clean dorms-only operation below Signal Hill; guests have access to common showers, TV and laundry facilities, and breakfast is included. ②, dorm beds RM18.

Borneo Wildlife Youth Hostel, Lot 4, Block L, Sinsuran Complex (☎088/213668). Next door to the *Trekkers Lodge*, but forgoing its neighbour's free breakfasts and movies to keep costs to a minimum; downstairs are the friendly staff of Borneo Wildlife (see box on p.456). ①, dorm beds RM15 (RM10 with YHA or student card).

Farida's B&B, 413 Jalan Saga, Mile 4.5, Kampung Likas (☎088/428733). A delightful family-run concern, fifteen minutes away from the minibus terminal – catch a "Kg Likas" minibus – and perfect if you want a quiet life. The rooms and dorms are wonderfully airy, and fitted out in varnished wood. ②, dorm beds RM12.

Jack's B&B, no. 17, Block B, Jalan Karamunsing (☎088/232367). One kilometre southwest of the minibus terminus (take a Sembulan minibus), *Jack's* is as spotless and as friendly a place as you could want, its dorms fitted with air-con and fan; breakfast is included and there are heaps of latest-release videos to watch. Jack will also lay on island and fishing trips on request. ②, dorm beds RM18.

Trekkers Lodge, Lot 5/6, Block L, Sinsuran Complex (☎088/252263). The city's best budget choice: the dorms and rooms are small but clean and cheery, and there are numerous maps, laundry facilities and Internet access. Very supportive atmosphere – ideal for women travelling alone. Highly recommended. ②, dorm beds RM12.

The City

Downtown KK was almost totally obliterated by World War II bombs, and only in the northeastern corner of the city centre – an area known as **KK Lama**, or old KK – are there even the faintest remains of its colonial past. KK Lama is bordered by **Jalan Pantai** (Beach Rd), formerly the waterfront, and **Jalan Gaya**, an attractive street whose chief landmark is the old general post office building which now houses the STPC. A lively **street market** is held along Jalan Gaya every Sunday morning, with stalls selling herbal teas, handicrafts, orchids and rabbits, and streetside coffee shops doing a roaring trade in *dim sum* and noodles.

A block east, under the shadow of Bukit Bendera (Signal Hill), stands the **Atkinson Clock Tower**, a quaint wooden landmark built in 1905 in memory of a district officer in the Chartered Company. From here, you can take the fifteen-minute walk up to the breezy **Signal Hill Observatory**, which provides a good overview of KK's matrix of dreary buildings and of the infinitely more attractive bay. Early photographs of the city show colonial officers playing cricket on the **padang**, an area you'll pass as you head up Jalan Istana, just west of the clock tower, on the way up to the observatory.

It's a five-minute stroll from the padang west across town to KK's waterfront markets, the most diverting of which is the **Filipino Market**, opposite blocks K and M of the Sinsuran Complex. Its numerous stalls are run by Filipino immigrants, who stock Sabahian ethnic wares beside their Filipino baskets, shells and trinkets. Next door is the dark and labyrinthine **general market** – the first floor has a number of superb food stalls – and, behind that, the manic waterfront **fish market** – worth investigating if you can stomach the odours.

To the Sabah State Museum

The **Sabah State Museum** (Mon–Thurs 10am–6pm, Sat & Sun 9am–6pm; free), KK's most rewarding sight, can be reached on the State Museum bus (50 sen) from opposite the GPO or by taxi (RM5), though the twenty-minute walk there is interesting enough, taking you southwest along Jalan Tunku Abdul Rahman, past the pyramidal Catholic **Sacred Heart Cathedral** and – slightly further on – the **Sabah State Mosque**, whose eye-catching dome sits, like a Fabergé egg, on top of the main body of the complex.

The museum buildings are styled after Murut and Rungus longhouses and set in exotic grounds that are home to several splendid steam engines. Its highlight is its **ethnographic collection** which features a *bangkaran*, or cluster of human skulls, dating from Sabah's head-hunting days; and a *sininggazanak*, a totemic wooden figurine which would have been placed in the field of a Kadazan man who had died leaving no heirs. Photographs in the history gallery trace the development of Kota Kinabalu – look out for an intriguing picture of Jesselton at a time when Jalan Gaya still constituted the waterfront, lined with lean-tos thatched with *nipah*-palm leaves. There are old snaps of Chartered Company officials, Sabahian natives and Chinese pioneers, while beyond, in the Merdeka Gallery, newspaper cuttings trace the story of Malaysia's path to independence. Of rather less interest is the tired collection of stuffed animals in the natural-history section, while only a fine old wooden coffin from Batu Putih (see p.492) stands out among the clay shards of the archaeology gallery. Most of the Islamic Civilization Gallery comprises photographs of objects from other museums around the world, though it does boast an exquisite nineteenth-century Ottoman chess board crafted from mother-of-pearl, ebony and ivory, and several antique Korans. Beside the museum entrance is a souvenir shop selling handicrafts and postcards.

The **Science and Technology Centre** (same hours as museum; free), next door to the museum, houses less-than-gripping exhibitions on oil-drilling and broadcasting technology, so head upstairs to the **Art Gallery** (Mon–Thurs 10am–4.30pm, Sat & Sun

9.30am–5pm; free) instead. Many of the works on display here are unadventurous, picture-postcard images of Sabah, though there are exceptions – notably the impressionistic paintings of Suzie Majikol and a dreamlike work in oil of four women dancing by Nazric Said. The gallery's centrepiece is a giant string of Rungus beads, created by Chee Sing Teck, hanging from the ceiling.

Fronting the museum is an **Ethno-botanical Garden** (daily 6am–6pm), whose huge range of tropical plants is best experienced on one of the free guided tours (daily except Fri at 9am & 2pm). Exquisitely crafted traditional houses representing all Sabah's major tribes border the garden, in the Kampung Warisan, or Heritage Village.

Past the museum, Jalan Tunku Abdul Rahman continues on for another 2.5km (becoming Jalan Mat Salleh) to the beach at **Tanjung Aru**, site of the swanky *Shangri-La Resort*, a highly impressive development. But as the long, narrow beach itself isn't spectacular, and given that there are so many beautiful islands just off the coast, there's no great incentive to visit other than to try its **food and drink stalls**, busiest and best at weekends, when large numbers of locals come for satay and barbecued seafood. To reach Tanjung Aru direct from the centre, take a red Luen Thung Company bus from opposite the GPO.

Eating, drinking and nightlife

Finding somewhere to eat in KK causes no headaches, with a big range of Malay, Chinese and Indian **restaurants**, and a good selection of central **hawker stalls**; there are also stalls at Tanjung Aru beach (see above). It's problematic, though, if you want to sample Sabahian cuisine: while the indigenous peoples all have their own dishes, the total absence of such fare at KK eating places is a big disappointment. Note that quite a few restaurants are closed by mid-evening, so be prepared for an early dinner; specific opening hours (daily unless otherwise stated) are given below. Opening hours for hawker stalls listed below are usually daily 6–11pm; the exception is the general market, whose stalls operate daily 9am–6pm. KK has an increasing number of **bars** and **clubs**, the best of which are listed opposite.

Hawker stalls

Asia City Food Court, Asia City. Near Jalan Duabelas. Featuring a wide selection of dishes, from hamburgers to delicious prawns, this is an excellent place to sit and while away the evening with its mixture of hip KK youth, friendly Asia City day workers, the odd grizzled expat and the occasional tourist.

General Market, Jalan Tun Fuad Stephens. The *nasi campur* stalls on the upper floor provide filling, good-value meals during the day.

Night Market, behind the Filipino Market, Jalan Tun Fuad Stephens. Fried chicken and barbecue fish are the specialities here.

SEDCO Square, SEDCO complex, between Jalan Sepuluh and Jalan Duabelas. Restaurant-lined square, with outdoor tables; a fine place for barbecued meat and fish.

Cafés and restaurants

Angela's, Block G, Asia City (☎088/252281). Ignore the gooey pink decor and endless cat pictures – the Nonya cooking here is really rather good. Try the *otak otak* (fish-head curry), or plump for a less exotic choice from the Western menu. Mon–Sat 11.30am–2.30pm & 6.30–10.30pm.

Restoran Bilal, Block B, Segama Complex. A classic North Indian Muslim eating house, with a buffet-style range of tasty and inexpensive curries. Daily 6am–9pm.

Eat & Chat Cyber Café, 63 Jalan Gaya. Rivalling *Pete's Corner* as the place to go for breakfast, this has the additional attraction of Internet access, along with the Western fry-ups or *mee goreng*.

Restoran Haj Anuar, Block H, Sinsuran Complex. Cosy, open-fronted place opposite the *Sinsuran Inn*, with a Malay menu including *mee soto*, *nasi lemak* and *nasi campur*. Daily 7am–7pm.

Jothy's Banana Leaf, 1/G9, Api-Api Centre (☎088/261595). Besides its mountainous *daun pisang* (banana leaf) meals, *Jothy's* has *biriyani*s and curries, though for proper *naan* you're better off at *Rana Sahib's*. Daily 10am–10pm.

Naluwan, 16–17 Jalan Haji Saman. A huge, cavernous place, and a porker's paradise: a modest outlay (RM7 lunch, RM15 dinner) buys you all you can eat from a buffet that's constantly replenished with all manner of tasty Asian dishes. Daily 11am–2.30pm & 6.30–11.30pm.

Nan Xing Restaurant, 33–35 Jalan Haji Saman. A decent Cantonese menu that includes a range of *dim sum* as well as steaks and chops. Daily noon–2.30pm & 6–9pm.

New Fortune Eating House, Block 36, Jalan Laiman Diki, Kampung Air. A busy place housing several stalls, the best of which serves superb *dim sum* at breakfast and later. Open 6am–7pm.

Pete's Corner, Block B, Asia City. Neatly tiled, open-fronted corner shop serving egg, sausage and baked-bean breakfasts, omelettes and sandwiches, as well as more substantial Western meals such as steaks and chops and Malaysian favourites, all at very affordable prices. Daily 7am–5.30pm.

Phoenix Court Restaurant, *Hyatt Hotel*, Jalan Datuk Salleh Sulong (☎088/221234). Superior Cantonese and Szechuan food, and elegant surroundings. Expect to pay RM30–40 a head, and reserve in advance. Daily 11am–2pm & 7–11pm.

Port View Restaurant, Jalan Haji Saman. Lively at night, when the roadside tables fill up with locals choosing from a wide range of (live) seafood. Daily 6pm–2am, Sat until 3am.

Prosperous Szechuan Restaurant, 103 Jalan Gaya (☎088/264666). Hot and spicy Chinese food, pleasing decor, smartly attired staff and a good range of set meals from RM36. Daily 11.30am–2.30pm & 5.30–10.30pm.

Rana Sahib's, Block G, Asia City (☎088/231354). Tasty North Indian food experience marred by high prices and over-attentive owner. The *sag gosh* and *chicken Kashmir* are both superb, and there's mango *lassi* to die for. Daily 11.30am–2.30pm & 6.30–11.00pm.

Sri Latha Curry House, Jalan 4 no. 33, Bandaran Berjaya. The banana-leaf curry in this no-frills South Indian restaurant is a mountainous, all-you-can-eat feast (RM3.50 for vegetarian, RM6 for meat), served by really friendly staff. There's chicken *biriyani* on a Saturday, and *masala dosai* on Sunday mornings. Daily 6.30am–2am.

Sri Melaka, 9 Jalan Laiman Diki, Kampung Air. A popular establishment that's great for Malay and Nonya food; try the excellent *asam* fish-head (RM10 portion feeds two). Open 11.00am–10.00pm.

Restoran Sri Rahmat, Lot 7, Block D, Segama Complex. A basic Malay restaurant – though with an air-con room – that's worth frequenting for the delicious *laksa* alone. Open Mon–Sat 7am–9pm, Sun 7am–5pm.

Tain Ran Vegetarian Restaurant, Block A, Ruang Singgah Mata 1, Asia City. Spartan coffee shop with a mouthwatering array of veggie dishes served from a tin-tray buffet counter. Daily 9am–7pm.

Tam Nak Thai, 5/G5, Api-Api Centre (☎088/257328). Authentic Thai cuisine unavailable elsewhere in the city, and a pleasing ambience. Daily 11.30am–3pm & 6–10pm.

Bars and clubs

Crash, below *New Sabah Inn*, Jalan Pantai. Lively enough bar set behind a facade crafted to resemble the chassis of a jet-plane.

Fun Sen, Block 37, Kampung Air. A few doors down from the *Diamond Inn* hotel. Guinness stout is the staple here for a boozy, let-it-all-hang-out local clientele. An atmospheric hangout. Daily noon–midnight.

Shenanigan's, *Hyatt Kinabalu*, Jalan Datuk Salleh Sulong. Slick and central bar whose overall-wearing staff pull English pints as well as local lagers. Features live rock music. Mon–Thurs 11am–1am, Fri & Sat 11am–2am, Sun 4pm–midnight.

Something Else, *Shangri-La Tanjung Aru Resort*, Tanjung Aru Beach. Likeable (if pricey) bar, frequented mainly by expats, with good pool tables and decent range of music on the jukebox.

Tiffiny 2020, Block A, Jalan Karamunsing. Mixture of 70s disco, live music and karaoke. Happy hour runs from 7.30 to 9.30pm; cover charge RM12–15. Open till 2am, Sat till 3am.

Yaaha Cowboy Lounge, Block C, Asia City. Despite the hick name this is a superb bar, with a friendly atmosphere, good jukebox and karaoke.

TOUR OPERATORS IN KK

A large number of **tour operators** are based in KK, and though prices are often high, many of the itineraries on offer are only possible on a tour; some of the best are listed below. Expect to pay around RM40 for a half-day KK city tour; RM100 for day-trips to Tunku Abdul Rahman Park or the Rafflesia Centre; RM180 for a day's white-water rafting; and RM600 upwards for extended tours into the forested interior.

Abdullah Sipadan Paradise, second floor, Block A, Taman Fortuna Shoplots, Jalan Penampang (☎088/258105). Pulau Sipadan diving experts; one of only five companies with accommodation on the coral paradise.

Api Tours, 13 Jalan Punai Kedut, Mile 5, Jalan Tuaran (☎088/421963). Offers rafting trips, longhouse tours and the Mount Trus Madi Trek.

Borneo Divers, ninth floor, Menara Jubili, 53 Jalan Gaya (☎088/222226). The most prestigious outfit for diving trips and scuba courses; three days (two nights) on Sipadan with them costs RM700.

Borneo Eco Tours, 12a, second floor, Lorong Bernam 3, Taman Soon Kiong, 5km west of town (☎088/234009, *www.borneoecotours.com*). Run by Sabah ecotourism pioneer and nature photographer, Albert Teo, they own *Sukau Lodge* on Sungei Kinabatangan. Their tours include the Sabah Wildlife Safari, a seven-day trip around the state taking in the Tunku Rahman and Turtle Islands, *Sukau Lodge*, Sepilok Orang Utan sanctuary, Kudat and Mount Kinabalu; and a four-day jungle trek in the Crocker Mountain Range, the best way of experiencing this inaccessible region where there are as yet no facilities for tourists.

Borneo Expeditions, *Shangri-La Tanjung Aru Resort* (☎088/222721). Specialists in white-water rafting, they organize some tours around Sapulut too.

Borneo Sea Adventures, first floor, 8A Karamunsing Warehouse (☎088/230000). One-day trips to Sipadan out of Semporna (RM200) for groups of four or more.

Borneo Wildlife Adventure, Block L, Sinsuran Complex (☎088/213668). Tailor-made adventure tours along the Sarawak and Kalimantan borders.

Discovery Tours, Shopping Arcade, *Shangri-La Tanjung Aru Resort* (☎088/221224). Half- and full-day tours in the KK area.

Journey World Travel, Taman Fortuna, Jalan Penampang (☎088/221586). Imaginative operator devising tailor-made adventure tours along the Sarawak and Kalimantan borders.

Seaventures, fourth floor, Wisma Sabah (☎088/251669). Sipadan diving packages from around RM1200 for two nights.

Sipadan Dive Centre, tenth floor, Wisma Merdeka (☎088/240584). Their two-day (one-night) diving excursions to Sipadan cost nearly RM1300 per person, and an extra night is a further RM250 a head; prices include return transfer from KK to Sipadan by air, land and sea, three daily boat dives plus unlimited shore dives.

Trekkers Lodge, Block L, Sinsuran Complex (☎088/240625). Offering the most competitive rates for trips to Tunku Abdul Rahman park, they can also help arrange trips further afield.

Listings

Airlines MAS, tenth floor, Kompleks Karamunsing, Jalan Tuaran (☎088/213555), and eleventh floor, Gaya Centre, north of Wisma Sabah (☎088/213555). Dragon Air (☎088/254733), Royal Brunei (☎088/242193), Singapore Airlines (☎088/255444) and Thai Airways (☎088/232896) are all on the ground floor, Block C, Kompleks Kuwasa, Jalan Karamunsing.

American Express Lot 3.50 and 3.51, third floor, Kompleks Karamunsing, Jalan Tuaran (Mon–Fri 8.30am–5.30pm; ☎088/241200).

Banks and exchange Hong Kong & Shanghai Bank, 56 Jalan Gaya; Sabah Bank, Block K, Sinsuran Complex; Standard Chartered Bank, 20 Jalan Haji Saman. Moneychangers (Mon–Sat 10am–7pm) include Ban Loong Money Changer and Travellers' Money Changer, both on the ground floor of Wisma Merdeka; there's also an office in the Taiping Goldsmith, Block A, Sinsuran Complex.

Bookshops Arena Book Centre (Block L, Sinsuran Complex), Iwase Bookshop (Wisma Merdeka) and the Yaohan bookstore (second floor, Centrepoint) all have a few shelves of English-language novels. For an unparalleled array of books on Southeast Asia, head for Borneo Crafts (Wisma Merdeka), or to their branch at the Sabah State Museum; the *Hyatt*'s bookshop stocks a modest range of international newspapers and magazines.

Car rental Ais Rent-A-Car, Lot 1, Block A, Sinsuran Complex (☎088/238954); Kinabalu Rent-A-Car, Lot 3.60, third floor, Kompleks Karamunsing (☎088/232602), and at the *Hyatt Hotel*; Sabah Holiday Rent-A-Car, Lot 20, Wisma Sabah, Jalan Tun Razak (☎088/245106). Rates start from around RM170 per day, though four-wheel-drives (from RM250) are advisable if you plan to get off the beaten track.

Cinemas The Poring and Kilan Cinema, and the Capitol Theatre, below the SEDCO Centre at the western edge of downtown KK, both have regular screenings of English-language movies. Programme listings are in the *Borneo Mail* or *Daily Express*.

Consulates Konsulat Jenderal Indonesia, Jalan Kemajuan (☎088/218600), issues one-month visas for Kalimantan. The nearest consular representation for most nationalities is in KL; see p.119.

Hospital Queen Elizabeth Hospital is beyond the Sabah State Museum, on Jalan Penampang (☎088/218166). In an emergency, dial ☎999.

Internet access *City Internet Café*, Lot 41, ground floor, City Parade, Jalan Centrepoint; *Cyber Café Centre*, Lot 4, Wisma Butaya; *Eat & Chat*, 63 Jalan Gaya; *Vision de Net Café*, 1st floor, 91 Jalan Gaya.

Laundry Meba Laundry Services, Block B, Sinsuran Complex (7.30am–8pm).

Pharmacies Centrepoint Pharmacy, Centrepoint; Farmasi Gaya, 122 Jalan Gaya; Metropharm, Block A, Sinsuran Complex.

Police The main police station, Balai Polis KK (☎088/247111), is below Atkinson Clock Tower on Jalan Padang. In an emergency, dial ☎999.

Post office The GPO (Mon–Sat 8am–5pm, Sun 10am–1pm) lies between the Sinsuran and Segama complexes, on Jalan Tun Razak; poste restante/general delivery is just inside the front doors.

Rural Development Corporation, Km 9, Jalan Tuaran (☎088/426051), Call to book a room at the *Batu Punggul Lodge*.

Shopping Borneo Handicraft, first floor, Wisma Merdeka, has a good choice of woodwork, basketry and gongs; Borneo Handicraft & Ceramic Shop (ground floor, Centrepoint) stocks ceramics, antiques and primitive sculptures. Also good are the souvenir shops at the Sabah State Museum and the STPC, while the Filipino Market's scores of stalls sell both local and Filipino wares.

Telephones There are IDD facilities at Kedai Telekom (daily 8am–10pm), in Centrepoint. Phonecards, available at the GPO and any shops displaying the "Uniphone Kad" sign, can be used for international calls in orange booths, but not yellow, public phone booths.

Taxis Book a taxi on either ☎088/252113 or 251863.

Train information Call ☎088/254611 for up-to-date timetable details.

Visa extensions Immigration Department, fourth floor, Wisma Dang Bandang, Jalan Haji Yaakob (Mon–Fri 8am–12.30pm & 2–4.15pm, Sat 8am–12.45pm; ☎088/216711). Visa extensions of up to a month are available and cost RM2.

Around Kota Kinabalu

The main attraction around KK is undoubtedly the beaches and wildlife of **Tunku Abdul Rahman Park**. It's also worth considering a day-trip south to the **Monsopiad Cultural Village** and on to **Kinarut**, a quaint village nestling below the Crocker Mountain Range.

Tunku Abdul Rahman Park

Named after Malaysia's first prime minister, and situated just a stone's throw from central Kota Kinabalu, the **five islands** of **Tunku Abdul Rahman Park** (sometimes written "TAR Park") represent the most westerly ripples of the undulating Crocker Mountain Range (see p.460). All five islands, their forests, beaches and coral reefs West Sabah's most visited treasure, lie within an eight-kilometre radius of downtown KK, with park territory as close as 3km off the mainland.

The site of the British North Borneo Chartered Company's first outpost in the region, **Pulau Gaya** is the closest of the islands to KK and also the largest, its name derived from *goyoh*, the Bajau word for "big". Although a native chief granted the island's timber rights to a certain Mr White in 1879, they were never fully exploited, and so lowland rainforest still blankets Gaya, a twenty-kilometre system of trails snaking across it. Most of these trails start on the southern side of the island at **Camp Bay**, which is adjacent to a mangrove forest whose crabs and mud-skippers can be viewed from the boardwalk that intersects it. While Camp Bay offers pleasant enough swimming, a more secluded and alluring alternative is **Police Beach**, on the north coast. Boatmen demand extra for circling round to this side of Gaya, but it's money well spent: the bay is idyllic, its dazzling white sand running gently down to the water, lined by trees. The wildlife on Gaya includes hornbills, wild pigs, lizards, snakes and macaques – which have been known to swim over to nearby **Pulau Sapi** (Cow Island), an islet just northwest of Gaya. Though far smaller than Gaya, Sapi too is ringed by trails and home to macaques and hornbills; with the best beaches of any of the islands, it's popular with swimmers, snorkellers and picnickers.

The park's three other islands cluster together a few kilometres west of Gaya. The park headquarters is situated on crescent-shaped **Pulau Manukan** – site of a former stone quarry and now the most developed of all the park's islands. Manukan's fine beaches and coral have led to the construction of chalets, a restaurant, a swimming pool, and tennis and squash courts, which draw large numbers of locals. Across a narrow channel from Manukan is tiny **Pulau Mamutik**, which can be crossed on foot in fifteen minutes and has excellent sands on either side of its jetty. The last of the group, **Pulau Sulug**, is the most remote and consequently the quietest, though its good coral makes it popular with divers.

PRACTICALITIES

There's a **boat service** to Pulau Manukan, which goes from the jetty at Jalan Tun Fuad Stephens. It's regular and easy to use – boats depart hourly on the half-hour between 7.30am and 11.30am inclusive, and hourly on the hour between 2pm and 4pm inclusive; the trip takes twenty minutes to Manukan, returning between 8am and 4pm (RM10 return, children RM5). Chartering a boat to go island-hopping costs RM50 a head (minimum six people).

The four **chalets** on Pulau Manukan, located in dense forest at the beach, are the only accommodation in the park. Each chalet, which must be reserved as a whole (RM140), contains two double rooms; book in advance in KK through Kinabalu Gold Resorts, third floor, Block C, Kompleks Karamunsing, Jalan Tuaran (Mon–Fri 8am–5pm, Sat 8am–2pm; ☎088/257941). There's only one place to eat on any of the islands – the **Coral Garden Seafood Restaurant** (7am–9pm) near the chalets.

South to Donggongon and Monsopiad Cultural Village

Regular minibuses from Jalan Tun Fuad Stephens leave the city for the suburb of **Donggongon**, around 10km to the south. From the bus station here, it's only a ten-minute local bus ride past rice fields and winding streams to **KAMPUNG MONSOPIAD**, where 39 of the 42 skulls cleaved by legendary Kadazan warrior, Monsopiad, provide the centrepiece of the **Monsopiad Cultural Village** (daily 9am–5pm; RM15), a Kadazan theme park nestled in an attractive rustic setting. The village comprises a museum, handicraft workshop, granary and main hall, in which cultural performances and native feasts are held (the latter by prior arrangement). Monsopiad's grisly harvest of skulls is displayed in a row along a rafter in his ancestral house and decked with *hisad* (palm) leaves signifying the victims' hair. Among them is a thigh bone, attesting to one of several legends about the great man which are recounted by resident guide Wenidy Moujadi: visiting a neighbouring village for a large feast, Monsopiad ended up in a dancing competition with a relative, called Gantang. When this ended unresolved, they had a drinking competition, before finally beginning to fight. His head fuzzy from the rice wine, Monsopiad forgot himself and unfairly resorted to using a bamboo spear, instead of his sword, to kill Gantang, whose thigh bone – rather than his head – was awarded to Monsopiad to remind him of his moment of dishonour. Monsopiad eventually grew too fond of harvesting heads and constituted a public menace; killed by a group of friends, he was buried beneath a stone that still stands near the house, with his own head left intact out of respect. Once a year (usually in May), a Kadazan priestess, or *bobohizan*, is called in to communicate with the skulls' spirits, whose job it is to watch over Monsopiad's descendants.

Once you're out in Donggongon, you might as well take the opportunity to see Sabah's oldest church, **St Michael's Catholic Church**, only a twenty-minute walk (or short bus ride) beyond the bus terminus and along the main road. Built in 1897, the sturdy granite building stands on a hillock above peaceful Kampung Dabak, its red roof topped by a simple stone cross. Inside, the church is undecorated, save a mural depicting the Last Supper and framed paintings of the Stations of the Cross.

On to Kinarut and Papar

Further down the main road south, KK's suburbs yield to a carpet of paddy fields that stretches away to the foothills of the Crocker Mountain Range (see overleaf). From the minibus terminal in KK, and also from Donggongon, there are frequent departures to the village of **KINARUT**, 21km away, the starting point for an enjoyable half-hour stroll along a quiet road to **Kampung Tampasak**, where there's a replica of the *sininggazanak* in the State Museum (see p.453). From the two faded old shophouses that form the centre of Kinarut, walk across the train line, cross the bridge to your left and turn right – the turning to the kampung is signposted by an overgrown tyre. On your way, you'll see two or three mysterious menhirs, upright stones, thought to have been erected centuries ago either as status symbols or boundary stones, or to mark the burial places of shamans.

Two to three kilometres away at **KINARUT LAUT** (take a Papar minibus from KK), the *Seaside Travellers' Inn* (☎088/750313; ③ including breakfast) has become a popular retreat for KK weekenders, its dorms (RM20) and rooms a little overpriced but otherwise hard to fault; a balcony off the dining room looks out to the nearby islands of Dinawan and Muntukat, and over the inn's own unspectacular stretch of beach. The slightly plusher *Langkah Syabas Beach Resort* (☎088/752000; ⑥), next door, has fourteen welcoming chalets around a swimming pool, just 100m from the shore.

The one town of any size between KK and Beaufort, **Papar**, is another 20km or so further south; buses run here all through the day from KK's minibus terminal. Unless you're in Papar on Sunday for the decent weekly market, the only reason to break your journey here is to visit the nearby beach – **Pantai Manis** – reached by minibus (RM1) from the centre of Papar.

Southwestern Sabah and the interior

Sabah's **southwestern** reaches are dominated by the ridge of the **Crocker Mountain Range**, which divides the state's west coast and swampy Klias Peninsula from the area christened the **interior** in the days of the Chartered Company. At one time, this sparsely populated region was effectively isolated from the west coast by the mountains. This changed at the turn of the century, when a railway was built between Jesselton (modern-day KK) and the interior in order to transport the raw materials being produced by the region's thriving rubber industry. Today, logging takes precedence, though the Kadazan/Dusun and Murut peoples still look to the interior's fertile soils for their living, cultivating rice, maize and cocoa.

Travelling by bus and train, it's possible to circumnavigate the region from KK, starting with a drive southeast over the mountains to the Kadazan/Dusun town of

Tambunan, which sits on a plain chequered with paddy fields. From Tambunan, the road continues further south to **Keningau**, the centre of the interior's timber industry and also the launch pad for more adventurous detours deeper into the heart of the interior. Following the circular route to KK entails travelling south on to **Tenom** which, along with Keningau, marks the start of Murut territory, which stretches down to the Kalimantan border. The traditional ways of the Murut are fast dying out, but those prepared to venture into the less accessible areas south of Keningau and Tenom – using remote **Sapulut** as a base – will come across isolated tribes to whom home is still a longhouse, albeit a modernized one.

Tenom itself sits on the bank of the Sungei Padas, whose turbulent waters you have to negotiate if you sign up for a white-water rafting tour. The train line connects Tenom with **Beaufort**, from where you can head one of three ways: north to KK; south to Sipitang, the terminus for buses and taxis into Sarawak; or west into the **Klias Peninsula**, an infertile former swamp forest that forms the northeastern reach of Brunei Bay. From Kuala Penyu, in the northern corner of the peninsula, boats travel to **Pulau Tiga Park**, which mostly comprises beaches and short trails; on the peninsula's southern side, Menumbok is linked by ferries and speedboats with the duty-free island of **Pulau Labuan**.

Sinsuron Pass and the Rafflesia Complex

Unless you take a Tenom-bound train from Beaufort (see p.465), the only way to reach the interior of Sabah is to follow the 80km of road from KK southeast to Tambunan (see opposite); buses plying this route leave regularly from Jalan Tunku Abdul Rahman in KK. Ten kilometres out of the city, paddy fields give way to the rolling foothills of the **Crocker Mountain Range**, and cars and buses start the long, twisting haul up to the 1649-metre-high **Sinsuron Pass**. From here, there are views of mighty Mount Kinabalu (see p.478), weather permitting. The occasional lean-to shack sits by the side of the road, piled with pineapples, bananas and vegetables; often no one attends to the produce, as some locals believe that anyone pilfering risks death by black magic. Should you wish to dally for a little longer in the bracing chill of the Sinsuron Pass, you can consider spending a night at the *Gunung Emas Highlands Resort* (☎011/811562), at the 52km mark of the KK–Tambunan road: guests choose between dormitory beds (RM15), double rooms (②) sharing common toilets, treetop cabins (②) "for those who want to experience the lifestyle of Tarzan and Jane", and more luxurious suites (③). Jungle trails from the resort lead to a picturesque waterfall, and to a look-out point from which KK is visible on a clear day.

The Rafflesia Complex

A few kilometres southeast of the pass, the **Rafflesia Complex** (Mon–Fri 8am–12.45pm & 2–5pm, Sat & Sun 8am–5pm; free) houses examples of the **Rafflesia**, a parasitic plant whose rubbery blooms can reach up to one metre in diameter – making it the world's largest flower. Its full name, *Rafflesia arnoldi*, recalls its discovery, in Sumatra in 1818, by Sir Stamford Raffles (see p.554) and his physician, the naturalist Dr Joseph Arnold; the latter collected a seven-kilo specimen and promptly sent it to the Royal Society in London. The blooms, which smell of rotting meat, are pollinated by carrion flies, while the petals, as Raffles recorded, "are of a brick-red with numerous pustular spots of a lighter colour. The whole substance of the flower is not less than half an inch thick, and of a firm fleshy consistence." The flower buds have been very much in demand by *bomoh*s (practitioners of traditional Malay medicine) and their Chinese *sinseh* counterparts for use in medicine, particularly as an aid to accelerate the shrinking of a woman's womb after she's given birth. With no predictable flowering season, and each flower lasting only a few days, there's a certain amount of luck involved in see-ing this strange plant in bloom; if you're making a trip here just to see the flowers, it's a good idea to phone their hotline (☎011/861499) before leaving KK to avoid a wasted journey. However, there's no need to hire one of the guides (RM20) advertised at the complex's Visitor Centre, as the park's paths are simple to follow and you're not going to miss a plant that size; someone at the centre should be able to direct you to any plant that happens to be in bloom.

Tambunan and around

Seventeen kilometres short of Tambunan, a kink in the road reveals the gleaming emerald paddy fields of **Tambunan Plain** below. Flanked by groves of bamboo – the result of a colonial regulation that for every pole cut, twenty more be planted – and threaded by the Sungei Pegalam, the plain is thought to have been named after two warriors, Tamadons and Gombunan, whose peoples joined forces centuries ago to expel invading tribes. **Gunung Trus Madi**, Sabah's second highest mountain (2642m), towers above the plain's eastern flank; climbing it (see overleaf) is an exciting alterna-tive to ascending Mount Kinabalu. Less ambitiously, it's possible to hike to the forest-framed **Mawar waterfall**, northeast of Tambunan, either on a tour from Tambunan itself or, if you're heading to Tambunan on a bus from KK, by getting off the bus when you hit the main Ranau–Tambunan road; see overleaf for details.

After such a wonderful approach, the small Kadazan settlement of **TAMBUNAN**, centred on an ugly square of modern shophouses, is bound to disappoint. The most generous thing that can be said about the place, the administrative centre of Tambunan District, is that it's a quiet, spacious town, the site, every Thursday morning, of a lively *tamu*, for which a smart new market building has been erected.

Although now a sleepy agricultural district, Tambunan featured in one of the more tur-bulent periods in Sabah's history, when it witnessed the demise of folk hero and rebel, **Mat Salleh**. In 1897, he burned down the British settlement on Pulau Gaya in protest at taxes being levied by the Chartered Company; branded an outlaw, with a price on his head, Salleh finally negotiated a deal with William Clarke Cowie of the Chartered Company that allowed him and his men to settle in Tambunan. The outcome outraged other members of the company and Salleh hurriedly withdrew to Tambunan Plain, where he erected a fort of bamboo and stone. Sure enough, British forces descended into the plain at the beginning of 1900 and besieged Salleh's fort; by the end of January, Salleh was dead, killed by a stray bullet. It's said that had Salleh been wearing his "invul-nerable jacket", inscribed with verses from the Koran (it's exhibited at the Sabah State Museum; see p.453), he would have lived to fight another day. At **Kampung Tibabar**, a few kilometres north of Tambunan, a stone memorial marks the site of his fort.

Practicalities

Buses to and from KK, Ranau and Keningau stop in the main square, around which are several unspectacular eating houses. There are two **places to stay** in town: the *Government Rest House* (☎087/774339; ②), a five-minute walk from the main road up a small hill which overlooks the Tambunan Plain; or the *Tambunan Village Resort Centre* (TVRC; ☎087/774076), 1km north of town, with ten rooms (②) and twin-bed chalets (③). To get there, catch a minivan (RM1) from the town square going along the KK road and ask to be dropped at the TVRC turning on the right. The centre, in a lovely location beside a fast running river, has a **restaurant** serving basic Chinese and Malay dishes, and also boasts a cottage industry producing *lihing* – the rice wine for which Tambunan is locally renowned. Kayaking and buffalo riding are available here too, though for residents only.

Around Tambunan: Mawar Waterfall and Gunung Trus Madi

The *Tambunan Village Resort Centre* arranges tours to the forest-framed **Mawar Waterfall** at Kampung Patau (for residents only; RM50), though it's possible to get there by catching the Ranau bus the 7km from Tambunan to **Kampung Patau** (hourly; RM2). Here there's a wide gravel trail leading to the waterfall, a two-hour hike away through an idyllic bowl of hills stepped with groves of fern and bamboo.

The centre also arranges treks up **Gunung Trus Madi**, an exciting and demanding overnight trip (RM150) whose first part involves a one-hour journey by minibus to **Kampung Kengaran**, at the base of the mountain. The climb up to the summit, where you camp in the cool conditions for the night, takes five hours up a rough, and often-times steep, path, which shouldn't be attempted without a guide. En route you come across the insectivorous *Nepenthes* (also called the pitcher plant), and enjoy stunning views over the Crocker Range.

Keningau

A fifty-kilometre jaunt south down the road from Tambunan brings you to the rapidly expanding town of **KENINGAU**, the interior's forestry capital. It's a hectic, noisy place, streets crammed with tooting buses and taxis, pavements lined by women hawking cigarettes and children offering "shoeshine, boss" from morning to night. At the weekend, the town attracts crowds of labourers from the sawmills and logging camps that have scarred the hills around it – a phenomenon in part responsible for a burgeoning prostitution trade which puts several of the town's hotels off-limits.

Keningau's single attraction is its **Chinese temple**, situated right beside the bus terminus. The brightly painted murals that cover its walls and ceilings are more reminiscent of those in a Hindu temple, while in the forecourt is a statue of a fat, smiling Buddha, resplendent in red-and-yellow gown. If you're in town on a Thursday morning, check out Keningau's weekly **tamu**, a short walk up the main Keningau–Tambunan road. The only other distraction is the minibus ride twenty minutes northeast of town, through paddy fields and small kampungs, to **Taman Bandukan**. This pleasant riverside park is packed with picnicking locals on Sundays, but at other times grazing cows and scores of butterflies are your only company; the river is clean and good for swimming, while from above its far banks – reached by a wobbly suspension bridge – there's a good view of the surrounding hills. To get to the park, take a Bingkor-bound minibus from the central square, telling the driver where you're headed.

Rather than **heading on**, to either Tenom or Tambunan, a more exciting alternative is to head for Sapulut (see opposite) to explore Sabah's Murut heartland; this remote region is effectively a dead end and accessible only from Keningau, to which you'll have to backtrack afterwards. It's also possible to take a Land Cruiser and strike east along the logging roads which connect the interior with Tawau (see p.497), the largest town in southern Sabah, though this really is a tough route.

PRACTICALITIES

There are minibuses here from Tambunan (RM7) and from KK (RM13), with buses and taxis terminating in and around the town's central square. It isn't possible to reserve a seat on a Land Cruiser to Tawau (RM100) and drivers only set off with a full load, so turn up early – around 7am – if you want to head out on this route.

A couple of adequate **hotels** – *Hotel Hiap Soon* (☎087/331541; ②), with small, simple air-con rooms, and the even more basic *Hotel Tai Wah* (☎087/332092; ①) – are near the centre, though the majority are found in the new part of town, five minutes' walk behind the Chinese temple, up Jalan Masuk Spur. It's here that you'll find Keningau's friendliest budget choice, *Wah Hin* (☎087/332506; ①), whose rooms are small and have fans and shared bathrooms; and the town's poshest address, *Hotel Perkasa* (☎087/331045, fax 334800; ④), which boasts an in-house fitness centre and restaurants, 1km out of town on the Tambunan road.

Locals congregate at the *Yung On* coffee shop, which serves cakes and pastries; it's at the northeastern edge of town, a five-minute walk to the east of the Chinese temple's neighbour, the Yuk Yin School. Nearby are *Restoran Shahrizal*, which serves fine *roti*s and curries behind its bamboo facade; and Keningau's best **restaurant**, the *Mandarin*, where one of the specialities is freshwater fish. Across town, near the *Hotel Wah Hin*, the *People Restaurant* dishes up *dim sum* and noodles. For a more economical meal, try the cluster of **food stalls** beside the bus stop, bearing in mind that most are closed by dusk.

The interior: Sapulut and beyond

One or two buses (RM20) a day make the 116-kilometre journey from Keningau southeast to **Sapulut**, deep in the heart of Murut country – the departure point for some exhilarating river expeditions. The time honoured customs of Sabah's indigenous peoples are dying out at an alarming rate, but along the rivers around Sapulut you can still witness traditional longhouse community life, little changed over the centuries. Moreover, the experience of sitting at the prow of a boat that's inching up a churning Bornean river under a dense canopy of forest is one that's hard to beat. If you do make the trip, bear in mind that it takes a few days and that you'll have to retrace your steps to Keningau, as the road runs out at Sapulut.

The trip starts inauspiciously: the terrain towards Sapulut has been so scarred by logging that, for much of the journey, you wonder why you bothered coming; on the way, endless logging trucks loom terrifyingly out of the dust cloud that hangs permanently over the route. Around an hour out of Keningau is tiny **Kampung Sook**, barely more than a wide stretch of the road, with a few stalls and split bamboo houses and a huge district office. Beyond Sook, keep your eyes peeled for roadside shelters, erected by the Murut over their buried dead and draped with painted cloths. While crosses decorate several of these cloths, others feature more unorthodox designs, such as portraits of soccer players.

Sapulut

From Keningau, it takes four hours to reach **SAPULUT**, situated at the convergence of the Sapulut and Talankai rivers, and hemmed in by densely forested hills. It remains an appealing place in spite of its ugly tapioca mill, and though the main reason for coming here is to continue up- or downriver, there's enough of interest to warrant a day in the village itself. Across the pedestrian suspension bridge that spans Sungei Talankai is Sapulut's former schoolhouse (dating back to the Japanese occupation, and now overgrown) and its **Mahkamah**, or native court building. The hollowed sandstone rock you can see outside the court is the *batu kelasan*, or spirit stone, by which men who were accused were entitled to test their innocence, the theory being that if they touched it and took an oath of honesty (a *sumpah*), and didn't subsequently die, they were telling the truth. A two-hour climb through the secondary forest above the mill brings you to a panoramic view of the surrounding kampungs and countryside.

The one **place to stay** in Sapulut is at the home of Lantir Bakayas (②), the boatman who arranges trips to Batu Punggul (see overleaf). Lantir's wife serves up simple but filling **meals** (RM5) throughout the day, and Lantir himself will happily show you around the village. Minibus drivers can drop you at Lantir's house, which is on the left-hand side of the road, beyond the mill.

Beyond Sapulut

The best trip out of Sapulut is up Sungei Sapulut to **Batu Punggul**, a 250-metre-high limestone cliff that rears out of virgin jungle. The climb to the summit is rewarded by outstanding views of the forest, while another few minutes' walk brings you to the impressive **Tinahas Caves**, whose walls are lined with swifts' nests and roosting bats. The Korporasi Pembangunan Desa (Rural Development Corporation, or KPD for short), which controls Sapulut's tapioca mill, operates the *Batu Punggul Lodge*, twenty minutes' walk from the cliff. As well as its resthouse (②), guests can stay in a traditional Murut longhouse (①) or camp out (RM5), and there's a canteen, too. For an extra RM30 per person, villagers from a nearby longhouse will lay on a Murut cultural evening, complete with jars of lethal *tapai* (rice wine, similar to Sarawak's *tuak*).

The **boat** trip from Sapulut to Batu Punggul (it costs around RM200 to charter a boat for six passengers) takes around two and a half hours, though it can take twice as long, depending on the weather, passing isolated riverside kampungs and longhouses on the way. Both the boat and accommodation are best booked ahead at the KPD's office at Km 9, Jalan Tuaran, Kota Kinabalu (☎088/428910), though arrangements can be made directly with Lantir when you arrive in Sapulut, subject to there being space at the lodge.

The going gets tougher – and pricier – if you travel downriver from Sapulut to visit one of the kampungs towards the Kalimantan border. The first settlement of any size, forty minutes south of Sapulut, is **Kampung Pagalongan**, a surprisingly large community, where local villagers pick up supplies. It's another ten minutes to the bend in the river commanded by **Kampung Silungai**'s huge 120-metre longhouse. Despite its jarring zinc roof, the longhouse is an appealing construction of green-and-white wooden slats, centring on a ceremonial hall, and home to around six hundred extremely friendly villagers. More traditional longhouses can be seen at nearby **Pensiangan**, but their future is uncertain since the logging industry is moving unerringly towards this settlement – already there's reputed to be a track from Sapulut, though minibuses don't run this far. Finally, provided you have an Indonesian visa, it's possible to follow the Sungei Sapulut **into Kalimantan**, though renting a boat for such a journey is prohibitively expensive.

The person to contact if you want to explore the territory south of Sapulut is Lantir, who arranges tailor-made **trips** to these parts, though at a price: chartering a boat for a day's river meandering – say to Pensiangan and back – costs RM400 for up to six people. Very occasionally, much cheaper **passenger launches** ply this stretch of the river – ask Lantir to check with the KPD office in Salong, 5km south of Sapulut, before you charter a boat, though bear in mind that you could have a long wait for a boat back again.

Tenom and around

After Keningau, the small town of **TENOM**, 42km to the southwest, comes as a great relief. The heady days when Tenom was the bustling headquarters of the Interior District of British North Borneo are now long gone, and today it's a peaceful, friendly backwater. Lying within a mantle of lushly forested hills, the town boasts a selection of charismatic wooden shophouses and a blue-domed mosque. The surroundings are extremely fertile, supporting maize, cocoa and soybean – predominantly cultivated by the indigenous Murut people.

The **Tenom Agricultural Research Station** (Mon–Thurs 8am–2pm, Fri & Sat 8–11am) in Lagud Sebrang, a 25-minute bus ride (RM2) from below the padang, is where the state's Agricultural Department carries out feasibility studies on a wide range of crops. The research station is renowned for its **Orchid Centre**, where a profusion of orchids cascade from trees and tree trunks. Less tempting, though actually much better than it sounds, is the nearby **Crop Museum** (free), where you can easily spend an hour strolling through the groves of exotic fruit trees and tropical plants, such as durian, rambutan, jackfruit, coffee and okra – all tended by women in wide-brimmed hats. The research station's own **resthouse** (☎087/735661; ②), a fair walk from the station headquarters, has large, if slightly shoddy, rooms with shared bathrooms, though it offers lovely views across a low valley.

Practicalities

Tenom marks the end of Sabah's only stretch of railway, the track skirting the southeast edge of town. The **train station** (☎087/735514) is on the southern edge of the padang – call for reservations to be sure of a railcar seat (see p.467 for timetable and details). **Minibuses** congregate on the town's main street, Jalan Padas, which runs along the north side of the padang. The journey northwest to Beaufort is best done by train, though it's possible to get a **minibus** there. **Buses** north to Keningau (RM5) – from where you can continue on to KK – and south to Kuala Tomani (RM4), circle around Tenom all day long, looking for passengers; you can always pick a bus up on the main street, at the western edge of the padang. **Shared taxis** to Keningau also cost RM5 and leave from the main street whenever they've assembled four passengers.

   Accommodation here includes the friendly *Hotel Kim San* (☎087/735485; ②), one street north of Jalan Tun Mustapha, about 500m southwest of the padang, to the spick-and-span rooms of the *Hotel Sri Jaya* (☎087/735077; ②) on Tenom's main street. The classiest place in town though, is the *Hotel Perkasa* (☎087/735811; ④), a RM3 taxi ride (or strenuous short hike) up the hill above town, its pleasing rooms affording great views of the surrounding countryside. **Places to eat** are plentiful, with a clutch of coffee shops and restaurants in the area around the *Hotel Kim San*. For a tasty *mee* soup, try the *Restoran Double Happiness*, below the padang; or, for something a bit more lavish, head 2km south of town along the Tomani road to the cavernous *YNL Restaurant* (daily 6pm–midnight), where the speciality is fresh fish caught in the nearby Sungei Padas. There's decent Chinese food at the *Perkasa*, and at the market on Saturday evenings, hawker stalls are set out on the hotel's front lawn.

South of Tenom: Murut villages

A string of tiny **Murut villages** runs along the road south of Tenom, most of them accessible by catching a bus bound for Kuala Tomani, 37km from Tenom. The Murut are Christians – the result of some fairly vigorous missionary work early in the twentieth century – which accounts for the area's several powder-blue churches, made of wood and bearing names like True Jesus Church. Traditional longhouses have disappeared from the region, but a few **ceremonial halls** still stand, inside which you'll find *lansaran*: Murut trampolines, made of planks and pliant logs, and used for dancing jigs on special occasions. To see one, ask your bus driver to stop at **Kampung Mamai Tom** (around 28km from Tenom) or, better still, at **Kampung Kaparungan**, close to Kuala Tomani, where the bamboo benches in the ceremonial hall have gaps in them to take *tapai* jars. Sadly, the Murut rarely don their traditional costumes these days, unless tourists pay them to do so.

Beaufort

Named after the elaborately monikered Leicester P. Beaufort, one of the early governors of British North Borneo, **BEAUFORT** is a quiet, uneventful town whose commercial importance has declined markedly since the laying of a sealed road from KK into the interior lessened the importance of its rail link with Tenom. The town's position on the banks of the Sungei Padas leaves it prone to flooding, which explains why its shophouses are raised on steps – early photographs show Beaufort looking like a sort of Southeast Asian Venice. But once you've poked around in the town market, inspected angular St Paul's Church at the top of town and taken a walk past the stilt houses on the river bank, you've exhausted its sights; tourists normally only stop by as part of the train ride to Tenom (see p.464), or on their way to the white-water rafting on Sungei Padas.

The **train** station is on the southern side of town, next to the river. **Buses** stop in the centre itself, beside the market, while **taxis** congregate outside the train station. Internet access is available at the *Multimedia Cyber Café*, first floor, Lot 9, Lo Chung Park.

Beaufort's two **hotels** are the *Beaufort* (☎087/211911; ②), east of the market, and the *Mandarin Inn* (☎087/212798; ②), five minutes' walk across the river – they're practically identical, each with shabby rooms and shared bathrooms, though the rooms at the *Mandarin* just have the edge in terms of freshness. When it comes to **eating**, you could do a lot worse than *Christopher's Corner Parking*, across from the train station, whose friendly owner will rustle you up a really good Western breakfast – toast, mar-

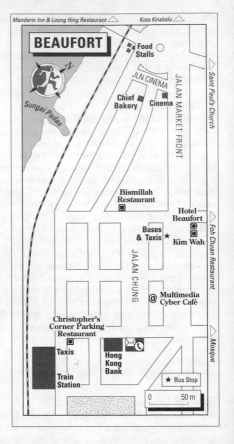

malade, sausage, beans and egg. *Restoran Kim Wah*, a sizeable establishment below the *Hotel Beaufort*, serves simple Chinese food, though better is to be found at the *Foh Chuan*, sited in one of the new blocks just north of the *Beaufort*, which is famed locally for its noodle dishes. The *Loong Hing*, 250m over the bridge and out of town, is another establishment that comes highly recommended, though if it's curries and *roti*s you're after, the *Bismillah* in the town centre is hard to beat. There are also hawker stalls next to the bridge.

West of Beaufort: the Klias Peninsula and Pulau Tiga Park

Immediately west of Beaufort, and served by regular minibuses from the centre of town, is the **Klias Peninsula**, from whose most westerly settlement, tiny **Menumbok**, several ferries depart daily for Pulau Labuan (see p.468). Meanwhile, it's a jarring, hour-long bus ride from Beaufort northwest to **KUALA PENYU**, at the northern point of the peninsula, the departure point for **Pulau Tiga Park** and not a place to visit for its own sake. The only place to stay is the *Government Rest House* (☎087/884231; ③) with large, airy, en-suite rooms; it's five minutes beyond the Shell garage on the water-

SABAH'S RAILWAY LINE

Over the metals all rusted brown,
Thunders the "Mail" to Jesselton Town;
Tearing on madly, reck'ning not fate,
Making up time – she's two days late
See how the sparks from her smokestack shower,
Swaying on wildly at three miles an hour.

As this 1922 rhyme illustrates, Sabah's only **railway line** (information on ☎088/254611) is more a curiosity than a practical mode of transport. Although the line runs all the way from KK to Tenom, travel between Beaufort and the capital is far quicker by **bus**, and it's only the journey from **Beaufort to Tenom** (2hr 15min) – a bone-shaking ride tracing the twists and turns of the Sungei Padas – that's really worth making. Here, the train passes tiny stations and winds through dramatic jungle that at times arches right over the track. Three types of train – diesel, cargo and railcar – ply this part of the route daily; the fastest, most comfortable and most expensive option is the compact **railcar** (RM8.35 one way; on the other types of train, the one-way fare is RM2.75), whose front windows afford an unimpeded view of the oncoming countryside; it only holds a handful of passengers, so phone or call in at the station to book ahead.

TIMETABLE

Beaufort–Tenom
Mon–Sat: 8.30am (railcar); 10.00am (diesel); 12.30pm (cargo); 3.55pm (cargo)
Sun: 6.45am (diesel); 10.50am (diesel); 2.30pm (diesel); 4.05pm (railcar).

Tenom–Beaufort
Mon–Sat: 6.40am (railcar); 8am (cargo); 10.15am (diesel); 2.50pm (cargo).
Sun: 7.20am (railcar); 7.55am (diesel); 12.10pm (diesel); 3.05pm (diesel).

front. Leaving Kuala Penyu, you can either get a direct bus to Beaufort, or take a local bus 5km to **Kampung Kayul** and, at the junction of two equally dusty – or muddy – unpaved roads, wave down a bus coming from Menumbok heading either for KK or Beaufort.

Pulau Tiga Park

In the South China Sea, north of Kuala Penyu, **Pulau Tiga Park** once comprised three islands, but wave erosion has reduced one of them, Pulau Kalampunian Besar, to a sand bar. The remaining two, Tiga and Kalampunian Damit, offer good **snorkelling**, plus the chance to see some unusual **wildlife**.

Pulau Tiga itself was formed by erupting mud volcanoes; you can still see smaller versions, occasionally squirting strings of mud into the air, at the top of the island. Circled by fine-sand beaches and good coral, and crisscrossed by lengthy trails, Tiga's forested interior harbours wild pigs and monitor lizards; if you're down on the sands, look out for Tiga's most famous inhabitants, its megapodes – rotund incubator birds, so called because they lay their eggs in mounds of sand and leaves.

Pulau Kalampunian Damit, 1km northeast of Pulau Tiga, is known locally as Pulau Ular, or "Snake Island", as it attracts a species of sea snake called the yellow-lipped sea krait in huge numbers – on an average day, at least a hundred of these metallic-grey and black creatures come ashore to rest, mate and lay their eggs. Though dozy in the heat of the day, the sea kraits are poisonous, so you're best off accompanied by a ranger if you want to see them.

To arrange boat transport **to the park**, call the Sabah Parks officer at the park itself (☎011/810636). The return journey costs RM30 per passenger as long as there are five or more in all. From Tiga, bank on RM30 more for a boat to visit Kalampunian Damit.

The only **accommodation** is on Tiga itself; hostels are RM30 a bed or twin-share chalets (③). Bookings are handled by Sabah Parks in KK (☎088/211188).

Pulau Labuan

Around 10km west of the Klias Peninsula, **PULAU LABUAN** is a small, arrowhead-shaped island whose size bears no relation to its significance. The terms of a treaty with the Sultan of Brunei yielded the island to the British Crown long before neighbouring Sabah was procured by the Chartered Company, and on Christmas Eve, 1846, Captain G.R. Mundy took possession of it in the name of Queen Victoria. In addition to Labuan's fine anchorage and consequent potential as a trading post, it was its **coal deposits** – the northern tip of the island is still called Tanjung Kubong, or Coal Point – which attracted the British, who were keen to establish a coaling station for passing steamships. With trade in mind, they made the island a free port in 1848; by 1889, it had been incorporated into British North Borneo, a state of affairs that lasted until it joined the Straits Settlements a few years into the twentieth century.

World War II brought the focus of the world upon Labuan. Less than a month after the bombing of Pearl Harbour, the island was occupied by the invading Japanese army on New Year's Day, 1942, and it was through Labuan that the Japanese forces penetrated British North Borneo. During the war years the island was known as **Maida Island**, in memory of General Maida, commander-in-chief of the Japanese forces in British Borneo, who was killed in a plane crash near Bintulu on his way to declare its airport open. In June 1945, the men of the Ninth Australian Infantry Division landed on Labuan and three and a half years of occupation came to an end. Having witnessed the arrival of Japanese forces, it was only fitting that Labuan should also witness their surrender, which took place on September 9, 1945. Labuan, along with Sabah, reverted to the British Crown in July 1946, though it was a further seventeen years before it actually became part of Sabah. Then, in 1984, the island was declared part of Malaysian Federal Territory, governed directly by Kuala Lumpur. Today, Labuan – with a population fast approaching fifty thousand – is still a duty-free port, though its present status as both a sordid getaway for Bruneians and Sabahians after prostitutes and cheap beer, and a base for Filipino smugglers, is at odds with its pretensions to become an offshore banking centre and tourist hot spot. Still, the main settlement, **Labuan Town**, has its own small charm, with some reasonable beaches and diving opportunities nearby; given that ferries from KK and Brunei interconnect at Labuan, you may well end up spending some time here.

The island

The centre of Labuan, previously known as Victoria but now referred to simply as **LABUAN TOWN**, lies on the southeastern side of the island, its central streets thronging with Malaysian businessmen and Russian sailors, Bruneian shoppers and Filipino traders. The *gerai*, or permanent **market**, at the far western end of town, is rather downbeat, though its upper level affords good views of Kampung Patau Patau, the modest **water village** northwest of town whose surrounding waters bristle with rotting foundations. Below the market is a gathering of tin shacks, where Filipinos sell seashell models, stuffed turtles, leather bags, brassware, cloths and silks.

Just 500m north of town, the dome of the **An-Nur Jamek Mosque** resembles a concrete shuttlecock. Further north is Labuan's **war memorial**, next to a sleepy kampung 4km out of town; you can get there on a Layang Layangan minibus from the bus area (see p.470). Occupying a serene seaside site within the aptly named **Peace Park**, the memorial – a concave concrete bridge covered in grass – commemorates all those who died in Borneo in World War II; just below, an enclosure marks the site of the Japanese

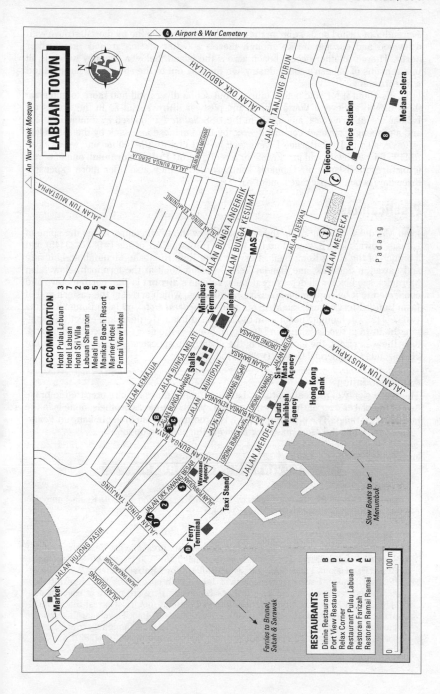

LABUAN TOWN

△ △, Airport & War Cemetery

△ An 'Nur Jamek Mosque

N

ACCOMMODATION

Hotel Pulau Labuan	3
Hotel Labuan	7
Hotel Sri Villa	2
Labuan Sheraton	8
Melati Inn	5
Manikar Beach Resort	4
Mariner Hotel	6
Pantai View Hotel	1

RESTAURANTS

Dinnie Restaurant	B
Port View Restaurant	D
Relax Corner	F
Restaurant Pulau Labuan	C
Restoran Farizah	A
Restoran Ramai Ramai	E

Medan Selera

Police Station

Telecom

Padang

MAS

Minibus Terminal

Cinema

Mawar Stalls

Wawasan Agency

Taxi Stand

Duta Agency

Muhibbah Agency

Siti Mata Agency

Hong Kong Bank

Ferry Terminal

Market

Slow Boats to Menumbok

Ferries to Brunei, Sabah & Sarawak

0   100 m

surrender of 1945. Locals swim on the narrow **beach** beside the memorial, strewn with driftwood and coconut husks, though there's a better stretch around 1km further north. There's another decent beach across the island, below a chimney which is all that remains of Labuan's coal industry. On the way out to the airport is a large **Allied war cemetery**.

That's about it for land-bound tourists, but scuba divers will find more to entertain them offshore. Several World War II and postwar **shipwrecks** lie in the waters off Labuan's southern coast, among them the USS *Salute* (scuppered by a mine in 1945) and a passenger steamer commandeered by the Japanese and sunk by the Australian airforce, also in 1945. Borneo Divers (see below) charge RM100 for one wreck dive, RM185 for two dives, and just RM65 for a reef dive off **Pulau Kuraman**, one of several picturesque islands off Labuan's southern coast; they also offer more expensive three-day/two-night packages out of KK.

Practicalities

Jalan Merdeka, running along the seafront below the town centre, forms the spine of Labuan Town; along it, you'll find the **tourist information office** (☎087/423445) and a branch of the Hong Kong Bank. **Ferries** from Kota Kinabalu, Menumbok, Limbang and Lawas in Sarawak, and Bandar Seri Begawan dock at the terminal below Jalan Merdeka; see box for all departure details. Labuan's **airport** is 3km north of town and connected to it by regular, inexpensive **minibuses**, which arrive at the eastern end of Jalan Bunga Melati; there's an MAS office in the *Federal Hotel*, on Jalan Bunga Kesuma (☎087/412263). Running north from the middle of Jalan Merdeka, and effectively splitting the town in two, is Jalan Tun Mustapha, home to the new post office building and, near the waterfront, the local office of the diving trip specialist, Borneo Divers, at Lot 2F, Lazenda Commercial Centre (☎087/415867).

Accommodation

There are plenty of **places to stay** in Labuan, though unless you're prepared to brave one of the places over at the east end of town, which double as brothels, none is in the budget price range. The best deal in town is a room with a fan in the Indian-run *Pantai View Hotel*, while the *Manikar Beach Resort* is the plushest option.

MOVING ON FROM LABUAN

BY AIR
There are regular **flights** from Labuan Town to KK (around RM50), Kuala Lumpur (RM370), Kuching (RM200) and Miri (RM70).

BY BOAT AND FERRY
Although schedules are susceptible to change, there are presently five departures a day to **Kota Kinabalu** (RM28), at 8.30am, 1pm (two boats) and 3.30pm (two boats); and four to **Brunei** at 8.30am, 11am, noon and 3pm (RM24). For **Limbang**, a ferry leaves daily at 12.30pm, while a **Lawas** ferry departs at 1pm – both cost RM20. For **Menumbok**, from where it's a two-hour bus ride to Kota Kinabalu, there are plenty of speedboats (RM10; 30min) as well as three daily car ferries (RM5 for foot passengers) that depart from the jetty behind the Hong Kong Bank at 8am, 1pm and 4pm. Tickets for the ferries and boats are sold at the arrival points at the ferry terminal area, though there are a couple of outlets nearby: Duta Muhibbah Agency (daily 8am–4pm; ☎087/413827) and Sin Matu Agency (Mon–Sat 8am–5pm, Sun 8am–noon; ☎087/412261), at 52 and 55 Jalan Merdeka respectively.

Labuan, Jalan Merdeka (☎087/412502). One of the more expensive options, with large, en-suite rooms boasting air-con and TV, and its own swimming pool. ⑥.

Labuan Sheraton, Jalan Merdeka (☎087/422000). Fine rooms and a range of stylish restaurants and bars. ⑦ including breakfast.

Manikar Beach Resort (☎087/418700). A free shuttle bus makes the 20min trip to the resort from the airport and waterfront. Set in fifteen acres of private beach and gardens up on the northwestern tip of the island, this is Labuan's last word in swank, with 250 rooms overlooking the sea, and classy business, recreational and water-sports facilities. ⑥.

Mariner, Jalan Tanjung Purun (☎087/418822). Its well-appointed rooms, with TV and air-con, represent excellent value. ⑤.

Melati Inn, Jalan OKK Awang Besar (☎087/416307). Right opposite the ferry terminal. Their double rooms come with TV, air-con and (for an extra RM3) bathroom. ②.

Pantai View, Jalan Bunga Tanjung (☎087/411339). Good-value Indian-run hotel; the rooms are small, with fans and shared bathrooms. ②.

Pulau Labuan, Jalan Perpaduan (☎087/416288). A comfortable option, with air-con en-suite rooms. ④.

Sri Villa, Jalan OKK Awang Besar (☎087/416369). Slightly pricier than the similar *Pantai View*, but good value nonetheless. ②.

Eating and drinking

Along Jalan Merdeka and Jalan OKK Awang Besar you'll find a number of no-frills, Chinese and Indian **restaurants** – the latter featuring American wrestling videos day and night. Particularly good for *rotis*, *murtabaks* and curries is *Restoran Farizah*, next to the *Pantai View* (see above) – though many locals swear by the *Fuizul*, which serves up similar fare a short way west along the same street. Two blocks north, facing each other on Jalan Bunga Mawar, there's the Muslim *Dinnie Restaurant* and the *Restaurant Pulau Labuan*, an air-con restaurant with a wide Chinese menu. For great *dim sum* and Chinese tea, try *Restoran Ramai Ramai* at the intersection of Jalan Merdeka and Jalan Tun Mustapha; also good for Chinese cuisine is Jalan Merdeka's waterfront *Port View Restaurant* where diners enjoy great sea views. At night, make a beeline for the stalls west of the town cinema, above Jalan Muhibbah, where you'll find *nasi campur* and delicious barbecued chicken wings. Altogether more upmarket is the *Hotel Labuan*'s *Nagalang Chinese & Japanese Restaurant*, while below it is the 24-hour *Kiamsam Terrace* coffee shop. For a quick sharpener before dining, there's *Relax Corner*, a friendly **pub** opposite *Hotel Labuan*, serving cold and incredibly cheap beer.

To Sarawak: Sipitang

On the bumpy gravel road 47km southwest of Beaufort, **SIPITANG** is a sleepy seafront town worth bearing in mind if you need a place to stay en route to Sarawak. As you approach from the north, a bridge marks the start of town – look out for the pretty stilt houses to your left as you cross. Just over the bridge, there's a jetty from where a **boat** leaves (daily 7.30am; RM20) for Labuan; 250m beyond that, you're in the town centre. Buses from Beaufort, KK and Lawas (see p.421) congregate at the terminus in the centre of town, right next door to which is the taxi stand. Except for a trip to **Taman Negara** – a beachside picnic spot a few kilometres south of town, and favoured by locals at the weekend, when there'll probably be a minibus service – there's nothing to do in Sipitang. On the bright side, there are stacks of **restaurants** and eating houses in the centre of town, a couple of which, the *Kami* and the *Rina*, have used their sunset-facing positions on the shore of Brunei Bay to good advantage by erecting balconies over the water's edge; both serve a range of Malay and Chinese dishes, including good seafood. Across the main road, *Restoran Bismillah* does good

---

CROSSING INTO SARAWAK

The easiest way to travel from Sipitang **to Sarawak** by public transport is to get the Lawas Express bus (RM6), which leaves KK daily at 1pm, passing through Sipitang around 4pm and getting to **Lawas** some time after 5pm; an alternative is to catch a minibus to Sindumin (RM2), on the Sabah side of the border, and connect with a Lawas bus there. Whichever you choose, the driver will wait while you pass through the passport controls flanking the border – one in Sindumin, the other a couple of hundred metres away at Merapok in Sarawak, where you're given a permit entitling you to remain in Sarawak for a month (for more on Sarawak's rules on visas, which differ from those in the rest of Malaysia, see p.20).

---

curries and breakfast *roti*s; a minute or so further south, the *Asandong* puts on a superb Malay buffet every night. A number of satay and fried-chicken sellers set up stalls on the waterfront at dusk. Of the **hotels** along the main road, the *Hotel Asanol* (☎087/821506; ②), just 200m from the centre, is the friendliest and most affordable with compact, en-suite rooms; the similar *Hotel Shangsan* (☎087/821800; ③) nearby has air-con to boot.

North of Kota Kinabalu

North of Kota Kinabalu, Sabah's trans-state road hurries through the capital's drab suburbs and past the timber yards of **Tepilok**, en route to the more pastoral environs of **Tuaran**. From here, the *atap* houses of the Bajau water villages, **Mengkabong** and **Penambawang**, are both a stone's throw away. Although the main road veers eastwards to Ranau (see p.482) just outside Tuaran, a lesser fork runs north, through the foothills of Mount Kinabalu, before reaching **Kota Belud**, the site of a weekly market that attracts tribespeople from all over the region. The landscape really heats up north of Kota Belud: jewel-bright paddy fields line the road for much of the way up to the **Kudat Peninsula**, with Mount Kinabalu beyond. Journey's end is signalled by the coconut groves and beaches of **Kudat**, formerly capital of British North Borneo, and now a focal point for the **Rungus** people who dwell in modernized longhouses in the surrounding countryside.

Buses for Tuaran and Kota Belud leave KK throughout the day, and both destinations make for decent day-trips out of the capital. However, it's worth thinking twice before committing yourself to the longer trip to the Kudat Peninsula, as the region's inaccessible beaches and modern longhouses leave many visitors disappointed.

Tuaran, Mengkabong and Penambawang

It takes just under an hour to travel the 34km from Kota Kinabalu to **TUARAN**, from where it's possible to visit two water villages. On the way, you'll pass the **Yayasan Sabah Building** – a vast glass cylinder in Likas Bay housing the Sabah Foundation, an organization that channels profits from its huge timber concession into schools, hospitals and a flying doctor service.

Of the two villages, **MENGKABONG**, ten minutes out of Tuaran on a local bus, is the most accessible and a favourite destination with KK's tour agencies. The sight of a village built out over the sea on stilts is usually a compelling one, but Mengkabong is a noisy, charmless example, and you'd do well to make the extra effort to reach **PENAMBAWANG**. Minibuses to Kampung Surusup – the tiny settlement from where you can catch a boat to Penambawang – leave from the road west of Tuaran's brown clock tower; it's a twenty-minute drive (on a nightmarish road) through idyllic paddy fields. Once in Surusup, you need to ask around for a boat (RM10–15 return) – Penambawang is fifteen minutes northeast, across a wide bay skirted with mangroves. Except for a handful of zinc roofs, it's a timeless village, its welcoming inhabitants Muslim Bajau, with houses of *atap*, bamboo and wood interconnected by labyrinthine boardwalks – called *jambatan* – along which fish are laid out to dry.

While **hotels** in Tuaran are nothing to write home about, the *Rasa Ria Resort* (☎088/792888, ⑦), 5km west on Dalit Bay, is as classy a place to stay as any in Sabah, and worth considering if you've got money to spare. The sister resort to Kota Kinabalu's *Shangri-La Tanjung Aru*, it's sandwiched between its own patch of forest and the South China Sea, and boasts over three hundred luxury rooms, most with sea views, as well as a golf course and private nature reserve. Several shuttle buses leave daily from the *Tanjung Aru Resort*, taking around 45 minutes to reach Dalit Bay, and there's also a bus service to the bay from Tuaran.

Kota Belud

For six days of the week, **KOTA BELUD**, 75km northeast of KK on the road to Kudat, is a drab little town, its main street the haunt of listless teenagers and packs of scraggy dogs. Each Sunday though, it springs to life as hordes of villagers from the surrounding countryside congregate at its weekly **market**, said to be the biggest in Sabah, ten minutes' walk out of town along Jalan Hasbollah. The *tamu* fulfils a social, as much as a commercial, role, and draws – among others – Rungus, Kadazan/Dusun and Bajau, the last of which occasionally ride in on horseback and in traditional apparel. Though Kota Belud's popularity among KK's tour operators means there are always tourists about here, you're far more likely to see dried fish, chains of yeast beads (used to make rice wine), buffalo, betel nut and *tudung saji* (colourful food covers) for sale, than souvenirs. To catch the *tamu* at its best, you should get here in the morning; if heading here from KK, plan to leave the city by 7am at the latest.

At Kota Belud's annual **tamu besar**, or "big market", usually held in November, there are cultural performances, traditional horseback games and handicraft demonstrations in addition to the more typical stalls. For specific details each year, call in at the STPC in KK.

Practicalities

Buses for Kota Belud (RM5) leave from the far side of the Shell garage near KK's GPO, and it's also possible to catch a Kudat-bound bus here from the long-distance station (RM5); the journey is a scenic ninety-minute trip. The buses stop beside the district office in the centre of town, and with onward connections so good, there's really no need to spend the night here. A far better idea is to book a bed at the Kinabalu National Park (see p.477), which can be reached via Tamparuli, or to carry on to Kudat (see p.474). There's not much in the way of **restaurants**; for Malay food, try *Restoran Rahmat* below the district office, or one of the lean-to stalls beyond the far side of the office. Otherwise, *Kedai Makan Sin Hing*, 1km south on the KK road, serves up basic Chinese meals. Of the coffee shops over in the newer part of Kota Belud (to the west of the Kudat road), the *Restoran Zam Zam*, 50m north of the main street and on the edge of the old market, does good curries and fried chicken.

On to Kudat

The journey from Kota Belud to Kudat takes in some of Sabah's most dramatic scenery, with the grand peaks of Mount Kinabalu reflected – rice harvest allowing – in the still waters of the paddy fields to the east. At the base of Marudu Bay, the road forks, the right turn leading to **Kota Marudu** – a town with two hotels and several restaurants, but with nothing to entice you to stop and try them out. The left turn, bringing you up the badly surfaced road that runs northwest of Marudu Bay, is lined by coconut groves and paddy fields along its northern section. Many of the coconuts end up at the desiccated-coconut factory 9km out of Kudat, right on Borneo's northern tip – piles of discarded husks can be seen, resembling bleached skulls.

The Kudat Peninsula is home to the **Rungus** people, whose **longhouse** dwellings, or *binatang*, were until recently the region's main attraction. These buildings still exist, and their size still impresses, but today they're often made with sheets of corrugated zinc, whose durability makes it preferable to traditional materials like timber, tree bark, *rattan* and *nipah* leaves. At **Kampung Matunggong**, a footpath leads eastwards over a wire suspension bridge, through bamboo groves, to **Kampung Mompilis**, which has two dilapidated longhouses; it's really the walk that makes the trip worthwhile. Further north, 37km short of Kudat, **Kampung Tinanggol**, set back from the main road through the peninsula, boasts three 25-family longhouses and a quaint white church. The STPC in KK (☎088/212121, *www.jaring.my/sabah*) has constructed a longhouse (②) in the village, allowing visitors to stay in a traditional Rungus environment.

Kudat and around

The natural harbour at **KUDAT**, on the western shore of Marudu Bay, led to it being declared the administrative capital of British North Borneo in 1881, though two years later the capital was switched to Sandakan. Although Kudat is lively and indisputably friendly, there's not much to bring you here, save for a peek at the town centre's lurid orange **Chinese temple**, a stroll around the busy **waterfront** – where wiry old men carry sacks to and from the godowns which back Jalan Lo Thien Chock's shophouses – and a visit to the adjacent **stilt village** at the southern end of town.

Kudat's most famous **beach** is **Bak Bak**, 12km north of town, though **Tajau**, a few kilometres to the north, is favoured by some locals. Quite a few locals visit Bak Bak on a Sunday; otherwise local buses to kampungs near Kudat's beaches are so erratic as to be totally impractical. Taking a taxi is the only practical solution, but prices start at around RM16 for the return journey. Across on the west coast, there's **Bangau Beach**, near the town of **Sikuati** – any bus headed for KK can drop you at the turning, but then it's a six-kilometre hike to the beach. Sikuati itself is only a small coastal settlement, some 20km west of Kudat, though it hosts a good-sized Sunday *tamu*. Further south, green turtles are said to come ashore to lay their eggs, at attractive **Kelambu Beach**. There's no public transport to Kelambu other than taxis from Sikuati; to get to the beach by car, turn west onto Jalan Indarasan Laut, some 12km south of Sikuati, and push on for another 8km.

It's also possible to take a ferry to **Pulau Banggi**, off Sabah's north coast, though only if you've got a few days to spare, as departures are unpredictable, and the only way to get around the island once you're there is to hitch on local boats. The island boasts forest and beaches, and there's a small government **resthouse** (☎088/612511; ②) at **Kampung Kalaki**, the main settlement.

Practicalities

Downtown Kudat centres on the intersection of Jalan Ibrahim Arshad and Jalan Lo Thien Chock – the latter is Kudat's main street, with most of its shops and a Standard Chartered Bank. **Minibuses** to and from Kota Belud and KK congregate a few yards east of the intersection, as do the town's **taxis**, though KK **buses** (outward journey daily at 7.30am and noon) stop along Lorong Empat west of Jalan Lo Thien Chock. For **ferries** to Pulau Banggi, head for the jetty at the southern end of Jalan Lo Thien Chock.

For **accommodation** there's the *Hotel Oriental* (☎088/611045; ②), at the port end of Jalan Lo Thien Chock, whose bright and clean rooms are marred by an insalubrious hallway, shared toilets and a noisy snooker hall downstairs. In the middle of the same street, *Hotel Sunrise* (☎088/611517; ②) has small rooms with fans and shared bathrooms. For a bit more comfort, your best bet is the *Hotel Greenland* (☎088/613211; ③), five minutes' walk east of the town centre, in Block E of the SEDCO shophouse development on Jalan Lo Thien Chock.

The best **restaurant** in town is the *Restoran Sungei Wang*, two minutes beyond the *Greenland Hotel*, serving such delights as scallops in black-bean sauce and tofu with crabmeat for around RM6 each; there are tables outside on the patio, which is strung with fairy lights. Back in the town centre, *Sri Mutiara*, opposite the *Sunrise* on Jalan Lo Thien Chock, is a spruce joint that serves tasty Malay food and fried chicken. At the *Keng Nam Tong Coffee Shop*, opposite the *Silver Inn*, you can have coffee and cake at a marble-topped table, and there's passable North Indian food at *Restoran Mawar* near the turning to Lorong Empat.

Kinabalu National Park

There's no more astounding sight in Borneo than the cloud-encased summit of **Mount Kinabalu** – at 4101 metres, half the height of Everest – shooting skywards from the 750 square kilometres of **KINABALU NATIONAL PARK**. Eighty-five kilometres northeast of KK and plainly visible from Sabah's west coast, Kinabalu's jagged peaks appear impossibly daunting at first sight, but in favourable conditions, the trek up can actually be straightforward for fit climbers. For the 20,000 or so a year who come here to haul themselves up, the process is made simpler by a well-defined, 8.5-kilometre-long path which weaves up its southern side to the bare granite of the summit, passing a vast range of flora and fauna. It's no wonder that climbing the mountain has become one of the must-dos of a Malaysian itinerary, as much an essential activity for package tourists from China as for the independent traveller from Europe or Australasia. But the mountain's fiercest fans are the Malaysian and Singaporean students who return time and again to sprint up the mountain, mostly to try to beat their own previous best times. Consequently, the trail can get pretty full, especially in good weather, so don't expect an alone-with-the-elements kind of experience.

Limbs that are weary from the climb up the mountain will welcome the warm, sulphurous waters of the **Poring Hot Springs**, around 40km away, just outside the park's southeastern border, and one of the few places in Sabah where camping is permitted. Between these two sites is the small, nondescript town of **Ranau**, which has a couple of places to stay and transport links to KK.

Practicalities

There's a morning **bus** to the park, leaving KK's long-distance terminal daily at 7.30am and arriving about two hours later; it's also straightforward to get a minibus here. You need at least two days to ascend and descend Mount Kinabalu – allow an extra day in the park's vicinity if you want to drop by Poring – though you'll be glad of a spare day or two, in the event of cloud cover spoiling the view from the summit, whereupon you may decide to postpone the climb. Groups of climbers leave headquarters for the mountain from around 8.30am, the last group usually setting off by 11am. Most climbers spend their first night at the park around the park headquarters and set off for the mountain next morning; a good ploy is to arrive in the early afternoon, giving yourself some time to acclimatize on the **trails** (see opposite) around the park head-quarters, before undertaking the mountain the following day. That said, it is possible to take an early-morning **taxi** from KK to the park (RM50) in order to begin your ascent that very morning.

Arrival and information

Buses drop you opposite the park gates (RM2 entry) on the KK–Ranau road. Directly inside are an extended cluster of lodgings, restaurants and offices known as the park **headquarters**; the **reception** office (daily 7am–7.30pm) is where you check into park accommodation. Staff here provide you with useful **maps** and information sheets, and can also arrange charter buses to Poring (RM40) or the *Mesilau Nature Resort* (RM65;

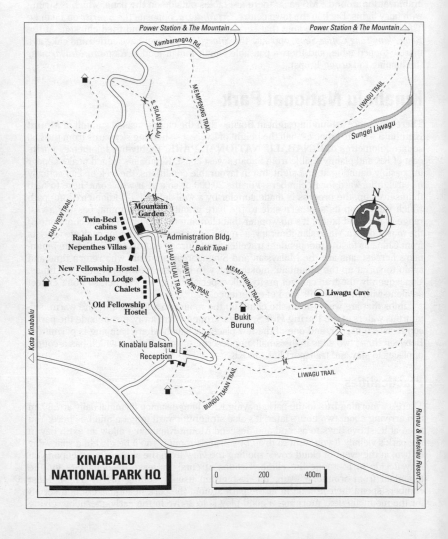

KINABALU NATIONAL PARK HQ.

Power Station & The Mountain △

Kambarangoh Rd.

MEMPENING TRAIL

S. SILAU SILAU

LIWAGU TRAIL

Sungei Liwagu

N

KIAU VIEW TRAIL

Mountain Garden

Twin-Bed cabins

Rajah Lodge

Nepenthes Villas

Administration Bldg.

Bukit Tupai

New Fellowship Hostel

Kinabalu Lodge

Chalets

Old Fellowship Hostel

SILAU SILAU TRAIL

BUKIT TUPAI TRAIL

MEMPENING TRAIL

Liwagu Cave

Bukit Burung

Kinabalu Balsam

Reception

BUNDU TUHAN TRAIL

LIWAGU TRAIL

△ Kota Kinabalu

Ranau & Mesilau Resort △

0   200   400m

see below), the latter just within the park perimeter, though if you've a reservation to stay at the latter, transport will have been arranged from KK to take you straight there. Also at headquarters is a souvenir shop with a wide range of T-shirts, postcards and Borneo-related books.

Twenty kilometres of **trails** loop the montane forest around the headquarters, with a free guided tour leaving daily from the reception office at 11.15am. Less dramatic, but still interesting, are the labelled plants of the **Mountain Garden** (Mon–Fri 8am–4.30pm, Sat 8am–5pm, Sun 9am–4pm), a ten-minute walk below the administration office. The **Multivision Show** (daily at 1.30pm; RM1), screened in the office itself, and the **Slide Show** (Mon, Fri & Sat at 7.30pm; RM1) are less informative – instead, go upstairs for the photos, visuals and mounted exhibits of park flora and fauna in the **Exhibit Centre** (look out, in particular, for the monster stick insect).

Accommodation and eating

It's essential to book a **place to stay** in the park if you're planning to be here at the weekend, when it's at its busiest, though during the week you can usually get accommodation without a reservation. To **book** accommodation at the park headquarters, the *Mesilau Nature Resort* or at Poring, contact Kinabalu Gold Resorts, third floor, Block C, Kompleks Karamunsing, Jalan Tuaran, KK (Mon–Fri 8am–5am, Sat 8am–2am; ☎088/257941); accommodation up the mountain, however, must be booked at the park itself.

AROUND THE PARK HEADQUARTERS

A cluster of **budget hotels** and **resthouses** has sprung up along the main road outside the park, but there's a perfectly adequate range of choices in the park itself, marked on the map opposite. For those on tight budgets, the *Fellowship* **hostels** are basic, friendly dormitory set-ups (RM10) with cooking facilities. From there, prices take a hike, with twin-bed **cabins** (③) commanding magnificent views and four-person **chalets**, the *Nepenthes Villa* and *Kinabalu Lodge*, perched dramatically up the sides of a small valley (RM50–80). Top of the range is the swish *Rajah Lodge,* which sleeps ten people and can only be booked as a whole (RM800).

There are two **restaurants** in the vicinity of the park headquarters; *Kinabalu Balsam* (daily 6am–10pm, Sat until 11pm) is the more basic, but has a nice balcony with fine views of the mountaintop. Inside the entrance is a little shop selling **provisions** for the climb and other essentials. Alternatively, close by the administration office there's the *Liwagu Restaurant* (daily 6am–11pm), which is altogether cosier, serving nicely prepared Western and Asian dishes.

THE MESILAU NATURE RESORT

Opened in 1998, **Mesilau Nature Resort** is located 2000m up in montane rainforest 17km east of the headquarters. Kinabalu Gold Resorts arranges transport there (RM50) from KK; alternatively minivans there can be hired for around this price from the park headquarters. However, once you're at the resort, you have to rely on its own minivans or private drivers to get around.

The advantage of being based at the resort is that it's a lot quieter than at the headquarters, with far fewer people starting their trek from here. It also offers a more interesting first leg to the summit trail, reached by a narrow path which gently curls up slopes before joining the main path at Layang Layang. Along this route you can see the largest *Nepenthes* plants in the world as the area's ecology changes from temperate to mossy cloudforest. Accommodation comprises a 96-bed dormitory (dorm beds RM30), lodges (RM320 for an eight-bed lodge) and chalets (RM350 for a four-bed chalet). For food, there's a restaurant, the *Kedamaian* (daily 8am–10pm) and a café, the *Malaxi* (daily 7am–6pm); there's also a small conservation centre and a gift shop.

UP MOUNT KINABALU
The **huts** on the mountain itself are generally basic; the *Laban Rata Rest House* (dorm beds RM25) at 3300m has its own restaurant (daily 7am–8pm & 2am–3.30am), as well as central heating and hot showers, while the others, *Gunting Lagadan, Panar Laban* and *Waras* huts (dorm beds RM10 at each) have electricity and cooking facilities but no heat. *Sayat-Sayat Hut* (dorm beds RM10), only 1500m from the summit, is an hour further up the mountain, and lacks even an electricity supply.

Mount Kinabalu

Conquering **Mount Kinabalu** today is far easier than it was in 1858, when Spenser St John, British consul-general to the native states of Borneo, found his progress blocked by Kadazan "shaking their spears and giving us other hostile signs". Hugh Low, at the time British colonial secretary on Pulau Labuan, had made the first recorded ascent of the mountain seven years earlier, though he baulked at climbing its highest peak, considering it "inaccessible to any but winged animals". The peak – subsequently named after Low, as was the mile-deep gully that cleaves the mountaintop – was finally conquered in 1888 by John Whitehead. **Low's Gully** (see box, below) splits the summit into a U-shape, which led early explorers to conclude that Kinabalu was volcanic; in fact, the mountain is a granite pluton – an enormous ball of molten rock which has solidified and forced its way through the Crocker Mountain Range over millions of years. This process continues today, with the mountain gaining a few millimetres annually.

The origin of the mountain's name is uncertain; one legend tells how a Chinese prince travelled to Borneo to seek out a huge pearl, guarded by a dragon at the summit of the mountain. Having slain the dragon and claimed the pearl, the prince married a Kadazan girl, only to desert her and return to China. His wife was left to mourn him on the slopes of the mountain – hence *Kina* (China) and *balu* (widow) – where she eventually turned to stone. Another idea is that the name derives from the Kadazan words *Aki Nabalu* – "the revered place of the dead". Nineteenth-century climbs had to take into account the superstitions of local porters, who believed the mountain to be a sacred ancestral home. When Low climbed it, his guides brought along charms, quartz crystals and human teeth to protect the party, and Kadazan porters still offer up chickens, eggs, cigars, betel nut and rice to the mountain's spirits at an annual ceremony.

LOW'S GULLY

Mount Kinabalu grabbed the world's headlines in March 1993, when two British army officers and three Hong Kong soldiers went missing on a training exercise down **Low's Gully** – described by Spenser St John as "a deep chasm, surrounded on three sides by precipices, so deep that the eye could not reach the bottom. . . . There was no descending here." Defeated by impassable waterfalls and boulders, the men set up camp in a mountain cave and left out an SOS marked out with white pebbles. Treacherous weather conditions and inhospitable terrain repeatedly thwarted rescue attempts, but the men were finally found, on day thirty of what should have been a ten-day mission – by which time they were surviving on a diet of Polo mints.

Five years later another British expedition, in perfect weather conditions, succeeded in abseiling down the gully and finding their way out. Climber Steve Long remembers tackling Commando Cauldron, part of the vertical wall of the gully. "We were in a boulder-choked gully only 5m wide, dwarfed by one-thousand-metre high cliffs towering back towards the summit rim. It was an awe-inspiring place. We spoke in whispers, anxious to avoid triggering rock falls. All around us pulverized granite and uprooted trees bore stark and silent witness to the devastation this would wreak. A final abseil, a leap into the last lagoon, and we were out."

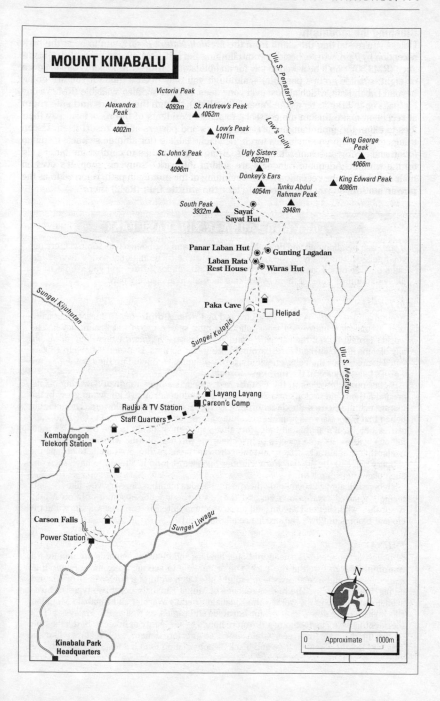

MOUNT KINABALU

Victoria Peak
4093m

Alexandra
Peak
4002m

St. Andrew's Peak
4052m

Low's Peak
4101m

King George
Peak
4066m

St. John's Peak
4096m

Ugly Sisters
4032m

Donkey's Ears
4054m

Tunku Abdul
Rahman Peak
3948m

King Edward Peak
4086m

South Peak
3932m

Sayat
Sayat Hut

Ulu S. Penataran

Low's Gully

Panar Laban Hut

Gunting Lagadan

Laban Rata
Rest House

Waras Hut

Paka Cave

Helipad

Sungei Kijuhutan

Sungei Kulopis

Ulu S. Mesilau

Radio & TV Station

Layang Layang
Carson's Camp

Staff Quarters

Kembarongoh
Telekom Station

Carson Falls

Power Station

Sungei Liwagu

N

0   Approximate   1000m

**Kinabalu Park
Headquarters**

Climbing the mountain

Unless you're starting the climb from the *Mesilau Nature Resort*, aim to be at the park reception by 7am, where, besides your climbing **permit** (RM50) and compulsory insurance (RM3.50), you'll be asked to pay for an obligatory **guide** (RM35 per group of seven or eight; smaller groups possible) – although you only need a guide if you are going beyond Labah Rata, which almost everyone does. Porters are also available (RM25 a day for loads up to 11kg as far as the Panar Laban huts), though the **lockers and safe room** at reception make this an unnecessary expense. Residents of the resort can pay their fees to climb the mountain and arrange guides and porters at the resort itself. Useful things to take with you include a torch, headache tablets (for altitude sickness), suntan lotion and strong shoes or hiking boots. Bring warm clothes to combat the bitter cold on the summit. Adequate raincoats are sold at the park's souvenir shop. It's over an hour's walk from the reception to the beginning of the mountain path, referred to as the **power station**, so you might prefer to take the **shuttle bus** (RM2) there.

FLORA AND FAUNA IN KINABALU PARK

If you dash headlong up and down Mount Kinabalu and then depart, as some visitors do, you'll miss out on many of the region's natural riches. The national park's diverse terrains have spawned an incredible variety of **plants** and **wildlife**, and you are far more likely to glimpse some of them by walking its trails at a leisurely pace.

FLORA

Around a third of the park's area is covered by **lowland dipterocarp forest**, characterized by massive, buttressed trees, allowing only sparse growth at ground level. The world's largest flower, the parasitic – and very elusive – *Rafflesia* (see p.460), occasionally blooms in the lowland forest around Poring Hot Springs. Between 900m and 1800m, you'll come across the oaks, chestnuts, ferns and mosses (including the *Dawsonia* – the world's tallest moss) of the **montane forest**.

Higher up (1800–2600m), the **cloudforest** supports a huge range of flowering plants: around a thousand orchids and 26 varieties of rhododendron are known to grow in the forest, including Low's Rhododendron, with its enormous yellow flowers. The hanging lichen that drapes across branches of stunted trees lends a magical feel to the landscape at this height. It's at this altitude, too, that you're most likely to see the park's most famous plants – its nine species of insectivorous **pitcher plants**, whose cups secrete a nectar that first attracts insects and then drowns them, as they are unable to escape the slippery sides of the pitcher. Early climber Spenser St John is alleged to have seen one such plant digesting a rat.

Higher still, above 2600m, only the most tenacious plantlife can survive – like the agonizingly gnarled *sayat-sayat* tree, and the heath rhododendron found only on Mount Kinabalu – while beyond 3300m, soil gives way to granite. Here, grasses, sedges and the elegant blooms of Low's Buttercup are all that flourish.

FAUNA

Although orang-utans, Bornean gibbons, tarsiers and clouded leopards are among the **mammals** which dwell in the park, you're unlikely to see anything more exotic than squirrels, rats and tree shrews – you might just catch sight of a mouse deer or a bearded pig, if you're lucky. The higher reaches of Mount Kinabalu boast two types of **birds** seen nowhere else in the world – the Kinabalu Friendly Warbler and Kinabalu Mountain Blackbird. Lower down, look out for hornbills and eagles, as well as the Malaysian Tree Pie, identifiable by its foot-long tail. You're bound to see plenty of **insects**: butterflies and moths flit through the trees, while down on the forest floor are creatures like the Trilobite Beetle, whose orange-and-black armour plating lend it a fearsome aspect.

Pulau Perhentian Kecil

Salang Beach, Pulau Tioman

Granite pinnacles known as "dragon's horns", Pulau Tioman

Express boat dock, Sibu, Sarawak

River in the interior, Sarawak

The south peak of Mount Kinabalu, Sabah

Sandakan seafront market, Sabah

View from main mosque, Bandar Seri Begawan

Financial District, Singapore

Antique shop, Chinatown

Temple monks, Phar Kark See Temple, Singapore

Climbing to your first night's accommodation, at around 3350m, takes between three and six hours, depending on your fitness. Roots and stones along the **trail** serve as steps, with wooden "ladders" laid up the muddier stretches. The air gets progressively cooler as you climb, but the walk is still a hard and sweaty one, and you'll be glad of the regular water tanks and **sheltered rest points** en route. Two or three hours into the climb, incredible views of the hills, sea and clouds below you start to unfold (if the weather is kind); higher up, at just above 3000m, a detour to the left brings you to **Paka Cave** – no more than a large overhanging rock, and the site of overnight camps on early expeditions. The end of your first day's climbing is heralded by the appearance of the mighty granite slopes of the **Panar Laban** rock face, veined by trickling waterfalls.

From the resthouses (see p.478) at the foot of Panar Laban (the name is a corruption of a Dusun word meaning "place of sacrifice"), the views of the sun setting over the South China Sea are exquisite. It's here that you spend your night on the mountain, though you should plan to get up at 2.30am the next day to join the procession to the top. Although ropes have been strung up much of this segment of the trail, none of the climbing is really hairy. That said, the air is quite thin, so headaches, nausea and breathlessness are a possibility. The spectacle of sunrise will rob you of any remaining breath, and then it's back down to Panar Laban for a hearty breakfast before the two-hour amble down to park headquarters. When you finally arrive back at headquarters, reflect on the fact that the Nepalese Kusang Gurung, the winner of the annual **Kinabalu Climbathon** in 1991, ran up *and* down the mountain in a staggering 2 hours, 42 minutes and 33 seconds.

Poring Hot Springs

Sited 43km from park headquarters, on the southeastern side of Kinabalu National Park, are the **Poring Hot Springs** (RM2; free for overnight guests). The complex – whose name derives from the giant bamboo found in the area (*poring* means "bamboo" in the local Dusun dialect) was developed by the Japanese during World War II, though the wooden tubs they installed have since been replaced by a clutch of round and square outdoor hot tubs, set in well-landscaped grounds, and large enough to seat two people at a time.

After a few days' hiking up the mountain, a soak in Poring's hot (48–60°C), sulphurous waters is just the ticket. The baths (daily 7am–6pm; from RM15 an hour) are a couple of minutes from the main gates, across a suspension bridge that spans Sungei Mamut; here there are two enclosed baths with jacuzzi and an adjacent plunge pool.

A fifteen-minute walk beyond the baths brings you to Poring's **canopy walk** (daily 6.30am–5.30pm; RM2, camera RM5), where five tree huts connected by suspended walkways afford you a monkey's-eye view of the surrounding lowland rainforest. Views from the walkways – 60m above ground at their highest point – are tremendous, though the shouts of giddy tourists negotiating them thwart your chances of seeing anything more interesting than birds, butterflies and ants. If you're set on witnessing some wildlife, arrange a more expensive trip at night or in the early morning, when it's cooler and quieter – or make do with the low-key but beautiful residents of the newly constructed **butterfly enclosures**, just to the south of the springs.

A more conventional trail strikes off to the east of the baths, reaching the 150-metre-high **Langanan Waterfall** about an hour and a half later. On its way, the trail passes the smaller **Kepungit Waterfall** – whose icy pool is ideal for swimming – and a cave lined with squealing, fluttering bats, as well as groves of towering bamboo. Be warned: if it's been raining, there'll be leeches (see p.75) on the trail.

Practicalities

To get to Poring from Kinabalu Park headquarters, it's best to charter a **minibus** if you're in a group (RM200 for four passengers) – the alternative is to wave down a passing minibus bound for Ranau (see below) and change there. The journey to Poring takes around half an hour. Minibuses drop you beside Poring's **reception** hut, inside the complex gates, where you can arrange an onward minibus when you leave.

For **accommodation**, there's a large campsite (RM6) and two hostels (dorm beds RM12), as well as a range of cabins and chalets, each of which must be booked as a whole: the *Tempua* and *Enggang* cabins (each RM60) sleep four, while the *Rajawali* lodge (RM50) sleeps six. All these places to stay must be booked in advance in KK at Kinabalu Gold Resorts, third floor, Block C, Kompleks Karamunsing, Jalan Tuaran (Mon–Fri 8am–5pm, Sat 8am–2pm; ☎088/257941, *www.nature.kinabalu.net*).

The springs' new **café** is the best **place to eat** at Poring; the only alternatives are the two unspectacular operations just outside the gates: the *Poring Restoran* (daily 8am–8pm), which serves uninspiring Chinese food; and the *Kedai Makanan Melayu* (daily 8am–6pm), three doors along, whose simple Malay dishes take an age to reach your table.

To Ranau

Set in a pleasant valley, the small town of **RANAU** huddles around a square on the south side of the main KK–Sandakan road, 20km from Kinabalu National Park. There's nothing to do here, but it's a handy stopping point if it's too late in the day to find transport to Poring. En route to Ranau from the park, you come to **Kundasang** after around 5km. Here, a **war memorial** signposted 150m off the main road commemorates the victims of the "Death March" of September 1944, when Japanese troops marched 2400 POWs from Sandakan to Ranau (see p.626).

Ranau is based around a grid of ugly, lettered blocks, with street names in short supply, though one exception is Jalan Kibarambang – the first turning on the right if you're coming from KK, and home to both a rickety old market and a new Chinese temple, its pale-cream walls striped by red pillars. The first day of every month sees a lively *tamu*, around one kilometre out of town towards Sandakan.

Practicalities

Minibuses stop at the eastern edge of town, on a patch of land beside Block A. **Long-distance buses** between KK and Sandakan stop on Jalan Kibarambang, also the site of Ranau's **shared taxi** stand. There's **Internet access** at Cyber City Centre, Lot 4, Wisma Budaya, right in the centre.

Ranau has three **hotels**, the best of which is the quiet, six-room *View Motel* (☎088/876445; ②) in Block L, with good-sized en-suite rooms. The *Hotel Ranau* (☎088/875661; ②), next to the Bank Bumiputra on the north side of the square, has a range of rooms, from box-like singles to more spacious air-con doubles with bathrooms. The *Kinabalu Hotel* (☎088/876028; ③), south of the square in Block A, is a smartly painted place with cosy rooms and shared bathrooms.

Jalan Kibarambang has several **restaurants** and **coffee shops**, including the excellent *Restoran Muslim* (daily 6.30am–10pm), where you can feast on great fried chicken to the strains of wrestling videos on the TV; the next-door *Yeong Hing* does good *pow*. Interesting Chinese food is in short supply in Ranau, though the *Sin Mui Mui Restoran* (closed Fri afternoon) at the southern edge of the square has a good menu; also recommended is the *Mien Mien Restoran*, opposite. For Malay food, make for the *Restoran Sugut* (daily 7am–10pm), below the *View Motel*.

Sandakan and around

Sandwiched between sea and cliffs, **SANDAKAN** – like Kota Kinabalu – was all but destroyed during World War II, and its postwar reconstruction was worked around an unimaginative – and, in Sabah, all too familiar – grid system of indistinguishable concrete blocks, without the sense of space you find in KK. That said, the town is the springboard to several of Sabah's most fascinating destinations, including the offshore **Turtle Islands Park** and the **Sepilok Orang-utan Rehabilitation Centre** to the west of town, and further afield, **Sungei Kinabatangan** (see p.490) and the **Danum Valley Conservation Area** (see p.494).

A little history

Although there are eighteenth-century accounts of a trading outpost called Sandakan within the Sultanate of Sulu (whose centre was in what's now the Philippines), the town's modern history began in the early 1870s, with the arrival of a group of European adventurers. Except for the identity of one, a moustachioed Scot called William Clarke Cowie, who ran guns for the Sultan of Sulu, nothing is known about these men, though Kampung German, the name of the settlement they established on Pulau Timbang, does point to their predominant nationality. The area of northeast Borneo between Brunei Bay and Sungei Kinabatangan had been leased by the Sultan of Brunei to the American Trading Company in 1865. The company's attempt to establish a settlement here failed, and in 1877 the Anglo-Austrian partnership of Baron Von Overbeck and Alfred Dent took up the lease, naming Englishman **William Pryer** as the first Resident of the east coast. After Kampung German burned down a year later, nearby Buli Sim-Sim was chosen by Pryer as the site of his new town, which he named Elopura, or "Beautiful City", although locals persisted in referring to it as Sandakan (in Sulu, "to be pawned"). By 1885, Sandakan was the **capital** of British North Borneo, its natural harbour and proximity to sources of timber, beeswax, rattan and edible birds' nests transforming it into a thriving commercial centre. Sabahian timber was used in the construction of Beijing's Temple of Heaven, and much of Sandakan's early trade was with Hong Kong; there's still a strong Cantonese influence in the town.

In January 1942 the Japanese army took control, establishing a POW camp from where the infamous Death March to Ranau commenced. What little of the town was left standing after intensive Allied bombing was burned down by the Japanese, and the end of the war saw the administration of Sabah shift to KK. Nevertheless, by the 1950s a rebuilt Sandakan had become the economic engine of the state, while the **timber** boom of the 1960s and 1970s generated such wealth that the town was reputed to have the world's greatest concentration of millionaires. When the region's decent timber had been exhausted in the 1980s, Sandakan looked to oil palm and cocoa, crops which now dominate the surrounding landscape.

Arrival, information and transport

The **long-distance bus station** is 5km west of the town, from where local buses (75 sen) and taxis (RM8) travel into the centre. The **airport** is 11km north of town; you can get a minibus (RM1.50) to the southern end of Jalan Pelabuhan throughout the day, or a taxi into the centre (RM12). The boat from Zamboanga in the Philippines docks at **Karamunting Jetty**, 3km west of town – buses await new arrivals.

Downtown Sandakan **addresses** take a little getting used to, as they rely on numbers rather than street names; indeed, less central addresses are pinpointed according to their distances out of the downtown area, hence "Mile 1 1/2", "Mile 3", and so on.

There's no tourist office as such, but you can pick up a map and a few leaflets from a travel agency, Crystal Quest, on the twelfth floor of Wisma Khoo Siak Chiew (☎089/212711, *cquest@tm.net.my*); you need to contact them if you want to stay at Turtle Islands National Park (see p.489), as Crystal Quest has taken over the running of the accommodation on Pulau Selingan.

Transport

Sandakan's two **local bus stations** are within a couple of minutes' walk of each other, in the centre of town. The scheduled services of the Labuk Road Bus Company leave from the waterfront **Labuk Road Station** – blue-and-white buses travel up Labuk Road itself, while those sporting red, yellow and green stripes are bound for points west, along Jalan Leila. A short walk west along Jalan Pryer brings you to the **local minibus**

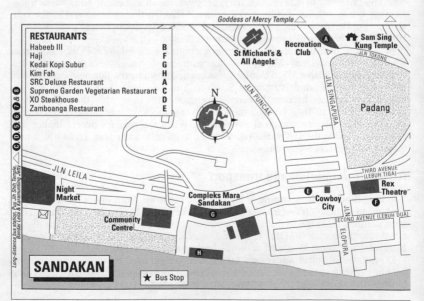

RESTAURANTS

Habeeb III	B
Haji	F
Kedai Kopi Subur	G
Kim Fah	H
SRC Deluxe Restaurant	A
Supreme Garden Vegetarian Restaurant	C
XO Steakhouse	D
Zamboanga Restaurant	E

SANDAKAN

★ Bus Stop

area. The two stations have many destinations in common, so it's worth checking both to find the earliest bus to your destination. **Taxis** speed around town throughout the day and gather in numbers at the southern end of Fourth Street.

Accommodation

The majority of **hotels** are in the blocks forming the town centre, with several also in the suburb of **Bandar Leila**, which can be reached in five minutes on any westbound bus. Sandakan's only central budget **hostel** is in Bandar Leila, though there are a few dormitory set-ups way out of town – one on the Labuk Road, another three near the Sepilok Orang-utan Rehabilitation Centre (p.488).

Hotel City View, Block 23, Third Ave (☎089/271122). Central hotel whose spacious and appealing rooms, furnished with TV and minibar, lie off rather gloomy corridors; downstairs on the ground floor is the smart *Hawaii* coffee shop. ④.

Hotel London, Block 10, Jalan Buli Sim-Sim (☎089/216366). The bare but presentable rooms in this friendly hotel have air-con and private bathrooms. ③.

Hotel Mayfair, 24 Jalan Pryer (☎089/219855). Boasts clean rooms with excellent showers. ③.

Hotel Paris, Third Ave (☎089/218488). Tatty Chinese-run hotel; air-con rooms cost fifty percent more than the ordinary rooms with fans. ②.

Ramada Renaissance, Jalan Utara (☎089/213299). Sandakan's five-star finest, with swish restaurants, a business centre, a swimming pool and sports facilities. ⑦.

Hotel Ramai, Mile 1 1/2 Jalan Leila (☎089/273222). Real effort has been made in this excellent mid-range hotel, whose 44 spacious rooms, complete with bathrooms, TV and air-con, are within striking distance of downtown Sandakan; recommended. ④.

Hotel Sanbay, Mile 1 1/2 Jalan Leila (☎089/275000). Smart new hotel west of the centre, with spacious en-suite rooms. ⑤.

Hotel Sandakan, Wisma Sandakan (☎089/221122). The town's most popular hotel for business folk and visiting local families. It's good value, given the top-of-the-range service, large rooms and good facilities. ⑤.

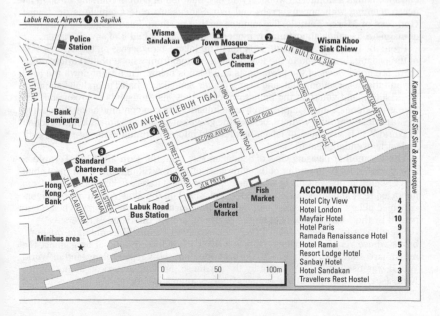

ACCOMMODATION	
Hotel City View	4
Hotel London	2
Mayfair Hotel	10
Hotel Paris	9
Ramada Renaissance Hotel	1
Hotel Ramai	5
Resort Lodge Hotel	6
Sanbay Hotel	7
Hotel Sandakan	3
Travellers Rest Hostel	8

Travellers' Rest Hostel, second floor, Apartment 2, Block E, Bandar Leila (☎089/221460). Clean, bargain-priced dorms and small rooms with breakfast included. The staff can arrange trips to the Turtle Islands Park and the orang-utan sanctuary, and operate a jungle camp along Sungei Kinabatangan (see p.490). ②, dorm beds RM10.

The Town

Sandakan town stands on the northern lip of Sandakan Bay, much of it on land reclaimed from the sea early in the twentieth century. Just inland from the town centre is the **padang** – one of the few reminders of Sandakan's colonial heritage. Your first stop should be the spectacular **waterfront market** (daily 7am–6pm) along Jalan Pryer, down whose dark aisles can be found exquisite conches and turtle eggs, illegally imported from the Philippines, and fish bigger than shovels. To the east is the anarchic fish market, Sabah's largest, just behind which a row of weather-beaten old fishing boats is moored.

A fifteen-minute walk east of the town centre, along Jalan Buli Sim-Sim, deposits you in front of Sandakan's modern, minimalist **mosque**, which stands on a promontory and commands fine views of the bay. Flanking its eastern side is **Kampung Buli Sim-Sim**, the water village around which Sandakan expanded in the nineteenth century, whose countless photogenic shacks spread like lilies out into the bay, crisscrossed by walkways. There's a marked contrast between the dilapidation of the water village and the well-tended surroundings of Sandakan's colonial remnants, especially the quintessentially English **St Michael's and All Angels Church**, a five-minute walk north up Jalan Puncak, one block west of the padang. Here, varnished pews, memorial plaques and faded photographs give a sense of the past rarely felt in Sabah. Steps lead down from the far side of the church grounds to Jalan Singapura, across which, on Jalan Tokong, the **Sam Sing Kung Temple** rears up above the padang. Inside, its smoke-stained walls are lined with wooden boards etched with gold Chinese characters; above the entrance hangs a wonderful woodcarving of a boat full of people coursing through an ocean teeming with prawns, crabs and fish. Sandakan's oldest temple is the Taoist **Goddess of Mercy Temple**, five minutes further north up Jalan Singapura in a grove of magnificent palms; unfortunately modernization has robbed it of any character.

From the temple, a ten-minute walk north up Jalan Utara, across on the eastern side of the padang, brings you to the foot of Jalan Astana, from whose **observation point** there are good views of the town, boats and islands below. Turn right down the road beyond the observation point, and bear left after Sandakan's half-Tudor, half-kampung-like **Astana**, and you're in the huge town **cemetery**, its thousands of green and sky-blue gravestones banked impressively up a hillside. You can continue along the path to the **Japanese cemetery** where, besides the graves of Japanese soldiers killed in action in World War II, are those of Japanese girls sold into prostitution in the late nineteenth and early twentieth centuries.

There's another pleasing view of Sandakan Bay from the **Puu Jih Shih Temple**, a new complex high up on the cliffs, 4km west of town; a Sibuga bus from the Labuk Road Station drops you off nearby. Inside, three tall statues of Buddha, carved from imported teak and embellished with gold leaf, stand on the altar, ringed by 32 dragon-entwined pillars – also of teak. Come early in the morning and your visit will be accompanied by the songs of scores of birds that swoop around the temple's rafters.

Speedboats from below Jalan Pryer run across to **Pulau Berhala** 4km offshore, below whose vertical sandstone cliffs is a decent beach; with a lot of bargaining, the return fare should come to RM20. Berhala once housed a leper colony, and in World War II was used as a POW camp by the Japanese, housing American author Agnes Keith (see "Books", p.646) and her son George, among others.

Eating, drinking and nightlife

Sandakan may not be able to match KK's variety of **restaurants**, but there's still enough choice here to suit most people, with Malay, Chinese, Indian and Western food all well represented. Most places are in the town centre or along Jalan Leila, though several renowned **seafood** restaurants open every evening on Trig Hill, high up above the town, with fine views of Sandakan Bay. For **hawker stalls**, try the market on Jalan Pryer, where stalls open during the day, or the grandstand near the Rex Cinema on Jalan Singapura, under which a makeshift cluster of *satay* stalls sets up every evening.

Beer is widely available in Chinese restaurants and coffee shops. For those who haven't the money for a night at the *Illusions Discotheque* at the *Renaissance Hotel*, **nightlife** in Sandakan is limited to Jalan Lelia's *Cowboy City*, a big, bare air-con bar that gets lively and raucous late in the evening.

Habeeb III, cnr of Jalan Buli Sim-Sim and Third St. Despite a menu that's full of tempting Indonesian, Malay and Western dishes (including breakfasts), only a handful of choices seem to be available at any one time in this cheap and cheerful air-con restaurant.

Haji. One of several restaurants just south of the Rex Cinema. The fresh juices and *roti*s at this popular Muslim Indian place are memorable, as is the creamy chicken korma. There's an air-con dining room upstairs. Daily 8am–9pm.

Kedai Kopi Subur, Kompleks Mara Sandakan, Jalan Leila. No-frills coffee shop specializing in *coto makassar* – a tasty, meaty broth with chunks of rice cake. Daily 8am–9pm.

Kim Fah, behind the long-distance bus station, off Jalan Leila. Rough-and-ready Chinese seafood restaurant, with views of the bay. Daily 11am–2pm & 5pm–3am.

SRC Deluxe Restaurant, *Sandakan Recreation Club*, Jalan Singapore. Among the Cantonese dishes here is the delicious whole baked duck in plum sauce (RM35), which serves three. At night, steamboat (RM9 per person) is served on the second-floor terrace. Daily 11.30am–2pm & 5–10pm.

Supreme Garden Vegetarian Restaurant, Block 30, Jalan Leila, Bandar Leila. Affordable and welcoming establishment, where the imaginative menu runs to mock-meat dishes like fried vegetarian frog with black-bean sauce. A vegetarian steamboat (RM3 per person) is available Mon–Fri. Daily 10am–2pm & 5.30–10pm.

XO Steakhouse, Hsiang Garden Estate, Mile 1 1/2 Jalan Leila. Sandakan's premier Western food restaurant, serving fish and seafood as well as Australian steaks. Daily 11am–2pm & 6–11pm.

Zamboanga Restaurant, Jalan Leila, between Jalan Puncak and Jalan Singapore. Faceless Malay coffee shop that's enlivened by the arrival of a Filipino chef after 7pm, when the menu widens to include Filipino seafood dishes. Daily 10am–10pm.

Listings

Airline MAS, Sabah Bldg, Jalan Pelabuhan (Mon–Fri 8am–4.30pm, Sat 8am–3pm, Sun 8am–noon; ☎089/273966).

Banks and exchange Bank Bumiputra, opposite Standard Chartered Bank, Third Ave; Hong Kong, cnr of Third Ave and Jalan Pelabuhan; Standard Chartered Bank, Sabah Bldg, Jalan Pelabuhan.

Hospital Sandakan Hospital, Jalan Leila (☎089/212111).

Internet access *Internet Cyber Café*, second floor, Lot 219, Wisma Sandakan; Infokom Cyber Shop, Block 21, Lot 1A, second floor, Third St.

Laundry Sandakan Laundry, Third Ave, between Third St and Fourth St.

Pharmacy Borneo Dispensary, cnr of Fifth St and Second Ave.

Police The main police station is on Jalan Bulu Sim-Sim (☎089/211222).

Post office Sandakan's GPO is five minutes' walk west of town, on Jalan Leila (Mon–Fri 8am–5pm, Sat 10am–1pm).

Telephones At the Telekom office, sixth floor, Wisma Khoo Siak Chiew, Jalan Buli Sim-Sim (daily 8.30am–4.45pm); IDD calls can presently only be made on cardphones.

Tour operators Borneo Eco Tours, c/o *Hotel Hsiang Garden*, Jalan Leila, PO Box 82 (☎089/220210); SI Tours, third floor, Yeng Yo Hong Bldg (☎089/271513); Wildlife Expeditions, Lot 903, ninth floor, Wisma Khoo Siak Chiew, Jalan Buli Sim-Sim (☎089/219616), and Discovery Tours, Lot 908, Wisma Khoo Siak Chiew (☎089/274106) all do tours to their respective lodges on Sungei Kinabatangan. For budget trips to the Turtle Islands Park, Gomantong caves and the Kinabatangan river, contact the *Travellers' Rest Hostel* (see p.486) or *Uncle Tan's* (see opposite). To arrange accommodation on Turtle Islands, contact Crystal Quest, twelfth floor, Wisma Khoo Siak Chiew (☎089/212711, *cquest@tm.net.my*).

Visa extensions Immigration Office, Wisma Secretariat, Batu 7, Ranau Rd (☎089/666552).

To Sepilok

Orang-utans – tailless, red-haired apes (their name means "man of the forest" in Malay) – can reach a height of around 1.65m, and can live to be as old as thirty. Solitary but not aggressively territorial animals, they live a largely arboreal existence, eating fruit, leaves, bark and the occasional insect. There are just four designated sanctuaries for these creatures in the world, one of which, the **Sepilok Orang-utan Rehabilitation Centre** (daily 9–11am & 2–3.30pm; feeding times 10am & 3pm; RM10, use of camcorder RM10; ☎089/531180), occupies a 43-square-kilometre patch of lowland rainforest 25km west of Sandakan. At the centre, young and domesticated orang-utans whose survival instincts are undeveloped are trained to fend for themselves. When the centre was established in 1964, the orang-utans it trained had been liberated by a law prohibiting the catching and keeping of them as pets, though nowadays the creatures here have been found by oil-palm planters or other groups clearing the forest. Although not always successful, the training process has so far seen around a hundred orang-utans reintroduced to their natural habitat. To aid the integration process, there are two **feeding stations** where those still finding their forest feet can find bananas and milk; the diet is never varied, as a way of encouraging orang-utans to forage for other food in the trees.

At the **information centre** that fronts the Sepilok sanctuary, a blackboard outlines the day's events, while inside there's an exhibition on forest preservation. A **video** outlining the work carried out at the centre is shown here twice daily and, since it's sometimes screened before feeding time, it's wise to turn up early if you want to catch it. Close to feeding time a warden leads you for ten minutes along a wooden boardwalk, passing the **nursery**, where baby orang-utans are taught elementary climbing skills on ropes and branches, to one of the feeding stations, **Station A**. Nothing prepares you for the thrill of seeing young orang-utans swinging, shimmying and strolling towards their breakfast, jealously watched by gangs of macaques that loiter around for scraps; the more cunning orang-utans take away enough bananas for a picnic lunch in the trees. There's a better chance of seeing semi-mature and more independent orang-utans a thirty-minute hike from the visitor information centre at **Station B**, though this feeding station is only open to tourists sporadically; ask at reception when you arrive.

Sepilok is also a halfway house for honey bears, elephants and other wild animals that are either sick or en route for other reserves in Sabah. You can't see any of these, though the four extremely rare **Sumatran rhinos** kept for breeding at the centre can be viewed by up to fifteen people at a time, at 10am, 10.30am and 11.30am (RM2).

Practicalities

Buses (RM1.40) leave for the centre daily at 9.20am, 11.30am, 1.30pm and 3pm from Sandakan's Labuk Road Station, but if you want an earlier start, take a "Batu 14" minibus (RM1.80). Minibuses ply the route regularly throughout the day; you can easily get to Sandakan by flagging down a bus from the main road.

There are four **places to stay** in the vicinity. Just 100m from the centre is the *Sepilok Resthouse*, Sepilok Road (☎089/534900, *sephse@tm.net.my*; ③ including breakfast), with spacious en-suite rooms and Internet access. Five minutes' walk away along the same road is the *Wildlife Lodge* (☎089/533031; ②), a welcoming, family-run operation set in delightful grounds. Its rooms are slightly overpriced though, and there's a surcharge of RM10 for one with a private bathroom, while you pay RM25 a night extra for an air-con room; the dorm beds (RM20) are better value. A very short distance further down the same road is *Sepilok B&B* (☎089/532288; ③ including breakfast), rougher and rather more basic than the *Sepilok Resthouse*, its dorms and rooms signposted down a dirt track. About 5km further west of the centre, along the Labuk road, is the perenially popular guesthouse, *Uncle Tan's*, Mile 17 1/2 Labuk Rd (☎089/531917, *tansulim@tm .net.my*; ②, including three meals a day). Uncle Tan himself arranges tours to his Sungei Kinabatangan jungle camp (see overleaf).

For **food**, there are two canteens, one at the rehabilitation centre, serving basic rice and noodle dishes and some Western snacks, and the other at the *Sepilok B&B*, offering a limited range of meals and snacks. The *Banana Café* at the *Wildlife Lodge* serves burgers, hot dogs, curries and noodle soups.

Taman Buaya and the War Memorial Park

On your way to or from Sandakan, you might consider a couple of minor diversions – neither of them thrilling – near Labuk Road. At **Taman Buaya** (daily 7am–5pm; RM2), Sabah's only crocodile farm, over a thousand crocodiles languish in dreary concrete moats. If this wasn't bad enough, the stuffed crocodiles, eggs and foetuses on sale in the souvenir shop are a study in tastelessness.

About 1500m further in towards Sandakan, north along Jalan Rimba, the **War Memorial Park** marks the site of the World War II POW camp where the Death March of 1944 originated. In 1942, 2750 British and Australian soldiers were transported from Singapore to Sandakan and set to work building an airstrip. By early in 1945, many had died, but the surviving 1800 Australians and 600 British troops were force-marched to Ranau, where they were to start work on a new project. Just six Australian soldiers survived the 240-kilometre march through mud and jungle. Dominating the park is a simple white block dedicated to the Allied soldiers who fought in North Borneo, as well as the locals who helped POWs and those involved in the Sandakan underground movement. Remnants of the camp are scattered around the sadly neglected grounds of the park.

Turtle Islands National Park

Peeping out of the Sulu Sea some 40km north of Sandakan, three tiny islands comprise Sabah's **Turtle Islands National Park**, the favoured egg-laying sites of the green and hawksbill turtles, varying numbers of which haul themselves laboriously above the high-tide mark to bury their clutches of eggs. To protect them, a turtle closed-season was introduced as early as 1927 by the British North Borneo Chartered Company. In 1966, Malaysia's first turtle **hatchery** was established here and today all three of the park's islands (Pulau Selingan, Pulau Bakkungan Kecil and Pulau Gulisaan) have a hatchery – though only Selingan has amenities for tourists. As at Malaysia's other protected turtle-watching site – Rantau Abang (see p.280), on the Peninsula's east coast – you're guaranteed an extraordinary sight, especially as the newly hatched turtles are liberated on the beach, to waddle, Chaplin-like, into the sea.

While turtles visit the park every day of the year, the peak nesting time falls between July and October. Turtles begin to come ashore around 7.30pm – **rangers** scout the island after dark and alert you once a sighting has been made. Typically, it takes half an hour for sea turtles to lurch up the sand, dig a nesting pit and lay their slimy, ping-pong ball **eggs** – an average clutch will contain upwards of a hundred eggs. All the egg-laying turtles are tagged, to aid research into the distribution and size of Southeast Asia's turtle population; their eggs, meanwhile, are taken for reburial to the hatchery, where they are safeguarded from hungry rats. With hatchings a nightly event, you're almost guaranteed the stirring sight of scores of determined little turtles wriggling up through the sand. In the meantime, Seligan's quiet **beaches** are good for swimming and sunbathing, or you can go snorkelling off nearby Bakkungan Kecil (RM25 per person, minimum four people; details from park headquarters).

On your way to Turtle Islands Park, you pass scores of **bagang**, or fish traps (called *kelong*s on the Peninsula). At night, the light of the kerosene lamps hung from their bamboo frames attracts shoals of anchovies, which are then caught in nets – though on certain days of the month the moon is too full and bright for the process to work. The *bagang* are washed away by the annual storms of the November monsoon and rebuilt early the next year.

Practicalities

You can only visit the park as part of a **tour**. Just Pulau Selingan has **accommodation**, with room for a mere twenty visitors a night, all of whom are put up in the island's four comfortable **chalets** (RM300 per person for accommodation, meals and transport to the park); to stay here, visit on a tour run by Crystal Quest in Sandakan (see p.488). While *Uncle Tan's* (see p.489; RM200) and the *Travellers' Rest Hostel* (see p.486; RM260) also organize tours to the park, they overnight on islands outside the park, where it's much less likely that you'll see the turtles. The *Roses Café* inside the visitor centre provides **meals** for chalet residents in the evening and for visitors in general during the day.

Sungei Kinabatangan and around

South of Sandakan Bay, Sabah's longest river, the 560-kilometre **Kinabatangan**, ends its northeasterly journey from the interior to the Sulu Sea. Whereas logging has had an adverse impact on the river's ecology upstream, the dual threats of piracy and flooding have kept its lower reaches largely free of development, and the area consequently has a wealth of Bornean **wildlife**. Despite Sabah's rather haphazard approach to making the most of its superb natural resources, the designation of the area as a wildlife sanctuary in 1999 is an encouraging step. That said, sanctuary status is one level below that of a national park, and so villages and agricultural development have been allowed to crisscross the protected sections.

Asian elephants, orang-utans, gibbons, macaques and crocodiles all dwell in the forest flanking the river, and the resident **birdlife** is equally impressive. With luck, visitors here get glimpses of hornbills, Brahminy kites, crested serpent eagles, egrets, exquisite blue-banded and stork-billed kingfishers, and oriental darters, which dive underwater to find food and then sit on the shore, their wings stretched out to dry. In the river itself are rare freshwater sharks and rays, irriwaddy dolphins and a great variety of fish species too. The Kinabatangan's greatest natural assets though – apart from the small but often visible population of orang-utans – are its **proboscis monkeys** (see box, opposite).

The only effective way to see the Kinabatangan is on a tour (see opposite), with each operator offering similar activities: **boat trips** along the river and its tributaries in the early morning, early evening or at night; short **hikes** away from the river on narrow

PROBOSCIS MONKEYS

For many, a trip to Borneo would not be complete without an encounter with a **proboscis monkey**, a shy animal found nowhere except the riverine forests and mangrove swamps of the Bornean coast. The monkey derives its name from the enlarged, drooping, red nose of the adult male monkey; females and young animals are snub-nosed. The role of the drooping nose, which seems to straighten out when the animal is issuing its curious honking call, is unclear, although it is likely that it helps in attracting a mate. The monkeys are reddish-brown in colour, with a dark red cap, long, thick, white tails and white rumps; in addition, the adult males have a cream-white collar and large bellies, giving them a rather portly, "old gentleman" appearance. Males are significantly heavier than females, weighing up to 23kg, compared with the female's maximum weight of around 10kg. All in all, this combination of features has earned male proboscis monkeys the (not necessarily complimentary) name of *orang Belanda*, or "Dutchman", in parts of Borneo.

The monkeys live in loose groups, spending their days in trees close to the water, though they will walk across open areas when necessary, and can swim proficiently, aided by their partly webbed feet. The creatures are most active at dawn and dusk, when moving to and from feeding sites. Feeding on young leaves, shoots and fruit, they are quite choosy eaters, preferring the leaves of the *Sonneraita* mangrove tree, a rather specialist diet which means that large areas of forest need to be protected to provide groups of monkeys with sufficient food. This fact, coupled with the restricted range of the proboscis monkey, makes the species vulnerable to habitat loss and hunters.

Visitors can hope to see proboscis monkeys in several of the national parks in Sabah and Sarawak, apart from the Kinabatangan area. In Sarawak in particular, the animals can be seen in Bako National Park (p.379).

paths in search of orang-utan nests (catching sight of a new nest usually means the orang-utan isn't far behind, as the solitary animal builds a different nest every day); and a stay in the operator's jungle lodge or rest camp.

Practicalities

There are two categories of **accommodation** along the river – the upmarket **jungle lodges** on the river's lower reaches around the small kampung of **Sukau**, 10km from the river mouth, and the upriver **rest camps** run by *Uncle Tan's* of Sepilok (see p.489) and the *Travellers' Rest Hostel* in Sandakan (see p.486). Although it's inexpensive to stay at the rest camps (the tours run by *Uncle Tan's* and the *Travellers' Rest Hotel* cost around RM150 including transport from their respective premises, plus RM15 a night for accommodation), they offer a real back-to-nature experience and won't be to your liking if you value creature comforts. Both camps are superbly positioned though, along narrow paths which weave away from the river. Upon arriving at the *Travellers' Rest Hostel's* camp you could be jumping into the pages of the best-selling children's novel *Swallows and Amazons*; its tree-houses and tiny wooden huts straight out of an alternative reality where the modern world scarcely intrudes. Lizards skulk around the camp as monkeys screech in conversation and elephants hoot their hefty presence 100m away in the jungle.

The riverside *Sukau Rainforest Lodge* (⑦), run by Borneo Eco Tours, comprises twenty twin-bed chalets on stilts just 200m from Sukau. It's built to be self-sufficient, harnessing solar power for its electricity and water supply. Although this pricey, this lodge is a fine example of ecotourism in practice and well worth a visit. Another tour operator, Sipidan Dive Centre (☎088/240584), runs *Proboscis Lodge* (⑥), which is even closer to the Sukau jetty. The three other places to stay around Sukau are run by Discovery Tours (p.456), SI Tours (p.488) and Wildlife Expeditions (p.488); all of these companies are a little cheaper than Borneo Eco Tours. Each lodge has its own restaurant or café.

Although the tour operators arrange transport to their lodges and campsites, it's easy to get to Sukau by public transport (but you must book in advance to stay here). Regular minibuses go to Sukau from 50m west of Sandakan's Labuk Road bus station (daily 6am–2pm; 3hr; RM10). Once in Sukau, you can charter a boat for the ten-minute ride (RM20) from the jetty to *Sukau Rainforest Lodge*. Alternatively, catch a Lahad Datu bus from Sandakan and get off at the Sukau junction, from where you catch an open-backed truck along the final 30km of untarred road to the village.

Batu Putih and Gomantong Caves

Within the limestone outcrop of **Batu Putih** (known locally as Batu Tulug), 1km north of the Kinabatangan Bridge on the road between Sandakan and Lahad Datu, small **caves**, visible from the road, contain wooden coffins well over a hundred years old. When the former curator of the Sarawak Museum, Tom Harrisson, explored the caves in the 1950s, he found many hardwood coffin troughs and lids, as well as a wooden upright, grooved with notches that were thought to represent a genealogical record. It was from here that the two-hundred-year-old coffin lid with a buffalo's head carved into its handle, displayed at the Sabah State Museum, was taken; other coffins are still in their original spots, though unless archeology is your passion, think twice about making the detour to see them. All buses running between Sandakan and Lahad Datu pass by the caves (no admission charge).

Gomantong Caves

Off the Sukau road, the **Gomantong Caves** are inspiring enough to warrant a visit at any time of the year, though you'll get most out of the trip when you can see the edible **nests** of their resident swiftlets being harvested. Sabah's Wildlife Department, which administers the caves, permits just two harvests a year – one between February and April, allowing the birds time to rebuild before the egg-laying season, the other between July and September, when the young have hatched and left. Harvesting the nests is a dangerous business: workers scale impossibly precarious rattan ladders and ropes – some up to 60m high – to collect the nests, and there are occasional fatalities. The nests are made into bird's-nest soup, long a Chinese culinary speciality – Chinese merchants have been coming to Borneo to trade for the nests for at least twelve centuries.

Outside the caves there's a picnic site and canteen, and an **information centre** that will fill you in on the caves' ecosystem. Of the two major caves, **Simud Hitam** is easiest to visit, reached by following the trail that runs off behind the staff quarters to the right of the reception building, taking a right fork after five minutes, and continuing on for a further ten minutes – the stench of ammonia will tell you when you are getting near. Reaching a height of 90m, with bug-ridden piles of compacted guano on the floor, Simud Hitam supports a colony of **black-nest** swiftlets, whose nests – a mixture of saliva and feathers – sell for RM40 a kilogram. Above Simud Hitam is the larger but less accessible **Simud Putih**, home to the **white-nest** swiftlet, whose nests are of pure, dried saliva and can fetch prices of over RM500 a kilogram. To reach Simud Putih, take the left fork, five minutes along the trail originating from the reception building, and start climbing. If you travel here independently, be sure to bring a torch, so that you can experience the full effect of the caves. Ringing the whole area is a patch of virgin jungle supporting orang-utans and elephants – neither of which you're likely to see.

It's easiest to visit the caves as part of a tour; both *Uncle Tan's* (see p.489) and the *Travellers' Rest Hostel* (see p.486) can organize day-trips here (around RM75 per person) from their premises, and can include a detour to the caves as part of their tours around Sungei Kinabatangan (this adds around RM50 per person to the cost of the tour). To get to the caves under your own steam from Sandakan, get a Sukau-bound minibus and ask to be dropped at the junction for Gomantong (20km before Sukau), from where it's a five-kilometre hike down a former logging road to the caves. Alternatively, if you're on a bus to or from Lahad Datu (see below), get off at the turning for Sukau, and catch a motorbike taxi (RM5) or open-backed truck the 20km to the Gomantong junction (RM10). There is nowhere to stay in and around Gomantong, so plan to leave the caves well before dark, if you are not on a tour.

South to Semporna

Below Sandakan Bay, the horseshoe of Sabah's main road continues southwards over the Kinabatangan Bridge to the towns of **Lahad Datu** and **Tawau**. This far east, the state's central mountain ranges taper away, to be replaced by lowland – and sometimes swampy – coastal regions lapped by the **Sulu** and **Celebes** seas, and dominated by oil-palm plantations. Archeological finds around **Madai**, off the road between Lahad Datu and Tawau, prove that this area of Borneo has been inhabited for well over ten thousand years. Nowadays, this is Sabah's "wild east": pirates working out of islands in the nearby Filipino waters pose a real threat to fishermen, and the streets teem with Filipino and Indonesian immigrants trying to eke out a living, their influx beginning in the 1950s (when they were drawn by the prospect of work on Sabah's plantations) and rising sharply in the 1970s as a result of the civil unrest in Mindanao.

The lowland rainforest runs riot at the **Danum Valley Conservation Area**, which can be reached via Lahad Datu. Closer to Kalimantan, and around the southern lip of wide **Darvel Bay**, the oceanic island of **Sipadan** is acclaimed as one of the world's top **diving** spots, its flawless coral ablaze with exotic fishes and sea creatures. More prosaically, you'll find yourself this far around the state if you're heading to **Indonesia**: a boat from Tawau is the cheapest way to reach northeastern Kalimantan.

If you're heading back to KK, there is an alternative to retracing your steps around the crown of the state. From Tawau, Land Cruisers depart daily for Keningau (p.462), travelling on logging roads that complete a **ring road** of sorts around Sabah.

Lahad Datu and east to Bandar Sahabat

LAHAD DATU, 175km south of Sandakan, has something of a frontier feel, the conspicuous consumption in the town resulting from the oil-palm and timber industry money which has underpinned its growth. In the 1990s, this unattractive boom town was flooded by immigrants – many of whom have now ended up hawking cigarettes and nuts. The Celebes Sea coastline is famous for a certain degree of lawlessness. In 1986 a mob of heavily armed pirates stormed the Standard Chartered Bank and MAS office on Jalan Teratai, Lahad Datu's main street, and made off with RM100,000; of more recent notoriety, in April 2000 a group of tourists on Pulau Sipadan were kidnapped and held for several months by Filipino Muslim separatists before being released). The only tourist sight is **Kampung Panji**, a run-down water village on the western edge of town, with a small daily market worth visiting for its handicrafts.

Practicalities

Buses from Sandakan, Semporna and Tawau stop at the **bus station** on Jalan Bunga Raya, a couple of minutes' walk east of the town centre. From the **airport**, north of town, it's only a short taxi ride into the centre (there are no buses on this route). The MAS office (☎089/881707) is at the *Hotel Mido*, a tall, green-and-white building at the northeastern end of Jalan Teratai, easily spotted by looking inland from the bus station.

As Lahad Datu is the jumping-off point for trips to the Danum Valley Conservation Area (see below), your first port of call will probably be the **Innoprise office**, Block D, Sadong Jaya Complex, KK (Mon–Fri 8am–12.45pm & 2–4.15pm, Sat 8am–12.45pm; ☎088/243245), where you can book trips to the valley or pick up the bus there (Mon, Wed & Fri at 3pm; RM30).

Budget **accommodation** centres on the northeastern (bus terminus) end of Jalan Teratai: the *Ocean Hotel* (☎089/881700; ③) has reasonably spruce air-con rooms with attached bathrooms. Up the side street 20m southwest is the best deal in town, the *Malaysia Venus Hotel II* (no phone; ②), whose clean, if spartan, rooms have attached bathrooms. You could also try the nicely furnished *Hotel Jago Kota* (☎089/882000; ④) on Jalan Kampong Panji, or Jalan Teratai's slightly shoddier *Hotel Mido* (☎089/881800; ④), both of which have en-suite air-con rooms. Top of the tree is the new *Executive Hotel* (☎089/881333; ⑥), whose gleaming white colonnades and welcoming, elegant rooms stand proudly beside the entrance to Kampong Panji, at the southwestern end of Jalan Teratai.

A handful of decent **restaurants** make a stay in Lahad Datu more bearable. There's the cave-like Chinese *Restoran Melawar*, a block southwest of the *Hotel Mido*; the *Restoran Auliah* (closes at 7pm), 50m away on Jalan Kiambang, does a fine *biriyani*. Otherwise, go for the *Executive Hotel's* harmonious *Spring Palace Chinese Restaurant*, which specializes in Cantonese and Szechuan cuisine, and boasts a memorable *dim sum* menu. The town's swish new **market**, also on Jalan Kiambang, has upstairs stalls commanding pleasant views out to sea.

To Bandar Sahabat

Although good stretches of beach do exist along the coastline east of Lahad Datu, the threat of piracy puts them off-limits. The only exception is the beach at **Tungku**, a seaside village that has its own police station – though 70km is a long way to go for a dip in the sea; look for a Tungku minibus at Lahad Datu's terminus.

A wiser plan is to continue east into **Sahabat**, a vast area of land which Sabah's Federal Land Development Agency (FELDA) has blanketed with oil palms. Here, the plantation settlement of **BANDAR SAHABAT** provides the unlikely backdrop to a tasteful seafront hotel, the *Sahabat Beach Resort* (⑤). While the hotel's palm-fringed beach can't be called idyllic (abutting it is a jetty where boats are loaded with palm oil), it's breezy and clean enough. Plans afoot include a water-sports complex and tours of local plantations. Those on a tighter budget should stay instead at the adjacent *Sahabat Resort Annexe* (③), with pleasant en-suite rooms that offer views over patches of jungle. Bookings at both hotels can be made on ☎089/776533.

Danum Valley Conservation Area

Spanning 438 square kilometres of primary lowland rainforest west of Lahad Datu, Sabah's **Danum Valley Conservation Area** (DVCA) lies within the boundaries of the **Yayasan Sabah Concession Area**, the vast tract of forest whose sustained-yield logging subsidizes the Sabah Foundation's charitable works across the state (see p.472). Established in 1981 for the purpose of rainforest-related "conservation, research, education and recreation", the DVCA supports a wealth of wildlife from bearded pigs to orang-utans, Sumatran rhinos to Asian elephants, and hornbills to pheasants.

Appealing as the DVCA sounds, it's unfortunately only possible to visit as part of an expensive package arranged by Innoprise (see opposite). All visitors base themselves at the **Borneo Rainforest Lodge**, sited on a bend in Sungei Danum 10km away. Staffed by guides who possess a mind-boggling knowledge of the local environment, this major new initiative aims to show that ecotourism can positively aid the protection of the rainforests; to this end, it offers what it calls "a high-quality natural history interpretative service", giving visitors the chance "not only to experience the Borneo rainforest, but to understand today's conservation realities": wildlife treks and marked nature trails weave through the surrounding forest, while a canopy walkway, video and slide shows illustrate how the rainforest functions. Other activities include trips to the **Danum Valley Field Centre** on the DVCA's eastern edge, where there are well-labelled botanical and ecology exhibits, night safaris by jeep, or you can see the recently unearthed coffins and jars of a Dusun burial site at a two-hundred-metre escarpment near the lodge.

Practicalities

Guests of the *Borneo Rainforest Lodge* are brought here from Lahad Datu by air-conditioned jeep (2hr; free) – staff can pick you up either at the airport, or at the Innoprise office (see opposite) at 9.30am. There are daily trips out to the Field Centre, where it's obligatory to hire a guide (RM20 for a half-day) for walks into the forest, while at the *Rainforest Lodge* the fee for jungle activities is RM50 a day.

Accommodation at the *Borneo Rainforest Lodge* (☎088/243245; ⑧), consists of comfortable (though not lavish) twin rooms built around a central lodge whose first-floor bar-cum-restaurant affords breathtaking views across Sungei Danum; prices include three hearty set meals a day, a mixture of Western and Asian dishes. Jeeps leave the lodge for Lahad Datu at 1.30pm daily.

Madai Caves

Roughly midway between Lahad Datu and Semporna, the **Madai Caves**, 13km west of the unremarkable coastal town of Kunak, are worth a stop, particularly if you aren't able to get to Gomantong Caves (see p.492). Minibuses between Tawau and Lahad Datu will drop you in the Madai area for RM5, though with the caves 3km off the main road, it's worth paying an extra RM2 to be driven all the way.

Although humans have dwelt in them for over ten thousand years, the caves of the Madai limestone massif are most remarkable for the birdlife they support; here, as at Gomantong, the **nests** of swiftlets are harvested for bird's-nest soup (see p.414). The nests can reach as much as RM500 a kilogram if in good condition. The entrance to the cave system is marked by a motley gathering of fragile stilt huts – home, in season, to Idahan nest-harvesters. Once beyond the front aperture, you'll discover a succession of vast chambers in which swiftlets dive, bats squeak and guano lies ankle-deep. In season, harvesters will offer to show you the remnants of old Idahan coffins in the caves – at a price. The caves are pitch-black, so a torch is essential.

Semporna and around

Named after the Malay word for perfect, the sleepy fishing village of **SEMPORNA** seems in danger of spilling into the sea. Bajau stilt houses are clustered in front and either side of the town; even its chaotic market, where buses stop, is built half on land and half on stilts. Though the centre (like Sandakan's) comprises predominantly

Chinese box-style buildings, not even the town's more important edifices, like the offices of the Semporna Ocean Tourism Centre, have escaped this water-focused existence, balancing as the town does on a causeway jutting out into the sea.

For generations Muslim Bajau and Suluk peoples have roamed the waters of East Sabah, farming the seas for fish, sea cucumbers, shells and other marine products. Often dubbed "sea gypsies", these people were originally nomads who lived on board their intricately-carved wooden boats, called *lipa-lipa*, with colourful, rectangular sails. Although they are now mostly settled in and around Semporna, their love of, and dependence upon, the sea remains strong today; some Bajau can still be seen living on traditional boats drifting across the bay east of Semporna.

Until recently Semporna, like Lahad Datu 80km to the north, was worth visiting only as a springboard to better things – in this case, **Pulau Sipadan** and the other Celebes Sea islands (see below). But the village is now awakening to the needs of tourist who want to experience the fragile beauty of these largely untouched islands.

Practicalities

Though not served by long-distance buses, Semporna is linked by minibus with Lahad Datu, Sandakan and Tawau. The **minibus station** is 100m east of the waterfront. There is no tourist office, though the Semporna Ocean Tourism Centre (**SOTC**; ☎089/781088), dangling out from the harbour, can provide lots of information on diving off the coast; also within the same building is Today Travel Service, Semporna's MAS agent.

For **accommodation**, the SOTC has basic, clean doubles (④) with communal bathrooms, as well as a dorm (RM20). Opposite, the *Seafest Inn*, Seafest Complex (☎089/782399, *seafestinn@hotmail.com*; ③, dorm beds RM20), has excellent en-suite rooms with air-con and TV. The rooms at the *Darmai Lodge* (☎089/782011; ③, dorm beds RM20), in the centre of town above the market, are small, with TV and attached bathrooms. The most expensive place to stay is the *Dragon Inn* (☎089/781088; ⑦), built on stilts over the sea directly across from the *Seafest Inn*.

Some of the best **eating** in town is at the cafés in the hotels we've mentioned. That said, the classy *Pearl City Restaurant* (part of the SOTC) has views out to sea and excellent seafood, as does the flimsy but highly atmospheric *Floating Restaurant*, which bobs in the water in between the SOTC and the harbour.

The islands off Semporna

The islands off Semporna – also Bajau territory – are exquisitely beautiful and, with the exception of **Sipadan**, rarely visited. **Sibuon**, for example, just over half an hour by boat from Semporna, has a breathtaking beach and shallow coral reefs; **Sabangkat**, twenty minutes from town, likewise has coral, as well as small villages and a seaweed farm. A lovely spot for diving and snorkelling, Sabangkat remains almost solely the preserve of the local Bajaus. On the outer island of **Pasir** (40min by boat from Semporna), there's a nice little resort, and on **Mataking** and **Boheian**, coral, turtle and magnificent rays in the water. **Bohaydulong** is the site of a fascinating restoration project – the revival of an old pearl farm which went out of business forty years ago. Most of these islands have few facilities for tourists, though it's hoped that recent plans to make Pulau Bohaydulong into a national park by 2002 will swiftly lead to the creation of some infrastructure for visitors. For some terrestrial wildlife, the large island of **Timbun Mata** has a population of birds, deer, monkeys, wild boat and bats.

Pulau Sipadan and Pulau Mabul

In the past few years, a trip to tiny **Pulau Sipadan** – 30km south of Semporna in the Celebes Sea – has become *de rigueur* for the hardcore scuba-diving fraternity.

Acclaimed by the late marine biologist Jacques Cousteau as "an untouched piece of art", Sipadan is a cornucopia of marine life, its waters teeming with turtles, moray eels, sharks, barracuda, vast schools of gaily coloured tropical fish, and a diversity of coral that's been compared to that at Australia's Great Barrier Reef.

Pulau Sipadan is at the crown of a limestone spire, which rises 600m from the seabed and widens at the top to form a coral shelf shaped like an artist's palette. Among the highlights for divers here is a network of marine caves, the most eerie of which is **Turtle Cavern**, a watery grave for the skeletal remains of turtles which have strayed in and become lost. **White-tip Avenue** and **Barracuda Point** are frequented, respectively, by basking white-tip sharks and spiralling shoals of slender barracuda, while the **Hanging Gardens** is an extraordinarily elegant profusion of soft coral hanging from the underside of the reef ledge. Snorkellers accompanying divers to the island can expect to see reef sharks and white-tips, lion fish, barracudas and scores of turtles, without having to leave the surface; the **Drop-off**, just beyond the jetty, is a good place to wade out and don goggles. Be aware, though, that on a boat dive, dive-master and divers will quickly disappear below the surface, leaving snorkellers to their own devices for forty minutes.

The island itself is carpeted by lush forest and fringed by flawless white-sand **beaches**, up which green **turtles** drag themselves to lay their eggs. Spare moments between dives are spent idling in the sun on hammocks or lounges, playing a little badminton or joining one of the ad hoc volleyball matches that start up from time to time. A walk around Sipadan, a good idea at sunset, takes around twenty minutes.

Nearby **Pulau Mabul** (20min by boat from Semporna) is becoming an increasingly popular destination because of its muck dives, where the silted water means you can't see the fish and marine flora until they suddenly loom up a short distance away from you.

Practicalities

It is possible to make **independent day-trips** to the islands: locals with boats (and snorkelling equipment) for rent can be found on the SOTC causeway in Semporna or direct from Setarawarni Tourism (☎089/782366, *setarawarni@hotmail.com*), at the *Seafest Inn*. The cost of chartering a boat for four passengers runs to RM220–450 a day – add around RM20 more for the snorkelling equipment. Setarawarni also offers an excellent package (RM650) comprising three days and two nights of diving off Sipadan and Mabul, with accommodation in Semporna, and a separate trip to Pulau Mabul, where you stay in dorms in kampung-style houses (RM400 to hire boat for two days, plus RM20 per person for accommodation).

Sipadan accommodation, run by five dive operators, is pricey and limited to 180 people all told. The largest place to stay is the *Pulau Sipadan Resort*, whose owner is based in Tawau (see below); all the other places are run by KK-based companies. The resort with the biggest reputation is, however, on Pulau **Mabul**: its *Smart Diver Resort* is a very plush hotel, with a swimming pool, good restaurant and fine beaches nearby. To contact the dive operators for bookings at the various resorts, see the box on p.456 or head to the SOTC and *Dragon Inn*, where these companies have branch offices.

Tawau and around

Sabah's southernmost town of any size, **TAWAU**, is 150km southwest of Lahad Datu. Tawau was originally a small Bajau settlement, until the British North Borneo Chartered Company, attracted by its fine harbour and rich volcanic soil, transformed it into the thriving commercial port it is today. While the town's prosperity relied at first upon the cultivation of cacao, nowadays oil-palm plantations and timber logging are in the ascendancy (as in so many parts of Sabah), attracting many Filipino and Indonesian immigrants. Tawau's demographics are changing faster than perhaps any town in Malaysia, as it's a major departure point for the **Kalimantan** ports of Nunakan and Tarakan – and hundreds of Indonesians arrive daily on the ferry. But amid the boom, there's also highly visible poverty, with beggars clustering around the squalid but unquestionably vibrant harbour area.

Central Tawau in contrast is an orderly blend of wooden shophouses and concrete buildings. There are numerous **markets** worth a stroll around; the clothes and trinkets stalls in the crowded building beside *Hotel Soon Yee* are especially worth a browse, while the sprawling produce market on the square of reclaimed land in front of Jalan Chen Fook is certainly diverting.

Practicalities

Long-distance buses use the **station** below the eastern end of Tawau's main street, Jalan Dunlop, with Land Cruisers to Keningau (see p.462) leaving from the same site. However, the four, daily buses to and from Sandakan have their own stop, one block south from here, just in front of Jalan Chen Fook. The **local bus station** is on Jalan Stephen Tan, in the centre of town, while **shared taxis** park at the southern end of Jalan Domenic. The **airport** is 3km northwest of town, from where a taxi to the centre costs RM8. **Ferries** from Indonesia arrive at Customs Wharf, Jalan Pelabuhan, 150m south of Jalan Dunlop's Shell station.

As well as several **banks**, the commercial estate known as the Fajar Centre, east of Jalan Masjid, houses both the Telekom building in Block 35, and the MAS office in Wisma Sasco; you'll find the **post office** across the southern side of Jalan Dunlop. One of provincial Sabah's busiest **Internet** cafés, *Datcom Cyber Café*, is right in the centre of town on the second floor of Suhindo Plaza, Jalan Dunlop. The *Pulau Sipadan Resort* (see p.497) has an office here on the first floor of 484 Bandar Sabindo (☎089/242262).

ACCOMMODATION

Most of Tawau's budget **hotels**, the best of which is the *Soon Yee*, are along Jalan Stephen Tan or Jalan Chester.

Belmont Marco Polo, Jalan Stephen Tan (☎089/777988). The classiest address in town is still this swish place above the mosque, with large air-con rooms. ⑦.

Dunlop, Jalan Dunlop (☎089/770733). Average Chinese-run place with small, quite adequate rooms. ②.

Loong, 3868 Jalan Abaca (☎089/765308). Another bargain, with air-con en-suite rooms, friendly staff and a great location – central, yet off the busy main drags. ③.

Merdeka, Jalan Masjid (☎089/776655). Mid-range air-con hotel; smart and good value. Ask about promotions and the price might go down a bit. ④.

Murah, Jalan Stephen Tan. Small rooms, each with air-con, TV and bathroom. ②.

North Borneo, Jalan Dunlop (☎089/763060). A mid-range establishment located behind Tawau's cinema. ④.

Sanctuary, 4263 Jalan Chester (☎089/751155). A smart place, with spacious rooms furnished with TV, hot showers and air-con. ④.

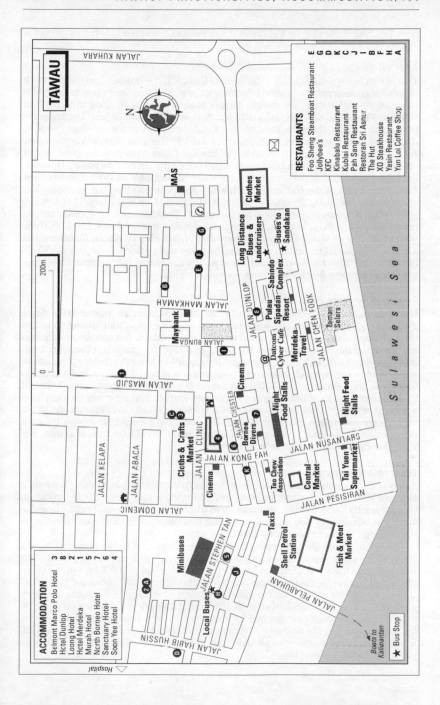

TAWAU

JALAN KUHARA

N

200m

0

MAS

Clothes Market

ACCOMMODATION

Belmont Marco Polo Hotel	3
Hotel Dunlop	8
Loong Hotel	2
Hotel Merdeka	1
Murah Hotel	5
North Borneo Hotel	7
Sanctuary Hotel	6
Soon Yee Hotel	4

RESTAURANTS

Foo Sheng Steamboat Restaurant	E
Jollybee's	G
KFC	D
Kinabalu Restaurant	K
Kublai Restaurant	C
Pah Sang Restaurant	J
Restoran Sri Asnur	I
The Hut	B
XO Steakhouse	F
Yasin Restaurant	H
Yun Loi Coffee Shop	A

JALAN MAKKAMAH

Maybank

JALAN BUNGA

JALAN MASJID

JALAN KELAPA

JALAN ABACA

Cloths & Crafts Market

JALAN CLINIC

Cinema

JALAN DOMENIC

Minibuses

JALAN STEPHEN TAN

Taxis

Shell Petrol Station

Local Buses

JALAN HABIB HUSSIN

Hospital

JALAN DUNLOP

Long Distance Buses & Landcruisers

★ Buses to Sandakan

Sabindo Complex

Pulau Sipadan Resort

Merdeka Travel

Datcom Cyber Café

@

Night Food Stalls

Cinema

JALAN CHESTER

Borneo Divers

JALAN KONG FAH

Teo Chew Association

Central Market

JALAN NUSANTARS

Night Food Stalls

Tai Yuen Supermarket

JALAN CHEN FOOK

Taman Selera

JALAN PESISIRAN

Fish & Meat Market

JALAN PELABUHAN

Boats to Kalimantan

S u l a w e s i   S e a

★ Bus Stop

Soon Yee, Jalan Stephen Tan (☎089/772447). A very friendly Chinese hotel; the best bargain option in town. ①.

EATING

Two blocks below Jalan Dunlop in the Sabindo Complex, the two-hundred-metre stretch of open-air **restaurants** and **stalls** collectively known as Taman Selera sets up daily; best value are the Malay stalls, and at night bargain seafood is available, along with cold beer and satay. You'll find several good Indian Muslim restaurants above Jalan Dunlop in the town centre, among them the *Yasin* and the *Kinabalu*; as well as the excellent *Pah Sang Restaurant*, which specializes in aromatic *bak kut teh*. North of here, below the *Loong Hotel*, the extensive (English) menu at the *Yun Loi Coffee Shop* includes good claypot dishes, and at night there's a BBQ seafood stall out on the covered forecourt. However, the Fajar Centre, east of the town centre, has a virtual monopoly on more stylish venues. Pick of the bunch is the *Hut* in Block 29, which has generous Western set meals. The open-fronted *Foo Sheng Restaurant*, in Block 41, couldn't be above more basic, but is still a good option if you fancy a steamboat pig-out; the *XO Steakhouse*, on the opposite corner, provides a protein fix. Otherwise, you might try the *Restoran Sri Asnur*, Block 38, if you want to go Thai or Malay. Finally, the *Marco Polo Hotel*'s elegant *Kublai Restaurant* has a *dim sum* breakfast on Sunday morning. The cakes and pastries at the *Jolly Bee's* bakery make fine desserts. Tawau's only bar of note is the *Marco Polo*'s pleasant lobby bar where you can hear fine karaoke renditions most nights.

Tawau Hills State Park

Out of town, an hour's drive north, is the 270-square-kilometre **Tawau Hills State Park**, an exuberant stretch of lowland rainforest with one major trail leading up 1000m through thick, damp, mossy forest and another, easier hike to hot springs and a waterfall. Reaching the park, however, is trickier than it's worth – no buses come here and most taxi drivers haven't a clue how to get here as it's only approachable via a maze of steep, muddy tracks which crisscross an agricultural estate; if you can find a taxi able to get you here, expect to pay RM60. It's a great pity that Sabah Parks haven't seen fit to set up even the most basic signposting to help tourists find their way through such a tropical labyrinth. Only the occasional local science students ever seem to get to the park. **Accommodation** (③, dorm beds RM10), oddly, is plentiful, as though the park management is patiently preparing for the day when there'll be a rush of people. For food, there's a canteen which sells basic meals.

West into the interior

A network of **logging roads** spanning the southern portion of Sabah makes it possible to travel back to KK overland, without having to retrace your steps. While not cheap, the journey by **Land Cruiser** (vehicles leave when full; RM70) from Tawau's long-distance bus terminus to Keningau, along a track that parallels the Kalimantan border, is worth taking for excitement value alone.

The journey is comfortable enough as you leave Tawau, as passengers are taken in two vehicles past the police roadblock outside town that checks on overcrowding – but then you're all transferred into one Land Cruiser. At **Merotai**, some 20km out of Tawau, the sealed road ends and the jolting ride begins, taking you past cocoa and palm plantations, lush forest and vast timber mills. Two-thirds of the way to Keningau, a quarry marks the left turn for Sapulut (see p.463), though if it's dark you're better off going on to Keningau, as vehicles are few and far between. Closer to **Kampung Sook**, look out for Murut graves by the roadside. Assuming your Land Cruiser doesn't experience difficulties – to be optimistic – you should reach Keningau in the early evening as long as you leave Tawau before 11am.

travel details

Trains

See box on p.467.

Beaufort to: KK (2 daily; 4hr); Tenom (4 daily; 2hr 30min).

KK to: Beaufort (2 daily; 4hr); Tenom (2 daily; 7hr).

Tenom to: Beaufort (4 daily; 2hr 30min); KK (2 daily; 7hr).

Buses

Beaufort to: KK (15 daily; 2hr); Kuala Penyu (8 daily; 1hr); Menumbok (8 daily; 1hr 30min); Sipitang (9 daily; 50min).

Keningau to: KK (15 daily; 2hr 30min); Sapulut (2 daily; 4hr); Tambunan (10 daily; 1hr); Tawau (2 daily; 6–8hr); Tenom (20 daily; 50min).

KK to: Beaufort (15 daily; 2hr); Keningau (15 daily; 2hr 30min); Kinabalu National Park (8 daily; 2hr); Kota Belud (16 daily; 2hr 10min); Kudat (10 daily; 4hr); Lawas, Sarawak (1 daily; 4hr); Menumbok (6 daily; 2hr 30min); Papar (20 daily; 40min); Ranau (10 daily; 2hr); Sandakan (12 daily; 5hr 30min); Tambunan (11 daily; 1hr 30min); Tawau (2 daily; 9hr); Tuaran (10 daily; 50min).

Sandakan to: KK (12 daily; 5hr 45min); Lahad Datu (6 daily; 2hr 30min); Ranau (8 daily; 3hr 30min); Tawau (6 daily; 4hr 30min).

Tawau to: Keningau (1–2 daily; 6–8hr); KK (2 daily; 9hr); Lahad Datu (8 daily; 2hr); Sandakan (6 daily; 4hr 30min); Semporna (14 daily; 1hr 30min).

Tenom to: Beaufort (20 daily, 50min).

Ferries

KK to: Labuan (3 daily; 3hr).

Labuan to: Brunei (4 daily; 1hr 30min); KK (3 daily; 2hr); Menumbok (at least 10 daily; 25min); Sipitang (1 daily; 1hr 10min).

Tawau to: Nunukan (Indonesia; 2 daily; 1hr); Tarakan (Indonesia; 2 daily; 3hr).

Flights

KK to: Johor Bahru (5 daily; 2hr 15min); Kuala Lumpur (11 daily; 4hr); Kuching (5 daily; 2hr 15min); Kudat (2 weekly; 40min); Labuan (7 daily; 30min); Lahad Datu (3 daily; 50min); Sandakan (6 daily; 50min); Singapore (7 daily; 2hr 15min); Tawau (7 daily; 45min).

Sandakan to: KK (6 daily; 50min); Kudat (5 weekly; 45min); Lahad Datu (1 weekly; 1hr 5min); Tawau (2 weekly; 1hr 40min).

Tawau to: Tarakan (Indonesia; 2 weekly; 30min).

CHAPTER EIGHT

BRUNEI

The tiny Islamic Sultanate of **BRUNEI** perches on the northwestern coast of Borneo, surrounded – and at one point even split in two – by the meandering border of Sarawak. At its height in the sixteenth century, Brunei was the seat of the proudest empire in Borneo, its sultans receiving tribute from as far away as Manila; elephants imported from India patrolled its jungle pathways from the South China to the Sulu seas. But Brunei's glory days were long past by the end of the nineteenth century, when the country feared for its very existence, European adventurers having methodically chipped away at its territory, absorbing it into their new colonies.

Today, however, the Sultanate of Brunei is thriving. Its 320,000 inhabitants (of which Malays account for seventy percent, the rest being Chinese, Indians, indigenous tribes and expatriates) enjoy a quality of life almost unparalleled in Southeast Asia. Education and healthcare are free; houses, cars, and even pilgrimages to Mecca are subsidized; taxation on personal income is unheard of. The explanation for this dramatic turn-around is simple: **oil**, first discovered in 1903 at the site of what is now the town of Seria. Although it wasn't until 1931 that the reserves yielded solid financial returns, the sultanate's natural resources (oil was later supplemented by natural gas) have produced a national wealth that's the envy of surrounding states – oil has made Bruneians rich, none more so than Brunei's twenty-ninth **sultan**, Hassanal Bolkiah (whose full title is 31 words long). Recently rated the fourth richest man in the world – and the richest non-American – by *Fortune* magazine, he holds assets estimated at US$30 billion. The sultan himself disputes such claims, asserting that he doesn't have unlimited access to state funds and emphasizing thrift and prudence when addressing the nation. Nevertheless, he has managed to acquire hotels in Singapore, London and Beverly Hills; a magnificent residence, the US$350-million Istana Nurul Iman; a collection of a few hundred cars and a private fleet of aircraft; and over two hundred fine polo horses, kept at his personal country club.

The sultanate's full name is *Negara Brunei Darussalam*, the "Country of Brunei, the Abode of Peace", and indeed "peaceful" is a fair, if rather polite, description of the state; the quality of life enjoyed by Bruneians has engendered an acquiescence towards the royal family's extravagance that extends to the country's **political climate**. Popular involvement in government decision-making remains minimal: the sultan fulfils the dual roles of prime minister and defence minister, while the posts of minister of foreign affairs and minister of finance were held for many years by his brothers, respectively Prince Mohamed and Prince Jefri (the latter, however, was sacked in 1999; see p.507).

Brunei lies on a slim coastal plain threaded by several substantial rivers. Most of the country is less than 150m above sea level, its rainforest, peat swamp and heath forest running down to sandy beaches and mangrove swamps. The country is divided into four districts: **Brunei Muara**, which contains the capital, **Bandar Seri Begawan** (known locally simply as Bandar); agricultural **Tutong**; oil-rich **Belait**; and **Temburong**, a beautiful, sparsely populated backwater severed from the rest of Brunei by the Limbang district of Sarawak. Thanks to its oil, Brunei has never needed to exploit its forestry to any great degree, with the result that primary and secondary tropical forest still cover around seventy percent of the total land area.

BRUNEI PRACTICALITIES

Brunei is most commonly visited as a stepping stone to either Sabah or Sarawak, but if you are having to watch your **budget** carefully, you may find an internal MAS flight between the two Malaysian states a less expensive alternative. Flying from Miri to Labuan and proceeding from there to Sabah, for instance, can work out only marginally pricier – and far more time effective – than bussing through Brunei and taking to the sea from there, once you've taken into account the inevitable overnighter in Bandar, where accommodation is generally pricey. However, food in Brunei is reasonably priced and public transport improving, making a few days' stopover in the sultanate both feasible and enjoyable.

GETTING THERE
There are regular **flights** from Malaysian cities and from Singapore to Bandar Seri Begawan; the prices given here are approximate one-way fares. Both Royal Brunei and MAS fly daily from **Kuala Lumpur** (RM550), **Kota Kinabalu** (RM100) and **Kuching** (RM320). From Singapore, there are daily Singapore Airlines and Royal Brunei flights (S$400).

Boats to Brunei depart daily from **Lawas** and **Limbang** in northern Sarawak, and from **Pulau Labuan**, itself connected by boat to Kota Kinabalu in Sabah. From **Miri** in Sarawak, several **buses** travel daily to Kuala Belait, in the far western corner of Brunei. The overland route from Sipitang in Sabah to Brunei necessitates taking a bus through Lawas to Brunei's Temburong District, from where it's only a short boat trip (see p.519) to Bandar.

GETTING AROUND
If you intend to explore Brunei in some depth, you've little option but to **rent a car**. Car rental is not overly expensive in Brunei, starting at $50 a day ($300 a week; see p.516 for agencies). South of the main coastal roads, **bus** services are nonexistent, while **taxis** are expensive if you want to cover much ground outside the capital. Apart from short hops across Sungei Brunei in Bandar's river taxis, the only time you're likely to use a **boat** is to get to Temburong District (see p.519), which is cut off from the rest of Brunei by the Limbang area of Sarawak.

ACCOMMODATION
All **hotels** in Brunei are up in the mid- to upper-range price brackets; there is little accommodation outside of this price range, though Bandar has one hostel that's a little cheaper. While **longhouses** do exist in the interior, there are only a few which offer accommodation, for which a small gratuity is asked. **Homestay** programmes in rural areas, where visitors stay in a kampung house with a local family, are being set up; here you pay substantially less for a room than in a hotel.

Throughout the Singapore and Brunei chapters we've used the following **price codes** to denote the cheapest available room for two people. Single occupancy should cost less than double, though this is not always the case. Some guesthouses provide dormitory beds, for which the dollar price is given.

① $25 and under	④ $61–100	⑦ $201–300
② $26–40	⑤ $101–150	⑧ $301–400
③ $41–60	⑥ $151–200	⑨ $401 and above

While many visitors have hitherto regarded the sultanate as little more than a stopover on the way to more exciting Sabah or Sarawak, just recently there have been signs that Brunei's neglect of tourism is starting to change. The sultanate's **natural attractions**, in particular, are being promoted and sections of pristine rainforest like **Ulu Temburong National Park** in the eastern section of the country can now be vis-

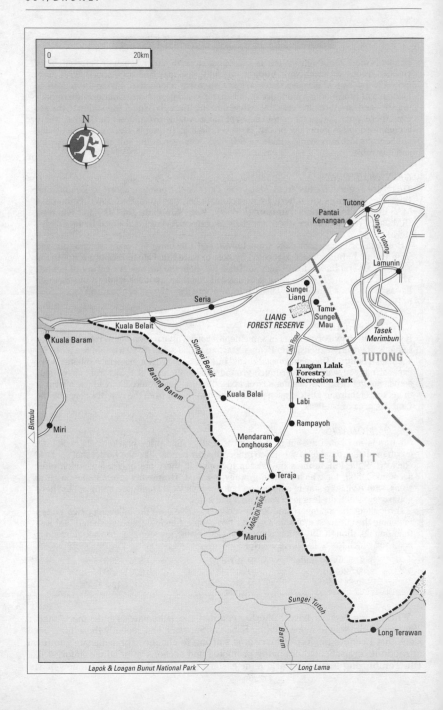

0   20km

N

Tutong
Pantai
Kenangan
Sungei Tutong
Lamunin
Seria
Sungei
Liang
*LIANG
FOREST RESERVE*
Tamu
Sungei
Mau
Kuala Belait
Labi Road
Tasek
Merimbun
Kuala Baram
Sungei Belait
Barang Baram
**Luagan Lalak
Forestry
Recreation Park**
TUTONG
Miri
Kuala Balai
Labi
Rampayoh
Mendaram
Longhouse
B E L A I T
Teraja
MARUDI TRAIL
Marudi
Sungei Tutoh
Baram
Long Terawan
Lapok & Loagan Bunut National Park   Long Lama
Bintulu

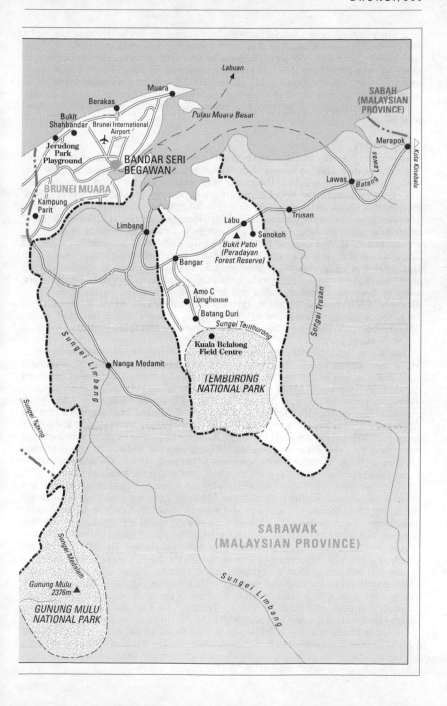

ited. The relative lack of a tourist infrastructure outside the capital is being tackled by the recently initiated **homestay** programme, whereby travellers overnight in Malay and Murut kampungs and Iban longhouses, affording an appealing opportunity to share in rural life. These developments are happening in parallel with a slow emergence from the introspection that has characterized the country, a change borne out in a small way by the building of smart new plazas – with requisite coffee bars – in Bandar, a small, attractive city with two exquisite **mosques** and the fascinating Kampung Ayer **stilt village**.

Some history

Contemporary Brunei's modest size belies its pivotal role in the formative centuries of Borneo's history. Little is known of the sultanate's **early history**, though trade was always the powerhouse behind the growth of its empire. Tang and Sung dynasty coins and ceramics, found in the Kota Batu area, a few kilometres from Bandar Seri Begawan, suggest that China was trading with Brunei as long ago as the seventh century, while allusions in ninth-century Chinese records to tributary payments to China by the ruler of an Asian city called Puni are thought to refer to Brunei. In subsequent centuries, Brunei benefited from its strategic position on the trade route between India, Melaka and China, and exercised a lucrative control over merchant traffic in the South China Sea. As well as being a staging post, where traders could stock up on supplies and offload some of their cargo, Brunei was commercially active in its own right; local produce such as beeswax, camphor, rattan and brasswork was traded by the *nakhoda*, or Bruneian sea traders, for ceramics, spices, woods and fabrics. By the fourteenth century, this commercial clout led to Brunei being brought under the sway of the Majapahit Empire, though by the end of that century the first sultan had taken the reins of independent power.

Islam had begun to make inroads into Bruneian society by the mid-fifteenth century, as the sultanate courted the business of foreign Muslim merchants. The religion's presence was accelerated by the decamping to Brunei of wealthy Muslim merchant families after the fall of Melaka to the Portuguese in 1511. Brunei was certainly an Islamic sultanate by the time it received its first **European visitors** in 1521. When Antonio Pigafetta, travelling to Southeast Asia with Ferdinand Magellan, arrived at the head of the Sungei Brunei, he found a thriving city ruled over by a splendid and sophisticated royal court. Pigafetta and his companions were taken by elephant to an audience with the sultan, whom they met in a hall "all hung with silk stuffs" – though not before they were taught "to make three obeisances to the king, with hands joined above the head, raising first one then the other foot, and then to kiss the hands to him".

Pigafetta's sojourn in Brunei coincided with the sultanate's **golden age**. In the first half of the sixteenth century, Brunei was Borneo's foremost kingdom, its influence stretching along the island's northern and western coasts, and even as far as territory belonging to the modern-day Philippines. Such was the extent of Bruneian authority that Western visitors found the sultanate and the island interchangeable: the word "Borneo" is thought to be no more than a European corruption of Brunei. The fall of Melaka did much to bolster the importance of Brunei, though the foundation of its success was a strong and efficient form of government based upon traditional Islamic frameworks, headed by the sultan himself and represented in the outer regions of Bruneian territories by his *pengiran*, or noblemen. But by the close of the sixteenth century, things were beginning to turn sour for the sultanate. Trouble with Catholic Spain, now sniffing around the South China and Sulu seas with a view to colonization, led to a sea battle off the coast at Muara in 1578; the battle was won by Spain, whose forces took the capital, only to be chased out days later by a cholera epidemic. The threat of piracy caused more problems, scaring off passing trade. Worse still, at home the sultans began to lose control of the *pengiran*, as factional struggles ruptured the court.

Western entrepreneurs arrived in this self-destructive climate, keen to take advantage of trade gaps left by Brunei's decline. One such fortune-seeker was **James Brooke**, whose arrival off the coast of Kuching in August 1839 was to change the face of Borneo for ever. For helping the sultan quell a Dyak uprising, Brooke demanded and was given the governorship of Sarawak; Brunei's contraction had begun. Over subsequent decades, the state was to shrink steadily, as Brooke and his successors used the suppression of piracy as the excuse they needed to siphon off more and more territory into the familial fiefdom. This trend culminated in the cession of the Limbang region in 1890 – a move which literally split Brunei in two.

Elsewhere, more Bruneian land was being lost to other powers. In January 1846, a court faction unsympathetic to foreign land-grabbing seized power in Brunei and the chief minister was murdered. British gunboats quelled the coup and Pulau Labuan was ceded to the British crown. A **treaty** signed the following year, forbidding the sultanate from ceding any of its territories without the British Crown's consent, underlined the decline of Brunei's power. In 1865, American consul Charles Lee Moses negotiated a treaty granting a ten-year lease to the American Trading Company of the portion of northeast Borneo that was later to become Sabah. By 1888, the British had declared Brunei a **protected state**, which meant the responsibility for its foreign affairs lay with London.

The start of the twentieth century was marked by the **discovery of oil**; given what little remained of Bruneian territory, it could hardly have been altruism that spurred the British to set up a Residency here in 1906. Initially, though, profits from the fledgling oil industry were slow to come, and the early decades of the century saw rubber estates springing up at Berakas, Gadong and Temburong. However, by 1931, the Seria Oil Field was on stream and profits were soon such that, despite the British appropriating a hefty slice, the sultanate was able to pay off debts from the lean years of the late nineteenth century.

The **Japanese invasion** of December 1941 temporarily halted Brunei's path to recovery. As in Sabah, Allied bombing over the three and a half years of occupation that followed left much rebuilding to be done. While Sabah, Sarawak and Pulau Labuan became Crown Colonies in the early postwar years, Brunei remained a **British protectorate** and retained its British Resident. Only in 1959 was the Residency finally withdrawn and a new constitution established, with provisions for a democratically elected legislative council. At the same time, Sultan Omar Ali Saifuddien (the present sultan's father) was careful to retain British involvement in matters of defence and foreign affairs – a move whose sagacity was made apparent when, in 1962, an armed coup led by Sheik Azahari's pro-democratic Brunei People's Party was crushed by British Army Gurkhas. Ever since the attempted coup, which resulted from Sultan Omar's refusal to convene the first sitting of the legislative council, Brunei has been ruled by the decree of the sultan, in his role as non-elected prime minister, and emergency powers – including provisions for detention without trial – have been in place. Despite showing interest in joining the planned **Malaysian Federation** in 1963, Brunei suffered a last-minute attack of cold feet, choosing to opt out rather than risk losing its new-found oil wealth and compromise the pre-eminence of its monarchy. Instead, Brunei remained a British Protectorate until January 1, 1984, when it attained full **independence**.

While the economy remains booming, oil revenues having exceeded all expectations, the Bolkiah family's control of the country has come under the spotlight recently. In 2000, an unprecedented **law suit** was launched by the Sultan against his youngest brother, Jefri, concerning the alleged mismanagement of the Brunei Investments Agency's funds when it was headed by Jefri. Although settled out of court, the case may well have led the inhabitants of Brunei to start questioning the way the Bolkiah family runs the country without any real accountability. Another anachronistic aspect to the sultan's tenure as exclusive arbiter of Bruneian life has been his attitude towards the largest ethnic minority (comprising a fifth of the population), the **Chinese**, who are not automatically classed as citizens; to enjoy the perks accorded to all other Bruneians, the Chinese must prove their citizenship, a process that demands not only a lengthy history of familial residence, but also a rigorous and humiliating written test in Malay language and customs.

Economic changes appear to be on the cards too; in July 2000, mindful that its oil resources may run out around 2020, the government announced sweeping **economic reforms**, including plans to impose income taxes, slash subsidies and set up a regional financial hub. The Sultan has been investing globally on a massive scale and is attempting to diversify the economy into areas like hi-tech industries and ecotourism, reflecting a less self-contained outlook. The Asian financial crisis of 1997 and the resulting restructuring of regional economies may well have jolted the sultanate into realizing it has to shed its almost total dependence on oil and gas revenues and bring Brunei closer into line with the economic approach of its neighbours.

Bandar Seri Begawan

The capital of Brunei, **BANDAR SERI BEGAWAN** is the sultanate's only settlement of any real size. Until 1970, Bandar was known simply as Brunei Town; the present name means "Town of the Seri Begawan", Seri Begawan being the title Sultan Omar Ali Saifuddien took after abdicating in favour of his son Hassanil Bolkiah in 1967. Straddling the northern bank of a twist in the Sungei Brunei, the city is characterized by its unlikely juxtaposition of striking modern buildings – such as its two grand **mosques** and the twin malls of the Yayasan Sultan Haji Hassanil Bolkiah shopping complex – with its traditional stilt houses.

Brunei's original seat of power was **Kampung Ayer**, the water village which is still home to around half Bandar's population. After the arrival of the British Residency in 1906, the streets which form downtown Bandar were laid out on reclaimed land, but the kampung dwellers stayed put, preferring to retain their traditional way of life despite an attempt to coax them onto dry land. As recently as the middle of the twentieth century, Brunei's capital was still a sleepy water village; the novelist Anthony Burgess, posted here as a teacher in the late 1950s, observed that onshore Bandar comprised "a single street of shops, run by Chinese, which sold long-playing records and old copies of the *Daily Mirror Weekly*".

That contemporary Bandar has become the attractive, clean and modern waterfront city it is today is due, inevitably, to oil. With the new-found wealth of the 1970s came large-scale urbanization north of the Sungei Brunei, resulting in housing schemes, shopping centres and, more obviously, the magnificent **Omar Ali Saifuddien Mosque**, which dominates the skyline of Bandar. First-time visitors to Bandar are pleasantly surprised by a sense of space that's rare among Southeast Asian cities. Unfortunately, though, Bandar isn't cheap to visit; the fact that most visitors to Brunei are businesspeople means room prices can be prohibitively high. Nevertheless, the sights of Bandar are interesting enough to warrant a day or two's stopover.

Arrival, information and city transport

Flying into Bandar, you land at plush **Brunei International Airport**, 11km north of the city. There are free public phones to your right beyond passport control, handy for booking a room upon arrival. To the left, as you walk out of the arrivals concourse and into the car park, is a **tourist information booth**, whose staff will furnish you with the glossy and mildly interesting 100-page *Explore Brunei* booklet. You can **change money**

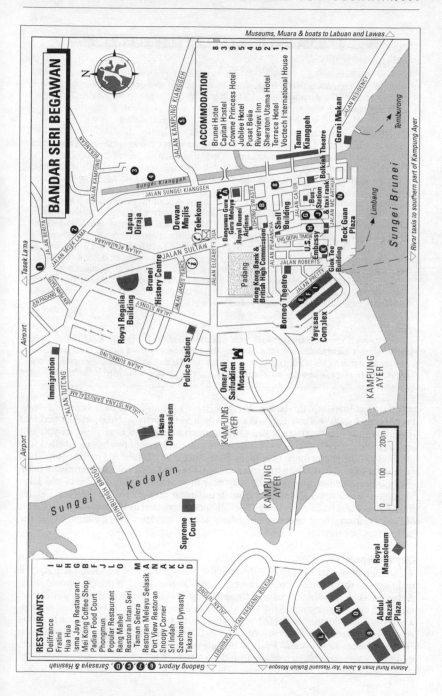

BANDAR SERI BEGAWAN

Museums, Muara & boats to Labuan and Lawas

ACCOMMODATION

Brunei Hotel	8
Capital Hostel	3
Crowne Princess Hotel	9
Jubilee Hotel	5
Pusat Belia	4
Riverview Inn	6
Sheraton Utama Hotel	2
Terrace Hotel	1
Voctech I'nternational House	7

RESTAURANTS

Delifrance	I
Fratini	E
Hua Hua	H
Isma Jaya Restaurant	G
Mei Kong Coffee Shop	B
Padian Food Court	F
Phongmun	J
Popular Restaurant	L
Rang Mahel	O
Restoran Intan Seri	
Taman Selera	M
Restoran Melayu Selasik	A
Port View Restoran	N
Snoopy Corner	A
Sri Indah	K
Szechuan Dynasty	C
Takara	D

Tasek Lana

Airport

Airport

JLN PADANG

JALAN ISTANA DARUSSALAM

JALAN TUTONG

Immigration

Istana Darussalem

JLN. JA.EN BERITA

JALAN TASEK LAMA

JALAN BENJNAHARA

Royal Regalia Building

JALAN SUMBILING

Police Station

Omar Ali Saifuddien Mosque

Supreme Court

EDINBURGH BRIDGE

Sungei Kedayan

Brunei 'History Centre'

JALAN SULTAN

Lapau Diraja

Dewan Majlis

Telekom

JALAN KAMPONG

BERTANGAN

JALAN KAMPUNG KIANGGEH

Sungei Kianggeh

JALAN SUNGEI KIANGGEH

Bangunan Guru Guru Melayu

Royal Brunei Airlines

JALAN ELIZABETH DUA

JAMES PEARLE

JALAN STONEY

Padang

Hong Kong Bank & British High Commission

Borneo Theatre

JALAN PEMANCHA

JALAN ROBERTS

Yayesan Complex

KAMPUNG AYER

KAMPUNG AYER

KAMPUNG AYER

LHG GERAI TIMOR

Shell Building

JALAN CATOR

U.S. Embassy

Giok Tee Building

JALAN MC ARTHUR

JALAN PRETTY

Bus Station & taxi rank

Bolkiah Theatre

Teck Guan Plaza

Tamu Kianggeh

Gerai Makan

JALAN RESIDENCY

Sungei Brunei

Tembburong

Limbang

River taxis to southern part of Kampung Ayer

0 100 200m

Royal Mausoleum

Abdul Razak Plaza

JALAN SULTAN HASSANIL BOLKIAH

LEBUHRAYA

Gadong Airport, ⑥⑦⑧⑥, Sarasaya & Hasinah

Astana Nurul Iman & Jame 'Asr Hassanil Bolkiah Mosque

MOVING ON FROM BANDAR SERI BEGAWAN

BY AIR

Central and Northern line buses ($1) run to the airport from the bus station at least every fifteen minutes between 6.30am and 6pm; you can also get a taxi there ($15) from the bus station. The **airport tax** is $5 for flights to Malaysia and Singapore, $12 for all other destinations.

BY BOAT

Boats for **Lawas** and **Labuan** leave from the Serasa wharf, 25km northeast of the city in Muara. To get there, take the Muara bus from the bus station (every 30min; 30min; $2). Tickets for Labuan (daily at 8am, 8.30am, 1pm & 2pm; $20) and Lawas (daily at 11.30am; $15) are sold by New Island Shipping, first floor, Giok Tee Building, Jalan McArthur (☎02/243059), and Halim Tours, Lorong Gerai Timor, off Jalan McArthur (☎02/226688). **Limbang** boats (frequent departures 7am–5.30pm according to demand; 30min; $10) leave from Bandar's main jetty; tickets for this route are sold at the stalls on Jalan MacArthur, just beside the entrance to the jetty. From Labuan, there are daily connections on to Kota Kinabalu and Menumbok in Sabah, though to ensure you catch one, it's wise to leave Bandar early in the day. Note that tickets to Labuan should be booked as early as possible – especially if you want to travel over a weekend or a holiday. Also be aware that schedules change, so double-check departure times to all destinations.

Boats to **Bangar** in Temburong (daily 6.30am–4.30pm; hourly; $7) depart from 300m east along Jalan Residency; tickets are sold beside the jetty. From Bangar, it's possible to travel overland to both Lawas and Limbang (see p.519).

BY BUS

Given how skimpy the **bus network** is, if you want to make a day-trip out of Bandar, you have to start early in the morning. Among the main routes from the bus station, there are buses north to Muara ($2), and west to Tutong ($3) and separately to Seria ($4) – the latter where you can change for Kuala Belait, served by buses for Miri in Sarawak.

at the airport branch of the Islamic Bank of Brunei (Mon–Thurs 9am–noon & 2–3pm, Fri 8–11am & 2.30–3.30pm, Sat 9–11am) located in the arrivals concourse. A **taxi** into Bandar from the airport costs $15–20; it's much cheaper to bear right as you exit arrivals, into the free parking zone, where you can catch one of two **buses** labelled simply Central Line or Northern Line (daily 8am–8pm; every 15min; $1) to the central **bus station** on Jalan Cator. Buses from Sarawak and the west of Brunei also terminate here.

Boats from Limbang dock at the jetty near the junction of Jalan Roberts and Jalan McArthur, while small speedboats from Temburong arrive 200m to the east. Ferries from Labuan and boats from Lawas dock at Serasa terminal in Muara, 25km northeast of the city, from where buses run regularly (daily 7am–5pm; every 30min; $4) to the Jalan Cator bus station.

City transport

With much of Bandar's population living in the villages that make up Kampung Ayer, it makes sense that the most common form of **public transport** in the city should be its **water taxis**. A veritable armada of these skinny speedboats plies the Sungei Brunei night and day, charging only $1–2 for a short hop – pay your fare on board. You can hire a water taxi for a longer tour of the water villages, or to see the Sultan's palace from the river; a half-hour round trip costs around $15–20 per person. The jetty below the intersection of Jalan Roberts and Jalan McArthur is the best place to catch a water taxi, though it's also possible to hail one from Jalan Residency.

Though user-friendly and inexpensive, Bandar's local **bus** network has the drawback of closing down at 6pm (it's largely geared to getting people to and from work). The bus terminal on Jalan Cator is very well organized, with maps alongside every bay. Services to points north, east and west of the city centre leave (daily 6.30am–6pm; every 15–20min; $1) from the bus station, underneath the multistorey car park just south of the eastern end of Jalan Cator. Three bus services ply the roads in and around the capital, their names pilfered from London's Underground system; the most useful to tourists are Central Line buses, which run between the airport and the Brunei and Malay Technology museums, crossing the city en route; and Circle Line services, which do a loop taking in the Jame 'Asr Hassanil Bolkiah mosque and the suburb of Gadong. For destinations outside the capital, bus details are given throughout the chapter.

Bandar has two distinct types of **taxi**: the CTS service, whose purple cars run around and within the city only, are useful for districts like Gadong and Batu 1 – but not, infuriatingly, the museums or the airport. They charge a flat rate of $3 and an extra $1 if you book by phone. The other type are the regular, metered, yellow taxis which congregate beside the bus station and outside swisher shopping centres and hotels. Fares start from $3, and a short journey – say, from the city centre to the Brunei Museum – costs $5–7, with a $2 surcharge between 9pm and 6am and another surcharge of $5 on trips to the airport. For longer journeys, out to Seria or Kuala Belait for instance, you can haggle with drivers and fix a price. **Car rental** agencies are listed on p.516, though note that a car is only really useful to get around outside Bandar.

Accommodation

Brunei is almost bereft of budget **accommodation**, with the *Pusat Belia* (youth hostel) and *VOCTECH International House* the only options at the lower end of the price range. There's a fair selection of comfortable **hotels** to choose from, though.

Brunei, 95 Jalan Pemancha (☎02/242372). Comfortable, with spacious, air-con en-suite rooms, this is Bandar's most central hotel. ⑥

Capital Hostel, Jalan Kampung Berangan (☎02/223561). A budget option by Bruneian standards, and a useful standby if you can't get into the neighbouring *Pusat Belia*. The rooms, though small, are clean and have attached bathrooms. ④

Crowne Princess, Jalan Tutong (☎02/241128). Situated away over Edinburgh Bridge; regular shuttle buses run between here and the city centre. With over a hundred well-appointed rooms, this place also has a restaurant serving decent Asian cuisine. ⑤

Jubilee, Jubilee Plaza, Jalan Kampung Kianggeh (☎02/228070). East of Sungei Kianggeh, this midrange hotel has large en-suite rooms with TV and air-con. It's set opposite a patch of traditional kampung houses, giving it a pleasant neighbourhood feel. ④

Pusat Belia, Jalan Sungai Kianggeh (☎02/222900). Brunei's youth hostel, and by far the cheapest option in town. The dorms sleep four, and there's a swimming pool ($1) downstairs. Dorm beds $10 a night for first three nights, $5 for each night thereafter.

Riverview, Km 1, Jalan Gadong (☎02/238238). Just as good as the *Brunei*, with large, pleasant, airy rooms with TV, air-con and attached bathrooms. ⑥

Sheraton Utama, Jalan Tasek Lama (☎02/244272). Brunei's earliest international-standard hotel, with over 150 swanky rooms and suites, plus a well-equipped business centre with Internet access. ⑦

Terrace, Jalan Tasek Lama (☎02/243554). Reasonable hotel, whose rooms are slightly worn and dated but full of charm; outside is a lovely, quiet swimming pool. ④

VOCTECH International House, Jalan Pasar Baharu (☎02/447992, fax 447955). To get there, take the Circle Line bus from the Jalan Cator terminal. This massive, comfortable place, ostensibly set up for international student groups, is now increasingly used by tour groups and independent travellers. Rooms are large and simply decorated, with balconies and attached bathrooms. It's got a well-priced café, a kitchen which can be used by guests and a library with Internet access. Five minutes' walk away is an excellent night market serving cheap, tasty food. ③

The City and around

Downtown Bandar is hemmed in by water: to the east is Sungei Kianggeh; to the south, the wide Sungei Brunei; and to the west, Sungei Kedayan, which runs under **Edinburgh Bridge**. The **Omar Ali Saifuddien Mosque**, overlooking the compact knot of central streets, is Bandar's most obvious point of reference, sitting in a cradle formed by **Kampung Ayer** (water village), a collection of settlements protruding from the river. Over Edinburgh Bridge, **Jalan Tutong** runs westwards and past the Batu 1 area (a grid of shopping complexes and hotels), reaching Astana Nurul Iman 3km later; branching off to the northwest is **Lebuhraya Sultan Hassanal Bolkiah**, one of several routes for the restaurants of the commercial suburb of **Gadong** and for the airport. On the eastern end of the centre, **Jalan Residency** hugs the river bank on its way to the **Brunei Museum** and its neighbouring attractions.

The Omar Ali Saifuddien Mosque

At the very heart of both the city and the sultanate's Muslim faith is the magnificent **Omar Ali Saifuddien Mosque** (Mon–Wed, Sat & Sun 8am–noon, 1–3.30pm & 4.30–5.30pm, Thurs open to Muslims only, Fri 4.30–5.30pm). Built in classical Islamic style, and mirrored in the circular lagoon surrounding it, it's a breathtaking sight, whether viewed dazzling in the sun or seen illuminated a lurid green at night. Commissioned by and named after the father of the present sultan, the mosque was completed in 1958 and makes splendid use of opulent yet tasteful fittings – Italian marble, granite from Shanghai, Arabian and Belgian carpets, and English chandeliers and stained glass. Topping the cream-coloured building is a 52-metre-high golden dome whose curved surface is adorned with a mosaic comprising over three million pieces of Venetian glass. Anthony Burgess described the mosque's construction in his autobiography, *Little Wilson and Big God*: "The dome had been covered with gold leaf," he wrote, "which, owing to the contraction and expansion of the structure with comparative cool and large heat, fell to the ground in flakes and splinters which were taken by the fisherfolk to be a gift from Allah." It's sometimes possible to ride the elevator up the 44-metre-high minaret and look out over the water village below; ask to speak to the person in charge at the mosque if you're interested in doing this. In the lagoon is a replica of a sixteenth-century royal barge, or *mahligai*, used on special religious occasions. The usual dress codes – modest attire, and shoes to be left at the entrance – apply when entering the mosque.

Kampung Ayer

Stilt villages have occupied this stretch of the Sungei Brunei for hundreds of years: Antonio Pigafetta, visiting Borneo in 1521, described a city, "entirely built on foundations in the salt water . . . it contains twenty-five thousand fires or families. The houses are all of wood, placed on great piles to raise them high up". Today, an estimated thirty thousand people live in the scores of sprawling villages that compose **Kampung Ayer**, their dwellings connected by a maze of wooden promenades. These villages now feature their own clinics, mosques, schools, a fire brigade and even a police station; homes here have piped water, electricity and TV. There's a strong sense of community, as a result of which government attempts to move the inhabitants into modern housing schemes on dry land have met with little success.

The meandering ways of Kampung Ayer make it an intriguing place to explore on foot, especially on Friday afternoons when everyone goes to the mosques and visits one another's homes afterwards. For a more panoramic impression of its dimensions though, it's best to charter one of the water taxis that zip around the river (see p.510). A handful of traditional **cottage industries** continue to turn out copperware and brassware (at Kampung Ujong Bukit), and exquisite sarongs and boats (Kampung Saba Darat); the boatmen should know the whereabouts of some of them.

Jalan Sultan and north to Tasek Lama

A short way east of the Omar Ali Saifuddien Mosque, Bandar's main drag, the broad **Jalan Sultan**, runs north past several of the city's lesser sights. First is the **Brunei History Centre** (Mon–Thurs & Sat 7.45am–12.15pm & 1.30–4.30pm; free), a research institution whose dull displays – maps showing Brunei's changing shape over the centuries, and tables outlining the genealogy of past sultans – will have you hurrying on to the **Royal Regalia Building** (Mon–Thurs 8.30am–5pm, Fri 9–11.30am & 2.30–5pm, Sat & Sun 8.30am–5pm; free) next door, opened in 1992 as part of the sultan's silver jubilee celebrations. A magnificent semicircular building fitted out with lavish carpets and marble, it contains an exhibition charting the life of the present sultan. The sycophantic labelling apart ("Since childhood His Majesty has a very cheerful, generous and benign personality"; of schooldays: "He picked up his lessons very fast within a short time"; of Sandhurst: "popular with fellow cadets as well as higher officers"), there's some quite interesting stuff here, including a surprisingly happy, smiling shot of the sultan taken during his circumcision ceremony, as well as a golden hand and forearm used to support his chin during the coronation, and a beautifully ornate crown. The **Constitutional Gallery** in the same building is inevitably drier, but its documents and treaties are worth a scan. Fronting the whole collection is the **coronation carriage**, or *usungan*, ringed by regalia from the coronation ceremony – which took place right across Jalan Sultan in the **Lapau Diraja** (Royal Ceremonial Hall) on August 1, 1968. The hall's slightly tacky exterior belies the grandeur of its huge inner chamber, whose western side is approached by a mini escalator. Beyond this, rows of red, black, pink and white pillars run up to the golden *patarana*, or royal throne. Although the hall is not officially open to the public, it's usually possible to take a peek at its lavish interior. Next door is the parliament building, the **Dewan Majlis**, which used to house the Legislative Assembly.

East of the Lapau Diraja and parallel to Jalan Sultan is **Jalan Sungei Kianggeh**, which runs past the daily produce market, **Tamu Kianggeh**, and Bandar's most central **Chinese temple**, before arriving at Jalan Tasek, the turning to tranquil **Tasek Lama Park** which is five-minutes' walk from the main road. Bear left and you pass through the pretty gardens to a small waterfall; bear right along the sealed road and right again at the fork and you end up at a bottle-green reservoir.

East to the Brunei Museum

Jalan Residency runs eastwards from Sungei Kianggeh, bordered to the south by the Sungei Brunei and to the north by a hillside Muslim cemetery whose scores of decrepit stones are shaded by an orchard of gnarled frangipani trees. After a little less than a kilometre, the road reaches the **Brunei Arts and Handicrafts Training Centre** (Mon–Thurs & Sat 7.45am–12.15pm & 1.30–4.30pm, Fri & Sun 8.30am–2pm; free), an organization dedicated to perpetuating the sultanate's cultural heritage. Here, young Bruneians are taught traditional skills, such as weaving, basketry and bamboo-working, brass casting and the crafting of the *kris* (traditional dagger). Apart from the occasional weaving demonstration though, you can't watch the proceedings unless you've sought permission to do so in advance. You'll probably have to make do with browsing through the **craft shop**'s decent selection of reasonably priced basketry, silverware and spinning tops.

From here it's 4km to the **Brunei Museum** (eastbound Central Line buses run, occasionally, from the stop opposite the handicrafts centre, or catch a Circle Line bus from the city centre), shortly before which is the **tomb of Sultan Bolkiah** (1473–1521), Brunei's fifth sultan, who held sway at the very peak of the state's power.

It's worth setting aside an hour or two for the museum (Tues–Thurs 9am–5pm, Fri 9.30–11.30am & 2.30–5pm, Sat & Sun 9am–5pm; free), which has several outstanding galleries. In the inevitable Oil and Gas Gallery, set up by Brunei Shell Petroleum, exhibits, graphics and captions recount the story of Brunei's oil reserves, from the drilling of the first well in 1928, to current extraction and refining techniques. Also interesting, though tantalizingly sketchy, is the **Muslim Life Gallery**, whose dioramas allow glimpses of social traditions such as the sweetening of a new-born baby's mouth with honey or dates, and the disposal of its placenta in a *bayung*, a palm-leaf basket either hung on a tree or floated downriver. At the back of the gallery, a small collection of early photographs shows riverine hawkers trading from their boats in Kampung Ayer. The museum's undoubted highlight, though, is its superb Islamic Art Gallery where, among the riches on display are beautifully illuminated antique Korans from India, Iran, Egypt and Turkey, exquisite prayer mats, and quirkier items like a pair of ungainly wooden slippers.

Steps around the back of the museum drop down to the riverside **Malay Technology Museum** (daily 9am–5pm except Fri 9–11.30am & 2.30–5pm, closed Tues; free), whose three galleries provide a mildly engaging insight into traditional Malay life. Of greatest interest is Gallery Three, whose exhibits include the *pelarik gasing*, a machine which evenly cuts spinning tops; the *lamin keleput*, used for boring blowpipes; and other devices worked from forest materials by Brunei's indigenous people. In the same gallery are authentic examples of Kedayan, Murut and Dusun dwellings, while elsewhere in the building you see dioramas highlighting stilt-house and *atap*-roof construction, boat-making and fishing methods.

The Jame 'Asr Hassanil Bolkiah Mosque

Many people reckon that the **Jame 'Asr Hassanil Bolkiah Mosque** (Mon–Wed, Sat & Sun 8am–noon, 1–3.30pm & 4.30–5.30pm; Thurs & Fri open to Muslims only), constructed to commemorate the silver jubilee of the sultan's reign in 1992, has a distinct edge over the Omar Ali Saifuddien Mosque both in style and grandeur. Teams of Bangladeshi workers busily clip and sweep outside, below the mosque's sea-blue roof, golden domes and slender minarets, while silk-clad Bruneians go about their prayers. The mosque, Brunei's largest, is referred to as the Kiarong Mosque (after a neighbouring kampung) by locals, who find its full name rather a mouthful. You can get an impression of the building, set in harmonious gardens close to the commercial suburb of Gadong, on your way to and from the airport, though to visit the mosque you need to get a Circle Line **bus**, whose route skirts the grounds of the mosque on the way to Gadong. Directly across from the mosque in Kampung Kiarong is a useful cybercafé (see p.517).

The Astana Nurul Iman

The **Astana Nurul Iman**, the official residence of the sultan, is sited at a superb riverside spot 4km west of the centre. Bigger than either Buckingham Palace or the Vatican, the astana is a monument to self-indulgence. Its design, by Filipino architect Leandro Locsin, is a sinuous blend of traditional and modern, with Islamic motifs such as arches and domes, and sloping roofs fashioned on traditional longhouse designs, combined with all the mod cons you'd expect of a house whose owner is estimated to earn millions of dollars a day. James Bartholomew's book, *The Richest Man in the World*, lists some of the mind-boggling figures relating to the palace which, over half a kilometre long, contains a grand total of 1778 rooms, including 257 toilets. Illuminating these rooms requires 51,000 light bulbs, many of which are consumed by the palace's 564 chandeliers; simply getting around the rooms requires 18 lifts and 44 staircases. The throne room is said to be particularly sumptuous: twelve one-ton chandeliers hang from its ceiling, while its four grand thrones stand against the backdrop of an eighteen-metre arch, tiled in 22-carat gold. In addition to the throne room, there's a royal banquet hall that seats 4000 diners, a prayer hall where 1500 people can worship at any one time, an underground car park for the sultan's hundreds of vehicles, a state-of-the-art sports complex, and a helipad.

Inevitably, the palace is not open to the general public, apart from two days every year during *Hari Raya Aidilfitri*, at the end of Ramadan (see p.71). Otherwise, nearby **Taman Persiaran Damuan**, a kilometre-long park sandwiched between Jalan Tutong and Sungei Brunei, offers the best view, or you can fork out for a boat trip ($30) and see the palace lit up at night from the water. Opposite the park is **Pulau Ranggu**, where monkeys congregate on the shore towards dusk.

All westbound buses travel along Jalan Tutong, over the Edinburgh Bridge and past the astana, though it is possible to walk there. En route you'll pass the city's **Batu 1** area, in the southwestern corner of which the **Royal Mausoleum and Graveyard** are tucked away. Brunei's sultans have been buried at this site since 1786, though only the last four were laid to rest in the mausoleum.

Eating

Fortunately, Bandar's **restaurants** are more reasonably priced than its hotels; there's an increasingly wide range of decent eating establishments, reflecting the multicultural make-up of the city's population. Several of Bandar's better eating places are situated in the area a little way west of Edinburgh Bridge, a short taxi-ride – or an interesting walk beyond the Omar Ali Saifuddien Mosque and through Kampung Ayer – from downtown Bandar. Several kilometres northwest of the centre, the booming suburb of **Gadong** has a number of interesting restaurants, including a sensational Japanese one, as well as superb Indian cafés and branches of *McDonald's* and *Pizza Hut*; Gadong's Abdul Razak Complex (not to be confused with the Abdul Razak Plaza west of the centre) has quite a concentration of eating places. It's straightforward to get to Gadong using a CTS taxi, which is a good thing given that buses stop running at 6pm.

Especially if you're on a tight budget, it's worth heading for the **night stalls** situated in the car park of the main market across the road from VOCTECH on the way to Gadong. Malay favourites are laid out buffet-style here, but food has to be taken away for consumption are there are no tables and chairs. There are also cheap stalls behind the Chinese temple on Jalan Sungei Kianggeh, where the bursting flames and billowing smoke of chicken being barbecued over charcoal fires have a rather dramatic aspect. A third location is the cluster of stalls behind the Temburong jetty on Jalan Residency, whose lack of panache is somewhat redeemed by good and cheap *soto ayam* (rice cubes served with shredded chicken and broth), *nasi campur* and other Malay staples.

One thing you won't find in Bandar, or for that matter in Brunei, is a bar. Drinking **alcohol** in public has been outlawed in Brunei since New Year's Day, 1991.

Café Melati, *Sheraton Utama Hotel*, Jalan Sungei Kianggeh. The generous buffet lunch ($25) in this bright and breezy establishment fills you up for the day; their buffet dinner ($35) features a different international culinary theme every night. Mon–Sat noon–2pm & 7–10pm, Sun 7–10pm.

Delifrance, ground floor, Yayasan Complex, Jalan Kumbang Pasang. Slick, French-style coffee and croissant joint. Very popular with Brunei's well-heeled youth. Daily 9am–9pm.

Fratini, G24 Block C, Yayasan Complex, Jalan Kumbang Pasang (☎02/232892). Italian-run expat oasis, adding a dash of sophistication to Bandar's dining scene; choose from a decent range of pizzas and pastas ($15), then round things off with a cappuccino. Daily 11.30am–2pm & 6–10pm.

Hasinah Restoran, Block 1, Unit 9, Abdul Razak Complex, Gadong. Excellent, inexpensive Malay and South Indian daytime café. With nine types of *dosai* and a mouthwatering *nasi campur* spread.

Hua Hua Restaurant, 48 Jalan Sultan. Steamed chicken with sausage is one of the highlights in this simple, no-frills Chinese establishment, where $15 feeds two people. Daily 7am–9pm.

Isma Jaya, 27 Jalan Sultan. One of several good Indian restaurants along Jalan Sultan; lip-smacking *korma* and *biriyani* sell well here. Daily 6am–8pm.

Mei Kong Coffee Shop, 108 Jalan Pemancha. Fronted by a chicken-rice bar, this unmarked coffee shop, right beside the Hong Kong Bank, also serves noodles, *roti*s and *panggang* (rice and prawns cooked in banana leaves). Daily 5am–8pm.

Padian Food Court, first floor, Yayasan Complex, Jalan Kumbang Pasang. Snow-bright, air-con food court whose spotless stalls serve Thai, Arabic, Japanese and Indian fare and several other regional cuisines. Daily 9am–10pm.

Phongmun Restaurant, second floor, Teck Guan Plaza, Jalan Sultan. Classy and centrally located Cantonese restaurant serving *dim sum*, with wall panels depicting roses and dragons. Daily 6.30am–11pm; *dim sum* served 6.30am–4.00pm.

Popular Restaurant, Shop 5, Block 1, Putri Anak Norain Complex, Batu 1, Jalan Tutong. Bare but clean Indian restaurant, serving lovely *dosai*, tandoori breads and curries. Mon 4–10pm, Tues–Sun 8am–10pm.

Port View Restaurant, Jalan McArthur. Quite expensive Western and Asian fare in a relaxing setting overlooking the harbour and Kampung Ayer. The pasta dishes are usually tasty and filling, and the rice-based Malay and Chinese food is good as well. Bands play Fri & Sat from 10pm–2am.

Rang Mahel, first floor, 3a Bangunan Mas Panchawarna, Batu 1, Jalan Tutong. Cosy and well-respected North Indian place; below is the *Regent's Den*, where cheaper Indian snacks are available. Both open daily 7.30am–10.30pm.

Restoran Intan Seri Taman Selera, 1–2 Bangunan Mas Panchawarna, Batu 1, Jalan Tutong. Popular, buffet-style Malay restaurant with a satay stall outside at night. Daily 9am–9.30pm.

Restoran Melayu Selasik, top floor, Bangunan Guru Guru Melayu, Jalan Sungei Kianggeh. Malay/Bruneian restaurant that verges on the chintzy, but boasts friendly staff and well-cooked dishes for $5. The house speciality, the *ambuyat* ($20 for two), is a sago mush which is served with fish, vegetables, shrimp and beef dishes; it's eaten by wrapping, candy-floss style, around chopsticks, and dipping it in *sambal belacan*, a spicy, pungent chilli and fermented prawn puree.

Sarasaya, Block C, Abdul Razak Complex, Gadong. Excellent Japanese restaurant, owned by and popular with Japanese expats.

Snoopy Corner & Fast Food, 108 Bangunan Guru Guru Melayu, Jalan Sungei Kianggeh. Small and simple Indian joint, producing good curries and a delicious chicken *biriyani*. Mon–Sat 6am–8.30pm, Sun 6am–1.30pm.

Sri Indah, 66 Jalan McArthur. Sweaty, cramped place churning out *murtabak*s and *roti*s that hit the spot. Daily 7am–9pm.

Szechuan Dynasty, Centrepoint, Abdul Razak Complex, Gadong. A truly elegant dining experience, though one which won't necessarily be to all tastes – the prevalence of chilli, pepper and ginger means the emphasis here is firmly on hot, spicy Chinese food. Daily noon–2.30pm & 6–10pm.

Takara, Centrepoint, Abdul Razak Complex, Gadong. Top-rank Japanese restaurant serving such classics as sashimi and *teppanyaki*; groups might consider dining the authentic Japanese way – cross-legged on the floor, in a *tatami* room. Daily 11.30am–2.30pm & 6–10pm.

Listings

Airlines British Airways, Lot 100, Jalan McArthur/Jalan Kianggeh (☎02/225871); Garuda Indonesia, 49 Wisma Jaya, Jalan Pemancha (☎02/235870); MAS, 144 Jalan Pemancha (☎02/224141); Philippine Airlines, first floor, Wisma Haji Fatimah, Jalan Sultan (☎02/224075, Royal Brunei Airlines, RBA Plaza, Jalan Sultan (☎02/242222); Singapore Airlines, 49–50 Jalan Sultan (☎02/244901); Thai Airways, fourth floor, Komplek Jalan Sultan, 51–55 Jalan Sultan (☎02/242991).

Airport For flight information call ☎02/331747.

American Express Unit 401–03, fourth floor, Shell Building, Jalan Sultan (Mon–Fri 8.30am–5pm, Sat 8.30am–1pm; ☎02/228314).

Banks and exchange Hong Kong Bank, Jalan Sultan; International Bank of Brunei, Jalan Roberts; Overseas Union Bank, RBA Plaza, Jalan Sultan; Standard Chartered Bank, Jalan Sultan. Banking hours are Mon–Fri 9am–3pm, Sat 9–11am.

Bookshops Best Eastern Books, G4 Teck Guan Plaza, Jalan Sultan, stocks a modest range of English-language books and magazines; Times Bookshop, first floor, Yayasan Complex, isn't bad either.

Car rental Avis, 16 Haji Daud Complex, Jalan Gadong (☎02/426345); Ellis, 3a Gadong Proprietors Bldg, Jalan Gadong (☎02/427237); Hertz, Unit 6, ground floor, Badiah Bldg, Jalan Tutong

(☎02/223355); Sukma, Lot 26, 69 Jalan Kiarong (☎02/427238); Syarikat Yuran Rent-A-Car, 144a Jalan Pemancha (☎02/224054).

Cinemas Borneo Theatre, on Jalan Roberts, and Bolkiah Theatre, on Jalan Sungei Kianggeh, both screen English-language movies; tickets around $4.

Embassies and consulates Australia, fourth floor, Teck Guan Plaza, Jalan Sultan (☎02/229435); Indonesia, Simpang 528, Lot 4498, Sungei Hanching Baru, Jalan Muara (☎02/330180); Malaysia, Lot 27 and 29, Simpang 396-39, Kampong Sungai Akar, Jalan Kebangsaan (☎02/3456520); Philippines, fourth and fifth floor, Badi'ah Bldg, Mile 1, Jalan Tutong (☎02/241465); Singapore, fifth floor, RBA Plaza, Jalan Sultan (☎02/227583); Thailand, no. 2, Simpang 682, Kampung Bunut, Jalan Tutong (☎02/653108); UK, Unit 2.01, Block D, Complex Yayasan Sultan Hassanal Bolkiah (☎02/222231); US, third floor, Teck Guan Plaza, Jalan Sultan (☎02/229670).

Hospital The Raja Isteri Pengiran Anak Saleha Hospital (RIPAS) is across Edinburgh Bridge on Jalan Putera Al-Muhtadee Billah (☎02/222366); or there's the 24hr Katong Clinic, 6, first floor, Block B, Abdul Razak Complex, Jalan Gadong (☎02/428715). For an ambulance, call ☎991.

Internet access *Cyber Café*, 8, Block A, Kiarong Complex, opposite the Kiarong mosque (daily noon–10pm).

Laundry Superkleen, opposite *Brunei Hotel*, Jalan Pemancha.

Pharmacies Khong Lin Dispensary, G3A, Wisma Jaya, Jalan Pemancha; Sentosa Dispensary, 42 Jalan Sultan.

Police Central Police Station, Jalan Stoney (☎02/222333).

Post office The GPO (Mon–Thurs & Sat 8am–4.30pm) is at the intersection of Jalan Elizabeth Dua and Jalan Sultan. Poste restante/general delivery is at the Money Order counter.

Telephones Telekom (daily 8am–midnight) is next to the GPO on Jalan Sultan; international calls can be made from here, or else buy a phonecard (in $5, $10, $20 or $50 denominations) and use a public booth.

Travel agents A number of travel agents around the city offer tours around the state; Sunshine Borneo Tours, Block C, Unit 1, second floor, Abdul Razak Complex, Jalan Gadong, opposite Centrepoint (☎02/441791, *www.sunshineborneo.com*); is among Brunei's most established agents, offering a wide range of tours including a two-night Ulu Temburong Park and homestay trips ($200). Other major firms include Freme Travel Services, fourth floor, Wisma Jaya, Jalan Pemancha (☎02/234277), who offer a three-hour city tour ($40) and a countryside tour ($50); J. Wildman Tours, PO Box 263, Salambigar BC 1515 (☎02/786987, *mrdmdg@brunet.bn*), who can take you to longhouses; and Borneo Outdoors, 3B Kiarong Apartments, Simpang 163, Jalan Kiarong (☎02/454764, *tjsjringrose@brunet.bn*) who specialize in the Tutong District.

Visa extensions At the Immigration Office (Mon–Thurs & Sat 7 45am–12.15pm & 1.45–4 30pm), Jalan Menteri Besar (☎02/383106).

Brunei Muara

Once you've exhausted all that Bandar has to offer, you may consider going further afield in **Brunei Muara** – the district of Brunei that contains the capital. Principal among the attractions that ring Bandar are **Kampung Parit** and **Bukit Shahbandar Forest Recreation Park**, the former an evocation of how Bruneians lived in the days before oil and concrete, the latter a sizeable nature reserve; both make for pleasant day-trips. For a glimpse of Brunei's countryside, head to the cultivated land that flanks Jalan Mulaut, though this requires a little determination; you may prefer simply to head for one of the area's several **beaches** or to the **Jerudong Park Playground**, a theme park which makes for an entertaining day out.

Kampung Parit

Some 15km west of Bandar along the inland road to Tutong, a mosque marks the turning southwards onto **Jalan Mulaut**. From here, it's a further 10km to a small show park, **Kampung Parit** (daily 8am–6pm; free), where a number of old-style Bornean dwellings have been erected to shed light on traditional Bruneian village life. Among the exhibits, which were built by local village artisans using only forest materials, is a replica of Kampung Ayer, the way it was before the advent of zinc and manufactured timber. The park's playground, picnic site and cluster of food stalls make it popular with Bruneian weekenders. Even so, access is not easy: unless you take a taxi, the only public transport is by Tutong-bound bus from the central bus terminus in Bandar; get off after 15km, at Jalan Mulaut, and make your own way from there.

North to Muara

Northeast of the city, beyond the Brunei Museum, Jalan Kota Batu stretches all the way up to **MUARA**, an oil town and Brunei's main port. The town was originally established to serve the now-defunct Brooketon Coal Mine, which was situated a few kilometres to the west. While there's nothing to bring you to Muara itself, nearby **Muara Beach** boasts a reasonable stretch of sand, as well as food stalls and changing rooms. At Serasa Beach, a few kilometres south of Muara, a recently built water-sports complex has facilities for sailing, windsurfing, water-skiing and fishing. **Buses** ($2) to Muara from the Bandar bus station pass along Jalan Kota Batu, skirting Sungei Brunei's north bank.

Crocodile Beach, Bukit Shahbandar and Jerudong Park Playground

From Muara, a highway more or less follows the northern coast 50km west to Tutong. A few kilometres from Muara, there's a turning to Pantai Meragang, known locally as **Crocodile Beach**, and considered by many to be the best in the area. The closest you can get to the beach by public transport is the intersection of the Bandar–Muara road and the Muara–Tutong Highway, from where the beach is a couple of kilometres west. You can reach this junction from Muara on the Berakas-bound bus ($1) from the main street behind Muara jetty (daily 8am–4pm; every 2hr), or from Bandar on the Muara-bound bus.

Around 20km west of Muara is the **Bukit Shahbandar Forest Recreation Park** (daily 8am–6pm; free), a compact area of acacia, pine and heath forest scored by unchallenging trails, and dotted with shelters and lookout points over Bandar and the South China Sea. Marking the entrance into the park is an information centre with displays on the surrounding terrain; it's also possible to **camp** here (free). Unfortunately, Bukit Shahbandar is tricky to reach; unless you're prepared to pay for a taxi, you'll have to take the bus to Berakas ($2) and try to hitch from there.

Several kilometres west of Bukit Shahbandar, on the road to Tutong, the district of **Jerudong** was long remarkable only for being the playground of the sultan, whose polo stadium and stables are located here. The 1994 opening of the **Jerudong Park Playground** (grounds daily 2pm–2am; games and rides Mon, Tues & Wed 5pm–midnight, Thurs & Sat 5pm–2am, Fri & Sun 2pm–midnight; during Ramadan daily 8pm–2am; free) on the occasion of the sultan's 48th birthday, changed all this. Conceived as a "lasting testimony to His Majesty's generosity to his *rakyat* (people)", the park has since been improved and expanded into a cracking funfair/adventure park whose scores of rides make it that rarest of treats, a Bruneian must-see. Although daily gates can average over a thousand, there's very little queuing for rides, and you'll find enough of interest to keep you amused for a long evening. For strong stomachs there's the **Boomerang** roller coaster or the heart-in-the-mouth vertical fall, the **giant drop**, while those of a more delicate constitution might enjoy the shooting galleries, boat rides, space-ride simulators, bumper cars and carousels. Beyond the excellent **hawker centre** that abuts the park are the yellow towers and green floodlights of the polo stadium.

To get to Jerudong Park Playground, catch the Jerudong **bus** from Bandar's bus station (daily: outward services 8am–4pm, return buses 9am–5pm; every 2hr; $3). To get back once buses have stopped in the early evening, you have to take a taxi (around $30) or try to share a taxi with some locals to cut the cost. There is no bus to Jerudong via Muara or Berakas.

Temburong District

Hilly **Temburong District** has been isolated from the rest of Brunei since 1884, when the strip of land to its west was ceded to Sarawak. Sparsely populated by Malay, Iban and Murut groups, this rainforest-dominated region is worth a visit to see the 500-square-kilometre **Ulu Temburong National Park**, with its canopy walkway and trails. While in the region, you can stay in the Malay and Murut **kampung** at Labu, or at the Iban **longhouse** in Amo. Temburong has over 60km of good roads, providing links into Sarawak – with Limbang (see p.420) to the west and Lawas (p.421) to the east.

Bangar

The starting point for all the above trips in Temburong is the district's only town, **BANGAR**. Standing on the Sungei Temburong, Bangar can only be reached by a rapid speedboat journey from Bandar (daily 6.30am to 4.30pm; every 45min; 40min; $7). The boats, known as flying coffins because of their shape, scream through narrow mangrove estuaries that are home to crocodiles and proboscis monkeys, swooping around corners and narrowly missing vessels travelling the opposite way, before shooting off down Sungei Temburong. The waterway makes for a beautiful journey passing by mangroves, their roots snaking out from the river banks. After all that, you'll find the town of Bangar is nothing much to write home about; its main street, which runs west from the jetty to the town mosque, is lined mainly by a handful of coffee shops and provision stores. Also on the main road, across the bridge from the jetty, is Bangar's grandest building, its new District Office, whose waterfront **café** is the town's most salubrious place to eat. There's nowhere to stay in Bangar and no local public buses except the daily Lawas Express (see box, below).

Amo C

From Bangar, a short taxi ride (20min; $15) brings you to **Amo C**, a five-door Iban **longhouse** (no phone) whose inhabitants offer it as a "homestay". There are always people around here to welcome you and invite you in (most of the young ones speak some English), and it's always best to take some small gifts for the children (while this isn't expected, it certainly makes you even more friends). The longhouse is just a few kilometres north of **Batang Duri** (see p.520) where boats leave for Ulu Temburong National Park; it's quite feasible to make a day-trip to the park and then spend the night at Amo C.

CROSSING INTO SARAWAK FROM TEMBURONG

If you're planning to cross from Temburong into Sarawak, either to **Limbang** or **Lawas**, you first have to make for the immigration post a few metres from the border beside the turning for Kampung Puni, 5km west of Bangar. Here your passport is checked and stamped; you then return to Bangar and await buses either way, which leave from the main road 200m from Bangar jetty. The eastbound **Lawas Express** bus ($10) leaves at 8.30am, getting to the Senokoh junction at 9am and arriving at Lawas – after a $1 river crossing – at around 10am. Going west towards Limbang, the bus gets to Bangar around 2pm, arriving at Limbang an hour later.

Unlike in Sarawak, where longhouses have rooms at the back for visitors, guests here sleep on the veranda, using simple mattresses. It's expected that you pay a modest sum towards your board and lodging (typically $5 per night, plus $3 for breakfast, $6 each for lunch and dinner).

Around the longhouse are some pleasant forest trails which the Ibans use for hunting; you need to hire a local as a guide if you want to explore these (day-trip $20–30; overnight $50). If you choose an overnight trip, ask the people at the longhouse to prepare food for you, or bring your own provisions.

Ulu Temburong National Park

Constituting a tenth of the area of Brunei, **Ulu Temburong National Park** is the finest example of the sultanate's successful forest protection policy (although the border region, to the south of the park, suffers some illegal logging from Malaysian companies). The park is reached by hiring a longboat from **Batang Duri** (see below), south of Bangar, up Sungei Temburong to the park headquarters; when the water level is especially shallow upriver you may have to get out and help pull the boat over rocks. En route, dense jungle cloaks the hills on either side and birds and monkeys abound in the trees, an atmospheric journey that sets the tone for the park itself.

The main attraction of the park is the **canopy walkway**, reached by an hour-long trek taking in a hanging bridge and a plankway, followed by a giddying climb up the stairs around a near-vertical, sixty-metre-high aluminium structure. The view from the top, of Brunei Bay to the north and Sarawak's Gunung Mulu Park to the south, is quite breathtaking. At this height, on a good day you can see in the trees four types of hornbill and gibbon, as well as numerous kinds of squirrel and small birds. According to a University of Brunei Darussalam survey, fifty species of birds use the fine "mist" netting around the walkway, and flying lizards, frogs and snakes feed regularly at ground level. Other activities in the park include chartering a small **longboat** (around $50 return) to go further upstream to a tree house where a few trails weave for short distances into the surrounding jungle, and **night walks**, conducted from time to time by the park office staff.

Along the trails or at the park HQ, you may well run into visiting scientists from the nearby Kuala Belalong Field Centre (not open to the public), established in 1991 to house the Brunei Rainforest Project. The primary goal of the project's research, involving seventy scientists, has been to document the biodiversity of the forest; the results show that the park contains many hitherto unknown species among its 170 different types of ferns, 700 tree species and tens of thousands of types of insect.

Practicalities

Batang Duri, the kampung from where longboats leave for the park, is a twenty-minute drive south from Bangar (a taxi here from Bangar costs around $15). At the village jetty, chartering a four-passenger longboat for the ninety-minute trip to the park costs $50; boatmen can be found at the jetty, or else ask at any of the houses close by.

The park headquarters (daily 8am–6.30pm), set on a spit of land at the junction of Sungei Temburong and an unnamed river, consists of a small office and a cramped area for eating, though food isn't yet served. Ten minutes' walk from the headquarters along a plankway above the river is the park's **accommodation**, seven wooden cabins nestling in the forest (④), comprising small rooms and simple bathrooms with cold showers. A new, expanded complex, which will have its own cafeteria, is expected to be finished some time in 2001.

To Labu

Twenty kilometres east of Bangar, on the road to Lawas in Sarawak, is the **Labu** region of Temburong. The area used to be largely comprised of rubber plantations until the bottom dropped out of the rubber market in the 1950s; today, paddy fields line the road on the north side, while the forest creeps down to the road on the other. Fifteen kilometres out of Bangar, you come to the **Peradayan Forest Reserve**, a small park containing a strenuous three-hour trek along an uphill plankway to the **Bukit Patoi** (310m), passing unusual rock formations and caves on the way. From the top of the hill there are great views across Brunei's spectacular, largely undisturbed rainforests south towards Sarawak. There are no amenities in the park, so bring your own food and drink.

Five kilometres further east, a signposted road to the right leads to **SENOKOH**, a Malay and Murut village comprising a few dozen stilt dwellings. In a rare move, the inhabitants of this kampung were able to buy their part of the former rubber estate from the Sultan to develop a **homestay** programme. The Muruts and Malays here take turns putting people up, thereby sharing the fun of having foreigners in their isolated kampung. You need to volunteer payment of around $10 per night and another $10 for a meal (an extra $5 if you want three meals a day). While there's little to do besides walking around the kampung, meeting people and having local fruit trees pointed out to you, a visit to a homestay like this allows a rare insight into the lifestyle of traditional, rural Bruneians; it's well worth making the effort to get here for that alone.

The only **bus** service through Labu is the Lawas Express, which stops on request at the forest reserve and Senokoh.

Tutong District

West of Muara District is wedge-shaped **Tutong District**, whose main settlement, **Tutong**, is a little over 40km west of Bandar. The wide range of mountains that runs down through Borneo from Sabah misses all but the Temburong District of Brunei; accordingly, the terrain of Tutong District never manages more than a gentle roll. This makes it ideal for the agriculturalism the government is presently trying to develop in the area (in preparation for the eventual demise of the oil reserves); the district contains coffee, tapioca and cinnamon plantations and a research station, at **Birau**, which develops new strains of cereal crops.

Though a coastal highway connects Tutong with Muara District, buses (daily from 8.30am–3pm; every 2hr; $3) from Bandar's Jalan Cator terminal only travel along the inland route along Jalan Tutong, which is skirted by scrublands and grasslands.

Tutong and around

Bruneian settlements don't come any sleepier than **TUTONG**, which has witnessed none of the oil-related development seen further west. Though it makes no real demands upon tourists' time, Tutong is an amiable enough place to break the trip between Sarawak and Bandar. The one street of any size, Jalan Enche Awang (buses drop you at the end beside the river), is flanked by rows of shophouses on one side, and on the other by the broad Sungei Tutong, its far bank massed with palm trees. Tutong has no places to stay, though it does have several **restaurants**: try the *Haji K-K-Koya* at Jalan Enche Awang 14, or the Chinese *Ho Yuen* at no. 12.

If you're in town on a Friday morning, you should visit the animated **Tamu Tutong**, which draws fruit and vegetable vendors from the interior of Brunei. The market takes place on a patch of land 1km south of central Tutong at Kampung Serambagaun, and is reached by walking out of town along Jalan Enche Awang and taking a left turn at the fork in the road. Ignoring this fork and continuing on across the coastal highway brings you, after fifteen minutes, to the best stretch of beach in the area, the peninsular **Pantai Seri Kenangan**, whose yellow sands divide Sungei Tutong from the South China Sea. Its name translates as "Memorable Beach", and though this may be rather stretching the point, the beach is pleasant enough, with a basic café. The royal family have a house nearby, which is less opulent than you may expect. If you want to take a peek at it, turn off at Tamu Tutong.

Tasek Merimbun

Tutong District's most impressive geographical feature is **Tasek Merimbun**, an S-shaped lake which is the largest in Brunei. Wooden boardwalks run from the attractively landscaped shore across to Pulau Jelandung, a tiny wooded island which has a profusion of **birdlife**, and pathways and picnic spots are to be found around the lake itself. Bird species easily spotted in the vicinity include egrets, falcons and eagles and a host of smaller ones. Unless you've rented a car, however, you aren't likely to get here, since the lake is around 25km inland from Tutong and not served by buses (the return taxi fare is well over $50). If you're driving, follow Jalan Tutong out of Bandar and after around 30km take the left turn to Lamunin. From there, signposts lead you to Tasek Merimbun, along roads that traverse glistening paddy fields. There is no accommodation at the lake.

Belait District

Belait District, west of Tutong and over Sungei Tutong, is oil and gas country, and has been the economic heart of the sultanate ever since the Seria Oil Field was established in 1931. The oil boom led directly to the rise of the region's two main coastal towns, **Seria** and **Kuala Belait**. Inland, though, it's a different story: down the fifty-kilometre-long **Labi Road**, a few Iban **longhouses** and tiny kampungs survive in the face of the tremendous changes brought about by the sultanate's wealth and the substantial population shift to the coast. Along with Temburong, this is the most serene and attractive part of Brunei to visit.

The coastal road west from Tutong is lined with flat scrubland, the sands along this stretch of Brunei's coast a brilliant white due to their high silica content. In time, as Brunei looks for moneymaking alternatives to its finite oil reserves, these sands could well spawn a glass industry. Around 20km west of Tutong at Kampung Sungei Liang, a turning south marks the start of **Labi Road**, which offers the chance to explore the interior (though there's no public transport along this road); continue west however, and you head towards Seria (see opposite).

To Labi and beyond

Just 500m from the northern end of Labi Road is the **Sungei Liang Forest Reserve**, whose thick lowland forest can be explored by following one of the well-kept walking trails leading from the lakes, information centre and picnic shelters clustered around the entrance. Several kilometres south is the bustling **Tamu Sungei Mau**, held on Sundays, while another 15km further along is the **Luagan Lalak Forestry Recreation Park**, whose freshwater swamp swells into a lake with the onset of the monsoon rains, flooding the area around it.

Some 35km south of Sungei Liang is **LABI** itself, a small agricultural settlement relying on harvests of durian and rambutan for its livelihood. Despite much speculative drilling, its surrounding hills have so far refused to yield any oil, though it was Labi's oil potential which led to the construction of the road here in the first place. There's nowhere to stay or eat in Labi. Shortly after Labi, the roads turns to a laterite track; around 300m along, a trail off to the east leads, after two hours, to **Wasai Rampayoh**, a large waterfall. Back on the track, continue south and you pass the first of several Iban longhouses here, **Rumah Mendaram Besar**, where around a hundred people live. Like most Iban longhouses in Brunei, this is a modern structure with electricity and running water. The people here are very friendly and happy to guide you along the trail to **Wasai Mendaram**, a small waterfall twenty minutes' walk away with a rock pool perfect for swimming.

A few kilometres further on, and around half-an-hour's drive from Labi, there is a second longhouse, **Rumah Teraja**, which marks the end of Labi Road, with only swamp forest beyond. The locals can point out a trail, which runs alongside a stream eastwards, to another small waterfall and on up to the largest hill in the region, Bukit Teraja, where there are spectacular views across Brunei and Sarawak; this route takes around 45 minutes. It is quite possible to visit these longhouses and some local travel agents (see p.517) are arranging homestays there. Another trip which can be made from Teraja longhouse is the **Marudi trail** across the border into Sarawak and down to **Marudi** (see p.423), a trek lasting four to six hours, for which you need to hire a local as a guide (expect to pay around $150 for the trip there and back). Though the final hour's walk into Marudi poses no particular difficulties, other parts of the path through steep rainforest can be hard to follow, and it's practically impassable in the wet season (Nov–Jan).

Seria

At the very centre of Brunei's oil and gas wealth is **SERIA**, 65km west of Bandar. Until oil was first discovered here at the start of the twentieth century, the area where the town now stands was nothing more than a malarial swamp, known locally as Padang Berawa, or "Wild Pigeon's Field"; an oil prospector in the area in 1926 reported that "walking here means really climbing and jumping over naked roots, and struggling and cutting through air roots of mangroves of more than man's height". It took until 1931 for S1, the sultanate's first well, to deliver commercially, after which Seria expanded rapidly, followed by offshore drilling in the 1950s, the construction of a gas-processing plant in 1955 and the opening of an oil refinery in 1983. Despite its mineral wealth, Seria remained an isolated settlement for several decades, unlinked by road with the capital. Driving along the shore on their way here four decades ago, Anthony Burgess and his wife "misjudged the table of the tides. We raced the incoming waves but lost. . . . Crocodiles, which had adapted themselves to shore life in order to prey on monkeys, lazily considered swimming across the *sungei* that joined the sea to examine us. The water had risen to our waists and was still rising. Lynne, always courageous, stripped and swam to the nearest kampung. Twenty men produced a rope and hauled us out. This sort of thing had happened before." At this time, Shell were still employing crocodile hunters to safeguard drilling sites.

As you approach from Tutong, you see numbers of small oil wells called "nodding donkeys" because of their rocking motion, though they actually bear a closer resemblance to praying mantises. Around the town are green-roofed housing units and bungalows, constructed by Brunei Shell for their employees, while on the waterfront is the **Billionth Barrel Monument**, whose interlocking arches celebrate the huge productivity of the first well.

Practicalities

Seria town centre is a hectic place, dominated by the Plaza Seria shopping mall, across from the **bus station** where the regular buses from Bandar (hourly 7am–3pm) terminate. Though there are no places to stay, budget **restaurants** and coffee shops abound.

On Jalan Sultan Omar Ali (left of the plaza when viewed from the bus station), you'll find the *Universal Café* at no. 11, a sleepy retreat that's good for coffee. Next door, the air-con *Restoran Sayang Merah* sells Asian and Western dishes such as spaghetti, Spanish omelettes and T-bone steaks. For a more upmarket meal, try the *New China Restaurant* in Plaza Seria.

Kuala Belait and Kuala Balai

It's a little under 20km from Seria to the neighbouring oil town of **KUALA BELAIT**. There's nothing very enticing about the place, but with all buses to and from Miri in Sarawak stopping here, it's a spot you may have to visit. The town is ringed by suburban development that caters for the expat community, while central Kuala Belait is characterized by the many workshops and businesses that the local oil industry has spawned. If Kuala Belait seems sleepy today, pity the poor expats consigned to its drilling stations in the early part of the twentieth century. A contemporary rhyme encapsulated the torpor and isolation they felt:

Work of course gets sometimes weary
Up in Belait
And the evenings long and dreary
Up in Belait
But when again New Year draws nigh
Let's go to Miri, they all cry.

Practicalities
Buses stop at the intersection of Jalan Bunga Raya and Jalan McKerron, across which is the town's **taxi** stand. There are just two **hotels**, one of which, *Hotel Sentosa* (☎03/334342; ⑤) at 93 Jalan McKerron, has capacious, well-appointed and welcoming rooms. The alternative is the slightly less expensive *Sea View Hotel* (☎03/332651; ④), 3–4km back along the coastal road towards Seria. You can **change money** in town at the Hong Kong Bank (Mon–Fri 9am–3pm, Sat 9–11am).

Jalan McKerron houses several good **restaurants**, the best of which are the tastefully decorated *Buccaneer Steakhouse* at no. 94, whose mid-priced international food is aimed squarely at the expat market; and the *Akhbar Restaurant*, at no. 99a, with a Malay and North Indian menu which includes excellent *dosai*. Of Kuala Belait's handful of other restaurants, two in particular, the first-floor *Healthy Way Tandoori* at 30 Jalan Pretty (the town's main drag, a block east of McKerron), and Jalan Bunga Raya's *Orchid Room*, are worth a visit – the former for its storming *naans*, *tikka masalas* and *lassis*, the latter for it's good-value three-course Western set lunches (Mon–Fri; $5).

CROSSING WEST INTO SARAWAK

Buses to **Miri** (see p.415) in Sarawak leave Kuala Belait's bus station on the main street at 7.30am, 9.30am, 11am, 1.30pm and 3.30pm; the fare ($10) includes the ferry across Sungei Belait and the connecting Sarawakian bus over the border. After going through Brunei customs you board a Malaysian bus for the short trip to the Malaysian customs and on to Miri. **Taxi** drivers charge around $100 for a full car (four passengers) to Miri, though you should be able to bargain them down substantially. It's worth avoiding the trip to Miri on a Friday afternoon when there are often long queues at the border resulting from Bruneians heading there for weekend shopping and for its lavish hotels.

Up Sungei Belait: Kuala Balai

Kuala Belait squats on the eastern bank of calm **Sungei Belait**, and motorboats moored at the back of the central market on Jalan McKerron can take you upriver – it costs at least $150 return for six passengers. However, unless it's the river travel itself you're interested in, there's very little reason to make the trip.

After around forty minutes, **KUALA BALAI** comes into sight. Once a thriving centre for sago processing, Kuala Balai has seen its population dwindle from hundreds to just a handful, as its inhabitants have left in search of work on the oil fields; it's now little more than a ghost town. As you approach Balai, look out for the wooden cage of human skulls on stilts over the river – a grim remnant of Borneo's head-hunting days.

travel details

Buses

Bandar Seri Begawan to: Jerudong (5 daily; 40min); Muara (every 30min until 4.30pm; 30min); Seria (hourly until 3pm; 1hr 45min); Tutong (hourly until 3pm; 1hr).

Kuala Belait to: Miri (5 daily; 2hr 30min); Seria (every 30min until 6.30pm; 45min).

Muara to: Berakas (5 daily; 20min).

Seria to: Bandar Seri Begawan (every 45min until 3pm; 1hr 45min); Kuala Belait (every 30min; 45min); Miri (5 daily; 2hr).

Ferries

Bandar Seri Begawan to: Bangar (11 daily; 40min); Labuan (4 daily; 1hr 30min); Lawas (1 daily; 2hr); Limbang (10 daily; 30min).

Muara to: Lawas (1 daily; 2hr); Pulau Labuan (4 daily; 1hr 30min).

Flights

Bandar Seri Begawan to: Kota Kinabalu (11 weekly; 40min); Kuala Lumpur (3 daily; 2hr 30min); Kuching (6 weekly; 1hr); Singapore (3 daily; 2hr).

CHAPTER NINE

SINGAPORE

Singapore is certainly the handiest city I ever saw, as well planned and carefully executed as though built entirely by one man. It is like a big desk, full of drawers and pigeon-holes, where everything has its place, and can always be found in it.

W. Hornaday, 1885.

Despite the immense changes the past century has wrought upon the tiny island of Singapore, natural historian William Hornaday's succinct appraisal is as valid today as it was in 1885. Since gaining full independence from Malaysia in 1965, this absorbing city-state, just 580 square kilometres in size and linked by two causeways to the southern tip of Malaysia, has been transformed from a sleepy colonial backwater to a pristine, futuristic shrine to consumerism. It's one of Southeast Asia's most accessible destinations, its downtown areas dense with towering skyscrapers and gleaming shopping malls, while sprawling new towns ring the centre, with their own separate communities and well-planned facilities. Yet visitors prepared to peer beneath the state's squeaky-clean surface will discover a profusion of age-old buildings, values and traditions that have survived in the face of profound social and geographical change. And the island has not been overwhelmed by development – as you make your way around the island, you're struck immediately by Singapore's abundance of parks, nature reserves, and lush, tropical greenery. Inevitably, given its geographical position, the state is seen by most people as a mere stopover and its compactness means you can gain an impression of the place in just a few hours. However, a lengthier stay is easily justified. Quite apart from enjoying its cultural highlights, you'll find several days spent in Singapore invaluable for arranging financial transfers, seeing to medical problems and generally gathering strength before continuing on to the region's less affluent – and often more demanding – areas.

Singapore's progress over the past three decades has been remarkable. Lacking any noteworthy natural resources, its early prosperity was based on a vigorous **free trade** policy, put in place in 1819 when Sir Stamford Raffles first set up a British trading post here. In the twentieth century, mass industrialization bolstered the economy, and today the state boasts the world's second busiest port after Rotterdam, minimal unemployment, and a superefficient infrastructure. Almost the entire population has been moved from unsanitary kampungs into swish new apartments, and the average per capita income is over US$20,000.

ACCOMMODATION PRICE CODES

Throughout the Singapore and Brunei chapters we've used the following **price codes** to denote the cheapest available room for two people. Single occupancy should cost less than double, though this is not always the case. Some guesthouses provide dormitory beds, for which the dollar price is given.

① Under $25	④ $61–100	⑦ $201–300
② $26–40	⑤ $101–150	⑧ $301–400
③ $41–60	⑥ $151–200	⑨ $401 and above

Yet none of this was achieved without considerable compromise – indeed, the state's detractors claim it has sold its soul in return for prosperity. Put simply, at the core of the Singapore success story is an unwritten bargain between its government and population, which stipulates the loss of a certain amount of personal freedom, with the government orchestrating the economy and society, in return for levels of affluence and comfort that would have seemed unimaginable thirty years ago. Lee Kuan Yew (the long-serving former prime minister, now "senior minister") has gone on record as saying, "When you are hungry, when you lack basic services, freedom, human rights and democracy do not add up to much." Outsiders often bridle at these sentiments, and it's true that some of the regulations in force here can seem extreme: neglecting to flush a public toilet, jaywalking and eating on the subway all carry sizeable fines, while chewing gum has been outlawed. The case of American teenager, Michael Fay, caught the world's headlines in early 1994, when he was given four strokes of the *rotan* (cane) for vandalizing cars. But far more telling is the fact that these punishments are rarely, if ever, inflicted, as Singaporeans have learned not to break the law. The population, trusting the wisdom of its leaders, seems generally content to acquiesce to a **paternalistic** form of government that critics describe as soft authoritarianism. Consequently, Singaporeans have earned a reputation for cowed, unquestioning subservience, a view that can be overstated, but which isn't without an element of truth. The past has taught Singaporeans that, if they follow their government's lead, they reap the benefits. In addition, they take a pride in their country that occasionally extends to smugness – witness the huge celebrations that accompany National Day, Singapore's annual collective pat on the back. Yet there is good reason to be proud: Singapore is a clean, safe place to visit, its amenities are second to none and its public places are smoke-free and hygienic. And as the nation's youth (who don't remember a time before the improvements they take for granted) begin to find a voice, public life should become increasingly, if gradually, more liberal and democratic.

Whatever the political ramifications of the state's economic success, of more relevance to the seven million annual visitors to Singapore is the fact that improvements in living conditions have been shadowed by a steady loss of the state's **heritage**, as historic buildings and streets are bulldozed to make way for shopping centres. Singapore undoubtedly lacks the personality of some Southeast Asian cities, but its reputation for being sterile and sanitized is unfair. Shopping on state-of-the-art Orchard Road is undoubtedly a major draw for many tourists, but under the long shadows cast by giddy towers and spires you still find the dusty temples, fragrant medicinal shops, and colonial buildings of old Singapore, neatly divided into enclaves, each home to a distinct ethnic culture. Much of Singapore's fascination springs from its **multicultural population**: of the 3.87 million inhabitants, 77 percent are Chinese (a figure reflected in the predominance of Chinese shops, restaurants and temples across the island), 14 percent Malay, and 7 percent Indian, the remainder being from other ethnic groups. This diverse ethnic mix textures the whole island, and often turns a ten-minute walk into what seems like a hop from one country to another. One intriguing by-product of this ethnic melting pot is **Singlish** (see p.653), or Singaporean English, a patois which blends English with the speech patterns, exclamations and vocabulary of Chinese and Malay.

The entire state is compact enough to be explored exhaustively in just a few days. Forming the core of downtown Singapore is the **Colonial District**, around whose public buildings and lofty cathedral the island's British residents used to promenade. Each surrounding enclave has its own distinct flavour, from the aromatic spice stores of **Little India**, to the tumbledown backstreets of **Chinatown**, where it's still possible to find calligraphers and fortune tellers, or the **Arab Quarter**, whose cluttered stores sell fine cloths and silks. **North** of the city, you'll find the country's two nature reserves – Bukit Timah Nature Reserve and the Central Catchment Area – and the splendid

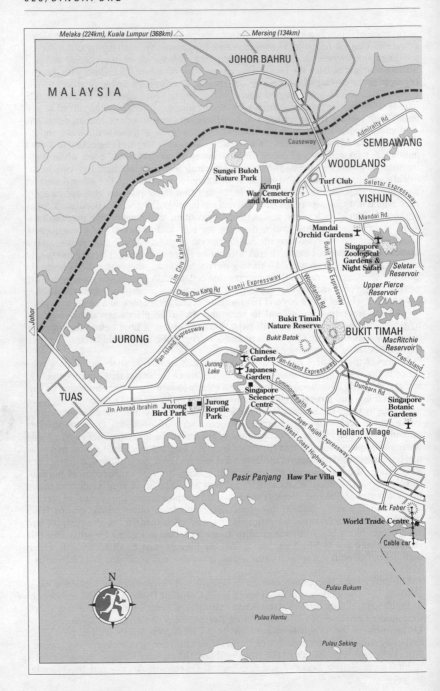

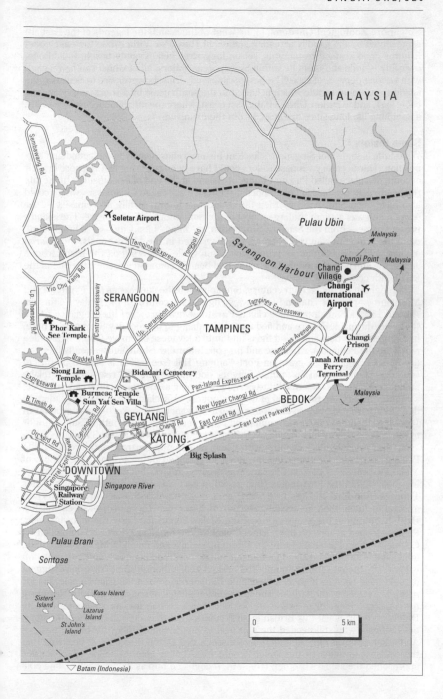

MALAYSIA

Sembawang Rd

✈ Seletar Airport

Tampines Expressway

Pongol Rd

Serangoon Harbour

Pulau Ubin

Malaysia ✈

Changi Point   Malaysia ✈

Changi Village ●

Changi International Airport ✈

Yio Chu Kang Rd

L.p. Thomson Rd

SERANGOON

U/p. Serangoon Rd

Central Expressway

Tampines Expressway

TAMPINES

🛕 **Phor Kark See Temple**

Braddell Rd

Tampines Avenue

■ **Changi Prison**

Siong Lim Temple 🛕

Bidadari Cemetery ■

Expressway

Pan-Island Expressway

Tanah Merah Ferry Terminal ■

🛕 **Burmese Temple**

B. Timah Rd

◆ **Sun Yat Sen Villa**

Serangoon Expressway

New Upper Changi Rd

BEDOK

Malaysia ↶

GEYLANG

Geylang   Changi Rd

East Coast Rd

East Coast Parkway

Orchard Rd

Central Expressway

KATONG

DOWNTOWN

■ **Big Splash**

Singapore Railway Station

Singapore River

Pulau Brani

Sentosa

Sisters' Island

Kusu Island

Lazarus Island

St John's Island

0 ————————— 5 km

▽ *Batam (Indonesia)*

Singapore Zoological Gardens. In the **west** of the island, the legends of the East are represented by the gaudily arresting statues of **Haw Par Villa**, while the **east coast** features good seafood restaurants, set on long stretches of sandy beach. In addition, over fifty islands and islets lie within Singaporean waters, all of which can be reached with varying degrees of ease. The best offshore day-trips, however, are to **Sentosa**, the island amusement arcade which is linked to the south coast by a short causeway (and cable car), and to **Pulau Ubin**, off the east coast, where the inhabitants continue to live a kampung life long since eradicated from the mainland.

Some history

What little is known of Singapore's ancient history relies heavily upon legend and supposition. Third-century Chinese sailors could have been referring to Singapore in their account of a place called Pu-Luo-Chung, or "island at the end of a peninsula". In the late thirteenth century, Marco Polo reported seeing a place called Chiamassie, which could also have been Singapore: by then the island was known locally as Temasek – "sea town" – and was a minor trading outpost of the Sumatran Srivijaya empire. The island's present name – from the Sanskrit **Singapura**, meaning "Lion City" – was first recorded in the sixteenth century, when a legend narrated in the Malay annals, the *Sejarah Melayu*, told how a Sumatran prince saw a lion while sheltering on the island from a storm; the annals reported that the name had been in common use since the end of the fourteenth century.

Throughout the fourteenth century, Singapura felt the squeeze as the Ayuthaya and Majapahit empires of Thailand and Java struggled for control of the Malay Peninsula. Around 1390, a Sumatran prince called **Paramesvara** threw off his allegiance to the Javanese Majapahit Empire and fled from Palembang to present-day Singapore. There, he murdered his host and ruled the island until a Javanese offensive forced him to flee north, up the Peninsula, where he and his son, **Iskandar Shah**, subsequently founded the Melaka Sultanate. A grave on Fort Canning Hill (see p.558) is said to be that of Iskandar Shah, though its authenticity is doubtful. With the rise of the Melaka Sultanate, Singapore devolved into a peripheral fishing settlement of little consequence; a century or so later, the arrival of the Portuguese in Melaka forced Malay leaders to flee southwards to modern-day Johor Bahru for sanctuary. A Portuguese account of 1613 described the razing of an unnamed Malay outpost at the mouth of Sungei Johor to the ground, after which began two centuries of historical limbo for Singapore.

By the late eighteenth century, with China opening up for trade with the West, the British East India Company felt the need to establish outposts along the Straits of Melaka to protect its interests. Penang was secured in 1786, but with the Dutch expanding their rule in the East Indies (Indonesia), a port was needed further south. Enter **Thomas Stamford Raffles** (see p.554) who, in 1818 was authorized by the governor-general of India, then lieutenant-governor of Bencoolen (in Sumatra), to establish a **British colony** at the southern tip of the Malay Peninsula. Early the following year, Raffles stepped ashore on the northern bank of the Singapore River accompanied by Colonel William Farquhar, former resident of Melaka and fluent in Malay. At the time, inhospitable swampland and tiger-infested jungle covered Singapore, and its population is generally thought to have numbered around 150, although some historians suggest it could have been as high as a thousand. Raffles recognized the island's potential for providing a deep-water harbour, and immediately struck a treaty with **Abdul Rahman**, *temenggong* (chieftain) of Singapore, establishing a British trading station there. The Dutch were furious at this British incursion into what they considered their territory, but Raffles – who still needed the approval of the Sultan of Johor for his outpost, as Abdul Rahman was only an underling – disregarded Dutch sensibilities. Realizing that the Sultan's loyalties to the Dutch would make such approval impossible, Raffles approached the sultan's brother, **Hussein**, recognized him as the true sultan, and concluded a second treaty with both the *temenggong* and His Highness the Sultan Hussein Mohammed Shah. The Union Jack was raised, and Singapore's future as a free trading post was set.

With its **strategic position** at the foot of the Straits of Melaka and below the South China Sea, and with no customs duties on imported or exported goods, Singapore's expansion was meteoric. The population had reached ten thousand by the time of the first census in 1824, with Malays, Chinese, Indians and Europeans arriving in search of work as coolies and merchants. In 1822, Raffles set about drawing up the demarcation lines that divide present-day Singapore. The area south of the Singapore River was earmarked for the Chinese; a swamp at the mouth of the river was filled and the commercial district established there. Muslims were settled around the Sultan's Palace in today's Arab Quarter. The Singapore of those times was a far cry from the pristine city of the present. "There were thousands of rats all over the district" wrote Abdullah bin Kadir, scribe to Stamford Raffles, "some almost as large as cats. They were so big that they used to attack us if we went out walking at night and many people were knocked over."

In 1824, Sultan Hussein and the *temenggong* were bought out, and Singapore ceded outright to the British. Three years later, the fledgling state united with Penang and Melaka (now under British rule) to form the **Straits Settlements**, which became a British Crown Colony in 1867. For forty years the island's *laissez-faire* economy boomed, though life was chaotic, and disease rife. More and more immigrants poured into the island; by 1860 the population had reached eighty thousand, with each ethnic community bringing its attendant cuisines, languages and architecture. Arabs, Indians, Javanese and Bugis all came, but most populous of all were the **Chinese** from the southern provinces of China, who settled quickly, helped by the clan societies (*kongsis*) already establishing footholds on the island. The British, for their part, erected impressive Neoclassical theatres, courts and assembly halls, and in 1887 Singapore's most quintessentially British establishment, the *Raffles Hotel*, opened for business.

In 1877, Henry Ridley began his one-man crusade to introduce the **rubber plant** into Southeast Asia, a move which further bolstered Singapore's importance as the island soon became the world centre of rubber exporting. By the end of the nineteenth century, the opening of the Suez Canal and the advent of the steamship had consolidated Singapore's position at the hub of international trade in the region, with the port becoming a major staging post on the Europe–East Asia route. This status was further enhanced by the slow but steady drawing of the Malay Peninsula under British control – a process begun with the Treaty of Pangkor (see p.623) in 1874 and completed in 1914 – which meant that Singapore gained further from the mainland's tin- and rubber-based economy. Between 1873 and 1913 trade increased eightfold, a trend which continued well into the twentieth century.

Singapore's Asian communities found their political voice in the 1920s. In 1926, the Singapore Malay Union was established, and four years later, the Malayan Communist Party (MCP), backed by local Chinese. But grumblings of independence had risen to no more than a faint whisper before an altogether more immediate problem reared its head.

In December 1941, the Japanese had bombed Pearl Harbour and invaded the Malay Peninsula. Less than two months later they were at the northern end of the causeway, a direction from which "Fortress Singapore" had not been prepared for an attack – Singapore's artillery were pointed south from what is now Sentosa Island. On February 15, 1942, the **fall of Singapore** (which the Japanese then renamed Syonan, or "Light of the South") was complete. Winston Churchill called the British surrender "the worst disaster and the largest capitulation in British history"; ironically, it later transpired that the Japanese forces had been outnumbered and their supplies hopelessly stretched immediately prior to the surrender.

Three and a half years of brutal **Japanese** rule ensued, during which thousands of civilians were executed in vicious anti-Chinese purges and Europeans were either herded into **Changi Prison** or marched up the Peninsula to work on Thailand's infamous "Death Railway". Less well known is the vicious campaign, known as Operation Sook Ching, mounted by the military police force, or *Kempeitai*, during which upwards of 25,000 Chinese males between 18 and 50 years of age were shot dead at Punggol and Changi beaches as enemies to the Japanese. Following the destruction of Hiroshima and Nagasaki in 1945, Singapore was passed back into British hands, but things were never to be the same. Singaporeans now wanted a say in the government of the island, and in 1957 the British government agreed to the establishment of an elected, 51-member legislative assembly. Full internal **self-government** was achieved in May 1959, when the **People's Action Party** (PAP), led by Cambridge law graduate **Lee Kuan Yew**, won 43 of the 51 seats. Lee became Singapore's first prime minister, and quickly looked for the security of a merger with neighbouring Malaya (what's now called Peninsular Malaysia). For its part (despite reservations about aligning with Singapore's predominantly Chinese population) anti-Communist Malaya feared that extremists within the PAP would turn Singapore into a Communist base, and accordingly preferred to have the state under its wing.

In 1963, Singapore combined with Malaya, Sarawak and British North Borneo (modern-day Sabah) to form the **Federation of Malaysia**. The alliance, though, was an uneasy one, and within two years Singapore was asked to leave the federation, in the face of outrage in Kuala Lumpur at the PAP's attempts to break into Peninsular politics in 1964. Hours after announcing Singapore's **full independence**, on August 9, 1965, a tearful Lee Kuan Yew went on national TV and described the event as "a moment of anguish". One hundred and forty-six years after Sir Stamford Raffles had set Singapore on the world map, the tiny island, with no natural resources of its own, faced the prospect of being consigned to history's bottom drawer of crumbling colonial ports.

Instead, Lee's personal vision and drive transformed Singapore into an Asian economic heavyweight, though this position was achieved at a price. Heavy-handed **censorship** of the media was introduced, and even more disturbing was the government's attitude towards **political opposition**. When the opposition Worker's Party won a by-election in 1981, the candidate, J.B. Jeyaretham, found himself charged with several criminal offences, and chased through the Singaporean law courts for the next decade. The archaic **Internal Security Act**, which grants the power to detain without trial anyone the government deems a threat to the nation, kept political prisoner Chia Thye Poh under lock and key from 1966 until 1989 for allegedly advocating violence. Singapore's population policies, too, have brought charges of social engineering from foreign critics. These measures began in the early 1970s, with a **birth-control campaign** which proved so successful that it had to be reversed: the 1980s saw the introduction of the "Go For Three" project, which offered tax incentives for those having more than two children in an attempt to boost the national – and some say, more specifically the Chinese Singaporean – birth rate. Lee Kuan Yew also made clear his conviction that Singapore's educated elite should intermarry in order that they might create highly intelligent future generations.

At other times, Singapore tries so hard to reshape itself that it falls into self-parody. "We have to pursue this subject of fun very seriously if we want to stay competitive in the twenty-first century" was the reaction of government minister George Yeo, when confronted with the fact that some foreigners find Singapore dull. The government's annual courtesy campaign, which in 1996 urged the population to hold lift doors open for neighbours and prevent their washing from dripping onto passers-by below, appears equally risible to outsiders. Whether Singaporeans will continue to suffer their government's foibles remains to be seen. Adults beyond a certain age remember how things were before independence and, more importantly, before the existence of the island's metro system, housing projects and saving schemes, and so particularly appreciate how the standard of living has improved. But their children and grandchildren have no such perspective, and telltale signs – presently nothing more extreme than putting one's feet up on metro train seats and jaywalking – suggest that the government can expect more **dissent** in future years. Already a substantial brain drain is afflicting the country, as skilled Singaporeans choose to move abroad in the pursuit of heightened civil liberties.

The man charged with leading Singapore into the new millennium is **Goh Chok Tong**, who became prime minister upon Lee's retirement in 1990. Goh has made it clear that he favours a more open form of government, though whether he will be able to break the mould set by Lee – who still looms over the political scene in his role as senior minister, and whose son, Brigadier-General Lee Hsien Loong, is deputy prime minister – remains open to question. Recent events do suggest that Goh has a mandate for change. Though in 1991's elections he suffered the relative setback of seeing an unprecedented four opposition members voted into parliament, in the campaign of December 1996 however (which the PAP had won even before the polling stations opened, as opposition candidates contested fewer than half of the seats), he clawed back two of these seats – partly thanks to insinuations that constituencies failing to return their PAP candidate would drop down the waiting list for housing-estate renovations. Singapore's next general elections are due by mid-2002.

Arrival and information

The diamond-shaped island of Singapore is 42km from east to west at its widest points, and 23km from north to south. The downtown city areas huddle at the southern tip of the diamond, radiating out from the mouth of the **Singapore River**. Two northeast–southwest roads form a dual spine to the central area, both of them traversing the river. One starts out as **North Bridge Road**, crosses the river and becomes **South Bridge Road**; the other begins as **Victoria Street**, becomes Hill Street and skirts Chinatown as **New Bridge Road**.

The island has developed a system of expressways, of which the main ones are the east–west **Pan Island Expressway** and the **East Coast Parkway/Ayer Rajah Expressway**, both of which run from Changi to Jurong, and the **Bukit Timah Expressway**, which branches off north from the Pan Island Expressway at Bukit Timah new town, running north to Woodlands. At Woodlands, the road (shadowed by the train from the railway station near Chinatown) crosses the 1056-metre **causeway** linking Singapore with Johor Bahru in Malaysia (see p.325). A **second causeway**, at Singapore's far western end, links Johor with the Ayer Raja Expressway.

Most people's first glimpse of Singapore is of Changi Airport in the east of the island, and a telling glimpse it is. Its two terminals, connected by the Skytrain monorail, are modern, efficient and air-conditioned – a Singapore in microcosm. Other arrivals are from over the causeway from the Malaysian city of Johor Bahru, or by boat from the Indonesian archipelago. Wherever you arrive, the well-oiled public transport infrastructure, including a **bus** network and **MRT** metro **trains**, means that you'll have no problem getting into the centre.

By air
Changi Airport is at the far eastern end of Singapore, 16km from the city centre. As well as duty-free shops, moneychanging and left-luggage facilities, the airport boasts a 24-hour post office and telephone service, hotel reservations counters, day rooms for a quick snooze, saunas, business centres and Internet cafés. There are also **car rental**

MOVING ON FROM SINGAPORE

For Changi Airport flight enquiries, and the addresses and telephone numbers of airlines, travel agencies and the Malay, Indonesian and Thai consulates in Singapore, see "Listings", p.610.

BY TRAIN

There are air-conditioned trains **to KL** via JB from Singapore's train station at 8am, 2.45pm and 10.10pm, with an additional service at 6.10pm which terminates in JB. You can make seat reservations up to one month in advance of departure at the station's information kiosk (daily 8.30am–2.30pm & 3–7pm; ☎2225165).

BY BUS AND TAXI

To Malaysia: the easiest way across the causeway is to get the **#170** JB-bound bus from the Ban San Terminal (daily 6am–12.30am; $1.20) or the plusher air-con **Singapore–Johore Express** (daily 6.30am–11.30pm; $2.40), both of which leave every ten minutes or so and take around an hour (including border formalities) to reach their destination. These buses terminate at JB's bus station, though it's easier to reach the town centre by leaving the bus at the causeway. From the taxi stand next to the Ban San Terminal, a shared taxi to JB (seating four passengers) costs $30. The Singapore–KL Express leaves from the Ban San Terminal daily at 9am, 1pm, 5pm and 10pm ($23). For other destinations in west Malaysia, go to the Lavender Street Terminal or the Golden Mile Complex – the former offers the greater choice, as the operators at the Golden Mile focus more on destinations in Thailand. Buses to Butterworth ($29), Penang ($30), Kota Bharu ($30) and Ipoh ($27) tend to leave in the late afternoon; those to Melaka ($11), Mersing ($11) and Kuantan ($17) depart in the early morning and afternoon. For KL ($17) there are both morning and night departures. Book as far in advance as possible – operators at the terminal include Pan Malaysia Express (☎2947034), Hasry Express (☎2949306), Malacca–Singapore Express (☎2935915) and Transnational Travel (☎2947034). It's slightly cheaper to travel to JB and then catch an onward bus from the bus terminal there – though it still pays to make an early start from Singapore.

---

agencies at the airport (see "Listings", p.610), though you'd be advised not to drive around Singapore (see "Transport", p.537, for better alternatives). For **food**, there's a *McDonald's*, a *Swenson's* ice-cream parlour and, in Terminal One's basement, a food centre – the cheapest and most authentically Singaporean option for a bite. That said, the likelihood is that you'll barely get the chance to take in the place at all – baggage comes through so quickly at Changi that you can be on a bus or in a taxi within fifteen minutes of arrival. Before you leave the building, be sure to pick up one of the free maps and weekly *This Week Singapore* guides that the Singapore Tourism Board leaves at the airport.

Since Singapore's underground train system doesn't extend as far as the airport, you'll have to take either a taxi or a public bus into the centre. The **bus** departure points in the basements of both terminals are well signposted – but make sure you've got the right money before you leave the concourse, as Singapore bus drivers don't give change; take the #36 (daily 6am–midnight; every 10min; $1.50). The bus heads west to Stamford Road, before skirting the southern side of Orchard Road. Ask the driver to give you a shout at the old Capitol Cinema stop for Beach Road, or at the YMCA stop, where you need to cross over Bras Basah Park if you are staying in Bencoolen Street.

Taxis from the airport levy a $3 surcharge on top of the fare. Again, pick-up points are well signposted: a trip into downtown Singapore costs around $15 and takes twen-

To Thailand: buses leave early morning from Beach Road's Golden Mile Complex. You can buy a ticket all the way to Bangkok (though it may be cheaper just to buy one as far as Hat Yai and pay for the rest of the journey in Thai currency once there). Fares to Hat Yai start at around $30, while Bangkok will set you back around $80. Try Phya Travel Service (☎2936692) or Grassland Express (☎2921166), and don't forget to allow two working days for securing a Thai visa (needed for stays of over 15 days).

BY BOAT

To Malaysia: From Changi Point (bus #2 to Changi Village), bumboats run to **Kampung Pengerang**, on the southeastern tip of Johor (for access to the beach resort of Desaru; p.331) boats leave when they're full (daily 7am–4pm; $5 one way). A service departs for **Tanjung Belungkor**, also in Johor, daily at 7.30am, 11.30am, 4pm and 8pm from the new Changi Ferry Terminal (bus #2 to Changi Village, and then a taxi). Run by Ferrylink (☎5453600), the service costs $20 one way, or $32 return; check in one hour before departure. Finally, from the Tanah Merah Ferry Terminal (bus #35 from Bedok MRT), there's an 8.30am service (March–Oct daily except Wed; $168 return) to **Tioman Island** (p.334). Information and tickets from Auto Batam (☎5427105). Again, check-in is one hour before departure.

To Indonesia: Boats to **Batam** in the Riau archipelago depart throughout the day from the World Trade Centre (7.45am–6.20pm; $17 one way; info and tickets from Channel Holidays; ☎2702228), docking at Sekupang, from where you take a taxi to Hangnadim airport for internal Indonesian flights. There are also four boats a day from the Tanah Merah Ferry Terminal ($49 one way; info and tickets from Dino Shipping; ☎2769722) to **Tanjung Pinang** on Pulau Bintan, from where cargo boats leave three times a week for Pekanbaru in Sumatra. There are also boat services from Kijang Port, south of Tanjung Pinang, to Jakarta.

BY AIR

There are **flights** from Changi Airport to, among other Malaysian destinations, KL, Melaka, Kota Kinabalu and Kuching. A departure tax of $15 is levied on all flights out of the island. If you're planning to head for either Malaysia or Indonesia by air, it's often quite a bit cheaper to go to JB or Batam, the nearest Indonesian island, and buy a flight from there.

ty minutes or so. Another option is to take a **MaxiCab** shuttle into town. These six-seater taxis, equipped to take wheelchairs, depart every fifteen minutes, or when full, and will take you to any hotel in the city for a flat fare of $7 (children $5).

By road

Drivers using the second causeway from Johor arrive in Singapore along the Ayer Rajah Expressway in the west of the island. All buses and trains from Malaysia use the old causeway from JB into Woodlands town in the north, with the **buses** stopping at one of three terminals in Singapore. Local buses from JB arrive at **Ban San Terminal** at the junction of Queen and Arab streets, from where a two-minute walk along Queen Street, followed by a left along Rochor Road, takes you to Bugis MRT station. Buses from elsewhere in **Malaysia** and **from Thailand** terminate at one of two sites, Lavender Street Terminal and the Golden Mile Complex. **Lavender Street Terminal**, at the corner of Lavender Street and Kallang Bahru, is around five-minutes' walk from Lavender MRT; alternatively, for the guesthouses of Bencoolen Street, walk a short way northwest until you come to the eastern end of Jalan Besar, and hop on bus #139. In addition, bus #145 passes the Lavender Street Terminal on its way down North Bridge and South Bridge roads. From outside the Golden Mile Complex, a host of buses run up Beach Road to Raffles City, where you can hop on the MRT. Should a bus or a walk seem like a lot of trouble, you'll have no trouble hailing a cab at either terminal.

By train

Trains from Malaysia end their journey at the **Singapore Railway Station** on Keppel Road, southwest of Chinatown. Oddly, you haven't officially arrived in Singapore until you step out of the station – the train line is Malaysian territory – and into the street, as a sign above the main station entrance saying "Welcome to Malaysia" testifies. The grounds of Singapore's railway system were sold lock, stock and barrel to the Federal Malay States in 1918, though recently the Singapore government has been buying back segments of it piecemeal. From Keppel Road, bus #97 travels past Tanjong Pagar MRT and on to Selegie and Serangoon roads, and you can usually find a cab in the forecourt.

By sea

Boats **from Batam**, in the Indonesian archipelago of Riau (through which travellers from Sumatra approach Singapore) dock at the World Trade Centre, off Telok Blangah Road, roughly 5km east of the centre. From Telok Blangah Road, bus #97 runs to Tanjong Pagar MRT, the #65 goes to Selegie and Serangoon roads via Orchard Road, and #166 heads for Chinatown. It's also possible to reach Singapore by boat **from Malaysia**. Bumboats from Kampung Pengerang on the southeastern coast of Johor moor at Changi Village, beyond the airport, from where bus #2 travels into the centre, via Geylang, Victoria and New Bridge roads. Swisher ferries from Tanjung Belungkor, also in Johor, dock at the Changi ferry terminal, from where you can take a taxi a short way west to Changi Village in order to connect with the #2. Ferries from Tioman Island dock at the new Tanah Merah Ferry Terminal, from where bus #35 will run you up to Bedok MRT station. The Tanah Merah Ferry Terminal is also your arrival point if you are coming from Indonesia's Pulau Bintan.

Information

The Singapore Tourism Board (STB; *www.newasia-singapore.com.sg*) maintains three **Tourist Information Centres**. One is at Tourism Court, 1 Orchard Spring Lane (Mon–Fri 8.30am–5pm, Sat 8.30am–1pm; toll-free ☎1-800/7362000); another is at Liang Court Shopping Centre, Level 1, 177 River Valley Rd (daily 10.30am–9.30pm; ☎3362888); and the third is at #01-35 Suntec City Mall, 3 Temasek Blvd (daily

---

THE EASTERN & ORIENTAL EXPRESS

There's no more luxurious way to cover the 1900km from **Singapore to Bangkok** than on the sumptuous **Eastern & Oriental Express**, a fairy-tale trip that unashamedly re-creates the pampered days of the region's colonial past. Departing once or twice weekly from Singapore, the Express takes approximately 41 hours to wend its unhurried way to Bangkok's Hualamphong Station, stopping at Kuala Lumpur, Ipoh and Butterworth en route. At Butterworth, passengers disembark for a whistle-stop **tour of Penang** by bus and trishaw. On board, guests enjoy breakfast in bed, lunch, tea and dinner, all served by attentive Thai and Malaysian staff in traditional or period garb. There are two bars – one is in the observation carriage at the rear of the train – as well as two luxurious restaurant cars serving Western and Oriental cuisine of a high standard; fortune tellers, Chinese opera singers and musicians keep you entertained. A word of warning: many guests dress up lavishly for the occasion, so be sure to have suitably **smart clothes** with you or you'll feel decidedly uncomfortable.

The two-night Singapore–Bangkok experience costs from US$1350 per person. **Bookings** can be made in Singapore at E&O Services, #32-01/3 Shaw Towers, 100 Beach Rd (☎3223500), or in Bangkok through Sea Tours Co. Ltd, c/o *Tong Poon Hotel*, 130 Rong Muang Soi 4, Rama IV Rd (☎662/2468661). Alternatively, contact the specialist tour operators listed in "Basics" before leaving home.

8am–8pm; toll-free ☎1-800/3325066). It's worth dropping in to pick up the free handouts, the biggest of which – the *Singapore Official Guide* – is very informative and features some handy maps. Other **maps** worth having include the slender *Map of Singapore* endorsed by the Singapore Hotel Association, and the *Singapore Street Directory* – a snip at around $6 (with a searchable online version at *www.streetdirectory.com*) and invaluable if you're going to rent a car.

A number of publications offer listings of events. Two of these, *Where Singapore* and *This Week Singapore* are available free at hotels all over the island. The "Life!" section of the *Straits Times* has a decent listings section, but best of all are *8 Days* magazine, published weekly ($1.50), and *IS*, a free paper published fortnightly.

Transport

All parts of the island are accessible by bus or MRT – the metro train network – and fares are reasonable; consequently, there's little to be gained by renting a car. However you travel, it's best to avoid rush hour (8–9.30am & 5–7pm) if at all possible; outside these times, things are relatively uncongested. The *Transitlink Guide* ($1.50), available from bus interchanges, MRT stations and major bookshops, outlines every bus and MRT route on the island in exhaustive detail – there's even a five-step explanation of how to board a train. Singapore also has thousands of **taxis** which are surprisingly affordable. Though getting around **on foot** is the best way to do justice to the central areas, bear in mind, though, that you are in the tropics: apply sun screen if you're fair-skinned, and stay out of the midday sun. Strolling through the remaining pockets of old Singapore entails negotiating uneven five-foot ways (the covered pavements that front Singapore's old shophouses) and yawning storm drains, so watch where you walk.

Most Singaporeans avoid the rigmarole of buying tickets for each bus or MRT journey by purchasing a **Transitlink Farecard** – a stored-value card that's valid on all MRT and bus journeys in Singapore, and is sold at MRT stations and bus interchanges for $12 (including a $2 deposit). The cost of each journey you make is automatically deducted from the card when you pass it through the turnstile; any credit on the card when you leave Singapore will be reimbursed if you take it to a Farecard outlet at an MRT station. The **Tourist Day Ticket**, available for $10 from leading hotels and central MRT stations, allows you to take up to twelve bus or MRT rides a day, regardless of distance travelled – though you'd have to do an awful lot of travelling to make this ticket pay.

The MRT (Mass Rapid Transit) System

Singapore's **MRT** system, opened in March 1988, currently boasts 48 stations, with more under construction. In terms of cleanliness, efficiency and value for money, the system is second to none – compared to London's tubes or New York's subways, a trip on the MRT is a joy. Nor is there any possibility of delays owing to a passenger falling on the line – the automatic doors dividing the platform from the track open only when a train arrives and is stationary.

FINDING AN ADDRESS

With so many of Singapore's shops, restaurants and offices located in vast high-rise buildings and shopping centres, deciphering **addresses** can sometimes be tricky. The numbering system generally adhered to is as follows: #02-15 means room number 15 on the second storey; #10-08 is room number 8 on the tenth storey. ground level is referred to as #01.

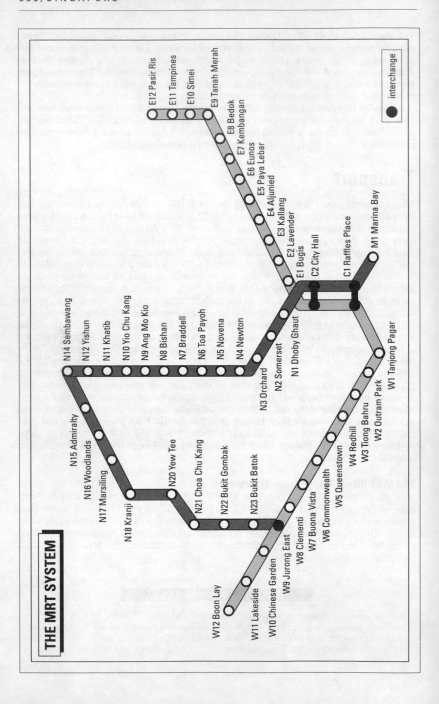

THE MRT SYSTEM

● interchange

E12 Pasir Ris
E11 Tampines
E10 Simei
E9 Tanah Merah
E8 Bedok
E7 Kembangan
E6 Eunos
E5 Paya Lebar
E4 Aljunied
E3 Kallang
E2 Lavender
E1 Bugis
C2 City Hall
C1 Raffles Place
M1 Marina Bay

N14 Sembawang
N12 Yishun
N11 Khatib
N10 Yio Chu Kang
N9 Ang Mo Kio
N8 Bishan
N7 Braddell
N6 Toa Payoh
N5 Novena
N4 Newton
N3 Orchard
N2 Somerset
N1 Dhoby Ghaut

N15 Admiralty
N16 Woodlands
N17 Marsiling
N18 Kranji
N20 Yew Tee
N21 Choa Chu Kang
N22 Bukit Gombak
N23 Bukit Batok

W1 Tanjong Pagar
W2 Outram Park
W3 Tiong Bahru
W4 Redhill
W5 Queenstown
W6 Commonwealth
W7 Buona Vista
W8 Clementi
W9 Jurong East
W10 Chinese Garden
W11 Lakeside
W12 Boon Lay

The system has two main lines: the north–south line, which runs a vaguely horse-shoe-shaped route from Marina Bay up to the north of the island and then southwest to Jurong, and the east–west line, connecting Boon Lay to Pasir Ris; see the MRT map opposite for more details. Trains run every four to five minutes on average, daily from 6am until midnight. For **information**, enquire at the station control room on any ticket concourse, or call the **MRT Information Centre** (toll-free; ☎1-800/3368900). A **no-smoking** rule applies on all trains, and eating and drinking is also outlawed. Signs in the ticket concourse appear to ban hedgehogs from the MRT; in fact, they signify "no durians" – not an unreasonable request if you've ever spent any time in a confined space with one of these pungent fruits. **Tickets** cost between 60¢ and $1.60 for a one-way journey. You need coins for the ticket machines, found inside the main hall at each station; adjacent change machines break $1 and $2 notes, while larger notes can be changed at the station control room.

Buses

Singapore's **bus** network is slightly cheaper to use than the MRT system, and far more comprehensive – you'll probably spend more time on buses than on trains, and there are several routes which are particularly useful for sightseeing (see box, below). There are two bus operators, both offering route information by phone and on the Internet: the **Singapore Bus Service** (SBS; ☎1-800/2872727, *www.i-one.net/onlineinfo/sbs*

USEFUL BUS ROUTES

Below is a selection of **bus routes** which connect Singapore's major points of interest; note that buses which serve Orchard Road always head up Penang Road/Somerset Road instead when on the other leg of their journey, as these are all one-way streets.

#2 passes along Eu Tong Sen Street (in Chinatown) and Victoria Street (past the Arab Quarter) en route to Changi Prison and Changi Village.

#7 runs along Orchard Road, Bras Basah Road and Victoria Street; its return journey takes in North Bridge Road, Stamford Road, Penang Road and Somerset Road en route to Holland Village.

#36 loops between Orchard Road and Changi airport.

#65 terminates at the World Trade Centre, after passing down Jalan Besar, Bencoolen Street, Penang Road and Somerset Road.

#97 runs along Stamford Road to Little India, then on to Upper Serangoon Road; returns via Bencoolen Street and Collyer Quay.

#103 runs between New Bridge Road Terminal (Chinatown) and Serangoon Road (Little India).

#105 runs along Stevens Road and Scotts Road on its way to Holland Road (for Holland Village).

#124 connects Scotts Road, Orchard Road and North Bridge Road with South Bridge Road and New Bridge Road in Chinatown; in the opposite direction, travels along Eu Tong Sen Street, Hill Street, Stamford Road and Somerset Road.

#139 heads past Tai Gin Road, via Dhoby Ghaut, Selegie Road, Serangoon Road and Balestier Road.

#167 passes down Scotts Road, Orchard Road and Bras Basah Road, Collyer Quay, Shenton Way and Neil Road (for Chinatown).

#170 starts at the Ban San Terminal at the northern end of Queen Street, passing Bukit Timah Nature Reserve and Kranji War Cemetery on its way to JB in Malaysia.

#190 is the most direct service between Orchard Road and Chinatown, via Scotts Road, Orchard Road, Bras Basah Road, Victoria Street, Hill Street and New Bridge Road; returns via Eu Tong Sen Street, Hill Street, Stamford Road, Penang Road, Somerset Road and Scotts Road.

/newinternetsbs/around.htm) and **Trans-Island Bus Services** (TIBS; ☎4825433, *www.tibs.com.sg*).

On most buses, fares are related to the distance you're travelling, ranging from 60¢–$1.20 (70¢–$1.50 for air-con buses, which comprise the majority of services), though some buses charge a flat fare as displayed on the destination plates on the front of the bus. Once you've told the driver where you want to go, he'll tell you how much money to drop into the metal chute at the front of the bus. Change isn't given, so make sure you have coins. Transitlink Farecards and Tourist Day Tickets (see p.537) should be inserted into the validator as you board; press the button to select your fare, which is deducted from the stored value on the card. Unless you are on a route rarely frequented by tourists, the driver is likely to know of anywhere you could possibly be heading for, and signs at bus stops will alert you.

The **Singapore Trolley** (for information call ☎3396833) is a mock-antique bus that loops between the Botanic Gardens, the Colonial District, the Singapore River and Suntec City throughout the day; one day's unlimited travel on it costs around $15.

Taxis

There are more than ten thousand **taxis** on the streets of Singapore, so you'll hardly ever have trouble hailing a cab, day or night. Taxis, which come in various colours and are always clearly marked "TAXI", are all metered, the fare starting at $2.40 for the first kilometre, after which it rises 10¢ for every 240m. However, there are **surcharges** to bear in mind, most notably the fifty-percent extra charged on journeys between midnight and 6am. Journeys from Changi airport and telephone taxi bookings each incur a $3 surcharge. Electronic tolls levied on journeys along expressways and within the CBD (see below) are also reflected in taxi fares.

On the whole, Singaporean taxi drivers are a friendly enough bunch, but their English isn't always good, so it's a good idea to have your destination written down on a piece of paper if you are heading off the beaten track. If a taxi displays a red destination sign on its dashboard, it means the driver is changing shift and will accept customers only if they are going in his direction. Finally, tourists confined to **wheelchairs** should note that TIBS Taxis (☎4811211) have ten wheelchair-accessible cabs.

Driving and cycling

The Singapore government has introduced huge disincentives to driving in order to combat traffic congestion. One of these measures is an Electronic Road Pricing (ERP) programme within the city's Central Business District (**CBD**) – encompassing Chinatown, Orchard Road and the financial zone – between 7.30am and 7pm. If you want to drive into the CBD during these hours, you have to buy a stored-value **CashCard**, available at petrol stations, to cover the electronic tolls that are now automatically levied. Parking, too, is expensive and requires that you purchase coupons from a licence booth, post office or shop.

With all these charges, and given the efficiency of public transport, the only worthwhile reason for **renting a car** in Singapore is to travel up into Malaysia – and even then it's far cheaper to rent in JB, as Singaporean firms levy a $25 Malaysia surcharge (though note that you can't drive a Malaysian vehicle into the CBD without having an In-Vehicle Unit for CashCards installed at the causeway, an expensive task). If you're still keen on driving in Singapore itself, see the list of rental companies on p.611. For details of prices, documentation and road rules, see Basics, p.40.

Bike rental is possible along the East Coast Parkway, where the cycle track that skirts the seashore is always crowded with Singaporeans zooming around in full cycling gear. Expect to pay around $4–8 an hour for a mountain bike, and bring some

SINGAPORE RIVER, ISLAND AND HARBOUR CRUISES

Fleets of **cruise boats** ply Singapore's southern waters every day and night. The best of these, Singapore River Cruises (daily 9am–11pm; every 10min; $7), use traditional bumboats and cast off from Boat Quay, Clarke Quay, Raffles' landing site and Riverside Point Landing Steps, passing the old godowns upriver where traders once stored their merchandise. Several cruise companies – the ones we've listed are all recommended by the STB – also operate out of Clifford Pier, offering a whole host of seaborne possibilities, from luxury catamaran trips around Singapore's southern isles to dinner on a *tongkang* (Chinese sailing boat). On average, a straightforward cruise will set you back around $20, and a dinner special $35–80. It's quite possible to **charter** your own boat – a few companies are listed below – but you can bank on forking out up to $1000 a day for the privilege. If you don't relish the idea of an organized cruise, you can haggle with a bumboat man on Clifford Pier: if you're lucky, you might get a trip around the southern isles (see p.591) for $25 an hour.

Cruise companies	**Charter companies**
Eastwind Organisation (☎5333432).	Amaril Cruises (☎4759688).
Singapore River Boat (☎3389205).	Fantasy Cruises (☎2840424).
Singapore River Cruises (☎3366111).	J&N Cruises (☎2707100).
Watertours (☎5339811).	Pacific Seacraft (☎2706665).

form of ID to leave at the office. The dirt tracks that crisscross Pulau Ubin, off Changi Point at the eastern tip of the island, are ideal for biking a day's rental at one of the cluster of shops near the jetty costs $4–8, though the price doubles in school holidays (June, Nov & Dec). Finally, there's a range of bikes – including tandems – available for rent next to the ferry terminal on Sentosa Island ($2–5 an hour), providing by far the best way to see the island.

Organized tours

Usefully if you're pushed for time, several reputable operators in Singapore offer **sightseeing tours**. The main ones are listed on p.612, or ask at your hotel or the tourist office. Tours vary from one operator to the next, but four-hour city tours typically take in Orchard Road, Chinatown and Little India, and cost around $30. For a Round the Island Tour (8hr) – visiting places of interest on all of Singapore's coasts, and including a trip to one of the many new towns that have sprung up across the island – expect to pay $70. There are also **specialist tours** on Raffles, horse racing, Singapore by night and World War II sights – and even an "In Harmony with Feng Shui" tour – costing $30–80 per person; for more details on these, contact the STB. For **nature trips** and **bird-watching**, contact R. Subharaj at 8 Jalan Buloh Perindu (☎7874733), whose tours range from three-hour birding sessions ($20) to personalized nature trips spanning Singapore and Malaysia, at around $600 a day for a group of up to five people.

Members of the Registered Tourist Guides Association (☎3392110) charge $25–50 an hour (minimum 4hr) for a **personalized tour**. Finally, free sightseeing tours of Singapore, arranged by the STB, are available to transit passengers at Changi Airport – call in at the tour desk in the transit lounge if you're interested.

Trishaws – three-wheeled bicycles with a carriage on the back – were once a practical transport option in Singapore, though they're a bit of an anachronism these days. You'll still see a few trishaws providing a genuine service around Little India and Chinatown, but most drivers now congregate on the open land below Bugis Village (p.557), from where they'll give you a 45-minute sightseeing ride for $25–40.

Accommodation

Room rates take a noticeable leap when you cross the causeway from Malaysia into Singapore, but good deals still abound if your expectations aren't too high or, at the budget end of the scale, if you don't mind sharing. Singapore's status as one of the main gateways to Southeast Asia means that occupancy rates are permanently high. Even so, you shouldn't encounter too many difficulties in finding a room, and advance booking isn't really necessary unless your visit coincides with Chinese New Year (usually January/February) or one of the *Hari Raya* festivals.

The **Singapore Hotel Association** has a booking counter at each of Changi airport's two terminals (daily 7am–2am); these counters will find you a room in the city free of charge, though they only represent Singapore's official hotels, all of which are listed in two free STB booklets, *Hotels Singapore* and *Budget Hotels Singapore*. Touts at the airport hand out flyers advertising rooms in guesthouses and hostels. It's possible to book a room at an official hotel online (go to *www.newasia-singapore.com* or *www.stayinsingapore.com.sg*).

The cheapest beds are in the communal **dormitories** of many of Singapore's resthouses, where you'll pay $10 or less a night. The next best deals are at **guesthouses**, most of which are situated along Bencoolen Street and Beach Road, with an increasing number in nearby Little India and some also south of the river, in Chinatown. Singapore's classic guesthouse address is Peony Mansions on Bencoolen Street, where a cluster of establishments is shoehorned into several floors of a decrepit apartment building, though the Bencoolen area is becoming less fashionable with every passing year. Guesthouses aren't nearly as cosy as their name suggests: costing $20–30, the rooms are tiny, bare, and divided by paper-thin partitions; toilets are shared and showers are cold. However, another $10–20 secures a bigger, air-con room, and often TV, laundry and cooking facilities, lockers and breakfast are included. Always check that the room is clean and secure, and that the shower and air-con work before you hand over any money. It's always worth asking for a discount, too, and you stand a better chance of a reduction if you are staying a few days. Finally, since guesthouses aren't subject to the same safety checks as official hotels, it's a good idea – without sounding alarmist – to check for a fire escape.

The appeal of Singapore's **Chinese-owned hotels**, similar in price to guesthouses, is their air of faded grandeur – some haven't changed in forty years. Sadly, faded grandeur is something the government frowns upon, with the result that there are not too many of these places left. In more modern, **mid-range hotels**, a room for two with air-con, private bathroom and TV will set you back around $60–90 a night. From there, prices rise steadily; at the top end of the scale, Singapore boasts some extraordinarily opulent hotels, ranging from the colonial splendour of *Raffles* to the awesome spectacle of the *Westin Stamford* – the world's second tallest hotel. Though you'll find the greatest concentration of upmarket hotels around Orchard Road, most of the new breed of **boutique hotels** – mid-range places which use antique furniture and fittings to create an air of Oriental nostalgia – are based in Chinatown.

Most mid-range and upmarket hotels in Singapore make no charge for children under 12 years old if they are occupying existing spare beds in rooms. However, if you require an extra bed to be put in your room, there's usually an additional charge of ten to fifteen percent of the roomrate, though cots are provided free.

Bencoolen Street and around

Bencoolen Street has long been the mainstay of Singapore's backpacker industry – so long, in fact, that its buildings are beginning to show their age, while others have already fallen to the demolition ball. Still, the location is handy for all parts of central

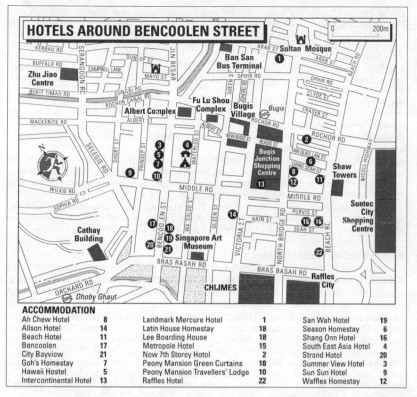

HOTELS AROUND BENCOOLEN STREET

0 — 200m

KERBAU RD
BUFFALO RD
Zhu Jiao Centre
BUKIT TIMAH RD
MACKENZIE RD
SERANGOON RD
CAMPBELL LANE
ROCHOR CANAL RD
Albert Complex
ALBERT ST
DUNLOP ST
MAYO ST
CUNGAI RD
JLN BESAR
Fu Lu Shou Complex
ALBERT ST
NEW BUGIS ST
Ban San Bus Terminal
OPHIR RD
QUEEN ST
Bugis Village
Bugis
ROCHOR RD
ARAB ST Sultan Mosque ❶
ARAB ST
OPHIR RD
CLYDE ST
FRASER ST
ROCHOR RD ❷
BEACH RD

SELEGIE RD
SHORT ST
PRINSEP ST
WILKIE RD
SOPHIA RD
Cathay Building
❸
❹
❺
❼
❾
❿
WATERLOO ST
MIDDLE RD
BUGIS ST
Bugis Junction Shopping Centre
❽ ⑬
⑫
TAN QUEE LAN ST
LIANG SEAH ST
❻
❶
Shaw Towers
NICOLL HIGHWAY
MIDDLE RD
BENCOOLEN ST
WA ERLOO S
QUEEN ST
VICTORIA ST
⑰
⑱
⑲ Singapore Art
⑳ Museum
㉑
BRAS RASAH RD
BAIN ST
⑭
PURVIS ST
SEAH ST
NORTH BRIDGE RD
⑯ ⑯
㉒
BEACH RD
Suntec City Shopping Centre
ORCHARD RD
DHOBY GHAUT
Dhoby Ghaut
CHIJMES
BRAS BASAH RD
Raffles City
Raffles

ACCOMMODATION

Ah Chew Hotel	8	Landmark Mercure Hotel	1	San Wah Hotel	19
Allson Hotel	14	Latin House Homestay	18	Season Homestay	6
Beach Hotel	11	Lee Boarding House	18	Shang Onn Hotel	16
Bencoolen	17	Metropole Hotel	15	South East Asia Hotel	4
City Bayview	21	New 7th Storey Hotel	2	Strand Hotel	20
Goh's Homestay	7	Peony Mansion Green Curtains	18	Summer View Hotel	3
Hawaii Hostel	5	Peony Mansion Travellers' Lodge	10	Sun Sun Hotel	9
Intercontinental Hotel	13	Raffles Hotel	22	Waffles Homestay	12

Singapore, and the proliferation of guesthouses makes it a great place for meeting people. All the places listed here are keyed on the map above.

Hotel Bencoolen, 47 Bencoolen St (☎3360822, *www.hotelbencoolen.com.sg*). Great-value, fairly upmarket option, with business centre, laundry service, air-ticketing facilities and smart rooms equipped with all mod cons. ④.

City Bayview, 30 Bencoolen St (☎3372882, fax 3382880). Bencoolen St's poshest hotel, with very comfortable rooms, a compact rooftop swimming pool and a friendly, modern café. ⑤.

Goh's Homestay, fourth floor, 169d Bencoolen St (☎3396561, fax 3398606). The smartest guest-house in town, with fresh and inviting (if slightly cell-like) rooms, pricier dorm beds than usual, laundry service, a bright, comfortable lounge/canteen area serving great breakfasts Recommended unless you are allergic to cats – the place is teeming with them. ③, dorm beds $14.

Hawaii Hostel, second floor, 171b Bencoolen St (☎3384187). Small, tidy, air-con rooms with breakfast included. ②, dorm beds $10.

Latin House Home Stay, #03-46 Peony Mansions, 46–52 Bencoolen St (☎3396308). The budget-priced dorms are adequate, but the rooms are a little run-down. ①, dorm beds $7.

Lee Boarding House, #07-52 Peony Mansions, 46–52 Bencoolen St (☎3383149). The brightest place in Peony Mansions: clean, simple dorms (a dollar more for air-con) and rooms, a pleasant breakfast area and laundry facilities. There's another *Lee*'s on Beach Rd (see p.544). ①, dorm beds $9.

Peony Mansion Green Curtains, #04-46 Peony Mansions, 46–52 Bencoolen St (☎3385638). A travel-consultant's desk, notice board and Internet access make this a handy place to stay. The dorms are cramped, while rooms range from basic to more comfortable doubles with TV, fridge, air-con and toilet. ②.

Peony Mansion Travellers' Lodge, second floor, 131a Bencoolen St (☎3348697). Actually a couple of hundred metres down the road from its parent guesthouse, *Green Curtains* in Peony Mansions, this place has lots of clean featureless rooms (the cheapest share common showers) and an air-con dorm. Conveniently, the Airpower travel agency operates right beside the lodge's friendly reception area. ②, dorm beds $10.

San Wah Hotel, 36 Bencoolen St (☎3362428). Shabby though rather charming Chinese hotel which benefits from being set back slightly from the road, and from being run by a friendly family. $5 surcharge for air-con. ③.

South East Asia Hotel, 190 Waterloo St (☎3382394, *web.singnet.com.sg/~seahotel*). Spotless doubles with air-con, TV and phone for those yearning for a few creature comforts. Downstairs is a vegetarian restaurant serving Western breakfasts, and right next door is Singapore's liveliest Buddhist temple. ④.

Strand Hotel, 25 Bencoolen St (☎3381866, fax 3363149). Excellent-value hotel with clean, welcoming rooms and a laundry service. ④.

Summer View Hotel, 173 Bencoolen St (☎3381122, fax 3366346). The future face of Bencoolen St: a smart but unpretentious one-hundred-room hotel with all the facilities the budget-minded business traveller or tourist might need (café, car rental, valet services, currency exchange and tour desk), but none of the needless frills that push up prices. ⑤.

Sun Sun Hotel, 260–262 Middle Rd (☎3384911). Housed in a splendid 1928 building, this hotel has decent rooms, some with air-con, and plenty of communal bathrooms, and isn't overpriced. Ask for one of the rooms with a balcony. Downstairs is the wonderful *L.E. Café & Confectionery*. ③.

Beach Road to Victoria Street

A few blocks east of Bencoolen Street, **Beach Road** boasts a mixture of charismatic old Chinese hotels and smart new guesthouses. What's more, you can brag about having stayed down the road from *Raffles Hotel* (or even in it) when you get home. The hotels in this area are shown on the map on p.543.

Ah Chew Hotel, 496 North Bridge Rd (☎8370356). Simple but charismatic rooms, and air-con dorms, with "Wild West" swing doors, crammed with period furniture and run by a gang of T-shirted old men lounging on ornate wooden benches which would once have been used by opium smokers. Despite its address, it's just around the corner from North Bridge Rd, on Liang Seah St. ②, dorm beds $12.

Allson Hotel, 101 Victoria St (☎3360811, fax 3397019). Reasonable 450-room hotel with shopping arcade, health and business centres and a clutch of restaurants. Some effort has been made to cater for the disabled: there are low counters and phones and adapted toilets, but you'll need to book well ahead for the hotel's sole bedroom specifically designed for disabled travellers. ⑥.

Beach Hotel, 95 Beach Rd (☎3367712, *bhotel@singnet.com.sg*). Professionally run and really tidy, with small, cheery rooms, though you'd expect a few more amenities for the price. ④.

Intercontinental, 80 Middle Rd (☎3387600, fax 3387366, *hotels.singapore.interconti.com*). Smashing hotel within the thriving Bugis Junction development, convenient and sumptuously furnished, with business centre, swimming pool, health club and an array of excellent restaurants including *Pimai Thai* and *Olive Tree* (see "Eating", p.599). ⑦.

Landmark Mercure Hotel, 390 Victoria St (☎2972828, fax 2982038). Very pleasant, once you get past the dated shopping centre downstairs; it has its own swimming pool and a baby-sitting service, and is handy for Bugis MRT Station and Arab St. ⑤.

Metropole Hotel, 41 Seah St (☎3363611, fax 3393610, *www.metrohotel.com*). Friendly, great-value establishment just across the road from *Raffles*, with roomy lodgings above the intriguing *Imperial Herbal Restaurant*. ⑤.

New 7th Storey Hotel, 229 Rochor Rd (☎3370251, fax 3343550). Despite its rather old-fashioned exterior, this is a clean hotel with perfectly respectable rooms, all with TV. Rooms with en-suite bathrooms are available, though the communal ones are fine. ③.

Raffles Hotel, 1 Beach Rd (☎3371886, fax 3397650, *www.raffles.com*). The flagship of Singapore's hotel industry, *Raffles* takes shameless advantage of its reputation: $25 buys you a Singapore Sling and a glass to take home, while the souvenir shop stocks *Raffles* golf balls, socks and cuddly tigers. Still, it's a beautiful place, dotted with frangipani trees and palms, and the suites (there are no rooms) are as tasteful as you would expect at these prices. See p.555 for more details. ⑨.

Season Homestay, 26a Liang Seah St (☎3372400). Occupying one of the last few shophouses along Liang Seah not to have been turned into a trendy café, this place has dorm beds and a modest range of private rooms, all sharing only two common bathrooms. Breakfast is included in the price. ②, dorm beds $9.

Shang Onn Hotel, 37 Beach Rd (☎3384153). Set in a quaint old building sporting attractive green shutters, the *Shang Onn* has reasonable, if rather spartan, rooms and a friendly manager/owner. ②.

Waffles Home Stay, third floor, 490 North Bridge Rd (☎3341608). Pleasantly tiled and painted crashpad, where prices include breakfast and a free flow of hot drinks. There are discounts if you introduce new guests; oodles of travel advice are pinned up on notice boards around the walls. To enter, walk through to the back of the curry house below, and up the stairs to your left. Recommended. ②, dorm beds $9.

The Colonial District

A handful of expensive hotels squat at the edges of the Padang, just north of the Singapore River. Several of them – including the *Marina Mandarin* and *Oriental* hotels – stand on the reclaimed land which robbed Beach Road of its beach. The places below are marked on the "Colonial District" map on p.553.

Excelsior Hotel, 5 Coleman St (☎3387733, fax 3393847). Sister to the *Peninsula* (whose gymnasium guests here can use), the *Excelsior's* 271 rooms enjoy a swimming pool, 24hr room service, TV, a safe and a secretarial service, and are as handy for the Financial District as for Orchard Rd's shopping centres. The excellent *Annalakshmi* Indian vegetarian restaurant is the best of the hotel's several food outlets. ⑥.

Marina Mandarin Hotel, 6 Raffles Blvd (☎3383388, fax 3394977). Top-flight hotel, architecturally interesting and affording great harbour views; the atrium is particularly impressive. ⑦.

Oriental Singapore, 5 Raffles Ave (☎3380066, fax 3399537). Housed, like the *Marina Mandarin*, in what's claimed to be Southeast Asia's largest shopping centre and hotel complex, Marina Square, the *Oriental* is one of Singapore's priciest hotels, but with very good reason: the rooms are exquisitely furnished, the views out over Marina Bay are breathtaking, and all the luxuries you could want are on hand. For a real treat, try their *Oriental Club*, whose two floors of luxury rooms have complimentary breakfast, evening cocktails and laundry service. Recommended. ⑨.

Ritz-Carlton Millennia Singapore, 7 Raffles Ave (☎3378888, fax 3380001). This recent arrival has elbowed its way into the very top ranks of the island's hotels; all imaginable comfort can be found within its monolithic structure. ⑧.

Westin Stamford, 2 Stamford Rd (☎3388585, fax 3365117). Upper-floor rooms aren't for those with vertigo, though the views are as splendid as you'd expect. There are over a thousand classy rooms here, some sixteen restaurants and an MRT station downstairs. Recommended. ⑦.

Orchard Road and around

Sumptuous hotels abound in and around **Orchard Road**; unless you opt for a dorm bed at the *YMCA* or tiny *Cavenagh Garden*, you have to be prepared to spend a bare minimum of $80 a double. You can multiply that figure by four or five, though, if you decide to treat yourself. See the map on p.536 for the location of hotels in this district.

Cavenagh Garden, Block 73 Cavenagh Rd #03-376 (☎7374600). At the northern end of Cuppage Rd, cross the Expressway bridge and walk to the left for 300m. A homestay in the literal sense of the word: various rooms are dotted around a family home. It's a steep $20 extra for a private shower. ③.

The Elizabeth, 24 Mount Elizabeth (☎7381188, fax 7324173). Within its toy-town exterior, this boutique hotel oozes panache; the rooms are delightful and well appointed. ⑥.

Goodwood Park Hotel, 22 Scotts Rd (☎7377411, fax 7328558, *www.goodwoodparkhotel.com.sg*). Don't be surprised if this opulent hotel reminds you of *Raffles* – both were designed by the same architect. The building is a study in elegance, its arching facades fronting exquisitely appointed rooms. ⑨.

Holiday Inn Park View, 11 Cavenagh Rd (☎7338333, fax 7344593, *www.holidayinn.com.sg*). While at this smart hotel with all the trimmings, the guests are next-door neighbours of Singapore's president – the istana is just across the road. ⑦.

Lloyd's Inn, 2 Lloyd Rd (☎7377309, fax 7377847). Motel-style building boasting attractive rooms and a fine location, just five-minutes' walk up Killiney Road from Orchard Road. ④.

Mandarin Hotel, 333 Orchard Rd (☎7374411, fax 7322361). Every luxury you could hope for; even if you don't stay, take a trip up to the top floors for the magnificent view of central Singapore. ⑧.

Metro-Y Lodge, 60 Stevens Rd (☎7377755, fax 2355528, *www.mymca.org.sg*). Not as central as the *YMCA* on Orchard Rd, but perfectly adequate, and suitable for travellers in wheelchairs. ④.

Mitre Hotel, 145 Killiney Rd (☎7373811). Reasonable old Chinese hotel, set amid overgrown grounds, and with an endearingly shabby air about it; there's a great lobby bar downstairs. ②.

Sandy's Place, 3c Sarkies Rd (☎7341431). Rooms are a touch overpriced in this friendly, laid-back place, set across a field from Newton MRT. Expect to pay $15 over the basic rate for air-con. The price includes a fruit breakfast. It's best to phone ahead. ②.

Sheraton Towers, 39 Scotts Rd (☎7376888, fax 7371072). Faultless hotel voted one of the top ten in the world by *Business Traveller* magazine. The lobby area is dazzling and there's even a waterfall out the back. ⑨.

Singapore Marriott, 320 Orchard Rd (☎7355800, fax 7359800, *marriotthotels.com/SINDT/*). A superior hotel and a Singapore landmark, housed in a 33-storey pagoda-style building next to the C.K.Tang department store. ⑧.

Sloane Court Hotel, 17 Balmoral Rd (☎2353311, fax 7339041). As close to a Tudor house as you get in Singapore, the *Sloane Court* is tucked away in a prime residential area, near Newton MRT. ④.

Hotel Supreme, 15 Kramat Rd (☎7378333, fax 7337404). A budget hotel, well placed at the eastern end of Orchard Rd, which levies a hefty $200 deposit at check in. ④.

Hotel VIP, Balmoral Crescent (☎2354277, fax 2352824). Within walking distance of Orchard Rd, this quiet, affordable hotel has its own swimming pool. ⑤.

YMCA International House, 1 Orchard Rd (☎3366000, fax 3373140, *ymca-hotels .com/singapore/ymca/*). Plush but overpriced rooms, excellent sports facilities (including roof-top pool) and free room service from the *McDonald's* downstairs. The dorm beds are the most expensive in town, though, and there's a first-day charge of $5 for non-members. Bus #36 from the airport stops right outside. ④, dorm beds $25.

Little India

The hotels and guesthouses of Little India used not to attract many Western visitors, though many more backpackers have been holing up here of late. All the places below are marked on the map on p.570.

Albert Court Hotel, 180 Albert St (☎3393939, fax 3393252). This charmingly conceived boutique hotel, designed around the restaurants of lively Albert Court Mall, is just a short walk from both Bugis Village and Little India; rooms have all the standard embellishments. ⑧.

Boon Wah Hotel, 43a Jalan Besar (☎2991466, fax 2942176). This decent Chinese hotel offers clean, if slightly cramped, rooms with TV, air-con and shower. The entrance is around the corner, on Upper Dickson Rd. ④.

Broadway Hotel, 195 Serangoon Rd (☎2924661, fax 2916414). Ugly-looking hotel in the heart of Little India, boasting pleasant enough rooms with air-con, bathroom and TV. ④.

Dickson Court, 1 Dickson Rd (☎2977811, fax 2977833). With smart, well-furnished rooms off light courtyard corridors, the *Dickson Court* represents pretty good value; most corners of central Singapore are accessible from the bus stop across the road on Jalan Besar. ④.

Fortuna Hotel, 2 Owen Rd (☎2953577). Mid-range hotel offering brilliant value for money; facilities include a health centre and secretarial services. ④.

Kerbau Hotel, 54–62 Kerbau Rd (☎2976668). Friendly, somewhat vault-like place, with spruce and welcoming rooms; discounts for stays of three days or more. ④.

Little India Guest House, 3 Veerasamy Rd (☎2942866, fax 2984866). A smart guesthouse with excellent, spick-and-span rooms and spotless toilets. ③.

Mount Emily Hotel, 10a Upper Wilkie Rd, Mount Emily Park (☎3389151, fax 3396008). A five-minute walk up from Selegie Rd. Rooms here are pricey and just starting to show their age, but the hotel's location beside a lovely park above the city makes it a quiet, relaxing option. ⑤.

Perak Lodge, 12 Perak Rd (☎2969072, fax 3920919, *www.peraklodge.net*). One of the new breed of upper-bracket guesthouses, set within a blue-and-white shophouse in a backstreet behind the Little India arcade and run by friendly staff. The rooms are secure, well-appointed and welcoming, and the price includes a continental breakfast. Downstairs there's an airy, residents-only living area. Recommended. ④.

Chinatown and around

Despite being such a big tourist draw, **Chinatown** isn't very well furnished with budget accommodation. On the other hand, the area does contain a mass of upmarket hotels which benefit from their proximity to the business district. The following places are all shown on the map on p.560.

Chinatown Guest House, fifth floor, 325d New Bridge Rd (☎2200671). This friendly, no-frills place is a popular choice, offering varied rooms, free breakfast and luggage storage. However, the cheapest rooms are tiny, the dorms pretty cramped and there are just three bathrooms. ②, dorm beds $12.

Chinatown Hotel, 12–16 Teck Lim Rd (☎2255166, fax 2253912, *www.chinatownhotel.com*). Decent boutique hotel with very smart rooms and a well-stocked business centre. ⑤.

Damenlou Hotel, 12 Ann Siang Rd (☎2211900, fax 2258500). Given its lovingly restored 1925 facade, the twelve compact but well-appointed rooms in this friendly hotel are surprisingly modern. After a pre-dinner drink overlooking Chinatown on the rooftop garden, head down to the excellent *Swee Kee* restaurant on the ground floor (see p.597). ④.

Dragon Inn, 18 Mosque St (☎2200671, fax 2227227). Sizeable, comfortable double rooms in the middle of Chinatown, all with air-con, TV, fridge and bathroom, and set in attractive shophouses. Try to avoid rooms backing onto the central air shaft, which houses many noisy air-con units. ⑤.

The Duxton, 83 Duxton Rd (☎2277678, fax 2271232, *www.duxtonhotels.com.sg*). Elegant rooms in the renovated shophouses that make up this hotel don't come cheap. ⑦.

Majestic Hotel, 31–37 Bukit Pasoh Rd (☎2223377, fax 2230907). Scrupulously clean and enormously friendly hotel within strolling distance of the sights of Chinatown. All rooms have air-con and private bathroom, while those at the front boast little balconies. Try and secure a room on the top floor – the noise from the KTV lounge next door carries maddeningly at night. ④.

Royal Peacock Hotel, 55 Keong Saik Rd (☎2233522, fax 2211770). The silky, sassy elegance of this place recalls the days when Keong Said Rd was a red-light district. Sculpted from ten shophouses, it's a superb boutique hotel, with great rooms, a bar, café and business services. ⑥.

Geylang and Katong

Geylang and Katong, along Singapore's southeastern coast, have traditionally both been Malay-dominated areas. If you can't face the noise and the bustle of central Singapore, this region might appeal – certainly its cool sea breezes and Malay markets are an advantage. MRT and buses connect you quickly with downtown Singapore.

Amber Hotel, 42 Amber Rd (☎3442323). Comfortable rooms with TV, air-con and bathroom just a short walk from the east coast's beaches. ④.

Hotel 81, 305 Joo Chiat Rd (☎3488181, *www.hotel81.com.sg*). Housed in a beautifully restored Peranakan building in cream and burgundy, *Hotel 81* offers rooms pleasant enough for any self-respecting business person, but at a fraction of the prices of the heavyweights downtown. Great place. ④.

Sing Hoe Hotel, 759 Mountbatten Rd (☎4400602). Beautifully kept colonial house, with attractive reliefs on its external walls, but its unmemorable, air-con rooms are overpriced. Look out for the amazing "gingerbread house" next door. ③.

Soon Teck Hotel, 57a Koon Seng Rd (☎3440240). A peaceful Chinese-run hotel with just five air-con rooms. Communal facilities are clean, and downstairs is a sleepy coffee shop. Recommended. ②.

Sentosa Island

Three luxury hotels on the island of **Sentosa** allow you to bypass the bustle of downtown Singapore. You can get a taxi direct from the airport to Sentosa (though note that from 7am to 10pm a $6 surcharge is levied for this); for details of public transport to the island, see p.589.

The Beaufort (☎2750331, fax 2750228, *www.beaufort-hotels.com/singapore/*). A swanky hotel, elegantly appointed and fitted out in varnished wood and bounded by two 18-hole golf courses and a beach. Prices go up by $40 on Fri and Sat. ⑧.

Shangri-La's Rasa Sentosa Resort (☎2750100, fax 2750355). Opened in 1993, the *Rasa Sentosa* is the first hotel in Singapore to have its own beachfront, and its situation on Sentosa island makes it a good option if you've got kids to amuse. As at the *Beaufort*, a $40 price rise applies on Fri and Sat; and rooms with a sea view also cost an extra $40. ⑧.

Sijori Resort Sentosa (☎2712002, fax 2740220). Sentosa's latest accommodation option, the *Sijori* is slap-bang in the middle of the island, making it an ideal base for exploring. ⑦.

Downtown Singapore

Ever since Sir Stamford Raffles first landed on its northern bank, in 1819, the area around the Singapore River, which strikes into the heart of the island from the island's south coast, has formed the hub of Singapore. All of Singapore's central districts lie within a three-kilometre radius of the mouth of the river – which makes **downtown Singapore** an extremely convenient place to tour. Although buses do run between these districts (see bus-route information on p.539), you might find that you prefer to explore the whole central region on foot. You need at least two days to do full justice to the main areas: the **Colonial District**, **Chinatown** and the **Financial District**, **Little India** and the **Arab Quarter**; while Singapore's commercial mecca, **Orchard Road**, can occupy a single morning, or several days, depending on how much you enjoy shopping.

The Colonial District

The Padang, north of the Singapore River, is the very nexus of the **Colonial District**, flanked by dignified reminders of British rule. The view from here is a panorama that defines Singapore's past and present. In the foreground is the Singapore Cricket Club – the epitome of colonial man's stubborn refusal to adapt to his surroundings. Behind that, the river snakes westwards and inland, passing the last few surviving godowns from Singapore's original trade boom. Towering high above all this are the spires of the modern business district; also to the south are Empress Place Building and Parliament House. To the north is the grand old *Raffles Hotel*, beyond which a string of nineteenth- and twentieth-century churches leads to Singapore's most famous entertainment centre, Bugis Village. Heading west, you pass City Hall and the Supreme Court before climbing the slopes of Fort Canning Hill, ten-minutes' walk from the Padang, and one of the few hills in Singapore not yet lost to land reclamation. The twenty-first century seems strangely absent amid all these echoes of the past, though the district's most notable modern building doesn't do things by half – the *Westin Stamford*, on Stamford Road, was until recently the world's tallest hotel.

Along the northern bank of the Singapore River

As the colony's trade grew in the last century, the **Singapore River** became its main artery, clogged with bumboats – traditional cargo boats with eyes painted on their prows, as if they are looking where they are going. The boat pilots ferried coffee, sugar and rice to the godowns, where coolies loaded and unloaded sacks. Indeed, in the 1880s the river itself was so busy it was practically possible to walk from one side of it to the other without getting your feet wet. A recent campaign to clean up the waters of the river relocated the bumboats to the west coast, though a handful still remain and offer trips downriver and around Marina Bay (see p.541). These days, with the bumboats gone, the river is quieter, cleaner and inevitably less charismatic, though parts of both banks have undergone a profound commercial revitalization as new restaurants and bars move into the formerly abandoned buildings.

From the Raffles Place MRT station, it's just a couple of minutes' walk past the former GPO, to the elegant suspension struts of **Cavenagh Bridge** – a good place to start a tour of Singapore's colonial centre. Named after Major General Orfeur Cavenagh, Governor of the Straits Settlements from 1859 to 1867, the bridge was constructed in 1869 by Indian convict labourers using imported Glasgow steel. Times change, but not necessarily on the bridge, where a police sign still maintains: "The use of this bridge is prohibited to any vehicle of which the laden weight exceeds 3cwt and to all cattle and horses."

Stepping off the bridge, you're confronted by **Empress Place Building**, a robust Neoclassical structure named for Queen Victoria and completed in 1865. It served for ten years as a courthouse before the Registry of Births and Deaths and the Immigration Department moved in. Latterly it's housed cultural exhibitions, and when renovations are completed, the building will reopen with a permanent **Asian Civilization** collection, whose focus upon the island's Indian and Malay heritage will complement the Asian Civilization Museum in Armenian Street (see p.558); ask at the STB for further details. The pyramid-shaped time capsule in the grounds in front of the building was sealed in 1990 as part of Singapore's silver-jubilee celebrations and is due to be opened in 2015. It contains "significant items" from Singapore's first 25 independent years: the smart money says that when opened it'll yield a Lee Kuan Yew speech or two.

Next door to Empress Place Building, two fine, off-white examples of colonial architecture, the **Victoria Concert Hall** and adjoining **Victoria Theatre**, are home to some of Singapore's most prestigious cultural events. The theatre was originally completed in 1862 as Singapore's town hall, while the Concert Hall was added in 1905 as a tribute to the monarch's reign. During the Japanese occupation, the clock tower here was altered to Tokyo time, while the statue of Raffles that once stood in front of the tower narrowly escaped being melted down. As luck would have it, the newly installed Japanese curator of the National Museum – where the statue was sent – valued it sufficiently to hide it and report it destroyed.

Further inland, along North Bank Quay, a copy of the statue marks the **landing site** where, in January 1819, the great man apparently took his first steps on Singaporean soil. Sir Stamford now stares contemplatively across the river towards the business district. The Singapore River cruise boats (see p.541) depart from a tiny jetty a few steps along from Raffles' statue.

North of the statue up Parliament Lane, the dignified white Victorian building on the left ringed by fencing is **Parliament House**, built as a private dwelling for a rich merchant by Singapore's pre-eminent colonial architect, the Irishman George Drumgould Coleman, who was named the settlement's Superintendent of Public Works in 1833. It is sometimes possible to watch Singapore's parliament in session from up in the Strangers' Gallery – call ☎3368811 for details. The bronze elephant in front of Parliament House was a gift to Singapore from King Rama V of Thailand (upon whose father *The King and I* was based) after his trip to the island in 1871 – the first foreign visit ever made by a Thai monarch.

The Padang

The **Padang**, earmarked by Raffles as a recreation ground shortly after his arrival, is the very essence of colonial Singapore; such is its symbolic significance that its borders have never been encroached upon by speculators and so it remains much as it was in 1907, when G.M. Reith wrote in his *Handbook to Singapore*, "Cricket, tennis, hockey, football and bowls are played on the plain . . . beyond the carriage drive on the other side, is a strip of green along the sea-wall, with a foot-path, which affords a cool and pleasant walk in the early morning and afternoon." Once the last over of the day had been bowled, the Padang would have assumed a more social role: the image of Singapore's European community hastening to the corner once known as Scandal Point to catch up on the latest gossip is pure Somerset Maugham. Today the Padang is still kept pristine by a bevy of gardeners on state-of-the-art lawnmowers.

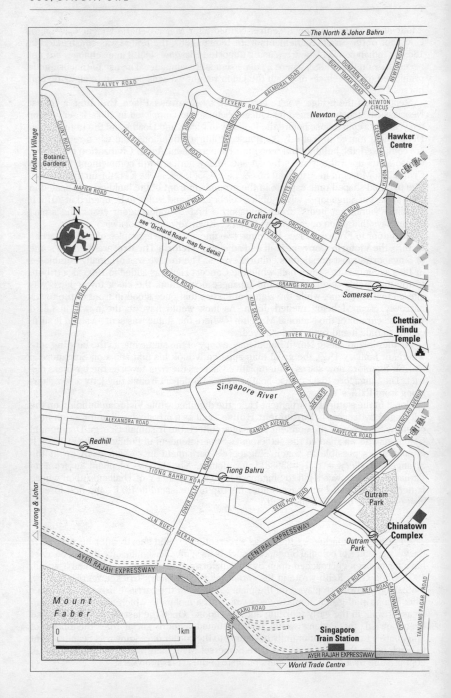

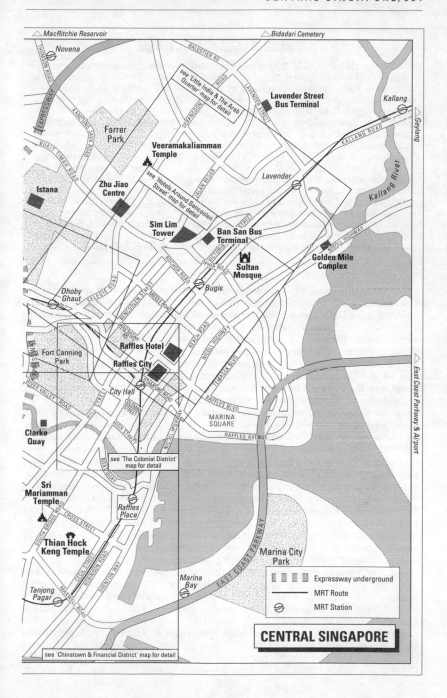

△MacRitchie Reservoir   △Bidadari Cemetery

Novena

BALESTIER RD

THOMSON ROAD

see 'Little India & The Arab Quarter' map for detail

Lavender Street Bus Terminal

Kallang

KALLANG ROAD

Seylang

Farrer Park

KAMPONG JAVA ROAD

Lavender

Veeramakaliamman Temple

Kallang River

BUKIT TIMAH ROAD

see 'Hotels Around Bencoolen Street' map for detail

Istana

Zhu Jiao Centre

Sim Lim Tower

Ban San Bus Terminal

NICOLL HIGHWAY

Golden Mile Complex

ROCHOR ROAD

OPHIR ROAD

Sultan Mosque

Dhoby Ghaut

SELEGIE ROAD

BENCOOLEN STREET

MIDDLE ROAD

Bugis

BEACH ROAD

NICOLL HIGHWAY

BRAS BASAH

Raffles Hotel

Raffles City

TEMASEK BLVD

Fort Canning Park

City Hall

STAMFORD ROAD

COLEMAN STREET

RAFFLES BLVD

RIVER VALLEY ROAD

HILL STREET

HIGH STREET

MARINA SQUARE

NICOLL HIGHWAY

RAFFLES AVENUE

Clarke Quay

see 'The Colonial District' map for detail

△East Coast Parkway & Airport

Sri Mariamman Temple

BOAT QUAY

CROSS STREET

Raffles Place

SOUTH BRIDGE ROAD

Thian Hock Keng Temple

CECIL STREET

ROBINSON ROAD

SHENTON WAY

Marina City Park

Tanjong Pagar

MAXWELL ROAD

Marina Bay

EAST COAST PARKWAY

	Expressway underground
——	MRT Route
⊖	MRT Station

CENTRAL SINGAPORE

see 'Chinatown & Financial District' map for detail

THE SEPOY MUTINY

Plaques on the west wall of St Andrew's Cathedral commemorate the victims of one of Singapore's bloodiest episodes, the **Sepoy Mutiny** of 1915. The mutiny began when a German warship, the *Emden*, was sunk by an Australian ship off the Cocos Islands: its survivors were brought to Singapore and imprisoned at Tanglin Barracks, at the western end of Orchard Road. With almost all of Singapore's troop contingent away in Europe fighting the Kaiser, soldiers of the Fifth Light Infantry, called **sepoys** – whose members were all Muslim Punjabis – were sent to guard the prisoners. Unfortunately, these men's allegiance to the British had recently been strained by the news that Muslim Turkey had come out against the Allies in Europe. A rumour that they were soon to be sent to Turkey to fight fellow Muslims upset them still further, and the German prisoners were able to incite the sepoys to mutiny. In the ensuing rampage through the city on February 15, 1915, the sepoys killed forty soldiers and civilians before they were finally rounded up by some remaining European sailors and a band of men led by the Sultan of Johor. All were court-martialled and 36 sepoys were executed before huge crowds. As for the Germans, they took the opportunity to effect an escape. Nine of them finally got back to Germany via Jakarta and one, Julius Lauterbach, received an Iron Cross in recognition of his daring and rather convoluted flight home through China and North America.

The brown-tiled roof, whitewashed walls and dark green blinds of the **Singapore Cricket Club**, at the southwestern end of the Padang, have a nostalgic charm. Founded in the 1850s, the club was the hub of colonial British society and still operates a "members only" rule, though there's nothing to stop you watching the action from outside on the Padang. The Singapore Rugby Sevens are played here, as well as a plethora of other big sporting events and parades; a timetable of forthcoming events is available at the club's reception. Eurasians who were formerly ineligible for membership of the Cricket Club founded their own establishment instead in 1883: the **Singapore Recreation Club**, which lies across on the north side of the Padang.

Just to the west of the Cricket Club, Singapore's Neoclassical **Supreme Court** (formerly the site of the exclusive *Hotel de L'Europe*, whose drawing rooms allegedly provided Somerset Maugham with inspiration for many of his Southeast Asian short stories) was built between 1937 and 1939, and sports a domed roof of green lead and a splendid, wood-panelled entrance hall – which is as far as you'll get unless you're appearing in front of the judges, as it's not open to the public. Next door is the older **City Hall**, whose uniform rows of grandiose Corinthian columns lend it the austere air of a mausoleum and reflect its role in recent Singaporean history. It was on the steps of this building that Lord Louis Mountbatten (then Supreme Allied Commander in Southeast Asia) announced Japan's surrender to the British in 1945; fourteen years later, Lee Kuan Yew chose the same spot from which to address his electorate at a victory rally celebrating self-government for Singapore. Nowadays, rather less dramatic photographs are taken on the steps as newlyweds line up to have their big day captured in front of one of Singapore's most imposing buildings.

The final building on the west side of the Padang, **St Andrew's Cathedral** (services Sun 7am, 8am, 11am, 2pm, 5pm & 7pm) on Coleman Street, gleams even brighter than the rest. The third church on this site, the cathedral was built in high-vaulted, Neo-Gothic style, using Indian convict labour, and was consecrated by Bishop Cotton of Calcutta on January 25, 1862. Its exterior walls were plastered using Madras *chunam* – an unlikely composite of eggs, lime, sugar and shredded coconut husks which shines brightly when smoothed – while the small cross behind the pulpit was crafted from two fourteenth-century nails salvaged from the ruins of England's Coventry Cathedral after it was razed to the ground during World War II. Closed-cir-

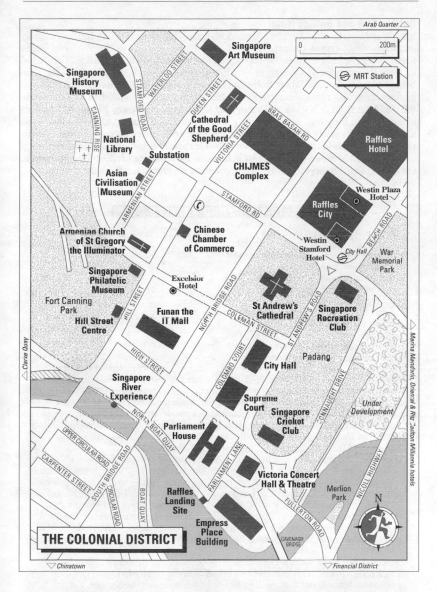

THE COLONIAL DISTRICT

cuit TVs allow the whole congregation to view proceedings up at the altar – a reflection of the Chinese fascination with all things hi-tech, which the cathedral's size hardly requires.

Land reclamation has widened the Padang to the east, but much of the waterside **Esplanade Park** is presently off-limits, while work continues on the ambitious **Theatres by the Bay** project, aimed at making Singapore the arts capital of the east.

Raffles City and Raffles Hotel

Immediately north of St Andrew's Cathedral, across Stamford Road, is **Raffles City**, an enormous development comprising two hotels – one of which is the 73-storey *Westin Stamford* – as well as a multilevel shopping centre and floor upon floor of offices. Completed in 1985, the complex was designed by Chinese-American architect I.M. Pei – the man behind the glass pyramid which fronts the Louvre in Paris – and required the highly contentious demolition of the venerable Raffles Institution, a school established by Raffles himself and built in 1835 by George Drumgould Coleman. The **Westin Stamford** holds an annual vertical marathon, in which hardy athletes attempt to run up to the top floor in as short a time as possible: the current record stands at under seven minutes. Elevators transport lesser mortals to admire the view from the *Compass Rose* bar and restaurant on the top floor. The open land east of Raffles City is home to the imposing **Civilian War Memorial**, comprising four seventy-metre-high white columns; it's known locally as the chopsticks.

SIR STAMFORD RAFFLES

Let it still be the boast of Britain
to write her name in characters of light;
let her not be remembered as the tempest
whose course was desolation,
but as the gale of spring reviving
the slumbering seeds of mind and
calling them to life
from the winter of ignorance and oppression.
If the time shall come
when her empire shall have passed away,
these monuments will endure when her triumphs
shall have become an empty name.

This verse, written by **Sir Stamford Raffles** himself, speaks volumes about the man whom history remembers as the founder of modern Singapore. Despite living and working in a period of imperial arrogance and self-motivated land-grabbing, Raffles maintained an unfailing concern for the welfare of the people under his governorship, and a conviction that British colonial expansion was for the general good – that his country was, as Jan Morris says in her introduction to Maurice Collis's biography *Raffles*, "the chief agent of human progress . . . the example of fair Government."

Fittingly for a man who was to spend his life roaming the globe, Thomas Stamford Raffles was born at sea on July 6, 1781, on the *Ann*, whose master was his father Captain Benjamin Raffles. By his fourteenth birthday, the young Raffles was working as a clerk for the **East India Company** in London, his schooling curtailed due to his father's debts. Even at this early age, Raffles' ambition and self-motivation was evident as, faced with a lifetime as a clerk, he resolved to educate himself, staying up through the night to study and developing a hunger for knowledge which would later spur him to learn Malay, amass a vast treasure trove of natural-history artefacts, and write his two-volume *History of Java*.

Abdullah bin Kadir, Raffles' clerk while in Southeast Asia, described him in his autobiography, the *Hikayat Abdullah*: "He was broad of brow, a sign of his care and thoroughness; round-headed with a projecting forehead, showing his intelligence. He had light brown hair, indicative of bravery; large ears, the mark of a ready listener. . . He was solicitous of the feelings of others, and open-handed with the poor. He spoke in smiles. He took the most active interest in historical research. Whatever he found to do he adopted no half-measures, but saw it through to the finish."

Raffles' diligence and hard work showed through in 1805, when he was chosen to join a team going out to Penang, then being developed as a British entrepôt; overnight, his

Across the way are the lofty halls, restaurants, bars, and peaceful gardens of the legendary **Raffles Hotel**, almost a byword for colonialism, prompting Somerset Maugham to remark that it "stood for all the fables of the exotic East". Oddly, though, this most inherently British of hotels started life as a modest seafront bungalow belonging to an Arab trader, Mohamed Alsagoff. After a spell as a tiffin house run by an Englishman called Captain Dare, the property was bought in 1886 by the Sarkies brothers, enterprising Armenians who eventually controlled a triumvirate of quintessentially colonial lodgings: the *Raffles*, the *Eastern and Oriental* in Penang, and the *Strand* in Rangoon.

Raffles Hotel opened for business on December 1, 1887, and quickly began to attract an impressive list of guests. It is thought that Joseph Conrad stayed in the late 1880s, and certainly Rudyard Kipling visited soon after, though at that stage the hotel couldn't, it seems, boast such sumptuous rooms as in later years. "Let the traveller take note," wrote Kipling, "feed at *Raffles* and stay at the *Hotel de l'Europe*". The hotel had its heyday dur-

annual salary leapt from £70 to £1500. Once in Southeast Asia, Raffles' rise was meteoric: by 1807 he was named chief secretary to the governor in Penang. Soon Lord Minto, the governor-general of the East India Company in India, was alerted to Raffles' Oriental expertise. Meeting Minto on a trip to Calcutta in 1810, Raffles was appointed secretary to the governor-general in Malaya, a promotion quickly followed by his becoming governor of Java in 1811. Raffles' rule of Java was wise, libertarian and compassionate, his economic, judicial and social reforms transforming an island bowed by Dutch rule.

Post-Waterloo European rebuilding saw the East Indies returned to the Dutch in 1816 – to the chagrin of Raffles, who foresaw problems for British trade should the Dutch regain their hold on the area. From Java, Raffles transferred to the governorship of Bencoolen, on the southern coast of Sumatra, but not before he had returned home for a break, stopping at St Helena en route to meet Napoleon ("a monster"). While in England he met his second wife, Sophia Hull (his first, Olivia, had died in 1814), and was knighted.

Raffles and Sophia sailed to Bencoolen in early 1818, Sophia reporting that her husband spent the four-month journey deep in study. Once in Sumatra, Raffles found the time to study the region's flora and fauna as tirelessly as ever, discovering the *Rafflesia arnoldi* – "perhaps the largest and most magnificent flower in the world" – on a jungle field trip. By now, Raffles felt strongly that Britain should establish a base in the Straits of Melaka, meeting Hastings – Minto's successor – in late 1818, he was given leave to pursue this possibility and in 1819 duly sailed to the southern tip of the Malay Peninsula, where his securing of Singapore early that year was a daring masterstroke of diplomacy.

For a man whose name is inextricably linked with Singapore, Raffles spent a remarkably short time on the island. His first stay was for one week, the second for three weeks, during which time he helped delineate the new settlement. Subsequent sojourns in Bencoolen ended tragically with the loss of four of his five children to tropical illnesses, and his own health began to deteriorate. Raffles visited Singapore one last time in late 1822, his final public duty there being to lay the foundation stone of the Singapore Institution (later the Raffles Institution), an establishment created to educate local Malays, albeit upper-class ones.

By August 1824, he was back in England. Awaiting news of a possible pension award from the East India Company, Raffles spent his free time founding the **London Zoo** and setting up a farm in Hendon. But the new life he had planned for Sophia and himself never materialized. Days after hearing that a Calcutta bank holding £16,000 of his capital had folded, his pension application was refused; worse still, the company was demanding £22,000 for overpayment. Three months later, the brain tumour that had caused him headaches for several years took his life on July 4, 1826. Buried at Hendon, he was honoured by no memorial tablet – the vicar had investments in slave plantations in the West Indies and was unimpressed by Raffles' friendship with William Wilberforce. Only in 1832 was Raffles commemorated, by a statue in Westminster Abbey.

ing the first three decades of the twentieth century, a time which saw it firmly establish its reputation for luxury and elegance – it was the first building in Singapore with electric lights and fans. In 1902, a little piece of Singaporean history was made at the hotel, according to an apocryphal tale, when the last tiger to be killed on the island was shot inside the building. Thirteen years later another *Raffles* legend, the "Singapore Sling" cocktail, was created by bartender Ngiam Tong Boon. The rich, famous and influential have always patronized the hotel, but despite a guest list heavy with politicians and film stars, the hotel is proudest of its literary connections. Herman Hesse, Somerset Maugham, Noel Coward and Günter Grass all stayed at *Raffles* at some time – Maugham is said to have written many of his Asian tales under a frangipani tree in the garden.

During World War II, British expatriates who had gathered in *Raffles* as the Japanese swept through the island in 1942 were quickly made POWs, and the hotel became a Japanese officers' quarters. After the Japanese surrender in 1945, *Raffles* became a transit camp for liberated Allied prisoners. Postwar deterioration earned it the affectionate but melancholy soubriquet, "grand old lady of the East", and the hotel was little more than a shabby tourist diversion when the government finally declared it a national monument in 1987. A $160-million facelift followed and the hotel reopened on September 16, 1991.

The new-look *Raffles* gets a very mixed reception. Though the hotel retains much of its colonial grace, the shopping arcade which now curves around the back of the building lacks class, selling *Raffles*-related souvenirs, exclusive garments, leatherware and perfume. Still, if you're in Singapore, there's no missing *Raffles* and, assuming you can't afford to stay here, there are other ways to soak up the atmosphere: a Singapore Sling in one of the hotel's several bars will cost you around $17, and upstairs at the back of the hotel complex is a free **museum** (daily 10am–9pm) crammed with memorabilia, much of which was recovered in a nationwide heritage search which encouraged Singaporeans to turn in souvenirs that had found their way up sleeves and into handbags over the years.

Bras Basah Road and the Singapore Art Museum

Bras Basah Road cuts northwest from *Raffles*, crossing North Bridge Road and then passing one of Singapore's newest and most aesthetically pleasing eating places, the **CHIJMES** complex. Based around the Neo-Gothic husk of the former Convent of the Holy Infant Jesus (from whose name the acronym for the complex is derived), CHIJMES is a rustic version of London's Covent Garden, given a sense of spatial dynamics – rare indeed in Singapore – by its lawns, courtyards, waterfalls, fountains and sunken forecourt. The shops and boutiques here open between 9am and 10pm, the restaurants and bars from 11am to 1am. Beyond CHIJMES, Bras Basah crosses Victoria and Queen streets, where elderly trishaw drivers in yellow T-shirts tout for custom, before arriving at the **Singapore Art Museum** (Tues & Thurs–Sun 9am–5.30pm, Wed 9am–9pm; $3 including free tour) on 71 Bras Basah Rd. A long-overdue replacement for the tired art wing of the National Museum, the Art Museum has a peerless location in the former St Joseph's Institution, Singapore's first Catholic school, whose impressive semicircular front facade and silvery dome rang to the sounds of school bells and rote learning until 1987. Though extensions have been necessary, many of the original rooms survive, among them the school chapel (now an auditorium), whose holy-water receptacles, stations of the cross and mosaic floor remain intact. In the school quad, the former gymnasium, glass sculptures by the American designer Dale Chihuly sprout off the walls like luminescent mushrooms.

Though the Art Museum's rolling schedule of visiting collections brings work by such acclaimed artists as Marc Chagall and the sculptor Carl Milles to Singapore, greater emphasis is placed on contemporary local and Southeast Asian artists and artwork. Indeed, the museum's real strength lies in its mapping of the Asian experience –

from Bui Xian Phai's *Coalmine*, an unremittingly desolate memory of his labour in a Vietnam re-education camp, to Srihadi Sudarsono's *Horizon Dan Prahu*, in which traditional Indonesian fishing boats ply a Mark Rothkoesque canvas. Fronted by a scattering of broken pottery, Montien Boonma's *The Pleasure of Being, Crying, Dying and Eating* comprises a tall stack of ceramic rice bowls decorated with jawbones.

Guides conduct free **tours** (Tues–Fri 11am & 2pm, Sat & Sun 11am, 2pm & 3.30pm) around the museum's major works. Outside these times, you can better get to grips with exhibits by visiting the **E-Mage Multimedia Gallery**, which gives background to the ASEAN artists and artworks featured. Outside the museum, the souvenir shop stocks prints and postcards, and there's a classy branch of *Dôme*, where you can have a coffee under the watchful gaze of a statue of the seventeenth-century saint John Baptist de la Salle, which stands over the museum's porch.

Waterloo Street and Bugis Village

Sunday sees **Waterloo Street**, flanking the Art Museum's western wall, at its best, the street springing to life as worshippers throng to its temples, churches and synagogue. The modern **Kuan Yim Temple**, named after the Buddhist Goddess of Mercy, may not have the cluttered altars, dusty rafters and elaborate roofs of Chinatown's temples, but is still extremely popular; all along the pavement outside, old ladies in floppy, wide-brimmed hats sell fresh flowers from baskets. Religious artefact shops on the ground floor of the apartment building opposite are well placed to catch worshippers on their way out – one shop specializes in small shrines for the house: the deluxe model boasts flashing lights and an extractor fan to expel unwanted incense smoke. **Fortune-tellers** and street traders operate along this stretch of the road, too, and look out for the cage containing turtles and a sleepy old snake: make a donation, touch one of the creatures inside, and it's said that good luck will come your way.

One block east of Waterloo Street's shops and temples, at the junction of Rochor Road and Victoria Street sits **Bugis Village** – a rather tame manifestation of infamous Bugis Street. Until it was demolished to make way for an MRT station, Bugis Street embodied old Singapore: after dark it was a chaotic place, crawling with rowdy sailors, transvestites and prostitutes – anathema to a Singapore government keen to clean up its country's reputation. However, Singaporean public opinion demanded a replacement, though when Bugis Village opened in 1991 with its beer gardens, seafood restaurants and pubs, it was a shadow of its former self. Although local reaction has been largely negative, a steady stream of tourists passes through nightly. The transvestites are notable only by their absence, the sole reminder of their heritage a weak cabaret show in the *Boom Boom Room* nightclub.

Hill Street and Armenian Street

From Stamford Road, **Hill Street** heads south to the river, flanking the eastern side of Fort Canning Park as it does so. A short way down Hill Street, at no. 47, is the **Singapore Chinese Chamber of Commerce**, a brash, Chinese-style building from 1964 featuring a striking pagoda roof. Along its facade are two large panels, each depicting nine intricately crafted porcelain dragons flying from the sea up to the sky. By way of contrast, the tiny Armenian **Church of St Gregory the Illuminator**, across the road and next to the former American Embassy, was designed by George Drumgould Coleman in 1835 (which makes it one of the oldest buildings in Singapore). Inside is a single, circular chamber, fronted by a marble altar and a painting of the Last Supper. Among the white gravestones and statues in the church's grounds is the tombstone of Agnes Joaquim, a nineteenth-century Armenian resident of Singapore, after whom the national flower, the delicate, purple Vanda Miss Joaquim Orchid is named; she discovered the orchid in her garden, and had it registered at the Botanic Gardens (see p.577).

The **Singapore Philatelic Museum** (Tues–Sun 9am–4.30pm; free tours at 11am and 2pm; $2), straight across Canning Rise at 23b Coleman St, makes a valiant stab at lending universal appeal to the wacky world of stamp collecting, aided by interactive games, an audiovisual theatre, and a "mail-maze".

Around the corner at 45 Armenian St, the **Substation**, a disused power station, has been converted into a multimedia arts centre, with classes, discussions and performances (see p.609 for details), and a pleasant coffee shop. A market takes place in the courtyard every Sunday afternoon, with stalls selling everything from local crafts to secondhand Russian watches.

Given that it was once home to the Tao Nan School, the first Hokkien school in Singapore, it seems appropriate that the spectacular 1910 mansion next door, fronted by two black eagles, should house so worthy a tenant as the **Asian Civilization Museum** (Tues & Thurs–Sun 9am–5.30pm, Wed 9am–9pm; $3; ☎3323015). The ten permanent galleries here together provide a cultural and historical context to Singapore's Chinese population (the museum's second phase, due to open in Empress Place Building in 2001 or so, will focus on the heritages of the island's Indian and Malay communities). After kicking off with a breakdown of China's various imperial dynasties, the galleries walk visitors through Chinese architecture, religions, and arts and crafts; the Symbolism Gallery, for instance, explains the bats, dragons and other auspicious motifs featured in Oriental art. There is much of beauty too, nowhere more so than in the Ceramics Gallery, which yields some exquisite cobalt-blue Ming pieces. Free guided tours of the museum are conducted regularly (Tues–Fri 11am & 2pm, Sat & Sun 11am, 2pm & 3.30pm).

The Singapore History Museum

Back on Stamford Road, a little way north of Armenian Street, an eye-catching dome of stained glass tops the entrance to the **Singapore History Museum** (Tues & Thurs–Sun 9am–5.30pm, Wed 9am–9pm; $3 including free tour). The museum's forerunner, the Raffles Museum and Library, was opened in 1887 and soon acquired a reputation for the excellence of its natural-history collection. In 1969, the place was renamed the National Museum in recognition of Singapore's independence, and subsequently altered its bias towards local history and culture. It's a fairly low-key collection, but one from which you can expect to wring an hour or two's enjoyment. Following a recent shake-up, the only permanent exhibitions are the **History of Singapore Gallery**, which features twenty dioramas depicting formative events in the state's history – from the arrival of Raffles in 1819 up to the first session of parliament in 1965; and the **Rumah Baba**, or Peranakan house, where the lifestyle and culture of the Straits Chinese is brought to life. Other exhibitions on disparate topics – such as the Hakka people, Chinese secret societies in Singapore, and nineteenth-century botanical prints – come and go; check the local press for details. Free **guided tours** (Tues–Fri 11am & 2pm, Sat & Sun 11am, 2pm & 3.30pm) start downstairs at the ticket counter, and the free film shows in the **AV Theatrette** (daily at 10am, noon, 2pm & 4pm), examining subjects like old Chinatown and Little India, the Singapore River and traditional kampung life, are also worth catching. From the museum, a short walk brings you to the heart of Fort Canning Park.

Fort Canning Park and around

When Raffles first caught sight of Singapore, **Fort Canning Park** was known locally as Bukit Larangan (Forbidden Hill). Malay annals tell of the five ancient kings of Singapura, said to have ruled the island from here six hundred years ago, and archeological digs have unearthed artefacts which prove it was inhabited as early as the fourteenth century. The last of the kings, Sultan Iskandar Shah, reputedly lies here, and a *keramat*, or auspicious place, on the eastern slope of the hill marks the supposed site of his grave – though the simple stone tomb doesn't look very auspicious. It was out of respect for – and fear of – his spirit that the Malays decreed the hill forbidden, and these days the *keramat* still attracts a trickle of Singaporean Muslims, as well as childless couples who offer prayers here for fertility.

However, when the British arrived, Singapore's first British Resident, William Farquhar, displayed typical colonial tact by promptly having the hill – then named Government Hill – cleared and building a bungalow, Government House, on the summit. The bungalow was subsequently replaced in 1859 by a fort named after Viscount George Canning, governor-general of India, but of this only a gateway, guardhouse and adjoining wall remain today. An early European **cemetery** survives, however, upon whose stones are engraved intriguing epitaphs to nineteenth-century sailors, traders and residents, among them pioneering colonial architect George Coleman.

History apart, Fort Canning Park is spacious and breezy and offers respite from, as well as fine views of, Singapore's crowded streets. There's a "back entrance" to the park which involves climbing the exhausting flight of steps that begins opposite the western end of High Street. Once you reach the top, there's a brilliant view along High Street towards the Merlion. The hill, which houses two theatres, is ringed by two walks, signs along which illuminate aspects of the park's fourteenth- and nineteenth-century history. Also here is the **Battle Box** (Tues–Sun 10am–6pm; adults $8, children $5), the underground operations complex from which the Allied war effort in Singapore was masterminded. Using audio and video effects and animatronics, the complex brings to life the last hours before the Japanese occupation began in February, 1942.

River Valley Road skirts the southwestern slope of Fort Canning Park, passing the **River Valley Swimming Complex** (daily 8am–9.30pm; $1; bus #32 from North Bridge Road or #54 from Scotts Rd). Evidence of the recent Singapore River development drive which initiated the beautification of Boat Quay itself can be seen across the road, where **Clarke Quay**, a chain of nineteenth-century godowns, has been converted into an attractive shopping and eating complex, though it seems gimmicky and not quite as appealing as Boat Quay (see p.568). That said, its street performers, souvenir stalls and arcades make it a reasonably buzzy place. It's possible to reach Clarke Quay by river taxi (daily 11am–11pm; every 5min; $2 return) from the quayside above the Standard Chartered Bank, two-minutes' walk from Raffles Place MRT.

The **Chettiar Hindu Temple** (daily 8am–noon & 5.30–8.30pm), a minute's walk further west at the intersection of River Valley and Tank roads, is the goal of every participant in Singapore's annual Thaipusam Festival (see p.68). This large temple, dwarfed by the pink *Imperial Hotel*, is dedicated to Lord Subramaniam and boasts a wonderful *gopuram* or bank of sculpted gods and goddesses. Built in 1984, it replaced a nineteenth-century temple built by Indian chettiars (moneylenders); inside, 48 glass panels etched with Hindu deities line the roof.

Chinatown

The two square kilometres of **Chinatown**, bounded by New Bridge Road to the west, Neil and Maxwell roads to the south, Cecil Street to the east and the Singapore River to the north, once constituted the focal point of Chinese life and culture in Singapore. Nowadays the area is on its last traditional legs, scarred by the wounds of demolition and dwarfed by the Financial District, in which the island's yuppies oversee the machinations of one of Asia's most dynamic money markets. Even so, a wander through the surviving nineteenth-century streets unearths aged craft shops, restaurants unchanged in decades and provision stores crammed with birds' nests, dried cuttlefish, ginger, chillies, mushrooms and salted fish; it's best visited in the morning, when the sun isn't yet hot enough to make walking around unpleasant.

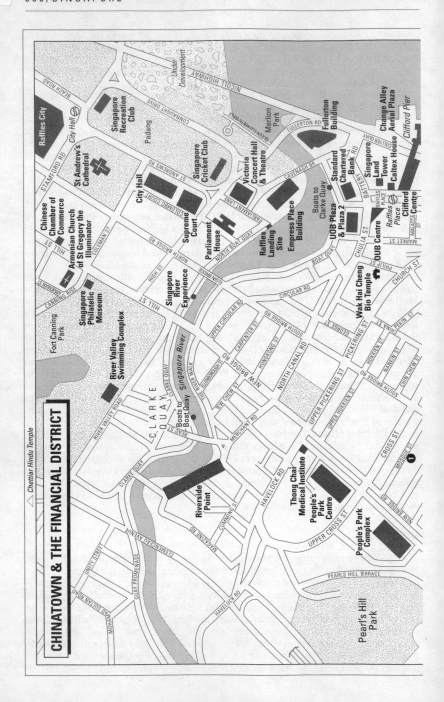

CHINATOWN & THE FINANCIAL DISTRICT

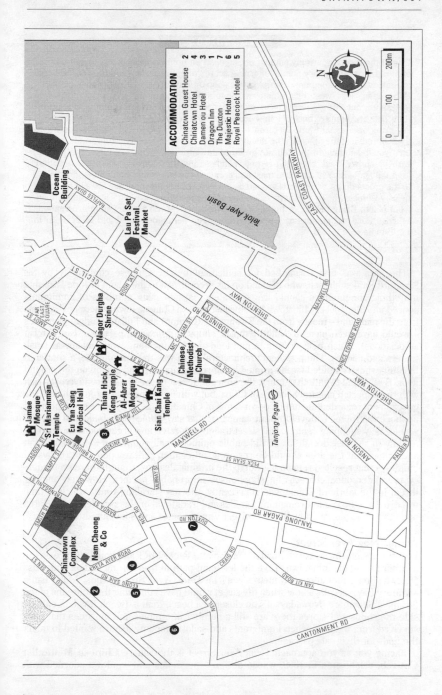

SONGBIRDS

One of the most enduringly popular of Singaporean hobbies is the keeping and training of **songbirds**, and every Sunday morning scores of enthusiasts – and their birds – congregate at an unnamed nondescript coffee shop on the corner of Tiong Bahru and Seng Poh roads, just west of Chinatown. Songbird competitions are commonplace in Singapore, but this gathering is an informal affair with bird owners coming to show off their pets and admire those of fellow collectors. The exquisite cages that house the birds are hung on a metal frame that fronts the coffee shop. Birds are grouped according to their breed, lest they pick up the distinctive songs of other breeds. The various types of bird you'll see include the delicate green Mata Puteh, or "white-eye bird"; the Jambul, with its showy black crest and red eye-patches; and the Sharma, which has beautiful, long tail feathers. You can have toast and coffee at the café while watching and listening to the proceedings, which start around 6am – a good early-morning start to a tour around nearby Chinatown. To get there, catch bus #851, which passes along Tiong Bahru Road, from North Bridge Road, or hop in a cab. The other central Sunday songbird venue is Sturdee Road, off Petain Road, which lies between Serangoon Road and Jalan Besar in Little India (see p.569).

The area was first earmarked for settlement by the Chinese community by Sir Stamford Raffles himself, who decided on his second visit to the island in June 1819 that the ethnic communities should live separately. As increasing numbers of immigrants poured into Singapore, Chinatown became just that – a Chinese town, where new arrivals from the mainland – mostly from the Kwangtong (Canton) and Fujian (Fukien) provinces – would have been pleased to find temples, shops and, most importantly, *kongsi* (clan associations), which helped them to find food and lodgings and work, mainly as small traders and coolies. The prevalent architectural form was the **shophouse**, a shuttered building whose moulded facade fronted living rooms upstairs and a shop on the ground floor. By the mid-twentieth century, the area southwest of the Singapore River was rich with the imported cultural heritage of China, but with independence came ambition: the government regarded the tumbledown slums of Chinatown as an eyesore and embarked upon a catastrophic **redevelopment** campaign that saw whole roads bulldozed to make way for new shopping centres, and street traders relocated into organized complexes.

Only in the last decade or so did public opinion finally convince the Singaporean authorities that the area should be restored rather than redeveloped. The renovated buildings that resulted remain faithful to the original designs, though there's a tendency to render once characterful shophouses improbably perfect. However, another threat to the fabric of Chinatown has recently arisen – spiralling rents, which in time will drive out the last few remaining families and traditional businesses, leaving the area open for full exploitation by bistros, advertising agencies and souvenir shops.

Along Telok Ayer Street

Follow the signs for Maxwell Road out of Tanjong Pagar MRT and you'll surface on the southern edge of Chinatown. Take the left-hand path in front of the station and cross Maxwell Road; after about fifty metres you'll hit **Telok Ayer Street**, whose Malay name – Watery Bay – recalls a time when the street would have run along the shoreline of the Straits of Singapore. Nowadays it's no closer to a beach than is Beach Road, but alongside the shops and stores there are still a number of temples and mosques that have survived from the time when immigrants and sailors stepping ashore wanted to thank the gods for their safe passage.

Facing you as you approach Telok Ayer Street is the square **Chinese Methodist Church**, established in 1889, whose design – portholes and windows adorned with white crosses and capped by a Chinese pagoda-style roof – testifies to its multicultural nature. Further up, shortly beyond McCallum Street, the enormous **Thian Hock Keng Temple**, the Temple of Heavenly Happiness, is a hugely impressive Hokkien building. Its construction begun in 1839 using materials imported from China, the temple was built on the site of a small joss house where immigrants made offerings to Ma Chu Por (also known as Tian Hou), the Queen of Heaven. A statue of the goddess, shipped in from southern China in time for the temple's completion in 1842, still stands in the centre of the main hall, flanked by the God of War on the right and the Protector of Life on the left. From the street, the temple looks spectacular: dragons stalk its broad roofs, while the entrance to the temple compound bristles with ceramic flowers, foliage and figures. Two stone lions stand guard at the entrance, and door gods, painted on the front doors, prevent evil spirits from entering. Look out, too, for the huge ovens, always lit, in which offerings to either gods or ancestors are burnt.

A block west of Telok Ayer Street is **Amoy Street**, which, – together with China Street (see below) and Telok Ayer Street, was also designated a Hokkien enclave in the colony's early days. Long terraces of shophouses flank the street, all featuring characteristic **five-foot ways**, or covered verandas, so called simply because they jut five feet out from the house. Some of the shophouses are in a ramshackle state, while others have been marvellously renovated, only to be bought by companies in need of some fancy office space. It's worth walking down to the **Sian Chai Kang Temple**, at 66 Amoy St, its eaves painted a shade of red as fiery as the dragons on its roof – it's a musty, open-fronted place dominated by huge urns, full to the brim with ash from untold numbers of burned incense sticks.

Telok Ayer Street continues north over Cross Street to **Far East Square**, a new shopping-cum-dining centre which taps Chinatown's heritage for its inspiration, and which boasts the **Fuk Tak Ch'i Street Museum** as its party piece. It's the surest sign yet of the gentrification of Chinatown that one of its oldest temples has had to suffer the ignominy of being turned into a tourist attraction – and a fairly dull one at that. The Fuk Tak Ch'i Temple was established by Singapore's Hakka and Cantonese communities in 1824. The temple has scrubbed up nicely – too nicely, in fact: none of the musty ambience that once made it such an interesting place has survived its $200,000 renovation.

On Philip Street, the **Wak Hai Cheng Bio Temple** completes Chinatown's string of former waterfront temples, fronted by an ugly concrete courtyard crisscrossed by a web of ropes supporting numerous spiralled incense sticks. Its name means "Temple of the Calm Sea", which made it a logical choice for early worshippers who had arrived safely in Singapore; an effigy of Tian Hou, the Queen of Heaven and protector of seafarers, is housed in the temple's right-hand chamber. This temple, too, has an incredibly ornate roof, crammed with tiny models of Chinese village scenes. The temple cat meanders across here sometimes, dwarfing the tableaux like a creature from a Godzilla movie.

From China Street to Ann Siang Hill

Around **China Street** and its offshoots, Chinatown becomes more residential, the roads affording at least an insight into how the area might have appeared in its prime. The old ways still survive – though only just – in this part of Singapore. In the upper windows of tumbledown shophouses, wizened old men in white T-shirts and striped pyjama trousers stare out from behind wooden gates, flanked by songbird cages and laundry poles hung with washing. Down at street level, the trishaw is still a recognized form of transport. But the traditional trades and industries – medicine shops, bakers, *popiah*-skin makers – which operated here as recently as the mid-1990s, are now a thing of the past, their shophouses converted into architects' studios, marketing agencies and the like.

At the southern end of China Street, Club Street rises up steeply, a thoroughfare once noted for its **temple-carving shops**, although these too fell to the demolition ball a couple of years ago. An impromptu **flea market** often takes shape on the far side of the car park opposite, where traders squat on their haunches surrounded by catalogues, old coins, sleeveless records and phonecards.

Even the **clan associations** and **guilds** that gave Club Street its name are fast disappearing, though there are still a few to be seen, higher up the hill. These are easy to spot; black-and-white photos of old members cover the walls, and behind the screens which almost invariably span the doorway, old men sit and chat. From upstairs, the clacking sound of mah-jong tiles reaches the street. Having laboured up Club Street to the brow of Ann Siang Hill, you may be ready for a refreshing drink in the *Ann Siang Hill Chinese Teahouse* (see box, below, for more on teahouses).

Tanjong Pagar

The district of **Tanjong Pagar**, at the southern tip of South Bridge Road and between Neil and Tanjong Pagar roads, is another area that's changed beyond recognition in recent years. Once a veritable sewer of brothels and opium dens, it was earmarked by the authorities as a conservation area, following which over two hundred shophouses were painstakingly restored, painted in sickly pastel hues and converted into bars catering to the Financial District crowd, or restaurants and shops which prey on passing tourists. The highlight of a trip around Tanjong Pagar is a stop at one of the traditional **teahouses** along Neil Road. At *Tea Chapter*, at nos. 9a–11a (daily 11am–11pm), you can have tea in the very chair in which Queen Elizabeth sat when she visited in 1989 – the shop is plastered with photographs of the occasion. The Chinese take tea-drinking very seriously – buy a bag of tea here and one of the staff will teach you all the attached rituals (see box, below). One-hundred-gramme bags go for anything from $5 to over $65; tea sets are also on sale, though they don't come cheap.

Along South Bridge Road

During the Japanese occupation, roadblocks were set up at the point where **South Bridge Road** meets Cross Street, and here Singaporeans were vetted at an interroga-

---

TAKING CHINESE TEA

If you're in need of a quick, thirst-quenching drink, avoid **Chinese teahouses**: the art of tea-making is heavily bound up in ritual, and the unhurried preparation time is crucial to the production of a pleasing brew. What's more, when you do get a cup, it's barely more than a mouthful and then the whole process kicks off again.

Tea drinking in China goes back thousands of years. Legend has it that the first cuppa was drunk by Emperor Shen Nong, who was pleasantly surprised by the aroma produced by some dried tea leaves falling into the water he was boiling; he was even more pleased when he tasted the brew. By the eighth century, making tea was such a complex art that Chinese scholar Lu Yu produced a three-volume tome on the processes involved.

Teahouses normally have conventional tables and chairs, but the authentic experience involves kneeling at a much lower traditional table. The basic procedure is as follows: the server places a towel in front of himself and his guest, with the folded edge facing the guest, and stuffs leaves into the pot with a bamboo scoop. Water, boiled over a flame, has to reach an optimum temperature, depending on which type of tea is being made; experts can tell its heat by the size of the bubbles rising, which are described variously, and rather confusingly, as "sand eyes", "prawn eyes", "fish eyes", etc. Once the pot has been warmed inside and out, the first pot of tea is made, transferred into the pouring jar and then, frustratingly, poured back *over* the pot – the thinking being that over a period of time, the porous clay of the pot becomes infused with the fragrance of the tea. Once a second pot is ready, a draught is poured into the sniffing cup, from which the aroma of the brew is savoured. Only now is it time to actually drink the tea and if you want a second cup, the complete procedure starts again.

tion post for signs of anti-Japanese feeling. Those whose answers failed to satisfy the guards either ended up as POWs or were never seen again. Nowadays – in stark contrast to the Tanjong Pagar conservation area – South Bridge Road is lined with numerous dingy shops that look as if they've seen no custom since the war.

Turn right (east) out of Ann Siang Hill and you'll see the beautifully renovated **Eu Yan Sang Medical Hall** at 267–271 South Bridge Rd (Mon–Sat 8.30am–6pm), first opened in 1910 and geared up for the tourist trade to an extent – some of the staff speak good English. The smell is the first thing you'll notice (a little like a compost heap on a hot day), the second, the weird assortment of ingredients on the shelves, which to the uninitiated look more likely to kill than cure. Besides the usual herbs and roots favoured by the Chinese are various dubious remedies derived from exotic and endangered species. Blood circulation problems and external injuries are eased with centipedes and insects, crushed into a "rubbing liquor"; the ground-up gall bladders of snakes or bears apparently work wonders on pimples; monkey's gallstones aid asthmatics; while deer penis is supposed to provide a lift to any sexual problem. Antlers, sea horses, scorpions and turtle shells also feature regularly in Chinese prescriptions, though the greatest cure-all of Oriental medicine is said to be **ginseng**, a clever little root that will combat anything from weakness of the heart to acne and jet lag. If you need a pick-me-up, or are just curious, the shop administers free glasses of ginseng tea.

Across the road from the front doors of Eu Yan Sang, the compound of the **Sri Mariamman Hindu Temple** bursts with primary-coloured, wild-looking statues of deities and animals, and there's always some ritual or other being attended to by one of the temple's priests, drafted in from the subcontinent and dressed in simple loincloths. A wood and *atap* hut was first erected here in 1827, on land belonging to Naraina Pillay – a government clerk who arrived on the same ship as Stamford Raffles, when Raffles first came ashore at Singapore. The present temple was completed in around 1843 and boasts a superb *gopuram* over the front entrance. Once inside the temple, look up at the roof and you'll see splendidly vivid friezes depicting a host of Hindu deities, including the three manifestations of the Supreme Being: Brahma the Creator (with three of his four heads showing), Vishnu the Preserver, and Shiva the Destroyer (holding one of his sons). The main sanctum, facing you as you walk inside, is devoted to Goddess Mariamman, who's worshipped for her powers to cure disease. Smaller sanctums dotted about the open walkway circumnavigating the temple honour a host of other deities. In that dedicated to Goddess Periachi Amman, a sculpture portrays her with a queen lying on her lap, whose evil child she has ripped from her womb; it's odd, then, that the Periachi Amman is the Protector of Children, to whom babies are brought when one month old. Sri Aravan, with his bushy moustache and big ears, is far less intimidating; his sanctum is at the back on the right-hand side of the complex.

To the left of the main sanctum there's an unassuming patch of sand which, once a year during the festival of **Thimithi** (see p.69), is covered in red-hot coals, which male Hindus run across to prove the strength of their faith. The participants, who line up all the way along South Bridge Road waiting for their turn, are supposedly protected from the heat of the coals by the power of prayer, though the presence of an ambulance parked round the back of the temple suggests that some aren't praying quite hard enough.

Chinatown Complex and beyond

After the crumbling Telok Ayer and China streets, much of the section of Chinatown **west of South Bridge Road** seems far less authentic. This is tour-bus Chinatown, heaving with gangs of holiday-makers plundering souvenir shops. However, until as recently as the 1950s, **Sago Street**, across South Bridge Road from Ann Siang Hill, was home to several death houses – rudimentary hospices where skeletal citizens saw out their final hours on rattan camp beds. These houses were finally deemed indecent and

SHOPPING IN CHINATOWN

As well as the markets and stores covered in the text, look out for the following, all either on or near to New Bridge Road and Eu Tong Sen Street.

Chinatown Point, 133 New Bridge Rd. One of its two buildings houses bright, fashionable, Orchard-Road-style shop units; the other is a handicraft centre, with scores of tourist-oriented businesses.

Hong Lim Complex, 531–531a Upper Cross St. Several Chinese provisions stores, fronted by sackfuls of dried mushrooms, cuttlefish, chillies, garlic cloves, onions, fritters and crackers. Other shops sell products ranging from acupuncture accessories to birds' nests.

Lucky Chinatown Complex, 11 New Bridge Rd. Fairly upmarket place with lots of jewellery shops, and even an Oriental-style *McDonalds*.

New Bridge Centre, 336 Smith St. The Da You Department Store (second floor) sells Chinese religious artefacts, tea sets and crockery.

Pearl's Centre, 100 Eu Tong Sen St. A centre for Chinese medicine. The Chinese Patent Medicines and Medicated Liquors Centre at #03-19 (daily 10am–9.30pm) and TCM Chinese Medicines at #02-21 (daily 10am–9pm) both have a Chinese clinic, where a consultation will cost you $5.

People's Park Centre, 101 Upper Cross St. Stall-like shop units selling cheap shoes, cassettes, electronics and gold. Look into Nison Department Store (daily 9.30am–10pm), on the first and second floors, which has some beautiful statues and rosewood screens.

People's Park Complex, 1 Park Rd. The Overseas Emporium is at #02-70 (daily 10am–9.30pm), and warrants a browse through its shelves of Chinese instruments, calligraphy pens, lacquerwork and jade. Cobblers set up stall in the courtyard beside the complex, behind which is a market and food centre.

have all now gone, replaced by lifeless restaurants and shops stacked to the rafters with cheap Chinese vases, teapots, cups and saucers. Sago, Smith, Temple and Pagoda streets only really recapture their youth around Chinese New Year, when they're crammed to bursting with stalls selling festive branches of blossom, oranges, sausages and waxed chickens – which look as if they have melted to reveal a handful of bones inside.

At other times of the year, give yourself an hour or so for the few things worth seeing. The hideous concrete exterior of the **Chinatown Complex**, at the end of Sago Street, belies the charm of the teeming market it houses. Walk up the front steps, past the garlic, fruit and nut hawkers, and once inside, the market's many twists and turns reveal stalls selling silk, kimonos, rattan, leather and clothes. There are no fixed prices, so you'll need to haggle. Deep in the market's belly is Yun Shi Services (shop #01-03) – where a calligrapher can quickly draw an oriental ink sign for you – while the Capitol Plastics stall (#01-16) specializes in mah-jong sets. There's a food centre on the second floor, while the wet market within the complex gets pretty packed early in the morning, when locals come to buy fresh fish or meat. Here, abacuses are still used to tally bills, and sugar canes lean like spears against the wall.

Despite **Trengganu Street**'s hordes of tourists, and the shops selling Singapore Airlines uniforms, presentation chopstick sets and silk hats with false pony tails, there are occasional glimpses of Chinatown's old trades and industries, such as Nam's Supplies at no. 22. It offers shirts, watches, mobile phones, money and passports – all made out of paper – which the Chinese burn to ensure their ancestors don't want for creature comforts in the next life, and even has "Otherworld Bank" credit cards and "Hell Airlines" plane tickets. Nam Cheong and Co, off nearby Kreta Ayer Street, takes this industry to its logical conclusion, producing huge houses and near-life-size safes, servants and Mercedes for the self-respecting ghost about town; the shop is at #01-04, Block 334, Keong Saik Road, between Chinatown Complex and New Bridge Road.

Trengganu's cross streets – Smith, Temple and Pagoda – lead west to Chinatown's main shopping drag, comprising two one-way streets, the southbound **New Bridge Road** and northbound **Eu Tong Sen Street**, along which are lined a handful of large malls. Try to pop into one of the barbecue pork vendors around the intersection of Smith, Temple and Pagoda streets with New Bridge Road – the flat squares of red, fatty, delicious meat that they cook on wire meshes over fires produce a rich, smoky odour that is pure Chinatown.

The **Thong Chai Medical Institute** has been sited at the top of Eu Tong Sen Street since 1892, when it first opened its doors with the avowed intention of dispensing free medical help regardless of race, colour or creed. Listed as a national monument, this beautiful southern Chinese-style building has recently been turned into a bar-disco (p.605) – a criminal waste of its wonderful serpentine gables and wooden inscribed pillars.

The Financial District

Until an early exercise in land reclamation in the mid-1820s rendered the zone fit for building, the patch of land south of the mouth of the Singapore River, where Raffles Place now stands, was swampland. However, within just a few years Commercial Square (later renamed Raffles Place) was the colony's busiest business address, boasting the banks, ship's chandlers and warehouses of a burgeoning trading port. The square now forms the nucleus of the **Financial District** (see map, p.560) – the commercial heart of the state, home to many of its 140 banks and financial institutions. Cutting through the district is **Battery Road**, whose name recalls the days when Fort Fullerton (named after Robert Fullerton, first Governor of the Straits Settlements) and its attendant battery of guns used to stand on the site of the Fullerton Building (until recently Singapore's GPO).

THE BARINGS BANK SCANDAL

Singapore hit the international headlines early in 1995 when the City of London's oldest merchant bank, **Barings**, collapsed as a result of what the London *Evening Standard* called "massive unauthorized dealings" in derivatives on the Japanese stock market. The supposed culprit – "the man who broke the bank", as the press dubbed him – was named as Nick Leeson, an Englishman dealing out of the bank's offices in the Financial District of Singapore. Leeson, it was alleged, had gambled huge funds in the hope of recouping losses made through ill-judged trading, only calling it a day when the bank's losses were approaching one billion pounds. One of his colleagues claimed that Leeson made "other fraudsters look like Walt Disney", although many have questioned the quality of Barings' management and financial controls which allowed such a catastrophe to happen.

By the time the scandal broke, Leeson was missing, and a manhunt across Southeast Asia was in full swing when he finally turned up – and was promptly arrested – six days later in Frankfurt. News of his capture was greeted with cheers from dealers in the Singapore Stock Exchange when it flashed across their screens. In the weeks that followed, Dutch bank ING bought Barings for one pound sterling, while Nick Leeson languished in a Frankfurt jail. In time, Singapore's application for extradition was duly granted, and less than two weeks after being passed into Singaporean custody, on December 2, 1995, Leeson pleaded guilty to two charges of deceit, receiving a six-and-a-half-year sentence, three and a half years of which he served out before he was released. In 1999, Leeson's story formed the basis of the movie *Rogue Trader*, in which he was played by Ewan McGregor.

Raffles Place and the river's south bank

Until superseded by Orchard Road in the late 1960s, **Raffles Place** was Singapore's central shopping area. Two department stores, *Robinsons* and *John Little*, dominated the area until then, but subsequent development turned Raffles Place into Singapore's financial epicentre, ringed by buildings so tall that pedestrians crossing the square feel like ants in a canyon. The most striking way to experience the giddy heights of the Financial District is by surfacing from Raffles Place MRT, following the signs for Raffles Place itself out of the station, and looking up to gleaming towers, blue skies and racing clouds. To your left is the soaring metallic triangle of the **OUB Centre** (home to the Overseas Union Bank), and to its right, the rocket-shaped **UOB Plaza 2** (United Overseas Bank); in front of you are the rich brown walls of the **Standard Chartered Bank**, and to your right rise sturdy **Singapore Land Tower** and the almost Art Deco **Caltex House**. A smallish statue, entitled *Progress and Advancement*, stands at the northern end of Raffles Place. Erected in 1988, it's a miniature version of what was then the skyline of central Singapore. Inevitably, the very progress and advancement it celebrates has already rendered it out of date – not featured is the **UOB Plaza**, a vast monolith of a building only recently built beside its twin, the UOB Plaza 2. The three roads that run southwest from Raffles Place – Cecil Street, Robinson Road and Shenton Way – are all choc-a-block with more high rise banks and financial houses; to the west is Chinatown.

Just north of Raffles Place, and beneath the "elephant's trunk" curve of the Singapore River, the pedestrianized row of shophouses known as **Boat Quay** is enjoying a renaissance. Derelict until a few years ago, it's Singapore's most fashionable hangout, sporting a huge collection of thriving restaurants and bars (see p.604), and is an excellent spot for an alfresco meal or drink.

East of Raffles Place

Branching off the second floor of the Clifford Centre, on the eastern side of Raffles Place, is **Change Alley Aerial Plaza**. The original Change Alley was a cheap, bustling street-level bazaar, wiped off the face of Singapore by redevelopment; all that remains is a sanitized, modern-day version, housed on a covered footbridge across Collyer Quay. The tailors here have a persuasive line in patter – you have to be very determined if you aren't going to waste half an hour being convinced that you need a new suit.

Walking east through Change Alley Aerial Plaza deposits you at **Clifford Pier**, long the departure point for trips on the Singapore River and to the southern islands. There are still a few bumboats tied up here, though these days they're rented out for cruises rather than as cargo boats. Visible from the pier to the north is the elegant **Fullerton Building**, fronted by sturdy pillars. Remarkably once one of Singapore's tallest buildings, it was built in 1928 as the headquarters for the General Post Office (a role it fulfilled until the mid-1990s). Old photographs of Singapore depict Japanese soldiers marching past it after the surrender of the Allied forces during World War II.

Opposite the Fullerton Building is **Merlion Park** (daily 6am–midnight; free), in which Singapore's national symbol, the statue of the mythical Merlion, presides. Half-lion, half-fish, and wholly ugly, the creature reflects Singapore's name – in Sanskrit, *Singapura* means "Lion City" – and its historical links with the sea. There are good views of Singapore's colonial buildings from the park, while beside the entrance to the park is a tacky souvenir shop shifting truck loads of Merlion T-shirts, paperweights and paperknives to passing tourists.

Back at Clifford Pier, it's just a short walk to the south along Raffles Quay to Telok Ayer Market, recently renamed **Lau Pa Sat Festival Market**. Originally built in 1894 on land reclaimed from the sea, its octagonal cast-iron frame has been turned into Singapore's most tasteful food centre (daily 24hr), which offers a range of Southeast Asian cuisines, as well as laying on free entertainment such as local bands and Chinese opera performances. After 7pm Boon Tat Street, on the south side of the market, is closed to traffic between Robinson Road and Shenton Way, and traditional hawker stalls take over the street.

One of Singapore's most ambitious land reclamation projects, **Marina South**, is plainly visible from Raffles Quay and Shenton Way. This has all the makings of a splendid folly – the entertainment and recreation park which was built on it during the 1980s has already gone bankrupt and the large patch of land now seems to serve no other purpose than to carry the East Coast Parkway on its journey west – making it surely the world's biggest bridge support. Marina South is a ghost town, its only real asset an imaginative children's playground within a pleasant park; access is by MRT from Raffles Place, or bus #400 from Tanjong Pagar MRT. Below Marina South, Singapore's **port** – the second busiest in the world after Rotterdam – begins its sprawl westwards. Hundreds of ships are docked south of the island at any one time, waiting for permission from the Port of Singapore Authority to enter one of the state's seven terminals.

Little India

A tour around **Little India** amounts to an all-out assault on the senses: Indian pop music blares out from gargantuan speakers outside cassette shops; the air is heavily perfumed with sweet incense, curry powder and jasmine garlands; Hindu women promenade in bright sarees; and a wealth of "hole-in-the-wall" restaurants serve up superior curries. The district's backbone is the north–south **Serangoon Road**, whose southern end is alive with shops, restaurants and fortune-tellers. To the east, stretching as far as Jalan Besar, is a tight knot of roads that's ripe for exploration, while parallel to Serangoon Road, **Race Course Road** boasts a clutch of fine restaurants and some temples. Little India is only a ten-minute walk from Bencoolen Street and Beach Road; to get there from Orchard Road, take bus #65 or #111 and ask for Serangoon Road. Alternatively, take the MRT to Dhoby Ghaut, hop on bus #64, #65 or #111 and, again, get off at Serangoon Road.

Indians did not always dominate this convenient central niche of Singapore, just fifteen minutes from the colonial district. The original occupants were Europeans and Eurasians who established country houses here, and for whom a race course was built (on the site of modern-day Farrer Park) in the 1840s. Only when Indian-run **brick kilns** began to operate here did an Indian community start to take shape. The enclave grew when a number of **cattle and buffalo yards** opened in the area in the latter half of the nineteenth century, and more Hindus were drawn in search of work. Street names hark back to this trade: side by side off the southern end of Serangoon Road are Buffalo Road and Kerbau (confusingly, "buffalo" in Malay) Road, along both of which cattle were kept in slaughter pens. Buffalo Road itself was once home to Singapore's largest maternity hospital (now moved a short way north to Bukit Timah Road), called Kandang Kerbau (Buffalo Pen) Hospital. Indians featured prominently in the development of Singapore, though not always out of choice: from 1825 onwards, convicts were transported from the subcontinent and by the 1840s there were over a thousand Indian prisoners labouring on buildings such as St Andrew's Cathedral and the istana.

Along Serangoon Road

Dating from 1822 and hence one of the island's oldest roadways, **Serangoon Road** is a kaleidoscopic whirl of Indian life, its shops selling everything from nostril studs and ankle bracelets to incense sticks and *kum kum* powder (used to make the red dot Hindus wear on their foreheads). Little stalls, set up in doorways and under "five-foot ways", sell garlands, gaudy posters of Hindu gods and gurus, movie soundtracks and newspapers like *The Hindu* and *India Today*. Look out for parrot-wielding **fortune-**

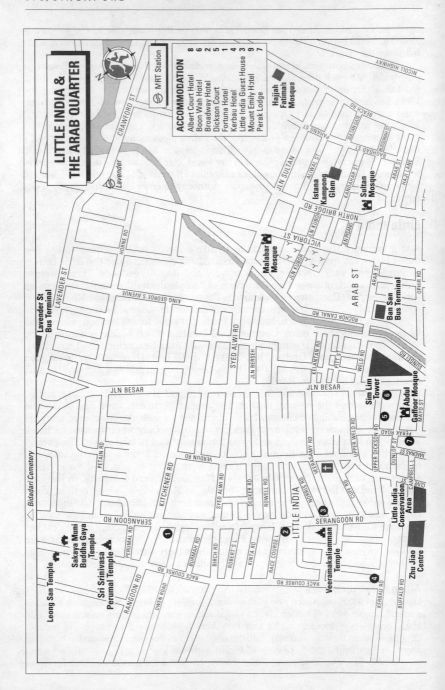

LITTLE INDIA &
THE ARAB QUARTER

MRT Station

ACCOMMODATION

Albert Court Hotel	8
Boon Wah Hotel	6
Broadway Hotel	2
Dickson Court	5
Fortuna Hotel	1
Kerbau Hotel	4
Little India Guest House	3
Mount Emily Hotel	9
Perak Lodge	7

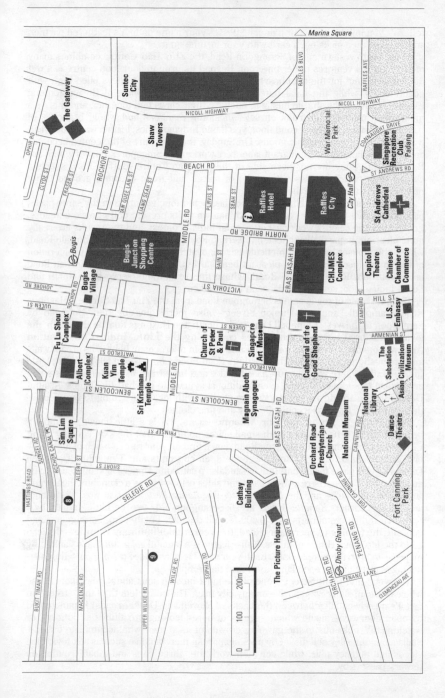

tellers – you tell the man your name, he passes your name on to his feathered partner, and the bird then picks out a card with your fortune on it.

At the southwestern end of Serangoon Road, the **Zhu Jiao Centre** combines many of Little India's ventures under one roof. Beyond its ground-floor food centre is a wet market that's not for the faint-hearted – traders push around trolleys piled high with goats' heads, while the halal butchers go to work in full view of the customers. Elsewhere, live crabs shuffle busily in buckets, their claws tied together, and there's a mouthwatering range of fruits on sale, including mangoes and whole branches of bananas. Upstairs, on the second floor, you'll find Indian fabrics, leatherware, footwear, watches and cheap electronic goods. On Sunday, the forecourt of the centre becomes an ad hoc social club for immigrant labourers working in Singapore, most of whom are Bangladeshi. Along the northern side of the Zhu Jiao Centre, Buffalo Road sports a cluster of provisions stores with sacks of spices and fresh coconut, ground using primitive machines out on the road.

Little India's remaining shophouses are fast being touched up from the same pastel paintbox as that which has "restored" Chinatown to its present doll's-house cuteness. Fortunately the colours work far better in an Indian context, and the results are really quite pleasing. In particular, check out Kerbau Road, one block north of Buffalo Road, whose shophouses have been meticulously renovated and now harbour a proliferation of Indian produce stores and a pleasant beer garden. (A right turn from Kerbau Road takes you onto **Race Course Road**, whose fine restaurants serve both North and South Indian food; several specialize in fish-head curry.)

The little braid of roads across Serangoon Road from the Zhu Jiao Centre – Hastings Road, Campbell Lane and Dunlop Street – also merits investigation. Bounded by Serangoon to the west, Campbell Lane to the north and Hastings Road to the south, the lovingly restored block of shophouses comprising the **Little India Conservation Area** was opened recently as a sort of Little India in microcosm: behind its cream walls and green shutters you'll find the Hastings Road Food Court (see p.595) and the Little India Arcade, where you can purchase textiles and tapestries, bangles, religious statuary, Indian tapes and CDs, and even traditional ayurvedic (herbal) medicines. Around Deepavali, the arcade's narrow ways are choked with locals hastening to buy decorations, garlands, traditional confectionery and fine clothes.

Dunlop Street's **Abdul Gaffoor Mosque** (at no. 41) is a little-known, crumbling beauty, built in 1910, bristling with small spires pointing up at the sky. Walking along Clive Street towards Upper Dickson Road, you'll find on your right a batch of junk dealers patiently tinkering with ancient cookers, air-con units and TVs, while Campbell Lane is a good place for buying Indian sandals. West along Upper Dickson Road – past an old barber's shop where a short back and sides is followed by a crunching head yank "to relieve tension" – are the *Madras New Woodlands Restaurant*, at nos. 12–14 and, around the corner, *Komala Villas* at 76 Serangoon Rd, two of Little India's best Southern Indian restaurants (see p.600 for full details). Further up, Serangoon Road opposite the turning to Veerasamy Road, the **Veeramakaliamman Temple** – dedicated to the ferocious Hindu goddess, Kali – features a fanciful *gopuram* that's flanked by majestic lions on the temple walls. Each year over Deepavali (see p.70), a pulsating market takes place on the open land just above the temple.

You won't find **Pink Street** – one of the most incongruous and sordid spots in the whole of clean, shiny Singapore – on any city map. The entire length of the "street" (in fact it's merely an alley between the backs of Rowell and Desker roads) is punctuated by open doorways, inside which gaggles of bored-looking prostitutes sit knitting or watching TV, oblivious to the gawping crowds of local men who accumulate outside. Stalls along the alley sell distinctly un-Singaporean merchandise such as sex toys, blue videos and potency pills, while con-men work the "three cups and a ball" routine on unwary passers-by.

North of Desker Road

Beyond Desker Road, a five-minute walk north takes you to the edge of Little India, a diversion worth making to see three very different temples. Each year, on the day of the Thaipusam festival (Jan/Feb), the courtyard of the **Sri Srinivasa Perumal Temple**, at 397 Serangoon Rd, witnesses a gruesome melee of activity, as Hindu devotees don huge metal frames (*kavadis*) topped with peacock feathers, which are fastened to their flesh with hooks and prongs. The devotees then leave the temple, stopping only while a coconut is smashed at their feet for good luck, and parade all the way to the Chettiar Temple on Tank Road, off Orchard Road. Even if you miss the festival, it's worth a trip to see the five-tiered *gopuram* with its sculptures of the various manifestations of Lord Vishnu the Preserver. On the wall to the right of the front gate, a sculpted elephant, its leg caught in a crocodile's mouth, trumpets silently.

Just beyond the Sri Srinivasa temple complex, a small path leads northwest to Race Course Road, where the **Sakaya Muni Buddha Gaya Temple** (also called the Temple of the Thousand Lights) is on the right at no. 366. Slightly kitsch, the temple betrays a strong Thai influence – which isn't surprising as it was built entirely by a Thai monk, Vutthisasala. On the left of the temple as you enter is a huge replica of Buddha's footprint, inlaid with mother-of-pearl; beyond sits a huge Buddha ringed by the thousand electric lights from which the temple takes its alternative name; while 25 scenes from the Buddha's life decorate the pedestal on which he sits. It is possible to walk inside the Buddha, through a door in his back; inside is a smaller representation, this time of Buddha reclining. The left wall of the temple features a sort of wheel of fortune – to discover your fortune, spin it (for 30¢) and take the numbered sheet of paper that corresponds to the number at which the wheel stops. Further along the left wall, a small donation entitles you to a shake of a tin full of numbered sticks, after which, again, you get a corresponding sheet of forecasts.

Back on Serangoon Road, a five-minute walk southeast along Petain Road towards Jalan Besar takes in some immaculate examples of **Peranakan shophouses**, their facades covered with elegant ceramic tiles reminiscent of Portuguese *azulejos*. There's more Peranakan architecture on display on Jalan Besar itself, a little way south (right) of the junction with Petain Road. Further south, a daily **flea market** takes place around Pitt Street, Weld Road, Kelantan Lane and Pasar Lane – secondhand tools, odd shoes and foreign currency are all laid out for sale on plastic sheets at the side of the road.

The Arab Quarter and around

Before the arrival of Raffles, the area of Singapore west of the Rochor River housed a Malay village known as Kampung Glam, after the Gelam tribe of sea gypsies who lived there. After signing a dubious treaty with the newly installed "Sultan" Hussein Mohammed Shah (see p.531), Raffles allotted the area to the sultan and designated the land around it as a Muslim settlement. Soon the zone was attracting Arab traders, as the road names in today's **Arab Quarter** – Baghdad Street, Muscat Street and Haji Lane – suggest. Even now, descendants of Sultan Hussein live in the grounds of the Istana Kampong Glam, a palace right in the centre of the district, bounded by Arab Street, Beach Road, Jalan Sultan and Rochor Canal Road.

The Arab Quarter is no more than a ten-minute walk from Bencoolen Street. To get there from Orchard Road, take bus #7 to Victoria Street and get off when you spot the *Landmark Mercure Hotel* on your right; alternatively, head for Bugis MRT.

Arab Street to North Bridge Road

While Little India is memorable for its fragrances, it's the vibrant colours of the shops of **Arab Street** and its environs that stick in the memory. The street boasts the highest concentration of shops in the Arab Quarter; its pavements are an obstacle course of carpets, cloths, baskets and bags. Most of the shops have been modernized, though one or two (like Shivlal & Sons at no. 77, and Aik Bee at no. 73) still retain their original dark wood and glass cabinets, and wide wooden benches where the shopkeepers sit. Textile stores are most prominent, their walls, ceilings and doorways draped with cloths and batiks. Elsewhere you'll see leather, basketware, gold, gemstones and jewellery for sale, while the most impressive range of basketware and rattan work – fans, hats and walking sticks – is found at Rishi Handicrafts, at no. 58. It's easy to spend a couple of hours weaving in and out of the stores, but don't expect a quiet window-shopping session – the traders here are masters of the forced sale, and will have you loaded with sarongs, baskets and leather bags before you know it.

The quarter's most evocative patch is the stretch of **North Bridge Road** between Arab Street and Jalan Sultan. Here, the men sport long sarongs and Abe Lincoln beards, the women fantastically colourful shawls and robes, while the shops and restaurants are geared more towards locals than tourists: Jamal Kazura Aromatics at 728 North Bridge Rd, for instance, sells alcohol-free perfumes, while neighbouring stores stock rosaries, prayer mats, the *songkok* hats worn by Muslim males in mosques, and *miswak* sticks – twigs the width of a finger used by some locals to clean their teeth.

Several roads run off the western side of North Bridge Road, including Jalan Pisang (Banana St), on which a street barber works under a tarpaulin. A walk up Jalan Kubor (Grave St) and across Victoria Street takes you to an unkempt Muslim **cemetery** where, it is said, Malay royalty are buried. On Sundays, Victoria Street throngs with children in full Muslim garb on their way to study scripture at the religious school, **Madrasah Al Junied Al-Islamiah**, on North Bridge Road.

Sultan Mosque and Istana Kampung Glam

Along the eastern side of North Bridge Road (though the best initial views of its golden domes are from pedestrianized Bussorah St to the east) is the **Sultan Mosque** or Masjid Sultan (daily 9am–1pm), the beating heart of the Muslim faith in Singapore. An earlier mosque stood on this site, finished in 1825 and constructed with the help of a $3000 donation from the East India Company. The present building was completed a century later, according to a design by colonial architects Swan and MacLaren; if you look carefully at the necks of the domes, you can see that the glistening effect is created by the bases of thousands of ordinary glass bottles attached flush against the surface, an incongruity which sets the tone for the rest of the building. In the wide lobby, reached by steps at the top of Bussorah Street, a digital display lists current prayer times. Beyond, though out of bounds to non-Muslims, is the main prayer hall, a large, bare chamber fronted by two more digital clocks which enable the faithful to time their prayers to the exact second.

An exhaustive set of rules applies to visitors wishing to enter the lobby: shoes must be taken off and shoulders and legs covered; no video cameras are allowed inside the mosque and entry is not permitted during the Friday mass congregation (11.30am–2.30pm). The best time to come is in the Muslim fasting month of **Ramadan** (see p.70) – when the faithful can only eat after dusk, and Muskat and Kandahar streets are awash with stalls selling *biriyani*, barbecued chicken and cakes.

Squatting between Kandahar and Aliwal streets, the **Istana Kampong Glam** was built as the royal palace of Sultan Ali Iskandar Shah, son of Sultan Hussein who negotiated with Raffles to hand over Singapore to the British; the sultan's descendants live here to this day, and continue to share an annual government allowance. Despite its royal provenance, the istana is a modest, colonial-style building, run-down and dingy, its grounds dotted with huts. This could change, though, if plans to turn the property into a Malay heritage museum come to fruition. Until this happens, tourists have to make do with glimpsing the building from the front gates. Outside there's a **stonemason's** shop on the corner of Baghdad Street and Sultan Gate, which chips out the lions that stand outside Chinese temples, and Muslim graves – uniformly shaped stones that look remarkably like chess pawns.

Beach Road

It's only a five-minute walk on to the **Hajjah Fatimah Mosque** on **Beach Road**, just outside the quarter proper, where a collection of photographs in the entrance porch show the mosque through the years following its construction in 1846 – first surrounded by shophouses, then by open land, and finally by huge housing projects. Across from the mosque, the **Golden Mile Complex** at 5001 Beach Rd attracts so many Thai nationals that locals refer to it as "Thai Village". Numerous bus firms selling tickets to Thailand operate out of here, while inside, the shops sell Thai foodstuffs, cafés sell Singha beer and Mekong whisky, and authentic restaurants serve up old favourites. On a Sunday, Thais come down here in hordes to meet up with their compatriots, listen to Thai pop music, and have a few drinks.

Beach Road still maintains shops – ships' chandlers and fishing-tackle specialists – which betray its former proximity to the sea. It's worth taking the time to walk southwest along Beach Road to see the two logic-defying office buildings that together comprise **The Gateway**. Designed by I.M. Pei, they rise magnificently into the air like vast razor blades, appearing two-dimensional when viewed from certain angles.

Orchard Road and around

It would be hard to conjure an image more diametrically opposed to the reality of modern-day **Orchard Road** than C.M. Turnbull's description of it during early colonial times as "a country lane lined with bamboo hedges and shrubbery, with trees meeting overhead for its whole length". One hundred years ago, a stroll down Orchard Road would have passed row upon row of nutmeg trees, and would have been enjoyed in the

ORCHARD ROAD SHOPPING CENTRES

The main Orchard Road shopping centres are detailed below; see map on p.576.

Centrepoint Dependable all-round complex, whose seven floors of shops include Marks and Spencers and Robinsons, the latter Singapore's oldest department store.

C.K. Tang's Singapore's most famous department store, whose pagoda-style construction provides Orchard Road with one of its most recognizable landmarks. Unlike other malls, it's closed on Sunday.

Delfi Orchard Good for crystalware, glassware and art galleries.

Forum the Shopping Mall Kids' clothes, toyshops, modelling specialists and clothes stores.

Lucky Plaza Crammed with tailors and electronics, this is Orchard Road's classic venue for haggling.

Ngee Ann City A brooding twin-towered complex – Singapore meets Gotham City – with a wealth of good clothes shops and Kinokuniya, the biggest bookstore on the island.

Orchard Plaza Tailors, leather jackets and silks galore, as well as a glut of audio, video and camera stores where haggling is par for the course.

Palais Renaissance One of Singapore's classiest complexes, featuring Prada, Versace, Ralph Lauren, Gucci, Christian Dior and other heavyweights.

Plaza Singapura Sportswear and sports equipment, musical instruments, audio, video and general electrical equipment, and the Yaohan department store.

Tanglin Shopping Centre Unsurpassed for art, antiques and curios.

Wheelock Place One of the newer shopping centres on the block, this impressive pyramid of a building boasts a well-stocked Border's bookshop.

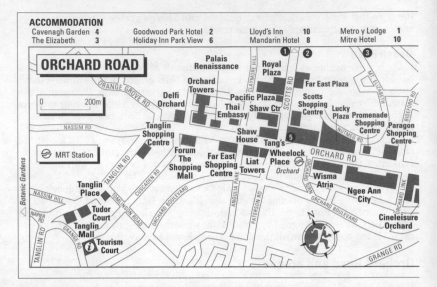

company of merchants taking their daily constitutionals, followed at a discreet distance by their trusty manservants. Today, Orchard Road is synonymous with shopping – indeed, tourist brochures refer to it as the "Fifth Avenue, the Regent Street, the Champs Elysées, the Via Veneto and the Ginza of Singapore". Huge malls, selling everything you can imagine, line the road, though don't expect shopping here to be relaxing; hordes of dawdling tourists from the numerous hotels along the road make browsing difficult. The road runs northwest from Fort Canning Park and is served by three MRT stations, Dhoby Ghaut, Somerset and Orchard, of which the last is the most central for shopping expeditions; the pick of the malls are listed in the box overleaf.

From Dhoby Ghaut to the Istana

In the **Dhoby Ghaut** area (at the eastern tip of Orchard Road), Indian *dhobies*, or laundrymen, used to wash clothes in the Stamford Canal, which once ran along Orchard and Stamford roads. Three minutes' walk west along Orchard Road from Dhoby Ghaut MRT takes you past Plaza Singapura, beyond which stern-looking soldiers guard the gate of the **Istana Negara Singapura**. Built in 1869, the istana, with its ornate cornices, elegant louvred shutters and high mansard roof, was originally the official residence of Singapore's British governors, though on independence it became the residence of the president of Singapore – currently Ong Teng Cheong, whose portrait you'll see in banks, post offices and shops across the state. The shuttered istana is only open to visitors on public holidays and is probably worth a visit if your trip coincides with one – the president goes walkabout at some point during every open day as thousands of Singaporeans flock to picnic on the well-landscaped sweeps and dips of its lawns, and brass bands belt out jaunty tunes. There's also a **changing of the guard** ceremony, which takes place at the gates onto Orchard Road (first Sun of every month at 5.45pm).

The **Tan Yeok Nee Mansion**, across the road at 207 Clemenceau Ave, is currently closed and its future is unclear. Built in traditional southern Chinese style for a wealthy Teochew merchant who traded in pepper and gambier (a resin used in tanning), and featuring ornate roofs and massive granite pillars, the mid-1880s mansion served as headquarters to the Singapore Salvation Army from 1940 until 1991.

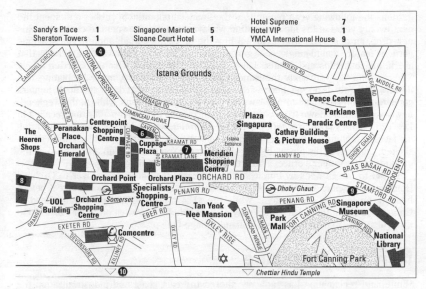

Sandy's Place   **1**   Singapore Marriott   **5**   Hotel Supreme   **7**
Sheraton Towers   **1**   Sloane Court Hotel   **1**   Hotel VIP   **1**
                                                       YMCA International House   **9**

Cuppage Road, Emerald Hill and the Goodwood Hotel

Further along Orchard Road, most of **Cuppage Road** has been pedestrianized, making it a great place to sit out and have a beer or a meal. **Cuppage Terrace**, halfway along on the left, is an unusually (for Orchard Road) old row of shophouses, where a burgeoning restaurant and bar scene has developed. A number of even more architecturally notable houses have also survived the bulldozers in Emerald Hill Road, parallel to Cuppage Road. **Emerald Hill** was granted to Englishman William Cuppage in 1845 and for some years afterwards was the site of a large nutmeg plantation. After Cuppage's death in 1872, the land was subdivided and sold off, much of it bought by members of the Peranakan community (see p.60). A walk up Emerald Hill Road takes you past a number of exquisitely crafted houses dating from this period, built in a decorative architectural style known as Chinese Baroque, typified by highly coloured ceramic tiles, carved swing doors, shuttered windows and pastel-shaded walls with fine plaster mouldings.

West of Emerald Hill Road, the **shopping centres** of Orchard Road begin to come thick and fast. Once you reach Orchard MRT station, a couple of minutes' walk north up Scotts Road brings you to the gleaming white walls of the impressive **Goodwood Hotel**, which started life in 1900 as the Teutonia Club for German expats. With the start of war across Europe in 1914, the club was commandeered by the British Custodian of Enemy Property and didn't open again until 1918, after which it served for several years as a function hall. In 1929 it became a hotel, though by 1942 the Goodwood – like *Raffles* – was lodging Japanese officers. It's fitting, then, that the hotel was chosen, after the war, as one of the venues for a war crimes court.

The Botanic Gardens

A ten-minute walk from the western end of Orchard Road are the open spaces of the **Singapore Botanic Gardens** (daily 5am–midnight; free) on Cluny Road. Founded in 1859, it was where the Brazilian seeds that gave rise to the great **rubber plantations** of Malaysia were first nurtured in 1877. Henry Ridley, named director of the botanic gardens the following year, recognized the financial potential of rubber and spent the next twenty years of his life persuading Malayan plantation-owners to convert to this new crop, an obsession which earned him the nickname "Mad" Ridley. The spacious gardens feature a mini-jungle, rose garden, topiary, fernery, palm valley, and lakes that are home to turtles and swans. There's also the **National Orchid Garden** (daily 8.30am–7pm; $2) with sixty thousand plants; orchid jewellery, made by plating real flowers with gold, is on sale here – at around $100 per piece. At dawn and dusk, joggers and students of t'ai chi haunt the lawns and paths of the gardens, while at the weekend, newlyweds bundle down from church for their photos to be taken – a ritual recalled in Lee Tzu Pheng's poem, *Bridal Party at the Botanics*, whose bride's "two hundred dollar face/is melting in the sun", while beside her is her groom, "black-stuffed, oil-slicked, fainting/in his finery, by the shrubbery". You can pick up a free **map** of the grounds at the ranger's office, a little to the right of the main gate.

To get to the gardens by bus from the Orchard Road area, cross over to Orchard Boulevard and catch #7, #106 or #174. The #106 passes down Bencoolen Street before heading on towards the gardens, while the #174 originates in New Bridge Road in Chinatown. From the gardens, it's only a short ride further west on bus #7 or #106 to the restaurants and craft shops of Holland Village (see p.587).

Northern Singapore

While land reclamation has radically altered the east coast and industrialization the west, the **northern** expanses of the island up to the Straits of Johor still retain pockets of the **rainforest** and mangrove swamp which blanketed Singapore on Raffles' arrival in 1819. Today, these are interspersed with sprawling **new towns** like Toa Payoh, maze-like Bishan and Ang Mo Kio, built in the 1970s. The name of the last, meaning "red-haired one's bridge" refers to the nineteenth-century British surveyor, John Turnbull Thomson, under whose supervision the transport network of Singapore began to penetrate the interior of the island. Man-eating tigers roamed these parts well into the twentieth century, and it was here that Allied forces confronted the invading Japanese army in 1942, a period of Singaporean history movingly recalled by the **Kranji War Memorial** on Woodlands Road. What remains of Singapore's agricultural past still clings tenaciously to the far northern sweep of the island: you'll see prawn and poultry farms, orchards and vegetable gardens when travelling in these parts.

Dominating the central northern region are two nature reserves, divided by the Bukit Timah Expressway, the main road route to Malaysia. West of the expressway is **Bukit Timah Nature Reserve**, an accessible slice of primary rainforest, while to the east, the four reservoirs of the Central Catchment Area are one of Singapore's main sources of water. North of here, the zone's principal tourist attraction is the excellent **Singapore Zoological Gardens**, sited on a finger of land pointing into the Seletar Reservoir. To the east are two of Singapore's most eye-catching Buddhist temples – **Siong Lim Temple** and the **Kong Meng San Phor Kark See** temple complex – as well as tiny Tai Gin Road, which houses both the former occasional residence of Chinese nationalist leader Dr Sun Yat Sen, and Singapore's Burmese temple.

Exploring the north is a matter of pinpointing the particular sight you want to see and heading straight for it; the bus trip to the zoo, for instance, takes around 45 minutes from downtown Singapore. Travel between all these places is decidedly tricky unless you are driving or in a cab, so don't expect to take in everything in a day. However, Siong Lim Temple, Sun Yat Sen Villa and the Burmese Temple all nestle around the outskirts of Toa Payoh new town and could be incorporated into a single expedition; as could the zoo, Mandai Orchid Gardens and the Kranji cemetery and memorial. The Kong Meng San Phor Kark See temple complex really requires a separate journey.

Bukit Timah

Bukit Timah Road shoots northwest from the junction of Selegie and Serangoon roads, arriving at the faceless suburb of **Bukit Timah** 8km later. Bukit Timah boasts Singapore's last remaining pocket of primary rainforest, which now comprises **Bukit Timah Nature Reserve** (daily 7am–7pm; free). Several **buses** head here from the city: #171 passes down Somerset and Scotts roads en route to Bukit Timah Reserve, while the #181 can be picked up on North Bridge Road, South Bridge Road or New Bridge Road; a third option is to take the #170 from the Ban San Terminal on Queen Street.

Visiting this area of Singapore in the mid-eighteenth century, natural-historian Alfred Russell Wallace reported seeing "tiger pits, carefully covered with sticks and leaves and so well concealed, that in several cases I had a narrow escape from falling into them . . . Formerly a sharp stake was stuck erect in the bottom," he continued, "but after an unfortunate traveller had been killed by falling into one, its use was forbidden." Today the 81-hectare reserve, established in 1883 by Nathaniel Cantley, then superintendent of the Botanic Gardens, yields no such hazards and provides a refuge for the dwindling numbers of species still extant in Singapore – only 25 types of mammal now inhabit the island. Creatures you're most likely to see in Bukit Timah are long-tailed macaques, butterflies, insects, and birds like the dark-necked tailorbird, which builds its nest by sewing together leaves. Scorpions, snakes, flying lemurs and pangolins (anteaters, whose name is derived from the Malay word *peng-goling*, meaning "roller", a reference to the animal's habit of rolling into a ball when threatened) can be found here too.

Recent alterations have vastly improved the reserve, which now has an informative visitor centre (daily 8.30am–6pm) full of displays, specimens and photos relating to the wildlife beyond. Four main paths from the centre twist and turn through the forest around and up to the top of **Bukit Timah** itself, a hill which – at a paltry 162.5m – is actually Singapore's highest. The paths are all well signposted, colour-coded and dotted with rest and shelter points, and clearly mapped on the free leaflet handed out to all visitors. You'd do best to visit in the early morning (when it's cooler) and during the week (when there are fewer visitors). Dramatic **Hindhede Quarry** (five-minutes' walk up the slope to the left of the visitor centre) is a fine place to head for once you've explored the forest – its deep green waters are ideal for a cooling swim.

West across Bukit Timah Road from the reserve is another forested hill, **Bukit Batok**, where British and Australian POWs were forced to erect a fifteen-metre-high wooden shrine, the Syonan Tyureito, for their Japanese captors. Only the steps at its base now remain. Legend has it that the shrine itself was destroyed by termites which the prisoners secretly introduced to the structure. Gone, too, is the wooden cross erected by the POWs to honour their dead. Any of the buses from the city centre to Bukit Timah continue to the entrance to Bukit Batok; get off the bus when you see Old Jurong Road on your left, a few hundred metres beyond the turning for Bukit Timah Nature Reserve. The hill is located at the end of Lorong Sesuai, the next turning left, the road itself laid by the same prisoners who constructed the shrine.

The zoo and Mandai Orchid Gardens

On Mandai Lake Road off the Bukit Timah Expressway, the **Singapore Zoological Gardens** (daily 8.30am–6pm; $10.30, children $4.60) are spread over a promontory jutting into peaceful Seletar Reservoir. The gardens attract over one million visitors a year – a fact perhaps explained by their status as one of the world's few open zoos, where moats are preferred to cages. The zoo manages to approximate the natural habitats of the animals it holds, and though leopards, pumas and jaguars still have to be kept behind bars, this is a thoughtful, humane place, described as "one of the really beautiful zoos" by the conservationist Sir Peter Scott.

There are over two thousand animals here, representing more than 240 species, so it's best to allow a whole day for your visit. A **tram** ($2) circles the grounds on a one-way circuit, but as it won't always be going your way, be prepared for a lot of legwork. Highlights include the komodo dragons, the polar bears (which you view underwater from a gallery) and the primate kingdom; also worth checking out is the **special loan enclosure**, which has recently played host to a giant panda, an Indian white tiger and a golden monkey. Two **animal shows** are featured daily – a primate and reptile show (10.30am & 2.30pm) and an elephant and sea lion show (11.30am & 3.30pm), the sea lions skidding, swimming and jumping to the theme from *Hawaii Five-O*. Kids tend to get most out of these shows, and the **Children's World** enclosure offers them the chance to ride a camel, hold young chicks and see a milking demonstration; at 9am and 4pm daily they can even share a meal with an **orang-utan** (see p.594).

On the **Night Safari** (daily 7.30pm–midnight; $15.45, children $10.30), over a hundred species of animals – among them elephants, rhinos, giraffes, leopards, hyenas, otters, and incredibly cute fishing cats – play out their nocturnal routines under a forest of standard lamps. Only five of the safari's eight zones are walkable – to see the rest you'll need to take a fifty-minute Jurassic Park-style tram ride ($3), and tolerate the intrusive chattering of its taped commentary.

PRACTICALITIES

To get to the zoo, take **bus** #171 from Stamford Road, Orchard Boulevard or Bukit Timah to Mandai Road, then transfer to the #138; alternatively, take the MRT to Ang Mo Kio station and catch the #138 from there. The $1 *Guide to S'pore Zoo* booklet, which you can buy on arrival, suggests itineraries which take in all the major shows and attractions, and contains riding and feeding times as well as a helpful map. At the other end of your trip, drop by the **gift shop** next to the exit, which stocks cuddly toys and rather less tempting bags of "zoo poo" compost.

Several **food** and drink kiosks are dotted around the zoo, or you can head for the reasonable *Makan Terrace*, bang in the centre of the grounds, where there are one or two hawker stalls. A meal at one of two fast-food outlets outside the entrance passes the time between the zoo's closing and the safari's opening.

Mandai Orchid Gardens

It's only a ten-minute walk from the zoo down Mandai Lake Road to the **Mandai Orchid Gardens** (daily 8.30am–5.30pm; $2), or you can take the #138 bus from the zoo, which stops right outside. Orchids are big business in Singapore: in 1991 alone, over $20 million of cut orchid flowers were exported from 56 orchid farms across the state. Here, four hectares of flowers are cultivated on a gentle slope, tended by old ladies in wide-brimmed hats. Unless you are a keen horticulturist, the place will be of only limited interest, since little effort has been taken to make it instructive. Still, the gardens make a colourful detour, and the cost of a gift box of orchids (under $70) compares favourably with prices charged by central flower shops.

North to Woodlands and the Sungei Buloh Nature Park

Five kilometres north of the zoo is the bustling town of **WOODLANDS**, from where the **causeway** spanning the Strait of Johor links Singapore to Johor Bahru in Malaysia. At peak hours (6.30–9.30am & 5.30–7.30pm) and at weekends, the roads leading to the causeway seethe with cars and trucks – all full of petrol, after a law passed in the early 1990s banned Singaporeans from driving out of the country on an empty tank.

Previously, people crossed into Malaysia, filled up with cut-price fuel and then headed home; now, signs line the roads approaching the causeway requesting that "Singapore cars please top up to 3/4 tank" – or risk a $500 fine.

Kranji War Memorial

Bus #170 from Ban San Terminal on Queen Street heads towards Woodlands on its way to JB, passing the **Kranji War Cemetery and Memorial** on Woodlands Road, where only the sound of birds and insects breaks the silence in the immaculate grounds. This is the resting place of the many Allied troops who died in the defence of Singapore; as you enter, row upon row of graves slope up the landscaped hill in front of you, some identified only as "known unto God". The graves are bare: placing flowers is banned because still water encourages mosquitoes to breed. Above the simple stone cross which stands over the cemetery is the **memorial**, around which are recorded the names of more than twenty thousand soldiers (including personnel from Britain, Canada, Australia, New Zealand, Malay and South Asia) who died in this region during World War II. Two unassuming **tombs** stand on the wide lawns below the cemetery, belonging to Yusof Bin Ishak and Dr Benjamin Henry Sheares, independent Singapore's first two presidents. As well as the #170, bus #181 from New Bridge Road and #182 from Stamford Road or Orchard Boulevard pass the cemetery; the journey takes at least 45 minutes.

The Turf Club

Singapore's only racecourse (reached on bus #170) is at **Singapore Turf Club**, a short way beyond the war memorial. As gambling in Singapore outside the course is severely restricted by law, the annual racing calendar here is very popular; the most prestigious events include the Lion City Cup, the Singapore Gold Cup and the Singapore Derby. Race dates change from year to year, so it's worth calling the information hotline (☎8791000) if you want to time your visit to coincide with a big race day. An evening's racing viewed from the enclosure can be booked in advance, but you'd do far better to just turn up, eat at the course's decent food centre and soak up the atmosphere in the stands. There's a fairly strict dress code – sandals, jeans, shorts and T-shirts are out – and foreign visitors have to take their passports with them. When there's no racing in Singapore, a giant video screen links the racecourse to various courses across the causeway in Malaysia.

Sungei Buloh Nature Park

Singapore's newest wildlife sanctuary, **Sungei Buloh Nature Park** (daily 7am–7pm; $1; ☎7941401) lies some 4–5km northwest of Kranji Cemetery, on the north coast. Beyond its visitor centre, café and video theatre (shows daily 9am, 11am, 1pm & 3pm) stretch 87 hectares of mangrove, mud flats, orchards and grassland hosting creatures such as kingfishers and mudskippers, herons and sea eagles. Between September and March, among the birds you're likely to catch sight of are migratory birds from around Asia roosting and feeding. To reach the park, take the MRT to either Woodlands or Kranji station, then transfer to bus #925, which stops at Kranji car park from Monday to Friday, and right at the park's entrance on Saturday and Sunday.

Tai Gin Road: the Sun Yat Sen Villa and Burmese Temple

Between Jalan Toa Payoh to the north and Balestier Road to the south is the **Sun Yat Sen Villa** (Mon–Fri 9am–4pm, Sat 9am–3pm; free), on tiny Tai Gin Road. Built to house the mistress of a wealthy Chinese businessman, this attractive bungalow changed hands in 1905, when one Teo Eng Hock bought it for his mother. Chinese nationalist leader Dr Sun Yat Sen paid his first of eight visits to Singapore the following year, and was invited by Teo to stay at Tai Gin Road, where he quickly established a Singapore branch of the Tong Meng Hui – a society dedicated to replacing the Manchu dynasty in China with a modern republic. After serving as a communications camp for the Japanese during World War II, the villa fell into disrepair until 1966, when it was opened to the public. Sadly, the collection of photographs inside is fairly dull unless you are familiar with that period of Chinese history; of more interest is the second-floor gallery with photos of Singapore during World War II, and an accompanying collection of combs, keys, pipes, glasses and other personal effects of victims of the Japanese occupation.

Next door is the **Sasanaramsi Burmese Buddhist Temple** (daily 6am–10pm), reconstructed in just two years having been moved from its previous site at Kinta Road because of redevelopment. Decorated by craftsmen from Burma, the temple's ground floor is dominated by a large, white-marble statue of the Buddha brought over from Burma in 1932; upstairs is another Buddha statue, this time standing, and ringed by blue sky painted on the wall behind. Tiny Buddha images have been "bought" by worshippers at $1000 a throw and mounted on the painted sky.

Bus #139 from Selegie Road comes out this way. You'll see a BP service station on the right of Balestier Road after about ten minutes – get off at the next stop, where Tai Gin Road is across the road and down a short footpath.

The Siong Lim and Phor Kark See temples

Two of Singapore's largest Chinese temples are situated in the island's central region, east of the Central Catchment Area. Both are rather isolated, but have plenty to interest temple enthusiasts, and buzz with activity at festival times.

The name of the popular **Siong Lim Temple**, at 184e Jalan Toa Payoh (bus #8 from outside Toa Payoh MRT), means "Twin Groves of the Lotus Mountain" – a reference to the Buddha's birth in a grove of trees and his death under a Bodhi tree. A Chinese abbot, Sek Hean Wei, established the temple at the start of the twentieth century when, passing through Singapore on his way home after a pilgrimage to Sri Lanka, he was waylaid by wealthy Hokkien merchant and philanthropist, Low Kim Pong, who supplied both the land and finances for the venture. Several renovations haven't robbed the temple of its grandeur, though the urban development of Toa Payoh's outskirts around it hardly enhances its appearance. Set behind a rock garden that combines a water cascade, ponds, streams and bridges, the temple is guarded by statues of the **Four Kings of Heaven**, each posted to keep evil out of the temple, symbolized by the demons on which they are treading. The highly regarded collection of carved and sculpted gods inside the temple's several halls includes a **Laughing Buddha**, believed to grant good luck if you rub his stomach; a shrine to Kuan Yin, Goddess of Mercy (in the rear hall); and a number of Thai-style Buddha figures.

Phor Kark See Temple

The largest temple complex in Singapore – and one of the largest in Southeast Asia – lies north of MacRitchie Reservoir, right in the middle of the island. Take bus #130 up Victoria Street to reach the complex, alighting at the far end of Sin Ming Drive, or #410 from Bishan MRT station.

Phor Kark See Temple (known in full as the Kong Meng San Phor Kark See Temple Complex), at 88 Bright Hill Drive, spreads over nineteen acres and combines temples, pagodas, pavilions, a Buddhist library and a vast crematorium to such impressive effect that it has been used several times as a backdrop to Chinese kung fu movies. More modern than Siong Lim, Phor Kark See boasts none of the faded charm of Singapore's older temples, but relies instead on its sheer magnitude and exuberant decor for effect. Multitiered roofs bristle with ceramic dragons, phoenixes, birds and human figures, while around the complex are statues of various deities, including a nine-metre-high marble statue of Kuan Yin, Goddess of Mercy. A soaring pagoda capped by a golden *chedi* (a reliquary tower) renders the complex even more striking. Even the **crematorium** – conveniently placed for the nearby Bright Hill Evergreen Home for the elderly – is huge and able to cope with five ceremonies at one time; it's housed below a Thai-style facade of elaborately carved, gilt wood. Below the crematorium is a pair of ponds, where thousands of turtles sunbathe precariously on wooden planks that slant into the water. Letting new turtles into the ponds is supposed to bring good luck, though worshippers are forbidden from doing so by a nearby sign. Beside the viewing gallery, old ladies sell bunches of vegetables, which purchasers then throw to the lucky turtles.

Upper Serangoon Road: Bidadari Cemetery

One of Singapore's more offbeat attractions, **Bidadari Cemetery**, lies some 10km northeast of the city, on Upper Serangoon Road. It's a Christian graveyard and the majority of its aged gravestones are in typical Western style, but there are Chinese graves here, too, their semicircular design affording a kneeling place to pray for the well-being of one's ancestors. Buried somewhere in the area is A.P. Williams, a British sailor upon whose life Joseph Conrad based his novel, *Lord Jim*. In his travelogue *In Search of Conrad*, Gavin Young describes how he tracked down Williams' burial plot in the depths of Singapore's public records offices – but seeking out the number he quotes (2559) yields no sign of the grave. Many species of birds flourish in the long grass of the grounds, making this a good destination for ornithologists – indeed, the Nature Society of Singapore periodically visits the cemetery. A word of warning, though: don't go wading into tall grass unless you are wearing ankle-high boots, as snakes also inhabit the grounds.

Bus #97 from Stamford, Selegie and Serangoon roads, and #106 from Orchard, Selegie and Serangoon roads both pass by the cemetery. Bus drivers aren't all familiar with the location of Bidadari, so tell them you want the better-known Youngberg Hospital, which is just across the road from the cemetery. It takes around fifteen minutes to get to Bidadari from Selegie Road.

Eastern Singapore

Thirty years ago, **eastern Singapore** was largely rural, dotted with Malay kampungs which perched on stilts over the shoreline and harbouring the odd weekend retreat owned by Europeans or moneyed locals. Massive **land reclamation** and development programmes have altered the region beyond recognition, wiping out all traces of the kampungs and throwing up huge housing projects in their place. Today, former seafront suburbs like Bedok are separated from the Straits of Singapore by a broad crescent of man-made land, much of which constitutes the **East Coast Park**, whose five kilometres incorporate leisure and water-sports facilities, imported sand beaches and seafood restaurants. Yet despite the massive upheavals that have ruptured the communities of the east coast, parts of it, including the suburbs of **Geylang** and **Katong**, have managed to retain a strong Malay identity.

Dominating the eastern tip of the island is Changi Airport and, beyond that, **Changi Village**, in whose prison the Japanese interned Allied troops and civilians during World War II. From Changi Point, it's possible to take a boat to **Pulau Ubin**, a small island with echoes of pre-development Singapore. If your schedule allows for only one trip out of downtown Singapore, Changi and its environs should definitely be on your shortlist.

Geylang and Katong

Malay culture has held sway in and around the adjoining suburbs of **GEYLANG** and **KATONG** since the mid-nineteenth century, when Malays and Indonesians first arrived to work in the local *copra* (dried coconut kernel) processing factory and later on its *serai* (lemon grass) farms; even now many of the shophouses, restaurants and food centres in the area are Malay-influenced. The thriving trade in prostitution here isn't kept in check by the local authorities, though it remains very localized along Geylang Road.

The continuation of Victoria Street and Kallang Road, **Geylang Road** – the main thoroughfare of Geylang – runs east from the Kallang River. Off Geylang Road's main stem shoot 42 lorongs (lanes), down which are clusters of brothels, recognizable by their exterior fairy lights. At its far end, 2km east and near Paya Lebar MRT station, Geylang Road meets **Joo Chiat Road**, which runs south and has a refreshingly laid-back and shambolic air after the restrictions of downtown Singapore. In the **Joo Chiat Complex**, at the northern end of Joo Chiat Road, textile merchants drape their wares on any available floor and wall space, transforming the drab interior. More market than shopping centre, it's a prime destination for anyone interested in buying cheap silk, batik, rugs or muslin.

Before striking off down Joo Chiat Road, cross over to the north side of Changi Road, where a hawker centre and wet market provide more Malay atmosphere, from the smell of clove cigarettes to the line of sarong sellers beyond the food stalls. The contrast between this authentic slice of life, and the **Malay Village** (daily 10am–10pm; $10 for its three attractions, otherwise free) is huge. Opened in 1990, and conceived as a celebration of the cuisine, music, dance, arts and crafts of the Malay people, the village conspicuously failed either to woo tourists or to rent out its replica wooden-kampung-style shops to locals, and seemed to be dying a slow death until a Hong Kong-based company took it over. Sadly, the three new tourist lures unveiled at the relaunch pack very little punch: the **Lagenda Fantasi**, an audiovisual presentation of Islamic and Malay legends such as Aladdin, Ali Baba and Sang Nila Utama, is geared squarely at kids, but probably won't impress them; the **Cultural Museum** features a humdrum array of household instruments, cloths, kites and *krises*, and a mock-up of a Malay wedding scene; and the dismal **Kampung Days** exhibition reproduces a traditional Malay kampung homestead, complete with fishing and rice-pounding scenes, a *wayang kulit* stage, an open-air cinema, and the seemingly obligatory wedding scene. If you give these attractions a miss, you're left with the village's numerous **shops**, selling batik, kites, spinning tops, bird cages and textiles, and the evening **food court** with free cultural performances on Saturday and Sunday nights (7.30–9.30pm). Nightly Malay cultural shows are on offer at the village's two restaurants, the halal Chinese *Floating Seafood* restaurant and the open-air *Temenggong* restaurant.

As you walk south down Joo Chiat Road you'll have to negotiate piles of merchandise that spill out of shophouses and onto the pavement. In particular, there's cane and wood furniture in the Phoon Fang Cheong shop at no. 175, while the store at no. 86 specializes in Chinese religious paraphernalia. Of the buildings, none are as magnificent as the immaculate **Peranakan shophouses** on Koon Seng Road (on your left about 600m down Joo Chiat Road), where painstaking work has restored their multicoloured facades, eaves and mouldings.

To get to the western end of Geylang Road, take the MRT to the Kallang stop, from where Geylang Road is a short walk south. Two stops east is Paya Lebar station, from where a short walk left out of the station, across Sims Avenue and left again onto Geylang Road, brings you to the Joo Chiat Complex. Alternatively, bus #16 from Orchard and Bras Basah roads deposits you right in the middle of Joo Chiat Road.

Changi

Bus #2, from the southern end of Victoria Street or from Tanah Merah MRT, drops you right outside **Changi Prison**. Still in use (drug offenders are periodically executed here), the prison is the infamous site of a World War II POW camp in which Allied prisoners were subjected to the harshest of treatment by their Japanese jailers. On the prison's north side, through the outer gates, is the hugely moving prison **museum** (Mon–Sat 10am–5pm, Sun open for 5.30pm religious service only; free), where sketches and photographs plot the Japanese invasion of Singapore and the fate of the soldiers and civilians subsequently incarcerated here and in nearby camps. Predominant are photos by George Aspinall, which record the appalling living conditions and illnesses suffered by POWs in Malaya and Thailand during the occupation. Then a young Australian trooper, Aspinall took his photographs using a folding Kodak 2 camera, later developing them with a stock of processing materials which he found while working on a labour gang in Singapore's docks. Novelist James Clavell was a young British artillery officer in Singapore at the time of the Japanese invasion; his *King Rat* evokes the "obscene forbidding prison" at Changi, describing the cells of the prison camp, where ". . . the stench was nauseating. Stench from rotting bodies. Stench from a generation of confined human bodies." Elsewhere in the museum, sketches drawn by W.R.M. Haxworth of prisoners playing bridge betray a dry sense of humour and some stiff upper lips in the face of adversity.

Beyond the museum is a replica of a simple wooden chapel, typical of those erected in Singapore's wartime prisons; its brass cross was crafted from spent ammunition casings, while the north wall carries poignant messages, penned by former POWs and relatives.

On a lighter note, among the war-related books stocked in the souvenir shop is *The Happiness Box*, the first copy of which was written, illustrated and bound by POWs in Changi in 1942 as a Christmas present for children in the prison. The Japanese became suspicious of the POWs' motives when they noticed one of the book's central characters was called Winston, but it was buried in the prison grounds before the Japanese could confiscate it.

Changi Village

Journey's end for bus #2 is at the terminal at **CHANGI VILLAGE**, ten minutes further on from the prison. There's little to bring you out here, save to catch a boat from **Changi Point**, behind the bus terminal, for Pulau Ubin (see below), or to the coast of Johor in Malaysia (see p.331); the left-hand jetty is for Ubin, the right-hand one for bumboats to Johor.

A stroll over the footbridge to the right of the two jetties takes you to **Changi Beach**, the execution site of many thousands of Singaporean civilians by Japanese soldiers in World War II. As a beach it wins few prizes, its most pleasant aspect being the view. To your left as you look out to sea is Pulau Ubin, slightly to the right is the island of Tekong (a military zone), behind which you can see a hill on mainland Malaysia. In the water you'll see *kelong*s and boats galore, from bumboats to supertankers. Changi Village Road, the village's main drag, has a smattering of good restaurants and a hawker centre near the bus terminal.

Pulau Ubin

Pulau Ubin, 2km offshore, gives visitors a pretty good idea of what Singapore would have been like fifty years ago. A lazy backwater tucked into the Straits of Johor, it's a great place to head for when you get tired of shops, high-rises and traffic, and it's almost worth coming for the boat trip alone, made in an old oil-stained bumboat which chugs noisily across Serangoon Harbour, belching fumes all the way. From 6am, boats depart from Changi Point throughout the day when full ($1.50 one way); the last boat back to Changi leaves as late as 10pm depending on demand, but plan to be at the jetty by 8.30pm at the latest, just in case. The boats dock at a rickety old pier in **Ubin Village**, where Malay stilt houses teeter over the sludgy, mangrove beach. The main road is lined with scores of battered old mopeds, while locals sit around watching the day take its course and chickens run free in the dirt.

The best, and most enjoyable, way to explore the dirt tracks of Ubin is by **mountain bike**. At Universal Adventure, on the left-hand side of the road leading west from the jetty, you pay $5–15 for a day's rental, depending on the type of bike and the season (it's most expensive during school holidays – June, Nov & Dec). They give you a baffling map of the island's labyrinthine network of tracks, though it's more fun to strike off and see where you end up – Ubin is only a small island (just 7km by 2km) so you won't get lost.

Just five-minutes' ride away is a deep, impressive **quarry**, from which granite was taken to build the causeway linking Singapore to Malaysia (hence the name "Ubin", which is Malay for granite). To reach the quarry, cycle through the village until you come to a basketball court, where you take a right turn past raised kampung houses and rubber trees to the eastern side of the island (a left turn instead takes you to the centre of the island). Further north along this track is a rather incongruous **Thai Buddhist Temple**, complete with portraits of the King and Queen of Thailand, and a bookcase full of Thai books. Pictures telling the story of the life of Buddha ring the inner walls of the temple, along with images of various Buddhist hells, the most disturbing of which is that of demons pouring molten liquid down the mouths of "those who always drink liquor". If you follow the left track out of Ubin Village for twenty or thirty minutes, you'll come to a steep slope: a right turn at the top takes you straight to the temple, just beyond which is another quarry, where you can take a swim and cool off.

Ignoring the right turn to the temple at the top of the steep slope and continuing straight ahead takes you towards the island's best restaurant, the *Ubin Restaurant*; it's a bit tricky to find, though – you'll have to look out for a taxi taking Singaporean diners there, to discover which track to turn down.

Western Singapore

Since the government's industrialization programme began in the late 1960s, far **western Singapore** has developed into the manufacturing heart of the state, and today thousands of companies occupy units within the towns of Jurong and Tuas. Manufacturing has proven the backbone of Singapore's economic success – the state presently produces a sizeable proportion of the world's hard-disk drives, for example. Despite this saturation, much of the western region – crafted from former swampland and wasteland – remains remarkably verdant, and perhaps surprisingly, given the industrial surroundings, several major tourist attractions are located here, including **Haw Par Villa**, as garish a theme park as you'll ever set eyes on, though the pick of the bunch is fascinating **Jurong Bird Park**. Slightly further east, the **Singapore Science Centre** is packed with imaginative and informative exhibitions, and is not to be missed if you've got kids to entertain. All of these places are easily reached from the city centre, using either buses or the MRT.

Telok Blangah, the World Trade Centre and Mount Faber

A twenty-minute walk west of Chinatown is the area known as **Telok Blangah**. Here stands Singapore's **World Trade Centre** (WTC), a splendid shopping centre-cum-marine terminal, where boats depart Singapore for Indonesia's Riau Archipelago. Lots of buses come this way: #97 and #166 travel down Bencoolen Street, #65 continues on from Bencoolen Street to Orchard Boulevard; from Scotts and Orchard roads, take bus #143. You'll know when to get off, because you'll see cable cars rocking across the skyline in front of you, on their way to and from Mount Faber, and across to Sentosa Island (p.589).

Mount Faber – 600m north of the WTC – was named in 1845 after Government Engineer Captain Charles Edward Faber. The top of the "mount" (hillock would be a better word) commands fine views of Keppel Harbour and, to the northeast, central Singapore – views which are even more impressive at night, when the city is lit up. It's a long, steep walk from Telok Blangah Road up to the top of Mount Faber – it's better to take the **cable car** from the World Trade Centre complex (daily 8.30am–9pm; $6.90 return, children $3.90). An accident in 1983, when a ship's mast clipped the cables on which the cars are suspended, cost seven passengers their lives, but today laser eyes ensure history won't repeat itself. As you'd expect, there's a correspondingly strong souvenir shop presence up here, though you can escape this by moving away from the area immediately around the cable-car station and up into the nearby park.

In the early days of colonial rule, Temenggong Abdul Rahman played prime minister to Sultan Hussein Shah's president, and his signature graced the treaty authorizing the East India Company to operate out of Singapore. All that's left of his settlement on the southern slopes of Mount Faber is its pillared mosque – the **State of Johor Mosque** – and, behind that, a small Malay cemetery and a portion of the brickwork that once housed the *temenggong*'s baths. The mosque lies five minutes' walk east of the World Trade Centre, and can be reached on any WTC-bound bus.

Haw Par Villa

As an entertaining exercise in bad taste, **Haw Par Villa** (daily 9am–6pm; $5, children $2.50) has few equals. Located at 262 Pasir Panjang Rd, 7km from downtown Singapore, it describes itself as an "aesthetically arresting . . . park which promises you the unfolding of Chinese legends and mythologies" – for which read a gaudy parade of over a thousand grotesque statues that take their inspiration from Chinese mythology. Previously known as Tiger Balm Gardens, the park now takes its name from its original owners, the Aw brothers, Boon Haw and Boon Par, who made a fortune early this century selling Tiger Balm – a cure-all unction created by their father. When the British government introduced licensing requirements for the possession of large animals, the private zoo which the brothers maintained on their estate here was closed down and replaced by statues. A few years ago, rides, theatrical shows and multimedia attractions added to broaden the appeal of the place actually did no such thing. All have now been closed, leaving only the hundreds of statues – gaudy, primary-coloured characters from the pantheon of Chinese tradition – for which the park is famous.

To get to Haw Par Villa, take the MRT to Buona Vista and change on to a #200 bus to Pasir Panjang Road, or get bus #51, which trundles down North Bridge Road on its way to the park, or the #143, which can be picked up on Scotts, Orchard and New Bridge roads.

Holland Village

A couple of kilometres north of Haw Par Villa and west of the Botanic Gardens (see p.577), **Holland Village**, previously home to some of the British soldiers based in Singapore, continues to be an expat stronghold, with a whole row of Western restaurants and shops. The **Holland Road Shopping Centre** at 211 Holland Ave is the place to head for if you want to buy Asian art, crafts or textiles: there are shops on two levels where you can buy anything from an Indian pram to a Chinese opium pipe, while outside, cobblers, key-cutters and newsagents set up stall. Off Lorong Liput, the small road alongside the shopping centre, shoots Lorong Mambong, home to a thriving restaurant scene and to **craft shops** that specialize in ceramic elephants, dragon pots, porcelain, rattan and bamboo products. **Pasar Holland**, opposite the shops on Lorong Mambong, is a small, tumbledown market selling fruit, flowers, fish and meat, as well as housing a handful of hawker stalls.

To reach Holland Village by MRT, head to the Buona Vista station, from where you walk up Commonwealth Avenue and then turn left onto Holland Avenue. Alternatively, buses #7 and #106 from Orchard Boulevard both pass the top of Holland Avenue – ring the bell when you see the Esso garage.

Around Jurong Lake and beyond

Several tourist destinations are dotted around the environs of tranquil **Jurong Lake**, about 4km northwest of the new town of Clementi. You're far more likely to want to come out this way if you've got children in tow; of all the area's attractions, only the **Tang Dynasty City** is of universal appeal.

Singapore Science Centre

At the **Singapore Science Centre** (Tues–Sun 10am–6pm; $3), seven exhibition galleries hold over six hundred hands-on exhibits designed to inject interest into even the most impenetrable scientific principles. The majority of the centre's visitors are local schoolchildren, who sweep around the galleries in vast, deafening waves, frantically trying out each interactive display. The exhibits variously allow you to experience sight through an insect's eyes, to write in Braille, and to see a thermal heat reflection of yourself. Within the centre's grounds, the **Omnimax-Theatre** (planetarium show $6, movie $10; ☎5603316) has entertaining features about science, space and history shown on a huge, engulfing domed screen. It takes ten minutes at most to reach the Science Centre on foot from Jurong East MRT – or hop onto either bus #66 or #335.

Chinese and Japanese Gardens

The **Chinese and Japanese gardens** (daily 9am–6pm; $4.50), situated just south of Jurong Lake, defy categorization, being too expensive and too far out to visit for just a sit-down in the park and too dull to be a fully fledged tourist attraction. To get there, head for Chinese Garden MRT Station, northeast of Jurong Lake, from where you follow signs to the Chinese Garden's back entrance, three or four minutes down a footpath.

In the **Chinese Garden** (or Yu Hwa Yuan), pagodas, pavilions, bridges, arches and weeping willows attempt to capture the style of Beijing's Summer Palace – and fail. If you visit at the weekend, be prepared to be confronted by hordes of newlyweds scouring the garden for a decent photo opportunity. The Chinese Garden is best explored on the day of the annual Moon Cake Festival (see p.69), when children parade with their lanterns after dark.

Across from the Chinese Garden, over the impressive, 65-metre "Bridge of Double Beauty", is the **Japanese Garden** (or Seiwaen, "Garden of Tranquillity"), whose wooden bridges, carp ponds, pebble footpaths and stone lanterns do much to help you forget the awful formica chairs and tables in the central pavilion.

The Bird Park and Reptile Park

On Jalan Ahmad Ibrahim, the **Jurong Bird Park** (Mon–Fri 9am–6pm, Sat & Sun 8am–6pm; $10.30, children $4.12) has one of the world's largest bird collections, with more than eight thousand birds representing over six hundred species, ranging from

Antarctic penguins to New Zealand kiwis. A ride on its **Panorail** ($2.50) is a good way to get your bearings; the bullet-shaped monorail skims over, past or through all the main exhibits, with its running commentary pointing out the attractions.

Be sure at least to catch the **Waterfall Walk-in Aviary**, which allows visitors to walk amongst 1500 free-flying birds in a specially created tropical rainforest, dominated by a thirty-metre-high waterfall. Other exhibits to seek out are the colourful **Southeast Asian Birds**, where a tropical thunderstorm is simulated daily at noon; the **Penguin Parade** (feeding times 10.30am & 3.30pm); and the **World of Darkness**, a fascinating exhibit which swaps day for night with the aid of a system of reversed lighting, in order that its cute collection of nocturnal residents doesn't snooze throughout the park's opening hours. The best of the **bird shows** is undoubtedly the "Kings of the Skies" show (4pm) – a *tour de force* of speed-flying by a band of trained eagles, hawks and falcons. Entrance to this, and to the similar "World of Hawks" show (10am) and "All Star Bird Show" (11am & 3pm), is free. To get to the Bird Park, take either bus #194 or #251 from the bus interchange outside Boon Lay MRT station, a ten-minute ride.

Across the car park in front of the Bird Park, **Jurong Reptile Park** (daily 9am–6pm; $7, children $3.50) houses the biggest gathering of crocodiles in Singapore among its fifty-plus species of reptile. The park has wisely jettisoned its previous name, the Crocodile Paradise: it's certainly no paradise for the poor beasts forced to feature in the daily shows, in which crocs are pushed, pulled and sat on in the name of entertainment by a character swathed in crocodile hide and dripping with crocodile teeth. Given the scant respect shown by the park for its reptilian inmates, it comes as no surprise to find the *Seafood Paradise Restaurant* serving up croc meat in the main entrance building.

Sentosa and the southern isles

Of the many little **islands** that stud the waters immediately south of Singapore, some, like Pulau Bukom, are owned by petrochemical companies and are off-limits to tourists; three others – **Sentosa, St John's and Kusu** – are served by ferries and can be visited without difficulty, though their accessibility has geared them very much to tourism. If you crave a more secluded spot, you'll have to charter a bumboat to one of the more remote islands from the World Trade Centre or Clifford Pier (see p.541 for details) or head for Pulau Ubin, off Singapore's east coast (p.585).

Sentosa

Given the rampant development that has transformed **SENTOSA** into the most developed of Singapore's southern islands over the past 25 years, it's ironic that its name means "tranquil" in Malay. The island has come a long way since World War II, when it was a British military base known as Pulau Blakang Mati, or the "Island of Death Behind". Promoted for its beaches, sports facilities, hotels (see p.547) and attractions, and ringed by a speeding monorail, Sentosa is a contrived but enjoyable place. Sentosa is also big business: millions of visitors descend on this tiny island, which measures just 3km by 1km, every year, though reports of the place are mixed. Ultimately, it's as enjoyable as you make it; there's certainly plenty to do (though few of the attractions would make the grade at Disneyland), so much so that it's a good idea to arrive early, with a clear plan of action. It's wise to avoid coming at the weekend, while the island should be avoided at all costs on public holidays.

Travel practicalities
Ferries for Sentosa (9.30am–9pm; every 20min; $2.30 return) depart from the **World Trade Centre** (see p.586). However, the most spectacular way there is by one of the

cable cars (daily 8.30am–9pm; $6.90 return, children $3.90) which travel on a loop between Mount Faber (see p.587) and Sentosa.

The island is linked to a spot just east of the WTC by a brand new five-hundred-metre **causeway**, which is free to cross on foot, a five-minute walk. Bus A from the WTC bus terminal runs across the bridge every ten to fifteen minutes (daily 7am–12.30am; $6, children $3). Service C, meanwhile, shuttles between Tiong Bahru MRT station and the ferry terminal on Sentosa (daily 7am–12.30am; $6, children $3), while bus E runs from Orchard Road to Sentosa's Gateway monorail station (daily 10am–10.45pm; $7, children $5). All these bus services include the basic **admission** fee for the island (otherwise $5, children $3; pay once you cross the bridge), which gives unlimited rides on Sentosa's **monorail** (daily 9am–10pm) and **bus** systems. A ride on the monorail upon arrival helps you get your bearings, while bus #2 circles the island between 9am and 7pm and services A, C and M are often handy too; we've mentioned which service to use for each of the sights. But the best way to get about is to **rent a bike** for the day ($4–8 an hour depending on the machine) from the kiosk beside the ferry terminal; tandems are also available. You can pick up a **map** of the island, showing the sights and transport routes, at the WTC or upon arrival on Sentosa.

The attractions

Two attractions outshine all others on Sentosa. At the **Underwater World** (daily 9am–9pm; $13, children $7; monorail station 2), a moving walkway carries you the length of a hundred-metre acrylic tunnel that snakes through two large tanks: sharks lurk menacingly on all sides, huge stingrays drape themselves languidly above you, and immense shoals of gaily coloured fish dart to and fro. This may not sound all that exciting, but the sensation of being engulfed by sea life of all descriptions is a really breathtaking one, and the nearest you'll get to being on the ocean floor without donning a wet suit. A **touchpool** beside the entrance allows you to pick up starfish and sea cucumbers – the latter rather like socks filled with wet sand – while beyond is the **Marine Theatre**, screening educational films throughout the day.

The other major-league attraction is the nearby **Images of Singapore Exhibition** (daily 9am–9pm; $5, children $3; monorail station 2). Here, life-sized dioramas present the history and heritage of Singapore from the fourteenth century through to the surrender of the Japanese in 1945. Though some of the wax dummies look like they've been pinched from clothes-shop windows, the effect is fascinating. The highlight of the exhibition is the Surrender Chambers, where audiovisual effects, videos, dioramas and artefacts combine to recount the events of World War II as experienced in Singapore. There are more wax dummies on parade in the Festivals of Singapore gallery, this time dolled up in all manner of festive costumes to represent Singapore's various ethnic celebrations.

A trip up to the new improved **Fort Siloso** (daily 9am–7pm, $3; monorail station 3), on the far western tip of the island, ties in nicely with a visit to the Surrender Chambers. The fort – actually a cluster of buildings and gun emplacements above a series of tunnels bored into the island – guarded Singapore's western approaches from the 1880s until 1956, but its obsolescence was revealed in 1942, when the Japanese moved down into Singapore from Malaysia. Today, the recorded voice of Battery Sergeant Major Cooper talks you through a mock-up of a nineteenth-century barracks, complete with living quarters, a laundry and an assault course. You can explore the complex's hefty gun emplacements and tunnels, and sit in on the battle for Singapore, when British soldiers were forced to surrender to the Japanese.

The rest of Sentosa is crammed with less interesting options. **The Asian Village** (daily 10am–9pm; free), next to the ferry terminal, showcases Asian life by way of restaurants, craft shops and street performances – little more than a vehicle for shifting overpriced arts, crafts and food. Within the village are the fairground rides of

Adventure Asia ($10) and the **Thai Pavilion Theatre**, in which the "Colours of Asia" (10.15am & 4pm; $5) and "Fascinating Asia" (6.30pm & 7.15pm; $18 including dinner) cultural shows are staged daily. Otherwise, you might consider one of Sentosa's three latest attractions: **Volcanoland** (daily 10am–7pm; $12, children $6), with a simulated eruption and trip to the earth's core; **Fantasy Island** (daily 10am–6.30pm; $16, children $10), with hi-tech water rides – "Flashflood", "Blackhole" and, for small children, "Pygmy Puddle"; or **Wondergolf** (9am–9pm; $8, children $4), with 45 crazy holes. If you end up at the **Maritime Museum** (daily 10am–7pm; free), you're really scraping the barrel – you'd do better strolling in the elegant grounds of the **Sentosa Orchid Gardens** near monorail station 1. For something slightly more exciting, head for the **Butterfly Park and Insect Kingdom Museum** (daily 9am–6.30pm; $6, children $3; monorail station 5), stuffed with all sorts of creepy crawlies.

Probably the best option, though, after a trip on the monorail and a visit to one or two attractions, is to head for the three **beaches**, named Siloso, Central and Tanjong (monorail station 2 or 5, or take bus A or M), on Sentosa's southwestern coast. Created with thousands of cubic metres of imported white sand and scores of coconut palms, they offer canoes, surfboards and aqua bikes for rent – as well as plain old deckchairs. The water here is great for swimming and Singapore does not demand the same modesty on its beaches as Malaysia, although topless and nude bathing are out. In recent years, Singapore's annual Dragonboat Racing Festival (see p.69) has been held off Siloso Beach.

By 7pm, many of Sentosa's attractions are closed, but not so the **Musical Fountain** (shows at 5pm, 5.30pm, 7.30pm, 8.30pm & 9.30pm), which is either cute or appalling, depending on your point of view. The fountain dances along to such classics as the *1812 Overture*, with colourful lights and lasers adding to the effect. Recently, the display has been overlooked by a new, 37-metre-high statue of Singapore's tourism totem, the **Merlion**, which itself takes centre-stage in the laser-illuminated "Rise of the Merlion" portions of the shows.

Eating and drinking

The *Rasa Sentosa Food Centre*, beside the ferry terminal, is the cheapest **eating** option; otherwise, try the nearby *Sentosa Riverboat* for fast food, or monorail station 5's *Sweetimes Café*. There's a *Burger King* and a coffee house at the ferry terminal as well as a beer garden.

Kusu, St John's and other islands

Well kept and clean as they are, Sentosa's beaches do tend to get overcrowded, and so you may do better to head for the decent sand beaches of either **St John's** or **Kusu** islands, which are 6km south of Singapore and connected to the mainland by a **ferry** ($9, children $6; for current ferry times call ☎8628322) from the WTC. This reaches Kusu in thirty minutes and then continues on to St John's, arriving shortly afterwards. There are just two departures from the WTC on weekdays and Saturdays, though the number rises to six on Sundays and public holidays.

The more interesting of the two is Kusu, also known as **Turtle Island**. Singaporean legend tells of a Chinese and a Malay sailor who were once saved from drowning by a turtle which transformed itself into an island; a sizeable pool of turtles is still kept on the island in commemoration of the tale. Another legend describes how an epidemic afflicting a ship moored off Kusu was banished by the God Tua Pek Kong. Whatever the truth in these tales, once a year during the ninth lunar month (October or November), tens of thousands of Singaporean pilgrims descend upon the **Chinese temple** and **Malay shrine**, a few minutes' walk from the jetty on Kusu, to pray for prosperity. The island is impossibly crowded during this time, but for the rest of the year it offers a tranquil escape from the mainland. There is a modest cafeteria on St John's, but if you're going to Kusu it's wise to take a picnic.

Other southern islands

Since no regular ferries run to any of Singapore's other southern islands, you'll have to **charter a bumboat** from Jardine Steps (beside the World Trade Centre) or from Clifford Pier. Boats take up to twelve passengers, and cost at least $30–40 an hour. Unless you rent a boat for the whole day, don't forget to arrange to be picked up again.

Lazarus Island and attractive **Sisters Islands**, which lie in the same cluster of isles as St John's and Kusu, are both popular snorkelling and fishing haunts, as is **Pulau Hantu** ("Ghost Island" in Malay), 12km further west and under the shadow of Pulau Bukum, its oil refineries reflecting the fact it's owned by Shell. Most interesting of all, though, is **Pulau Seking**, around 4km east of Hantu, where a handful of Malays continue to live in traditional stilt houses that teeter over the sea, their lifestyle almost untouched by the progress that has transformed the mainland. These islands have few amenities, so take a picnic and a day's supply of bottled water with you.

Eating

Along with shopping, **eating** ranks as the Singaporean national pastime – the country offers the chance to sample the whole spectrum of Asia's dishes – and an enormous number of food outlets cater for this obsession. However, eating out is not afforded the same reverence that it receives in the West. Often, you find yourself eating off plastic plates in bare, unpretentious restaurants that ring to the sound of agitated conversation (invariably about food) – it's the fare, and not the surroundings, that's important. What's more, strict government regulations ensure that food outlets are consistently hygienic – you don't need to worry about eating food cooked at a street stall. You may want to choreograph your visit to coincide with July's **Singapore Food Festival**, a celebration of regional cuisines during which food outlets across the island whip up especially interesting local specialities.

The mass of establishments serving **Chinese** food throughout the island reflects the fact that Chinese residents account for around three-quarters of the population. You're most likely to come across Cantonese, Beijing and Szechuan restaurants, though there's not a region of China whose specialities you can't sample. **North and South Indian** cuisines give a good account of themselves too, as do restaurants serving **Malay**, **Indonesian**, **Korean**, **Japanese** and **Vietnamese** food. One thing you won't find, however, is a Singaporean restaurant: the closest Singapore comes to an indigenous cuisine is **Nonya**, a hybrid of Chinese and Malay food that developed following the intermarrying of nineteenth-century Chinese immigrants with Malay women (see p.59).

Naturally, it's possible to eat **Western food** in Singapore – venture beyond the ubiquitous burger chains and pizza parlours, and you'll find a host of excellent restaurants serving anything from haggis to jambalaya. These and other dishes may be enjoyed at establishments geared to the dishes of a particular nation, or at **international restaurants**, whose menus are a patchwork of Western cuisines. A more informal alternative is to opt for a plate of **British** food – fish and chips, say – at a pub or bar.

Several specialist Chinese restaurants and a number of Indian restaurants serve **vegetarian food**, but otherwise vegetarians need to tread very carefully: chicken and seafood will appear in a whole host of dishes unless you make it perfectly clear that you don't want them. **Halal food** is predictably easy to find, given the number of Muslims in Singapore; the Arab Street end of North Bridge Road and Serangoon Road's Zhu Jiao Centre both have proliferations of restaurants and stalls. There are no **kosher** restau-

MARKETS AND SUPERMARKETS

Some guesthouses do have cooking facilities, and if you want to buy your own food or fancy a bag of fresh fruit, you're most likely to go to a **wet market** – so called due to the pools of water perpetually covering the floor. Vendors are usually very helpful even if you don't know a mango from a mangosteen. Singapore also has plenty of **supermarkets**, most of which have a delicatessen counter and bakery – some offer familiar beers from back home, too.

MARKETS

Little India is served by the large wet market in the Zhu Jiao Centre, at the southern end of Serangoon Road; the Chinatown Complex market in **Chinatown** rewards a visit as well. All of Singapore's new towns have their own wet markets too.

SUPERMARKETS

Cold Storage, branches at Centrepoint, Orchard Road and 293 Holland Rd. Local chain which stocks a wide range of Western products.

Daimaru, Liang Court Shopping Complex, 177 River Valley Rd. Across from River Valley Swimming Complex. Japanese department store with a large food hall featuring takeaway counters.

Good Gifts Emporium, Golden Mile Complex, 5001 Beach Rd. A smallish supermarket with a leaning towards Thai produce.

NTUC Fairprice, Rochor Centre, 1 Rochor Rd. Basic supermarket that's handy for Bencoolen Street.

Sogo, Raffles City Shopping Centre, 252 North Bridge Rd. Near City Hall MRT. Japanese department store where you can buy groceries and takeaway snacks.

Yaohan, Plaza Singapura, 68 Orchard Rd. Near Dhoby Ghaut MRT. Japanese department store and supermarket similar to Daimaru and Sogo.

rants, but you could try one of the delis listed above, or the food store at the Maghain Aboth Synagogue opposite the Church of St Peter and Paul, on Waterloo Street.

By far the cheapest and most fun place to dine in Singapore is in a **hawker centre** or **food court**, where scores of stalls let you mix and match dishes at really low prices. For a few extra dollars you graduate into the realm of proper **restaurants**, ranging from no-frills, open-fronted eating houses and coffee shops to sumptuously decorated establishments – often, though not always, located in swanky hotels. Restaurant **opening hours**, on average, are 11.30am–2.30pm and 6–10.30pm daily; hawker stall owners tend to operate to their own schedules, but are invariably open at peak eating times.

Breakfast, brunch and snacks

Guesthouses sometimes include coffee or tea and toast in the price of the room but the chances are you'll want to head off elsewhere for breakfast. **Western breakfasts** are available, at a price, at all bigger hotels, most famously at the *Hilton* or *Raffles*. Otherwise, there are a number of cafés serving continental breakfasts, while *McDonald's*, *Kentucky Fried Chicken* and *Burger King* all rustle up breakfasts before reverting to burgers and chicken after 11am. For a really cheap fry-up, though, you can't beat a Western food stall in a hawker centre. Here, $8 will buy enough steak, chops and sausage for even the most starving carnivore.

Many visitors to Singapore find the **local breakfasts** a little hard to stomach, but there are some tasty possibilities. The classic Chinese breakfast is *congee*, a watery rice porridge augmented with chopped spring onion, crispy fried onion and strips of meat, though the titbits that comprise *dim sum* tend to be more palatable to Western tastes.

Among the Malays, an abiding favourite is *nasi lemak*, while curry and bread breakfasts are served up by scores of Indian establishments.

Bengawan Solo. Excellent cake shop, specializing in Malay *kueh* (cakes), with branches at Centrepoint, 176 Orchard Rd, and at Clifford Centre, 24 Raffles Place. Daily 10am–8pm.

Breakfast With An Orang-Utan, Singapore Zoo, 80 Mandai Lake Rd (☎3608509). A bumper American-style spread with seasonal tropical fruits, shared with whichever orang-utan is on duty, costs around $15.50 (children $11.30). Daily 9–10am.

Breakfast With The Birds, Jurong Bird Park, Jalan Ahmad Ibrahim (☎2650022). A buffet of local and Western breakfast favourites, eaten to the accompaniment of the caged songbirds hanging above you; $12. Daily 8–11am.

Brooklyn Bagels, 235 River Valley Rd (☎7320056). Opposite Mohamad Sultan Rd. Tiny takeaway joint where you choose from plain, egg, onion, garlic, sesame or pumpernickel bagels, filled with pastrami, salmon or roast beef, or make do with a plain old muffin. All produce is baked in-house daily. Mon–Thurs 7am–8pm, Fri & Sat 7am–midnight, Sun 7am–6pm.

Champagne Brunch At The Hilton, *Hilton Hotel*, 581 Orchard Rd (☎7372233). Around $60 buys a superb free flow of delicacies – oysters, salmon, curry and cakes – washed down with litres of champagne and orange juice. Reservations are essential. Sun 11.30am–2.30pm only.

De Boa (HK) Restaurant, 42 Smith St. Set right opposite the Chinatown Complex, this smashing little café offers *dim sum*, *pow* and Chinese tea. Daily 7.30am–5pm.

Delifrance, #01-03 Peranakan Place, 180 Orchard Rd. Next to Centrepoint. This stylish café is one of a chain of French delis specializing in filled croissants and pastries; recommended. Daily 7.30am–10pm.

Dôme, ground floor, UOB Plaza, Financial District (☎5333266). Slick café – one of a global chain – boasting an impressive list of coffees and teas. Their muffins, toast and croissants are reasonable, and a selection of international papers are on hand. There's also a branch at the National Art Museum. Daily 7.30am–10pm.

Famous Amos, #01-05 Specialists' Shopping Centre, 277 Orchard Rd. Sublime handmade cookies to take away. Daily 10am–9pm.

Mr Bean's Café, 30 Selegie Rd. Based in the same wedge-shaped colonial building as the Selegie Arts Centre, *Mr Bean's* draws an interesting crowd, who breakfast on muffins, croissants, toast and coffee. Open 24hr.

HIGH TEA AND TIFFIN

Many of Singapore's swisher hotels advertise that most colonial of traditions, **high tea**, in the local press; below are a few of the more permanent choices. Typically, a Singapore high tea comprises local and Western snacks, both sweet and savoury. If you really want to play the part of a Victorian settler, Singapore's most splendid food outlet at the *Raffles* still serves **tiffin** – the colonial term for a light curry meal (derived from the Hindi word for luncheon).

Alkaff Mansion, 10 Telok Blangah Green (☎2786979). Bus #145 from Redhill MRT. The veranda bar at this restored building hosts a sweet and savoury local high tea on Saturday and Sunday only (2.30–4.30pm).

Café l'Espresso, *Goodwood Park Hotel*, 22 Scotts Rd (☎7377411). A great array of English cakes and pastries. Daily 2.30–6pm.

Café Vienna, *Royal Holiday Inn Crowne Plaza*, 25 Scotts Rd (☎7377966). Tremendously popular among Singaporeans, so get here early and wait in line to avoid disappointment. Mon–Fri 3–5.30pm, Sat & Sun 3–6pm.

Hilton Lounge, *Hilton Hotel*, 581 Orchard Rd (☎7372233). Afternoon tea ($22) at the *Hilton* is taken overlooking Orchard Road from the second-floor mezzanine lounge. Daily noon–5pm.

Tiffin Room, *Raffles Hotel*, 1 Beach Rd (☎3371886). Tiffin lunch (noon–2pm) and dinner (7–10pm) both cost over $30 per person, though the spread of edibles, and the charming colonial surroundings make them worth considering. Between tiffin sittings, high tea ($25) is served 3.30–5pm.

Mr Cucumber, #02-02 Clifford Centre, 24 Raffles Place (☎5340363). Sandwich bar with a wide variety of fillings, catering for the business crowd. Sandwiches from $3 upwards, or try one of the bagels supplied by *Brooklyn Bagels*. Mon–Fri 10am–6pm, Sat 11am–3pm.

Red Lantern Beer Garden, Basement, 60a Change Alley Aerial Plaza, Collyer Quay. The continental set breakfast in this enclosed beer garden is great value at under $5. Daily 7–10.30am.

Spinelli Coffee Company, #01-15 Bugis Junction, 230 Victoria St. San Francisco-based outfit that's riding on the crest of Singapore's current mania for fresh coffee; the narrow bar is ideal for a quick espresso. Daily 10am–10pm.

Starbucks Coffee, #01-46 Raffles City Shopping Centre, 252 North Bridge Rd (☎3333083). Central branch of the American coffee chain that's spreading like wildfire across the island. Mon–Fri 7.30am–10.30pm, Sat & Sun 8am–midnight.

Tan Hock Seng Cake Shop, 88 Telok Ayer St. They've been baking cakes and biscuits on site for more than 50 years at this famous Hokkien shop, just next door to the Fuk Tak Ch'i Street Museum. Daily 10am–8pm.

Tiffin Room, *Raffles Hotel*, 1 Beach Rd (☎3371886). Have your buffet breakfast here and you won't eat again until dinner; $25 per person. Daily 7.30–10am.

Yasinn Restaurant, 127 Bencoolen St. Does a roaring trade in *roti prata* (fried bread) with curry sauce each morning. Open 24hr.

Hawker centres and food courts

Although **hawker centres** are kept scrupulously clean, they are often housed in functional buildings, which tend to get extremely hot and, if you are seated next to a stall cooking fried rice or noodles, extremely smoky. As a consequence, an increasing number of smaller, air-conditioned **food courts** are popping up, where eating is a slightly more civilized, if less atmospheric affair. Hawker centres and food courts are open from lunchtime through to dinnertime and sometimes beyond, though individual stalls open and shut as they please. Avoid the peak lunching (12.30–1.30pm) and dining (6–7pm) periods, when hungry Singaporeans go to their nearest hawker centre, and you should have no problems in finding a seat.

Bugis Village, New Bugis St. Off Rochor Rd. A handful of evening hawkers dish up Asian specialities like satay, *laksa*, *kueh* and sushi.

Chinatown Complex, Smith St, at end of New Bridge Rd, Chinatown. A huge range of dishes with a predictably Chinese bias.

Food Junction, B1, Seiyu Department Store, Bugis Junction, 200 Victoria St. By Bugis MRT. Happening food court whose trendy piped music provides a stirring soundtrack to your dinner. Culinary themes as diverse as Thai, Japanese, *nasi padang* and claypot are represented, and there's a choice of local desserts or Häagen-Dazs ice creams.

Geylang Serai Food Centre, Geylang Serai. Turn left out of Paya Lebar MRT and left again onto Sims Ave; the centre is five-minutes' walk along, on your right. In the heart of Singapore's Malay quarter, this place has a corresponding range of stalls offering Malay staples like *nasi lemak* and *nasi campur*.

Hastings Road Food Court, Little India Arcade, Serangoon Rd, Little India. Diminutive food court whose handful of stalls are labelled by region – Keralan, Mughlai, Sri Lankan and so on.

Hill Street Centre, 64 Hill St. On the southeastern flank of Fort Canning Park. Boasts a number of fine Chinese and Indian stalls on two floors; on the far right-hand side as you enter is a stall serving excellent *popiah*.

Lau Pa Sat Festival Market, 18 Raffles Quay, Financial District. The smartest hawker stalls in Singapore, and now open round the clock. At lunchtime the place is full to bursting with suits from the city; at night the clubbers take over.

Newton Circus Hawker Centre, north end of Scotts Rd, a short walk from Newton MRT. Prices are a little higher than other centres because it's on the mainstream tourist trail, but it has the advantage of staying open until late. Noted for its seafood stalls.

Orchard Emerald Food Court, basement, Orchard Emerald, 218 Orchard Rd. Smart food court, bang in the centre of Orchard Rd, where the Indonesian buffet is great value.

Picnic Food Court, Scotts Shopping Centre, 6 Scotts Rd. Orchard MRT. Slap-bang in the middle of Orchard Rd, squeaky clean, and with lots of choice.

Satay Club, Clarke Quay. A Singapore institution not to be missed, serving inexpensive chicken and mutton satay. Open evenings only, from around 7pm.

Sim Lim Square Food Centre, 1 Rochor Canal Rd, on the southern edge of Little India. Convenient if you are staying on Bencoolen St; it's under the Sim Lim Square building.

Taman Serasi, junction of Napier and Cluny rds, opposite the main entrance to the Botanical Gardens. The speciality here is *roti john*.

Zhujiao Hawker Centre, cnr of Bukit Timah and Serangoon rds, Little India. The bulk of the stalls here, naturally enough, serve Indian food.

Coffee shops and restaurants

Below is a representative selection of the thousands of **coffee shops** and **restaurants** that span Singapore, with the **cuisines** listed alphabetically. **Meal prices**, where quoted, are fairly arbitrary – even in the most extravagant restaurant in Singapore it's possible to snack on fried rice and a soft drink. Equally, a delicacy such as shark's-fin or bird's-nest soup will send a bill soaring, no matter how unpretentious the restaurant. Individual **opening hours** are given below. If possible, try to book ahead at more upmarket restaurants, particularly on Saturday nights and Sunday lunchtimes, when they are at their busiest. Moreover, bear in mind that many restaurants close over Chinese New Year, and those that don't are often bursting at the seams. There aren't too many establishments that enforce a dress code, though it's always best to dress up a little if you're heading for a hotel restaurant.

Chinese

The majority of the **Chinese** restaurants in Singapore are Cantonese, that is, from the province of Canton (Guangdong) in southern China, though you'll also come across northern Peking (Beijing) and western Szechuan (Sichuan) cuisines, as well as the Hokkien specialities of the southeastern province of Fukien (Fujian); and Teochew dishes from the area east of Canton. Whatever the region, it's undoubtedly the real thing – Chinese food as eaten by the Chinese – which means it won't always sound particularly appealing to foreigners: the Chinese eat all parts of an animal, from its lips to its undercarriage, and it's important to retain a sense of adventure when exploring menus. Fish and seafood is nearly always outstanding in Chinese cuisine, with prawns, crab, squid and a variety of fish on offer. Noodles, too, are ubiquitous, and come in wonderful variations. For something a little more unusual, try a steamboat or a claypot. The other thing to note is that at many Cantonese restaurants (and in other regional restaurants, too), lunch consists of **dim sum** – steamed and fried dumplings served in little bamboo baskets.

CANTONESE

Bugis Village, New Bugis St. Touts at the several seafood restaurants here hassle you incessantly to take a seat and a menu. The furious competition ensures prices are reasonable, despite the high proportion of tourists; all restaurants work from similar, mainstream menus. Daily 5pm–3am.

Capital, #01-207, Block 2, Cantonment Rd, Chinatown (☎2213516). The friendly staff in this spotless restaurant recommend fried deer meat with ginger; also worth a try are the fried prawns rolled in bean-curd skin. A feast for two costs less than $35. Daily noon–2.30pm & 6–10.30pm.

Fatty's Wing Seong Restaurant, #01-31 Burlington Complex, 175 Bencoolen St, Colonial District (☎3381087). A Singapore institution, where every dish on the wide Cantonese menu is well cooked and speedily delivered. Around $20 a head. Daily noon–11pm.

Hai Tien Lo, 37th floor, *Pan Pacific Hotel*, 7 Raffles Blvd, Marina Square (☎4348338). East of City Hall MRT. If you have money enough for just one blowout, come here for exquisitely presented food and stunning views of downtown Singapore. Extravagant set meals are available, while Sunday lunchtimes are set aside for *dim sum* (10.30am–2.30pm). Daily noon–2.30pm & 6.30–10.30pm.

Hillman, #01-159, Block 1, Cantonment Rd, Chinatown (☎2215073). Extremely popular for its rich-tasting earthen pots of flavoursome stews featuring various meats and seafood; small pots (around $10) are enough to fill two people. Daily 11.30am–2.30pm & 5.30–10.30pm.

Mitzi's, 24–26 Murray Terrace, Chinatown (☎2220929). The cracking Cantonese food in this simple place, situated in a row of restaurants known as "Food Alley", draws crowds, so be prepared to wait in line. Two can eat for $30, drinks extra. Daily 11am–3pm & 6–10pm.

Mouth, #02-01 Chinatown Point, 133 New Bridge Rd (☎5344233). Beside a popular *dim sum* menu, this jam-packed restaurant offers classy Hong Kong new-wave Cantonese food, at under $20 a head. Daily 11am–4am (*dim sum* 11.30am–5pm).

Soup Restaurant, 25 Smith St, Chinatown (☎2229923). Traditional Cantonese double-boiled and simmered soups are the speciality in this steam-heat-dependent soup shop whose elegant tables and low-hung lights recall old Chinatown. The samsui ginger chicken comes recommended. Daily 11.30am–10.30pm.

Swee Kee, *Damenlou Hotel*, 12 Ann Siang Rd, Chinatown (☎2211900). A Cantonese restaurant with real pedigree: Tang Swee Kee hawked the first bowl of his trademark *ka shou* fish-head noodles more than sixty years ago, and now his son sells this and other well-cooked dishes from the attractive coffee shop on the ground floor of his Chinatown hotel. Daily 11am–2.30pm & 5.30–11pm.

Thye Choon Huan Restaurant and Bar, cnr of New Bridge and Upper Cross sts, Chinatown. Old-style coffee shop whose fittings ooze antiquity, from its marble-topped tables to its huge, liver-spotted mirror; *wan ton* and noodle soups, chicken, and duck rice can all be whistled up in a trice.

Ubin Seafood, 2161 Pulau Ubin (☎5458202). One of the finest seafood restaurants in Singapore – and with a great view of Johor. Take bus #2 from Victoria St to Changi Village, and hop on a bumboat to Pulau Ubin, then catch a taxi or rent a bike. Daily 11.30am–9pm.

Union Farm Eating House, 435a Clementi Rd, Western Singapore (☎4662776). This was a poultry farm until thirty years ago, and palms and bamboo lend the restaurant a pleasantly rural feel. The house special, *chee pow kai* (marinated chicken wrapped in greaseproof paper and deep-fried – $14 buys enough for two), is messy and wonderful. From Clementi MRT, take bus #154 and get off when you see Maju army camp. Daily 11.30am–8.30pm.

Wang Jiang Lou, Block A, Clarke Quay (☎3383001). Slick Cantonese–Teochew restaurant where the ingredients of a full seafood menu eye you suspiciously from tanks on the walls. Also available is a medley of *dim sum* (weekday lunchtime; $14), and night-time steamboat (from $11). Daily 11.30am–2.30pm & 6.30–10.30pm.

HAINANESE

Mooi Chin Palace, #B1-03 Funan the IT Mall, 109 North Bridge Rd (☎3397766). Hainanese immigrants often worked as domestics to colonial families, resulting in crossover dishes like Hainanese mutton soup and Hainanese pork chop – both cooked to perfection in this 60-year-old place, where whole *pomfret sambal* ($24) is a speciality, and set menus start at $32 for two. Daily 7.30–9am (*dim sum*), 11.30am–3pm & 6–10pm.

Yet Con Chicken Rice Restaurant, 25 Purvis St (☎3376819). A couple of streets north of Bras Basah Rd. Cheap and cheerful, old-time restaurant: try "crunchy, crispy" roast pork with pickled cabbage and radish, or chicken rice, washed down with barley water, for two people. Daily 10.30am–9.30pm.

HOKKIEN

Bee Heong, fourth floor, Pil Bldg, 140 Cecil St, Financial District (☎2229075). Customers are pumped through at a rate of knots in this lunchtime-only, cafeteria-style place; there's no menu, but the *beggar chicken* and dried chilli prawn come recommended, or ask the friendly staff for advice. Daily 11am–2.30pm.

Beng Hiang, 115 Amoy St, Chinatown (☎2216695). The Hokkien chef relies heavily upon robust soups and sauces, though his most popular dish is a superbly cooked fried *mee*; the lack of a menu makes ordering distinctly tricky, but persistence is rewarded by well-cooked food at good-value prices – you can eat well for under $15. Daily 11.30am–2pm & 6–9pm.

Beng Thin Hoon Kee, #05-02 OCBC Centre, 65 Chulia St, Financial District (☎5332818). Hidden inside the OCBC car park, this minty green restaurant is very popular at lunchtime with city slickers from the nearby business district. Big portions make it a good and filling introduction to Hokkien cuisine. Daily 11.30am–3pm & 6–10pm.

SZECHUAN AND HUNANESE

Cherry Garden, *The Oriental*, 5 Raffles Ave, Marina Square (☎3380066 ext 3538). Elegant restaurant, designed to resemble a Chinese courtyard, and serving tasty Szechuan and Hunanese dishes. The Hunanese honey-glazed ham is delectable, as is the Szechuan house speciality, camphor-smoked duck and bean-curd crust (both under $30); the set lunch costs $44 a head. Daily noon–2.30pm & 6.30–10.30pm.

Min Jiang, *Goodwood Park Hotel*, 22 Scotts Rd (☎7375337). This restaurant's reputation for fine Szechuan classics – like camphor and tea-smoked duck – makes reservations a good idea. A meal for two costs around $60. Daily noon–2.30pm & 6.30–10.30pm.

TEOCHEW

Ban Seng, #B1-44 The Riverwalk, 20 Upper Circular Rd, Chinatown (☎5331471). Road-widening caused this venerable, mid-price restaurant to decamp to just around the corner not long ago, and the traditional charcoal ovens didn't survive the move. The food is still top-notch, however: try the steamed crayfish, braised goose or stuffed sea cucumber. Daily noon–2pm & 6–10pm.

Liang Kee, 16 Murray Terrace, Chinatown (☎5341029). An unpretentious, popular local restaurant that thwarts tourists with its lack of any written clues as to the food on offer. Good quality, though. Open noon–2.30pm & 6–9.30pm; closed Wed.

Teochew City Seafood Restaurant, #05-16 Centrepoint, 176 Orchard Rd (☎7333338). Somerset MRT. Standard Teochew restaurant whose karaoke facilities are, mercifully, confined to two private rooms; $50 suffices for a meal for two. Daily 11.30am–2.30pm & 6.30–11pm.

VEGETARIAN

Fut Sai Kai, 147 Kitchener Rd, Little India (☎2980336). Old-fashioned Cantonese restaurant with a strongly Oriental atmosphere and fiery red decor; $20 is sufficient for two. Bean-curd forms the backbone of Chinese vegetarian cooking, though it reaches your table shaped to resemble meat or fish. Tues–Sun 10am–9pm.

Happy Realm Vegetarian Food Centre, #03-16 Pearls Centre, 100 Eu Tong Sen St, Chinatown (☎2226141). "The way to good health and a sound mind", boasts the restaurant's card; tasty and reasonably priced vegetarian dishes. Daily 11am–8.30pm.

Kwan Yim Vegetarian Restaurant, 190 Waterloo St (☎3382394). A huge display of sweet and savoury *pow* (Chinese-style buns) is the highlight of this unfussy establishment, sited close to Bencoolen St. Daily 8am–8.30pm.

Lingzhi, #B1-17/18 Orchard Towers, 400 Orchard Rd (☎7343788). A real treat, where skewers of vegetables served with satay sauce are the highlight of an imaginative menu; there's also a take-away counter. Daily 11.30am–10pm.

OTHER SPECIALITY RESTAURANTS

Doc Cheng's, *Raffles Hotel*, 328 North Bridge Rd (☎3311612). East meets West in the most recent addition to *Raffles*, an ice-cool joint themed around the global travels of imagined local *bon viveur*, Doc Cheng. Though the menu betrays Alaskan, Japanese, Cajun and Spanish influences, Chinese culinary ideology provides the backbone to much of the food; the decor presents a similarly eclectic blend of Oriental, Art Deco and modernist influences. Two pay around $60. Daily noon–10.30pm.

House of Mao, #03-02 China Square Food Centre, 51 Telok Ayer St (☎5330660). Really rather a good restaurant, once you get over the shock of being served by waitresses in full Red Guard fatigues, and the eerie sense of being watched by the scores of images of Mao on the walls. The Hunan shredded pork comes recommended, though it seems churlish not to try Chairman Mao's favourite braised garlic pork. Daily 11.30am–2.30pm & 6–10pm.

Imperial Herbal Restaurant, third floor, *Metropole Hotel*, 41 Seah St (☎3370491 ext 212). One street north of Bras Basah Rd. The place to go if you are concerned about your yin and yang balance: after checking your pulse and tongue, a resident Chinese physician recommends either a cooling or a "heaty" dish from the menu. For migraine sufferers the drunken scorpions are, by all accounts, a must; rheumatics should opt for crispy black ants. Daily 11.30am–2.30pm & 6.30–10.30pm.

Moi Kong Hakka, 22 Murray St, Chinatown (☎2217758). Hakka food relies heavily on salted and preserved ingredients and dishes here, in the best Hakka food outlet in Singapore, encompass abacus yam starch beads ($6) and stewed pork belly with preserved vegetables. Daily 10.30am–2.30pm & 6–10pm.

Pine Court, 35th floor, *Mandarin Hotel*, 333 Orchard Rd (☎7374411). Three elegant pine trees dominate this beautiful restaurant serving Beijing cuisine; their speciality is whole Peking duck ($70) – enough for three hungry people. Cheaper set meals are available, too. You need to reserve in advance. Daily noon–2.30pm & 6.30–10.30pm.

Shanghai Palace Seafood Restaurant, *Excelsior Hotel*, 5 Coleman St (☎3393428). Just west of the Padang. Authentic Shanghai dishes – drunken chicken, fried hot and sour chicken, bean-curd claypot – and a smattering of Cantonese and Szechuan favourites are served here in unfussy surroundings; two people pay upwards of $50. Daily noon–2.30pm & 6.30–10.30pm.

Snackworld, #01-12/13 Cuppage Plaza, 5 Koek Rd, off Orchard Rd. Hectic terrace restaurant where the Chinese menu is enlivened by hot-plate crocodile meat ($25) and emu. Daily 11am–midnight.

Superbowl, 80 Boat Quay (☎5386066). An affordable range of 47 *congee*s, served at marble-topped tables recalling a 1950s coffee shop. Daily 11am–11pm.

Top Flight Mongolian BBQ, #04-01 Park Mall, 9 Penang Rd (☎3344888). Just south of Orchard Rd, near Dhoby Ghaut MRT. Create your own combination from an array of meats, vegetables and sauces and hand it in at the open kitchen, where it's cooked for you on a hot griddle. Unlimited visits to the food bar cost under $20 (lunchtime) and $25 (dinner), and include starters and desserts. Daily 11.30am–2.30pm & 6–10pm.

European and international

Compass Rose, 69th floor, *Westin Stamford Hotel*, 2 Stamford Rd (☎3388585). An expensive place, but one that boasts a panoramic view of central Singapore. Buffet lunch ($48) is the cheapest way to experience the international cuisine. Daily noon–2.30pm & 6.30–10.30pm.

Don Noodle Bistro, #01-16 Tanglin Mall, Tanglin Rd (☎7383188). Opposite Nassim Hill, off the western end of Orchard Rd. Minimalist yet chic, Don is something of a paradox – a Western-style take on the noodle bar, imported back to the East. The menu is not country-specific, meaning that you can enjoy Indonesian *kway teow goreng* while your dining partner tucks into Japanese *ramen* noodles. Daily 11.30am–10.30pm.

Gordon Grill, *Goodwood Park Hotel*, 22 Scotts Rd (☎7301744). Upmarket restaurant lent a Scottish feel by the tartan decor and the haggis with tatties: excellent food – but at a price. The set lunch ($32) is your best bet. Daily noon–3pm & 7–11pm.

Hot Stones, 53 Boat Quay (☎5345188). A healthy and novel twist on dining: steaks, chicken and seafood grilled at table on non-porous alpine rock heated to 200° – no oil, but bags of flavour. Daily noon–2.30pm & 6–10.30pm.

Louis' Oyster Bar, 36 Boat Quay (☎5330534). The Louis in question is Louis Armstrong, who beams down from all the walls. Oysters cost around $18 per half-dozen, but the High Society Platter (crayfish, crab, mussels, oysters and prawns on ice; $55 for two) is hard to resist. Mon–Fri 11am–1am, Sat & Sun 6pm–1am.

Maison Basque, Suntec City Mall, 3 Temasek Blvd (☎3385308). About 250m south of The Gateway on Beach Rd. French food cooked with half an eye over the border into Spain: come and have a crack at the filling Paella San Sebastian (a chicken, monkfish, prawn, mussel and squid feast); or settle for the *Ttoro* (seafood soup), washed down with mouthfuls of sangria ($20 per half-litre). Daily 11am–3pm & 6–11pm.

Milano's, Funan the IT Mall, North Bridge Rd. Near High St. Their "All you can eat – all day, every day" policy makes *Milano's* unbeatable value: choose from soups, pizzas, pastas and salad. Then choose again. And again. $11 a head. Daily 11.30am–11.30pm.

Nooch, #02-16 Wheelock Place, 501 Orchard Rd (☎2350880). The blurb on its menu calls this cool and popular, crescent-shaped joint overlooking Orchard Blvd a "non-destinational" restaurant – meaning that the idea is to order and scoff your MSG-free Thai or Japanese noodles on the double, and be on your way. The *tub tim krob*, or chestnuts in syrup and coconut milk, is a good way to douse the fires after a Thai *tom yam* soup. Mon–Fri noon–3pm & 6–10.30pm, Sat & Sun noon–11pm.

Olive Tree, *Hotel Inter-Continental*, 80 Middle Rd (☎3387600). Anything goes in this stylish joint as long as there's a sun-kissed, Mediterranean connection: kick off with *bruschetta* or *gambas ceviche* (prawns marinated in tomato sauce, lime juice and olive oil), move on to *merguez* sausages with couscous, complemented by a Lebanese durum-wheat salad, and end with Andalucian chocolate mousse. Buffet-style set lunches ($40) and dinners ($50) ease the choosing process.

Pasta Fresca, 30 Boat Quay (☎5326283). Match up fresh pasta and a sauce from the menu, and sit out on the riverside terrace. Around $20 a head, drinks extra. Daily 11am–10pm.

Paulaner Bräuhaus, #01-01 Millenia Walk, 9 Raffles Blvd (☎3377123). German-theme restaurant-cum-brewery, serving generous platters of wurst, *kartoffeln* and sauerkraut; two pay $60, including a stein of beer each. Dinner 11am–2.30pm & 6.30–9.30pm, then drinks only (see p.604).

Indian and Nepali

Annalakshmi, *Excelsior Hotel*, 5 Coleman St (☎3399993). Terrific North and South Indian vegetarian food in sumptuous surroundings, with all profits going to Kala Mandhir, an Indian cultural association next door. Many of the staff are volunteers from the Hindu community, so your waiter might just be a doctor or a lawyer. Dishes from $10. Daily 11.30am–3pm & 6–9.30pm.

Azmi Muslim Food Stall, 168–170 Serangoon Rd. Set within the *Thye Chong Restaurant* on the corner of Norris Rd. Here, *chapatis* are hand-cooked on a griddle in front of you; brains, liver and goats' legs flank more conventional dishes on the accompanying curry menu. Daily 10am–9pm.

Banana Leaf Apolo, 54–58 Race Course Rd, Little India (☎2938682). Pioneering fish-head curry ($30 for two people) restaurant where a wide selection of South Indian dishes are all served on banana leaves. Despite its recently refurbishment (the place is now resplendent in marble), eating with your hands is still the order of the day here. Daily 10.30am–10pm.

Gandhi Eating House, 29 Chandler Rd, Little India. Many locals reckon this open-fronted place off Race Course Road knocks out the best chicken curries in Little India; meals come on banana leaves, water in metal jugs. Daily 9am–9.30pm.

Gorkha Grill, 21 Smith St, Chinatown (☎2270806). There are fish, mutton and chicken dishes galore at this enchanting Nepali place, but be sure to start with *momo* (minced chicken dumplings) and end with *kheer* (rice pudding), a tasty blend of cream, rice and cardamom. Daily 11.30am–11.30pm.

Islamic Restaurant, 791–797 North Bridge Rd (☎2987563). Near the junction with Jalan Sultan. Aged Muslim restaurant manned by a gang of old men who plod solemnly up and down between the tables. It boasts the best chicken *biriyani* in Singapore, cooked in the traditional way – heated from above and below with charcoal. $10 for two. Daily except Fri 9.30am–9.30pm.

Kinara, 57 Boat Quay (☎5330412). Exquisite restaurant boasting antique fittings imported from the subcontinent and a marvellous view of the river from upstairs; the food comprises elegantly presented Punjabi dishes. Around $50 for two. Daily noon–2.30pm & 6.30–10.30pm.

Komala Villas, 76–78 Serangoon Rd, Little India (☎2936980). A cramped, popular vegetarian establishment specializing in fifteen varieties of *dosai*. The "South Indian Meal", served upstairs on a banana leaf, is great value at $4.50. Daily 7am–10pm.

Madras New Woodlands, 12–14 Upper Dickson Rd, Little India (☎2971594). Functional, canteen-style place serving up decent vegetarian food at bargain prices. House specialities are the hali set meal ($4) and the VIP Thali ($6); samosas, bhajis and other snacks are available after 3pm, and there's a big selection of sweets, too. Recommended. Daily 8am–11pm.

Maharani, #05-36 Far East Plaza, Scotts Rd (☎2358840). Orchard Rd's pioneering North Indian restaurant grades each dish's "heatiness" with star ratings. Around $25 a head, with beer. Daily noon–3pm & 6.30–11pm.

Moti Mahal, 18 Murray St, Chinatown (☎2214338). Not cheap, but one of Singapore's very best, serving tasty tandoori dishes in pleasant surroundings. The special is *murg massalam*, a whole chicken stuffed with rice ($50 – must be ordered in advance). Daily 11am–3pm & 6.30–10.30pm.

Muthu's Curry Restaurant, 76/78 Race Course Rd, Little India (☎2932389) This rough-and-ready South Indian restaurant, without a written menu, is famous for its fish-head curry. Daily 10am–10pm.

Orchard Maharajah, 25 Cuppage Terrace, Cuppage Rd (☎7326331). Off Orchard Rd. Set in a wonderful old Peranakan house, this splendid North Indian restaurant has a large terrace and a tempting menu that includes the sublime fish *mumtaz* – fillet of fish stuffed with minced mutton, almonds, eggs, cashews and raisins – worth the extra few dollars. The set lunch is good value at $16. Daily 11.30am–3pm & 6.30–11pm.

Selera Restaurant, 15 Mackenzie Rd (☎3385687). Off Selegie Rd. The best curry puffs – curried meat and boiled egg folded into a pastry semicircle – in Singapore. Two will fill you up for around a dollar. Daily noon–11.30pm.

Sri Vijayah, 229 Selegie Rd (☎3361748). Hole-in-the-wall vegetarian banana-leaf joint offering unbeatable value for money: $3 buys a replenishable mountain of rice and vegetable curries, and there's a mouthwatering display of sweetmeats at the front door. Daily 6am–10pm.

Taj Jazzaurant, #02-01 Little India Arcade, 48 Serangoon Rd, Little India (☎2914680). Fine North and South Indian food until 10pm (signature dishes: prawn and *brinjal* curry at $12, and *raan pasinda*, leg of lamb in yogurt, for $18), after which the bar (see p.604) continues to serve.

Zam Zam, 699 North Bridge Rd, Arab Quarter (☎2987011). A simple curry house, though worth a visit to see the award-winning *murtabak* maker in action. Daily 7am–11pm.

Indonesian

Alkaff Mansion, 10 Telok Blangah Green, Western Singapore (☎2786979). Bus #145 from Redhill MRT. Built in the 1920s as a weekend retreat for the Alkaff family, this splendidly restored mansion offers a superb *rijstaffel* ($66), ten dishes served by a line of ten women in traditional *kebayas*. Or just have a beer in the bar, worth the exorbitant price for an hour or two of colonial grandeur. Daily noon–midnight.

House of Sundanese Food, 55 Boat Quay (☎5343775). Spicy salads and barbecued seafood characterize the cuisine of Sunda (West Java), served here in simple yet tasteful surroundings. Try the tasty *ikan sunda* (grilled Javanese fish) – an $18 fish serves two to three people. Mon–Fri 11am–2.30pm & 5–10pm, Sat & Sun 5–10pm.

Rendezvous, #02-02 Hotel Rendezvous, 9 Bras Basah Rd (☎53397508). Revered *nasi padang* – highly spiced Sumatran cuisine – joint that still turns in lip-smacking curries, *rendang*s and *sambal*s; the weighing machine in the corner is an unusual touch. Daily 11am–9.30pm.

Rumah Makan Minang, 18a Kandahar St, Arab Quarter. Fiery *nasi padang* in the heart of the Arab Quarter; $4 ensures a good feed, while $3 buys the popular barbecued fish. Daily noon–2.30pm & 6–10.30pm.

Sanur, #04-17/18 Centrepoint, 176 Orchard Rd (☎7342192). Hearty, reasonably priced food served by waitresses in traditional batik dress; the beef *rendang* is terrific. It's best to book ahead. Daily 11.30am–2.45pm & 5.45–10pm.

Tambuah Mas Indonesian Restaurant, #04-10, Tanglin Shopping Centre, 19 Tanglin Rd, off the western end of Orchard Rd (☎7333333). Friendly restaurant, approached through a Minangkabau-style entrance, and offering spicy food and a smattering of Chinese dishes. Daily 11.30am–2.30pm & 6–10.30pm.

Japanese

Inagiku, third floor, *Westin Plaza Hotel*, 2 Stamford Rd, Colonial District (☎3388585). More of a maze than a restaurant, with four sections serving expensive, quality tempura, *teppanyaki*, sushi, and an à la carte menu – the latter the cheapest alternative. Open Mon–Sat noon–2.30pm & 6.30–10.30pm.

Japanese stalls, *Food Junction*, B1, Seiyu Department Store, Bugis Junction, 200 Victoria St. *Sumo* has sashimi, tempura and teriyaki sets around $9; while nearby *Express-Teppanyaki*'s "big-value meal" ($6.20) offers your choice of meats and vegetables flash-fried on the U-shaped hot bar.

Sakae Sushi, #02-13 Wheelock Place, 501 Orchard Rd (☎7376281). In between Angullia Park and Paterson Rd. Cheery sushi and sashimi bar, bang in the centre of Orchard Rd, where lunch sets start from $12. Diners choose to sit up at the conveyor-belt bar, or at diner-style booths around the restaurant's outer walls. Daily noon–10pm.

Senbazuru, *Hotel New Otani*, 177a River Valley Rd (☎3383333). Across from the River Valley Swimming Complex on the southern edge of Fort Canning Park. If the wide menu here proves too mind-boggling, choose from the selection of set lunches; for real gastronomes, there's the *kaiseki ryori*, or traditional eleven-course meal. Daily 11.30am–2.30pm & 6.30–10.30pm.

Sushi Tei, 20 Lorong Mambong, Holland Village (☎4632310). A cross-fertilization of Tokyo sushi bar and airport baggage reclaim: diners snatch sushi sets ($1.50–4) from the conveyor belt looping the bar. Daily 11.30am–2.30pm & 6–10pm.

Tatsu Sushi, #01-16, CHIJMES, 30 Victoria St (☎3325868). *Tatsu* is already a veteran relative to the notoriously fluid CHIJMES restaurant scene. Owner Ronny Chia's expertise, and the high quality of ingredients used (all fish is flown in from Japan) draw a clientele that's around 75 percent Japanese. Mon–Sat noon–2.30pm & 6.30–11pm.

Korean

Haebok's Korean Restaurant, 44–46 Tanjong Pagar Rd, Chinatown (☎2239003). All the standard dishes, served by indifferent staff in a plain dining room. Plastic models of the meals available displayed in the front window lend a few pointers. Daily 11.30am–3pm & 5.30–10.30pm.

Korean Restaurant Pte Ltd, #05-35 Specialists' Centre, 277 Orchard Rd (☎2350018). Somerset MRT. Singapore's first Korean restaurant, beautifully furnished and serving up a wide range of dependably good dishes at around $16–20 per dish. Daily 11am–11pm.

Seoul Garden Korean Restaurant, #03-119 Marina Square, 6 Raffles Blvd (☎3391339). Entertaining, busy restaurant with daily set lunches from $7.90; best value is the "all you can eat" Korean barbecue – a buffet of twenty seasoned meats, seafoods and vegetables which you cook at your table. Mon–Fri 11am–3pm & 5.30–10.30pm, Sat & Sun 11am–10.30pm.

Malay and Nonya

Bintang Timur, #02-08/13 Far East Plaza, 14 Scotts Rd (☎2354539). A perennial favourite, thanks to its reliable cooking; the sticks of satay here are bigger than usual, so take care not to overorder. Around $12 a head without beer. Daily 11am–9.45pm.

Blue Ginger, 97 Tanjong Pagar Rd, Chinatown (☎2223928). Housed in a renovated shophouse, this trendy Peranakan restaurant is proving a yuppie favourite, thanks to such dishes as *ikan masal asam gulai* (mackerel simmered in a tamarind and lemon-grass gravy), and that benchmark of Nonya cuisine, *ayam buah keluak* – braised chicken with Indonesian black nuts. Daily 11.30am–3pm & 6.30–11pm.

Guan Hoe Soon, 214 Joo Chiat Rd, Katong (☎3442761). Over fifty years old, this place still turns out fine Nonya cuisine; try the *chendol* (coconut milk, red beans, sugar, green jelly and ice), a refreshing end to a meal. Around $35 for two, with beer. Daily 11am–3pm & 6–9.30pm; closed Tues.

Mum's Kitchen, 314 Joo Chiat Rd, Katong (☎3460969). The emphasis here, as you'd imagine, is on home-cooked food, Nonya-based, though with other Asian incursions. Their house speciality, Mum's Curry, is wonderful, and best chased down by home-made barley water; special business lunches (Mon–Fri) offer three courses at $18 for two people. Daily 11am–10pm.

Nonya & Baba, 262 River Valley Rd (☎7341382). Near the Chettiar Hindu Temple. Greatly respected Nonya restaurant lent character by its marble tables and tasteful decor; the *otak otak* (fish mashed with coconut milk and chilli paste, then wrapped in banana leaf) and the *ayam buah keluak* (chicken with black nuts) are both terrific; other dishes cost around $7 a head. Daily 11.30am–10pm.

Spring Blossoms Café, *Bayview Inn*, 30 Bencoolen St (☎3372882 ext 281). This faceless hotel café's buffet lunch is a great introduction to Nonya cuisine, and very reasonable at around $15. Wed, Sat & Sun noon–5pm.

Thai, Vietnamese and Filipino

Cuppage Thai Food Restaurant, 49 Cuppage Terrace, off Orchard Rd (☎7341116). Dhoby Ghaut MRT. Nondescript inside, but boasting a great outdoor terrace, this cheap and cheerful restaurant offers quality Thai dishes at around the $8 mark. Daily 11am–3pm & 6–11pm.

Indochine, 49 Club St, Chinatown (☎3230503). One of Singapore's most elegant restaurants, its beautiful fixtures complemented by a truly great menu embracing Vietnamese, Laotian and Cambodian cuisine. Try the Laotian *larb kai* (spicy chicken salad) or the Vietnamese *nha trang* roast duck and mango salad from Vietnam. Mon–Sat noon–2.30pm & 6–10pm.

Kabayan Filipino Restaurant, #03-25 Lucky Plaza, 304 Orchard Rd. Big, dark chamber crammed with tables to cater for the Sunday melee of Filipino maids; dishes are laid out buffet-style, and best washed down with San Miguel beer. Daily 10am–9pm.

Pornping Thai Seafood Restaurant, #01-96/98 Golden Mile Complex, 5001 Beach Rd, Arab Quarter (☎2985016). Set in a complex known locally as "Thai Village" and always full of Thais waiting to catch buses home. All the standard dishes at cheap prices – $25 buys a meal for two, washed down with Singha beer. Daily 10am–10pm.

Shingthai Palace, 36 Purvis St (☎3371161). A couple of streets north of Bras Basah Rd. Good but characterless restaurant serving reasonably priced Thai dishes; try the *peek kai sord sai* (chicken wings with asparagus, prawns, mushrooms and meat). Around $15–20 a head. Daily 11am–2pm & 6–10.30pm.

Sukhothai, 47 Boat Quay (☎5382422). Chef's recommendations include fried cotton fish topped with sliced green mangoes, but you can't go far wrong whatever you plump for; the dining room is rather understated, so take advantage of the riverside tables. Daily 6.30–11pm, Mon–Fri also noon–3pm.

Viet Café, #01-76 UE Square, Unity St (☎3336453). Off the southern end of Clemenceau Ave. The heady aromas of Vietnamese *pho* (soup) – mint, basil and citrus – hang heavy in the air at this sleek establishment. Follow the pebble path that leads up to the balcony or, better still, sit out on the fore-court and enjoy the night air. Daily noon–3am.

US

Billy Bombers, #02-52 Bugis Junction, 200 Victoria St (☎3378018). Shades of *Arnold's* diner in *Happy Days*: reasonably priced burgers and bowls of chilli eaten in speakeasy booths upholstered in red leather. Daily 11.30am–2.30pm & 6.30–10.30pm.

Bobby Rubino's, #B1-03 Fountain Court, CHIJMES, 30 Victoria St (☎3375466). Ribs are their spe-ciality, but steaks, burgers and other big-boy platters are available; eschew the "wine-rack" parti-tions and rough hewn red-brick interior and make for the terrace, superbly located below CHI-JMES' looming convent. Daily 12.30–4pm & 6–10pm.

Cha Cha Cha, 32 Lorong Mambong, Holland Village (☎4621650). Classic Mexican dishes in this vibrantly coloured restaurant range from $10 to $22; outside are a few open-air patio tables, ideal for posing with a bottle of Dos Equis beer, but book ahead for these. Daily 11.30am–10pm.

Chico's N Charlie's, #05-01 Liat Towers, 541 Orchard Rd (☎7341753). Faithfully re-created Mexican decor and food ($11–38), as well as a good-value set lunch ($15 for main course, soup, gar-lic bread, dessert and coffee or tea). Daily 11am–11pm.

Dan Ryan's Chicago Grill, #B1-01 Tanglin Mall, Tanglin Rd (☎7383800). Chug back a Budweiser and get stuck into "American portions" of ribs, burgers and chicken in a dining room that's crammed with Americana; main courses cost around $15. Daily 11am–midnight.

El Pollo Loco, #01-75 Millennia Walk, 9 Raffles Blvd (☎3397377); branch at 2 Lorong Mambong, Holland Village. Flame-broiled chicken are served with tortillas and salsa at this health-conscious, Los Angeles-based chain; it's surely the only Singaporean restaurant to boast an endorsement from the American Heart Association.

Ponderosa, #02-20 Raffles City Shopping Centre, 252 North Bridge Rd (☎3344926). Near City Hall MRT. The perfect cure for vitamin deficiency – chicken, steak and fish set meals come with baked potato, sundae and as much salad as you can eat, all for $25. Daily noon–10.30pm.

Seah Street Deli, *Raffles Hotel*, 1 Beach Rd (☎3371886). New York-style deli boasting the most mountainous sandwiches in Asia, at around $10 each. Huge crayons, bagels and wristwatches on the walls make this the most un-colonial establishment in *Raffles Hotel*. Daily 11am–10pm, Fri & Sat until 11pm.

Drinking and nightlife

Singapore has much more to offer in the way of **nightlife** than it's often given credit for. The island's burgeoning **bar and pub** scene means there is now a wide range of drink-ing holes to choose from, with the Colonial District, Boat Quay and Orchard Road areas offering particularly good pub-crawl potential. With competition hotting up, more and more bars are turning to **live music** to woo punters, though this is usually no more than cover versions performed by local bands. That said, big-name groups do occa-sionally make forays here. **Clubs** also do brisk business; glitzy yet unpretentious, they feature the latest imported pop, rock and dance music, though don't expect anything like a rave scene – Ecstasy isn't in the Singaporean dictionary.

Bars and pubs

With the **bars and pubs** of Singapore ranging from slick cocktail joints through elegant colonial chambers to boozy dives, you're bound to find a place that suits you.

Establishments open either in the late morning (to catch the lunchtime dining trade) or in the early evening, and usually close around midnight. On Friday and Saturday, opening hours almost invariably extend by an hour or two. Many serve snacks throughout the day, and a few offer more substantial dishes. It's possible to buy a small glass of beer in most places for around $6–7, but **prices** can be double or treble that amount, especially in the Orchard Road district. A glass of wine usually costs much the same as a beer, and spirits a dollar or two more. One way of cutting costs is to arrive in time for **happy hour** in the early evening, when bars offer local beers and house wine either at half price, or "one for one" – you get two of whatever you order, but one is held back for later.

Singaporeans adore rock **music**, and a plethora of bars panders to this, presenting nightly performances by local or Filipino covers bands. These are picked out below, but for more details see p.606. Also hugely popular is **karaoke**, which almost reaches an art form in some Singapore bars.

Boat Quay and Clarke Quay

Bernie Goes to Town, 82a/b Boat Quay (☎5363533). This laid-back, roadhouse-style joint is just a short walk down Boat Quay from the yuppie haunt of *Harry's*, but a whole world away from it in terms of atmosphere. Reggae, blues and R&B are the preferred sounds here, and there is a live band nightly. Beers and margheritas are discounted during happy hour (3–8pm). Mon–Thurs & Sun 11am–1am, Fri & Sat 3pm–3am.

Crazy Elephant, #01-07 Trader's Market, Clarke Quay. The only bar with any real clout along Clarke Quay, playing decent rock music on the turntable between live sessions by the house band; regulars prefer the tables out by the water's edge. Mon–Thurs & Sun 5pm–1am, Fri & Sat till 2am.

Harry's Quayside, 28 Boat Quay. There's live jazz and R&B Tuesday to Saturday in this upmarket place, and a blues jam every Sunday evening. Light lunches are served too. Daily 1pm–1am.

Mambo No 5, 60 Boat Quay. Cramped and sweaty bar, rocking over the weekend, whose DJ's catholic tastes embrace soul, Motown, funk, hip-hop, reggae and R&B; not the place for a quiet chat. Daily 3pm–2am.

Molly Malone's, 42 Circular Rd. Just west of Boat Quay. With Kilkenny and Guinness on tap, sounds courtesy of Van Morrison and the Pogues, and a menu offering Connemara oysters and Irish stew, this is hardly your quintessential Singaporean boozer, but the craic's good when full. Daily 11am–1am.

The Colonial District

Bar and Billiards Room, *Raffles Hotel*, 1 Beach Rd. A Singapore Sling ($18.50), in the colonial elegance of the hotel where Ngiam Tong Boon invented it in 1915, is required drinking on a visit to Singapore. Snacks are available through the afternoon, and billiards costs another $15 an hour. Daily 11.30am–midnight.

Compass Rose Bar, seventieth floor, *Westin Stamford Hotel*, 2 Stamford Rd. Tasteful bar from whose floor-to-ceiling windows you can see as far as southern Malaysia. Happy hour 5.30–8.30pm; minimum charge $15 after 8.30pm. Daily 11am–12.30am.

Lot, Stock and Barrel Pub, 29 Seah St. North of Bras Basah Rd. Frequented by a daytime office crowd and later a backpacker crowd (Beach Rd's homestays are just around the corner), who come for the rock classics on the jukebox. Happy hour 4–8pm; open daily 4pm–midnight.

Paulaner Bräuhaus, #01-01 Millenia Walk, 9 Raffles Blvd. Wurst and sauerkraut might be a priority upstairs (see p.600), but down in the bar of this themed micobrewery, lager is very much in the forefront of the punter's minds. It's predictably busy around Oktoberfest-time. Daily noon–midnight.

Little India and around

Leisure Pub, #B1-01 Selegie Centre, 189 Selegie Rd. Tame but endearing, darts-orientated establishment that's ideal for a quiet chat. Happy hour daily 3–8pm; open daily 5pm–midnight.

Pirate's Well Pub, #01-275 Selegie Complex, Selegie Rd. Indian-run hideaway catering to the Little India community, with dim lighting conjuring up a moody atmosphere. Daily 5pm–midnight.

Taj Jazzaurant, #02-01 Little India Arcade, 48 Serangoon Rd. Once the plates and cutlery have been cleared away, there's swinging Hindi and Tamil dance music deep into the night. Disco 10pm–2am.

Orchard Road

Anywhere, #04-08/09 Tanglin Shopping Centre, 19 Tanglin Rd. Off the western end of Orchard Rd. Tania, Singapore's most famous covers band, plays nightly to a boozy roomful of expats that's at its rowdiest on Friday nights. Happy hour Mon–Fri 6–8pm; open Mon–Sat 6pm–2am.

Excalibur Pub, #B1-06 Tanglin Shopping Centre, 19 Tanglin Rd. Wonderfully cluttered and cramped British-style pub that's full of weather-beaten expats. Daily 11am–10.30pm.

Ice Cold Beer, 9 Emerald Hill Rd. Just north of Somerset MRT. Noisy, hectic and happening place where the beers are kept on ice under the glass topped bar. Happy hour daily 5–9pm; open daily 5pm–2am.

No 5 Emerald Hill, 5 Emerald Hill Rd. Quite a pleasant Peranakan-style bar/restaurant, if you can stomach the posing bar staff and the constant crunch of monkey nuts underfoot. There's nightly live jazz in the upstairs bar. Happy hour daily noon–9pm and 1–2am; open daily noon–2am.

Observation Lounge, 38th floor, *Mandarin Hotel*, 333 Orchard Rd. Swanky cocktail bar offering awesome views over downtown Singapore. Daily 11am–1am (Fri & Sat until 2am).

Saxophone, 23 Cuppage Rd. Just north of Somerset MRT. The coolest address in town, and a magnet for the beautiful people, who relax on the terrace to the sounds of the house jazz band. Happy hour daily 6–8pm; open daily 6pm–2am.

The Sportsman, #02-01 Far East Shopping Centre, 545 Orchard Rd. One for homesick British footie fans, this: the walls are plastered with pictures of the likes of Gazza and Beckham, big matches are screened live, and Tiger beer is $5 a mug. Daily 11am–midnight.

Vintage Rock Café, #03-18 Cuppage Plaza, 5 Koek Rd. Just north of Somerset MRT. Friendly staff and locals, great R&B music on the speakers and cheapish beer: recommended. Happy hour 5–8pm; open 5pm–midnight.

River Valley Road and around

The Mitre, 145 Killiney Rd. Marvellously shabby old hotel bar, with TV and dartboard.

Next Page Pub, 15 Mohamed Sultan Rd. Cool, popular pub, with pool table, scatter cushions and R&B sounds. The decor is a mixture of Chinese wooden screens, lanterns and rough brick wall. Daily 3pm–1am.

Wong San's, 12 Mohamed Sultan Rd. Stylish pub in a beautifully decorated Peranakan-style building, popular with local journalists and white-collar workers. Daily 3pm–1am.

The Yard, 294 River Valley Rd. Busy English pub with bar snacks available. Happy hour daily 3–8pm; open daily 3pm–midnight.

Chinatown and Tanjong Pagar

Bar Sa Vanh, 49 Club St (☎3230503). Candlelit, and crammed with Buddha effigies, scatter cushions and plants, the *Sa Vanh* (the name means "Heaven" in Lao) is a chilled-out bar if ever there was one. The cool acid-jazz sounds round things off nicely. Happy hour 5–8pm. Daily 5pm–1am.

Flag and Whistle Public House, 10 Duxton Hill. Predictable British pub, complete with Bass beer, bar snacks and a large Union Jack. Daily 11am–midnight.

J.J. Mahoney Pub, 58 Duxton Rd. A popular haunt for karaoke-hungry local yuppies; the bar serves Bass beer and snacks throughout the night. Happy hour is 11am–8pm, but doesn't include Bass. Daily 11am–1am.

Lang Kwai Fong, 50 Eu Tong Sen St. While it's a shame to see such a beautiful building turned into a bar, it must be said that the end result is most impressive – a blend of flashing lights, gleaming bars and elegant Chinese fittings. Happy hour 6–9pm, open Mon–Sat 6pm–3am.

Clubs

Singaporean **clubs** are refreshingly unpretentious, their customers more intent on enjoying themselves than on posing. European and American dance music dominates (though some play Cantonese pop songs, too), and many feature live bands playing cover versions of current hits and pop classics. Clubs tend to open around 9pm, though some start earlier in the evening with a happy hour. Indeed, the difference between bars and discos has recently begun to blur, and some now include bars or restaurants that kick off at lunchtime. Most have a **cover charge**, at least on busy Friday and Saturday nights, which fluctuates between $10 and $30, depending on what day it is, and almost invariably entitles you to a drink or two. It's worth checking the local press to see which venues are currently in favour; a scan through *8 Days* or *IS* magazines will bring you up to date.

Singapore also has a plethora of seedy hostess clubs, in which aged Chinese hostesses working on commission try to hassle you into buying them a drink. Extortionately expensive, these joints are to be avoided, not least because they attract a decidedly unsavoury clientele. Fortunately, they are easy to spot: even if you get beyond the heavy wooden front door flanked by brandy adverts, the pitch darkness inside gives the game away.

Boom Boom Room, #02-04, 3 New Bugis St (☎3398187). The comedy and dance on show every night is tame by old Bugis St standards, though still well attended and enjoyed by locals and tourists. Cover charge Tues–Sat; 9pm–2am.

Brix, 10–12 Scotts Rd (☎7307107). Formally known as *Brannigan's*, this large basement bar has shed its pick-up joint reputation, roughed up its decor a bit, and moved up into the premier league of Singapore clubs. There's loud R&B nightly. Daily 9pm–2am.

Sparks Disco, seventh floor, Ngee Ann City, 391 Orchard Rd (☎7356133). Soccer pitch-sized and multichambered nightspot whose slick Art Deco fittings are aimed squarely at the yuppie market. Three live bands play jazz, pop and Canto-pop. Daily Mon–Sat 6pm–3am.

Sugar, 13 Mohamed Sultan Rd (☎8360010). If Elton John were to decorate Marie Antoinette's bedroom it'd probably look something akin to the front bar at *Sugar*. Most of the dancing goes on out back, though, where Singapore's beautiful people dance to house and garage. Mon–Sat 8pm–3am.

Sultan of Swing, #01-01 Central Mall, 5 Magazine Rd (☎5570828). Southwest of Clarke Quay and across the Singapore River. Draws a substantial enough crowd of young executives to fill the huge dance hall that lies behind the quieter wine bar out front. There's a retro Eighties theme to the music till midnight, after which house takes over. Cover charges apply Sat & Sun only. Daily 5pm–2am.

Tajie, 27 Mohamed Sultan Rd (☎8870007). "Chinese funky" is how its staff describe this popular bar-cum-disco, whose decor comprises rough brick walls and red Chinese lanterns. The actual dance floor is modest – most punters prefer to dance where they stand; cover charges apply at weekends only. Daily 7pm–1am.

Zouk, 17–21 Jiak Kim St (☎7382988). Slightly over 1km west of Clarke Quay, on the south side of the Singapore river; reached off Kim Seng Rd. Singapore's trendiest club, fitted out to create a Mediterranean feel. World-renowned DJs guest occasionally. Happy hour 8–9pm; open Mon–Sat 6pm–3am.

Live music

Singapore is too far off the European and North American tour trail to attract many big-name performers, but there are occasional visits to rally the troops. Rivalling Western music in terms of popularity in Singapore is **Canto-pop**, a bland hybrid of Cantonese lyrics and Western disco beats; Hong Kong Canto-pop superstars visit periodically, and the rapturous welcomes they receive make their shows quite an experience. No matter who else is in town, you can always catch a set of cover versions at one of Singapore's bars and clubs; main venues are picked out on pp.604–605.

Anywhere, #04-08/09 Tanglin Shopping Centre, 19 Tanglin Rd (☎7348233). Off the western end of Orchard Rd. Good-time rock music by local favourites Tania.

Bernie Goes to Town, 82a/b Boat Quay (☎5363533). Depending on which night you come, there'll be either reggae, blues or R&B played live.

Crazy Elephant, #01-07 Trader's Market, Clarke Quay. Live blues and rock throughout the week.

Harry's Quayside, 28 Boat Quay (☎5383029). Live jazz Wednesday to Saturday, and a blues jam on Sunday evening.

Molly Malone's, 42 Circular Rd. Two guitar and fiddle sets nightly.

Saxophone, 23 Cuppage Rd (☎2358385). Off Orchard Rd, just north of Somerset MRT. Slick jazz played on a cramped stage behind the bar.

Singapore Indoor Stadium, Stadium Walk. On the east bank of the Kallang River and south off Nicoll Highway. The usual venue for big-name bands in town; tickets are available through Sistic or Ticketcharge (see below).

World Trade Centre, 1 Maritime Square (☎3212717). Hosts international acts from time to time, as well as presenting free local gigs in its amphitheatre (check press for details).

The arts and culture

Of all the performing arts, **drama** gets the best showing in Singapore, the island's theatres staging productions that range from English farces to contemporary productions by local writers. **Dance** – Western or Asian – performances crop up only occasionally, though if your trip coincides with the annual **Singapore Festival of Arts** in June you may see something memorable. **Asian culture** is showcased in Singapore's major venues from time to time, but tends to appear more often on the street than in the auditorium, particularly around the time of the bigger festivals. Outstripping all other forms of entertainment in terms of popularity is **film**, with up-to-the-minute Asian and Western movies all drawing big crowds, and the annual **Singapore International Film Festival** in April.

For **information** on cultural events and performances, pick up a copy of either the *Singapore Straits Times* (whose daily "Life!" supplement has a good "what's on" section), *8 Days* magazine, or the free magazines *IS* (fortnightly) and *Where Singapore* (monthly), available at most hotel lobbies. Tickets for music shows, theatre and dance are sold either at the venue itself, or through two ticketing agencies, Sistic (☎3485555, *www.sistic.co.sg*) and Ticketcharge (☎2962929, *www.ticketcharge.net*). You can expect to pay at least $10 to attend a performance, though international acts command substantially higher prices.

Classical music

At the heart of the **Western** classical music scene in Singapore is the **Singapore Symphony Orchestra**. Performances by this 85-member multinational orchestra take place at the Victoria Concert Hall and often feature guest soloists, conductors and choirs from around the world; occasional **Chinese** classical music shows are included in the programme. From time to time, ensembles from the orchestra also give **lunchtime concerts** at various spots around the island. In addition, the Singapore Symphony Orchestra gives occasional free performances in Singapore's parks, while Sentosa Island also plays host to regular Sunday concerts – the shows themselves are free, but the usual Sentosa entry fee applies (see p.590).

Nanyang Academy of Fine Arts Chinese Orchestra, 111 Middle Rd (☎3382790). Chinese classical and folk music.

Singapore Symphony Orchestra, Victoria Concert Hall, Empress Place (☎3381230). Performances on Fri and Sat evenings throughout the year.

Cultural performances

If you walk around Singapore's streets for long enough, you're likely to come across some sort of streetside **cultural event**, most usually a *wayang*, or Chinese opera, played out on tumbledown outdoor stages that spring up overnight next to temples and markets, or just at the side of the road. *Wayang*s are highly dramatic and stylized affairs, in which garishly made-up and costumed characters enact popular Chinese legends to the accompaniment of the crashes of cymbals and gongs. They're staged throughout the year, but the best time to catch one is during the Festival of the Hungry Ghosts, when they are held to entertain passing spooks, or during the Festival of the

Nine Emperor Gods (see p.69). The STB may also be able to help you track down a *wayang*, and as usual the local press is worth checking. Another fascinating traditional performance, **lion dancing**, takes to the streets during Chinese New Year, and **puppet theatres** appear around then, as well.

The Kala Mandhir cultural association, based at the *Excelsior Hotel* on Coleman Street, is dedicated to perpetuating traditional **Indian** art, music and dance. Less spontaneous displays of Asian culture can be seen at **theme parks** such as Asian Village on Sentosa Island (p.590) and the Malay Village in Geylang Serai (p.584).

Film

With over fifty **cinemas** on the island, you should have no trouble finding a movie that appeals to you, and at a price ($5–8) that compares favourably with cinemas in Europe and America. As well as the latest Hollywood blockbusters, a wide range of Chinese, Malay and Indian movies, all with English subtitles, are screened. **Chinese** productions tend to be a raucous blend of slapstick and martial arts, while **Malay** and **Indian** movies are characterized by exuberant song and dance routines. **European** movies in languages other than English also pop up occasionally. The Alliance Française (1 Sarkies Rd; ☎7378422) screens free French movies (Tues 7.15pm, Wed 9.15pm) and holds an annual film festival in November. There are also regular presentations at the British Council, Napier Road (☎4731111) and the Goethe Institute, #05-01, 163 Penang Rd (☎7354555). The annual **Singapore International Film Festival** screens over 150 films and shorts – mostly by Asian directors – over two weeks in April; smaller festivals are occasionally mounted by the Singapore Film Society.

Cinema-going is a popular pastime here, so if you plan to catch a newly released film, turn up early to secure your tickets – and take along a sweater, as the air-con units are perpetually on full blast. Be prepared, also, for a lot of noise during shows: Singaporeans are great ones for talking all the way through the movie, and the sound of a bag of popcorn being rustled pales next to the sound of melon seeds being cracked and crunched. The most central cinemas are listed below, but check the local press for a full rundown of any special events or one-offs that might be taking place.

Cathay Cineleisure Orchard, 8 Grange Rd (☎2358386). Just off Orchard Rd. Central and recently renovated cinema, with a swish new shopping centre constructed around it.

Cathay Cinema, 11 Dhoby Ghaut (☎3383400). Singapore's oldest cinema, now a multiscreen affair.

Jade Classics, fourth floor, Shaw Leisure Gallery, 100 Beach Rd (☎2942568). Like the Picture House, this screens slightly more cerebral movies than most.

Lido Cineplex, Level 5, Shaw House, 1 Scotts Rd (☎7324124). Five screens, including the luxurious Lido Classic.

The Picture House, Cathay Bldg, 11 Dhoby Ghaut (☎3383400). A new cinema, pricier than most, screening interesting new releases.

United Artists Bugis Junction, 200 Victoria St (☎3379522). Posh and central new cinema.

Yangtse, Pearl Centre, 100 Eu Tong Sen St (☎2237529). In the heart of Chinatown, this place shows Western and Oriental films.

Theatre and the performing arts

Though modest, Singapore's **drama** scene is thriving, with most local productions, predominantly in English, debuting at either the Black Box, Substation or Drama Centre, and graduating to the Victoria Theatre if they are successful. Prices of tickets range from about $15 to $45. Foreign companies occasionally visit and usually perform at the Victoria or Kallang theatres. Performances of **dance** crop up from time to time – most notably by the Singapore Dance Theatre (☎3380611), which performs periodically at various venues, and even in local parks.

Singapore's annual **Festival of the Arts** attracts class acts from all over the world, spreading over two months between June and August; a schedule of events is published a month before the festival begins so, unless you are in Singapore for quite a while, you'll probably have trouble getting tickets for the more popular events. Still, an accompanying **fringe festival** takes place concurrently, and its programme always includes free street and park performances. Singapore also hosts an annual **Festival of Asian Performing Arts**, showcasing the cultures of neighbouring nations.

The Black Box, Fort Canning Centre, Cox Terrace, Fort Canning Park (☎3384077). Local productions by the Theatreworks Company.

Boom Boom Room, #02-04, 3 New Bugis St (☎3398187). Stand-up comedy hasn't really taken off in Singapore, though the Boom Boom Room's vaguely saucy revue, with a camp Malay comedian whose jokes are delivered in broad Singlish (see p.653), is worth checking out.

Drama Centre, Canning Rise (☎3360005). On the eastern side of Fort Canning Park. Drama by local companies.

Hilton-British Airways Playhouse, *Hilton Hotel*, 581 Orchard Rd (☎7372233). Light comedy imported from London's West End theatres.

Kallang Theatre, 1 Stadium Walk (☎3454888). Hosts visiting companies such as the Bolshoi Ballet and touring musical productions.

The Substation, 45 Armenian St (☎3377800). Self-styled "home for the arts" with a multipurpose hall that presents drama and dance, as well as art, sculpture and photography exhibitions in its gallery.

Victoria Theatre, 9 Empress Place (☎3377490). Visiting performers and successful local performances that graduate here from lesser venues.

Shopping

For many stopover visitors, Singapore is synonymous with **shopping**, though prices aren't necessarily much cheaper than in Western cities, due to the consistently strong Singaporean dollar and a rising cost of living. Good deals can, however, be found on watches, cameras, electrical and computer equipment, fabrics and antiques, and cut-price imitations – Rolexes, Lacoste polo shirts and so on – are rife. What's more, come during the **Great Singapore Sale** (usually between May and July), and you'll find seriously marked-down prices in many outlets across the island. Choice and convenience make the Singapore shopping experience a rewarding one, with scores of shopping centres and department stores meaning that you're rarely more than an air-con escalator ride away from what you want to buy. Usual **shopping hours** are daily 10am–9pm, though some shopping centres, especially those along Orchard Road, stay open until 10pm.

Singapore operates a three-percent sales tax (called GST) on all goods and services. Tourists can claim a GST refund on purchases of $300 or over (receipts of $100 or more can be pooled for this purpose) at retailers displaying a blue-and-grey **Tax Free Shopping** sticker; ask them to draft you a Tax Free Shopping Cheque to the value of the tax you're claiming back, which you can redeem subsequently at the airport or have credited to your credit card.

If you have any complaints to lodge, contact the Retail Promotions Centre on ☎4502114 – or write to them at second floor, Block 528, Ang Mo Kio Ave 10. Better still, go to Singapore's **Small Claims Tribunal**, Subordinate Courts, Apollo Centre, 2 Havelock Rd (☎5356922), which has a fast-track system for dealing with tourists' complaints; to have your case heard costs $10.

For clothes (either by Western or local designers – the latter are far more reasonably priced), tailor-made suits, sports equipment, electronic goods or antiques, the shopping malls of **Orchard Road** have all you could possibly want; the main shopping centres are listed on p.575. At **Arab Street** (p.573), you find exquisite textiles and batiks, robust basketware and some good deals on jewellery, as well as more unusual Muslim items. From here, make a beeline for **Little India** (p.569), where the silk stores and goldsmiths spoil you for choice; en route you pass the intersection of **Bencoolen Street and Rochor Road**, where a gaggle of shopping centres stocks electrical goods galore. As well as its souvenir shops, **Chinatown** boasts some more traditional outlets stocking Chinese foodstuffs, medicines, instruments and porcelain – Chinatown's shopping highlights are listed on p.566. For souvenirs, head for the Singapore Handicraft Centre (see below) in New Bridge Road or for the recently renovated Tanjong Pagar district (see p.564) whose restored shophouses feature oriental goods a cut above the normal tourist tat. Pick up any tourism leaflet in Singapore, and you are sure to find plenty of suggestions as to where to spend your hard-earned cash. The free monthly, *Where Singapore*, has a decent selection, and the STB publishes a *Merchants of the Gold Circle* booklet, which lists those shops deemed courteous and reliable enough to display the "Gold Circle Promise of Excellence" logo in their windows. As well as the various shops and outlets picked out in the text, check out any of the following as you travel around Singapore.

Antiques Antiques of the Orient, #02-40 Tanglin Shopping Centre, 19 Tanglin Rd, specializes in antiquarian books, maps and prints; Far East Inspiration, 33 Pagoda St, Chinatown, is the classiest of several antique shops along this street, stocking Asian furniture, porcelain-based lamps, prints and watercolours; Katong Antiques House, 208 East Coast Rd, Katong, is an Aladdin's cave of tiffin carriers, Peranakan slippers and cloths, and Chinese porcelain; One Price Store, 3 Emerald Hill Rd, off Orchard Rd, carries everything from carved camphorwood chests to Chinese snuff bottles; Tong Mern Sern Antiques, Block D, Clarke Quay has postcards, abacuses, lamps, old 78s; Wong's Collections, 13 Ann Siang Hill, Chinatown, sells everything from antique furniture and wartime food coupons to matchboxes and MRT cards.

Buddhist goods Nanyang Buddhist Culture Service, #01-13 Block 333, Kreta Ayer Rd, Chinatown, sells effigies, trinkets, necklaces and books.

Computers and software Funan the IT Mall, 109 North Bridge Rd, at the junction with High St.

Electronic equipment Sim Lim Tower, 10 Jalan Besar; Lucky Plaza, 304 Orchard Rd.

Fabrics and silk Dakshaini Silks, 164 Serangoon Rd, Little India, sells premier Indian embroidered silks; Goodwill Trading Co, 56 Arab St, has Indonesian batik sarongs heaped on varnished wood shelves.

Jewellery The entire first floor of the Pidemco Centre, 95 South Bridge Rd, is a jewellery market.

Music Beethoven Record House, #03-41 Centrepoint, 176 Orchard Rd, for classical sounds; HMV Singapore, #01-11 The Heeren Shops, 260 Orchard Rd; Lata Music Centre, 42 Race Course Rd, for Indian music on tape; Roxy Records, #03-36 Funan the IT Mall, 109 North Bridge Rd; Supreme Record Centre, #03-28 Centrepoint, 175 Orchard Rd; Tower Records, fourth floor, Pacific Plaza, junction of Scotts Rd and Orchard Rd.

Porcelain New Ming Village, 32 Pandan Rd (Clementi MRT and then bus #78), where all the work on Ming and Qing Dynasty reproductions is done by hand, according to traditional methods – most fascinating is the painstaking work of the painters.

Rubber-stamp makers Stamps made to order at Poh Hwa Stamp Maker, #02-50 Hong Lim Complex, Block 531, Upper Cross St, make inexpensive gifts.

Souvenirs China Mec, #03-31/32 Raffles City Shopping Centre, 250 North Bridge Rd, for Beijing cloisonné goods; Eng Tiang Huat, 284 River Valley Rd, for oriental musical instruments, *wayang* costumes and props; Funan Stamp and Coin Agency, #03-03 Funan the IT Mall, 109 North Bridge Rd; Selangor Pewter, #02-38 Raffles City Shopping Centre, 252 North Bridge Rd, for fine pewterwork; Singapore Handicraft Centre, Chinatown Point, 133 New Bridge Rd, gathers around fifty souvenir shops under one roof; Zhen Lacquer Gallery, 17 Duxton Rd, Chinatown.

Listings

Airlines Aeroflot, #01-02/#02-00 Tan Chong Tower, 15 Queen St (☎3361757); Air Canada, #01-08 United Square, 101 Thompson Rd (☎2561198); Air India, #B1-10/12 UIC Bldg, 5 Shenton Way (☎2259411); Air Lanka, #13-01a/b Keck Seng Tower, 133 Cecil St (☎2236026); Air New Zealand, #24-

08 Ocean Bldg, 10 Collyer Quay (☎5358266); American Airlines, #04-02 The Promenade, 300 Orchard Rd (☎8397766); British Airways, #04-02 The Promenade, 300 Orchard Rd (☎8397788); Cathay Pacific, #16-01 Ocean Building, 10 Collyer Quay (☎5331333); Garuda, #13-03 United Square, 101 Thompson Rd (☎2505666); KLM, #12-06 Ngee Ann City Tower A, 391a Orchard Rd (☎7377622); Lufthansa, #05-07 Palais Renaissance, 390 Orchard Rd (☎2455600); MAS, #02-09 Singapore Shopping Centre, 190 Clemenceau Ave (☎3366777); Pelangi Air, #02-09 Singapore Shopping Centre, 190 Clemenceau Ave (☎3366777); Philippine Airlines, #01-10 Parklane Shopping Mall, 35 Selegie Rd (☎3361611); Qantas, #06-05/08 The Promenade, 300 Orchard Rd (☎7309222); Royal Brunei, #01-4a/4b/5 *Royal Holiday Inn Crowne Plaza*, 25 Scotts Rd (☎2354672); Royal Nepal Airlines, #03-09 Peninsula Shopping Centre, 3 Coleman St (☎3395535); Singapore Airlines, Airline House, 25 Airline Rd (☎5423333), also at #01-01 SIA Bldg, 77 Robinson Rd (☎2238888), *Mandarin Hotel*, 333 Orchard Rd (☎2297293), and Raffles City Shopping Centre, 252 North Bridge Rd (☎2297274); Thai Airways, #02-00 The Globe, 100 Cecil St (☎2249977); Silkair, see Singapore Airlines; United Airlines, #44-02 Hong Leong Bldg, 16 Raffles Quay (☎8733525).

Airport For Changi Airport flight information, call ☎1-800/5424422 (toll-free).

American Express Travel services at #18-01 The Concourse, 300 Beach Rd (☎2998133) and #01-04/05 Winsland House, 3 Killiney Rd (☎2355788).

Banks and exchange All Singapore's banks change traveller's cheques, with the UOB and Posbank charging the lowest commission; normal banking hours are Mon–Fri 10am–3pm & Sat 11am–1pm. Licensed moneychangers, offering slightly more favourable rates also abound – particularly in Arab St, Serangoon Rd's Mustafa Centre, and the Orchard Rd shopping centres.

Bookshops Times bookshops stock a wide choice of titles, and crop up all over town: useful branches are at #04-08/15 Centrepoint, 175 Orchard Rd, and #02-24/25 Raffles City Shopping Centre, 252 North Bridge Rd. MPH shops are also well stocked, especially the flagship store on Stamford Rd. For secondhand books, your best bet is to check out the shelves in the backpacker crashpads of Bencoolen St. Select Books, #03-15 Tanglin Shopping Centre, 19 Tanglin Rd (☎7321515), has a huge array of specialist books on Southeast Asia, while Packir Mohamed & Sons, #01-20/21 Orchard Plaza, 150 Orchard Rd, boasts a vast selection of magazines.

Car rental Avis, *Boulevard Hotel*, 200 Orchard Blvd (☎7371668), Airport Terminal 1 (☎5432331) and Terminal 2 (☎5428855); Hertz, #01-20 Tanglin Shopping Centre, 19 Tanglin Rd (☎7344646) – to pick up at airport, phone the downtown branch; Sintat, Terminals 1 and 2, Changi Airport (☎5459086 or 5427288).

Credit-card helplines American Express (☎2998133); Diners Club (☎2944222); MasterCard and Visa (☎1-800/3451345).

Dentists Listed in the *Singapore Buying Guide* (equivalent to the *Yellow Pages*) under "Dental Surgeons", and "Dentist Emergency Service".

Disabled travellers *Access Singapore*, an informative booklet published by the National Council of Social Service, details hotels, banks, shopping centres and hospitals with facilities for the disabled. For a copy of the booklet write to the Council at 11 Penang Lane (☎3361544).

Embassies and consulates Australia, 25 Napier Rd (☎8384100); Brunei, 235 Tanglin Hill (☎7339055); Canada, #14-00 IBM Towers, 80 Anson Rd (☎3253200); France, 5 Gallop Rd (☎4664866); Germany, #14-00 Far East Shopping Centre, 545 Orchard Rd (☎7371355); India, 31 Grange Rd (☎7376777); Indonesia, 7 Chatsworth Rd (☎7377422); Ireland, #08-06 Tiong Bahru Rd (☎2768935); Malaysia, 301 Jervois Rd (☎2350111); New Zealand, 15-06, Ngee Ann City Tower A, 391a Orchard Rd (☎2359966); Philippines, 20 Nassim Rd (☎7373977); Sri Lanka, #13-07/13 Goldhill Plaza, 51 Newton Rd (☎2544595); Thailand, 370 Orchard Rd (☎7372644); UK, 100 Tanglin Rd (☎4739333); US, 27 Napier Rd (☎4789100); Vietnam, 10 Leedon Park (☎4625938).

Emergencies Police ☎999; Ambulance and Fire Brigade ☎995; larger hotels have doctors on call at all times.

Hospitals Singapore General, Outram Rd (☎2223322); Alexandra Hospital, Alexandra Rd (☎4735222); and National University Hospital, Kent Ridge (☎7795555). All are state hospitals and all have casualty departments.

Internet access There are numerous Internet cafés, among them Cyberarena, 39 Cuppage Terrace (daily 10am–11.30pm); e-den, #02-08 Wheelock Place, 501 Orchard Rd (daily noon–midnight); PICity@Capitol, #01-19 Capitol Bldg, 11 Stamford Rd (daily 10am–10pm); *Travel Café*, 50 Prinsep St, just northwest of Bencoolen St (Mon–Thurs & Sun 11am–11pm, Fri & Sat 11am–2am). Typical charges are $3 per half-hour or $5 per hour.

Laundry Washington Dry Cleaning, #02-22 Cuppage Plaza, 5 Koek Rd (Mon–Sat 9am–7.45pm); Washy Washy, #01-18 Cuppage Plaza, 5 Koek Rd (Mon–Sat 10am–7pm).

Pharmacies Guardian Pharmacy has over forty outlets, including ones at Centrepoint, 176 Orchard Rd; Raffles City Shopping Centre, 252 North Bridge Rd; and Clifford Centre, 24 Raffles Place. Usual hours are 9am–6pm, but some stay open until 10pm.

Police Report stolen property at Tanglin Police Station, 17 Napier Rd, off Orchard Rd (☎7330000). In an emergency, dial ☎999.

Post offices The GPO (Mon–Fri 8am–6pm, Sat 8am–2pm) is beside Paya Lebar MRT; poste restante/general delivery is here (take your passport). Branches at Raffles City and Changi Airport.

Swimming The most central public pool is on River Valley Rd, though Katong Swimming Complex, on Wilkinson Rd, and Buona Vista Swimming Complex, on Holland Drive, are better. For something more adventurous, try Sentosa's Fantasy Island (see p.591).

Telephones Local calls from private phones cost next to nothing; calls from public phones cost 10¢ for three minutes, though Changi Airport's courtesy phones are free. Singapore has no area codes – the only time you'll punch more than seven digits for a local number is if you're dialling a toll-free (☎1-800) number or a pager. Cardphones are taking over from payphones: cards are available from the Comcentre on Killiney Rd, post offices, 7-Elevens, stationers and bookshops and come in denominations rising from $2. International calls can be made from all public cardphones. Otherwise, use a credit-card phone. IDD calls from hotel rooms in Singapore carry no surcharge. For directory enquiries, call ☎100 and for IDD information, call ☎100 or ☎1607, or ☎104 for international enquiries.

Tour operators Gray Line of Singapore (☎3318203), Holiday Tours (☎7382622), RMG Tours (☎2201661), SH Tours (☎7349923) and Singapore Sightseeing (☎3323755) can all arrange sightseeing tours of Singapore.

Travel agents The following organizations are good for discounted airfares and buying bus tickets to Malaysia and Thailand: Airpower Travel, 131a Bencoolen St (☎3346571); Harharah Travel, first floor, 171a Bencoolen St (☎3372633); STA Travel, Cuppage Terrace (☎7377188).

Vaccinations Vaccinations can be arranged through the Government Vaccination Centre, Institute of Health, 226 Outram Rd (☎3572222).

Visa extensions Contact the Singapore Immigration and Registration Department, 10 Kallang Rd (Mon–Fri 9am–5pm; ☎3916100).

Water sports Asia Aquatic, 7 Circular Rd (☎5368116); Cowabunga Ski Centre, 10 Kallang Stadium Lane (☎3448813); Europa Sailing Centre, 1210 East Coast Parkway (☎4495118); Great Blue Dive Shop, #03-05 Holland Rd Shopping Centre, 211 Holland Ave (☎4670767); Pro Diving Service, 32 Bali Lane (☎2912261).

Women's helpline AWARE is a women's helpline (☎1-800/7745935).

travel details

Trains

Singapore Railway Station to:

Gemas (4 daily; 4hr); Kuala Lumpur (3 daily; 6hr 30min); Seremban (3 daily; 5hr).

Buses

Ban San Terminal to:

Johor Bahru (every 10min; 40min); Kuala Lumpur (4 daily; 6hr).

Golden Mile Complex to:

Bangkok (8 daily; 38hr); Hat Yai (8 daily; 28hr).

Lavender Street Terminal to:

Butterworth (at least 2 daily; 12hr 30min); Ipoh (2 daily; 8hr 30min); Kota Bharu (1 daily; 12hr 30min); Kuala Lumpur (8 daily; 5hr 30min); Kuantan (5 daily; 6hr 30min); Melaka (6 daily; 3hr 30min); Mersing (at least 2 daily; 3hr).

Ferries

From Changi Ferry Terminal to:

Tanjung Belungkor (Johor; 4 daily; 45min).

From Changi Point to:

Kampung Pengerang (for Desaru; hourly; 45min); Pulau Ubin (every 45min; 25min).

From Tanah Merah Ferry Terminal to:

Tanjung Pinang (Indonesia; 4 daily; 1hr); Tioman (March–Oct 1 daily except Wed; 4hr 30min).

From the World Trade Centre to:

Batam (Indonesia; every 30min; 40min).

Flights

From Changi Airport to:

Bandar Seri Begawan (2 daily; 2hr); Butterworth (8 daily; 1hr 15min); Kota Kinabalu (2 daily; 2hr 30min); Kuala Lumpur (11 daily; 55min); Kuantan (2 weekly; 50min); Kuching (2 daily; 1hr 20min); Melaka (6 weekly; 55min).

PART THREE

THE

CONTEXTS

THE HISTORICAL FRAMEWORK

The modern-day nations of Malaysia, Singapore and Brunei only acquired independent status in 1963, 1965 and 1984 respectively. Before that, the history of these countries was inextricably linked with events in the larger Malay archipelago, from Sumatra, across Borneo to the Philippines.

The problem for any historian is the lack of reliable source material for the region: there's little hard archeological evidence pertaining to the prehistoric period, while the events prior to the foundation of Melaka are known only from unreliable written accounts by Chinese and Arab traders. However, there are two vital sources for an understanding of events in the formative fourteenth and fifteenth centuries: the **Suma Oriental** (*Treatise of the Orient*), by Tomé Pires, a Portuguese emissary who came to Melaka in 1512 and wrote a history of the Orient based upon his own observations, and the **Sejarah Melayu**, the seventeenth-century "Malay Annals", which recorded oral historical tales recounted in a poetic, rather than strictly chronological, style. Although differing in many respects, not least in time scale, both volumes describe similar events.

Portuguese and Dutch **colonists** who arrived in the sixteenth and seventeenth centuries provided **written records**, though these tended to concern commercial rather than political or social matters. The wealth of information from **British colonial** times (from the early nineteenth century onwards), though giving detailed insights into Malay affairs, is imprinted with an imperialistic bias. It is only in the twentieth century, when Malay sources come into play, that a complete picture can be presented.

BEGINNINGS

The oldest remains of *homo sapiens* in the region were discovered in the Niah Caves in Sarawak in 1958 (see p.413), and are thought to be those of hunter-gatherers, between 35,000 and 40,000 years old; other finds in the Peninsular state of Kedah are only 10,000 years old. The variety of **ethnic groups** found in both East and West Malaysia – from small, dark-skinned Negritos through to paler Austronesian Malays – has led to the theory of a slow filtration of peoples through the Malay archipelago from southern Indochina – a theory backed by an almost universal belief in animism, celebration of fertility and ancestor worship among the various peoples.

The development of the Malay archipelago owed much to the importance of the **shipping trade**, which flourished as early as the first century AD. This was engendered by the region's strategic geographical position, linking the two major markets of the early world – India and China – and by the richness of its own resources. From the dense jungle of the Peninsula and from northern Borneo came aromatic woods, timber and *nipah* palm thatch, traded by the forest-dwelling Orang Asli with the coastal Malays, who then bartered or sold it on to Arab and Chinese merchants. The region was also rumoured to be rich in **gold**, leading to its description by Greek explorers as "The Golden Chersonese" (peninsula), a phrase that was used by later travellers, bowled over by the spectacular scenery and culture. Although gold was never found in the quantities supposed to exist, ornaments made of the precious metal helped to develop decorative traditions among craftsmen, and still survive today. More significant, however, were the **tin fields** of the Malay Peninsula, mined in early times to provide an alloy used for temple sculptures. Chinese traders were also attracted by the medicinal properties of various sea products, such as sea slugs, collected by the Orang Laut (sea people), as well as the aesthetic value of pearls and tortoise shells.

In return, the indigenous peoples acquired cloth, pottery and glass from foreign traders, and came into contact with new ideas, religions and cultural practices. From as early as 200 AD, **Indian traders** brought with them their Hindu and Buddhist practices, and archeological evidence from later periods, such as the tenth-century temples at Lembah Bujang (p.191), suggests that the indigenes not only tolerated these new belief systems, but adapted them to suit their own experiences. Perhaps the most striking contemporary example of such cultural interchange is the traditional entertainment of *wayang kulit* (shadow plays), still commonly performed in the eastern Peninsular states, whose stories are drawn from the Hindu *Ramayana*.

Contact with **China**, the other significant trading source, was initially much less pronounced due to the pre-eminence of the overland silk route, further to the north. It wasn't until much later, in the eighth and ninth centuries, that Chinese ships ventured into the archipelago.

There's little evidence to reveal the **structure of society** in these early times. All that is certain is that by the time Srivijaya (see below) appeared on the scene, there were already a number of states – particularly in the Kelantan and Terengganu areas of the Peninsula – that were sending envoys to China. This suggests a well-developed social system, complete with chiefs and diplomats, who were perhaps the forebears of the later Malay nobility.

SRIVIJAYA

The calm channel of the Melaka Straits provided a refuge for ships which were forced to wait several months for a change in the monsoon winds. The inhabitants of the western Peninsula and eastern Sumatra were quick to realize their geographical advantage, and from the fifth century onwards a succession of **entrepôts** (storage ports) were created to cater for the needs of passing vessels.

One entrepôt stood head and shoulders above the rest to become the mighty empire of **Srivijaya**, eminent from the beginning of the seventh century until the end of the thirteenth, and encompassing all the shores and islands surrounding the Straits of Melaka. Since records are fragmentary, the exact location of Srivijaya is still a matter for debate, although most sources point to **Palembang** in southern Sumatra. The empire's early success was owed primarily to its favourable relationship with China, which it plied with tributes to ensure profitable trade. The entrepôt's stable administration attracted commerce when insurrection elsewhere frightened traders away, while its wealth was boosted by extracting tolls and taxes from passing ships. With such valuable cargoes bound for the port, **piracy** in the surrounding oceans was rife, but was kept in check in Srivijayan waters by the fearsome Orang Laut who formed the linchpin of the navy. Indeed, they might otherwise have turned to piracy themselves had not the prestige of association with the empire been so great.

Significant political concepts developed during the period of Srivijayan rule were to form the basis of Malay government in future centuries. Unquestioning **loyalty** among subjects was underpinned by the notion of *daulat*, the divine force of the ruler (who was called the Maharaja, further evidence of Indian influence in the region), which would strike down anyone guilty of *derhaka* (treason) – a powerful means of control over a deeply superstitious people. Srivijaya also became known as an important centre for **Mahayana Buddhism** and learning. Supported by a buoyant economy, centres for study sprang up all over the empire, and monks and scholars were attracted from afar by Srivijaya's academic reputation. When the respected Chinese monk, I Ching, arrived in 671 AD, he found more than a thousand monks studying the Buddhist scriptures.

The decision made between 1079 and 1082 to shift the capital (for reasons unknown) from Palembang to **Melayu**, in the Sungei Jambi area to the north, seems to have marked the start of Srivijaya's decline. Piracy became almost uncontrollable, with even the loyal Orang Laut turning against their rulers, and soon both local and foreign traders began to seek safer ports, with the area that is now Kedah becoming one of the main beneficiaries. Other regions were soon able to replicate the peaceable conditions and efficient administration conducive to commercial success. One such was **Puni** in northwest Borneo, thought to be the predecessor of Brunei, which had been trading with China since the ninth century. Over the next three hundred years Puni continued to prosper until its capital numbered more than ten thousand people, drawn by the hospitable reception given to visiting merchants and by the entrepôt's considerable wealth.

Srivijaya's fate was sealed when it attracted the eye of envious foreign rivals, among them the Majapahit empire of Java, the Cholas of India and, latterly, the Thai kingdom of Ligor. In 1275, the Majapahits invaded Melayu and made inroads into many of Srivijaya's peninsular territories. The Cholas raided Sumatra and Kedah, while Ligor enforced its territorial claims by the instigation of a **tribute system**, whereby local Malay chiefs sent gifts of gold to their Thai overlords as recognition of their vassal status, a practice which continued until the nineteenth century (see p.192). Moreover, trading restrictions in China were relaxed from the late twelfth century onwards, which made it more lucrative for traders to go directly to the source of their desired products, bypassing the once mighty entrepôt. Around the early fourteenth century Srivijaya's name disappears from the record books.

THE MELAKA SULTANATE

With the collapse of Srivijaya came the beginning of the Malay Peninsula's most significant historical period, the establishment of the **Melaka Sultanate**. Both the *Sejarah Melayu* and the Portuguese *Suma Oriental* document the story of a Sumatran prince from Palembang named **Paramesvara**, who fled the collapsing empire of Srivijaya to set up his own kingdom, finally settling on the site of present-day Melaka (see p.302 for more).

As well placed as its Sumatran predecessor, with a deep, sheltered harbour and good riverine access to its own lucrative jungle produce, Melaka set about establishing itself as an international marketplace. The securing of a special agreement in 1405 with the new Chinese Emperor, Yung-lo, guaranteed trade to Melaka and protected it from its main warring rivals: the kingdom of Samudra-Pasai in northeast Sumatra, and that of Aru further to the south. To further ensure its prosperity, Melaka's second ruler, Paramesvara's son **Iskandar Shah** (1414–24), took the precaution of acknowledging the neighbouring kingdoms of Ayuthaya and Majapahit as overlords. In return, Melaka received vital supplies and much-needed immigrants which bolstered the expansion of the settlement.

New laws empowered an **effective administration** to meet the needs of passing traders, guaranteeing their safety in pirate-infested waters and offering ample space in which to store their cargo and refit their vessels. Port taxes and market regulations were managed by four **Shahbandars** (harbour masters). Each was in charge of a group of nations: one for the northwest Indian state of Gujarat alone; another for southern India, Bengal, Samudra-Pasai and Burma; the third for local neighbours such as Java, Palembang and Borneo; and the fourth for the eastern nations, including China and Japan. Intimately concerned with the physical and commercial requirements of his group, the Shahbandar also supervised the giving of gifts to the ruler and his ministers, an important method of boosting the kingdom's wealth.

Melaka began to amplify its reputation by territorial expansion which, by the reign of its last ruler **Sultan Mahmud** (1488–1528), included the west coast of the Peninsula as far as Perak, Pahang, Singapore, and most of east-coast Sumatra. But although this made it strong enough to reject the patronage of Java and Ayuthaya, it never really controlled the far north or east of the Peninsula, nor did it make inroads into its competitors' territories in northern Sumatra.

Hand in hand with the trade in commodities went the exchange of ideas. By the thirteenth century, Arab merchants had begun to frequent Melaka's shores, bringing with them their religion, **Islam**, which their Muslim Indian counterparts helped to propagate among the Malays. The sultanate's **conversion** helped to increase its prestige by placing it within a worldwide community which worked to maintain profitable trade links.

The legacy of **Melaka's golden age** reaches far beyond memories of its material wealth. One of the most significant developments was the establishment of a **court structure** (see p.305), which was to lay the foundations for a system of government lasting until the nineteenth century. According to Malay royal tradition, the **sultan**, as head of state, traced his ancestry back through Paramesvara to the Maharajas of ancient Srivijaya; in turn Paramesvara was believed to be descended from Alexander the Great (Iskandar Zulkarnain). The sultan also claimed divinity, a claim strengthened by the sultanate's conversion to Islam, which held Muslim rulers to be Allah's representatives on earth. To secure further his power, which was always under threat from the over-zealous nobility, the sultan embarked on a series of measures to emphasize his "otherness": no one but he could wear gold unless it was a royal gift, and yellow garments were forbidden among the general population.

The Melaka Sultanate also allowed the **arts** to flourish; the principal features of the courtly dances and music of this period can still be distinguished in traditional entertainments today. Much more significant, however, was the refinement of **language**, adapting the primitive Malay – itself of Austronesian roots – that had been used in the kingdom of Srivijaya into a language of the elite. Such was Melaka's prestige that all who passed through the entrepôt sought to imitate it, and by the sixteenth century, Malay was the most widely used language in the archipelago. Tellingly, the word *bahasa*, although literally meaning "language", came to signify Malay culture in general.

THE PORTUGUESE CONQUEST OF MELAKA

With a fortune as tempting as Melaka's, it wasn't long before Europe set its sights on the acquisition of the empire. At the beginning of the sixteenth century, the **Portuguese** began to take issue with Venetian control of the Eastern market. They planned instead to establish direct contacts with the commodity brokers of the East by gaining control of crucial regional ports.

The key player in the subsequent **conquest** of Melaka was Portuguese viceroy **Alfonso de Albuquerque**, who led the assault on the entrepôt in 1511, forcing its surrender after less than a month's siege. Sultan Mahmud Shah fled to the island of Bentan in the Riau archipelago, and Albuquerque himself departed a year later, leaving behind eight hundred officers to administer the new colony. There are few physical reminders of their time in Melaka, apart from the gateway to their fort, A Famosa (see p.309), and the small **Eurasian** community, descendants of intermarriage between the Portuguese and local Malay women. The colonizers had more success with religion, however, converting large num-

bers of locals to **Catholicism**; their churches still dominate the city. Aloof and somewhat effete in their high-necked ruffs and stockings, the Portuguese were not well liked, but despite the almost constant attacks from upriver Malays, the Portuguese controlled Melaka for the next 130 years.

MELAKA'S CONTEMPORARY RIVALS

During the period of Melaka's meteoric rise, **Brunei** had been busily establishing itself as a trading port of some renown. Ideally poised on the sea route to China, it had for a long time benefited from its vassal status to successive Ming emperors, and with its arch rival's capture set about filling its place. The Brunei Sultanate's conversion to **Islam**, no doubt precipitated by the arrival of wealthy Muslim merchants fleeing from the Portuguese in Melaka, also helped to increase its international prestige. When geographer Antonio Pigafetta, travelling with Ferdinand Magellan's expedition of 1521, visited Brunei, he found the court brimming with visitors from all over the world. This, indeed, was Brunei's "golden age", with its borders embracing land as far south as present-day Kuching in Sarawak, and as far north as the lower islands of the modern-day Philippines. Brunei's efforts, however, were soon curtailed by Spanish colonization in 1578, which, although lasting only a matter of weeks, enabled the Philippine kingdom of Sulu to gain a hold in the area – a fact which put paid to Brunei's early expansionist aims.

The ambitious Thai kingdom of **Ayuthaya** had been initially willing to strike bargains with Melaka, but by 1455 had tired of its competitor's unhindered progress and launched a full-scale attack. Sources are vague as to the outcome, though it can reasonably be assumed that Ayuthaya was emphatically defeated, since the Thai kingdom made no further attempts on the entrepôt for the next forty years. It was only when Melaka's last ruler, Sultan Mahmud Shah, sought to include the Thai vassal state of Kelantan in his own territories that he provoked Ayuthaya to retaliate with another unsuccessful foray into the Peninsula in 1500, though it was to be another 35 years – well after the fall of Melaka to the Portuguese – before they tried again.

THE KINGDOM OF JOHOR

Johor's rise to pre-eminence in the Malay world began as a direct consequence of the fall of Melaka to the Portuguese. Fleeing Melaka, Sultan Mahmud Shah made for Pulau Bentan in the Riau archipelago, south of Singapore, where he established the first **court of Johor**. When, in 1526, the Portuguese attacked and razed the settlement, Mahmud fled once again, this time to Sumatra, where he died in 1528. It was left to his son, Alauddin Riayat Shah, to found a new court on the upper reaches of the Johor river, though the capital of the kingdom then shifted repeatedly, during a century of assaults on Johor territory by Portugal and the Sumatran Sultanate of Aceh.

The **arrival of the Dutch** in Southeast Asia towards the end of the sixteenth century marked a distinct upturn in Johor's fortunes. Hoping for protection from its local enemies, the court aligned itself firmly with the new European arrivals, and was instrumental in the successful siege of Portuguese Melaka by the Dutch in 1641 (see below). Such loyalty was rewarded by trading privileges and by assistance in securing a treaty with Aceh, the main aggressive force in Sumatra at that time, which at last gave Johor the breathing space to develop. Soon it had grown into a thriving kingdom, its sway extending some way throughout the Peninsula.

Johor was the supreme Malay kingdom for much of the seventeenth century, but by the 1690s its empire was fraying under the irrational and despotic rule of another Sultan Mahmud. Lacking strong leadership, Johor's Orang Laut turned to piracy, scaring off the trade upon which the kingdom relied, while wars with the Sumatran kingdom of Jambi, one of which resulted in the total destruction of Johor's capital, weakened it still further. No longer able to tolerate his cruel regime, Mahmud's nobles stabbed him to death in 1699. Not only did this change the nature of power in Malay government – previously, law deemed that the sultan could only be punished by Allah – but it marked the end of the Melaka dynasty.

THE DUTCH IN MELAKA

Already the masters of Indonesia's valuable spice trade, the Vereenigde Oostindische Compagnie (VOC), or **Dutch East India Company**, began a bid to gain control of its most potent rival, Melaka. After a five-month siege, the Dutch flag was hoisted over Melaka in 1641. Instead of ruling from above as their predecessors had tried to do, the Dutch cleverly wove their subjects into the fabric of government: each racial group was represented by a *Kapitan*, a respected figure from the community who mediated between his own people and the new administrators – often becoming a very wealthy and powerful person in his own right. The Dutch were also responsible for the rebuilding of Melaka, much of which had been turned to rubble during the protracted takeover of the city. Many of these structures, in their distinctive Northern European style, still survive today. The narrow houses and godowns backing on to the network of canals are reminiscent of Amsterdam, and the headquarters of the administration, the Stadthuys, is one of Melaka's main tourist attractions.

By the mid-eighteenth century, the conditions for trade with **China** were at their peak: the relaxation of maritime restrictions in China itself had opened up the Straits for their merchants, while Europeans were eager to satisfy the growing demand for tea. Since the Chinese had no interest in the native goods that Europe could supply in exchange, and the Dutch themselves had no knowledge of indigenous products, European traders found themselves more and more reliant on Indian items, such as cloth and opium, as bartering tools. The Chinese came to Melaka in droves and soon established themselves as the city's foremost entrepreneurs. Chinese intermarriage with local Malay women created a new cultural blend, known as **Peranakan** (literally, "Straits-born") or Baba-Nonya – the legacies of which are the opulent mansions and unique cuisine of Melaka (see box, p.314).

But a number of factors prevented Dutch Melaka from fulfilling its potential. Since their VOC salary was hardly bountiful, Dutch administrators found it more lucrative to trade on the black market, taking backhanders from grateful merchants, a situation which severely damaged Melaka's commercial standing. High taxes forced traders to more economical locations such as the newly established British port of **Penang**, whose foundation in 1786 heralded the awakening of British interest in the Straits. A more significant sign of Dutch loss of control was their reliance on military rather than governmental means to sustain their supremacy, which ultimately made them vulnerable to anyone of greater strength. In the end, given the VOC's overall strategy in the archipelago, Melaka never stood a chance: Batavia (modern-day Jakarta) was the VOC capital, and Johor's penchant for commerce suited Dutch purposes too much for it to put serious effort into maintaining Melaka's fortunes.

THE BUGIS AND THE MINANGKABAUS

Through the second half of the seventeenth century, a new ethnic group, the **Bugis** – renowned for their martial and commercial skills – had been trickling into the Peninsula, seeking refuge from the civil wars which wracked their homeland of Sulawesi (in the mid-eastern Indonesian archipelago). By the beginning of the eighteenth century, there were enough of them to constitute a powerful court lobby, and in 1721 they took advantage of factional struggles to capture the kingdom of Johor – now based in Riau. Installing a Malay puppet sultan, Sulaiman, the Bugis ruled for over sixty years, making Riau an essential port of call on the eastern trade route; they even almost succeeded in capturing Melaka in 1756. Although their ousting had long been desired by discontented Malay vassals, Bugis supremacy in the Straits was put paid to by the Dutch: when Riau-Johor made another bid for Melaka in 1784, the Dutch held on with renewed vigour and finally forced a treaty placing all Bugis territory in Dutch hands.

In spiritual terms, the **Minangkabaus** (see p.300), hailing from western Sumatra, had what the Bugis lacked, being able to claim cultural affinity with the ancient kingdom of Srivijaya. Although this migrant group had been present in the Negeri Sembilan region since the fifteenth century, the second half of the seventeenth century brought them to the Malay Peninsula in larger numbers. Despite professing allegiance to their Sumatran ruler, the Minangkabaus were prepared to accept Malay overlordship, which in practice gave them a great deal of autonomy. Accredited with supernatural powers, the warrior Minangkabaus were not natural allies of the Bugis or the Malays, although they did occasionally join forces in order to defeat a common enemy. In fact, over time the distinction between various migrant groups became less obvious, as inter-marriage blurred clan demarcations, and Malay influence, such as the adoption of Malay titles, became more pronounced.

THE ARRIVAL OF THE BRITISH

At the end of the eighteenth century, Dutch control in Southeast Asia was more widespread than ever, and the VOC empire should have been at its height. Instead, its coffers were bare and it faced the superior trading and maritime skills of the British. The disastrous defeat of the Dutch in the fourth Anglo-Dutch war (1781–83) lowered their morale still further, and when the British, in the form of the **East India Company** (EIC), moved in on Melaka and the rest of the Dutch Asian domain in 1795, the VOC barely demurred.

Initially, the British agreed to a caretaker administration, whereby they would assume sovereignty over the entrepôt to prevent it falling under French control, now that Napoleon had conquered Holland. The end of the Napoleonic wars in Europe put the Dutch in a position to retake Melaka between 1818 and 1825, but in the meantime, the EIC had established the stable port of **Penang** and – under the supervision of **Sir Thomas Stamford Raffles** (see p.554) – founded the new settlement of **Singapore** as their own regional entrepôt, signing a formal agreement to this effect with the Sultanate of Riau-Johor in 1819.

The strategic position and free-trade policy of Singapore – backed by the impressive industrial developments of the British at home – instantly threatened the viability of both Melaka and Penang, forcing the Dutch finally to relinquish their hold on the former to the British, and leaving the latter to dwindle to a backwater. In the face of such stiff competition, smaller Malay rivals inevitably linked their fortunes to the British.

THE CONSOLIDATION OF BRITISH POWER IN THE PENINSULA

To a degree, the British presence in Malay lands was only the most recent episode in a history of foreign interference that stretched back centuries. What differed this time, however, was the rapidity and extent of the takeover – aided by technological developments in the West that improved communications.

The British assumption of power was sealed by the **Anglo-Dutch Treaty** of 1824, which divided territories between the two countries using the Straits of Melaka and the equator as the dividing lines, thereby splitting the Riau-Johor kingdom as well as ending centuries of cultural interchange with Sumatra. This was followed in 1826 by the unification of Melaka, Penang (together with its mainland counterpart Province Wellesley) and Singapore into one administration, known as the **Straits Settlements**, with Singapore replacing Penang as its capital in 1832. Even with this more cohesive power base, the official British line was minimum interference for maximum trading opportunity, a policy that was brought into sharp conflict with the desires of local empire builders by the **Naning Wars of 1831**. These erupted when the governor of the Straits Settlements, Robert Fullorton, tried to impose Melaka's tax laws on a somewhat uppity local chief, Abdul Said. A year-long battle ensued, and though the British were finally able to add Naning to Melaka's territories, their pyrrhic victory brought home the costs of too close an involvement in complex Malay politics.

Raffles had at first hoped that **Singapore** would act as a market to sell British goods to traders from all over Southeast Asia, but it soon became clear that **Chinese** merchants, the linchpin of Singapore's trade, were interested only in Malay products such as birds' nests, seaweed and camphor. But passing traders were not the only Chinese to come to the Straits. Although settlers had trickled into the Peninsula since the early days of Melaka, new pepper and gambier (an astringent product used in tanning and dyeing) **plantations**, and the rapidly expanding **tin mines**, attracted floods of willing workers eager to escape a life of poverty in China. By 1845, the Chinese formed over half of Singapore's population, while principal towns along the Peninsula's west coast (site of the world's largest tin field) and, for that matter, Kuching, became predominantly Chinese.

CIVIL CONFLICT

Allowed a large degree of commercial independence by both the British and the Malay chiefs, the Chinese carried their traditions into the social and political arena with the formation of **kongsis**, or clan houses (see p.178), and secret societies (triads). Struggles between clan groups were rife, sometimes resulting in large-scale riots, such as those in Penang in 1867 (see p.179), where the triads allied themselves with Malay groups in a bloody street battle lasting several days.

Malays, too, were hardly immune from factional conflicts, which frequently became intertwined with Chinese squabbles, causing a string of **civil wars**. In **Negeri Sembilan** (1824–69), conflict was largely brought about by contending Minangkabau heirs, although most worrying to British administrators were arguments over the control of the tin trade (see p.295). **Pahang's** skirmishes (1858–63) also involved rival political claims by two brothers, Mutahir and Ahmad, although this time the British were much more directly involved: on hearing that the Thais had backed Ahmad, the Straits Governor Cavenagh hastily aligned himself with Mutahir by attacking Kuala Terengganu – then a Thai vassal town – in order to ward off further foreign involvement in the Peninsula. But the British government was outraged by this decision and forbade any other action to prevent Ahmad's succession.

Perak was riven (1861–73) with the disputes of rival Chinese clans in the central region of Larut, with tin once again a major contributing factor. In **Selangor**, tax claims between Malay chiefs were the basis of the wars (1867–73). The British again intervened, this time to support Tengku Kudin, the person they thought most likely to assure a peaceful resolution to the conflict. However, he was a weak figure, little respected by his own people, and effect was to underline to the Malays that British help could be secured even for a lacklustre regime such as Kudin's.

Lawlessness like this was detrimental to commerce, giving the British an excuse to increase their involvement in local affairs. A meeting involving the chiefs of the Perak Malays was arranged by the new Straits Governor, Andrew Clarke, on Pulau Pangkor, just off the west coast of the Peninsula. In the meantime, Raja Abdullah, the man most likely to succeed to the Perak throne, had written to Clarke asking for the appointment of a British **Resident** (or advisor), in return for his own guaranteed position as sultan. On January 20, 1874, the **Pangkor Treaty** (p.153) was signed between the British and Abdullah, formalizing British intervention in the political affairs of the Malay people.

BRITISH MALAYA

By 1888 the name **British Malaya** had been brought into use – a term which reflected the intention to extend British control over the whole Peninsula. Over subsequent decades, the Malay sultans' economic and administrative powers were gradually eroded, while the introduction of rubber estates during the first half of the twentieth century made British Malaya one of the most productive colonies in the world.

Each state soon saw the arrival of a **Resident** (see p.160), a senior British civil servant whose main function was to act as advisor to the local sultan, but who also oversaw the collecting of local taxes. The first Resident, J.W.W. Birch, posted in Perak, was not sympathetic to the ways of the Malays, and was soon out of favour. Perak's Sultan Abdullah in particular opposed Birch's centralizing tendencies, and senior British officials, fearful of a Malay rebellion, announced that judicial decisions would from now on be in the hands of the British, which was against the letter of the Pangkor Treaty. Furious Malays soon found a vent for their frustration: on November 2, 1875, Birch was killed on an upriver visit. The British brought in troops from India and Hong Kong to quell the trouble, although the attack on Birch was not followed by further assaults on colonial staff. The third Resident of Perak, the respected Hugh Low, got the system working far more smoothly after these early problems.

Agreements along the lines of the Pangkor Treaty were drawn up with Selangor, Negeri Sembilan and Pahang in the 1880s, and in 1896 these three became bracketed together under the title of the **Federated Malay States**, with the increasingly important town of Kuala Lumpur made the regional capital.

The gradual extension of British power brought further unrest, particularly in the east-coast states, where the Malays proved just as resentful of British control as in Perak. In Pahang a set of skirmishes took place in the early 1890s, when Malay chiefs protested about the reduction of their former privileges. One powerful chief, Dato' Bahaman, was stripped of his title by Pahang's Resident, Hugh Clifford, as a result of which the Dato' led a small rebellion which – though never a serious military threat to the British – soon became the stuff of legends. One fighter, **Mat Kilau**, gained a place in folklore as a heroic figure who stood up to the British in the name of Malay nationalism. From this time onwards, Malays would interpret the uprisings as a valiant attempt to safeguard Malay traditions and preserve Malay autonomy.

By 1909, the northern Malay states of Kedah and Perlis were brought into the colonial fold. In 1910, Johor accepted a British General-Adviser; a 1914 treaty between Britain and Johor made his powers equal to those of Residents elsewhere. Terengganu, which was under Thai control, was the last state to accept a British Adviser, in 1919. These four states were sometimes referred to as the Unfederated Malay States, though they shared no common administration.

By the outbreak of World War I, British political control was more or less complete. The Peninsula was subdivided into groups of states and regions with the seat of power split between Singapore and Kuala Lumpur.

THE EXPANSION OF BRITISH INTERESTS IN BORNEO

The Anglo-Dutch Treaty (see p.623) did not include **Borneo**, where official expansion was discouraged by the EIC, who preferred to concentrate on expanding their trading contacts rather than geographical control. The benefits of Borneo did not, however, elude the sights of one British explorer, **James Brooke** (1803–68). Finding lawlessness throughout the territories, Brooke persuaded the Sultan of Brunei to award him his own area – **Sarawak** – in 1841, becoming the first of a line of "**White Rajahs**" that ruled the state until the start of World War II. By involving formerly rebellious Malay chiefs in government, he quickly managed to assert his authority, although the less congenial Iban tribes in the interior proved more of a problem. Despite the informal association of the British with Rajah Brooke (Sarawak was not granted the status of a protectorate, and Brooke was careful not to encourage European contacts that might challenge his hold on the state), trade between Singapore and Sarawak flourished. By the mid-nineteenth century, however, the British attitude had mellowed considerably; they chose Brooke as their agent in Brunei, and found him a useful deterrent against French and Dutch aspirations towards the valuable trade routes. (For a fuller history of the Brooke lineage see p.507)

In 1888, the three states of Sarawak, Sabah and Brunei were transformed into **protectorates**, a status which handed over the responsibility for their foreign policy to the British in exchange for military protection. The legacy of James Brooke was furthered by his nephew Charles in the closing years of the nineteenth century. New regions – the Baram and Trusan valleys and Limbang – were bought, or rather wrested, from the Sultan of Brunei, while the British North Borneo Chartered Company handed over to Brooke the Lawas Valley in 1905. The Chartered Company had assumed control over Northern Borneo (later renamed Sabah) in 1878 when an Austrian, Baron von Overbeck, with the backing of British businessmen, paid the sultans of Brunei and Sulu an annuity to administer and develop the region.

Like his uncle before him, **Charles Brooke** ruled Sarawak in a paternalistic fashion, recruiting soldiers, lowly officials and boatmen from the ranks of the ethnic groups and leaving the Chinese to get on with running commercial enterprises and opening out the interior. Although the British government in London and the colonial administrators in Singapore were concerned about Brooke's territorial expansions, they accepted that the indigenous peoples were not being oppressed and that Brooke's rule was not despotic.

The rule of the last White Rajah, **Vyner Brooke**, Charles' eldest son (1916–41), saw no new territorial acquisitions, but there was a steady development in rubber, pepper and palm oil production. The ethnic peoples mostly continued living a traditional lifestyle in longhouses along the river systems and, with the end of groups' practice of head-hunting, there was some degree of integration among the country's varied racial groups.

By way of contrast, the **British North Borneo Chartered Company**'s writ in what became Sabah encountered some early obstacles. Its plans for economic expansion involved clearing the rainforest and **planting rubber and tobacco** over large areas, and levying taxes on the ethnic groups. Resistance followed, with the most vigorous action, in 1897, led by a Bajau chief, **Mat Salleh**, whose men rampaged through the company's outstation on Pulau Gaya. Another rebellion by the Murut tribespeople in 1915 resulted in a heavy-handed response from British forces, who killed hundreds.

By the start of the twentieth century, the majority of the lands of the erstwhile powerful **Sultanate of Brunei** had been dismembered – the sultanate was now surrounded by Sarawak. But the sultan's fortunes had not completely disappeared and with the discovery of **oil** in 1929, the British thought it prudent to appoint a Resident. Exploitation of the small state's oil beds picked up pace in the 1930s following investment from British companies; see p.507 for more details.

ECONOMIC DEVELOPMENT AND ETHNIC RIVALRIES

In the first quarter of the twentieth century hundreds of thousands of **immigrants** from China and India were encouraged by the British to emigrate to sites across Peninsular Malaysia, Sarawak, North Borneo and Singapore. They came to work as tin miners or plantation labourers, and Malaya's population in this period doubled to four million.

The main impact of what was effectively a recruitment drive by the British was to fuel resentment among the Malays, who believed that they were being denied the economic opportunities advanced to others. The situation was made worse under the British **education system**, since schooling was offered at a very basic level to only small numbers of Malays, Chinese and Indians. The British barely noticed the deepening differences between the ethnic groups – a factor which contributed to resentment and racial violence in later years.

A further deterioration in Malay–Chinese relations followed the success of the mainland Chinese revolutionary groups in Malaya. Chinese-educated Chinese, who joined the **Malayan Communist Party** (MCP) from 1930 onwards, formed the backbone of the politicized Chinese movements after World War II, which demanded an end to British rule and to what they perceived as special privileges extended to the Malays. For their part, the Malays – specifically those influenced by radical Islamic movements – saw better education as the key to their future. The establishment of the **Singapore Malay Union** in 1926 gradually gained support in Straits Settlement areas where Malays were outnumbered by Chinese. It held its first conference in 1939 and advocated a Malay supremacist line. A year earlier, the first All-Malaya Malays Conference, organized by the Selangor

Malays Association, had been held in Kuala Lumpur.

Despite the argument put forward by the British in the 1930s that a Union for Malaya (incorporating the Unfederated Malay States) would decentralize power and integrate the regional state groupings, little progress had been made on the burning issue of independence by the time Malaya was **invaded** by the Japanese in late 1941.

JAPANESE OCCUPATION

By February 1942, the whole of Malaya and Singapore was in Japanese hands and most of the British were POWs. The **surrender** of the British forces in Singapore (see p.531) ushered in a Japanese regime which proceeded to brutalize the Chinese, largely because of Japan's history of conflict with China; up to fifty thousand people were tortured and killed in the two weeks immediately after the surrender of the island by the British military command. Allied POWs were rounded up into prison camps; many of the troops were subsequently sent to build the infamous "Death Railway" in Burma.

In **Malaya**, towns and buildings were destroyed as the Allies attempted to bomb strategic targets. But with the Japanese firmly in control, the occupiers ingratiated themselves with some of the Malay elite by suggesting that after the war the country would be given independence. Predictably, it was the Chinese activists in the MCP, more so than the Malays, who organized **resistance** during wartime; in the chaotic period directly after the war it was the MCP's armed wing, the **Malayan People's Anti-Japanese Army** (MPAJA), who maintained order in many areas.

The Japanese invasion of **Sarawak** in late 1941 began with the capture of the Miri oil field and spread south, encountering little resistance. Although the Japanese invaders never penetrated the interior, they quickly established complete control over the populated towns along the coast. The Chinese in Miri, Sibu and Kuching were the main targets: the Japanese put down rebellions against their rule brutally, and there was no organized guerrilla activity until late in the occupation. What resistance there was arose from the presence of Major **Tom Harrisson** and his team of British and Australian commandos, who parachuted into the remote Kelabit Highlands to gauge the feelings of the indigenous tribespeople; they later managed to recruit Kayan, Kenyah and Kelabit warriors in an uprising.

In **North Borneo**, the Japanese invaded Pulau Labuan on New Year's Day, 1942 (see p.468). Over the next three years the main suburban areas were bombed by the Allies, and by the time of the Japanese surrender in September 1945, most of Jesselton (modern-day KK) and Sandakan had been destroyed. Captured troops and civilians suffered enormously – the worst single outrage being the Death March in September 1944 when 2400 POWs were forced to walk from Sandakan to Ranau. Only six prisoners had survived.

The Allies had been preparing to retake Singapore, but just prior to the planned invasion the **Japanese surrendered** on September 9, 1945, on Pulau Labuan, following the dropping of atom bombs on Nagasaki and Hiroshima. The surrender led to a power vacuum in the region, with the British initially left with no choice but to work with the MPAJA to exert political control. Violence occurred between the MPAJA and Malays, with those who were accused of collaborating with the Japanese during the occupation specifically targeted.

THE IMMEDIATE POSTWAR PERIOD

Immediately after the war, the British introduced the **Malayan Union**, in effect turning the Malay States from a Protectorate into a colony, as part of which the Malay rulers had their sovereignty removed. One impact of these new arrangements was to make the Chinese and Indian inhabitants full citizens and give them equal rights with the Malays. This erosion of their superior position quickly aroused opposition among the Malays, with Malayan nationalists forming the **United Malays National Organization** (UMNO) in 1946. Its main tenet was that Malays should retain their special privileges, largely because they were the region's first inhabitants. UMNO also pushed the customary Malay line that the uniquely powerful position of the sultans should not be tampered with – indeed, they still exerted immense influence despite the administrative changes wrought by the British.

UMNO supporters displayed widespread resistance to the British plan, and the idea of union was subsequently replaced by the **Federation of Malaya** which restored the sovereign position of the rulers. Established in 1948, this upheld the sultans' power and privileges and brought all the regional groupings together under one government, with the exception of Chinese-dominated Singapore, whose inclusion would have led to the Malays being in a minority overall. Protests erupted in Singapore at its exclusion, with the **Malayan Democratic Union** (MDU), a multiracial party, calling for integration with Malaya – a position that commanded little support among the Chinese population. After the communists took control of China in 1949, most of the Malayan Chinese ceased to look to China and the most political among them founded a new political party, the **Malayan Chinese Association**, in Kuala Lumpur.

In **Borneo**, after the Japanese surrender, the Colonial Office in London stepped into the breach and made Sarawak and North Borneo **Crown Colonies**, with Vyner Brooke offering no objection. Britain also signed a Treaty of Protection with the Sultan of Brunei, making Sarawak's high commissioner the Governor of Brunei – a purely decorative position, as the sultan remained the chief power in the state. Brunei's most lucrative resource – its oil fields – sustained considerable damage during the Japanese invasion, and much of the immediate postwar period was spent in rebuilding the installations.

Although Sarawak's ruling body, the Council Negeri (composed of Malays, Chinese, Iban and British) had voted to transfer power to Britain, some Malays and prominent Iban in Kuching opposed their country's new status. Protests reached a peak with the assassination in Sibu in 1949 of the senior official in the new administration, Governor Duncan Stewart. But on the whole, resentment at the passing of the Brooke era was short-lived, and as the population gradually got used to the new political alignments, the economy expanded. The infrastructure of both Sarawak and north Borneo steadily improved, with new roads and a limited air service helping to open out the country to commercial development.

THE EMERGENCY

In the Peninsular, many Chinese were angered by the change of the status of the country from a colony to a federation, in which they effectively became second-class citizens. According to the new laws, non-Malays could only qualify as citizens if they had lived in the country for fifteen out of the last twenty-five years, and they also had to prove they spoke Malay or English.

More Chinese began to identify with the MCP, which, under its new leader, **Chin Peng**, declared its intention of setting up a Malayan republic. Peng fused the MCP with the remains of the wartime resistance movement, the MPAJA, and using the arms supplies which the latter had dumped in the forests, he recruited a secret central committee, set up **guerrilla cells** deep in the jungle and, from June 1948, launched sporadic attacks on rubber estates, killing planters and employees as well as spreading fear among rural communities.

The period of unrest, which lasted for twelve years (1948–60), was referred to as **the Emergency**, rather than the civil war it undoubtedly was. This was mainly for insurance purposes – planters would have had their premiums cancelled if war had been officially declared. Although the Emergency was never fully felt in the main urban areas (life went on as normal in Kuala Lumpur), the British rubber-estate owners would arrive for steaks and *sten gahs* (whisky and water, from the Malay word for "half") at the *Coliseum Hotel* in central KL with harrowing stories of how the guerrillas (dubbed Communist terrorists) had hacked off the arms of rural Chinese workers who had refused to support the cause, and of armed attacks on plantations.

The British were slow to respond to the threat, but once lieutenant-general Sir Harold Briggs was put in command of police and army forces, Malaya was on a war footing. The most controversial policy Briggs enacted was the **resettlement** of 400,000 rural Chinese – mostly squatters who had moved to areas bordering the jungle to escape victimization by the Japanese during the war – as well as thousands of Orang Asli, seen as potential MCP sympathizers, to four hundred "New Villages", scattered across the country. Although these forced migrations were successful in breaking down many of the guerrillas' supply networks, they had the effect of making both Chinese and Orang Asli more sympathetic to the idea of a Communist republic replacing British rule.

The violence peaked in 1950 with ambushes and attacks on plantations near Ipoh, Kuala Kangsar, Kuala Lipis and Raub. The most notorious incident occurred in 1951 on the road to Fraser's Hill, when the British high commissioner to Malaya, **Sir Henry Gurney**, was assassinated (see p.230). Under the new commissioner, Sir Gerald Templer, a new policy was introduced to win hearts and minds. "White Areas", regions perceived as free of guerrilla activity, were established; communities in these areas had food restrictions and curfews lifted, a policy which began to dissipate guerrilla activity over the next three years. At the same time, the British army – bolstered by conscripted British National Servicemen and assisted by Gurkha contingents and the Malay police force – successfully hunted down most of the Chinese leaders, although not Chin Peng. The leaders were offered an amnesty in 1956, which was refused, and Chin Peng and most of the remaining cell members fled over the border to Thailand where they received sanctuary.

TOWARDS INDEPENDENCE

The Emergency had the effect of speeding up the political processes prior to independence. Although UMNO stuck to its "Malays first" policy (its founder Dato' Onn bin Jaafar resigned because his call to include non-Malays was rejected), **Tunku Abdul Rahman** (the Chief Minister of Malaya and brother of the Sultan of Kedah), won the 1955 election by co-operating with the Malayan Chinese Association (MCA) and the Malayan Indian Association. The result was called the **UMNO Alliance**, and it swept into power under the rallying cry of **Merdeka** (Freedom). The hope was that ethnic divisions would no longer be a major factor if **Malayan independence** was granted, though the deep-seated differences between the various ethnic groups' positions still hadn't been eradicated.

With British backing, *Merdeka* was promulgated on August 31, 1957 in a ceremony in Kuala Lumpur's padang – promptly renamed Merdeka Square. The British high commissioner signed a treaty which decreed that under British and Malay law, the Federation of Malaya was now independent of the Crown, with Tunku Abdul Rahman as the first Prime Minister. The new **constitution** allowed for the nine Malay sultans to alternate as king, and established a two-tier **parliament**, comprising a house of elected representatives and a Senate with delegates from each of the states. Although the system was, in theory, a democracy, the Malay-dominated UMNO remained by far the most influential element in the political equation.

Under Rahman, the country was fully committed to economic expansion and full employment; foreign investment was actively encouraged. Arguments between the two dominant Alliance parties, UMNO and the MCA, were mostly over the allocation of seats in parliament and in the area of education, but Rahman refused to compromise the pre-eminent position of the Malays, and the MCA remained far less powerful than UMNO. Despite the Alliance's aim of creating a new citizen, whose loyalties would be to the country and not to their particular ethnic group, age-old communal divisions had still not been obliterated.

Similarly, in **Singapore** the process of gaining independence gained momentum throughout the 1950s. In 1957 the British gave the go-ahead for the setting up of an elected 51-member assembly, and full **self-government** was attained in 1959, when the People's Action Party (PAP) under **Lee Kuan Yew** won most of the seats. Lee immediately entered into talks with Tunku Abdul Rahman over the notion that Singapore and Malaya should be joined administratively – Rahman initially agreed, although he feared the influence of pro-Communist extremists in the PAP.

In 1961 Tunku Abdul Rahman announced that the two Crown Colonies of Sarawak and North Borneo should join Malaya and Singapore in a revised federation. Many in Borneo would have preferred the idea of a separate Borneo Federation, but the advent of the Konfrontasi, an armed struggle launched by newly independent Indonesia to wrest control of the two colonies from Malaya (see p.629) played into Rahman's hands – those against his proposals could see how vulnerable the states were to attack from Indonesia.

Behind Rahman's proposal was the concern that demographic trends would in time lead to Malaya having a greater Chinese population than Malay. Consequently he campaigned hard for the inclusion of the two Malay-dominated Borneo colonies into the proposed federation, to act as a demographic balance to the Chinese in Singapore.

FEDERATION AND THE KONFRONTASI

In September 1963 North Borneo (quickly renamed Sabah), Sarawak and Singapore joined Malaya in the **Federation of Malaysia** – "Malaysia" being a term first coined by the British in the 1950s when the notion of a Greater Malaya had been propounded. Both Indonesia, which laid claim to Sarawak (the border of Indonesian Kalimantan ran alongside the state), and the Philippines, which argued it had jurisdiction over Sabah as it had originally been part of the Sulu Sultanate, reacted angrily to the new federation. Although the Philippines backed down (while to this day not dropping its claim on Sabah), Indonesia didn't, and border skirmishes known as the **Konfrontasi** ensued. The conflict intensified as Indonesian soldiers crossed the border, and a wider war was only just averted when Indonesian President Sukarno backed away from costly confrontations with British and Gurkha troops brought in to boost Sarawak's small armed forces.

Differences soon developed between Lee Kuan Yew and the Malay-dominated Alliance party over the lack of egalitarian policies – although the PAP had dominated recent elections in Singapore, many Chinese were concerned that UMNO's overall influence in the Federation was too great. Tensions rose on the island and ugly racial incidents developed into full-scale **riots** in 1964, in which several people were killed.

These developments were viewed with great concern by Tunku Abdul Rahman, and when the PAP subsequently attempted to enter Peninsular politics, he decided it would be best if Singapore left the Federation. This was emphatically not in Singapore's best interests, since it was an island without any obvious natural resources; Lee cried on TV when the expulsion was announced and Singapore acquired full **independence** soon after on August 9, 1965 (see p.532 for details). The severing of the bond between Malaysia and Singapore soured relations between the countries for some years.

BRUNEI

The British Governor of Brunei was withdrawn in 1959, although Britain was still responsible for defence matters and foreign relations. The sultan's autocratic rule was tested in 1962 when, in the state's first ever general election, the left-wing **Brunei People's Party** (BPP) came to power. Sultan Omar, however, viewed democracy suspiciously and refused to let the BPP form a government. A rebellion followed, when the BPP – backed by the Communist North Kalimantan Army – gained control of parts of Seria, Kuala Belait, Tutong and Bandar, but the revolt was crushed within four days by British and Gurkha forces. Sultan Omar's powers remained unchanged and the autocratic royal rule of Brunei continues to this day. Although Abdul Rahman had wanted Brunei to join the Malaysian Federation, too, along with neighbouring Sarawak and Sabah, Omar refused when he realized Rahman's price – a substantial proportion of Brunei's oil and gas revenues. Brunei remained under nominal British jurisdiction until **independence** was declared on December 31, 1983. For more on Brunei's history, in particular recent developments, see p.506.

ETHNIC CONFLICT

The exclusion of Singapore from the Malaysian Federation was not enough to quell the ethnic conflicts. Resentment built among the Malaysian Chinese over the principle that Malay be the main language taught in schools and over the privileged employment opportunities offered to Malays. In 1969 the Malay-dominated UMNO Alliance lost regional power in parliamentary elections, and Malays in major cities reacted angrily to a perceived increase in power of the Chinese, who had commemorated their breakthrough with festivities in the streets, triggering counter-demonstrations by Malays. Hundreds of people, mostly Chinese, were killed and injured in the **riots** which followed, with Kuala Lumpur in particular becoming a war zone where large crowds of youths went on the rampage. Rahman kept the country under a state of emergency for nearly two years, during which the draconian **Internal Security Act** (ISA) was used to arrest and imprison activists, as well as many writers and artists.

THE NEW ECONOMIC POLICY

Rahman never recovered full political command after the riots and resigned in 1970. In September that year, the new Prime Minister, **Tun Abdul Razak**, also from UMNO, took up the reins with a less authoritarian stance – though still implementing the ISA. He brought the parties in Sarawak and Sabah into the political process and initiated a broad set of directives, called the **New Economic Policy** (NEP). This set out to restructure the management of the economy so that it would be less reliant on the Chinese, who previously dominated its most lucrative sectors. Ethnic Malays were now to be considered **bumiputras** (Malay for "sons of the soil") and thus given favoured positions in business, commerce and other professions (see p.58 for more details). The NEP also requires all state secondary schools to use Malay as the main language of instruction.

DEVELOPMENTS IN SINGAPORE

Lee Kuan Yew continued to rule **Singapore** in a similarly draconian style, also using Internal Security legislation to detain anyone said to be a threat to the nation. Yet despite earlier doubts, Lee's transformation of the island's **economy** was amazing. Political alignments were made to maximize business opportunities – the government was non-Communist, ethnically mixed and (in theory at least) democratic, although like Malaysia's UMNO, no other party seriously rivalled the PAP.

The economy grew fast: per capita income increased an astonishing fourfold between 1965 and 1977, with huge profits being made in financial services, hi-tech manufacturing, information technology and the petroleum industry. The high taxes these boom areas produced were used to bolster the island's infrastructure and housing, and by 1980 the impossible had been achieved: Singapore stood on the verge of becoming a **Newly Industrialized Economy** (NIE), along with Hong Kong, Taiwan and South Korea. Lee had converted a tiny, highly populated country with no inherent assets into a dynamic crossroads between East and West.

But these developments came at a price. Through the 1970s and 1980s the image of Singapore as a humourless, dull place where everyone worked within the confines of a Big Brother civic apparatus started to take shape, and political intolerance became a fact of life. The **Opposition Worker's Party** won a by-election in 1984 and yet the candidate, J.B. Jeyaretnam, was unable to take his seat as he found himself charged under five offences. Although cleared, further investigations sullied his chances of developing his political career – clearly even one voice proffering criticism of Lee's policies could not be tolerated. For more details of Singapore's history, in particular recent developments, see p.530.

MALAYSIA UNDER MAHATHIR

For the last two decades Malaysian politics has been dominated by the present prime minister, **Dr Mahathir Mohamad**, who has triumphed at every election since winning the leadership of UMNO in 1981. UMNO is the dominant party in a coalition, the **Barisan Nasional (BN)**, which was formed in 1974 under Razak and includes representatives from the other mainstream Chinese and Indian parties and – from the 1990s – members of the indigenous parties in Sabah and Sarawak.

During Mahathir's first ten years in power, UMNO's prime concern had been to extend the concept of the NEP as well as maintaining the concept of *bumiputra* and overall Malay political dominance. Initially, the NEP had been underwritten by oil and timber revenues, while Malaysia looked away from the West, preferring to rely on other Southeast Asian countries, especially Singapore, as economic partners. But as the costs of the NEP started to bite, Mahathir galvanized Western investment, offering juicy financial incentives like low tax rates and cheap labour' the UK soon became the main foreign investor in Malaysia.

Although the NEP was understandably popular with Malays, many of whom got richer through its tax, educational and financial breaks, it was deeply resented by the Chinese and Indians, although outspoken critics of the government were few. In 1991, the NEP was succeeded by the **National Development Policy**. Critics say the favoured position of the Malays was just being continued under a new name, but Mahathir has been careful to remove some of the most ill-regarded elements, such as the use of quotas to push Malays into powerful positions. Despite the lighter touch, *bumiputras* are still protected, and the Chinese and Indians have to work substantially harder for a commensurate reward in most spheres of Malaysian economic and educational life.

The structure of Malaysia's expanding **economy** has changed over the last twenty years. Manufacturing output overtook agriculture as the biggest earner in the late 1980s, while the shift to export-dominated areas, notably hi-tech industries and the service sector, has changed the landscape of regions like the Klang Valley, Petaling Jaya and Johor, where industrial zones have mushroomed. During the 1990s, Mahathir again set out to attract international money by launching a massive IT project, the Multimedia Super Corridor, whereby a large area south of Kuala Lumpur will be developed into a hi-tech industrial zone by 2020.

The development patterns which took shape in the nineteenth century still hold true today: the most productive areas of the Peninsula, with the highest per capita income, remain the west coast, particularly the urban areas of Kuala Lumpur, Ipoh, Penang, Melaka and Johor, with the east coast and interior lagging far behind, although revenue from **tourism** is changing the picture slightly.

On the political front, the only serious threat to Mahathir during his first decade in office was in 1987, when Tunku Razaleigh Hamzah, the then trade and industry minister and member of the Kelantan royal family, challenged the prime minister's leadership of UMNO. In the wake of his narrow defeat, Razaleigh formed his own party **Semangat '46** (meaning Spirit of '46, after the year in which UMNO had been founded), which went on to make an alliance with the opposition Islamist party PAS. In the October 1990 election, this combination of Semangat and PAS helped reap all 13 parliamentary and 39 state seats in Kelantan.

But by the next election in April 1995, the strains between Semangat and PAS were beginning to show. Although PAS managed to hold on to power in Kelantan with fewer seats, the Barisan National coalition went on to its greatest victory since independence. The falling out with Semangat became public when PAS attempted to push through controversial new regulations on entertainment in the state. A year later, the split with PAS was official and Semangat was in negotiations for its members to rejoin UMNO. This reunification of the parties happened in October 1996, underlining Mahathir's skill at neutering political opposition by embracing former enemies and bringing them within the BN fold.

Although both East Malaysian states have local parties whose membership is drawn from the various ethnic groups, Sabah and Sarawak have largely been governed by parties loyal to the BN. **Sarawak**'s politics are dominated by Muslims in the Sarawak Alliance (part of the BN), though the **Parti Bansa Dayak Sarawak** (PBDS), formed by defecting Iban representatives from the Sarawak Alliance, has provided the indigenous population of the state (which makes up roughly fifty percent of the population) with an important voice – albeit one allied with the BN. In **Sabah**, the **Parti Bersatu Sabah** (PBS), dominated by the Kadazan/Dusan, actually opposed Mahathir on many issues for several years, beginning in the mid-1980s. Led by a Christian, Joseph Pairin Kitingan, who was for many years the only non-Muslim to hold political power in Malaysia, the PBS is critical of central government's bleeding of 95 percent of the profits from the state's crude-oil exports, and of its blatant pro-Muslim propaganda – Christians have even been offered cash incentives to convert to Islam. Pairin however lost power in the 1994 elections: a BN-allied Muslim, Tan Sri Sakaran Dandai, is now the state's chief minister.

THE ANWAR AFFAIR

Soon after the 1996 election, pressures began to build within Malaysian politics. The **Asian economic crisis** which had begun in Thailand and Korea sucked Malaysia in, leading to a major devaluation of the ringgit, a drop in living standards for many of the population and the cancelling of a number of high-profile projects. Although the impact on the economy was not catastrophic, the chief fallout of the crisis was to heighten the growing rift between Mahathir and his deputy **Anwar Ibrahim**, who had for some years been groomed to succeed Mahathir.

Ostensibly, the quarrel between the two focused on their different approaches to dealing with the crisis, Anwar urging a free-market approach while Mahathir was in favour of fiscal stringency and currency controls. But behind this debate lay a leadership struggle: Mahathir believed Anwar was a threat to his control of UMNO, Anwar having earlier been the leader of the influential UMNO youth party and enjoying a significant following among both secular Malay youth and those with Islamist leanings.

In September 1998, Mahathir sacked Anwar from the government; within a week, Anwar was arrested on corruption and sexual misconduct charges which stunned the nation. The former involved alleged interference with an Anti-

Corruption Agency investigation, while the latter alleged that Anwar had engaged in a homosexual act with his driver. A succession of demonstrations in support of Anwar ensued. When Anwar appeared in court on the corruption charge he had a black eye, prompting concern to be expressed over his treatment in detention. Anwar was subsequently found guilty – leading many observers to question the independence of the judiciary – and sentenced to six years in prison. His trial on the sexual misconduct charge began in June 1999, though it wasn't until August 2000 that a verdict was reached: Anwar was found guilty of sodomy and sentenced to nine years in prison on top of his jail term for corruption. In the opinion of most observers, this effectively ends his political career.

THE 1999 ELECTIONS AND THEIR AFTERMATH

Throughout 1999, Anwar's wife **Wan Azizah Wan Ismail** became the focus of opposition to Mahathir for many Malay youths, who rallied behind the Anwar campaign. Azizah formed a new party, **Keadilan** ("Justice"), which contested the November 1999 elections in direct opposition to UMNO and in alliance with other opposition parties including the ethnic Chinese dominated Democratic Action Party (DAP) and PAS.

The battle for Malay hearts and minds between UMNO and PAS had meanwhile been intensifying, particularly over PAS's intention to bring strict Islamic, or **Syariat**, law into force in Kelantan. The harsh penalties the Syariat prescribes for crimes cannot become law unless passed by a two-thirds majority in the Federal Parliament – a highly unlikely event. Mahathir, while opposing Syariat, could not be seen to be too un-Islamic, so he has found other ways of dealing with this political thorn, in particular, by doing little to assist the economy of Kelantan, which remains the poorest state in Malaysia.

Resentment to the government had built up, and during the November elections PAS made significant gains, leading critics to view the election as a watershed in Malaysian politics and quite possibly the start of a profound slide in UMNO's grip over the Malay vote (and corre-

spondingly, the BN's control over the nation). Although UMNO retained a three-quarters majority in parliament, it lost nearly twice as many seats as in the previous election, going down from 94 MPs to 72, with the BN parties' overall share of the vote dropping ten percent to 55 percent. The gains mostly went to PAS, which swept through **Terengganu**, hitherto an UMNO state. This was despite the exclusion from the election of some 680,000 mainly younger voters who had registered to vote over the previous year and who the government feared would favour the opposition. Keadilan, for its part, won six seats, which was viewed as a triumph for a party which hadn't even existed fourteen months earlier.

In **East Malaysia**, however, the trend went the other way, with UMNO's position strengthened. The 1999 elections left not one seat in Sarawak for the smaller opposition parties, and only three in the hands of the opposition in Sabah.

Observers of the 1999 election say that the gains made by PAS occurred not so much because the electorate supported Islamic revivalism, but more because of the growing disillusionment with UMNO, most notably in Mahathir's handling of the Anwar affair, and in the continued suggestions of cronyism which periodically afflict the party. Despite these rumblings of discontent, the opposition, its divisions never far below the surface, faces an uphill task: in recent times, Keadilan has already lost much grassroots support as election fervour has subsided and as the economic recovery has continued.

Furthermore, at the UMNO annual conference in 2000, Mahathir sent out a message that many wanted to hear, hinting more plainly than ever before that he would resign soon, probably at around the time of the next election (which will most likely be held in 2003). His Deputy Prime Minister **Abdullah Ahmad Badawi**, although clearly not a charismatic figure with his own independent power base like Mahathir or Anwar, looks like an interim caretaker rather than a replacement of the same calibre. As Malaysia moves into the new millennium, a shake-up in the political arena looks more likely than at any time since independence.

DEVELOPMENT AND THE ENVIRONMENT

Malaysia is slowly becoming more environmentally friendly, largely as a result of well-organized and scientifically persuasive organizations within the country, but the pace of change is slow.

Although there has not been substantial internal opposition, some of Malaysia's economic policies have been condemned internationally, while the issues surrounding **logging** and **large-scale development** projects, in particular, have brought severe criticism. Environmental groups both within and outside the country have fought to highlight the irretrievable loss of biodiversity caused by the systematic felling of the rainforest. But the issue which has most embarrassed the authorities is the impact of development, whether in the form of logging, oil-palm cultivation or large-scale projects, on the lifestyles of the **indigenous groups**. For ordinary Malaysians though, the most tangible environmental problem is the **haze**, thought to be caused by forest fires in Indonesia, which periodically blankets the region.

LOGGING AND DEFORESTATION

The **sustainable exploitation** of forest products by the indigenous population has always played a vital part in the domestic and export economy of the region – for almost two thousand years, the ethnic tribes have bartered products like rattan, wild rubber and forest plants with foreign traders. Nowadays, the government suggests that the **slash-and-burn** agricultural practices of the indigenous groups in Sarawak, and to a lesser degree, in Sabah and the interior of Peninsular Malaysia, are the cause of substantial deforestation, not **logging**. But researchers have found that the bulk of this agricultural activity occurs in secondary rather than primary (untouched) forest. Indeed, environmental groups believe that only around one hundred square kilometres of primary forest – a tiny proportion compared to the haul by commercial timber companies – is cleared by the indigenous groups annually.

SABAH

Commercial logging started in **Sabah** (then North Borneo) in the late nineteenth century, when the British Borneo Trading and Planting Company began to extract large trees from the area around Sandakan to satisfy the demand for timber sleepers for the expanding railway system in China. By 1930 the larger **British Borneo Timber Company** (BBTC) was primarily responsible for the extraction of 178,000 cubic metres of timber, rising to nearly five million cubic metres by the outbreak of World War II, and Sandakan became one of the world's main timber ports. Most areas were logged indiscriminately, and the indigenous tribal groups who lived there were brought into the economic system to work on North Borneo's rubber, tobacco and, later, oil-palm plantations. The process intensified as the main players in Sabah tapped the lucrative Japanese market, where postwar reconstruction costing billions of dollars was underway.

By the early 1960s, timber had accelerated past rubber as the region's chief export and by 1970 nearly thirty percent of Sabah had been extensively logged, with oil palm and other plantation crops replacing around a quarter of the degraded forest. Timber exports had accounted for less than ten percent of all exports from Sabah in 1950; by the 1970s, this had rocketed to over seventy percent.

The current picture in Sabah indicates that over 40,000 square kilometres (well over sixty percent of the state) has been exploited for timber. However, there is a low level of tribal protest, simply because fewer of Sabah's indigenous people live in the deep interior where most of the logging takes place.

SARAWAK

A much larger share of contemporary logging takes place in **Sarawak** – eighty percent of the total Malaysian output by the late 1990s, or 2700 square kilometres a year. The development of large foreign-run plantations in the state was hindered initially by the White Rajahs, James and Charles Brooke, who largely kept foreign investment out of their paternalistically run fiefdom. However, small indigenous timber concerns run by Chinese and Malay merchants were allowed to trade. But once the BBTC was given rights to start logging in northern Sarawak in the 1930s, timber extraction grew rapidly, especially since the third White Rajah, Vyner Brooke, was less stringent in his opposition to the economic development of the state. Timber was viewed as a vital commercial resource to be utilized in the massive reconstruction of the state, following the devastating Japanese occupation. During its short postwar period as a Crown Colony and, after 1963, as a Malaysian state, logging in Sarawak grew to become one of its chief revenue earners, alongside oil extraction. The state government encouraged foreign investment and issued timber concessions to rich individuals, who were encouraged to carve up ever more remote areas. Today, most of the **Baram** basin in the north of the state has been logged – the river is now a soupy brown sludge due to the run-off of earth and silt caused by the extraction process – and attention has switched to the remote Balui river and its tributaries in the east of the state, where the Bakun dam project (see p.403) is also underway.

Accurate figures as to the current state of Sarawak's forests are, however, notoriously hard to come by. Suaram, a coalition of East Malaysian environmental NGOs, says that less than half of Sarawak's 124,000 square kilometres remains as forest; the state claims the figure is more like three-quarters – though it includes oil palm and other plantation zones in its calculations.

In principle, **customary land tenure**, which was enshrined in law throughout the White Rajah period and forms the basis of the 1958 **Sarawak Land Code**, protects the land claimed by the state's indigenous tribal groups. In practice, much commercial logging ignores this. If illegal logging is to be stopped, then the government has to give teeth to what have hitherto been a complex, largely symbolic system of logging regulations.

THE PENINSULA

Peninsular Malaysia's pre-independence economy was not as reliant on timber revenues as those of Sabah and Sarawak. Although one-sixth of the region's 120,000 square kilometres of forest, predominantly in Johor, Perak and Negeri Sembilan states, had been cut down by 1957, most of the logging had been done gradually and on a small, localized scale. As in Sabah, it was the demand for rail sleepers – for the expansion of the Malayan train network in

the 1920s – which had first attracted the commercial logging companies, but wide-scale clearing and conversion to rubber and palm-oil plantations in the more remote areas of Pahang, Perlis, Kedah and Terengganu didn't intensify until the 1960s. By the end of the 1970s, more efficient extraction methods, coupled with a massive increase in foreign investment in the logging industry, had led to over forty percent of the Peninsula's remaining forests being either cleared for plantation purposes or partially logged. Only in the last decade has logging in West Malaysia slowed significantly, with more stringent assessments of the environmental impact being carried out before logging is allowed to proceed.

GOVERNMENT INITIATIVES

During the 1990s logging has slowed down as a result of the **National Forestry Policy** (NFP). This has led to deforestation being reduced to 900 square kilometres a year, almost a third slower than the previous rate, with a further target of reducing timber harvesting by ten percent each year, although critics say this isn't enough to save the forests, which within 25 years will cover less than twenty percent of the surface of the country instead of the current 55 percent.

The Malaysian government is naturally keen to deflect attention away from the accusation that the timber concessions it grants are solely responsible for unsustainable timber production. Reafforestation schemes within the Permanent Forest Estates – government-run tracts of land given over to tree cultivation – are on the increase. And organizations like the Forest Resource Institute of Malaysia (FRIM), which sustains an area of secondary forest on the edge of Kuala Lumpur, prove how rainforest habitats can be renewed. FRIMS' ecological management plan ensures that a comprehensive range of flora, including tree species and a wide spectrum of plants, are planted and monitored over a long period. It must be stressed, however, that FRIM is the exception rather than the rule, and most environmentalists within Malaysia don't believe that renewable forestry can offset the damage caused by current timber extraction techniques, which seldom aid regrowth. As a rule, logging devastates over seventy percent of all the flora, topsoil and root structures in a given area.

LARGE-SCALE PROJECTS: DAM CONSTRUCTION

Deforestation is not the only hot topic on the environmental agenda in Malaysia; massive **dam constructions** are another. One example in Sarawak is the **Bakun dam** (see p.403) in the Belaga district, in preparation for whose construction ten thousand people from the Kenyah, Kayan, Ukit and other ethnic groups have been moved from their longhouses along the Balui river to Asap. Environmentalists opposed to the scheme say it flies in the face of scientific evidence indicating the adverse effects of flooding of an area the size of Singapore, not just the uprooting of ethnic peoples but also the eradication of the region's unique biodiversity.

The convoluted economic processes at work in modern Malaysia were highlighted most pointedly in early 1994 when it became clear that £1.3 billion's worth of defence contracts awarded to British companies had been linked to £234 million of British aid money for the building of a hydroelectric dam at **Pergau** in northern Kelantan. British civil servants declared the dam "a bad buy", but the British government went ahead, it was suggested, because the Malaysians had made the arms purchases conditional on the massive injection of funds to underwrite the dam. A Parliamentary Committee in Britain launched an inquiry, but the issue was firmly swept under the carpet in Malaysia where the press stood right behind Mahathir. Indeed, the British press coverage incensed the Malaysian government, which threatened to withhold contracts from British companies as a result. In 2000 the dam was near to being finished and the earlier frosty relations between the two countries over the controversy have been long forgotten.

THE THREAT TO TRADITIONAL LIFESTYLES

While large-scale projects such as the **Bakun dam** are a glaring example of how the land rights of indigenous peoples have been ignored, **logging** is also a huge threat to the tribespeople's way of life. Given that customary land rights are being ignored by Sarawak's loggers, it is not only locations of special importance – burial places, access routes and sections of rivers used for fishing – that are not respected, but even areas in which the indigenous people

can prove they have lived and farmed for generations have been abused; forests around Bintulu, Belaga and Limbang have suffered in this way.

Unlike many of the ethnic groups who can base their customary land claims on a settled history of farming, the nomadic lifestyle of the **Penan**, and the particular ways in which they utilize the land, makes it harder for their land rights to be defined and recognized. An additional factor in the case of the Penan has been that since the mid-1980s the Sarawak state government's avowed policy has been to bring them into what it views as the development process (as has been applied to the more settled Dayak and Orang Ulu groups for many decades), urging them to move to permanent longhouses, work in the cash economy and send their children to school.

The Penan have proved resilient to these attempts to assimilate them into the wider Malaysian social system, largely because the government diktats seem to go suspiciously hand in hand with an expansion of logging in their customary land areas. Very often, there's been no warning that Penan land has been earmarked for logging until the extraction actually begins – examples in remote areas of the Belaga district have been well documented by the environmental group **Sahabat Alam Malaysia**. Subsequently, the Penan have had to watch the destruction of their traditional living areas: trees are cut down; wildlife disappears along with its habitat; and the rivers become polluted by soil erosion, topsoil run-off and siltation.

In retaliation, some Penan tribespeople have applied for **communal forest areas** (so-called "Penan zones") to be designated, so that some of their land would receive protection, but until now, all such applications have been refused. Throughout the 1980s and early 1990s the Penan in some areas became a well organized passive resistance force with the help of Swiss environmentalist Bruno Manser, who for a time topped Malaysia's most-wanted persons list. Today, few Penan are continuing to resist the government's resettlement programmes, with the majority of people resigned to their fate.

Another hot issue in Sarawak in recent years has been **oil-palm cultivation**, the state government launching joint ventures with private companies to open up new plantations in the state. There have been many examples of plantations taking over thousands of acres of customary tenure, with the authorities compelling longhouse communities to resettle in model villages nearby. The communities are then offered work at a low rate in the emerging oil-palm cash economy.

The authorities are quick to defend themselves, insisting that areas like Sarawak must progress. Monoagricultural enterprises, like oil palm, and massive energy projects like Bakun generate, so their argument goes, substantial profits which in turn fund initiatives like new housing and education for the poorer sections of society. Indigenous groups argue that most profits from these businesses are in fact not ploughed back into social policies but return to private company accounts, often in Peninsular Malaysia.

REGIONAL HAZE

For the inhabitants of Peninsular Malaysia and Singapore, the environmental issue which has affected them most has not been forest depletion or land rights, but the **haze** which has plagued Kuala Lumpur, Singapore and much of the Peninsula. Though such hazes had occurred sporadically during the 1990s, in 1997/8 the region suffered a severe, prolonged episode, when the haze was so bad that for long periods motorists were warned to keep their distance from one another and there was an alarming rise in respiratory illnesses. Visibility in the Straits of Melaka – the world's busiest shipping route – dropped to as little as 2km.

The Malaysian government originally suggested that the agricultural methods of the indigenous peoples – which involve the burning of excess vegetation at the end of growing cycles – were to blame. However, further research indicated that small longhouse communities could not have caused such extensive fires and that larger agencies must be the culprits. It's now thought that the haze is caused by Indonesian plantation companies **starting fires** to clear large areas of **forest** to facilitate the planting of a range of crops, including oil palm and acacia. The Indonesian government does not appear to have been able to change the habits of its forest developers given that the 1997 catastrophe was repeated, albeit to a considerably lesser extent, in 2000.

WILDLIFE

There's an extraordinary tropical biodiversity in the Malay Peninsula and in Borneo, with over six hundred species of birds; more than two hundred mammal species, including the tiger, Asian elephant, orangutan and tapir; many thousands of flowering plant species, among them the insectivorous pitcher plant and scores of others of known medicinal value; and over one thousand species of brightly coloured butterflies. This enormous variety of bird, plant and animal life makes any trip to a tropical rainforest a memorable experience. Wherever you visit, it's important to remember that observing wildlife in tropical forests requires much patience, and on any one visit it is unlikely that you will encounter more than a fraction of the wildlife living in the forest; many of the mammals are shy and nocturnal.

Although Malaysia is divided into two distinct parts – Peninsular and East Malaysia (the states of Sabah and Sarawak on the island of Borneo) – the wildlife and plant communities of both areas are very similar, since Borneo was joined to the mainland by a land bridge until after the last ice age. Nonetheless, there are some specific differences. The forests of the Peninsula support populations of several large mammal species, such as tiger, tapir and *gaur* (forest-dwelling wild cattle), which are absent from Borneo. Other large mammals, like the Asian elephant, and birds like the hornbill, occur both on Borneo and on the Peninsula; while Borneo features the orang-utan (the "man of the

forest") and the proboscis monkey. Indeed, this latter species is endemic to the island of Borneo.

Below we feature two of the most exciting – and accessible – areas in Peninsular Malaysia in which to view wildlife, namely **Taman Negara** and **Fraser's Hill**; the round-ups of bird, plant and animal life at these two sites should be read in conjunction with the general accounts of both places in the *Guide*. East Malaysia and Brunei also offer many opportunities for observing wildlife. It's easy to spot **proboscis monkeys** along **Sungei Kinabatangan** in Sabah and at **Bako National Park** in Sarawak, the former also a good place to watch orang-utans. Those with an interest in **birdlife** should head for Sarawak's **Loagan Bunut National Park**, whose shallow lake is home to many different bird species, or to Brunei's **Ulu Temburong National Park**.

Downtown Singapore, on the other hand, is not the sort of place you would expect to find much plant or animal life. The rapid urbanization of Singapore has had a major impact on its indigenous wildlife, and the state has consequently lost many of its original forest plant species, all its large mammals and many of its ecologically sensitive bird species such as hornbills. However, two remnant patches of tropical forest still survive amid the rampant development – at Bukit Timah Nature Reserve and the Botanic Gardens.

The following **books** are useful references, best obtained in Malaysia and Singapore: the Sabah Society's *Pocket Guide to the Birds of Borneo* (Sabah Society, Malaysia); M. Strange and A. Jeyarajasingam's *Photographic Guide to the Birds of Peninsular Malaysia and Singapore* (Sun Tree Publishing, Singapore); J. Payne, C. Francis and K. Phillipp's *Field Guide to the Mammals of Borneo* (Sabah Society, Malaysia); M. Tweedie's *Mammals of Malaysia* (Longman, Malaysia); and Lord Medway's *Wild Mammals of Malaya and Singapore* (Oxford University Press).

TAMAN NEGARA

The vast expanse (4343 square kilometres) of **Taman Negara** contains one of the world's oldest tropical rainforests, and is generally regarded as one of Asia's finest national parks. It has an **equatorial climate**, with rainfall throughout the year and no distinct dry season.

Temperatures can reach 35°C during the day, with the air often feeling very muggy. Most rain falls as heavy convectional showers in the afternoon, following a hot and sunny morning – from November to February, heavy rains may cause flooding in low-lying areas.

FOREST TREES

The natural richness of the habitat is reflected in the range of forest types found within the park. Only a small proportion of Taman Negara is true **lowland forest**, though it's here that most of the trails and hides are located. The lowlands support **dipterocarp** (meaning "two-winged fruit") evergreen forest, featuring tall tropical hardwood species and thick-stemmed lianas. There are more than four hundred dipterocarp species in Malaysia, and it's not uncommon to find up to forty in just one small area of forest. Among other trees present at Taman Negara are the majestic fifty-metre tall *tualang*, Southeast Asia's tallest tree; many others have broad, snaking buttress roots and leaves the size of dinner plates. Several species of **fruit trees**, such as durian, mango, guava and rambutan also grow wild here.

Montane forest predominates above 1000m, mainly oak and native conifers with a shrub layer of rattan and dwarf palm. Above 1500m on Gunung Tahan is **cloudforest**, where trees are often cloaked by swirling mist, and the damp boughs bear thick growths of mosses and ferns; at elevations of over 1700m, miniature montane forest of rhododendron and fan palms is found.

MAMMALS

The best method of trying to see some of the larger herbivorous (grazing) **mammals** is to spend the night in a **hide** overlooking a salt lick – the animals visit these natural and artificial "salt sites" to consume salt. There are six hides in the park, and to maximize your chances of spotting mammals you need to stay overnight at one.

Animals commonly encountered include the Malayan **tapir**, a species related to horses and rhinos, though pig-like in appearance with a short, fat body, a long snout and black-and-white colouring. The **gaur** (wild cattle) is dark in colour apart from its white leg patches, which look like ankle socks. There are also several species of **deer**: the larger *sambar*, the *kijang* or

barking deer, the size of a roe deer; and the lesser and greater mouse deer, these last two largely nocturnal, and not much bigger than rabbits.

Primates (monkeys and gibbons) are found throughout the park, although they are quite shy since they have traditionally been hunted for food by the park's indigenous groups. The dawn chorus of a white-handed **gibbon** troupe – making a plaintive whooping noise – is not a sound which will be quickly forgotten. Other primates include the long-tailed and pig-tailed **macaques**, which come to the ground to feed, the latter identified by its shorter tail, brown fur and pinkish-brown face. There are dusky (or spectacled – with white patches around the eyes) and banded **leaf monkeys**, too, which can be recognized by their long, drooping tails (gibbons are tailless) and their habit of keeping their bodies hidden among the foliage. Whereas macaques sometimes feed on the ground, both leaf monkeys and gibbons keep to the trees.

Several **squirrel** species, including the black and common giant squirrels, are present in the park, and towards dusk there's a chance of seeing the nocturnal red flying squirrel shuffling along the highest branches of a tree before launching itself to glide across the forest canopy to an adjacent tree. This squirrel can make continuous glides of up to 100m at a time.

Other mammals you might encounter by – admittedly fairly remote – chance are the Asian **elephant**, with smaller ears and a more humped back than the African; **tigers**, of which a reasonably healthy population exists due to an abundance of prey and the relatively large size of the protected area; and **sun bears**. The bears are an interesting species: standing about 70cm high on all fours, and around 1.5m in length, they are dark brown or black, with muzzle and breast marked dirty white to dull orange, and live on fruit, honey and termites. Their behaviour towards humans can be unpredictable, particularly if there are cubs nearby.

Also present are **clouded leopards**, a beautifully marked cat species with a pattern of cloud-like markings on the sides of the body. They live mostly in the trees, crossing from bough to bough in their search for food, eating monkeys, squirrels and birds, which they swat with their claws; they're most active at twilight. Smaller predators include the **leopard cat** (around the size of a large domestic cat) and several species of nocturnal **civet**, some of which have been known to enter the hides at night in search of tourists' food. Smooth **otters** may also sometimes be seen, in small family groups along Sungei Tembeling.

BIRDS

Over 250 species of bird – including some of the most spectacular forest-dwelling birds in the world – have been recorded in Taman Negara, though many species are shy or only present in small numbers. Birds are at their most active from early to mid-morning, and again in the late afternoon and evening periods; the areas around Kuala Keniam, and the Kumbang and Tabing hides are particularly worth visiting.

Resident forest birds include several species of **green pigeon**, which feed on the fruiting trees; **bulbuls**, vocal, fruit-eating birds which often flock to feed; **minivets**, slender, colourful birds with long, graduated tails, white, yellow or red bands in the wings and outer tail feathers of the same colour; and **babblers**, various short-tailed, round-winged, often ground-dwelling species. The period from September to March is when the visitor can hope to encounter the greatest diversity of birds, with resident species joined by **wintering birds** from elsewhere in Asia, such as warblers and thrushes. At this time of year, up to seventy species altogether can be seen near the park headquarters, particularly if the trees are in fruit.

Pittas, brilliantly coloured in hues of red, yellow, blue and black, are ground-dwelling birds generally occurring singly or in pairs, though they are notoriously shy and difficult to approach. The resident species are the giant, garnet and banded pittas, with blue-winged and hooded pittas being winter visitors.

In addition, several species of pheasant may be seen along the trails, including the **Malaysian peacock pheasant**, a shy bird with a blue-green crest and a patch of bare, orange facial skin; the feathers of the back and tail have green *ocelli* (eye-spots). The crested and crestless **fireback** are similar species of pheasant, differing in the crested fireback's black crest, white tail-plumes, blue-sheen upper parts and white-streaked (rather than plain black) belly. The **great argus** is the largest pheasant species present in the area, with the male birds reaching a maximum of 1.7m in length including their long tail feathers; its pen-etrating "kwow wow" series of call notes is audible most days in the park. Finally, the **mountain peacock pheasant** – very similar in plumage to the Malaysian peacock pheasant and endemic to Malaysia – is found high on Gunung Tahan.

You may also see birds of prey, with two of the most common species, the **crested serpent eagle** and the **changeable hawk eagle**, often spotted soaring over gaps in the forest canopy. The crested serpent eagle (with a 75cm wingspan; about the size of a buzzard) can be identified by the black and white bands on the trailing edge of the wings and on the tail.

Other species confined to tropical forests are **trogons** (brightly coloured, mid-storey birds), of which five species are present at Taman Negara; and several species of **hornbill** – large, broad-winged, long-tailed forest birds with huge, almost outlandish bills.

REPTILES AND AMPHIBIANS

Reptiles and amphibians are well represented in the area. **Monitor lizards** (which can grow to be over 2m long) can be found close to the park headquarters, as can **skinks** (rather short-legged types of lizard which wriggle as much as run among the leaf litter).

Several species of snake are present, too, including the reticulated **python** (which feeds on small mammals and birds and can grow to a staggering 9m in length), and the king and common **cobras**; king cobras, the largest venomous snake in the world, grow up to five metres long. These are all pretty rare in Taman Negara, though, and you're more likely to come across **whip snakes** (which eat insects and lizards) and – most common of all – harmless green **tree snakes** (which, not surprisingly, live in the trees, and eat small lizards).

FRASER'S HILL

At **Fraser's Hill**, visitors can escape the stultifying tropical heat of the lowlands and venture into the cool breezes and fogs of the mountain forests, where ferns and pitcher plants cling to damp, moss-covered branches. It's a noted area for bird-watching, with the hill itself harbouring several montane species of bird, while mammals represented in the area include those normally restricted to more mountainous regions, in addition to some lowland species.

Much of the **forest** at Fraser's Hill is in pristine condition and the route there takes you from lowland forest through sub-montane to montane forest. Higher up on the hill, there are more evergreen tree species present, while the very nature of the vegetation changes: the trees are more gnarled and stunted, and the boughs heavily laden with dripping mosses and colourful epiphytic orchids (ie, orchids which grow on other plants and trees).

MAMMALS

The more strictly montane mammal species at Fraser's Hill include the **siamang gibbon**, a large, all-black gibbon lacking any pale facial markings, that spends its time exclusively in trees. There are also several species of **bat**, including the montane form of the Malayan fruit bat and the grey fruit bat; and several **squirrel** species such as the mountain red-bellied squirrel and the tiny Himalayan striped squirrel, the latter species having a pattern of black-and-yellow stripes running along the length of its back. Lowland mammal species which may be encountered are the tiger, clouded leopard, sun bear and leaf monkeys (see the "Taman Negara" section of this piece). However, most of these are scarce here, and you can realistically expect to encounter only monkeys, squirrels and, possibly, *siamangs*.

BIRDS

A feature of montane forest bird flocks is the **mixed feeding flock**, which may contain many different species. These pass rapidly through an area of forest searching for insects as they go, and it's quite likely that different observers will see entirely different species in one flock. Species which commonly occur within these flocks are the **lesser racket-tailed drongo**, a black crow-like bird with long tail streamers; the **speckled piculet**, a small spotted woodpecker; and the **blue nuthatch**, a small species – blue-black in colour with a white throat and pale eye ring – which runs up and down tree trunks. Several species of brightly coloured **laughing thrushes**, small thrush-sized birds which spend time foraging on the ground or in the understorey, also occur in these flocks. One sound to listen out for is the distinctive cackling "took" call of the **helmeted hornbill** echoing up from the lowlands – see p.435 for more on these birds.

Fraser's Hill itself peaks at 1310m at the High Pines, where a ridge trail begins. Here, there's the possibility of encountering rare species unlikely to be seen at lower altitudes, including the brown bullfinch and the **cutia** – a striking bird, with blue cap, black eyeline and tail, white underparts barred black and a chestnut-coloured back.

Tony Stones, with additional contributions by Charles de Ledesma

MALAYSIAN MUSIC

Like much of the region, Malaysia is rapidly Westernizing at the expense of its own traditions, though there's still a lot to enjoy, from traditional ensembles to local diva Sheila Majid, as well as the hidden delights of the indigenous music of Sarawak and Sabah.

The peoples of Malaysia share in the wider heritage of Indonesia and the Philippines, the cultures of the three nations having borrowed and adapted elements from one another from pre-Islamic times down to the present day. Malaysia lies at the hub of global trade routes which have brought a rich mixture of cultural influences, most significantly Islam from the Middle East. Consequently, its music betrays a wide range of sources, having been enriched over the centuries by instruments and tunes brought by Chinese, Indian and Arab traders.

The aboriginal inhabitants of the Peninsula and Borneo contributed strong rhythms, reed flutes, and a wooden xylophone to the modern-day "national music". The bronze gong is thought to be part of the **Chinese** influence, the Indonesian gamelan being one of its most refined derivatives. The skin drum in its many forms was first brought in by seafaring Arabs, who also introduced the three-string spiked fiddle (*rebab*), lute (*gambus*) and the choral tradition of *hadrah* (religious songs accompanied by tambourines). A species of oboe (*serunai*) is thought to be of Indian origin.

Portuguese music was quickly adapted after the fifteenth century: its Moorish intervals and rhythms sounded familiar to the Indian–Arab trading communities, even if the "Franks" – all Europeans – were sometimes treated as enemies or scarcely tolerated competition. The policy of borrowing and adapting has continued, and today, traditional styles like *asli*, *ronggeng* and *joget* are still played on "foreign" violins, accordions, clarinets and hand drums. Contemporary bands perform them on electric guitars, electronic keyboards and a battery of percussion, but the old tunes remain.

TRADITIONAL STYLES

Authentic **traditional** Malaysian music exists but is hard to find – it doesn't have a big popular following and is generally performed by and among connoisseurs. For example, each of the former royal courts of Kedah, Perak, Selangor and Trengganu has its ceremonial **nobat** ensemble of oboe, drums, valveless trumpet and gongs, though these only perform their mournful strains for ceremonial occasions from which the public is usually excluded.

Easier to hear is **asli** (literally "original"), a slow traditional music played by small ensembles which also play the faster *joget* and **zapin** dances, the former with Portuguese roots, the latter considered typically Malay (and popular throughout the peninsula), though actually of Arabic origin. In their traditional form, both *asli* and *zapin* dances or songs are accompanied by the *gambus* and a couple of two-headed frame drums beating out an interlocking rhythm. These are often supplemented by violin and harmonium (or accordion), flute, keyboards and guitars. The *zapin* begins slowly, but quickens abruptly as the accordion provides the cue for the dancers to improvise around their steps.

THE EAST COAST

Kelantan, **Terengganu** and southeastern Thailand share a distinctive Malay culture, seaborne traffic having linked this region more to the cultures of the South China Sea and less to Western influence than is the case with the west coast of the Peninsula. At Pantai Batu Burok in Kuala Terengganu, performances of traditional dance, the fighting-dance *silat* and occasionally the *wayang kulit* shadow-puppet plays are given at weekends from April to

September, before the monsoon puts a seasonal stop to these open-air shows; in Kota Bharu, such shows are held two or three times a week.

Its moves resembling those of t'ai chi, **silat** is generally called "the Malay art of self-defence", though it isn't unique to the Peninsula. A Kelantan *silat* performance is accompanied by a small ensemble of long drums, Indian oboes and gongs, which generate a loose set of cross rhythms. Two Malay men in baggy dark costumes, topped by a draped head-cloth, face each other in the sandpit where this dance-exercise is usually held, though for weddings and other entertainment it can be performed on a mat indoors. The initial passes are dignified, almost slow, but as the music intensifies, the flowing movements change; the combatants grip each other and the first to throw his opponent to the ground is the winner. The music rises to a crescendo as the *silat* intensifies, the *serunai* screeching atonally while the drums and gongs quicken their loose rhythm.

Kertok, a form of music which originated with the Orang Asli, is played by a very different sort of ensemble, in which six to twelve men play pentatonically tuned wooden xylophones. The rhythmic melody they hammer out in unison is fast and jolly and all the players end each piece at precisely the same time, raising their beaters overhead as they do so.

The **wayang kulit** (shadow-puppet play), an ancient artistic tradition of Southeast Asia, serves as a good example of the meeting and intermingling of cultures in the Malay Peninsula: the *wayang's* roots are in the Hindu epic, the *Ramayana*; the craftsmanship of the puppets is Indonesian/Malay; and the core of the accompanying music is Arabic – each element distilled and refracted through a Malaysian prism. The music is produced by something similar to a *silat* ensemble, enhanced by the wood xylophone and sometimes small hand drums. The puppet master sits onstage beside the musicians, hidden by a screen. As he chants the epic, he manipulates the leather puppets to act out the dramatic sequence for the audience seated in front.

Another form of Malaysian drama, **mak yong**, is of east-coast origin but hardly ever seen there today. A dance-drama, *mak yong* was traditionally performed as entertainment for the court ladies of Kelantan; it's accompanied by the music of *rebab* or violin, oboes and

percussion. Before each show the stage has to be ritually cleansed with incense and incantations. Both male and female characters in the romantic drama are portrayed by women, with the exception of one aged clown whose lines tend to be ribald. A pre-Islamic art form, *mak yong* is disapproved of by many; in religiously conservative Kelantan, it is currently banned. Moderate Muslims, however, challenge this ban and advocate performances without the preliminary ritual (which approaches spirit-worship), without bawdy ad-libs, and with more modest costumes. Traditional drama enthusiasts in Kuala Lumpur get up a performance of *mak yong* once in a while, but even here these shows are becoming more and more rare. On the cultural scale, *wayang kulit* and *mak yong* are considered highbrow, to be enjoyed on special occasions only.

The popular traditional music of the east coast is **Zikir Barat**. After evening prayers, when villagers stroll along the outdoor food stalls, some of the more musically inclined may strike up an impromptu *zikir*. *Zikir Barat* is an Islamic, particularly Sufi, style of singing. In its traditional form two singers perform, alternating verses in praise of Allah, to the beat of a single tambourine, sometimes accompanied by hand-clapping. As practised at evening markets or neighbourhood parties, teams of men sing the impromptu verses on topics of local politics, village gossip, or any subject of general interest. *Zikir Barat* has its own stars, like Drahman, Dollah, Mat Yeh, and the style of singing is also frequently recorded by Indian and Chinese vocalists.

KUALA LUMPUR

The shopping malls and markets of **Kuala Lumpur** are awash with music: Western, Eastern and anywhere in between – the quality measured almost exclusively in decibels. Shopkeepers, it seems, firmly believe that music will attract customers, but most shoppers put up with the ear-splitting noise without paying the slightest attention to it. Besides the music blaring forth from shops, there are teams of blind buskers who sing and accompany themselves on electronic keyboards; most of them will produce anything from Christmas carols to Country and Western, as well as a sentimental form of folk pop derived from Indian *ghazals* – the poetic love songs of Indian light-classical music.

More professional **ghazal** artists are to be heard on cassette or in concert. The great star of this genre remains the late **Kamariah Noor** whose tapes are still available and whose voice, both intense and languid, enabled her to bend and hold notes, milking them for every last drop of emotion. Kamariah often sang with her husband **Hamzah Dolmat**, Malaysia's greatest *rebab* player, famous for his slow rather mournful style combined with a wonderful melodic creativity. As well as Kuala Lumpur, *ghazal* is associated particularly with Johor.

Alongside the *rebab*, the other stringed instrument of Arabic origin is the **gambus**, used as an accompanying instrument for singers of *ghazal* and *asli* music as well as in ensembles for dance music. In the right hands, this six-stringed lute has a beautifully refined tone redolent of intimate, domestic music-making. Malaysia's recognized master of the gambus is **Fadzil Ahmad**, who started performing in the 1950s and later assisted in the formation of several cultural groups dedicated to preserving traditional Malay-Arabic music.

MELAKA

Like its buildings, a strange mix of Portuguese, Dutch and Chinese architecture, **Melaka**'s music is a confluence and compromise between styles. Modern Malaysia accepts the Malaccan **ronggeng** as its own "folk music" – a music played on the violin and the button accordion, accompanied by frame drums, hand drums and sometimes a brass gong. The melodies speak of their Portuguese origin, with faint echoes of Moorish intervals and motifs. The fiddle holds the floor until the singers join in, when it recedes to a plaintive accompaniment.

The Portuguese introduced the European custom of mixed dancing, now best known as the **joget**: couples move gracefully with and around each other but never actually touch. *Joget* is a lively dance, ending in a final passage where the beat quickens, and the dancers skip heel-toe from one leg to the other like dancing cockerels. The traditional ensembles might contain flute, *gambus*, harmonium and drums, but there's also a ten-instrument *joget*-gamelan of gongs and metallophones in Terengganu which originally came from the Riau islands of Indonesia.

Perhaps Melaka's most prominent group are the ensemble **Kumpulan Sri Maharani**, who play **dondang sayang**, a slow, intense, majestic music led by sharp percussive drum rolls which trigger a shift in melody or a change in the pace of rhythm. This is a typically Malaysian style, in fact an amalgam of Hindu, Arabic, Chinese and Portuguese instruments and musical styles. Tabla and harmonium, double-headed *gendang* drum and tambourine create the rhythm, while the violin (and sometimes the accordion) carries the melody. *Dondang* traditionally accompanies classical singing, usually duets with romantic lyrics. Maharani's band integrates electric keyboard and snippets of guitar into the traditional framework. Once incredibly long though shorter nowadays, the songs start with fast, expressive drumming which slows down when the soloists enter, only to accelerate for dramatic emphasis towards the finale.

EAST MALAYSIA

The music of the various tribal groups of **Borneo** has been preserved almost pure, without the admixtures of European and other Asian styles that have entered into Malay music. That said, the music now fights for survival against social change and against the radios, televisions and cassettes that have made their way into the remotest river tributary or mountain valley. It is unusual to find a young person proficient in his or her people's traditional music nowadays.

However, a recent interest in Borneo's culture – both on the part of tourists and the "root searching" urban middle classes in East Malaysia – may yet help to reverse this decline. There has been a conscious attempt to revive the art of playing the **sapé**, the guitar or lute of the Orang Ulu people (though the only place where children can take organized traditional music lessons is in a midtown office block in Kuching).

Traditional **Iban** music is played on the bossed gongs that are widespread all over Southeast Asia. The lead instruments are heirloom pieces in sets of six or eight, laid in a wooden frame over a bed of string and played with two beaters – these are the "melody gongs". The larger gongs are suspended singly, and beaten to keep the rhythm. Gong ensembles play for traditional dancing, and in a longhouse everybody and his grandmother can play the gongs.

The principal **Orang Ulu** instrument, the *sapé*, is one of the real joys of Sarawak music when played by a real master. Tusau Padan, the man usually cited as the best, died in 1996; Kesing Nyipa from Belaga is one of the most famous living sapé players, but he is one of a rare breed. The body of the sapé is hollowed out from one block of wood, and often painted with geometric designs resembling jungle ferns. The instrument has three or four strings, of which the lowest is the melody string and the others drones. *Sapés* are commonly played in pairs, or even larger groups, possibly because they are rather soft in tone despite their large size. In an ensemble, they are sometimes joined by a wooden xylophone, whose top end can be fastened to an upright support (in a longhouse, one of the house pillars) while the lower end tied to the performer's waist. In the Orang Ulu longhouses you often see old "mouth-organs", called *keluré* or *kediri*, made from a gourd into which are fixed bamboo pipes; these instruments were once used to accompany dances or processions, though nowadays you really have to hunt to find anyone who can play one.

There are, however, many types of mouth and nose flute all over Borneo. The **Lun Bawang** people are particularly active players and have formed "bamboo bands" incorporating every flute known to man, including a "bass flute" that looks more like a bamboo tuba than anything else. Schools and villages of east Sarawak and west Sabah have resounding bamboo bands, playing anything from *Onward Christian Soldiers* to the patriotic march *Malaysia Berjaya*.

The ethnic music of Sarawak and Sabah may be heard during **harvest festivals** (in June; see the chapters on these two states for more details). At other times, your best bet is to visit Kuching's Sarawak Museum (see p.366), which has excellent examples of tribal houses and artefacts, including musical instruments; *sapé* players can often be found in its Orang Ulu house, while tapes of *sapé* and other indigenous music are on sale at its shop.

CROONERS AND POP SINGERS

Modern music in Malay was almost entirely Indonesian – of the sentimental **kroncong** variety – until the late **P. Ramlee**'s mellifluous baritone sang its way into Malaya's heart in the 1950s. Penang-born Ramlee used popular melodies, new and old, or adapted from the Western crooners of the day, usually supplying new lyrics which catered for popular taste. Musically, he adapted the folk instrument repertoire, often recording with a dance hall orchestra, and reflecting the influence of the Latin ballroom music favoured in the postwar period. He also launched a new movement in modernizing traditional Malay singing, not just by largely employing Western instruments but also by abbreviating the songs. Ramlee's great duets with his wife, Saloma, are regarded as Malaysian pop's glorious dawn. His critics felt, however, that the purity of Malay music was desecrated by its performance in popular halls devoted to such wickedness as drinking and mixed dancing. Their descendants still make themselves heard today, and manage to get rock and rap concerts banned on religious grounds.

Today's best known singer of "modern classical" Malay songs is **Sharifah Aini**, whose strong, sweet voice seems to improve with the years. Younger musicians tend towards more modern styles, though many intersperse a softrock or *balada* (ballad) disc with a few P. Ramlee covers.

Young Malaysians, however, buy a lot more rock and pop than traditional music. The Malaysian pop/rock scene today is dominated by young musicians singing in Malay, or English, following the world's styles with their own individual interpretations, often with a shot of tradition cleverly injected. A weekly TV programme, *Asia Bagus*, is worth watching for the new talent – not to mention the presenters' adolescent antics.

Sheila Majid is Malaysia's best-known pop star and was the first Malaysian to penetrate the Asian market, particularly in Indonesia. Her foundation in classical music has stood her in good stead as she sings her way from soft rock towards jazz – mostly in the Malay *balada* genre, though she is equally at home in English.

Recently, a young singer, **Siti Nurhaliza**, has adopted a much rootsier style with a band featuring *rebana* (drums), tabla and bamboo flutes. Her album *Cindai* sold 200,000 copies in 1998, a year when economic problems meant that music wasn't supposed to be selling.

Rock singers **Awie** and **Ella** keep their standing in the local and ASEAN charts, as does the enfant terrible of Malaysian music, M. Nasir, a singer-poet-writer-director given to public criticism of political figures, or anything else that arouses his ire. His *Ghazal Untok Rabiah* (Love

Song for Rabiah), sung in duet with Jamal Abdillah, has won awards, and is a moving example of what *ghazal* means to a creative, modern Malay mind. While M. Nasir is an outstanding talent that can't be silenced, "socially unacceptable" bands like the rapping brothers **KRU** have been banned from performing – the objection being to their "irreverent" demeanour, mode of dress and rapped comment on social issues.

The two new sounds on the Malaysian scene today are *dangdut* and *nasyid*, which are about as far apart as musical genres can be. Both have been around for a long time – at the village party and mosque level respectively – and have now suddenly blossomed out and hit the charts with a bang. **Dangdut**, long a great success in Indonesia, is in its Malaysian incarnation a sensuous, pulsing, frankly amorous music generally sung by women. Singer **Amelina** is Malaysia's recognized *dangdut* queen, while everywhere in the country *dangdut* lounges and similar venues advertise Indonesian artistes. **Nasyid**, sung chastely by all-male or all-female groups to the accompaniment of drums and tambourines, is the Muslim equivalent of gospel pop – religious songs in Arabic or Malay rendered to appeal to the young, pop-fed generation. In this vein, the group **Raihan** sold an unprecedented 600,000 copies of their album *Puji-Pujian*, a smoothly produced debut which owed quite a debt to percussionist Yusuf Islam (Cat Stevens).

There are quite a number of Web sites, such as *www.music.upm.edu.my/malaysia*, where you can get more information about Malaysian music and musicians. To buy Malaysian music, it's best to head for a major record store in a big town or city – Tower Records in KL is not a bad starting point.

Heidi Munan
Abridged from
The Rough Guide to World Music

DISCOGRAPHY

TRADITIONAL

Fadzil Ahmad *Raja Gambus Malaysia* (Ahas Productions, Malaysia). "King of the Gambus" goes the title of this album, a great illustration of Fadzil's art, featuring instrumental tracks as well as songs.

Siti Nurhaliza *Cindai* (SRC, Malaysia). On which Nurhaliza is accompanied by an acoustic band for that traditional feel.

Tusau Padan *Masters of the Sarawakian Sapé*, featuring Tusau Padan (Pan, Netherlands). These are the only recordings of his that have been preserved – traditional dances played on the *sapé* plus a couple of duets with younger players

Various *Muzik Tarian Malaysia* (Life, Singapore). Two-CD set of *joget*, *zapin* and other traditional dances played by a small instrumental ensemble. Classical and refined.

MODERN

Sharifah Aini *Nostalgia Aidil Fitri* (EMI, Malaysia). Released just in time for the feast of *Hari Raya Puasa* in 1997, this album contains sentimental, nostalgic, uplifting numbers like the very popular *Dendang Perantau*.

Amelina *Cinta O Cinta* (Warner Music, Malaysia). *Dangdut* for dancing, *dangdut* ballads, *dangdut* cha-cha-cha.

KRU *KRUmania* (EMI, Malaysia). The record of the tour which created a sensation; a mix of straight-out pop, rap and a few more sedate ballads.

Sheila Majid *Ratu* (Warner Music, Malaysia). Easy-listening Malaysian style, and superbly produced. The album justifies her claim to being one of Malaysia's few jazz singers. *Ratu*, suitably enough, means "queen".

M. Nasir *Suratan Kasih* (Warner Music, Malaysia). His best collection, including the famous *Ghazal Untok Rabiah* with Jamal Abdillah.

Raihan *Puji-pujian* (Warner Music, Malaysia). Fresh young voices, sophisticated percussion. Their more recent *Syukur* (Warner Music, Malaysia) has a couple of tracks in English, perhaps with more of an eye on the international audience.

P. Ramlee *Sri Kenangan Abadi* Vols I–III (EMI, Malaysia). Any of these volumes are recommended as an introduction to P. Ramlee's most popular tunes.

BOOKS

There's no shortage of books written about Malaysia, Singapore and Brunei, though as the selection below demonstrates, the majority have tended to be penned by Western visitors to the region, rather than by local writers. Only in the latter part of the twentieth century did writing about Malaysia and Singapore, by Malaysians and Singaporeans themselves, begin to gather momentum.

Though Skoob Books of London (*www.skoob.com/pacificat.htm*) is doing much to introduce Southeast Asian literature to the West, many of the books we've listed – indeed, the best selection of local writing – are produced by publishers in Malaysia, Singapore and Brunei. It's best to buy these books while you are travelling around the countries concerned, though it may be possible to order them from bookshops at home or on the Internet.

In the reviews below, we either give both UK and US publisher details in that order, or mention one publisher when the book appears in both countries under the same imprint or is available in one country only. For books published outside the UK and US, we've given the country or city of publication. Where a book is listed as o/p, this signifies it is out of print, though it may be available in secondhand bookshops and in libraries.

TRAVEL, IMPRESSIONS, EXPLORATION AND ADVENTURE

James Barclay, *A Stroll Through Borneo* (Hodder & Stoughton, UK; o/p). A seminal tour of Sarawak and Indonesian Kalimantan by the doyen of travel writers; particularly perceptive on the Kayan ethnic group.

John Bastin (ed), *Travellers' Singapore* (Oxford University Press, Kuala Lumpur). Singapore-related vignettes from as early as 1819 and as late as the Japanese conquest of 1942.

Isabella Bird, *The Golden Chersonese* (Oxford University Press; o/p). Delightful epistolary romp through old Southeast Asia, penned by the intrepid Bird, whose adventures in the Malay states in 1879 ranged from strolls through Singapore's streets to elephant-back rides and encounters with alligators.

Margaret Brooke, *My Life in Sarawak* (Oxford University Press, Singapore). Engaging account by White Rajah Charles Brooke's wife of nineteenth-century Sarawak, which reveals a sympathetic attitude to her subjects (which extended to rubbing eau de cologne into a Dyak warrior's forehead). Her eye for detail conveys the wonder of an unprejudiced colonial embracing an alien culture.

Anthony Burgess, *Little Wilson and Big God* (Penguin; Weidenfeld & Nicolson; o/p). An application for a teaching post in Malaya while drunk on cider took Burgess ("novelist, composer, traveller, teacher, raconteur, linguist, soldier, husband, boozer, and amorous adventurer") to Kuala Kangsar's Malay College in 1954. His unerring eye for extraordinary characters and customary relish for cultural and semantic detail make the Asian segment of this autobiography an entertaining time capsule of 1950s Malaysia.

Spencer Chapman, *The Jungle is Neutral* (Mayflower; Time Life; o/p). This riveting first-hand account of being lost, and surviving, in the Malay jungle during World War II reads like a breathless novel.

Oscar Cook, *Borneo, the Stealer of Hearts* (Borneo Publishing Company). Written by a young district officer in the North Borneo Civil Service, this piece of Imperial literature is interesting but insufferably plummy.

G.M. Gullick, *They Came To Malaya* (Oxford University Press, UK). A cornucopia of accounts and of people, places and events, written by the governors, planters and explorers who tamed Malaya.

Eric Hansen, *Stranger In The Forest* (Abacus; Houghton Mifflin; o/p). A gripping book, the result of a seven-month tramp through the forests of Sarawak and Kalimantan in 1982, that almost saw the author killed by a poison dart.

Judith M. Heimann, *The Most Offending Soul Alive: Tom Harrisson And His Remarkable Life* (University of Hawaii Press). From his first expedition there in 1932 onwards, Tom Harrisson's life was inextricably linked with Sarawak. Heimann's biography tracks Harrisson's many dealings with Borneo, from his wartime exploits raising a headhunter army against the Japanese, to his subsequent work as curator of the Sarawak Museum.

Victor T. King, *The Best of Borneo Travel* (Oxford University Press). Compendium of extracts from Bornean travel writing since the sixteenth century; an interesting travelling companion.

Dennis Lau, *Borneo: a Photographic Journey* (Travelcom Asia). You won't find a more moving nor a more beautiful memento of East Malaysia in all the souvenir shops of Kuching. Lau's black-and-white shots of the tribespeople of Sarawak and Sabah get to the very heart of Bornean society.

Andro Linklater, *Wild People* (Sphere; Grove-Atlantic). As telling and as entertaining a glimpse into the lifestyle of the Iban as you could pack, depicting their age-old traditions surviving amid the T-shirts, baseball caps and rock posters of Western influence.

Redmond O'Hanlon, *Into The Heart of Borneo* (Picador; Vintage). A hugely entertaining yarn recounting O'Hanlon's refreshingly amateurish romp through the jungle to a remote summit on the Sarawak/Kalimantan border, partnered by the English poet James Fenton.

Ambrose B. Rathborne, *Camping and Tramping in Malaya* (Oxford University Press, Singapore; o/p). Lively nineteenth-century account with insights into the colonial personalities and working conditions of the leading figures of the day; many of Rathborne's impressions of the country still ring true today.

The Rev G.M. Reith, *1907 Handbook to Singapore* (Oxford University Press, UK; o/p). Intriguing period piece which illuminates colonial attitudes in Singapore c.1900: drill hall, juil and docks are detailed in preference to Chinatown, while the list of useful Malay phrases includes such essentials as "harness the horse" and "off with you".

Margaret Shennan, *Out in the Midday Sun* (John Murray, UK). An enlightening snapshot of the British in Malaya, Shennan's book breathes life into the days of Singapore slings, tiffin and rubber planters so memorably documented in the fiction of Somerset Maugham.

Spenser St John, *Life in the Forests of the Far East* (Oxford University Press, UK). A description of an early ascent of Mount Kinabalu is a highlight of this animated nineteenth-century adventure, written by the personal secretary to Rajah Brooke.

Michael Wise (ed), *Travellers' Tales of Old Singapore* (In Print Publishing, UK). Identical in theme to Bastin's *Travellers' Singapore* (opposite), though Wise's selection of tales is the more catholic and more engrossing of the two.

Gavin Young, *In Search of Conrad* (Penguin, UK). In which Young plays detective and historian, tracing Joseph Conrad's footsteps around Southeast Asia in search of the stories and locations that inspired him. Young's time in Singapore takes him from the National Library to Bidadari cemetery in search of A.P. Williams – Conrad's Lord Jim.

HISTORY AND POLITICS

S. Robert Aiken, *Imperial Beldeveres* (Oxford University Press, UK). Sketches, photographs and contemporary accounts enliven this compact examination of the development, landscapes and attractions of the hill stations of Malaya.

Syed Husin Ali, *Two Faces (Detention without Trial)* (Insan, Malaysia). In 1974, Syed, a sociology professor at Universiti Malaya, was taken from his home and detained under the Internal Security Act. For six years he languished in Kamunting, Malaysia's own gulag. This is his harrowing, eye-opening story.

Barbara Watson Andaya and Leonard Andaya, *The History of Malaysia* (Macmillan; St Martin's Press; o/p in UK). Unlike more paternalistic histories, penned by former colonists, this standard text on the region takes a more even-handed view of Malaysia, and finds time for cultural coverage, too.

Noel Barber, *War of the Running Dogs* (Arrow, UK; o/p). Illuminates the Malayan Emergency with a novelist's eye for mood.

James Bartholomew, *The Richest Man in the World* (Penguin, UK). Despite an obvious (and admitted) lack of sources, Bartholomew's study of the Sultan of Brunei makes fairly engaging reading – particularly the mind-bending facts and figures used to illustrate the sultan's wealth.

David Brazil, *Street Smart Singapore* (Times Editions, Singapore). An Aladdin's cave of Singaporean history and trivia that remains fascinating throughout.

Maurice Collis, *Raffles* (Century; o/p). The most accessible and enjoyable biography of Sir Stamford Raffles – very readable.

Peter Elphick, *Singapore The Pregnable Fortress* (Coronet, UK). Drawing on documents only made available in 1993, Elphick has produced the definitive history of the fall of Singapore, showing the gaffes, low morale and desertion that led to it; a scholarly *tour de force*.

Stephen Fay, *The Fall of Barings* (Arrow; Norton). A fascinating and surprisingly readable tale by an authoritative financial writer, of how one of London's oldest and most prestigious banking houses was brought to ruin by the reckless though inadequately controlled derivatives trading in Singapore (see p.567).

Roy Follows, *The Jungle Beat* (TravellersEye). The Malaysian jungle proved as unforgiving an enemy as the Malayan Communist insurgents when Follows joined the Malay police in the 1950s. His story engages from beginning to end.

Images of Asia series (Oxford University Press). Maya Jayapal's *Old Singapore* and Sarnia Hayes Hoyt's *Old Malacca* and *Old Penang* chart the growth of three of the region's most important outposts, drawing on contemporary maps, sketches and photographs to engrossing effect.

Robert Jackson, *The Malayan Emergency* (Routledge, UK; o/p). Thorough account of the conflict between the Chinese Communist guerrillas and the security forces in postwar Malaya.

Abdullah bin Kadir, *The Hikayat Abdullah* (Oxford University Press, UK). Raffles' one-time clerk, Melaka-born Abdullah, later turned diarist of some of the most formative years of Southeast Asian history; his first-hand account is crammed with illuminating vignettes and character portraits.

Lee Kuan Yew, *The Singapore Story* (Times Editions, Singapore). Spanning the first 42 years of Lee Kuan Yew's life, up to Singapore's separation from Malaysia in 1965, this first volume of memoirs by the grand-daddy of contemporary Singapore is essential reading for anyone wanting the inside story on the island's huge economic expansion over the past fifty years.

Nick Leeson, *Rogue Trader* (Warner; Little, Brown). Leeson's own account of his beginnings, his ambitions and of the whirlpool of deceit in which he floundered as the result of his covert trading in Singapore. The inadequacies of Barings' systems and controls are revealed as contributing factors, though Leeson's apparent lack of penitence wins him little sympathy.

Eric Lomax, *The Railway Man* (Vintage; Ballantine). Such is the power of Lomax's artless, redemptive and moving story of capture during the fall of Singapore, torture by the Japanese and reconciliation with his tormentor after fifty years, that many reviewers were moved to tears.

James Minchin, *No Man Is An Island* (Allen & Unwin; Paul & Co). A well-researched, and at times critical study of Lee Kuan Yew, which refuses to kowtow to Singapore's ex-PM and is hence unavailable in Singapore itself, but gleefully sold in shops throughout Malaysia.

Anthony Oei, *What If There Had Been No Lee Kuan Yew* (Mandarin Paperbacks, Singapore). Ignore the sycophantic tone of this readable enough overview of the life and works of Singapore's pre-eminent statesman; for a more opinionated account, see Minchin, above.

Steven Runciman, *The White Rajahs* (Cambridge University Press; o/p). A ponderous, blow-by-blow chronicle of the Brookes' private fiefdom, whose attention to detail compensates for its lack of colour.

Sterling Seagrave, *Lords of the Rim* (Corgi; Putnam). History and hard economics are the tools Seagrave uses as he highlights the extent to which the "offshore Chinese" have shouldered their way into the vanguard of Pacific Rim economies.

C. Mary Turnbull, *A Short History of Malaysia, Singapore & Brunei* (Graham Brash, Singapore). Decent, informed introduction to the region, touching on the major issues that have shaped it. Its big brother, Turnbull's *History of Singapore 1819–1988* (Oxford University Press, Singapore) is, in contrast, as scholarly an approach to Singapore as you could wish to read.

C.E. Wurtzburg, *Raffles of the Eastern Isles* (Oxford University Press, UK). A weighty and learned tome that's the definitive study of the man who founded modern Singapore; not for the marginally interested, who should opt for Collis's more accessible volume (opposite).

WORLD WAR II AND THE JAPANESE OCCUPATION

Noel Barber, *Sinister Twilight* (Arrow, UK). Documents the fall of Singapore to the Japanese, by reimagining the crucial events of the period.

Russell Braddon, *The Naked Island* (Penguin; Simon & Schuster; o/p). Southeast Asia under the Japanese: Braddon's disturbing yet moving first-hand account of the POW camps of Malaya, Singapore and Siam displays courage in the face of appalling conditions and treatment; worth scouring secondhand stores for.

Chin Kee Onn, *Malaya Upside Down*. A coherent analysis of the impact of the Japanese occupation on Malaysian society; difficult to find in the UK and US, but available in Malaysian bookshops.

Agnes Keith, *Three Came Home* (Eland; Little, Brown; o/p). Pieced together from scraps of paper secreted in latrines and teddy bears, this is a remarkable story of survival in the face of Japanese attempts to eradicate the "proudery and arrogance" of the West in the World War II prison camps of Borneo.

CULTURE AND SOCIETY

Salleh Ben Joned, *As I Please* (Skoob; Atrium). Named after his occasional column in the *New Straits Times*, Salleh's articles are candid observations on Malaysian society with titles such as "The Art of Pissing" and "Kiss My Arse – In the Name of Common Humanity". Don't let this mislead you. Although he's outspoken, Salleh is thoughtful and intensely proud of his Malay roots.

Iskandar Carey, *The Orang Asli* (Oxford University Press, o/p). The only detailed anthropological work on the indigenes of Peninsular Malaysia.

Culture Shock! Malaysia and **Culture Shock! Singapore** (Kuperard; Graphic Arts Center Publishing). Cultural dos and don'ts for the leisure and business traveller to the region, spanning subjects as diverse as hand-

ing over business cards and belching after a fine meal.

Tom Harrisson, *A World Within* (Oxford University Press, US; o/p). The only in-depth description of the Kelabit peoples of Sarawak, and a cracking good World War II tale courtesy of Harrisson, who parachuted into the Kelabit Highlands to organize resistance against the Japanese.

William Krohn, *In Borneo Jungles* (Oxford University Press; o/p). An interwar-years description of the infamous head-hunters of Sarawak.

Leslie Layton, *Songbirds in Singapore* (Oxford University Press, US). A delightful examination of songbird-keeping in Singapore, detailing all facets of the pastime, from its growth in the nineteenth century.

Rahman Rashid, *A Malaysian Journey*. Excellent autobiographical account by a journalist returning to Malaysia in the 1990s after self-imposed exile; look it up in KL's bookshops.

Karim Raslan, *Ceritalah: Malaysia in Transition* (Times). Collection of the young lawyer-turned-journalist's articles from local newspapers and magazines, providing an insight into modern Malaysia. Raslan may at times be sentimental and an apologist for the excesses of Malaysia's political and social set-up, but he is always entertaining. The essay "Roots", about his family, is excellent.

Owen Rutter, *The Pagans of North Borneo* (Oxford University Press; o/p). Dry, scholarly examination of the lifestyles and traditions of Sabah's non-Muslim peoples, which suffers from a tendency towards cultural chauvinism.

Sabah Women Action Resource Group, *Women in Sabah* (SAWO, Malaysia). Occasionally interesting profile of the status and contribution of women in Sabahan society; available in KK shops.

Tan Kok Seng, *Son Of Singapore* (Heinemann, Singapore; o/p). Tan Kok Seng's candid and sobering autobiography on the underside of the Singaporean success story, telling of hard times spent as a coolie.

NATURAL HISTORY AND ECOLOGY

For specific field guides to the birds and mammals of Malaysia, Singapore, Sabah and Sarawak, see p.637.

Odoardo Beccari, *Wanderings in the Great Forests of Borneo* (Oxford University Press; o/p US). Vivid c.1900 account of the natural and human environment of Sarawak.

John Briggs, *Parks of Malaysia* (Longman, Malaysia). Top tips and maps for the serious naturalist or hiker in Malaysia.

Mark Cleary and Peter Eaton, *Borneo Change and Development* (Oxford University Press, Singapore). A very readable composite of Bornean history, economy and society, that's rounded off by a section dealing with issues such as logging, conservation and the future of the Penan.

G.W.H. Davison and Chew Yen Fook, *A Photographic Guide to Birds of Peninsular Malaysia and Singapore* (New Holland; R. Curtis). Well-keyed and user-friendly, this slender volume carries oodles of glossy plates that make positive identifying a breeze. The companion volume, *A Photographic Guide to Birds of Borneo*, is also excellent.

Robin Hanbury-Tenison, *Mulu: The Rain Forest* (Arrow; o/p). Hanbury-Tenison's overview of the flora, fauna and ecology of the rainforest, the result of a 1977 Royal Geographical Society field trip into Sarawak's Gunung Mulu National Park; makes enlightening reading.

Jeffrey McNeely, *Soul of the Tiger* (OUP; Doubleday). Synoptic, multidisciplinary overview of the importance of the various facets of nature and the environment to the peoples of the region.

Alfred Russel Wallace, *The Malay Archipelago* (Oxford University Press; Dover; o/p). Wallace's peerless account of the flora and fauna of Borneo, based on travels made between 1854 and 1862 – during which time he collected over one hundred thousand specimens. Still required reading for nature lovers.

World Rainforest Movement, *The Battle For Sarawak's Forests* (Sahabat Alam Malaysia, Penang; o/p). A worthy collection of writings on the acrimonious, and sometimes violent, confrontations between the state government-sponsored loggers and tribespeople in east Malaysia.

ART AND ARCHITECTURE

Jacques Dumarcay, *The House in Southeast Asia* (Oxford University Press; o/p US); *Palaces of Southeast Asia* (Oxford University Press; o/p US). The former is a pocket-sized overview of regional domestic architecture, covering the rituals and techniques of house construction; the latter is more specialist, but has only ten pages on Malaysia.

Norman Edwards, *Singapore House and Residential Life* (Oxford University Press, o/p US). The development of the Singapore detached house, traced from early plantation villas, through colonial bungalows to Chinese landowners' mansions; beguiling photographs.

Roxana Waterson, *The Living House* (Oxford University Press). More authoritative than Dumarcay's slender introduction to Southeast Asian dwellings, and required reading for anyone with an interest in the subject.

LITERATURE

Charles Allen, *Tales from the South China Seas* (Futura; David Charles; o/p). Memoirs of the last generation of British colonists, in which predictable Raj attitudes prevail, though some of the drama of everyday lives, often in inhospitable conditions, is evinced with considerable pathos.

Gopal Baratham, *Moonrise, Sunset* (Serpent's Tail). When How Kum Menon's fiancée is murdered while sleeping by his side in Singapore's East Coast Park, it seems everyone he knows has a motive. How Kum turns detective, and an engaging whodunnit emerges. In the earlier a *Candle or the Sun*, Baratham swallows hard and tackles the thorny issue of political corruption.

Noel Barber, *Tanamera* (Coronet, UK). Romantic saga based in mid-twentieth-century Singapore.

Anthony Burgess, *The Long Day Wanes* (Minerva; Norton). Burgess's Malayan trilogy – *Time for a Tiger*, *The Enemy in the Blanket* and *Beds in the East* – published in one volume, provides a witty and acutely observed vision of 1950s Malaya, underscoring the racial prejudices of the period. *Time for a Tiger*, the first novel, is worth reading for the Falstaffian Nabby Adams alone.

James Clavell, *King Rat* (Hodder; Dell). Set in Japanese-occupied Singapore, a gripping tale of survival in the notorious Changi Prison.

Joseph Conrad, *Lord Jim* (Penguin). Southeast Asia provides the backdrop to the story of Jim's desertion of an apparently sinking ship and subsequent efforts to redeem himself; modelled upon the sailor, A.P. Williams, Jim's character also yields echoes of Rajah Brooke of Sarawak.

Alastair Dingwall (ed), *South-east Asia Traveller's Literary Companion* (In Print Publishing, UK). Among the bite-sized essays in this gem of a book are enlightening segments on Malaysia and Singapore, into which are crammed biopics, a recommended reading list, historical, linguistic and literary backgrounds. Excerpts range from classical Malayan literature to the nations' leading contemporary lights.

J.G. Farrell, *The Singapore Grip* (Phoenix Press; Orion). Lengthy novel – Farrell's last – of World War II Singapore in which real and fictitious characters flit from tennis to dinner party as the countdown to the Japanese occupation begins.

Henri Fauconnier, *The Soul of Malaya* (Oxford University Press, UK; o/p). Fauconnier's semi-autobiographical novel is a lyrical, sensory tour of the plantations, jungle and beaches of early twentieth-century Malaya, and pierces deeply into the underside of the country.

Lloyd Fernando, *Scorpion Orchid* (Heinemann Educational, Kuala Lumpur; o/p); *Green is the Colour* (Landmark Books, Singapore). Social politics form the basis of Fernando's works. In *Scorpion Orchid*, he concerns himself with the difficulties of adjusting to the move towards Merdeka and new nationhood; *Green is the Colour* is a remarkable novel, exploring the deep-seated racial tensions brought to light by the Kuala Lumpur demonstrations of May 1969.

Chin Kee Onn, *The Grand Illusion* (Aspatra Quest, Kuala Lumpur). A novel with a difference, exploring the Emergency from the perspective of a Communist guerrilla cell; also good is his *Twilight of the Nyonyas* (Aspatra Quest, Kuala Lumpur), a historical novel about the life and culture of a Nonya family. Both are widely available in Malaysia.

K.S. Maniam, *The Return* (Skoob), *In A Far Country* (Skoob); *Haunting the Tiger* (Skoob). The purgative writings of this Tamil-descended Malaysian author are strong, highly descriptive and humorous – essential reading.

Wong Phui Nam, *Ways of Exile* (Skoob). Chinese-Malaysian poet's first collection published outside Malaysia; evocative works rooted in the interaction of cultures and ethnicity.

William Riviere, *Borneo Fire* (Sceptre). As he spins his tale of family fortunes and forest fires in contemporary Sarawak, Riviere highlights both the state's staggering beauty, and its environmental plight.

Rex Shelley, *The Shrimp People* (Times Books, Singapore). Eurasian family saga, critically acclaimed in Singapore, that's played out against the backdrop of the years of race riots and confrontation in Singapore, Malaysia and Indonesia.

Skoob Pacifica Anthology No. 1 and No. 2 (Skoob). These two thorough compendia of writings from the Pacific Rim together comprise an invaluable introduction to the contemporary literatures of Singapore and Malaysia.

W. Somerset Maugham, *Short Stories Volume 4* (Mandarin; Penguin). Peopled by hoary sailors, bored plantation-dwellers and colonials wearing mutton-chop whiskers and topees, Maugham's short stories resuscitate Malaya c.1900; quintessential colonial literature graced by an easy style and a steady eye for a story.

Paul Theroux, *Saint Jack* (Penguin; Ballantine; o/p); *The Consul's File* (Penguin; Pocket Books; o/p). *Saint Jack* tells the compulsively bawdy tale of Jack Flowers, an ageing American who supplements his earnings at a Singapore ship's chandlers by pimping for Westerners; Jack's jaundiced eye and Theroux's rich prose open windows on Singapore's past. In *The Consul's File*, the fictitious American consul to interior Malaya recounts a series of short stories.

Leslie Thomas, *The Virgin Soldiers* (Penguin; Little Brown; o/p). The bawdy exploits of teenage British Army conscripts snatching all the enjoyment they can, before being sent to fight in troubled 1950s Malaya.

Beth Yahp, *The Crocodile Fury* (Women's Press, UK). Described by one reviewer as a "spicy Malaysian curry" to Amy Tan's "lightly seasoned Chinese soup", Yahp has produced a garlicky, rambunctious storytelling treat that shadows the lives of three women – grandmother, mother and daughter – in colonial and post-colonial Malaysia.

LANGUAGE

The national language of Malaysia, Singapore and Brunei is Bahasa Malaysia, which means, simply, "Malay language". It's an old language, with early roots in the Central and South Pacific, and one which was refined by its use in the ancient kingdom of Srivijaya and during the fifteenth-century Melaka Sultanate into a language of the elite. Indeed, the very word bahasa (language) came to signify Malay culture in general.

The situation is slightly complicated by the presence of several other racial groups and languages in all three countries: in Singapore, for example, Mandarin, Tamil and English all have the status of official languages, as well as Malay; in Malaysia itself, Cantonese, Mandarin, other Chinese languages like Hokkien and Hakka, and Tamil all form significant minority languages. In practice, however, you'll be able to get by with **English** in all but the most remote areas, since this is the common means of communication between the different races, as well as the language of business.

Nevertheless, it always helps to pick up a few words, especially since basic *Bahasa* is simple enough to learn. Understanding the quick-fire, staccato speech is a different matter altogether, particularly since the spoken word is often corrupted. For example, Malays will often use *-lah* at the end of a word or sentence – hence *Minumlah Coca-cola* – a meaningless, though pervasive, suffix.

MANGLISH

"To *lah* or not to *lah*, that is the question." This slogan, spotted on a T-shirt in Melaka, sums up what most visitors notice first off about English as it's spoken in Malaysia – the indiscriminate addition of the meaningless *lah* to the end of many words. But the development of **Manglish** – as the combination of Malay and English is called – doesn't stop with *lah*. Courtesy of the Chinese-Malaysian satirical writer and poet Kit Leee, Manglish has taken on a life of its own. In his book *Adoi* (meaning "ouch"), Leee explains how Manglish should be written exactly as it sounds; hence *debladigarmen* – a contraction of "the bloody government" and *olafasudden* for "all of a sudden". Leee is quick to point out that he didn't invent Manglish, but that it has been evolving ever since the end of British rule, when the previously imposed rules of spoken English were thrown out. On a more serious note, with Malaysia aiming for developed nation status, the government is aware of the need to raise the level of **English proficiency** in the country. But in the meantime, writers and performers such as Leee, Julian Mokhtar and Rafique Rashid, entertain their fellow countrymen with this unique language, some examples of which are below:

ackchwurly	"Actually", used as a sentence starter	*tingwat*	"What do you think?"
aidontch-main	"I don't mind"	*watudu*	"What can we do?", a rhetorical question
baiwanfriwan	"Buy one and you'll get one free", a sales ploy	*yusobadwan*	"You're such a bad one!" meaning "that's not very nice!"
betayudon	"You'd better not do that!"		

Leee advises that *Mat Salleh's* (white-skinned *furriers*) should not attempt to speak Manglish as it might cause offence, but that it is worthwhile studying the language so as to understand *wat peeple are saying about you lah*.

SINGLISH

Upon first hearing the machine-gun rattle of Singaporean English, or **Singlish**, you could easily be forgiven for thinking you're listening to a language other than English. Pronunciation is so staccato that many words are rendered almost unrecognizable – especially monosyllabic words such as "cheque" and "book", which together would be spoken "che-boo". In contrast, in two-syllable words the second syllable is lengthened, and stressed by a rise in tone: ask a Singaporean what they've been doing, and you'll variously be told "wor-king", "shop-ping", and "slee-ping".

But it's the **unorthodox rhythms** of phrasing that make Singlish so memorable. Conventional English syntax is twisted and wrung, and tenses and pronouns discarded. Ask a Singaporean if they've ever seen Michael Jackson, and you might be answered, "I ever see him", while enquiring whether they've just been shopping might yield "go come back already".

Responses are almost invariably reduced to their bare bones, with single-word replies often repeated for stress. Request something in a shop and you'll hear "have, have", or "got, got".

Suffixes and **exclamations** drawn from Malay, Hokkien and English complete this patois, the most distinctive being "lah", as in "okay lah", and "so cheap one lah" (which translates as "this is really inexpensive, isn't it?"). Also commonly heard are "is it?" (pronounced "eezeet?"), which expresses "really?" and "ah", which means "yes" if on its own and accompanied by a nod of the head, but can imply a question if set at the end of a phrase.

If Singlish has you totally baffled, you might try raising your eyes to the heavens, and crying either "ay yor" (with a drop of tone on "yor") or "Allama" – both expressions of annoyance or exasperation.

GRAMMAR

Nouns have no genders and don't require an article, while the **plural** form is constructed just by saying the word twice; thus "child" is *anak*, while "children" is *anak anak* – occasionally you'll see this written as if to the power of two, as in *anak2*. Doubling a word can also indicate

COMMON WORDS AND PHRASES IN BAHASA MALAYSIA

CIVILITIES AND BASIC PHRASES

Selamat is the all-purpose greeting derived from Arabic, which communicates a general goodwill.

Good morning	*Selamat pagi*	My name is...	*Nama saya...*
Good afternoon	*Selamat petang*	Where are you from?	*Dari mana?*
Good evening	*Selamat malam*	I come from...	*Saya dari...*
Good night	*Selamat tidur*	...England	*...Inggeris* (also
Goodbye	*Selamat tinggal*		means "English")
Bon voyage	*Selamat jalan*	...America	*...Amerika*
Welcome	*Selamat datang*	...Australia	*...Australia*
Bon appetit	*Selamat makan*	...Canada	*...Kanada*
How are you?	*Apa khabar?*	...New Zealand	*...Zealandia Baru*
Fine/OK	*Baik*	...Ireland	*...Irlandia*
See you later	*Jumpa lagi*	...Scotland	*...Skotlandia*
Please	*Tolong*	Do you speak	*Bisa bercakap bahasa*
Thank you	*Terima kasih*	English?	*Inggeris?*
You're welcome	*Sama-sama*	I don't understand	*Saya tidak mengerti*
Sorry/excuse me	*Maaf*	I want...	*Saya mahu...*
No worries/never mind	*Tidak apa-apa*	I like...	*Saya suka...*
Yes	*Ya*	What is this/that?	*Apa ini/itu?*
No	*Tidak*	Can you help me?	*Bolekah anda tolong*
What is your name?	*Siapa nama anda?*		*saya?*

continued overleaf

What?	*Apa?*	Why?	*Mengapa?*
When?	*Bila?*	How?	*Berapa?*
Where?	*Dimana?*		

GETTING AROUND AND DIRECTIONS

Where is the...?	*Dimana...?*	Front	*Hadapan*
I want to go to...	*Saya mahu naik ke...*	Behind	*Belakang*
How do I get there?	*Bagaimanakah saya*	North	*Utara*
	boleh ke sana?	South	*Selatan*
How far?	*Berapa jauh?*	East	*Timur*
How long will it take?	*Berapa lama?*	West	*Barat*
When will the bus		Street	*Jalan*
leave?	*Bila bas berangkat?*	Train station	*Stesen keratapi*
What time does	*Jam berapa keratapi*	Bus station	*Stesen bas*
the train arrive?	*sampai?*	Airport	*Lapangan terbang*
Stop	*Berhenti*	Ticket	*Tiket*
Wait	*Tunggu*	Hotel	*Hotel/rumah penginapan*
Go up	*Naik*	Post office	*Pejabat pos*
Go down	*Turun*	Restaurant	*Restoran*
Turn	*Belok*	Shop	*Kedai*
Right	*Kanan*	Market	*Pasar*
Left	*Kiri*	Taxi	*Teksi*
Straight	*Terus*	Trishaw	*Becak*

ACCOMMODATION

How much is...?	*Berapa...?*	Please clean my	*Tolong bersikan bilik*
I need a room	*Saya perlu satu bilik*	room	*saya*
Cheap/expensive	*Murah/mahal*	Can I store my	
I'm staying for one	*Saya mahu tinggal*	luggage here?	*Bisa titip barang?*
night	*satu hari*	I want to pay	*Saya nak bayar*

SHOPPING

I want to buy...	*Saya mahu beli...*	I'll give you no	*Saya bayar tidak*
Can you reduce		more than...	*lebih dari...*
the price?	*Boleh kurang?*	I'm just looking	*Saya hanya lihat-lihat*

PERSONAL PRONOUNS AND TITLES

You'll often see the word *Dato'* placed before the name of a government official or some other worthy. It's an honorific title of distinction roughly equivalent to the British "Sir". Royalty are always addressed as *Tuanku*.

I/my	*Saya*	They	*Mereka*
You	*Anda/awak*	Mr	*Encik*
S/he	*Dia*	Mrs	*Puan*
We	*Kami*	Miss	*Cik*

USEFUL ADJECTIVES

Good	*Bagus*	Hot	*Panas*
A lot/very much	*Banyak*	Sweet	*Manis*
A little	*Sedikit*	Salty	*Garam*
Cold (Object)	*Sejuk*	Spicy	*Pedas*
Cold (Person)	*Dingin*	Big	*Besar*

Small	Kecil	Thirsty	Haus
Enough	Cukup	Tired	Lelah
Closed	Tutup	Ill/sick	Sakit
Hungry	Laparad		

USEFUL NOUNS

Entrance	Masuk	Drink	Minum
Exit	Keluar	Fork	Garpu
Toilet	Tandas	Knife	Pisau
Bath/shower	Mandi	Spoon	Sudu
Man	Lelaki	Boyfriend/girlfriend	Pacar
Woman	Perempuan	Husband	Suami
Water	Air	Wife	Istri
Money	Wang/duit	Friend	Kawan
Food	Makan		

USEFUL VERBS

Malay verbs do not conjugate, and often double as nouns or adjectives. Here, they are given in the form in which you'd use the verb, rather than in the strictly grammatical infinitive.

Come	Datang	Give	Beri
Go	Pergi	Take	Gambil
Do	Buat	Sit	Duduk
Have	Punya	Sleep	Tidur

NUMBERS

0	Nul	7	Tujuh	21	Dua puluh satu
1	Satu	8	Lapan	100	Seratus
2	Dua	9	Sembilan	143	Seratus empatpuluh tiga
3	Tiga	10	Sepuluh	200	Duaratus
4	Empat	11	Sebelas	1000	Scribu
5	Lima	12	Duabelas	1 Million	Sejuta
6	Enam	20	Duapuluh	A half	Setengah

TIME AND DAYS OF THE WEEK

What time is it?	Jam berapa?	Year	Tahun
It's...		Today	Hari Ini
three o'clock	Jam tiga	Tomorrow	Besok
ten past four	Jam empat lewat sepuluh	Yesterday	Kemarin
quarter to five	Jam lima kurang seperempat	Now	Sekarang
		Ago	Yang Lalu
six-thirty	Jam setengah tujuh (lit. "half to seven")	Not Yet	Belum
		Never	Tidak Perna
7am	Tujuh pagi		
8pm	Lapan malam	Monday	Hari Isnin
Second	Detik	Tuesday	Hari Selasa
Minute	Menit	Wednesday	Hari Rabu
Hour	Jam	Thursday	Hari Kamis
Day	Hari	Friday	Hari Jumaat
Week	Minggu	Saturday	Hari Sabtu
Month	Bulan	Sunday	Hari Ahad/minggu

For more Malay words, see the glossary of words and terms in the next section.

"doing"; for example, *jalan jalan* is used to mean "walking". **Verbs** have no tenses either, the meaning being indicated either by the context, or by the use of "time" words such as *sedang, akan* and *sudah* for the present, future and past. **Sentence order** is the same as in English, though adjectives usually follow their corresponding nouns.

PRONUNCIATION

The **pronunciation** of *Bahasa Malaysia* is broadly the same as the English reading of Roman script, with a few exceptions:

VOWELS AND DIPHTHONGS

a as in c**u**p

e a short indeterminate vowel when unstressed, though more as in "h**ey**" when stressed, eg in the word *kelong*

i as in bout**i**que

o as in g**o**t

u as in b**oo**t

ai as in f**i**ne

au as in h**ow**

CONSONANTS

c as in **ch**eap

g as in **g**irl

j as in **j**oy

k hard, as in English, except at the end of the word, when it becomes a glottal stop (ie you should stop just short of pronouncing it). In writing, this is frequently indicated by an apostrophe at the end of the word; for example, *beso'* for *besok*

ngg as in bo**ng**o

sy as in **sh**ut

A GLOSSARY OF WORDS AND TERMS

AIR PANAS Hot springs.

AIR TERJUN Waterfall.

ATAP Palm thatch.

BABA Straits-born Chinese (male).

BANDAR Town.

BANGUNAN Building.

BATANG River system.

BATIK Wax and dye technique of cloth decoration.

BATU Rock/stone.

BEJALAI Period in an Iban youth's life when he ventures out from the longhouse to experience life in the towns.

BELIAN A hardwood traditionally used to construct Sarawak longhouses.

BOMOH Traditional healer.

BUKIT Hill.

BUMBUN Hide.

BUMIPUTRA Indigenous Malay person (lit. "son of the soil").

CANDI Temple.

DAULAT Divine force possessed by a ruler that commands unquestioning loyalty.

DERHAKA Treason; punished severely even in contemporary Malaysia.

EKSPRES Express (used for boats and buses).

GASING Spinning top.

GAWAI Annual festivals celebrated by indigenous groups in Sarawak.

GELANGGANG SENI Cultural centre.

GEREJA Church.

GODOWN Warehouse.

GONGSI Chinese clan-house.

GOPURAM Sculpted deities over the entrance to a Hindu temple.

GUA Cave.

GUNUNG Mountain.

HALAL Something that's permissible in Islam.

HUTAN Forest.

IKAT Woven fabric.

ISTANA Palace.

JALAN Road/street.

JAMBATAN Bridge.

KAMPUNG Village.

KEDAI KOPI Coffee shop.

KELONG Large marine fish trap.

KERANGAS Sparse forest (lit. "poor soil").

KHALWAT Close proximity; forbidden between people of the opposite sex under Islamic law.

KONGSI Chinese clan-house/temple.

KOTA Fort.

KRIS Wavy-bladed dagger.

KUALA River confluence or estuary.

LAUT Sea.

LEBUH Avenue.

LEBUHRAYA Highway/expressway.

LORONG Lane.

MAK YONG Epic courtly dance drama.

MAKAM Grave or tomb.

MANDI Asian method of bathing by dousing with water from a tank using a small bucket.

MASJID Mosque.

MAT SALLEH Malaysian colloquial term for a foreigner.

MEDAN SELERA Food centre.

MENARA Minaret or tower.

MERDEKA Freedom (and therefore applied to Malaysian independence).

MINANGKABAU Matriarchal people from Sumatra.

MUZIUM Museum.

NEGARA National.

NIPAH Palm tree.

NONYA Straits-born Chinese (female); sometimes *Nyonya*.

ORANG ASLI Peninsular Malaysia aborigines (lit. "original people"); also Orang Ulu (upriver people) and Orang Laut (sea people).

PADANG Field/square; usually the main town square.

PANTAI Beach.

PARANG Machete.

PASAR Market (pasar malam, night market).

PASIR Sand.

PEJABAT DAERAH District office.

PEJABAT POS Post office.

PEKAN Town.

PELABUHAN Port/harbour.

PENGHULU Chief/leader.

PENGKALAN Port/harbour.

PERANAKAN Straits-born Chinese.

PERIGI Well.

PINTU Arch/gate.

PONDOK Hut/shelter; used as religious schools.

PULAU Island.

PUSAT BANDAR Town centre.

RAJAH Prince (often spelled Raja).

RAMADAN Muslim fasting month.

REBANA Drum.

ROTAN Rattan cane; used in the infliction of corporal punishment.

RUMAH PERSINGGAHAN Lodging house.

RUMAH REHAT Resthouse (usually government-run).

RUMAH TUMPANGAN Boarding house used mainly by migrant workers.

SAREE Traditional Indian woman's garment, worn in conjunction with a *choli* (short-sleeved blouse).

SEKOLAH School.

SILAT Malay art of self-defence.

SONGKET Woven cloth.

STESEN BAS Bus station.

STESEN KERATAPI Train station.

SULTAN Ruler.

SUNGEI River.

T'AI CHI Chinese martial art; commonly performed as an early-morning exercise.

TAMAN Park.

TAMU Market/fair.

TANJUNG Cape/headland.

TASIK (or Tasek) Lake.

TELAGA Freshwater spring or well.

TELUK Bay/inlet.

TOKONG Chinese temple.

TOWKAY Chinese merchant.

TUAI Tribal headman (Sarawak).

WAU Kite.

WAYANG KULIT Shadow-puppet play.

ACRONYMS

ASEAN Association of SouthEast Asian Nations, an economic and political grouping of ten regional states, including Malaysia, Singapore and Brunei.

BN Barisan Nasional or National Front – the coalition, dominated by UMNO, that has governed Malaysia since 1974.

KTMB Keretapi Tanah Melayu Berhad, the Malaysian national railway company.

MAS Malaysian national airline.

MCP Malayan Communist Party.

MRT Singapore's Mass Rapid Transit system.

PAP Singaporean People's Action Party.

PAS Parti Islam SeMalaysia, the Pan-Malaysian Islamic Party.

UMNO United Malays National Organization.

INDEX

Stay in touch with us!

ROUGH*NEWS* **is Rough Guides' free newsletter.
In four issues a year we give you news, travel
issues, music reviews, readers' letters and the
latest dispatches from authors on the road.**

I would like to receive ROUGH*NEWS*: please put me on your free mailing list.

NAME . . . .

ADDRESS . . . .

Please clip or photocopy and send to: Rough Guides, 62–70 Shorts Gardens, London WC2H 9AH,
England or Rough Guides, 375 Hudson Street, New York, NY 10014, USA.

ROUGH GUIDES: Travel

Alaska
Amsterdam
Andalucia
Argentina
Australia
Austria

Bali & Lombok
Barcelona
Belgium &
  Luxembourg
Belize
Berlin
Brazil
Britain
Brittany &
  Normandy
Bulgaria
California
Canada
Central America
Chile
China
Corsica
Costa Rica
Crete
Croatia
Cuba
Cyprus
Czech & Slovak
  Republics

Dodecanese &
  the East Aegean
Devon &
  Cornwall
Dominican
  Republic
Dordogne & the
  Lot
Ecuador
Egypt
England
Europe
Florida
France
French Hotels &
  Restaurants
  1999
Germany
Goa
Greece
Greek Islands
Guatemala
Hawaii
Holland
Hong Kong &
  Macau
Hungary

Iceland
India
Indonesia
Ionian Islands
Ireland

Israel & the
  Palestinian
  Territories
Italy
Jamaica
Japan
Jordan
Kenya
Lake District
Languedoc &
  Roussillon
Laos
London
Los Angeles
Malaysia,
  Singapore &
  Brunei
Mallorca &
  Menorca
Maya World
Mexico
Morocco
Moscow
Nepal
New England
New York
New Zealand
Norway
Pacific
  Northwest
Paris
Peru
Poland
Portugal
Prague
Provence & the
  Côte d'Azur
The Pyrenees
Romania
St Petersburg
San Francisco

Sardinia
Scandinavia
Scotland
Scottish
  highlands and
  Islands
Sicily
Singapore
South Africa
South India
Southeast Asia
Southwest USA
Spain
Sweden
Switzerland
Syria

Thailand
Trinidad &
  Tobago
Tunisia
Turkey
Tuscany &
  Umbria
USA
Venice
Vienna
Vietnam
Wales
Washington DC
West Africa
Zimbabwe &
  Botswana

AVAILABLE AT ALL GOOD BOOKSHOPS